Which
carclub.om
convenient way to save time and money when
you buy a new car or truck. Simple as that.

Just tell us the vehicle and options you want
(any make or model-foreign or domestic) and
we'll get you a lower price than you can get
on your own. Guaranteed in writing.
We can factory order any domestic vehicle
and usually save you even more.

No haggling. No hassles. No games.

Don't forget to ask about our loans, leases,
extended service contracts, gas discounts,
deductible reimbursement, and more. It's
a terrific way to save even more money
on the purchase of your new car

For more information, call carclub.com at
1-800-carclub (1-800-227-2582)

1-800-CARCLUB
or visit us on the web at carclub.com

All new cars arranged for sale are subject to price and availability
from the selling franchised new car dealer

carclub^{SM}
.com

You're not alone.^{SM}

Edmunds.com In The News

YAHOO! "Fire up your Web browser and make a beeline for Edmunds Online. Edmunds has been publishing those handy pocket-sized automotive price guides since 1966. You'll find buying strategies, information on current rebates and incentives, and plenty of auto prices." —*Yahoo! For Newspapers, April 10, 2000*

"A good example of a metamediary in the automobile market is Edmunds, which has created a valuable data franchise by giving **BUSINESS 2.0** away information about new and used auto pricing, dealer cost and holdbacks, reliability, auto-buying advice, and auto reviews. Edmund's generates tremendous traffic on its site, which has been ranked as one of the most heavily trafficked as well as one of the most usable Web sites." —*Business 2.0, March 2000*

THE WALL STREET JOURNAL. "Edmunds.com Inc., an auto-information company, has a well-trafficked Web site and a brand name car buyers trust, a rarity in the automotive universe." —*The Wall Street Journal, July 11, 2000*

"In the process of going online, they've (Edmunds.com has) trans- **www.THECARCONNECTION.com** formed their corporate identity from print powerhouse into a dot-com destination for auto information and discussion, where even some top auto executives admit they lurk to see what people are talking about." —*The Car Connection, August 7, 2000*

Forbes.com "...when you start to haggle, Edmunds' information is invaluable... Ample info on both new and used cars." -*Forbes, February 28, 2000*

"Edmunds.com, the site of the automotive publisher, is packed with information, including photos and reviews **GANNETT** of various models.". —*Gannett News Service, April 30, 2000*

Consumer Reports "At Edmunds.com you can get a free list of competing cars, specifications, safety features and prices for the vehicle and for every available option." —*Editors of Consumer Reports, April 17, 2000*

The Internet is big. Your phone is small. Don't worry, Nextel has a solution.

ACCESS ESSENTIAL INFORMATION
Receive priority email through MSN Hotmail. And with MSN Mobile, you can be alerted about important things like stock quotes, weather updates, news headlines — even check flight information.

SEND SHORT MESSAGES
With Nextel Online Two-Way Messaging,℠ receive and send text messages during meetings or any time you can't break away to make calls.

MOBILE ECOMMERCE
Purchase software, books, electronics, even construction tools and equipment. Right from your phone.

FIND IT ALL IN ONE PHONE
Get critical information your business requires. Designed to fit comfortably in your pocket.

RELAX
Business just got easier.

Nextel phones are manufactured by Motorola, Inc.

Nextel. How business gets done.™   1-800-NEXTEL 9   nextel.com

Most people have three things in common when they buy a car.

They pay too much,
They waste time,
and
They hate the experience.

2001

edmunds.com
where smart car buyers start

USED CARS & TRUCKS

PRICES & RATINGS

"WHERE SMART CAR BUYERS START"

Cover photo:
1999 Volvo S70

ISBN: 0-87759-666-2
ISSN: 1523-8024

USED CARS & TRUCKS

T A B L E O F C O N T E N T S

SPRING 2001

VOL. U3501-0004

Publisher:
Peter Steinlauf
Editor-in-Chief:
Christian Wardlaw
Director, Data Coordination:
Alison Cooper
Production Manager:
Lynette Archbold
Executive Editor:
Karl Brauer
Managing Editor:
Deborah Gordon
Detroit Editor:
John Clor

Sr. Features Editor:
Brent Romans
Features Editor:
Miles Cook
Technical Editor:
Scott Memmer
News Editor:
Carmen Tellez
Road Test Editor:
Neil Chirico
Photography Editor:
Scott Jacobs
Associate Editors:
Liz Kim

Erin Mahoney
Edward Hellwig
Senior Layout and Design Artist:
Robert Archbold
Car Buying Consultant:
Phil Reed
Researcher:
Erin Riches
Director, New Car Data:
Garth Nalleweg
Senior New Car Data Editor:
Charlie Schiavone

New Vehicle Data Editors:
Richard Milenkovich
KJ Jones
Roxane Ishimaru
Used Vehicle Editor:
John DiPietro
Used Vehicle Data Editor:
Wandile Kunene
Maintenance Data Editor:
Jose Luis Munoz
Acquisition Specialist:
Steven Petrecca
Photo Archivist:
Letitia Poteet

Printed in U.S.A.

Edmunds® books are available at special quantity discounts when purchased in bulk by credit
unions, corporations, organizations, and other special interest groups. Custom covers and/
or customized copy on available pages may also be prepared to fit particular needs.

INTRODUCTION

Thanks for consulting *Edmunds® Used Cars & Trucks Prices & Ratings*! You've made a wise purchase, because the values contained within this publication represent a current snapshot of the U.S. used car market as it exists for the consumer. Unlike other guides, we aren't publishing data sourced strictly from dealer-only auction houses or dealership sales records. Our values are based on advertised and actual transaction prices between private parties, between private owners and dealers, and between dealers. You won't find a dealer slant to our data, because one doesn't exist.

The Edmunds® Philosophy

For years Edmunds® followed tradition and published wholesale and retail values for vehicles. But we found that the commonly accepted method of providing a wholesale value and a retail value was based on a dealer's market, making such a system unreliable for and misleading to the average consumer. Dealers and private owners almost never sell a car for retail, and dealers almost never give wholesale value when assessing a trade-in. In years past we based our pricing on actual dealer advertised prices and auction data to generate retail and wholesale price. Our current pricing is gathered using a similar methodology, but we've modified the process to arrive at what we call Market Value and Trade-in Value.

Market Value

Market Value is a national average of prices asked by private sellers and dealers. Our source compiles hundreds of thousands of advertised prices nationwide, and interviews thousands of sellers by phone each week to find out their bottom-line price (the take price, as it is referred to in the industry), or the actual transaction price if the car has been sold. Data gleaned from telephone interviews, combined with national averages from the advertised price database, is used to create the Market Value. By including private sellers in the tabulation, we've effectively generated a more accurate, more reliable average value for any given make and model.

Trade-in Value

Trade-in Value is the amount that a consumer might expect to get from a dealer for a trade-in. Most dealers won't give a customer wholesale value (the average value a dealer could expect to receive at an auction) on a trade-in unless there is profit to be made from some other aspect of the deal. Why won't they? Because the dealer is assuming the customer's risk. If the car has a problem, the dealer must fix it. If the car is only in fair condition, the dealer must recondition it. If the car won't pass emissions inspection, the dealer must repair it. Then there is no guarantee that the car will sell on the dealer's used car lot, so the dealer must anticipate taking the car to the auction house, where a profit, no matter how meager, will be expected. So, when assessing a customer's trade-in, the dealer will value it lower than wholesale price.

Our Trade-in Value, calculated as a percentage of Market Value, is designed to provide consumers with a more realistic guide to valuing a trade-in.

When buying or selling a car, a price close to Market Value is a fair price. When trading a car, a price close to Trade-in Value is a fair price. Keep in mind that dealers will use whatever regional price guide favors them the most to value your trade-in and price the used cars on their lot. Sometimes, they will consult two different guides; one that undervalues trades, and one that overvalues retail prices for used cars. Since Edmunds® does not cater to the dealer or sell dealer-specific value guides like many of our competitors, expect initial resistance by the dealer to the prices we publish, but don't give in to dealer claims that our numbers are wrong. Also, keep the following guideline in mind: *A car is only worth as much as someone is willing to pay for it.*

Where's the Recall Data?

We've stopped publishing recall data, and here's the reason why. If you have Internet access, go to www.nhtsa.dot.gov, which is the address for the National Highway and Traffic Safety Administration's website. There you can search archives of recalls, technical service bulletins, and crash tests. The data found at this website is much more comprehensive and detailed than we could ever hope to provide, and you'll be better off arming yourself with this information before heading down to the local dealership for a chat with the service advisor.

How Do I Use Edmunds® Data?

As an example, we'll use a 1999 Mazda Miata with 32,500 miles on it. Options include air conditioning and the leather package. We would value the car like this:

	Trade-in Value	Market Value
1999 Mazda Miata	**$13,860**	**$16,235**
Air Conditioning	$565	$565
Leather Package	$960	$960
Mileage Adjustment	-$621	-$621
TOTAL:	**$14,764**	**$17,139**

Since these figures are for a car in average shape, we could adjust the numbers slightly upward since this car is in showroom condition. Also keep in mind that the value of this type of car increases during "top-down" season (when demand is higher) and decreases as the colder months approach (when demand is lower).

Remember that vehicle condition affects the car's value, as does having receipts for all the maintenance done on the car. Obviously, a car in excellent condition with receipts proving strict maintenance will be worth more than an average car without records. Other variables can affect the price as well, such as demand for this particular model and the time of year that the car is sold.

However, just because our book claims a fair value for this car of about $17,139, that doesn't mean we can automatically sell it for that amount of money. *A used car is only worth as much as someone is willing to pay for it.*

Contact Us

We believe that this guide is much more accurate and easy-to-understand than ever before. If you have questions, comments, suggestions, or complaints, you can write to us at the following address:

> Automotive Editors
> Edmunds.com
> P.O. Box 25906
> Los Angeles, CA 90025-9998

Or, you can send us e-mail to editors@edmunds.com. We look forward to your feedback!

HOW TO USE THIS GUIDE

Understanding the Layout

Finding the Right Model

We've listed all makes and models in alphabetical order, from Acura to Volvo. To find the make and model you want to value, look at the title bar at the top of each page. The title bar defines each section of the book by listing the *Automobile Make* and *Model Year* covered on each page. When the proper section has been found, you can find the right model by looking at the gray shaded title bars that begin each model listing. In this gray bar, you will find the *Model Name* and *Model Year*. To distinguish cars from trucks, we've printed truck data over a gray background.

What's New and Ratings

Beneath the model title bar is a section of text, called a *Yearly Feature Update*, which explains what changed on the model for that particular model year. Next is a *Ratings Chart*, containing a synopsis of heavily researched data about the model you're valuing. Most of the vehicles covered in this book have a ratings chart, but some vehicles cannot be rated because there is not enough data to calculate accurate ratings. Below the ratings chart is a *Mileage Category Designation*.

Mileage Categories

Each vehicle in this guide has been assigned to a specific mileage category, which contains other vehicles with similar characteristics. For example, Category C contains mid-sized American cars like the Ford Contour. Category E contains economy cars like the Toyota Tercel. And, Category G contains compact pickups, compact SUVs, and minivans like the Chevrolet S-10, the Nissan Pathfinder, and the Dodge Caravan. The mileage adjustment table is keyed to each vehicle by category. Sometimes, different versions of the same model may fall into different categories. In this event, versions belonging to different categories will be listed separately within the individual model listing section.

Data Presentations

The first column of data contains a *Model Description* for each individual model that has pricing data. The number of doors, trim level, drive system (if something other than two-wheel drive), and body style are described here. The middle column is the baseline *Trade-in Value*, which is used to calculate the amount of money you might expect a dealership to offer you if you traded the car in. The third column is the baseline *Market Value*, which is used to calculate the amount of money you might expect to receive for your car on the open market, or the amount of money you might pay a dealership for a used car. Beneath the pricing data for each individual model you might find values for *Optional Equipment*. Conveniently located on the last page of this book is a *Mileage Adjustment Table*.

Pricing a Vehicle

Market or Trade-in Value?

To find an accurate value for a vehicle, you must make adjustments to the baseline values for equipment and mileage. Realistically, you should use Market Value if selling to a private party or buying from a private party or dealer, and use Trade-in Value if selling to a dealer.

Options and Packages

Below the baseline pricing data for most vehicles are lists of optional equipment that require price adjustments. If the vehicle you're valuing is equipped with any of these items, you must add the appropriate value to the baseline values. Also listed with the options are expensive option packages. For example, a BMW might be equipped with a Luxury Package that includes power leather seats, cruise control, an onboard computer, wood trim, special aluminum wheels, and special trim. Some of these items might be found separately in the equipment list, and some might not. The published package price includes the intrinsic value for those items that are not otherwise listed as options. Most private sellers will be able to tell you if a vehicle is equipped with a certain package, but don't expect a dealer to know much about a used car except the price. Do your homework!

Transmissions

Our Market Value and Trade-in Value includes the standard transmission on that model, whether manual shift or automatic. Keep in mind that sometimes manufacturers would install a 3-speed automatic transmission as standard equipment, but would offer an upgraded 4-speed automatic transmission as an option. Newer Chevrolet Cavalier LS sedans provide an excellent example of this practice; the 3-speed automatic is standard, and the 4-speed automatic is optional. Don't assume that a listing for an optional automatic transmission means that the basic vehicle came with a stick shift.

Engines

There are five basic engine types: gasoline; diesel; supercharged gasoline; turbocharged gasoline and turbocharged diesel. Some engines appear in the optional equipment listings. Each vehicle record is listed including the standard gasoline engine. Similarly, models with standard turbocharged or supercharged engines are listed individually. The only engines contained in the optional equipment lists are optional gasoline- or diesel-powered powerplants. Make sure you find out what engine is under the hood of the vehicle you're valuing. If the vehicle you're buying or selling has an optional engine, look for the value in the optional equipment list.

The Mileage Table

Once the proper adjusted value has been determined, you must further modify the price of the vehicle using the Mileage Table on the last page of this book. Edmunds links mileage adjustments directly to each vehicle category and presents the data in a single table. The table features an average mileage range for each category and model year, and provides an exact value to be added or subtracted **per mile** over or under the average mileage range. No other value guide provides such detailed, or realistic, mileage adjustments. Because the acceptable mileage range is based on an actual average mileage of all vehicles within a given category, an exotic car like the Acura NSX will be valued according to a substantially lower and tighter average mileage range than a mid-sized import like the Honda Accord. If the vehicle you're valuing has excessively high or low mileage, you should not add or subtract value in excess of half of the vehicle's adjusted trade-in value.

The Disclaimer

That's all there is to valuing a used car with Edmunds.com. Now you've got accurate ballpark values for trade-in value and market value. *Keep the following in mind, however. Regional price differences, seasonal price differences, seasonal demand, vehicle condition, and the economic laws of supply and demand all help determine the actual worth of a used car. The values calculated using this guide are designed to represent average values nationwide for a used car in average condition, and should be used only as a guide to set an acceptable price range for selling or purchasing. None of the values published herein are intended to represent absolute values.*

Pricing Examples

	Trade-in Value	Market Value
1. 1996 Ford Explorer XLT 4WD	**$12,690**	**$15,300**
Automatic Transmission	345	345
Aluminum Alloy Wheels	120	120
AM/FM Stereo Tape	80	80
Dual Power Seats	150	150
JBL Sound System	280	280
Keyless Entry System	70	70
Leather Seats	285	285
Luggage Rack	60	60
Value before Mileage Adjustment	$14,080	$ 16,690
70,500 miles (Category G)	0	0
TOTAL ADJUSTED VALUE:	**$14,080**	**$16,690**
2. 1993 Nissan Altima GXE	**$4,300**	**$5,545**
Automatic Transmission	165	165
Air Conditioning	170	170
Cruise Control	50	50
Value before Mileage Adjustment	$4,685	$5,930
117,200 miles (Category D)	-300	-300
TOTAL ADJUSTED VALUE:	**$4,385**	**$5,630**
3. 1991 BMW 325i Sedan	**$7,930**	**$9,720**
Leather Seats	85	85
Power Sunroof	90	90
Value before Mileage Adjustment	$8,105	$9,895
87,250 miles (Category F)	+1,518	+1,518
TOTAL ADJUSTED VALUE:	**$9,623**	**$11,413**

HOW WE RATE THE CARS

Each spring, we update our ratings for used cars. Currently, we offer ratings for many vehicles built between 1991 and 1999. Edmund's ratings are presented in chart form, on a 1 to 10 numerical scale where 10 is best. Some ratings data is supplied by IntelliChoice, Inc., 471 Division Street, Campbell, CA 95008. IntelliChoice, a respected automotive data provider, has contributed information to our Safety and Reliability ratings for used cars and trucks.

Safety Rating

We examine nine factors that determine vehicle safety. First, we check frontal impact crash test data from the National Highway and Traffic Safety Administration (NHTSA). The NHTSA selects several models each year for crash testing, which is conducted at 35 mph into a fixed barrier. Federal standards require that all cars pass a 30 mph test to be sold in the United States. The higher speed used by the NHTSA allows for comparison outside of federal regulations. By crashing into a fixed barrier, the NHTSA simulates a head-on collision with another vehicle of similar size and weight traveling at the same rate of speed. The NHTSA assigns specific scores to the driver and front passenger. The higher the score, the more likely a person is to escape such a crash with minimal injuries. *If a vehicle has not been crash tested, we do not rate the vehicle in this category.* Crash test data is the most important ingredient of our safety score. Without it, a safety rating means little.

Other factors that are used to determine a safety rating include the number of times the model has been recalled for non-emissions-related issues and the presence of safety equipment like airbags and anti-lock brakes (ABS). On later model vehicles, offset crash test scores, which the Insurance Institute for Highway Safety (IIHS) began conducting in 1994, are rolled into the tabulation if available. In 1996, Volvo equipped their entire model lineup with side-impact airbags. Therefore, all 1996 through 1999 Volvos include side-impact airbags in the safety calculation. If a 1995 model that is identical to a 1996 model but is not equipped with side-impact airbags has a slightly lower safety rating than the newer vehicle, now you know why.

Important Note About Airbags and ABS:
These days, it seems like everybody is talking about how unsafe these systems are. Edmund's® does not consider airbags or ABS to be unsafe. In defense of airbags, they have saved approximately 25 people for every one person they have killed. True, they shouldn't be killing anyone. Unfortunately, airbags were designed to protect a 165-lb. person not wearing a seatbelt. To accomplish this mandate, airbags must inflate rapidly, expanding at a rate of approximately 200 mph. Children and adults are getting hurt or killed because of these rapid inflation rates, but it is important to note that in almost all cases involving death, the person killed was not properly restrained by a seatbelt.

Problems with airbags seem particularly acute in low-speed collisions, such as tapping a car in a parking lot, which do not require the protection the airbag provides. The sensors that control the airbag may not be without fault or flaw, but neither are most other sophisticated systems in today's cars. The best way to avoid injury or loss with airbag-equipped cars is to sit as far away from the airbag as possible, wear your seat belt and strap youngsters into the back seat.

The lawmakers who forced automobile manufacturers to install airbags may have gone about doing so in a misguided and uneducated fashion, but the fact of the matter is that these supplemental restraints do save lives and are improved with each passing model year. In fact, many 1998 model year cars and trucks came equipped with airbags that deploy at lower speeds. This recently accepted lower deployment speed will save more properly belted vehicle occupants, but those who do not wear a seatbelt will be more at risk than if they rode in a vehicle with airbags that deployed at higher speeds.

Recent reports claim that vehicles equipped with anti-lock brakes are more likely to be involved in single vehicle crashes than cars that are not equipped with anti-lock brakes. Why is this? ABS is misunderstood, and is misused in general by the driving public.

Here are the facts. ABS will not shorten stopping distances. ABS will not prevent all skids. What ABS is designed to do, and it does this very well, is allow the driver to steer around danger while simultaneously using maximum braking ability. A car without ABS will skid when the wheels lock up, and when the car is skidding all steering ability is lost. So, in such a car, it is highly likely that the driver will lock up the brakes, and slide into whatever situation or object caused him to apply the brakes in the first place.

With ABS, the driver can hit the brakes hard and steer around the situation or object in the road because the front wheels are not locked up. However, it is important that the driver steer carefully and not wildly. Once the car begins to change direction, it may begin to skid sideways, or laterally, if direction is changed too quickly. ABS cannot help control a lateral skid. One theory says that

drivers of ABS-equipped cars are steering around immediate danger successfully, but then skidding laterally off the road and hitting a tree, a road sign, or a building. Also, some drivers of ABS-equipped cars may be pumping the brakes in moments of panic, because that's what has been taught for decades to stop a car without ABS.

Owners of ABS-equipped cars should practice using the system in a vacant parking lot before the need to use ABS in a panic situation arises. For the record, Edmund's staff members prefer ABS on all surfaces except narrow dirt or gravel roads, where there is little room to steer and a locked tire can dig into the earth and drop speed more rapidly.

Finally, consider this. Bob Bondurant (famed racing legend and operator of the acclaimed Bob Bondurant School of High Performance Driving in Phoenix, AZ) told us that when ABS-equipped Mustangs were introduced to his fleet of student cars, the accident rate on his track dropped a whopping 40 percent. Bondurant believes in ABS, but concedes that most drivers have no idea how to use them. Do all of us a favor – learn.

Reliability Rating

Our reliability rating is based on three factors that determine how trouble-free a vehicle is likely to be. Intellichoice, Inc. tracks complaints from vehicle owners. For any given make and model, we combine data regarding specific reported problem areas with the number of mechanically-related recalls issued by NHTSA. Finally, we consult our records regarding build quality inside and out when the car was new.

Performance Rating

We take into consideration a vehicle's ability to accelerate, stop, and turn, then compare it to other models in the same vehicle class. So, the performance rating for the Dodge Neon is to be compared to the Chevrolet Cavalier or Ford Escort rather than the Chevrolet Camaro or Ford Mustang. Additionally, we toss transmission performance and steering ability into the recipe. Since performance often means different things to different people, we'll define it this way. A fast car with good brakes, communicative steering, a smooth-shifting transmission, and the ability to get around a turn without keeling over and begging for mercy gets a higher rating than a car that, uh, doesn't.

Comfort Rating

Another subjective category, rated by our staffers, is overall comfort. We look for a comfortable position behind the steering wheel on a supportive seat with a clear view of gauges and an easy stretch to controls that operate with minimum amounts of concentration. A car or truck with a quiet ride that doesn't jar occupants, clear sightlines front and rear, and easy ingress and egress will get a better score than one that rattles teeth and requires a stepladder to enter. So, if your idea of comfort is a rolling Barcalounger surrounded by look-alike chrome buttons and switches, you can ignore our rating.

Value Rating

To determine value, we examine nationally averaged theft rates, parts costs if purchased at the dealership, the likelihood that a vehicle will break down or run reliably and average insurance rates based on claims losses from a nationally-known insurance company. The icing on the value cupcake is the vehicle's degree of versatility. A full-size 4WD Suburban is infinitely more useable than a Mazda Miata, and therefore, offers better overall versatility.

Overall Rating

Add 'em all together, and you come up with an overall rating. We do not weight the overall rating, allowing each factor to count equally toward the final tally. If any of the five factors is missing from the equation due to insufficient data, we do not provide an overall rating.

Important Note: If data was unavailable for more than two of the five factors, we did not rate the vehicle at all. For those cars without ratings, the reason a rating is not given in any category is because of scarce data for at least three of the rating factors listed above.

Car Buying and Selling Tips

Buying a Used Car

- Visually inspect the car in daylight. If buying from a dealer, request that any items that are broken or damaged be repaired. If buying from a private seller, devalue the vehicle for broken or damaged items. Signs of paint overspray may indicate a history of bodywork.

- Have the car thoroughly inspected by a mechanic. If mechanical repair is necessary, devalue the vehicle accordingly.

- Have the car looked at by a body shop technician for signs of accident repair. Inspect the title, too. If the car has been wrecked and repaired, but has a clear title, chances are good that the vehicle is still in sound condition. If the vehicle is saddled with a salvage title, you should steer clear of it. This means it has been damaged so badly that the insurance company totaled it, and an enterprising person has repaired the vehicle for sale.

- Do a VIN search to help determine if the car has a clear title. Visit our website at www.edmunds.com to run a CarFax VIN report on any used car you're considering.

- Pay for the car with a cashier's check.

- Prepare a bill of sale. The bill of sale can be written in crayon on the back of a paper towel as long as a notary public witnesses the signatures of both parties. If the owner of the car has a lien against it, the bill of sale, when properly notarized, will serve as proof of purchase until the owner's loan is paid and you receive the title.

Selling a Used Car

- Clean the vehicle thoroughly, and make sure it is in good operating condition.

- Make sure all paperwork related to the vehicle is in order, particularly the title and registration.

- Advertise, advertise, advertise in major newspapers and used car magazine classifieds. If possible, park the car in high-traffic areas with For Sale signs in the windows and flyers tucked under the wiper blade that explain why someone would want your car. However, beware of local ordinances prohibiting the display of vehicles for sale.

- Realize that Japanese cars are generally in more demand than most American and European cars on the used car market.

Trading a Used Car

- Clean the vehicle thoroughly, and make sure it is in good operating condition.

- Make sure all paperwork related to the vehicle is in order, particularly the title and registration.

- Expect the dealer to offer far less than the car is worth. Negotiate as close to Trade-in Value as possible.

- Make sure the trade-in value doesn't get lost in the purchase or lease contract. Keep your eye on the ball.

1999
VOLVO
S70 AWD

VOLVO'S GREEN BERET

John DiPietro

There's a war a raging in the automotive marketplace. The two armies are the ever-popular sport-utility vehicles and a fairly new crop of all-wheel-drive cars. Yeah, we know, Subaru has been blowing the AWD horn (all their current models feature AWD) for some time now, and in the past Toyota offered AWD on the Corolla and Camry models. But we're talking high-end stuff here; upscale sedans and wagons for those folks who don't cotton to an SUV's bulk, clumsiness and fuel appetite, but who do like the secure feeling of AWD traction and control, especially in poor-weather driving conditions.

Those vehicles trying to steal some sales away from the SUVs include Mercedes-Benz with their 4matic AWD E-class sedan and wagon, Audi's quattro sedans and wagons, and now Volvo with AWD versions of their V70 GLT wagon and S70 GLT sedan called simply the V70 AWD and S70 AWD. Actually, the V70 AWD was introduced last year, as was the "Cross Country"; Volvo's more rugged, raised suspension version of the V70 AWD wagon. This review focuses on the S70 AWD sedan.

When Volvo facelifted their 850 line last year and renamed it the 70 series, the makeover was a success. The corners of the traditionally Volvo boxy body were softened, and along with the smoothly integrated lamp clusters front and rear, make for a pleasing design.

The style of these Volvos is purposeful, classy and well-proportioned.

The interior is a nice place to log miles. Volvos have had a reputation for making some of the best seats in the car biz (in terms of comfort and proper support) for ages. And the latest chairs support this theory as well as your back. For those folks residing in colder climates, the ever-important seat heaters are top notch; heating up quickly and providing even distribution of said heat. In more recent years, Volvo's stereos have garnered a reputation for kickin' sound. Go ahead, blast that U2 CD if the mood strikes you; you'll swear Bono and the lads are playing in the back seat!

Of course, there are safety features galore; front and side airbags, front/rear crumple zones, antilock disc brakes, three-point belts for all occupants, daytime running lights, and others too numerous to mention. You could say that Volvo's priority for safety is alive and well. And yes, a lot of other carmakers have the same safety equipment. Isn't competition great?!

Featuring the same light-pressure turbocharged, four valves-per-cylinder, inline five-cylinder engine as the S70 GLT, the AWD sedan has the same crisp performance in spite of the slight weight gain of the AWD system. In fact, even the V70 AWD wagon gets to 60 mph in less than eight seconds, a performance on par with the quicker sport coupes and sedans.

Using a low-boost setting for the turbo means it's not necessary to zing the tach needle towards redline to get the most out of the five-banger. Maximum torque of 199 foot-pounds is attained at only 1800 rpm, translating into sprightly around-town pickup and good passing power on the highway. This engine's power curve mates nicely to the four-speed automatic gearbox; the only tranny available with this powerplant. Those enthusiast types (like us) who like to shift for themselves can opt for the hot-rod R wagon. This conservative shoe box features a high-pressure turbo that has even more power (247 horsepower versus 190 horsepower in the light-pressure turbo), and is a blast when hooked up to a five-speed manual box. I recall, when evaluating the V70 R wagon, surprising the hell out of some tailgating hotshot in a Thunderbird supercoupe…oh the look on his face as the Volvo wagon dusted him was priceless, but we digress. The binders of the S70 AWD are up to the task of scrubbing off the easily gotten velocity; as a stopping distance of only

125 feet from 60 mph attests.

Volvo's suspension team did a good job of striking a balance in the handling and ride equation. Due to those pesky laws of physics, there is an inverse relationship between a car's handling ability and ride comfort on bumpy roads. A softer suspension gives a smoother ride but handling suffers due to too much body lean and wallow in corners, whereas firmer suspension settings provide better handling by keeping body motion in check, but the ride tends to be less compliant over the bumps. The S70 AWD handles just fine, and though the ride is a touch on the firm side, it is not stiff by any stretch. The only gripe we had was over highway expansion joints; for some reason these weren't damped as well as other bumps that the car simply dismissed.

We'd like to say that we were able to test the mettle of the AWD system, but alas, the roads were dry during my brief time with the car. Earlier this year, however, we had the chance to try the S70 AWD in Canada, on snowy and icy

roads, and reported that the AWD and traction-control systems were confidence-inspiring on the slippery stuff. And this high-tech wizardry doesn't call attention to itself, its just goes about its

business automatically, stopping wheelspin and transferring power to the wheel(s) with the best grip.

So, what would it be if it were our $35 to $40 large, a Volvo AWD car or an SUV? Hmmm... Performance, comfort, 21 miles to a gallon and parking ease versus a typical SUV's lack of athleticism, stiffer ride, 14-15 mpg and parking woes. Unless we really needed that towing capacity it'd be a no brainer; give us the Volvo AWD.

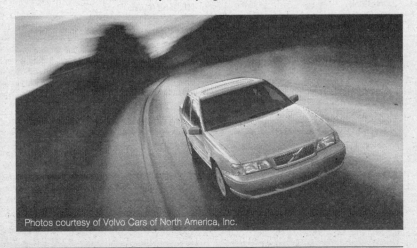

Photos courtesy of Volvo Cars of North America, Inc.

Model Description	Trade-in Value	Market Value

ACURA · Japan

1997 Acura TL

2000 ACURA

INTEGRA · 2000

The Type R is baaack, thankfully, and it arrives with two more color choices. The four-speed automatic transmission has been enhanced for better shift quality, and all Integras now have a tune-up interval of 100,000 miles.

Category E

Model	Trade-in	Market
2 Dr GS Hbk	15865	18505
4 Dr GS Sdn	16275	18980
2 Dr GS-R Hbk	16790	19585
4 Dr GS-R Sdn	17015	19845
2 Dr LS Hbk	14645	17080
4 Dr LS Sdn	15235	17770
2 Dr Type R Hbk	18385	21445

OPTIONS FOR INTEGRA
Auto 4-Speed Transmission +655
Fog Lights +125
Gold Package +300
Keyless Entry System +135

NSX · 2000

For 2000 the NSX gets improvements to its six-speed manual transmission, an upgraded, perforated leather interior, and a cleaner engine that now qualifies it as a low-emission vehicle.

Category K

Model	Trade-in	Market
2 Dr STD Cpe	64655	73925
2 Dr NSX-T Cpe	67705	77415

RL-SERIES · 2000

A new Vehicle Stability Assist system keeps the RL pointed straight, a new navigation system offers a larger screen and more information, and the 3.5-liter V6 now meets low-emission vehicle standards.

Category A

Model	Trade-in	Market
4 Dr STD Sdn	31870	36740

OPTIONS FOR RL-SERIES
Navigation System +1635

TL-SERIES · 2000

The real scoop is that the 2000 TL gets a bit faster, thanks to a new five-speed sequential SportShift automatic transmission and free-flowing intake manifold. A side-airbag system becomes standard as does a dual-stage inflator for the front-passenger airbag. The optional navigation system now features a DVD database.

Category A

Model	Trade-in	Market
4 Dr 3.2 Sdn	22970	26480

OPTIONS FOR TL-SERIES
Navigation System +1635

1999 ACURA

CL-SERIES · 1999

The previously optional Premium package, consisting of leather seats, is now standard.

RATINGS (SCALE OF 1-10)

Overall	Safety	Reliability	Performance	Comfort	Value
N/A	N/A	N/A	7.8	7.5	N/A

Category J

Model	Trade-in	Market
2 Dr 2.3 Cpe	16175	18835
2 Dr 3.0 Cpe	18270	21275

OPTIONS FOR CL-SERIES
Auto 4-Speed Transmission[Std on 3.0] +535

INTEGRA · 1999

In a small step up-market, Acura has decided to kill the Integra's entry-level RS trim. The LS gets leather accents and 15-inch wheels, and the sporty GS-R now comes with leather seats. Type R will return in limited numbers later in the year.

RATINGS (SCALE OF 1-10)

Overall	Safety	Reliability	Performance	Comfort	Value
N/A	6.9	N/A	8.6	7.8	N/A

Category E

Model	Trade-in	Market
2 Dr GS Hbk	15280	17820
4 Dr GS Sdn	15275	17880
2 Dr GS-R Hbk	15765	18450
4 Dr GS-R Sdn	15975	18700
2 Dr LS Hbk	14045	16390
4 Dr LS Sdn	14295	16735

Don't forget to refer to the Mileage Adjustment Table at the back of this book!

Model Description	Trade-in Value	Market Value	Model Description	Trade-in Value	Market Value

OPTIONS FOR INTEGRA
Auto 4-Speed Transmission +535
Fog Lights +100
Keyless Entry System +110

NSX 1999

An Alex Zanardi Edition of the NSX is new this year, but get your orders in early: only 50 will be made for sale in North America. The special edition car features a fixed roof, lighter rear spoiler and manual steering in its quest to shed nearly 150 pounds. For flair, the Zanardi Edition adds BBS alloy wheels, a titanium shifter and softer red-stitched leather seats. And it wouldn't be a tribute to the CART champion without a stiffer suspension and lower height. Hang on for the ride.

Category K
	Trade-in	Market
2 Dr NSX-T Cpe	63985	73250
2 Dr STD Cpe	61100	69950

RL-SERIES 1999

There are more than 300 changes to the RL this year, so we'll just touch on the important ones: the suspension has been revised for better handling and a firmer ride, brake rotors have added mass, side air bags are standard, styling is more aggressive, the Premium features have been incorporated into one trim level, and, best of all, the price has been slashed.

RATINGS (SCALE OF 1-10)

Overall	Safety	Reliability	Performance	Comfort	Value
N/A	N/A	N/A	7.8	8.9	N/A

Category A
	Trade-in	Market
4 Dr STD Sdn	29970	34660

OPTIONS FOR RL-SERIES
Navigation System +1335

SLX 1999

The SLX is carried over unchanged from a year ago.

RATINGS (SCALE OF 1-10)

Overall	Safety	Reliability	Performance	Comfort	Value
N/A	7.3	N/A	N/A	7.6	N/A

Category G
	Trade-in	Market
4 Dr STD 4WD Wgn	23335	27050

TL-SERIES 1999

The TL has been redesigned for 1999, with everything just getting better. The 2.5-liter engine is gone, making way for an all-new 3.2-liter V6. The transmission has been refined, the interior design makes better use of space, and the exterior is updated with a less stodgy appearance.

RATINGS (SCALE OF 1-10)

Overall	Safety	Reliability	Performance	Comfort	Value
N/A	7.6	9.6	7.8	N/A	N/A

Category A
	Trade-in	Market
4 Dr 3.2 Sdn	21925	25355

OPTIONS FOR TL-SERIES
Navigation System +1335

1998 ACURA

CL-SERIES 1998

A new 2.3L engine replaces last year's 2.2L unit. All CL models get a revised grille and new alloy wheels.

RATINGS (SCALE OF 1-10)

Overall	Safety	Reliability	Performance	Comfort	Value
N/A	N/A	9.1	7.8	7.5	N/A

Category J
	Trade-in	Market
2 Dr 2.3 Cpe	15240	17835
2 Dr 2.3 Premium Cpe	15940	18660
2 Dr 3.0 Cpe	17170	20095
2 Dr 3.0 Premium Cpe	18070	21150

OPTIONS FOR CL-SERIES
Auto 4-Speed Transmission[Opt on 2.3, 2.3 Premium] +435
Rear Spoiler +220

INTEGRA 1998

A slight nose job, designed for a more aerodynamic approach, is added this year. LS, GS and GS-R models get a little more comfortable with a tilt- and height-adjustable driver's seat and new alloy wheels appear on the LS and GS-R. The performance edition Type R is available again this year.

RATINGS (SCALE OF 1-10)

Overall	Safety	Reliability	Performance	Comfort	Value
7.4	6.9	9.1	9.2	7.8	4

Category E
	Trade-in	Market
2 Dr GS Hbk	14390	16915
4 Dr GS Sdn	14135	16725
2 Dr GS-R Hbk	14695	17270
4 Dr GS-R Sdn	14895	17510
2 Dr LS Hbk	13275	15600
4 Dr LS Sdn	13815	16235
2 Dr RS Hbk	11245	13220
2 Dr Type R Hbk	16180	19020

OPTIONS FOR INTEGRA
Auto 4-Speed Transmission +435
Air Conditioning[Opt on RS, Type R] +455
Aluminum/Alloy Wheels[Opt on RS] +185
Fog Lights +85
Keyless Entry System +90
Leather Seats[Std on GS] +480

Don't forget to refer to the Mileage Adjustment Table at the back of this book!

EDMUNDS® USED CARS & TRUCKS   www.edmunds.com   21

Model Description	Trade-in Value	Market Value

NSX 1998

No changes for 1998.

Category K

	Trade-in Value	Market Value
2 Dr NSX-T Cpe	60845	69625
2 Dr STD Cpe	58100	66490

RL-SERIES 1998

Slight suspension enhancements provide more sporty handling without sacrificing the ride.

RATINGS (SCALE OF 1-10)

Overall	Safety	Reliability	Performance	Comfort	Value
N/A	N/A	9.6	8.2	8.9	4.2

Category A

	Trade-in Value	Market Value
4 Dr Premium Sdn	27120	31445
4 Dr STD Sdn	25975	30115
4 Dr Special Edition Sdn	25900	30030

OPTIONS FOR RL-SERIES

Navigation System +1130
Compact Disc Changer[Opt on STD] +410

SLX 1998

Acura's rebadged Isuzu Trooper gets more power and torque, a trick new 4WD system and revised styling for 1998.

RATINGS (SCALE OF 1-10)

Overall	Safety	Reliability	Performance	Comfort	Value
6.9	6.5	9.2	6.8	7.6	4.6

Category G

	Trade-in Value	Market Value
4 Dr STD 4WD Wgn	21095	24520

TL-SERIES 1998

The premium level is gone, but the TL-Series gets more standard equipment.

RATINGS (SCALE OF 1-10)

Overall	Safety	Reliability	Performance	Comfort	Value
7.6	7.6	9.6	7.4	8	5.3

Category A

	Trade-in Value	Market Value
4 Dr 2.5 Sdn	20120	23325
4 Dr 3.2 Sdn	19800	23260

1997 ACURA

CL-SERIES 1997

Introduced as a 1997 model, the CL is supposed to compete in the growing personal coupe segment. Like many Acura products, the CL is based on a Honda platform, in this case the Honda Accord. The CL's sights are aimed squarely at BMW's 3-Series coupes.

RATINGS (SCALE OF 1-10)

Overall	Safety	Reliability	Performance	Comfort	Value
N/A	N/A	8.8	7.8	7.5	N/A

Category J

	Trade-in Value	Market Value
2 Dr 2.2 Cpe	13565	15970
2 Dr 2.2 Premium Cpe	14195	16710
2 Dr 3.0 Cpe	15220	17920
2 Dr 3.0 Premium Cpe	16025	18865

OPTIONS FOR CL-SERIES

Auto 4-Speed Transmission[Opt on 2.2CL] +355

INTEGRA 1997

No major changes to what may be the last Acura Integra. The good news is that prices for Special Edition (now called GS), LS and RS models remain the same as last year.

RATINGS (SCALE OF 1-10)

Overall	Safety	Reliability	Performance	Comfort	Value
7.2	6.9	9.1	9.2	7.8	3

Category E

	Trade-in Value	Market Value
2 Dr GS Hbk	12855	15175
4 Dr GS Sdn	13190	15575
2 Dr GS-R Hbk	12895	15225
4 Dr GS-R Sdn	13345	15755
2 Dr LS Hbk	11785	13915
4 Dr LS Sdn	12275	14490
2 Dr RS Hbk	10105	11930
2 Dr Type R Hbk	13160	15535

OPTIONS FOR INTEGRA

Auto 4-Speed Transmission +355
AM/FM Stereo Tape[Std on LS] +135
Air Conditioning[Opt on RS, Type R] +370
Aluminum/Alloy Wheels[Opt on LS] +150
Leather Seats[Std on GS] +390

NSX 1997

The six-speed NSX comes to us this year with a larger, 3.2-liter V6 engine that makes 290- ponies. Automatic NSXs continue with the 3.0-liter, 252-horse V6.

Category K

	Trade-in Value	Market Value
2 Dr NSX-T Cpe	50940	58425
2 Dr STD Cpe	48645	55790

RL-SERIES 1997

No changes for the 1997 3.5RL.

RATINGS (SCALE OF 1-10)

Overall	Safety	Reliability	Performance	Comfort	Value
N/A	N/A	9.5	8.2	8.9	4.2

Category A

	Trade-in Value	Market Value
4 Dr Premium Sdn	23820	27790
4 Dr STD Sdn	22215	25915

Don't forget to refer to the Mileage Adjustment Table at the back of this book!

Model Description	Trade-in Value	Market Value

Model Description	Trade-in Value	Market Value

OPTIONS FOR RL-SERIES
Elect. Navigation System +895
Alarm System +130
Compact Disc Changer[Opt on STD] +335
Compact Disc W/fm/tape +285

SLX   1997

No changes to Acura's upscale Isuzu Trooper twin.

RATINGS (SCALE OF 1-10)

Overall	Safety	Reliability	Performance	Comfort	Value
6.7	6.5	8	6.8	7.6	4.6

Category G

	Trade-in	Market
4 Dr Premium 4WD Wgn	19825	23125
4 Dr STD 4WD Wgn	18290	21335

TL-SERIES   1997

The TL is unchanged for 1997.

RATINGS (SCALE OF 1-10)

Overall	Safety	Reliability	Performance	Comfort	Value
7.5	7.6	9.5	7.4	8	5

Category A

	Trade-in	Market
4 Dr 2.5 Sdn	16420	19150
4 Dr 2.5 Premium Sdn	17585	20510
4 Dr 3.2 Sdn	18975	22135
4 Dr 3.2 Premium Sdn	20425	23825

1996 ACURA

INTEGRA   1996

All Integras get new wheel cover and alloy wheel designs this year, as well as green tinted glass. LS models receive body-colored moldings. Three new colors can be applied to the 1996 Integra: pearls in red, green or black.

RATINGS (SCALE OF 1-10)

Overall	Safety	Reliability	Performance	Comfort	Value
7.3	6.9	9	9.2	7.8	3.4

Category E

	Trade-in	Market
2 Dr GS-R Hbk	11810	14010
4 Dr GS-R Sdn	11975	14205
2 Dr LS Hbk	10575	12545
4 Dr LS Sdn	11015	13065
2 Dr RS Hbk	9065	10755
4 Dr RS Sdn	9485	11250
2 Dr Special Edition Hbk	11540	13685
4 Dr Special Edition Sdn	11840	14045

OPTIONS FOR INTEGRA
Auto 4-Speed Transmission +290
Air Conditioning[Opt on RS] +305

Aluminum/Alloy Wheels[Opt on LS] +125
Leather Seats[Opt on GS-R] +320

NSX   1996

The hardtop NSX is reintroduced to the Acura lineup.

Category K

	Trade-in	Market
2 Dr NSX-T Cpe	46485	53365
2 Dr STD Cpe	44280	50830

OPTIONS FOR NSX
Auto 4-Speed Transmission +1275

RL-SERIES   1996

The replacement for the Legend arrives wearing Acura's new alphanumeric naming system: the 3.5 RL. The 3.5 refers to the Acura's engine size. Detractors claim that the RL stands for little more than "Revised Legend." While the 3.5 RL is definitely luxurious, we think that many will miss the Legend's sporty feel. The front wheels of the 3.5 RL are powered by a torquey V6 engine mated to an electronic four-speed automatic transmission. Other changes include 101 ways to isolate bumps, vibrations and road noise. Acura's new flagship promises to be about as noisy as a sensory-deprivation chamber.

RATINGS (SCALE OF 1-10)

Overall	Safety	Reliability	Performance	Comfort	Value
N/A	N/A	9.5	8.2	8.9	3.1

Category A

	Trade-in	Market
4 Dr 3.5 Sdn	19545	22910
4 Dr 3.5 Premium Sdn	20960	24570

OPTIONS FOR RL-SERIES
Navigation System +730
AM/FM Compact Disc Player +170
Compact Disc Changer[Opt on 3.5] +275

SLX   1996

In typical Acura form, the SLX is one of the first luxury-badged sport-utes to be released in this country. Based on the successful Isuzu Trooper, the SLX is very similar to its twin.

RATINGS (SCALE OF 1-10)

Overall	Safety	Reliability	Performance	Comfort	Value
N/A	N/A	7	6.8	7.6	5.5

Category G

	Trade-in	Market
4 Dr STD 4WD Wgn	15855	18635

OPTIONS FOR SLX
Premium Pkg +1065
Dual Power Seats +150
Leather Seats +285
Limited Slip Diff +100
Power Moonroof +315

ACURA 96-94

TL-SERIES — 1996

Vigor replacement designed to do battle with new Infiniti I30 and the Lexus ES300 in the near-luxury segment. Cleanly styled with room for four, the new TL-Series comes with either a 2.5-liter, inline five- cylinder, or a smooth, 3.2-liter V6.

RATINGS (SCALE OF 1-10)

Overall	Safety	Reliability	Performance	Comfort	Value
N/A	N/A	9.4	7.4	8	5

Category A

	Trade-in	Market
4 Dr 2.5 Sdn	14340	16810
4 Dr 2.5 Premium Sdn	15380	18025
4 Dr 3.2 Sdn	16900	19805
4 Dr 3.2 Premium Sdn	18190	21320

OPTIONS FOR TL-SERIES
Compact Disc Changer +275

1995 ACURA

INTEGRA — 1995

A Special Edition model debuts, sporting leather interior, spoiler and larger tires. All LS models receive a sunroof.

RATINGS (SCALE OF 1-10)

Overall	Safety	Reliability	Performance	Comfort	Value
7.3	7.1	8.9	9.2	7.8	3.4

Category E

	Trade-in	Market
2 Dr GS-R Hbk	10000	12030
4 Dr GS-R Sdn	10155	12220
2 Dr LS Hbk	8935	10750
4 Dr LS Sdn	9320	11215
2 Dr RS Hbk	7645	9200
4 Dr RS Sdn	8010	9640
2 Dr Special Edition Hbk	9775	11765
4 Dr Special Edition Sdn	10040	12085

OPTIONS FOR INTEGRA
Auto 4-Speed Transmission +225
AM/FM Compact Disc Player +130
Air Conditioning[Opt on RS] +250
Alarm System +125
Aluminum/Alloy Wheels[Std on GS-R] +100
Compact Disc W/fm/tape +145
Leather Seats[Opt on GS-R] +260

LEGEND — 1995

Last year for the Acura flagship, the 1996 model will bear Acura's new alphanumeric nomenclature. No changes for this year's model.

RATINGS (SCALE OF 1-10)

Overall	Safety	Reliability	Performance	Comfort	Value
7.9	8	9.6	8.6	8	5.4

Category A

	Trade-in	Market
4 Dr GS Sdn	18175	21260
2 Dr L Cpe	17060	19960
4 Dr L Sdn	15770	18450
2 Dr LS Cpe	18690	21865
4 Dr LS Sdn	17190	20110
4 Dr SE Sdn	17140	20055

OPTIONS FOR LEGEND
Auto 4-Speed Transmission[Opt on GS,L,Cpe] +240
Compact Disc Changer[Opt on L] +225
Leather Seats[Opt on L Sdn] +205

1994 ACURA

INTEGRA — 1994

Redesigned for 1994, the Integra sports a distinctive four-headlight front end. All models receive four-wheel disc brakes to aid stopping; LS and GS-R models get antilock brakes. GS-Rs get a 10-horsepower boost over last year to improve performance. Dual airbags finally replace the annoying motorized seat belts as the passive restraint system on the Integra.

RATINGS (SCALE OF 1-10)

Overall	Safety	Reliability	Performance	Comfort	Value
7.2	7.1	8.1	9.2	7.8	3.8

Category E

	Trade-in	Market
2 Dr GS-R Hbk	8775	10760
4 Dr GS-R Sdn	8830	10830
2 Dr LS Hbk	7820	9590
4 Dr LS Sdn	7735	9480
2 Dr RS Hbk	6660	8165
4 Dr RS Sdn	6920	8485

OPTIONS FOR INTEGRA
Auto 4-Speed Transmission +185
Air Conditioning[Opt on RS] +205
Alarm System +100
Aluminum/Alloy Wheels[Opt on LS] +80

LEGEND — 1994

The base Legend is dropped from the lineup and a GS sedan is added. The new sedan offers the same 230-horsepower engine found in the coupe as well as traction control and a sport-tuned suspension. A new grille and bumpers find their way to all Legends and the LS coupe gets a new chin-spoiler. An automatically tilting steering wheel raises as soon as the key is removed from the ignition. Further improvements include a steering wheel position memory that is incorporated into the seat memory feature.

Don't forget to refer to the Mileage Adjustment Table at the back of this book!

Model Description	Trade-in Value	Market Value	Model Description	Trade-in Value	Market Value

RATINGS (SCALE OF 1-10)

Overall	Safety	Reliability	Performance	Comfort	Value
7.9	8	9.6	8.6	8	5.4

Category A
4 Dr GS Sdn	15360	18125
2 Dr L Cpe	14235	16805
4 Dr L Sdn	13205	15585
2 Dr LS Cpe	15655	18480
4 Dr LS Sdn	14570	17200

OPTIONS FOR LEGEND
Auto 4-Speed Transmission[Opt on GS,L,Cpe] +195
Leather Seats[Std on GS,LS,Cpe] +170

NSX   1994

Still no changes for the four-year-old NSX.
Category K
2 Dr STD Cpe	37710	43390

OPTIONS FOR NSX
Auto 4-Speed Transmission +975

VIGOR   1994

Dual airbags are now standard on all Vigors. Burled walnut trim replaces the Zebrano wood trim and GS models get a standard CD player. This is the final year for the Vigor.
Category D
4 Dr GS Sdn	12195	14670
4 Dr LS Sdn	11060	13300

OPTIONS FOR VIGOR
Auto 4-Speed Transmission +185

1993 ACURA

INTEGRA   1993

An LS Special model is introduced to the Integra line-up. Standard leather upholstery, rear spoiler and bigger tires make this midlevel Integra attractive to luxury-oriented buyers. An improved warranty boosts coverage to four years/45,000 miles.

RATINGS (SCALE OF 1-10)

Overall	Safety	Reliability	Performance	Comfort	Value
N/A	N/A	8.8	8.8	7.9	3.7

Category E
2 Dr GS Hbk	6265	7905
4 Dr GS Sdn	6460	8150
2 Dr GS-R Hbk	6720	8475
2 Dr LS Hbk	5485	6920
4 Dr LS Sdn	5755	7260
2 Dr LS Special Hbk	6025	7600
2 Dr RS Hbk	4795	6050
4 Dr RS Sdn	5130	6470

OPTIONS FOR INTEGRA
Auto 4-Speed Transmission +150
Air Conditioning +165
Leather Seats[Opt on GS] +175

LEGEND   1993

Thirty more horsepower and a six-speed manual transmission make the Legend coupe a viable luxury-performance contender. A passenger airbag is now standard on the base Legend. Upgraded stereos are standard on the L and LS models. Warranty coverage is extended to four years/45,000 miles.

RATINGS (SCALE OF 1-10)

Overall	Safety	Reliability	Performance	Comfort	Value
7.8	8	9.1	8.6	8	5.3

Category A
2 Dr L Cpe	10965	13085
4 Dr L Sdn	10745	12820
2 Dr LS Cpe	11885	14180
4 Dr LS Sdn	11940	14245
4 Dr STD Sdn	10310	12300

OPTIONS FOR LEGEND
Auto 4-Speed Transmission +160
AM/FM Compact Disc Player +95
Compact Disc W/fm/tape +125
Leather Seats[Opt on L] +140

NSX   1993

A passenger airbag is introduced this year, as is a cupholder for the center console. Warranty coverage is improved from three years/36,000 miles to four years/ 45,000 miles.
Category K
2 Dr STD Cpe	32050	36890

OPTIONS FOR NSX
Auto 4-Speed Transmission +795

VIGOR   1993

A passenger airbag debuts on the up-level GS Vigor. Restyled front grille and sound insulation mark the other changes to this car. Warranty coverage increases to four years/45,000 miles.
Category D
4 Dr GS Sdn	9465	11615
4 Dr LS Sdn	8600	10550

OPTIONS FOR VIGOR
Auto 4-Speed Transmission +150

Don't forget to refer to the Mileage Adjustment Table at the back of this book!

ACURA 92-91

Model Description	Trade-in Value	Market Value	Model Description	Trade-in Value	Market Value

1992 ACURA

INTEGRA 1992

A minor facelift and more horsepower are the only changes for the '92 Integra. A GS-R performance model is introduced with a 160 horsepower VTEC engine.

RATINGS (SCALE OF 1-10)

Overall	Safety	Reliability	Performance	Comfort	Value
N/A	N/A	8.6	8.8	7.9	5.1

Category E

2 Dr GS Hbk	5715	7255
4 Dr GS Sdn	5895	7485
2 Dr GS-R Hbk	6135	7790
2 Dr LS Hbk	4985	6330
4 Dr LS Sdn	5235	6650
2 Dr RS Hbk	4345	5515
4 Dr RS Sdn	4655	5910

OPTIONS FOR INTEGRA
Auto 4-Speed Transmission +120
Air Conditioning +135

LEGEND 1992

A passenger airbag joins the standard equipment list on LS models. Cupholders are finally available to front-seat passengers. LS models are now available with heated front seats.

RATINGS (SCALE OF 1-10)

Overall	Safety	Reliability	Performance	Comfort	Value
7.7	7.5	8.2	8.6	8	6.1

Category A

2 Dr L Cpe	9875	11915
4 Dr L Sdn	9430	11375
2 Dr LS Cpe	10475	12640
4 Dr LS Sdn	10810	13040
4 Dr STD Sdn	8690	10490

OPTIONS FOR LEGEND
Auto 4-Speed Transmission +130

NSX 1992

No changes for the sweetest looking car since the Ferrari 308.

Category K

2 Dr STD Cpe	20240	23365

OPTIONS FOR NSX
Auto 4-Speed Transmission +650

VIGOR 1992

The Vigor is introduced to broaden Acura's market. It is a midsized near-luxury sedan based on the Honda Accord. Offered in two trim levels, the Vigor can be had with an automatic or manual transmission. Power comes via an inline five-cylinder engine. Antilock brakes, power everything and a security system are standard on the Vigor.

Category D

4 Dr GS Sdn	7660	9640
4 Dr LS Sdn	7065	8890

OPTIONS FOR VIGOR
Auto 4-Speed Transmission +120

1991 ACURA

INTEGRA 1991

No significant changes are made to the 1991 Integra.

RATINGS (SCALE OF 1-10)

Overall	Safety	Reliability	Performance	Comfort	Value
N/A	N/A	7.5	8.8	7.9	4.1

Category E

2 Dr GS Hbk	4850	6510
4 Dr GS Sdn	5005	6725
2 Dr LS Hbk	4220	5670
4 Dr LS Sdn	4440	5960
2 Dr LS Special Hbk	4485	6020
2 Dr RS Hbk	3660	4915
4 Dr RS Sdn	3930	5275

OPTIONS FOR INTEGRA
Auto 4-Speed Transmission +95
Air Conditioning +110

LEGEND 1991

Redesigned for 1991, the Legend gets longer and larger. A more powerful (200 horsepower) engine keeps this car competitive with domestic and import rivals.

RATINGS (SCALE OF 1-10)

Overall	Safety	Reliability	Performance	Comfort	Value
7.6	7.4	7.5	8.6	8	6.6

Category A

2 Dr L Cpe	8460	10335
4 Dr L Sdn	8295	10130
2 Dr LS Cpe	8745	10680
4 Dr LS Sdn	9145	11170
4 Dr STD Sdn	7335	8960

OPTIONS FOR LEGEND
Auto 4-Speed Transmission +105
Compact Disc W/fm/tape +85
Leather Seats[Opt on L] +90

Don't forget to refer to the Mileage Adjustment Table at the back of this book!

AUDI 00

Model Description	Trade-in Value	Market Value	Model Description	Trade-in Value	Market Value

AUDI · Germany

1997 Audi A8

2000 AUDI

A4 · 2000

All A4 models receive minor updates to the interior, exterior and chassis. The front styling has been changed with new headlights, a new grille, new door handles, and new mirror housings. Inside, there's a revised instrument cluster and center console, along with other minor interior changes. The rear seats have been modified to improve comfort. There are now optional head airbags and xenon headlights. The chassis has been reworked for improved ride comfort and responsiveness.

Category J

Model Description	Trade-in Value	Market Value
4 Dr Avant Quattro 2.8 4WD Wgn	24450	28085
4 Dr Avant Quattro 1.8T 4WD Wgn	20790	23880
4 Dr Quattro 1.8T 4WD Sdn	20025	23005
4 Dr Quattro 2.8 4WD Sdn	23685	27210
4 Dr STD 2.8 Sdn	22355	25675
4 Dr STD 1.8T Sdn	18695	21470

OPTIONS FOR A4
Auto Manual Transmission +880
Navigation System +900
Automatic Dimming Mirror +370
Bose Sound System +670
Heated Front Seats +355
Leather Seats +1025
Power Moonroof +775
Ski Sack[Std on Avant Quattro] +155

A6 · 2000

There are two new models joining the A6 2.8 and A6 2.8 Avant. The first is the A6 2.7T powered by a turbocharged V6 engine. The second model is the A6 4.2 powered by a powerful V8.

Category J

Model Description	Trade-in Value	Market Value
4 Dr Quattro 2.7T 4WD Sdn	29005	33315
4 Dr Quattro 4.2 4WD Sdn	36685	42140
4 Dr Avant 2.8 4WD Wgn	27780	31905
4 Dr Quattro 2.8 4WD Sdn	26890	30885
4 Dr STD 2.8 Sdn	25590	29390

OPTIONS FOR A6
Navigation System +900
Sport Handling Pkg +815
Warm Weather Pkg +785
Automatic Dimming Mirror[Std on 4.2 Quattro] +370
Bose Sound System[Std on 4.2 Quattro] +670
Heated Seats +410
Leather Seats[Std on 4.2 Quattro] +1025
Metallic Paint +530
Power Moonroof[Std on 4.2 Quattro] +775
Rear Side Air Bags +315
Ski Sack[Std on 4.2 Quattro,Avant] +155

A8 · 2000

Updated styling in the form of a revised grille, enlarged headlights, added chrome and aluminum trim and reshaped bumpers provides a subtle new look. Inside, new interior surfaces and standard Valcona leather intensify an already richly appointed cabin. Revised switchgear makes it easier to pilot the A8, and a new navigation system is available. A new 4.2-liter, 40-valve V8 resides under the hood, and aluminum suspension components reduce unsprung weight and enhance handling. A long wheelbase version (A8L) is now available for increased comfort of rear passengers, and comes standard with an electronic stability control system and GPS.

Category L

Model Description	Trade-in Value	Market Value
4 Dr L Quattro 4WD Sdn	50745	58290
4 Dr Quattro 4WD Sdn	46370	53265

OPTIONS FOR A8
10-Spoke Polished Wheels +1225
Alcantara & Leather Pkg +2860
Navigation System +900
Polished Alloy Wheels +815
Premium Comfort Pkg +980
Solar Sun Roof +695
Warm Weather Pkg +980

S4 · 2000

The Audi S4 is a new sport sedan based off the excellent A4 platform. Highlights include a turbocharged, 250-

AUDI 00-98

Model Description	Trade-in Value	Market Value	Model Description	Trade-in Value	Market Value

horsepower engine, all-wheel drive and improved handling and braking.

Category J

4 Dr Quattro Turbo 4WD Sdn	31190	35825

OPTIONS FOR S4

Navigation System +900
Automatic Dimming Mirror +370
Bose Sound System +670
Heated Front Seats +355
Power Moonroof +775
Ski Sack +155

TT 2000

Audi introduces the funky-looking TT Coupe for the 2000 model year. A turbocharged, 1.8-liter engine squeezes out 180-horsepower for this avant-garde sports car.

Category D

2 Dr Quattro Turbo 4WD Cpe	26190	30080
2 Dr STD Turbo Cpe	24790	28475

OPTIONS FOR TT

Performance Pkg +780
Bose Sound System +640
Compact Disc Changer +535
Heated Front Seats +305
Trip Computer +210
Xenon Headlamps +410

1999 AUDI

A4 1999

Audi introduces the 1.8T Avant wagon to its lineup, while other A4 models gain standard equipment and new options.

RATINGS (SCALE OF 1-10)

Overall	Safety	Reliability	Performance	Comfort	Value
N/A	8.7	9.6	8.8	8.1	N/A

Category J

4 Dr Avant Quattro 2.8 4WD Wgn		
	22585	26140
4 Dr Avant Quattro 1.8T 4WD Wgn		
	19290	22325
4 Dr Quattro 1.8T 4WD Sdn	18575	21500
4 Dr Quattro 2.8 4WD Sdn	21870	25310
4 Dr STD 2.8 Sdn	20685	23945
4 Dr STD 1.8T Sdn	17395	20130

OPTIONS FOR A4

Auto Manual Transmission +720
Compact Disc Changer +625
Heated Front Seats +290
Leather Seats +840
Power Moonroof +635

A6 1999

The A6 continues basically unchanged after last year's redesign.

RATINGS (SCALE OF 1-10)

Overall	Safety	Reliability	Performance	Comfort	Value
N/A	9.3	N/A	8.2	8.1	N/A

Category J

4 Dr Avant 4WD Wgn	25860	29930
4 Dr Quattro 4WD Sdn	25025	28960
4 Dr STD Sdn	23875	27630

OPTIONS FOR A6

Enhanced Security Pkg +635
Warm Weather Pkg +845
Automatic Dimming Mirror +300
Compact Disc Changer +625
Heated Seats +335
Leather Seats +840
Power Moonroof +635
Ski Sack[Std on Avant] +130

A8 1999

The A8's warm weather package is modified to improve electronic accessory performance, while dual pane laminated glass replaces insulated glass. Standard on the A8 is a larger right outside mirror, a first aid kit and a CD changer. A premium leather/alcantra trim package and a new volcano black exterior paint color are optional. A8 prices will remain unchanged from 1998.

RATINGS (SCALE OF 1-10)

Overall	Safety	Reliability	Performance	Comfort	Value
N/A	N/A	N/A	7.6	8	N/A

Category L

4 Dr Quattro 4WD Sdn	42645	49355
4 Dr STD Sdn	37695	43630

OPTIONS FOR A8

Alcantara & Leather Pkg +2340
Electronics Pkg +935
Polished Alloy Wheels +670
Warm Weather Pkg +800

1998 AUDI

A4 1998

The 2.8 sedan gets a valve job resulting in 18 more horsepower and additional torque. Side-impact airbags are standard, as is traction control. Opt for the automatic and you'll get the same Tiptronic technology that allows Biff to manually shift Buffy's 911 Cabriolet. A new station wagon called Avant debuts, while the A4 1.8T gets new wheels, a sport package and an ambient

AUDI 98-97

Model Description	Trade-in Value	Market Value	Model Description	Trade-in Value	Market Value

temperature gauge. New colors and stereo improvements round out the changes for 1998.

RATINGS (SCALE OF 1-10)

Overall	Safety	Reliability	Performance	Comfort	Value
7.9	8.6	9.3	8.8	8.1	4.9

Category J

	Trade-in	Market
4 Dr Avant 2.8 Wgn	21395	24825
4 Dr Avant 2.8 4WD Wgn	21790	25285
4 Dr Quattro 1.8T 4WD Sdn	16925	19795
4 Dr Quattro 2.8 4WD Sdn	21100	24485
4 Dr STD 1.8T Sdn	15815	18510
4 Dr STD 2.8 Sdn	19960	23160

OPTIONS FOR A4

Bose Sound System +450
Compact Disc Changer +515
Heated Front Seats +235
Leather Seats +685
Power Moonroof +520
Special Factory Paint +965

A6   1998

Stretch an A4 platform, add rounded styling with plenty of edges for character, toss in a sumptuously comfortable interior available in several "atmosphere" styles, blend it all with traditional Germanic handling, and what do you get? The excellent new Audi A6 sedan. Our only quibble is the with the dorky taillights, which appear to have been inspired by the Chevrolet S-10 pickup. The wagon is carried over from 1997.

RATINGS (SCALE OF 1-10)

Overall	Safety	Reliability	Performance	Comfort	Value
N/A	9.1	N/A	8.6	8.1	N/A

Category J

	Trade-in	Market
4 Dr Quattro 4WD Sdn	23945	27785
4 Dr Quattro 4WD Wgn	24345	28245
4 Dr STD Sdn	22845	26505
4 Dr STD Wgn	23275	27010

OPTIONS FOR A6

Enhanced Security Pkg +520
Warm Weather Pkg +820
Bose Sound System +450
Compact Disc Changer +515
Dual Power Seats +405
Heated Front Seats +235
Leather Seats +685
Metallic Paint +355
Power Moonroof +520

A8   1998

Tiptronic automanual gear shifting is standard, as is a glass sunroof, dual-pane laminated window glass, an improved stereo and an upgraded antilock braking system.

Category L

	Trade-in	Market
4 Dr Quattro 4WD Sdn	36455	41890
4 Dr STD Sdn	32225	37030

OPTIONS FOR A8

Polished Alloy Wheels +545
Warm Weather Pkg +1090
Bose Sound System[Opt on STD] +305

CABRIOLET   1998

Here's an argument for euthanasia. Based on the ancient 80/90 platform from the late 80s, the Cabriolet soldiers on with minimal change. A new steering wheel design is standard, and the Audi logo disappears from the side moldings.

Category F

	Trade-in	Market
2 Dr STD Conv	22630	26245

OPTIONS FOR CABRIOLET

Premium Equipment Pkg +1485

1997 AUDI

A4   1997

A cheaper Audi A4 1.8T debuts, featuring a 150-horsepower, 20-valve, turbocharged inline four-cylinder engine and a base price in the low 20s. The 2.8 gains a revised decklid and expanded central locking features. All models have new cloth upholstery, and the console and armrests are trimmed with the same fabric as the seats. Three new colors debut for 1997.

RATINGS (SCALE OF 1-10)

Overall	Safety	Reliability	Performance	Comfort	Value
7.7	7.6	9	8.8	8.1	4.9

Category J

	Trade-in	Market
4 Dr Quattro 2.8 4WD Sdn	18640	21740
4 Dr Quattro 1.8T 4WD Sdn	15840	18470
4 Dr STD 2.8 Sdn	17630	20560
4 Dr STD 1.8T Sdn	14890	17365

OPTIONS FOR A4

Auto 5-Speed Transmission +435
Bose Sound System +365
Heated Front Seats +195
Leather Seats +560
Power Moonroof +425
Special Factory Paint +785
Sport Seats +320

A6   1997

A new Quattro Value Package is available with a power glass sunroof, larger alloy wheels, bigger tires, and, of course, the quattro all-wheel drive system. Selective unlocking capability expands to the remote keyless

AUDI 97-96

Model Description	Trade-in Value	Market Value	Model Description	Trade-in Value	Market Value

entry fob, and the alarm system now features interior monitoring. Jacquard cloth upholstery is new, and three new colors debut: Tornado Red, Volcano Black metallic and Byzantine metallic.

RATINGS (SCALE OF 1-10)

Overall	Safety	Reliability	Performance	Comfort	Value
N/A	8.2	N/A	8	8	5.8

Category J

4 Dr Quattro 4WD Sdn	19840	23135
4 Dr Quattro 4WD Wgn	20870	24335
4 Dr STD Sdn	18925	22070
4 Dr STD Wgn	19955	23270

OPTIONS FOR A6

Bose Sound System +365
Dual Power Seats +330
Headlight Washers +105
Heated Front Seats +195
Leather Seats +560
Metallic Paint +290
Power Moonroof +425

A8 1997

Audi revolutionizes luxury sedan construction with the Audi Space Frame, which employs seven new aircraft-grade aluminum alloys to lighten weight and provide a tighter, more crashworthy structure. The new A8 is also the first passenger car equipped with six airbags. The usual accouterments associated with a premium German sedan are all in place.

Category L

4 Dr Quattro 4WD Sdn	32645	37770
4 Dr STD Sdn	28830	33355

OPTIONS FOR A8

Cold Weather Pkg +335
Polished Alloy Wheels +445
Warm Weather Pkg +895
Bose Sound System [Opt on STD] +250
Heated Seats +225
Metallic Paint +260

CABRIOLET 1997

Base price drops a couple grand, but at the expense of the power top, burled walnut wood trim, and leather seats. Opt for the Premium Equipment Package, and these items magically reappear. Casablanca White and Cactus Green join the list of paint colors, and three new top colors debut. Leather seats can be had in two new shades, too.

Category F

2 Dr STD Conv	19910	23165

OPTIONS FOR CABRIOLET

Premium Equipment Pkg +1325

1996 AUDI

A4 1996

All-new, the A4 replaces the compact 90. This car performs better than the lackluster 90, and features a full load of standard features. Plus, it's drop-dead gorgeous. For the first time, a five-speed automatic transmission is available with the optional Quattro all-whee-drive system.

RATINGS (SCALE OF 1-10)

Overall	Safety	Reliability	Performance	Comfort	Value
N/A	N/A	8.4	8.8	8.1	6.1

Category J

4 Dr Quattro 2.8 4WD Sdn	15675	18385
4 Dr STD 2.8 Sdn	14850	17415

OPTIONS FOR A4

Auto 5-Speed Transmission +340
Bose Sound System +300
Heated Front Seats +160
Leather Seats +460
Metallic Paint +235
Power Moonroof +345

A6 1996

Traction control systems have been improved this year. Fans of the manual transmission will mourn the loss of it; all 1996 A6 models are saddled with an automatic shifter.

RATINGS (SCALE OF 1-10)

Overall	Safety	Reliability	Performance	Comfort	Value
N/A	8.2	N/A	8	8	5.7

Category J

4 Dr Quattro 4WD Sdn	16765	19660
4 Dr Quattro 4WD Wgn	17595	20635
4 Dr STD Sdn	16005	18775
4 Dr STD Wgn	16835	19745

OPTIONS FOR A6

Bose Sound System +300
Dual Power Seats +270
Headlight Washers +85
Heated Front Seats +160
Leather Seats +460
Metallic Paint +235
Power Moonroof +345

CABRIOLET 1996

Better acceleration, a new radio, a new color and revised alloy wheels are the only changes.

Category F

2 Dr STD Conv	19255	22540

Don't forget to refer to the Mileage Adjustment Table at the back of this book!

1995 AUDI

90 1995

Sport 90 model introduced, featuring lowered suspension.

Category D

	Trade-in	Market
4 Dr Quattro 4WD Sdn	11430	13555
4 Dr STD Sdn	10810	12820
4 Dr Sport Sdn	10975	13015

OPTIONS FOR 90

Auto 4-Speed Transmission +270
Heated Front Seats +110
Keyless Entry System +95
Leather Seats +340
Power Sunroof +235

A6 1995

Subtle restyle of last year's 100 brings new name. Sedan or wagon available in either front- or all-wheel drive. Wagon comes only with an automatic transmission.

RATINGS (SCALE OF 1-10)

Overall	Safety	Reliability	Performance	Comfort	Value
N/A	9	N/A	8	8	7

Category J

	Trade-in	Market
4 Dr Quattro 4WD Sdn	13765	16250
4 Dr Quattro 4WD Wgn	14850	17530
4 Dr STD Sdn	13130	15500
4 Dr STD Wgn	14215	16780

OPTIONS FOR A6

Auto 4-Speed Transmission[Std on Wgn] +270
Bose Sound System +245
Dual Power Seats +220
Heated Front Seats +130
Leather Seats +375
Power Moonroof +285

CABRIOLET 1995

No changes.

Category F

	Trade-in	Market
2 Dr STD Conv	16660	19365

S6 1995

Category F

	Trade-in	Market
4 Dr STD Turbo 4WD Sdn	21125	24565

OPTIONS FOR S6

Compact Disc Changer +190

1994 AUDI

100 1994

Base sedan dropped. CS sedan gets standard automatic transmission. Rear ashtrays and cigarette lighters disappear from all models.

RATINGS (SCALE OF 1-10)

Overall	Safety	Reliability	Performance	Comfort	Value
N/A	N/A	N/A	8	8.1	7

Category D

	Trade-in	Market
4 Dr CS Sdn	12620	15085
4 Dr CS Quattro 4WD Sdn	13375	15985
4 Dr CS Quattro 4WD Wgn	14605	17455
4 Dr S Sdn	11475	13720
4 Dr S Wgn	11850	14165

OPTIONS FOR 100

Auto 4-Speed Transmission[Std on CS,Wgn] +195
Bose Sound System[Opt on S Sdn] +190
Heated Front Seats[Opt on S,Sdn] +90
Leather Seats[Opt on S Sdn] +275

90 1994

Passenger airbag newly standard. S model can be equipped with leather and a power sunroof.

Category D

	Trade-in	Market
4 Dr CS Sdn	10535	12590
4 Dr CS Quattro 4WD Sdn	11765	14060
4 Dr S Sdn	9540	11400

OPTIONS FOR 90

Auto 4-Speed Transmission +195
Heated Front Seats +90
Power Sunroof[Opt on S] +190

CABRIOLET 1994

Based on 90 platform. Features dual airbags, ABS and 2.8-liter V6 engine. No manual transmission available. Rear window is plastic.

Category F

	Trade-in	Market
2 Dr STD Conv	14210	16615

OPTIONS FOR CABRIOLET

Heated Front Seats +95

S4 1994

Category F

	Trade-in	Market
4 Dr STD Turbo 4WD Sdn	16740	19575

V8 1994

Category F

	Trade-in	Market
4 Dr Quattro 4WD Sdn	19445	22740

Don't forget to refer to the Mileage Adjustment Table at the back of this book!

Model Description	Trade-in Value	Market Value

1993 AUDI

100 — 1993

Passenger airbag standard.

RATINGS (SCALE OF 1-10)

Overall	Safety	Reliability	Performance	Comfort	Value
N/A	N/A	N/A	8	8.1	6.9

Category D

Model	Trade-in	Market
4 Dr CS Sdn	10075	12270
4 Dr CS Quattro 4WD Sdn	10670	12990
4 Dr CS Quattro 4WD Wgn	11520	14025
4 Dr S Sdn	9295	11315
4 Dr STD Sdn	8510	10360

OPTIONS FOR 100
Auto 4-Speed Transmission[Std on CS, Wgn] +160
Heated Front Seats +75
Leather Seats[Opt on S] +225

90 — 1993

All-new 90 model debuts, with 2.8-liter V6 under the hood. ABS and driver airbag standard. Quattro AWD system still available.

Category D

Model	Trade-in	Market
4 Dr CS Sdn	8190	9970
4 Dr CS Quattro 4WD Sdn	9190	11185
4 Dr S Sdn	7390	8995

OPTIONS FOR 90
Auto 4-Speed Transmission +160
Heated Front Seats +75
Power Sunroof[Opt on S] +155

S4 — 1993

Passenger airbag standard.
Category F

Model	Trade-in	Market
4 Dr STD Turbo 4WD Sdn	13745	16145

V8 — 1993

Category F

Model	Trade-in	Market
4 Dr Quattro 4WD Sdn	14535	17075

1992 AUDI

100 — 1992

Sheetmetal redesigned, and 2.8-liter V6 replaces five-cylinder motor. Quattro models available with automatic transmission. Driver airbag and ABS standard. All wagons are Quattro-equipped.

RATINGS (SCALE OF 1-10)

Overall	Safety	Reliability	Performance	Comfort	Value
N/A	N/A	N/A	8	8.1	6.9

Category D

Model	Trade-in	Market
4 Dr CS Sdn	8250	10270
4 Dr CS Quattro 4WD Sdn	8165	10165
4 Dr CS Quattro 4WD Wgn	9325	11610
4 Dr S Sdn	7505	9345
4 Dr STD Sdn	6960	8665

OPTIONS FOR 100
Auto 4-Speed Transmission[Std on Wgn] +130
Pearlescent Met. Paint +150
Heated Front Seats[Std on Wgn] +60
Leather Seats[Std on Wgn] +185

80 — 1992

90 model discontinued. Coupe Quattro disappears. Antilock brakes made standard on 80, and optional power sunroof replaces last year's manual one.
Category D

Model	Trade-in	Market
4 Dr Quattro 4WD Sdn	6375	7935
4 Dr STD Sdn	5515	6865

OPTIONS FOR 80
Auto 4-Speed Transmission +145
Power Sunroof +125

S4 — 1992

200 designation dropped in favor of S4. Driver airbag and ABS standard.
Category F

Model	Trade-in	Market
4 Dr STD Turbo Sdn	14870	17375

V8 — 1992

Category F

Model	Trade-in	Market
4 Dr Quattro 4WD Sdn	12595	14715

1991 AUDI

100 — 1991

100E dropped. New programmable four-speed automatic transmission for 100 models.
Category D

Model	Trade-in	Market
4 Dr Quattro 4WD Sdn	5695	7450
4 Dr STD Sdn	5260	6880

OPTIONS FOR 100
Bose Sound System +105
Heated Front Seats +50
Leather Seats +150

200 — 1991

New 20-valve turbo engine installed in 200 Quattro models.
Category F

Model	Trade-in	Market
4 Dr Quattro Turbo 4WD Sdn	7880	9700
4 Dr Quattro Turbo 4WD Wgn	10000	12300
4 Dr STD Turbo Sdn	7825	9625

Don't forget to refer to the Mileage Adjustment Table at the back of this book!

Model Description	Trade-in Value	Market Value

OPTIONS FOR 200
Heated Front Seats +50

80   1991

Programmable four-speed automatic transmission introduced. 80 dumps weak, 2.0-liter, four-cylinder engine in favor of more powerful, 2.3-liter, five-cylinder engine.
Category D

4 Dr Quattro 4WD Sdn	5125	6705
4 Dr STD Sdn	4360	5700

OPTIONS FOR 80
Auto 4-Speed Transmission +110
Sunroof +60

Model Description	Trade-in Value	Market Value

90   1991

Programmable four-speed automatic transmission introduced.
Category D

4 Dr Quattro 4WD Sdn	5065	6625
4 Dr STD Sdn	4560	5960

OPTIONS FOR 90
Heated Front Seats +50
Leather Seats +150

COUPE   1991
Category F

2 Dr Quattro 4WD Cpe	9015	11095

V8   1991
Category F

4 Dr Quattro 4WD Sdn	9855	12125

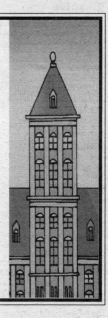
Don't forget to refer to the Mileage Adjustment Table at the back of this book!

BMW 00

Model Description	Trade-in Value	Market Value	Model Description	Trade-in Value	Market Value

BMW — Germany

1990 BMW M3 Coupe

2000 BMW

3-SERIES — 2000

3-Series coupes, convertibles and wagons are all-new for 2000; the hatchback has been discontinued. After last year's complete redesign, 2000 sedans see only minor improvements.

Category D

Model	Trade-in Value	Market Value
2 Dr 323Ci Conv	29340	33860
2 Dr 323Ci Cpe	24390	28145
4 Dr 323i Sdn	22740	26240
4 Dr 323iT Wgn	24560	28345
2 Dr 328Ci Cpe	28515	32905
4 Dr 328i Sdn	28030	32345

OPTIONS FOR 3-SERIES
Auto 5-Speed Transmission +1010
Navigation System +1390
Premium Pkg +630
Radio Navigation System +1065
AM/FM Compact Disc Player +380
Automatic Dimming Mirror +200
Cruise Control[Opt on 323i,323iT] +205
Dual Power Seats[Std on 328Ci,328i,Conv] +695
Fog Lights[Opt on 323i,323iT] +205
Heated Power Mirrors[Opt on 323i,323iT] +65
Leather Seats +925
Leather Steering Wheel[Opt on 323i,323iT] +105
Onboard Computer[Opt on 323i,323iT] +350
Power Moonroof +690

5-SERIES — 2000

The 5-Series cars carryover from last year with small changes and no price increase.

Category J

Model	Trade-in Value	Market Value
4 Dr 528i Sdn	32420	37245
4 Dr 528iT Wgn	33900	38940
4 Dr 540i Sdn	42440	48755
4 Dr 540iT Wgn	44395	51000

OPTIONS FOR 5-SERIES
6-Speed Transmission +2290
Auto 5-Speed Transmission[Opt on 528i 528iT] +1040
Comfort Seats +980
Navigation System +1380
Premium Hi-fi Sound +980
Premium Pkg +635
Sport Handling Pkg +1895
Sport Premium Pkg +4425
Automatic Dimming Mirror[Std on 540i,540iT] +370
Heated Front Seats +355
Leather Seats[Std on 540i,540iT] +1025
Metallic Paint +530
Spoke Wheels +1160

7-SERIES — 2000

The Premium Package is standard on the 740i and 740iL and the Cold Weather Package now includes heated rear seats. Two new "Protection" trim levels are also available that provide light armor, bullet-resistant glass and run-flat tires.

Category L

Model	Trade-in Value	Market Value
4 Dr 740iA Sdn	52265	59810
4 Dr 740iL Sdn	55585	63610
4 Dr 740iL Protection Sdn	82045	93895
4 Dr 750iL Sdn	76055	87040
4 Dr 750iL Protection Sdn	102565	117375

OPTIONS FOR 7-SERIES
Active Comfort Seats +1300
Adaptive Ride Pkg +1450
Park Distance Control +690
Security Glass +1985
Sport Handling Pkg +1855
Heated Front Seats +405

M5 — 2000

The M5 is a powerful (400-horsepower), all-new sport sedan based on the 540i.

Category J

Model	Trade-in Value	Market Value
4 Dr M5 Sdn	58000	66630

X5 — 2000

BMW joins the SUV craze with its all-new X5 SAV (sport activity vehicle), powered by the same superb V8 fitted to the 540i.

Category H

Model	Trade-in Value	Market Value
4 Dr STD AWD Wgn	41315	47585

Don't forget to refer to the Mileage Adjustment Table at the back of this book!

34   www.edmunds.com   **EDMUNDS® USED CARS & TRUCKS**

Model Description	Trade-in Value	Market Value

OPTIONS FOR X5

Navigation System +1625
Premium Audio System +980
Sport Handling Pkg +2020
Power Moonroof +795

Z3 COUPE/CONVERTIBLE 2000

Z3

Category F

Model	Trade-in	Market
2 Dr 2.3 Conv	26370	30350
2 Dr 2.8 Conv	31005	35680
2 Dr 2.8 Cpe	30715	35350

OPTIONS FOR Z3 COUPE/CONVERTIBLE

Auto 4-Speed Transmission +795
Cross-Spoke Wheels +920
Extended Leather Trim +980
Radial Alloy Wheels +920
AM/FM Compact Disc Player +380
Cruise Control[Std on 2.8] +180
Leather Seats[Std on 2.8] +520
Power Convertible Top +615

Z8 2000

BMW has created an all-new sports car with philosophical and styling elements gleaned from its original 1955 507 roadster.

Category J

Model	Trade-in	Market
2 Dr STD Conv	103135	118480

1999 BMW

3-SERIES 1999

3-Series sedans redesigned for 1999, offering 5-Series style along with more room for rear seat passengers.

RATINGS (SCALE OF 1-10)

Overall	Safety	Reliability	Performance	Comfort	Value
N/A	8.5	9.4	8.8	8.4	N/A

Category D

Model	Trade-in	Market
2 Dr 318ti Hbk	18575	21505
2 Dr 323i Conv	27450	31775
4 Dr 323i Sdn	20990	24300
2 Dr 323is Cpe	22780	26370
2 Dr 328i Conv	32740	37900
4 Dr 328i Sdn	26440	30605
2 Dr 328is Cpe	26285	30425

OPTIONS FOR 3-SERIES

Auto 4-Speed Transmission +650
Auto 5-Speed Transmission[Opt on Sedans, M3] +750
California Roof +1050
Navigation System +1265
Premium Pkg +655
Sport Handling Pkg +605
Alarm System[Std on 328i,Sdn] +355

Aluminum/Alloy Wheels[Opt on 323i Sedan] +310
Automatic Dimming Mirror +165
Compact Disc Changer +440
Cruise Control[Opt on 318ti,323i Sedan] +165
Dual Power Seats[Opt on 323i] +570
Fog Lights[Opt on 323i,323is] +165
Heated Front Seats +250
Leather Seats +760
Onboard Computer[Std on 328i Sedan] +285
Power Sunroof +520
Sport Suspension[Std on 318ti] +210
Xenon Headlamps[Opt on Sedans] +335

5-SERIES 1999

This fall, new 528i and 540i sport wagons debut, all 5-Series models achieve Low Emission Vehicle (LEV) status, and consumers will find extensive new standard and optional equipment on the cars.

RATINGS (SCALE OF 1-10)

Overall	Safety	Reliability	Performance	Comfort	Value
N/A	N/A	N/A	9.4	8.8	N/A

Category J

Model	Trade-in	Market
4 Dr 528i Sdn	30635	35240
4 Dr 528iT Wgn	32035	36845
4 Dr 540i Sdn	40105	46135
4 Dr 540iT Wgn	41955	48260

OPTIONS FOR 5-SERIES

6-Speed Transmission +1870
Auto 4-Speed Transmission +650
Comfort Seats +800
Navigation System +1185
Premium Hi-fi Sound +800
Premium Pkg +1045
Sport Handling Pkg +1495
Sport Premium Pkg +2575
Automatic Dimming Mirror[Std on 540i Sedan,540iT Sport Wagon] +300
Leather Seats[Std on 540i Sedan,540iT Sport Wagon] +840
Metallic Paint +435
Power Moonroof[Std on 540i Sedan,540iT Sport Wagon] +635
Premium Sound System[Std on 540iT Sport Wagon] +860

7-SERIES 1999

All 7-Series engines achieve LEV (Low Emission Vehicle) status. Revised standard and optional equipment add to the cars' appeal.

Category L

Model	Trade-in	Market
4 Dr 740i Sdn	48120	55195
4 Dr 740iL Sdn	51175	58700
4 Dr 750iL Sdn	69405	79610

OPTIONS FOR 7-SERIES

Comfort Seats +800
Elect. Damping Control Susp. +1000
Navigation System +1205

Don't forget to refer to the Mileage Adjustment Table at the back of this book!

BMW 99-98

Model Description	Trade-in Value	Market Value

Park Distance Control +600
Security Glass +1735
Security Sun Roof +1735
Sport Handling Pkg +1620
Compact Disc Changer[Std on 750iL] +725
Headlight Washers[Std on 750iL] +220
Heated Front Seats[Std on 750iL] +330
Power Sunroof +640

M3   1999

Production of M3 four-door sedans ends this year as BMW concentrates on selling the M3 coupe and recently introduced M3 convertible. These models go unchanged for 1999.

Category J

	Trade-in	Market
2 Dr M3 Conv	35680	41040
2 Dr M3 Cpe	30920	35565

OPTIONS FOR M3

Auto 5-Speed Transmission +800
Forged Alloy Wheels +970
Cruise Control +325
Dual Power Seats +495
Harman Kardon Sound Sys +920
Heated Front Seats +290
Power Moonroof +635

Z3 COUPE/CONVERTIBLE 1999

RATINGS (SCALE OF 1-10)

Overall	Safety	Reliability	Performance	Comfort	Value
N/A	N/A	N/A	8.8	7.6	N/A

M

Category F

	Trade-in	Market
2 Dr M Conv	33785	38990
2 Dr M Cpe	33080	38180

Z3

Category F

	Trade-in	Market
2 Dr 2.3 Conv	24425	28190
2 Dr 2.8 Conv	29430	33960
2 Dr 2.8 Cpe	29430	33960

OPTIONS FOR Z3 COUPE/CONVERTIBLE

Auto 4-Speed Transmission +650
Extended Leather Trim +800
Round Spoke Alloy Wheels +750
AM/FM Compact Disc Player +310
Cruise Control[Opt on 2.3] +150
Leather Seats[Opt on 2.3] +425
Power Convertible Top[Std on M] +500

1998 BMW

3-SERIES   1998

BMW adds a 2.5-liter inline-six engine to their entry-level coupe and convertible, making them the cheapest six-cylinder BMWs in years. Also new are standard side-impact airbags for front seat passengers in all models except the 318ti, in which they're optional.

RATINGS (SCALE OF 1-10)

Overall	Safety	Reliability	Performance	Comfort	Value
7.7	8.4	9.4	9.4	8	3.5

Category D

	Trade-in	Market
4 Dr 318i Sdn	19570	22680
2 Dr 318i Hbk	15945	18480
2 Dr 323i Conv	25830	29940
2 Dr 323is Cpe	21435	24845
2 Dr 328i Conv	30810	35715
4 Dr 328i Sdn	24660	28580

Category F

	Trade-in	Market
2 Dr 328i Cpe	25410	29395

Category J

	Trade-in	Market
2 Dr M3 Conv	34120	39315
2 Dr M3 Cpe	30280	34890
4 Dr M3 Sdn	30280	34890

OPTIONS FOR 3-SERIES

Auto 4-Speed Transmission +530
Auto 5-Speed Transmission[Opt on M3] +690
California Roof +875
Forged Alloy Wheels +820
Rollover Protection System[Opt on Conv) +790
Sport Handling Pkg +1160
Aluminum/Alloy Wheels[Opt on 318i,318ti] +255
Compact Disc Changer +350
Cruise Control[Opt on 318ti,M3] +135
Dual Power Seats[Opt on M3] +405
Heated Front Seats +205
Keyless Entry System +100
Leather Seats[Std on M3] +345
Metallic Paint +155
Onboard Computer +205
Power Sunroof +365
Side Air Bag Restraint[Opt on 318ti] +160
Sport Suspension[Std on M3] +105

5-SERIES   1998

Side-impact airbags are now available for rear-seat passengers, as is break-resistant glass for the windows and moonroof.

RATINGS (SCALE OF 1-10)

Overall	Safety	Reliability	Performance	Comfort	Value
N/A	N/A	9.1	9.4	8.8	N/A

Category J

	Trade-in	Market
4 Dr 528i Sdn	30210	34950
4 Dr 540i Sdn	38260	44080

OPTIONS FOR 5-SERIES

6-Speed Transmission[Opt on 540i] +1530
Auto 4-Speed Transmission +530
Comfort Seats +655

Don't forget to refer to the Mileage Adjustment Table at the back of this book!

Model Description	Trade-in Value	Market Value	Model Description	Trade-in Value	Market Value

BMW 98-97

Navigation System +1415
Premium Pkg +1355
Sport Handling Pkg +1260
Heated Front Seats +235
Leather Seats[Opt on 528i] +685
Metallic Paint +355
Power Moonroof[Opt on 528i] +520
Premium Sound System +705
Sport Suspension +230

7-SERIES   1998

BMW introduces Dynamic Stability Control (DSC) to the big Bimmer. DSC is designed to automatically correct the yaw on all 7-Series cars, preventing plowing and fishtailing. Guess this means no more smoky burnouts in the Beverly Hilton's parking lot.

Category L

	Trade-in	Market
4 Dr 740i Sdn	39505	45445
4 Dr 740iL Sdn	42050	48375
4 Dr 750iL Sdn	57055	65635

OPTIONS FOR 7-SERIES
Comfort Seats +655
Elect. Damping Control Susp. +1090
Navigation System +1365
Park Distance Control +490
Security Sun Roof +1420
Auto Load Leveling[Opt on 740iL] +620
Compact Disc W/fm/tape[Std on 750iL] +345
Heated Front Seats[Std on 750iL] +270
Metallic Paint +320
Power Sunroof +525

Z3   1998

The M Roadster, a 240-horsepower version of the Z3 convertible, arrives for 1998. An electric top also becomes available this year.

RATINGS (SCALE OF 1-10)

Overall	Safety	Reliability	Performance	Comfort	Value
N/A	N/A	8.9	9	7.5	N/A

Category F

	Trade-in	Market
2 Dr 1.9 Conv	22195	25675
2 Dr 2.8 Conv	26985	31220
2 Dr M Conv	30750	35575

OPTIONS FOR Z3
Auto 4-Speed Transmission +530
Alloy Wheels W/17in. Tires +615
Extended Leather Trim +655
Heated Front Seats[Std on M] +210
Heated Power Mirrors[Std on M] +115
Leather Seats[Opt on 1.9] +345
Metallic Paint[Std on M] +210
Onboard Computer +205
Power Convertible Top[Std on M] +410
Premium Sound System[Opt on 1.9] +210
Side Air Bag Restraint +215

1997 BMW

3-SERIES   1997

An M3 sedan has arrived at a store near you. Those of you claiming to want power and practicality no longer have an excuse for driving that old jalopy currently parked in your driveway. Buy one now. Also, All-Season Traction is now standard on all models.

RATINGS (SCALE OF 1-10)

Overall	Safety	Reliability	Performance	Comfort	Value
7.3	7.4	9	9.4	8	2.9

Category D

	Trade-in	Market
2 Dr 318i Conv	22490	26155
4 Dr 318i Sdn	17690	20570
2 Dr 318ti Hbk	14545	16915
2 Dr 328i Conv	27705	32215
4 Dr 328i Sdn	22325	25960
2 Dr 328i Luxury Conv	32320	37580

Category F

	Trade-in	Market
2 Dr 318is Cpe	19415	22560
2 Dr 328is Cpe	23050	26780

Category J

	Trade-in	Market
2 Dr M3 Cpe	27455	31710
4 Dr M3 Sdn	27455	31710

OPTIONS FOR 3-SERIES
Auto 4-Speed Transmission +435
Forged Alloy Wheels +645
Luxury Pkg +975
Rollover Protection System(Opt on Conv) +645
Sports Pkg +595
AM/FM Compact Disc Player +210
Aluminum/Alloy Wheels[Opt on 318ti,318i] +210
Compact Disc W/fm/tape +345
Heated Front Seats +165
Leather Seats[Std on M3,Luxury,328i STD Conv] +285
Onboard Computer +165
Power Sunroof +300
Premium Sound System +165
Sport Seats +220

5-SERIES   1997

The 5-Series is redesigned and introduced midway through 1996 as a 1997 model. Bearing a strong resemblance to its 3- and 7-Series siblings, the 5-Series offers a lot of car for a lot of money. The Touring wagons are no longer available, and the 3.0-liter V8 is history. New 5-Series models can be had as a six-cylinder 528i or a V8 540i. Both models feature new engines, all-aluminum suspensions, improved brakes and available side impact airbag protection.

Don't forget to refer to the Mileage Adjustment Table at the back of this book!

Model Description	Trade-in Value	Market Value

Model Description	Trade-in Value	Market Value

RATINGS (SCALE OF 1-10)

Overall	Safety	Reliability	Performance	Comfort	Value
N/A	N/A	8.9	9.4	8.8	N/A

Category J
4 Dr 528i Sdn	26875	31225
4 Dr 540i Sdn	33580	38785

OPTIONS FOR 5-SERIES
6-Speed Transmission[Opt on 540i] +970
Auto 4-Speed Transmission +385
Comfort Seats +475
Navigation System +1150
Premium Pkg +445
Heated Front Seats +195
Leather Seats[Opt on 528i] +560
Power Moonroof[Opt on 528i] +425
Premium Sound System +575
Sport Suspension +190

7-SERIES   1997

BMW reintroduces the regular length 740i after the uproar caused over its cancellation for the 1996 model year. Like the rest of the 7-Series, the 740i has a standard equipment list that will leave the Sultan of Brunei drooling with desire.

Category L
4 Dr 740i Sdn	35140	40455
4 Dr 740iL Sdn	37400	43055
4 Dr 750iL Sdn	50780	58455

OPTIONS FOR 7-SERIES
Cold Weather Pkg +355
Comfort Seats +520
Elect. Damping Control Susp. +865
Navigation System +1210
Park Distance Control +390
Auto Load Leveling[Opt on 740iL] +505
Headlight Washers[Std on 750iL] +145
Heated Front Seats[Std on 750iL] +220

8-SERIES   1997

Engine displacement is bumped, making the 1997 840Ci and 850Ci a bit stronger than last year's models. BMW's five-speed Steptronic is now standard on both models.

Category J
2 Dr 850Ci Cpe	53335	61600

Category L
2 Dr 840Ci Cpe	42335	48735

OPTIONS FOR 8-SERIES
Forged Alloy Wheels +540

Z3   1997

Hooray, the market for sports cars is alive and kicking. Despite the ever-increasing number of minivans and sport-utes on our clogged highways, there are still enough of us that like to drive to support this wonderful little car. As a reward for keeping the segment alive, BMW makes its 190-horsepower six-cylinder engine available in the Z3 2.8.

RATINGS (SCALE OF 1-10)

Overall	Safety	Reliability	Performance	Comfort	Value
N/A	N/A	8.3	9	7.5	N/A

Category F
2 Dr 1.9 Conv	19830	23040
2 Dr 2.8 Conv	24455	28415

OPTIONS FOR Z3
Auto 4-Speed Transmission +435
Extended Leather Trim +535
Compact Disc Changer +285
Heated Front Seats +175
Leather Seats[Opt on 1.9] +285
Onboard Computer +165
Traction Control System[Opt on 1.9] +165

1996 BMW

3-SERIES   1996

BMW's highly acclaimed 3-series receives new engines across the board. The 318 remains a 318 despite an increase in displacement to 1.9 liters. The six-cylinder model becomes the 328 with an improved engine that increases torque by a whopping 14 percent. Vented rear disc brakes aid the 328's stopping power by reducing brake fade. Automatic climate control is standard, except in the 318ti, and improved sound systems are optional on all models.

RATINGS (SCALE OF 1-10)

Overall	Safety	Reliability	Performance	Comfort	Value
7.4	7.4	8.7	9.4	8	3.3

Category D
2 Dr 318i Conv	19990	23340
4 Dr 318i Sdn	15745	18390
2 Dr 318ti Hbk	12615	14730
2 Dr 328i Conv	24910	29090
4 Dr 328i Sdn	20075	23445

Category F
2 Dr 318is Cpe	17515	20460
2 Dr 328is Cpe	20790	24285

Category J
2 Dr M3 Cpe	24620	28430

OPTIONS FOR 3-SERIES
Auto 4-Speed Transmission +355
Rollover Protection System(Opt on Conv) +530
Sports Pkg +340
AM/FM Compact Disc Player +170
Air Conditioning[Opt on 318ti] +315
Aluminum/Alloy Wheels[Opt on 318ti,318i Sdn] +170

Don't forget to refer to the Mileage Adjustment Table at the back of this book!

BMW 96-95

Model Description	Trade-in Value	Market Value	Model Description	Trade-in Value	Market Value

Cruise Control[Opt on 318ti,M3] +90
Heated Front Seats +135
Keyless Entry System +115
Leather Seats[Std on M3,328i Conv] +230
Onboard Computer +135
Power Sunroof[Opt on 318ti,M3] +285
Premium Sound System +135
Sport Seats +180
Traction Control System +135

7-SERIES   1996

BMW's flagship gets stretched; the only 7-Series models available for 1996 are long wheelbase models. The 740iL receives a larger V8 that substantially increases torque. BMW's killer 440-watt sound system is now standard on the 750iL and optional on the 740iL. A sophisticated interior-motion theft-deterrent system is now available.

Category L

4 Dr 740iL Sdn	31000	35765
4 Dr 750iL Sdn	42985	49590

OPTIONS FOR 7-SERIES
Comfort Seats +440
Park Distance Control +330
Headlight Washers[Std on 750iL] +120

8-SERIES   1996

Category J

2 Dr 850CSi Cpe	52570	60710
2 Dr 850Ci Cpe	47675	55055

Category L

2 Dr 840Ci Cpe	37550	43320

OPTIONS FOR 8-SERIES
Forged Alloy Wheels +455
Aluminum/Alloy Wheels[Std on 850Ci] +155

Z3   1996

BMW follows Mazda's lead and introduces a roadster. This dreamy two-seater made its debut in the James Bond movie, *Golden Eye*, and has had enthusiasts across the country drooling over its smart styling and impressive refinement. Featured as the perfect Christmas gift in the 1995 Neiman Marcus Christmas catalog, BMW sold out of Z3s before the first one was released to the public.

RATINGS (SCALE OF 1-10)

Overall	Safety	Reliability	Performance	Comfort	Value
N/A	N/A	8.3	8.6	7.5	N/A

Category F

2 Dr STD Conv	18300	21375

OPTIONS FOR Z3
Auto 4-Speed Transmission +355
Heated Front Seats +140
Leather Seats +230

Onboard Computer +135
Traction Control System +135

1995 BMW

3-SERIES   1995

A new M3 coupe debuts with blistering performance and exceptional grace. Available only as a five-speed manual, the M3 has Z-rated tires, a limited-slip differential and 17-inch wheels. The 318 series gains a convertible. Two new packages debut that allow a driver to choose between a sports or luxury orientation.

RATINGS (SCALE OF 1-10)

Overall	Safety	Reliability	Performance	Comfort	Value
7.1	7.9	7.4	9.2	8	3.1

Category D

2 Dr 318i Conv	16375	19230
4 Dr 318i Sdn	13220	15525
2 Dr 318ti Hbk	10645	12500
2 Dr 325i Conv	20465	24035
4 Dr 325i Sdn	17155	20150

Category F

2 Dr 318is Cpe	14660	17210
2 Dr 325is Cpe	17995	21125

Category J

2 Dr M3 Cpe	20870	24245

OPTIONS FOR 3-SERIES
Auto 4-Speed Transmission +275
Luxury Pkg +370
Rollover Protection Sys. +425
Sports Pkg +580
AM/FM Compact Disc Player +140
Heated Front Seats +110
Keyless Entry System +95
Leather Seats[Opt on 318i,318is,318ti] +190
Onboard Computer +110
Power Sunroof[Opt on 318ti,M3] +235
Sport Seats +140
Traction Control System +110

5-SERIES   1995

BMW sports up its 540i by making a six-speed manual transmission available. That option includes 12-way power sport seats, a sport suspension and beefy anti-roll bars. Unfortunately, all models lose their V-rated tires in favor of wimpy H-rated tires in an attempt to improve fuel economy.

RATINGS (SCALE OF 1-10)

Overall	Safety	Reliability	Performance	Comfort	Value
N/A	N/A	8.6	8.8	8	N/A

Category J

4 Dr 525i Sdn	18905	21965
4 Dr 525i Touring Wgn	19280	22405

Don't forget to refer to the Mileage Adjustment Table at the back of this book!

Model Description	Trade-in Value	Market Value
4 Dr 530i Sdn	21115	24530
4 Dr 530i Touring Wgn	23215	26975
4 Dr 540i Sdn	23655	27485

OPTIONS FOR 5-SERIES
6-Speed Transmission[Opt on 540i] +270
Auto 4-Speed Transmission[Std on Touring] +310
Premium Pkg +655
AM/FM Compact Disc Player +115
Heated Front Seats +130
Leather Seats[Opt on 525i] +375
Onboard Computer[Opt on 525i] +130
Power Sunroof[Std on 530i,540i] +335
Traction Control System +350

7-SERIES   1995

The big Bimmer is totally redesigned for 1995. The flagship sedan now features sleek styling and a lengthened wheelbase. Three models are available for 1995, including a new 740i regular-wheelbase model. The V12 engine found in the 750iL gains 27 horsepower and 30 foot-pounds of torque. New interior refinements include a residual heat system which will continue to heat the car after the power has been turned off, and 14-way power seats.

Category L

Model Description	Trade-in Value	Market Value
4 Dr 740i Sdn	26430	30565
4 Dr 740iL Sdn	27335	31610
4 Dr 750iL Sdn	38525	44555

OPTIONS FOR 7-SERIES
Comfort Seats +300
Park Distance Control +245
Compact Disc Changer[Std on 750iL] +325
Heated Front Seats[Std on 750iL] +150
Traction Control System[Std on 750iL] +405

8-SERIES   1995

No changes for the 8-Series.

Category J

Model Description	Trade-in Value	Market Value
2 Dr 850CSi Cpe	44770	52020
2 Dr 850Ci Cpe	39050	45370

Category L

Model Description	Trade-in Value	Market Value
2 Dr 840Ci Cpe	30610	35400

OPTIONS FOR 8-SERIES
Electronic Damp Control +565
Forged Alloy Wheels +330

1994 BMW

3-SERIES   1994

Dual airbags appear on all 3-series models. A new six-cylinder convertible joins the stable and traction control becomes optional for all cars.

RATINGS (SCALE OF 1-10)

Overall	Safety	Reliability	Performance	Comfort	Value
7	7.9	7.5	9.2	8	2.6

Category D

Model Description	Trade-in Value	Market Value
4 Dr 318i Sdn	11635	13785
2 Dr 325i Conv	18245	21445
4 Dr 325i Sdn	14490	17170

Category F

Model Description	Trade-in Value	Market Value
2 Dr 318i Conv	14800	17395
2 Dr 318is Cpe	12800	15045
2 Dr 325is Cpe	15920	18715

OPTIONS FOR 3-SERIES
Auto 4-Speed Transmission +220
Rollover Protection System(Opt on Conv) +340
AM/FM Compact Disc Player +115
Heated Front Seats +90
Leather Seats[Opt on 318is,Sdn] +155
Onboard Computer +90
Sport Seats +115
Traction Control System +90

5-SERIES   1994

A passenger airbag debuts on all models and two new V8s join the lineup. The 535i and M5 are dropped. BMW's traction control system becomes standard on the 530i Touring and optional on other models. Both 525i models gain a premium sound system.

RATINGS (SCALE OF 1-10)

Overall	Safety	Reliability	Performance	Comfort	Value
N/A	N/A	8.7	8.8	8	N/A

Category J

Model Description	Trade-in Value	Market Value
4 Dr 525i Sdn	15825	18505
4 Dr 525i Touring Wgn	15970	18680
4 Dr 530i Sdn	17750	20760
4 Dr 530i Touring Wgn	19570	22885
4 Dr 540i Sdn	20290	23725

OPTIONS FOR 5-SERIES
Auto 4-Speed Transmission[Std on Touring] +220
AM/FM Compact Disc Player +95
Heated Front Seats +105
Onboard Computer[Std on 540i] +105
Traction Control System[Opt on 525i,540i] +285

7-SERIES   1994

No changes for the 7-Series.

Category L

Model Description	Trade-in Value	Market Value
4 Dr 740i Sdn	19795	23110
4 Dr 740iL Sdn	21200	24745
4 Dr 750iL Sdn	27875	32540

OPTIONS FOR 7-SERIES
Elect. Damping Control Susp. +365
Heated Front Seats[Std on 750iL] +120
Traction Control System[Std on 750iL] +330

Don't forget to refer to the Mileage Adjustment Table at the back of this book!

Model Description	Trade-in Value	Market Value	Model Description	Trade-in Value	Market Value

BMW 94-92

8-SERIES 1994

Two new models are introduced to the 8-Series: the 840Ci and the 850CSi. The 840Ci has the same V8 power found in the 740 and 540. The 850CSi gets an increased displacement V12 that offers a whopping 372-horsepower. The CSi comes standard with a sports suspension and a six-speed manual transmission. Unfortunately, the introduction of the CSi takes away from the sportiness of the 850Ci, which is now saddled with a four-speed automatic as the only transmission choice.

Category J

	Trade-in	Market
2 Dr 850CSi Cpe	38210	44685
2 Dr 850Ci Cpe	33165	38790

Category L

2 Dr 840Ci Cpe	25900	30235

OPTIONS FOR 8-SERIES
Elect. Damping Control Susp. +365
Forged Alloy Wheels +270

1993 BMW

3-SERIES 1993

Four-bangers can now be equipped with an automatic transmission. Six-cylinder models get a variable valve timing system that improves low-end torque.

RATINGS (SCALE OF 1-10)

Overall	Safety	Reliability	Performance	Comfort	Value
6.7	6.5	7.4	9.2	8	2.4

Category D

	Trade-in	Market
4 Dr 318i Sdn	9280	11085
2 Dr 325i Conv	13865	16495
4 Dr 325i Sdn	11565	13815

Category F

2 Dr 318is Cpe	10275	12230
2 Dr 325is Cpe	12780	15205

OPTIONS FOR 3-SERIES
Auto 4-Speed Transmission +170
Sports Pkg +170
Heated Front Seats +75
Leather Seats[Opt on Sdn] +125
Onboard Computer[Std on Conv] +75
Sport Seats +95

5-SERIES 1993

Bad news for trees and cows: wood trim and leather upholstery are now standard on the 525i. The 525i gets a variable valve timing system that improves low-end torque. The M5 gets new wheels for 1993.

RATINGS (SCALE OF 1-10)

Overall	Safety	Reliability	Performance	Comfort	Value
N/A	N/A	8.5	8.6	8	N/A

Category J

	Trade-in	Market
4 Dr 525i Sdn	14035	16425
4 Dr 525i Touring Wgn	15045	17610
4 Dr 535i Sdn	16745	19600
4 Dr M5 Sdn	22865	26760

OPTIONS FOR 5-SERIES
Auto 4-Speed Transmission[Std on Touring] +170
Auto Stab Cntrl Susp. +255
Heated Front Seats[Opt on 525i] +85
Leather Seats[Opt on Touring] +250
Onboard Computer[Opt on 525i] +85

7-SERIES 1993

The 7-Series' cheapest model swaps I-6 for V8 power. The entry-level 7-Series is now called the 740 to denote this change. The new engine has 282-horsepower that is mated to a five-speed automatic transmission. More wood for the interior, Z-rated tires, and an upgraded stereo round out the changes for the 1993 7-Series.

Category L

	Trade-in	Market
4 Dr 740i Sdn	16200	19040
4 Dr 740iL Sdn	17390	20440
4 Dr 750iL Sdn	22430	26365

OPTIONS FOR 7-SERIES
Elect Damp Cntrl Susp. +295
Heated Seats[Opt on 740i] +100
Traction Control System[Std on 750iL] +270

8-SERIES 1993

The 850i is now called the 850Ci. A passenger airbag is added to the standard equipment list, as is a split-fold rear seat. All interior materials have been upgraded over previous models.

Category J

	Trade-in	Market
2 Dr 850Ci Cpe	28520	33385

OPTIONS FOR 8-SERIES
Forged Alloy Wheels +200

1992 BMW

3-SERIES 1992

New sheetmetal for the 3-series; all the corners are rounded and the wheelbase is stretched. Interior space is marginally greater than previous models. Interior space is marginally greater than previous models. A driver airbag is added to the equipment list. Buyers can choose between a sports or luxury package, depending on their predilections.

BMW 92-91

RATINGS (SCALE OF 1-10)

Overall	Safety	Reliability	Performance	Comfort	Value
6.7	6.4	6.7	9.2	8	3.3

Category D

Model Description	Trade-in Value	Market Value
2 Dr 318i Conv	10140	12160
4 Dr 318i Sdn	8070	9675
2 Dr 325i Conv	11860	14215
4 Dr 325i Sdn	9835	11795

Category F

Model Description	Trade-in Value	Market Value
2 Dr 318is Cpe	8795	10595
2 Dr 325is Cpe	10815	13025

OPTIONS FOR 3-SERIES
Auto 4-Speed Transmission +130
Appearance Pkg +300
Compact Disc W/fm/tape +125
Heated Front Seats[Std on 318i STD Conv] +60
Leather Seats[Opt on Sdn] +105
Onboard Computer[Std on Conv] +60

5-SERIES   1992

The 525 loses some luxury items from its standard equipment list; the steering wheel is now wrapped in leatherette instead of leather and the spare tire is shod with a steel wheel instead of an alloy. The 535 gains options like a nifty on-board computer and a power-adjustable steering wheel with a position memory. A security system is now standard. The M5 gets better power steering and a higher final-drive ratio. A Touring model is introduced as a wagon body style.

RATINGS (SCALE OF 1-10)

Overall	Safety	Reliability	Performance	Comfort	Value
N/A	N/A	8.1	8.6	8	N/A

Category J

Model Description	Trade-in Value	Market Value
4 Dr 525i Sdn	10950	12940
4 Dr 525i Touring Wgn	11865	14020
4 Dr 535i Sdn	13615	16085

OPTIONS FOR 5-SERIES
Auto 4-Speed Transmission[Std on 535i, Touring] +130
Auto Stability Control +210
Wood & Leather Pkg +195
Heated Front Seats +70
Leather Seats[Opt on 525i] +205
Onboard Computer[Opt on Touring] +70

7-SERIES   1992

7-Series cars equipped with an automatic transmission now have a shift interlock that prevents the car from being shifted out of park without simultaneously applying the brake. The one-touch-down power window feature now applies to all windows, not just the driver's. The 750iL model receives double-paned windows to improve noise reduction. All 1992 7-Series cars get a new Infinity stereo.

Category L

Model Description	Trade-in Value	Market Value
4 Dr 735i Sdn	13405	15935
4 Dr 735iL Sdn	14400	17120
4 Dr 750iL Sdn	17470	20770

OPTIONS FOR 7-SERIES
Auto Stability Control +210
Elect. Damping Control Susp. +240
Heated Front Seats[Std on 750iL] +80

8-SERIES   1992

BMW's most expensive coupe gets a few tweaks for 1992. Models equipped with an automatic transmission now have a shift interlock to prevent the car from unintentionally being shifted out of "park". BMW's Electronic Damping System is improved for 1992 as well, offering greater diversity between the sports and comfort settings.

Category J

Model Description	Trade-in Value	Market Value
2 Dr 850i Cpe	23900	28245

OPTIONS FOR 8-SERIES
Auto Stability Control +245
Elect. Damping Control Susp. +240
Forged Alloy Wheels +165

M5   1992

Category J

Model Description	Trade-in Value	Market Value
4 Dr STD Sdn	21000	24815

1991 BMW

3-SERIES   1991

No changes for the 3-Series.

Category D

Model Description	Trade-in Value	Market Value
2 Dr 318i Conv	8325	10205
4 Dr 318i Sdn	5845	7165
2 Dr 325i Conv	9095	11150
2 Dr 325i Sdn	7700	9435
4 Dr 325i Sdn	7930	9720

Category F

Model Description	Trade-in Value	Market Value
2 Dr 318is Sdn	6975	8415
2 Dr 325iX 4WD Sdn	10150	12245
4 Dr 325iX 4WD Sdn	10175	12275

Category J

Model Description	Trade-in Value	Market Value
2 Dr M3 Sdn	9840	11690

OPTIONS FOR 3-SERIES
Auto 3-Speed Transmission +95
Sport Handling Pkg +255
Leather Seats[Std on Conv] +85
Power Sunroof +90

5-SERIES   1991

No changes for the 1991 5-Series.

Don't forget to refer to the Mileage Adjustment Table at the back of this book!

Model Description	Trade-in Value	Market Value

RATINGS (SCALE OF 1-10)

Overall	Safety	Reliability	Performance	Comfort	Value
N/A	N/A	7.8	8.6	8	N/A

Category J

	Trade-in Value	Market Value
4 Dr 525i Sdn	9855	11705
4 Dr 535i Sdn	11790	14005
4 Dr M5 Sdn	16355	19425

OPTIONS FOR 5-SERIES
Auto 4-Speed Transmission +95
Stability Control +170
Heated Front Seats +55
Leather Seats[Opt on 525i] +165

7-SERIES   1991

No changes for the 7-Series.

Category L

	Trade-in Value	Market Value
4 Dr 735i Sdn	10915	13225
4 Dr 735iL Sdn	11890	14410
4 Dr 750iL Sdn	13850	16780

OPTIONS FOR 7-SERIES
Elect. Damping Control Susp. +170
Electronic Susp. +195
Stability Control +170
Heated Front Seats[Std on 750iL] +65

8-SERIES   1991

BMW's replacement for the 635CSi, the 850i offers V12 power, a six-speed manual transmission and rear-wheel drive. Standard traction control, a driver airbag, antilock brakes and power head restraints are a few of the safety features found on this expensive BMW coupe. A four-speed automatic transmission is optional.

Category J

	Trade-in Value	Market Value
2 Dr 850i Cpe	17630	20945

OPTIONS FOR 8-SERIES
Electronic Susp. +195
Forged Alloy Wheels +135
Stability Control +200

Don't forget to refer to the Mileage Adjustment Table at the back of this book!

BUICK 00-99

Model Description	Trade-in Value	Market Value	Model Description	Trade-in Value	Market Value

BUICK USA

1995 Buick Riviera

2000 BUICK

CENTURY 2000

Buick's midsize Century heads into the new millennium with a Special Edition model commemorating the turn of the century and more horsepower in all three models from a revised 3.1-liter 3100 V6.

Category C

4 Dr Custom Sdn	13960	16300
4 Dr Limited Sdn	15310	17875

OPTIONS FOR CENTURY
AM/FM Stereo Tape +135
Aluminum/Alloy Wheels +255
Climate Control for AC +135
Compact Disc W/fm/tape +265
Cruise Control +180
Dual Power Seats +475
Leather Steering Wheel +80
Power Drivers Seat +245

LESABRE 2000

The best-selling U.S. full-size car for seven straight years, Buick's LeSabre has been totally redesigned for the 2000 model year. Though it looks a lot like a '99, this car has undergone a remarkable transformation, riding on a new platform with mildly tweaked sheetmetal and an entirely reworked cabin. Better ride, steering and seats, plus side airbags and integrated seatbelts, make it an even better value than before.

Category B

4 Dr Custom Sdn	16890	19665
4 Dr Limited Sdn	19485	22680

OPTIONS FOR LESABRE
AM/FM Stereo Tape[Opt on Custom] +140
Aluminum/Alloy Wheels[Opt on Custom] +270
Compact Disc W/fm/tape +305
Leather Seats +560
Traction Control System +145

PARK AVENUE 2000

Enjoying mild sales success since its 1997 redesign, Buick's full-size Park Avenue gets only minor refinements in the areas of safety, stability and comfort for 2000. The biggest news is the addition of StabiliTrak, GM's advanced vehicle stability control system.

Category A

4 Dr STD Sdn	21950	25305
4 Dr Ultra Sprchgd Sdn	25325	29200

OPTIONS FOR PARK AVENUE
Compact Disc W/fm/tape +520
Leather Seats[Opt on STD] +565

REGAL 2000

For the 2000 model year, the "Official Car of the Supercharged Family" gets new alloy wheels, a standard body-colored grille on the GS and two new colors, Gold Metallic and Sterling Silver. Inside, there's now a split-folding rear seat and an optional side airbag for the driver on leather-lined Regals.

Category C

4 Dr GS Sprchgd Sdn	17845	20835
4 Dr LS Sdn	15870	18530
4 Dr LSE Sdn Sdn	16205	18925

OPTIONS FOR REGAL
Touring Pkg +715
Aluminum/Alloy Wheels[Std on GS] +255
Automatic Dimming Mirror +90
Climate Control for AC +135
Compact Disc W/fm/tape +265
Leather Seats[Std on GS] +505
Power Drivers Seat[Opt on LS] +245
Power Moonroof +560
Steer. Whl. Radio Cntrls +125

1999 BUICK

CENTURY 1999

After a complete redesign in 1997 put the Century into carryover status last year, 1999 brings a host of safety feature improvements, many of them standard. Additionally, the suspension has been retuned for less body roll, the sound systems have been upgraded and one new paint color, called Auburn Nightmist, has been added.

Model Description	Trade-in Value	Market Value

RATINGS (SCALE OF 1-10)

Overall	Safety	Reliability	Performance	Comfort	Value
N/A	7.3	8.7	8	7.9	N/A

Category C
4 Dr Custom Sdn	12025	14150
4 Dr Limited Sdn	12880	15155

OPTIONS FOR CENTURY
AM/FM Stereo Tape +110
Aluminum/Alloy Wheels +205
Automatic Dimming Mirror +75
Climate Control for AC +110
Cruise Control +145
Dual Power Seats +390
Leather Seats +415

LESABRE 1999

Buick's LeSabre celebrates its 40th year in the marketplace as a carryover model for 1999. Perhaps deciding there's no need to mess with success (more than 6 million LeSabres have been sold since the nameplate's 1959 introduction), Buick has merely made some emissions system improvements for '99, and added two exterior metallic paint choices, Sterling Silver and Dark Bronzemist.

RATINGS (SCALE OF 1-10)

Overall	Safety	Reliability	Performance	Comfort	Value
N/A	7.6	8.9	8.6	8.1	N/A

Category B
4 Dr Custom Sdn	14675	17150
4 Dr Limited Sdn	16785	19610

OPTIONS FOR LESABRE
AM/FM Stereo Tape[Opt on Custom] +115
Aluminum/Alloy Wheels[Opt on Custom] +220
Compact Disc W/fm/tape +250
Leather Seats +460
Power Drivers Seat +210
Power Mirrors +65

PARK AVENUE 1999

Riding a wave of sales success since its 1997 redesign, Buick didn't feel like fiddling much with its Park Avenue recipe for 1999. One noticeable change is a revision of the Park Avenue's taillamps, which are now similar to those found on the upscale Ultra model. Also new this year is an enhanced eight-speaker audio system dubbed Concert Sound III, a new hood-to-fender seal for improved appearance, an adjustable rubber bumper for the decklid, and four new exterior colors.

RATINGS (SCALE OF 1-10)

Overall	Safety	Reliability	Performance	Comfort	Value
N/A	N/A	9	8.4	8.4	N/A

Category A
4 Dr STD Sdn	19370	22605
4 Dr Ultra Sprchgd Sdn	22355	26085

OPTIONS FOR PARK AVENUE
Chrome Wheels +655
Compact Disc W/fm/tape +425
Leather Seats[Opt on STD]+460
Power Moonroof +850

REGAL 1999

Performance-oriented changes, such as more power, sporty tweaks to the steering and suspension, firmer motor mounts and the addition of a strut tower brace underhood, lead the news for the '99 Regal. Other changes include enhancements to the ABS and traction control systems, as well as the addition of a tire inflation monitor, perimeter lighting and the Concert Sound II audio system to Regal's already long list of standard equipment. New options include a self-dimming electrochromic outside rearview mirror, redesigned 15-inch alloy wheels and the eight-speaker, 220-watt Monsoon audio system. And that's all in addition to a new exterior paint color, Auburn Nightmist.

RATINGS (SCALE OF 1-10)

Overall	Safety	Reliability	Performance	Comfort	Value
N/A	N/A	8.8	8.4	7.8	N/A

Category C
4 Dr GS Sprchgd Sdn	15595	18350
4 Dr LS Sdn	13910	16365

OPTIONS FOR REGAL
LSE Pkg +860
Aluminum/Alloy Wheels[Std on GS] +205
Bucket Seats +110
Compact Disc W/fm/tape +220
Leather Seats[Std on GS] +415
Power Drivers Seat[Std on GS] +200

RIVIERA 1999

We were going to mention that traction control is now standard on the Riviera and that this year brings the choice of four new paint colors (Sterling Silver, Titanium Blue, Gold Firemist and Dark Bronzemist), but that was before Buick decided to pull the plug on the big coupe soon after production began. Now you also need to know that only approximately 2,000 Riveras will be built for the 1999 model year, along with a special run of 200 special edition models dubbed Silver Arrow."

RATINGS (SCALE OF 1-10)

Overall	Safety	Reliability	Performance	Comfort	Value
N/A	N/A	N/A	8.6	8	N/A

BUICK 99-98

Model Description	Trade-in Value	Market Value	Model Description	Trade-in Value	Market Value

Category B
2 Dr STD Sprchgd Cpe   20710   24200

OPTIONS FOR RIVIERA
Chrome Wheels +455
Power Moonroof +650

1998 BUICK

CENTURY   1998

The addition of second-generation airbags, three new exterior colors, one new interior color and the availability of OnStar mobile communications are this year's changes.

RATINGS (SCALE OF 1-10)

Overall	Safety	Reliability	Performance	Comfort	Value
8.1	7.2	8.4	8	7.9	8.8

Category C
4 Dr Custom Sdn   10775   12790
4 Dr Limited Sdn   11555   13715

OPTIONS FOR CENTURY
AM/FM Compact Disc Player +190
Aluminum/Alloy Wheels +170
Climate Control for AC +90
Cruise Control +120
Heated Power Mirrors[Opt on Custom] +55
Leather Seats +340
Power Drivers Seat +165
Power Moonroof +375

LESABRE   1998

Cruise control is standard on base models, OnStar Mobile Communications is a dealer-installed option, Limited models get a couple of electrochromic mirrors, and new colors are on tap inside and out. Second-generation airbags are made standard.

RATINGS (SCALE OF 1-10)

Overall	Safety	Reliability	Performance	Comfort	Value
8.5	7.6	9.1	8.6	8.1	8.9

Category B
4 Dr Custom Sdn   12980   15230
4 Dr Limited Sdn   14855   17435

OPTIONS FOR LESABRE
AM/FM Compact Disc Player +180
Aluminum/Alloy Wheels[Opt on Custom] +180
Auto Load Leveling +100
Dual Power Seats[Opt on Custom] +210
Keyless Entry System[Opt on Custom] +95
Leather Seats +375
Power Mirrors +55
Traction Control System +95

PARK AVENUE   1998

Exterior mirrors can be folded away, a new optional feature tilts the exterior mirrors down for curb viewing during reversing, dealers can install an OnStar Communications system and new colors are available inside and out. Second-generation airbags are made standard.

RATINGS (SCALE OF 1-10)

Overall	Safety	Reliability	Performance	Comfort	Value
N/A	N/A	9	8.4	8.4	8.9

Category A
4 Dr STD Sdn   16700   19550
4 Dr Ultra Sprchgd Sdn   19295   22595

OPTIONS FOR PARK AVENUE
AM/FM Compact Disc Player[Opt on STD] +255
Heads-up Display +150
Heated Front Seats[Opt on STD] +115
Heated Power Mirrors[Opt on STD] +55
Leather Seats[Opt on STD] +375
Power Moonroof +695
Traction Control System[Opt on STD] +115

REGAL   1998

Regal LS gets a new standard four-speed automatic transmission, and three new exterior colors are available. Dealers will install an OnStar Mobile Communications system if the buyer desires, and second-generation airbags are added.

RATINGS (SCALE OF 1-10)

Overall	Safety	Reliability	Performance	Comfort	Value
N/A	N/A	8.2	8.4	7.8	8.2

Category C
4 Dr 25TH Anniversary Sdn   14145   16785
4 Dr GS Sprchgd Sdn   14000   16620
4 Dr LS Sdn   12415   14735

OPTIONS FOR REGAL
Aluminum/Alloy Wheels[Opt on LS] +170
Chrome Wheels[Opt on GS,LS] +330
Climate Control for AC +90
Compact Disc W/fm/tape[Opt on GS,LS] +180
Dual Power Seats +315
Heated Front Seats +105
Leather Seats[Opt on LS] +340
Power Drivers Seat[Opt on LS] +165
Power Moonroof +375

RIVIERA   1998

Supercharged power is standard, OnStar satellite communications system is a new option and de-powered airbags debut. Four exterior colors are new, suspension and steering have been massaged and a

---

Don't forget to refer to the Mileage Adjustment Table at the back of this book!

BUICK 98-97

Model Description	Trade-in Value	Market Value	Model Description	Trade-in Value	Market Value

heated passenger seat with lumbar support has been added to the options list.

RATINGS (SCALE OF 1-10)

Overall	Safety	Reliability	Performance	Comfort	Value
N/A	N/A	8.4	8.6	8	8.1

Category B

	Trade-in	Market
2 Dr STD Sprchgd Cpe	17435	20460

OPTIONS FOR RIVIERA

Chrome Wheels +370
Heated Front Seats +150
Power Moonroof +530
Special Factory Paint +110
Traction Control System +95

SKYLARK   1998

Skylark was sold strictly to fleets for 1998. If you're buying one used, chances are good that it was once a rental car.
Category C

	Trade-in	Market
4 Dr Custom Sdn	8620	10230

OPTIONS FOR SKYLARK

6 cyl 3.1 L Engine +245
Cruise Control +120
Power Windows +175

1997 BUICK

CENTURY   1997

After a decade and a half, Buick finally redesigns its bread-and-butter mid-size sedan, dropping the wagon variant in the process. A spunky 3.1-liter V6 engine, roomier interior, larger trunk and traditional Buick styling cues should convince Grandpa to trade the old warhorse in on a new one.

RATINGS (SCALE OF 1-10)

Overall	Safety	Reliability	Performance	Comfort	Value
7.4	7.2	8	8	7.9	5.9

Category C

	Trade-in	Market
4 Dr Custom Sdn	9510	11445
4 Dr Limited Sdn	10220	12300

OPTIONS FOR CENTURY

Prestige Pkg +385
AM/FM Compact Disc Player +155
Aluminum/Alloy Wheels +140
Automatic Dimming Mirror +50
Climate Control for AC +75
Compact Disc W/fm/tape +145
Cruise Control +95
Dual Power Seats +260
Leather Seats +275
Power Drivers Seat +135
Power Moonroof +305

LESABRE   1997

Buick freshens the somewhat stale LeSabre with new front and rear styling. Redesigned wheel selections, new seats on Custom models, and walnut instrument panel appliques round out the visual changes. Structurally, the LeSabre now meets side-impact standards.

RATINGS (SCALE OF 1-10)

Overall	Safety	Reliability	Performance	Comfort	Value
8.2	7.5	8.3	8.6	8.1	8.3

Category B

	Trade-in	Market
4 Dr Custom Sdn	11045	12975
4 Dr Limited Sdn	12700	14920

OPTIONS FOR LESABRE

Prestige Pkg +335
AM/FM Compact Disc Player +150
Aluminum/Alloy Wheels[Opt on Custom] +150
Automatic Dimming Mirror +35
Cruise Control[Opt on Custom] +100
Dual Power Seats[Opt on Custom] +175
Keyless Entry System[Opt on Custom] +80
Leather Seats +305
Power Drivers Seat +140
Power Mirrors[Opt on Custom] +45
Traction Control System +80

PARK AVENUE   1997

Buick engineers substantially improve the Park Avenue for 1997 by strengthening the body structure, improving interior ergonomics, and introducing a sleek new look. Powertrains are carried over, and two models are available: base and Ultra. Prices have risen, but the Park Avenue represents real value in comparison to other traditional luxury sedans.

RATINGS (SCALE OF 1-10)

Overall	Safety	Reliability	Performance	Comfort	Value
N/A	N/A	8.2	8.4	8.4	8.3

Category A

	Trade-in	Market
4 Dr STD Sdn	14325	16855
4 Dr Ultra Sprchgd Sdn	16665	19600

OPTIONS FOR PARK AVENUE

AM/FM Compact Disc Player[Opt on STD] +210
Automatic Dimming Mirror +75
Chrome Wheels +440
Compact Disc Changer +335
Heated Front Seats[Opt on STD] +95
Heated Power Mirrors[Opt on STD] +45
Leather Seats[Opt on STD] +310
Power Moonroof +570
Traction Control System[Opt on STD] +95

Don't forget to refer to the Mileage Adjustment Table at the back of this book!

Model Description	Trade-in Value	Market Value

REGAL 1997

Long overdue, the complete redesign of the Regal means Buick finally has a viable entry in the midsized sedan marketplace. The standard equipment list is a mile long, including ABS, traction control, dual-zone climate controls, heated exterior mirrors, retained accessory power and battery rundown protection.

RATINGS (SCALE OF 1-10)

Overall	Safety	Reliability	Performance	Comfort	Value
N/A	N/A	7.7	8.4	7.8	8.1

Category C
4 Dr GS Sprchgd Sdn	12185	14660
4 Dr LS Sdn	10940	13165

OPTIONS FOR REGAL

Aluminum/Alloy Wheels[Opt on LS] +140
Automatic Dimming Mirror +50
Chrome Wheels +270
Climate Control for AC +75
Compact Disc W/fm/tape +145
Heated Front Seats +85
Leather Seats[Opt on LS] +275
Power Drivers Seat +135
Power Moonroof +305

RIVIERA 1997

Upgraded transmissions, several new colors inside and out, additional standard equipment and new options summarize minimal changes to the Riviera.

RATINGS (SCALE OF 1-10)

Overall	Safety	Reliability	Performance	Comfort	Value
N/A	N/A	8.1	8.6	8	7.5

Category B
2 Dr STD Cpe	14535	17075
2 Dr STD Sprchgd Cpe	15100	17735

OPTIONS FOR RIVIERA

Automatic Dimming Mirror +35
Chrome Wheels +305
Heated Front Seats +125
Leather Seats +305
Power Moonroof +435
Traction Control System +80

SKYLARK 1997

Skylark gets minimal revisions this year. The standard equipment list is expanded.

RATINGS (SCALE OF 1-10)

Overall	Safety	Reliability	Performance	Comfort	Value
7.8	7.7	8.5	7.2	7.3	8.2

Category C
2 Dr Custom Cpe	7455	8970
4 Dr Custom Sdn	7455	8970
2 Dr Gran Sport Cpe	8500	10225
4 Dr Gran Sport Sdn	8500	10225

OPTIONS FOR SKYLARK

6 cyl 3.1 L Engine[Opt on Custom] +190
AM/FM Stereo Tape[Opt on Custom] +75
Aluminum/Alloy Wheels[Opt on Custom] +140
Cruise Control[Opt on Custom] +95
Keyless Entry System +85
Leather Seats +275
Power Drivers Seat +135
Power Mirrors[Opt on Custom] +50
Power Moonroof +305
Power Windows[Opt on Custom] +140

1996 BUICK

CENTURY 1996

In many states, this design is just a decade away from antique car status. Wagons get the V6 as standard equipment. Power windows, cassette player, rear window defogger and a remote trunk release make the standard equipment list as this ancient A-body rolls into its final year of production.

RATINGS (SCALE OF 1-10)

Overall	Safety	Reliability	Performance	Comfort	Value
7.5	6.5	7.7	7.4	7.3	8.4

Category C
4 Dr STD Sdn	6850	8430
4 Dr STD Wgn	7415	9120

OPTIONS FOR CENTURY

6 cyl 3.1 L Engine[Opt on Sdn] +170
Auto 4-Speed Transmission[Opt on Sdn] +70
AM/FM Stereo Tape +60
Cruise Control +80
Keyless Entry System +70
Leather Seats +225
Luggage Rack +40
Power Drivers Seat +110
Wire Wheel Covers +85

LESABRE 1996

Finally, the Series II engine is standard on LeSabre. Order the Gran Touring suspension, and get the same magnetic variable effort steering found on the Park Avenue Ultra. Now standard on the Custom is an electric rear window defogger and storage armrest. Limited trim levels get Twilight Sentinel, dual automatic ComforTemp climate controls, and a rear seat center armrest.

RATINGS (SCALE OF 1-10)

Overall	Safety	Reliability	Performance	Comfort	Value
8.1	7.5	8.1	8.6	8.1	8.3

Model Description	Trade-in Value	Market Value	Model Description	Trade-in Value	Market Value
Category B			4 Dr Limited Sdn	9065	11155
4 Dr Custom Sdn	9350	11090	4 Dr Olympic Gold Sdn	8820	10850
4 Dr Limited Sdn	10945	12975			

OPTIONS FOR LESABRE
Prestige Pkg +415
AM/FM Compact Disc Player +120
Cruise Control[Opt on Custom] +80
Keyless Entry System[Opt on Custom] +65
Leather Seats +250
Power Drivers Seat +115
Power Passenger Seat +130

OPTIONS FOR REGAL
6 cyl 3.8 L Engine[Opt on Custom] +135
AM/FM Compact Disc Player +130
Keyless Entry System +70
Leather Seats +225
Power Drivers Seat[Std on Gran Sport] +110
Power Moonroof +250
Premium Sound System +140

PARK AVENUE 1996

Ultra gets new Series II supercharged engine as standard equipment, as well as magnetic variable effort steering gear. Colors and trim are revised, battery rundown protection is added, and long-life engine components keep the Park going longer between maintenance stops.

RATINGS (SCALE OF 1-10)

Overall	Safety	Reliability	Performance	Comfort	Value
8.1	7.4	7.9	8.6	8.1	8.3

Category A

4 Dr STD Sdn	11595	13845
4 Dr Ultra Sprchgd Sdn	13450	16060

OPTIONS FOR PARK AVENUE
Luxury Pkg +580
Prestige Pkg +690
AM/FM Compact Disc Player +170
Automatic Dimming Mirror +60
Heated Front Seats +75
Keyless Entry System[Opt on STD] +100
Leather Seats[Opt on STD] +250
Power Moonroof +465
Traction Control System +75

REGAL 1996

The Series II 3.8-liter V6 is standard on Limited and Gran Sport, optional on base Custom models. Standard equipment now includes dual ComforTemp climate controls and a cassette player. Revised wheels, available in chrome, are standard on the Gran Sport. Base V6 is upgraded, and both engines feature long-life engine components.

RATINGS (SCALE OF 1-10)

Overall	Safety	Reliability	Performance	Comfort	Value
N/A	N/A	8	7.4	7.6	8.1

Category C

2 Dr Custom Cpe	8335	10255
4 Dr Custom Sdn	8460	10410
2 Dr Gran Sport Cpe	9125	11230
4 Dr Gran Sport Sdn	9320	11465

RIVIERA 1996

Series II supercharged engine gives top-of-the-line Riv 240 horsepower. There are new colors inside and out, real wood on the dash, and revised climate and radio controls. Chrome wheels are optional.

RATINGS (SCALE OF 1-10)

Overall	Safety	Reliability	Performance	Comfort	Value
N/A	N/A	7.5	8.6	8	8

Category B

2 Dr STD Cpe	12300	14585
2 Dr STD Sprchgd Cpe	12750	15120

OPTIONS FOR RIVIERA
Prestige Pkg +265
Chrome Wheels +250
Heated Front Seats +100
Leather Seats +250
Power Moonroof +355
Traction Control System +65

ROADMASTER 1996

Last year for 260 hp land yacht. All models are designated Collector's Editions.

RATINGS (SCALE OF 1-10)

Overall	Safety	Reliability	Performance	Comfort	Value
7.6	7.2	6.5	7.8	8.4	8.3

Category B

4 Dr Estate Wgn	12595	14935
4 Dr Limited Sdn	12555	14890
4 Dr STD Sdn	11695	13865

OPTIONS FOR ROADMASTER
Limited Pkg +405
Prestige Pkg +280
Auto Load Leveling +65
Camper/Towing Package +135
Compact Disc W/frn/tape +135
Heated Front Seats +100
Keyless Entry System[Std on Limited] +65
Leather Seats +250
Power Drivers Seat +115
Power Passenger Seat +130

Model Description	Trade-in Value	Market Value

Model Description	Trade-in Value	Market Value

SKYLARK 1996

Styling changes inside and out make the Skylark far more marketable, and credible. Dual airbags are new, as are three-point seatbelts mounted to the B-pillar where they should be. A new twin-cam engine replaces the 2.3-liter Quad 4, and automatic transmissions include traction control. Air conditioning, a rear window defroster, and a tilt wheel are now standard. Long-life engine components round out the long list of improvements to Buick's lame duck.

RATINGS (SCALE OF 1-10)

Overall	Safety	Reliability	Performance	Comfort	Value
7.8	7.8	8.2	7.2	7.3	8.5

Category C

2 Dr Custom Cpe	6200	7625
4 Dr Custom Sdn	6200	7625
4 Dr Olympic Gold Sdn	6360	7825

OPTIONS FOR SKYLARK

6 cyl 3.1 L Engine +170
Gran Sport Pkg +485
AM/FM Stereo Tape +60
Cruise Control[Opt on Custom] +80
Keyless Entry System +70
Leather Seats +225
Power Drivers Seat +110
Power Moonroof +250
Power Windows +115

1995 BUICK

CENTURY 1995

Instruments newly backlit, and seats are revised.

RATINGS (SCALE OF 1-10)

Overall	Safety	Reliability	Performance	Comfort	Value
7.3	7	7.3	7.4	7.3	7.4

Category C

4 Dr Custom Sdn	5725	7245
4 Dr Limited Sdn	6270	7935
4 Dr Special Sdn	5410	6845
4 Dr Special Wgn	5455	6905

OPTIONS FOR CENTURY

6 cyl 3.1 L Engine[Opt on Special] +145
Auto 4-Speed Transmission[Opt on Special] +60
AM/FM Stereo Tape[Std on Limited] +50
Cruise Control[Std on Limited] +65
Keyless Entry System[Std on Limited] +55
Power Drivers Seat[Std on Limited] +90
Power Windows[Opt on Special] +95

LESABRE 1995

New climate controls and radios are major changes.

RATINGS (SCALE OF 1-10)

Overall	Safety	Reliability	Performance	Comfort	Value
8.2	8.3	7.9	8.6	8.1	8.2

Category B

4 Dr Custom Sdn	7930	9560
4 Dr Limited Sdn	8670	10455

OPTIONS FOR LESABRE

AM/FM Compact Disc Player +100
Cruise Control[Opt on Custom] +65
Keyless Entry System[Opt on Custom] +50
Leather Seats +205
Power Drivers Seat[Opt on Custom] +95

PARK AVENUE 1995

Base engine upgraded to 3800 Series II status; makes 35 more horsepower than previous year. Base models get styling tweaks front and rear. New climate controls and radios are added.

RATINGS (SCALE OF 1-10)

Overall	Safety	Reliability	Performance	Comfort	Value
8.2	8.3	7.9	8.6	8.1	8.2

Category A

4 Dr STD Sdn	9495	11395
4 Dr Ultra Sprchgd Sdn	11085	13305

OPTIONS FOR PARK AVENUE

Luxury Pkg +370
Prestige Pkg +665
AM/FM Compact Disc Player +140
Heated Front Seats +60
Keyless Entry System[Opt on STD] +80
Leather Seats[Opt on STD] +205
Power Moonroof +380

REGAL 1995

New interior has dual airbags housed in revised instrument panel. Gauges are actually legible. Seats are new, too. Fake wood has been chopped from door panels. Exterior styling is updated.

RATINGS (SCALE OF 1-10)

Overall	Safety	Reliability	Performance	Comfort	Value
N/A	N/A	5.6	7.4	7.6	8.1

Category C

2 Dr Custom Cpe	7105	8990
4 Dr Custom Sdn	7220	9135
4 Dr Custom Select Sdn	6775	8570
2 Dr Gran Sport Cpe	7590	9605
4 Dr Gran Sport Sdn	7545	9550
4 Dr Limited Sdn	7335	9280

OPTIONS FOR REGAL

6 cyl 3.8 L Engine[Opt on Custom] +110
AM/FM Compact Disc Player +105

Don't forget to refer to the Mileage Adjustment Table at the back of this book!

Model Description	Trade-in Value	Market Value
Keyless Entry System[Std on Custom Select] +55		
Leather Seats +185		
Power Drivers Seat[Std on Custom Select] +90		
Power Moonroof +205		

RIVIERA 1995

All-new Riv debuts with controversial styling. Dual airbags and ABS are standard. Base engine is 3800 Series II V6; optional is a supercharged 3.8-liter. Traction control is optional.

RATINGS (SCALE OF 1-10)

Overall	Safety	Reliability	Performance	Comfort	Value
N/A	N/A	7.3	8.6	8	7

Category B		
2 Dr STD Cpe	9795	11805
2 Dr STD Sprchgd Cpe	10375	12505

OPTIONS FOR RIVIERA

AM/FM Compact Disc Player +100		
Heated Front Seats +80		
Leather Seats +205		
Power Moonroof +290		

ROADMASTER 1995

New radios and larger rearview mirrors are added. Cassette player is made standard. Wagon gets standard alloy wheels. New options are heated front seats and memory feature for power driver's seat.

RATINGS (SCALE OF 1-10)

Overall	Safety	Reliability	Performance	Comfort	Value
7.5	7.9	5.2	7.8	8.4	8.3

Category B		
4 Dr Estate Wgn	10315	12435
4 Dr Limited Sdn	10495	12650
4 Dr STD Sdn	9640	11620

OPTIONS FOR ROADMASTER

Limited Wagon Pkg +265		
Camper/Towing Package +110		
Compact Disc W/fm/tape +110		
Keyless Entry System[Std on Limited] +50		
Leather Seats +205		
Power Drivers Seat[Std on Limited] +95		

SKYLARK 1995

Rear suspension is revised. New base engine is 150-horsepower Quad 4, packing 35 more ponies than previous base engine. GS gets 3.1-liter V6 standard. Power sunroof is a new option.

RATINGS (SCALE OF 1-10)

Overall	Safety	Reliability	Performance	Comfort	Value
7.3	7.2	7.7	7.2	7	7.2

Category C		
2 Dr Custom Cpe	4625	5855
4 Dr Custom Sdn	4815	6090
2 Dr Gran Sport Cpe	5760	7290
4 Dr Gran Sport Sdn	5760	7290

OPTIONS FOR SKYLARK

6 cyl 3.1 L Engine[Opt on Custom] +145		
Auto 4-Speed Transmission[Opt on Custom] +60		
AM/FM Stereo Tape[Opt on Custom] +50		
Air Conditioning[Opt on Custom] +245		
Cruise Control[Opt on Custom] +65		
Keyless Entry System +55		
Power Drivers Seat +90		
Power Moonroof +205		
Power Windows[Opt on Custom] +95		

1994 BUICK

CENTURY 1994

A driver airbag and ABS are standard on all models. This marks the first time ABS is offered on the Century. Coupe trimmed from lineup. The 2.2-liter engine gains 10 horsepower, and the optional 3.3-liter V6 is replaced by a 3.1-liter unit. When transmission is shifted into "Park," automatic door locks unlock themselves. Defeat this feature by removing a fuse. Tilt steering is standard on Special. New gauges debut.

RATINGS (SCALE OF 1-10)

Overall	Safety	Reliability	Performance	Comfort	Value
7	6.5	5.8	7.4	7.3	7.8

Category C		
4 Dr Custom Sdn	4805	6175
4 Dr Special Sdn	4555	5855
4 Dr Special Wgn	4795	6160

OPTIONS FOR CENTURY

6 cyl 3.1 L Engine +125		
Auto 4-Speed Transmission +50		
AM/FM Stereo Tape +40		
Cruise Control +55		
Keyless Entry System +45		
Power Drivers Seat +75		
Power Windows +80		

LESABRE 1994

Passenger airbag installed. Traction control system now cuts engine power to slipping wheels in addition to applying brake. Front seat travel increased one inch.

RATINGS (SCALE OF 1-10)

Overall	Safety	Reliability	Performance	Comfort	Value
8.3	8.4	7.9	8.6	8.1	8.5

Don't forget to refer to the Mileage Adjustment Table at the back of this book!

Model Description	Trade-in Value	Market Value	Model Description	Trade-in Value	Market Value

Category B

	Trade-in	Market
4 Dr Custom Sdn	6340	7850
4 Dr Limited Sdn	7205	8920

OPTIONS FOR LESABRE

AM/FM Stereo Tape[Opt on Custom] +40
Keyless Entry System[Opt on Custom] +45
Leather Seats +165
Power Drivers Seat[Opt on Custom] +75

PARK AVENUE   1994

Passenger airbag debuts, and Ultra model gets 20 more horsepower. Traction control system now cuts engine power to slipping wheels in addition to applying brake, and can be turned off if desired. Remote keyless entry, power trunk pull-down and auto dimming rearview mirror added to Ultra standard equipment list. Front seat travel increased one inch. Heated front seats are newly optional.

RATINGS (SCALE OF 1-10)

Overall	Safety	Reliability	Performance	Comfort	Value
8.4	8.4	8.4	8.6	8.1	8.6

Category A

	Trade-in	Market
4 Dr STD Sdn	7625	9365
4 Dr Ultra Sprchgd Sdn	8925	10960

OPTIONS FOR PARK AVENUE

Prestige Pkg +285
AM/FM Compact Disc Player +115
Astro Roof +355
Keyless Entry System[Opt on STD] +65
Leather Seats[Opt on STD] +170

REGAL   1994

Driver airbag and ABS standard on all Regals. 3.1-liter V6 gets 20 more horsepower. Power windows standard across the board, and automatic door locks automatically unlock when car is shifted into "Park." Defeat this feature by removing a fuse.

RATINGS (SCALE OF 1-10)

Overall	Safety	Reliability	Performance	Comfort	Value
7.4	6.5	6.3	8.2	7.3	8.5

Category C

	Trade-in	Market
2 Dr Custom Cpe	5475	7040
4 Dr Custom Sdn	5465	7030
2 Dr Gran Sport Cpe	6055	7785
4 Dr Gran Sport Sdn	6145	7895
4 Dr Limited Sdn	6000	7710

OPTIONS FOR REGAL

6 cyl 3.8 L Engine[Opt on Custom] +95
AM/FM Stereo Tape +40
Cruise Control +55
Leather Seats +150

Power Drivers Seat +75
Power Moonroof +165

ROADMASTER   1994

Detuned Corvette engine transplanted into big Buick, giving Roadmaster 80 additional horsepower. Dual airbags housed in redesigned dashboard with new gauges.

RATINGS (SCALE OF 1-10)

Overall	Safety	Reliability	Performance	Comfort	Value
7.9	8	5.7	7.8	8.4	9.4

Category B

	Trade-in	Market
4 Dr Estate Wgn	7495	9280
4 Dr Limited Sdn	7775	9630
4 Dr STD Sdn	6625	8200

OPTIONS FOR ROADMASTER

AM/FM Compact Disc Player +80
Camper/Towing Package +90
Keyless Entry System[Std on Limited] +45
Leather Seats +165
Power Drivers Seat[Opt on STD] +75

SKYLARK   1994

Driver airbag added to all models. New 3.1-liter V6 replaces 3.3-liter V6 from 1993. Automatic transmission gets overdrive gear. Gran Sport and Limited gain standard equipment including air conditioning, power windows, cruise control and tilt steering wheel. Automatic door locks automatically unlock when car is put in "Park." Defeat this feature by removing a fuse.

RATINGS (SCALE OF 1-10)

Overall	Safety	Reliability	Performance	Comfort	Value
7.1	7.2	7.3	7.2	7	7

Category C

	Trade-in	Market
2 Dr Custom Cpe	3905	5020
4 Dr Custom Sdn	3880	4990
2 Dr Gran Sport Cpe	5200	6680
4 Dr Gran Sport Sdn	5200	6680
4 Dr Limited Sdn	4620	5940

OPTIONS FOR SKYLARK

6 cyl 3.1 L Engine[Std on Gran Sport] +125
Auto 4-Speed Transmission[Std on Gran Sport] +50
AM/FM Stereo Tape +40
Air Conditioning[Opt on Custom] +200
Cruise Control[Opt on Custom] +55
Power Drivers Seat +75
Power Windows[Opt on Custom] +80

Model Description	Trade-in Value	Market Value	Model Description	Trade-in Value	Market Value

1993 BUICK

CENTURY 1993

Driver airbag standard on Custom and Limited; optional on Special. New 2.2-liter four-cylinder replaces old 2.5-liter unit with no loss of power. Fuel tank capacity increased.

RATINGS (SCALE OF 1-10)

Overall	Safety	Reliability	Performance	Comfort	Value
7	4.6	7.4	7.4	7.3	8.3

Category C

	Trade-in	Market
2 Dr Custom Cpe	3800	5050
4 Dr Custom Sdn	3870	5140
4 Dr Custom Wgn	4185	5565
4 Dr Limited Sdn	4095	5440
4 Dr Special Sdn	3470	4610
4 Dr Special Wgn	3645	4845

OPTIONS FOR CENTURY
6 cyl 3.3 L Engine +105
Auto 4-Speed Transmission +40
Premium Pkg +150
Prestige Pkg +200
Cruise Control +45
Keyless Entry System +35
Power Drivers Seat +60
Power Windows +65

LESABRE 1993

Engine gets more torque, and both ABS and power door locks standard on all models. Limited offers variable-assist steering.

RATINGS (SCALE OF 1-10)

Overall	Safety	Reliability	Performance	Comfort	Value
7.8	7.2	7.2	8.6	8.1	8

Category B

	Trade-in	Market
4 Dr 90th Anniversary Sdn	4740	5940
4 Dr Custom Sdn	4965	6225
4 Dr Limited Sdn	5200	6520

OPTIONS FOR LESABRE
Luxury Pkg +185
Prestige Pkg +200
Aluminum/Alloy Wheels +65
Cruise Control[Opt on Custom,Limited] +45
Leather Seats +135
Power Drivers Seat[Opt on Custom,Limited] +65

PARK AVENUE 1993

Base V6 gains power. Revisions made to grilles and taillights. An automatic ride control system adjusts the suspension between three different modes ranging from soft to firm.

RATINGS (SCALE OF 1-10)

Overall	Safety	Reliability	Performance	Comfort	Value
N/A	N/A	7.5	8.6	8.1	8.5

Category A

	Trade-in	Market
4 Dr STD Sdn	6380	7930
4 Dr Ultra Sprchgd Sdn	7185	8930

OPTIONS FOR PARK AVENUE
Luxury Pkg +240
Prestige Pkg +255
AM/FM Compact Disc Player +95
Leather Seats[Opt on STD] +140
Power Sunroof +305

REGAL 1993

A new transmission, grille and taillights debut. The 3.8-liter V6 gains torque. 15-inch wheels replace 14-inch wheels. Optional on Limited and Gran Sport is a steering wheel with radio controls.

RATINGS (SCALE OF 1-10)

Overall	Safety	Reliability	Performance	Comfort	Value
7.1	4.8	6.6	8.2	7.3	8.4

Category C

	Trade-in	Market
2 Dr Custom Cpe	4260	5665
4 Dr Custom Sdn	4325	5750
2 Dr Gran Sport Cpe	4880	6485
4 Dr Gran Sport Sdn	4935	6555
2 Dr Limited Cpe	4675	6210
4 Dr Limited Sdn	4725	6275

OPTIONS FOR REGAL
6 cyl 3.8 L Engine[Std on Gran Sport] +75
AM/FM Stereo Tape +35
Aluminum/Alloy Wheels[Std on Gran Sport] +60
Anti-Lock Brakes[Opt on Custom] +120
Cruise Control +45
Leather Seats +125
Power Drivers Seat +60
Power Sunroof +135
Power Windows +65

RIVIERA 1993

Gran Touring model gets larger wheels and tires from defunct Reatta.

Category B

	Trade-in	Market
2 Dr STD Cpe	6125	7680

OPTIONS FOR RIVIERA
AM/FM Compact Disc Player +65
Aluminum/Alloy Wheels +65
Leather Seats +135
Power Sunroof +215

Don't forget to refer to the Mileage Adjustment Table at the back of this book!

Model Description	Trade-in Value	Market Value

ROADMASTER 1993

Wagons get Solar-Ray tinted windshield. Both models receive power window lockout switch and more sound deadening.

RATINGS (SCALE OF 1-10)

Overall	Safety	Reliability	Performance	Comfort	Value
N/A	N/A	7.3	7.4	8.4	9.3

Category B

	Trade-in	Market
4 Dr Estate Wgn	5935	7440
4 Dr Limited Sdn	6195	7765
4 Dr STD Sdn	5620	7045

OPTIONS FOR ROADMASTER

Prestige Pkg +175
AM/FM Compact Disc Player +65
Aluminum/Alloy Wheels[Std on Estate] +65
Camper/Towing Package +75
Leather Seats +135
Power Drivers Seat[Std on Limited] +65

SKYLARK 1993

New entry-level Custom model debuts. Base engine loses five horsepower. Split-folding rear seat optional on Limited; not available on Custom. Adjustable Ride Control moves to GS options list from standard equipment roster.

RATINGS (SCALE OF 1-10)

Overall	Safety	Reliability	Performance	Comfort	Value
6.5	4.1	7	7.2	7	7

Category C

	Trade-in	Market
2 Dr Custom Cpe	3195	4245
4 Dr Custom Sdn	3195	4245
2 Dr Gran Sport Cpe	3865	5135
4 Dr Gran Sport Sdn	3865	5135
2 Dr Limited Cpe	3415	4535
4 Dr Limited Sdn	3415	4535

OPTIONS FOR SKYLARK

6 cyl 3.3 L Engine[Std on Gran Sport] +105
AM/FM Stereo Tape +35
Air Conditioning +160
Cruise Control +45
Power Drivers Seat +60
Power Windows +65

1992 BUICK

CENTURY 1992

Power door locks made standard.

RATINGS (SCALE OF 1-10)

Overall	Safety	Reliability	Performance	Comfort	·Value
6.8	4.1	7	7.4	7.3	8.2

Category C

	Trade-in	Market
2 Dr Custom Cpe	2850	4050
4 Dr Custom Sdn	2890	4105
4 Dr Custom Wgn	3065	4350
4 Dr Limited Sdn	3070	4355
4 Dr Limited Wgn	3205	4545
4 Dr Special Sdn	2710	3845

OPTIONS FOR CENTURY

6 cyl 3.3 L Engine +90
Auto 4-Speed Transmission +35
Cruise Control +35
Power Drivers Seat +50
Power Windows +50

LESABRE 1992

All-new car debuts based on 1991 Park Avenue redesign. ABS is standard on Limited, optional on Custom. Driver airbag is standard. Coupe dropped; all LeSabres are sedans. 3.8-liter V6 gets more power. Theft-deterrent system, power windows, and child-proof rear door locks are standard.

RATINGS (SCALE OF 1-10)

Overall	Safety	Reliability	Performance	Comfort	Value
7.6	6.6	6.7	8.6	8.1	7.9

Category B

	Trade-in	Market
4 Dr Custom Sdn	3985	5160
4 Dr Limited Sdn	4240	5490

OPTIONS FOR LESABRE

Anti-Lock Brakes[Opt on Custom] +110
Leather Seats +110
Power Drivers Seat +50

PARK AVENUE 1992

Ultra gets 205-horsepower supercharged V6. Traction control is a new option. Variable-effort power steering and dual cupholders are new for all Park Avenues.

RATINGS (SCALE OF 1-10)

Overall	Safety	Reliability	Performance	Comfort	Value
N/A	N/A	7	8.6	8.1	7.9

Category A

	Trade-in	Market
4 Dr STD Sdn	5030	6475
4 Dr Ultra Sprchgd Sdn	5710	7350

OPTIONS FOR PARK AVENUE

Premium Pkg +125
Prestige Pkg +245
AM/FM Compact Disc Player +75
Astro Roof +240
Leather Seats[Opt on STD] +115

REGAL 1992

Gran Sport no longer an option package; becomes a full-fledged model designation. ABS newly standard

Don't forget to refer to the Mileage Adjustment Table at the back of this book!

BUICK 92-91

Model Description	Trade-in Value	Market Value	Model Description	Trade-in Value	Market Value

on Gran Sport and Limited. Power door locks made standard on all Regals. Power front passenger seat is new option.

RATINGS (SCALE OF 1-10)

Overall	Safety	Reliability	Performance	Comfort	Value
7	4.9	6.2	8.2	7.3	8.3

Category C
2 Dr Custom Cpe	3320	4710
4 Dr Custom Sdn	3370	4780
2 Dr Gran Sport Cpe	3705	5260
4 Dr Gran Sport Sdn	3840	5450
2 Dr Limited Cpe	3545	5035
4 Dr Limited Sdn	3610	5125

OPTIONS FOR REGAL
6 cyl 3.8 L Engine[Std on Gran Sport] +80
Anti-Lock Brakes[Opt on Custom] +95
Leather Seats +100
Power Drivers Seat +50
Power Sunroof +110
Power Windows +50

RIVIERA 1992

Solar-control glass is standard. Brake system gets larger rotors and calipers.
Category B
2 Dr STD Cpe	5065	6550

OPTIONS FOR RIVIERA
Astro Roof +220
Leather Seats +110
Power Passenger Seat +60

ROADMASTER 1992

Wagon gets 5.7-liter engine. Sedan debuts.

RATINGS (SCALE OF 1-10)

Overall	Safety	Reliability	Performance	Comfort	Value
N/A	N/A	5.7	7.4	8.4	8.6

Category B
4 Dr Estate Wgn	4570	5915
4 Dr Limited Sdn	4795	6200
4 Dr STD Sdn	4340	5620

OPTIONS FOR ROADMASTER
Cruise Control[Opt on Estate] +35
Leather Seats +110
Power Drivers Seat[Std on Limited] +50

SKYLARK 1992

Redesign meant to bring younger buyers into showrooms backfires. Choice of four- or six-cylinder engines available. Automatic transmission, ABS, power door locks and split-folding rear seat are standard. Still has door-mounted seatbelts. Adjustable Ride Control,

standard on GS and optional on other Skylarks, allows driver to select one of three suspension settings.

RATINGS (SCALE OF 1-10)

Overall	Safety	Reliability	Performance	Comfort	Value
6.4	4.1	6.7	7.2	7	6.9

Category C
2 Dr Gran Sport Cpe	2930	4160
4 Dr Gran Sport Sdn	2930	4160
2 Dr STD Cpe	2565	3645
4 Dr STD Sdn	2565	3645

OPTIONS FOR SKYLARK
6 cyl 3.3 L Engine[Opt on STD] +90
Air Conditioning +135
Power Drivers Seat +50
Power Windows +50

1991 BUICK

CENTURY 1991

Remote keyless entry and steering wheel radio controls are newly available.

RATINGS (SCALE OF 1-10)

Overall	Safety	Reliability	Performance	Comfort	Value
6.7	3.7	7	7.4	7.3	8.1

Category C
2 Dr Custom Cpe	2600	3785
4 Dr Custom Sdn	2580	3760
4 Dr Custom Wgn	2740	3990
4 Dr Limited Sdn	2650	3860
4 Dr Limited Wgn	2900	4225

OPTIONS FOR CENTURY
6 cyl 3.3 L Engine +85
Auto 4-Speed Transmission +25
Prestige Pkg +110
Power Door Locks +35
Power Drivers Seat +40
Power Windows +40

LESABRE 1991

New 3.8-liter V6 engine replaces old one.
Category B
4 Dr Custom Sdn	3025	4080
2 Dr Limited Cpe	3240	4365
4 Dr Limited Sdn	3260	4390
2 Dr STD Cpe	3045	4100

OPTIONS FOR LESABRE
Anti-Lock Brakes +90
Leather Seats +90
Power Door Locks +35
Power Drivers Seat +40
Power Windows +40

Don't forget to refer to the Mileage Adjustment Table at the back of this book!

Model Description	Trade-in Value	Market Value	Model Description	Trade-in Value	Market Value

PARK AVENUE   1991

All-new design debuts. New 3.8-liter V6 engine installed under the hood. Driver airbag and ABS are standard. Ultra gets standard dual-zone climate controls; this feature is optional on base car.

RATINGS (SCALE OF 1-10)

Overall	Safety	Reliability	Performance	Comfort	Value
N/A	N/A	7	8.6	8.1	7.9

Category A
4 Dr STD Sdn	4345	5765
4 Dr Ultra Sdn	4755	6305

OPTIONS FOR PARK AVENUE
Luxury Pkg +120
Prestige Pkg +160
Astro Roof +195
Leather Seats[Opt on STD] +90

REATTA   1991

New transmission and alloy wheels debut. New 3.8-liter V6 installed under the hood. Final year for slow-selling sportster.
Category C
2 Dr STD Conv	5400	7860
2 Dr STD Cpe	4970	7240

OPTIONS FOR REATTA
Power Sunroof +90

REGAL   1991

Teensy analog gauges replace yucky digital readouts, except on Custom coupe. New 3.8-liter V6 is optional on Regal except Gran Sport, on which it is standard. ABS optional on all Regals.

RATINGS (SCALE OF 1-10)

Overall	Safety	Reliability	Performance	Comfort	Value
6.7	4.6	5.3	8.2	7.3	8.3

Category C
2 Dr Custom Cpe	2810	4090
4 Dr Custom Sdn	2755	4015
2 Dr Limited Cpe	2940	4285
4 Dr Limited Sdn	2995	4360

OPTIONS FOR REGAL
6 cyl 3.8 L Engine +55
Anti-Lock Brakes +80
Leather Seats +85
Power Door Locks +35
Power Drivers Seat +40
Power Sunroof +90
Power Windows +40

RIVIERA   1991

Improved 3.8-liter V6 powers Riviera. Concert Sound II speaker system made standard. Retained accessory power means windows and sunroof can be shut after car is turned off.
Category B
2 Dr STD Cpe	4045	5445

OPTIONS FOR RIVIERA
Prestige Pkg +110
Astro Roof +180
Leather Seats +90

ROADMASTER   1991

Buick revives legendary moniker for huge new rear-drive wagon with glass Vista Roof over rear seat. ABS and driver airbag are standard. Powered by 5.0-liter V8.

RATINGS (SCALE OF 1-10)

Overall	Safety	Reliability	Performance	Comfort	Value
N/A	N/A	5.9	7.4	8.4	7.6

Category B
4 Dr Estate Wgn	3590	4835

OPTIONS FOR ROADMASTER
Leather Seats +90
Power Door Locks +35
Power Drivers Seat +40

SKYLARK   1991

No changes.
Category C
2 Dr Custom Cpe	1955	2845
4 Dr Custom Sdn	1955	2845
2 Dr Gran Sport Cpe	2210	3220
4 Dr Luxury Sdn	2240	3265
2 Dr STD Cpe	1900	2765
4 Dr STD Sdn	1750	2550

OPTIONS FOR SKYLARK
4 cyl 2.3 L Quad 4 Engine +90
6 cyl 3.3 L Engine +85
Air Conditioning +110
Power Door Locks +35
Power Drivers Seat +40
Power Windows +40

Model Description	Trade-in Value	Market Value

CADILLAC · USA

1997 Cadillac DeVille

2000 CADILLAC

CATERA — 2000

Mildly successful front and rear styling enhancements and a revised interior update Catera for 2000. Side airbags are standard on all models, and an optional sport package finally arrives with 17-inch wheels, heated sport seats, a spoiler, rocker panel extensions, xenon HID headlights and brushed-aluminum interior trim. Electronic drive-by-wire throttle control and a revised torque converter improve oomph off the line. Revised suspension tuning better controls ride motions and body roll, while tightened steering improves road feel. Two new colors round out the changes.

Category A

Model	Trade-in	Market
4 Dr STD Sdn	22630	26135
4 Dr Sport Sdn Sdn	24065	27795

OPTIONS FOR CATERA
Luxury Pkg +725
Alarm System[Opt on STD] +240
Bose Sound System +505
Compact Disc W/fm/tape +520
Dual Power Seats[Opt on STD] +390
Power Moonroof +1040

DEVILLE — 2000

The 2000 DeVille is all-new inside and out and showcases new automotive technologies such as Night Vision, Ultrasonic Rear Parking Assist and the newest generation of GM's StabiliTrak traction-control system. It also boasts improvements to the Northstar V8 that not only improve fuel economy, but make this engine operate even smoother than before.

Category A

Model	Trade-in	Market
4 Dr DHS Sdn	33740	38960
4 Dr DTS Sdn	33740	38960
4 Dr STD Sdn	30215	34890

OPTIONS FOR DEVILLE
Adaptive Front Seats +815
Navigation System +1155
Night Vision +1405
Safety/Security Pkg +640
Leather Seats[Opt on STD] +565

ELDORADO — 2000

The Northstar V8s have been improved, and the standard Eldorado gets a new logo, ESC (for Eldorado Sport Coupe). The racy Eldorado Touring Coupe (ETC) lands exterior enhancements such as body-color fascia moldings and side inserts (replacing chrome), new seven-spoke wheels with Cadillac logos in the center caps, and a new ETC decklid logo.

Category A

Model	Trade-in	Market
2 Dr ESC Cpe	28375	32770
2 Dr ETC Cpe	30900	35685

OPTIONS FOR ELDORADO
Bose Sound System[Std on ETC] +505
Chrome Wheels +805
Compact Disc W/fm/tape[Std on ETC] +520
Heated Front Seats[Std on ETC] +170
Power Moonroof +1040

ESCALADE — 2000

The big change for 2000 is the availability of vertical-split rear cargo doors in addition to the standard split-tailgate rear-hatch design.

Category G

Model	Trade-in	Market
4 Dr STD 4WD Wgn	33520	38495

SEVILLE — 2000

The Northstar V8s have been improved, and all models get a new airbag suppression system and the revised version of GM's StabiliTrak. A new ultrasonic rear parking assist feature and an advanced navigation system is optional on both STS and SLS. There are also two new exterior colors, Midnight Blue and Bronzemist.

Category A

Model	Trade-in	Market
4 Dr SLS Sdn	30475	35195
4 Dr STS Sdn	33580	38775

OPTIONS FOR SEVILLE
Adaptive Seat Pkg +1220
Bose Mini Disc Player +1020
Navigation System +1545
Personalization Pkg +950
Bose Sound System[Std on STS] +505
Chrome Wheels +805

Don't forget to refer to the Mileage Adjustment Table at the back of this book!

CADILLAC 00-99

Model Description	Trade-in Value	Market Value	Model Description	Trade-in Value	Market Value

Compact Disc Changer +615
Power Moonroof +1040

Category A

4 Dr Concours Sdn	27620	31955
4 Dr D'elegance Sdn	27305	31595
4 Dr STD Sdn	24725	28610

1999 CADILLAC

CATERA   1999

Catera's "black chrome" grille will be darkened this year, while new electronics and emissions systems make the '99 Catera the first Cadillac to meet the federal Low Emissions Vehicle (LEV) standards. There's also a redesigned fuel cap and tether with an instrument cluster telltale to indicate a loose fuel cap. Up to four remote entry key fobs can now be programmed for separate memory settings, all with enhanced automatic door lock/unlock functions. Cadillac is rumored to be working on a special Sport Edition planned for later in the model year.

RATINGS (SCALE OF 1-10)

Overall	Safety	Reliability	Performance	Comfort	Value
N/A	N/A	N/A	8.6	8.6	N/A

Category A

4 Dr STD Sdn	22030	25490

OPTIONS FOR CATERA
Sport Handling Pkg +530
Bose Sound System +410
Chrome Wheels +655
Compact Disc W/fm/tape +425
Power Moonroof +850

DEVILLE   1999

Comfort is big with Cadillac, so who else would offer massaging lumbar seats? Sure enough, this industry-first option is available on '99 d'Elegance and Concours models. All DeVilles get an electrochromic inside rearview mirror with compass added to the standard equipment list, in addition to an audible theft deterrent system. There are three new exterior colors this year, and one different shade of leather inside. As if that weren't enough, side airbag deployment now communicates with the optional OnStar communications system, so the outside world will know when you've taken a broadside hit. Comforting, indeed. Look for a limited run of about 2000 specially badged and optioned Golden Anniversary Edition DeVilles, painted White Diamond with gold trim, to celebrate the nameplate's 50th anniversary.

RATINGS (SCALE OF 1-10)

Overall	Safety	Reliability	Performance	Comfort	Value
N/A	8.9	9.1	N/A	8.3	N/A

OPTIONS FOR DEVILLE
Chrome Wheels[Std on D'elegance] +655
Compact Disc W/fm/tape[Opt on STD] +425
Leather Seats[Opt on STD] +460
Power Moonroof +850

ELDORADO   1999

Colors are big each year with Cadillac, and 1999 is no different. Cashmere, Parisian Blue and Sterling Silver replace Frost Beige, Baltic Blue Silver Mist and Shale on Eldorado's exterior color chart. Oatmeal leather replaces Cappuccino Cream as an interior color, while Pewter cloth has been deleted, leaving only Shale and Blue cloth available. In the hardware department, an electrochromic inside rearview mirror with compass and an audible theft deterrent system are now standard equipment. The Eldorado Touring Coupe (ETC) also gets the Bose four-speaker AM/FM cassette/single-slot CD & Weather Band audio system standard, with the option of adding massaging lumbar seats that provide a gentle back rub as you drive.

RATINGS (SCALE OF 1-10)

Overall	Safety	Reliability	Performance	Comfort	Value
N/A	8	N/A	8.6	7.6	N/A

Category A

2 Dr STD Cpe	25105	29050
2 Dr Touring Cpe	27520	31845

OPTIONS FOR ELDORADO
Bose Sound System[Opt on STD] +410
Chrome Wheels +655
Compact Disc Changer +505
Leather Seats[Opt on STD] +460
Power Moonroof +850

ESCALADE   1999

The new Cadillac Escalade is really more a 1999 GMC Yukon Denali than it is a Cadillac. (And GMC's Yukon Denali is really more Yukon than anything else-except, perhaps, a Chevrolet Tahoe, but that's another story) Regardless of its origins, think of the Escalade as a big, four-wheel-drive Cadillac limo for well-heeled, outdoorsy types. Loaded with luxury touches and every possible convenience (even GM's OnStar mobile communications system), Escalade comes in four special colors and lacks only one thing: an options list. Why? It's got it all.

Model Description	Trade-in Value	Market Value

Model Description	Trade-in Value	Market Value

RATINGS (SCALE OF 1-10)

Overall	Safety	Reliability	Performance	Comfort	Value
N/A	N/A	N/A	6	8	N/A

Category G

	Trade-in	Market
4 Dr STD 4WD Wgn	31205	35925

SEVILLE   1999

The Seville sees only minor changes after its successful redesign in 1998. Cadillac's new massaging lumbar seats are offered as an option on the STS. Heated seats become part of the adaptive seat package, which is now available on both SLS and STS trim levels. And the optional OnStar mobile communications system will automatically notify the OnStar customer assistance center in the case of any airbag deployment, front or side, so that the center can dispatch emergency services to the scene. Previously, notification occurred only with a front airbag deployment. There are also three new exterior colors, Cashmere, Parisian Blue and Sterling Silver, and one new interior shade called Oatmeal.

RATINGS (SCALE OF 1-10)

Overall	Safety	Reliability	Performance	Comfort	Value
N/A	N/A	9.2	8.8	8.6	N/A

Category A

	Trade-in	Market
4 Dr SLS Sdn	27270	31555
4 Dr STS Sdn	30055	34775

OPTIONS FOR SEVILLE

Adaptive Seat Pkg +1130
Personalization Pkg +785
Bose Sound System[Std on STS] +410
Chrome Wheels +655
Compact Disc Changer +505
Garage Door Opener +75
Power Moonroof +850

1998 CADILLAC

CATERA   1998

New radios are available across the board, and a new option is a power rear sunshade. Second-generation airbags arrived during the middle of the model year.

RATINGS (SCALE OF 1-10)

Overall	Safety	Reliability	Performance	Comfort	Value
N/A	N/A	9.3	8.6	8.6	N/A

Category A

	Trade-in	Market
4 Dr STD Sdn	17460	20265

OPTIONS FOR CATERA

Leather Pkg +1390
Bose Sound System +335
Chrome Wheels +535

Dual Power Seats +260
Heated Seats +190
Leather Seats +375
Power Moonroof +695

DEVILLE   1998

StabiliTrak, an integrated chassis control system that corrects four-wheel lateral skids, is available on base and d'Elegance. New radio systems debut, and door lock programmability is enhanced. An idiot light is added to warn about loose fuel caps, and new colors are available inside and out. Heated seats are added to the d'Elegance and Concours while the Concours also gets a much-needed alloy wheel redesign. Second-generation airbags debut as standard equipment.

RATINGS (SCALE OF 1-10)

Overall	Safety	Reliability	Performance	Comfort	Value
8.2	8.7	8.5	8.2	8.3	7.4

Category A

	Trade-in	Market
4 Dr Concours Sdn	23490	27260
4 Dr D'elegance Sdn	23150	26870
4 Dr STD Sdn	21165	24565

OPTIONS FOR DEVILLE

Alarm System +160
Chrome Wheels[Std on D'elegance] +535
Compact Disc W/fm/tape[Opt on STD] +345
Heated Front Seats[Opt on STD] +115
Leather Seats[Opt on STD] +375

ELDORADO   1998

New radios, a revised interior electrochromic mirror, enhanced programmable features, second-generation airbags and the addition of StabiliTrak to the base model's option list are the major improvements for 1998.

RATINGS (SCALE OF 1-10)

Overall	Safety	Reliability	Performance	Comfort	Value
7.5	7.9	8.4	8.6	7.6	4.9

Category A

	Trade-in	Market
2 Dr STD Cpe	22165	25725
2 Dr Touring Cpe	24460	28385

OPTIONS FOR ELDORADO

Bose Sound System[Opt on STD] +335
Chrome Wheels +535
Compact Disc Changer +410
Heated Front Seats[Opt on STD] +115
Leather Seats[Opt on STD] +375
Power Moonroof +695

Model Description	Trade-in Value	Market Value

Model Description	Trade-in Value	Market Value

SEVILLE   1998

Cadillac redefines the American luxury car by debuting an athletic sedan that boasts the performance, style, refinement and technological innovation necessary to play ball on a global level.

RATINGS (SCALE OF 1-10)

Overall	Safety	Reliability	Performance	Comfort	Value
N/A	N/A	8.6	8.8	8.8	6.2

Category A

4 Dr SLS Sdn	24435	28355
4 Dr STS Sdn	26980	31310

OPTIONS FOR SEVILLE

Adaptive Seat Pkg +600
Personalization Pkg +650
Bose Sound System[Opt on SLS] +335
Chrome Wheels +535
Compact Disc Changer +410
Heated Seats +190
Power Moonroof +695

1997 CADILLAC

CATERA   1997

Cadillac leaps into the near luxury segment of the market with a stylish, German-engineered sedan that features a 200-horsepower V6, an impressive load of standard equipment, and proper rear-wheel drive.

RATINGS (SCALE OF 1-10)

Overall	Safety	Reliability	Performance	Comfort	Value
N/A	N/A	8.8	8.6	8.6	N/A

Category A

4 Dr STD Sdn	15120	17640

OPTIONS FOR CATERA

Leather Pkg +735
Bose Sound System +275
Chrome Wheels +440
Dual Power Seats +215
Heated Seats +155
Leather Seats +310
Power Moonroof +570

DEVILLE   1997

DeVille undergoes a substantial revamp for 1997, including revised styling, the addition of standard side-impact airbags, and a fresh interior that is actually functional. Concours receives stability enhancement and road texture detection as part of its Integrated Chassis Control System (ICCS), while a new D'elegance model picks up where the defunct Fleetwood left off. Finally, the OnStar Services package provides DeVille owners with security and convenience features that will pinpoint the car's location at any given time or allow you to book a flight to Paris from the comfort of your driver's seat.

RATINGS (SCALE OF 1-10)

Overall	Safety	Reliability	Performance	Comfort	Value
8.3	8.9	8.6	8.2	8.3	7.3

Category A

4 Dr Concours Sdn	20550	23975
4 Dr D'elegance Sdn	19690	22975
4 Dr STD Sdn	18240	21280

OPTIONS FOR DEVILLE

Alarm System +130
Chrome Wheels[Std on D'elegance] +440
Compact Disc W/fm/tape +285
Leather Seats[Opt on STD] +310

ELDORADO   1997

Structural, suspension, and brake system enhancements are made across the board. Base models get MagnaSteer variable effort steering, while the Eldorado Touring Coupe (ETC) receives a new Integrated Chassis Control System (ICCS) that includes stability enhancement and road texture detection. All Eldos have slightly revised stereo and climate controls, and the OnStar services package is a slick new option that can notify emergency personnel where your disabled car is located or can allow you to book dinner reservations from the driver's seat.

RATINGS (SCALE OF 1-10)

Overall	Safety	Reliability	Performance	Comfort	Value
7.3	7.9	7.9	8.6	7.6	4.6

Category A

2 Dr STD Cpe	19430	22670
2 Dr Touring Cpe	21170	24700

OPTIONS FOR ELDORADO

Automatic Dimming Mirror +75
Bose Sound System +275
Chrome Wheels +440
Compact Disc Changer +335
Heated Front Seats +95
Leather Seats[Opt on STD] +310
Power Moonroof +570

SEVILLE   1997

All Sevilles receive body structure, suspension, brake system, and interior enhancements. STS models get a new stability enhancement feature designed to correct lateral skids, and road texture detection, which helps modulate the ABS more effectively on rough roads. Enhanced, programmable memory systems are new to both models, as is a revised rear seatback and the availability of OnStar, a vehicle information and

Don't forget to refer to the Mileage Adjustment Table at the back of this book!

Model Description	Trade-in Value	Market Value
communications service. SLS models get MagnaSteer variable-effort steering.		

RATINGS (SCALE OF 1-10)

Overall	Safety	Reliability	Performance	Comfort	Value
7.7	7.6	8.4	8.2	8.1	6.1

Category A

	Trade-in	Market
4 Dr SLS Sdn	19990	23320
4 Dr STS Sdn	22405	26140

OPTIONS FOR SEVILLE
Automatic Dimming Mirror +75
Bose Sound System +275
Chrome Wheels +440
Compact Disc Changer +335
Heated Front Seats +95
Leather Seats[Opt on SLS] +310
Power Moonroof +570

1996 CADILLAC

DEVILLE 1996

Northstar V8 is installed in base DeVille, along with a new transmission, Integrated Chassis Control System, and Road-Sensing Suspension. Concours gets 25 horsepower boost to 300, along with a higher final-drive ratio for quicker pickup and an improved continuously-variable Road-Sensing Suspension. Automatic windshield wipers and new variable-effort steering are standard on the Concours. Daytime running lights debut on both of these monsters.

RATINGS (SCALE OF 1-10)

Overall	Safety	Reliability	Performance	Comfort	Value
8	8	8.4	8.2	8.3	7.2

Category A

	Trade-in	Market
4 Dr Concours Sdn	16860	19795
4 Dr STD Sdn	15095	17725

OPTIONS FOR DEVILLE
Alarm System +105
Leather Seats[Opt on STD] +250

ELDORADO 1996

Sea Mist Green is a new interior and exterior color, and daytime running lights are standard. Eldorado gets new seats and revised audio systems. Touring Coupe interior is revised, with a center-stack console, bigger gauges, and seamless passenger airbag. Rainsense, an automatic windshield wiper system, is standard on the ETC, as is an updated continuously-variable Road-Sensing Suspension.

RATINGS (SCALE OF 1-10)

Overall	Safety	Reliability	Performance	Comfort	Value
7.2	7.7	7.3	8.6	7.6	4.6

Category A

	Trade-in	Market
2 Dr STD Cpe	16770	19685
2 Dr Touring Cpe	18185	21350

OPTIONS FOR ELDORADO
Bose Sound System +225
Chrome Wheels +360
Compact Disc Changer +275
Heated Front Seats +75
Leather Seats[Opt on STD] +250
Power Moonroof +465

FLEETWOOD 1996

Final year for the longest production car sold in the U.S. Updates are limited to a new audio system, revised center storage armrest, and pre-wiring for Cadillac's Dual Mode cellular phone.

RATINGS (SCALE OF 1-10)

Overall	Safety	Reliability	Performance	Comfort	Value
N/A	N/A	7.3	7.6	8.1	6.7

Category A

	Trade-in	Market
4 Dr STD Sdn	15725	18460

OPTIONS FOR FLEETWOOD
Camper/Towing Package +115
Chrome Wheels +360
Compact Disc W/fm/tape +230
Heated Seats +130
Leather Seats +250
Power Moonroof +465

SEVILLE 1996

All Sevilles get new seats and seat trim, redesigned sound systems, an (optional) integrated voice-activated cellular phone, daytime running lights, and programmable door lock functions and seating positions. The STS also receives an updated instrument panel with big gauges and a new center console, the Cadillac-exclusive Rainsense Wiper System (which detects rainfall and turns the wipers on automatically) and a newly improved continuously-variable Road-Sensing Suspension. Magnasteer variable-assist steering replaces the old speed-sensitive gear on last year's STS.

RATINGS (SCALE OF 1-10)

Overall	Safety	Reliability	Performance	Comfort	Value
7.6	7.4	8.1	8.2	8.1	6

Category A

	Trade-in	Market
4 Dr SLS Sdn	17745	20835
4 Dr STS Sdn	19575	22980

OPTIONS FOR SEVILLE
Bose Sound System +225
Chrome Wheels +360
Compact Disc Changer +275

Model Description	Trade-in Value	Market Value

Model Description	Trade-in Value	Market Value

Heated Front Seats +75
Leather Seats[Opt on SLS] +250
Power Moonroof +465

1995 CADILLAC

DEVILLE 1995

Traction control (which can be shut off) is standard on base DeVille. Headlights come on automatically when windshield wipers are activated. Chrome wheels can be ordered on Concours. Garage door opener is optional on DeVille; standard on Concours.

RATINGS (SCALE OF 1-10)

Overall	Safety	Reliability	Performance	Comfort	Value
8.1	8.6	8.4	8.2	8.3	7.1

Category A

	Trade-in	Market
4 Dr Concours Sdn	13755	16295
4 Dr STD Sdn	12310	14580

OPTIONS FOR DEVILLE
Compact Disc W/fm/tape +190
Leather Seats[Opt on STD] +205

ELDORADO 1995

Northstar V8 power is increased. Electronic chassis controls now evaluate steering angle when deciding what to do with the Road Sensing Suspension, traction control, and ABS. Styling is slightly revised front and rear. Headlights come on automatically when windshield wipers are activated.

RATINGS (SCALE OF 1-10)

Overall	Safety	Reliability	Performance	Comfort	Value
7.9	8.5	8	8.6	7.6	6.6

Category A

	Trade-in	Market
2 Dr STD Cpe	13615	16130
2 Dr Touring Cpe	14775	17505

OPTIONS FOR ELDORADO
Chrome Wheels +295
Compact Disc W/fm/tape +190
Heated Front Seats +60
Leather Seats[Opt on STD] +205
Power Moonroof +380

FLEETWOOD 1995

Traction control gets on/off switch. Platinum-tipped spark plugs are added, allowing tune-ups to occur every 100,000 miles. Anti-lockout feature added. Remote keyless entry, central unlocking, and fold-away outside mirrors are added. Garage door opener is new option.

RATINGS (SCALE OF 1-10)

Overall	Safety	Reliability	Performance	Comfort	Value
N/A	N/A	7.2	7.6	8.1	6.6

Category A

	Trade-in	Market
4 Dr STD Sdn	12115	14350

OPTIONS FOR FLEETWOOD
Camper/Towing Package +95
Chrome Wheels +295
Compact Disc W/fm/tape +190
Heated Front Seats +60
Leather Seats +205
Power Moonroof +380

SEVILLE 1995

Northstar V8 power is increased. Electronic chassis controls now evaluate steering angle when deciding what to do with the Road Sensing Suspension, traction control, and ABS. Headlights come on automatically when windshield wipers are activated. Chrome wheels are new option.

RATINGS (SCALE OF 1-10)

Overall	Safety	Reliability	Performance	Comfort	Value
7.6	8.5	7.9	8.2	8.1	5.5

Category A

	Trade-in	Market
4 Dr SLS Sdn	14560	17250
4 Dr STS Sdn	15925	18870

OPTIONS FOR SEVILLE
Chrome Wheels +295
Compact Disc W/fm/tape +190
Heated Front Seats +60
Leather Seats[Opt on SLS] +205
Power Moonroof +380

1994 CADILLAC

DEVILLE 1994

Redesigned with dual airbags, height-adjustable seat belts, and side-impact protection meeting 1997 standards. Base and Concours models available, with Concours replacing Touring Sedan. Concours comes with Northstar V8 and Road Sensing Suspension. Coupe DeVille and Sixty Special are retired. Base DeVille powered by 1993's 4.9-liter V8. Remote keyless entry is standard.

RATINGS (SCALE OF 1-10)

Overall	Safety	Reliability	Performance	Comfort	Value
N/A	N/A	7.7	8.2	8.3	8

Category A

	Trade-in	Market
4 Dr Concours Sdn	11215	13500
4 Dr STD Sdn	9895	11910

OPTIONS FOR DEVILLE
Compact Disc W/fm/tape +155
Leather Seats[Opt on STD] +170

Don't forget to refer to the Mileage Adjustment Table at the back of this book!

Model Description	Trade-in Value	Market Value

ELDORADO 1994

Base model gets Northstar V8, Road Sensing Suspension, and traction control. Remote keyless entry and automatic door locks are made standard.

RATINGS (SCALE OF 1-10)

Overall	Safety	Reliability	Performance	Comfort	Value
7.5	8.4	7.3	8.6	7.6	5.5

Category A
	Trade-in	Market
2 Dr STD Cpe	11245	13535
2 Dr Touring Cpe	12215	14700

OPTIONS FOR ELDORADO
Astro Roof +355
Chrome Wheels +240
Compact Disc W/fm/tape +155
Leather Seats[Opt on STD] +170

FLEETWOOD 1994

Detuned Corvette 5.7-liter engine makes its way under Fleetwood's gargantuan hood. Performance is much improved. New transmission comes with new engine. Brougham package includes padded vinyl roof and alloy wheels. Flash-to-pass is a new feature, and a battery saver is installed.

RATINGS (SCALE OF 1-10)

Overall	Safety	Reliability	Performance	Comfort	Value
N/A	N/A	7.4	7.6	8.1	7.1

Category A
	Trade-in	Market
4 Dr STD Sdn	10265	12360

OPTIONS FOR FLEETWOOD
Cloth Brougham Pkg +340
Leather Brougham Pkg +310
Astro Roof +355
Camper/Towing Package +75
Chrome Wheels +240
Compact Disc W/fm/tape +155
Leather Seats +170

SEVILLE 1994

Base model now called SLS. SLS gets Northstar V8, traction control, and Road Sensing Suspension. Remote keyless entry is standard this year.

RATINGS (SCALE OF 1-10)

Overall	Safety	Reliability	Performance	Comfort	Value
7.5	8.4	6.9	8.2	8.1	5.8

Category A
	Trade-in	Market
4 Dr STD Sdn	11850	14265
4 Dr STS Sdn	12950	15590

OPTIONS FOR SEVILLE
Astro Roof +355
Chrome Wheels +240

Compact Disc W/fm/tape +155
Leather Seats[Opt on STD] +170

1993 CADILLAC

60 SPECIAL 1993

Speed-sensitive steering debuts. Speed Sensitive Suspension is standard on all models. Grille is revised.

Category A
	Trade-in	Market
4 Dr STD Sdn	8225	10005

OPTIONS FOR 60 SPECIAL
Ultra Seating Pkg +470
AM/FM Compact Disc Player +95
Astro Roof +290
Chrome Wheels +195
Keyless Entry System +55
Leather Seats +140
Power Passenger Seat +65

ALLANTE 1993

Final year for ill-fated convertible, and this is the year to buy. Why? This is the only Allante with Northstar V8 engine. Along with the superb engine, Allante gets a new transmission, new traction control system, and a Road Sensing Suspension. Rear suspension is redesigned, and tires are rated to 155 mph. Audio system is revised, dual cupholders are added, alloy wheels are restyled, and seats are all-new. Buy one. Store it.

Category J
	Trade-in	Market
2 Dr STD Conv	19010	22165

DEVILLE 1993

Fleetwood tag moved to big new rear-drive sedan. Speed-sensitive steering debuts. Speed Sensitive Suspension is standard on all models. Grille is revised. Special Edition option packages include really cool stuff like gold trim and Phaeton roof.

RATINGS (SCALE OF 1-10)

Overall	Safety	Reliability	Performance	Comfort	Value
N/A	N/A	7.6	8	8	7.4

Category A
	Trade-in	Market
2 Dr STD Cpe	7680	9340
4 Dr STD Sdn	7470	9085
4 Dr Touring Sdn	7845	9540

OPTIONS FOR DEVILLE
Leather Seats[Opt on STD] +140

ELDORADO 1993

Touring Coupe gets stellar Northstar V8, Road Sensing Suspension, and traction control. Passenger airbag debuts. Rear suspension redesigned. Speed-sensitive steering made standard. Base Eldo gets

Model Description	Trade-in Value	Market Value

Speed Sensitive Suspension standard. Sport Performance package is a blend of base model and TC with detuned Northstar. Sport Appearance package gives look of Sport Performance package with 4.9-liter V8 from base coupe. Got that?

RATINGS (SCALE OF 1-10)

Overall	Safety	Reliability	Performance	Comfort	Value
7.3	8.4	6.7	8.6	7.6	5.4

Category A

	Trade-in	Market
2 Dr STD Cpe	8720	10605
2 Dr Touring Cpe	9715	11815

OPTIONS FOR ELDORADO

Sport Appearance Pkg +175
Astro Roof +290
Chrome Wheels +195
Compact Disc W/fm/tape +125
Leather Seats +140
Traction Control System +40

FLEETWOOD 1993

Dual airbags and rounded styling characterize this Brougham replacement, which is based on stretched Chevy Caprice chassis. Length is up 4.1 inches. Yowza! Traction control and ABS are standard. Optional trailer tow group gives car a 7,000-lb. towing capacity. Goofy digital dashboard standard.

RATINGS (SCALE OF 1-10)

Overall	Safety	Reliability	Performance	Comfort	Value
N/A	N/A	6.8	7.2	8.1	7.9

Category A

	Trade-in	Market
4 Dr STD Sdn	8575	10430

OPTIONS FOR FLEETWOOD

AM/FM Compact Disc Player +95
Astro Roof +290
Leather Seats +140

SEVILLE 1993

STS gets Northstar V8, Road Sensing Suspension, and traction control. Passenger airbag added to all Sevilles. Base Seville gets Speed Sensitive Suspension. Bigger fuel tank is added, rear suspension is redesigned, and a cupholder is added to center console. ABS and speed-sensitive steering standard on all Sevilles.

RATINGS (SCALE OF 1-10)

Overall	Safety	Reliability	Performance	Comfort	Value
7.5	8.4	7	8.2	8.1	5.9

Category A

	Trade-in	Market
4 Dr STD Sdn	9040	10990
4 Dr STS Sdn	10240	12455

OPTIONS FOR SEVILLE

AM/FM Compact Disc Player +95
Astro Roof +290
Bose Sound System +125
Chrome Wheels +195
Keyless Entry System[Opt on STD] +55
Leather Seats[Opt on STD] +140

1992 CADILLAC

ALLANTE 1992

No changes.
Category J

	Trade-in	Market
2 Dr STD Conv	12810	15080

OPTIONS FOR ALLANTE

Hardtop Roof +515

BROUGHAM 1992

5.7-liter V8 escapes gas-guzzler tax. Towing capacity increased 2,000 lbs. Final edition.
Category A

	Trade-in	Market
4 Dr STD Sdn	5915	7395

OPTIONS FOR BROUGHAM

8 cyl 5.7 L Engine +40
D'Elegance Pkg +305
Astro Roof +240
Leather Seats +115

DEVILLE 1992

Traction control optional on base DeVille; standard on all others. Platinum-tipped spark plugs mean tune-ups happen every 100,000 miles. Power passenger seat made standard on DeVille. Electrochromic rearview mirror made standard on all models.

RATINGS (SCALE OF 1-10)

Overall	Safety	Reliability	Performance	Comfort	Value
N/A	N/A	7.5	8	8	7.3

Category A

	Trade-in	Market
2 Dr STD Cpe	6125	7660
4 Dr STD Sdn	6125	7660
4 Dr Touring Sdn	6295	7875

OPTIONS FOR DEVILLE

Phaeton Roof +180
Astro Roof +240
Bose Sound System +100
Leather Seats[Opt on STD] +115

ELDORADO 1992

Complete makeover results in distinctly European-flavored coupe. Powertrains are carried over from 1991. ABS and driver airbag are standard. Sport interior option includes analog gauges rather than digital gauges.

Don't forget to refer to the Mileage Adjustment Table at the back of this book!

Model Description	Trade-in Value	Market Value

Model Description	Trade-in Value	Market Value

RATINGS (SCALE OF 1-10)

Overall	Safety	Reliability	Performance	Comfort	Value
7.2	7.5	6.9	8.2	7.6	5.8

Category A

2 Dr STD Cpe	7020	8780

OPTIONS FOR ELDORADO
Touring Pkg +405
Astro Roof +240
Compact Disc W/fm/tape +105
Leather Seats +115

FLEETWOOD 1992

Traction control standard. Platinum-tipped spark plugs mean tune-ups happen every 100,000 miles. Electrochromatic rearview mirror made standard on all models.

Category A

2 Dr STD Cpe	6035	7545
4 Dr STD Sdn	6035	7545
4 Dr Sixty Special Sdn	6605	8260

OPTIONS FOR FLEETWOOD
Astro Roof +240
Bose Sound System +100
Leather Seats[Opt on STD] +115

SEVILLE 1992

Complete makeover results in distinctly European-flavored sedan. Powertrains are carried over from 1991. ABS and driver airbag are standard. Sport interior option includes analog gauges rather than digital gauges. Leather upholstery and analog gauges are standard on STS.

RATINGS (SCALE OF 1-10)

Overall	Safety	Reliability	Performance	Comfort	Value
7.6	7.5	7.6	8	8.1	6.8

Category A

4 Dr STD Sdn	6955	8695
4 Dr STS Sdn	7540	9430

OPTIONS FOR SEVILLE
Phaeton Roof +180
Astro Roof +240
Leather Seats[Opt on STD] +115

1991 CADILLAC

ALLANTE 1991

Traction control debuts. Power latching mechanism added to manual top.

Category J

2 Dr STD Conv	10875	12875

OPTIONS FOR ALLANTE
Hardtop Roof +420

BROUGHAM 1991

Standard and optional engines gain more power. Optional 5.7-liter motor slapped with gas-guzzler tax for city rating of 15 mpg.

Category A

4 Dr STD Sdn	5050	6515

OPTIONS FOR BROUGHAM
8 cyl 5.7 L Engine +35
D'elegance Pkg +240
Astro Roof +195
Leather Seats +90
Wire Wheels +135

DEVILLE 1991

Engine upgraded to 200-horsepower, 4.9-liter V8 from 180-horsepower, 4.5-liter V8. DeVille Touring Sedan debuted late in model year, with monotone exterior paint, performance tires, quicker-ratio steering, and thicker stabilizer bars.

RATINGS (SCALE OF 1-10)

Overall	Safety	Reliability	Performance	Comfort	Value
N/A	N/A	7	8	8	7.8

Category A

2 Dr STD Cpe	5100	6580
4 Dr STD Sdn	5140	6630
4 Dr Touring Sdn	5580	7205

OPTIONS FOR DEVILLE
Phaeton Roof +145
Astro Roof +195
Bose Sound System +80
Leather Seats[Opt on STD] +90

ELDORADO 1991

Engine upgraded to 200-horsepower, 4.9-liter V8 from 180-horsepower, 4.5-liter V8. Transmission modified to generate better acceleration. Touring Coupe debuts, featuring Seville STS styling and suspension modifications.

Category A

2 Dr Biarritz Cpe	5335	6885
2 Dr STD Cpe	5395	6965

OPTIONS FOR ELDORADO
Touring Coupe Pkg +210
Astro Roof +195
Bose Sound System +80
Leather Seats[Opt on STD] +90

Don't forget to refer to the Mileage Adjustment Table at the back of this book!

CADILLAC 91

Model Description	Trade-in Value	Market Value	Model Description	Trade-in Value	Market Value

FLEETWOOD 1991

Engine upgraded to 200-horsepower, 4.9-liter V8 from 180-horsepower, 4.5-liter V8.

Category A

2 Dr STD Cpe	4945	6380
4 Dr STD Sdn	4980	6425
4 Dr Sixty Special Sdn	5455	7040

OPTIONS FOR FLEETWOOD
Astro Roof +195
Bose Sound System +80
Leather Seats[Opt on STD] +90

SEVILLE 1991

Engine upgraded to 200-horsepower, 4.9-liter V8 from 180-horsepower, 4.5-liter V8. Transmission modified to generate better acceleration.

Category A

4 Dr STD Sdn	4845	6250
4 Dr STS Sdn	5295	6830

OPTIONS FOR SEVILLE
Phaeton Roof +160
Astro Roof +195
Bose Sound System +80
Leather Seats[Opt on STD] +90

Don't forget to refer to the Mileage Adjustment Table at the back of this book!

Model Description	Trade-in Value	Market Value	Model Description	Trade-in Value	Market Value

CHEVROLET 00

CHEVROLET · USA

1995 Chevrolet Suburban

2000 CHEVROLET

ASTRO 2000

Retained accessory power and additional warning chimes are added to this ancient van for 2000. Also new are automatic headlights with a flash-to-pass feature, remote keyless entry, battery rundown protection, lockout protection, and a tow/haul trailering mode for the transmission. The ABS, engine and exhaust have been improved, and a plastic 27-gallon fuel tank is standard.

Category G

	Trade-in	Market
2 Dr LS Pass. Van Ext	16510	19270
2 Dr LS 4WD Pass. Van Ext	17780	20750
2 Dr LT Pass. Van Ext	19780	23085
2 Dr LT 4WD Pass. Van Ext	21405	24980
2 Dr STD Pass. Van Ext	15655	18270
2 Dr STD 4WD Pass. Van Ext	17275	20165

OPTIONS FOR ASTRO

AM/FM Compact Disc Player +260
AM/FM Stereo Tape[Std on LS] +180
Aluminum/Alloy Wheels[Std on LT] +265
Cruise Control[Opt on STD] +170
Luggage Rack[Opt on STD] +130
Power Door Locks[Opt on STD] +190
Power Mirrors[Opt on STD] +110
Power Windows[Opt on STD] +200
Privacy Glass[Std on LS,LT] +225
Rear Window Defroster[Opt on LS,STD] +140
Rear Window Wiper[Std on LT] +125
Tilt Steering Wheel[Opt on STD] +145
Tutone Paint +210

ASTRO CARGO 2000

Retained accessory power and additional warning chimes are added to this ancient van for 2000. Also new are automatic headlights with a flash-to-pass feature, battery rundown protection, and a tow/haul trailering mode for the transmission. The ABS, engine and exhaust have been improved, and a plastic 27-gallon fuel tank is standard.

Category G

	Trade-in	Market
2 Dr STD Cargo Van Ext	14535	16965
2 Dr STD 4WD Cargo Van Ext	16205	18915

OPTIONS FOR ASTRO CARGO

AM/FM Compact Disc Player +260
Compact Disc W/fm/tape +365
Cruise Control +170
Power Door Locks +190
Power Windows +200
Rear Heater +155
Rear Window Defroster +140
Tilt Steering Wheel +145
Trailer Hitch +230

BLAZER 2000

Base models are dropped as Chevy learns SUV buyers prioritize goodies and a luxury image rather than rugged go-anywhere capability. The engine, exhaust and ABS are refined for increased durability, and exterior trim on some models is modified. Two new colors are available.

Category G

	Trade-in	Market
2 Dr LS Utility	14135	16425
2 Dr LS 4WD Utility	15800	18440
4 Dr LS Wgn	17625	20570
4 Dr LS 4WD Wgn	19030	22210
4 Dr LT Wgn	18890	22045
4 Dr LT 4WD Wgn	20430	23845
4 Dr Trailblazer Wgn	21135	24665
4 Dr Trailblazer 4WD Wgn	22535	26300

OPTIONS FOR BLAZER

Auto 4-Speed Transmission[Opt on Utility] +815
ZR2 Suspension Pkg +1285
AM/FM Compact Disc Player[Opt on LS] +260
Bucket Seats[Std on LS 4WD 2-Door,LT 4WD,TrailBlazer 2WD] +285
Center Console[Std on Utility,LT 4WD] +135
Climate Control for AC[Opt on LT] +160
Compact Disc W/fm/tape +365
Cruise Control[Opt on LS] +170
Dual Power Seats[Opt on LS,LT] +340
Heated Front Seats +225
Heated Power Mirrors[Opt on LS] +65
Keyless Entry System[Opt on LS] +160
Leather Seats[Opt on LT] +640
Power Door Locks[Opt on LS] +190

Model Description	Trade-in Value	Market Value
Power Drivers Seat[Std on LT] +230		
Power Windows[Opt on LS] +200		
Privacy Glass[Opt on LS] +225		
Rear Window Defroster[Opt on LS] +140		
Rear Window Wiper[Opt on LS] +125		
Remote Trunk Release[Opt on LS] +55		
Tilt Steering Wheel[Opt on LS] +145		

C/K 2500   2000

Literally, one new paint color. The C/K is a dead duck after this model year.

Category H

Model Description	Trade-in Value	Market Value
4 Dr LS Crew Cab SB	18495	21460
4 Dr LS 4WD Crew Cab SB	20585	23880
2 Dr LS Ext Cab SB	15890	18435
2 Dr LS 4WD Ext Cab LB 4WD Ext Cab LB	18015	20900
2 Dr LS 4WD Ext Cab SB 4WD Ext Cab SB	17935	20805
2 Dr LS Std Cab LB	14770	17135
2 Dr LS 4WD Std Cab LB	16580	19235
4 Dr STD Crew Cab SB	16085	18660
4 Dr STD 4WD Crew Cab SB	18170	21080
2 Dr STD Ext Cab LB	14385	16690
2 Dr STD 4WD Ext Cab LB	16515	19155
2 Dr STD 4WD Ext Cab SB	16430	19060
2 Dr STD Std Cab LB	13265	15390
2 Dr STD 4WD Std Cab LB	15080	17490

OPTIONS FOR C/K 2500

8 cyl 6.5 L Turbodsl Engine +2310
8 cyl 7.4 L Engine +490
Auto 4-Speed Transmission[Std on Crew Cab] +885
AM/FM Compact Disc Player +255
AM/FM Stereo Tape[Std on LS] +165
Air Conditioning[Std on LS] +665
Bucket Seats +305
Compact Disc W/fm/tape +255
Cruise Control[Std on LS] +155
Power Drivers Seat +230
Privacy Glass +130
Tilt Steering Wheel[Std on LS] +155

C/K 3500   2000

Literally, one new paint color. The C/K is a dead duck after this model year.

Category H

Model Description	Trade-in Value	Market Value
4 Dr LS Crew Cab LB	18195	21110
4 Dr LS 4WD Crew Cab LB	20285	23535
4 Dr LS Crew Cab SB	19170	22240
4 Dr LS 4WD Crew Cab SB	21260	24665
2 Dr LS Ext Cab LB	17350	20130
2 Dr LS 4WD Ext Cab LB	19200	22275
2 Dr LS Standard Cab LB	15095	17515
2 Dr LS 4WD Std Cab LB	17070	19800

Model Description	Trade-in Value	Market Value
4 Dr STD Crew Cab LB	15780	18310
4 Dr STD 4WD Crew Cab LB	17870	20730
4 Dr STD Crew Cab SB	16755	19440
4 Dr STD 4WD Crew Cab SB	18845	21860
2 Dr STD Ext Cab LB	15910	18460
2 Dr STD 4WD Ext Cab LB	17760	20605
2 Dr STD Std Cab LB	13590	15770
2 Dr STD 4WD Std Cab LB	15565	18060

OPTIONS FOR C/K 3500

8 cyl 6.5 L Turbodsl Engine +2310
8 cyl 7.4 L Engine[Std on SB] +490
Auto 4-Speed Transmission +895
AM/FM Stereo Tape[Std on LS] +165
Air Conditioning[Std on LS] +665
Camper/Towing Package +270
Cruise Control[Std on LS] +155
Dual Rear Wheels[Std on SB] +645
Power Drivers Seat +230
Tilt Steering Wheel[Std on LS] +155

CAMARO   2000

New interior colors and fabrics, redundant steering-wheel radio controls, new alloy wheels, and a new exterior color spruce up the aging Camaro. V6 and V8 engines meet California's Low-Emission Vehicle (LEV) standards.

Category F

Model Description	Trade-in Value	Market Value
2 Dr STD Conv	17750	20620
2 Dr STD Cpe	12525	14545
2 Dr Z28 Conv	20885	24255
2 Dr Z28 Cpe	15890	18455
2 Dr Z28 SS Conv	23710	27540
2 Dr Z28 SS Cpe	18625	21635

OPTIONS FOR CAMARO

Auto 4-Speed Transmission[Opt on STD] +665
Sport Appearance Pkg +1155
AM/FM Compact Disc Player +380
Alarm System[Opt on Cpe] +150
Aluminum/Alloy Wheels[Opt on STD] +250
Cruise Control[Opt on Cpe] +180
Fog Lights[Opt on Cpe] +145
Glass Panel T-tops +810
Keyless Entry System[Opt on Cpe] +150
Leather Seats +520
Leather Steering Wheel[Opt on Cpe] +130
Lighted Entry System[Opt on Cpe] +115
Power Door Locks[Opt on Cpe] +170
Power Drivers Seat[Opt on STD,Cpe] +195
Power Mirrors[Opt on Cpe] +95
Power Windows[Opt on Cpe] +190
Rear Window Defroster[Opt on Cpe] +140
Remote Trunk Release[Opt on Cpe] +55

Model Description	Trade-in Value	Market Value	Model Description	Trade-in Value	Market Value

CAVALIER 2000

Still available as a coupe, sedan or convertible, Chevy's best-selling car gets several subtle changes for 2000. Outside it has new body-colored front and rear facias, new headlamp/taillamp assemblies, new badging and restyled wheel covers/alloy wheels. Inside, the instrument panel now features an electronic odometer and tripmeter, a revamped center console with three front cupholders and an improved storage area. Functionally, it gets a better-shifting five-speed manual transaxle, smoother-operating ABS, Passlock II security system and standard air-conditioning.

Category E

4 Dr LS Sdn	10725	12645
2 Dr STD Cpe	9570	11285
4 Dr STD Sdn	9640	11370
2 Dr Z24 Conv	14245	16795
2 Dr Z24 Cpe	11815	13935

OPTIONS FOR CAVALIER
4 cyl 2.4 L Engine[Opt on LS] +370
Auto 3-Speed Transmission +530
Auto 4-Speed Transmission[Std on LS] +635
AM/FM Compact Disc Player[Std on Z24] +355
AM/FM Stereo Tape[Std on LS] +250
Compact Disc W/fm/tape +395
Power Door Locks[Std on Z24] +205
Power Mirrors[Std on Z24] +90
Power Moonroof +475
Power Windows[Std on Z24] +215

CORVETTE 2000

Minor refinements improve the Corvette for 2000. The Z51 performance-handling package has larger front and rear stabilizer bars for improved handling, while new, thin-spoke alloy wheels with optional high-polish finish subtly change the outward appearance. Two new colors are available on coupe and convertible: extra-cost Millennium Yellow and no-cost Dark Bowling Green Metallic. A garish Torch Red interior can be ordered, the stupendous LS1 5.7-liter V8 engine meets LEV regulations in California, the remote keyless-entry system has been upgraded, and the passenger door-lock cylinder has been deleted.

Category J

2 Dr STD Conv	37810	44135
2 Dr STD Cpe	32570	38020
2 Dr STD Hardtop	31940	37285

OPTIONS FOR CORVETTE
6-Speed Transmission[Std on Hardtop] +665
Damping Suspension +1385
Magnesium Wheels +1635
Polished Alloy Wheels +730
AM/FM Compact Disc Player +320

Climate Control for AC +230
Dual Power Seats +605
Fog Lights +55
Heads-up Display +305
Telescopic Steering Whl +285

EXPRESS 2000

Chevy updates the basic V6 for quieter operation, enhanced durability and reduced emissions. New exterior colors and side striping debut, and a new rear defogger for models with fixed rear glass and swing-out vent windows improves visibility.

Category H

2 Dr G1500 Cargo Van	13815	16030
2 Dr G2500 Cargo Van	14070	16320
2 Dr G2500 Cargo Van Ext	14660	17005
2 Dr G3500 Cargo Van	15230	17670
2 Dr G3500 Cargo Van Ext	15820	18355

OPTIONS FOR EXPRESS
8 cyl 5.0 L Engine +400
8 cyl 5.7 L Engine[Std on G3500 Cargo Van, G3500 Ext.
  Cargo Van HD] +975
8 cyl 6.5 L Turbodsl Engine +2310
8 cyl 7.4 L Engine +490
Air Conditioning +665

EXPRESS PASSENGER 2000

Chevy updates the basic V6 for quieter operation, enhanced durability and reduced emissions. New exterior colors and side striping debut, and a new rear defogger for models with fixed rear glass and swing-out vent windows improves visibility.

Category H

2 Dr G1500 LS Pass. Van	17290	20055
2 Dr G1500 Pass. Van	16170	18760
2 Dr G2500 LS Pass. Van	18980	22015
2 Dr G2500 Pass. Van	17860	20720
2 Dr G2500 LS Pass. Van Ext	19585	22725
2 Dr G2500 Pass. Van Ext	18470	21425
2 Dr G3500 LS Pass. Van	19175	22245
2 Dr G3500 Pass. Van	18055	20945
2 Dr G3500 LS Pass. Van Ext	19815	22985
2 Dr G3500 Pass. Van Ext	18695	21685

OPTIONS FOR EXPRESS PASSENGER
8 cyl 5.0 L Engine +400
8 cyl 5.7 L Engine[Opt on G1500, G1500 Base LD] +975
8 cyl 6.5 L Turbodsl Engine +2310
8 cyl 7.4 L Engine +490

IMPALA 2000

GM has resurrected the Impala nameplate (a staple in Chevy's lineup from 1959 to the early '80s and then briefly from 1994 to '96) and put it on an all-new, full-sized sedan body that rides on the Lumina front-drive

CHEVROLET 00

Model Description	Trade-in Value	Market Value	Model Description	Trade-in Value	Market Value

platform. Although the Lumina itself is back for the 2000-model year, Impala will eventually replace it as Chevy's large-car entry to battle the likes of Ford's Crown Victoria, Buick's LeSabre and Chrysler's LH cars.

Category B

4 Dr LS Sdn	16735	19480
4 Dr STD Sdn	13985	16285

OPTIONS FOR IMPALA
6 cyl 3.8 L Engine[Std on LS] +65
AM/FM Stereo Tape[Std on LS] +140
Bucket Seats +230
Compact Disc W/fm/tape +305
Cruise Control[Std on LS] +185
Leather Seats +560

LUMINA   2000

Base models receive additional standard equipment, while the standard 3.1-liter V6 gets more power and torque. The sporty LTZ and upscale LS models are dropped. This is the final year for the Lumina.

Category C

4 Dr STD Sdn	12560	14765

MALIBU   2000

Revised front styling ties Malibu to Impala, while the 1999's perfectly good brushed-aluminum wheels have been redesigned to look like Prizm hubcaps. The 3.1-liter V6 engine is standard this year, and has been improved to offer more horsepower while meeting low-emission vehicle (LEV) standards. And hold on to your hats - a spoiler and a gold package are available. Yikes! Where are the landau roof and whitewall tires, Chevy?

Category C

4 Dr LS Sdn	13090	15385
4 Dr STD Sdn	11250	13225

OPTIONS FOR MALIBU
AM/FM Stereo Tape +135
Cruise Control[Std on LS] +180
Power Door Locks[Std on LS] +210
Power Mirrors[Std on LS] +85
Power Windows[Std on LS] +260
Rear Window Defroster[Std on LS] +140

METRO   2000

Two new colors help buyers differentiate between 1999 and 2000 Metros.

Category E

2 Dr LSi Hbk	6960	8210
4 Dr LSi Sdn	7345	8660
2 Dr STD Hbk	6395	7540

OPTIONS FOR METRO
Auto 3-Speed Transmission +485
AM/FM Stereo Tape +250
Air Conditioning +680

Power Steering +210
Rear Window Defroster +135

MONTE CARLO   2000

Chevy's large personal-luxury coupe is all-new for 2000, based on the Impala platform and sporting distinctive, heritage styling cues.

Category C

2 Dr LS Cpe	14230	16730
2 Dr SS Cpe	15985	18790

OPTIONS FOR MONTE CARLO
Aluminum/Alloy Wheels[Std on SS] +255
Compact Disc W/fm/tape +265
Cruise Control[Std on SS] +180
Keyless Entry System[Std on SS] +150
Leather Seats +505
Power Moonroof +560

PRIZM   2000

New standard features improve the Prizm's value quotient, and variable valve timing boosts power and torque. The tweaked engine now meets low-emission vehicle status in California, and three new colors freshen the exterior.

Category E

4 Dr LSi Sdn	11340	13375
4 Dr STD Sdn	9925	11705

OPTIONS FOR PRIZM
Auto 3-Speed Transmission +405
Auto 4-Speed Transmission +655
AM/FM Compact Disc Player +355
AM/FM Stereo Tape[Std on LSi] +250
Anti-Lock Brakes +545
Cruise Control[Std on LSi] +185
Power Door Locks[Std on LSi] +205
Power Sunroof +510
Power Windows[Std on LSi] +215
Rear Window Defroster[Std on LSi] +135
Side Air Bag Restraint +235

S-10   2000

Performance and durability enhancements have been made to the engine, exhaust system, manual transmission, and antilock braking system, but they don't result in more horsepower. Trucks equipped with the ZR2 package get a new axle ratio designed to improve acceleration. Extended cabs are available in Base trim this year, and LS models have revised exterior moldings.

Category G

2 Dr LS Xtreme Ext Cab SB	13500	15755
2 Dr LS Ext Cab SB	11895	13885
2 Dr LS Wide Stance 4WD Ext Cab SB	17985	20990

Don't forget to refer to the Mileage Adjustment Table at the back of this book!

Model Description	Trade-in Value	Market Value	Model Description	Trade-in Value	Market Value
2 Dr LS 4WD Ext Cab SB	14895	17385	2 Dr LT 4WD Ext Cab LB	21905	25410
2 Dr LS Ext Cab Stepside SB	12240	14285	2 Dr LT Ext Cab SB	19530	22660
2 Dr LS Xtreme Ext Cab Stepside SB			2 Dr LT 4WD Ext Cab SB	21700	25175
	13845	16155	2 Dr LT Ext Cab Stepside SB	20070	23280
2 Dr LS 4WD Ext Cab Stepside SB			2 Dr LT 4WD Ext Cab Stepside SB		
	15240	17785		22240	25800
2 Dr LS Std Cab LB	10485	12240	2 Dr STD Ext Cab LB	14470	16785
2 Dr LS Xtreme Std Cab SB	12050	14065	2 Dr STD 4WD Ext Cab LB	16565	19215
2 Dr LS Std Cab SB	10235	11945	2 Dr STD Ext Cab SB	13795	16005
2 Dr LS 4WD Std Cab SB	13415	15655	2 Dr STD 4WD Ext Cab SB	16360	18980
2 Dr LS Std Cab Stepside SB	10575	12345	2 Dr STD Ext Cab Stepside SB	14400	16705
2 Dr LS 4WD Std Cab Stepside SB			2 Dr STD 4WD Ext Cab Stepside SB		
	13760	16060		16965	19685
2 Dr STD Ext Cab SB	11580	13515	2 Dr STD Std Cab LB	11240	13040
2 Dr STD 4WD Ext Cab SB	13945	16275	2 Dr STD 4WD Std Cab LB	13350	15485
2 Dr STD Std Cab LB	9750	11375	2 Dr STD Std Cab SB	11040	12805
2 Dr STD Std Cab SB	9495	11080	2 Dr STD 4WD Std Cab SB	13145	15250
2 Dr STD 4WD Std Cab SB	12555	14650	2 Dr STD Std Cab Stepside SB	11645	13510
			2 Dr STD 4WD Std Cab Stepside SB		
				13750	15955

OPTIONS FOR S-10

6 cyl 4.3 L Engine[Std on 4WD] +1060
Auto 4-Speed Transmission +895
AM/FM Compact Disc Player +260
AM/FM Stereo Tape[Opt on STD] +180
Air Conditioning[Opt on STD,LS 2WD Regular Cab LB] +670
Cruise Control +170
Hinged Third Door[Std on LS Wide Stance 4WD Ext Cab SB] +275
Power Door Locks[Std on LS Wide Stance 4WD Ext Cab SB] +190
Power Windows[Std on LS Wide Stance 4WD Ext Cab SB] +200
Privacy Glass[Std on LS Wide Stance 4WD Ext Cab SB] +225
Tilt Steering Wheel +145

SILVERADO   2000

SILVERADO 1500

Category H

Model Description	Trade-in Value	Market Value
2 Dr LS Ext Cab LB	16340	18960
2 Dr LS 4WD Ext Cab LB	18440	21390
2 Dr LS Ext Cab SB	15670	18180
2 Dr LS 4WD Ext Cab SB	18235	21155
2 Dr LS Ext Cab Stepside SB	16205	18800
2 Dr LS 4WD Ext Cab Stepside SB		
	18775	21780
2 Dr LS Std Cab LB	14015	16255
2 Dr LS 4WD Std Cab LB	16110	18690
2 Dr LS Std Cab SB	13810	16020
2 Dr LS 4WD Std Cab SB	15905	18455
2 Dr LS Std Cab Stepside SB	14345	16645
2 Dr LS 4WD Std Cab Stepside SB		
	16445	19075
2 Dr LT Ext Cab LB	19735	22895

SILVERADO 2500

Category H

Model Description	Trade-in Value	Market Value
2 Dr LS Extended Cab LB HD	17660	20490
2 Dr LS 4WD Ext Cab LB	19735	22895
2 Dr LS Ext Cab SB	17725	20565
2 Dr LS 4WD Ext Cab SB	19535	22665
2 Dr LS Std Cab LB	16285	18895
2 Dr LS Std Cab LB	16020	18585
2 Dr LS 4WD Std Cab LB	16090	18665
2 Dr LT Ext Cab LB	20305	23555
2 Dr LT 4WD Ext Cab LB	22630	26255
2 Dr LT Ext Cab SB	19640	22780
2 Dr LT 4WD Ext Cab SB	22430	26025
2 Dr STD Extended Cab LB HD	15805	18335
2 Dr STD 4WD Ext Cab LB	17880	20745
2 Dr STD Ext Cab SB	15870	18410
2 Dr STD 4WD Ext Cab SB	17680	20510
2 Dr STD Std Cab LB	14430	16740
2 Dr STD Std Cab LB	14165	16435
2 Dr STD 4WD Std Cab LB	16240	18840

OPTIONS FOR SILVERADO

8 cyl 4.8 L Engine +570
8 cyl 5.3 L Engine +910
8 cyl 6.0 L Engine +290
Auto 4-Speed Transmission +895
AM/FM Stereo Tape +165
Air Conditioning +665
Aluminum/Alloy Wheels[Std on LT,LT 4WD Ext Cab Step SB, LT Ext Cab Step SB] +255
Bucket Seats +305
Camper/Towing Package +270
Cruise Control +155

Don't forget to refer to the Mileage Adjustment Table at the back of this book!

CHEVROLET 00

Model Description	Trade-in Value	Market Value	Model Description	Trade-in Value	Market Value

Dual Power Seats[Std on LT,LT 4WD Ext Cab Step SB,LT Ext Cab Step SB] +385
Power Door Locks +155
Skid Plates +85
Trailer Hitch +135

SUBURBAN 2000

The 2000 Chevrolet Suburban is completely redesigned. It's roomier, safer, more comfortable and a more powerful ride.
Category H

4 Dr C1500 Wgn	20250	23490
4 Dr C2500 Wgn	21690	25165
4 Dr K1500 4WD Wgn	22480	26080
4 Dr K2500 4WD Wgn	23990	27830
4 Dr C1500 LS Wgn	25935	30090
4 Dr C2500 LS Wgn	27380	31765
4 Dr K1500 LS 4WD Wgn	28190	32705
4 Dr K2500 LS 4WD Wgn	29680	34430
4 Dr C1500 LT Wgn	29055	33705
4 Dr C2500 LT Wgn	30165	34995
4 Dr K1500 LT 4WD Wgn	31290	36300
4 Dr K2500 LT 4WD Wgn	32465	37660

OPTIONS FOR SUBURBAN
AM/FM Compact Disc Player +255
Bucket Seats +305
Camper/Towing Package +270
Center Console +110
Compact Disc W/fm/tape +255
Cruise Control +155
Dual Power Seats +385
Limited Slip Diff +215
Luggage Rack +125
Rear Window Defroster +125
Rear Window Wiper +100
Trailer Hitch +135

TAHOE LIMITED/Z71 2000

All old-style Tahoes are dropped, except these two four-door special editions. The rugged 4WD Z71 is for the rock-hopping weekend warrior set, while the swanky 2WD Limited appeals to those who'd otherwise have a truck reworked by Earl Sheib and Tirerack.com.
Category H

4 Dr Limited Wgn	21660	25125
4 Dr Z71 4WD Wgn	23625	27410

OPTIONS FOR TAHOE LIMITED/Z71
Bucket Seats +305
Camper/Towing Package +270
Compact Disc W/fm/tape +255
Leather Seats +815
Limited Slip Diff +215
Power Moonroof +795
Rear Window Wiper +100

Skid Plates +85
Trailer Hitch +135

TRACKER 2000

After a complete redesign in 1999, new colors sum up the changes for 2000.
Category G

2 Dr STD Conv	10440	12185
2 Dr STD 4WD Conv	11240	13120
4 Dr STD Wgn	11330	13225
4 Dr STD 4WD Wgn	12135	14160

OPTIONS FOR TRACKER
4 cyl 2.0 L Engine[Std on Wgn] +325
Auto 4-Speed Transmission +815
AM/FM Compact Disc Player +260
Air Conditioning +670
Aluminum/Alloy Wheels +265
Cruise Control +170
Luggage Rack +130
Power Door Locks +190
Power Mirrors +110
Power Windows +200
Rear Window Wiper +125
Tilt Steering Wheel +145

VENTURE 2000

Chevy adds two new models on either end of the price spectrum for 2000. On the low end, a new Value Van includes basic equipment for a low price, while on the high end, a Warner Bros. Edition provides leather and a video entertainment system. New radios include RDS (radio data system) on uplevel versions. Three-door models die this year, while remaining models get new interior fabric patterns and a redesigned gauge cluster with a scratch-resistant lens. Smokey Carmel is a new paint color.
Category G

4 Dr LS Pass. Van	17705	20660
4 Dr LS Pass. Van Ext	18215	21255
4 Dr LT Pass. Van Ext	19885	23205
4 Dr Plus Pass. Van	17000	19840
4 Dr Plus Pass. Van Ext	17705	20660
4 Dr STD Pass. Van	16155	18855
4 Dr Value Pass. Van	14960	17460
4 Dr Warner Bros. Ed. Pass. Van Ext	20745	24215

OPTIONS FOR VENTURE
8 Passenger Seating +330
AM/FM Stereo Tape[Std on LS] +180
Auto Load Leveling[Std on LT] +190
Camper/Towing Package +245
Captain Chairs (4)[Std on LT] +505
Compact Disc W/fm/tape[Opt on LS,Plus,STD] +365
Dual Air Conditioning[Opt on LS,Plus] +755

Don't forget to refer to the Mileage Adjustment Table at the back of this book!

72   www.edmunds.com   EDMUNDS® USED CARS & TRUCKS

Model Description	Trade-in Value	Market Value	Model Description	Trade-in Value	Market Value

CHEVROLET 00-99

Leather Seats[Opt on LT] +640
Luggage Rack[Opt on LS,Plus] +130
Power Drivers Seat +230
Power Sliding Door[Opt on LS,Plus] +340
Rear Window Defroster[Opt on Value] +140
Traction Control System[Std on LT] +220

1999 CHEVROLET

ASTRO   1999

A new, all-wheel-drive active transfer case replaces the previous AWD system, and includes a new control module and service light. There are two new interior roof consoles: one with storage is optional on base model, another with trip computer is standard on LS and LT trim. A new LT stripe design comes in three new colors. Dealer-installed running boards are available, as are new optional aluminum wheels. Three exterior paint colors are added for '99, while depowered airbags finally arrive this year. Finally, the outside mirrors are redesigned, available heated and with or without electrochromatic glare reduction.

RATINGS (SCALE OF 1-10)

Overall	Safety	Reliability	Performance	Comfort	Value
N/A	7	8.5	5.8	6.1	N/A

Category G

	Trade-in	Market
2 Dr LS Pass. Van Ext	14885	17540
2 Dr LS 4WD Pass. Van Ext	16060	18930
2 Dr LT Pass. Van Ext	16735	19720
2 Dr LT 4WD Pass. Van Ext	18225	21475
2 Dr STD Cargo Van Ext	13250	15615
2 Dr STD 4WD Cargo Van Ext	14820	17465
2 Dr STD Pass. Van Ext	14085	16600
2 Dr STD 4WD Pass. Van Ext	15590	18370

OPTIONS FOR ASTRO

AM/FM Stereo Tape[Opt on STD] +150
Compact Disc W/fm/tape +295
Cruise Control[Opt on STD] +140
Luggage Rack[Opt on STD] +110
Power Door Locks[Opt on STD] +155
Power Mirrors[Opt on STD] +90
Power Windows[Opt on STD] +160
Privacy Glass[Opt on STD] +185
Rear Heater +125
Rear Window Defroster[Opt on LS,STD,4WD] +115
Rear Window Wiper +105
Tilt Steering Wheel[Opt on STD] +120
Tutone Paint +170

BLAZER   1999

Blazer gets automatic transmission improvements, new exterior colors and larger outside mirrors, while four-wheel-drive versions can be equipped with GM's

AutoTrac active transfer case. Inside, there're new power-seating features, upgraded sound system options and available redundant radio controls in the steering wheel. On the safety side, the '99 Blazer now offers a vehicle content theft alarm, flash-to-pass headlamp feature, and a liftgate ajar warning lamp. What's more, a new TrailBlazer trim package is available on four-door versions, featuring monochrome paint with gold accents, unique aluminum wheels, touring suspension and leather-lined interior.

RATINGS (SCALE OF 1-10)

Overall	Safety	Reliability	Performance	Comfort	Value
N/A	7.3	8.7	8	7.9	N/A

Category G

	Trade-in	Market
2 Dr LS Utility	13085	15520
2 Dr LS 4WD Utility	14685	17470
4 Dr LS Wgn	15195	18355
4 Dr LS 4WD Wgn	17440	20830
4 Dr LT Wgn	16480	19900
4 Dr LT 4WD Wgn	17910	21560
2 Dr STD Utility	13200	15405
2 Dr STD 4WD Utility	12790	15325
4 Dr STD Wgn	15555	18335
4 Dr STD 4WD Wgn	16775	19765
4 Dr Trailblazer Wgn	19920	23480
4 Dr Trailblazer 4WD Wgn	21335	25145

OPTIONS FOR BLAZER

Auto 4-Speed Transmission[Opt on Utility] +670
ZR2 Suspension Pkg +1135
AM/FM Compact Disc Player[Std on Utility] +210
AM/FM Stereo Tape[Std on LS,LT,Trailblazer,Utility] +150
Aluminum/Alloy Wheels[Std on LS,LT,Trailblazer,Utility] +215
Compact Disc W/fm/tape +295
Cruise Control[Opt on STD] +140
Heated Front Seats +190
Luggage Rack[Std on LS,LT,Trailblazer,Utility] +110
Overhead Console[Opt on LS,STD] +105
Power Door Locks[Opt on STD] +155
Power Drivers Seat[Opt on Wgn] +190
Power Sunroof[Opt on LS] +530
Power Windows[Opt on STD] +160
Rear Window Defroster[Opt on STD] +115
Rear Window Wiper[Opt on STD] +105
Swing Out Tire Carrier +125
Tilt Steering Wheel[Opt on STD] +120

C/K PICKUP   1999

C/K 1500 SERIES

Category H

	Trade-in	Market
2 Dr LS Ext Cab SB	14595	17005
2 Dr LS 4WD Ext Cab SB	16565	19295

Don't forget to refer to the Mileage Adjustment Table at the back of this book!

Model Description	Trade-in Value	Market Value

C/K 2500 SERIES
Category H

Model Description	Trade-in Value	Market Value
4 Dr LS 4WD Crew Cab SB	18585	21650
2 Dr LS Ext Cab LB	14370	16740
2 Dr LS 4WD Ext Cab LB	16385	19030
2 Dr LS 4WD Ext Cab SB	16255	18940
2 Dr LS Std Cab LB	13395	15605
2 Dr LS 4WD Std Cab LB	15070	17555
4 Dr STD Crew Cab SB	14425	16805
4 Dr STD 4WD Crew Cab SB	16355	19055
2 Dr STD Ext Cab LB	12980	15120
2 Dr STD 4WD Ext Cab LB	14945	17410
2 Dr STD 4WD Ext Cab SB	14865	17320
2 Dr STD Std Cab LB	12005	13985
2 Dr STD 4WD Std Cab LB	13680	15935

C/K 3500 SERIES
Category H

Model Description	Trade-in Value	Market Value
4 Dr LS Crew Cab LB	16320	19010
4 Dr LS 4WD Crew Cab LB	18245	21255
4 Dr LS Crew Cab SB	17215	20055
4 Dr LS 4WD Crew Cab SB	19145	22305
2 Dr LS Ext Cab LB	15595	18170
2 Dr LS 4WD Ext Cab LB	17305	20160
2 Dr LS Std Cab LB	13575	15815
2 Dr LS 4WD Std Cab LB	15395	17935
4 Dr STD Crew Cab LB	14090	16410
4 Dr STD 4WD Crew Cab LB	16015	18660
4 Dr STD Crew Cab SB	14990	17460
4 Dr STD 4WD Crew Cab SB	16915	19705
2 Dr STD Ext Cab LB	14265	16620
2 Dr STD 4WD Ext Cab LB	15975	18610
2 Dr STD Std Cab LB	12185	14195
2 Dr STD 4WD Std Cab LB	14010	16320

OPTIONS FOR C/K PICKUP
8 cyl 5.7 L Engine[Opt on C/K 1500] +675
8 cyl 6.5 L Turbodsl Engine +1910
Auto 4-Speed Transmission[Std on C/K 1500] +665
AM/FM Compact Disc Player +205
Air Conditioning[Opt on STD] +545
Aluminum/Alloy Wheels +210
Bed Liner +150
Camper/Towing Package +220
Cruise Control[Opt on STD] +130
Keyless Entry System +115
Leather Seats +670
Power Door Locks[Opt on STD] +125
Power Drivers Seat +190
Privacy Glass +105
Skid Plates +70
Sliding Rear Window +80
Tilt Steering Wheel[Opt on STD] +125

CAMARO 1999

Traction control (Acceleration Slip Regulation in Chevrolet parlance) is available on all models in 1999, and on the Z28 ASR allows for some tire slip before killing the power to the rear wheels. Electronic throttle control is newly standard on V6 models, a new engine oil-life monitor tracks specific driving conditions to determine when the next change should occur and a Zexel Torsen differential is employed in the limited-slip rear axle.

RATINGS (SCALE OF 1-10)

Overall	Safety	Reliability	Performance	Comfort	Value
N/A	8	N/A	9	6.8	N/A

Category F

Model Description	Trade-in Value	Market Value
2 Dr STD Conv	15725	18360
2 Dr STD Cpe	11965	13970
2 Dr Z28 Conv	19540	22815
2 Dr Z28 Cpe	14855	17345
2 Dr Z28 SS Conv	21625	25250
2 Dr Z28 SS Cpe	16975	19820

OPTIONS FOR CAMARO
Auto 4-Speed Transmission[Opt on STD] +545
Performance Pkg +910
Sport Appearance Pkg +980
AM/FM Compact Disc Player +310
Alarm System[Opt on STD,Cpe] +120
Aluminum/Alloy Wheels[Opt on STD] +205
Cruise Control[Opt on STD,Cpe] +150
Fog Lights[Opt on STD,Cpe] +120
Glass Panel T-tops +660
Keyless Entry System[Opt on STD,Cpe] +120
Leather Seats +425
Power Door Locks[Opt on STD,Cpe] +135
Power Drivers Seat[Opt on STD,Cpe] +160
Power Mirrors[Opt on STD,Cpe] +75
Power Windows[Opt on STD,Cpe] +155
Rear Window Defroster[Opt on Cpe] +115

CAVALIER 1999

Chevrolet changes little on this slow-selling compact for 1999. The 2.4 twin cam engine benefits from reliability, emissions and fuel economy enhancements, and new front brake linings increase pad life. Minor interior and exterior revisions have been made, and Fern Green Metallic and Sandrift Metallic replace Bright Aqua and Deep Purple on the paint chart.

RATINGS (SCALE OF 1-10)

Overall	Safety	Reliability	Performance	Comfort	Value
N/A	6.8	8.8	6.6	7.5	N/A

Category E

Model Description	Trade-in Value	Market Value
4 Dr LS Sdn	9635	11560
2 Dr RS Cpe	8810	10570

Model Description	Trade-in Value	Market Value
2 Dr STD Cpe	7995	9595
4 Dr STD Sdn	8060	9670
2 Dr Z24 Conv	12965	15560
2 Dr Z24 Cpe	10640	12770

OPTIONS FOR CAVALIER

4 cyl 2.4 L Engine[Opt on LS] +300
Auto 3-Speed Transmission +400
Auto 4-Speed Transmission[Std on LS] +520
AM/FM Compact Disc Player +290
AM/FM Stereo Tape[Std on LS,Z24] +200
Air Conditioning[Std on LS,Z24] +555
Bucket Seats +80
Power Door Locks[Std on Z24] +165
Power Mirrors[Std on Z24] +75
Power Sunroof +415
Power Windows[Std on Z24] +180
Rear Window Defroster[Std on Conv] +110

CORVETTE   1999

A hardtop model aimed at enthusiasts is introduced, and it's options list is short. Other Corvettes can be equipped with numerous options including a new heads-up display and a power tilt/telescope steering wheel.

RATINGS (SCALE OF 1-10)

Overall	Safety	Reliability	Performance	Comfort	Value
N/A	N/A	N/A	8.8	7.1	N/A

Category J

Model	Trade-in	Market
2 Dr STD Conv	35685	41070
2 Dr STD Cpe	30665	35295
2 Dr STD Hardtop	30360	34940

OPTIONS FOR CORVETTE

6-Speed Transmission[Std on Hardtop] +545
Damping Suspension +1130
Sport Magnesium Wheels +2005
AM/FM Compact Disc Player +260
Bose Sound System +550
Climate Control for AC +190
Dual Power Seats +495
Fog Lights +45
Power Drivers Seat[Opt on Hardtop] +235

EXPRESS   1999

The Chevy Express line of full-size vans now include both the Passenger Van version and the newly renamed Cargo Van, in a variety of configurations, including the G1500 (1/2-ton), G2500 (3/4-ton) and G3500 (1-ton) series. Two wheelbases (135-inches and 155-inches) are available on 2500 and 3500 models. For '99, all Express vans get automatic transmission enhancements to increase durability and improve sealing, plus de-powered dual front airbags. There are also two new exterior paint colors and one new interior shade for the 1999 model year.

RATINGS (SCALE OF 1-10)

Overall	Safety	Reliability	Performance	Comfort	Value
N/A	N/A	N/A	4.8	6.5	N/A

Category H

Model	Trade-in	Market
2 Dr G1500 Cargo Van	12665	14755
2 Dr G1500 LS Pass. Van	15585	18160
2 Dr G1500 Pass. Van	14565	16970
2 Dr G2500 Cargo Van	12945	15080
2 Dr G2500 Cargo Van Ext	13500	15730
2 Dr G2500 LS Pass. Van	17130	19955
2 Dr G2500 Pass. Van	16110	18765
2 Dr G2500 LS Pass. Van Ext	17685	20600
2 Dr G2500 Pass. Van Ext	16665	19410
2 Dr G3500 Cargo Van	13890	16185
2 Dr G3500 Cargo Van Ext	14450	16830
2 Dr G3500 LS Pass. Van	17305	20160
2 Dr G3500 Pass. Van	16285	18975
2 Dr G3500 LS Pass. Van Ext	17860	20810
2 Dr G3500 Pass. Van Ext	16840	19620

OPTIONS FOR EXPRESS

8 cyl 5.0 L Engine +330
8 cyl 5.7 L Engine[Opt on G15,G25] +675
8 cyl 6.5 L Turbodsl Engine +1910
8 cyl 7.4 L Engine +400
15 Passenger Seating +545
AM/FM Compact Disc Player +205
Air Conditioning[Opt on Cargo Van,Cargo Van Ext] +545
Aluminum/Alloy Wheels +210
Cruise Control[Std on LS] +130
Dual Air Conditioning +860
Keyless Entry System +115
Power Door Locks[Std on LS] +125
Power Drivers Seat +190
Power Windows[Std on LS] +130
Rear Heater +140
Tilt Steering Wheel[Std on LS] +125

LUMINA   1999

Chevrolet adds standard equipment to the LTZ and introduces Auburn Nightmist Medium Metallic to the base and LS models.

RATINGS (SCALE OF 1-10)

Overall	Safety	Reliability	Performance	Comfort	Value
N/A	7.8	7.9	7.4	7.3	N/A

Category C

Model	Trade-in	Market
4 Dr LS Sdn	12225	14485
4 Dr LTZ Sdn	12485	14795
4 Dr STD Sdn	11190	13260

OPTIONS FOR LUMINA

AM/FM Compact Disc Player +235
Aluminum/Alloy Wheels[Opt on STD] +205
Anti-Lock Brakes[Opt on STD] +395
Keyless Entry System +125

Don't forget to refer to the Mileage Adjustment Table at the back of this book!

CHEVROLET 99

Model Description	Trade-in Value	Market Value	Model Description	Trade-in Value	Market Value

Leather Seats +415
Power Drivers Seat +200
Power Mirrors[Opt on STD] +70

MALIBU   1999

The 1999 Malibu is identical to the 1998 model, unless you consider the addition of Medium Bronzemist Metallic to the paint chart big news.

RATINGS (SCALE OF 1-10)

Overall	Safety	Reliability	Performance	Comfort	Value
N/A	N/A	N/A	8	8.3	N/A

Category C
4 Dr LS Sdn	11695	13860
4 Dr STD Sdn	9915	11750

OPTIONS FOR MALIBU
6 cyl 3.1 L Engine[Std on LS] +395
AM/FM Stereo Tape[Std on LS] +110
Cruise Control[Std on LS] +145
Power Door Locks[Std on LS] +170
Power Mirrors[Std on LS] +70
Power Windows[Std on LS] +215
Rear Window Defroster[Std on LS] +115

METRO   1999

After getting a makeover last year to mark its move from the old Geo nameplate to the Chevrolet model family, the Metro is a carryover product for 1999, save for the addition of two new exterior colors: Dark Green Metallic and Silver Metallic.

RATINGS (SCALE OF 1-10)

Overall	Safety	Reliability	Performance	Comfort	Value
N/A	6.3	N/A	5.2	6.4	N/A

Category E
2 Dr LSi Hbk	6160	7390
4 Dr LSi Sdn	6530	7835
2 Dr STD Hbk	5675	6810

OPTIONS FOR METRO
Auto 3-Speed Transmission +395
AM/FM Stereo Tape +200
Air Conditioning +555
Power Steering +170
Rear Window Defroster +110

MONTE CARLO   1999

Deep Purple is gone. No, we're not talking about '70s rock bands here, just metallic paint. Meaning that, except for Medium Auburn Nightmist replacing Deep Purple on Chevy's color availability chart (we could guess what Deep Purple looked like, but Medium Auburn Nightmist?), the Monte Carlo is a carryover model. Unless, of course, you count the availability of the optional OnStar communications system, a 24-hour roadside assistance network that is accessed through a dealer-installed cellular phone.

RATINGS (SCALE OF 1-10)

Overall	Safety	Reliability	Performance	Comfort	Value
N/A	7.6	N/A	7.4	7.5	N/A

Category C
2 Dr LS Cpe	11745	13915
2 Dr Z34 Cpe	12990	15395

OPTIONS FOR MONTE CARLO
AM/FM Compact Disc Player +235
Aluminum/Alloy Wheels[Opt on LS] +205
Bucket Seats[Opt on LS] +110
Leather Seats +415
Power Drivers Seat +200
Power Moonroof +460
Rear Spoiler +120

PRIZM   1999

After a thorough revision last year, the only changes for 1999 are four new paint colors.

RATINGS (SCALE OF 1-10)

Overall	Safety	Reliability	Performance	Comfort	Value
N/A	7.2	9.2	7.2	7.8	N/A

Category E
4 Dr LSi Sdn	9535	11440
4 Dr STD Sdn	7930	9515

OPTIONS FOR PRIZM
Auto 3-Speed Transmission +330
Auto 4-Speed Transmission +535
AM/FM Compact Disc Player +290
Air Conditioning[Std on LSi] +555
Power Windows +180
Rear Window Defroster +110
Tilt Steering Wheel +100

S-10   1999

An all-new sport package called the Xtreme replaces the old SS model. All S-10s get automatic transmission enhancements to improve sealing and durability and larger outside mirrors with an optional power heated mirror. Other changes for '99 include a content theft alarm, headlamp flash-to-pass feature, three new exterior paint choices and the availability of GM's AutoTrac electronic push-button transfer case on select four-wheel-drive models.

RATINGS (SCALE OF 1-10)

Overall	Safety	Reliability	Performance	Comfort	Value
N/A	6.5	N/A	6.6	8.1	N/A

Category G
2 Dr LS Xtreme Ext Cab SB	12340	14545
2 Dr LS Ext Cab SB	10895	12840

Model Description	Trade-in Value	Market Value
2 Dr LS Wide Stance 4WD Ext Cab SB		
	16865	19880
2 Dr LS 4WD Ext Cab SB	13945	16435
2 Dr LS Ext Cab Stepside SB	11220	13220
2 Dr LS Xtreme Ext Cab Stepside SB		
	12665	14925
2 Dr LS 4WD Ext Cab Stepside SB		
	14235	16780
2 Dr LS Std Cab LB	9730	11465
2 Dr LS 4WD Std Cab LB	12900	15205
2 Dr LS Xtreme Std Cab SB	11130	13115
2 Dr LS Std Cab SB	9485	11180
2 Dr LS Wide Stance 4WD Std Cab SB		
	15335	18070
2 Dr LS 4WD Std Cab SB	12610	14860
2 Dr LS Std Cab Stepside SB	9710	11445
2 Dr LS 4WD Std Cab Stepside SB		
	12935	15245
2 Dr STD Std Cab LB	9135	10765
2 Dr STD 4WD Std Cab LB	12020	14165
2 Dr STD Std Cab SB	8680	10225
2 Dr STD 4WD Std Cab SB	11795	13900

OPTIONS FOR S-10
6 cyl 4.3 L Engine[Std on 4WD] +730
6 cyl 4.3 L Vortec Engine[Std on LS Wide Stance] +615
Auto 4-Speed Transmission +715
AM/FM Compact Disc Player +210
Air Conditioning[Std on ZR2] +550
Aluminum/Alloy Wheels[Std on ZR2] +215
Cruise Control[Std on LS Wide Stance,2 Dr LS 4WD
    Extended Cab Stepside SB] +140
Hinged Third Door[Opt on LS Xtreme,2,LS 4WD Extended
    Cab SB] +225
Power Door Locks[Opt on LS,LS Xtreme] +155
Power Windows[Opt on LS,LS Xtreme] +160
Privacy Glass[Std on LS Wide Stance,2 Dr LS 4WD
    Extended Cab Stepside SB] +185
Tilt Steering Wheel[Std on LS Wide Stance,2 Dr LS 4WD
    Extended Cab Stepside SB] +120

SILVERADO   1999

Finally, after having the same basic design since 1988, Chevy brings out a new line of pickups. Dubbed Silverado, which was a former trim level, the new trucks are more refined, stylish and powerful than before.

RATINGS (SCALE OF 1-10)

Overall	Safety	Reliability	Performance	Comfort	Value
N/A	N/A	N/A	7.6	8.5	N/A

SILVERADO 1500

Category H

Model Description	Trade-in Value	Market Value
2 Dr LS Ext Cab LB	15125	17625
2 Dr LS 4WD Ext Cab LB	17105	19925

Model Description	Trade-in Value	Market Value
2 Dr LS Ext Cab SB	14555	16960
2 Dr LS 4WD Ext Cab SB	16910	19700
2 Dr LS Ext Cab Stepside SB	14935	17400
2 Dr LS 4WD Ext Cab Stepside SB		
	17290	20145
2 Dr LS Std Cab LB	12995	15140
2 Dr LS 4WD Std Cab LB	14970	17440
2 Dr LS Std Cab SB	12805	14915
2 Dr LS 4WD Std Cab SB	14780	17220
2 Dr LS Std Cab Stepside SB	13185	15360
2 Dr LS 4WD Std Cab Stepside SB		
	15160	17660
2 Dr LT Ext Cab LB	18115	21100
2 Dr LT 4WD Ext Cab LB	20160	23485
2 Dr LT Ext Cab SB	17920	20880
2 Dr LT 4WD Ext Cab SB	19965	23260
2 Dr STD Ext Cab LB	13470	15695
2 Dr STD 4WD Ext Cab LB	15445	17995
2 Dr STD Ext Cab SB	12900	15030
2 Dr STD 4WD Ext Cab SB	15255	17770
2 Dr STD Ext Cab Stepside SB	13345	15545
2 Dr STD 4WD Ext Cab Stepside SB		
	15700	18290
2 Dr STD Std Cab LB	10385	12100
2 Dr STD 4WD Std Cab LB	12370	14410
2 Dr STD Std Cab SB	10195	11875
2 Dr STD 4WD Std Cab SB	12180	14190
2 Dr STD Std Cab Stepside SB	10635	12390
2 Dr STD 4WD Std Cab Stepside SB		
	12625	14705

SILVERADO 2500

Category H

Model Description	Trade-in Value	Market Value
2 Dr LS Ext Cab SB	16310	19000
2 Dr LS Std Cab LB	14760	17195
2 Dr LT Ext Cab SB	18025	21000
2 Dr STD Ext Cab SB	14665	17085
2 Dr STD Std Cab LB	13120	15285

OPTIONS FOR SILVERADO
8 cyl 4.8 L Engine[Opt on Std Cab, 2WD Ext. Cab SB] +395
8 cyl 5.3 L Engine[Std on Silverado 2500,LT] +680
8 cyl 6.0 L Engine +335
Auto 4-Speed Transmission[Std on Silverado 2500,LT] +665
AM/FM Stereo Tape +135
Air Conditioning[Opt on STD] +545
Aluminum/Alloy Wheels[Std on LT] +210
Bucket Seats +250
Camper/Towing Package +220
Chrome Wheels[Std on LS] +200
Cruise Control[Opt on STD] +130
Locking Differential +170
Power Door Locks[Opt on STD] +125
Privacy Glass[Std on LT] +105
Skid Plates +70

CHEVROLET 99

Model Description	Trade-in Value	Market Value	Model Description	Trade-in Value	Market Value

SUBURBAN 1999

A couple of new colors are the only modifications to the Suburban as Chevrolet prepares a redesigned model for 2000.

RATINGS (SCALE OF 1-10)

Overall	Safety	Reliability	Performance	Comfort	Value
N/A	8.2	8.1	7	7.9	N/A

Category H

	Trade-in	Market
4 Dr C1500 Wgn	18950	22075
4 Dr C2500 Wgn	20090	23405
4 Dr K1500 4WD Wgn	20915	24365
4 Dr K2500 4WD Wgn	21970	25595

OPTIONS FOR SUBURBAN

8 cyl 6.5 L Turbodsl Engine +1910
8 cyl 7.4 L Engine +400
AM/FM Compact Disc Player +205
Air Conditioning +545
Aluminum/Alloy Wheels +210
Camper/Towing Package +220
Center & Rear Bench Seat +765
Center Console +90
Cruise Control +130
Dual Air Conditioning +860
Keyless Entry System +115
Leather Seats +670
Luggage Rack +105
Overhead Console +90
Power Drivers Seat +190
Power Mirrors +70
Power Windows +130
Privacy Glass +105
Rear Heater +140
Rear Window Defroster +105
Rear Window Wiper +85
Tilt Steering Wheel +125

TAHOE 1999

The standard cargo net is deleted, and new colors are added as Tahoe cruises into final model year in current guise.

RATINGS (SCALE OF 1-10)

Overall	Safety	Reliability	Performance	Comfort	Value
N/A	N/A	N/A	7.4	8	N/A

Category H

	Trade-in	Market
2 Dr LS Utility	20440	23815
2 Dr LS 4WD Utility	22280	25955
4 Dr LS Wgn	21455	24990
4 Dr LS 4WD Wgn	23385	27240
2 Dr LT Utility	21395	24925
2 Dr LT 4WD Utility	23235	27065
4 Dr LT Wgn	22500	26210
4 Dr LT 4WD Wgn	24340	28355

	Trade-in	Market
2 Dr STD Utility	17350	20215
2 Dr STD 4WD Utility	19190	22355

OPTIONS FOR TAHOE

8 cyl 6.5 L Turbodsl Engine +1910
Special Z-71 Pkg +1530
Air Conditioning[Opt on STD] +545
Aluminum/Alloy Wheels[Opt on STD] +210
Bucket Seats +250
Camper/Towing Package +220
Compact Disc W/fm/tape[Std on LT] +210
Cruise Control[Opt on STD] +130
Dual Air Conditioning +860
Dual Power Seats +315
Rear Window Defroster[Opt on STD] +105
Running Boards +235
Tilt Steering Wheel[Opt on STD] +125

TRACKER 1999

The redesigned-for-1999 Tracker, available in either two-door convertible or four-door hardtop versions and in two- or four-wheel drive, features sporty new looks, more power, improved ride and handling and a roomier, more comfortable interior.

RATINGS (SCALE OF 1-10)

Overall	Safety	Reliability	Performance	Comfort	Value
N/A	N/A	N/A	6.6	7.4	N/A

Category G

	Trade-in	Market
2 Dr STD Conv	9305	10970
2 Dr STD 4WD Conv	10040	11830
4 Dr STD Wgn	10105	11910
4 Dr STD 4WD Wgn	10835	12770

OPTIONS FOR TRACKER

4 cyl 2.0 L Engine[Std on Wgn] +265
Auto 4-Speed Transmission +670
AM/FM Compact Disc Player +210
AM/FM Stereo Tape +150
Air Conditioning +550
Aluminum/Alloy Wheels +215
Cruise Control +140
Luggage Rack +110
Power Door Locks +155
Power Mirrors +90
Power Windows +160
Rear Window Wiper +105
Tilt Steering Wheel +120

VENTURE 1999

Venture gets some performance and safety enhancements. Other changes include additional seating choices, four new exterior and two new interior colors, as well as fatter standard tires. What's more, there's a newly badged LT model that packages an upgraded audio system with a touring suspension,

CHEVROLET 99-98

Model Description	Trade-in Value	Market Value	Model Description	Trade-in Value	Market Value

traction control and captain's seats with available leather.

RATINGS (SCALE OF 1-10)

Overall	Safety	Reliability	Performance	Comfort	Value
N/A	8	8.5	7.4	7.9	N/A

Category G
4 Dr LS Pass. Van	16035	18895
4 Dr LS Pass. Van Ext	16500	19445
4 Dr LT Pass. Van Ext	18045	21265
2 Dr STD Pass. Van	13885	16365
4 Dr STD Pass. Van	14730	17360
4 Dr STD Pass. Van Ext	15380	18130

OPTIONS FOR VENTURE

AM/FM Stereo Tape[Std on LS] +150
Compact Disc W/fm/tape[Std on LT] +295
Cruise Control[Opt on STD] +140
Keyless Entry System[Opt on STD] +130
Luggage Rack[Opt on STD] +110
Power Windows[Opt on STD] +160
Privacy Glass[Opt on STD] +185

1998 CHEVROLET

ASTRO   1998

New colors, improved clearcoating, a standard theft deterrent system (like anybody wants to steal one of these) and the addition of composite headlights and an uplevel grille to base models are all that's different on this year's Astro. Full-power airbags continue for 1998.

RATINGS (SCALE OF 1-10)

Overall	Safety	Reliability	Performance	Comfort	Value
7.4	6.9	8.1	6.8	6.5	8.5

Category G
2 Dr LS Pass. Van Ext	13620	16130
2 Dr LS 4WD Pass. Van Ext	14715	17425
2 Dr LT Pass. Van Ext	14605	17295
2 Dr LT 4WD Pass. Van Ext	15925	18855
2 Dr STD Cargo Van Ext	11615	13755
2 Dr STD 4WD Cargo Van Ext	13015	15410
2 Dr STD Pass. Van Ext	12100	14330
2 Dr STD 4WD Pass. Van Ext	13440	15915

OPTIONS FOR ASTRO

AM/FM Compact Disc Player +175
Aluminum/Alloy Wheels[Std on LT] +175
Cruise Control[Opt on STD] +115
Dual Air Conditioning +505
Dual Power Seats +230
Keyless Entry System[Std on LT] +105
Leather Seats +430
Power Door Locks[Opt on STD] +130
Power Drivers Seat[Std on LT] +155

Power Mirrors[Opt on STD] +70
Power Windows[Opt on STD] +135
Rear Heater +105
Rear Window Defroster[Std on LT] +95
Tilt Steering Wheel[Opt on STD] +100

BLAZER   1998

Blazer gets a nose job and an interior redesign. New standard equipment includes a theft deterrent system, automatic headlight control, four-wheel disc brakes and dual airbags incorporating second-generation technology to reduce the bags' inflation force. New radios, colors, and a column-mounted automatic shift selector round out the major changes.

RATINGS (SCALE OF 1-10)

Overall	Safety	Reliability	Performance	Comfort	Value
7.6	7.4	7.7	8	7.9	7

Category G
2 Dr LS Utility	13860	16415
2 Dr LS 4WD Utility	14800	17525
4 Dr LS Wgn	14935	17685
4 Dr LS 4WD Wgn	16085	19045
4 Dr LT Wgn	16160	19140
4 Dr LT 4WD Wgn	17310	20500
2 Dr STD Utility	11405	14105
2 Dr STD 4WD Utility	11505	14115
4 Dr STD Wgn	13900	16460
4 Dr STD 4WD Wgn	14840	17570

OPTIONS FOR BLAZER

Auto 4-Speed Transmission[Opt on Utility] +485
Wide Stance Suspension +935
AM/FM Compact Disc Player +175
Aluminum/Alloy Wheels[Opt on STD] +175
Cruise Control[Opt on STD] +115
Fog Lights[Opt on LS] +80
Heated Front Seats +150
Keyless Entry System[Opt on LS] +105
Power Door Locks[Opt on STD] +130
Power Drivers Seat[Opt on LS] +155
Power Mirrors +70
Power Sunroof +430
Power Windows[Opt on STD] +135
Rear Window Defroster[Opt on STD] +95
Rear Window Wiper[Opt on STD] +85
Sport Suspension +245
Tilt Steering Wheel[Opt on STD] +100

C/K PICKUP   1998

This year's big news is a standard theft deterrent system, revised color choices, and fresh tailgate lettering. The Sport package has been dropped from the option list. Second generation airbags are standard on models under 8,600 GVWR.

Model Description	Trade-in Value	Market Value

Overall	Safety	Reliability	Performance	Comfort	Value
N/A	8	6.9	7.8	8.4	N/A

C/K 1500 SERIES

Category H

Model Description	Trade-in Value	Market Value
2 Dr C1500 Cheyenne Ext Cab LB	12845	15855
2 Dr C1500 Cheyenne Ext Cab SB	12545	14725
2 Dr C1500 Cheyenne Std Cab LB	11125	13055
2 Dr C1500 Cheyenne Std Cab SB	11010	12920
2 Dr C1500 Cheyenne Std Cab Stepside SB	10825	12705
2 Dr C1500 Silverado Ext Cab LB	13400	15630
2 Dr C1500 Silverado Ext Cab SB	13230	15530
2 Dr C1500 Silverado Ext Cab Stepside SB	13380	15700
2 Dr C1500 Silverado Std Cab LB	11025	12920
2 Dr C1500 Silverado Std Cab SB	10850	12710
2 Dr C1500 Silverado Std Cab Stepside SB	11590	13605
2 Dr C1500 WT Std Cab LB	9440	11030
2 Dr C1500 WT Std Cab SB	9250	10810
2 Dr K1500 Cheyenne 4WD Ext Cab LB	14400	16825
2 Dr K1500 Cheyenne 4WD Ext Cab SB	14310	16715
2 Dr K1500 Cheyenne 4WD Std Cab LB	12795	14950
2 Dr K1500 Cheyenne 4WD Std Cab SB	12710	14845
2 Dr K1500 Cheyenne 4WD Std Cab Stepside SB	12950	15045
2 Dr K1500 Silverado 4WD Ext Cab LB	14575	17030
2 Dr K1500 Silverado 4WD Ext Cab SB	14405	16825
2 Dr K1500 Silverado 4WD Ext Cab Stepside SB	14465	16900
2 Dr K1500 Silverado 4WD Std Cab LB	13100	15305
2 Dr K1500 Silverado 4WD Std Cab SB	12920	15100
2 Dr K1500 Silverado 4WD Std Cab Stepside SB	13260	15495
2 Dr K1500 WT 4WD Std Cab LB	11630	13585
2 Dr K1500 WT 4WD Std Cab SB	11440	13365

C/K 2500 SERIES

Category H

Model Description	Trade-in Value	Market Value
2 Dr C2500 Cheyenne Ext Cab SB	12170	14220
2 Dr C2500 Cheyenne Std Cab LB	10665	12465
2 Dr C2500 HD Cheyenne Ext Cab LB	12190	14245
2 Dr C2500 HD Cheyenne Std Cab LB	11270	13170
2 Dr C2500 HD Silverado Ext Cab LB	13505	15780
2 Dr C2500 HD Silverado Std Cab LB	12585	14705
2 Dr C2500 Silverado Ext Cab SB	13485	15755
2 Dr C2500 Silverado Std Cab LB	11980	14000
2 Dr K2500 HD Cheyenne 4WD Ext Cab LB	14050	16415
2 Dr K2500 HD Cheyenne 4WD Ext Cab SB	13980	16330
2 Dr K2500 HD Cheyenne 4WD Std Cab LB	12855	15020
2 Dr K2500 HD Silverado 4WD Ext Cab LB	15365	17950
2 Dr K2500 HD Silverado 4WD Ext Cab SB	15290	17865
2 Dr K2500 HD Silverado 4WD Std Cab LB	14170	16555

C/K 3500 SERIES

Category H

Model Description	Trade-in Value	Market Value
4 Dr C3500 Cheyenne Crew Cab LB	14275	16750
2 Dr C3500 Cheyenne Ext Cab LB	13315	15550
2 Dr C3500 Cheyenne Std Cab LB	12145	14255
4 Dr C3500 Silverado Crew Cab LB	15260	17830
2 Dr C3500 Silverado Ext Cab LB	14240	16715
2 Dr C3500 Silverado Std Cab LB	12665	14795
4 Dr K3500 Cheyenne 4WD Crew Cab LB	14975	17495

Model Description	Trade-in Value	Market Value
2 Dr K3500 Cheyenne 4WD Ext Cab LB	13960	16385
2 Dr K3500 Cheyenne 4WD Std Cab LB	13075	15275
4 Dr K3500 Silverado 4WD Crew Cab LB	17065	20025
2 Dr K3500 Silverado 4WD Ext Cab LB	16190	18915
2 Dr K3500 Silverado 4WD Std Cab LB	14390	16810

OPTIONS FOR C/K PICKUP

8 cyl 5.0 L Engine[Std on C1500 Silverado Ext. Cab, C2500, K1500] +270
8 cyl 5.7 L Engine[Opt on C1500, C2500, K1500, K2500 LD] +545
8 cyl 6.5 L Turbodsl Engine +1645
8 cyl 7.4 L Engine +330
Auto 4-Speed Transmission +530
AM/FM Compact Disc Player +170
Air Conditioning[Std on Silverado] +445
Aluminum/Alloy Wheels +170
Bed Liner +125
Camper/Towing Package +180
Cruise Control[Std on Silverado] +105
Hinged Third Door +230
Keyless Entry System +95
Leather Seats +545
Power Door Locks[Opt on Cheyenne] +105
Power Drivers Seat +155
Rear Window Defroster +85
Skid Plates +60
Sliding Rear Window +65
Tilt Steering Wheel[Std on Silverado] +105

CAMARO   1998

Chevrolet dumps a 305-horsepower version of the Corvette's V8 engine under a new front end, adds standard four-wheel disc brakes on all models, adds a couple of new colors, makes second generation airbags standard, and revises trim levels. The midyear SS package makes 320 horsepower. Uh, why were you considering that Mustang again?

RATINGS (SCALE OF 1-10)

Overall	Safety	Reliability	Performance	Comfort	Value
7.2	8	7.8	9.2	6.8	4.1

Category F
2 Dr STD Conv	14430	16910
2 Dr STD Cpe	10930	12805
2 Dr Z28 Conv	17635	20665
2 Dr Z28 Cpe	13380	15675
2 Dr Z28 SS Conv	20425	23935
2 Dr Z28 SS Cpe	15895	18625

OPTIONS FOR CAMARO

Auto 4-Speed Transmission[Opt on STD] +445
Performance Pkg +640
Sport Appearance Pkg +810
AM/FM Compact Disc Player +255
Aluminum/Alloy Wheels[Opt on STD] +170
Chrome Wheels +320
Cruise Control[Opt on STD, Cpe] +120
Fog Lights[Opt on STD, Cpe] +100
Glass Panel T-tops +540
Keyless Entry System[Opt on STD, Cpe] +100
Leather Seats +345
Limited Slip Diff[Opt on STD] +180
Power Door Locks[Opt on STD, Cpe] +110
Power Drivers Seat[Opt on STD, Cpe] +130
Power Mirrors[Opt on STD, Cpe] +65
Power Windows[Opt on STD, Z28, Cpe] +125
Rear Window Defroster[Opt on Cpe] +90

CAVALIER   1998

A Z24 convertible is introduced, cruise control is standard on all but base models, power windows and remote keyless entry are no longer available on base cars, and...hold on to your seats, buyers can no longer delete the AM/FM radio. Second-generation airbags debut on all models.

RATINGS (SCALE OF 1-10)

Overall	Safety	Reliability	Performance	Comfort	Value
7.1	6.8	8.3	7	7.6	5.8

Category E
4 Dr LS Sdn	8735	10585
2 Dr RS Cpe	7920	9595
2 Dr STD Cpe	7175	8690
4 Dr STD Sdn	7290	8830
2 Dr Z24 Conv	11795	14285
2 Dr Z24 Cpe	9600	11630

OPTIONS FOR CAVALIER

4 cyl 2.4 L Engine[Opt on LS] +245
Auto 3-Speed Transmission +330
Auto 4-Speed Transmission[Std on LS] +425
AM/FM Compact Disc Player +235
Air Conditioning[Opt on RS, STD] +455
Aluminum/Alloy Wheels[Std on Z24] +185
Cruise Control[Opt on STD] +125
Keyless Entry System[Std on Z24] +90
Power Door Locks[Std on Z24] +135
Power Mirrors[Std on Z24] +60
Power Sunroof +340
Power Windows[Std on Z24] +145
Rear Window Defroster[Std on Conv] +90
Tilt Steering Wheel[Opt on STD] +80
Traction Control System[Std on LS] +25

Model Description	Trade-in Value	Market Value

CHEVY VAN/EXPRESS   1998

All vans equipped with airbags switch to mini-module bag designs for the driver, but they still deploy with more force than second-generation types. A theft-deterrent system is standard, and three new colors debut.

CHEVY VAN

Category H

Model Description	Trade-in Value	Market Value
2 Dr G1500 Chevy Van	11515	13455
2 Dr G2500 Chevy Van	11760	13740
2 Dr G2500 Chevy Van Ext	12275	14340
2 Dr G3500 Chevy Van	12635	14765
2 Dr G3500 Chevy Van Ext	13150	15365

EXPRESS

Category H

Model Description	Trade-in Value	Market Value
2 Dr G1500 Express Van	13820	16145
2 Dr G1500 LS Express Van	14440	16875
2 Dr G2500 Express Van	14930	17445
2 Dr G2500 Express Van Ext	15450	18050
2 Dr G2500 LS Express Van	15885	18560
2 Dr G2500 LS Express Van Ext	16405	19165
2 Dr G3500 Express Van	15095	17640
2 Dr G3500 Express Van Ext	15615	18245
2 Dr G3500 LS Express Van	16050	18755
2 Dr G3500 LS Express Van Ext	16570	19360

OPTIONS FOR CHEVY VAN/EXPRESS

8 cyl 5.0 L Engine +270
8 cyl 5.7 L Engine[Opt on G15, G25 Chevy Van] +545
8 cyl 6.5 L Turbodsl Engine +1645
8 cyl 7.4 L Engine +330
15 Passenger Seating +445
8 Passenger Seating[Std on G15] +200
AM/FM Compact Disc Player +170
Air Conditioning[Opt on Chevy Van, Chevy Van Ext] +445
Aluminum/Alloy Wheels +170
Cruise Control[Std on LS] +105
Dual Air Conditioning +705
Heated Power Mirrors +50
Keyless Entry System +95
Power Door Locks[Std on LS] +105
Power Drivers Seat +155
Power Windows[Std on LS] +105
Rear Heater +115
Tilt Steering Wheel[Std on LS] +105

CORVETTE   1998

Two fresh colors are available, but the new convertible model steals the show. Equipped with a manual folding top, a hard tonneau that extends along the rear wall of the passenger compartment and a real live trunk that holds golf bags, this new drop top should prove quite popular. Lower-powered airbags are not available on the Corvette.

Category J

Model Description	Trade-in Value	Market Value
2 Dr STD Conv	34680	39940
2 Dr STD Cpe	29555	34040

OPTIONS FOR CORVETTE

6-Speed Transmission +445
Selective Damping System +925
Sport Magnesium Wheels +1640
AM/FM Compact Disc Player +215
Climate Control for AC +155
Dual Power Seats +405
Fog Lights +40
Glass Targa Top +355

LUMINA   1998

Last year's aborted LTZ sport sedan comes on strong for 1998, with a 200-horsepower 3800 V6 engine and machine-faced aluminum wheels. Four new exterior colors and one new interior color are also available on all Lumina models. To help give Lumina a more upscale image than Malibu, an OnStar Mobile Communications system is a dealer-installed option. Second-generation airbags are standard equipment.

RATINGS (SCALE OF 1-10)

Overall	Safety	Reliability	Performance	Comfort	Value
7.9	7.8	8	7.6	7.3	8.8

Category C

Model Description	Trade-in Value	Market Value
4 Dr LS Sdn	10670	12730
4 Dr LTZ Sdn	10940	13050
4 Dr STD Sdn	9590	11445

OPTIONS FOR LUMINA

6 cyl 3.8 L Engine[Opt on LTZ] +235
AM/FM Compact Disc Player +190
Aluminum/Alloy Wheels[Opt on STD] +170
Anti-Lock Brakes[Opt on STD] +325
Cruise Control +120
Keyless Entry System +100
Leather Seats +340
Power Drivers Seat +165
Power Mirrors[Opt on STD] +60
Power Moonroof +375
Power Windows[Opt on STD] +175
Rear Window Defroster +90

MALIBU   1998

Leather trim is newly optional on LS models, aluminum wheels are revised, a sunroof can be ordered and Base models can be equipped with Medium Oak colored interior. Second-generation airbags debut.

RATINGS (SCALE OF 1-10)

Overall	Safety	Reliability	Performance	Comfort	Value
N/A	N/A	8.3	8	8.3	7.5

Don't forget to refer to the Mileage Adjustment Table at the back of this book!

Model Description	Trade-in Value	Market Value
Category C		
4 Dr LS Sdn	10690	12755
4 Dr STD Sdn	9040	10790

OPTIONS FOR MALIBU

6 cyl 3.1 L Engine[Std on LS] +245
AM/FM Compact Disc Player +190
Aluminum/Alloy Wheels[Std on LS] +170
Cruise Control[Std on LS] +120
Keyless Entry System[Std on LS] +100
Leather Seats +340
Power Door Locks[Std on LS] +140
Power Drivers Seat[Std on LS] +165
Power Mirrors[Std on LS] +60
Power Sunroof +365
Power Windows[Std on LS] +175
Rear Window Defroster[Std on LS] +90

METRO   1998

The Geo badge is replaced with a Chevy bowtie. Styling is updated front and rear. The LSi's four-cylinder engine gets four valves per cylinder for more power and better acceleration. Second-generation airbags are standard equipment. Wheel covers are revised, new radios, new interior fabrics, and the addition of California Gold Metallic to the paint palette round out the changes.

RATINGS (SCALE OF 1-10)

Overall	Safety	Reliability	Performance	Comfort	Value
6.1	6.3	8	5.2	6.4	4.8

	Trade-in	Market
Category E		
2 Dr LSi Hbk	5285	6400
4 Dr LSi Sdn	5605	6790
2 Dr STD Hbk	4905	5940

OPTIONS FOR METRO

Auto 3-Speed Transmission +320
AM/FM Compact Disc Player +235
Air Conditioning +455
Anti-Lock Brakes +365
Power Door Locks +135
Power Steering +140
Rear Window Defroster +90
Rear Window Wiper +70

MONTE CARLO   1998

The Z34 model gets a different engine and fresh wheels. Second-generation airbags are added. New paint colors and one new interior hue round out the changes.

RATINGS (SCALE OF 1-10)

Overall	Safety	Reliability	Performance	Comfort	Value
7.5	7.6	7.7	7.4	7.5	7.1

Model Description	Trade-in Value	Market Value
Category C		
2 Dr LS Cpe	10365	12370
2 Dr Z34 Cpe	11780	14055

OPTIONS FOR MONTE CARLO

AM/FM Compact Disc Player +190
Aluminum/Alloy Wheels[Opt on LS] +170
Cruise Control[Opt on LS] +120
Keyless Entry System[Opt on LS] +100
Leather Seats +340
Power Drivers Seat +165
Power Moonroof +375
Rear Window Defroster +90

PRIZM   1998

Chevy replaces the Geo badge with their own on the completely redesign- ed Prizm. Among the improvements are a larger standard engine, optional side airbags, an optional handling package for LSi models and new colors inside and out. Front airbags are of the de-powered variety.

RATINGS (SCALE OF 1-10)

Overall	Safety	Reliability	Performance	Comfort	Value
7.5	7.2	9.2	7.2	7.8	6

	Trade-in	Market
Category E		
4 Dr LSi Sdn	8560	10365
4 Dr STD Sdn	7130	8640

OPTIONS FOR PRIZM

Auto 3-Speed Transmission +270
Auto 4-Speed Transmission +435
AM/FM Compact Disc Player +235
Air Conditioning +455
Aluminum/Alloy Wheels +185
Anti-Lock Brakes +365
Cruise Control +125
Power Door Locks[Opt on STD] +135
Power Sunroof +340
Power Windows +145
Rear Window Defroster +90
Side Air Bag Restraint +155
Tilt Steering Wheel +80

S-10   1998

The S-10 gets a sheetmetal makeover and a new interior with dual airbags that incorporate second-generation technology for reduced force deployments. The basic four-cylinder engine benefits from Vortec technology this year, while 4WD models now have four-wheel disc brakes and a more refined transfer case on trucks with an automatic transmission. New radios, automatic headlight control, and a standard theft-deterrent system sum up the changes.

Don't forget to refer to the Mileage Adjustment Table at the back of this book!

Model Description	Trade-in Value	Market Value

RATINGS (SCALE OF 1-10)

Overall	Safety	Reliability	Performance	Comfort	Value
N/A	6.6	7.3	6.6	8.1	N/A

Category G

Model Description	Trade-in Value	Market Value
2 Dr LS Ext Cab SB	10010	11855
2 Dr LS 4WD Ext Cab SB	12810	15170
2 Dr LS Ext Cab Stepside SB	10315	12210
2 Dr LS 4WD Ext Cab Stepside SB	13095	15510
2 Dr LS Std Cab LB	8930	10575
2 Dr LS 4WD Std Cab LB	11875	14060
2 Dr LS Std Cab SB	8705	10310
2 Dr LS 4WD Std Cab SB	11600	13740
2 Dr LS Std Cab Stepside SB	9010	10670
2 Dr LS 4WD Std Cab Stepside SB	11890	14075
2 Dr STD Std Cab LB	8375	9920
2 Dr STD 4WD Std Cab LB	11055	13090
2 Dr STD Std Cab SB	7955	9420
2 Dr STD 4WD Std Cab SB	10845	12840
2 Dr ZR2 4WD Ext Cab SB	15705	18600
2 Dr ZR2 4WD Std Cab SB	14670	17375

OPTIONS FOR S-10

6 cyl 4.3 L Engine[Opt on 2WD] +595
6 cyl 4.3 L Vortec Engine[Std on ZR2] +440
Auto 4-Speed Transmission[Std on ZR2] +585
AM/FM Compact Disc Player +175
Air Conditioning[Std on ZR2] +450
Aluminum/Alloy Wheels[Opt on LS] +175
Cruise Control[Std on ZR2] +115
Fog Lights +80
Heavy Duty Suspension +80
Hinged Third Door +185
Keyless Entry System[Opt on LS] +105
Power Door Locks[Opt on LS] +130
Power Mirrors[Opt on LS] +70
Power Windows[Opt on LS] +135
Premium Sound System +185
Skid Plates[Std on ZR2] +75
Sliding Rear Window +65
Sport Suspension +245
Tilt Steering Wheel[Std on ZR2] +100

SUBURBAN   1998

New colors, a standard theft deterrent system, optional heated seats, second generation airbags, and an automatic 4WD system improve the 1998 Suburban.

RATINGS (SCALE OF 1-10)

Overall	Safety	Reliability	Performance	Comfort	Value
7.6	8.1	7.8	7	7.9	7.4

Category H

Model Description	Trade-in Value	Market Value
4 Dr C1500 Wgn	17885	20840
4 Dr C2500 Wgn	18665	21810
4 Dr K1500 4WD Wgn	19360	22620
4 Dr K2500 4WD Wgn	20445	23885

OPTIONS FOR SUBURBAN

8 cyl 6.5 L Turbodsl Engine[Opt on 2500] +1645
8 cyl 7.4 L Engine[Opt on 2500] +330
LS Pkg +1875
LT Pkg +2290
AM/FM Compact Disc Player +170
Air Conditioning +445
Aluminum/Alloy Wheels +170
Camper/Towing Package +180
Cruise Control +105
Dual Air Conditioning +705
Heated Front Seats +200
Keyless Entry System +95
Leather Seats +545
Power Drivers Seat +155
Power Mirrors +55
Power Windows +105
Privacy Glass +85
Rear Heater +115
Rear Window Defroster +85
Rear Window Wiper +70
Tilt Steering Wheel +105

TAHOE   1998

Autotrac is a new optional automatic four-wheel drive system that switches from 2WD to 4WD automatically as conditions warrant. A new option package includes heated seats and heated exterior mirrors. Second generation airbags deploy with less force than last year. A theft deterrent system is standard, and color selections are modified.

RATINGS (SCALE OF 1-10)

Overall	Safety	Reliability	Performance	Comfort	Value
7.7	8.2	7.7	7.4	8	7.4

Category H

Model Description	Trade-in Value	Market Value
2 Dr LS Utility	19350	22610
2 Dr LS 4WD Utility	21110	24665
4 Dr LS Wgn	20320	23745
4 Dr LS 4WD Wgn	22080	25800
2 Dr LT Utility	20265	23680
2 Dr LT 4WD Utility	22025	25735
4 Dr LT Wgn	21235	24810
4 Dr LT 4WD Wgn	22995	26865
2 Dr STD Utility	16605	19400
2 Dr STD 4WD Utility	18155	21210

OPTIONS FOR TAHOE

8 cyl 6.5 L Turbodsl Engine[Opt on 2 Dr] +1645
AM/FM Compact Disc Player +170
Air Conditioning[Opt on STD] +445
Aluminum/Alloy Wheels[Opt on STD] +170
Camper/Towing Package +180
Cruise Control[Opt on STD] +105

Don't forget to refer to the Mileage Adjustment Table at the back of this book!

CHEVROLET 98-97

Model Description	Trade-in Value	Market Value
Model Description	Trade-in Value	Market Value

Heated Front Seats +200
Rear Window Defroster[Opt on STD] +85
Rear Window Wiper[Opt on STD] +70
Running Boards +190
Tilt Steering Wheel[Opt on STD] +105

TRACKER   1998

Geo is gone, so all Trackers are now badged as Chevrolets. The LSi models are dropped, though an LSi equipment package is available on Base models. Two new colors are available. Second-generation airbags are standard.

RATINGS (SCALE OF 1-10)

Overall	Safety	Reliability	Performance	Comfort	Value
6.2	5.8	8.6	5.8	6.8	4.2

Category G

2 Dr STD Conv	8110	9600
2 Dr STD 4WD Conv	8690	10290
4 Dr STD Wgn	8805	10430
4 Dr STD 4WD Wgn	9240	10940

OPTIONS FOR TRACKER

Auto 3-Speed Transmission +340
Auto 4-Speed Transmission +545
AM/FM Compact Disc Player +175
Air Conditioning +450
Aluminum/Alloy Wheels +175
Anti-Lock Brakes +320
Auto Locking Hubs (4WD) +145
Cruise Control +115
Power Door Locks +130
Power Mirrors +70
Power Steering[Std on Wgn,4WD] +155
Power Windows +135
Rear Window Wiper +85

VENTURE   1998

Venture is the first minivan to get side-impact airbags. Other changes include the availability of a cargo van edition, a wider variety of dual door models, and an optional power sliding door on regular wheelbase vans. Power rear window vents are also added for 1998. Front airbags deploy with less force thanks to second-generation technology.

RATINGS (SCALE OF 1-10)

Overall	Safety	Reliability	Performance	Comfort	Value
7.6	7.8	7.7	7.8	7.9	7

Category G

2 Dr LS Pass. Van	13610	16120
2 Dr LS Pass. Van Ext	14335	16975
2 Dr STD Pass. Van	12675	15010
2 Dr STD Pass. Van Ext	13540	16030

OPTIONS FOR VENTURE

AM/FM Compact Disc Player +175
Aluminum/Alloy Wheels +175
Cruise Control[Std on LS] +115
Keyless Entry System[Std on LS] +105
Power Drivers Seat +155
Power Windows[Std on LS] +135
Privacy Glass +150
Rear Window Defroster +95
Sliding Driver Side Door +290
Traction Control System +145

1997 CHEVROLET

ASTRO   1997

Daytime running lights debut, and LT models can be equipped with leather upholstery. Also optional this year is a HomeLink three-channel transmitter. Delayed entry/exit lighting is now standard on all Astro passenger vans. Transmission refinements mean smoother shifts, and electronic variable orifice steering eases steering effort at low speeds.

RATINGS (SCALE OF 1-10)

Overall	Safety	Reliability	Performance	Comfort	Value
7.2	6.8	7.4	6.8	6.5	8.4

Category G

2 Dr LS Pass. Van Ext	11930	14195
2 Dr LS 4WD Pass. Van Ext	12880	15320
2 Dr LT Pass. Van Ext	13115	15600
2 Dr LT 4WD Pass. Van Ext	14275	16980
2 Dr STD Cargo Van Ext	10550	12550
2 Dr STD 4WD Cargo Van Ext	11735	13955
2 Dr STD Pass. Van Ext	10865	12925
2 Dr STD 4WD Pass. Van Ext	12045	14330

OPTIONS FOR ASTRO

8 Passenger Seating[Opt on STD] +180
AM/FM Compact Disc Player +140
Aluminum/Alloy Wheels[Std on LT] +145
Child Seats (2) +115
Cruise Control[Opt on STD] +95
Dual Air Conditioning +410
Keyless Entry System[Std on LT] +85
Leather Seats +350
Power Door Locks[Opt on STD] +105
Power Drivers Seat[Std on LT] +125
Power Mirrors[Std on LT] +60
Power Windows[Opt on STD] +110
Privacy Glass[Opt on STD] +120
Rear Heater +85
Tilt Steering Wheel[Opt on STD] +80

BLAZER   1997

Those who prefer a liftgate over a tailgate have that option on 1997 four-door Blazers. A power sunroof is

CHEVROLET 97

Model Description	Trade-in Value	Market Value	Model Description	Trade-in Value	Market Value

a new option for all Blazers, and models equipped with LT decor are equipped with a HomeLink transmitter that will open your garage, among other things. All-wheel drive Blazers get four-wheel disc brakes, and automatic transmissions are revised for smoother shifting. Early production 4WD two-door Blazers could be ordered with a ZR2 suspension package, but by the time we got pricing, Chevrolet had cancelled the option. Base Blazers get a chrome grille, while LT four-door models have body-color grilles in six exterior colors. Two new paint colors round out the changes.

RATINGS (SCALE OF 1-10)

Overall	Safety	Reliability	Performance	Comfort	Value
7.1	5.3	7.4	8	7.9	6.9

Category G
2 Dr LS Utility	12165	14470
2 Dr LS 4WD Utility	12915	15365
4 Dr LS Wgn	13065	15540
4 Dr LS 4WD Wgn	14035	16695
4 Dr LT Wgn	14250	16950
4 Dr LT 4WD Wgn	15160	18035
2 Dr STD Utility	11255	13390
2 Dr STD 4WD Utility	12180	14485
4 Dr STD Wgn	12070	14360
4 Dr STD 4WD Wgn	13010	15475

OPTIONS FOR BLAZER

Auto 4-Speed Transmission[Std on Wgn] +395
Wide Stance Suspension +825
AM/FM Compact Disc Player +140
Aluminum/Alloy Wheels[Opt on STD] +145
Cruise Control[Opt on STD] +95
Keyless Entry System[Opt on LS] +85
Power Door Locks[Opt on STD] +105
Power Drivers Seat[Opt on LS] +125
Power Mirrors[Opt on STD] +60
Power Sunroof +355
Power Windows[Opt on STD] +110
Running Boards +175
Skid Plates +60
Swing Out Tire Carrier[Opt on 4WD,Utility] +85
Tilt Steering Wheel[Opt on STD] +80

C/K PICKUP   1997

Order a truck under 8,600 lbs. GVWR, and you'll get a passenger airbag. The airbag can be deactivated when a rear-facing child safety seat is installed. Low-speed steering effort is reduced this year, and a refined transmission fluid pump results in smoother shifts. An alternative fuel version of the Vortec 5700 is available, but only on a specific model. K1500's get a tighter turning radius, and three new colors debut. The third door option will be more widely available, because it is now a required option on all C/K 1500 shortbed extended cab trucks.

RATINGS (SCALE OF 1-10)

Overall	Safety	Reliability	Performance	Comfort	Value
N/A	8	6.7	7.8	8.4	N/A

C/K 1500 SERIES

Category H
2 Dr C1500 Cheyenne Ext Cab LB	11950	14020
2 Dr C1500 Cheyenne Ext Cab SB	11345	13310
2 Dr C1500 Cheyenne Ext Cab Stepside SB	11425	13410
2 Dr C1500 Cheyenne Std Cab LB	10225	12000
2 Dr C1500 Cheyenne Std Cab SB	10145	11905
2 Dr C1500 Cheyenne Std Cab Stepside SB	10325	12115
2 Dr C1500 Silverado Ext Cab LB	12740	15010
2 Dr C1500 Silverado Ext Cab SB	11815	13865
2 Dr C1500 Silverado Ext Cab Stepside SB	12855	15090
2 Dr C1500 Silverado Std Cab LB	11425	13405
2 Dr C1500 Silverado Std Cab SB	9610	11560
2 Dr C1500 Silverado Std Cab Stepside SB	9705	11620
2 Dr C1500 WT Std Cab LB	8195	9620
2 Dr C1500 WT Std Cab SB	8100	9505
2 Dr K1500 Cheyenne 4WD Ext Cab LB	13520	15795
2 Dr K1500 Cheyenne 4WD Ext Cab SB	13390	15645
2 Dr K1500 Cheyenne 4WD Ext Cab Stepside SB	13400	15725
2 Dr K1500 Cheyenne 4WD Std Cab LB	10870	12695
2 Dr K1500 Cheyenne 4WD Std Cab SB	10760	12570
2 Dr K1500 Cheyenne 4WD Std Cab Stepside SB	10785	12600
2 Dr K1500 Silverado 4WD Ext Cab LB	13175	15390
2 Dr K1500 Silverado 4WD Ext Cab SB	13075	15275

Model Description	Trade-in Value	Market Value	Model Description	Trade-in Value	Market Value
2 Dr K1500 Silverado 4WD Ext Cab Stepside SB			2 Dr C3500 Silverado Ext Cab LB		
	13120	15325		12875	15110
2 Dr K1500 Silverado 4WD Std Cab LB			2 Dr C3500 Silverado Std Cab LB		
	11860	13855		12105	14205
2 Dr K1500 Silverado 4WD Std Cab SB			4 Dr K3500 Cheyenne 4WD Crew Cab LB		
	11755	13730		14060	16500
2 Dr K1500 Silverado 4WD Std Cab Stepside SB			2 Dr K3500 Cheyenne 4WD Ext Cab LB		
	11805	13790		11940	14015
2 Dr K1500 WT 4WD Std Cab LB	9890	11550	2 Dr K3500 Cheyenne 4WD Std Cab LB		
2 Dr K1500 WT 4WD Std Cab SB	9785	11430		12990	15300

C/K 2500 SERIES

Category H

Model Description	Trade-in Value	Market Value	Model Description	Trade-in Value	Market Value
2 Dr C2500 Cheyenne Ext Cab SB			4 Dr K3500 Silverado 4WD Crew Cab LB		
	11045	12960		15425	18100
2 Dr C2500 Cheyenne Std Cab LB			2 Dr K3500 Silverado 4WD Ext Cab LB		
	9950	11675		14370	16865
2 Dr C2500 HD Cheyenne Ext Cab LB			2 Dr K3500 Silverado 4WD Std Cab LB		
	11175	13110		13075	15345
2 Dr C2500 HD Cheyenne Std Cab LB					
	10305	12095			

OPTIONS FOR C/K PICKUP

2 Dr C2500 HD Silverado Ext Cab LB		
	12430	14590
2 Dr C2500 HD Silverado Std Cab LB		
	11365	13335
2 Dr C2500 Silverado Ext Cab SB		
	12120	14225
2 Dr C2500 Silverado Std Cab LB		
	11460	13450
2 Dr K2500 HD Cheyenne 4WD Ext Cab LB		
	12520	14695
2 Dr K2500 HD Cheyenne 4WD Ext Cab SB		
	12420	14575
2 Dr K2500 HD Cheyenne 4WD Std Cab LB		
	11250	13205
2 Dr K2500 HD Silverado 4WD Ext Cab LB		
	13725	16105
2 Dr K2500 HD Silverado 4WD Ext Cab SB		
	13635	16000
2 Dr K2500 HD Silverado 4WD Std Cab LB		
	12745	14955

8 cyl 5.0 L Engine +220
8 cyl 5.7 L Engine +465
8 cyl 6.5 L Turbodsl Engine +1365
8 cyl 7.4 L Engine +270
Auto 4-Speed Transmission +435
AM/FM Compact Disc Player +140
Air Conditioning[Std on Silverado] +365
Aluminum/Alloy Wheels +140
Automatic Dimming Mirror[Std on Crew Cab] +65
Bed Liner +100
Camper/Towing Package +150
Cruise Control[Std on Silverado] +85
Hinged Third Door +185
Keyless Entry System +80
Leather Seats +445
Power Door Locks[Opt on Cheyenne] +85
Power Drivers Seat +125
Tilt Steering Wheel[Std on Silverado] +85

C/K 3500 SERIES

Category H

Model Description	Trade-in Value	Market Value
4 Dr C3500 Cheyenne Crew Cab LB		
	13110	15390
2 Dr C3500 Cheyenne Ext Cab LB		
	12095	14195
2 Dr C3500 Cheyenne Std Cab LB		
	11260	13215
4 Dr C3500 Silverado Crew Cab LB		
	14120	16570

CAMARO 1997

Chevrolet celebrates the Camaro's 30th Anniversary with a special-edition Z28 that emulates the appearance of the 1969 SS Indy Pace Car with white paint, Hugger Orange stripes, and black-and-white houndstooth seat inserts. Interior revisions to seats, center console and dashboard freshen the look inside for 1997. Two new shades of gray are available for interiors, while exteriors get new green and purple hues. Tri-color taillamps debut, and new five-spoke alloy wheels are optional. On the safety front, daytime running lights are standard and side-impact regulations are met.

RATINGS (SCALE OF 1-10)

Overall	Safety	Reliability	Performance	Comfort	Value
7.2	7.9	7.4	9.2	6.8	4.5

Don't forget to refer to the Mileage Adjustment Table at the back of this book!

Model Description	Trade-in Value	Market Value
Category F		
2 Dr RS Conv	13485	15965
2 Dr RS Cpe	10675	12635
2 Dr STD Conv	12870	15235
2 Dr STD Cpe	9660	11440
2 Dr Z28 Conv	14820	17545
2 Dr Z28 Cpe	11915	14105
2 Dr Z28 SS Conv	17100	20240
2 Dr Z28 SS Cpe	14020	16600

OPTIONS FOR CAMARO
Auto 4-Speed Transmission[Std on Z28,SS] +350
Performance Pkg +505
Sport Suspension Pkg +525
Torsen Torque Sensing Axle +445
AM/FM Compact Disc Player +205
Aluminum/Alloy Wheels[Opt on STD] +135
Cruise Control +100
Fog Lights +80
Glass Panel T-tops +440
Keyless Entry System +80
Leather Seats +285
Limited Slip Diff[Opt on RS,STD] +145
Power Door Locks +90
Power Drivers Seat +110
Power Mirrors +50
Power Windows +105

CAVALIER   1997

The historically on-again off-again Rally Sport (RS) trim level is evidently on-again, attached for 1997 to the coupe and slotted between base and Z24 editions of the Cavalier. RS trim nets buyers the rear spoiler from the Z24, 15-inch tires, AM/FM stereo, tachometer, interior and exterior trim goodies, and a really cool (yeah, right) 3D rear quarter panel decal. Base coupes have new wheel covers and safety belt guide loops. All 1997 Cavaliers meet federal side-impact standards for the first time. One new interior color and three new exterior colors freshen the lineup.

RATINGS (SCALE OF 1-10)

Overall	Safety	Reliability	Performance	Comfort	Value
6.7	6.5	7.3	7	7.6	5.3

Model Description	Trade-in Value	Market Value
Category E		
2 Dr LS Conv	9800	11845
4 Dr LS Sdn	7450	9000
2 Dr RS Cpe	6830	8250
2 Dr STD Cpe	6270	7575
4 Dr STD Sdn	6270	7575
2 Dr Z24 Cpe	8030	9705

OPTIONS FOR CAVALIER
4 cyl 2.4 L Engine[Opt on LS, Z24] +190
Auto 3-Speed Transmission[Std on LS] +235
Auto 4-Speed Transmission[Std on LS] +345

AM/FM Compact Disc Player +195
Air Conditioning[Opt on RS,STD] +370
Aluminum/Alloy Wheels[Std on Z24] +150
Cruise Control +100
Keyless Entry System +75
Power Door Locks +110
Power Mirrors +50
Power Sunroof +280
Power Windows +120
Tilt Steering Wheel[Std on Z24] +65

CHEVY VAN/EXPRESS   1997

Dual airbags appear on the G3500 model, while daytime running lights and three fresh exterior colors make this van easier to see. (Editor's Note: If you can't see this monster van without DRL's, perhaps you should consider surrendering your driver's license.) Electronic variable orifice steering reduces effort at low speeds for easier parking, and automatic transmissions shift more smoothly.

CHEVY VAN

Model Description	Trade-in Value	Market Value
Category G		
2 Dr G1500 Chevy Van	10945	12845
2 Dr G2500 Chevy Van	11180	13120
2 Dr G2500 Chevy Van Ext	11680	13710
2 Dr G3500 Chevy Van	11945	14020
2 Dr G3500 Chevy Van Ext	12450	14610

EXPRESS

Model Description	Trade-in Value	Market Value
Category H		
2 Dr G1500 Express Van	12210	14330
2 Dr G1500 LS Express Van	12665	14860
2 Dr G2500 Express Van	13150	15430
2 Dr G2500 Express Van Ext	13615	15975
2 Dr G2500 LS Express Van	13970	16395
2 Dr G2500 LS Express Van Ext	14435	16940
2 Dr G3500 Express Van	13230	15525
2 Dr G3500 Express Van Ext	13695	16075
2 Dr G3500 LS Express Van	14055	16490
2 Dr G3500 LS Express Van Ext	14520	17040

OPTIONS FOR CHEVY VAN/EXPRESS
8 cyl 5.0 L Engine +220
8 cyl 5.7 L Engine[Opt on G1500] +465
8 cyl 6.5 L Turbodsl Engine +1365
8 cyl 7.4 L Engine +270
15 Passenger Seating +365
8 Passenger Seating[Std on G1500] +165
AM/FM Compact Disc Player +140
Aluminum/Alloy Wheels +140
Cruise Control[Std on LS] +85
Dual Air Conditioning +575
Keyless Entry System +80
Power Door Locks[Std on LS] +85
Power Drivers Seat +125
Power Windows[Std on LS] +85

Model Description	Trade-in Value	Market Value	Model Description	Trade-in Value	Market Value

Privacy Glass +70
Rear Heater +95
Tilt Steering Wheel[Std on LS] +85

CORVETTE 1997

Fifth-generation Corvette debuts 44 years after the original, and is better than ever with world-class build quality and performance at a bargain price.
Category J

2 Dr STD Cpe	27365	31590

OPTIONS FOR CORVETTE
6-Speed Transmission +400
Selective Damping System +835
AM/FM Compact Disc Player +175
Climate Control for AC +125
Dual Power Seats +330
Fog Lights +30
Glass Targa Top +290
Solid & Glass Targa Tops +425
Sport Seats +320

LUMINA 1997

Performance-oriented Lumina LTZ debuts, though a spoiler, special front and rear styling, graphics, and alloy wheels don't amount to performance in our book. Daytime running lamps are standard on all Luminas, and the power sunroof expected last year finally arrives. New colors and an oil life monitor round out changes to Lumina for 1997.

RATINGS (SCALE OF 1-10)

Overall	Safety	Reliability	Performance	Comfort	Value
7.7	7.8	7.8	7.6	7.3	8.2

Category C

4 Dr LS Sdn	9545	11445
4 Dr LTZ Sdn	9690	11620
4 Dr STD Sdn	8480	10170

OPTIONS FOR LUMINA
6 cyl 3.4 L Engine +490
AM/FM Compact Disc Player +155
Aluminum/Alloy Wheels[Opt on STD] +140
Anti-Lock Brakes[Opt on STD] +265
Child Seat (1) +55
Cruise Control[Std on LS] +95
Keyless Entry System +85
Leather Seats +275
Power Drivers Seat +135
Power Moonroof +305
Power Windows[Opt on STD] +140

MALIBU 1997

Malibu returns after consumer clinics tell Chevrolet they want a tight, solid, roomy, fun-to-drive midsize sedan. Guess what? Chevrolet delivers.

RATINGS (SCALE OF 1-10)

Overall	Safety	Reliability	Performance	Comfort	Value
N/A	N/A	7.3	8	8.3	N/A

Category C

4 Dr LS Sdn	9175	11000
4 Dr STD Sdn	7840	9400

OPTIONS FOR MALIBU
6 cyl 3.1 L Engine[Std on LS] +190
AM/FM Compact Disc Player +155
Aluminum/Alloy Wheels[Std on LS] +140
Cruise Control[Std on LS] +95
Keyless Entry System[Std on LS] +85
Power Door Locks[Std on LS] +115
Power Drivers Seat[Std on LS] +135
Power Mirrors[Std on LS] +50
Power Windows[Std on LS] +140
Rear Window Defroster[Std on LS] +75

MONTE CARLO 1997

Hot-rod Z34 gets a new transmission, while all models have daytime running lights. Newly optional is a power sunroof. Two new colors freshen the rather dull sheetmetal.

RATINGS (SCALE OF 1-10)

Overall	Safety	Reliability	Performance	Comfort	Value
7.3	7.6	7.5	7.4	7.5	6.5

Category C

2 Dr LS Cpe	9115	10930
2 Dr Z34 Cpe	10385	12450

OPTIONS FOR MONTE CARLO
AM/FM Compact Disc Player +155
Aluminum/Alloy Wheels[Opt on LS] +140
Cruise Control[Opt on LS] +95
Keyless Entry System[Opt on LS] +85
Leather Seats +275
Power Drivers Seat +135
Power Sunroof +295

S-10 1997

Chevy strengthens the 2WD S-10 frame by using tougher components. Refinements to the automatic transmission result in improved efficiency and smoother shifts. Four-wheel drive models have lighter-weight plug-in half shafts. Two new colors are available.

RATINGS (SCALE OF 1-10)

Overall	Safety	Reliability	Performance	Comfort	Value
N/A	5	7.1	6.6	8.1	N/A

Category G

2 Dr LS Ext Cab SB	8825	10495
2 Dr LS 4WD Ext Cab SB	11595	13795
2 Dr LS Ext Cab Stepside SB	9090	10810

Model Description	Trade-in Value	Market Value
2 Dr LS 4WD Ext Cab Stepside SB	11860	14110
2 Dr LS Std Cab LB	7820	9305
2 Dr LS 4WD Std Cab LB	10725	12760
2 Dr LS Std Cab SB	7645	9095
2 Dr LS 4WD Std Cab SB	10475	12460
2 Dr LS Std Cab Stepside SB	7910	9410
2 Dr LS 4WD Std Cab Stepside SB	10740	12775
2 Dr STD Std Cab LB	7320	8705
2 Dr STD 4WD Std Cab LB	10140	12060
2 Dr STD Std Cab SB	7145	8495
2 Dr STD 4WD Std Cab SB	9945	11830

OPTIONS FOR S-10

6 cyl 4.3 L Engine[Opt on 2WD] +440
6 cyl 4.3 L Vortec Engine +335
Auto 4-Speed Transmission +480
Wide Stance Suspension +750
AM/FM Compact Disc Player +140
Air Conditioning +365
Aluminum/Alloy Wheels +145
Cruise Control +95
Heavy Duty Suspension +65
Hinged Third Door +150
Keyless Entry System +85
Power Door Locks +105
Power Mirrors +60
Power Windows +110
Skid Plates +60
Tilt Steering Wheel +80

SUBURBAN   1997

Dual airbags debut, and a cargo area power lock switch makes locking up the vehicle after unloading cargo more convenient. Electronic Variable Orifice power steering lightens low-speed steering effort, and automatic transmissions are improved. Two new exterior colors are added to the paint roster.

RATINGS (SCALE OF 1-10)

Overall	Safety	Reliability	Performance	Comfort	Value
7.5	8.1	7.3	7	7.9	7.2

Category H

	Trade-in Value	Market Value
4 Dr C1500 Wgn	16710	19765
4 Dr C2500 Wgn	18465	21675
4 Dr K1500 4WD Wgn	19420	22790
4 Dr K2500 4WD Wgn	20290	23810

OPTIONS FOR SUBURBAN

8 cyl 6.5 L Turbodsl Engine +1365
8 cyl 7.4 L Engine +270
AM/FM Compact Disc Player +140
Air Conditioning +365
Aluminum/Alloy Wheels +140
Automatic Dimming Mirror[Std on K2500] +65

Camper/Towing Package +150
Cruise Control +85
Dual Air Conditioning +575
Keyless Entry System +80
Leather Seats +445
Power Drivers Seat +125
Power Mirrors +45
Power Windows +85
Privacy Glass +70
Rear Heater +95
Tilt Steering Wheel +85

TAHOE   1997

A passenger-side airbag is added, and the automatic transmission is improved. Electronic Variable Orifice steering debuts, and cargo areas have a power door lock switch. A new center console comes with high-back bucket seats, and two new paint colors are available.

RATINGS (SCALE OF 1-10)

Overall	Safety	Reliability	Performance	Comfort	Value
7.7	8.2	7.4	7.4	8	7.3

Category H

	Trade-in Value	Market Value
2 Dr LS Utility	17280	20280
2 Dr LS 4WD Utility	18910	22195
4 Dr LS Wgn	18160	21310
4 Dr LS 4WD Wgn	19760	23190
2 Dr LT Utility	18230	21390
2 Dr LT 4WD Utility	19860	23305
4 Dr LT Wgn	19105	22425
4 Dr LT 4WD Wgn	20705	24300
2 Dr STD Utility	14850	17430
2 Dr STD 4WD Utility	16480	19345

OPTIONS FOR TAHOE

8 cyl 6.5 L Turbodsl Engine +1365
AM/FM Compact Disc Player +140
Air Conditioning[Opt on STD] +365
Aluminum/Alloy Wheels[Opt on STD] +140
Camper/Towing Package +150
Cruise Control[Opt on STD] +85
Keyless Entry System[Std on LT,LS Utility] +80
Power Drivers Seat[Opt on LS] +125
Privacy Glass[Opt on STD] +70
Tilt Steering Wheel[Opt on STD] +85
Velour/Cloth Seats[Std on LS] +50

VENTURE   1997

Complete redesign of Chevy's minivan results in a new name, a left-side sliding door, optional traction control, a powerful standard engine, and a fun-to-drive demeanor. Nice van, except for the big chrome grille.

Don't forget to refer to the Mileage Adjustment Table at the back of this book!

Model Description	Trade-in Value	Market Value

Model Description	Trade-in Value	Market Value

RATINGS (SCALE OF 1-10) *

Overall	Safety	Reliability	Performance	Comfort	Value
7.4	7	7.6	7.8	7.9	6.8

Category G
2 Dr LS Pass. Van	12115	14410
2 Dr LS Pass. Van Ext	12575	14960
2 Dr STD Pass. Van	11370	13525
2 Dr STD Pass. Van Ext	12015	14290

OPTIONS FOR VENTURE

AM/FM Compact Disc Player +140
Aluminum/Alloy Wheels +145
Child Seat (1) +75
Cruise Control +95
Dual Air Conditioning +410
Keyless Entry System +85
Power Drivers Seat +125
Power Windows +110
Privacy Glass +120
Sliding Driver Side Door +235
Traction Control System +120

1996 CHEVROLET

ASTRO   1996

A new interior with dual airbags, new radio systems, an improved V6, and three new paint colors are the changes for this year.

RATINGS (SCALE OF 1-10)

Overall	Safety	Reliability	Performance	Comfort	Value
7.2	6.9	7.5	6.8	6.5	8.3

Category G
2 Dr LS Pass. Van Ext	9810	11885
2 Dr LS 4WD Pass. Van Ext	10500	12720
2 Dr LT Pass. Van Ext	10695	12960
2 Dr LT 4WD Pass. Van Ext	11670	14140
2 Dr STD Cargo Van Ext	8730	10575
2 Dr STD 4WD Cargo Van Ext	9730	11790
2 Dr STD Pass. Van Ext	8995	10900
2 Dr STD 4WD Pass. Van Ext	10000	12115

OPTIONS FOR ASTRO

8 Passenger Seating[Opt on STD] +145
AM/FM Compact Disc Player +115
Aluminum/Alloy Wheels[Std on LT] +120
Child Seats (2) +90
Cruise Control[Opt on STD] +75
Dual Air Conditioning +335
Keyless Entry System[Std on LT] +70
Power Door Locks[Opt on STD] +85
Power Drivers Seat[Std on LT] +105
Power Mirrors[Std on LT] +50
Power Windows[Opt on STD] +90
Privacy Glass[Opt on STD] +100

Rear Heater +70
Tilt Steering Wheel[Opt on STD] +65

BERETTA   1996

Final year for Beretta. Only change is the addition of long-life coolant to the engine.

RATINGS (SCALE OF 1-10)

Overall	Safety	Reliability	Performance	Comfort	Value
6.8	6.4	7.7	7.8	7	5

Category E
2 Dr STD Cpe	5930	7365
2 Dr Z26 Cpe	7290	9050

OPTIONS FOR BERETTA

6 cyl 3.1 L Engine[Opt on STD] +175
Auto 3-Speed Transmission +195
Auto 4-Speed Transmission[Opt on STD] +270
AM/FM Compact Disc Player +160
Aluminum/Alloy Wheels +125
Cruise Control +85
Power Windows +95
Sunroof +130
Tilt Steering Wheel +55

BLAZER   1996

More power, available all-wheel drive, and five new colors improve the 1996 Blazer. A five-speed manual transmission is optional on two-door models.

RATINGS (SCALE OF 1-10)

Overall	Safety	Reliability	Performance	Comfort	Value
6.4	4.9	6.6	8	7.9	4.8

Category G
2 Dr LS Utility	10590	12825
2 Dr LS 4WD Utility	11270	13655
4 Dr LS Wgn	11250	13630
4 Dr LS 4WD Wgn	12000	14540
4 Dr LT Wgn	12360	14970
4 Dr LT 4WD Wgn	12660	15340
2 Dr STD Utility	9410	11400
2 Dr STD 4WD Utility	10240	12405
4 Dr STD Wgn	10215	12375
4 Dr STD 4WD Wgn	10950	13260

OPTIONS FOR BLAZER

Auto 4-Speed Transmission[Std on Wgn] +315
AM/FM Compact Disc Player +115
Cruise Control[Opt on STD] +75
Keyless Entry System[Std on LT] +70
Power Door Locks[Opt on STD] +85
Power Drivers Seat[Std on LT] +105
Power Mirrors[Opt on STD] +50
Power Windows[Opt on STD] +90
Running Boards +140
Skid Plates +50
Tilt Steering Wheel[Opt on STD] +65

Don't forget to refer to the Mileage Adjustment Table at the back of this book!

Model Description	Trade-in Value	Market Value

C/K PICKUP   1996

Major engine improvements result in more horsepower and torque. Extended-cab models can be equipped with an access panel that opens to the rear of the cab from the passenger side of the truck. Daytime running lights are added, and K1500 models offer an optional electronic shift transfer case.

RATINGS (SCALE OF 1-10)

Overall	Safety	Reliability	Performance	Comfort	Value
N/A	7.4	6	7.8	8.4	N/A

C/K 1500 SERIES

Category H

Model Description	Trade-in Value	Market Value
2 Dr C1500 Cheyenne Ext Cab LB	11050	13035
2 Dr C1500 Cheyenne Ext Cab SB	10505	12390
2 Dr C1500 Cheyenne Ext Cab Stepside SB	10650	12500
2 Dr C1500 Cheyenne Std Cab LB	9470	11170
2 Dr C1500 Cheyenne Std Cab SB	9380	11010
2 Dr C1500 Cheyenne Std Cab Stepside SB	9440	11080
2 Dr C1500 Silverado Ext Cab LB	11865	13925
2 Dr C1500 Silverado Ext Cab SB	10960	12860
2 Dr C1500 Silverado Ext Cab Stepside SB	11915	14050
2 Dr C1500 Silverado Std Cab LB	10500	12320
2 Dr C1500 Silverado Std Cab SB	10240	12015
2 Dr C1500 Silverado Std Cab Stepside SB	10420	12230
2 Dr C1500 WT Std Cab LB	7075	8345
2 Dr C1500 WT Std Cab SB	6915	8155
2 Dr K1500 Cheyenne 4WD Ext Cab LB	12140	14320
2 Dr K1500 Cheyenne 4WD Ext Cab SB	11975	14125
2 Dr K1500 Cheyenne 4WD Ext Cab Stepside SB	12045	14205
2 Dr K1500 Cheyenne 4WD Std Cab LB	9470	11170
2 Dr K1500 Cheyenne 4WD Std Cab SB	9380	11065
2 Dr K1500 Cheyenne 4WD Std Cab Stepside SB	9420	11110
2 Dr K1500 Silverado 4WD Ext Cab LB	12105	14275
2 Dr K1500 Silverado 4WD Ext Cab SB	12000	14150
2 Dr K1500 Silverado 4WD Ext Cab Stepside SB	12055	14215
2 Dr K1500 Silverado 4WD Std Cab LB	10645	12555
2 Dr K1500 Silverado 4WD Std Cab SB	10540	12430
2 Dr K1500 Silverado 4WD Std Cab Stepside SB	10585	12485
2 Dr K1500 WT 4WD Std Cab LB	9005	10620
2 Dr K1500 WT 4WD Std Cab SB	8940	10545

C/K 2500 SERIES

Category H

Model Description	Trade-in Value	Market Value
2 Dr C2500 Cheyenne Ext Cab SB	9430	11125
2 Dr C2500 Cheyenne Std Cab LB	8480	10005
2 Dr C2500 HD Cheyenne Ext Cab LB	9360	11040
2 Dr C2500 HD Silverado Ext Cab LB	11530	13600
2 Dr C2500 Silverado Std Cab LB	10820	12760
2 Dr K2500 Cheyenne 4WD Ext Cab LB	11260	13285
2 Dr K2500 Cheyenne 4WD Ext Cab SB	11150	13155
2 Dr K2500 Cheyenne 4WD Std Cab LB	10265	12110
2 Dr K2500 Silverado 4WD Ext Cab LB	12625	14895
2 Dr K2500 Silverado 4WD Ext Cab SB	12525	14775
2 Dr K2500 Silverado 4WD Std Cab LB	11235	13255
2 Dr Silverado Ext Cab SB	12865	15175

C/K 3500 SERIES

Category H

Model Description	Trade-in Value	Market Value
4 Dr C3500 Cheyenne Crew Cab LB	11995	14150
2 Dr C3500 Cheyenne Ext Cab LB	11070	13060
2 Dr C3500 Cheyenne Std Cab LB	10125	11945
4 Dr C3500 Silverado Crew Cab LB	12920	15245
2 Dr C3500 Silverado Ext Cab LB	11835	13985

Don't forget to refer to the Mileage Adjustment Table at the back of this book!

Model Description	Trade-in Value	Market Value
2 Dr C3500 Silverado Std Cab LB	10375	12240
4 Dr K3500 Cheyenne 4WD Crew Cab LB	12745	15035
2 Dr K3500 Cheyenne 4WD Ext Cab LB	11860	13995
2 Dr K3500 Cheyenne 4WD Std Cab LB	11020	13000
4 Dr K3500 Silverado 4WD Crew Cab LB	14580	17200
2 Dr K3500 Silverado 4WD Ext Cab LB	13780	15785
2 Dr K3500 Silverado 4WD Std Cab LB	12040	14205

OPTIONS FOR C/K PICKUP
8 cyl 5.0 L Engine +205
8 cyl 5.7 L Engine +370
8 cyl 6.5 L Turbodsl Engine +1195
8 cyl 7.4 L Engine +225
Auto 4-Speed Transmission +350
Silverado Pkg 2 +555
AM/FM Compact Disc Player +115
Air Conditioning[Std on Silverado] +300
Automatic Dimming Mirror +55
Bed Liner +85
Camper/Towing Package +120
Cruise Control[Std on Silverado] +70
Hinged Third Door +155
Keyless Entry System +65
Leather Seats +365
Power Door Locks[Std on Silverado] +70
Power Drivers Seat +105
Tilt Steering Wheel[Std on Silverado] +70

CAMARO 1996

Hot, new, 200 hp base V6 whumps the Mustang. Z28's 285 hp, LT1 V8 (with 10 more horsepower this year), whumps the Mustang GT. SLP Engineering provides a 305-horse Z28 SS, which ties the new Mustang Cobra for horsepower. The RS trim level returns, and chrome aluminum wheels are optional.

RATINGS (SCALE OF 1-10)

Overall	Safety	Reliability	Performance	Comfort	Value
7.2	8	7.4	9.2	6.8	4.4

Category F

Model	Trade-in	Market
2 Dr RS Conv	11755	14010
2 Dr RS Cpe	9290	11070
2 Dr STD Conv	11240	13395
2 Dr STD Cpe	8000	9530
2 Dr Z28 Conv	12650	15075
2 Dr Z28 Cpe	10270	12235
2 Dr Z28 SS Conv	14675	17490
2 Dr Z28 SS Cpe	12095	14410

OPTIONS FOR CAMARO
Auto 4-Speed Transmission +280
Performance Pkg +430
R1 Wheels/tires Pkg +695
Suspension Pkg +365
Torque-sensing Axle +365
AM/FM Compact Disc Player +170
Air Conditioning[Opt on STD Cpe] +305
Aluminum/Alloy Wheels[Opt on STD] +110
Bose Sound System +165
Cruise Control +80
Fog Lights +65
Glass Panel T-tops +360
Keyless Entry System +65
Leather Seats +230
Limited Slip Diff[Opt on RS,STD] +120
Power Door Locks +75
Power Drivers Seat +90
Power Mirrors +40
Power Windows +85

CAPRICE 1996

Zero changes as Caprice enters final year of production.

RATINGS (SCALE OF 1-10)

Overall	Safety	Reliability	Performance	Comfort	Value
7.7	7.2	6.3	8.2	8.3	8.4

Category B

Model	Trade-in	Market
4 Dr STD Sdn	10530	12400
4 Dr STD Wgn	11965	14090

OPTIONS FOR CAPRICE
8 cyl 5.7 L Engine[Opt on Sdn] +190
Special Value Pkg 3 +295
Auto Load Leveling +65
Cruise Control +80
Dual Power Seats +140
Keyless Entry System +65
Leather Seats +250
Power Windows +105

CAVALIER 1996

The 2.3-liter Quad 4 is replaced after just one year by a 2.4-liter twin-cam engine. Four-speed automatic transmission includes traction control. Daytime running lights debut, remote keyless entry is optional on LS and Z24, and base models get new interior fabrics and an Appearance Package.

RATINGS (SCALE OF 1-10)

Overall	Safety	Reliability	Performance	Comfort	Value
6.8	6.4	6.7	7	7.6	6.1

Category E

Model	Trade-in	Market
2 Dr LS Conv	8165	10135
4 Dr LS Sdn	6080	7545
2 Dr STD Cpe	4990	6195

Model Description	Trade-in Value	Market Value
4 Dr STD Sdn	5080	6305
2 Dr Z24 Cpe	6670	8280

OPTIONS FOR CAVALIER
4 cyl 2.4 L Engine[Opt on LS] +125
Auto 3-Speed Transmission[Std on LS] +190
Auto 4-Speed Transmission +275
Preferred Equipment Grp-3 +275
AM/FM Compact Disc Player +160
Air Conditioning[Opt on STD] +305
Cruise Control +85
Keyless Entry System +60
Power Door Locks +90
Power Mirrors +40
Power Sunroof +230
Power Windows +95
Tilt Steering Wheel[Std on Z24] +55

CHEVY VAN/EXPRESS   1996

First all-new full-size cargo van for Chevrolet in 25 years sports dual airbags, standard four-wheel antilock brakes, up to 317 cubic feet of cargo room and 10,000 pounds of towing capacity. Full-frame construction replaces the less rugged unibody configuration of the previous model. Sportvan replacement, the Express, carries up to 15 passengers and offers full-frame rather than unibody construction. Dual airbags and four-wheel antilock brakes are standard. Long-wheelbase models can carry 317 cubic feet of cargo with the rear seats removed. 3500 models can tow up to 10,000 pounds.

CHEVY VAN
Category H

Model	Trade-in	Market
2 Dr G1500 Chevy Van	10830	12770
2 Dr G2500 Chevy Van	11065	13050
2 Dr G2500 Chevy Van Ext	11570	13650
2 Dr G3500 Chevy Van	11840	13965
2 Dr G3500 Chevy Van Ext	12345	14560

EXPRESS VAN
Category H

Model	Trade-in	Market
2 Dr G1500 Express Van	11255	13275
2 Dr G2500 Express Van	12130	14305
2 Dr G2500 Express Van Ext	12565	14820
2 Dr G3500 Express Van	12210	14400
2 Dr G3500 Express Van Ext	12645	14910

OPTIONS FOR CHEVY VAN/EXPRESS
8 cyl 5.0 L Engine +205
8 cyl 5.7 L Engine[Opt on G1500] +370
8 cyl 6.5 L Turbodsl Engine +1195
8 cyl 7.4 L Engine +225
15 Passenger Seating +300
AM/FM Compact Disc Player +115
Aluminum/Alloy Wheels +115
Cruise Control +70
Dual Air Conditioning +470

Power Door Locks +70
Power Drivers Seat +105
Power Windows +70
Privacy Glass +60
Rear Heater +75
Tilt Steering Wheel +70

CHEVY VAN/SPORTVAN CLASSIC 1996

Final year for ancient GM vans dating to 1971.

CHEVY VAN CLASSIC
Category H

Model	Trade-in	Market
2 Dr G30 Chevy Van	10210	12045
2 Dr G30 Chevy Van Ext	10735	12665

SPORTVAN
Category H

Model	Trade-in	Market
2 Dr G30 Sportvan	11155	13155
2 Dr G30 Sportvan Ext	11230	13245
2 Dr G30 Beauville Sportvan	11690	13785
2 Dr G30 Beauville Sportvan Ext	12125	14300

OPTIONS FOR CHEVY VAN/SPORTVAN CLASSIC
8 cyl 6.5 L Dsl Engine +605
8 cyl 7.4 L Engine +225
15 Passenger Seating +300
AM/FM Stereo Tape[Opt on STD] +75
Air Conditioning[Opt on STD] +300
Cruise Control[Opt on STD] +70
Dual Air Conditioning +470
Power Door Locks[Opt on STD] +70
Power Windows[Opt on STD] +70
Privacy Glass +60
Rear Heater +75
Tilt Steering Wheel[Opt on STD] +70

CORSICA   1996

Chevy's fleet favorite rolls into the sunset with long-life coolant.

RATINGS (SCALE OF 1-10)

Overall	Safety	Reliability	Performance	Comfort	Value
6.7	5.3	7.4	8	7.5	5.1

Category C

Model	Trade-in	Market
4 Dr STD Sdn	5570	6910

OPTIONS FOR CORSICA
6 cyl 3.1 L Engine +170
AM/FM Stereo Tape +60
Cruise Control +80
Power Windows +115
Tilt Steering Wheel +55

CORVETTE   1996

New 330-horsepower LT4 engine debuts on all manually shifted Corvettes. Two special editions are available, the Collector Edition and the Grand Sport, to

---

Don't forget to refer to the Mileage Adjustment Table at the back of this book!

CHEVROLET 96

Model Description	Trade-in Value	Market Value	Model Description	Trade-in Value	Market Value

send the fourth-generation Vette off in style. Next year, an all-new Corvette debuts. Other additions for 1996 include a Selective Real Time Damping system for the shock absorbers, and a tooth-jarring Z51 suspension setup.

Category J

2 Dr Grand Sport Conv	25890	30015
2 Dr Grand Sport Cpe	21905	25395
2 Dr STD Conv	24355	28230
2 Dr STD Cpe	20680	23975

OPTIONS FOR CORVETTE

8 cyl 5.7 L LT4 Engine[Opt on STD, Conv] +505
Electronic Suspension +590
Bose Sound System +300
Climate Control for AC +105
Compact Disc W/fm/tape +260
Dual Power Seats +270
Power Drivers Seat +130
Solid & Glass Targa Tops +350
Sport Seats[Opt on STD] +265
Sport Suspension +155

IMPALA   1996

Big surprise. The car is finally correct with the addition of a tachometer and floor shifter, and General Motors kills it. Take note collectors: the 1996 Impala SS should be on your list.

RATINGS (SCALE OF 1-10)

Overall	Safety	Reliability	Performance	Comfort	Value
7.8	7.2	6.3	9	8.3	8.1

Category B

4 Dr SS Sdn	14155	16665

OPTIONS FOR IMPALA

AM/FM Compact Disc Player +120
Keyless Entry System +65
Power Passenger Seat +130

LUMINA   1996

The ultimate family sedan is now available with an integrated child safety seat. Driver and passenger get their own climate controls. LS models offer available leather, and four-wheel disc brakes when equipped with the 3.4-liter V6.

RATINGS (SCALE OF 1-10)

Overall	Safety	Reliability	Performance	Comfort	Value
7.8	7.7	7.2	7.6	7.3	9.1

Category C

4 Dr LS Sdn	7440	9225
4 Dr STD Sdn	6760	8380

OPTIONS FOR LUMINA

6 cyl 3.4 L Engine +380
AM/FM Compact Disc Player +130

Anti-Lock Brakes[Std on LS] +215
Child Seat (1) +45
Cruise Control +80
Keyless Entry System +70
Leather Seats +225
Power Drivers Seat +110
Power Windows[Std on LS] +115

LUMINA MINIVAN   1996

Last year for sloped-nose, plastic-bodied van. A 3.4-liter V6 good for 180 horsepower replaces standard and optional V6 engines from last year. Air conditioning, seven-passenger seating, and an electronically controlled four-speed automatic transmission are standard.

RATINGS (SCALE OF 1-10)

Overall	Safety	Reliability	Performance	Comfort	Value
7.6	6.3	8.1	7.6	7.3	8.5

Category G

2 Dr STD Cargo Van	8020	9715
2 Dr STD Pass. Van	8900	10780

OPTIONS FOR LUMINA MINIVAN

AM/FM Stereo Tape +80
Aluminum/Alloy Wheels +120
Child Seat (1) +60
Cruise Control +75
Keyless Entry System +70
Power Door Locks +85
Power Drivers Seat +105
Power Mirrors +50
Power Sliding Door +150
Power Windows +90
Privacy Glass +100
Tilt Steering Wheel +65

MONTE CARLO   1996

Dual-zone climate controls reduce marital spats. The 3.4-liter V6 makes more power this year, and four-wheel disc brakes, standard on the Z34, are optional on the LS.

RATINGS (SCALE OF 1-10)

Overall	Safety	Reliability	Performance	Comfort	Value
7.4	7.5	6.3	7.4	7.5	8.5

Category C

2 Dr LS Cpe	7540	9350
2 Dr Z34 Cpe	8470	10510

OPTIONS FOR MONTE CARLO

AM/FM Compact Disc Player +130
Cruise Control[Opt on LS] +80
Keyless Entry System[Opt on LS] +70
Leather Seats +225
Power Drivers Seat +110
Power Sunroof +245

S10 PICKUP 1996

Improved V6 engines make more power and torque this year. A new five-speed manual gives four-cylinder models better acceleration, and four-bangers also get four-wheel antilock brakes. Extended-cab models get third-door access panel on the driver's side to make loading cargo and passengers easier. A new sport suspension turns the S-10 into a competent sports truck, and the new Sportside cargo box allows the S-Series to go head-to-head with the Ford Ranger Splash.

RATINGS (SCALE OF 1-10)

Overall	Safety	Reliability	Performance	Comfort	Value
N/A	5.1	6.3	6.6	8.1	N/A

Category G

2 Dr LS Ext Cab SB	7300	8840
2 Dr LS 4WD Ext Cab SB	9635	11670
2 Dr LS Ext Cab Stepside SB	7905	9575
2 Dr LS 4WD Ext Cab Stepside SB	9835	11915
2 Dr LS Std Cab LB	6590	7985
2 Dr LS 4WD Std Cab LB	9165	11100
2 Dr LS Std Cab SB	6440	7805
2 Dr LS 4WD Std Cab SB	8880	10755
2 Dr LS Std Cab Stepside SB	6645	8050
2 Dr LS 4WD Std Cab Stepside SB	9080	11000
2 Dr STD Std Cab LB	6085	7375
2 Dr STD 4WD Std Cab LB	8660	10490
2 Dr STD Std Cab SB	5930	7185
2 Dr STD 4WD Std Cab SB	8370	10140

OPTIONS FOR S10 PICKUP

6 cyl 4.3 L Engine[Opt on 2WD] +360
6 cyl 4.3 L Vortec Engine +275
Auto 4-Speed Transmission +360
Wide Stance Suspension +580
AM/FM Compact Disc Player +115
Air Conditioning +300
Aluminum/Alloy Wheels +120
Anti-Lock Brakes[Opt on 2WD] +210
Cruise Control +75
Heavy Duty Suspension +55
Hinged Third Door +125
Keyless Entry System +70
Power Door Locks +85
Power Mirrors +50
Power Windows +90
Tilt Steering Wheel +65

SUBURBAN 1996

Improved engines generate lots of horsepower and torque. Four-wheel-drive models get an optional electronic shift transfer case. Daytime running lights, rear seat heating ducts, and two new paint colors summarize the changes to Chevy's Texas Cadillac.

RATINGS (SCALE OF 1-10)

Overall	Safety	Reliability	Performance	Comfort	Value
7.2	6.6	6.9	7	7.9	7.6

Category H

4 Dr C1500 Wgn	15910	18765
4 Dr C2500 Wgn	16705	19700
4 Dr K1500 4WD Wgn	17395	20515
4 Dr K2500 4WD Wgn	18135	21385

OPTIONS FOR SUBURBAN

8 cyl 6.5 L Turbodsl Engine +1195
8 cyl 7.4 L Engine +225
AM/FM Compact Disc Player +115
Air Conditioning +300
Automatic Dimming Mirror +55
Camper/Towing Package +120
Cruise Control +70
Dual Air Conditioning +470
Keyless Entry System +65
Leather Seats +365
Power Door Locks +70
Power Drivers Seat +105
Power Mirrors +40
Power Windows +70
Privacy Glass +60
Rear Heater +75
Tilt Steering Wheel +70

TAHOE 1996

For 1996, Tahoe gets 50 additional horsepower and more torque out of a new 5700 V8. Other improvements include rear seat heating ducts, quieter-riding P-metric tires, improved automatic transmissions, and extended interval service schedules. Daytime running lights are new for 1996.

RATINGS (SCALE OF 1-10)

Overall	Safety	Reliability	Performance	Comfort	Value
7.4	6.9	6.9	7.4	8	7.6

Category H

2 Dr LS Utility	15405	18170
2 Dr LS 4WD Utility	16665	19660
4 Dr LS Wgn	16825	19840
4 Dr LS 4WD Wgn	18105	21355
2 Dr LT Utility	16175	19080
2 Dr LT 4WD Utility	17440	20570
4 Dr LT Wgn	16300	19220
4 Dr LT 4WD Wgn	18270	21545
2 Dr STD Utility	13690	16145
2 Dr STD 4WD Utility	15000	17695

OPTIONS FOR TAHOE

8 cyl 6.5 L Turbodsl Engine +1195
Auto 4-Speed Transmission[Std on STD Utility,Wgn] +340

Model Description	Trade-in Value	Market Value

AM/FM Compact Disc Player +115
Air Conditioning[Opt on STD] +300
Aluminum/Alloy Wheels[Opt on STD] +115
Camper/Towing Package +120
Cruise Control[Opt on STD] +70
Keyless Entry System[Opt on LS] +65
Power Drivers Seat[Opt on LS] +105
Privacy Glass[Opt on STD] +60
Tilt Steering Wheel[Opt on STD,LS Utility] +70

1995 CHEVROLET

ASTRO 1995

Front sheetmetal is restyled. Regular-length versions are dropped from the lineup, leaving only the extended-length model. Multi-leaf steel springs replace single-leaf plastic springs. One engine is available, the 190-horsepower, 4.3-liter V6. Air conditioning is newly standard, and remote keyless entry is a new option.

RATINGS (SCALE OF 1-10)

Overall	Safety	Reliability	Performance	Comfort	Value
7	6	6.3	7.2	6.6	8.7

Category G

2 Dr CL Pass. Van Ext	8415	10290
2 Dr CL 4WD Pass. Van Ext	9025	11035
2 Dr CS Pass. Van Ext	7910	9670
2 Dr CS 4WD Pass. Van Ext	8855	10825
2 Dr LT Pass. Van Ext	9060	11075
2 Dr LT 4WD Pass. Van Ext	9975	12195
2 Dr STD Cargo Van	7545	9225
2 Dr STD 4WD Cargo Van	8495	10385
2 Dr STD Pass. Van Ext	7795	9530
2 Dr STD 4WD Pass. Van Ext	8700	10635

OPTIONS FOR ASTRO
8 Passenger Seating[Std on CL,LT] +120
AM/FM Compact Disc Player +95
Cruise Control[Opt on STD] +65
Dual Air Conditioning +275
Keyless Entry System[Std on LT] +60
Power Door Locks[Std on CL,LT] +70
Power Drivers Seat +85
Power Mirrors[Std on LT] +40
Power Windows[Opt on CS,STD,CL Pass. Van Ext] +70
Privacy Glass[Opt on CS,STD,CL Pass. Van Ext] +80
Rear Heater +55
Tilt Steering Wheel[Opt on STD] +55

BERETTA 1995

Daytime running lights are newly standard. 170-horse Quad 4 engine is dropped, and 3.1-liter V6 loses five horsepower. Platinum-tipped spark plugs are standard on both engines.

RATINGS (SCALE OF 1-10)

Overall	Safety	Reliability	Performance	Comfort	Value
6.9	7	7.8	7.8	7	4.9

Category E

2 Dr STD Cpe	4895	6235
2 Dr Z26 Cpe	6095	7760

OPTIONS FOR BERETTA
6 cyl 3.1 L Engine[Opt on STD] +80
Auto 3-Speed Transmission +165
Auto 4-Speed Transmission[Opt on STD] +300
AM/FM Compact Disc Player +130
Cruise Control +70
Power Windows +80
Sunroof +105
Tilt Steering Wheel +45

BLAZER 1995

All-new SUV appears based on revamped S10. S10 nomenclature is dropped, and full-size Blazer becomes Tahoe. Four-wheel-drive models have electronic transfer case as standard equipment. Spare tire on four-door model is mounted beneath cargo bay instead of in it. Five different suspension packages are available. One engine, a 195-horsepower 4.3-liter V6, is available. All-wheel drive is optional. Driver airbag and air conditioning are standard equipment.

RATINGS (SCALE OF 1-10)

Overall	Safety	Reliability	Performance	Comfort	Value
6.5	5.3	5.3	8	7.9	6.1

Category G

2 Dr LS Utility	8955	10945
2 Dr LS 4WD Utility	9455	11560
4 Dr LS Wgn	9325	11400
4 Dr LS 4WD Wgn	10000	12225
4 Dr LT Wgn	10310	12605
4 Dr LT 4WD Wgn	10990	13435
2 Dr STD Utility	7940	9710
2 Dr STD 4WD Utility	9690	11625
4 Dr STD Wgn	8805	10770
4 Dr STD 4WD Wgn	9320	11395

OPTIONS FOR BLAZER
AM/FM Compact Disc Player +95
Cruise Control[Opt on STD] +65
Keyless Entry System[Std on LT] +60
Power Door Locks[Opt on STD] +70
Power Drivers Seat[Std on LT] +85
Power Mirrors[Opt on STD] +40
Power Windows[Opt on STD] +70
Skid Plates +40
Swing Out Tire Carrier +55
Tilt Steering Wheel[Opt on STD] +55

Don't forget to refer to the Mileage Adjustment Table at the back of this book!

Model Description	Trade-in Value	Market Value

C/K PICKUP 1995

New interior with driver airbag (models under 8,500-lb. GVWR) and standard four-wheel ABS debut. New dashboard features modular design with controls that are much easier to read and use. Power mirrors and remote keyless entry are new options. Uplevel radios come with automatic volume control that raises or lowers the volume depending on vehicle speed.

RATINGS (SCALE OF 1-10)

Overall	Safety	Reliability	Performance	Comfort	Value
N/A	8.1	6	7.6	8.4	N/A

C/K 1500 SERIES
Category H

Model Description	Trade-in Value	Market Value
2 Dr C1500 Cheyenne Ext Cab LB	9390	11180
2 Dr C1500 Cheyenne Ext Cab SB	8910	10610
2 Dr C1500 Cheyenne Ext Cab Stepside SB	9170	10920
2 Dr C1500 Cheyenne Std Cab LB	8005	9530
2 Dr C1500 Cheyenne Std Cab SB	7835	9330
2 Dr C1500 Cheyenne Std Cab Stepside SB	8250	9825
2 Dr C1500 Silverado Ext Cab LB	10390	12370
2 Dr C1500 Silverado Ext Cab SB	9910	11800
2 Dr C1500 Silverado Ext Cab Stepside SB	10170	12110
2 Dr C1500 Silverado Std Cab LB	9080	10810
2 Dr C1500 Silverado Std Cab SB	8935	10640
2 Dr C1500 Silverado Std Cab Stepside SB	9185	10940
2 Dr C1500 WT Std Cab LB	7350	8750
2 Dr C1500 WT Std Cab SB	7145	8505
2 Dr K1500 Cheyenne 4WD Ext Cab LB	10535	12545
2 Dr K1500 Cheyenne 4WD Ext Cab SB	10330	12300
2 Dr K1500 Cheyenne 4WD Ext Cab Stepside SB	10350	12325
2 Dr K1500 Cheyenne 4WD Std Cab LB	9330	11110
2 Dr K1500 Cheyenne 4WD Std Cab SB	9155	10900
2 Dr K1500 Cheyenne 4WD Std Cab Stepside SB	9440	11240
2 Dr K1500 Silverado 4WD Ext Cab LB	11535	13735
2 Dr K1500 Silverado 4WD Ext Cab SB	11345	13510
2 Dr K1500 Silverado 4WD Ext Cab Stepside SB	11355	13520
2 Dr K1500 Silverado 4WD Std Cab LB	10255	12210
2 Dr K1500 Silverado 4WD Std Cab SB	10105	12030
2 Dr K1500 Silverado 4WD Std Cab Stepside SB	10390	12370
2 Dr K1500 WT 4WD Std Cab LB	8895	10590
2 Dr K1500 WT 4WD Std Cab SB	8795	10470

C/K 2500 SERIES
Category H

Model Description	Trade-in Value	Market Value
2 Dr C2500 Cheyenne Ext Cab LB	10235	12185
2 Dr C2500 Cheyenne Ext Cab SB	10205	12150
2 Dr C2500 Cheyenne Std Cab LB	8580	10215
2 Dr C2500 Silverado Ext Cab LB	11260	13410
2 Dr C2500 Silverado Ext Cab SB	11230	13375
2 Dr C2500 Silverado Std Cab LB	9160	10910
2 Dr K2500 Cheyenne 4WD Ext Cab LB	11630	13850
2 Dr K2500 Cheyenne 4WD Ext Cab SB	11075	13190
2 Dr K2500 Cheyenne 4WD Std Cab LB	9720	11570
2 Dr K2500 Silverado 4WD Ext Cab LB	12590	14990
2 Dr K2500 Silverado 4WD Ext Cab SB	12040	14340
2 Dr K2500 Silverado 4WD Std Cab LB	10825	12890

C/K 3500 SERIES
Category H

Model Description	Trade-in Value	Market Value
4 Dr C3500 Cheyenne Crew Cab LB	11800	13210
2 Dr C3500 Cheyenne Ext Cab LB	11425	12790
2 Dr C3500 Cheyenne Std Cab LB	9330	11110

Don't forget to refer to the Mileage Adjustment Table at the back of this book!

Model Description	Trade-in Value	Market Value
4 Dr C3500 Silverado Crew Cab LB	12400	14765
2 Dr C3500 Silverado Ext Cab LB	12145	13595
2 Dr C3500 Silverado Std Cab LB	10550	12560
4 Dr K3500 Cheyenne 4WD Crew Cab LB	12150	14470
2 Dr K3500 Cheyenne 4WD Ext Cab LB	12160	13610
2 Dr K3500 Cheyenne 4WD Std Cab LB	10650	12680
4 Dr K3500 Silverado 4WD Crew Cab LB	13955	16620
2 Dr K3500 Silverado 4WD Ext Cab LB	13610	15235
2 Dr K3500 Silverado 4WD Std Cab LB	11730	13970

OPTIONS FOR C/K PICKUP
8 cyl 5.0 L Engine +180
8 cyl 5.7 L Engine +225
8 cyl 6.5 L Dsl Engine +670
8 cyl 6.5 L Turbodsl Engine +950
8 cyl 7.4 L Engine +170
Auto 4-Speed Transmission +280
AM/FM Compact Disc Player +90
Air Conditioning +245
Bed Liner +70
Cruise Control[Opt on STD,WT] +55
Keyless Entry System +50
Leather Seats +300
Power Door Locks[Opt on STD] +55
Power Drivers Seat +85
Power Mirrors +30
Tilt Steering Wheel[Opt on STD,WT] +55

CAMARO 1995

Z28 gets optional traction control. Z28 can now be ordered with body-color roof and side mirrors (standard color is gloss black). Chrome-plated alloys are newly optional.

RATINGS (SCALE OF 1-10)

Overall	Safety	Reliability	Performance	Comfort	Value
7.3	8.7	6.9	9.2	6.8	4.9

Category F

2 Dr STD Conv	8520	10275
2 Dr STD Cpe	7170	8645
2 Dr Z28 Conv	10665	12860
2 Dr Z28 Cpe	8520	10275

OPTIONS FOR CAMARO
6 cyl 3.8 L Engine +125
Auto 4-Speed Transmission +225
AM/FM Compact Disc Player +140
Air Conditioning +250
Bose Sound System +135
Cruise Control +65
Fog Lights +55
Glass Panel T-tops +295
Keyless Entry System +55
Leather Seats +190
Power Door Locks +60
Power Drivers Seat +70
Power Mirrors[Std on Cpe] +35
Power Windows +70

CAPRICE 1995

Impala SS styling treatment for C-pillar is carried over to more mainstream sedan. New seats and radios debut. Outside mirrors can be folded in, and a new option is a radio with speed-compensated volume control.

RATINGS (SCALE OF 1-10)

Overall	Safety	Reliability	Performance	Comfort	Value
7.7	7.9	5.7	8.2	8.3	8.3

Category B

4 Dr STD Sdn	7855	9390
4 Dr STD Wgn	8705	10410

OPTIONS FOR CAPRICE
8 cyl 5.7 L Engine[Std on Wgn] +165
AM/FM Stereo Tape[Std on Wgn] +50
Auto Load Leveling +55
Cruise Control +65
Keyless Entry System +50
Leather Seats +205
Power Drivers Seat +95
Power Mirrors +30
Power Windows +85

CAVALIER 1995

First redesign since 1982 debut. Sedan, coupe and convertible are available. Wagon is dropped. Sedan comes in base and LS trim. Coupe comes in base and Z24 trim. Convertible is available as LS only. Dual airbags and ABS are standard. Base engine is a 2.2-liter, 120-horsepower four-cylinder engine. Optional on LS sedan and convertible is the Z24's standard powerplant; a 2.3-liter, DOHC four-cylinder making 150 horsepower.

RATINGS (SCALE OF 1-10)

Overall	Safety	Reliability	Performance	Comfort	Value
7.3	7.2	7	7	7.6	7.9

Category E

2 Dr LS Conv	6670	8495
4 Dr LS Sdn	4880	6215
2 Dr STD Cpe	3975	5065

CHEVROLET 95

Model Description	Trade-in Value	Market Value
4 Dr STD Sdn	4050	5160
2 Dr Z24 Cpe	5390	6865

OPTIONS FOR CAVALIER

4 cyl 2.3 L Quad 4 Engine[Opt on LS] +120
Auto 3-Speed Transmission[Std on LS] +150
Auto 4-Speed Transmission +110
AM/FM Compact Disc Player +130
Air Conditioning[Opt on STD] +250
Cruise Control +70
Power Door Locks +75
Power Mirrors +35
Power Sunroof +185
Power Windows +80
Tilt Steering Wheel[Std on Z24] +45

CHEVY VAN/SPORTVAN 1995

No changes.

CHEVY VAN

Category H

Model Description	Trade-in Value	Market Value
2 Dr G10 Chevy Van	7365	8770
2 Dr G10 Chevy Van Ext	7440	8860
2 Dr G20 Chevy Van	7310	8705
2 Dr G20 Chevy Van Ext	7435	8855
2 Dr G30 Chevy Van	7460	8885
2 Dr G30 Chevy Van Ext	8400	10000

SPORTVAN

Category H

Model Description	Trade-in Value	Market Value
2 Dr G20 Sportvan	8765	10435
2 Dr G20 Beauville Sportvan	9560	11385
2 Dr G30 Sportvan	9365	11150
2 Dr G30 Sportvan Ext	9435	11235
2 Dr G30 Beauville Sportvan	9725	11580
2 Dr G30 Beauville Sportvan Ext	10055	11975

OPTIONS FOR CHEVY VAN/SPORTVAN

8 cyl 5.0 L Engine +180
.8 cyl 5.7 L Engine[Opt on G20,Chevy Van] +225
8 cyl 6.5 L Dsl Engine +670
8 cyl 7.4 L Engine +170
16 Passenger Seating +110
AM/FM Stereo Tape[Opt on G10,STD] +60
Air Conditioning[Opt on G10,STD] +245
Cruise Control[Opt on G10,STD] +55
Dual Air Conditioning +385
Power Door Locks[Opt on G10,STD] +55
Power Windows[Opt on G10,STD] +55
Privacy Glass +45
Rear Heater +65
Tilt Steering Wheel[Opt on G10,STD] +55

CORSICA 1995

Daytime running lights debut. Rear suspension is revised, and larger tires are standard.

RATINGS (SCALE OF 1-10)

Overall	Safety	Reliability	Performance	Comfort	Value
6.8	5.8	7.5	8	7.5	5

Category C

Model Description	Trade-in Value	Market Value
4 Dr STD Sdn	4430	5675

OPTIONS FOR CORSICA

6 cyl 3.1 L Engine +145
AM/FM Stereo Tape +50
Cruise Control +65
Power Windows +95
Tilt Steering Wheel +45

CORVETTE 1995

ZR-1's brakes trickle down to base models. Front fenders get revised gills. Only 448 ZR-1s were produced in 1995.

Category J

Model Description	Trade-in Value	Market Value
2 Dr STD Conv	21365	24785
2 Dr STD Cpe	18535	21500
2 Dr ZR1 Cpe	33675	39065

OPTIONS FOR CORVETTE

Handling Pkg +610
Selective Ride Suspension +505
Bose Sound System +245
Climate Control for AC[Opt on STD] +85
Compact Disc W/fm/tape[Opt on STD] +215
Power Drivers Seat[Opt on STD] +105
Solid & Glass Targa Tops +285

IMPALA 1995

Dark Cherry and Green Gray paint colors join basic black. New seats and radios debut. Outside mirrors can be folded in, and a new option is a radio with speed-compensated volume control.

RATINGS (SCALE OF 1-10)

Overall	Safety	Reliability	Performance	Comfort	Value
7.8	7.9	5.7	9	8.3	8

Category B

Model Description	Trade-in Value	Market Value
4 Dr SS Sdn	11860	14180

OPTIONS FOR IMPALA

AM/FM Compact Disc Player +100
Keyless Entry System +50
Power Passenger Seat +110

LUMINA 1995

Midsize sedan is redesigned; features dual airbags. Base and LS trim levels are available. ABS is optional on base model; standard on LS. Standard powerplant is a 160-horsepower, 3.1-liter V6. Optional on LS is a 210-horsepower, 3.4-liter V6. Air conditioning is standard.

Don't forget to refer to the Mileage Adjustment Table at the back of this book!

EDMUNDS® USED CARS & TRUCKS

CHEVROLET 95

Model Description	Trade-in Value	Market Value	Model Description	Trade-in Value	Market Value

RATINGS (SCALE OF 1-10)

Overall	Safety	Reliability	Performance	Comfort	Value
7.2	7.9	5.6	7.6	7.3	7.5

Category C
4 Dr LS Sdn	5920	7590
4 Dr STD Sdn	5415	6935

OPTIONS FOR LUMINA
6 cyl 3.4 L Engine +285
AM/FM Compact Disc Player +105
Anti-Lock Brakes[Std on LS] +175
Cruise Control +65
Keyless Entry System +55
Power Drivers Seat +90
Power Windows[Std on LS] +95

LUMINA MINIVAN   1995

Transmission gets brake/shift interlock.

RATINGS (SCALE OF 1-10)

Overall	Safety	Reliability	Performance	Comfort	Value
6.9	6.9	6	7.6	7.3	6.6

Category G
2 Dr STD Cargo Van	6405	7830
2 Dr STD Pass. Van	6920	8465

OPTIONS FOR LUMINA MINIVAN
6 cyl 3.8 L Engine +125
Auto 4-Speed Transmission +60
AM/FM Stereo Tape +65
Air Conditioning +245
Child Seat (1) +50
Cruise Control +65
Keyless Entry System +60
Power Door Locks +70
Power Drivers Seat +85
Power Mirrors +40
Power Windows +70
Privacy Glass +80
Tilt Steering Wheel +55

MONTE CARLO   1995

Chevy slaps revered moniker on coupe version of Lumina. Available in LS or Z34 trim levels. Dual airbags and ABS are standard. LS comes with 160-horsepower, 3.1-liter V6, while Z34 is powered by 3.4-liter, twin-cam V6 good for 210 horsepower. All Monte Carlos have automatic transmissions. Air conditioning is standard.

RATINGS (SCALE OF 1-10)

Overall	Safety	Reliability	Performance	Comfort	Value
7	7.8	5.4	7.4	7.5	7.1

Category C
2 Dr LS Cpe	6170	7905
2 Dr Z34 Cpe	6955	8910

OPTIONS FOR MONTE CARLO
Cruise Control[Opt on LS] +65
Keyless Entry System[Opt on LS] +55
Leather Seats +185
Power Drivers Seat +90
Power Mirrors[Opt on LS] +30

S10 PICKUP   1995

Driver airbag is added, and daytime running lights are standard. ZR2 off-road package can be ordered on the extended-cab. Power window and lock buttons are illuminated at night. Remote keyless entry is a new option. A single key operates both the door locks and the ignition. A manual transmission can now be ordered with the 191-horsepower, 4.3-liter V6.

RATINGS (SCALE OF 1-10)

Overall	Safety	Reliability	Performance	Comfort	Value
N/A	5.1	5.7	6.6	8.1	N/A

Category G
2 Dr LS Ext Cab SB	6005	7345
2 Dr LS 4WD Ext Cab SB	7975	9750
2 Dr LS Std Cab LB	5555	6790
2 Dr LS 4WD Std Cab LB	7640	9345
2 Dr LS Std Cab SB	5420	6625
2 Dr LS 4WD Std Cab SB	7385	9030
2 Dr STD Std Cab LB	5100	6240
2 Dr STD 4WD Std Cab LB	7195	8795
2 Dr STD Std Cab SB	4960	6065
2 Dr STD 4WD Std Cab SB	6935	8475

OPTIONS FOR S10 PICKUP
6 cyl 4.3 L Engine[Opt on 2WD] +240
6 cyl 4.3 L CPI Engine +245
Auto 4-Speed Transmission +300
Wide Stance Suspension +515
AM/FM Compact Disc Player +95
AM/FM Stereo Tape +65
Air Conditioning +245
Anti-Lock Brakes[Opt on 2WD] +175
Cruise Control +65
Heavy Duty Suspension +45
Keyless Entry System +60
Power Door Locks +70
Power Windows +70
Tilt Steering Wheel +55

SUBURBAN   1995

New interior with driver airbag debuts. New dashboard features modular design with controls that are much easier to read and use. 1500 models can now be ordered with turbodiesel engine. Brake/transmission shift interlock is added to automatic transmission. Seats and door panels are revised. New console on models with bucket seats features pivoting writing surface,

Don't forget to refer to the Mileage Adjustment Table at the back of this book!

EDMUNDS® USED CARS & TRUCKS   www.edmunds.com   101

CHEVROLET 95-94

Model Description	Trade-in Value	Market Value	Model Description	Trade-in Value	Market Value

along with rear cupholders and storage drawer. Uplevel radios come with automatic volume controls that raise or lower the volume depending on vehicle speed.

RATINGS (SCALE OF 1-10)

Overall	Safety	Reliability	Performance	Comfort	Value
6.9	6.9	5.2	6.8	7.9	7.5

Category H

4 Dr C1500 Wgn	13430	15990
4 Dr C2500 Wgn	14165	16865
4 Dr K1500 4WD Wgn	14805	17630
4 Dr K2500 4WD Wgn	15305	18225

OPTIONS FOR SUBURBAN

8 cyl 6.5 L Turbodsl Engine +950
8 cyl 7.4 L Engine +170
AM/FM Compact Disc Player +90
Air Conditioning +245
Automatic Dimming Mirror +45
Camper/Towing Package +100
Cruise Control +55
Dual Air Conditioning +385
Keyless Entry System +50
Leather Seats +300
Power Door Locks +55
Power Drivers Seat +85
Power Mirrors +30
Power Windows +55
Privacy Glass +45
Rear Heater +65
Tilt Steering Wheel +55

TAHOE   1995

Full-size SUV gets a new name as S10-based model takes Blazer moniker. New interior with driver airbag debuts. New dashboard features modular design with controls that are much easier to read and use. New five-door model is added midyear, nicely sized between Blazer and Suburban. New model is offered only in LS or LT trim with a 5.7-liter V8 and an automatic transmission in either 2WD or 4WD. Brake/transmission shift interlock is added to automatic transmission. New console on models with bucket seats features pivoting writing surface, along with rear cupholders and storage drawer.

RATINGS (SCALE OF 1-10)

Overall	Safety	Reliability	Performance	Comfort	Value
7.2	7.6	5.6	7.2	8	7.6

Category H

2 Dr LS 4WD Utility	13400	15955
4 Dr LS Wgn	14280	17005
4 Dr LS 4WD Wgn	15445	18390
2 Dr LT 4WD Utility	14340	17075
4 Dr LT Wgn	14470	17230

4 Dr LT 4WD Wgn	15585	18560
2 Dr STD 4WD-Utility	11870	14135

OPTIONS FOR TAHOE

8 cyl 6.5 L Turbodsl Engine +950
Auto 4-Speed Transmission[Std on Wgn] +275
AM/FM Compact Disc Player +90
AM/FM Stereo Tape[Opt on STD] +60
Air Conditioning[Opt on STD] +245
Cruise Control[Opt on STD] +55
Keyless Entry System[Std on LT] +50
Power Door Locks[Opt on STD] +55
Power Drivers Seat[Opt on LS] +85
Privacy Glass[Opt on STD] +45
Tilt Steering Wheel[Opt on STD] +55

1994 CHEVROLET

ASTRO   1994

Driver airbag is made standard. Side-door guard beams are stronger, and air conditioners use CFC-free refrigerant. A high-mount center brake light is added. Analog gauges get new graphics, and carpet is treated with Scotchgard.

RATINGS (SCALE OF 1-10)

Overall	Safety	Reliability	Performance	Comfort	Value
7.1	5.8	6.5	7.2	6.6	9.2

Category G

2 Dr CL Pass. Van	6380	7995
2 Dr CL 4WD Pass. Van	7210	9035
2 Dr CL Pass. Van Ext	6490	8130
2 Dr CL 4WD Pass. Van Ext	7320	9170
2 Dr LT Pass. Van	7025	8805
2 Dr LT 4WD Pass. Van	7550	9460
2 Dr LT Pass. Van Ext	7135	8940
2 Dr LT 4WD Pass. Van Ext	7655	9595
2 Dr STD Cargo Van	5660	7095
2 Dr STD 4WD Cargo Van	6575	8240
2 Dr STD Cargo Van Ext	5830	7305
2 Dr STD 4WD Cargo Van Ext	6745	8450
2 Dr STD Pass. Van	5995	7510
2 Dr STD 4WD Pass. Van	6825	8550
2 Dr STD Pass. Van Ext	6100	7645
2 Dr STD 4WD Pass. Van Ext	6930	8685

OPTIONS FOR ASTRO

6 cyl 4.3 L CPI Engine[Opt on 2WD] +135
8 Passenger Seating +100
AM/FM Stereo Tape +55
Air Conditioning +200
Cruise Control +50
Dual Air Conditioning +225
Power Door Locks +55
Power Drivers Seat +70
Power Windows +60

Model Description	Trade-in Value	Market Value	Model Description	Trade-in Value	Market Value

Privacy Glass[Std on LT] +65
Tilt Steering Wheel +45

BERETTA 1994

GT and GTZ are dropped in favor of Z26 model, which offers a standard 170-horsepower Quad 4 engine. Base models get 10 more horsepower, and the 3.1-liter V6 makes an additional 20 horsepower, up to 160. Automatic transmission is unavailable with Quad 4; manual transmission is unavailable with V6. Door-mounted seat belts are added. Automatic door locks lock doors once Beretta is underway, and unlock when car is stopped. Disable this feature by yanking a fuse. Interior lights shut off after 10 minutes to save battery. Warning chime reminds driver that turn signal has been left on.

RATINGS (SCALE OF 1-10)

Overall	Safety	Reliability	Performance	Comfort	Value
6.8	6.6	7.5	7.8	7	4.9

Category E

2 Dr STD Cpe	3860	5370
2 Dr Z26 Cpe	4390	6105

OPTIONS FOR BERETTA
6 cyl 3.1 L Engine +180
Auto 3-Speed Transmission +135
Auto 4-Speed Transmission +165
AM/FM Stereo Tape[Opt on STD] +75
Cruise Control +55
Power Windows +65
Sunroof +85
Tilt Steering Wheel +35

BLAZER 1994

Air conditioning receives CFC-free coolant. Side-door guard beams are added. A new grille appears, and models equipped with a decor package get composite headlamps. A turbocharged diesel is newly optional. Third brake light is added.

Category H

2 Dr STD 4WD Utility	8655	10500
2 Dr Silverado 4WD Utility	11495	13940
2 Dr Sport 4WD Utility	12080	14650

OPTIONS FOR BLAZER
8 cyl 6.5 L Turbodsl Engine +755
Auto 4-Speed Transmission +215
AM/FM Stereo Tape +50
Air Conditioning[Opt on STD] +200
Cruise Control[Opt on STD] +45
Power Door Locks[Std on Sport] +45
Power Drivers Seat +70
Power Windows[Std on Sport] +45
Tilt Steering Wheel[Opt on STD] +45

C/K PICKUP 1994

454 SS dropped. Grilles are restyled, side-door guard beams are added, and a third brake light is installed. Leather seats are available. Front seatback on extended-cab models gets memory feature to improve entry and exit to rear seat. A 6.5-liter diesel replaces last year's 6.2-liter unit, and a turbocharged version is also available for 1500 and 2500 models.

RATINGS (SCALE OF 1-10)

Overall	Safety	Reliability	Performance	Comfort	Value
N/A	6	6.4	7.4	8.4	N/A

C/K 1500 SERIES

Category H

2 Dr C1500 Cheyenne Ext Cab LB	8070	9790
2 Dr C1500 Cheyenne Ext Cab SB	7685	9320
2 Dr C1500 Cheyenne Ext Cab Stepside SB	7875	9550
2 Dr C1500 Cheyenne Std Cab LB	6975	8460
2 Dr C1500 Cheyenne Std Cab SB	6845	8300
2 Dr C1500 Cheyenne Std Cab Stepside SB	7150	8670
2 Dr C1500 Silverado Ext Cab LB	8650	10490
2 Dr C1500 Silverado Ext Cab SB	8265	10020
2 Dr C1500 Silverado Ext Cab Stepside SB	8450	10250
2 Dr C1500 Silverado Std Cab LB	7555	9160
2 Dr C1500 Silverado Std Cab SB	7425	9005
2 Dr C1500 Silverado Std Cab Stepside SB	7730	9375
2 Dr C1500 Work Truck Std Cab LB	6170	7485
2 Dr C1500 Work Truck Std Cab SB	6080	7370
2 Dr K1500 Cheyenne 4WD Ext Cab LB	9105	11040
2 Dr K1500 Cheyenne 4WD Ext Cab SB	8750	10610
2 Dr K1500 Cheyenne 4WD Ext Cab Stepside SB	8940	10840
2 Dr K1500 Cheyenne 4WD Std Cab LB	8105	9825
2 Dr K1500 Cheyenne 4WD Std Cab SB	7635	9260

Model Description	Trade-in Value	Market Value
2 Dr K1500 Cheyenne 4WD Std Cab Stepside SB		
	8225	9975
2 Dr K1500 Silverado 4WD Ext Cab LB		
	9685	11745
2 Dr K1500 Silverado 4WD Ext Cab SB		
	9330	11315
2 Dr K1500 Silverado 4WD Ext Cab Stepside SB		
	9520	11545
2 Dr K1500 Silverado 4WD Std Cab LB		
	8680	10530
2 Dr K1500 Silverado 4WD Std Cab SB		
	8545	10365
2 Dr K1500 Silverado 4WD Std Cab Stepside SB		
	8800	10675
2 Dr K1500 Sport 4WD Std Cab Stepside SB		
	9420	11425
2 Dr K1500 Work Truck 4WD Std Cab LB		
	7590	9205
2 Dr K1500 Work Truck 4WD Std Cab SB		
	7495	9090

C/K 2500 SERIES

Category H

Model Description	Trade-in Value	Market Value
2 Dr C2500 Cheyenne Ext Cab LB		
	8995	10910
2 Dr C2500 Cheyenne Ext Cab SB		
	8675	10520
2 Dr C2500 Cheyenne Std Cab LB		
	7395	8970
2 Dr C2500 Silverado Ext Cab LB		
	9610	11650
2 Dr C2500 Silverado Ext Cab SB		
	9285	11265
2 Dr C2500 Silverado Std Cab LB		
	7685	9320
2 Dr K2500 Cheyenne 4WD Ext Cab LB		
	9990	12115
2 Dr K2500 Cheyenne 4WD Ext Cab SB		
	9525	11550
2 Dr K2500 Cheyenne 4WD Std Cab LB		
	8345	10120
2 Dr K2500 Silverado 4WD Ext Cab LB		
	10595	12850
2 Dr K2500 Silverado 4WD Ext Cab SB		
	10135	12295
2 Dr K2500 Silverado 4WD Std Cab LB		
	9005	10925

C/K 3500 SERIES

Category H

Model Description	Trade-in Value	Market Value
4 Dr C3500 Cheyenne Crew Cab LB		
	9805	11895

Model Description	Trade-in Value	Market Value
2 Dr C3500 Cheyenne Ext Cab LB		
	10065	12210
2 Dr C3500 Cheyenne Std Cab LB		
	8495	10305
4 Dr C3500 Silverado Crew Cab LB		
	10065	12205
2 Dr C3500 Silverado Ext Cab LB		
	10115	12270
2 Dr C3500 Silverado Std Cab LB		
	8870	10755
4 Dr K3500 4WD Crew Cab LB	10675	12945
2 Dr K3500 Cheyenne 4WD Ext Cab LB		
	11105	13470
2 Dr K3500 Cheyenne 4WD Std Cab LB		
	9760	11835
4 Dr K3500 Silverado 4WD Crew Cab LB		
	11465	13905
2 Dr K3500 Silverado 4WD Ext Cab LB		
	11215	13600
2 Dr K3500 Silverado 4WD Std Cab LB		
	10085	12230

OPTIONS FOR C/K PICKUP

8 cyl 5.0 L Engine +145
8 cyl 5.7 L Engine +175
8 cyl 6.5 L Dsl Engine +640
8 cyl 6.5 L Turbodsl Engine +755
8 cyl 7.4 L Engine +150
Auto 4-Speed Transmission +220
LT Pkg +200
AM/FM Stereo Tape[Std on Sport] +50
Air Conditioning[Opt on STD, Work Truck] +200
Bed Liner +55
Camper/Towing Package +80
Cruise Control[Std on Sport] +45
Power Door Locks[Std on Sport] +45
Power Drivers Seat +70
Power Windows[Std on Sport] +45
Tilt Steering Wheel[Std on Sport] +45

CAMARO 1994

Convertible returns in base and Z28 trim. First-to-fourth shift pattern added to six-speed manual transmission to meet fuel economy regulations. Z28 with manual transmission gets revised gearing for better acceleration.

RATINGS (SCALE OF 1-10)

Overall	Safety	Reliability	Performance	Comfort	Value
7.2	8.7	7	9.2	6.8	4.4

Category F

Model	Trade-in	Market
2 Dr STD Conv	8140	9905
2 Dr STD Cpe	5880	7150
2 Dr Z28 Conv	9315	11335
2 Dr Z28 Cpe	7310	8890

Model Description	Trade-in Value	Market Value

Model Description	Trade-in Value	Market Value

OPTIONS FOR CAMARO

Auto 4-Speed Transmission +165
Air Conditioning +205
Bose Sound System +110
Fog Lights +45
Glass Panel T-tops +240
Keyless Entry System +45
Leather Seats +155
Power Door Locks +50
Power Drivers Seat +60
Power Windows +55

CAPRICE 1994

Passenger airbag added. New base engine for sedan is a 200-horsepower, 4.3-liter V8. Optional on sedan and standard on wagon is a more powerful 260-horsepower, 5.7-liter V8. Automatic transmissions get electronic controls. Pass-Key II is a standard theft-deterrent system, and CFC-free refrigerant is added to air conditioning systems.

RATINGS (SCALE OF 1-10)

Overall	Safety	Reliability	Performance	Comfort	Value
7.9	8	6	8.2	8.3	8.8

Category B

4 Dr LS Sdn	6765	8340
4 Dr STD Sdn	6170	7605
4 Dr STD Wgn	6735	8300

OPTIONS FOR CAPRICE

8 cyl 5.7 L Engine[Std on Wgn] +80
AM/FM Stereo Tape[Std on LS,Wgn] +40
Cruise Control[Std on LS] +55
Leather Seats +165
Power Door Locks[Std on LS] +65
Power Drivers Seat[Std on LS] +75
Power Windows[Std on LS] +70

CAVALIER 1994

Wagon is sold without trim designation. Base engine is up 10 horsepower to 120. Automatic door locks unlock when ignition is turned off. Feature is defeated by yanking a fuse.

RATINGS (SCALE OF 1-10)

Overall	Safety	Reliability	Performance	Comfort	Value
N/A	N/A	6.7	6.4	6.8	8.5

Category E

2 Dr RS Conv	5135	7145
2 Dr RS Cpe	3290	4580
4 Dr RS Sdn	3465	4825
4 Dr STD Wgn	3510	4885
2 Dr VL Cpe	2740	3815
4 Dr VL Sdn	2785	3875
2 Dr Z24 Conv	6015	8375
2 Dr Z24 Cpe	4255	5920

OPTIONS FOR CAVALIER

6 cyl 3.1 L Engine[Std on Z24] +180
Auto 3-Speed Transmission[Opt on VL,Z24,RS Cpe] +120
AM/FM Stereo Tape[Std on Z24] +75
Air Conditioning[Opt on VL] +205
Cruise Control +55
Power Windows[Std on Conv] +65
Sunroof +85
Tilt Steering Wheel[Std on Z24] +35

CHEVY VAN / SPORTVAN 1994

Driver airbag is added to all models under 8,500-lb. GVWR. Side-door guard beams are installed in front doors and a high-mount center brake light is added.

CHEVY VAN

Category H

2 Dr G10 Chevy Van	5685	6890
2 Dr G10 Chevy Van Ext	5745	6970
2 Dr G20 Chevy Van	5670	6880
2 Dr G20 Chevy Van Ext	5745	6965
2 Dr G30 Chevy Van	5790	7020
2 Dr G30 Chevy Van Ext	6525	7915

SPORTVAN

Category H

2 Dr G20 Sportvan	7480	9070
2 Dr G20 Beauville Sportvan	8170	9905
2 Dr G30 Sportvan	8090	9815
2 Dr G30 Sportvan Ext	8060	9770
2 Dr G30 Beauville Sportvan	8290	10050
2 Dr G30 Beauville Sportvan Ext	8715	10570

OPTIONS FOR CHEVY VAN/SPORTVAN

8 cyl 5.0 L Engine +145
8 cyl 5.7 L Engine[Opt on G20] +175
8 cyl 6.5 L Dsl Engine +640
8 cyl 7.4 L Engine +150
15 Passenger Seating +200
AM/FM Stereo Tape +50
Air Conditioning[Opt on G10,STD] +200
Cruise Control[Opt on G10,STD] +45
Dual Air Conditioning +315
Power Door Locks[Opt on G10,STD] +45
Power Windows[Opt on G10,STD] +45
Privacy Glass +40
Tilt Steering Wheel[Opt on G10,STD] +45

CORSICA 1994

Door mounted seatbelts are added. Engines gain power; the 2.2-liter unit is up to 120 horsepower, and the optional, 3.1-liter V6 now makes 160 horsepower. Sport Handling Package dropped from options list. Manual transmission dropped. Automatic door locks now unlock when car is shut off. This feature can be disabled by pulling a fuse. Interior lights will shut off automatically after 10 minutes to save the battery. Warning chime sounds if turn signal is left on.

Model Description	Trade-in Value	Market Value

Model Description	Trade-in Value	Market Value

RATINGS (SCALE OF 1-10)

Overall	Safety	Reliability	Performance	Comfort	Value
6.9	5.8	7.3	8	7.5	6.1

Category C

	Trade-in	Market
4 Dr STD Sdn	3370	4570

OPTIONS FOR CORSICA

6 cyl 3.1 L Engine +125
AM/FM Stereo Tape +40
Cruise Control +55*
Power Windows +80
Tilt Steering Wheel +35

CORVETTE   1994

Passenger airbag is added. Traction control is standard. A new steering wheel and redesigned seats are added inside. Leather upholstery is standard. Automatic transmission gets electronic shift controls and brake/transmission shift interlock. Convertible gets glass rear window with defogger. ZR-1 has new five-spoke alloys. Power windows gain express-down feature for driver's side. Selective Ride Control system has softer springs.

Category J

	Trade-in	Market
2 Dr STD Conv	18765	21815
2 Dr STD Cpe	16395	19055
2 Dr ZR1 Cpe	29975	34845

OPTIONS FOR CORVETTE

Adjustable Handling Pkg +500
Selective Ride & Handling +415
Bose Sound System[Opt on STD] +200
Power Drivers Seat[Opt on STD] +85
Power Passenger Seat[Opt on STD] +85
Solid & Glass Targa Tops +230

IMPALA   1994

Caprice-based sedan powered by 260-horsepower, 5.7-liter V8 and sporting monochromatic black paint debuts to critical acclaim. Has four-wheel disc brakes, dual airbags, ABS, five-spoke alloys, and restyled C-pillars.

RATINGS (SCALE OF 1-10)

Overall	Safety	Reliability	Performance	Comfort	Value
8	8	6	9	8.3	8.5

Category B

	Trade-in	Market
4 Dr SS Sdn	10010	12340

OPTIONS FOR IMPALA

AM/FM Compact Disc Player +80
Keyless Entry System +45

LUMINA   1994

Base coupe is dropped from lineup. Manual transmission disappears.

RATINGS (SCALE OF 1-10)

Overall	Safety	Reliability	Performance	Comfort	Value
N/A	N/A	7.8	8.2	7.6	7.9

Category C

	Trade-in	Market
2 Dr Euro Cpe	4785	6490
4 Dr Euro Sdn	4690	6355
4 Dr STD Sdn	4355	5905
2 Dr Z34 Cpe	5455	7400

OPTIONS FOR LUMINA

6 cyl 3.4 L Engine[Std on Z34] +275
AM/FM Stereo Tape[Opt on STD] +40
Anti-Lock Brakes[Opt on STD] +145
Cruise Control[Std on Z34] +55
Power Drivers Seat +75
Power Windows[Opt on STD] +80

LUMINA MINIVAN   1994

APV designation dropped in favor of more descriptive "Minivan" nomenclature. Front styling is revised; overall length drops three inches. Driver airbag is standard. Integrated child seats and remote keyless entry are newly optional. Midyear, traction control becomes available on LS model.

RATINGS (SCALE OF 1-10)

Overall	Safety	Reliability	Performance	Comfort	Value
7.3	6.9	6.3	7.6	7.5	8.4

Category G

	Trade-in	Market
2 Dr STD Cargo Van	5305	6645
2 Dr STD Pass. Van	5745	7195

OPTIONS FOR LUMINA MINIVAN

6 cyl 3.8 L Engine +150
Auto 4-Speed Transmission +50
AM/FM Stereo Tape +55
Air Conditioning +200
Cruise Control +50
Power Door Locks +55
Power Drivers Seat +70
Power Windows +60
Privacy Glass +65
Tilt Steering Wheel +45

S10 BLAZER   1994

Side-door guard beams and a high-mount center brake light are added. Front bench seat is now standard on four-door models.

RATINGS (SCALE OF 1-10)

Overall	Safety	Reliability	Performance	Comfort	Value
6	5.1	6.6	6.8	7.1	4.6

Category G

	Trade-in	Market
2 Dr STD Utility	5795	7260
2 Dr STD 4WD Utility	6435	8060
4 Dr STD Wgn	6110	7655

Don't forget to refer to the Mileage Adjustment Table at the back of this book!

Model Description	Trade-in Value	Market Value
4 Dr STD 4WD Wgn	6905	8650
2 Dr Tahoe Utility	6285	7875
2 Dr Tahoe 4WD Utility	6910	8660
4 Dr Tahoe Wgn	6345	7945
4 Dr Tahoe 4WD Wgn	6975	8735
2 Dr Tahoe LT Utility	7315	9165
2 Dr Tahoe LT 4WD Utility	7710	9665
4 Dr Tahoe LT Wgn	7460	9350
4 Dr Tahoe LT 4WD Wgn	7890	9890

OPTIONS FOR S10 BLAZER

6 cyl 4.3 L CPI Engine +135
Auto 4-Speed Transmission +220
AM/FM Stereo Tape[Std on Tahoe LT] +55
Air Conditioning[Std on Tahoe LT] +200
Cruise Control[Opt on Tahoe LT] +50
Keyless Entry System[Std on Tahoe LT] +50
Power Door Locks[Std on Tahoe LT] +55
Power Drivers Seat[Std on Tahoe LT] +70
Power Windows[Std on Tahoe LT] +60
Tilt Steering Wheel[Opt on STD] +45

S10 PICKUP   1994

All-new truck debuts with more powerful engines and available four-wheel ABS. Side-door guard beams are standard. Rear ABS is standard on four cylinder models; V6 trucks get the new, four-wheel ABS system that works in both two- and four-wheel drive. ZR2 package is for serious off-roaders. Available only on regular-cab shortbed models, the ZR2 package includes four-inch wider track, three-inch height increase, off-road suspension and tires, wheel flares and thick skid plates. Base engine is 118-horse, 2.2-liter four cylinder. Standard on 4WD models is a 165-horsepower 4.3-liter V6. Optional on all models is a 195-horsepower, high-output 4.3-liter V6. SS package available with high-output engine, sport suspension and alloy wheels.

RATINGS (SCALE OF 1-10)

Overall	Safety	Reliability	Performance	Comfort	Value
N/A	5.2	6.5	6.6	8.1	N/A

Category G
2 Dr LS Ext Cab SB	4930	6180
2 Dr LS 4WD Ext Cab SB	6750	8460
2 Dr LS Std Cab LB	4760	5965
2 Dr LS 4WD Std Cab LB	6575	8235
2 Dr LS Std Cab SB	4530	5675
2 Dr LS 4WD Std Cab SB	6340	7945
2 Dr STD Std Cab LB	4195	5255
2 Dr STD 4WD Std Cab LB	6005	7525
2 Dr STD Std Cab SB	3885	4865
2 Dr STD 4WD Std Cab SB	5885	7370

OPTIONS FOR S10 PICKUP

6 cyl 4.3 L Engine[Opt on 2WD] +205
Auto 4-Speed Transmission +225
Wide Stance Pkg +410
AM/FM Stereo Tape +55
Air Conditioning +200
Anti-Lock Brakes[Opt on 2WD] +140
Cruise Control +50
Power Door Locks +55
Power Windows +60
Tilt Steering Wheel +45

SUBURBAN   1994

Side-door guard beams are added, as well as a high-mounted center brake light. A turbocharged diesel is newly optional on 2500 models. A new grille appears.

RATINGS (SCALE OF 1-10)

Overall	Safety	Reliability	Performance	Comfort	Value
6.7	6.4	6.7	6.8	7.5	6.3

Category H
4 Dr C1500 Wgn	10765	13055
4 Dr C2500 Wgn	11250	13640
4 Dr K1500 4WD Wgn	11770	14270
4 Dr K2500 4WD Wgn	12380	15015

OPTIONS FOR SUBURBAN

8 cyl 6.5 L Turbodsl Engine +755
8 cyl 7.4 L Engine +150
Silverado Pkg +495
AM/FM Stereo Tape +50
Air Conditioning +200
Camper/Towing Package +80
Cruise Control +45
Dual Air Conditioning +315
Leather Seats +245
Power Door Locks +45
Power Drivers Seat +70
Power Windows +45
Tilt Steering Wheel +45

1993 CHEVROLET

APV   1993

Category G
2 Dr STD Cargo Van	4840	6405

OPTIONS FOR APV

AM/FM Stereo Tape +45
Air Conditioning +165
Power Door Locks +45

ASTRO   1993

Base 4.3-liter V6 gets 15 additional horsepower. Automatic transmission gets electronic shift controls and second-gear start feature. New speedometer

Model Description	Trade-in Value	Market Value

reads to 100 mph. Driver airbag is offered as an option midyear.

RATINGS (SCALE OF 1-10)

Overall	Safety	Reliability	Performance	Comfort	Value
6.6	4	6.3	7.2	6.6	9

Category G

2 Dr CL Pass. Van	4850	6420
2 Dr CL 4WD Pass. Van	5220	6910
2 Dr CL Pass. Van Ext	4960	6565
2 Dr CL 4WD Pass. Van Ext	5290	7000
2 Dr LT Pass. Van	5340	7070
2 Dr LT 4WD Pass. Van	5650	7480
2 Dr LT Pass. Van Ext	5455	7215
2 Dr LT 4WD Pass. Van Ext	5740	7600
2 Dr STD Cargo Van	4285	5675
2 Dr STD 4WD Cargo Van	4935	6530
2 Dr STD Cargo Van Ext	4475	5920
2 Dr STD 4WD Cargo Van Ext	5115	6770
2 Dr STD Pass. Van	4285	5675
2 Dr STD 4WD Pass. Van	5445	7205
2 Dr STD Pass. Van Ext	4650	6155

OPTIONS FOR ASTRO

6 cyl 4.3 L CPI Engine[Opt on CL,Pass. Van Ext,2WD] +100
8 Passenger Seating +80
AM/FM Stereo Tape +45
Air Conditioning +165
Cruise Control +40
Dual Air Conditioning +185
Power Door Locks +45
Power Drivers Seat +55
Power Windows +50
Privacy Glass[Std on LT] +55

BERETTA   1993

Standard engine on the GT is now a ridiculous 110-horsepower four-cylinder from the base car. The V6 is optional. GTZ's Quad 4 engine loses five horsepower to emissions regulations. A brake/shift interlock has been added to automatic transmissions. Manuals get an improved clutch.

RATINGS (SCALE OF 1-10)

Overall	Safety	Reliability	Performance	Comfort	Value
6.9	6.6	7.7	7.8	7	5.3

Category E

2 Dr GT Cpe	3250	4570
2 Dr GTZ Cpe	3975	5585
2 Dr STD Cpe	2865	4025

OPTIONS FOR BERETTA

6 cyl 3.1 L Engine +120
Auto 3-Speed Transmission +110
AM/FM Stereo Tape +60
Air Conditioning[Std on GTZ] +165

Cruise Control +45
Power Door Locks +50
Power Windows +55
Tilt Steering Wheel +30

BLAZER   1993

No changes.

Category H

2 Dr STD 4WD Utility	7790	9595
2 Dr Silverado 4WD Utility	9285	11435
2 Dr Sport 4WD Utility	9700	11945

OPTIONS FOR BLAZER

Auto 4-Speed Transmission +175
AM/FM Stereo Tape +40
Air Conditioning[Opt on Sport,STD] +165
Cruise Control[Opt on Sport,STD] +40
Power Door Locks +40
Power Drivers Seat +55
Power Windows +40
Tilt Steering Wheel[Opt on Sport,STD] +35

C/K PICKUP   1993

Solar-Ray tinted glass is made standard. Cloth interior surfaces are now protected by Scotchgard fabric protection. Automatic transmissions get electronic shift controls. Base V6 gets five additional horsepower.

RATINGS (SCALE OF 1-10)

Overall	Safety	Reliability	Performance	Comfort	Value
N/A	5.6	7.1	7.4	8	N/A

C/K 1500 SERIES

Category H

2 Dr C1500 454SS Std Cab SB	8855	10905
2 Dr C1500 Cheyenne Ext Cab LB		
	6645	8185
2 Dr C1500 Cheyenne Ext Cab SB		
	6535	8050
2 Dr C1500 Cheyenne Ext Cab Stepside SB		
	6705	8255
2 Dr C1500 Cheyenne Std Cab LB		
	6020	7415
2 Dr C1500 Cheyenne Std Cab SB		
	5895	7260
2 Dr C1500 Cheyenne Std Cab Stepside SB		
	6060	7465
2 Dr C1500 Indy Pace Std Cab SB		
	7305	9000
2 Dr C1500 Silverado Ext Cab LB	7175	8835
2 Dr C1500 Silverado Ext Cab SB	7065	8700
2 Dr C1500 Silverado Ext Cab Stepside SB		
	7230	8905
2 Dr C1500 Silverado Std Cab LB	6540	8055
2 Dr C1500 Silverado Std Cab SB	6415	7905

Model Description	Trade-in Value	Market Value
2 Dr C1500 Silverado Std Cab Stepside SB		
	6585	8110
2 Dr C1500 Sport Std Cab Stepside SB		
	6980	8600
2 Dr C1500 Work Truck Std Cab LB		
	5070	6245
2 Dr K1500 Cheyenne 4WD Ext Cab LB		
	7595	9350
2 Dr K1500 Cheyenne 4WD Ext Cab SB		
	7470	9200
2 Dr K1500 Cheyenne 4WD Ext Cab Stepside SB		
	7640	9405
2 Dr K1500 Cheyenne 4WD Std Cab LB		
	6950	8560
2 Dr K1500 Cheyenne 4WD Std Cab SB		
	6830	8410
2 Dr K1500 Cheyenne 4WD Std Cab Stepside SB		
	6995	8615
2 Dr K1500 Silverado 4WD Ext Cab LB		
	8120	10005
2 Dr K1500 Silverado 4WD Ext Cab SB		
	8000	9855
2 Dr K1500 Silverado 4WD Ext Cab Stepside SB		
	8170	10060
2 Dr K1500 Silverado 4WD Std Cab LB		
	7475	9205
2 Dr K1500 Silverado 4WD Std Cab SB		
	7355	9055
2 Dr K1500 Silverado 4WD Std Cab Stepside SB		
	6690	8235
2 Dr K1500 Work Truck 4WD Std Cab LB		
	6415	7900

C/K 2500 SERIES
Category H

Model Description	Trade-in Value	Market Value
2 Dr C2500 Cheyenne Ext Cab LB		
	6790	8365
2 Dr C2500 Cheyenne Ext Cab SB		
	6680	8230
2 Dr C2500 Cheyenne Std Cab LB		
	6345	7815
2 Dr C2500 Silverado Ext Cab LB	7720	9510
2 Dr C2500 Silverado Ext Cab SB	7645	9410
2 Dr C2500 Silverado Std Cab LB	6660	8200
2 Dr K2500 Cheyenne 4WD Ext Cab LB		
	7865	9685
2 Dr K2500 Cheyenne 4WD Ext Cab SB		
	7745	9540
2 Dr K2500 Cheyenne 4WD Std Cab LB		
	7085	8730
2 Dr K2500 Silverado 4WD Ext Cab LB		
	8195	10095

Model Description	Trade-in Value	Market Value
2 Dr K2500 Silverado 4WD Ext Cab SB		
	8320	10250
2 Dr K2500 Silverado 4WD Std Cab LB		
	7665	9440

C/K 3500 SERIES
Category H

Model Description	Trade-in Value	Market Value
4 Dr C3500 Crew Cab LB	8525	10500
2 Dr C3500 Ext Cab LB	8380	10320
2 Dr C3500 Cheyenne Std Cab LB		
	7820	9630
4 Dr C3500 Silverado Crew Cab LB		
	8845	10895
2 Dr C3500 Silverado Ext Cab LB		
	8830	10875
2 Dr C3500 Silverado Std Cab LB		
	8125	10005
4 Dr K3500 4WD Crew Cab LB	9035	11125
2 Dr K3500 Cheyenne 4WD Ext Cab LB		
	9430	11615
2 Dr K3500 Cheyenne 4WD Std Cab LB		
	8805	10845
4 Dr K3500 Silverado 4WD Crew Cab LB		
	9920	12220
2 Dr K3500 Silverado 4WD Ext Cab LB		
	9615	11840
2 Dr K3500 Silverado 4WD Std Cab LB		
	8895	10955

OPTIONS FOR C/K PICKUP
8 cyl 5.0 L Engine +120
8 cyl 5.7 L Engine +165
8 cyl 6.2 L Dsl Engine +425
8 cyl 6.5 L Turbodsl Engine +570
8 cyl 7.4 L Engine +170
Auto 4-Speed Transmission[Std on 454SS] +175
AM/FM Stereo Tape[Std on Sport] +40
Air Conditioning[Opt on Cheyenne,STD,Work Truck] +165
Bed Liner +45
Camper/Towing Package +65
Cruise Control[Std on 454SS,Sport,Silverado] +40
Power Door Locks[Std on 454SS,Sport] +40
Power Drivers Seat +55
Power Windows[Std on 454SS,Sport] +40

CAMARO   1993

All-new sports coupe is redesigned for the first time in 12 years. Dual airbags and ABS are standard. Convertible disappears for one year. Available in base and Z28 trim. Base model powered by 3.4-liter V6; Z28 gets 5.7-liter V8 rated at 275 horsepower (115 more than base Camaro). Z28 has a six-speed manual transmission standard.

Model Description	Trade-in Value	Market Value

RATINGS (SCALE OF 1-10)

Overall	Safety	Reliability	Performance	Comfort	Value
7.4	8.7	6.9	9.2	6.8	5.3

Category F

2 Dr STD Cpe	5010	6205
2 Dr Z28 Cpe	6230	7715

OPTIONS FOR CAMARO

Auto 4-Speed Transmission +120
Air Conditioning +170
Aluminum/Alloy Wheels[Opt on STD] +60
Bose Sound System +90
Glass Panel T-tops +195
Power Door Locks +40
Power Drivers Seat +50
Power Windows +45

CAPRICE   1993

Rear styling is revised, and rear wheel wells are opened up. Rear track is increased 1.6 inches. LTZ gets a 180-horsepower 5.7-liter V8 standard. Acoustical package added to reduce noise. LS trim level gets gold accents on wheels and trim.

RATINGS (SCALE OF 1-10)

Overall	Safety	Reliability	Performance	Comfort	Value
7.9	7	7.3	7.6	8.3	9.3

Category B

4 Dr LS Sdn	5465	6935
4 Dr LTZ Sdn	5640	7155
4 Dr STD Sdn	4930	6260
4 Dr STD Wgn	5355	6795

OPTIONS FOR CAPRICE

8 cyl 5.7 L Engine +50
AM/FM Stereo Tape +35
Cruise Control +45
Leather Seats +135
Power Door Locks[Std on LS,LTZ] +50
Power Drivers Seat +65
Power Windows[Std on LTZ] +55

CAVALIER   1993

Convertible gets glass rear window, and RS coupes and sedans can be equipped with the Z24's 3.1-liter V6. A CD player is a new option on VL models. RS gets Z24 interior trimmings.

RATINGS (SCALE OF 1-10)

Overall	Safety	Reliability	Performance	Comfort	Value
N/A	N/A	7.1	6.4	6.8	7.2

Category E

2 Dr RS Conv	3990	5605
2 Dr RS Cpe	2510	3530
4 Dr RS Sdn	2535	3565
4 Dr RS Wgn	2830	3975

Model Description	Trade-in Value	Market Value
2 Dr VL Cpe	2260	3175
4 Dr VL Sdn	2285	3210
4 Dr VL Wgn	2565	3605
2 Dr Z24 Conv	4720	6630
2 Dr Z24 Cpe	3260	4580

OPTIONS FOR CAVALIER

6 cyl 3.1 L Engine[Opt on RS] +120
Auto 3-Speed Transmission[Std on Wgn] +100
AM/FM Stereo Tape +60
Air Conditioning +165
Cruise Control +45
Power Windows[Std on Conv] +55

CHEVY VAN/SPORTVAN   1993

Solar-Ray tinted glass and Scotchgard fabric protectant are both standard. Four-wheel ABS is a new standard feature. Remote keyless entry joins the options list.

CHEVY VAN

Category H

2 Dr G10 Chevy Van	4825	5945
2 Dr G10 Chevy Van Ext	4885	6015
2 Dr G20 Chevy Van	4865	5990
2 Dr G20 Chevy Van Ext	4930	6070
2 Dr G30 Chevy Van	4965	6115
2 Dr G30 Chevy Van Ext	5760	7090

SPORTVAN

Category H

2 Dr G10 Sportvan	5650	6960
2 Dr G10 Sportvan Ext	5885	7250
2 Dr G10 Beauville Sportvan	6155	7580
2 Dr G10 Beauville Sportvan Ext	6625	8160
2 Dr G20 Sportvan Ext	5950	7325
2 Dr G20 Beauville Sportvan Ext	6220	7665
2 Dr G30 Sportvan	6535	8045
2 Dr G30 Sportvan Ext	6600	8130
2 Dr G30 Beauville Sportvan	6830	8410
2 Dr G30 Beauville Sportvan Ext	7295	8980

OPTIONS FOR CHEVY VAN/SPORTVAN

8 cyl 5.0 L Engine +120
8 cyl 5.7 L Engine[Opt on G10,G20,Chevy Van] +165
8 cyl 6.2 L Dsl Engine +425
8 cyl 7.4 L Engine +170
12 Passenger Seating +125
AM/FM Stereo Tape +40
Air Conditioning +165
Cruise Control +40
Dual Air Conditioning +255
Power Door Locks +40
Power Windows +40
Tilt Steering Wheel +35

Don't forget to refer to the Mileage Adjustment Table at the back of this book!

Model Description	Trade-in Value	Market Value

CORSICA 1993

Wow. A brake/transmission shift interlock is added. Larger muffler is supposed to make Corsica quieter.

RATINGS (SCALE OF 1-10)

Overall	Safety	Reliability	Performance	Comfort	Value
6.8	5.8	7.6	6.8	7.3	6.4

Category C

	Trade-in	Market
4 Dr LT Sdn	2540	3550

OPTIONS FOR CORSICA

6 cyl 3.1 L Engine +120
Auto 3-Speed Transmission +110
AM/FM Stereo Tape +35
Air Conditioning +160
Cruise Control +45
Power Door Locks +50
Power Drivers Seat +60
Power Windows +65
Tilt Steering Wheel +30

CORVETTE 1993

Base model gets narrower front tires and wider rear tires. LT1 V8 gets additional torque. ZR-1 horsepower is up to 405 this year. All models can be ordered in 40th Anniversary trim, consisting of Ruby Red paint and badging. Passive Keyless Entry is newly optional, and locks or unlocks the doors simply by having the key fob close to the car.

Category J

	Trade-in	Market
2 Dr STD Conv	16340	19035
2 Dr STD Cpe	14385	16760
2 Dr ZR1 Cpe	26830	31250

OPTIONS FOR CORVETTE

Adjustable Handling Pkg +270
Selective Ride Suspension +340
Bose Sound System +165
Leather Seats[Opt on STD] +250
Power Drivers Seat[Opt on STD] +70
Solid & Glass Targa Tops +190

LUMINA 1993

Base sedans get five more horsepower this year, and base coupes now have standard V6 power. Doors lock automatically when vehicle reaches eight mph.

RATINGS (SCALE OF 1-10)

Overall	Safety	Reliability	Performance	Comfort	Value
N/A	N/A	7.5	8.2	7.6	8.4

Category C

	Trade-in	Market
2 Dr Euro Cpe	3610	5045
4 Dr Euro Sdn	3655	5105
2 Dr STD Cpe	3405	4760
4 Dr STD Sdn	3115	4355
2 Dr Z34 Cpe	4235	5920

OPTIONS FOR LUMINA

6 cyl 3.1 L Engine[Std on Euro,Cpe] +120
6 cyl 3.4 L Engine[Std on Z34] +200
Auto 4-Speed Transmission +40
AM/FM Stereo Tape[Std on Z34] +35
Air Conditioning[Opt on STD Sdn] +160
Anti-Lock Brakes[Opt on STD] +120
Cruise Control[Std on Z34] +45
Power Drivers Seat +60
Power Windows +65
Tilt Steering Wheel[Std on Z34] +30

LUMINA MINIVAN 1993

Uplevel trim switches from CL to LS designation. Sunroof joins options list this year. Center console is redesigned to include dual cupholders.

RATINGS (SCALE OF 1-10)

Overall	Safety	Reliability	Performance	Comfort	Value
7.1	5.8	6.5	7.6	7.5	8.3

Category G

	Trade-in	Market
2 Dr LS Pass. Van	4960	6560
2 Dr STD Pass. Van	4165	5515

OPTIONS FOR LUMINA MINIVAN

6 cyl 3.8 L Engine +125
Auto 4-Speed Transmission +40
AM/FM Stereo Tape +45
Air Conditioning[Std on LS] +165
Cruise Control +40
Power Door Locks +45
Power Drivers Seat +55
Power Windows +50
Privacy Glass +55
Tilt Steering Wheel[Std on LS] +35

S10 BLAZER 1993

Two-door model available in LT trim. All models get two-tone paint scheme in LT trim. V6 engines get internal balance shaft designed to reduce vibration. Automatic transmission receives electronic shift controls and second-gear start feature. Manual lumbar adjusters are newly standard on front seats.

RATINGS (SCALE OF 1-10)

Overall	Safety	Reliability	Performance	Comfort	Value
5.9	5.1	6.1	6.8	7.1	4.3

Category G

	Trade-in	Market
2 Dr STD Utility	4470	5920
2 Dr STD 4WD Utility	4985	6600
4 Dr STD Wgn	4750	6290
4 Dr STD 4WD Wgn	5385	7130
2 Dr Tahoe Utility	4790	6345
2 Dr Tahoe 4WD Utility	5300	7010
4 Dr Tahoe Wgn	4940	6540
4 Dr Tahoe 4WD Wgn	5445	7210

Don't forget to refer to the Mileage Adjustment Table at the back of this book!

Model Description	Trade-in Value	Market Value
2 Dr Tahoe LT Utility	5730	7585
2 Dr Tahoe LT 4WD Utility	5990	7930
4 Dr Tahoe LT Wgn	5915	7830
4 Dr Tahoe LT 4WD Wgn	6110	8085

OPTIONS FOR S10 BLAZER
6 cyl 4.3 L CPI Engine +100
Auto 4-Speed Transmission +180
AM/FM Stereo Tape[Std on Tahoe LT] +45
Air Conditioning[Std on Tahoe LT] +165
Cruise Control[Std on Tahoe LT] +40
Leather Seats[Std on Tahoe LT] +155
Power Door Locks[Std on Tahoe LT] +45
Power Drivers Seat[Std on Tahoe LT] +55
Power Windows[Std on Tahoe LT] +50
Tilt Steering Wheel[Opt on STD] +35

S10 PICKUP   1993

V6 engines get internal balance shaft designed to reduce vibration. Automatic transmission gets electronic shift controls.

RATINGS (SCALE OF 1-10)

Overall	Safety	Reliability	Performance	Comfort	Value
N/A	3.4	6.6	7.2	7	N/A

Category G

	Trade-in	Market
2 Dr EL Std Cab SB	2970	3930
2 Dr EL 4WD Std Cab SB	4195	5555
2 Dr STD Ext Cab SB	3900	5165
2 Dr STD 4WD Ext Cab SB	5050	6685
2 Dr STD Std Cab LB	3415	4525
2 Dr STD 4WD Std Cab LB	4565	6045
2 Dr STD Std Cab SB	3415	4525
2 Dr STD 4WD Std Cab SB	4565	6045
2 Dr Tahoe Ext Cab SB	4100	5425
2 Dr Tahoe 4WD Ext Cab SB	5340	7070
2 Dr Tahoe Std Cab LB	3485	4610
2 Dr Tahoe 4WD Std Cab LB	4635	6135
2 Dr Tahoe Std Cab SB	3485	4610
2 Dr Tahoe 4WD Std Cab SB	4635	6135

OPTIONS FOR S10 PICKUP
6 cyl 2.8 L Engine +80
6 cyl 4.3 L Engine[Opt on 2WD] +125
Auto 4-Speed Transmission +175
AM/FM Stereo Tape[Opt on EL,STD] +45
Air Conditioning +165
Cruise Control +40
Power Windows +50
Tilt Steering Wheel +35

SUBURBAN   1993

No changes.

RATINGS (SCALE OF 1-10)

Overall	Safety	Reliability	Performance	Comfort	Value
6.9	6.6	6.9	6.8	7.5	6.7

Category H

	Trade-in	Market
4 Dr C1500 Wgn	9270	11415
4 Dr C2500 Wgn	9835	12110
4 Dr K1500 4WD Wgn	10080	12415
4 Dr K2500 4WD Wgn	10635	13095

OPTIONS FOR SUBURBAN
8 cyl 7.4 L Engine +170
Silverado Pkg +400
AM/FM Stereo Tape +40
Air Conditioning +165
Camper/Towing Package +65
Cruise Control +40
Dual Air Conditioning +255
Leather Seats +200
Power Door Locks +40
Power Drivers Seat +55
Power Windows +40
Tilt Steering Wheel +35

1992 CHEVROLET

ASTRO   1992

Dutch rear door treatment is available. With Dutch doors, a rear washer/wiper and rear defogger can be ordered. All-wheel-drive models get high-output, 200-horsepower, V6 standard. Engine is optional on 2WD models.

RATINGS (SCALE OF 1-10)

Overall	Safety	Reliability	Performance	Comfort	Value
6.5	3.6	6.9	7.2	6.6	8

Category G

	Trade-in	Market
2 Dr CL Pass. Van	4330	5710
2 Dr CL 4WD Pass. Van	4860	6410
2 Dr CL Pass. Van Ext	4500	5935
2 Dr CL 4WD Pass. Van Ext	5030	6635
2 Dr LT Pass. Van	4335	5720
2 Dr LT 4WD Pass. Van	4865	6420
2 Dr LT Pass. Van Ext	4505	5945
2 Dr LT 4WD Pass. Van Ext	5040	6645
2 Dr STD Cargo Van	3740	4935
2 Dr STD 4WD Cargo Van	4340	5725
2 Dr STD Cargo Van Ext	3915	5165
2 Dr STD 4WD Cargo Van Ext	4515	5955
2 Dr STD Pass. Van	4045	5340
2 Dr STD 4WD Pass. Van	4575	6040
2 Dr STD Pass. Van Ext	4220	5565
2 Dr STD 4WD Pass. Van Ext	4750	6265

CHEVROLET 92

Model Description	Trade-in Value	Market Value

OPTIONS FOR ASTRO

6 cyl 4.3 L CPI Engine +70
8 Passenger Seating +65
Air Conditioning +135
Power Door Locks +40
Power Drivers Seat +45
Power Windows +40

BERETTA 1992

ABS is standard. Base engine gains 15 horsepower. GTZ gets revised gearing for better off-the-line acceleration. Base V6 models get gearing change designed to save fuel. Order a GTZ with the V6, and you'll get touring tires instead of high-performance rubber. Front brakes are slightly larger on all models.

RATINGS (SCALE OF 1-10)

Overall	Safety	Reliability	Performance	Comfort	Value
6.8	6.6	6.7	7.8	7	5.7

Category E
2 Dr GT Cpe	2745	3935
2 Dr GTZ Cpe	3375	4845
2 Dr STD Cpe	2610	3660

OPTIONS FOR BERETTA

6 cyl 3.1 L Engine +100
Auto 3-Speed Transmission +90
Air Conditioning[Std on GT] +135
Cruise Control +35
Power Door Locks +40
Power Windows +45

BLAZER 1992

Totally redesigned and based on same platform and sheetmetal as C/K pickup. Six-passenger seating is standard. Cargo area gets fixed metal roof rather than fiberglass shell. Four-wheel ABS is standard and works in 4WD. New Sport appearance package includes two-tone paint and wheelwell flares. Diesel option is dropped. Five-speed manual is standard transmission. An automatic is optional. Shift-on-the-fly 4WD is standard.

Category H
2 Dr STD 4WD Utility	6910	8625
2 Dr Silverado 4WD Utility	7230	9025
2 Dr Sport 4WD Utility	7345	9170

OPTIONS FOR BLAZER

Auto 4-Speed Transmission +145
Air Conditioning +135
Cruise Control +30
Power Door Locks +30
Power Drivers Seat +45
Power Windows +30

C/K PICKUP 1992

Extended-cab models get Sportside box option. Crew Cab model is all-new, sporting same engineering and styling as rest of C/K line. Front buckets have been redesigned. Standard gauge cluster is restyled. Integral head restraints are added for outboard passengers. A new turbocharged, 6.5-liter diesel V8 is optional in C/K 2500 and regular cab C/K 3500 models. Four-speed manual transmission is dropped.

RATINGS (SCALE OF 1-10)

Overall	Safety	Reliability	Performance	Comfort	Value
N/A	5.6	6.8	7.4	8	N/A

C/K 1500 SERIES

Category H
2 Dr C1500 Ext Cab LB	5170	6455
2 Dr C1500 Ext Cab SB	5065	6325
2 Dr C1500 Ext Cab Stepside SB	5205	6495
2 Dr C1500 Std Cab LB	4840	6045
2 Dr C1500 Std Cab SB	4735	5915
2 Dr C1500 Std Cab Stepside SB	4875	6085
2 Dr C1500 454SS Std Cab SB	7015	8760
2 Dr C1500 Scottsdale Ext Cab LB	5400	6740
2 Dr C1500 Scottsdale Ext Cab SB	5295	6610
2 Dr C1500 Scottsdale Ext Cab Stepside SB	5435	6785
2 Dr C1500 Scottsdale Std Cab LB	5075	6340
2 Dr C1500 Scottsdale Std Cab SB	4975	6210
2 Dr C1500 Scottsdale Std Cab Stepside SB	5110	6380
2 Dr C1500 Silverado Ext Cab LB	5475	6835
2 Dr C1500 Silverado Ext Cab SB	5370	6705
2 Dr C1500 Silverado Ext Cab Stepside SB	5510	6880
2 Dr C1500 Silverado Std Cab LB	5140	6415
2 Dr C1500 Silverado Std Cab SB	5030	6280
2 Dr C1500 Silverado Std Cab Stepside SB	5170	6455
2 Dr C1500 Work Truck Std Cab LB	3875	4835
2 Dr K1500 4WD Ext Cab LB	5950	7425
2 Dr K1500 4WD Ext Cab SB	5845	7295
2 Dr K1500 4WD Ext Cab Stepside SB	5985	7470
2 Dr K1500 4WD Std Cab LB	5620	7015
2 Dr K1500 4WD Std Cab SB	5515	6885

Model Description	Trade-in Value	Market Value
2 Dr K1500 4WD Std Cab Stepside SB	5655	7060
2 Dr K1500 Scottsdale 4WD Ext Cab LB	6075	7585
2 Dr K1500 Scottsdale 4WD Ext Cab SB	6075	7585
2 Dr K1500 Scottsdale 4WD Ext Cab Stepside SB	6215	7760
2 Dr K1500 Scottsdale 4WD Std Cab LB	5855	7310
2 Dr K1500 Scottsdale 4WD Std Cab SB	5750	7180
2 Dr K1500 Scottsdale 4WD Std Cab Stepside SB	5890	7355
2 Dr K1500 Silverado 4WD Ext Cab LB	6250	7800
2 Dr K1500 Silverado 4WD Ext Cab SB	6145	7670
2 Dr K1500 Silverado 4WD Ext Cab Stepside SB	6285	7845
2 Dr K1500 Silverado 4WD Std Cab LB	5915	7385
2 Dr K1500 Silverado 4WD Std Cab SB	5810	7255
2 Dr K1500 Silverado 4WD Std Cab Stepside SB	5950	7425
2 Dr K1500 Work Truck 4WD Std Cab LB	4915	6140

C/K 2500 SERIES
Category H

Model Description	Trade-in Value	Market Value
2 Dr C2500 Ext Cab LB	5475	6840
2 Dr C2500 Ext Cab SB	5375	6710
2 Dr C2500 Std Cab LB	4990	6235
2 Dr C2500 Scottsdale Ext Cab LB	5590	6980
2 Dr C2500 Scottsdale Ext Cab SB	5490	6855
2 Dr C2500 Scottsdale Std Cab LB	5225	6525
2 Dr C2500 Silverado Ext Cab LB	5815	7260
2 Dr C2500 Silverado Ext Cab SB	5710	7130
2 Dr C2500 Silverado Std Cab LB	5325	6645
2 Dr K2500 4WD Ext Cab LB	6060	7565
2 Dr K2500 4WD Ext Cab SB	5960	7440
2 Dr K2500 4WD Std Cab LB	5595	6985
2 Dr K2500 Scottsdale 4WD Ext Cab LB	6175	7710
2 Dr K2500 Scottsdale 4WD Ext Cab SB	6075	7585
2 Dr K2500 Scottsdale 4WD Std Cab LB	5830	7280
2 Dr K2500 Silverado 4WD Ext Cab LB	6400	7990
2 Dr K2500 Silverado 4WD Ext Cab SB	6295	7860
2 Dr K2500 Silverado 4WD Std Cab LB	5930	7400

C/K 3500 SERIES
Category H

Model Description	Trade-in Value	Market Value
4 Dr C3500 Crew Cab LB	6145	7670
2 Dr C3500 Ext Cab LB	5885	7350
2 Dr C3500 Std Cab LB	5520	6895
2 Dr C3500 Scottsdale Ext Cab LB	6080	7590
2 Dr C3500 Scottsdale Std Cab LB	5755	7185
2 Dr C3500 Silverado Ext Cab LB	6225	7770
2 Dr C3500 Silverado Std Cab LB	5905	7375
4 Dr K3500 4WD Crew Cab LB	6860	8565
2 Dr K3500 4WD Ext Cab LB	6670	8325
2 Dr K3500 4WD Std Cab LB	6305	7875
2 Dr K3500 Scottsdale 4WD Ext Cab LB	6865	8570
2 Dr K3500 Scottsdale 4WD Std Cab LB	6425	8025
2 Dr K3500 Silverado 4WD Ext Cab LB	6710	8375
2 Dr K3500 Silverado 4WD Std Cab LB	6690	8355
4 Dr Silverado Crew Cab LB	6865	8570

OPTIONS FOR C/K PICKUP
8 cyl 5.0 L Engine +95
8 cyl 5.7 L Engine +135
8 cyl 6.2 L Dsl Engine +350
8 cyl 6.5 L Turbodsl Engine +460
8 cyl 7.4 L Engine +130
Auto 4-Speed Transmission[Std on 454SS] +145
Silverado Pkg +170
Sport Handling Pkg +145
Air Conditioning +135
Camper/Towing Package +55
Cruise Control[Std on 454SS, Silverado] +30
Power Door Locks[Std on 454SS] +30
Power Drivers Seat +45
Power Windows[Std on 454SS] +30

CAMARO   1992

Heritage Appearance option, essentially a couple of sport stripes and a dashboard plaque, commemorates Camaro's 25th anniversary. Z28 models get quicker steering and an improved suspension.
Category F

Model	Trade-in Value	Market Value
2 Dr RS Conv	5540	6995
2 Dr RS Cpe	3750	4740

Don't forget to refer to the Mileage Adjustment Table at the back of this book!

Model Description	Trade-in Value	Market Value
2 Dr Z28 Conv	6210	7845
2 Dr Z28 Cpe	4940	6240

OPTIONS FOR CAMARO
8 cyl 5.0 L Engine[Opt on RS] +60
8 cyl 5.7 L Engine +75
Auto 4-Speed Transmission +85
Air Conditioning +135
Bose Sound System +75
Glass Panel T-tops +160
Leather Seats +105
Power Door Locks +35
Power Drivers Seat +40
Power Windows +40

CAPRICE 1992

Station wagon gets more powerful V8 option. Speedometer now reads to 100 mph, tilt steering is standard, and wagon's quarter vent windows are power operated.

RATINGS (SCALE OF 1-10)

Overall	Safety	Reliability	Performance	Comfort	Value
7.2	6.6	5.5	7.6	8.3	8.1

Category B

4 Dr Classic Sdn	4215	5555
4 Dr STD Sdn	3800	5010
4 Dr STD Wgn	4095	5400

OPTIONS FOR CAPRICE
8 cyl 5.7 L Engine +40
Cruise Control +35
Leather Seats +110
Power Door Locks[Std on Classic] +45
Power Drivers Seat +50
Power Windows +45

CAVALIER 1992

ABS is standard, and base engines are bumped 15 horsepower to 110. RS and Z24 convertibles are back after two-year hiatus. Automatic door locks are added. VL and RS models get new wheelcovers. Z24 trades performance tires for touring.

RATINGS (SCALE OF 1-10)

Overall	Safety	Reliability	Performance	Comfort	Value
N/A	N/A	6.8	6.4	6.8	5.6

Category E

2 Dr RS Conv	3470	4980
2 Dr RS Cpe	2290	3285
4 Dr RS Sdn	2335	3350
4 Dr RS Wgn	2555	3660
2 Dr VL Cpe	2050	2940
4 Dr VL Sdn	2070	2970
4 Dr VL Wgn	2315	3315

Model Description	Trade-in Value	Market Value
2 Dr Z24 Conv	4105	5890
2 Dr Z24 Cpe	2945	4225

OPTIONS FOR CAVALIER
6 cyl 3.1 L Engine[Opt on RS] +100
Auto 3-Speed Transmission[Std on Wgn] +80
Air Conditioning +135
Cruise Control +35
Power Windows[Std on Conv] +45

CHEVY VAN / SPORTVAN 1992

Minor suspension modifications improve the ride.

CHEVY VAN

Category H

2 Dr G10 Chevy Van	4230	5280
2 Dr G10 Chevy Van Ext	4295	5365
2 Dr G20 Chevy Van	4290	5355
2 Dr G20 Chevy Van Ext	4375	5465
2 Dr G30 Chevy Van	4740	5915
2 Dr G30 Chevy Van Ext	4295	5365

SPORTVAN

Category H

2 Dr G10 Sportvan	5045	6295
2 Dr G10 Sportvan Ext	5350	6680
2 Dr G10 Beauville Sportvan	5290	6605
2 Dr G10 Beauville Sportvan Ext	5580	6965
2 Dr G20 Sportvan Ext	5390	6730
2 Dr G20 Beauville Sportvan Ext	5640	7040
2 Dr G30 Sportvan	5920	7390
2 Dr G30 Sportvan Ext	5960	7445
2 Dr G30 Beauville Dsl Sportvan	6200	7740
2 Dr G30 Beauville Sportvan Ext	6195	7735

OPTIONS FOR CHEVY VAN/SPORTVAN
8 cyl 5.0 L Engine +95
8 cyl 5.7 L Engine[Opt on G10,G20,Chevy Van Ext] +135
8 cyl 6.2 L Dsl Engine +350
8 cyl 7.4 L Engine +130
12 Passenger Seating +105
Air Conditioning +135
Cruise Control +30
Dual Air Conditioning +210
Power Door Locks +30
Power Windows +30

CORSICA 1992

Five-door hatchback is dropped. ABS is standard, and base engine makes more power. Manual transmission cannot be ordered with V6 this year. V6 models get more fuel-efficient gearing. Front brakes are larger, and optional CD player gets theft-deterrent system. Outside mirrors are body-color.

Model Description	Trade-in Value	Market Value

RATINGS (SCALE OF 1-10)

Overall	Safety	Reliability	Performance	Comfort	Value
6.6	5.8	6.5	6.8	7.3	6.8

Category C

4 Dr LT Sdn	2095	3035

OPTIONS FOR CORSICA

6 cyl 3.1 L Engine +105
Auto 3-Speed Transmission +90
Air Conditioning +135
Cruise Control +35
Power Door Locks +40
Power Windows +50

CORVETTE   1992

New base V8 is the LT1 engine, making 300 horsepower. ZR-1 gets fender badging to distinguish itself from lesser Corvettes. All Corvettes get traction control standard. Speedometer swaps spots with the fuel gauge for better readability. A Quiet Car option adds weather-stripping and sound insulation.

Category J

2 Dr STD Conv	13295	15565
2 Dr STD Cpe	12040	14100
2 Dr ZR1 Cpe	21870	25605

OPTIONS FOR CORVETTE

Handling Pkg +335
Selective Suspension +275
Bose Sound System +135
Compact Disc W/fm/tape[Opt on STD] +115
Leather Seats[Opt on STD] +205
Power Drivers Seat[Opt on STD] +60
Solid & Glass Targa Tops +155

LUMINA   1992

Euro sedan can be equipped with 3.4-liter twin-cam engine. Base engine loses five horsepower. ABS is standard on Z34 and Euro; optional on base models. A CD player joins the options sheet.

RATINGS (SCALE OF 1-10)

Overall	Safety	Reliability	Performance	Comfort	Value
N/A	N/A	6.6	8.2	7.6	8.3

Category C

2 Dr Euro Cpe	2965	4295
4 Dr Euro Sdn	3000	4345
2 Dr STD Cpe	2525	3655
4 Dr STD Sdn	2810	3820
2 Dr Z34 Cpe	3480	5040

OPTIONS FOR LUMINA

6 cyl 3.1 L Engine[Opt on STD] +105
6 cyl 3.4 L Engine[Std on Z34] +160
Auto 4-Speed Transmission +35
Euro 3.4 Pkg +275
Air Conditioning[Opt on STD] +135

Anti-Lock Brakes[Opt on STD] +95
Cruise Control[Std on Z34] +35
Power Door Locks +40
Power Drivers Seat +50
Power Windows +50

LUMINA MINIVAN   1992

An optional 165-horsepower, 3.8-liter V6 with a four-speed automatic is newly available. Wheels and tires are larger this year. Power mirrors and a four-way manual seat adjuster for the driver are new options.

RATINGS (SCALE OF 1-10)

Overall	Safety	Reliability	Performance	Comfort	Value
7.1	5.9	6.3	7.6	7.5	8.3

Category G

2 Dr CL Pass. Van	4070	5365
2 Dr STD Cargo Van	3390	4470
2 Dr STD Pass. Van	3660	4830

OPTIONS FOR LUMINA MINIVAN

6 cyl 3.8 L Engine +110
Auto 4-Speed Transmission +35
Air Conditioning[Std on CL] +135
Cruise Control +35
Power Door Locks +40
Power Drivers Seat +45
Power Windows +40

S10 BLAZER   1992

Four-wheel ABS is standard on all models. Electronic-shift transfer case is added to options list of 4WD models. A high-performance 4.3-liter V6 debuts with 40 additional horsepower, bringing total output to 200 ponies. Bucket seats are redesigned, a new speedometer is installed, and a four-spoke steering wheel is added.

RATINGS (SCALE OF 1-10)

Overall	Safety	Reliability	Performance	Comfort	Value
5.8	3.9	6.2	6.8	7.1	4.9

Category G

2 Dr STD Utility	3935	5190
2 Dr STD 4WD Utility	4385	5785
4 Dr STD Wgn	4180	5515
2 Dr Tahoe Utility	4155	5480
2 Dr Tahoe 4WD Utility	4595	6065
4 Dr Tahoe Wgn	4280	5645
4 Dr Tahoe 4WD Wgn	4835	6380

OPTIONS FOR S10 BLAZER

6 cyl 4.3 L CPI Engine +70
Auto 4-Speed Transmission +145
LT Pkg +135
Air Conditioning +135
Cruise Control +35

Don't forget to refer to the Mileage Adjustment Table at the back of this book!

Model Description	Trade-in Value	Market Value
Power Door Locks +40		
Power Windows +40		

S10 PICKUP   1992

Base EL model can be equipped with four-wheel drive. Baja package dropped. Front bucket seats are redesigned, integral head restraints are added, and Extended Cabs can be equipped with leather seats. New speedometer and four-spoke steering wheel are installed. Premium sound system with CD player is added to options list. Four-wheel-drive models can be equipped with an electronic-shift transfer case.

RATINGS (SCALE OF 1-10)

Overall	Safety	Reliability	Performance	Comfort	Value
N/A	3.5	6.6	7.2	7	N/A

Category G		
2 Dr EL Std Cab SB	2470	3255
2 Dr EL 4WD Std Cab SB	3420	4515
2 Dr STD Ext Cab SB	3175	4190
2 Dr STD 4WD Ext Cab SB	4135	5450
2 Dr STD Std Cab LB	2775	3660
2 Dr STD 4WD Std Cab LB	3730	4920
2 Dr STD Std Cab SB	2775	3660
2 Dr STD 4WD Std Cab SB	3730	4920
2 Dr Tahoe Ext Cab SB	3485	4595
2 Dr Tahoe 4WD Ext Cab SB	4375	5770
2 Dr Tahoe Std Cab LB	2970	3915
2 Dr Tahoe 4WD Std Cab LB	3865	5095
2 Dr Tahoe Std Cab SB	2970	3915
2 Dr Tahoe 4WD Std Cab SB	3865	5095

OPTIONS FOR S10 PICKUP

6 cyl 2.8 L Engine +65
6 cyl 4.3 L Engine[Opt on 2WD] +100
Auto 4-Speed Transmission +145
Air Conditioning +135
Cruise Control +35
Power Door Locks +40
Power Windows +40

SUBURBAN   1992

All-new design debuts based on platform and styling of C/K pickup. Cargo space and towing capacity are up. ABS works on all four wheels even in 4WD. Tailgate glass is lifted up instead of powered down. No diesel is offered. GM's Instatrac 4WD system is standard on K models.

RATINGS (SCALE OF 1-10)

Overall	Safety	Reliability	Performance	Comfort	Value
6.7	6.4	6.3	6.8	7.5	6.6

Category H		
4 Dr C1500 Wgn	6990	8730
4 Dr C2500 Wgn	7440	9290
4 Dr K1500 4WD Wgn	7480	9335
4 Dr K2500 4WD Wgn	7905	9870

OPTIONS FOR SUBURBAN

8 cyl 7.4 L Engine +130
Silverado Pkg +300
Air Conditioning +135
Cruise Control +30
Dual Air Conditioning +210
Power Door Locks +30
Power Drivers Seat +45
Power Windows +30

1991 CHEVROLET

ASTRO   1991

Cargo models gain the 4.3-liter V6 as standard equipment. A revised Sport Package is available with sport suspension, rally wheels, front air dam with fog lights, and a sport steering wheel. Side and rear windows now have swing-out glass. Extended-length models can be ordered with the Sport Package.

RATINGS (SCALE OF 1-10)

Overall	Safety	Reliability	Performance	Comfort	Value
6.2	3.4	6.2	7.2	6.6	7.6

Category G		
2 Dr CL Pass. Van	3715	5160
2 Dr CL 4WD Pass. Van	3960	5355
2 Dr CL Pass. Van Ext	3870	5370
2 Dr CL 4WD Pass. Van Ext	3275	5000
2 Dr LT Pass. Van	3825	5305
2 Dr LT 4WD Pass. Van	4185	5720
2 Dr LT Pass. Van Ext	3880	5425
2 Dr LT 4WD Pass. Van Ext	4415	6125
2 Dr STD Cargo Van	3210	4455
2 Dr STD 4WD Cargo Van	3735	5185
2 Dr STD Cargo Van Ext	3365	4670
2 Dr STD 4WD Cargo Van Ext	3890	5395
2 Dr STD Pass. Van	3475	4820
2 Dr STD 4WD Pass. Van	3350	4645
2 Dr STD Pass. Van Ext	3170	4520
2 Dr STD 4WD Pass. Van Ext	3295	4710

OPTIONS FOR ASTRO

6 cyl 4.3 L HO Engine +55
Sport Handling Pkg +120
8 Passenger Seating +55
Air Conditioning +110
Power Door Locks +30
Power Drivers Seat +40
Power Windows +30

Model Description	Trade-in Value	Market Value

Model Description	Trade-in Value	Market Value

BERETTA   1991

New dashboard debuts, and a driver airbag is added. Color-keyed lace-spoke alloys are available on GT, along with revised graphics. A CD player is newly optional. GTZ can be ordered with the more tame 3.1-liter V6 found in other Berettas so that folks who hate to shift their own gears can get a GTZ with an automatic transmission. All Quad 4 GTZs come with a five-speed only.

RATINGS (SCALE OF 1-10)

Overall	Safety	Reliability	Performance	Comfort	Value
6.5	5.5	6.9	7.8	7	5.1

Category E

	Trade-in	Market
2 Dr GT Cpe	2365	3775
2 Dr GTZ Cpe	2700	4315
2 Dr STD Cpe	1855	3125

OPTIONS FOR BERETTA

6 cyl 3.1 L Engine[Opt on STD] +90
Auto 3-Speed Transmission +75
Air Conditioning[Opt on STD] +110
Cruise Control +30
Power Door Locks +35
Power Windows +35

BLAZER   1991

Throttle-body fuel injection is improved, and more powerful alternator is standard.

Category H

	Trade-in	Market
2 Dr STD 4WD Utility	5300	7180
2 Dr Silverado 4WD Utility	5675	7685

OPTIONS FOR BLAZER

8 cyl 6.2 L Dsl Engine +315
Auto 4-Speed Transmission +115
Air Conditioning +110
Cruise Control +25
Power Door Locks +25
Power Windows +25

C/K PICKUP   1991

7.4-liter V8 is reworked, and can be mated to four-speed automatic transmission. 454 SS gets 25 more horsepower. New gauge cluster includes a tachometer. Bucket seats are a new option. Air conditioners get a new recirculation mode. Two-wheel-drive models add tow hooks to the options list. W/T gets new steering wheel and revised outside mirrors.

RATINGS (SCALE OF 1-10)

Overall	Safety	Reliability	Performance	Comfort	Value
N/A	5.7	6.8	7.4	8	N/A

C/K 1500 SERIES

Category H

	Trade-in	Market
2 Dr C1500 Ext Cab LB	3780	5120
2 Dr C1500 Ext Cab SB	3695	5005
2 Dr C1500 Std Cab LB	3425	4640
2 Dr C1500 Std Cab SB	3510	4755
2 Dr C1500 Std Cab Stepside SB	3525	4770
2 Dr C1500 454SS Std Cab SB	5545	7515
2 Dr C1500 Scottsdale Ext Cab LB	3950	5350
2 Dr C1500 Scottsdale Ext Cab SB	3865	5235
2 Dr C1500 Scottsdale Std Cab LB	3685	4990
2 Dr C1500 Scottsdale Std Cab SB	3600	4875
2 Dr C1500 Scottsdale Std Cab Stepside SB	3695	5005
2 Dr C1500 Silverado Ext Cab LB	4065	5510
2 Dr C1500 Silverado Ext Cab SB	3980	5395
2 Dr C1500 Silverado Ext Cab Stepside SB	4080	5525
2 Dr C1500 Silverado Std Cab LB	3800	5145
2 Dr C1500 Silverado Std Cab SB	3715	5030
2 Dr C1500 Silverado Std Cab Stepside SB	3810	5160
2 Dr C1500 WT Std Cab LB	3175	4300
2 Dr K1500 4WD Ext Cab LB	4420	5985
2 Dr K1500 4WD Ext Cab SB	4335	5870
2 Dr K1500 4WD Std Cab LB	4140	5605
2 Dr K1500 4WD Std Cab SB	4055	5490
2 Dr K1500 4WD Std Cab Stepside SB	4150	5620
2 Dr K1500 Scottsdale 4WD Ext Cab LB	4590	6215
2 Dr K1500 Scottsdale 4WD Ext Cab SB	4505	6100
2 Dr K1500 Scottsdale 4WD Std Cab LB	4310	5840
2 Dr K1500 Scottsdale 4WD Std Cab SB	4225	5725
2 Dr K1500 Scottsdale 4WD Std Cab Stepside SB	4320	5855
2 Dr K1500 Silverado 4WD Ext Cab LB	4620	6255
2 Dr K1500 Silverado 4WD Ext Cab SB	4795	6490
2 Dr K1500 Silverado 4WD Ext Cab Stepside SB	4890	6620
2 Dr K1500 Silverado 4WD Std Cab LB	4145	5610

Model Description	Trade-in Value	Market Value
2 Dr K1500 Silverado 4WD Std Cab SB		
	4340	5880
2 Dr K1500 Silverado 4WD Std Cab Stepside SB		
	4440	6010
2 Dr K1500 WT 4WD Std Cab LB	3745	5070

C/K 2500 SERIES
Category H

Model Description	Trade-in Value	Market Value
2 Dr C2500 Ext Cab LB	4040	5470
2 Dr C2500 Ext Cab SB	3955	5355
2 Dr C2500 Std Cab LB	3640	4935
2 Dr C2500 Scottsdale Ext Cab LB		
	4335	5870
2 Dr C2500 Scottsdale Ext Cab SB		
	4125	5585
2 Dr C2500 Scottsdale Std Cab LB		
	3810	5160
2 Dr C2500 Silverado Ext Cab LB		
	4320	5850
2 Dr C2500 Silverado Ext Cab SB	4235	5740
2 Dr C2500 Silverado Std Cab LB	3925	5315
2 Dr K2500 4WD Ext Cab LB	4515	6115
2 Dr K2500 4WD Ext Cab SB	4430	6000
2 Dr K2500 4WD Std Cab LB	4135	5600
2 Dr K2500 Scottsdale 4WD Ext Cab LB		
	4685	6340
2 Dr K2500 Scottsdale 4WD Ext Cab SB		
	4600	6230
2 Dr K2500 Scottsdale 4WD Std Cab LB		
	4305	5830
2 Dr K2500 Silverado 4WD Ext Cab LB		
	4795	6495
2 Dr K2500 Silverado 4WD Ext Cab SB		
	4715	6385
2 Dr K2500 Silverado 4WD Std Cab LB		
	4420	5985

C/K 3500 SERIES
Category H

Model Description	Trade-in Value	Market Value
2 Dr C3500 Ext Cab LB	4705	6370
2 Dr C3500 Std Cab LB	4405	5965
2 Dr C3500 Scottsdale Ext Cab LB		
	4795	6490
2 Dr C3500 Scottsdale Std Cab LB		
	4690	6355
2 Dr C3500 Silverado Ext Cab LB		
	4940	6690
2 Dr C3500 Silverado Std Cab LB		
	4800	6505
2 Dr K3500 4WD Ext Cab LB	5515	7470
2 Dr K3500 4WD Std Cab LB	5055	6845
2 Dr K3500 Scottsdale 4WD Ext Cab LB		
	5295	7175
2 Dr K3500 Scottsdale 4WD Std Cab LB		
	5175	7010
2 Dr K3500 Silverado 4WD Ext Cab LB		
	5435	7360
2 Dr K3500 Silverado 4WD Std Cab LB		
	5285	7160

OPTIONS FOR C/K PICKUP
8 cyl 5.0 L Engine +80
8 cyl 5.7 L Engine +110
8 cyl 6.2 L Dsl Engine +315
8 cyl 7.4 L Engine +115
Auto 4-Speed Transmission[Std on 454SS] +115
Sport Handling Pkg +120
Air Conditioning[Std on 454SS] +110
Cruise Control[Std on 454SS] +25
Power Door Locks[Std on 454SS] +25
Power Windows[Std on 454SS] +25

CAMARO — 1991

Chevy loses IROC sponsorship to Dodge, and right to use IROC name. Z28 nomenclature returns on top-level Camaro. Order your RS with the 5.0-liter V8 engine, and you can opt for a 16-inch wheel and tire combination. Z28 models have a revised hood, scooped rocker panels, and a more aggressive rear spoiler. Color-keyed alloys are available.

Category F

Model Description	Trade-in Value	Market Value
2 Dr RS Conv	5010	6590
2 Dr RS Cpe	3515	4620
2 Dr Z28 Conv	5475	7200
2 Dr Z28 Cpe	4325	5690

OPTIONS FOR CAMARO
8 cyl 5.0 L Engine[Opt on RS] +45
8 cyl 5.7 L Engine +65
Auto 4-Speed Transmission +70
Air Conditioning +110
Power Door Locks +25
Power Drivers Seat +30
Power Windows +30
T-Tops (solid/Colored) +125

CAPRICE — 1991

Shamu arrives! Sedan and wagon are totally re ...ahem, designed. Retain rear-wheel drive. Standard engine is a 5.0-liter V8. Driver airbag and ABS are standard. Wagon provides over 92 cubic feet of cargo volume. LTZ model added midyear sporting wider tires, sport suspension, and heavy-duty cooling and braking systems.

RATINGS (SCALE OF 1-10)

Overall	Safety	Reliability	Performance	Comfort	Value
7	6.7	4.7	7.6	8.3	7.5

Don't forget to refer to the Mileage Adjustment Table at the back of this book!

Model Description	Trade-in Value	Market Value
Category B		
4 Dr Classic Sdn	3450	4670
4 Dr STD Sdn	3335	4515
4 Dr STD Wgn	3485	4715

OPTIONS FOR CAPRICE
Cruise Control +30
Power Door Locks[Std on Classic] +35
Power Drivers Seat +40
Power Windows[Std on Classic] +40

CAVALIER   1991

Styling is revised front and rear for a more aerodynamic look. Cupholders and storage cubbies are added to a restyled dashboard. RS trim level reappears for coupe and sedan after two-year hiatus. Z51 Performance Handling Package is available on Cavalier RS coupe, and includes sport suspension, performance tires and gauge package. Scotchgard protectant covers cloth seats and door trim. Z24 gets new alloy wheels.

RATINGS (SCALE OF 1-10)

Overall	Safety	Reliability	Performance	Comfort	Value
N/A	N/A	6.6	6.4	6.8	5.4

Category E		
2 Dr RS Conv	2670	4265
2 Dr RS Cpe	1825	2915
4 Dr RS Sdn	1860	2965
4 Dr RS Wgn	1950	3115
2 Dr VL Cpe	1700	2710
4 Dr VL Sdn	1745	2785
4 Dr VL Wgn	1830	2920
2 Dr Z24 Cpe	2330	3725

OPTIONS FOR CAVALIER
6 cyl 3.1 L Engine[Opt on Wgn] +90
Auto 3-Speed Transmission[Std on Wgn] +65
Air Conditioning +110
Cruise Control +30
Power Door Locks[Std on Conv] +35
Power Windows[Std on Conv] +35

CHEVY VAN/SPORTVAN   1991

7.4-liter engine can be equipped with a four-speed automatic transmission.

CHEVY VAN

Category H		
2 Dr G10 Chevy Van	3440	4660
2 Dr G10 Chevy Van Ext	3500	4740
2 Dr G20 Chevy Van	3485	4720
2 Dr G30 Chevy Van	3995	5410
2 Dr G30 Chevy Van Ext	3500	4740

SPORTVAN

Category H		
2 Dr G10 Sportvan	4070	5515
2 Dr G20 Sportvan	4355	5895
2 Dr G20 Beauville Sportvan	4580	6200
2 Dr G30 Sportvan	4810	6515
2 Dr G30 Sportvan Ext	4780	6475
2 Dr G30 Beauville Sportvan	5035	6820
2 Dr G30 Beauville Sportvan Ext	5005	6780

OPTIONS FOR CHEVY VAN/SPORTVAN
8 cyl 5.0 L Engine +80
8 cyl 5.7 L Engine[Std on G30,Chevy Van Ext] +110
12 Passenger Seating +85
Air Conditioning +110
Cruise Control +25
Power Door Locks +25
Power Windows +25

CORSICA   1991

New dashboard debuts, and a driver airbag is added. LTZ model is dropped, leaving one trim level available. Sport Handling Package includes LTZ suspension, trim, and wheels. A CD player joins the options sheet.

RATINGS (SCALE OF 1-10)

Overall	Safety	Reliability	Performance	Comfort	Value
6.4	4.7	6.7	6.8	7.3	6.3

Category C		
4 Dr LT Hbk	1740	2700
4 Dr LT Sdn	1635	2540

OPTIONS FOR CORSICA
6 cyl 3.1 L Engine +70
Auto 3-Speed Transmission +70
Air Conditioning +110
Cruise Control +30
Power Door Locks +35
Power Windows +40

CORVETTE   1991

Styling is tweaked front and rear for a more aerodynamic appearance. All Corvettes get the ZR-1's rear styling treatment. New alloy wheels are standard across the line.

Category J		
2 Dr STD Conv	11650	13685
2 Dr STD Cpe	10855	12750
2 Dr ZR1 Cpe	19395	22780

OPTIONS FOR CORVETTE
Electronic Ride Select. +225
Electronic Ride Selection +225
Handling Pkg +285
Bose Sound System +110
Leather Seats[Opt on STD] +165
Power Drivers Seat[Opt on STD] +45
Solid & Glass Targa Tops +125

Model Description	Trade-in Value	Market Value	Model Description	Trade-in Value	Market Value

CHEVROLET 91

LUMINA 1991

Euro models get standard alloy wheels. Newly optional is a Delco/Bose sound system. Coupes can be ordered in new Z34 trim, which comes standard with a 3.4-liter twin-cam V6, sport suspension and louvered hood.

RATINGS (SCALE OF 1-10)

Overall	Safety	Reliability	Performance	Comfort	Value
N/A	N/A	6.1	8.2	7.6	8.2

Category C

2 Dr Euro Cpe	2405	3725
4 Dr Euro Sdn	2435	3775
2 Dr STD Cpe	2300	3565
4 Dr STD Sdn	1855	3125
2 Dr Z34 Cpe	2715	4215

OPTIONS FOR LUMINA

6 cyl 3.1 L Engine[Opt on STD] +70
Auto 4-Speed Transmission +25
Air Conditioning[Opt on STD] +110
Cruise Control[Std on Z34] +30
Power Door Locks +35
Power Drivers Seat +40
Power Windows +40

LUMINA MINIVAN 1991

A CD player is newly optional. Non-reflective carpet is added to the top of the dashboard.

RATINGS (SCALE OF 1-10)

Overall	Safety	Reliability	Performance	Comfort	Value
6.7	4.9	6.5	7	7.5	7.7

Category G

2 Dr CL Pass. Van	3255	4520
2 Dr STD Cargo Van	2865	3980
2 Dr STD Pass. Van	3100	4300

OPTIONS FOR LUMINA MINIVAN

Air Conditioning +110
Cruise Control +30
Power Door Locks +30
Power Drivers Seat +40
Power Windows +30

R3500 PICKUP 1991

Category H

4 Dr STD Crew Cab LB	4695	6360
4 Dr Silverado Crew Cab LB	4960	6715

OPTIONS FOR R3500 PICKUP

8 cyl 6.2 L Dsl Engine +315
8 cyl 7.4 L Engine +115
Auto 4-Speed Transmission +130
Air Conditioning +110
Cruise Control +25
Dual Rear Wheels +105

Power Door Locks +25
Power Windows +25

S10 BLAZER 1991

Four-door models get new Sport Package on the options list. It includes two-tone paint, alloy wheels and chrome trim. A heavy-duty battery is standard on all models, and 2WD Blazers can be equipped with 15-inch alloy wheels. Front bench seat option will give four-door models six-passenger capacity. Softer suspension available midyear with Tahoe LT trim.

RATINGS (SCALE OF 1-10)

Overall	Safety	Reliability	Performance	Comfort	Value
5.5	3.7	5.4	6.8	7.1	4.3

Category G

2 Dr STD Utility	3335	4625
2 Dr STD 4WD Utility	3735	5185
4 Dr STD Wgn	3625	5025
4 Dr STD 4WD Wgn	4120	5715
2 Dr Sport Utility	3570	4955
2 Dr Sport 4WD Utility	3975	5515
4 Dr Sport Wgn	3885	5390
4 Dr Sport 4WD Wgn	4385	6090
2 Dr Tahoe Utility	3590	4980
2 Dr Tahoe 4WD Utility	3985	5530
4 Dr Tahoe Wgn	3880	5385
4 Dr Tahoe 4WD Wgn	4385	6085

OPTIONS FOR S10 BLAZER

Auto 4-Speed Transmission +115
LT Pkg +130
Air Conditioning +110
Cruise Control +30
Power Door Locks +30
Power Windows +30

S10 PICKUP 1991

Exterior facelift that includes a new grille, fresh trim and restyled wheels debuted early in 1990. Four-wheel-drive models get the 4.3-liter V6 as standard equipment. Durango trim is dropped. Midyear, the base four-cylinder powerplant gets more horsepower.

RATINGS (SCALE OF 1-10)

Overall	Safety	Reliability	Performance	Comfort	Value
N/A	3.4	6	7.2	7	N/A

Category G

2 Dr Baja 4WD Ext Cab SB	3785	5250
2 Dr Baja 4WD Std Cab LB	3585	4975
2 Dr Baja 4WD Std Cab SB	3585	4975
2 Dr EL Std Cab SB	2150	2985
2 Dr STD Ext Cab SB	2780	3860
2 Dr STD 4WD Ext Cab SB	3475	4825

CHEVROLET 91

Model Description	Trade-in Value	Market Value
2 Dr STD Std Cab LB	2470	3430
2 Dr STD 4WD Std Cab LB	3280	4550
2 Dr STD Std Cab SB	2470	3430
2 Dr STD 4WD Std Cab SB	3280	4550
2 Dr Tahoe Ext Cab SB	2955	4105
2 Dr Tahoe 4WD Ext Cab SB	3640	5050
2 Dr Tahoe Std Cab LB	2615	3630
2 Dr Tahoe 4WD Std Cab LB	3410	4730
2 Dr Tahoe Std Cab SB	2615	3630
2 Dr Tahoe 4WD Std Cab SB	3410	4730

OPTIONS FOR S10 PICKUP
6 cyl 2.8 L Engine +50
6 cyl 4.3 L Engine[Opt on 2WD] +85
Auto 4-Speed Transmission +115
Air Conditioning +110
Cruise Control +30
Power Door Locks +30
Power Windows +30

SUBURBAN 1991

Manual transmission is dropped.

Category H	Trade-in Value	Market Value
4 Dr R1500 Wgn	5225	7075
4 Dr R2500 Wgn	5700	7720
4 Dr V1500 4WD Wgn	5825	7890
4 Dr V2500 4WD Wgn	5935	8035

OPTIONS FOR SUBURBAN
8 cyl 6.2 L Dsl Engine +315
8 cyl 7.4 L Engine +115
Silverado Pkg +195
Air Conditioning +110
Cruise Control +25
Dual Air Conditioning +170
Power Door Locks +25
Power Windows +25

V3500 PICKUP 1991

Category H	Trade-in Value	Market Value
4 Dr STD 4WD Crew Cab LB	5405	7320
4 Dr Silverado 4WD Crew Cab LB	5325	7210

OPTIONS FOR V3500 PICKUP
8 cyl 6.2 L Dsl Engine +315
8 cyl 7.4 L Engine +115
Auto 4-Speed Transmission +115
Air Conditioning +110
Cruise Control +25
Dual Rear Wheels +105
Power Door Locks +25
Power Windows +25

Don't forget to refer to the Mileage Adjustment Table at the back of this book!

CHRYSLER USA

1995 Chrysler Sebring

2000 CHRYSLER

300M 2000

There are five new colors, interior upgrades such as rear-seat cupholders and color-keyed switches, and a four-disc in-dash CD player. The rear suspension has been improved for less noise, vibration and harshness. The 2000 has the brake-shift interlock safety feature, which won't allow the driver to shift out of "park" unless his foot is on the brake.

Category A

	Trade-in	Market
4 Dr STD Sdn	21535	24815

OPTIONS FOR 300M
Chrome Wheels +805
Power Moonroof +1040

CIRRUS 2000

With a redesigned Cirrus modeled after the exceptionally attractive Concorde due in showrooms for 2001, the 2000 model is essentially a carryover model. Child-seat tethers have been added behind the back seat, four new colors debut, and an entry level LX arrives.

Category C

	Trade-in	Market
4 Dr LX Sdn	11620	13575

OPTIONS FOR CIRRUS
4 cyl 2.4 L Engine +370
Auto 4-Speed Transmission[Opt on LX] +860

CONCORDE 2000

All models are given a more refined touring suspension, and variable-assist, speed-proportional steering is standard on LXi. Five new colors come aboard, and the instrument panel has been freshened.

Category B

	Trade-in	Market
4 Dr LX Sdn	15210	17725
4 Dr LXi Sdn	18085	21075

OPTIONS FOR CONCORDE
Aluminum/Alloy Wheels[Opt on LX] +270
Chrome Wheels +555
Compact Disc W/fm/tape[Opt on LX] +305
Leather Seats[Opt on LX] +560
Power Moonroof +795

LHS 2000

Nothing dramatically changes for 2000. There are interior upgrades, including a four-disc in-dash CD changer, and a modified rear suspension for less noise, vibration and harshness. An automatic transaxle brake-shift interlock is now standard, and there are four more color choices.

Category A

	Trade-in	Market
4 Dr STD Sdn	20215	23295

SEBRING COUPE 2000

For 2000, the standard-equipment list has increased. Also, Ice Silver is the newest color, and the LX trim fabric has been updated.

Category C

	Trade-in	Market
2 Dr LX Cpe	14485	16925
2 Dr LXi Cpe	16145	18865

OPTIONS FOR SEBRING COUPE
Aluminum/Alloy Wheels[Opt on LX] +255
Anti-Lock Brakes +485
Power Sunroof +545

SEBRING COUPE/CONVERTIBLE 2000

Sebring Convertible

Category C

	Trade-in	Market
2 Dr JX Conv	16785	19615
2 Dr JXi Limited Conv	19415	22685
2 Dr JXi Conv	18255	21330

OPTIONS FOR SEBRING COUPE/CONVERTIBLE
Compact Disc Changer +385

TOWN & COUNTRY 2000

The model lineup changes this year, and telling the difference between the LX and LXi will be easier to the untrained eye, thanks to distinctive exterior and interior modifications. New colors for 2000 are Shale Green, Bright White, Patriot Blue, Bright Silver and Inferno Red.

Category G

	Trade-in	Market
4 Dr LX Pass. Van Ext	19520	22580
4 Dr LX 4WD Pass. Van Ext	21795	25215
4 Dr LXi Pass. Van Ext	21000	24290
4 Dr LXi 4WD Pass. Van Ext	23285	26935

Don't forget to refer to the Mileage Adjustment Table at the back of this book!

Model Description	Trade-in Value	Market Value
4 Dr Limited Pass. Van Ext	25210	29160
4 Dr Limited 4WD Pass. Van Ext	26920	31140

OPTIONS FOR TOWN & COUNTRY
6 cyl 3.8 L Engine[Opt on LXi FWD] +435
Alarm System[Opt on LX,LXi] +220
Aluminum/Alloy Wheels +265
Compact Disc W/fm/tape[Opt on LX,LXi] +365
Dual Air Conditioning[Opt on LX,LXi] +755
Dual Power Seats[Opt on LXi] +340
Garage Door Opener[Opt on LX,LXi] +120
Heated Front Seats[Opt on LXi] +225
Leather Seats[Opt on LXi] +640
Luggage Rack[Opt on LX,LXi] +130
Rear Heater[Opt on LX,LXi] +155
Traction Control System[Opt on LXi] +220

VOYAGER   2000

With Plymouth's impending death, the Voyager turns into a Chrysler this year, but it is otherwise unchanged. Four new colors and a new Value-Plus option package that includes a V6 and power goodies for about $20,000 are new this year.

Category G
	Trade-in	Market
4 Dr Grand Pass. Van	15835	18315
4 Dr Grand SE Pass. Van	17440	20175
4 Dr SE Pass. Van	16745	19365
4 Dr STD Pass. Van	13655	15795

OPTIONS FOR VOYAGER
6 cyl 3.0 L Engine[Opt on STD] +655
6 cyl 3.3 L Engine +465
6 cyl 3.3 L FLEX Engine[Opt on STD] +795
Auto 4-Speed Transmission[Opt on STD] +165
7 Passenger Seating[Opt on STD] +425
Air Conditioning[Opt on STD] +670
Cruise Control[Opt on Grand,STD] +170
Keyless Entry System +160
Lighted Entry System +120
Luggage Rack +130
Power Door Locks[Opt on Grand,STD] +190
Power Windows[Opt on Grand,STD] +200
Rear Window Defroster[Opt on Grand,STD] +140
Tilt Steering Wheel[Opt on Grand,STD] +145

1999 CHRYSLER

300M   1999

This all-new car from Chrysler will try to win some international recognition for the marque.

RATINGS (SCALE OF 1-10)
Overall	Safety	Reliability	Performance	Comfort	Value
N/A	N/A	N/A	8.4	8.3	N/A

Category A
	Trade-in	Market
4 Dr STD Sdn	19670	22895

OPTIONS FOR 300M
Chrome Wheels +655
Power Moonroof +850

CIRRUS   1999

A slightly revised suspension gives the Cirrus a softer ride, and the interior improvements include a new instrument cluster and lower NVH levels. Outside, 15-inch chrome wheel covers are standard, and a winged Chrysler badge now decorates the front grille.

RATINGS (SCALE OF 1-10)
Overall	Safety	Reliability	Performance	Comfort	Value
N/A	6.8	8.2	7.6	7.8	N/A

Category C
	Trade-in	Market
4 Dr LXi Sdn	12600	14795

OPTIONS FOR CIRRUS
Aluminum/Alloy Wheels +205

CONCORDE   1999

Bigger sway bar links and tubular rear trailing arms will be phased in during the model year, two changes that Chrysler promises will provide more road isolation for a more luxurious ride. Premium carpeting is added to the interior, and the LXi leather is improved.

RATINGS (SCALE OF 1-10)
Overall	Safety	Reliability	Performance	Comfort	Value
N/A	7.3	8.1	N/A	8.5	N/A

Category B
	Trade-in	Market
4 Dr LX Sdn	13475	15795
4 Dr LXi Sdn	15925	18670

OPTIONS FOR CONCORDE
Aluminum/Alloy Wheels[Opt on LX] +220
Compact Disc W/fm/tape +250
Dual Power Seats[Opt on LX] +260

LHS   1999

What a difference two years can make. The luxury-tuned LHS has been completely redesigned for 1999. In fact, it's such a new car, we're kinda' disappointed that they kept the name.

RATINGS (SCALE OF 1-10)
Overall	Safety	Reliability	Performance	Comfort	Value
N/A	7.8	8.3	7.8	8.3	N/A

Category A
	Trade-in	Market
4 Dr STD Sdn	19010	22125

SEBRING COUPE/CONVERTIBLE   1999

RATINGS (SCALE OF 1-10)
Overall	Safety	Reliability	Performance	Comfort	Value
N/A	7.5	N/A	6.8	7.5	N/A

Don't forget to refer to the Mileage Adjustment Table at the back of this book!

Model Description	Trade-in Value	Market Value

Sebring

Category C

	Trade-in	Market
2 Dr LX Cpe	11785	13840
2 Dr LXi Cpe	14580	17125

Sebring Convertible

Category C

	Trade-in	Market
2 Dr JX Conv	15130	17775
2 Dr JXi Conv	16560	19455

OPTIONS FOR SEBRING COUPE/CONVERTIBLE

6 cyl 2.5 L Engine[Opt on LX] +450
Auto 4-Speed Transmission[Opt on LX] +465
Aluminum/Alloy Wheels[Opt on JX,LX] +205
Anti-Lock Brakes[Opt on Sebring] +395
Cruise Control[Opt on LX] +145
Power Door Locks[Opt on LX] +170
Power Drivers Seat[Opt on Sebring] +200
Power Mirrors +70
Power Sunroof +445
Power Windows[Opt on LX] +215

TOWN & COUNTRY   1999

The top-of-the-line trim level is now called "Limited," and it offers more standard equipment (hence less options) than any other Chrysler minivan. Leather upgrades, steering wheel mounted stereo controls, and a center armrest in the rear bench are new this year, and new exterior features such details as 16-inch 15-spoke chrome wheels and chrome door handles.

RATINGS (SCALE OF 1-10)

Overall	Safety	Reliability	Performance	Comfort	Value
N/A	7	8.8	6.8	7.9	N/A

Category G

	Trade-in	Market
2 Dr LX Pass. Van Ext	19325	22430
2 Dr LX 4WD Pass. Van Ext	21480	24930
2 Dr LXi Pass. Van Ext	21845	25360
2 Dr LXi 4WD Pass. Van Ext	23885	27725
2 Dr Limited Pass. Van Ext	23470	27240
2 Dr Limited 4WD Pass. Van Ext	25085	29115
2 Dr SX Pass. Van	19000	22055

OPTIONS FOR TOWN & COUNTRY

6 cyl 3.8 L Engine[Opt on SX,LX FWD] +245
Aluminum/Alloy Wheels[Opt on LX] +215
Compact Disc W/fm/tape[Opt on LX,SX] +295
Dual Air Conditioning[Opt on LX] +615
Heated Front Seats[Opt on LXi] +180
Luggage Rack[Opt on LX] +110
Sunscreen Glass[Opt on LX,SX] +250
Traction Control System[Opt on SX,LX FWD] +180

CIRRUS   1998

There's just one model to choose from this year, as Chrysler says "goodbye" to the base LX, and "hello" to a higher price. That means that leather seats, a powered driver's seat, a 2.5-liter V6 engine, a tilt wheel, and power windows, locks, and mirrors are now standard equipment. The LXi also comes in five new colors and as with all other Chrysler products, depowered airbags are standard.

RATINGS (SCALE OF 1-10)

Overall	Safety	Reliability	Performance	Comfort	Value
7.6	6.8	8	7.6	7.6	8.1

Category C

	Trade-in	Market
4 Dr LXi Sdn	11275	13315

OPTIONS FOR CIRRUS

Chrome Wheels +330
Power Moonroof +375

CONCORDE   1998

The Concorde is all-new for 1998. The only thing they didn't change is the name.

RATINGS (SCALE OF 1-10)

Overall	Safety	Reliability	Performance	Comfort	Value
8.1	7.1	8.1	7.8	8.5	9

Category B

	Trade-in	Market
4 Dr LX Sdn	12120	14250
4 Dr LXi Sdn	14640	17210

OPTIONS FOR CONCORDE

Aluminum/Alloy Wheels[Opt on LX] +180
Anti-Lock Brakes[Opt on LX] +365
Compact Disc W/fm/tape +205
Dual Power Seats[Opt on LX] +210
Power Moonroof +530
Traction Control System[Opt on LX] +95

SEBRING   1998

Evolutionary, mostly aesthetic changes enhance the Sebrings this year. The Sebring Coupe LX and LXi now offer a black and gray interior, and the exterior color of the day is "Caffe Latte" (not to be confused with Macchiato or Cappuccino).

RATINGS (SCALE OF 1-10)

Overall	Safety	Reliability	Performance	Comfort	Value
7.2	7.5	7.7	7.6	7.5	5.5

Category C

	Trade-in	Market
2 Dr JX Conv	12545	14815
2 Dr JXi Conv	15215	17965

Model Description	Trade-in Value	Market Value
2 Dr LX Cpe	10325	12195
2 Dr LXi Cpe	12755	15060

OPTIONS FOR SEBRING
6 cyl 2.5 L Engine[Std on LXi] +370
Auto 4-Speed Transmission[Opt on LX] +380
Aluminum/Alloy Wheels[Opt on JX, LX] +170
Anti-Lock Brakes[Opt on JX, LX] +325
Chrome Wheels +330
Compact Disc W/fm/tape[Std on LXi] +180
Cruise Control[Opt on JX, LX] +120
Heated Power Mirrors[Opt on JX] +55
Keyless Entry System[Opt on JX, LX] +100
Power Door Locks[Opt on JX, LX] +140
Power Drivers Seat[Std on JXi] +165
Power Mirrors +60
Power Sunroof +365
Power Windows[Opt on LX] +175
Remote Trunk Release[Opt on JX] +50
Traction Control System +115

TOWN & COUNTRY   1998

Chrysler's luxury minivans get a few improvements this year, with the addition of a new Chrysler-signature grille, more powerful 3.8-liter V6, high-performance headlights, and three fancy new colors.

RATINGS (SCALE OF 1-10)

Overall	Safety	Reliability	Performance	Comfort	Value
7.9	6.9	8.5	7.4	7.9	8.8

	Trade-in	Market
Category G		
2 Dr LX Pass. Van Ext	16320	19085
2 Dr LX 4WD Pass. Van Ext	18075	21140
2 Dr LXi Pass. Van Ext	19105	22340
2 Dr LXi 4WD Pass. Van Ext	20495	23965
2 Dr SX Pass. Van	16050	18770

OPTIONS FOR TOWN & COUNTRY
6 cyl 3.8 L Engine[Std on LXi, 4WD] +225
Auto Load Leveling[Std on LXi, 4WD] +130
Camper/Towing Package +160
Compact Disc W/fm/tape[Std on LXi] +240
Dual Air Conditioning[Opt on LX] +505
Garage Door Opener[Std on LXi] +80
Heated Front Seats +150
Leather Seats[Std on LXi] +430
Power Drivers Seat +155
Rear Heater[Opt on LX] +105
Special Factory Paint +80

1997 CHRYSLER

CIRRUS   1997

New wheels for everyone; the LXi trim level gets chrome wheels and the LX gets optional aluminum wheels. The Gold Package is also available on the LX, for any driver who wants to be mistaken for Slick Jimmy, your friendly, neighborhood pimp. On a more positive note, an in-dash CD changer is now available on LX and LXi models, as is a trip computer.

RATINGS (SCALE OF 1-10)

Overall	Safety	Reliability	Performance	Comfort	Value
7.2	6.6	7	7.6	7.6	7.4

	Trade-in	Market
Category C		
4 Dr LX Sdn	9330	11085
4 Dr LXi Sdn	10430	12390

OPTIONS FOR CIRRUS
6 cyl 2.5 L Engine +405
AM/FM Compact Disc Player +155
Aluminum/Alloy Wheels +140
Child Seat (1) +55
Gold Package +165
Keyless Entry System[Opt on LX] +85
Power Drivers Seat[Opt on LX] +135
Trip Computer +85

CONCORDE   1997

The 3.5-liter engine is now standard on the LX trim level. An upgraded stereo debuts along with hood-mounted windshield-washer nozzles. The automatic transmission receives refinements.

RATINGS (SCALE OF 1-10)

Overall	Safety	Reliability	Performance	Comfort	Value
8.1	7.1	7.5	8.2	8.5	9.3

	Trade-in	Market
Category B		
4 Dr LX Sdn	9750	11675
4 Dr LXi Sdn	11610	13900

OPTIONS FOR CONCORDE
Aluminum/Alloy Wheels[Std on LXi] +150
Anti-Lock Brakes[Std on LXi] +300
Compact Disc W/fm/tape +165
Dual Power Seats +175
Leather Seats[Opt on LX] +305
Power Moonroof +435
Premium Sound System[Opt on LX] +165
Traction Control System[Opt on LX] +80

LHS   1997

What's new for 1997? Deep Amethyst Pearl Paint. Oh yeah, the automatic transmission receives some fine-tuning.

RATINGS (SCALE OF 1-10)

Overall	Safety	Reliability	Performance	Comfort	Value
8	7.5	7.7	8.4	8.1	8.2

	Trade-in	Market
Category A		
4 Dr STD Sdn	13650	16170

OPTIONS FOR LHS
Compact Disc W/fm/tape +285
Power Moonroof +570

SEBRING   1997

After just one year in production, the Sebring Convertible receives a rash of changes. The most significant are a quieter intake manifold for the 2.4-liter engine and the availability of Chrysler's AutoStick transmission. Other changes include the addition of new colors, auto-dimming mirror, trip computer, enhanced vehicle theft system, and damage resistant power antenna to the options list.

RATINGS (SCALE OF 1-10)

Overall	Safety	Reliability	Performance	Comfort	Value
6.9	7.4	6.7	7.6	7.5	5.4

Category C

2 Dr JX Conv	10940	12995
2 Dr JXi Conv	13290	15785
2 Dr LX Cpe	9030	10725
2 Dr LXi Cpe	11450	13600

OPTIONS FOR SEBRING

6 cyl 2.5 L Engine[Std on LXi] +405
Auto 4-Speed Transmission[Opt on LX] +310
Aluminum/Alloy Wheels[Opt on JX,LX] +140
Anti-Lock Brakes[Opt on JX,LX] +265
Compact Disc W/fm/tape[Std on LXi] +145
Cruise Control[Opt on JX,LX] +95
Keyless Entry System[Opt on JX,LX] +85
Leather Seats[Opt on LXi] +275
Power Door Locks[Opt on JX,LX] +115
Power Drivers Seat[Std on JXi] +135
Power Sunroof +295
Power Windows[Opt on LX] +140

TOWN & COUNTRY   1997

Chrysler's luxury minivans get a few improvements this year, as AWD extended length models are added to the lineup. Also new this year is a sporty SX model, which replaces last year's LX as the regular length Town & Country. Families with kids will love the standard left side sliding door on this vehicle.

RATINGS (SCALE OF 1-10)

Overall	Safety	Reliability	Performance	Comfort	Value
7.4	6.8	7.6	7.4	7.9	7.1

Category G

2 Dr LX Pass. Van Ext	14610	17150
2 Dr LX 4WD Pass. Van Ext	16200	19015
2 Dr LXi Pass. Van Ext	17095	20065
2 Dr LXi 4WD Pass. Van Ext	18355	21545
2 Dr SX Pass. Van	14455	16965

OPTIONS FOR TOWN & COUNTRY

6 cyl 3.8 L Engine[Std on LXi,LX 4WD] +185
Auto Load Leveling[Std on LXi,LX 4WD] +105
Child Seats (2) +115

Compact Disc W/fm/tape[Std on LXi] +200
Dual Air Conditioning[Std on LXi] +410
Leather Seats[Std on LXi] +350
Luggage Rack[Std on LXi] +70
Power Drivers Seat +125

1996 CHRYSLER

CIRRUS   1996

Base LX model gets a four-cylinder engine in a cost-cutting move. Uplevel LXi gets revised torque converter for better V6 response. A power sunroof, chrome-plated aluminum wheels, and new colors are available for 1996.

RATINGS (SCALE OF 1-10)

Overall	Safety	Reliability	Performance	Comfort	Value
6.6	6.3	5.4	7.6	7.6	6.1

Category C

4 Dr LX Sdn	7910	9550
4 Dr LXi Sdn	8580	10360

OPTIONS FOR CIRRUS

6 cyl 2.5 L Engine[Opt on LX] +365
AM/FM Compact Disc Player +130
Aluminum/Alloy Wheels +115
Child Seat (1) +45
Chrome Wheels +220
Power Drivers Seat[Opt on LX] +110
Power Sunroof +245

CONCORDE   1996

Improved headlight illumination, a revised exterior appearance, a quieter interior and new colors bow on all Concorde models. Base cars get standard 16-inch wheels. LXi models get gold accented wheels and trim.

RATINGS (SCALE OF 1-10)

Overall	Safety	Reliability	Performance	Comfort	Value
8	7.1	7.1	8.2	8.5	9.1

Category B

4 Dr LX Sdn	7910	9615
4 Dr LXi Sdn	9320	11325

OPTIONS FOR CONCORDE

6 cyl 3.5 L Engine +235
Child Seat (1) +35
Climate Control for AC[Opt on LX] +60
Compact Disc W/fm/tape +135
Dual Power Seats +140
Keyless Entry System +65
Power Moonroof +355
Premium Sound System[Opt on LX] +135
Traction Control System[Opt on LX] +65
Trip Computer[Opt on LX] +145

Don't forget to refer to the Mileage Adjustment Table at the back of this book!

CHRYSLER 96-95

Model Description	Trade-in Value	Market Value	Model Description	Trade-in Value	Market Value

LHS   1996

A quieter interior and new colors entice buyers for 1996. Revised sound systems and a HomeLink Universal transmitter that opens your garage door for you when you pull in the driveway debut.

RATINGS (SCALE OF 1-10)

Overall	Safety	Reliability	Performance	Comfort	Value
7.8	7.5	7.6	8.4	8.1	7.6

Category A
4 Dr STD Sdn	11400	13695

OPTIONS FOR LHS

AM/FM Compact Disc Player +170
Infinity Sound System +110
Power Moonroof +465

NEW YORKER   1996

Gets same changes as LHS, plus added standard equipment over last year's New Yorker. After a short 1996 production run, the New Yorker is axed from the lineup in favor of the more popular LHS.

RATINGS (SCALE OF 1-10)

Overall	Safety	Reliability	Performance	Comfort	Value
7.9	7.6	7.9	8.4	8.1	7.6

Category B
4 Dr STD Sdn	10245	12445

OPTIONS FOR NEW YORKER

Compact Disc Changer +165
Leather Seats +250
Power Moonroof +355
Power Passenger Seat +130
Traction Control System +65

SEBRING   1996

Remote keyless entry system gets a panic feature, and a HomeLink Universal Transmitter debuts on this suave sport coupe. Three new paint colors are also available. Chrysler dumps its final K-Car variant this year in favor of the fine looking Sebring Convertible. Based on the Cirrus platform and drivetrains, this drop top shares only the name of the Sebring coupe.

RATINGS (SCALE OF 1-10)

Overall	Safety	Reliability	Performance	Comfort	Value
6.4	6.7	6.4	7.6	7.5	3.8

Category C
2 Dr JX Conv	8945	10795
2 Dr JXi Conv	11160	13470
2 Dr LX Cpe	7595	9165
2 Dr LXi Cpe	9255	11170

OPTIONS FOR SEBRING

6 cyl 2.5 L Engine[Opt on JX,LX] +365
Auto 4-Speed Transmission[Opt on LX] +235
Anti-Lock Brakes[Opt on JX] +215
Compact Disc Changer +170
Compact Disc W/fm/tape +120
Cruise Control[Opt on JX,LX] +80
Keyless Entry System[Opt on JX,LX] +70
Leather Seats[Opt on LXi] +225
Power Door Locks[Opt on JX,LX] +95
Power Drivers Seat[Std on JXi] +110
Power Sunroof +245
Power Windows[Opt on LX] +115
Premium Sound System[Opt on LX] +140

TOWN & COUNTRY   1996

Totally redesigned for 1996, the T&C raises the bar for luxury minivans. In a departure from last year, the T&C is offered in a short wheelbase version, and is available in two trim levels: LX and LXi. New innovations include a driver's side passenger door, dual-zone temperature controls, and a one-hand latch system on the integrated child safety seats.

RATINGS (SCALE OF 1-10)

Overall	Safety	Reliability	Performance	Comfort	Value
7	6.5	6.1	7.4	7.9	6.9

Category G
2 Dr LX Pass. Van	12015	14230
2 Dr LXi Pass. Van Ext	14730	17445
2 Dr STD Pass. Van Ext	12020	14240

OPTIONS FOR TOWN & COUNTRY

6 cyl 3.8 L Engine[Std on LXi] +160
Captain Chairs (4)[Std on LXi] +225
Child Seats (2) +90
Compact Disc W/fm/tape[Std on LXi] +160
Dual Air Conditioning[Opt on STD] +335
Infinity Sound System +160
Keyless Entry System[Std on LXi] +70
Leather Seats[Std on LXi] +285
Luggage Rack[Std on LXi] +60
Power Drivers Seat +105
Sliding Driver Side Door[Std on LXi] +190
Sunscreen Glass[Std on LXi] +140

1995 CHRYSLER

CIRRUS   1995

The Cirrus is replacing the LeBaron sedan. A cab-forward design, a 164-horsepower V6 coupled with an automatic transmission, dual airbags, antilock brakes, air conditioning, power door locks, and power windows are just a few of the improvements this car has over the LeBaron.

Model Description	Trade-in Value	Market Value

RATINGS (SCALE OF 1-10)

Overall	Safety	Reliability	Performance	Comfort	Value
7	6.9	5.2	7.6	7.6	7.5

Category C

4 Dr LX Sdn	6525	8080
4 Dr LXi Sdn	7225	8950

OPTIONS FOR CIRRUS

4 cyl 2.4 L Engine +130
AM/FM Compact Disc Player +105
Child Seat (1) +35
Power Drivers Seat[Opt on LX] +90
Premium Sound System[Opt on LX] +115

CONCORDE   1995

No significant changes for the 1995 Concorde.

RATINGS (SCALE OF 1-10)

Overall	Safety	Reliability	Performance	Comfort	Value
7.9	7.8	6.7	8.2	8.5	8.5

Category B

4 Dr STD Sdn	7005	8595

OPTIONS FOR CONCORDE

6 cyl 3.5 L Engine +215
Aluminum/Alloy Wheels +100
Child Seat (1) +30
Infinity Sound System +190
Keyless Entry System +50
Leather Seats +205
Power Drivers Seat +95
Power Moonroof +290
Power Passenger Seat +110
Traction Control System +50

LE BARON   1995

The last of the K-cars, the LeBaron convertible rides into the sunset in GTC trim.

RATINGS (SCALE OF 1-10)

Overall	Safety	Reliability	Performance	Comfort	Value
7.8	8.5	7.8	7.8	6.6	8.4

Category C

2 Dr GTC Conv	6060	7505

OPTIONS FOR LE BARON

AM/FM Compact Disc Player +105
Anti-Lock Brakes +175
Cruise Control +65
Keyless Entry System +55
Leather Seats +185
Power Door Locks +75
Power Drivers Seat +90
Premium Sound System +115
Trip Computer +55

LHS   1995

No changes to the highly acclaimed LHS.

RATINGS (SCALE OF 1-10)

Overall	Safety	Reliability	Performance	Comfort	Value
8	8.4	7.7	8.4	8.1	7.4

Category A

4 Dr STD Sdn	9155	11245

OPTIONS FOR LHS

AM/FM Compact Disc Player +140
Power Moonroof +380

NEW YORKER   1995

No changes to the highly acclaimed New Yorker.

RATINGS (SCALE OF 1-10)

Overall	Safety	Reliability	Performance	Comfort	Value
7.9	8.4	7.4	8.4	8.1	7.4

Category B

4 Dr STD Sdn	8110	9955

OPTIONS FOR NEW YORKER

Climate Control for AC +50
Infinity Sound System +190
Keyless Entry System +50
Leather Seats +205
Power Moonroof +290
Power Passenger Seat +110
Traction Control System +50

SEBRING   1995

Chrysler's sporty replacement for the LeBaron coupe is the Sebring. Based on the Dodge Avenger, the Sebring offers more luxury than its corporate cousin. The Sebring is available as a four-cylinder LX or an upscale 2.5-liter V6 LXi; both come standard with an automatic transmission.

RATINGS (SCALE OF 1-10)

Overall	Safety	Reliability	Performance	Comfort	Value
7.2	7.8	6.9	7.6	7.5	6.3

Category C

2 Dr LX Cpe	6170	7640
2 Dr LXi Cpe	7560	9360

OPTIONS FOR SEBRING

6 cyl 2.5 L Engine[Opt on LX] +290
Auto 4-Speed Transmission[Opt on LX] +205
AM/FM Compact Disc Player +105
Cruise Control[Opt on LX] +65
Keyless Entry System[Opt on LX] +55
Leather Seats +185
Power Door Locks[Opt on LX] +75
Power Drivers Seat +90
Power Sunroof +200
Power Windows[Opt on LX] +95
Premium Sound System +115

Don't forget to refer to the Mileage Adjustment Table at the back of this book!

CHRYSLER 95-94

Model Description	Trade-in Value	Market Value	Model Description	Trade-in Value	Market Value

TOWN & COUNTRY 1995

There are no changes for the 1995 Town & Country.

RATINGS (SCALE OF 1-10)

Overall	Safety	Reliability	Performance	Comfort	Value
7.9	8.4	7.5	7.8	8	7.9

Category G

	Trade-in	Market
2 Dr STD Pass. Van	9385	11435
2 Dr STD 4WD Pass. Van	10080	12280

OPTIONS FOR TOWN & COUNTRY
AM/FM Compact Disc Player +95
Child Seats (2) +75

1994 CHRYSLER

CONCORDE 1994

The base 3.3-liter engine is upped to 161 horsepower. A flexible-fuel version of the Concorde is available that will allow the car to run on alternative fuels such as methanol. Variable-assist power steering and a touring suspension are also added to the standard equipment list.

RATINGS (SCALE OF 1-10)

Overall	Safety	Reliability	Performance	Comfort	Value
7.8	7.7	6.4	8.2	8.5	8.4

Category B

	Trade-in	Market
4 Dr STD Sdn	5630	7135

OPTIONS FOR CONCORDE
6 cyl 3.5 L Engine +175
AM/FM Compact Disc Player +80
Aluminum/Alloy Wheels +80
Infinity Sound System +155
Keyless Entry System +45
Leather Seats +165
Power Door Locks +65
Power Drivers Seat +75
Power Moonroof +235
Power Windows +70
Traction Control System +45

LE BARON 1994

The two-door coupe is cancelled, leaving the convertible and sedan in place. The 100-horsepower four-cylinder engine is dropped, leaving the 141-horsepower V6 as the sole powerplant.

RATINGS (SCALE OF 1-10)

Overall	Safety	Reliability	Performance	Comfort	Value
7.7	8.5	7.8	7.8	6.6	7.7

Category C

	Trade-in	Market
2 Dr GTC Conv	4495	6045
4 Dr LE Sdn	4005	5385
4 Dr Landau Sdn	4730	6355

OPTIONS FOR LE BARON
6 cyl 3.0 L Engine[Opt on LE] +165
Auto 4-Speed Transmission[Opt on LE] +40
AM/FM Compact Disc Player +85
Air Conditioning[Opt on LE] +200
Aluminum/Alloy Wheels +75
Anti-Lock Brakes +145
Cruise Control[Opt on GTC] +55
Infinity Sound System +150
Leather Seats +150
Power Door Locks[Opt on GTC,LE] +60
Power Drivers Seat +75
Premium Sound System +95
Trip Computer +45

LHS 1994

The de-chromed LHS model is the sporty edition of the New Yorker.

RATINGS (SCALE OF 1-10)

Overall	Safety	Reliability	Performance	Comfort	Value
7.7	8.2	6.5	8.4	8.1	7.4

Category A

	Trade-in	Market
4 Dr STD Sdn	7720	9665

OPTIONS FOR LHS
AM/FM Compact Disc Player +115

NEW YORKER 1994

An all-new New Yorker replaces the stodgy car of yesteryear. Improved handling, styling and luxury mark a significant change in direction for the once-ailing Chrysler corporation.

RATINGS (SCALE OF 1-10)

Overall	Safety	Reliability	Performance	Comfort	Value
8	8.4	7.7	8.4	8.1	7.4

Category B

	Trade-in	Market
4 Dr STD Sdn	6610	8380

OPTIONS FOR NEW YORKER
AM/FM Compact Disc Player +80
Aluminum/Alloy Wheels +80
Climate Control for AC +40
Keyless Entry System +45
Leather Seats +165
Power Moonroof +235
Power Passenger Seat +90
Premium Sound System +90
Traction Control System +45

Model Description	Trade-in Value	Market Value

TOWN & COUNTRY 1994

A passenger airbag joins the standard equipment list of the Chrysler Town & Country, once again pushing the envelope of the growing minivan segment. A larger engine is also available in the 1994 Town & Country.

RATINGS (SCALE OF 1-10)

Overall	Safety	Reliability	Performance	Comfort	Value
7.4	8.3	5.9	7.8	8	6.8

Category G
	Trade-in	Market
2 Dr STD Pass. Van	8260	10300
2 Dr STD 4WD Pass. Van	8880	11070

OPTIONS FOR TOWN & COUNTRY
AM/FM Compact Disc Player +75
Child Seats (2) +60

1993 CHRYSLER

CONCORDE 1993

Chrysler's new near-luxury sedan is designed to compete with cars like the Acura Vigor and the Lexus ES 300. Standard antilock brakes, dual airbags, an optional integrated child-seat, and optional traction control are some of the Concorde's available safety features. Cab-forward design and a long wheelbase insure good passenger space and a comfortable ride for all occupants. A 3.5-liter V6 engine that produces 214 horsepower is available instead of the standard 3.3-liter V6 that produces 153 horsepower.

RATINGS (SCALE OF 1-10)

Overall	Safety	Reliability	Performance	Comfort	Value
7.6	7.6	5.8	8.2	8.5	7.8

Category B
	Trade-in	Market
4 Dr STD Sdn	4290	5805

OPTIONS FOR CONCORDE
6 cyl 3.5 L Engine +125
AM/FM Compact Disc Player +65
Aluminum/Alloy Wheels +65
Cruise Control +45
Keyless Entry System +35
Leather Seats +135
Power Door Locks +50
Power Drivers Seat +65
Power Passenger Seat +70
Power Windows +55
Premium Sound System +75
Traction Control System +35

FIFTH AVENUE 1993

A new stereo is available on the Fifth Avenue; buyers can now choose between a CD player or a cassette player for their listening pleasure. A tamper-resistant odometer is also added.

Category C
	Trade-in	Market
4 Dr STD Sdn	4475	6060

OPTIONS FOR FIFTH AVENUE
6 cyl 3.8 L Engine +75
AM/FM Compact Disc Player +70
AM/FM Stereo Tape +35
Aluminum/Alloy Wheels +60
Anti-Lock Brakes +120
Infinity Sound System +125
Keyless Entry System +35
Leather Seats +125
Power Passenger Seat +55
Premium Sound System +75

IMPERIAL 1993

A new stereo is available on the Imperial. Buyers can choose between a CD player or a cassette player. A tamper-resistant odometer is also added; this means that the miles displayed should be true.

Category A
	Trade-in	Market
4 Dr STD Sdn	4265	5930

OPTIONS FOR IMPERIAL
AM/FM Compact Disc Player +95
Aluminum/Alloy Wheels +90
Dual Power Seats +95
Keyless Entry System +55
Leather Seats +140

LE BARON 1993

The turbocharged engine is dropped and a new grille is added.

RATINGS (SCALE OF 1-10)

Overall	Safety	Reliability	Performance	Comfort	Value
6.9	5.9	7.6	7.8	6.6	6.8

Category C
	Trade-in	Market
2 Dr GTC Conv	4610	6240
2 Dr GTC Cpe	3935	5325
4 Dr LE Sdn	3390	4590
2 Dr LX Conv	4650	6295
2 Dr LX Cpe	3895	5275
4 Dr Landau Sdn	3980	5390
2 Dr STD Conv	3925	5315
2 Dr STD Cpe	3290	4455

OPTIONS FOR LE BARON
6 cyl 3.0 L Engine[Opt on LE,STD] +140
Auto 4-Speed Transmission[Std on Landau,LX] +80
AM/FM Compact Disc Player +70
Air Conditioning[Opt on LE,STD] +160
Aluminum/Alloy Wheels[Std on GTC Conv] +60
Anti-Lock Brakes +120
Cruise Control[Opt on STD] +45
Leather Seats[Std on LX Conv] +125

CHRYSLER 93-92

Model Description	Trade-in Value	Market Value

Power Door Locks[Std on GTC,LX] +50
Power Drivers Seat[Std on LX Conv] +60
Power Windows[Opt on Landau,LE] +65
Premium Sound System +75
Sport Suspension[Opt on LX] +45
Trip Computer +35

NEW YORKER   1993

This is the last model year for the New Yorker in its current form. Interior changes include a six-way power seat and an upgraded stereo.
Category B

4 Dr Salon Sdn	3890	5260

OPTIONS FOR NEW YORKER
AM/FM Stereo Tape +35
Aluminum/Alloy Wheels +65
Anti-Lock Brakes +135
Cruise Control +45
Infinity Sound System +125
Keyless Entry System +35
Leather Seats +135
Power Door Locks +50
Power Passenger Seat +70

TOWN & COUNTRY   1993

A stainless-steel exhaust system, new wheels and adjustable front shoulder belts are the main changes for the 1993 Town & Country.

RATINGS (SCALE OF 1-10)

Overall	Safety	Reliability	Performance	Comfort	Value
6.7	6.2	4.8	7.8	8	6.7

Category G

2 Dr STD Pass. Van	6910	8640
2 Dr STD 4WD Pass. Van	7385	9230

OPTIONS FOR TOWN & COUNTRY
AM/FM Compact Disc Player +65
Air Conditioning +165
Leather Seats +155

1992 CHRYSLER

FIFTH AVENUE   1992

The Fifth Avenue gets revised front-end styling that includes a new hood, grille and headlights.
Category C

4 Dr STD Sdn	3745	5255

OPTIONS FOR FIFTH AVENUE
Electronic Features Pkg +165
Anti-Lock Brakes +95
Infinity Sound System +100
Leather Seats +100

IMPERIAL   1992

No changes for 1992.
Category A

4 Dr STD Sdn	3875	5180

OPTIONS FOR IMPERIAL
Electronic Features Pkg +295
Infinity Sound System +50
Leather Seats +115

LE BARON   1992

Antilock brakes become an available option on the 1992 LeBaron. A transmission interlock also joins the list of safety equipment. Designed to keep the car from being started while in gear, the interlock requires that the clutch be fully depressed before the car will start. This year there are three trim levels available for the LeBaron, including a Landau and base model that have a 100-horsepower four-cylinder engine.

RATINGS (SCALE OF 1-10)

Overall	Safety	Reliability	Performance	Comfort	Value
6.7	5.8	6.7	7.8	6.6	6.7

Category C

2 Dr GTC Conv	3550	4975
2 Dr GTC Turbo Conv	3550	4975
2 Dr GTC Cpe	3035	4255
2 Dr GTC Turbo Cpe	3035	4255
2 Dr LX Conv	3490	4900
2 Dr LX Cpe	3020	4240
4 Dr LX Sdn	2870	4025
4 Dr Landau Sdn	2945	4135
2 Dr STD Conv	3140	4400
2 Dr STD Turbo Conv	3165	4435
2 Dr STD Cpe	2550	3575
2 Dr STD Turbo Cpe	2675	3750
4 Dr STD Sdn	2635	3695

OPTIONS FOR LE BARON
6 cyl 3.0 L Engine[Std on GTC,LX] +115
Auto 4-Speed Transmission[Std on LX] +70
Air Conditioning[Opt on STD,LX Sdn] +135
Anti-Lock Brakes +95
Cruise Control[Std on GTC,Landau,LX,Sdn] +35
Leather Seats[Std on LX Conv] +100
Power Door Locks[Opt on Landau,STD,Sdn] +40
Power Drivers Seat[Std on LX Conv] +50
Power Windows[Opt on Landau,Sdn] +50

NEW YORKER   1992

Revised styling results in rounded front and rear corners on Chrysler's midsized luxury cars. The landau top is reintroduced and an electromagnetic mirror is added to the options list.

Model Description	Trade-in Value	Market Value
Category B		
4 Dr Salon Sdn	3395	4655

OPTIONS FOR NEW YORKER
Anti-Lock Brakes +110
Cruise Control +35
Infinity Sound System +105
Leather Seats +110
Power Door Locks +45

TOWN & COUNTRY 1992

The Town & Country can finally be ordered without the awful wood paneling that has "graced" previous year's models.

RATINGS (SCALE OF 1-10)

Overall	Safety	Reliability	Performance	Comfort	Value
6.6	5.5	4	7.8	8	7.6

	Trade-in	Market
Category G		
2 Dr STD Pass. Van	5515	7240
2 Dr STD 4WD Pass. Van	5930	7780

OPTIONS FOR TOWN & COUNTRY
Dual Air Conditioning +150
Leather Seats +130

1991 CHRYSLER

IMPERIAL 1991

No changes for 1991.

	Trade-in	Market
Category A		
4 Dr STD Sdn	3170	4405

OPTIONS FOR IMPERIAL
Electronic Features Pkg +185
Infinity Sound System +40
Leather Seats +90

LE BARON 1991

No major changes for the 1991 Chrysler LeBaron.

RATINGS (SCALE OF 1-10)

Overall	Safety	Reliability	Performance	Comfort	Value
6.5	5.8	5.7	7.8	6.6	6.6

	Trade-in	Market
Category C		
2 Dr GTC Conv	2360	3940
2 Dr GTC Turbo Conv	2575	4305
2 Dr GTC Cpe	2080	3475
2 Dr GTC Turbo Cpe	2150	3590
2 Dr Highline Conv	2070	3460
2 Dr Highline Turbo Conv	2165	3615
2 Dr Highline Cpe	1735	2900

Model Description	Trade-in Value	Market Value
2 Dr Highline Turbo Cpe	1885	3145
2 Dr Premium LX Conv	2500	4180
2 Dr Premium LX Cpe	2070	3455
4 Dr STD Sdn	2205	3680

OPTIONS FOR LE BARON
6 cyl 3.0 L Engine[Opt on Highline,STD] +90
Auto 4-Speed Transmission[Opt on GTC,Highline] +55
Air Conditioning[Opt on Highline] +110
Anti-Lock Brakes +80
Cruise Control[Opt on Highline] +30
Infinity Sound System +85
Leather Seats[Opt on GTC,STD] +85
Power Door Locks[Opt on Highline,STD] +35
Power Drivers Seat +40
Power Windows[Opt on STD] +40

NEW YORKER 1991

No changes for the 1991 New Yorker.

	Trade-in	Market
Category B		
4 Dr Fifth Avenue Sdn	3060	4450
4 Dr Salon Sdn	2720	3960

OPTIONS FOR NEW YORKER
Electronic Features Pkg +165
Luxury Pkg +170
Anti-Lock Brakes +90
Cruise Control[Opt on Salon] +30
Infinity Sound System +85
Leather Seats +90
Power Door Locks[Opt on Salon] +35
Power Drivers Seat[Opt on Salon] +40

TC 1991

	Trade-in	Market
Category J		
2 Dr STD Conv	5420	7095

OPTIONS FOR TC
Hardtop Roof +420

TOWN & COUNTRY 1991

Antilock brakes and a driver airbag are added to the all-new Town & Country option lists.

RATINGS (SCALE OF 1-10)

Overall	Safety	Reliability	Performance	Comfort	Value
6.6	5	3.8	7.8	8	8.6

	Trade-in	Market
Category G		
2 Dr STD Pass. Van	4250	5755

OPTIONS FOR TOWN & COUNTRY
Captain Chairs (4) +80
Dual Air Conditioning +125

DAEWOO 00-99

Model Description	Trade-in Value	Market Value	Model Description	Trade-in Value	Market Value

DAEWOO   S. Korea

1999 Daewoo Leganza

2000 DAEWOO

LANOS   2000

The three-door SX disappears, as does the SE Sedan. Daewoo picks up the tab for all scheduled maintenance during the warranty period and has added ownership peace of mind with 24-hour roadside assistance for three years or 36,000 miles.

Category E

2 Dr S Hbk	6780	8020
4 Dr S Sdn	7365	8715
2 Dr SE Hbk	7930	9385
4 Dr SX Sdn	9075	10740

OPTIONS FOR LANOS
Auto 4-Speed Transmission +655
Air Conditioning[Std on SX] +680

LEGANZA   2000

Content is pulled from the base SE model, but all Leganzas have new grilles and larger stereo knobs. New seat fabric on SE models, revised alloy wheels and a more convenient remote keyless-entry design debut, and buyers now get 24-hour roadside assistance and free scheduled maintenance for the duration of the basic warranty period. New colors round out the changes.

Category E

4 Dr CDX Sdn	13145	15555
4 Dr SE Sdn	9685	11460
4 Dr SX Sdn	11760	13915

OPTIONS FOR LEGANZA
Auto 4-Speed Transmission[Opt on SE] +655
Aluminum/Alloy Wheels[Std on CDX] +275
Power Moonroof[Opt on SX] +475

NUBIRA   2000

Nubira, already the most appealing choice from the Daewoo buffet, is restyled inside and out and becomes even more attractive to cash-strapped buyers. Firmer springs and a new rear stabilizer bar tighten handling, and the new SE trim level replaces last year's SX model. The five-door hatchback is dropped, but four new colors debut. Scheduled maintenance for the duration of the basic warranty, and three-year/36,000-mile 24-hour roadside assistance is standard.

Category E

4 Dr CDX Sdn	10040	11880
4 Dr CDX Wgn	10475	12390
4 Dr SE Sdn	8180	9680

OPTIONS FOR NUBIRA
Auto 4-Speed Transmission +655
Air Conditioning[Opt on SE] +680
Alarm System[Opt on SE] +340
Fog Lights[Opt on SE] +125
Heated Power Mirrors[Opt on SE] +110
Keyless Entry System[Opt on SE] +135
Power Door Locks[Opt on SE] +205
Power Windows[Opt on SE] +215
Tilt Steering Wheel[Opt on SE] +125

1999 DAEWOO

LANOS   1999

This entry into the subcompact class is Daewoo's attack on the Honda Civic.

Category E

2 Dr S Hbk	6035	7250
4 Dr S Sdn	6505	7815
2 Dr SE Hbk	7110	8540
4 Dr SE Sdn	7315	8785
2 Dr SX Hbk	7830	9405
4 Dr SX Sdn	8030	9645

OPTIONS FOR LANOS
Auto 4-Speed Transmission +535
Air Conditioning[Std on SX] +555

LEGANZA   1999

The whole car is new to the United States, as is the motor company that makes it.

Category E

4 Dr CDX Sdn	11955	14360
4 Dr SE Sdn	9350	11230
4 Dr SX Sdn	10690	12840

OPTIONS FOR LEGANZA
Auto 4-Speed Transmission[Opt on SE] +535
Power Drivers Seat +200
Power Moonroof[Opt on SX] +390

Don't forget to refer to the Mileage Adjustment Table at the back of this book!

Model Description	Trade-in Value	Market Value	Model Description	Trade-in Value	Market Value
NUBIRA		**1999**	*Category E*		
			4 Dr CDX Hbk	9025	10845
			4 Dr CDX Sdn	9025	10845
			4 Dr CDX Wgn	9250	11115
			4 Dr SX Hbk	8185	9835
			4 Dr SX Sdn	8185	9835
			4 Dr SX Wgn	8410	10105

In an attempt to lure consumer's away from the likes of Honda and Toyota, the new Korean upstart fields their loaded-with-features Nubira. A/C, power windows, keyless entry, four-wheel disc brakes, 129 horsepower and a funny name all come as standard equipment.

OPTIONS FOR NUBIRA
Auto 4-Speed Transmission +535

Don't forget to refer to the Mileage Adjustment Table at the back of this book!

DODGE 00

Model Description	Trade-in Value	Market Value	Model Description	Trade-in Value	Market Value

DODGE   USA

1994 Dodge Ram 1500 2WD

2000 DODGE

AVENGER   2000

Base Avengers get new standard equipment, including the 2.5-liter V6 and automatic transmission from the uplevel ES, new cloth fabric on the seats and standard 16-inch wheels with luxury wheelcovers. A sport package is newly optional. A power leather-trimmed driver's seat is included with ES trim for 2000. Two key fobs come with the remote keyless-entry system this year, and two new colors are available. The Avenger will be completely redesigned for 2001.

Category F

2 Dr ES Cpe	15530	18285
2 Dr STD Cpe	13935	16405

OPTIONS FOR AVENGER
Anti-Lock Brakes +530
Compact Disc W/fm/tape[Std on ES] +410
Power Moonroof +535

CARAVAN / GRAND CARAVAN   2000
CARAVAN

Category G

2 Dr Grand Pass. Van	15600	18230
2 Dr Grand ES Pass. Van	20865	24385
2 Dr Grand ES 4WD Pass. Van	22670	26490
2 Dr Grand LE Pass. Van	19340	22600
2 Dr Grand LE 4WD Pass. Van	21535	25165
2 Dr Grand SE Pass. Van	17180	20080
2 Dr Grand Sport 4WD Pass. Van	19950	23315

OPTIONS FOR CARAVAN/GRAND CARAVAN
6 cyl 3.3 L Engine[Opt on STD] +465
6 cyl 3.8 L Engine[Std on Grand ES,Grand Sport,4] +435

Aluminum/Alloy Wheels[Std on Grand ES] +265
Captain Chairs (4) +505
Cruise Control[Opt on Grand,STD] +170
Heated Power Mirrors[Opt on Grand,STD] +65
Leather Seats +640
Luggage Rack +130
Power Door Locks[Opt on Grand,STD] +190
Power Windows[Opt on Grand,STD] +200
Rear Window Defroster[Opt on Grand,STD] +140
Sunscreen Glass[Opt on Grand,Grand SE,SE,STD] +310
Tilt Steering Wheel[Opt on Grand,STD] +145

DAKOTA   2000

The biggest change this year is design oriented - the Dakota is now available with four full-size doors, and with that, a family name: Quad Cab. A 4.7-liter V8 has been added, but the 8-foot bed is gone. You can select from five more colors as well.

Category G

2 Dr R/T Sport Ext Cab SB	15875	18550
2 Dr R/T Sport Std Cab SB	13505	15780
2 Dr SLT Ext Cab SB	12710	14855
2 Dr SLT 4WD Ext Cab SB	15105	17650
4 Dr SLT Ext Cab SB	14640	17110
4 Dr SLT 4WD Ext Cab SB	16625	19430
2 Dr SLT Std Cab SB	11595	13555
2 Dr SLT 4WD Std Cab SB	14180	16570
2 Dr STD Ext Cab SB	12295	14365
2 Dr STD 4WD Ext Cab SB	14555	17010
2 Dr STD 4WD Std Cab SB	12400	14490
2 Dr Sport Ext Cab SB	12985	15175
2 Dr Sport 4WD Ext Cab SB	15365	17960
2 Dr Sport Std Cab SB	10640	12435
2 Dr Sport 4WD Std Cab SB	13220	15450

OPTIONS FOR DAKOTA
6 cyl 3.9 L Engine[Opt on SLT Std Cab SB,Sport Std Cab SB,Base 2WD Regular Cab SB] +460
8 cyl 4.7 L Engine +595
8 cyl 5.9 L Engine[Std on R/T Sport] +1130
Auto 4-Speed Transmission[Std on R/T Sport Ext Cab SB,R/T Sport Std Cab SB] +795
Air Conditioning +670
Compact Disc W/fm/tape +365
Cruise Control +170
Fog Lights[Std on R/T Sport Ext Cab SB,R/T Sport Std Cab SB] +120
Keyless Entry System +160
Overhead Console +130
Power Door Locks +190
Power Mirrors +110
Power Windows +200
Sliding Rear Window +100
Tilt Steering Wheel +145

Don't forget to refer to the Mileage Adjustment Table at the back of this book!

Model Description	Trade-in Value	Market Value	Model Description	Trade-in Value	Market Value

DURANGO 2000

The next-generation 4.7-liter V8 is now available on four-wheel-drive models and is linked to an all-new automatic transmission. Rack-and-pinion steering becomes standard for both two- and four-wheel-drives. A performance-oriented R/T model has been added to the lineup that already includes the SLT and the decked-out SLT Plus.

Category H		
4 Dr R/T 4WD Wgn	24110	27975
4 Dr SLT Wgn	19485	22605
4 Dr SLT 4WD Wgn	20900	24245
4 Dr STD Wgn	18840	21860
4 Dr STD 4WD Wgn	20255	23495

OPTIONS FOR DURANGO
8 cyl 5.9 L Engine[Std on R/T 4WD Wgn] +570
Bucket Seats[Opt on SLT Wgn] +305
Camper/Towing Package +270
Compact Disc W/fm/tape[Std on R/T 4WD Wgn] +255
Dual Air Conditioning +1055
Third Seat +515

INTREPID 2000

A performance R/T model is onboard for 2000. Intrepids get five new colors, new seat fabric in Base models, and added horsepower and torque to ES models powered by the 2.7-liter V6. AutoStick is newly available with that engine, and ES buyers can order an in-dash CD changer. Tether-ready child-seat anchors have been added behind the rear seat, and cars sold in California meet LEV standards.

Category B		
4 Dr ES Sdn	15295	17835
4 Dr R/T Sdn	16775	19555
4 Dr STD Sdn	14165	16510

OPTIONS FOR INTREPID
6 cyl 3.2 L Engine +410
Alarm System +130
Bucket Seats[Std on R/T] +230
Climate Control for AC +140
Dual Power Seats +320
Leather Seats +560

NEON 2000

Everything's new inside and out, as the second-generation Neon grows up, not old. A totally redesigned suspension and steering system, low-speed traction control, and a complete exterior redesign head up the notable changes.

Category E		
4 Dr ES Sdn	10270	12140
4 Dr Highline Sdn	8975	10615

OPTIONS FOR NEON
Auto 3-Speed Transmission +430
Air Conditioning[Std on ES Sdn] +680

RAM PICKUP 2000

RAM 1500
Category H

Model	Trade-in	Market
4 Dr SLT Ext Cab LB	15935	18485
4 Dr SLT 4WD Ext Cab LB	18045	20935
2 Dr SLT Ext Cab SB	15165	17590
2 Dr SLT 4WD Ext Cab SB	17280	20050
4 Dr SLT Ext Cab SB	15745	18265
4 Dr SLT 4WD Ext Cab SB	17825	20675
2 Dr SLT Std Cab LB	13475	15630
2 Dr SLT 4WD Std Cab LB	16055	18625
2 Dr SLT Std Cab SB	13280	15405
2 Dr SLT 4WD Std Cab SB	15825	18360
4 Dr ST Ext Cab LB	14380	16680
4 Dr ST 4WD Ext Cab LB	16580	19235
2 Dr ST Ext Cab SB	13610	15785
2 Dr ST 4WD Ext Cab SB	15815	18345
4 Dr ST Ext Cab SB	14190	16460
4 Dr ST 4WD Ext Cab SB	16355	18975
2 Dr ST Std Cab LB	11915	13825
2 Dr ST 4WD Std Cab LB	14500	16820
2 Dr ST Std Cab SB	11725	13600
2 Dr ST 4WD Std Cab SB	14270	16550
2 Dr WS Std Cab LB	10700	12415
2 Dr WS Std Cab SB	10520	12205

RAM 2500
Category H

Model	Trade-in	Market
4 Dr SLT Ext Cab LB	16760	19445
4 Dr SLT 4WD Ext Cab LB	18925	21955
4 Dr SLT Ext Cab SB	16635	19300
4 Dr SLT 4WD Ext Cab SB	18795	21805
2 Dr SLT Std Cab LB	15460	17935
2 Dr SLT 4WD Std Cab LB	17530	20335
4 Dr ST Ext Cab LB	15225	17660
4 Dr ST 4WD Ext Cab LB	17385	20170
4 Dr ST Ext Cab SB Ext Cab SB	15095	17515
4 Dr ST 4WD Ext Cab SB	17260	20020
2 Dr ST Std Cab LB	13920	16150
2 Dr ST 4WD Std Cab LB	15990	18550

RAM 3500
Category H

Model	Trade-in	Market
4 Dr SLT Ext Cab LB Ext Cab LB	18055	20945
4 Dr SLT 4WD Ext Cab LB	20195	23430
2 Dr SLT Std Cab LB	16195	18785
2 Dr SLT 4WD Std Cab LB	18275	21200
4 Dr ST Ext Cab LB	16935	19650
4 Dr ST 4WD Ext Cab LB	19075	22130

Don't forget to refer to the Mileage Adjustment Table at the back of this book!

Model Description	Trade-in Value	Market Value
2 Dr ST Std Cab LB	15075	17490
2 Dr ST 4WD Std Cab LB	17155	19905

OPTIONS FOR RAM PICKUP
10 cyl 8.0 L Engine +385
6 cyl 5.9 L Turbodsl Engine +3780
8 cyl 5.2 L Engine +480
8 cyl 5.9 L Engine[Opt on Ram 1500] +570
6-Speed Transmission +325
Auto 4-Speed Transmission +795
Off-Road Group +1005
AM/FM Stereo Tape[Opt on WS] +165
Air Conditioning +665
Bed Liner +185
Camper/Towing Package +270
Chrome Wheels[Opt on Ram 1500,SLT 4WD Ext Cab SB] +245
Cruise Control +155
Fog Lights +105
Overhead Console[Std on Ram 1500 2 Dr SLT 4WD Ext Cab SB 4WD Extended Cab SB] +110
Sliding Rear Window +95
Tilt Steering Wheel +155
Velour/Cloth Seats +90

RAM VAN — 2000

Minor changes come with the 2000 model year, including hood-mounted windshield-washer nozzles and chrome-clad wheels. Sealing has been improved to reduce noise and keep out the weather, and Ram vans get a six-speaker audio system as standard equipment.

Category H

Model Description	Trade-in Value	Market Value
2 Dr 1500 Maxi Cargo Van Ext	13850	16065
2 Dr 2500 Maxi Cargo Van Ext	14800	17170
2 Dr 3500 Maxi Cargo Van Ext	14905	17295
2 Dr 1500 STD Cargo Van	12440	14435
2 Dr 1500 STD Cargo Van Ext	12470	14470
2 Dr 2500 STD Cargo Van Ext	13450	15605
2 Dr 3500 STD Cargo Van Ext	14550	16880

OPTIONS FOR RAM VAN
8 cyl 5.2 L Engine[Opt on Cargo Van, 1500 Base Cargo LWB, 1500 Base Maxi LWB] +480
8 cyl 5.9 L Engine +570
Auto 4-Speed Transmission +245
Air Conditioning +665
Compact Disc W/fm/tape +255

RAM WAGON — 2000

Minor changes come with the 2000 model year, including hood-mounted windshield-washer nozzles and chrome-clad wheels. Sealing has been improved to reduce noise and keep out the weather, and Ram Wagons get a six-speaker audio system as standard equipment.

Category H

Model Description	Trade-in Value	Market Value
2 Dr 3500 Maxi Pass. Van Ext	20060	23275
2 Dr 1500 STD Pass. Van	16310	18925
2 Dr 2500 STD Pass. Van Ext	17815	20670

OPTIONS FOR RAM WAGON
8 cyl 5.2 L Engine[Opt on Pass. Van] +480
8 cyl 5.9 L Engine +570
Auto 4-Speed Transmission[Opt on Pass. Van] +245
Cruise Control +155
Power Door Locks +155
Power Mirrors +85
Power Windows +155
Rear Window Defroster +125

STRATUS — 2000

A new entry-level SE replaces last year's Base model and comes with so much standard equipment and free optional equipment that you'll have a whole new kind of sticker shock! The upper-level ES steps up to a 2.5-liter V6, and new colors also debut.

Category C

Model Description	Trade-in Value	Market Value
4 Dr ES Sdn	13400	15755
4 Dr SE Sdn	10935	12860

OPTIONS FOR STRATUS
4 cyl 2.4 L Engine +370
Auto 4-Speed Transmission[Std on ES] +860
Cruise Control[Std on ES] +180
Power Door Locks[Std on ES] +210
Power Drivers Seat +245
Power Windows[Std on ES] +260

VIPER — 2000

The 2000 Viper is available in a new Steel Gray color and the ACR version has been revised to further poison the snake's venomous bite.

Category K

Model Description	Trade-in Value	Market Value
2 Dr ACR Competition Cpe	66980	76585
2 Dr GTS Cpe	58655	67060
2 Dr RT/10 Conv	56570	64680

OPTIONS FOR VIPER
Dual Stripes +1635

1999 DODGE

AVENGER — 1999

One new color for the exterior: Shark Blue (replaces Silver Mist).

RATINGS (SCALE OF 1-10)

Overall	Safety	Reliability	Performance	Comfort	Value
N/A	7.7	N/A	7.6	7.4	N/A

Category F

Model Description	Trade-in Value	Market Value
2 Dr ES Cpe	12010	14205
2 Dr STD Cpe	10515	12435

Don't forget to refer to the Mileage Adjustment Table at the back of this book!

Model Description	Trade-in Value	Market Value	Model Description	Trade-in Value	Market Value

OPTIONS FOR AVENGER

6 cyl 2.5 L Engine +430
Auto 4-Speed Transmission +465
Air Conditioning[Std on ES] +565
Aluminum/Alloy Wheels[Std on ES] +205
Anti-Lock Brakes +435
Compact Disc W/fm/tape +335
Cruise Control[Std on ES] +150
Keyless Entry System +120
Leather Seats +425
Power Door Locks +135
Power Drivers Seat +160
Power Mirrors +75
Power Moonroof +440
Power Windows +155
Rear Spoiler[Std on ES] +160

CARAVAN/GRAND CARAVAN   1999

RATINGS (SCALE OF 1-10)

Overall	Safety	Reliability	Performance	Comfort	Value
N/A	6.6	8.4	6.6	7.4	N/A

CARAVAN

Category G

2 Dr LE Pass. Van	16885	19820
2 Dr SE Pass. Van	14585	17120
2 Dr STD Pass. Van	12070	14165

GRAND CARAVAN

Category G

2 Dr Grand Pass. Van	14050	16490
2 Dr Grand ES Pass. Van	18885	22170
2 Dr Grand ES 4WD Pass. Van	20555	24125
2 Dr Grand LE Pass. Van	17470	20505
2 Dr Grand LE 4WD Pass. Van	19505	22895
2 Dr Grand SE Pass. Van	15170	17805
2 Dr Grand SE 4WD Pass. Van	17050	20015

OPTIONS FOR CARAVAN/GRAND CARAVAN

6 cyl 3.0 L Engine +375
6 cyl 3.3 L Engine[Std on Grand] +650
6 cyl 3.8 L Engine[Std on Grand ES, 4WD] +245
Auto 4-Speed Transmission[Opt on STD] +135
7 Passenger Seating[Opt on STD] +350
AM/FM Stereo Tape[Opt on Grand, STD] +150
Air Conditioning[Opt on Grand, STD] +550
Captain Chairs (4) +410
Compact Disc W/fm/tape[Std on Grand ES] +295
Cruise Control[Opt on Grand, STD] +140
Dual Air Conditioning +615
Dual Power Seats +280
Leather Seats +525
Luggage Rack +110
Power Door Locks[Std on Grand ES, Grand LE, LE] +155
Power Windows[Std on Grand ES, Grand LE, LE] +160
Rear Window Defroster[Opt on Grand, STD] +115
Tilt Steering Wheel[Opt on Grand, STD] +120

DAKOTA   1999

Solar Yellow paint is now available for those who want their pickups to get noticed. Other un-pickup-like refinements include an express down feature for the driver's window, extra storage space for cassettes or CDs, and remote radio controls on the steering wheel.

RATINGS (SCALE OF 1-10)

Overall	Safety	Reliability	Performance	Comfort	Value
N/A	N/A	N/A	6.6	7.1	N/A

Category G

2 Dr R/T Sport Ext Cab SB	15015	17625
2 Dr R/T Sport Std Cab SB	12860	15095
2 Dr SLT Ext Cab SB	12035	14125
2 Dr SLT 4WD Ext Cab SB	14330	16820
2 Dr SLT Std Cab LB	11360	13335
2 Dr SLT Std Cab SB	11045	12965
2 Dr SLT 4WD Std Cab SB	13520	15870
2 Dr STD Ext Cab SB	11700	13730
2 Dr STD 4WD Ext Cab SB	13900	16315
2 Dr STD Std Cab LB	9825	11530
2 Dr STD Std Cab SB	9510	11160
2 Dr STD 4WD Std Cab SB	11860	13920
2 Dr Sport Ext Cab SB	11930	13975
2 Dr Sport 4WD Ext Cab SB	13795	16195
2 Dr Sport Std Cab LB	10430	12245
2 Dr Sport Std Cab SB	10115	11875
2 Dr Sport 4WD Std Cab SB	12265	14450

OPTIONS FOR DAKOTA

6 cyl 3.9 L Engine[Std on 4WD and Ext. Cab] +375
8 cyl 5.2 L Engine +595
8 cyl 5.9 L Engine[Std on R/T Sport] +1125
Auto 4-Speed Transmission[Std on R/T Sport] +650
AM/FM Compact Disc Player +210
Air Conditioning[Std on SLT] +550
Anti-Lock Brakes +390
Bed Liner +185
Cruise Control[Std on R/T Sport] +140
Fog Lights +95
Overhead Console +105
Power Door Locks +155
Power Mirrors +90
Power Windows +160
Sliding Rear Window +80
Tilt Steering Wheel[Std on R/T Sport] +120

DURANGO   1999

Two-wheel drive models finally show up for true flatlander use, and all Durangos gain a rear power outlet. Also available are steering wheel-mounted radio controls, heated mirrors, and two new colors: Bright Platinum Metallic and Patriot Blue.

Don't forget to refer to the Mileage Adjustment Table at the back of this book!

Model Description	Trade-in Value	Market Value

RATINGS (SCALE OF 1-10)

Overall	Safety	Reliability	Performance	Comfort	Value
N/A	N/A	N/A	6.6	7.6	N/A

Category H

4 Dr SLT Wgn	17150	19975
4 Dr SLT 4WD Wgn	18480	21525

OPTIONS FOR DURANGO

8 cyl 5.2 L Engine +395
8 cyl 5.9 L Engine +490
Compact Disc W/fm/tape +210
Dual Air Conditioning +860
Fog Lights +85
Leather Seats +670
Overhead Console +90
Power Drivers Seat +190
Third Seat +420

INTREPID   1999

Minor appearance tweaks such as chrome badging and improved floor carpeting debut for 1999. A new engine immobilizer is now available on the ES.

RATINGS (SCALE OF 1-10)

Overall	Safety	Reliability	Performance	Comfort	Value
N/A	7.2	8	8.2	8.5	N/A

Category B

4 Dr ES Sdn	14290	16790
4 Dr STD Sdn	12550	14740

OPTIONS FOR INTREPID

AM/FM Compact Disc Player +220
Anti-Lock Brakes[Std on ES] +450
Keyless Entry System[Std on ES] +120
Leather Seats +460
Power Drivers Seat[Std on ES] +210
Power Sunroof +720
Traction Control System +115

NEON   1999

One new color is available for the Neon Style Package: Inferno Red. Disco, anyone?

RATINGS (SCALE OF 1-10)

Overall	Safety	Reliability	Performance	Comfort	Value
N/A	6	7.6	7.4	7.6	N/A

Category E

2 Dr Competition Cpe	7405	8895
4 Dr Competition Sdn	7530	9045
2 Dr Highline Cpe	7665	9205
4 Dr Highline Sdn	7715	9265
2 Dr R/T Cpe	8870	10650
4 Dr R/T Sdn	8995	10800
2 Dr Sport Cpe	8475	10180
4 Dr Sport Sdn	8470	10170

OPTIONS FOR NEON

4 cyl 2.0 L DOHC Engine[Std on R/T,Sport] +100
Auto 3-Speed Transmission +400
Competition Pkg +1010
AM/FM Compact Disc Player +290
AM/FM Stereo Tape[Std on R/T] +200
Air Conditioning[Std on R/T,Sport] +555
Aluminum/Alloy Wheels[Std on R/T] +225
Cruise Control +155
Power Door Locks +165
Power Mirrors +75
Power Windows +180
Rear Window Defroster[Opt on Competition] +110
Tilt Steering Wheel +100

RAM PICKUP   1999

RATINGS (SCALE OF 1-10)

Overall	Safety	Reliability	Performance	Comfort	Value
N/A	N/A	N/A	7	8	N/A

RAM 1500

Category H

2 Dr Laramie SLT Ext Cab LB	14305	16655
2 Dr Laramie SLT 4WD Ext Cab LB	16330	19020
4 Dr Laramie SLT Ext Cab LB	14810	17250
4 Dr Laramie SLT 4WD Ext Cab LB	16840	19610
2 Dr Laramie SLT Ext Cab SB	14125	16450
2 Dr Laramie SLT 4WD Ext Cab SB	16120	18775
4 Dr Laramie SLT Ext Cab SB	14630	17040
4 Dr Laramie SLT 4WD Ext Cab SB	16630	19365
2 Dr Laramie SLT Std Cab SB	12635	14715
2 Dr Laramie SLT 4WD Std Cab LB	14940	17395
2 Dr Laramie SLT Std Cab SB	12455	14505
2 Dr Laramie SLT 4WD Std Cab SB	14720	17145
2 Dr ST Ext Cab LB	12765	14865
2 Dr ST 4WD Ext Cab LB	14875	17325
4 Dr ST Ext Cab LB	13335	15530
4 Dr ST 4WD Ext Cab LB	15450	17990
2 Dr ST Ext Cab SB	12650	14735
4 Dr ST Ext Cab SB	13160	15325
2 Dr ST 4WD Ext Cab SB	14730	17155
4 Dr ST 4WD Ext Cab SB	15240	17745
2 Dr ST Std Cab LB	11160	13000
2 Dr ST 4WD Std Cab LB	13465	15680
2 Dr ST Standard Cab SB	10980	12785
2 Dr ST 4WD Std Cab SB	13245	15430
2 Dr WS Std Cab LB	10015	11665
2 Dr WS Std Cab SB	9845	11465

Model Description	Trade-in Value	Market Value	Model Description	Trade-in Value	Market Value

RAM 2500

Category H

Model Description	Trade-in Value	Market Value
2 Dr Laramie SLT Ext Cab LB	15075	17555
2 Dr Laramie SLT 4WD Ext Cab LB	17110	19930
4 Dr Laramie SLT Ext Cab LB	15575	18135
4 Dr Laramie SLT 4WD Ext Cab LB	17610	20510
2 Dr Laramie SLT Ext Cab SB	14955	17415
2 Dr Laramie SLT 4WD Ext Cab SB	16995	19790
4 Dr Laramie SLT Ext Cab SB	15455	18000
4 Dr Laramie SLT 4WD Ext Cab SB	17555	20445
2 Dr Laramie SLT Std Cab LB	14210	16550
2 Dr Laramie SLT 4WD Std Cab LB	16110	18760
2 Dr ST Ext Cab LB	13655	15900
2 Dr ST 4WD Ext Cab LB	15695	18275
4 Dr ST Ext Cab LB	14215	16555
4 Dr ST 4WD Ext Cab LB	16255	18930
2 Dr ST Ext Cab SB	13535	15765
2 Dr ST 4WD Ext Cab SB	15575	18135
4 Dr ST Ext Cab SB	14100	16420
4 Dr ST 4WD Ext Cab SB	16135	18790
2 Dr ST Std Cab LB	12855	14970
2 Dr ST 4WD Std Cab LB	14750	17180

RAM 3500

Category H

Model Description	Trade-in Value	Market Value
4 Dr Laramie SLT Ext Cab LB	16890	19675
4 Dr Laramie SLT 4WD Ext Cab LB	18600	21665
2 Dr Laramie SLT Std Cab LB	15020	17495
2 Dr Laramie SLT 4WD Std Cab LB	16910	19695
4 Dr ST Ext Cab LB	15830	18440
4 Dr ST 4WD Ext Cab LB	17540	20430
2 Dr ST Std Cab LB	13965	16260
2 Dr ST 4WD Std Cab LB	15850	18460

OPTIONS FOR RAM PICKUP

10 cyl 8.0 L Engine +315
6 cyl 5.9 L Turbodsl Engine +3060
8 cyl 5.2 L Engine[Std on Ext Cab,4WD] +395
8 cyl 5.9 L Engine[Opt on Ram 1500] +490
Auto 4-Speed Transmission +650
AM/FM Compact Disc Player +205
Air Conditioning[Opt on ST,WS] +545
Anti-Lock Brakes[Std on Ram 3500] +330
Bed Liner +150
Camper/Towing Package +220
Cruise Control[Opt on ST,WS] +130
Fog Lights +85
Keyless Entry System +115
Leather Seats +670
Limited Slip Diff +175
Power Drivers Seat +190
Sliding Rear Window +80
Tilt Steering Wheel[Opt on ST,WS] +125
Tutone Paint +165

RAM VAN/WAGON   1999

RATINGS (SCALE OF 1-10)

Overall	Safety	Reliability	Performance	Comfort	Value
N/A	N/A	N/A	6.2	6.9	N/A

VAN

Category H

Model Description	Trade-in Value	Market Value
2 Dr 2500 Maxi Cargo Van Ext	13525	15750
2 Dr 3500 Maxi Cargo Van Ext	13805	16075
2 Dr 1500 STD Cargo Van	11345	13215
2 Dr 1500 STD Cargo Van Ext	11375	13245
2 Dr 3500 STD Cargo Van Ext	13220	15395

WAGON

Category H

Model Description	Trade-in Value	Market Value
2 Dr 3500 Maxi Pass. Van Ext	18035	21005
2 Dr 1500 STD Pass. Van	14885	17340
2 Dr 2500 STD Pass. Van Ext	16490	19205

OPTIONS FOR RAM VAN/WAGON

8 cyl 5.2 L Engine[Opt on 1500] +395
8 cyl 5.9 L Engine +490
Auto 4-Speed Transmission[Opt on 1500] +200
Tradesman Upfitter Pkg +665
AM/FM Stereo Tape[Opt on Van] +135
Air Conditioning[Opt on Van] +545
Aluminum/Alloy Wheels +210
Cruise Control +130
Keyless Entry System +115
Power Door Locks +125
Power Mirrors +70
Power Windows +130
Rear Heater +140
Rear Window Defroster +105
Sunscreen Glass +170

STRATUS   1999

The instrument panel gauges are now white-faced, wheels are better looking, and some work has been done to reduce the interior noise levels.

RATINGS (SCALE OF 1-10)

Overall	Safety	Reliability	Performance	Comfort	Value
N/A	6.4	N/A	6.4	7.9	N/A

Category C

Model Description	Trade-in Value	Market Value
4 Dr ES Sdn	11760	13900
4 Dr STD Sdn	9540	11275

Don't forget to refer to the Mileage Adjustment Table at the back of this book!

DODGE 99-98

Model Description	Trade-in Value	Market Value	Model Description	Trade-in Value	Market Value

OPTIONS FOR STRATUS

4 cyl 2.4 L Engine +300
Auto 4-Speed Transmission[Std on ES] +700
AM/FM Compact Disc Player +235
Cruise Control[Std on ES] +145
Keyless Entry System +125
Power Door Locks[Std on ES] +170
Power Drivers Seat +200
Power Windows[Std on ES] +215

VIPER   1999

Goodies for the '99 Viper include power mirrors, Connolly leather for various interior surfaces, a new shift knob, aluminum interior accents, and a remote release for the glass hatch on the GTS. Black is again an exterior color choice, available with or without silver stripes. New 18-inch aluminum wheels with the Viper logo on the caps round out the changes.

Category K

2 Dr GTS Cpe	55825	63925
2 Dr RT/10 Conv	53800	61605

OPTIONS FOR VIPER

Dual Stripes +1335

1998 DODGE

AVENGER   1998

Interior fabrics are new, as is a black and gray color scheme. The ES model gets a new Sport package that affects appearance, not performance. Also available for the ES are new 16-inch aluminum wheels and a rear sway bar that improves handling.

RATINGS (SCALE OF 1-10)

Overall	Safety	Reliability	Performance	Comfort	Value
7.2	7.5	7.1	7.6	7.6	6

Category F

2 Dr ES Cpe	10865	12880
2 Dr STD Cpe	9340	11065

OPTIONS FOR AVENGER

6 cyl 2.5 L Engine +350
Auto 4-Speed Transmission +380
Air Conditioning[Std on ES] +460
Aluminum/Alloy Wheels[Std on ES] +170
Anti-Lock Brakes +355
Compact Disc W/fm/tape +275
Cruise Control[Std on ES] +120
Keyless Entry System +100
Leather Seats +345
Leather Steering Wheel[Std on ES] +90
Power Door Locks +110
Power Drivers Seat +130
Power Mirrors +65
Power Sunroof +365
Power Windows +125

CARAVAN   1998

Available this year is a 3.8-liter V6 that puts out 180 horsepower and 240 foot-pounds of torque. And for convenience, Caravans come with rear-seat mounted grocery bag hooks, and driver's-side easy-entry Quad seating. All Chrysler products are equipped with "Next Generation" depowered airbags.

RATINGS (SCALE OF 1-10)

Overall	Safety	Reliability	Performance	Comfort	Value
7.6	6.8	8.1	6.6	7.4	9.3

Category G

2 Dr Grand Pass. Van	12245	14425
2 Dr Grand ES Pass. Van	15930	18765
2 Dr Grand ES 4WD Pass. Van	17745	20905
2 Dr Grand LE Pass. Van	15590	18365
2 Dr Grand LE 4WD Pass. Van	17440	20550
2 Dr Grand SE Pass. Van	13595	16020
2 Dr Grand SE 4WD Pass. Van	15370	18110
2 Dr LE Pass. Van	15010	17685
2 Dr SE Pass. Van	13010	15325
2 Dr STD Pass. Van	10715	12625

OPTIONS FOR CARAVAN

6 cyl 3.0 L Engine[Std on Grand, SE] +270
6 cyl 3.3 L Engine[Std on Grand ES, Grand LE, LE] +185
6 cyl 3.8 L Engine[Std on 4WD] +225
Auto 4-Speed Transmission[Opt on Grand, STD] +135
AM/FM Compact Disc Player +175
Air Conditioning[Std on Grand ES,Grand LE,4WD] +450
Aluminum/Alloy Wheels[Std on Grand ES] +175
Anti-Lock Brakes[Opt on Grand, STD] +320
Auto Load Leveling[Std on 4WD] +130
Captain Chairs (4) +335
Cruise Control[Opt on Grand, STD] +115
Dual Air Conditioning +505
Keyless Entry System[Opt on Grand SE, SE] +105
Leather Seats +430
Power Door Locks[Std on Grand ES, Grand LE, LE] +130
Power Drivers Seat +155
Power Mirrors[Opt on Grand, STD] +70
Power Windows[Opt on Grand SE, SE] +135
Rear Window Defroster[Std on Grand ES, Grand LE, LE] +95
Sliding Driver Side Door[Opt on STD] +290
Sunscreen Glass[Std on Grand ES,Grand LE,LE] +205
Tilt Steering Wheel[Opt on Grand, STD] +100
Traction Control System +145
Trip Computer[Opt on Grand SE, SE] +80

DAKOTA   1998

The Dakota R/T, featuring a 250-horsepower V8, is available for those seeking a performance pickup. The passenger airbag can now be deactivated in all Dakotas, so a rear-facing child seat is perfectly safe. The Dakota is also available in three new colors.

Don't forget to refer to the Mileage Adjustment Table at the back of this book!

Model Description	Trade-in Value	Market Value

Model Description	Trade-in Value	Market Value

RATINGS (SCALE OF 1-10)

Overall	Safety	Reliability	Performance	Comfort	Value
N/A	N/A	N/A	7	7.1	N/A

Category G

Model	Trade-in	Market
2 Dr R/T Sport Ext Cab SB	13490	15895
2 Dr R/T Sport Std Cab SB	11440	13480
2 Dr SLT Ext Cab SB	11610	13675
2 Dr SLT 4WD Ext Cab SB	13840	16305
2 Dr SLT Std Cab LB	10505	12375
2 Dr SLT Std Cab SB	10205	12020
2 Dr SLT 4WD Std Cab SB	12920	15220
2 Dr STD Ext Cab SB	10990	12950
2 Dr STD 4WD Ext Cab SB	13235	15590
2 Dr STD Std Cab LB	9205	10845
2 Dr STD Std Cab SB	8905	10490
2 Dr STD 4WD Std Cab SB	11505	13550
2 Dr Sport Ext Cab SB	11265	13325
2 Dr Sport 4WD Ext Cab SB	14015	16515
2 Dr Sport Std Cab LB	9850	11600
2 Dr Sport Std Cab SB	9550	11250
2 Dr Sport 4WD Std Cab SB	13090	15200

OPTIONS FOR DAKOTA

6 cyl 3.9 L Engine[Std on 4WD, SLT 2WD Ext Cab SB] +275
8 cyl 5.2 L Engine +475
8 cyl 5.9 L Engine[Std on R/T Sport] +865
Auto 4-Speed Transmission[Std on R/T Sport] +520
AM/FM Compact Disc Player +175
Air Conditioning[Std on SLT] +450
Anti-Lock Brakes +320
Bed Liner +155
Cruise Control[Std on R/T Sport] +115
Fog Lights +80
Keyless Entry System +105
Limited Slip Diff[Std on R/T Sport] +150
Power Door Locks +130
Power Drivers Seat +155
Power Mirrors +70
Power Windows +135
Sliding Rear Window +65
Tilt Steering Wheel[Std on R/T Sport] +100

DURANGO   1998

As the most recent addition to the Dodge truck lineup, the Durango makes quite an entry. Offering the most cargo space in its class, along with eight-passenger seating and three-and-a-half tons of towing capacity, the Durango is the most versatile sport-utility on the market.

RATINGS (SCALE OF 1-10)

Overall	Safety	Reliability	Performance	Comfort	Value
N/A	N/A	8.8	6.8	7.6	N/A

Category H

Model	Trade-in	Market
4 Dr SLT 4WD Wgn	17235	20160
4 Dr STD 4WD Wgn	16545	19355

OPTIONS FOR DURANGO

8 cyl 5.2 L Engine +320
8 cyl 5.9 L Engine +325
Anti-Lock Brakes +270
Camper/Towing Package +180
Compact Disc W/fm/tape +170
Fog Lights +70
Leather Seats +545
Limited Slip Diff +145
Power Drivers Seat +155
Third Seat +345

INTREPID   1998

Completely redesigned for 1998, the Intrepid is a sedan that has the graceful styling of a coupe, thanks to a continuation of Chrysler's cab-forward design. Dodge's trademark cross hair grille dominates the front end along with two large, sparkling headlights. And the new Intrepid is powered by your choice of two new V6 engines.

RATINGS (SCALE OF 1-10)

Overall	Safety	Reliability	Performance	Comfort	Value
8.1	7.1	7.8	8.2	8.5	9

Category B

Model	Trade-in	Market
4 Dr ES Sdn	12755	15110
4 Dr STD Sdn	11215	13285

OPTIONS FOR INTREPID

AM/FM Compact Disc Player +180
Anti-Lock Brakes[Std on ES] +365
Climate Control for AC +90
Dual Power Seats +210
Keyless Entry System[Std on ES] +95
Leather Seats +375
Power Drivers Seat[Std on ES] +175
Power Moonroof +530
Traction Control System +95

NEON   1998

An R/T appearance package makes people think you're driving a Viper! Improved option packages, LEV emissions and next-generation airbags round out the changes.

RATINGS (SCALE OF 1-10)

Overall	Safety	Reliability	Performance	Comfort	Value
7.1	6.1	7.7	7.4	7.6	6.8

Category E

Model	Trade-in	Market
2 Dr Competition Cpe	6465	7840
4 Dr Competition Sdn	6575	7975
2 Dr Highline Cpe	6605	8015
4 Dr Highline Sdn	6720	8150

Model Description	Trade-in Value	Market Value	Model Description	Trade-in Value	Market Value
2 Dr R/T Cpe	7690	9325	2 Dr ST 4WD Ext Cab SB	13855	16205
4 Dr R/T Sdn	7800	9460	4 Dr ST Ext Cab SB	12370	14470
2 Dr Sport Cpe	7220	8755	4 Dr ST 4WD Ext Cab SB	14335	16770
4 Dr Sport Sdn	7400	8975	2 Dr ST Std Cab LB	10400	12165
			2 Dr ST 4WD Std Cab LB	12620	14765
			2 Dr ST Std Cab SB	10230	11965
			2 Dr ST 4WD Std Cab SB	12415	14525
			2 Dr WS Std Cab LB	9275	10850
			2 Dr WS Std Cab SB	9160	10715

OPTIONS FOR NEON
Auto 3-Speed Transmission +330
Competition Pkg +825
AM/FM Compact Disc Player +235
Air Conditioning[Std on R/T, Sport] +455
Aluminum/Alloy Wheels[Std on R/T] +185
Anti-Lock Brakes +365
Cruise Control +125
Keyless Entry System +90
Power Door Locks +135
Power Mirrors +60
Power Windows +145
Rear Window Defroster[Opt on Competition] +90
Tilt Steering Wheel +80

RAM PICKUP   1998

All Rams get a totally redesigned interior, standard passenger-side airbag with cutoff switch, and all airbags are "depowered" for safety.

RATINGS (SCALE OF 1-10)

Overall	Safety	Reliability	Performance	Comfort	Value
N/A	N/A	8.9	7	8	N/A

RAM 1500
Category H

Model Description	Trade-in Value	Market Value
2 Dr Laramie SLT Ext Cab LB	13510	15805
2 Dr Laramie SLT 4WD Ext Cab LB	15430	18045
4 Dr Laramie SLT Ext Cab LB	13990	16365
4 Dr Laramie SLT 4WD Ext Cab LB	15905	18605
2 Dr Laramie SLT Ext Cab SB	13345	15610
2 Dr Laramie SLT 4WD Ext Cab SB	15230	17815
4 Dr Laramie SLT Ext Cab SB	13825	16170
4 Dr Laramie SLT 4WD Ext Cab SB	15710	18375
2 Dr Laramie SLT Std Cab LB	11850	13865
2 Dr Laramie SLT 4WD Std Cab LB	14070	16460
2 Dr Laramie SLT Std Cab SB	11680	13665
2 Dr Laramie SLT 4WD Std Cab SB	13870	16220
2 Dr SS/T Std Cab SB	13165	15400
2 Dr ST Ext Cab LB	12060	14105
2 Dr ST 4WD Ext Cab LB	14055	16440
4 Dr ST Ext Cab LB	12540	14665
4 Dr ST 4WD Ext Cab LB	14535	17000
2 Dr ST Ext Cab SB	11890	13910

RAM 2500
Category H

Model Description	Trade-in Value	Market Value
2 Dr Laramie SLT Ext Cab LB	14465	16920
2 Dr Laramie SLT 4WD Ext Cab LB	16390	19175
4 Dr Laramie SLT Ext Cab LB	14935	17475
4 Dr Laramie SLT 4WD Ext Cab LB	16865	19725
2 Dr Laramie SLT Ext Cab SB	14355	16790
2 Dr Laramie SLT 4WD Ext Cab SB	16280	19040
4 Dr Laramie SLT Ext Cab SB	14825	17340
4 Dr Laramie SLT 4WD Ext Cab SB	16750	19595
2 Dr Laramie SLT Std Cab LB	13295	15555
2 Dr Laramie SLT 4WD Std Cab LB	15325	17925
2 Dr ST Ext Cab LB	13125	15355
2 Dr ST 4WD Ext Cab LB	15050	17605
4 Dr ST Ext Cab LB	13595	15905
4 Dr ST 4WD Ext Cab LB	15520	18155
2 Dr ST Ext Cab SB	13010	15220
2 Dr ST 4WD Ext Cab SB	14935	17475
4 Dr ST Ext Cab SB	13485	15775
4 Dr ST 4WD Ext Cab SB	15410	18025
2 Dr ST Std Cab LB	12255	14205
2 Dr ST 4WD Std Cab LB	13985	16355

RAM 3500
Category H

Model Description	Trade-in Value	Market Value
4 Dr Laramie SLT Ext Cab LB	15680	18345
4 Dr Laramie SLT 4WD Ext Cab LB	17150	20060
2 Dr Laramie SLT Std Cab LB	13800	16140
2 Dr Laramie SLT 4WD Std Cab LB	15580	18225
4 Dr ST Ext Cab LB	14620	17105
4 Dr ST 4WD Ext Cab LB	16090	18820
2 Dr ST Std Cab LB	12735	14900
2 Dr ST 4WD Std Cab LB	14520	16985

OPTIONS FOR RAM PICKUP
10 cyl 8.0 L Engine +530
6 cyl 5.9 L Turbodsl Engine +2425

Don't forget to refer to the Mileage Adjustment Table at the back of this book!

Model Description	Trade-in Value	Market Value	Model Description	Trade-in Value	Market Value

8 cyl 5.2 L Engine[Std on Ext Cab, 4WD] +320
8 cyl 5.9 L Engine[Std on Ram 2500, Ram 3500, SS/T] +325
Auto 4-Speed Transmission +520
AM/FM Compact Disc Player +170
Air Conditioning[Opt on ST, WS] +445
Aluminum/Alloy Wheels[Opt on Ram 2500, ST] +170
Anti-Lock Brakes +270
Bed Liner +125
Camper/Towing Package +180
Cruise Control[Opt on ST, WS] +105
Fog Lights[Std on SS/T] +70
Heated Power Mirrors[Std on Ram 3500, Laramie SLT, SS/T] +50
Keyless Entry System +95
Leather Seats +545
Limited Slip Diff +145
Power Drivers Seat +155
Skid Plates[Std on Ram 3500] +60
Sliding Rear Window +65
Tilt Steering Wheel[Opt on ST, WS] +105
Tutone Paint +135

RAM VAN/WAGON 1998

A minor redesign this year includes better build quality, so we're told. Of note are the appearance of dual airbags in the revised dash and upgrades to the brakes and sound systems. The V8 engines have also been relocated forward to reduce the size of that annoying "doghouse."

RATINGS (SCALE OF 1-10)

Overall	Safety	Reliability	Performance	Comfort	Value
N/A	N/A	8.3	6.2	6.9	N/A

VAN

Category H

2 Dr 1500 Ram Van	10600	12400
2 Dr 1500 Ram Van Ext	10625	12430
2 Dr 2500 Ram Van Ext	11700	13690
2 Dr 2500 Maxi Ram Van Ext	12615	14760
2 Dr 3500 Ram Van Ext	12370	14470
2 Dr 3500 Maxi Ram Van Ext	12880	15070

WAGON

Category H

2 Dr 1500 Ram Wagon	13170	15405
2 Dr 1500 SLT Ram Wagon	13465	15750
2 Dr 2500 Ram Wagon Ext	14670	17160
2 Dr 2500 SLT Ram Wagon Ext	14965	17505
2 Dr 3500 Maxi Ram Wagon Ext	15945	18650
2 Dr 3500 SLT Maxi Ram Wagon Ext	16330	19100

OPTIONS FOR RAM VAN/WAGON

8 cyl 5.2 L Engine[Opt on 1500] +320
8 cyl 5.9 L Engine +325
Auto 4-Speed Transmission[Opt on 1500] +165
AM/FM Compact Disc Player +170
Air Conditioning[Opt on Ram Van, Ram Van Ext] +445
Aluminum/Alloy Wheels +170
Anti-Lock Brakes +270
Cruise Control +105
Keyless Entry System +95
Power Door Locks +105
Power Drivers Seat +155
Power Mirrors +55
Power Windows +105
Premium Sound System +205
Rear Heater +115
Rear Window Defroster +85
Sunscreen Glass +140

STRATUS 1998

The 2.4-liter engine with automatic transmission is now standard on the ES. New colors are available this year and numerous refinements were made to reduce noise and vibration.

RATINGS (SCALE OF 1-10)

Overall	Safety	Reliability	Performance	Comfort	Value
7.3	6.3	7.9	6.4	7.8	8.1

Category C

4 Dr ES Sdn	9955	11925
4 Dr STD Sdn	8410	10075

OPTIONS FOR STRATUS

4 cyl 2.4 L Engine[Std on ES] +245
6 cyl 2.5 L Engine +370
Auto 4-Speed Transmission[Std on ES] +575
AM/FM Compact Disc Player +190
Anti-Lock Brakes +325
Cruise Control[Std on ES] +120
Heated Power Mirrors[Std on ES] +55
Keyless Entry System +100
Leather Seats +340
Power Door Locks[Std on ES] +140
Power Drivers Seat +165
Power Sunroof +365
Power Windows[Std on ES] +175

VIPER 1998

Tubular, stainless steel exhaust manifolds help reduce emissions and weight. Silver Metallic paint is a new option and the powerful Dodge gets a passenger airbag cutoff switch and second-generation depowered airbags.

Category K

2 Dr GTS Cpe	50245	57600
2 Dr RT/10 Conv	48375	55460

OPTIONS FOR VIPER

Dual Painted Stripes +820

DODGE 97

Model Description	Trade-in Value	Market Value	Model Description	Trade-in Value	Market Value

1997 DODGE

AVENGER 1997

Front and rear styling is updated, while ES models lose the standard V6 engine. The V6 is available on base and ES models, and includes 17-inch wheels and tires on the ES. New colors inside and out and two additional speakers with cassette stereos further broaden the appeal of this roomy coupe.

RATINGS (SCALE OF 1-10)

Overall	Safety	Reliability	Performance	Comfort	Value
6.8	7.4	6.7	7.6	7.6	4.9

Category F

	Trade-in	Market
2 Dr ES Cpe	9975	11930
2 Dr STD Cpe	8340	9975

OPTIONS FOR AVENGER

6 cyl 2.5 L Engine +345
Auto 4-Speed Transmission +310
Air Conditioning[Std on ES] +375
Aluminum/Alloy Wheels[Std on ES] +135
Anti-Lock Brakes[Std on ES] +290
Compact Disc W/fm/tape +225
Cruise Control[Std on ES] +100
Keyless Entry System +80
Leather Seats +285
Power Door Locks +90
Power Drivers Seat +110
Power Sunroof +300
Power Windows +105

CARAVAN 1997

Traction control is a new option, so long as you get LE or ES trim, and an enhanced accident response system will automatically unlock the doors and illuminate the interior when an airbag deploys. Appearance and equipment refinements complete the modest changes to this best-in-class minivan.

RATINGS (SCALE OF 1-10)

Overall	Safety	Reliability	Performance	Comfort	Value
7	6.4	6.6	6.6	7.4	8.1

Category G

	Trade-in	Market
2 Dr ES Pass. Van	13870	16435
2 Dr Grand Pass. Van	10255	12150
2 Dr Grand ES Pass. Van	14230	16865
2 Dr Grand ES 4WD Pass. Van	15865	18795
2 Dr Grand LE Pass. Van	13920	16495
2 Dr Grand LE 4WD Pass. Van	15585	18465
2 Dr Grand SE Pass. Van	11415	13525
2 Dr Grand SE 4WD Pass. Van	13695	16225
2 Dr LE Pass. Van	13560	16065
2 Dr SE Pass. Van	10970	13000
2 Dr STD Pass. Van	9535	11295

OPTIONS FOR CARAVAN

6 cyl 3.0 L Engine +310
6 cyl 3.3 L Engine[Opt on Grand,Grand SE,SE,STD] +410
6 cyl 3.8 L Engine[Opt on ES,LE] +185
Auto 4-Speed Transmission[Opt on Grand,STD] +110
Sport Handling Pkg +425
7 Passenger Seating[Opt on STD] +235
Air Conditioning[Opt on Grand,Grand SE,SE,STD] +365
Aluminum/Alloy Wheels[Std on ES,Grand ES] +145
Anti-Lock Brakes[Opt on Grand,STD] +260
Auto Load Leveling +105
Captain Chairs (4) +275
Child Seats (2) +115
Compact Disc W/fm/tape +200
Cruise Control[Opt on Grand,STD] +95
Dual Air Conditioning +410
Keyless Entry System[Opt on Grand SE,SE] +85
Leather Seats +350
Luggage Rack +70
Power Door Locks[Opt on Grand,Grand SE,SE,STD] +105
Power Drivers Seat +125
Power Windows[Opt on Grand SE,SE] +110
Premium Sound System +155
Sliding Driver Side Door[Opt on Grand,Grand SE,SE, STD] +235
Traction Control System +120

DAKOTA 1997

What's new? Almost the entire truck, that's what. Powertrains are carried over, but everything else is new. Distinctions? Tightest turning circle in class, roomiest cabs and dual airbags are standard. Faux pas? No third door option, and the passenger airbag cannot be deactivated, so a rear-facing child seat is out of the question unless you cram it into the rear of the Club Cab.

RATINGS (SCALE OF 1-10)

Overall	Safety	Reliability	Performance	Comfort	Value
N/A	7.1	8.3	7	7.1	N/A

Category G

	Trade-in	Market
2 Dr SLT Ext Cab SB	10765	12755
2 Dr SLT 4WD Ext Cab SB	12845	15215
2 Dr SLT Std Cab LB	9445	11190
2 Dr SLT Std Cab SB	9170	10865
2 Dr SLT 4WD Std Cab SB	11965	14180
2 Dr STD Ext Cab SB	10200	12085
2 Dr STD 4WD Ext Cab SB	12170	14415
2 Dr STD Std Cab LB	8250	9775
2 Dr STD Std Cab SB	7970	9445
2 Dr STD 4WD Std Cab SB	10660	12635
2 Dr Sport Ext Cab SB	10215	12105
2 Dr Sport 4WD Ext Cab SB	12285	14555

Don't forget to refer to the Mileage Adjustment Table at the back of this book!

Model Description	Trade-in Value	Market Value	Model Description	Trade-in Value	Market Value
2 Dr Sport Std Cab LB	8805	10430	*Category E*		
2 Dr Sport Std Cab SB	8525	10105	2 Dr Highline Cpe	6190	7670
2 Dr Sport 4WD Std Cab SB	11360	13460	4 Dr Highline Sdn	6285	7790
			2 Dr STD Cpe	5395	6685
			4 Dr STD Sdn	5490	6800
			2 Dr Sport Cpe	6335	7850
			4 Dr Sport Sdn	6430	7965

OPTIONS FOR DAKOTA
6 cyl 3.9 L Engine +225
8 cyl 5.2 L Engine +375
Auto 4-Speed Transmission +425
Air Conditioning[Std on SLT] +365
Anti-Lock Brakes +260
Camper/Towing Package +135
Compact Disc W/fm/tape +200
Cruise Control +95
Keyless Entry System +85
Limited Slip Diff +125
Power Door Locks +105
Power Windows +110
Skid Plates +60
Velour/Cloth Seats[Opt on STD, Std Cab LB] +95

OPTIONS FOR NEON
4 cyl 2.0 L DOHC Engine +65
Auto 3-Speed Transmission +260
Competition Pkg +605
AM/FM Compact Disc Player +195
Air Conditioning[Opt on STD] +370
Aluminum/Alloy Wheels +150
Anti-Lock Brakes +295
Child Seat (1) +50
Cruise Control +100
Keyless Entry System +75
Power Door Locks +110
Power Moonroof +260
Power Windows +120
Tilt Steering Wheel +65

INTREPID 1997

Few changes as first-generation Intrepid enters final year of production. A Sport Group including the 3.5-liter V6 engine is optional on base models, which also get an upgraded cassette stereo standard. Bolt-on wheel covers debut, and a new exterior color is introduced. Automatic transmissions get new software.

RATINGS (SCALE OF 1-10)

Overall	Safety	Reliability	Performance	Comfort	Value
8.2	7.1	7.5	8.4	8.6	9.3

Category B

4 Dr ES Sdn	10565	12750
4 Dr STD Sdn	8985	10845

OPTIONS FOR INTREPID
6 cyl 3.5 L Engine[Std on ES] +85
Anti-Lock Brakes[Std on ES] +300
Climate Control for AC +75
Compact Disc W/fm/tape +165
Dual Power Seats +175
Keyless Entry System[Std on ES] +80
Power Moonroof +435
Premium Sound System +165
Traction Control System +80

NEON 1997

Sport trim level disappears in favor of Sport Package for Highline models. Twin-cam engine is now optional on Highline models. Federal side-impact standards are met for the first time. More work has been done to quiet the Neon's boisterous demeanor.

RATINGS (SCALE OF 1-10)

Overall	Safety	Reliability	Performance	Comfort	Value
7.1	6	7.6	7.4	7.6	6.8

RAM PICKUP 1997

No major changes to this popular truck for 1997. Refinements include available leather seating and wood-grain trim on SLT models, optional remote keyless entry, and standard deep-tinted quarter glass on Club Cab models. Newly available is a combination CD/cassette stereo. Items from the 1996 Indy 500 Special Edition are available in a new Sport Package upgrade. Fresh interior and exterior colors sum up the changes this year.

RATINGS (SCALE OF 1-10)

Overall	Safety	Reliability	Performance	Comfort	Value
N/A	5.9	8.2	7	8	N/A

RAM 1500

Category H

2 Dr LT Std Cab LB	10430	12245
2 Dr LT 4WD Std Cab LB	12405	14565
2 Dr LT Std Cab SB	10250	12040
2 Dr LT 4WD Std Cab SB	12190	14315
2 Dr Laramie SLT Ext Cab LB	12865	15105
2 Dr Laramie SLT 4WD Ext Cab LB		
	14525	17055
2 Dr Laramie SLT Ext Cab SB	12695	14910
2 Dr Laramie SLT 4WD Ext Cab SB		
	14330	16825
2 Dr Laramie SLT Std Cab LB	10765	12760
2 Dr Laramie SLT 4WD Std Cab LB		
	13375	15705
2 Dr Laramie SLT Std Cab SB	10895	12865

Model Description	Trade-in Value	Market Value
2 Dr Laramie SLT 4WD Std Cab SB	13170	15465
2 Dr SS/T Std Cab SB	11990	14280
2 Dr ST Ext Cab LB	11680	13700
2 Dr ST 4WD Ext Cab LB	14035	16480
2 Dr ST Ext Cab SB	11210	13215
2 Dr ST 4WD Ext Cab SB	12730	15340
2 Dr WS Std Cab LB	9000	10620
2 Dr WS Std Cab SB	8720	10320

RAM 2500

Category H

Model Description	Trade-in Value	Market Value
2 Dr LT Std Cab LB	11860	13930
2 Dr LT 4WD Std Cab LB	13745	16140
2 Dr Laramie SLT Ext Cab LB	14540	17075
2 Dr Laramie SLT 4WD Ext Cab LB	15680	18535
2 Dr Laramie SLT Ext Cab SB	14415	16925
2 Dr Laramie SLT 4WD Ext Cab SB	15855	18655
2 Dr Laramie SLT Std Cab LB	13440	15785
2 Dr Laramie SLT 4WD Std Cab LB	13950	16575
2 Dr ST Ext Cab LB	12510	14895
2 Dr ST 4WD Ext Cab LB	15050	17675
2 Dr ST Ext Cab SB	12685	14995
2 Dr ST 4WD Ext Cab SB	14335	16825
2 Dr ST Std Cab LB	11195	13385
2 Dr ST 4WD Std Cab LB	13980	16420

RAM 3500

Category H

Model Description	Trade-in Value	Market Value
2 Dr LT Std Cab LB	12755	14975
2 Dr LT 4WD Std Cab LB	14290	16780
2 Dr Laramie SLT Ext Cab LB	15255	17915
2 Dr Laramie SLT 4WD Ext Cab LB	16795	19720
2 Dr Laramie SLT Std Cab LB	14225	16705
2 Dr Laramie SLT 4WD Std Cab LB	15760	18505
2 Dr ST Ext Cab LB	14185	16655
2 Dr ST 4WD Ext Cab LB	15725	18465
2 Dr ST Std Cab LB	13140	15430
2 Dr ST 4WD Std Cab LB	14675	17230

OPTIONS FOR RAM PICKUP

10 cyl 8.0 L Engine +435
6 cyl 5.9 L Turbodsl Engine +1935
8 cyl 5.2 L Engine +250
8 cyl 5.9 L Engine +195
Auto 4-Speed Transmission +425
Sport Appearance Group +350
Air Conditioning[Opt on LT,ST,WS] +365
Aluminum/Alloy Wheels[Std on SS/T] +140
Anti-Lock Brakes +220
Camper/Towing Package +150
Chrome Wheels[Std on Laramie SLT] +135
Compact Disc W/fm/tape +140
Cruise Control[Opt on LT,ST,WS] +85
Keyless Entry System +80
Leather Seats +445
Limited Slip Diff +120
Power Drivers Seat +125
Premium Sound System +170
Rear Step Bumper[Std on Laramie SLT,SS/T] +65
Skid Plates[Std on Ram 3500 ST 4WD Ext Cab LB] +50

RAM VAN/WAGON 1997

New this year are wider cargo doors, upgraded stereo systems, and an improved ignition switch with anti-theft protection. Front quarter vent windows disappear for 1997, and underhood service points feature colored identification.

RATINGS (SCALE OF 1-10)

Overall	Safety	Reliability	Performance	Comfort	Value
N/A	6.5	7.8	6.2	6.9	N/A

VAN

Category H

Model Description	Trade-in Value	Market Value
2 Dr 1500 Ram Van	9350	10980
2 Dr 1500 Ram Van Ext	9705	11395
2 Dr 2500 Ram Van	9790	11495
2 Dr 2500 Ram Van Ext	9810	11520
2 Dr 2500 Maxi Ram Van Ext	10695	12560
2 Dr 3500 Ram Van Ext	11200	13150
2 Dr 3500 Maxi Ram Van Ext	11505	13510

WAGON

Category H

Model Description	Trade-in Value	Market Value
2 Dr 1500 Ram Wagon	11210	13160
2 Dr 1500 SLT Ram Wagon	12650	14855
2 Dr 2500 Ram Wagon Ext	12420	14585
2 Dr 2500 SLT Ram Wagon Ext	13410	15750
2 Dr 3500 Ram Wagon Ext	12640	14840
2 Dr 3500 Maxi Ram Wagon Ext	13600	15970
2 Dr 3500 SLT Ram Wagon Ext	14360	16860
2 Dr 3500 SLT Maxi Ram Wagon Ext	15320	17990

OPTIONS FOR RAM VAN/WAGON

8 cyl 5.2 L Engine[Std on 3500,2500 Ram Wagon Ext] +250
8 cyl 5.9 L Engine +195
Auto 4-Speed Transmission[Std on 3500,Ram Wagon Ext] +135
Tradesman Upfitter Pkg +445
AM/FM Compact Disc Player +140
Air Conditioning[Opt on Ram Van,Ram Van Ext] +365
Aluminum/Alloy Wheels +140
Anti-Lock Brakes +220
Camper/Towing Package +150
Chrome Bumpers[Std on SLT] +50

Don't forget to refer to the Mileage Adjustment Table at the back of this book!

DODGE 97-96

Model Description	Trade-in Value	Market Value	Model Description	Trade-in Value	Market Value

Chrome Wheels[Opt on STD] +135
Cruise Control[Opt on Maxi,STD] +85
Dual Air Conditioning[Opt on 1500,2500,Maxi,STD] +575
Keyless Entry System[Opt on Maxi,STD] +80
Limited Slip Diff +120
Power Door Locks[Opt on Maxi,STD] +85
Power Drivers Seat +125
Power Windows[Opt on Maxi,STD] +85
Premium Sound System +170

STRATUS   1997

Subtle styling revisions are the most obvious change to the Stratus for 1997. Sound systems have been improved, rear seat heat ducts benefit from improved flow, and the optional 2.4-liter engine runs quieter. New colors and a revised console round out changes.

RATINGS (SCALE OF 1-10)

Overall	Safety	Reliability	Performance	Comfort	Value
N/A	6.2	6.9	N/A	7.8	7.4

Category C

4 Dr ES Sdn	8430	10170
4 Dr STD Sdn	7610	9185

OPTIONS FOR STRATUS

4 cyl 2.4 L Engine +195
6 cyl 2.5 L Engine +405
Auto 4-Speed Transmission +405
Anti-Lock Brakes[Std on ES] +265
Child Seat (1) +55
Compact Disc W/fm/tape +145
Cruise Control[Std on ES] +95
Keyless Entry System +85
Leather Seats +275
Lighted Entry System +70
Power Door Locks[Std on ES] +115
Power Windows[Std on ES] +140

VIPER   1997

One new color, flame red, with or without white stripes, is available for 1997. Silver, sparkle gold or yellow gold wheels come with red Vipers. The original blue with white stripes paint scheme is available as an option, as are last year's standard polished aluminum wheels. The RT/10 roadster is set to return later this year, with dual airbags, power windows and door locks, and the 450-horsepower V10 from the GTS. Also set to debut on the revamped drop top are the four-wheel independent suspension and adjustable pedals from the GTS.

Category K

2 Dr GTS Cpe	42050	48250
2 Dr RT/10 Conv	40475	46440

OPTIONS FOR VIPER

Blue Pearlcoat Paint +535
Air Conditioning[Std on GTS] +505
Hardtop Roof +1115

1996 DODGE

AVENGER   1996

Dodge's sporty coupe gets a panic mode for the remote keyless entry system and a HomeLink transmitter that will open your garage door. ES models get new seat fabric, and three new colors are on the roster.

RATINGS (SCALE OF 1-10)

Overall	Safety	Reliability	Performance	Comfort	Value
6.5	7.4	6.3	7.6	7.6	3.7

Category F

2 Dr ES Cpe	9080	10830
2 Dr STD Cpe	7095	8460

OPTIONS FOR AVENGER

Auto 4-Speed Transmission[Std on ES] +235
Air Conditioning[Std on ES] +305
Anti-Lock Brakes[Std on ES] +235
Compact Disc W/fm/tape +185
Cruise Control[Std on ES] +80
Keyless Entry System +65
Leather Seats +230
Power Door Locks +75
Power Drivers Seat +90
Power Sunroof +245
Power Windows +85
Premium Sound System +140

CARAVAN   1996

A complete redesign yields a cavernous interior, best-in-class driveability, and new innovations such as the optional driver's side passenger door. And although the all-wheel drive version is discontinued for now, Caravan dethrones the Ford Windstar and once again reigns as king of the minivans.

RATINGS (SCALE OF 1-10)

Overall	Safety	Reliability	Performance	Comfort	Value
6.9	6.2	5.2	6.6	7.4	8.9

Category G

2 Dr ES Pass. Van	11630	14025
2 Dr Grand Pass. Van	8815	10630
2 Dr Grand ES Pass. Van	11860	14305
2 Dr Grand LE Pass. Van	11585	13970
2 Dr Grand SE Pass. Van	9860	11895
2 Dr LE Pass. Van	11355	13690
2 Dr SE Pass. Van	9535	11500
2 Dr STD Pass. Van	8245	9940

OPTIONS FOR CARAVAN

6 cyl 3.0 L Engine +265
6 cyl 3.3 L Engine[Opt on Grand SE,SE] +315
6 cyl 3.3 L CNG Engine +320
6 cyl 3.8 L Engine[Opt on LE, ES] +160

Don't forget to refer to the Mileage Adjustment Table at the back of this book!

DODGE 96

Model Description	Trade-in Value	Market Value	Model Description	Trade-in Value	Market Value

Auto 4-Speed Transmission[Opt on SE,STD] +75
7 Passenger Seating[Opt on STD] +190
Air Conditioning[Opt on Grand,Grand SE,SE,STD] +300
Anti-Lock Brakes[Opt on SE,STD] +210
Captain Chairs (4) +225
Child Seats (2) +90
Compact Disc W/fm/tape +160
Cruise Control[Opt on Grand,STD] +75
Dual Air Conditioning +335
Infinity Sound System +160
Keyless Entry System[Std on LE] +70
Leather Seats +285
Luggage Rack +60
Power Door Locks[Opt on Grand,Grand SE,SE,STD] +85
Power Drivers Seat +105
Power Windows[Opt on Grand SE,SE] +90
Sliding Driver Side Door +190

DAKOTA 1996

America's first midsized pickup gets a more powerful standard four-cylinder engine, revised sound system, and three new colors.

RATINGS (SCALE OF 1-10)

Overall	Safety	Reliability	Performance	Comfort	Value
N/A	6.5	7.7	7	7.1	N/A

Category G
2 Dr SLT Ext Cab SB	8375	10095
2 Dr SLT 4WD Ext Cab SB	10175	12270
2 Dr SLT Std Cab LB	7430	8960
2 Dr SLT 4WD Std Cab LB	9860	11890
2 Dr SLT Std Cab SB	7175	8655
2 Dr SLT 4WD Std Cab SB	9585	11560
2 Dr STD Ext Cab SB	8270	9970
2 Dr STD 4WD Ext Cab SB	9980	12030
2 Dr STD Std Cab LB	6020	7260
2 Dr STD 4WD Std Cab LB	9310	11225
2 Dr STD Std Cab SB	6745	8135
2 Dr STD 4WD Std Cab SB	9035	10895
2 Dr Sport Ext Cab SB	7710	9300
2 Dr Sport 4WD Ext Cab SB	9595	11570
2 Dr Sport Std Cab SB	6140	7405
2 Dr Sport 4WD Std Cab SB	8585	10355
2 Dr WS Std Cab LB	6015	7255
2 Dr WS 4WD Std Cab LB	8520	10275
2 Dr WS Std Cab SB	5715	6890
2 Dr WS 4WD Std Cab SB	8200	9890

OPTIONS FOR DAKOTA

6 cyl 3.9 L Engine +250
8 cyl 5.2 L Engine +270
Auto 4-Speed Transmission +335
AM/FM Compact Disc Player +115
Air Conditioning[Std on SLT] +300
Aluminum/Alloy Wheels[Opt on SLT] +120

Anti-Lock Brakes +210
Camper/Towing Package +110
Chrome Bumpers[Std on SLT] +55
Chrome Wheels[Std on SLT] +60
Cruise Control[Opt on Sport,STD] +75
Limited Slip Diff +100
Power Door Locks +85
Power Windows +90
Premium Sound System +125
Velour/Cloth Seats[Std on SLT,Sport,Ext Cab] +75

INTREPID 1996

ES carries over, but the base model gets several improvements to remain competitive with the new Ford Taurus. ES styling cues and 16-inch wheels come standard on the base Intrepid. New colors and seat fabrics update this full-size sedan, and all Intrepids get noise, vibration and harshness improvements.

RATINGS (SCALE OF 1-10)

Overall	Safety	Reliability	Performance	Comfort	Value
8.1	7.1	7.1	8.4	8.6	9.1

Category B
4 Dr ES Sdn	8795	10890
4 Dr STD Sdn	7320	9065

OPTIONS FOR INTREPID

6 cyl 3.5 L Engine +235
AM/FM Compact Disc Player +120
Aluminum/Alloy Wheels +120
*Anti-Lock Brakes[Std on ES] +245 ***
Child Seat (1) +35
Climate Control for AC +60
Keyless Entry System +65
Leather Seats +250
Power Drivers Seat +115
Power Moonroof +355
Power Passenger Seat +130
Traction Control System +65

NEON 1996

A raft of improvements make the sprightly Neon even more attractive to compact buyers. Base models get more equipment, and the ugly gray bumpers are history. A base coupe is newly available. Interior noise levels are supposedly subdued this year. ABS is available across the board this year.

RATINGS (SCALE OF 1-10)

Overall	Safety	Reliability	Performance	Comfort	Value
6.7	5.9	6.7	7.4	7.6	6.1

Category E
2 Dr Highline Cpe	4705	5995
4 Dr Highline Sdn	4780	6100
2 Dr STD Cpe	3985	5080
4 Dr STD Sdn	4185	5335

Don't forget to refer to the Mileage Adjustment Table at the back of this book!

Model Description	Trade-in Value	Market Value
2 Dr Sport Cpe	5605	7150
4 Dr Sport Sdn	5260	6710

OPTIONS FOR NEON
4 cyl 2.0 L DOHC Engine[Std on Sport] +55
Auto 3-Speed Transmission +200
AM/FM Compact Disc Player +160
Air Conditioning +305
Anti-Lock Brakes[Std on Sport] +245
Child Seat (1) +40
Cruise Control +85
Power Door Locks[Std on Sport] +90
Power Steering[Opt on STD] +95
Power Windows +95
Rear Spoiler[Std on Sport] +80
Tilt Steering Wheel[Std on Sport] +55

RAM PICKUP   1996

Best-selling Ram has a more powerful diesel engine option for 1996, an available "Camper Special" suspension package, and new wheels on the 1500 SLT and Sport. Two new colors, a revised sound system, and easy-to-find yellow under-hood service point identification all debut for 1996.

RATINGS (SCALE OF 1-10)

Overall	Safety	Reliability	Performance	Comfort	Value
N/A	N/A	7.8	7	8	N/A

RAM 1500

Category H

Model Description	Trade-in Value	Market Value
2 Dr LT Std Cab LB	9315	10990
2 Dr LT 4WD Std Cab LB	11315	13355
2 Dr LT Std Cab SB	9150	10795
2 Dr LT 4WD Std Cab SB	11120	13120
2 Dr Laramie SLT Ext Cab LB	11735	13845
2 Dr Laramie SLT 4WD Ext Cab LB	12590	14855
2 Dr Laramie SLT Ext Cab SB	11290	13320
2 Dr Laramie SLT 4WD Ext Cab SB	12410	14645
2 Dr Laramie SLT Std Cab LB	10120	11940
2 Dr Laramie SLT 4WD Std Cab LB	12005	14165
2 Dr Laramie SLT Std Cab SB	9965	11760
2 Dr Laramie SLT 4WD Std Cab SB	11820	13950
2 Dr ST Ext Cab LB	10910	12875
2 Dr ST 4WD Ext Cab LB	12375	14600
2 Dr ST Ext Cab SB	10745	12680
2 Dr ST 4WD Ext Cab SB	12180	14375
2 Dr WS Std Cab LB	8510	10045
2 Dr WS Std Cab SB	8355	9860

RAM 2500

Category H

Model Description	Trade-in Value	Market Value
2 Dr LT Std Cab LB	10110	11935
2 Dr LT 4WD Std Cab LB	11685	13790
2 Dr Laramie SLT Ext Cab LB	13275	15665
2 Dr Laramie SLT 4WD Ext Cab LB	14915	17600
2 Dr Laramie SLT Ext Cab SB	13160	15530
2 Dr Laramie SLT 4WD Ext Cab SB	14970	17665
2 Dr Laramie SLT Std Cab LB	11645	13740
2 Dr Laramie SLT 4WD Std Cab LB	13050	15400
2 Dr ST Ext Cab LB	12150	14335
2 Dr ST 4WD Ext Cab LB	13625	16080
2 Dr ST Ext Cab SB	12030	14200
2 Dr ST 4WD Ext Cab SB	13510	15945
2 Dr ST Std Cab LB	10340	12205
2 Dr ST 4WD Std Cab LB	11915	14060

RAM 3500

Category H

Model Description	Trade-in Value	Market Value
2 Dr LT Std Cab LB	12310	14530
2 Dr LT 4WD Std Cab LB	13940	16450
2 Dr Laramie SLT Ext Cab LB	14845	17520
2 Dr Laramie SLT 4WD Ext Cab LB	16405	19360
2 Dr Laramie SLT Std Cab LB	13810	16300
2 Dr Laramie SLT 4WD Std Cab LB	15505	18295
2 Dr ST Ext Cab LB	13750	16225
2 Dr ST 4WD Ext Cab LB	15235	17975
2 Dr ST Std Cab LB	12700	14985
2 Dr ST 4WD Std Cab LB	14330	16910

OPTIONS FOR RAM PICKUP
10 cyl 8.0 L Engine +170
6 cyl 5.9 L Turbodsl Engine +1500
8 cyl 5.2 L Engine +220
8 cyl 5.9 L Engine +155
Auto 4-Speed Transmission +335
Heavy Duty Pkg +420
AM/FM Compact Disc Player +115
Air Conditioning[Opt on LT,ST,WS] +300
Aluminum/Alloy Wheels[Std on Laramie SLT] +115
Anti-Lock Brakes +180
Bed Liner +85
Camper/Towing Package +120
Chrome Bumpers[Opt on ST] +40
Chrome Wheels[Opt on LT,ST] +110
Cruise Control[Opt on LT,ST,WS] +70
Limited Slip Diff +95
Power Door Locks[Opt on LT,ST] +70
Power Drivers Seat +105
Premium Sound System +140

DODGE 96

Rear Step Bumper[Std on Laramie SLT] +50
Skid Plates +40
Split Front Bench Seat +125

RAM VAN/WAGON 1996

New interior and exterior colors, a revised stereo system, and improved ventilation freshen this ancient design. Also new: a higher GVWR and new cruise control switches.

RATINGS (SCALE OF 1-10)

Overall	Safety	Reliability	Performance	Comfort	Value
N/A	6.5	7.6	6.2	6.9	N/A

RAM VAN
Category H

	Trade-in	Market
2 Dr 1500 Ram Van	9115	10755
2 Dr 1500 Ram Van Ext	9460	11165
2 Dr 2500 Ram Van	9495	11200
2 Dr 2500 Ram Van Ext	9525	11240
2 Dr 2500 Maxi Ram Van Ext	10375	12245
2 Dr 3500 Ram Van Ext	10875	12835
2 Dr 3500 Maxi Ram Van Ext	11190	13205

RAM WAGON
Category H

	Trade-in	Market
2 Dr 1500 Ram Wagon	9460	11165
2 Dr 1500 SLT Ram Wagon	10865	12825
2 Dr 2500 Ram Wagon Ext	10435	12315
2 Dr 2500 SLT Ram Wagon Ext	11335	13375
2 Dr 3500 Ram Wagon Ext	11020	13005
2 Dr 3500 Maxi Ram Wagon Ext	11370	13420
2 Dr 3500 SLT Ram Wagon Ext	12070	14240
2 Dr 3500 SLT Maxi Ram Wagon Ext	12960	15295

OPTIONS FOR RAM VAN/WAGON
8 cyl 5.2 L Engine[Std on B350] +220
8 cyl 5.9 L Engine +155
Auto 4-Speed Transmission[Std on B350] +90
AM/FM Compact Disc Player +115
Air Conditioning[Std on B350 Ram Wagon] +300
Anti-Lock Brakes[Opt on B350,Maxi,Ram Van,Ram Van Ext] +180
Camper/Towing Package +120
Chrome Bumpers[Std on SLT] +40
Chrome Wheels[Opt on STD] +110
Cruise Control[Opt on Maxi,STD] +70
Dual Air Conditioning[Opt on B150,B250,Maxi,STD] +470
Keyless Entry System[Std on SLT,SLT Maxi] +65
Limited Slip Diff +95
Power Door Locks[Opt on Maxi,STD] +70
Power Drivers Seat +105
Power Windows[Opt on Maxi,STD] +70
Premium Sound System +140
Velour/Cloth Seats[Opt on B150,STD] +40

STEALTH 1996

Final year for slow-selling Japanese-built sports car. A new rear spoiler and body-color roof mark the 1996 model. A chrome 18-inch wheel package is available with Pirelli P-Zero tires and base models get an optional Infinity sound system.

RATINGS (SCALE OF 1-10)

Overall	Safety	Reliability	Performance	Comfort	Value
N/A	N/A	7.8	N/A	N/A	N/A

Category F

	Trade-in	Market
2 Dr R/T Hbk	13425	16010
2 Dr R/T Turbo 4WD Hbk	16775	20010
2 Dr STD Hbk	11860	14145

OPTIONS FOR STEALTH
Auto 4-Speed Transmission +320
AM/FM Compact Disc Player +170
Anti-Lock Brakes +235
Chrome Wheels +215
Cruise Control[Std on 4WD] +80
Keyless Entry System[Std on 4WD] +65
Leather Seats +230
Power Door Locks[Std on 4WD] +75
Power Drivers Seat +90
Power Sunroof +245
Power Windows[Std on 4WD] +85

STRATUS 1996

Excellent midsized sedan gets a more responsive torque converter when equipped with the 2.5-liter V6. New colors and a power sunroof are also new for 1996.

RATINGS (SCALE OF 1-10)

Overall	Safety	Reliability	Performance	Comfort	Value
N/A	5.9	5.6	N/A	7.8	7.4

Category C

	Trade-in	Market
4 Dr ES Sdn	6920	8565
4 Dr STD Sdn	6235	7715

OPTIONS FOR STRATUS
4 cyl 2.4 L Engine +165
6 cyl 2.5 L Engine +365
Auto 4-Speed Transmission +300
AM/FM Compact Disc Player +130
Anti-Lock Brakes[Std on ES] +215
Child Seat (1) +45
Keyless Entry System +70
Leather Seats +225
Lighted Entry System +60
Power Door Locks[Std on ES] +95
Power Drivers Seat +110
Power Sunroof +245
Power Windows[Std on ES] +115
Premium Sound System +140

Model Description	Trade-in Value	Market Value	Model Description	Trade-in Value	Market Value

VIPER 1996

Final year for Viper in current form. More power is eked from the V10 engine via a low-restriction rear outlet exhaust system, and an optional hardtop with sliding side curtains is available. Five-spoke aluminum wheels and three exterior styling themes replace the trim on the 1995 Viper. GTS coupe begins production when convertibles have completed their run. Scheduled to pace the 1996 Indianapolis 500, the GTS will arrive in showrooms with dual airbags and air conditioning.

Category K

	Trade-in	Market
2 Dr GTS Cpe	38070	43710
2 Dr RT/10 Conv	33845	38860

OPTIONS FOR VIPER

Air Conditioning[Std on GTS] +410
Hardtop Roof +910

1995 DODGE

AVENGER 1995

New coupe is late replacement for Daytona. Based on a Mitsubishi Galant platform, the Avenger is about the size of a Camry coupe. Base and ES models are available. Base cars have a 2.0-liter, 140-horsepower four-cylinder engine underhood. ES gets a Mitsubishi-built 2.5-liter V6 making 155 horsepower. An automatic is the only transmission available on the ES. ABS is optional on base models; standard on ES. All Avengers have dual airbags, height-adjustable driver's seat, split-folding rear seat, rear defroster, and tilt steering wheel.

RATINGS (SCALE OF 1-10)

Overall	Safety	Reliability	Performance	Comfort	Value
7.4	8.4	7.2	7.6	7.6	6.3

Category F

	Trade-in	Market
2 Dr ES Cpe	7525	9120
2 Dr Highline Cpe	5890	7140

OPTIONS FOR AVENGER

Auto 4-Speed Transmission[Std on ES] +205
AM/FM Compact Disc Player +140
Air Conditioning[Std on ES] +250
Anti-Lock Brakes[Std on ES] +195
Cruise Control[Std on ES] +65
Infinity Sound System +185
Keyless Entry System +55
Leather Seats +190
Power Door Locks +60
Power Drivers Seat +70
Power Sunroof +200
Power Windows +70
Premium Sound System +115

CARAVAN 1995

Newly optional is a 3.3-liter V6 engine designed to operate on compressed natural gas. Sport and SE decor packages are available this year. The five-speed manual transmission, available only with the four-cylinder engine, has been canceled.

RATINGS (SCALE OF 1-10)

Overall	Safety	Reliability	Performance	Comfort	Value
7.8	8.2	6.6	7.4	8.3	8.5

Category G

	Trade-in	Market
2 Dr ES Pass. Van	8545	10545
2 Dr Grand Pass. Van	7030	8675
2 Dr Grand ES Pass. Van	8650	10675
2 Dr Grand ES 4WD Pass. Van	9375	11565
2 Dr Grand LE Pass. Van	8470	10455
2 Dr Grand LE 4WD Pass. Van	9195	11345
2 Dr Grand SE Pass. Van	7395	9125
2 Dr Grand SE 4WD Pass. Van	7980	9845
2 Dr LE Pass. Van	8365	10325
2 Dr SE Pass. Van	7125	8790
2 Dr STD Cargo Van	6130	7565
2 Dr STD Cargo Van Ext	6695	8260
2 Dr STD Pass. Van	6135	7570

OPTIONS FOR CARAVAN

6 cyl 3.0 L Engine[Opt on STD] +215
6 cyl 3.3 L Engine[Opt on ES,LE,SE] +70
6 cyl 3.3 L CNG Engine +260
6 cyl 3.8 L Engine +125
Auto 4-Speed Transmission[Opt on SE,Cargo Van, STD] +60
7 Passenger Seating[Opt on STD] +155
Air Conditioning[Opt on Grand,Grand SE,SE,STD] +245
Anti-Lock Brakes[Std on ES,Grand ES,Grand LE,LE,
    4WD] +175
Captain Chairs (4) +185
Child Seats (2) +75
Cruise Control[Opt on Grand,STD] +65
Dual Air Conditioning +275
Keyless Entry System[Opt on Grand SE,SE] +60
Leather Seats +235
Luggage Rack +50
Power Door Locks[Opt on Grand,Grand SE,SE,STD] +70
Power Drivers Seat +85
Power Windows +70
Premium Sound System +100

DAKOTA 1995

A 2WD Club Cab Sport is added to the model mix.

RATINGS (SCALE OF 1-10)

Overall	Safety	Reliability	Performance	Comfort	Value
N/A	7.1	7.7	7	7.1	N/A

Model Description	Trade-in Value	Market Value
Category G		
2 Dr SLT Ext Cab SB	6970	8600
2 Dr SLT 4WD Ext Cab SB	8610	10625
2 Dr SLT Std Cab LB	6400	7900
2 Dr SLT 4WD Std Cab LB	8195	10110
2 Dr SLT Std Cab SB	5880	7255
2 Dr SLT 4WD Std Cab SB	7955	9815
2 Dr STD Ext Cab SB	6900	8515
2 Dr STD 4WD Ext Cab SB	8425	10395
2 Dr STD Std Cab LB	6000	7405
2 Dr STD 4WD Std Cab LB	7740	9550
2 Dr STD Std Cab SB	5480	6760
2 Dr STD 4WD Std Cab SB	7475	9225
2 Dr Sport Ext Cab SB	6345	7830
2 Dr Sport 4WD Ext Cab SB	8010	9885
2 Dr Sport Std Cab SB	4955	6110
2 Dr Sport 4WD Std Cab SB	7115	8780
2 Dr WS Std Cab LB	5215	6435
2 Dr WS 4WD Std Cab LB	7125	8790
2 Dr WS Std Cab SB	4645	5735
2 Dr WS 4WD Std Cab SB	6820	8415

OPTIONS FOR DAKOTA
6 cyl 3.9 L Engine +205
8 cyl 5.2 L Engine +220
Auto 4-Speed Transmission +270
AM/FM Compact Disc Player +95
Air Conditioning[Std on SLT] +245
Anti-Lock Brakes +175
Camper/Towing Package +90
Chrome Wheels[Std on SLT] +50
Cruise Control[Std on SLT Ext Cab SB] +65
Limited Slip Diff +85
Power Door Locks +70
Power Windows +70
Premium Sound System +100
Rear Step Bumper[Opt on WS] +45
Sliding Rear Window[Std on SLT] +35
Velour/Cloth Seats[Std on SLT,Sport,Ext Cab] +65

INTREPID   1995

ABS is now standard on ES. Traction control is a new ES option.

RATINGS (SCALE OF 1-10)

Overall	Safety	Reliability	Performance	Comfort	Value
8	7.8	6.7	8.4	8.6	8.5

	Trade-in	Market
Category B		
4 Dr ES Sdn	6670	8460
4 Dr STD Sdn	5775	7325

OPTIONS FOR INTREPID
6 cyl 3.3 L FLEX Engine +45
6 cyl 3.5 L Engine +215
AM/FM Compact Disc Player +100
Anti-Lock Brakes[Std on ES] +200

Child Seat (1) +30
Climate Control for AC +50
Cruise Control[Std on ES] +65
Dual Power Seats +115
Keyless Entry System +50
Power Door Locks[Std on ES] +80
Power Drivers Seat +95
Power Moonroof +290
Power Windows[Std on ES] +85
Traction Control System +50

NEON   1995

This spunky Shadow replacement is cleverly designed, adequately powered, and cute to boot. Base, Highline and Sport models are available. Coupe and sedan body styles are offered. All except Sport Coupe have a 132-horsepower, 2.0-liter four-cylinder engine. Sport Coupe gets a 150-horsepower twin-cam edition of the base motor. Dual airbags are standard on all models; ABS is standard on Sport and optional on others. Integrated child seats are optional.

RATINGS (SCALE OF 1-10)

Overall	Safety	Reliability	Performance	Comfort	Value
6.5	5.6	5	7.4	7.6	6.9

	Trade-in	Market
Category E		
2 Dr Highline Cpe	4055	5330
4 Dr Highline Sdn	3865	5080
4 Dr STD Sdn	3270	4300
2 Dr Sport Cpe	4855	6385
4 Dr Sport Sdn	4390	5775

OPTIONS FOR NEON
4 cyl 2.0 L DOHC Engine[Std on Sport] +50
Auto 3-Speed Transmission +180
AM/FM Compact Disc Player +130
Air Conditioning +250
Anti-Lock Brakes[Std on Sport] +200
Child Seat (1) +35
Cruise Control +70
Power Door Locks[Std on Sport] +75
Power Steering[Opt on STD] +75
Power Windows +80
Premium Sound System +100
Rear Spoiler[Opt on Sdn] +65
Tilt Steering Wheel[Std on Sport] +45
Tinted Glass[Opt on STD] +30

RAM PICKUP   1995

A Club Cab model is added in 1500-, 2500-, and 3500-series levels with either two- or four-wheel drive. The Club Cab is available only in ST or Laramie SLT trim. Regular-cab models can be equipped with Sport trim midyear. Sport models have a sport suspension, chrome wheels, and a body-color grille with fog lights. Four-wheel ABS moves to the 3500 options list midyear.

Don't forget to refer to the Mileage Adjustment Table at the back of this book!

Model Description	Trade-in Value	Market Value

Model Description	Trade-in Value	Market Value

RATINGS (SCALE OF 1-10)

Overall	Safety	Reliability	Performance	Comfort	Value
N/A	N/A	7.5	7	8	N/A

RAM 1500

Category H

Model	Trade-in	Market
2 Dr LT Std Cab LB	7855	9355
2 Dr LT 4WD Std Cab LB	9440	11245
2 Dr LT Std Cab SB	7710	9185
2 Dr LT 4WD Std Cab SB	9405	11205
2 Dr Laramie SLT Ext Cab LB	10455	12450
2 Dr Laramie SLT 4WD Ext Cab LB	11500	13700
2 Dr Laramie SLT Ext Cab SB	10310	12285
2 Dr Laramie SLT 4WD Ext Cab SB	11425	13610
2 Dr Laramie SLT Std Cab LB	9090	10825
2 Dr Laramie SLT 4WD Std Cab LB	10680	12720
2 Dr Laramie SLT Std Cab SB	8945	10655
2 Dr Laramie SLT 4WD Std Cab SB	10645	12680
2 Dr ST Ext Cab LB	9385	11180
2 Dr ST 4WD Ext Cab LB	10660	12695
2 Dr ST Ext Cab SB	9240	11010
2 Dr ST 4WD Ext Cab SB	10585	12605
2 Dr WS Std Cab LB	6970	8300
2 Dr WS Std Cab SB	6830	8135

RAM 2500

Category H

Model	Trade-in	Market
2 Dr LT Std Cab LB	8825	10510
2 Dr LT 4WD Std Cab LB	10050	11970
2 Dr Laramie SLT Ext Cab LB	11465	13660
2 Dr Laramie SLT 4WD Ext Cab LB	12960	15440
2 Dr Laramie SLT 4WD Ext Cab SB	12685	15115
2 Dr Laramie SLT Std Cab LB	10215	12170
2 Dr Laramie SLT 4WD Std Cab LB	11440	13630
2 Dr ST Ext Cab LB	10470	12470
2 Dr ST 4WD Ext Cab LB	11630	13855
2 Dr ST Ext Cab SB	10365	12345
2 Dr ST 4WD Ext Cab SB	11525	13730
2 Dr ST Std Cab LB	9030	10760
2 Dr ST 4WD Std Cab LB	10255	12220
2 Dr Sport Ext Cab SB	11330	13500
2 Dr Sport 4WD Ext Cab SB	12620	15035

RAM 3500

Category H

Model	Trade-in	Market
2 Dr LT Std Cab LB	10750	12810
2 Dr LT 4WD Std Cab LB	12095	14410
2 Dr Laramie SLT Ext Cab LB	12915	15390
2 Dr Laramie SLT 4WD Ext Cab LB	14330	17070
2 Dr Laramie SLT Std Cab LB	12085	14395
2 Dr Laramie SLT 4WD Std Cab LB	13515	16100
2 Dr ST Ext Cab LB	11950	14235
2 Dr ST 4WD Ext Cab LB	13270	15805
2 Dr ST Std Cab LB	11105	13230

OPTIONS FOR RAM PICKUP

10 cyl 8.0 L Engine +140
6 cyl 5.9 L Turbodsl Engine +1225
8 cyl 5.2 L Engine +180
8 cyl 5.9 L Engine +135
Auto 4-Speed Transmission +275
Sport Appearance Grp +255
AM/FM Compact Disc Player +90
Air Conditioning[Std on Laramie SLT] +245
Aluminum/Alloy Wheels +95
Anti-Lock Brakes +145
Camper/Towing Package +100
Chrome Wheels[Opt on LT,ST] +90
Cruise Control[Std on Laramie SLT] +55
Limited Slip Diff +80
Power Door Locks[Opt on LT,ST] +55
Power Drivers Seat +85
Power Windows[Opt on ST] +55
Premium Sound System +115
Rear Step Bumper[Opt on Ram 3500,WS] +40
Skid Plates +30

RAM VAN/WAGON   1995

A driver airbag is added, and four-wheel ABS is now standard on Wagons and Vans sent to conversion outfitters. LE trim changes to SLT. Chrome wheels and a CD player are new options.

RATINGS (SCALE OF 1-10)

Overall	Safety	Reliability	Performance	Comfort	Value
N/A	7.2	7.4	6.2	6.9	N/A

RAM VAN

Category H

Model	Trade-in	Market
2 Dr 1500 Ram Van	6795	8095
2 Dr 1500 Ram Van Ext	8050	9590
2 Dr 2500 Ram Van	8025	9560
2 Dr 2500 Ram Van Ext	8115	9665
2 Dr 2500 Maxi Ram Van Ext	8720	10390
2 Dr 3500 Ram Van	8995	10715
2 Dr 3500 Ram Van Ext	9445	11250

Model Description	Trade-in Value	Market Value
RAM WAGON		
Category H		
2 Dr 1500 Ram Wagon	7210	8585
2 Dr 1500 SLT Ram Wagon	8685	10350
2 Dr 2500 Ram Wagon	8860	10555
2 Dr 2500 Maxi Ram Wagon Ext	9585	11420
2 Dr 2500 SLT Ram Wagon	9615	11455
2 Dr 2500 SLT Ram Wagon Ext	10310	12280
2 Dr 3500 Ram Wagon	9570	11400
2 Dr 3500 Ram Wagon Ext	9585	11420
2 Dr 3500 SLT Ram Wagon	10920	13005
2 Dr 3500 SLT Ram Wagon Ext	11560	13770

OPTIONS FOR RAM VAN/WAGON
8 cyl 5.2 L Engine[Std on 3500,Ram Wagon Ext] +180
8 cyl 5.9 L Engine +135
Auto 4-Speed Transmission[Std on 3500] +75
Rear A/C W/Rear Heater +245
AM/FM Compact Disc Player +90
Air Conditioning[Std on 2500 SLT] +245
Anti-Lock Brakes[Opt on Ram Van,Ram Van Ext] +145
Chrome Bumpers[Std on SLT] +35
Chrome Wheels[Std on SLT] +90
Cruise Control[Std on SLT] +55
Dual Air Conditioning[Opt on 2500,STD] +385
Keyless Entry System[Std on SLT] +50
Limited Slip Diff[Opt on 2500,3500] +80
Power Door Locks[Opt on Maxi,STD] +55
Power Drivers Seat +85
Power Windows[Opt on Maxi,STD] +55
Premium Sound System +115
Velour/Cloth Seats[Opt on 1500,Maxi,STD] +35

SPIRIT   1995

Flexible fuel model and optional four-speed automatic transmission are dropped. A three-speed automatic continues as standard equipment.

RATINGS (SCALE OF 1-10)

Overall	Safety	Reliability	Performance	Comfort	Value
7	6.7	7.5	6.8	7.4	6.8

Category C

4 Dr STD Sdn	4435	5685

OPTIONS FOR SPIRIT
6 cyl 3.0 L Engine +240
Power Door Locks +75
Power Drivers Seat +90
Power Windows +95

STEALTH   1995

Chromed 18-inch aluminum wheels are available on R/T Turbo.

RATINGS (SCALE OF 1-10)

Overall	Safety	Reliability	Performance	Comfort	Value
N/A	N/A	7.7	9.4	6.8	N/A

Model Description	Trade-in Value	Market Value
Category F		
2 Dr R/T Hbk	10860	13165
2 Dr R/T Turbo 4WD Hbk	15290	18540
2 Dr STD Hbk	9440	11445

OPTIONS FOR STEALTH
Auto 4-Speed Transmission +265
Anti-Lock Brakes[Std on 4WD] +195
Chrome Wheels +175
Compact Disc Changer +190
Cruise Control[Opt on STD] +65
Keyless Entry System +55
Leather Seats +190
Power Door Locks[Std on 4WD] +60
Power Sunroof +200
Power Windows[Std on 4WD] +70

STRATUS   1995

Spirit replacement features cutting-edge styling and class-leading accommodations. Dual airbags and ABS are standard. Base and ES models are available. Base model has 2.0-liter, four-cylinder engine making 132 horsepower and a five-speed manual transmission. ES is powered by 155-horsepower, Mitsubishi 2.5-liter V6. A credit option on the ES is the Neon's 2.0-liter four hooked to a five-speed manual transmission.

RATINGS (SCALE OF 1-10)

Overall	Safety	Reliability	Performance	Comfort	Value
N/A	6.5	5.2	N/A	7.8	7.5

Category C

4 Dr ES Sdn	6075	7790
4 Dr STD Sdn	4950	6345

OPTIONS FOR STRATUS
4 cyl 2.4 L Engine +130
Auto 4-Speed Transmission[Std on ES] +220
AM/FM Compact Disc Player +105
Anti-Lock Brakes[Std on ES] +175
Child Seat (1) +35
Keyless Entry System +55
Leather Seats +185
Lighted Entry System +45
Power Door Locks[Std on ES] +75
Power Drivers Seat +90
Power Windows[Std on ES] +95
Premium Sound System +115

VIPER   1995

No changes.

Category K

2 Dr RT/10 Conv	28990	33285

OPTIONS FOR VIPER
Air Conditioning +335

Don't forget to refer to the Mileage Adjustment Table at the back of this book!

DODGE 94

Model Description	Trade-in Value	Market Value	Model Description	Trade-in Value	Market Value

1994 DODGE

CARAVAN   1994

A passenger airbag is added to a redesigned dashboard, and new side-door guard beams meet 1997 passenger car safety standards. All-wheel drive is no longer available on regular-length models. Bumpers are restyled, and seats with integrated child seats can be reclined for the first time.

RATINGS (SCALE OF 1-10)

Overall	Safety	Reliability	Performance	Comfort	Value
7.6	8.2	6.2	7.4	8.3	7.9

Category G

2 Dr ES Pass. Van	6810	8635
2 Dr Grand Pass. Van	5875	7450
2 Dr Grand ES Pass. Van	7080	8980
2 Dr Grand ES 4WD Pass. Van	7870	9980
2 Dr Grand LE Pass. Van	6930	8785
2 Dr Grand LE 4WD Pass. Van	7720	9790
2 Dr Grand SE Pass. Van	6230	7900
2 Dr Grand SE 4WD Pass. Van	6665	8450
2 Dr LE Pass. Van	6660	8440
2 Dr SE Pass. Van	5865	7435
2 Dr STD Cargo Van	4665	5915
2 Dr STD Cargo Van Ext	5435	6890
2 Dr STD Pass. Van	4855	6155

OPTIONS FOR CARAVAN

6 cyl 3.0 L Engine[Opt on STD] +150
6 cyl 3.3 L Engine[Opt on Grand,SE] +25
6 cyl 3.8 L Engine +100
Auto 3-Speed Transmission[Opt on STD] +145
Auto 4-Speed Transmission[Opt on Grand,SE, STD] +95
7 Passenger Seating[Opt on SE,STD] +125
AM/FM Compact Disc Player +75
Air Conditioning[Std on Grand LE,LE] +200
Anti-Lock Brakes +140
Captain Chairs (4) +150
Child Seats (2) +60
Cruise Control[Opt on Grand,STD] +50
Dual Air Conditioning +225
Heavy Duty Suspension[Opt on LE] +35
Infinity Sound System +105
Keyless Entry System[Std on Grand LE,LE] +50
Leather Seats +190
Lighted Entry System[Opt on Grand SE] +35
Power Door Locks[Std on Grand LE,LE] +55
Power Drivers Seat +70
Power Windows[Std on LE] +60
Sport Suspension +110

COLT   1994

A driver airbag debuts. ES trim replaces GL nomenclature. Order ABS on an ES sedan and you'll get rear discs instead of drums. The optional 1.8-liter engine is available on the coupe this year, but only with ES trim. Sedans gain standard power steering. Air conditioners use CFC-free refrigerant.

RATINGS (SCALE OF 1-10)

Overall	Safety	Reliability	Performance	Comfort	Value
6.6	5.5	7.4	8	7.4	4.7

Category E

2 Dr ES Sdn	2585	3765
4 Dr ES Sdn	3105	4525
2 Dr STD Sdn	2350	3430
4 Dr STD Sdn	2920	4255

OPTIONS FOR COLT

4 cyl 1.8 L Engine[Opt on ES Sdn] +110
Auto 3-Speed Transmission +125
Auto 4-Speed Transmission +160
AM/FM Stereo Tape +75
Air Conditioning +205
Aluminum/Alloy Wheels +80
Anti-Lock Brakes +160
Cruise Control +55
Power Door Locks +60
Power Windows +65

DAKOTA   1994

Driver airbag is added, along with side-door guard beams. LE trim level now called SLT. A strengthened roof now meets passenger car crush standards. The 5.2-liter V8 loses horsepower but gains torque.

RATINGS (SCALE OF 1-10)

Overall	Safety	Reliability	Performance	Comfort	Value
N/A	7	7.3	7	7.1	N/A

Category G

2 Dr SLT Ext Cab SB	5985	7590
2 Dr SLT 4WD Ext Cab SB	7250	9190
2 Dr SLT Std Cab LB	5190	6580
2 Dr SLT 4WD Std Cab LB	6585	8350
2 Dr SLT Std Cab SB	4865	6170
2 Dr SLT 4WD Std Cab SB	6520	8270
2 Dr STD Ext Cab SB	5640	7150
2 Dr STD 4WD Ext Cab SB	6945	8805
2 Dr STD Std Cab LB	4870	6175
2 Dr STD 4WD Std Cab LB	6275	7960
2 Dr STD Std Cab SB	4560	5785
2 Dr STD 4WD Std Cab SB	6225	7890
2 Dr Sport Ext Cab SB	5540	7025
2 Dr Sport 4WD Ext Cab SB	6845	8680
2 Dr Sport Std Cab SB	4280	5430
2 Dr Sport 4WD Std Cab SB	6010	7625
2 Dr WS Std Cab LB	4415	5595
2 Dr WS 4WD Std Cab LB	5875	7450

Don't forget to refer to the Mileage Adjustment Table at the back of this book!

DODGE 94

Model Description	Trade-in Value	Market Value
2 Dr WS Std Cab SB	3830	4860
2 Dr WS 4WD Std Cab SB	5790	7345

OPTIONS FOR DAKOTA
6 cyl 3.9 L Engine +130
8 cyl 5.2 L Engine +175
Auto 4-Speed Transmission +220
AM/FM Stereo Tape[Opt on STD,WS] +55
Air Conditioning[Opt on Sport,STD,WS] +200
Anti-Lock Brakes +140
Camper/Towing Package +70
Chrome Bumpers[Std on SLT] +35
Chrome Wheels[Std on SLT] +40
Cruise Control[Opt on Sport,STD] +50
Limited Slip Diff +70
Power Door Locks +55
Power Windows +60
Premium Sound System +85
Rear Step Bumper[Opt on STD,WS] +35

INTREPID   1994

Base engine is upgraded with eight more horsepower. A flexible-fuel model is introduced to all states except California. Standard equipment now includes air conditioning and a touring suspension. ES models gain variable-assist power steering, which is optional on base models with the Wheel and Handling Group. New options include a power sunroof, security alarm and power passenger seat.

RATINGS (SCALE OF 1-10)

Overall	Safety	Reliability	Performance	Comfort	Value
7.9	7.7	6.4	8.4	8.6	8.4

Category B
Model	Trade-in	Market
4 Dr ES Sdn	5340	6950
4 Dr STD Sdn	4800	6250

OPTIONS FOR INTREPID
6 cyl 3.5 L Engine +175
Anti-Lock Brakes +165
Climate Control for AC +40
Compact Disc W/fm/tape +90
Cruise Control[Std on ES] +55
Dual Power Seats +95
Keyless Entry System +45
Leather Seats +165
Power Door Locks +65
Power Moonroof +235
Power Windows +70
Traction Control System +45

RAM PICKUP   1994

Brand-new truck replaces 22-year-old D-Series model. New truck sports big-rig styling, driver airbag, available V10 engine, and a commodious cabin. All 1994 Rams are regular-cab models in shortbed or longbed configuration with 2WD or 4WD. Optional on 1500 and 2500 models is four-wheel ABS that works in both 2WD and 4WD.

RATINGS (SCALE OF 1-10)

Overall	Safety	Reliability	Performance	Comfort	Value
N/A	N/A	7.4	7	8	N/A

RAM 1500
Category H
Model	Trade-in	Market
2 Dr LT Std Cab LB	7090	8590
2 Dr LT 4WD Std Cab LB	8500	10300
2 Dr LT Std Cab SB	6965	8435
2 Dr LT 4WD Std Cab SB	8350	10115
2 Dr Laramie SLT Std Cab LB	8015	9710
2 Dr Laramie SLT 4WD Std Cab LB	9430	11425
2 Dr Laramie SLT Std Cab SB	7890	9560
2 Dr Laramie SLT 4WD Std Cab SB	9280	11245
2 Dr ST Std Cab LB	7325	8875
2 Dr ST 4WD Std Cab LB	8550	10355
2 Dr ST Std Cab SB	7195	8720
2 Dr ST 4WD Std Cab SB	8490	10290
2 Dr WS Std Cab LB	6230	7545
2 Dr WS Std Cab SB	6100	7390

RAM 2500
Category H
Model	Trade-in	Market
2 Dr LT Std Cab LB	7695	9325
2 Dr LT 4WD Std Cab LB	8755	10610
2 Dr Laramie SLT Std Cab LB	8040	9740
2 Dr Laramie SLT 4WD Std Cab LB	10000	12115
2 Dr ST Std Cab LB	7885	9550
2 Dr ST 4WD Std Cab LB	8945	10840

RAM 3500
Category H
Model	Trade-in	Market
2 Dr LT Std Cab LB	9435	11430
2 Dr LT 4WD Std Cab LB	10650	12905
2 Dr Laramie SLT Std Cab LB	10720	12985
2 Dr Laramie SLT 4WD Std Cab LB	11815	14315
2 Dr ST Std Cab LB	9755	11820
2 Dr ST 4WD Std Cab LB	10865	13160

OPTIONS FOR RAM PICKUP
10 cyl 8.0 L Engine +115
6 cyl 5.9 L Turbodsl Engine +1090
8 cyl 5.2 L Engine +125
8 cyl 5.9 L Engine +120
Auto 4-Speed Transmission +220
Air Conditioning[Opt on LT,ST,WS] +200
Anti-Lock Brakes +120
Bed Liner +55
Camper/Towing Package +80

Model Description	Trade-in Value	Market Value
Chrome Bumpers[Opt on LT] +30		
Chrome Wheels[Opt on LT,ST] +75		
Compact Disc W/fm/tape +75		
Cruise Control[Opt on LT,ST,WS] +45		
Limited Slip Diff +65		
Power Drivers Seat +70		
Premium Sound System +90		
Rear Step Bumper +35		

RAM VAN/WAGON 1994

A reskinned full-size van debuted in mid-1993, featuring new front and rear styling. Early-build vans did not include side-door guard beams for the front doors or improved roof crush protection. Air conditioning now uses CFC-free refrigerant.

RATINGS (SCALE OF 1-10)

Overall	Safety	Reliability	Performance	Comfort	Value
N/A	6.3	7.7	6.2	6.9	N/A

RAM VAN
Category H

Model	Trade-in	Market
2 Dr 1500 Ram Van	5300	6425
2 Dr 1500 Ram Van Ext	6445	7805
2 Dr 2500 Ram Van	6460	7830
2 Dr 2500 Ram Van Ext	6605	8000
2 Dr 2500 Maxi Ram Van Ext	6990	8470
2 Dr 3500 Ram Van Ext	7105	8610
2 Dr 3500 Maxi Ram Van Ext	7485	9065

RAM WAGON
Category H

Model	Trade-in	Market
2 Dr 1500 Ram Wagon	5700	6910
2 Dr 1500 LE Ram Wagon	6915	8375
2 Dr 2500 Ram Wagon	7125	8635
2 Dr 2500 LE Ram Wagon	7865	9530
2 Dr 2500 Maxi Ram Wagon	7610	9220
2 Dr 3500 Ram Wagon	7615	9225
2 Dr 3500 Ram Wagon Ext	7995	9690
2 Dr 3500 LE Ram Wagon	8560	10370
2 Dr 3500 LE Ram Wagon Ext	9070	10985

OPTIONS FOR RAM VAN/WAGON
8 cyl 5.2 L Engine[Std on 3500] +125
8 cyl 5.9 L Engine +120
Auto 4-Speed Transmission[Std on 3500] +60
AM/FM Stereo Tape +50
Air Conditioning[Std on LE] +200
Aluminum/Alloy Wheels +75
Anti-Lock Brakes +120
Auxiliary Fuel Tank +35
Cruise Control[Opt on Maxi,STD] +45
Dual Air Conditioning[Opt on 2500] +315
Infinity Sound System +55
Keyless Entry System[Opt on Maxi,STD] +45
Limited Slip Diff +65
Power Door Locks[Opt on Maxi,STD] +45

Power Windows[Opt on Maxi,STD] +45		
Premium Sound System +90		
Velour/Cloth Seats[Std on LE,Maxi LE] +25		

SHADOW 1994

Four-door hatchback production stops midyear. Front passengers are now restrained by the dreaded motorized seatbelt to comply with federal regulations. Air conditioning runs on CFC-free coolant this year.

RATINGS (SCALE OF 1-10)

Overall	Safety	Reliability	Performance	Comfort	Value
6.5	6.5	6.9	7.2	6.8	5.1

Category E

Model	Trade-in	Market
2 Dr ES Hbk	2750	4005
4 Dr ES Hbk	2850	4155
2 Dr STD Hbk	2380	3465
4 Dr STD Hbk	2480	3615

OPTIONS FOR SHADOW
4 cyl 2.5 L Engine[Std on ES] +70
6 cyl 3.0 L Engine +195
Auto 3-Speed Transmission +135
Auto 4-Speed Transmission +180
AM/FM Compact Disc Player +105
Air Conditioning +205
Aluminum/Alloy Wheels +80
Anti-Lock Brakes +160
Cruise Control +55
Power Door Locks +60
Power Drivers Seat +75
Power Windows +65
Premium Sound System +80
Sunroof +85

SPIRIT 1994

Motorized seatbelt is introduced for front passengers. Highline and ES trim designations are retired in favor of ... well, nothing. All 1994 Spirits come equipped one way, with various option packages available.

RATINGS (SCALE OF 1-10)

Overall	Safety	Reliability	Performance	Comfort	Value
7.1	6.6	7.5	6.8	7.4	7.4

Category C

Model	Trade-in	Market
4 Dr STD Sdn	2950	4335

OPTIONS FOR SPIRIT
6 cyl 3.0 L Engine +165
Auto 4-Speed Transmission +40
AM/FM Stereo Tape +40
Anti-Lock Brakes +145
Power Door Locks +60
Power Drivers Seat +75
Power Windows +80

Don't forget to refer to the Mileage Adjustment Table at the back of this book!

Model Description	Trade-in Value	Market Value

STEALTH 1994

Passenger airbag is added. R/T Turbo gains 20 horsepower and a six-speed transmission. ES trim level is dropped. Styling is slightly revised front and rear, revealing the addition of projector-beam headlamps in place of the hidden lights used previously. CFC-free refrigerant is used in the air conditioning system, and R/T models can be painted a really bright shade of yellow.

RATINGS (SCALE OF 1-10)

Overall	Safety	Reliability	Performance	Comfort	Value
N/A	N/A	7.6	9.4	6.8	N/A

Category F
2 Dr R/T Hbk	7560	9080
2 Dr R/T Turbo 4WD Hbk	10980	13190
2 Dr R/T Luxury Hbk	10045	12065
2 Dr STD Hbk	7135	8575

OPTIONS FOR STEALTH
Auto 4-Speed Transmission +235
AM/FM Stereo Tape +55
Air Conditioning[Std on R/T Luxury,4WD] +205
Anti-Lock Brakes[Std on 4WD] +160
Chrome Wheels +145
Compact Disc Changer[Opt on R/T,STD] +155
Cruise Control[Std on R/T Luxury,4WD] +55
Keyless Entry System[Opt on R/T,STD] +45
Leather Seats +155
Power Door Locks[Std on R/T Luxury,4WD] +50
Power Sunroof +165
Power Windows[Std on R/T Luxury,4WD] +55
Premium Sound System[Std on R/T Luxury,4WD] +95
Rear Spoiler[Std on R/T Luxury,4WD] +60

VIPER 1994

Air conditioning with CFC-free refrigerant can be installed at the factory when the appropriate option box is checked. Green and yellow are added to the color chart. Green cars get a new black-and-tan interior.

Category K
2 Dr RT/10 Cpe	22995	26420

OPTIONS FOR VIPER
Air Conditioning +275

1993 DODGE

CARAVAN 1993

No changes.

RATINGS (SCALE OF 1-10)

Overall	Safety	Reliability	Performance	Comfort	Value
6.9	6	4.7	7.4	8.3	8.3

Category G
2 Dr ES Pass. Van	5380	7030
2 Dr ES 4WD Pass. Van	5960	7790
2 Dr Grand Pass. Van	4780	6245
2 Dr Grand ES 4WD Pass. Van	6120	7995
2 Dr Grand ES Pass. Van	5580	7295
2 Dr Grand LE Pass. Van	5470	7145
2 Dr Grand LE 4WD Pass. Van	5980	7815
2 Dr Grand SE Pass. Van	4875	6375
2 Dr Grand SE 4WD Pass. Van	5430	7095
2 Dr LE Pass. Van	5240	6845
2 Dr LE 4WD Pass. Van	5825	7610
2 Dr SE Pass. Van	4395	5745
2 Dr SE 4WD Pass. Van	5230	6840
2 Dr STD Cargo Van	3755	4910
2 Dr STD Cargo Van Ext	4400	5750
2 Dr STD Pass. Van	3705	4840

OPTIONS FOR CARAVAN
6 cyl 3.0 L Engine[Opt on SE,STD] +130
6 cyl 3.3 L Engine[Std on Grand ES,Grand LE,Grand SE, 4WD] +85
Auto 3-Speed Transmission[Opt on STD] +120
Auto 4-Speed Transmission[Opt on SE Pass. Van, LE Pass. Van] +45
7 Passenger Seating[Std on Grand ES] +105
AM/FM Compact Disc Player +65
Air Conditioning[Std on ES,Grand ES, Grand LE, LE] +165
Aluminum/Alloy Wheels +65
Anti-Lock Brakes +115
Captain Chairs (4) +125
Child Seats (2) +50
Cruise Control[Opt on Grand,Grand SE,SE,STD] +40
Dual Air Conditioning +185
Leather Seats +155
Luggage Rack +30
Power Door Locks[Opt on Grand,Grand SE,SE,STD] +45
Power Drivers Seat +55
Power Windows +50
Premium Sound System +70

COLT 1993

Complete redesign results in two- and four-door notchback models; the hatchback is dropped. Coupes and sedans come in base or GL trim. Coupe and base sedan are powered by same 1.5-liter engine from last year. GL has a stronger 113-horsepower, 1.8-liter engine; this powerplant is optional on base sedan. GL sedan is only Colt that can be equipped with optional ABS.

RATINGS (SCALE OF 1-10)

Overall	Safety	Reliability	Performance	Comfort	Value
N/A	N/A	6	8	7.4	6.6

Don't forget to refer to the Mileage Adjustment Table at the back of this book!

Model Description	Trade-in Value	Market Value
Category E		
2 Dr GL Sdn	1785	2805
4 Dr GL Sdn	2195	3445
2 Dr STD Sdn	1620	2545
4 Dr STD Sdn	1955	3070

OPTIONS FOR COLT
4 cyl 1.8 L Engine[Std on GL] +80
Auto 3-Speed Transmission +105
Auto 4-Speed Transmission +135
AM/FM Stereo Tape +60
Air Conditioning +165
Aluminum/Alloy Wheels +65
Anti-Lock Brakes +135
Cruise Control +45
Power Door Locks +50
Power Steering +50
Power Windows +55

DAKOTA   1993

Sport model gets new graphics.

RATINGS (SCALE OF 1-10)

Overall	Safety	Reliability	Performance	Comfort	Value
N/A	4.8	7.1	7	7.1	N/A

Model Description	Trade-in Value	Market Value
Category G		
2 Dr LE Ext Cab SB	4720	6170
2 Dr LE 4WD Ext Cab SB	5885	7690
2 Dr LE Std Cab LB	4115	5375
2 Dr LE 4WD Std Cab LB	5230	6830
2 Dr LE Std Cab SB	4115	5375
2 Dr LE 4WD Std Cab SB	5230	6830
2 Dr S Std Cab SB	3210	4195
2 Dr STD Ext Cab SB	4365	5705
2 Dr STD 4WD Ext Cab SB	5565	7275
2 Dr STD Std Cab LB	4010	5240
2 Dr STD 4WD Std Cab LB	5230	6830
2 Dr STD Std Cab SB	3950	5160
2 Dr STD 4WD Std Cab SB	5190	6780
2 Dr Sport Std Cab SB	3470	4540
2 Dr Sport 4WD Std Cab SB	4865	6360

OPTIONS FOR DAKOTA
6 cyl 3.9 L Engine +105
8 cyl 5.2 L Engine +170
Auto 4-Speed Transmission +180
Dakota Snowplow Prep Grp. +150
AM/FM Stereo Tape[Opt on S,STD] +45
Air Conditioning[Std on LE] +165
Aluminum/Alloy Wheels[Opt on STD] +65
Anti-Lock Brakes +115
Camper/Towing Package +60
Chrome Bumpers +30
Chrome Wheels +35
Cruise Control[Std on LE] +40
Limited Slip Diff +55

Power Door Locks +45
Power Steering[Std on LE,Sport,4WD] +55
Power Windows +50
Premium Sound System +70
Rear Step Bumper[Opt on S,STD] +30

DAYTONA   1993

ABS is now available on base model. IROC loses turbocharged engine, though the limited-edition IROC R/T continues with turbo power.

Model Description	Trade-in Value	Market Value
Category C		
2 Dr ES Hbk	2470	3615
2 Dr STD Hbk	2245	3285
Category F		
2 Dr IROC Hbk	3560	4610
2 Dr IROC R/T Turbo Hbk	5070	6570

OPTIONS FOR DAYTONA
6 cyl 3.0 L Engine[Std on IROC] +140
Auto 3-Speed Transmission +110
Auto 4-Speed Transmission +140
AM/FM Compact Disc Player +70
Air Conditioning[Std on IROC R/T] +160
Aluminum/Alloy Wheels[Opt on STD] +60
Anti-Lock Brakes[Opt on ES] +120
Cruise Control +45
Leather Seats +125
Power Door Locks +40
Power Drivers Seat +50
Power Windows +45
Premium Sound System +75
Tilt Steering Wheel +30

DYNASTY   1993

Audio system is upgraded, a tamper-resistant odometer is added, and a stainless steel exhaust system is installed.

Model Description	Trade-in Value	Market Value
Category C		
4 Dr LE Sdn	3255	4760
4 Dr STD Sdn	2960	4325

OPTIONS FOR DYNASTY
6 cyl 3.0 L Engine[Std on LE] +140
6 cyl 3.3 L Engine +105
Auto 4-Speed Transmission[Std on LE] +25
AM/FM Stereo Tape +35
Air Conditioning +160
Anti-Lock Brakes +120
Cruise Control +45
Keyless Entry System +35
Leather Seats +125
Power Door Locks +50
Power Drivers Seat +60
Power Passenger Seat +55
Power Windows +65
Premium Sound System +75
Wire Wheel Covers +45

Don't forget to refer to the Mileage Adjustment Table at the back of this book!

Model Description	Trade-in Value	Market Value

INTREPID 1993

This midsized car represents the beginning of a revolution at Chrysler. Introducing cab-forward styling, Intrepid is powered by one of two V6 engines and comes in base or ES trim. ES model has four-wheel disc brakes. ABS is optional on base and ES. All Intrepids are equipped with dual airbags and height-adjustable seatbelts, while an integrated child seat is optional.

RATINGS (SCALE OF 1-10)

Overall	Safety	Reliability	Performance	Comfort	Value
7.6	7.6	5.8	8.4	8.6	7.8

Category B
4 Dr ES Sdn	3980	5365
4 Dr STD Sdn	3695	4985

OPTIONS FOR INTREPID

6 cyl 3.5 L Engine +125
Air Conditioning +175
Aluminum/Alloy Wheels +65
Anti-Lock Brakes +135
Climate Control for AC +35
Compact Disc W/fm/tape +75
Cruise Control +45
Leather Seats +135
Power Door Locks +50
Power Drivers Seat +65
Power Passenger Seat +70
Power Windows +55
Premium Sound System +75
Traction Control System +35

RAM 50 PICKUP 1993

Rear-wheel ABS reappears as standard equipment on all models.

Category G
2 Dr SE Std Cab SB	3285	4295
2 Dr STD Std Cab LB	2920	3815
2 Dr STD Std Cab SB	2920	3815
2 Dr STD 4WD Std Cab SB	3890	5085

OPTIONS FOR RAM 50 PICKUP

Auto 4-Speed Transmission +140
AM/FM Stereo Tape +45
Air Conditioning +165
Cruise Control +40
Limited Slip Diff +55
Power Door Locks +45
Power Steering[Opt on 2WD] +55
Power Windows +50
Rear Step Bumper +30

RAM PICKUP 1993

The optional 5.9-liter V8 is upgraded. New steel and alloy wheel designs debut.

RAM 150

Category H
2 Dr LE Ext Cab LB	6440	7990
2 Dr LE 4WD Ext Cab LB	7515	9320
2 Dr LE Ext Cab SB	6440	7990
2 Dr LE Std Cab LB	5730	7105
2 Dr LE 4WD Std Cab LB	6500	8060
2 Dr LE Std Cab SB	5650	7010
2 Dr LE 4WD Std Cab SB	6500	8060
2 Dr STD Ext Cab LB	6015	7465
2 Dr STD 4WD Ext Cab LB	7090	8795
2 Dr STD Ext Cab SB	6060	7520
2 Dr STD Std Cab LB	5240	6500
2 Dr STD 4WD Std Cab LB	6125	7595
2 Dr STD Std Cab SB	5165	6405
2 Dr STD 4WD Std Cab SB	6080	7540

RAM 250

Category H
2 Dr LE Turbodsl Ext Cab LB	8570	10630
2 Dr LE 4WD Ext Cab LB	8240	10220
2 Dr LE Std Cab LB	6715	8325
2 Dr LE 4WD Std Cab LB	7705	9560
2 Dr STD Ext Cab LB	7100	8805
2 Dr STD 4WD Ext Cab LB	7960	9870
2 Dr STD Std Cab LB	6205	7695
2 Dr STD 4WD Std Cab LB	7225	8960

RAM 350

Category H
2 Dr LE Turbodsl Ext Cab LB	11765	14595
2 Dr LE Turbodsl 4WD Ext Cab LB	12965	16080
2 Dr LE Std Cab LB	8700	10790
2 Dr LE 4WD Std Cab LB	9975	12375
2 Dr STD Turbodsl Ext Cab LB	11145	13825
2 Dr STD Turbodsl 4WD Ext Cab LB	12315	15275
2 Dr STD Std Cab LB	8080	10025
2 Dr STD 4WD Std Cab LB	9355	11605

OPTIONS FOR RAM PICKUP

6 cyl 5.9 L Turbodsl Engine +780
8 cyl 5.2 L Engine +115
8 cyl 5.9 L Engine +105
Auto 3-Speed Transmission +130
Auto 4-Speed Transmission +180
Snow Plow Prep Pkg +165
AM/FM Stereo Tape[Opt on STD] +40
Air Conditioning[Opt on STD] +165
Aluminum/Alloy Wheels +60
Camper/Towing Package +65
Chrome Step Bumper +40
Cruise Control[Opt on STD,] +40
Dual Rear Wheels +160

EDMUNDS® USED CARS & TRUCKS

Model Description	Trade-in Value	Market Value

Limited Slip Diff +55
Power Door Locks[Opt on STD] +40
Power Windows[Opt on STD] +40
Premium Sound System +75
Rear Step Bumper[Opt on STD] +30

RAM VAN/WAGON   1993

The optional 5.9-liter V8 is upgraded.

RAM VAN
Category H

Model	Trade-in	Market
2 Dr 1500 Ram Van	4465	5540
2 Dr 1500 Ram Van Ext	4710	5840
2 Dr 2500 Ram Van	4625	5740
2 Dr 2500 Ram Van Ext	4830	5990
2 Dr 2500 Maxi Ram Van Ext	5125	6355
2 Dr 3500 Ram Van Ext	5210	6460
2 Dr 3500 Maxi Ram Van Ext	5495	6815

RAM WAGON
Category H

Model	Trade-in	Market
2 Dr 1500 Ram Wagon	5730	7105
2 Dr 1500 Ram Wagon Ext	5850	7255
2 Dr 1500 LE Ram Wagon	6820	8460
2 Dr 1500 LE Ram Wagon Ext	7115	8825
2 Dr 1500 Value Ram Wagon	6090	7550
2 Dr 1500 Value Ram Wagon Ext	6380	7915
2 Dr 2500 Ram Wagon Ext	6245	7745
2 Dr 2500 LE Ram Wagon Ext	6895	8555
2 Dr 2500 LE Maxi Ram Wagon Ext	7305	9065
2 Dr 2500 Maxi Ram Wagon Ext	6685	8290
2 Dr 2500 Value Ram Wagon Ext	6620	8210
2 Dr 2500 Value Maxi Ram Wagon Ext	7070	8770
2 Dr 3500 Ram Wagon	6685	8290
2 Dr 3500 Ram Wagon Ext	6990	8675
2 Dr 3500 LE Ram Wagon	7520	9330
2 Dr 3500 LE Ram Wagon Ext	7810	9685
2 Dr 3500 Value Ram Wagon	7100	8805
2 Dr 3500 Value Ram Wagon Ext	6920	8580

OPTIONS FOR RAM VAN/WAGON
8 cyl 5.2 L Engine[Std on 3500,LE Maxi,Value Maxi,2500 Maxi Ram Wagon Ext] +115
8 cyl 5.9 L Engine +105
Auto 3-Speed Transmission[Opt on 1500,Ram Van,Ram Van Ext] +65
Auto 4-Speed Transmission[Std on 3500] +85
8 Pass W/Travel Seat Pkg +180
AM/FM Stereo Tape +40
Air Conditioning[Opt on Maxi,STD,1500, LE Ram Wagon Ext] +165
Aluminum/Alloy Wheels +60
Cruise Control[Std on LE,LE Maxi] +40
Dual Air Conditioning +255

Limited Slip Diff +55
Power Door Locks[Opt on Value] +40
Power Windows[Opt on Value] +40
Premium Sound System[Opt on Value] +75

RAMCHARGER   1993

The optional 5.9-liter V8 is upgraded.

Category H

Model	Trade-in	Market
2 Dr Canyon Sport Utility	7690	9540
2 Dr Canyon Sport 4WD Utility	8240	10220
2 Dr LE Utility	7390	9165
2 Dr LE 4WD Utility	7940	9845
2 Dr S Utility	6425	7965
2 Dr S 4WD Utility	7250	8995
2 Dr STD Utility	7230	8970
2 Dr STD 4WD Utility	7450	9240

OPTIONS FOR RAMCHARGER
8 cyl 5.9 L Engine +105
Ramcharger Snow Plow Pkg +210
AM/FM Stereo Tape +40
Air Conditioning[Std on LE] +165
Aluminum/Alloy Wheels +60
Camper/Towing Package +65
Cruise Control[Std on LE] +40
Limited Slip Diff +55
Locking Differential +50
Power Door Locks[Std on LE] +40
Power Windows[Std on LE] +40
Premium Sound System +75

SHADOW   1993

America model is dropped. Convertible disappears midyear. ABS is newly optional.

RATINGS (SCALE OF 1-10)

Overall	Safety	Reliability	Performance	Comfort	Value
6.6	6.5	7.7	7.2	6.8	5

Category E

Model	Trade-in	Market
2 Dr ES Conv	2855	4490
2 Dr ES Hbk	2010	3160
4 Dr ES Hbk	2085	3275
2 Dr Highline Conv	2830	4445
2 Dr STD Hbk	1730	2720
4 Dr STD Hbk	1810	2845

OPTIONS FOR SHADOW
4 cyl 2.5 L Engine[Opt on STD] +55
6 cyl 3.0 L Engine +140
Auto 3-Speed Transmission +110
Auto 4-Speed Transmission +140
AM/FM Compact Disc Player +85
Air Conditioning +165
Aluminum/Alloy Wheels +65
Anti-Lock Brakes +135
Cruise Control +45
Power Door Locks +50

Don't forget to refer to the Mileage Adjustment Table at the back of this book!

DODGE 93-92

Model Description	Trade-in Value	Market Value	Model Description	Trade-in Value	Market Value

Power Drivers Seat +60
Power Windows[Opt on STD] +55
Premium Sound System +65
Sunroof +70

SPIRIT — 1993

LE and R/T models are dropped from lineup. Turbocharged engines are banished. Four thousand flexible-fuel models are produced. Grille is now color keyed. CD player is added to options list. Rear styling is revised.

RATINGS (SCALE OF 1-10)

Overall	Safety	Reliability	Performance	Comfort	Value
7.1	6.1	8	6.8	7.4	7.4

Category C
4 Dr ES Sdn	3075	4495
4 Dr Highline Sdn	2515	3675

OPTIONS FOR SPIRIT

6 cyl 3.0 L Engine +140
Auto 3-Speed Transmission[Std on ES] +110
Auto 4-Speed Transmission +80
AM/FM Stereo Tape +35
Air Conditioning +160
Aluminum/Alloy Wheels[Std on ES] +60
Anti-Lock Brakes +120
Cruise Control[Std on ES] +45
Power Door Locks +50
Power Drivers Seat +60
Power Windows +65
Premium Sound System +75

STEALTH 1993

Base model gets ES sill moldings, while R/T's spoiler is optional across the line. R/T Turbo can be ordered with chrome wheels. Remote keyless entry and a CD changer are new options.

RATINGS (SCALE OF 1-10)

Overall	Safety	Reliability	Performance	Comfort	Value
N/A	6.3	7.5	9.4	6.8	N/A

Category F
2 Dr ES Hbk	6235	8075
2 Dr R/T Hbk	7390	9575
2 Dr R/T Turbo 4WD Hbk	8920	11555
2 Dr STD Hbk	5380	6970

OPTIONS FOR STEALTH

Auto 4-Speed Transmission +170
AM/FM Stereo Tape +45
Air Conditioning[Std on R/T] +170
Anti-Lock Brakes[Std on R/T] +130
Chrome Wheels +120
Compact Disc Changer +125
Cruise Control[Std on R/T] +45
Keyless Entry System +35

Leather Seats +125
Power Door Locks[Std on R/T] +40
Power Sunroof +135
Power Windows[Std on R/T] +45
Premium Sound System[Std on R/T] +75
Rear Spoiler[Std on R/T] +50

VIPER 1993

Black is added to the paint palette. Production slowed due to problems with resin-transfer molded hood, keeping production level to a low 1500 units.
Category K
2 Dr RT/10 Cpe	17065	19665

1992 DODGE

CARAVAN 1992

Integrated child seats are a new option. Exterior door handles are flush-mounted, and new wheels debut.

RATINGS (SCALE OF 1-10)

Overall	Safety	Reliability	Performance	Comfort	Value
6.6	5.3	3.9	7.4	8.3	8.1

Category G
2 Dr ES Pass. Van	4495	6045
2 Dr ES 4WD Pass. Van	5060	6800
2 Dr Grand Pass. Van	4170	5600
2 Dr Grand ES Pass. Van	4765	6400
2 Dr Grand ES 4WD Pass. Van	5195	6980
2 Dr Grand LE Pass. Van	4650	6250
2 Dr Grand LE 4WD Pass. Van	5085	6835
2 Dr Grand SE Pass. Van	4225	5675
2 Dr Grand SE 4WD Pass. Van	4690	6305
2 Dr LE Pass. Van	4495	6040
2 Dr LE 4WD Pass. Van	4950	6655
2 Dr SE Pass. Van	3760	5050
2 Dr SE 4WD Pass. Van	4475	6010
2 Dr STD Cargo Van	3125	4200
2 Dr STD 4WD Cargo Van	3975	5340
2 Dr STD Cargo Van Ext	3695	4970
2 Dr STD 4WD Cargo Van Ext	4145	5565
2 Dr STD Pass. Van	3265	4385

OPTIONS FOR CARAVAN

6 cyl 3.0 L Engine[Opt on SE,STD] +125
6 cyl 3.3 L Engine[Std on Grand ES,Grand LE,Grand SE, Cargo Van,4WD] +65
Auto 3-Speed Transmission[Opt on STD] +95
Auto 4-Speed Transmission[Std on ES,Grand ES,Grand LE, Grand SE,LE,4WD] +95
7 Passenger Seating[Opt on STD] +85
Air Conditioning[Opt on Grand,Grand SE,SE,STD] +135
Captain Chairs (4) +100
Cruise Control[Opt on Grand,Grand SE,SE,STD] +35
Infinity Sound System +70

Don't forget to refer to the Mileage Adjustment Table at the back of this book!

Model Description	Trade-in Value	Market Value	Model Description	Trade-in Value	Market Value

Power Door Locks[Opt on Grand,Grand SE,SE,STD] +40
Power Drivers Seat +45
Power Windows[Opt on Grand SE,SE] +40

COLT 1992

GL models can be equipped with a digital clock, but all Colts lose options such as factory floor mats, intermittent wipers, wheel trim rings, and alloy wheels.

Category E

	Trade-in	Market
2 Dr GL Hbk	1450	2365
2 Dr STD Hbk	1310	2135

OPTIONS FOR COLT

Auto 3-Speed Transmission +90
Air Conditioning +135
Power Steering +40

DAKOTA 1992

V6 and V8 engines get more power. The V6 is up considerably, from 125 to 180 horsepower. V8 models add a whopping 65 horsepower and 30 foot-pounds of torque. Four-wheel drive models can be equipped with an optional Off-Road Appearance package.

RATINGS (SCALE OF 1-10)

Overall	Safety	Reliability	Performance	Comfort	Value
N/A	4.7	7.1	7	7.1	N/A

Category G

	Trade-in	Market
2 Dr LE Ext Cab SB	3920	5265
2 Dr LE 4WD Ext Cab SB	4800	6450
2 Dr LE Std Cab LB	3525	4735
2 Dr LE 4WD Std Cab LB	4225	5680
2 Dr LE Std Cab SB	3525	4735
2 Dr LE 4WD Std Cab SB	4165	5600
2 Dr S Std Cab SB	2625	3530
2 Dr STD Ext Cab SB	3480	4675
2 Dr STD 4WD Ext Cab SB	4370	5870
2 Dr STD Std Cab LB	3235	4345
2 Dr STD 4WD Std Cab LB	4225	5680
2 Dr STD Std Cab SB	3150	4230
2 Dr STD 4WD Std Cab SB	4135	5555
2 Dr Sport Ext Cab SB	3505	4710
2 Dr Sport 4WD Ext Cab SB	3930	5280
2 Dr Sport Std Cab SB	2800	3760
2 Dr Sport 4WD Std Cab SB	3930	5280

OPTIONS FOR DAKOTA

6 cyl 3.9 L Engine +85
8 cyl 5.2 L Engine +140
Auto 4-Speed Transmission +145
Snow Plow Prep Pkg +125
Air Conditioning +135
Cruise Control +35
Limited Slip Diff +45
Power Door Locks +40

Power Steering[Std on Sport,4WD] +45
Power Windows +40

DAYTONA 1992

Front and rear styling is revised, unsuccessfully. ABS is a new option. Shelby model is replaced midyear by IROC R/T model, powered by a 224-horsepower, 2.2-liter turbocharged engine and limited to a production run of 800 units.

Category C

	Trade-in	Market
2 Dr ES Hbk	1925	2960
2 Dr STD Hbk	1760	2700

Category F

	Trade-in	Market
2 Dr IROC Hbk	2990	3935
2 Dr IROC R/T Turbo Hbk	4235	5570

OPTIONS FOR DAYTONA

6 cyl 3.0 L Engine[Std on IROC] +115
Auto 3-Speed Transmission +90
Auto 4-Speed Transmission +105
Air Conditioning +135
Anti-Lock Brakes +95
Cruise Control +35
Power Door Locks +35
Power Drivers Seat[Std on IROC R/T] +40
Power Windows +40

DYNASTY 1992

Child-proof door locks are added, and options include an overhead console with storage bin and console with cassette storage.

Category C

	Trade-in	Market
4 Dr LE Sdn	2610	4005
4 Dr STD Sdn	2370	3640

OPTIONS FOR DYNASTY

6 cyl 3.0 L Engine[Std on LE] +115
Air Conditioning +135
Cruise Control +35
Power Door Locks +40
Power Drivers Seat +50
Power Windows +50

MONACO 1992

No changes.

Category C

	Trade-in	Market
4 Dr ES Sdn	2675	4105
4 Dr LE Sdn	2245	3445

OPTIONS FOR MONACO

Air Conditioning[Opt on LE] +135
Cruise Control +35
Power Door Locks +40
Power Drivers Seat +50
Power Windows +50

Don't forget to refer to the Mileage Adjustment Table at the back of this book!

Model Description	Trade-in Value	Market Value
RAM 50 PICKUP 1992		

The V6 engine, rear ABS, and extended-cab models are dropped from the lineup. Left are regular-cab trucks in 2WD or 4WD in base or SE trim.

Category G

Model Description	Trade-in Value	Market Value
2 Dr SE Std Cab LB	2590	3480
2 Dr SE Std Cab SB	2590	3480
2 Dr STD Std Cab LB	2290	3075
2 Dr STD Std Cab SB	2290	3075
2 Dr STD 4WD Std Cab SB	3080	4140

OPTIONS FOR RAM 50 PICKUP
Auto 4-Speed Transmission +115
Air Conditioning +135
Power Steering[Std on SE,4WD] +45

Model Description	Trade-in Value	Market Value
RAM PICKUP 1992		

Gasoline engines make more horsepower, and the Cummins Turbo Diesel engine is newly optional on Club Cab models. A one-ton duallie is introduced. Club Cabs have larger fuel tanks.

RAM 150

Category H

Model Description	Trade-in Value	Market Value
2 Dr LE Ext Cab LB	5605	7060
2 Dr LE 4WD Ext Cab LB	6545	8245
2 Dr LE Ext Cab SB	5605	7060
2 Dr LE Std Cab LB	5115	6445
2 Dr LE 4WD Std Cab LB	5725	7210
2 Dr LE Std Cab SB	5045	6355
2 Dr LE 4WD Std Cab SB	5725	7210
2 Dr STD Ext Cab LB	5185	6535
2 Dr STD 4WD Ext Cab LB	6055	7630
2 Dr STD Ext Cab SB	5115	6440
2 Dr STD Std Cab LB	4440	5590
2 Dr STD 4WD Std Cab LB	5310	6690
2 Dr STD Std Cab SB	4510	5680
2 Dr STD 4WD Std Cab SB	5240	6600

RAM 250

Category H

Model Description	Trade-in Value	Market Value
2 Dr LE Ext Cab LB	6240	7860
2 Dr LE 4WD Ext Cab LB	6950	8755
2 Dr LE Std Cab LB	5540	6980
2 Dr LE 4WD Std Cab LB	6440	8115
2 Dr STD Ext Cab LB	5690	7170
2 Dr STD 4WD Ext Cab LB	6400	8060
2 Dr STD Std Cab LB	5050	6360
2 Dr STD 4WD Std Cab LB	5895	7430

RAM 350

Category H

Model Description	Trade-in Value	Market Value
2 Dr LE Turbodsl Ext Cab LB	7455	9395
2 Dr LE Turbodsl 4WD Ext Cab LB	8210	10340

Model Description	Trade-in Value	Market Value
2 Dr LE Std Cab LB	5740	7230
2 Dr LE 4WD Std Cab LB	6600	8315
2 Dr STD Turbodsl Ext Cab LB	7035	8865
2 Dr STD Turbodsl 4WD Ext Cab LB	7790	9810
2 Dr STD Std Cab LB	5340	6730
2 Dr STD 4WD Std Cab LB	6200	7810

OPTIONS FOR RAM PICKUP
6 cyl 5.9 L Turbodsl Engine +635
8 cyl 5.2 L Engine +95
8 cyl 5.9 L Engine +75
Auto 3-Speed Transmission +105
Auto 4-Speed Transmission +145
Snow Plow Prep Pkg +135
Air Conditioning +135
Camper/Towing Package +55
Cruise Control +30
Dual Rear Wheels[Opt on 4WD] +130
Limited Slip Diff +45
Power Door Locks +30
Power Windows +30

Model Description	Trade-in Value	Market Value
RAM VAN / WAGON 1992		

Alloy wheels and moldings are revised, and two engines get an infusion of horsepower.

RAM VAN

Category H

Model Description	Trade-in Value	Market Value
2 Dr 1500 Ram Van	3890	4900
2 Dr 1500 Ram Van Ext	4115	5180
2 Dr 2500 Ram Van	4040	5085
2 Dr 2500 Ram Van Ext	4225	5325
2 Dr 2500 Maxi Ram Van Ext	4495	5660
2 Dr 3500 Ram Van Ext	4575	5760
2 Dr 3500 Maxi Ram Van Ext	4835	6090

RAM WAGON

Category H

Model Description	Trade-in Value	Market Value
2 Dr 1500 Ram Wagon	4280	5395
2 Dr 1500 LE Ram Wagon	4775	6015
2 Dr 2500 Ram Wagon Ext	4690	5910
2 Dr 2500 LE Ram Wagon Ext	5180	6525
2 Dr 2500 LE Maxi Ram Wagon Ext	5530	6970
2 Dr 2500 Maxi Ram Wagon Ext	5545	6985
2 Dr 3500 Ram Wagon Ext	5040	6350
2 Dr 3500 LE Ram Wagon Ext	5475	6895
2 Dr 3500 Maxi Ram Wagon Ext	5390	6790

OPTIONS FOR RAM VAN/WAGON
8 cyl 5.2 L Engine[Std on 3500] +95
8 cyl 5.9 L Engine[Opt on 1500,2500,3500] +75
Auto 3-Speed Transmission[Opt on 1500,Ram Van,Ram Van Ext] +55
Auto 4-Speed Transmission +75
Travel Seating Pkg +150

Don't forget to refer to the Mileage Adjustment Table at the back of this book!

DODGE 92

Model Description	Trade-in Value	Market Value	Model Description	Trade-in Value	Market Value

Air Conditioning[Opt on 1500,2500,Maxi,STD] +135
Cruise Control[Opt on 1500,2500,Maxi,STD] +30
Dual Air Conditioning +210
Limited Slip Diff +45
Power Door Locks[Opt on 1500,2500,Maxi,STD] +30
Power Windows[Opt on 1500,2500,Maxi,STD] +30

RAMCHARGER 1992

The 5.2-liter engine gains 50 horsepower, and manual transmissions have five speeds rather than four. A Canyon Sport trim level is available this year.

Category H

2 Dr Canyon Sport Utility	6025	7585
2 Dr Canyon Sport 4WD Utility	6260	7885
2 Dr LE Utility	5775	7275
2 Dr LE 4WD Utility	6015	7575
2 Dr S Utility	5185	6530
2 Dr S 4WD Utility	5610	7065
2 Dr STD Utility	5855	7380
2 Dr STD 4WD Utility	6110	7695

OPTIONS FOR RAMCHARGER

8 cyl 5.9 L Engine +75
Auto 4-Speed Transmission[Opt on 4WD] +145
Air Conditioning +135
Cruise Control +30
Limited Slip Diff +45
Power Door Locks +30
Power Windows +30

SHADOW 1992

ES model gets body-color bumpers. Midyear, the turbo engine found in the ES is swapped for a 3.0-liter V6.

RATINGS (SCALE OF 1-10)

Overall	Safety	Reliability	Performance	Comfort	Value
6.3	5.9	6.1	7.2	6.8	5.4

Category E

2 Dr America Hbk	1405	2290
4 Dr America Hbk	1470	2400
2 Dr ES Conv	2515	4100
2 Dr ES Turbo Conv	2635	4300
2 Dr ES Hbk	1890	3080
2 Dr ES Turbo Hbk	2010	3280
4 Dr ES Hbk	1940	3170
4 Dr ES Turbo Hbk	2065	3365
2 Dr Highline Conv	2310	3770
2 Dr Highline Turbo Conv	2435	3975
2 Dr Highline Hbk	1610	2630
4 Dr Highline Hbk	1680	2740

OPTIONS FOR SHADOW

4 cyl 2.5 L Engine[Std on ES,Conv] +45
6 cyl 3.0 L Engine +120
Auto 3-Speed Transmission +90
Auto 4-Speed Transmission +110

Air Conditioning +135
Cruise Control +35
Power Door Locks +40
Power Windows +45

SPIRIT 1992

R/T gets revised gear ratios to make it accelerate faster, and revised suspension tuning to make it handle better. V6 models can be equipped with either a three-speed automatic or a four-speed unit. Alloy wheels are restyled.

RATINGS (SCALE OF 1-10)

Overall	Safety	Reliability	Performance	Comfort	Value
7	6.1	7.1	6.8	7.4	7.7

Category C

4 Dr ES Sdn	2405	3690
4 Dr ES Turbo Sdn	2525	3880
4 Dr LE Sdn	2255	3465
4 Dr LE Turbo Sdn	2375	3645
4 Dr R/T Turbo Sdn	3085	4735
4 Dr STD Sdn	1925	2955

OPTIONS FOR SPIRIT

6 cyl 3.0 L Engine[Std on ES] +115
Auto 3-Speed Transmission[Std on LE] +90
Auto 4-Speed Transmission +70
Air Conditioning +135
Anti-Lock Brakes +95
Cruise Control[Opt on STD] +35
Power Door Locks +40
Power Drivers Seat +50
Power Windows +50

STEALTH 1992

A tilt/removable glass sunroof becomes available midyear.

RATINGS (SCALE OF 1-10)

Overall	Safety	Reliability	Performance	Comfort	Value
N/A	6.3	7.5	9.4	6.8	N/A

Category F

2 Dr ES Hbk	5065	6665
2 Dr R/T Hbk	6310	8300
2 Dr R/T Turbo 4WD Hbk	7625	10030
2 Dr STD Hbk	4575	6020

OPTIONS FOR STEALTH

Auto 4-Speed Transmission +135
Air Conditioning[Std on R/T] +135
Anti-Lock Brakes[Std on R/T] +105
Cruise Control[Std on R/T] +35
Leather Seats +105
Power Door Locks[Std on R/T] +35
Power Windows[Std on R/T] +40
Sunroof +65

Don't forget to refer to the Mileage Adjustment Table at the back of this book!

Model Description	Trade-in Value	Market Value

VIPER 1992

Monstrous V10 power, cartoonish styling, and red paint characterized Dodge's new mega-buck icon. Two hundred 1992 models were produced.

Category K

2 Dr RT/10 Cpe	14195	16345

1991 DODGE

CARAVAN 1991

Van is substantially reworked, with new styling, new interior, available all-wheel drive, and optional ABS. A driver airbag is standard on models built after February 1, 1991. All models have an automatic transmission, and the turbocharged model has been dropped.

RATINGS (SCALE OF 1-10)

Overall	Safety	Reliability	Performance	Comfort	Value
6.6	4.8	3.7	7.4	8.3	8.6

Category G

2 Dr ES Pass. Van	3965	5560
2 Dr ES 4WD Pass. Van	3985	5585
2 Dr Grand LE Pass. Van	3990	5590
2 Dr Grand LE 4WD Pass. Van	3995	5600
2 Dr Grand SE Pass. Van	3350	4695
2 Dr Grand SE 4WD Pass. Van	3725	5220
2 Dr LE Pass. Van	3665	5135
2 Dr LE 4WD Pass. Van	3890	5450
2 Dr SE Pass. Van	3000	4205
2 Dr SE 4WD Pass. Van	3585	5020
2 Dr STD Cargo Van	2645	3705
2 Dr STD 4WD Cargo Van	3350	4695
2 Dr STD Cargo Van Ext	2995	4200
2 Dr STD 4WD Cargo Van Ext	3350	4695
2 Dr STD Pass. Van	2770	3885

OPTIONS FOR CARAVAN

6 cyl 3.0 L Engine[Std on ES,Cargo Van Ext] +95
6 cyl 3.3 L Engine[Opt on ES,SE,LE,STD,Cargo Van Ext] +80
Luxury Pkg +130
Premium Decor Pkg +110
7 Passenger Seating[Std on ES,Grand LE,Grand SE,LE, SE] +70
Air Conditioning[Std on ES,Grand LE,LE] +110
Anti-Lock Brakes +75
Captain Chairs (4) +80
Cruise Control[Std on ES,Grand LE,LE] +30
Power Door Locks[Std on ES,Grand LE,LE] +30
Power Drivers Seat +40
Power Windows +30

COLT 1991

GT model dropped from lineup due to lack of interest.

Category E

2 Dr GL Hbk	1055	2115
2 Dr STD Hbk	940	1880
4 Dr STD Wgn	1670	3350
4 Dr STD 4WD Wgn	1795	3600

OPTIONS FOR COLT

Auto 3-Speed Transmission +70
Air Conditioning +110
Power Door Locks +35
Power Steering[Std on 4WD] +35
Power Windows +35

DAKOTA 1991

Base four-cylinder engine gets more horsepower. Club Cab can be ordered with four-wheel drive. Slow-selling convertible model is dropped from lineup. Front styling is freshened with composite headlamps (LE and Sport), new bumper, new grille, and extended sheetmetal to better accommodate the optional V8 engine. Exterior door handles are now metal instead of plastic. Front disc brake calipers are larger. Ignition and lock keys are double-sided.

RATINGS (SCALE OF 1-10)

Overall	Safety	Reliability	Performance	Comfort	Value
N/A	4.6	6.6	6.6	7.1	N/A

Category G

2 Dr LE Ext Cab SB	3275	4585
2 Dr LE 4WD Ext Cab SB	4060	5690
2 Dr LE Std Cab LB	2960	4145
2 Dr LE 4WD Std Cab LB	3585	5025
2 Dr LE Std Cab SB	2960	4145
2 Dr LE 4WD Std Cab SB	3790	5310
2 Dr S Std Cab SB	2265	3170
2 Dr SE Ext Cab SB	3290	4610
2 Dr SE 4WD Ext Cab SB	4085	5725
2 Dr SE Std Cab LB	2955	4140
2 Dr SE 4WD Std Cab LB	3875	5430
2 Dr SE Std Cab SB	2955	4140
2 Dr SE 4WD Std Cab SB	3800	5325
2 Dr STD Ext Cab SB	2965	4150
2 Dr STD 4WD Ext Cab SB	3735	5235
2 Dr STD Std Cab LB	2690	3770
2 Dr STD 4WD Std Cab LB	3510	4920
2 Dr STD Std Cab SB	2690	3770
2 Dr STD 4WD Std Cab SB	3510	4920
2 Dr Sport Ext Cab SB	3395	4755
2 Dr Sport 4WD Ext Cab SB	4080	5715
2 Dr Sport Std Cab LB	3310	4640
2 Dr Sport 4WD Std Cab LB	4110	5760
2 Dr Sport Std Cab SB	3135	4390
2 Dr Sport 4WD Std Cab SB	3910	5475

DODGE 91

Model Description	Trade-in Value	Market Value	Model Description	Trade-in Value	Market Value

OPTIONS FOR DAKOTA
6 cyl 3.9 L Engine +70
8 cyl 5.2 L Engine +130
Auto 4-Speed Transmission +120
Snow Plow Prep Pkg +100
Air Conditioning +110
Camper/Towing Package +40
Cruise Control +30
Limited Slip Diff +35
Power Door Locks +30
Power Steering[Std on 4WD] +40
Power Windows +30

DAYTONA   1991

No changes.
Category C

Model	Trade-in	Market
2 Dr ES Hbk	1635	3145
2 Dr STD Hbk	1305	2515
2 Dr STD Turbo Hbk	1525	2930

Category F

Model	Trade-in	Market
2 Dr IROC Hbk	2830	3715
2 Dr IROC Turbo Hbk	2885	3790
2 Dr Shelby Turbo Hbk	3225	4235

OPTIONS FOR DAYTONA
6 cyl 3.0 L Engine[Std on IROC] +90
Auto 3-Speed Transmission +80
Auto 4-Speed Transmission +95
CS Competition Pkg +285
Leather Enthusiast Seats +175
Air Conditioning +110
Anti-Lock Brakes +85
Cruise Control +30
Power Door Locks +25
Power Drivers Seat +30
Power Windows +30

DYNASTY   1991

Remote keyless entry is a new option, available with a security system and illuminated entry in an option package. Door glass is thicker, and front suspensions are improved.
Category C

Model	Trade-in	Market
4 Dr LE Sdn	1875	3610
4 Dr STD Sdn	1790	3445

OPTIONS FOR DYNASTY
6 cyl 3.0 L Engine[Std on LE] +90
Luxury Pkg +120
Air Conditioning +110
Anti-Lock Brakes +80
Cruise Control +30
Power Door Locks +35
Power Windows +40

MONACO   1991

No changes.

Category C

Model	Trade-in	Market
4 Dr ES Sdn	1740	3350
4 Dr LE Sdn	1550	2980

OPTIONS FOR MONACO
Air Conditioning[Opt on LE] +110
Cruise Control +30
Power Door Locks +35
Power Drivers Seat +40
Power Windows +40

RAM 50 PICKUP   1991

Rear-wheel ABS is standard on top models. V6 engine is infused with additional power. Upholstery is revised.
Category G

Model	Trade-in	Market
2 Dr LE Ext Cab SB	2810	3940
2 Dr LE 4WD Ext Cab SB	3675	5150
2 Dr SE 4WD Ext Cab SB	3445	4825
2 Dr SE Std Cab SB	2125	2980
2 Dr SE 4WD Std Cab SB	3150	4410
2 Dr STD Ext Cab SB	2330	3265
2 Dr STD Std Cab LB	1955	2740
2 Dr STD 4WD Std Cab LB	2775	3885
2 Dr STD Std Cab SB	1955	2740
2 Dr STD 4WD Std Cab SB	2630	3685

OPTIONS FOR RAM 50 PICKUP
6 cyl 3.0 L Engine +95
Auto 4-Speed Transmission +90
Air Conditioning +110
Power Steering[Std on LE,4WD] +40
Power Windows +30

RAM PICKUP   1991

New rear step bumper increases towing capacity from 3,000 to 5,000 pounds. An intercooler for turbodiesel models debuts midyear. Grille is revised, and Ram's-head hood ornament has been axed.

RAM 150

Category H

Model	Trade-in	Market
2 Dr LE Ext Cab LB	4540	5860
2 Dr LE 4WD Ext Cab LB	5310	6855
2 Dr LE Ext Cab SB	4540	5860
2 Dr LE Std Cab LB	3915	5055
2 Dr LE 4WD Std Cab LB	4565	5900
2 Dr LE Std Cab SB	3915	5055
2 Dr LE 4WD Std Cab SB	4565	5900
2 Dr S Std Cab LB	3120	4030
2 Dr S 4WD Std Cab LB	3705	4785
2 Dr S Std Cab SB	3120	4030
2 Dr S 4WD Std Cab SB	3705	4785
2 Dr SE Std Cab LB	3815	4930
2 Dr SE 4WD Std Cab LB	4470	5770
2 Dr SE Std Cab SB	3815	4930

Don't forget to refer to the Mileage Adjustment Table at the back of this book!

Model Description	Trade-in Value	Market Value
2 Dr SE 4WD Std Cab SB	4470	5770
2 Dr STD Ext Cab LB	4235	5465
2 Dr STD 4WD Ext Cab LB	4945	6390
2 Dr STD Ext Cab SB	4175	5395
2 Dr STD Std Cab LB	3160	4080
2 Dr STD 4WD Std Cab LB	3755	4850
2 Dr STD Std Cab SB	3100	4005
2 Dr STD 4WD Std Cab SB	3695	4775

RAM 250
Category H

Model Description	Trade-in Value	Market Value
2 Dr LE Ext Cab LB	5165	6670
2 Dr LE 4WD Ext Cab LB	5695	7355
2 Dr LE Std Cab LB	4355	5625
2 Dr LE 4WD Std Cab LB	5055	6530
2 Dr SE Std Cab LB	4345	5610
2 Dr SE 4WD Std Cab LB	4940	6385
2 Dr STD Ext Cab LB	4820	6225
2 Dr STD 4WD Ext Cab LB	5350	6910
2 Dr STD Std Cab LB	4050	5230
2 Dr STD 4WD Std Cab LB	4750	6135

RAM 350
Category H

Model Description	Trade-in Value	Market Value
2 Dr LE Std Cab LB	4800	6195
2 Dr LE 4WD Std Cab LB	5430	7010
2 Dr SE Std Cab LB	4685	6050
2 Dr SE 4WD Std Cab LB	5315	6865
2 Dr STD Std Cab LB	4495	5805
2 Dr STD 4WD Std Cab LB	5125	6620

OPTIONS FOR RAM PICKUP
6 cyl 5.9 L Turbodsl Engine +455
8 cyl 5.2 L Engine +80
8 cyl 5.9 L Engine +65
Auto 3-Speed Transmission +85
Auto 4-Speed Transmission +120
Snow Plow Pkg +140
Air Conditioning +110
Cruise Control +25
Dual Rear Wheels +105
Limited Slip Diff +35
Power Door Locks +25
Power Windows +25

RAM VAN/WAGON   1991

Cruise control buttons now located on steering wheel. A new air conditioning outlet next to the second rear seat of Wagons improves cooling.

RAM VAN
Category H

Model Description	Trade-in Value	Market Value
2 Dr 1500 Ram Van	3140	4055
2 Dr 1500 Ram Van Ext	3300	4260
2 Dr 2500 Ram Van	3195	4125
2 Dr 2500 Ram Van Ext	3345	4320

Model Description	Trade-in Value	Market Value
2 Dr 3500 Ram Van	3600	4650
2 Dr 3500 Ram Van Ext	3810	4920

RAM WAGON
Category H

Model Description	Trade-in Value	Market Value
2 Dr 1500 Ram Wagon	3785	4890
2 Dr 1500 LE Ram Wagon	4070	5255
2 Dr 1500 LE Ram Wagon Ext	4275	5520
2 Dr 2500 Ram Wagon	4145	5355
2 Dr 2500 Ram Wagon Ext	4455	5755
2 Dr 2500 LE Ram Wagon	4430	5725
2 Dr 2500 LE Ram Wagon Ext	4740	6125
2 Dr 3500 Ram Wagon	4455	5755
2 Dr 3500 Ram Wagon Ext	4765	6155
2 Dr 3500 LE Ram Wagon	4740	6125
2 Dr 3500 LE Ram Wagon Ext	4520	5840

OPTIONS FOR RAM VAN/WAGON
8 cyl 5.2 L Engine[Std on 3500] +80
8 cyl 5.9 L Engine[Std on Maxi] +65
Auto 3-Speed Transmission[Opt on 1500,Ram Van,Ram Van Ext] +45
Auto 4-Speed Transmission[Std on 3500,1500 STD Ram Van Ext] +60
Travel Seating Pkg +165
Air Conditioning +110
Captain Chairs (2) +70
Cruise Control +25
Dual Air Conditioning +170
Power Door Locks +25
Power Windows +25

RAMCHARGER   1991

Front styling is revised with a new grille and the exclusion of the Ram's head hood ornament. A stronger rear bumper provides more towing capacity. Models equipped with a manual transmission can be ordered with tilt steering.

Category H

Model Description	Trade-in Value	Market Value
2 Dr LE Utility	4770	6165
2 Dr LE 4WD Utility	4520	5835
2 Dr S Utility	3915	5055
2 Dr S 4WD Utility	4255	5495
2 Dr STD Utility	4450	5745
2 Dr STD 4WD Utility	4650	6010

OPTIONS FOR RAMCHARGER
8 cyl 5.9 L Engine +65
Auto 4-Speed Transmission[Opt on 4WD] +120
Snow Plow Pkg +130
Air Conditioning +110
Camper/Towing Package +45
Cruise Control +25
Limited Slip Diff +35
Power Door Locks +25
Power Windows +25

Don't forget to refer to the Mileage Adjustment Table at the back of this book!

SHADOW   1991

A bargain-basement America model is introduced, and convertible body style is added to the lineup.

RATINGS (SCALE OF 1-10)

Overall	Safety	Reliability	Performance	Comfort	Value
6.2	5.8	5.4	7.4	6.8	5.8

Category E

	Trade-in	Market
2 Dr America Hbk	1195	2395
4 Dr America Hbk	1230	2465
2 Dr ES Conv	1935	3880
2 Dr ES Turbo Conv	2025	4060
2 Dr ES Hbk	1485	2980
2 Dr ES Turbo Hbk	1575	3155
4 Dr ES Hbk	1525	3050
4 Dr ES Turbo Hbk	1610	3230
2 Dr Highline Conv	1800	3610
2 Dr Highline Turbo Conv	1895	3795
2 Dr Highline Hbk	1220	2450
4 Dr Highline Hbk	1305	2615

OPTIONS FOR SHADOW

4 cyl 2.5 L Engine[Std on ES,Conv] +40
Auto 3-Speed Transmission +75
Air Conditioning +110
Cruise Control +30
Power Door Locks +35
Power Windows[Std on Conv] +35

SPIRIT   1991

R/T trim level debuts with monochromatic paint scheme, sport-tuned suspension, 2.2-liter twin-cam turbocharged engine good for 224 horsepower, and 6.5 second zero-to-60 times. Four-wheel ABS is newly optional on all Spirit models.

RATINGS (SCALE OF 1-10)

Overall	Safety	Reliability	Performance	Comfort	Value
6.9	6	6.2	6.8	7.4	8.2

Category C

	Trade-in	Market
4 Dr ES Sdn	1790	3445
4 Dr ES Turbo Sdn	1870	3600
4 Dr LE Sdn	1640	3150
4 Dr LE Turbo Sdn	1720	3305
4 Dr R/T Turbo Sdn	2105	4055
4 Dr STD Sdn	1480	2850

OPTIONS FOR SPIRIT

6 cyl 3.0 L Engine[Std on ES] +90
Auto 3-Speed Transmission[Std on LE] +75
Auto 4-Speed Transmission +55
Air Conditioning[Std on R/T] +110
Cruise Control[Opt on STD] +30
Power Door Locks +35

Power Drivers Seat +40
Power Windows +40

STEALTH   1991

Brand-new sports car based on Mitsubishi 3000GT is available with front- or all-wheel drive. Four-wheel steering is standard with the all-wheel drive R/T Turbo model, powered by a twin-turbocharged 300-horsepower V6 engine. Base models have a 164-horse SOHC V6 engine, ES and R/T a DOHC V6 making 222 horsepower.

RATINGS (SCALE OF 1-10)

Overall	Safety	Reliability	Performance	Comfort	Value
N/A	6.2	7.1	9.4	6.8	N/A

Category F

	Trade-in	Market
2 Dr ES Hbk	4530	5945
2 Dr R/T Hbk	5630	7385
2 Dr R/T Turbo 4WD Hbk	6805	8930
2 Dr STD Hbk	4095	5375

OPTIONS FOR STEALTH

Auto 4-Speed Transmission +110
Air Conditioning[Std on R/T] +110
Anti-Lock Brakes[Std on R/T] +85
Cruise Control[Std on R/T] +30
Leather Seats +85
Power Door Locks[Std on R/T] +25
Power Windows[Std on R/T] +30

Don't forget to refer to the Mileage Adjustment Table at the back of this book!

EAGLE 98-97

Model Description	Trade-in Value	Market Value

EAGLE USA

1993 Eagle Talon

1998 EAGLE

TALON 1998

New silver exterior badging and a new black and gray interior mark the Eagle in its final year of production. A new four-speaker CD/cassette player is now optional on the ESi, and all Talons benefit from Chrysler's next generation depowered airbags.

RATINGS (SCALE OF 1-10)

Overall	Safety	Reliability	Performance	Comfort	Value
6.7	6.8	7.6	8.4	6.6	4.2

Category F
2 Dr ESi Hbk	9620	11375
2 Dr STD Hbk	9150	10820
2 Dr TSi Turbo Hbk	11555	13665
2 Dr TSi Turbo 4WD Hbk	12930	15285

OPTIONS FOR TALON
Auto 4-Speed Transmission +445
AM/FM Compact Disc Player +255
Air Conditioning +460
Aluminum/Alloy Wheels[Opt on ESi] +170
Anti-Lock Brakes +355
Cruise Control[Std on 4WD] +120
Infinity Sound System +340
Keyless Entry System +100
Leather Seats +345
Power Door Locks[Std on 4WD] +110
Power Drivers Seat +130
Power Mirrors[Opt on ESi] +65
Power Sunroof +365
Power Windows[Std on 4WD] +125
Rear Window Defroster[Std on TSi] +90

1997 EAGLE

TALON 1997

Eagle's sporty Talon sees a host of changes as Chrysler Corp. seeks to rescue this endangered species. New front and rear fascias, bodyside cladding, bright new paint colors and "sparkle" wheels and wheel covers are guaranteed to attract attention to this overshadowed model. A bargain-basement Talon is introduced with minimal standard equipment to serve as a value leader for the model.

RATINGS (SCALE OF 1-10)

Overall	Safety	Reliability	Performance	Comfort	Value
6.8	6.8	6.9	8.4	6.6	5.1

Category F
2 Dr ESi Hbk	8690	10355
2 Dr STD Hbk	8255	9835
2 Dr TSi Turbo Hbk	10495	12505
2 Dr TSi Turbo 4WD Hbk	11770	14025

OPTIONS FOR TALON
Auto 4-Speed Transmission +355
Air Conditioning +375
Aluminum/Alloy Wheels[Opt on ESi] +135
Anti-Lock Brakes +290
Compact Disc W/fm/tape +225
Cruise Control[Std on 4WD] +100
Keyless Entry System +80
Leather Seats +285
Limited Slip Diff +145
Power Door Locks[Std on 4WD] +90
Power Drivers Seat +110
Power Sunroof +300
Power Windows[Std on 4WD] +105
Premium Sound System +170

VISION 1997

The 3.5-liter engine formerly exclusive to the TSi is now available on the ESi. Automatic transmission refinements are intended to improve shifting. Eagle Vision ESis gets an improved stereo. A new color, Deep Amethyst Pearl, is now available.

RATINGS (SCALE OF 1-10)

Overall	Safety	Reliability	Performance	Comfort	Value
8.1	7.2	7.8	8.4	8.5	8.8

Category B
4 Dr ESi Sdn	8805	10550
4 Dr TSi Sdn	10380	12440

OPTIONS FOR VISION
Anti-Lock Brakes[Opt on ESi] +300
Compact Disc W/fm/tape +165
Keyless Entry System[Opt on ESi] +80
Leather Seats +305

Don't forget to refer to the Mileage Adjustment Table at the back of this

EAGLE 97-95

Model Description	Trade-in Value	Market Value	Model Description	Trade-in Value	Market Value

Lighted Entry System[Opt on ESi] +45
Power Drivers Seat +140
Power Moonroof +435
Trip Computer[Opt on ESi] +175

1996 EAGLE

SUMMIT   1996

Nothing new for the Mitsubishi-built Summit except a new choice of paint colors. The Summit wagon, a funky cross between a sedan and a minivan, gets new colors and seat fabrics.

RATINGS (SCALE OF 1-10)

Overall	Safety	Reliability	Performance	Comfort	Value
6.7	5.9	8.3	8.2	7	3.9

Category E
2 Dr DL Cpe   4270   5240
4 Dr DL Wgn   6040   7420
2 Dr ESi Cpe   4695   5765
4 Dr ESi Sdn   5575   6845
4 Dr LX Sdn   5255   6450
4 Dr LX Wgn   6540   8030
4 Dr STD 4WD Wgn   6795   8345

OPTIONS FOR SUMMIT

AM/FM Stereo Tape +110
Air Conditioning +305
Power Door Locks[Std on LX] +90
Power Mirrors[Std on LX,STD] +40
Power Steering[Opt on Cpe] +95
Rear Window Defroster[Std on STD,Wgn] +60
Rear Window Wiper[Opt on DL] +45
Remote Trunk Release[Opt on DL,LX,Cpe] +25
Tachometer[Std on Sdn] +30
Tilt Steering Wheel[Opt on ESi] +55
Tinted Glass[Opt on DL,ESi,Sdn] +35
Tutone Paint[Std on LX] +70

TALON   1996

Based on Mitsubishi mechanicals, Talon receives minor upgrades for 1996, including revised sound systems, a panic alarm, a HomeLink transmitter, and two new colors. ESi trim level gets standard 16-inch wheels.

RATINGS (SCALE OF 1-10)

Overall	Safety	Reliability	Performance	Comfort	Value
6.7	6.8	6.8	8.4	6.6	5

Category F
2 Dr ESi Hbk   7160   8675
2 Dr STD Hbk   6800   8240
2 Dr TSi Turbo Hbk   8645   10475
2 Dr TSi Turbo 4WD Hbk   9695   11745

OPTIONS FOR TALON

Auto 4-Speed Transmission +285
Air Conditioning +305
Aluminum/Alloy Wheels +110
Anti-Lock Brakes +235
Compact Disc W/fm/tape +185
Cruise Control[Std on 4WD] +80
Leather Seats +230
Power Door Locks[Std on 4WD] +75
Power Drivers Seat +90
Power Sunroof +245
Power Windows[Std on 4WD] +85

VISION   1996

An automanual transmission called AutoStick gives the 1996 Vision a feature to distinguish it as Chrysler's premier sport sedan. Interiors have been quieted down, and the ESi gets standard 16-inch wheels. Headlight illumination has been improved, new colors and seat fabrics are on board, and improved sound systems debut; all in the hope that some interest can be sparked in this slow-selling Eagle.

RATINGS (SCALE OF 1-10)

Overall	Safety	Reliability	Performance	Comfort	Value
8	7.2	7.4	8.4	8.5	8.6

Category B
4 Dr ESi Sdn   7240   8825
4 Dr TSi Sdn   8725   10635

OPTIONS FOR VISION

Anti-Lock Brakes[Opt on ESi] +245
Child Seat (1) +35
Compact Disc W/fm/tape +135
Keyless Entry System[Opt on ESi] +65
Leather Seats +250
Power Drivers Seat[Opt on ESi] +115
Power Moonroof +355
Premium Sound System +135

1995 EAGLE

SUMMIT   1995

Dual airbags for the slow-selling Eagle Summit are the only change for 1995.

RATINGS (SCALE OF 1-10)

Overall	Safety	Reliability	Performance	Comfort	Value
6.7	6.5	7.5	8.2	7	4.3

Category E
2 Dr DL Cpe   3260   4275
4 Dr DL Wgn   4600   6030
2 Dr ESi Cpe   3585   4700
4 Dr ESi Sdn   4275   5600
4 Dr LX Sdn   4020   5265

Don't forget to refer to the Mileage Adjustment Table at the back of this book!

Model Description	Trade-in Value	Market Value	Model Description	Trade-in Value	Market Value
4 Dr LX Wgn	4990	6535	*Category B*		
4 Dr STD 4WD Wgn	5195	6810	4 Dr ESi Sdn	5725	7360
			4 Dr TSi Sdn	6380	8200

OPTIONS FOR SUMMIT
4 cyl 1.8 L Engine[Opt on Wgn] +195
4 cyl 2.4 L Engine[Opt on DL] +55
Auto 3-Speed Transmission +155
Auto 4-Speed Transmission +210
AM/FM Stereo Tape +90
Air Conditioning +250
Anti-Lock Brakes +200
Cruise Control +70
Keyless Entry System +50
Luggage Rack +40
Power Door Locks[Std on LX] +75
Power Steering[Opt on Cpe] +75
Power Windows +80
Tilt Steering Wheel[Opt on ESi] +45
Tutone Paint[Std on LX] +55

OPTIONS FOR VISION
6 cyl 3.5 L Engine[Opt on ESi] +215
AM/FM Compact Disc Player +100
Anti-Lock Brakes[Opt on ESi] +200
Child Seat (1)[Opt on TSi] +30
Climate Control for AC[Opt on ESi] +50
Keyless Entry System[Opt on ESi] +50
Leather Seats +205
Power Drivers Seat[Opt on ESi] +95
Power Moonroof +290
Power Passenger Seat +110
Traction Control System +50

1994 EAGLE

TALON   1995

The Talon is redesigned for 1995. The new model features gorgeous curves and more power. Base engine creeps up to 140 horsepower, the turbo to 210 horsepower. Dual airbags replace the antiquated motorized seatbelts on the previous edition, and the Talon now meets 1997 federal side-impact standards.

RATINGS (SCALE OF 1-10)

Overall	Safety	Reliability	Performance	Comfort	Value
6.4	7.5	5.7	8.4	6.6	3.8

Category F
2 Dr ESi Hbk	5825	7210
2 Dr TSi Turbo Hbk	6870	8510
2 Dr TSi Turbo 4WD Hbk	7895	9780

OPTIONS FOR TALON
Auto 4-Speed Transmission +245
Air Conditioning +250
Anti-Lock Brakes +195
Compact Disc W/fm/tape +150
Cruise Control[Std on 4WD] +65
Keyless Entry System +55
Leather Seats +190
Power Door Locks[Std on 4WD] +60
Power Drivers Seat +70
Power Sunroof +200
Power Windows[Std on 4WD] +70

VISION   1995

No changes to the Vision.

RATINGS (SCALE OF 1-10)

Overall	Safety	Reliability	Performance	Comfort	Value
8.1	7.9	7	8.4	8.5	8.5

SUMMIT   1994

A driver airbag is added to the standard equipment list of the Eagle Summit. CFC-free air conditioning is now standard on all models equipped with air conditioning. Power steering is standard on all sedan models.

RATINGS (SCALE OF 1-10)

Overall	Safety	Reliability	Performance	Comfort	Value
N/A	N/A	7.2	8.2	7	4.7

Category E
2 Dr DL Cpe	2770	3695
4 Dr DL Wgn	3810	5085
2 Dr ES Cpe	3040	4060
4 Dr ES Sdn	3615	4825
2 Dr ESi Cpe	3155	4215
4 Dr ESi Sdn	3835	5125
4 Dr LX Sdn	3365	4495
4 Dr LX Wgn	4150	5545
4 Dr STD 4WD Wgn	4350	5805

OPTIONS FOR SUMMIT
4 cyl 2.4 L Engine[Opt on DL] +45
Auto 3-Speed Transmission +125
Auto 4-Speed Transmission +165
AM/FM Stereo Tape +75
Air Conditioning +205
Anti-Lock Brakes +160
Cruise Control +55
Keyless Entry System +40
Luggage Rack +30
Power Door Locks[Std on LX] +60
Power Steering[Opt on ES Cpe] +60
Power Windows +65
Tilt Steering Wheel[Opt on ES,ESi] +35

TALON   1994

No changes for the Talon.

Model Description	Trade-in Value	Market Value

RATINGS (SCALE OF 1-10)

Overall	Safety	Reliability	Performance	Comfort	Value
N/A	N/A	8	8.4	6.8	3.9

Category F

2 Dr DL Hbk	3545	4605
2 Dr ES Hbk	4255	5525
2 Dr TSi Turbo Hbk	4690	6095
2 Dr TSi Turbo 4WD Hbk	5295	6875

OPTIONS FOR TALON

Auto 4-Speed Transmission +190
Air Conditioning +205
Aluminum/Alloy Wheels[Std on 4WD] +75
Anti-Lock Brakes +160
Compact Disc W/fm/tape +125
Cruise Control +55
Leather Seats +155
Power Door Locks +50
Power Steering[Opt on DL] +85
Power Windows +55
Premium Sound System +95
Sunroof +95

VISION   1994

ESi models restyled to resemble their TSi stablemates by adding body cladding and a similar front fascia. The ESi's engine gains an increase in horsepower for 1994 as well. A flexible fuel version of the Vision is released in all states but California.

RATINGS (SCALE OF 1-10)

Overall	Safety	Reliability	Performance	Comfort	Value
8	7.9	6.7	8.4	8.5	8.4

Category B

4 Dr ESi Sdn	4900	6400
4 Dr TSi Sdn	5500	7180

OPTIONS FOR VISION

AM/FM Compact Disc Player +80
Climate Control for AC[Opt on ESi] +40
Infinity Sound System +155
Leather Seats +165
Overhead Console[Opt on ESi] +90
Power Drivers Seat[Opt on ESi] +75
Power Passenger Seat +90
Traction Control System +45

1993 EAGLE

SUMMIT   1993

The Eagle Summit is redesigned and in the process loses its hatchback. Offered as a coupe or sedan, the new Summit is longer than the one it replaces, which translates into more interior room for passengers. The Summit is now available as a base DL or upscale ES. Fortunately, the 113-horsepower engine can be had

on both models. Antilock brakes are a thoughtful option on the ES models and wagons. The minivan/station wagon hybrid is positioned to take advantage of those consumers who want the convenience of a minivan and the driveability of a car. There is seating for five in the Summit Wagon, which is available as a DL, LX or all-wheel-drive model.

RATINGS (SCALE OF 1-10)

Overall	Safety	Reliability	Performance	Comfort	Value
N/A	N/A	5.9	8.2	7	6.6

Category E

2 Dr DL Cpe	1850	2660
4 Dr DL Sdn	2230	3205
4 Dr DL Wgn	2640	3800
2 Dr ES Cpe	2040	2935
4 Dr ES Sdn	2500	3600
4 Dr LX Wgn	2845	4095
4 Dr STD 4WD Wgn	3105	4470

OPTIONS FOR SUMMIT

4 cyl 1.8 L Engine[Std on ES,Wgn] +80
4 cyl 2.4 L Engine[Opt on DL Wgn] +35
Auto 3-Speed Transmission +105
Auto 4-Speed Transmission +140
AM/FM Stereo Tape +60
Air Conditioning +165
Aluminum/Alloy Wheels +65
Anti-Lock Brakes +135
Cruise Control +45
Luggage Rack +25
Power Door Locks +50
Power Steering[Opt on ES,Sdn] +50
Power Windows +55
Tilt Steering Wheel[Opt on ES] +30

TALON   1993

The Talon gets a new base model to attract bargain shoppers. The new Talon DL comes standard with a disappointing 92-horsepower engine. Geez, that's just a little more than the base Summit. The former base model is renamed the ES.

RATINGS (SCALE OF 1-10)

Overall	Safety	Reliability	Performance	Comfort	Value
N/A	N/A	8.1	8.4	6.8	4.4

Category F

2 Dr DL Hbk	2740	4095
2 Dr ES Hbk	3290	4920
2 Dr TSi Turbo Hbk	3630	5430
2 Dr TSi Turbo 4WD Hbk	4095	6125

OPTIONS FOR TALON

Auto 4-Speed Transmission +155
Air Conditioning +170
Aluminum/Alloy Wheels[Std on 4WD] +60

Model Description	Trade-in Value	Market Value
Anti-Lock Brakes +130		
Compact Disc W/fm/tape +100		
Cruise Control +45		
Leather Seats +125		
Power Door Locks +40		
Power Steering[Opt on DL] +70		
Power Windows +45		
Premium Sound System +75		
Sunroof +80		

VISION   1993

Eagle receives its version of the Chrysler LH sedan in the form of the Vision. Available as an ESi or TSi, the Vision features cab-forward styling, dual airbags, V6 power, and available antilock brakes. TSi models are the sportier of the two, it comes equipped with a touring suspension, standard antilock brakes, a 214-horsepower engine, and sixteen-inch wheels.

RATINGS (SCALE OF 1-10)

Overall	Safety	Reliability	Performance	Comfort	Value
7.8	7.8	6.4	8.4	8.5	7.8

Category B	Trade-in	Market
4 Dr ESi Sdn	3495	4890
4 Dr TSi Sdn	4020	5625

OPTIONS FOR VISION

AM/FM Compact Disc Player +65		
Anti-Lock Brakes[Opt on ESi] +135		
Climate Control for AC[Opt on ESi] +35		
Cruise Control[Opt on ESi] +45		
Dual Power Seats +75		
Keyless Entry System +35		
Leather Seats +135		
Power Door Locks[Opt on ESi] +50		
Power Windows +55		
Premium Sound System +75		
Traction Control System +35		

1992 EAGLE

PREMIER   1992

Exterior tweaks to the Premier include a new grille, tail lights and new paint.

Category C	Trade-in	Market
4 Dr ES Sdn	1950	3850
4 Dr ES Limited Sdn	1950	3850
4 Dr LX Sdn	1705	3365

OPTIONS FOR PREMIER

Anti-Lock Brakes[Opt on ES,LX] +95	
Cruise Control[Opt on LX] +35	
Leather Seats[Opt on ES] +100	
Power Door Locks[Opt on LX] +40	
Power Drivers Seat[Opt on ES,LX] +50	
Power Windows[Opt on ES,LX] +50	

SUMMIT   1992

Cloth seats are now optional on base models for those who don't like the adhesive quality imparted by vinyl seats in the summer.

Category E	Trade-in	Market
4 Dr DL Wgn	2070	3405
2 Dr ES Hbk	1495	2455
4 Dr ES Sdn	1825	3000
4 Dr LX Wgn	2195	3610
2 Dr STD Hbk	1350	2220
4 Dr STD Sdn	1645	2705
4 Dr STD 4WD Wgn	2435	4005

OPTIONS FOR SUMMIT

4 cyl 2.4 L Engine +30	
Auto 3-Speed Transmission +90	
Auto 4-Speed Transmission +115	
Air Conditioning +135	
Anti-Lock Brakes +110	
Cruise Control +35	
Power Door Locks +40	
Power Windows +45	

TALON   1992

The Talon is redesigned for 1992, getting a new grille, headlights, taillights and sheetmetal.

RATINGS (SCALE OF 1-10)

Overall	Safety	Reliability	Performance	Comfort	Value
N/A	N/A	7.2	8.4	6.8	3.3

Category F	Trade-in	Market
2 Dr STD Hbk	2745	4145
2 Dr TSi Turbo Hbk	3035	4590
2 Dr TSi Turbo 4WD Hbk	3425	5175

OPTIONS FOR TALON

Auto 4-Speed Transmission +130	
Air Conditioning +135	
Anti-Lock Brakes +105	
Cruise Control +35	
Leather Seats +105	
Power Door Locks +35	
Power Windows +40	
Sunroof +65	

1991 EAGLE

PREMIER   1991

No changes for the Premier.

Category C	Trade-in	Market
4 Dr ES Sdn	1815	3440
4 Dr ES Limited Sdn	1835	3480
4 Dr LX Sdn	1590	3020

Don't forget to refer to the Mileage Adjustment Table at the back of this

Model Description	Trade-in Value	Market Value

OPTIONS FOR PREMIER
Leather Seats[Opt on ES] +85
Power Door Locks[Opt on LX] +35
Power Drivers Seat[Opt on ES,LX] +40
Power Windows[Opt on ES,LX] +40

SUMMIT 1991
No changes to the Summit.

Category E	Trade-in Value	Market Value
2 Dr ES Hbk	920	1985
4 Dr ES Sdn	1130	2435
2 Dr STD Hbk	815	1760
4 Dr STD Sdn	1010	2180

OPTIONS FOR SUMMIT
Auto 3-Speed Transmission +75
Auto 4-Speed Transmission +90
Air Conditioning +110
Power Door Locks +35
Power Windows +35

TALON 1991
Antilock brakes are now available on the Talon.

RATINGS (SCALE OF 1-10)

Overall	Safety	Reliability	Performance	Comfort	Value
N/A	N/A	6.7	8.4	6.8	4.2

Category F	Trade-in Value	Market Value
2 Dr STD Hbk	2555	3630
2 Dr TSi Turbo Hbk	2865	4075
2 Dr TSi Turbo 4WD Hbk	3235	4595

OPTIONS FOR TALON
Auto 4-Speed Transmission +105
Air Conditioning +110
Anti-Lock Brakes +85
Cruise Control +30
Leather Seats +85
Power Door Locks +25
Power Windows +30
Sunroof +55

Don't forget to refer to the Mileage Adjustment Table at the back of this book!

FORD 00

FORD   USA

1997 Ford F-150

2000 FORD

CARGO VAN   2000

The 5.4-liter V8 and the 6.8-liter V10 gas engines generate more horsepower and torque. Four-wheel antilock brakes are now standard on all models. The Light Convenience Group, including courtesy lights, a rear cargo light, a chime warning module, a "headlamps on" alert, and illuminated courtesy door lights, is now standard on all models. The handling package has been made standard on all Econolines. The towing package is standard on all wagons. The instrument panel has been simplified. Remote keyless entry and power sail-mount mirrors are standard on recreational vans.

Category H

	Trade-in	Market
2 Dr E-150 STD Cargo Van	14225	16450
2 Dr E-250 STD Cargo Van	14975	17320
2 Dr E-250 STD Cargo Van	16635	19240
2 Dr E-250 STD Cargo Van Ext	15545	17985
2 Dr E-350 STD Cargo Van Ext	17295	20005

OPTIONS FOR CARGO VAN
10 cyl 6.8 L Engine +500
8 cyl 4.6 L Engine +650
8 cyl 5.4 L Engine[Std on E-350] +1065
8 cyl 7.3 L Turbodsl Engine +3765
AM/FM Stereo Tape +165
Cruise Control +155
Dual Air Conditioning +1055
Keyless Entry System +145
Power Door Locks +155
Power Mirrors +85
Power Windows +155
Privacy Glass +130
Tilt Steering Wheel +155

CONTOUR   2000

The Contour LX is dropped, leaving either the Contour SE Sport or SVT Contour to pick from. New colors are offered and an emergency trunk-release handle is standard.

Category C

	Trade-in	Market
4 Dr SE Sdn	11510	13490
4 Dr SE Sport Sdn	11585	13575
4 Dr SVT Sdn	15470	18125

OPTIONS FOR CONTOUR
6 cyl 2.5 L Engine[Opt on SE] +405
Auto 5-Speed Transmission[Std on SE] +665
AM/FM Compact Disc Player +285
Aluminum/Alloy Wheels[Opt on SE] +255
Anti-Lock Brakes[Std on SVT] +485
Compact Disc W/fm/tape +265
Keyless Entry System[Opt on SE] +150
Power Drivers Seat[Std on SVT] +245
Power Moonroof +560
Traction Control System[Std on SVT] +175

CROWN VICTORIA   2000

New safety items have been added, including an emergency trunk release, child seat-anchor brackets, and the Belt Minder system. The rear-axle ratio for Crown Victorias with the handling package changes from 3.27 to 3.55, for quicker acceleration. Two new shades of green are offered—Tropical Green and Dark Green Satin.

Category B

	Trade-in	Market
4 Dr LX Sdn	17355	20115
4 Dr STD Sdn	15880	18405

OPTIONS FOR CROWN VICTORIA
AM/FM Compact Disc Player +270
Aluminum/Alloy Wheels +270
Climate Control for AC +140
Dual Power Seats +320
Keyless Entry System[Std on LX] +145
Leather Seats +560
Power Drivers Seat[Std on LX] +260
Traction Control System +145

ECONOLINE WAGON   2000

The 5.4-liter V8 and the 6.8-liter V10 gas engines generate more horsepower and torque. Four-wheel antilock brakes are now standard on all models. The Light Convenience Group, including courtesy lights, a rear cargo light, a chime warning module, a "headlamps on" alert, and illuminated courtesy door lights, is now standard on all models. The handling package has been made standard on all Econolines. The towing package is standard on all wagons. The instrument panel has been simplified. Remote keyless

---

Don't forget to refer to the Mileage Adjustment Table at the back of this book!

Model Description	Trade-in Value	Market Value

entry and power sail-mount mirrors are standard on recreational vans.

Category H

Model	Trade-in	Market
2 Dr E-150 Chateau Club Wgn Pass. Van	19400	22445
2 Dr E-150 Chateau Pass. Van	17520	20270
2 Dr E-150 XL Pass. Van	15525	17960
2 Dr E-350 XL Pass. Van	17460	20195
2 Dr E-350 XL Pass. Van Ext	18540	21450
2 Dr E-150 XLT Pass. Van	17600	20360
2 Dr E-350 XLT Pass. Van	19515	22575
2 Dr E-350 XLT Pass. Van Ext	19760	22855

OPTIONS FOR ECONOLINE WAGON
10 cyl 6.8 L Engine +500
8 cyl 4.6 L Engine +650
8 cyl 5.4 L Engine[Std on E-350] +1065
8 cyl 7.3 L Turbodsl Engine +3765
Aluminum/Alloy Wheels[Opt on XLT] +255
Compact Disc W/fm/tape +255
Cruise Control[Opt on XL] +155
Dual Air Conditioning[Opt on E-150 XL Wagon, E-350 SD XL Wagon] +1055
Keyless Entry System +145
Power Door Locks[Opt on XL] +155
Power Drivers Seat +230
Power Windows[Std on Chateau, XLT] +155
Privacy Glass +130
Tilt Steering Wheel[Opt on XL] +155

ESCORT 2000

The 2000 Escort line has been simplified. The station wagon is discontinued, and there is now only one trim level for the sedan and coupe models.

Category E

Model	Trade-in	Market
4 Dr STD Sdn	9220	10875
2 Dr ZX2 Cpe	9065	10690

OPTIONS FOR ESCORT
Auto 4-Speed Transmission +665
S/R Pkg +1220
Air Conditioning +680
Aluminum/Alloy Wheels[Std on ZX2] +275
Anti-Lock Brakes +545
Compact Disc W/fm/tape +395
Cruise Control +185
Keyless Entry System +135
Power Door Locks +205
Power Mirrors[Std on ZX2] +90
Power Moonroof +475
Power Windows +215
Tilt Steering Wheel +125

EXCURSION 2000

The Excursion is an entirely new SUV based on Ford's F-250 Super Duty truck platform. It is the largest vehicle

of its type, outgunning even the Chevy Suburban in terms of overall size and interior space.

Category H

Model	Trade-in	Market
4 Dr Limited Utility	25415	29395
4 Dr Limited 4WDUtility	27465	31770
4 Dr XLT Utility	22760	26330
4 Dr XLT 4WD Utility	24960	28875

OPTIONS FOR EXCURSION
10 cyl 6.8 L Engine[Std on 4WD] +500
8 cyl 5.4 L Engine[Std on 2WD] +1065
8 cyl 7.3 L Turbodsl Engine +3765
Compact Disc Changer +365
Leather Seats[Opt on XLT] +815
Power Drivers Seat[Opt on XLT] +230

EXPEDITION 2000

The Expedition receives power-adjustable foot pedals, a rear sonar system for when the vehicle is backing up, optional side airbags, a revised center console and restyled wheels.

Category H

Model	Trade-in	Market
4 Dr Eddie Bauer Utility	25150	29095
4 Dr Eddie Bauer 4WD Utility	27720	32065
4 Dr XLT Utility	20845	24110
4 Dr XLT 4WD Utility	22810	26385

OPTIONS FOR EXPEDITION
8 cyl 5.4 L Engine[Opt on XLT, 2WD] +1065
Aluminum/Alloy Wheels +255
Auto Load Leveling +575
Automatic Dimming Mirror[Opt on XLT] +120
Camper/Towing Package +270
Compact Disc Changer[Opt on XLT] +365
Dual Air Conditioning[Opt on XLT] +1055
Fog Lights[Opt on XLT] +105
Heated Front Seats +295
Heated Power Mirrors[Opt on XLT] +75
Leather Seats[Opt on XLT] +815
Privacy Glass[Opt on XLT] +130
Running Boards[Opt on XLT] +285

EXPLORER 2000

The recently introduced Reverse Sensing System continues to be an option. A color-keyed, two-spoke leather-wrapped steering wheel (with auxiliary audio, climate and speed control) is now standard on Eddie Bauer models. XLT Sport/Eddie Bauer/Limited models with 5.0-liter V8s receive a trailer-towing package as standard equipment. The XL is available only for fleet sales, and the XLS replaces the XL Appearance as the base retail model.

Category G

Model	Trade-in	Market
4 Dr Eddie Bauer Utility	23350	27220
4 Dr Eddie Bauer 4WD Utility	24765	28870
4 Dr Limited Utility	23530	27435

Don't forget to refer to the Mileage Adjustment Table at the back of this book!

Model Description	Trade-in Value	Market Value	Model Description	Trade-in Value	Market Value
4 Dr Limited 4WD Utility	24945	29085	4 Dr XL Ext Cab SB	13565	15695
2 Dr Sport Utility	14800	17255	4 Dr XL 4WD Ext Cab SB	16245	18795
2 Dr Sport 4WD Utility	17035	19860	4 Dr XL Ext Cab Stepside SB	14270	16505
4 Dr XL Utility	16445	19175	4 Dr XL 4WD Ext Cab Stepside SB		
4 Dr XL 4WD Utility	17800	20755		16950	19605
4 Dr XLS Utility	17260	20125	2 Dr XL Std Cab LB	11915	13780
4 Dr XLS 4WD Utility	19115	22205	2 Dr XL 4WD Std Cab LB	14230	16460
4 Dr XLT Utility	20065	23395	2 Dr XL Std Cab SB	11885	13750
4 Dr XLT 4WD Utility	21550	25125	2 Dr XL 4WD Std Cab SB	14020	16220
			2 Dr XL Std Cab Stepside SB	12405	14350

OPTIONS FOR EXPLORER

6 cyl 4.0 L SOHC Engine[Std on Eddie Bauer,Limited] +440
8 cyl 5.0 L Engine +440
Auto 5-Speed Transmission[Std on Eddie Bauer,Limited, XLT] +895
Comfort Group +690
Premium Sport Group +790
AM/FM Compact Disc Player[Std on XLT] +260
Compact Disc Changer +415
Compact Disc W/fm/tape[Std on Eddie Bauer,Limited] +365
Cruise Control[Std on Eddie Bauer,Limited,XLT] +170
Fog Lights[Opt on Sport] +120
Keyless Entry System[Opt on Sport,XLS] +160
Leather Seats[Opt on Sport,XLT] +640
Overhead Console[Opt on Sport] +130
Power Drivers Seat[Std on XLT] +230
Power Moonroof +710
Privacy Glass[Std on Limited,Sport,XLT] +225
Running Boards[Std on Eddie Bauer,Limited] +315
Tilt Steering Wheel[Std on Eddie Bauer,Limited,XLT] +145

F-SERIES PICKUP   2000

F-150

Category H

Model Description	Trade-in Value	Market Value
4 Dr Harley-Davidson Ext Cab Stepside SB		
	22875	26460
4 Dr Lariat Ext Cab LB	18480	21375
4 Dr Lariat 4WD Ext Cab LB	20765	24020
4 Dr Lariat Ext Cab SB	18270	21135
4 Dr Lariat 4WD Ext Cab SB	20555	23780
4 Dr Lariat Ext Cab Stepside SB		
	18970	21945
4 Dr Lariat 4WD Ext Cab Stepside SB		
	21255	24590
4 Dr Work Ext Cab LB	13055	15100
4 Dr Work 4WD Ext Cab LB	15640	18090
4 Dr Work Ext Cab SB	12855	14870
4 Dr Work 4WD Ext Cab SB	15440	17860
2 Dr Work Std Cab LB	11260	13025
2 Dr Work 4WD Std Cab LB	13490	15605
2 Dr Work Std Cab SB	11060	12790
2 Dr Work 4WD Std Cab SB	13290	15375
4 Dr XL Ext Cab LB	13775	15935
4 Dr XL 4WD Ext Cab LB	16455	19035

Model Description	Trade-in Value	Market Value
2 Dr XL 4WD Std Cab Stepside SB		
	14720	17030
4 Dr XLT Ext Cab LB	15855	18340
4 Dr XLT 4WD Ext Cab LB	18495	21395
4 Dr XLT Ext Cab SB	15940	18435
4 Dr XLT 4WD Ext Cab SB	18290	21155
4 Dr XLT Ext Cab Stepside SB	16350	18910
4 Dr XLT 4WD Ext Cab Stepside SB		
	19060	22045
2 Dr XLT Std Cab LB	13960	16145
2 Dr XLT 4WD Std Cab LB	16335	18900
2 Dr XLT Std Cab SB	13755	15910
2 Dr XLT 4WD Std Cab SB	16120	18650
2 Dr XLT Std Cab Stepside SB	14455	16720
2 Dr XLT 4WD Std Cab Stepside SB		
	16820	19460

F-150 SVT

Category H

Model Description	Trade-in Value	Market Value
2 Dr SVT Lightning Sprchgd Std Cab Stepside SB		
	25830	29875

F-250

Category H

Model Description	Trade-in Value	Market Value
4 Dr Lariat Crew Cab LB	20010	23150
4 Dr Lariat 4WD Crew Cab LB	22155	25630
4 Dr Lariat Crew Cab SB	19875	22990
4 Dr Lariat 4WD Crew Cab SB	22015	25465
4 Dr Lariat Ext Cab LB	18690	21620
4 Dr Lariat 4WD Ext Cab LB	20825	24090
4 Dr Lariat Ext Cab SB	18550	21460
4 Dr Lariat 4WD Ext Cab SB	20685	23930
2 Dr Lariat Std Cab LB	17325	20040
2 Dr Lariat 4WD Std Cab LB	19470	22520
4 Dr XL Crew Cab LB	16880	19525
4 Dr XL 4WD Crew Cab LB	19025	22005
4 Dr XL Crew Cab SB	16740	19365
4 Dr XL 4WD Crew Cab SB	18880	21840
4 Dr XL Ext Cab LB	15970	18470
4 Dr XL 4WD Ext Cab LB	18110	20950
4 Dr XL Ext Cab SB	15830	18310
4 Dr XL 4WD Ext Cab SB	17975	20790
2 Dr XL Std Cab LB	14320	16565

Don't forget to refer to the Mileage Adjustment Table at the back of this book!

Model Description	Trade-in Value	Market Value
2 Dr XL 4WD Std Cab LB	16465	19045
4 Dr XLT Crew Cab LB	18805	21750
4 Dr XLT 4WD Crew Cab LB	20950	24230
4 Dr XLT Crew Cab SB	18665	21590
4 Dr XLT 4WD Crew Cab SB	20810	24070
4 Dr XLT Ext Cab LB	17490	20235
4 Dr XLT 4WD Ext Cab LB	19635	22710
4 Dr XLT Ext Cab SB	17355	20075
4 Dr XLT 4WD Ext Cab SB	19495	22550
2 Dr XLT Std Cab LB	16120	18645
2 Dr XLT 4WD Std Cab LB	18260	21120

F-350

Category H

Model Description	Trade-in Value	Market Value
4 Dr Lariat Crew Cab LB	21215	24540
4 Dr Lariat 4WD Crew Cab LB	23190	26825
4 Dr Lariat Crew Cab SB	21075	24380
4 Dr Lariat 4WD Crew Cab SB	23050	26665
4 Dr Lariat Ext Cab LB	19985	23115
4 Dr Lariat 4WD Ext Cab LB	22125	25595
4 Dr Lariat Ext Cab SB	19845	22955
4 Dr Lariat 4WD Ext Cab SB	21985	25435
2 Dr Lariat Std Cab LB	18380	21260
2 Dr Lariat 4WD Std Cab LB	20525	23745
4 Dr XL Crew Cab LB	17690	20460
4 Dr XL 4WD Crew Cab LB	19835	22945
4 Dr XL Crew Cab SB	17550	20300
4 Dr XL 4WD Crew Cab SB	19695	22785
4 Dr XL Ext Cab LB	16865	19510
4 Dr XL 4WD Ext Cab LB	19015	21995
4 Dr XL Ext Cab SB	16725	19350
4 Dr XL 4WD Ext Cab SB	18875	21835
2 Dr XL Std Cab LB	14980	17330
2 Dr XL 4WD Std Cab LB	17125	19810
4 Dr XLT Crew Cab LB	19860	22975
4 Dr XLT 4WD Crew Cab LB	21845	25270
4 Dr XLT Crew Cab SB	19720	22815
4 Dr XLT 4WD Crew Cab SB	21705	25105
4 Dr XLT Ext Cab LB	18640	21565
4 Dr XLT 4WD Ext Cab LB	20790	24045
4 Dr XLT Ext Cab SB	18500	21400
4 Dr XLT 4WD Ext Cab SB	20650	23885
2 Dr XLT Std Cab LB	17025	19695
2 Dr XLT 4WD Std Cab LB	19180	22185

OPTIONS FOR F-SERIES PICKUP
10 cyl 6.8 L Engine +500
8 cyl 4.6 L Engine +650
8 cyl 5.4 L Engine[Std on F-250,F-350,Harley-Davidson Ext Cab Step] +1065
8 cyl 7.3 L Turbodsl Engine +3765
Auto 4-Speed Transmission[Opt on F-250,F-350, Work,XL,XLT] +895

Off-Road Pkg +725
AM/FM Compact Disc Player[Opt on XL,XLT] +255
Air Conditioning[Opt on Work,XL] +665
Aluminum/Alloy Wheels +255
Anti-Lock Brakes +400
Camper/Towing Package +270
Compact Disc Changer[Opt on F-150] +365
Compact Disc W/fm/tape +255
Cruise Control[Opt on Work,XL] +155
Fog Lights[Opt on XL] +105
Keyless Entry System +145
Limited Slip Diff +215
Power Drivers Seat +230
Power Mirrors +85
Sliding Rear Window[Std on F-150 SVT] +95
Tilt Steering Wheel[Opt on Work,XL] +155
Trailer Hitch[Std on F-150 SVT] +135

FOCUS   2000

This is Ford's all-new "world car" that will be sold concurrently with the Escort. Everything from interior room to performance has been addressed to make this European-engineered compact a winner in the small-car segment.

Category E

Model Description	Trade-in Value	Market Value
4 Dr LX Sdn	9435	11125
4 Dr SE Sdn	10355	12215
4 Dr SE Wgn	11695	13795
4 Dr Sony Limited Sdn	11535	13605
4 Dr ZTS Sdn	11540	13610
2 Dr ZX3 Hbk	9240	10900

OPTIONS FOR FOCUS
4 cyl 2.0 L ZETEC Engine[Opt on SE] +165
Auto 4-Speed Transmission[Std on Wgn] +665
Kona Mountain Bike Pkg +1075
AM/FM Compact Disc Player[Opt on LX,SE] +355
Air Conditioning[Opt on LX,ZX3] +680
Aluminum/Alloy Wheels[Opt on LX] +275
Anti-Lock Brakes[Std on ZTS] +545
Cruise Control[Std on ZTS] +185
Fog Lights[Std on ZX3] +125
Keyless Entry System[Opt on LX,ZX3] +135
Leather Seats +720
Power Door Locks[Opt on LX,ZX3] +205
Power Windows[Std on ZTS] +215
Tilt Steering Wheel[Std on ZTS] +125

MUSTANG   2000

The Mustang has three updated colors: Performance Red, Amazon Green and Sunburst Gold. A child-safety-seat anchoring system is standard on both the coupe and convertible. New 16-inch wheels and tires are offered as an option on appearance package-equipped V6 Mustangs. The 2000 Mustang also features a tri-color bar emblem on the sides of the front fenders.

Don't forget to refer to the Mileage Adjustment Table at the back of this book!

Model Description	Trade-in Value	Market Value	Model Description	Trade-in Value	Market Value
Category F			*Anti-Lock Brakes +475*		
2 Dr Cobra Conv	23645	27440	*Bed Liner +230*		
2 Dr Cobra Cpe	20710	24030	*Cruise Control +170*		
2 Dr GT Conv	19060	22120	*Fog Lights +120*		
2 Dr GT Cpe	15935	18490	*Keyless Entry System +160*		
2 Dr STD Conv	16195	18795	*Power Door Locks +190*		
2 Dr STD Cpe	12630	14655	*Power Mirrors +110*		
			Power Windows +200		
			Sliding Rear Window +100		
			Tilt Steering Wheel +145		

OPTIONS FOR MUSTANG
Auto 4-Speed Transmission +665
Anti-Lock Brakes[Opt on STD] +530
Cruise Control[Std on Cobra] +180
Leather Seats[Std on Cobra] +520
Power Drivers Seat[Std on Cobra] +195
Rear Window Defroster[Std on Cobra] +140
Traction Control System[Std on Cobra] +300

RANGER   2000

For 2000, the 2WD can be had with a "Trailhead" off-road style suspension package complete with larger tires and wheels, giving it the tough look of its 4WD cousin. All Ranger models have new wheel designs, and the XLT 4WD Off-Road Group receives a stainless steel front-suspension skid plate.

Category G		
2 Dr XL Ext Cab SB	11370	13255
2 Dr XL 4WD Ext Cab SB	13025	15185
2 Dr XL 4WD Ext Cab Stepside SB		
	11530	13435
2 Dr XL Std Cab LB	9430	10940
2 Dr XL 4WD Std Cab LB	12200	14225
2 Dr XL Std Cab SB	9285	10745
2 Dr XL 4WD Std Cab SB	11860	13830
2 Dr XL Std Cab Stepside SB	9360	10895
2 Dr XLT Ext Cab SB	11840	13800
2 Dr XLT 4WD Ext Cab SB	14655	17090
2 Dr XLT Ext Cab Stepside SB	11820	13780
2 Dr XLT 4WD Ext Cab Stepside SB		
	14640	17070
2 Dr XLT Std Cab LB	10620	12380
2 Dr XLT 4WD Std Cab LB	13830	16125
2 Dr XLT Std Cab SB	10290	11995
2 Dr XLT 4WD Std Cab SB	13415	15640
2 Dr XLT Std Cab Stepside SB	10560	12315
2 Dr XLT 4WD Std Cab Stepside SB		
	13755	16040

OPTIONS FOR RANGER
6 cyl 3.0 L FLEX Engine +325
6 cyl 4.0 L Engine +835
Auto 4-Speed Transmission +895
Auto 5-Speed Transmission +935
AM/FM Stereo Tape +180
Air Conditioning +670
Aluminum/Alloy Wheels[Std on XLT 4WD] +265

TAURUS   2000

Many changes are in store for the 2000 Taurus. Styling is the most obvious, with a new look for both the front and rear. Improved safety comes from a new airbag-deployment system, adjustable pedals, seatbelt pre-tensioners and child safety-seat anchors. The ride has been made more comfortable and the powertrain has been updated for more power and less noise. The V8-powered SHO has been dropped from the lineup.

Category C		
4 Dr LX Sdn	12700	14880
4 Dr SE Sdn	13530	15855
4 Dr SE Wgn	14335	16795
4 Dr SEL Sdn	15090	17685
4 Dr SES Sdn	14205	16645

OPTIONS FOR TAURUS
6 cyl 3.0 L DOHC Engine +545
Aluminum/Alloy Wheels[Opt on LX] +255
Anti-Lock Brakes[Opt on LX,SE] +485
Compact Disc Changer +385
Cruise Control[Opt on LX] +180
Keyless Entry System[Opt on LX] +150
Leather Seats +505
Power Door Locks[Opt on LX] +210
Power Drivers Seat[Opt on LX,SE] +245
Power Moonroof +560

WINDSTAR   2000

The Windstar now has standard power-adjustable pedals and an optional rear-seat video entertainment center. There's also a new trim level called the Limited. Available mid-year 2000, it will contain more standard features than the previously top-line SEL.

Category G		
2 Dr LX Pass. Van	17570	20485
2 Dr Limited Pass. Van	24070	28065
2 Dr SE Pass. Van	20000	23320
2 Dr SEL Pass. Van	22125	25795
2 Dr STD Pass. Van	15680	18280

OPTIONS FOR WINDSTAR
6 cyl 3.8 L Engine[Opt on STD] +435
Entertainment System +1060
Pwr Sliding Lh & Rh Doors +735
Alarm System[Std on Limited] +220

Don't forget to refer to the Mileage Adjustment Table at the back of this book!

FORD 00-99

Model Description	Trade-in Value	Market Value	Model Description	Trade-in Value	Market Value

Aluminum/Alloy Wheels[Opt on LX] +265
Compact Disc W/fm/tape[Opt on LX,SE] +365
Cruise Control[Opt on LX] +170
Dual Air Conditioning[Opt on LX] +755
Keyless Entry System[Opt on LX,STD] +160
Leather Seats[Opt on SE] +640
Luggage Rack[Opt on LX] +130
Power Drivers Seat[Std on SE] +230
Power Sliding Door[Opt on LX,SE] +340
Privacy Glass[Opt on LX,STD] +225
Sliding Driver Side Door[Opt on LX,STD] +430
Tilt Steering Wheel[Opt on STD] +145
Traction Control System[Std on Limited] +220

1999 FORD

CLUB WAGON/ECONOLINE 1999

RATINGS (SCALE OF 1-10)

Overall	Safety	Reliability	Performance	Comfort	Value
N/A	N/A	N/A	6.6	7.4	N/A

E-150
Category H

2 Dr STD Econoline	12505	14550

E-150 WAGON
Category H

2 Dr Chateau Club Wagon	16115	18745
2 Dr XL Pass. Van	14105	16410
2 Dr XLT Pass. Van	15255	17745

E-250
Category H

2 Dr STD Cargo Van	12740	14820
2 Dr STD Cargo Van Ext	13180	15330

E-350 SUPER DUTY
Category H

2 Dr STD Cargo Van	14585	16970
2 Dr STD Cargo Van Ext	15220	17710

E-350 SUPER DUTY WAGON
Category H

2 Dr E-350 Chateau Pass. Van	17495	20355
2 Dr XL Pass. Van	15885	18480
2 Dr XL Pass. Van Ext	16915	19680
2 Dr XLT Pass. Van	16985	19760
2 Dr XLT Pass. Van Ext	17515	20375

OPTIONS FOR CLUB WAGON/ECONOLINE
10 cyl 6.8 L Engine +250
8 cyl 4.6 L Engine +495
8 cyl 5.4 L Engine[Std on E-350] +650
8 cyl 7.3 L Turbodsl Engine +3080
AM/FM Stereo Tape +135
Air Conditioning[Std on XL, XLT, Chateau] +545
Aluminum/Alloy Wheels[Opt on XLT] +210
Anti-Lock Brakes[Std on XL, XLT, Chateau] +330

Cruise Control +130
Dual Air Conditioning +860
Keyless Entry System +115
Power Door Locks[Std on Chateau, XLT] +125
Power Drivers Seat +190
Power Mirrors +70
Power Windows[Std on Chateau, XLT] +130
Privacy Glass +105
Tilt Steering Wheel +125

CONTOUR   1999

All-speed traction control is a new option on V6 models equipped with ABS. Tropic Green and Medium Steel Blue replace Dark Green Satin, Light Denim Blue and Pacific Green on the color chart. The integrated child seat is dropped from the optional equipment list, as are the 15-inch wheel covers. The instrument panel receives a mild revision and the 10-way power seats become 6-way power seats thanks to the deletion of the power lumbar and recline adjustments. Ford increases rear seat room in the Contour for the third year in a row, desperately trying to shed this sedan's cramped car image.

RATINGS (SCALE OF 1-10)

Overall	Safety	Reliability	Performance	Comfort	Value
N/A	6.9	7.5	8.2	7.9	N/A

Category C

4 Dr LX Sdn	9070	10775
4 Dr SE Sdn	10270	12145
4 Dr SVT Sdn	13985	16615

OPTIONS FOR CONTOUR
6 cyl 2.5 L Engine[Opt on SE] +450
Auto 4-Speed Transmission +545
AM/FM Compact Disc Player +235
AM/FM Stereo Tape[Opt on LX] +110
Aluminum/Alloy Wheels[Std on SVT] +205
Anti-Lock Brakes[Std on SVT] +395
Cruise Control[Opt on LX] +145
Keyless Entry System[Std on SVT] +125
Leather Seats[Opt on SE] +415
Power Door Locks[Opt on LX] +170
Power Drivers Seat[Std on SVT] +200
Power Moonroof +460
Power Windows[Opt on LX] +215
Rear Window Defroster[Opt on LX] +115
Traction Control System[Opt on SE] +140

CROWN VICTORIA   1999

Antilock brakes are now standard on Base and LX models. A stereo with cassette player is also newly standard on the Base model. Deep Wedgewood Blue, Light Blue and Harvest Gold are new exterior colors. Medium Wedgewood Blue, Light Denim Blue and Light Prairie Tan are no longer available.

Don't forget to refer to the Mileage Adjustment Table at the back of this book!

FORD 99

Model Description	Trade-in Value	Market Value	Model Description	Trade-in Value	Market Value

RATINGS (SCALE OF 1-10)

Overall	Safety	Reliability	Performance	Comfort	Value
N/A	8.1	8.7	7.7	8.2	N/A

Category B
4 Dr LX Sdn	15465	18220
4 Dr STD Sdn	14195	16725

OPTIONS FOR CROWN VICTORIA

AM/FM Compact Disc Player +220
Aluminum/Alloy Wheels +220
Climate Control for AC +115
Dual Power Seats +260
Keyless Entry System[Std on LX] +120
Leather Seats +460
Power Drivers Seat[Std on LX] +210
Traction Control System +115

ESCORT   1999

Ford's entry-level car gets new colors, new interior fabrics, and revised options. An AM/FM stereo with cassette is now standard on the Escort SE. An interior trunk release is now standard on all models. The sedans and wagon get all-door remote keyless entry added to their standard equipment lists. An integrated child seat is no longer available.

RATINGS (SCALE OF 1-10)

Overall	Safety	Reliability	Performance	Comfort	Value
N/A	6.1	8.6	7.2	7.3	N/A

Category E
4 Dr LX Sdn	7805	9365
4 Dr SE Sdn	8775	10530
4 Dr SE Wgn	9560	11470
2 Dr ZX2 Cool Cpe	7910	9490
2 Dr ZX2 Hot Cpe	9010	10810

OPTIONS FOR ESCORT

Auto 4-Speed Transmission +545
AM/FM Stereo Tape[Std on SE,ZX2 Hot] +200
Air Conditioning[Std on SE,ZX2 Hot] +555
Aluminum/Alloy Wheels +225
Anti-Lock Brakes +445
Cruise Control +155
Fog Lights +100
Keyless Entry System[Std on SE,ZX2 Hot] +110
Power Door Locks +165
Power Moonroof +390
Power Windows +180
Rear Window Defroster[Std on SE,ZX2 Hot] +110
Tilt Steering Wheel +100

EXPEDITION   1999

Power output is improved for both Triton V8 engines on Ford's full-size sport-ute. Package content is added for both XLT and Eddie Bauer trim levels. Power adjustable accelerator and brake pedals have been added to the option list to make it easier for the vertically challenged to reach the stop and go pedals. An updated Command Trac four-wheel drive system allows automatic four-wheel drive operation when required. Spruce Green, Harvest Gold, Tropic Green and Deep Wedgewood Blue replace Light Prairie Tan, Vermont Green, Light Denim Blue and Pacific Green on the color chart.

RATINGS (SCALE OF 1-10)

Overall	Safety	Reliability	Performance	Comfort	Value
N/A	8.3	8.4	6.8	8.1	N/A

Category H
4 Dr Eddie Bauer Utility	23105	26880
4 Dr Eddie Bauer 4WD Utility	25540	29710
4 Dr XLT Utility	18920	22015
4 Dr XLT 4WD Utility	20595	23960

OPTIONS FOR EXPEDITION

8 cyl 5.4 L Engine[Opt on XLT,2WD] +650
Aluminum/Alloy Wheels[Opt on XLT] +210
Auto Load Leveling +470
Camper/Towing Package +220
Compact Disc Changer +300
Dual Air Conditioning[Opt on XLT] +860
Fog Lights[Opt on XLT] +85
Heated Front Seats +240
Heated Power Mirrors +60
Leather Seats[Opt on XLT] +670
Privacy Glass[Opt on XLT] +105
Running Boards[Opt on XLT] +235
Third Seat[Opt on XLT] +420

EXPLORER   1999

The Explorer gets exterior revisions including new fog lamps, rocker panel moldings, wheel moldings, running boards and wheels. Harvest Gold, Chestnut, Deep Wedgewood, Spruce Green and Tropic Green replaces Light Prairie Tan, Desert Violet, Light Denim Blue, Pacific Green and Evergreen Frost on the color chart. New options include a reverse sensing system and rear load leveling. Side impact airbags are also newly available.

RATINGS (SCALE OF 1-10)

Overall	Safety	Reliability	Performance	Comfort	Value
N/A	7.8	8.8	7.8	7.3	N/A

Category G
4 Dr Eddie Bauer Utility	21640	25440
4 Dr Eddie Bauer 4WD Utility	22970	27000
4 Dr Limited Utility	22115	25995
4 Dr Limited 4WD Utility	23440	27560
2 Dr Sport Utility	14020	16480
2 Dr Sport 4WD Utility	16050	18870
4 Dr XL Utility	15320	18010
4 Dr XL 4WD Utility	16600	19515

Don't forget to refer to the Mileage Adjustment Table at the back of this book!

Model Description	Trade-in Value	Market Value
4 Dr XLS Utility	16835	19790
4 Dr XLS 4WD Utility	18000	21160
4 Dr XLT Utility	18620	21890
4 Dr XLT 4WD Utility	19950	23455

OPTIONS FOR EXPLORER

6 cyl 4.0 L SOHC Engine[Opt on Sport,XL,XLS,XLT] +360
8 cyl 5.0 L Engine +360
Auto 5-Speed Transmission[Opt on Sport,XL,XLS] +710
Premium Sport Group +580
Sport Group +530
AM/FM Compact Disc Player[Opt on Sport,XL] +210
Aluminum/Alloy Wheels[Opt on XL] +215
Compact Disc Changer +340
Compact Disc W/fm/tape[Opt on Sport,XL,XLS,XLT] +295
Cruise Control[Opt on Sport,XL,XLS] +140
Fog Lights[Opt on Sport] +95
Keyless Entry System[Opt on Sport,XL,XLS] +130
Leather Seats[Std on Eddie Bauer,Limited] +525
Luggage Rack[Opt on XL] +110
Power Door Locks[Opt on XL] +155
Power Drivers Seat[Opt on Sport, XLT] +190
Power Mirrors[Opt on XL] +90
Power Moonroof +580
Power Windows[Opt on XL] +160
Privacy Glass[Opt on XL,XLS] +185
Running Boards[Std on Eddie Bauer,Limited] +260
Tilt Steering Wheel[Opt on XL,XLS] +120

F-SERIES PICKUP   1999

RATINGS (SCALE OF 1-10)

Overall	Safety	Reliability	Performance	Comfort	Value
N/A	N/A	N/A	6.6	7.8	N/A

F-150
Category H

Model	Trade-in	Market
4 Dr Lariat Ext Cab LB	17025	19810
4 Dr Lariat 4WD Ext Cab LB	19240	22380
4 Dr Lariat Ext Cab SB	16830	19580
4 Dr Lariat 4WD Ext Cab SB	19045	22155
4 Dr Lariat Ext Cab Stepside SB	17490	20350
4 Dr Lariat 4WD Ext Cab Stepside SB	19700	22920
2 Dr Lariat Std Cab LB	15180	17660
2 Dr Lariat 4WD Std Cab LB	17590	20465
2 Dr Lariat Std Cab SB	14985	17430
2 Dr Lariat 4WD Std Cab SB	17395	20240
2 Dr Lariat Std Cab Stepside SB	15640	18195
2 Dr Lariat 4WD Std Cab Stepside SB	18055	21005
4 Dr Work Ext Cab LB	12245	14245
4 Dr Work 4WD Ext Cab LB	14675	17075
4 Dr Work Ext Cab SB	12055	14025
4 Dr Work 4WD Ext Cab SB	14485	16855
2 Dr Work Std Cab LB	10490	12205
2 Dr Work 4WD Std Cab LB	12590	14650
2 Dr Work Std Cab SB	10305	11985
2 Dr Work 4WD Std Cab SB	12405	14430
4 Dr XL Ext Cab LB	12945	15060
4 Dr XL 4WD Ext Cab LB	15465	17990
4 Dr XL Ext Cab SB	12750	14830
4 Dr XL 4WD Ext Cab SB	15270	17765
4 Dr XL Ext Cab Stepside SB	13405	15600
4 Dr XL 4WD Ext Cab Stepside SB	15930	18530
2 Dr XL Std Cab LB	11130	12950
2 Dr XL 4WD Std Cab LB	13310	15485
2 Dr XL Std Cab SB	10935	12720
2 Dr XL 4WD Std Cab SB	13115	15255
2 Dr XL Std Cab Stepside SB	11595	13490
2 Dr XL 4WD Std Cab Stepside SB	13775	16025
4 Dr XLT Ext Cab LB	14835	17255
4 Dr XLT 4WD Ext Cab LB	17420	20265
4 Dr XLT Ext Cab SB	14635	17030
4 Dr XLT 4WD Ext Cab SB	17090	19885
4 Dr XLT Ext Cab Stepside SB	15295	17795
4 Dr XLT 4WD Ext Cab Stepside SB	17880	20805
2 Dr XLT Std Cab LB	12985	15105
2 Dr XLT 4WD Std Cab LB	15285	17780
2 Dr XLT Std Cab SB	12790	14880
2 Dr XLT 4WD Std Cab SB	15085	17550
2 Dr XLT Std Cab Stepside SB	13450	15645
2 Dr XLT 4WD Std Cab Stepside SB	15745	18315

F-150 SVT
Category H

Model	Trade-in	Market
2 Dr Lightning Std Cab Stepside SB	23615	27470

F-250
Category H

Model	Trade-in	Market
4 Dr Lariat Ext Cab SB	17730	20630
4 Dr Lariat 4WD Ext Cab SB	20065	23345
2 Dr Lariat Std Cab SB	15875	18470
2 Dr Lariat 4WD Std Cab LB	18265	21250
4 Dr Work Ext Cab SB	13440	15635
4 Dr Work 4WD Ext Cab SB	15440	17960
2 Dr Work Std Cab LB	11680	13590
2 Dr Work 4WD Std Cab LB	13685	15920
4 Dr XL Ext Cab SB	14185	16505
4 Dr XL 4WD Ext Cab SB	16260	18915
2 Dr XL Std Cab LB	12365	14385
2 Dr XL 4WD Std Cab LB	14440	16795
4 Dr XLT Ext Cab SB	16135	18770
4 Dr XLT 4WD Ext Cab SB	18270	21255

Model Description	Trade-in Value	Market Value	Model Description	Trade-in Value	Market Value
2 Dr XLT Std Cab LB	14275	16605	4 Dr XL 4WD Ext Cab LB	16655	19375
2 Dr XLT 4WD Std Cab LB	16470	19160	4 Dr XL Ext Cab SB	14490	16860

F-250 SUPER DUTY

Category H

Model Description	Trade-in Value	Market Value	Model Description	Trade-in Value	Market Value
4 Dr Lariat Crew Cab LB	16930	19695	4 Dr XL 4WD Ext Cab SB	16525	19225
4 Dr Lariat 4WD Crew Cab LB	18920	22010	2 Dr XL Std Cab LB	13120	15260
4 Dr Lariat Crew Cab SB	16800	19545	2 Dr XL 4WD Std Cab LB	15150	17625
4 Dr Lariat 4WD Crew Cab SB	18790	21860	4 Dr XLT Crew Cab LB	16825	19570
4 Dr Lariat Ext Cab LB	15685	18250	4 Dr XLT 4WD Crew Cab LB	18530	21560
4 Dr Lariat 4WD Ext Cab LB	17675	20565	4 Dr XLT Crew Cab SB	16690	19420
4 Dr Lariat Ext Cab SB	15560	18100	4 Dr XLT 4WD Crew Cab SB	18400	21405
4 Dr Lariat 4WD Ext Cab SB	17685	20570	4 Dr XLT Ext Cab LB	15780	18360
2 Dr Lariat Std Cab LB	14570	16950	4 Dr XLT 4WD Ext Cab LB	17655	20535
2 Dr Lariat 4WD Std Cab LB	16555	19260	4 Dr XLT Ext Cab SB	15650	18205
4 Dr XL Crew Cab LB	14720	17125	4 Dr XLT 4WD Ext Cab SB	17520	20385
4 Dr XL 4WD Crew Cab LB	16710	19440	2 Dr XLT Std Cab LB	14275	16605
4 Dr XL Crew Cab SB	14595	16975	2 Dr XLT 4WD Std Cab LB	16150	18785
4 Dr XL 4WD Crew Cab SB	16585	19290			
4 Dr XL Ext Cab LB	13615	15840			
4 Dr XL 4WD Ext Cab LB	15605	18155			
4 Dr XL Ext Cab SB	13485	15690			
4 Dr XL 4WD Ext Cab SB	15895	18495			
2 Dr XL Std Cab LB	12360	14380			
2 Dr XL 4WD Std Cab LB	14350	16695			
4 Dr XLT Crew Cab LB	15605	18155			
4 Dr XLT 4WD Crew Cab LB	17595	20470			
4 Dr XLT Crew Cab SB	15480	18010			
4 Dr XLT 4WD Crew Cab SB	17470	20320			
4 Dr XLT Ext Cab LB	14500	16870			
4 Dr XLT 4WD Ext Cab LB	16490	19185			
4 Dr XLT Ext Cab SB	14370	16720			
4 Dr XLT 4WD Ext Cab SB	16360	19035			
2 Dr XLT Std Cab LB	13245	15410			
2 Dr XLT 4WD Std Cab LB	15235	17725			

F-350

Category H

Model Description	Trade-in Value	Market Value
4 Dr Lariat Crew Cab LB	18030	20975
4 Dr Lariat 4WD Crew Cab LB	19900	23155
4 Dr Lariat Crew Cab SB	17900	20825
4 Dr Lariat 4WD Crew Cab SB	19770	23000
4 Dr Lariat Ext Cab LB	16985	19760
4 Dr Lariat 4WD Ext Cab LB	19020	22130
4 Dr Lariat Ext Cab SB	16855	19610
4 Dr Lariat 4WD Ext Cab SB	18890	21975
2 Dr Lariat Std Cab LB	15480	18010
2 Dr Lariat 4WD Std Cab LB	17515	20375
4 Dr XL Crew Cab LB	15665	18225
4 Dr XL 4WD Crew Cab LB	17535	20400
4 Dr XL Crew Cab SB	15535	18070
4 Dr XL 4WD Crew Cab SB	17405	20245
4 Dr XL Ext Cab LB	14625	17010

OPTIONS FOR F-SERIES PICKUP

10 cyl 6.8 L Engine +250
8 cyl 4.6 L Engine[Std on F-150 4WD, F250, Lariat] +495
8 cyl 5.4 L Engine[Std on F-250 Super Duty, F-350] +650
8 cyl 7.3 L Turbodsl Engine +3080
Auto 4-Speed Transmission +665
AM/FM Compact Disc Player +205
Air Conditioning[Std on Lariat] +545
Aluminum/Alloy Wheels[Std on XLT] +210
Anti-Lock Brakes[Std on XLT, Lariat] +330
Camper/Towing Package +220
Chrome Wheels[Std on Lariat] +200
Cruise Control[Std on XLT, Lariat] +130
Fog Lights[Std on F-150 SVT, Lariat 4WD] +85
Keyless Entry System +115
Leather Seats +670
Power Door Locks[Std on XLT, Lariat] +125
Power Drivers Seat +190
Power Mirrors[Std on XLT, Lariat, F-150 SVT] +70
Power Windows[Std on XLT, Lariat, F-150 SVT] +130
Sliding Rear Window[Std on F-150 SVT] +80
Tilt Steering Wheel[Std on XLT, Lariat, F-150 SVT] +125
Trailer Hitch +110

MUSTANG   1999

Following on the heels of the '98 Camaro update, Ford gives its sports car fresh styling and more motor. The 3.8-liter V6 engine makes 190 horsepower and 220 foot-pounds of torque, putting it within spitting distance of the V6 Camaro. The SOHC V8 found in GT models gets an 16-percent increase in horsepower, and a SVT Cobra model boasts 320 ponies and an independent rear suspension. Improvements to the V6 and GT suspension and steering gear, as well as a styling update, insure that this car will maintain its lead in the pony car wars.

RATINGS (SCALE OF 1-10)

Overall	Safety	Reliability	Performance	Comfort	Value
N/A	7	N/A	8.2	7.4	N/A

Don't forget to refer to the Mileage Adjustment Table at the back of this book!

Model Description	Trade-in Value	Market Value	Model Description	Trade-in Value	Market Value
Category F			2 Dr XLT Std Cab SB	9775	11495
2 Dr Cobra Conv	22140	25815	2 Dr XLT 4WD Std Cab SB	12370	14545
2 Dr Cobra Cpe	19370	22585	2 Dr XLT Std Cab Stepside SB	10155	11935
2 Dr GT Conv	17675	20605	2 Dr XLT 4WD Std Cab Stepside SB		
2 Dr GT Cpe	15015	17505		12680	14910
2 Dr STD Conv	15155	17670			
2 Dr STD Cpe	11925	13905			

OPTIONS FOR MUSTANG

Auto 4-Speed Transmission +545
Anti-Lock Brakes[Opt on STD] +435
Cruise Control[Std on Cobra] +150
Leather Seats +425
Power Drivers Seat[Opt on STD] +160
Rear Window Defroster[Std on Cobra] +115
Traction Control System[Std on Cobra] +245

RANGER   1999

The Ranger is "Built Ford Tough" according to its ads and we tend to agree. This year's changes include standard 15-inch silver styled wheels, a class III frame-mounted hitch receiver for V6 applications, and a spare tire access lock. All models get dual front cup holders and Dark Graphite has been added to the interior colors option list while Willow Green and Denim Blue have been removed as interior choices. Too bad for you folks who liked the splashy "Splash" model, it has been discontinued. Finally, a 3.0-liter V6 flexible fuel engine is available that is designed specifically for ethanol/gasoline fuel blends.

RATINGS (SCALE OF 1-10)

Overall	Safety	Reliability	Performance	Comfort	Value
N/A	N/A	N/A	7	7.8	N/A

Category G		
2 Dr XL Ext Cab SB	10715	12595
2 Dr XL 4WD Ext Cab SB	12100	14225
2 Dr XL Ext Cab Stepside SB	10825	12760
2 Dr XL 4WD Ext Cab Stepside SB		
	12410	14590
2 Dr XL Std Cab LB	8585	10110
2 Dr XL 4WD Std Cab LB	11325	13310
2 Dr XL Std Cab SB	8365	9835
2 Dr XL 4WD Std Cab SB	11005	12935
2 Dr XL Std Cab Stepside SB	8675	10195
2 Dr XL 4WD Std Cab Stepside SB		
	11315	13300
2 Dr XLT Ext Cab SB	11205	13170
2 Dr XLT 4WD Ext Cab SB	13525	15905
2 Dr XLT Ext Cab Stepside SB	11015	13035
2 Dr XLT 4WD Ext Cab Stepside SB		
	13845	16275
2 Dr XLT Std Cab LB	10150	11930
2 Dr XLT 4WD Std Cab LB	12760	15005

OPTIONS FOR RANGER

6 cyl 3.0 L Engine[Std on 4WD] +375
6 cyl 4.0 L Engine +675
Auto 4-Speed Transmission +730
Auto 5-Speed Transmission +755
4 Dr. Supercab (XLT only) +390
AM/FM Compact Disc Player +210
Air Conditioning +550
Aluminum/Alloy Wheels[Std on XLT 4WD] +215
Anti-Lock Brakes[Std on XLT 4WD] +390
Bed Liner +185
Cruise Control +140
Fog Lights +95
Keyless Entry System +130
Power Door Locks +155
Power Mirrors +90
Power Windows +160
Sliding Rear Window +80
Tilt Steering Wheel +120

TAURUS   1999

Against all odds, the Taurus SHO pulls through for another model year. The light group and speed control are now optional on LX level cars. Chrome wheels on the SE models have been replaced with five-spoke aluminum wheels.

RATINGS (SCALE OF 1-10)

Overall	Safety	Reliability	Performance	Comfort	Value
N/A	7.8	7.9	8	7.9	N/A

Category C		
4 Dr LX Sdn	11075	13160
4 Dr SE Sdn	11690	13890
4 Dr SE Wgn	12305	14620
Category F		
4 Dr SHO Sdn	19170	22350

OPTIONS FOR TAURUS

6 cyl 3.0 L DOHC Engine +350
Aluminum/Alloy Wheels +205
Anti-Lock Brakes[Std on SHO] +395
Compact Disc Changer[Opt on SE] +315
Keyless Entry System[Opt on LX] +125
Leather Seats[Opt on SE] +415
Power Door Locks[Opt on LX] +170
Power Drivers Seat +200
Power Moonroof[Opt on SE] +460

WINDSTAR   1999

Ford continues to battle it out with GM and Chrysler in the hotly contested minivan segment. This year the

---

Don't forget to refer to the Mileage Adjustment Table at the back of this book!

Model Description	Trade-in Value	Market Value

Windstar has been totally redesigned in yet another attempt to dethrone the hot pentastar prospects. The biggest news for '99, in addition to the completely new exterior and interior styling, is a left-hand sliding door. The second and third row seats are now on rollers for easier adjustment/interchangeability and the instrument panel has been redesigned for improved ergonomics. There's also a more powerful and cleaner-burning 3.8-liter V6 plus upgraded suspension, transmission, brakes and air conditioning components. Hot new options include side airbags and a trick reverse sensing system to keep you from banging into those short gas station poles.

RATINGS (SCALE OF 1-10)

Overall	Safety	Reliability	Performance	Comfort	Value
N/A	8.8	7.7	7	7.8	N/A

Category G

2 Dr LX Pass. Van	15820	18600
2 Dr SE Pass. Van	18110	21290
2 Dr SEL Pass. Van	19995	23505
2 Dr STD Cargo Van	13090	15390
2 Dr STD Pass. Van	13575	15960

OPTIONS FOR WINDSTAR

6 cyl 3.8 L Engine[Opt on STD] +245
Pwr Sliding Lh & Rh Doors +535
Air Conditioning[Opt on STD] +550
Aluminum/Alloy Wheels[Opt on LX] +215
Captain Chairs (4)[Opt on LX] +410
Compact Disc W/fm/tape[Std on SEL] +295
Cruise Control[Opt on STD] +140
Dual Air Conditioning[Opt on LX] +615
Keyless Entry System[Std on SE,SEL] +130
Leather Seats[Opt on SE] +525
Luggage Rack[Opt on LX] +110
Power Door Locks[Opt on STD] +155
Power Drivers Seat[Std on SE, SEL] +190
Power Mirrors[Opt on STD] +90
Power Windows[Opt on STD] +160
Privacy Glass[Std on SE,SEL] +185
Rear Window Defroster[Opt on STD] +115
Sliding Driver Side Door[Opt on LX,STD] +350
Tilt Steering Wheel[Opt on STD] +120

1998 FORD

CLUB WAGON/ECONOLINE 1998

New interior and exterior packages appear on the Club Wagon and Econoline vans.

RATINGS (SCALE OF 1-10)

Overall	Safety	Reliability	Performance	Comfort	Value
N/A	7.9	N/A	6.6	7.4	N/A

Model Description	Trade-in Value	Market Value

E-150

Category H

2 Dr Chateau Club Wagon	14775	17345
2 Dr STD Econoline	11535	13540
2 Dr XL Club Wagon	13050	15320
2 Dr XLT Club Wagon	14175	16645

E-250

Category H

2 Dr STD Econoline	11895	13965
2 Dr STD Econoline Ext	12310	14450

E-350

Category H

2 Dr Chateau Club Wagon	16285	19120
2 Dr STD Econoline	13265	15575
2 Dr STD Econoline Ext	13835	16240
2 Dr XL Club Wagon	14725	17285
2 Dr XL Club Wagon Ext	15720	18450
2 Dr XLT Club Wagon	15805	18555
2 Dr XLT Club Wagon Ext	16280	19110

OPTIONS FOR CLUB WAGON/ECONOLINE

10 cyl 6.8 L Engine +330
8 cyl 4.6 L Engine +355
8 cyl 5.4 L Engine[Std on E-350] +500
8 cyl 7.3 L Turbodsl Engine +2635
12 Passenger Seating[Std on XL,Club Wagon] +350
Air Conditioning[Std on Chateau, XL, XLT] +445
Aluminum/Alloy Wheels[Opt on XLT] +170
Anti-Lock Brakes[Std on Chateau, XL, XLT] +270
Cruise Control +105
Dual Air Conditioning +705
Keyless Entry System +95
Power Door Locks[Std on Chateau, XLT] +105
Power Drivers Seat +155
Power Mirrors +55
Power Windows[Std on Chateau, XLT] +105
Privacy Glass +85
Tilt Steering Wheel +105

CONTOUR   1998

A redesigned face gives this Ford more character, but the new taillight treatment is almost identical to the Contour's sibling, the Mercury Mystique. New alloy wheels and a slightly more commodious rear seat debut. The outstanding SVT model provides the performance of a BMW 328i at the price of a Buick Century. Mid-year changes included a model consolidation, the addition of de-powered airbags, as well as improved handling and new wheels for the SVT.

RATINGS (SCALE OF 1-10)

Overall	Safety	Reliability	Performance	Comfort	Value
7.4	6.7	6.7	8.2	7.9	7.4

Don't forget to refer to the Mileage Adjustment Table at the back of this book!

Model Description	Trade-in Value	Market Value
Category C		
4 Dr LX Sdn	8585	10300
4 Dr SE Sdn	9260	11285
4 Dr STD Sdn	7640	9165
4 Dr SVT Sdn	12495	15000

OPTIONS FOR CONTOUR
6 cyl 2.5 L Engine[Std on SE, SVT] +370
Auto 4-Speed Transmission +445
AM/FM Compact Disc Player +190
Air Conditioning[Std on SVT] +445
Aluminum/Alloy Wheels[Opt on GL, LX] +170
Anti-Lock Brakes[Std on SVT] +325
Cruise Control[Std on SVT] +120
Keyless Entry System[Std on SVT] +100
Leather Seats[Std on SVT] +340
Power Door Locks[Opt on GL, LX] +140
Power Drivers Seat[Std on SVT] +165
Power Moonroof +375
Power Windows[Std on SVT] +175
Rear Window Defroster[Std on SE, SVT] +90
Traction Control System[Opt on SE] +115

CROWN VICTORIA 1998

A formal roofline graces this favorite of police officers and taxi drivers. To further add to the Crown Victoria's driving excitement, the power steering and suspension have been improved.

RATINGS (SCALE OF 1-10)

Overall	Safety	Reliability	Performance	Comfort	Value
8.2	8.1	8.6	7.7	8.2	8.4

Category B		
4 Dr LX Sdn	13420	15980
4 Dr STD Sdn	12075	14380

OPTIONS FOR CROWN VICTORIA
Aluminum/Alloy Wheels +180
Anti-Lock Brakes +365
Climate Control for AC +90
Dual Power Seats +210
Keyless Entry System[Std on LX] +95
Leather Seats +375
Power Drivers Seat[Std on LX] +175
Traction Control System +95

ESCORT 1998

Packages are reshuffled on Ford's entry-level cars. Available this year as sedans, wagons or stylish coupes, the Ford Escort now qualifies as a low emissions vehicle, thanks to the car's split-port induction 2.0-liter four-cylinder engine.

RATINGS (SCALE OF 1-10)

Overall	Safety	Reliability	Performance	Comfort	Value
7.3	6.1	8.5	7.2	7.3	7.2

Model Description	Trade-in Value	Market Value
Category E		
4 Dr LX Sdn	7010	8460
4 Dr SE Sdn	7780	9390
4 Dr SE Wgn	8490	10245
2 Dr ZX2 Cool Cpe	7690	9280
2 Dr ZX2 Hot Cpe	8025	9685

OPTIONS FOR ESCORT
Auto 4-Speed Transmission +425
Air Conditioning[Std on SE] +455
Aluminum/Alloy Wheels +185
Anti-Lock Brakes +365
Cruise Control +125
Keyless Entry System[Std on SE] +90
Luggage Rack +70
Power Door Locks +135
Power Mirrors[Std on SE] +60
Power Moonroof +320
Power Windows +145
Premium Sound System +180
Rear Window Defroster[Std on SE] +90
Rear Window Wiper +70
Tilt Steering Wheel +80

EXPEDITION 1998

After an insanely successful first year, the Ford Expedition pounds its way into 1998 without changes.

RATINGS (SCALE OF 1-10)

Overall	Safety	Reliability	Performance	Comfort	Value
7.5	8.1	7.9	6.8	7.9	7

Category H		
4 Dr Eddie Bauer Utility	20305	23840
4 Dr Eddie Bauer 4WD Utility	21945	25760
4 Dr XLT Utility	17930	21045
4 Dr XLT 4WD Utility	19545	22945

OPTIONS FOR EXPEDITION
8 cyl 5.4 L Engine +500
Aluminum/Alloy Wheels[Opt on XLT] +170
Camper/Towing Package +180
Compact Disc Changer +245
Compact Disc W/fm/tape +170
Cruise Control[Opt on XLT] +105
Dual Air Conditioning +705
Fog Lights[Opt on XLT] +70
Heated Front Seats +200
Heated Power Mirrors +50
Leather Seats[Opt on XLT] +545
Power Drivers Seat[Opt on XLT] +155
Privacy Glass[Opt on XLT] +85
Running Boards +190
Third Seat +345

EXPLORER 1998

The Ford Explorer gets a restyled tailgate for 1998.

Model Description	Trade-in Value	Market Value

Model Description	Trade-in Value	Market Value

RATINGS (SCALE OF 1-10)

Overall	Safety	Reliability	Performance	Comfort	Value
7.4	7.7	7.9	7.8	7.1	6.7

Category G

Model	Trade-in	Market
4 Dr Eddie Bauer Utility	18635	21985
4 Dr Eddie Bauer 4WD Utility	19905	23485
4 Dr Limited Utility	20410	24080
4 Dr Limited 4WD Utility	21680	25580
2 Dr Sport Utility	13000	15335
2 Dr Sport 4WD Utility	14810	17475
4 Dr XL Utility	14070	16600
4 Dr XL 4WD Utility	15290	18040
4 Dr XLT Utility	15995	18870
4 Dr XLT 4WD Utility	17265	20370

OPTIONS FOR EXPLORER

6 cyl 4.0 L SOHC Engine[Opt on Sport, XLT] +295
8 cyl 5.0 L Engine +485
Auto 4-Speed Transmission +545
Auto 5-Speed Transmission[Std on Eddie Bauer, Limited] +580
Aluminum/Alloy Wheels[Opt on XL] +175
Climate Control for AC[Std on Limited] +105
Compact Disc Changer +275
Compact Disc W/fm/tape[Std on Limited] +240
Cruise Control[Opt on Sport, XL] +115
Dual Power Seats[Std on Limited] +230
Fog Lights[Std on Limited] +80
Keyless Entry System[Std on Limited] +105
Leather Seats[Std on Limited] +430
Power Drivers Seat[Opt on Sport, XLT] +155
Power Moonroof +475
Rear Heater[Std on Limited] +105
Rear Window Defroster[Opt on Sport, XL] +95
Rear Window Wiper[Opt on Sport, XL] +85
Running Boards[Std on Limited] +210
Tilt Steering Wheel[Opt on XL] +100
Tutone Paint[Opt on XLT] +140

F-SERIES PICKUP   1998

The 1998 F-150 celebrates its 50th Anniversary with a small decal on the windshield. Other changes include making the locking tailgate standard on XLT and Lariat trims, optional on XL and Standard models. Fog lights become optional this year on all four-wheel drive models except for the Lariat, which gets them standard. An STX package featuring 17-inch tires, aluminum wheels, and color-keyed grille debuts as an option for the XLT 2WD. The Lariat receives a color-keyed steering column, leather-wrapped steering wheel, and outside power signal mirrors. Silver Metallic paint replaces Silver Frost paint, and Light Denim Blue replaces Portofino Blue.

RATINGS (SCALE OF 1-10)

Overall	Safety	Reliability	Performance	Comfort	Value
N/A	7.4	8.5	6.6	7.8	N/A

F-150

Category H

Model	Trade-in	Market
2 Dr Lariat Ext Cab LB	15985	18610
2 Dr Lariat 4WD Ext Cab LB	16970	19925
2 Dr Lariat Ext Cab SB	15800	18395
2 Dr Lariat 4WD Ext Cab SB	17685	20605
2 Dr Lariat Ext Cab Stepside SB	16265	18940
2 Dr Lariat 4WD Ext Cab Stepside SB	18105	21100
2 Dr Lariat Std Cab LB	14295	16625
2 Dr Lariat 4WD Std Cab LB	16245	18910
2 Dr Lariat Std Cab SB	14110	16410
2 Dr Lariat 4WD Std Cab SB	16060	18695
2 Dr Lariat Std Cab Stepside SB	14730	17135
2 Dr Lariat 4WD Std Cab Stepside SB	16525	19245
2 Dr STD Ext Cab LB	11985	13910
2 Dr STD 4WD Ext Cab LB	14205	16520
2 Dr STD Ext Cab SB	11805	13700
2 Dr STD 4WD Ext Cab SB	14025	16310
2 Dr STD Std Cab LB	10570	12250
2 Dr STD 4WD Std Cab LB	12545	14570
2 Dr STD Std Cab SB	10390	12045
2 Dr STD 4WD Std Cab SB	12365	14360
2 Dr XL Ext Cab LB	12750	14810
2 Dr XL 4WD Ext Cab LB	15050	17510
2 Dr XL Ext Cab SB	12565	14595
2 Dr XL 4WD Ext Cab SB	14820	17295
2 Dr XL Ext Cab Stepside SB	13030	15140
2 Dr XL 4WD Ext Cab Stepside SB	15260	17755
2 Dr XL Std Cab LB	11205	13000
2 Dr XL 4WD Std Cab LB	13255	15405
2 Dr XL Std Cab SB	11025	12785
2 Dr XL 4WD Std Cab SB	13070	15190
2 Dr XL Std Cab Stepside SB	11640	13510
2 Dr XL 4WD Std Cab Stepside SB	13540	15740
2 Dr XLT Ext Cab LB	14490	16855
2 Dr XLT 4WD Ext Cab LB	16765	19525
2 Dr XLT Ext Cab SB	14305	16640
2 Dr XLT 4WD Ext Cab SB	16585	19310
2 Dr XLT Ext Cab Stepside SB	14775	17185
2 Dr XLT 4WD Ext Cab Stepside SB	17005	19805
2 Dr XLT Std Cab LB	12800	14870
2 Dr XLT 4WD Std Cab LB	14750	17160

Model Description	Trade-in Value	Market Value
2 Dr XLT Std Cab SB	12615	14655
2 Dr XLT 4WD Std Cab SB	14565	16940
2 Dr XLT Std Cab Stepside SB	13240	15385
2 Dr XLT 4WD Std Cab Stepside SB		
	15035	17495

F-250

Category H

Model Description	Trade-in Value	Market Value
2 Dr Lariat Ext Cab SB	16725	19445
2 Dr Lariat 4WD Ext Cab SB	18600	21650
2 Dr Lariat Std Cab LB	15180	17625
2 Dr Lariat 4WD Std Cab LB	17125	19915
2 Dr STD Ext Cab SB	13045	15120
2 Dr STD 4WD Ext Cab SB	14925	17330
2 Dr STD Std Cab LB	11815	13675
2 Dr STD 4WD Std Cab LB	13695	15885
2 Dr XL Ext Cab SB	13845	16060
2 Dr XL 4WD Ext Cab SB	15795	18350
2 Dr XL Std Cab LB	12490	14470
2 Dr XL 4WD Std Cab LB	14440	16760
2 Dr XLT Ext Cab SB	15615	18145
2 Dr XLT 4WD Ext Cab SB	17495	20350
2 Dr XLT Std Cab LB	14070	16325
2 Dr XLT 4WD Std Cab LB	16020	18615

OPTIONS FOR F-SERIES PICKUP
8 cyl 4.6 L Engine[Std on F-150 4WD, F-250, Lariat] +355
8 cyl 5.4 L Engine +500
Auto 4-Speed Transmission +545
AM/FM Compact Disc Player +170
Air Conditioning +445
Aluminum/Alloy Wheels[Std on Lariat] +170
Anti-Lock Brakes[Std on Lariat] +270
Camper/Towing Package +180
Chrome Wheels[Std on Lariat] +165
Cruise Control +105
Fog Lights[Std on Lariat] +70
Keyless Entry System +95
Leather Steering Wheel[Opt on XLT] +35
Power Drivers Seat +155
Power Mirrors[Std on Lariat, XLT Stepside] +55
Skid Plates +60
Sliding Rear Window +65
Tilt Steering Wheel +105

MUSTANG   •   1998

The Mustang gains standard equipment, such as power windows and door locks, air conditioning, and premium sound. Options are shuffled as well, making it easier to choose the car you want. GT models get a slight boost in power.

RATINGS (SCALE OF 1-10)

Overall	Safety	Reliability	Performance	Comfort	Value
6.9	6.7	7.8	8.8	7.3	3.7

Category F

Model Description	Trade-in Value	Market Value
2 Dr Cobra Conv	18965	22210
2 Dr Cobra Cpe	17130	20065
2 Dr GT Conv	16160	18930
2 Dr GT Cpe	13645	15980
2 Dr STD Conv	13975	16370
2 Dr STD Cpe	11005	12890

OPTIONS FOR MUSTANG
Auto 4-Speed Transmission +445
Anti-Lock Brakes[Std on Cobra] +355
Cruise Control[Std on Cobra] +120
Leather Seats +345
Power Drivers Seat[Opt on STD] +130
Rear Window Defroster[Std on Cobra] +90

RANGER   1998

The Ranger gets new sheetmetal, a new grille and revised headlamps. The wheelbase on regular cab models has been stretched to provide more cabin room and the displacement of the base engine has been increased. A short- and long-arm (SLA) suspension replaces the Twin-I-Beam suspension found on last year's models. A four-door Ranger join the lineup mid-year.

RATINGS (SCALE OF 1-10)

Overall	Safety	Reliability	Performance	Comfort	Value
N/A	N/A	8.7	7.2	7.3	N/A

Category G

Model Description	Trade-in Value	Market Value
2 Dr Splash Ext Cab Stepside SB		
	11005	12985
2 Dr Splash 4WD Ext Cab Stepside SB		
	12940	15265
2 Dr Splash Std Cab Stepside SB	9960	11755
2 Dr Splash 4WD Std Cab Stepside SB		
	12405	14640
2 Dr XL Ext Cab SB	9895	11675
2 Dr XL 4WD Ext Cab SB	11450	13510
2 Dr XL Ext Cab Stepside SB	9920	11705
2 Dr XL 4WD Ext Cab Stepside SB		
	11435	13495
2 Dr XL Std Cab LB	7980	9420
2 Dr XL 4WD Std Cab LB	10725	12650
2 Dr XL Std Cab SB	7680	9065
2 Dr XL 4WD Std Cab SB	10420	12295
2 Dr XL Std Cab Stepside SB	7765	9165
2 Dr XL 4WD Std Cab Stepside SB		
	10435	12315
2 Dr XLT Ext Cab SB	10215	12055
2 Dr XLT 4WD Ext Cab SB	12415	14650
2 Dr XLT Ext Cab Stepside SB	10235	12075
2 Dr XLT 4WD Ext Cab Stepside SB		
	12380	14605

Don't forget to refer to the Mileage Adjustment Table at the back of this book!

Model Description	Trade-in Value	Market Value
2 Dr XLT Std Cab LB	9200	10855
2 Dr XLT 4WD Std Cab LB	11845	13975
2 Dr XLT Std Cab SB	8845	10440
2 Dr XLT 4WD Std Cab SB	11465	13530
2 Dr XLT Std Cab Stepside SB	8900	10500
2 Dr XLT 4WD Std Cab Stepside SB	11450	13510

OPTIONS FOR RANGER
6 cyl 3.0 L Engine[Std on 4WD, Splash 2WD Ext Cab] +270
6 cyl 4.0 L Engine +490
Auto 4-Speed Transmission +600
Auto 5-Speed Transmission +615
AM/FM Compact Disc Player +175
Air Conditioning +450
Aluminum/Alloy Wheels[Opt on XL, XLT, Ext Cab] +175
Anti-Lock Brakes +320
Bed Liner +155
Chrome Wheels[Opt on XLT] +90
Cruise Control +115
Fog Lights +80
Keyless Entry System +105
Power Door Locks +130
Power Mirrors[Opt on XLT] +70
Power Windows +135
Sliding Rear Window[Opt on XL, XLT, Std Cab, 2WD] +65
Tilt Steering Wheel +100

TAURUS   1998

A mild facelift, revised trim levels and fewer options are the only changes to Ford's mid-size sedan.

RATINGS (SCALE OF 1-10)

Overall	Safety	Reliability	Performance	Comfort	Value
7.9	7.9	8.1	8	8	7.4

	Trade-in	Market
Category C		
4 Dr LX Sdn	10535	12595
4 Dr SE Sdn	10815	12980
4 Dr SE Wgn	11765	14115
Category F		
4 Dr SHO Sdn	16885	19780

OPTIONS FOR TAURUS
6 cyl 3.0 L DOHC Engine[Opt on LX, SE] +270
Aluminum/Alloy Wheels +170
Anti-Lock Brakes[Std on SHO] +325
Chrome Wheels[Opt on SE] +330
Climate Control for AC[Opt on SE] +90
Compact Disc Changer[Opt on SE] +255
Dual Power Seats[Opt on SE] +315
Heated Power Mirrors[Opt on SE] +55
Keyless Entry System[Opt on LX, Wgn] +100
Leather Seats +340
Power Door Locks[Opt on LX] +140
Power Drivers Seat +165
Power Moonroof[Opt on SE] +375

WINDSTAR   1998

Ford widens the driver's door as a stop-gap measure until the 1999 Windstar arrives with a fourth door. Subtle styling revisions and a new Limited model round out the changes for 1998.

RATINGS (SCALE OF 1-10)

Overall	Safety	Reliability	Performance	Comfort	Value
7.1	8.1	6.3	6.8	7.3	6.9

	Trade-in	Market
Category G		
2 Dr GL Pass. Van	12675	14950
2 Dr LX Pass. Van	15450	18230
2 Dr Limited Pass. Van	17340	20460
2 Dr STD Cargo Van	10955	12925
2 Dr STD Pass. Van	11635	13730

OPTIONS FOR WINDSTAR
6 cyl 3.8 L Engine[Std on Limited, LX] +225
AM/FM Compact Disc Player +175
Air Conditioning[Std on LX] +450
Aluminum/Alloy Wheels[Opt on GL] +175
Captain Chairs (4)[Opt on GL, LX] +335
Cruise Control[Opt on GL, STD] +115
Dual Air Conditioning[Opt on GL, LX] +505
JBL Sound System +420
Keyless Entry System +105
Leather Seats[Opt on LX] +430
Power Door Locks[Opt on GL, STD] +130
Power Drivers Seat[Opt on GL] +155
Power Mirrors[Opt on GL, STD] +70
Power Windows[Opt on GL, STD] +135
Privacy Glass +150
Rear Window Defroster[Std on Limited] +95
Tilt Steering Wheel[Opt on GL, STD] +100
Traction Control System +145

1997 FORD

AEROSTAR   1997

Ford's aging minivan gets a 5-speed automatic transmission this year. The sound systems are upgraded and the seats are restyled as well.

RATINGS (SCALE OF 1-10)

Overall	Safety	Reliability	Performance	Comfort	Value
7.3	5.8	7.7	6.8	7.5	8.5

	Trade-in	Market
Category G		
2 Dr STD Cargo Van	8895	10600
2 Dr XLT Pass. Van	9240	11010
2 Dr XLT Pass. Van Ext	10710	12760
2 Dr XLT 4WD Pass. Van Ext	11910	14190

OPTIONS FOR AEROSTAR
6 cyl 4.0 L Engine[Opt on 2WD] +365
AM/FM Compact Disc Player +140
AM/FM Stereo Tape +100

Don't forget to refer to the Mileage Adjustment Table at the back of this book!

FORD 97

Model Description	Trade-in Value	Market Value	Model Description	Trade-in Value	Market Value

Air Conditioning[Opt on STD] +365
Aluminum/Alloy Wheels +145
Captain Chairs (4) +275
Child Seat (1) +75
Cruise Control +95
Dual Air Conditioning +410
Luggage Rack +70
Power Door Locks +105
Power Windows +110
Running Boards +175

ASPIRE   1997

This Kia-built entry-level Ford gets a higher final drive ratio on models equipped with an automatic transmission. New wheel covers, paint choices and interior trim are the only other changes.

RATINGS (SCALE OF 1-10)

Overall	Safety	Reliability	Performance	Comfort	Value
6.9	6.6	8.7	7.2	7.3	4.9

Category E
2 Dr STD Hbk	4005	4975
4 Dr STD Hbk	4265	5300

OPTIONS FOR ASPIRE

Auto 3-Speed Transmission +295
AM/FM Stereo Tape +135
Air Conditioning +370
Anti-Lock Brakes +295
Power Steering +115
Rear Window Defroster +75

CLUB WAGON/ECONOLINE 1997

More power? Ford's full-size minivans are now the only ones in the segment to offer V10 power. Multiple overhead-cam engines also debut in models across the board. Econoline vans get standard four-wheel ABS this year.

RATINGS (SCALE OF 1-10)

Overall	Safety	Reliability	Performance	Comfort	Value
N/A	7.9	8.9	6.6	7.4	N/A

E-150
Category H
2 Dr Chateau Club Wagon	13795	16195
2 Dr STD Econoline	10795	12675
2 Dr XL Club Wagon	11925	14000
2 Dr XLT Club Wagon	13235	15535

E-250
Category H
2 Dr STD Cargo Van	11645	13675
2 Dr STD Cargo Van Ext	12120	14225
2 Dr STD Econoline	10875	12870
2 Dr STD Econoline Ext	11890	13960

E-350
Category H
2 Dr Chateau Club Wagon	15280	17940
2 Dr STD Econoline	12470	14640
2 Dr STD Econoline Ext	13015	15280
2 Dr XL Club Wagon	13175	15470
2 Dr XL Club Wagon Ext	14405	16915
2 Dr XLT Club Wagon	14720	17285
2 Dr XLT Club Wagon Ext	15165	17800

OPTIONS FOR CLUB WAGON/ECONOLINE

10 cyl 6.8 L Engine +185
8 cyl 4.6 L Engine +265
8 cyl 5.4 L Engine[Std on E-350] +365
8 cyl 7.3 L Turbodsl Engine +1870
AM/FM Stereo Tape[Std on Chateau] +90
Air Conditioning[Std on Chateau, XLT] +365
Aluminum/Alloy Wheels[Opt on XL, XLT] +140
Anti-Lock Brakes[Opt on STD] +220
Camper/Towing Package +150
Chrome Bumpers[Std on Chateau, XLT] +50
Cruise Control[Std on Chateau] +85
Dual Air Conditioning +575
Keyless Entry System +80
Limited Slip Diff +120
Power Door Locks[Std on Chateau, XLT] +85
Power Drivers Seat +125
Power Windows[Std on Chateau, XLT] +85
Velour/Cloth Seats[Std on Chateau, XLT] +50

CONTOUR   1997

The addition of a Sport Package for the GL and LX models and the inclusion of a standard trunk light are the only changes for the 1997 Contour.

RATINGS (SCALE OF 1-10)

Overall	Safety	Reliability	Performance	Comfort	Value
7.5	6.8	7.1	8.2	7.9	7.3

Category C
4 Dr GL Sdn	6975	8440
4 Dr LX Sdn	7270	8800
4 Dr SE Sdn	8070	9765

OPTIONS FOR CONTOUR

6 cyl 2.5 L Engine[Std on SE] +405
Auto 4-Speed Transmission +365
AM/FM Compact Disc Player +155
Air Conditioning +365
Aluminum/Alloy Wheels[Std on SE] +140
Anti-Lock Brakes +265
Cruise Control +95
Keyless Entry System +85
Leather Seats +275
Power Door Locks +115
Power Drivers Seat +135
Power Moonroof +305
Power Windows +140

Don't forget to refer to the Mileage Adjustment Table at the back of this book!

Rear Spoiler[Opt on GL] +80
Traction Control System +95

CROWN VICTORIA   1997

After a mild facelift last year, the Crown Vic soldiers on with a few color changes, improved power steering, and the addition of rear air suspension to the handling package.

RATINGS (SCALE OF 1-10)

Overall	Safety	Reliability	Performance	Comfort	Value
8	7.9	7.7	7.7	8.2	8.3

Category B

	Trade-in	Market
4 Dr LX Sdn	11280	13535
4 Dr STD Sdn	10565	12675

OPTIONS FOR CROWN VICTORIA

Handling/Performance Pkg +490
AM/FM Stereo Tape +75
Aluminum/Alloy Wheels +150
Anti-Lock Brakes +300
Climate Control for AC +75
Cruise Control +100
Dual Power Seats +175
Keyless Entry System +80
Leather Seats +305
Power Door Locks +115
Premium Sound System +165
Traction Control System +80
Trip Computer +175

ESCORT   1997

The Ford Escort is totally redesigned this year with improvements across the board. The most noticeable improvements are in the powertrain and ride quality. New sheetmetal gives the Escort a rounder, more aerodynamic appearance as well. To the chagrin of bargain-basement enthusiasts, the GT hatchback version is dropped.

RATINGS (SCALE OF 1-10)

Overall	Safety	Reliability	Performance	Comfort	Value
7.1	6.1	8.5	7.2	7.3	6.2

Category E

	Trade-in	Market
4 Dr LX Sdn	6025	7485
4 Dr LX Wgn	6345	7885
4 Dr STD Sdn	5640	7010

OPTIONS FOR ESCORT

Auto 4-Speed Transmission +335
AM/FM Stereo Tape +135
Air Conditioning +370
Aluminum/Alloy Wheels +150
Anti-Lock Brakes +295
Child Seat (1) +50
Compact Disc Changer +215
Cruise Control +100

Keyless Entry System +75
Luggage Rack +60
Power Door Locks +110
Power Windows +120
Tilt Steering Wheel +65

EXPEDITION   1997

Ford's replacement for the aging Bronco is the all-new Expedition. Based on the hugely successful 1997 F-150 platform, this full-size sport-utility vehicle is poised to do battle with the wildly popular Chevrolet Tahoe and GMC Yukon. Ford has priced the Expedition aggressively and hopes to steal some sales from GM customers who have been told that they'll have to wait four months for their full-size SUV.

RATINGS (SCALE OF 1-10)

Overall	Safety	Reliability	Performance	Comfort	Value
7.1	8.1	7.4	6.8	7.9	5.5

Category H

	Trade-in	Market
4 Dr Eddie Bauer Utility	19195	22540
4 Dr Eddie Bauer 4WD Utility	20770	24385
4 Dr XLT Utility	16085	18880
4 Dr XLT 4WD Utility	17570	20625

OPTIONS FOR EXPEDITION

8 cyl 5.4 L Engine +365
Aluminum/Alloy Wheels[Opt on XLT] +140
Camper/Towing Package +150
Chrome Wheels +135
Compact Disc W/fm/tape +140
Cruise Control[Opt on XLT] +85
Dual Air Conditioning +575
Leather Seats[Opt on XLT] +445
Limited Slip Diff +120
Luggage Rack[Opt on XLT] +70
Power Drivers Seat[Opt on XLT] +125
Power Moonroof +435
Running Boards +155
Skid Plates +50
Third Seat +280

EXPLORER   1997

Ford's best-selling Explorer receives a few appreciated improvements this year. A new SOHC V6 engine is now available, providing nearly as much power as the 5.0-liter V8. Also new is a five-speed automatic transmission, the first ever offered by an American auto manufacturer, which is standard on V6 models equipped with automatic.

RATINGS (SCALE OF 1-10)

Overall	Safety	Reliability	Performance	Comfort	Value
7.1	7.6	7.7	7.8	7.1	5.5

Don't forget to refer to the Mileage Adjustment Table at the back of this book!

Model Description	Trade-in Value	Market Value
Category G		
4 Dr Eddie Bauer Utility	16405	19550
4 Dr Eddie Bauer 4WD Utility	17520	20875
4 Dr Limited Utility	18435	21965
4 Dr Limited 4WD Utility	19700	23475
2 Dr Sport Utility	12240	14580
2 Dr Sport 4WD Utility	13265	15805
2 Dr XL Utility	11575	13790
2 Dr XL 4WD Utility	12680	15105
4 Dr XL Utility	12360	14730
4 Dr XL 4WD Utility	13270	15810
4 Dr XLT Utility	13720	16350
4 Dr XLT 4WD Utility	14835	17675

OPTIONS FOR EXPLORER

6 cyl 4.0 L SOHC Engine[Opt on Sport,XL,XLT] +190
8 cyl 5.0 L Engine +545
Auto 4-Speed Transmission +445
Auto 5-Speed Transmission[Opt on Sport,XL,XLT] +475
AM/FM Stereo Tape[Std on Eddie Bauer] +100
Camper/Towing Package +135
Child Seat (1) +75
Chrome Wheels[Opt on Sport] +75
Climate Control for AC[Std on Limited] +85
Compact Disc Changer +225
Cruise Control[Opt on XL] +95
Dual Power Seats[Opt on Sport,XLT] +185
JBL Sound System[Std on Limited] +340
Keyless Entry System[Std on Limited] +85
Leather Seats[Std on Limited] +350
Limited Slip Diff +125
Luggage Rack[Opt on Sport,XL,XLT] +70
Power Door Locks[Opt on XL] +105
Power Moonroof +385
Power Windows[Opt on XL] +110
Running Boards[Std on Limited] +175

F-SERIES PICKUP 1997

Everything is new (except for Heavy Duty models, which retain last year's chassis and body style). New engines, new sheetmetal, and a new suspension compliment dual airbags and class-leading side impact protection in this user-friendly heavy hauler. All SuperCab models get a third door for easy access to the rear compartment.

RATINGS (SCALE OF 1-10)

Overall	Safety	Reliability	Performance	Comfort	Value
N/A	7.4	8	6.6	7.8	N/A

F-150

Model Description	Trade-in Value	Market Value
Category H		
2 Dr Lariat Ext Cab LB	14935	17535
2 Dr Lariat 4WD Ext Cab LB	16920	19865
2 Dr Lariat Ext Cab SB	14765	17335
2 Dr Lariat 4WD Ext Cab SB	16700	19605
2 Dr Lariat Ext Cab Stepside SB	15245	17895
2 Dr Lariat 4WD Ext Cab Stepside SB	17180	20170
2 Dr Lariat Std Cab LB	13465	15810
2 Dr Lariat 4WD Std Cab LB	15155	17795
2 Dr Lariat Std Cab SB	13280	15590
2 Dr Lariat 4WD Std Cab SB	15030	17645
2 Dr Lariat Std Cab Stepside SB	14005	16440
2 Dr Lariat 4WD Std Cab Stepside SB	15510	18210
2 Dr STD Ext Cab LB	11005	12920
2 Dr STD 4WD Ext Cab LB	13440	15780
2 Dr STD Ext Cab SB	10825	12710
2 Dr STD 4WD Ext Cab SB	13225	15525
2 Dr STD Std Cab LB	9645	11325
2 Dr STD 4WD Std Cab LB	11875	13940
2 Dr STD Std Cab SB	9480	11125
2 Dr STD 4WD Std Cab SB	11675	13710
2 Dr XL Ext Cab LB	11815	13870
2 Dr XL 4WD Ext Cab LB	14420	16925
2 Dr XL Ext Cab SB	11515	13520
2 Dr XL 4WD Ext Cab SB	14190	16660
2 Dr XL Ext Cab Stepside SB	12115	14225
2 Dr XL 4WD Ext Cab Stepside SB	14670	17225
2 Dr XL Std Cab LB	10290	12080
2 Dr XL 4WD Std Cab LB	12420	14585
2 Dr XL Std Cab SB	10115	11875
2 Dr XL 4WD Std Cab SB	12295	14435
2 Dr XL Std Cab Stepside SB	10745	12620
2 Dr XL 4WD Std Cab Stepside SB	12720	14935
2 Dr XLT Ext Cab LB	13615	15985
2 Dr XLT 4WD Ext Cab LB	15730	18470
2 Dr XLT Ext Cab SB	13450	15790
2 Dr XLT 4WD Ext Cab SB	15555	18260
2 Dr XLT Ext Cab Stepside SB	13925	16350
2 Dr XLT 4WD Ext Cab Stepside SB	15985	18770
2 Dr XLT Std Cab LB	12010	14100
2 Dr XLT 4WD Std Cab LB	13775	16170
2 Dr XLT Std Cab SB	11795	13850
2 Dr XLT 4WD Std Cab SB	13650	16025
2 Dr XLT Std Cab Stepside SB	12525	14705
2 Dr XLT 4WD Std Cab Stepside SB	14070	16520

F-250

Model Description	Trade-in Value	Market Value
Category H		
2 Dr Lariat Ext Cab SB	15750	18495
2 Dr Lariat 4WD Ext Cab SB	17730	20815
2 Dr Lariat Std Cab LB	14230	16705
2 Dr Lariat 4WD Std Cab LB	16175	18990

Don't forget to refer to the Mileage Adjustment Table at the back of this book!

Model Description	Trade-in Value	Market Value
2 Dr STD Ext Cab SB	12040	14140
2 Dr STD 4WD Ext Cab SB	14100	16555
2 Dr STD Std Cab LB	10865	12755
2 Dr STD 4WD Std Cab LB	12985	15245
2 Dr XL Ext Cab SB	12935	15190
2 Dr XL 4WD Ext Cab SB	15105	17735
2 Dr XL Std Cab LB	11555	13565
2 Dr XL 4WD Std Cab LB	13705	16090
4 Dr XL Crew Cab SB HD	14150	16615
4 Dr XL 4WD Crew Cab SB HD	16150	18960
2 Dr XL Ext Cab LB HD	12925	15175
2 Dr XL 4WD Ext Cab LB HD	14930	17525
2 Dr XL Ext Cab SB HD	13040	15310
2 Dr XL 4WD Ext Cab SB HD	15045	17660
2 Dr XL Std Cab LB HD	11755	13800
2 Dr XL 4WD Std Cab LB HD	13680	16060
2 Dr XLT Ext Cab SB	14740	17305
2 Dr XLT 4WD Ext Cab SB	16655	19550
2 Dr XLT Std Cab LB	13245	15550
2 Dr XLT 4WD Std Cab LB	15095	17725
4 Dr XLT Crew Cab SB HD	15840	18595
4 Dr XLT 4WD Crew Cab SB HD	17840	20940
2 Dr XLT Ext Cab LB HD	14485	17005
2 Dr XLT 4WD Ext Cab LB HD	16490	19360
2 Dr XLT Ext Cab SB HD	14600	17140
2 Dr XLT 4WD Ext Cab SB HD	16600	19490
2 Dr XLT Std Cab LB HD	13355	15675
2 Dr XLT 4WD Std Cab LB HD	15275	17935

F-350

Category H

Model Description	Trade-in Value	Market Value
4 Dr XL Crew Cab LB	14295	16785
4 Dr XL 4WD Crew Cab LB	16300	19135
2 Dr XL Ext Cab LB	14075	16525
2 Dr XL Std Cab LB	12100	14205
2 Dr XL 4WD Std Cab LB	14085	16540
4 Dr XLT Crew Cab LB	15985	18770
4 Dr XLT 4WD Crew Cab LB	17990	21120
2 Dr XLT Ext Cab LB	15395	18075
2 Dr XLT Std Cab LB	13460	15800
2 Dr XLT 4WD Std Cab LB	15685	18415

OPTIONS FOR F-SERIES PICKUP
8 cyl 4.6 L Engine +265
8 cyl 5.4 L Engine +365
8 cyl 7.3 L Turbodsl Engine +1870
8 cyl 7.5 L Engine +170
Auto 4-Speed Transmission +410
Air Conditioning[Opt on F-150,F-250] +365
Aluminum/Alloy Wheels[Std on Lariat] +140
Anti-Lock Brakes[Std on Lariat] +220
Camper/Towing Package +150
Chrome Wheels[Opt on XL,XLT] +135
Compact Disc W/fm/tape +140

Cruise Control[Opt on F-150,F-250] +85
Dual Rear Wheels +355
Keyless Entry System +80
Limited Slip Diff +120
Power Drivers Seat +125
Rear Step Bumper +65
Skid Plates +50
Tutone Paint +110

MUSTANG   1997

While messing around with the rest of their models, Ford decided to take it easy with changes to the Mustang. GT models and base convertibles get new interior color options, and Stangs equipped with an automatic transmission (what fun) get a thicker shift lever. New 17-inch aluminum wheels are optional on the GT. Lastly, the Passive Anti-Theft System has been introduced to all Mustangs in an attempt decrease this vehicle's extremely high theft rating.

RATINGS (SCALE OF 1-10)

Overall	Safety	Reliability	Performance	Comfort	Value
6.9	7	8.3	8.8	7.3	3

Category F

Model Description	Trade-in Value	Market Value
2 Dr Cobra Conv	17025	20070
2 Dr Cobra Cpe	15365	18110
2 Dr GT Conv	14560	17165
2 Dr GT Cpe	11125	13115
2 Dr STD Conv	12780	15065
2 Dr STD Cpe	9540	11245

OPTIONS FOR MUSTANG
Auto 4-Speed Transmission +365
Air Conditioning[Std on Cobra] +375
Aluminum/Alloy Wheels[Opt on STD] +135
Anti-Lock Brakes[Std on Cobra] +290
Compact Disc W/fm/tape +225
Cruise Control[Std on Cobra] +100
Keyless Entry System[Std on Cobra] +80
Leather Seats +285
Limited Slip Diff[Std on Cobra] +145
Power Door Locks[Std on Cobra,Conv] +90
Power Drivers Seat[Std on Cobra] +110
Power Windows[Std on Cobra,Conv] +105
Premium Sound System +170
Rear Spoiler[Opt on STD,Cpe] +105

PROBE   1997

Ford adds a GTS Sport Appearance Package to the GT's option sheet. The package includes a rear spoiler, racing stripes and 16-inch chrome wheels.

RATINGS (SCALE OF 1-10)

Overall	Safety	Reliability	Performance	Comfort	Value
N/A	7.1	7.6	9	7.4	N/A

Model Description	Trade-in Value	Market Value
Category E		
2 Dr GT Hbk	8495	10560
2 Dr STD Hbk	7265	9030

OPTIONS FOR PROBE

Auto 4-Speed Transmission +400
AM/FM Compact Disc Player +195
Air Conditioning +370
Aluminum/Alloy Wheels[Std on GT] +150
Anti-Lock Brakes +295
Chrome Wheels +195
Cruise Control +100
Keyless Entry System +75
Leather Seats +390
Power Door Locks +110
Power Drivers Seat +135
Power Sunroof +280
Power Windows +120

RANGER 1997

Ford introduces its brand-new five-speed automatic transmission to the Ranger lineup. Available with the V6 engines, the five-speed automatic is designed to improve the Ranger's acceleration, towing, and hill climbing ability.

RATINGS (SCALE OF 1-10)

Overall	Safety	Reliability	Performance	Comfort	Value
N/A	6.7	8.9	7.2	7.3	N/A

Model Description	Trade-in Value	Market Value
Category G		
2 Dr STX 4WD Ext Cab SB	11165	13300
2 Dr STX 4WD Std Cab LB	10840	12920
2 Dr STX 4WD Std Cab SB	10510	12520
2 Dr Splash Ext Cab Stepside SB		
	9560	11390
2 Dr Splash 4WD Ext Cab Stepside SB		
	11740	13990
2 Dr Splash Std Cab Stepside SB		
	8635	10290
2 Dr Splash 4WD Std Cab Stepside SB		
	11200	13345
2 Dr XL Ext Cab SB	8335	9935
2 Dr XL 4WD Ext Cab SB	10410	12405
2 Dr XL Ext Cab Stepside SB	8675	10335
2 Dr XL 4WD Ext Cab Stepside SB		
	10680	12725
2 Dr XL Std Cab LB	6660	7935
2 Dr XL 4WD Std Cab LB	9765	11635
2 Dr XL Std Cab SB	6445	7675
2 Dr XL 4WD Std Cab SB	9495	11315
2 Dr XL Std Cab Stepside SB	6780	8080
2 Dr XL 4WD Std Cab Stepside SB		
	9765	11635
2 Dr XLT Ext Cab SB	8675	10340

Model Description	Trade-in Value	Market Value
2 Dr XLT 4WD Ext Cab SB	11210	13355
2 Dr XLT Ext Cab Stepside SB	8935	10645
2 Dr XLT 4WD Ext Cab Stepside SB		
	11470	13665
2 Dr XLT Std Cab LB	7745	9230
2 Dr XLT 4WD Std Cab LB	10705	12755
2 Dr XLT Std Cab SB	7445	8870
2 Dr XLT 4WD Std Cab SB	10370	12355
2 Dr XLT Std Cab Stepside SB	7705	9180
2 Dr XLT 4WD Std Cab Stepside SB		
	10625	12660

OPTIONS FOR RANGER

6 cyl 3.0 L Engine +310
6 cyl 4.0 L Engine +365
Auto 4-Speed Transmission +465
Auto 5-Speed Transmission +480
AM/FM Compact Disc Player +140
Air Conditioning +365
Aluminum/Alloy Wheels[Std on Splash] +145
Anti-Lock Brakes +260
Bed Liner +125
Chrome Wheels[Opt on XLT] +75
Cruise Control +95
Keyless Entry System +85
Limited Slip Diff +125
Power Door Locks +105
Power Drivers Seat +125
Power Steering[Std on Splash,STX,Ext Cab,4WD] +125
Power Windows +110

TAURUS 1997

After totally redesigning the Taurus for 1996, Ford is taking it slow with changes for '97. A few new exterior color choices are added and there are minor changes to a couple of optional equipment packages.

RATINGS (SCALE OF 1-10)

Overall	Safety	Reliability	Performance	Comfort	Value
8.1	7.8	7.7	8	8	9.1

Model Description	Trade-in Value	Market Value
Category C		
4 Dr G Sdn	8780	10625
4 Dr GL Sdn	9250	11195
4 Dr GL Wgn	9820	11885
4 Dr LX Sdn	9490	11680
4 Dr LX Wgn	11015	13330
Category F		
4 Dr SHO Sdn	13625	16060

OPTIONS FOR TAURUS

AM/FM Compact Disc Player +155
Aluminum/Alloy Wheels[Opt on G,GL] +140
Anti-Lock Brakes[Std on SHO] +265
Child Seat (1) +55
Chrome Wheels +265
Climate Control for AC +75

FORD 97-96

Cruise Control[Std on SHO] +95
Keyless Entry System +80
Leather Seats +275
Power Door Locks[Opt on G,GL] +115
Power Drivers Seat[Opt on GL] +135
Power Moonroof +290
Third Seat +75

THUNDERBIRD 1997

The Thunderbird receives few updates this year. A revised center console, a few new colors, and standard four-wheel disc brakes are the big news for 1997.

RATINGS (SCALE OF 1-10)

Overall	Safety	Reliability	Performance	Comfort	Value
7.6	7.9	7.8	8	7.9	6.2

Category C
2 Dr LX Cpe   8795   10640

OPTIONS FOR THUNDERBIRD
8 cyl 4.6 L Engine +330
Aluminum/Alloy Wheels +140
Anti-Lock Brakes +265
Chrome Wheels +270
Compact Disc W/fm/tape +145
Keyless Entry System +85
Leather Seats +275
Power Drivers Seat +135
Power Moonroof +305
Premium Sound System +170
Traction Control System +95

WINDSTAR 1997

Nothing is new for the 1997 Ford Windstar.

RATINGS (SCALE OF 1-10)

Overall	Safety	Reliability	Performance	Comfort	Value
7.6	8.4	7.5	6.8	7.3	8.1

Category G
2 Dr GL Pass. Van   10985   13085
2 Dr LX Pass. Van   13290   15830

OPTIONS FOR WINDSTAR
6 cyl 3.8 L Engine[Std on LX] +185
AM/FM Compact Disc Player +140
Air Conditioning[Std on LX] +365
Aluminum/Alloy Wheels[Opt on GL] +145
Child Seats (2) +115
Cruise Control[Std on LX] +95
Dual Air Conditioning +410
Keyless Entry System +85
Leather Seats +350
Luggage Rack +70
Power Door Locks[Std on LX] +105
Power Windows[Std on LX] +110
Traction Control System +120

1996 FORD

AEROSTAR 1996

Smoother shifting transmission debuts, along with revised A/C controls and a new radio with visible controls. Solar tinted glass is standard.

RATINGS (SCALE OF 1-10)

Overall	Safety	Reliability	Performance	Comfort	Value
7.4	5.7	7.7	6.8	7.5	9.1

Category G
2 Dr STD Cargo Van   7430   8960
2 Dr XLT Pass. Van   7695   9280
2 Dr XLT Pass. Van Ext   9120   10995
2 Dr XLT 4WD Pass. Van Ext   9625   11600

OPTIONS FOR AEROSTAR
6 cyl 4.0 L Engine[Opt on 2WD] +280
AM/FM Compact Disc Player +115
Air Conditioning[Opt on STD] +300
Aluminum/Alloy Wheels +120
Captain Chairs (4) +225
Child Seat (1) +60
Cruise Control[Opt on STD,Pass. Van] +75
Dual Air Conditioning +335
Luggage Rack +60
Power Door Locks +85
Power Windows +90

ASPIRE 1996

Korean-built minicompact loses the SE trim level and several items of standard and optional equipment. Four new colors debut.

RATINGS (SCALE OF 1-10)

Overall	Safety	Reliability	Performance	Comfort	Value
7.1	6.6	8.5	7.2	7.3	5.9

Category E
2 Dr STD Hbk   3080   3925
4 Dr STD Hbk   3285   4195

OPTIONS FOR ASPIRE
Auto 3-Speed Transmission +230
AM/FM Stereo Tape +110
Air Conditioning +305
Anti-Lock Brakes +245
Power Steering +95

BRONCO 1996

Trick new turn signal system is embedded in side view mirrors. Otherwise, minor trim changes mark the passing of the last Bronco.

RATINGS (SCALE OF 1-10)

Overall	Safety	Reliability	Performance	Comfort	Value
7.2	8	8.6	6.4	6.6	6.5

Don't forget to refer to the Mileage Adjustment Table at the back of this book!

Model Description	Trade-in Value	Market Value
Category H		
2 Dr Eddie Bauer 4WD Utility	14815	17560
2 Dr XL 4WD Utility	11865	14065
2 Dr XLT 4WD Utility	13260	15720

OPTIONS FOR BRONCO

8 cyl 5.8 L Engine +345
Auto 4-Speed Transmission[Opt on XL,XLT] +370
AM/FM Compact Disc Player +115
Air Conditioning[Opt on XL,XLT] +300
Camper/Towing Package +120
Chrome Wheels +110
Keyless Entry System +65
Leather Seats +365
Limited Slip Diff +95
Power Door Locks +70
Power Windows +70
Rear Window Defroster[Opt on XL,XLT] +55
Velour/Cloth Seats[Std on XLT] +40

CLUB WAGON/ECONOLINE 1996

For Club Wagon, the flip-out rear door glass is replaced by that of the fixed variety, four new colors are available, and E-150 models get plastic hubcaps. For Econoline, monster 14,050 GVWR E-350 van and van cutaway are introduced.

RATINGS (SCALE OF 1-10)

Overall	Safety	Reliability	Performance	Comfort	Value
N/A	7	8.5	6.4	7.8	N/A

E-150

Category H

Model Description	Trade-in Value	Market Value
2 Dr Chateau Club Wagon	12710	15065
2 Dr STD Econoline	8945	10605
2 Dr XL Club Wagon	9980	11830
2 Dr XL Econoline	9625	11410
2 Dr XLT Club Wagon	11135	13200

E-250

Category H

Model Description	Trade-in Value	Market Value
2 Dr STD Econoline	9290	11010
2 Dr STD Econoline Ext	9645	11435
2 Dr XL Econoline	9990	11840
2 Dr XL Econoline Ext	10350	12265

E-350

Category H

Model Description	Trade-in Value	Market Value
2 Dr Chateau Club Wagon	13775	16325
2 Dr STD Econoline	10620	12585
2 Dr STD Econoline Ext	11135	13195
2 Dr XL Club Wagon	11135	13200
2 Dr XL Club Wagon Ext	11880	14080
2 Dr XL Econoline	11355	13460
2 Dr XL Econoline Ext	11870	14070
2 Dr XLT Club Wagon	12225	14490
2 Dr XLT Club Wagon Ext	12660	15005

OPTIONS FOR CLUB WAGON/ECONOLINE

8 cyl 5.0 L Engine +205
8 cyl 5.8 L Engine +345
8 cyl 7.3 L Turbodsl Engine +1695
8 cyl 7.5 L Engine +310
Auto 4-Speed Transmission[Opt on E-250,E-350,STD] +110
AM/FM Stereo Tape[Std on Chateau] +75
Air Conditioning[Std on XLT] +300
Aluminum/Alloy Wheels[Std on Chateau] +115
Anti-Lock Brakes[Opt on Econoline,Econoline Ext] +180
Camper/Towing Package +120
Chrome Bumpers[Std on Chateau,XLT,E-150] +40
Cruise Control[Std on Chateau] +70
Dual Air Conditioning[Std on Chateau] +470
Keyless Entry System +65
Limited Slip Diff +95
Power Door Locks[Opt on STD, XL Club Wagon] +70
Power Drivers Seat +105
Power Windows[Opt on STD, XL Club Wagon] +70

CONTOUR 1996

Designers sculpt and adjust interior seating to make more leg and head room in the back seat. Five new colors are available and improvements to shift effort on manual transmission models make the 1996 Contour more competitive.

RATINGS (SCALE OF 1-10)

Overall	Safety	Reliability	Performance	Comfort	Value
7.2	6.8	6.5	8.2	7.9	6.6

Category C

Model Description	Trade-in Value	Market Value
4 Dr GL Sdn	5755	7080
4 Dr LX Sdn	6030	7420
4 Dr SE Sdn	6715	8260

OPTIONS FOR CONTOUR

6 cyl 2.5 L Engine[Std on SE] +365
Auto 4-Speed Transmission +285
AM/FM Compact Disc Player +130
Air Conditioning +295
Anti-Lock Brakes +215
Keyless Entry System +70
Leather Seats +225
Power Door Locks +95
Power Drivers Seat +110
Power Moonroof +250
Power Windows +115

CROWN VICTORIA 1996

A new steering wheel and gas cap are standard, and some equipment has been dropped from the roster, including the JBL sound system and trailer towing package.

RATINGS (SCALE OF 1-10)

Overall	Safety	Reliability	Performance	Comfort	Value
7.9	7.7	7	7.7	8.2	8.8

Don't forget to refer to the Mileage Adjustment Table at the back of this book!

Model Description	Trade-in Value	Market Value
Category B		
4 Dr LX Sdn	9220	11235
4 Dr STD Sdn	8635	10520

OPTIONS FOR CROWN VICTORIA
Handling/Performance Pkg +380
Preferred Equipment Pkg 2 +435
Anti-Lock Brakes +245
Climate Control for AC +60
Cruise Control +80
Dual Power Seats +140
Keyless Entry System +65
Leather Seats +250
Power Door Locks +95
Premium Sound System +135
Traction Control System +65
Trip Computer +145

ESCORT   1996

Last year for the second-generation Escort. The 1.9-liter engine gets 100,000-mile tune-up interval. Automatic transmissions have lower final drive ratio when coupled with 1.9-liter engine to improve acceleration. Sport/Appearance Group available on four-door models. Ultra Violet decor no longer offered on GT. Integrated child safety seat, added during 1995 model year, continues for 1996 on sedan and wagon.

RATINGS (SCALE OF 1-10)

Overall	Safety	Reliability	Performance	Comfort	Value
7.1	6.6	8.3	6.8	7.3	6.5

	Trade-in	Market
Category E		
2 Dr GT Hbk	5530	7055
2 Dr LX Hbk	4595	5860
4 Dr LX Hbk	4775	6090
4 Dr LX Sdn	4840	6175
4 Dr LX Wgn	5000	6375
2 Dr STD Hbk	4250	5425

OPTIONS FOR ESCORT
Auto 4-Speed Transmission +285
AM/FM Compact Disc Player +160
Air Conditioning +305
Anti-Lock Brakes +245
Child Seat (1) +40
Cruise Control +85
Luggage Rack +45
Power Door Locks +90
Power Moonroof +215
Power Steering[Std on GT] +95
Power Windows +95
Rear Spoiler[Opt on LX] +80
Tilt Steering Wheel +55

EXPLORER   1996

The long-awaited V8 AWD Explorers are available in XLT, Eddie Bauer or Limited Edition flavors. An integrated child safety seat is optional, and the Expedition model has been replaced by a Premium trim package for the Sport.

RATINGS (SCALE OF 1-10)

Overall	Safety	Reliability	Performance	Comfort	Value
6.8	7.4	7.1	7.6	7.1	4.9

	Trade-in	Market
Category G		
4 Dr Eddie Bauer Utility	13900	16760
4 Dr Eddie Bauer 4WD Utility	14870	17930
4 Dr Limited Utility	15665	18890
4 Dr Limited 4WD Utility	17065	20575
2 Dr Sport Utility	10490	12645
2 Dr Sport 4WD Utility	11175	13470
2 Dr XL Utility	9905	11945
2 Dr XL 4WD Utility	10875	13115
4 Dr XL Utility	10595	12775
4 Dr XL 4WD Utility	11325	13655
4 Dr XLT Utility	11720	14130
4 Dr XLT 4WD Utility	12690	15300

OPTIONS FOR EXPLORER
8 cyl 5.0 L Engine +350
Auto 4-Speed Transmission[Opt on Sport,XL,XLT] +345
Premium Sport Pkg +880
AM/FM Stereo Tape[Std on Eddie Bauer] +80
Aluminum/Alloy Wheels +120
Camper/Towing Package +110
Child Seat (1) +60
Chrome Wheels[Opt on Sport] +60
Climate Control for AC[Std on Limited] +70
Compact Disc Changer +185
Cruise Control[Opt on XL] +75
Dual Power Seats[Opt on XLT] +150
JBL Sound System[Std on Limited] +280
Keyless Entry System[Opt on Sport,XLT, Eddie Bauer] +70
Leather Seats[Std on Limited] +285
Limited Slip Diff +100
Luggage Rack[Opt on Sport,XL,XLT] +60
Power Door Locks[Opt on XL] +85
Power Moonroof +315
Power Windows[Opt on XL] +90
Running Boards[Std on Limited] +140

F-250 HEAVY DUTY   1996

	Trade-in	Market
Category H		
2 Dr XL Std Cab LB	9430	11175
2 Dr XLT Std Cab LB	10735	12725

OPTIONS FOR F-250 HEAVY DUTY
AM/FM Stereo Tape[Opt on XL] +75
Air Conditioning[Opt on XL] +300
Camper/Towing Package +120
Cruise Control[Opt on XL] +75
Tilt Steering Wheel[Opt on XL] +70
Velour/Cloth Seats[Opt on XL] +40

Don't forget to refer to the Mileage Adjustment Table at the back of this book!

Model Description	Trade-in Value	Market Value
F-SERIES PICKUP 1996		

Until an all-new truck goes into production for release in the spring, we're stuck with the same old truck that's been on the road since 1980. The Lightning has been axed from the 1996 lineup. Two new F-250 models debut, and both F-250 and F-350 models receive improvements.

RATINGS (SCALE OF 1-10)

Overall	Safety	Reliability	Performance	Comfort	Value
N/A	6.6	7.7	6.8	7.4	N/A

F-150

Category H

Model Description	Trade-in Value	Market Value
2 Dr Eddie Bauer Ext Cab LB	11990	14215
2 Dr Eddie Bauer 4WD Ext Cab LB	13025	15440
2 Dr Eddie Bauer Ext Cab SB	11855	14055
2 Dr Eddie Bauer 4WD Ext Cab SB	13035	15450
2 Dr Eddie Bauer Ext Cab Stepside SB	12250	14520
2 Dr Eddie Bauer 4WD Ext Cab Stepside SB	13370	15850
2 Dr Eddie Bauer Std Cab LB	10655	12630
2 Dr Eddie Bauer 4WD Std Cab LB	12180	14435
2 Dr Eddie Bauer Std Cab SB	10525	12475
2 Dr Eddie Bauer 4WD Std Cab SB	11980	14200
2 Dr Eddie Bauer Std Cab Stepside SB	11090	13140
2 Dr Eddie Bauer 4WD Std Cab Stepside SB	12350	14640
2 Dr Special Ext Cab LB	9260	10975
2 Dr Special Ext Cab SB	9125	10815
2 Dr Special Std Cab LB	8375	9925
2 Dr Special 4WD Std Cab LB	10100	11975
2 Dr Special Std Cab SB	8225	9750
2 Dr Special 4WD Std Cab SB	9915	11755
2 Dr XL Ext Cab LB	10045	11905
2 Dr XL 4WD Ext Cab LB	11395	13505
2 Dr XL Ext Cab SB	9910	11745
2 Dr XL 4WD Ext Cab SB	11315	13410
2 Dr XL Ext Cab Stepside SB	10305	12215
2 Dr XL 4WD Ext Cab Stepside SB	11660	13820
2 Dr XL Std Cab LB	8820	10455
2 Dr XL 4WD Std Cab LB	10395	12325
2 Dr XL Std Cab SB	8780	10410
2 Dr XL 4WD Std Cab SB	10200	12090
2 Dr XL Std Cab Stepside SB	9345	11075
2 Dr XL 4WD Std Cab Stepside SB	10570	12525
2 Dr XLT Ext Cab LB	11105	13160
2 Dr XLT 4WD Ext Cab LB	12375	14665
2 Dr XLT Ext Cab SB	11055	13105
2 Dr XLT 4WD Ext Cab SB	12240	14510
2 Dr XLT Ext Cab Stepside SB	11455	13575
2 Dr XLT 4WD Ext Cab Stepside SB	12580	14910
2 Dr XLT Std Cab LB	10000	11850
2 Dr XLT 4WD Std Cab LB	11025	13070
2 Dr XLT Std Cab SB	9885	11720
2 Dr XLT 4WD Std Cab SB	11835	14025
2 Dr XLT Std Cab Stepside SB	10435	12370
2 Dr XLT 4WD Std Cab Stepside SB	11195	13270

F-250

Category H

Model Description	Trade-in Value	Market Value
4 Dr XL Crew Cab LB	13145	15580
4 Dr XL 4WD Crew Cab LB	14890	17650
2 Dr XL Ext Cab LB	11975	14195
2 Dr XL 4WD Ext Cab LB	13830	16395
2 Dr XL Ext Cab SB	12085	14325
2 Dr XL 4WD Ext Cab SB	13845	16410
2 Dr XL Std Cab LB	9955	11800
2 Dr XL 4WD Std Cab LB	12555	14880
4 Dr XLT Crew Cab LB	14660	17375
4 Dr XLT 4WD Crew Cab LB	16485	19540
2 Dr XLT Ext Cab LB	13565	16075
2 Dr XLT 4WD Ext Cab LB	15210	18030
2 Dr XLT Ext Cab SB	13565	16080
2 Dr XLT 4WD Ext Cab SB	15315	18155
2 Dr XLT Std Cab LB	11295	13390
2 Dr XLT 4WD Std Cab LB	14135	16755

F-350

Category H

Model Description	Trade-in Value	Market Value
4 Dr XL Crew Cab LB	13690	16230
4 Dr XL 4WD Crew Cab LB	15575	18465
2 Dr XL Ext Cab LB	13550	16060
2 Dr XL Std Cab LB	11710	13880
2 Dr XL 4WD Std Cab LB	13510	16010
4 Dr XLT Crew Cab LB	15340	18180
4 Dr XLT 4WD Crew Cab LB	17240	20435
2 Dr XLT Ext Cab LB	14835	17580
2 Dr XLT Std Cab LB	12940	15340
2 Dr XLT 4WD Std Cab LB	15070	17860

OPTIONS FOR F-SERIES PICKUP

8 cyl 5.0 L Engine +205
8 cyl 5.8 L Engine +345
8 cyl 7.3 L Turbodsl Engine +1695
8 cyl 7.5 L Engine +310

Don't forget to refer to the Mileage Adjustment Table at the back of this book!

Model Description	Trade-in Value	Market Value

Auto 3-Speed Transmission +270
Auto 4-Speed Transmission +355
Air Conditioning[Opt on Special,XL] +300
Anti-Lock Brakes +180
Camper/Towing Package +120
Chrome Wheels[Opt on XL] +110
Compact Disc W/fm/tape +115
Cruise Control[Opt on Special,XL] +70
Dual Rear Wheels +290
Keyless Entry System +65
Limited Slip Diff +95
Power Door Locks[Opt on XL] +70
Power Drivers Seat +105
Power Windows[Opt on XL] +70
Rear Bench Seat +110
Skid Plates +40
Tilt Steering Wheel[Opt on Special,XL] +70

MUSTANG 1996

After much anticipation among enthusiasts, Ford plugs a 4.6-liter modular V8 into its pony car. Too bad it doesn't make any more power than the old 5.0-liter motor it replaces. Suspension and steering upgrades compliment the new engine, which does live up to its promise in the limited-edition 305-horsepower Cobra. Base cars also get engine improvements, and all Mustangs get minor styling revisions. Collectors tip: The GTS model, a midyear 1995 V8 base Mustang, has been dropped. Buy one if you can find one.

RATINGS (SCALE OF 1-10)

Overall	Safety	Reliability	Performance	Comfort	Value
6.8	6.9	7.7	8.8	7.3	3.4

Category F

Model Description	Trade-in Value	Market Value
2 Dr Cobra Conv	14505	17185
2 Dr Cobra Cpe	13075	15490
2 Dr GT Conv	12395	14685
2 Dr GT Cpe	9535	11300
2 Dr STD Conv	11355	13450
2 Dr STD Cpe	8255	9780

OPTIONS FOR MUSTANG

Auto 4-Speed Transmission +285
Mystic Metallic Paint +285
Air Conditioning[Std on Cobra] +305
Anti-Lock Brakes[Std on Cobra] +235
Compact Disc W/fm/tape +185
Cruise Control[Std on Cobra] +80
Keyless Entry System[Std on Cobra] +65
Leather Seats +230
Power Door Locks[Std on Cobra,Conv] +75
Power Drivers Seat[Std on Cobra] +90
Power Windows[Std on Cobra,Conv] +85
Premium Sound System +140
Rear Spoiler[Std on Cobra,Conv] +90

PROBE 1996

Ford concentrates on the SE and GT trim levels this year, revising and simplifying options lists and making minor cosmetic and trim revisions.

RATINGS (SCALE OF 1-10)

Overall	Safety	Reliability	Performance	Comfort	Value
6.9	7.1	7.5	9	7.4	3.5

Category E

Model Description	Trade-in Value	Market Value
2 Dr GT Hbk	6935	8845
2 Dr SE Hbk	5895	7520
2 Dr STD Hbk	5690	7255

OPTIONS FOR PROBE

Auto 4-Speed Transmission +285
AM/FM Compact Disc Player +160
Air Conditioning +305
Anti-Lock Brakes +245
Chrome Wheels +160
Cruise Control +85
Keyless Entry System +60
Leather Seats +320
Power Door Locks +90
Power Drivers Seat +110
Power Sunroof +230
Power Windows +95
Tilt Steering Wheel +55

RANGER 1996

An optional passenger-side airbag is available, and it comes with a switch that will disable the system if a child seat is installed in the truck. Cool, huh? Super Cab models get standard privacy glass, Splash models lose that putrid green tape stripe, and the Flareside box from the Splash is now available on two-wheel drive, four-cylinder XL and XLT models.

RATINGS (SCALE OF 1-10)

Overall	Safety	Reliability	Performance	Comfort	Value
N/A	6.7	8.7	7.2	7.3	N/A

Category G

Model Description	Trade-in Value	Market Value
2 Dr STX 4WD Ext Cab SB	9860	11885
2 Dr STX 4WD Std Cab LB	9560	11530
2 Dr STX 4WD Std Cab SB	9265	11170
2 Dr Splash Ext Cab Stepside SB	8155	9830
2 Dr Splash 4WD Ext Cab Stepside SB	10375	12505
2 Dr Splash Std Cab Stepside SB	7320	8825
2 Dr Splash 4WD Std Cab Stepside SB	9880	11915
2 Dr XL Ext Cab SB	7075	8530
2 Dr XL 4WD Ext Cab SB	9205	11095
2 Dr XL Ext Cab Stepside SB	7375	8895

Model Description	Trade-in Value	Market Value
2 Dr XL 4WD Ext Cab Stepside SB	9440	11380
2 Dr XL Std Cab LB	5695	6865
2 Dr XL 4WD Std Cab LB	8490	10235
2 Dr XL Std Cab SB	5565	6710
2 Dr XL 4WD Std Cab SB	8255	9950
2 Dr XL Std Cab Stepside SB	5865	7070
2 Dr XL 4WD Std Cab Stepside SB	8490	10235
2 Dr XLT Ext Cab SB	7320	8825
2 Dr XLT 4WD Ext Cab SB	9900	11940
2 Dr XLT Ext Cab Stepside SB	7550	9105
2 Dr XLT 4WD Ext Cab Stepside SB	10130	12215
2 Dr XLT Std Cab LB	6605	7960
2 Dr XLT 4WD Std Cab LB	9320	11240
2 Dr XLT Std Cab SB	6335	7640
2 Dr XLT 4WD Std Cab SB	9025	10880
2 Dr XLT Std Cab Stepside SB	6565	7915
2 Dr XLT 4WD Std Cab Stepside SB	9255	11155

OPTIONS FOR RANGER

6 cyl 3.0 L Engine +265
6 cyl 4.0 L Engine +280
Auto 4-Speed Transmission +380
AM/FM Compact Disc Player +115
Air Conditioning +300
Anti-Lock Brakes[Opt on 2WD] +210
Bed Liner +100
Chrome Wheels[Opt on XL,XLT] +60
Cruise Control +75
Dual Air Bag Restraints +160
Keyless Entry System +70
Limited Slip Diff +100
Power Door Locks +85
Power Drivers Seat +105
Power Steering[Std on Splash,STX,Ext Cab,4WD] +105
Power Windows +90

TAURUS   1996

All-new Taurus debuts in sedan and wagon format, available in GL, LX and SHO trim levels. New or substantially revised engines and suspensions improve the performance of the Taurus, while several functional innovations make the car easier and more enjoyable to drive.

RATINGS (SCALE OF 1-10)

Overall	Safety	Reliability	Performance	Comfort	Value
7.7	7.6	6.3	8	8	8.8

Category C

	Trade-in	Market
4 Dr GL Sdn	7785	9575
4 Dr GL Wgn	8225	10115
4 Dr LX Sdn	8750	10765
4 Dr LX Wgn	9165	11275

Category F

	Trade-in	Market
4 Dr SHO Sdn	11630	13780

OPTIONS FOR TAURUS

AM/FM Compact Disc Player +130
Anti-Lock Brakes[Std on SHO] +215
Child Seat (1) +45
Chrome Wheels[Opt on LX] +220
Climate Control for AC +60
Cruise Control[Std on SHO] +80
Keyless Entry System +65
Leather Seats[Opt on LX] +225
Power Door Locks[Opt on GL] +95
Power Drivers Seat[Opt on GL] +110
Power Moonroof +240
Premium Sound System +140
Third Seat +60

THUNDERBIRD   1996

Revised styling greatly improves the look of the Thunderbird for 1996. The Super Coupe is deleted, replaced by a Sport Package for the V8 model. Base V6 engines have been upgraded, and go 100,000 miles between tune-ups. Equipment rosters have been shuffled.

RATINGS (SCALE OF 1-10)

Overall	Safety	Reliability	Performance	Comfort	Value
7.4	7.7	7	8	7.9	6.6

Category C

	Trade-in	Market
2 Dr LX Cpe	7305	8985

OPTIONS FOR THUNDERBIRD

Preferred Equipment Pkg 2 +430
AM/FM Compact Disc Player +130
Anti-Lock Brakes +215
Climate Control for AC +60
Keyless Entry System +70
Leather Seats +225
Power Drivers Seat +110
Power Moonroof +250
Premium Sound System +140
Traction Control System +80

WINDSTAR   1996

Holy Smokes! That's just what the front tires will be doing, unless you find one with the optional traction control system. Ford boosted output on the 3.8-liter V6 from 155 to 200 horsepower. Trim and equipment have been revised, and four-wheel disc brakes come with traction control or the tow package. A new integrated child safety seat has been added to the options list. Tune-ups happen every 100,000 miles.

Don't forget to refer to the Mileage Adjustment Table at the back of this book!

Model Description	Trade-in Value	Market Value

Model Description	Trade-in Value	Market Value

RATINGS (SCALE OF 1-10)

Overall	Safety	Reliability	Performance	Comfort	Value
7.4	8.2	6.4	6.8	7.3	8.5

Category G

	Trade-in	Market
2 Dr GL Pass. Van	8925	10760
2 Dr LX Pass. Van	10740	12945
2 Dr STD Cargo Van	8340	10055

OPTIONS FOR WINDSTAR
6 cyl 3.8 L Engine[Std on LX] +160
AM/FM Compact Disc Player +115
Air Conditioning[Std on LX] +300
Child Seats (2) +90
Cruise Control +75
Dual Air Conditioning +335
Keyless Entry System +70
Luggage Rack +60
Power Door Locks[Std on LX] +85
Power Windows[Std on LX] +90
Traction Control System +100

1995 FORD

AEROSTAR   1995

The XL and Eddie Bauer trim levels are dropped; only the XLT remains. The AWD system is available only in extended-length versions. Antilock brakes become standard for the Aerostar.

RATINGS (SCALE OF 1-10)

Overall	Safety	Reliability	Performance	Comfort	Value
7.2	6.1	7.4	6.6	7.5	8.5

Category G

	Trade-in	Market
2 Dr STD Cargo Van	6370	7755
2 Dr XLT Pass. Van	6600	8040
2 Dr XLT Pass. Van Ext	7820	9520
2 Dr XLT 4WD Pass. Van Ext	8245	10040

OPTIONS FOR AEROSTAR
6 cyl 4.0 L Engine[Opt on 2WD] +225
AM/FM Stereo Tape[Std on 4WD] +65
Air Conditioning[Opt on STD] +245
Camper/Towing Package +90
Captain Chairs (4) +185
Child Seat (1) +50
Cruise Control[Opt on STD] +65
Dual Air Conditioning +275
Luggage Rack +50
Power Door Locks[Std on 4WD] +70
Power Windows[Std on 4WD] +70

ASPIRE   1995

Commonly referred to as the Expire, the latest runabout from Ford has little to offer but economy. Available as a two- or four-door hatchback, the Aspire comes with dual airbags and available antilock brakes.

RATINGS (SCALE OF 1-10)

Overall	Safety	Reliability	Performance	Comfort	Value
7.4	7.3	7.9	7.2	7.3	7.3

Category E

	Trade-in	Market
2 Dr SE Hbk	2700	3715
2 Dr STD Hbk	2430	3340
4 Dr STD Hbk	2600	3575

OPTIONS FOR ASPIRE
Auto 3-Speed Transmission +175
AM/FM Compact Disc Player +130
Air Conditioning +250
Anti-Lock Brakes +200
Power Steering +75
Premium Sound System +100
Rear Window Defroster +50

BRONCO   1995

An available Sport Package and new exterior styling for the Eddie Bauer model are the sole changes for 1995.

RATINGS (SCALE OF 1-10)

Overall	Safety	Reliability	Performance	Comfort	Value
7.2	8.8	7.3	6.4	6.6	7

Category H

	Trade-in	Market
2 Dr Eddie Bauer 4WD Utility	12640	15165
2 Dr XL 4WD Utility	9755	11700
2 Dr XLT 4WD Utility	10850	13020

OPTIONS FOR BRONCO
8 cyl 5.8 L Engine +275
Auto 4-Speed Transmission[Opt on XL,XLT] +310
AM/FM Compact Disc Player +90
Air Conditioning[Opt on XL,XLT] +245
Camper/Towing Package +100
Chrome Wheels +90
Keyless Entry System +50
Leather Seats +300
Limited Slip Diff +80
Power Door Locks +55
Power Windows +55
Velour/Cloth Seats +35

CLUB WAGON/ECONOLINE 1995

The optional diesel engine gets a turbocharger. Heavy-duty versions of the van receive the driver airbag that became standard on light-duty models in 1992.

RATINGS (SCALE OF 1-10)

Overall	Safety	Reliability	Performance	Comfort	Value
N/A	7.7	8.3	6.4	7.8	N/A

E-150

Category H

	Trade-in	Market
2 Dr Chateau Club Wagon	10990	13185
2 Dr STD Econoline	7785	9340

Don't forget to refer to the Mileage Adjustment Table at the back of this book!

Model Description	Trade-in Value	Market Value
2 Dr XL Club Wagon	8685	10420
2 Dr XL Econoline	8395	10070
2 Dr XLT Club Wagon	9595	11510

E-250
Category H
Model Description	Trade-in Value	Market Value
2 Dr STD Econoline	8315	9975
2 Dr STD Econoline Ext	8650	10375
2 Dr XL Econoline	8950	10740
2 Dr XL Econoline Ext	9285	11135

E-350
Category H
Model Description	Trade-in Value	Market Value
2 Dr Chateau Club Wagon	11495	13790
2 Dr STD Econoline	8685	10415
2 Dr STD Econoline Ext	9115	10935
2 Dr XL Club Wagon	9320	11180
2 Dr XL Club Wagon Ext	9875	11845
2 Dr XL Econoline	9290	11145
2 Dr XL Econoline Ext	9725	11665
2 Dr XLT Club Wagon	10175	12205
2 Dr XLT Club Wagon Ext	10550	12655

OPTIONS FOR CLUB WAGON/ECONOLINE
8 cyl 5.0 L Engine +180
8 cyl 5.8 L Engine +275
8 cyl 7.3 L Turbodsl Engine +1355
8 cyl 7.5 L Engine +255
Auto 4-Speed Transmission[Opt on E-250, E-350] +90
AM/FM Stereo Tape[Std on Chateau] +60
Air Conditioning[Opt on STD, XL] +245
Anti-Lock Brakes[Std on Club Wagon, Club Wagon Ext] +145
Camper/Towing Package[Opt on E-150, E-250, Club Wagon] +100
Chrome Bumpers +35
Cruise Control[Std on Chateau] +55
Dual Air Conditioning +385
Keyless Entry System +50
Limited Slip Diff +80
Power Door Locks[Opt on STD, XL] +55
Power Drivers Seat +85
Power Windows[Opt on STD, XL] +55
Velour/Cloth Seats[Std on XL] +35

CONTOUR   1995

The Contour replaces the much-maligned Tempo in an attempt to compete with European and Japanese compacts. Based on the European Mondeo, the Contour has front-wheel drive and dual airbags. Traction control and antilock brakes are available on all models, as is a V6 engine that produces an impressive 170 horsepower.

RATINGS (SCALE OF 1-10)
Overall	Safety	Reliability	Performance	Comfort	Value
7.1	7	5.3	8.2	7.9	7.1

Category C
Model Description	Trade-in Value	Market Value
4 Dr GL Sdn	4540	5855
4 Dr LX Sdn	4765	6145
4 Dr SE Sdn	5325	6865

OPTIONS FOR CONTOUR
6 cyl 2.5 L Engine[Std on SE] +290
Auto 4-Speed Transmission +245
Air Conditioning +245
Anti-Lock Brakes +175
Compact Disc W/fm/tape +95
Cruise Control +65
Keyless Entry System +55
Leather Seats +185
Power Door Locks +75
Power Drivers Seat +90
Power Moonroof +205
Power Windows +95
Premium Sound System +115

CROWN VICTORIA   1995

New grille, trunk lid, wheels, and bumpers freshen the Crown Victoria's styling. Rear window defroster and heated outside mirrors move from the options list to the standard equipment roster. A new interior includes a revised stereo, backlit door switches, restyled instrument panel, and a fresh climate control system.

RATINGS (SCALE OF 1-10)
Overall	Safety	Reliability	Performance	Comfort	Value
7.4	8.1	5.4	7.7	8.2	7.4

Category B
Model Description	Trade-in Value	Market Value
4 Dr LX Sdn	6910	8665
4 Dr STD Sdn	6570	8235

OPTIONS FOR CROWN VICTORIA
Handling/Performance Pkg +255
AM/FM Stereo Tape +50
Aluminum/Alloy Wheels +100
Anti-Lock Brakes +200
Camper/Towing Package +110
Climate Control for AC +50
Cruise Control +65
Dual Power Seats +115
Keyless Entry System +50
Leather Seats +205
Power Door Locks +80
Premium Sound System +110
Traction Control System +50

ESCORT   1995

A passenger airbag is now available but the motorized seatbelts mysteriously remain. A more powerful, optional air conditioner appears in the revised instrument panel. An integrated child seat is available on sedans and wagons.

Model Description	Trade-in Value	Market Value

RATINGS (SCALE OF 1-10)

Overall	Safety	Reliability	Performance	Comfort	Value
6.7	6.9	6.9	6.8	7.3	5.5

Category E

Model Description	Trade-in Value	Market Value
2 Dr GT Hbk	4240	5835
2 Dr LX Hbk	3500	4815
4 Dr LX Hbk	3645	5010
4 Dr LX Sdn	3700	5085
4 Dr LX Wgn	3820	5255
2 Dr STD Hbk	3225	4435

OPTIONS FOR ESCORT

Auto 4-Speed Transmission +245
AM/FM Compact Disc Player +130
Air Conditioning +250
Anti-Lock Brakes +200
Child Seat (1) +35
Cruise Control +70
Luggage Rack +40
Power Door Locks +75
Power Moonroof +175
Power Steering[Std on GT] +75
Power Windows +80
Premium Sound System +100
Rear Spoiler[Opt on LX] +65
Tilt Steering Wheel +45

EXPLORER   1995

Dual airbags top the changes for the redesigned Explorer. Integrated child safety seats are optional on four-door models. Exterior changes include new sheetmetal, headlights, grille, taillights, and side moldings. The Control-Trac four-wheel-drive system automatically sends power to front wheels if it senses rear-wheel slippage. This feature can be locked in for full-time four-wheeling.

RATINGS (SCALE OF 1-10)

Overall	Safety	Reliability	Performance	Comfort	Value
7.3	8	6.3	7.6	7.1	7.6

Category G

Model Description	Trade-in Value	Market Value
4 Dr Eddie Bauer Utility	11790	14360
4 Dr Eddie Bauer 4WD Utility	12640	15390
2 Dr Expedition 4WD Utility	11515	14025
4 Dr Limited Utility	13275	16165
4 Dr Limited 4WD Utility	14500	17660
2 Dr Sport Utility	8935	10880
2 Dr Sport 4WD Utility	9470	11535
2 Dr XL Utility	8425	10260
2 Dr XL 4WD Utility	9275	11295
4 Dr XL Utility	9030	10995
4 Dr XL 4WD Utility	9600	11695
4 Dr XLT Utility	9895	12050
4 Dr XLT 4WD Utility	10735	13075

OPTIONS FOR EXPLORER

Auto 4-Speed Transmission[Opt on Sport,XL,XLT] +280
Preferred Equipment Pkg +245
AM/FM Stereo Tape[Opt on Sport,XL,XLT] +65
Aluminum/Alloy Wheels +95
Camper/Towing Package +90
Climate Control for AC[Std on Limited] +60
Compact Disc Changer +150
Cruise Control[Opt on XL] +65
Dual Power Seats[Opt on Sport,XLT] +125
JBL Sound System[Std on Limited] +230
Keyless Entry System[Opt on Sport,XLT, Eddie Bauer] +60
Leather Seats[Std on Limited] +235
Limited Slip Diff +85
Luggage Rack[Opt on Sport,XL,XLT] +50
Power Door Locks[Opt on XL] +70
Power Moonroof +260
Power Windows[Opt on XL] +70
Running Boards[Std on Limited] +115

F-SERIES PICKUP   1995

The Lightning model returns after a one-year hiatus and a new turbodiesel engine is made available.

RATINGS (SCALE OF 1-10)

Overall	Safety	Reliability	Performance	Comfort	Value
N/A	7.3	7.4	6.8	7.4	N/A

F-150

Category H

Model Description	Trade-in Value	Market Value
2 Dr Eddie Bauer Ext Cab LB	10480	12570
2 Dr Eddie Bauer 4WD Ext Cab LB	11380	13650
2 Dr Eddie Bauer Ext Cab SB	10355	12425
2 Dr Eddie Bauer 4WD Ext Cab SB	11310	13565
2 Dr Eddie Bauer Ext Cab Stepside SB	10715	12855
2 Dr Eddie Bauer 4WD Ext Cab Stepside SB	11660	13985
2 Dr Eddie Bauer Std Cab LB	9220	11060
2 Dr Eddie Bauer 4WD Std Cab LB	10510	12610
2 Dr Eddie Bauer Std Cab SB	9110	10925
2 Dr Eddie Bauer 4WD Std Cab SB	10330	12390
2 Dr Eddie Bauer Std Cab Stepside SB	9555	11460
2 Dr Eddie Bauer 4WD Std Cab Stepside SB	10760	12910
2 Dr Lightning Std Cab SB	11480	13775
2 Dr Special Ext Cab LB	8055	9665
2 Dr Special Ext Cab SB	7940	9525
2 Dr Special Std Cab LB	7215	8655

Don't forget to refer to the Mileage Adjustment Table at the back of this book!

Model Description	Trade-in Value	Market Value
2 Dr Special 4WD Std Cab LB	8705	10440
2 Dr Special Std Cab SB	7075	8485
2 Dr Special 4WD Std Cab SB	8535	10240
2 Dr XL Ext Cab LB	8725	10465
2 Dr XL 4WD Ext Cab LB	9845	11810
2 Dr XL Ext Cab SB	8515	10215
2 Dr XL 4WD Ext Cab SB	9775	11725
2 Dr XL Ext Cab Stepside SB	8965	10755
2 Dr XL 4WD Ext Cab Stepside SB	10130	12155
2 Dr XL Std Cab LB	7675	9205
2 Dr XL 4WD Std Cab LB	9005	10800
2 Dr XL Std Cab SB	7560	9070
2 Dr XL 4WD Std Cab SB	8855	10620
2 Dr XL Std Cab Stepside SB	8005	9605
2 Dr XL 4WD Std Cab Stepside SB	9285	11140
2 Dr XLT Ext Cab LB	9720	11660
2 Dr XLT 4WD Ext Cab LB	10745	12895
2 Dr XLT Ext Cab SB	9595	11510
2 Dr XLT 4WD Ext Cab SB	10675	12805
2 Dr XLT Ext Cab Stepside SB	10040	12045
2 Dr XLT 4WD Ext Cab Stepside SB	11035	13235
2 Dr XLT Std Cab LB	8520	10220
2 Dr XLT 4WD Std Cab LB	9970	11960
2 Dr XLT Std Cab SB	8530	10230
2 Dr XLT 4WD Std Cab SB	9890	11865
2 Dr XLT Std Cab Stepside SB	8975	10765
2 Dr XLT 4WD Std Cab Stepside SB	10320	12385

F-250

Category F

Model Description	Trade-in Value	Market Value
2 Dr Special Ext Cab LB	9140	10965
2 Dr XL Ext Cab LB	9985	11975
2 Dr XL 4WD Ext Cab LB	11390	13665
2 Dr XL Std Cab LB	8225	9865
2 Dr XL 4WD Std Cab LB	10300	12355
2 Dr XLT Ext Cab LB	11170	13400
2 Dr XLT 4WD Ext Cab LB	12470	14955
2 Dr XLT Std Cab LB	9275	11125
2 Dr XLT 4WD Std Cab LB	11560	13865

F-350

Category H

Model Description	Trade-in Value	Market Value
4 Dr XL Crew Cab LB	11720	14060
4 Dr XL 4WD Crew Cab LB	13370	16040
2 Dr XL Ext Cab LB	11815	14175
2 Dr XL Std Cab LB	10505	12600
2 Dr XL 4WD Std Cab LB	11600	13920
4 Dr XLT Crew Cab LB	13155	15780

Model Description	Trade-in Value	Market Value
4 Dr XLT 4WD Crew Cab LB	14865	17830
2 Dr XLT Ext Cab LB	12925	15505
2 Dr XLT Std Cab LB	11710	14045
2 Dr XLT 4WD Std Cab LB	12960	15550

OPTIONS FOR F-SERIES PICKUP

8 cyl 5.0 L Engine +180
8 cyl 5.8 L Engine +275
8 cyl 7.3 L Turbodsl Engine +1355
8 cyl 7.5 L Engine +255
Auto 3-Speed Transmission +220
Auto 4-Speed Transmission[Std on Lightning] +290
AM/FM Compact Disc Player +90
Air Conditioning[Opt on Special,XL] +245
Camper/Towing Package +100
Chrome Wheels[Opt on XL] +90
Cruise Control[Opt on Special,XL] +55
Dual Rear Wheels +235
Keyless Entry System +50
Limited Slip Diff +80
Power Drivers Seat +85
Premium Sound System +115
Skid Plates +30

MUSTANG   1995

A power driver's seat moves from the standard equipment list to the options list. A powerful new stereo with a CD changer also debuts on the options list.

RATINGS (SCALE OF 1-10)

Overall	Safety	Reliability	Performance	Comfort	Value
6.8	7.3	6.4	8.8	7.3	4.4

Category F

Model Description	Trade-in Value	Market Value
2 Dr Cobra Conv	12845	15640
2 Dr Cobra Cpe	10375	12635
2 Dr Cobra R Cpe	16595	20210
2 Dr GT Conv	10475	12755
2 Dr GT Cpe	8540	10400
2 Dr GTS Cpe	8090	9850
2 Dr STD Conv	9885	12035
2 Dr STD Cpe	6880	8380

OPTIONS FOR MUSTANG

Auto 4-Speed Transmission +240
Air Conditioning +250
Anti-Lock Brakes[Std on Cobra] +195
Compact Disc W/frm/tape +150
Cruise Control +65
Keyless Entry System +55
Leather Seats[Opt on GT] +190
Power Door Locks[Std on Cobra,GT,Conv] +60
Power Drivers Seat +70
Power Windows[Std on Cobra,GT,Conv] +70
Rear Spoiler[Opt on STD] +70

Don't forget to refer to the Mileage Adjustment Table at the back of this book!

PROBE 1995

The SE Package becomes a trim level. Base and GT models receive new taillights. GTs receive 16-inch directional wheels. The rear-window wiper washer, four-way seat height adjuster and graphic equalizer have been deleted from the option list.

RATINGS (SCALE OF 1-10)

Overall	Safety	Reliability	Performance	Comfort	Value
6.9	7.8	7.1	9	7.4	3.3

Category E

	Trade-in	Market
2 Dr SE Hbk	4560	6610
2 Dr STD Hbk	4640	6385
Category F		
2 Dr GT Hbk	6395	7790

OPTIONS FOR PROBE

Auto 4-Speed Transmission +235
AM/FM Compact Disc Player +130
Air Conditioning[Std on SE] +250
Anti-Lock Brakes +195
Chrome Wheels +175
Cruise Control[Std on SE] +65
Keyless Entry System +50
Leather Seats +190
Power Door Locks[Std on SE] +60
Power Drivers Seat +70
Power Sunroof +185
Power Windows[Std on SE] +70

RANGER 1995

A driver airbag and optional four-wheel antilock brakes are two of the features added to the safety equipment roster of the capable Ford Ranger. SuperCab models can now be had with a power driver's seat.

RATINGS (SCALE OF 1-10)

Overall	Safety	Reliability	Performance	Comfort	Value
N/A	6.7	8.5	7.2	7.3	N/A

Category G

	Trade-in	Market
2 Dr STX 4WD Ext Cab SB	8590	10460
2 Dr STX 4WD Std Cab LB	8315	10130
2 Dr STX 4WD Std Cab SB	8050	9805
2 Dr Splash Ext Cab Stepside SB	6955	8470
2 Dr Splash 4WD Ext Cab Stepside SB	9050	11020
2 Dr Splash Std Cab Stepside SB	6245	7605
2 Dr Splash 4WD Std Cab Stepside SB	8605	10480
2 Dr XL Ext Cab SB	5985	7285
2 Dr XL 4WD Ext Cab SB	7995	9740
2 Dr XL Std Cab LB	5005	6095
2 Dr XL 4WD Std Cab LB	7370	8975
2 Dr XL Std Cab SB	4830	5885
2 Dr XL 4WD Std Cab SB	7155	8715
2 Dr XLT Ext Cab SB	6210	7560
2 Dr XLT 4WD Ext Cab SB	8625	10505
2 Dr XLT Std Cab LB	5820	7085
2 Dr XLT 4WD Std Cab LB	8105	9870
2 Dr XLT Std Cab SB	5580	6795
2 Dr XLT 4WD Std Cab SB	7835	9540
2 Dr XLT Std Cab Stepside SB	5785	7045

OPTIONS FOR RANGER

6 cyl 3.0 L Engine +215
6 cyl 4.0 L Engine +225
Auto 4-Speed Transmission +310
AM/FM Compact Disc Player +95
Air Conditioning +245
Anti-Lock Brakes[Opt on 2WD] +175
Chrome Wheels[Std on Splash] +50
Cruise Control +65
Limited Slip Diff[Std on Splash 4WD Ext Cab Stepside SB, STX 4WD Ext Cab SB,XLT 4WD Ext Cab SB] +85
Power Door Locks +70
Power Drivers Seat +85
Power Steering[Std on Splash,STX,Ext Cab,4WD] +85
Power Windows +70
Velour/Cloth Seats +65

TAURUS 1995

Sport edition model is introduced as an SE. The SE includes aluminum wheels, sport bucket seats, air conditioning, and a rear defroster. The base engine has been revised to decrease engine noise.

RATINGS (SCALE OF 1-10)

Overall	Safety	Reliability	Performance	Comfort	Value
7.6	7.4	6.8	8	7.8	8.2

Category C

	Trade-in	Market
4 Dr GL Sdn	5835	7520
4 Dr GL Wgn	6185	7975
4 Dr LX Sdn	6420	8275
4 Dr LX Wgn	6935	8940
4 Dr SE Sdn	6170	7955
Category F		
4 Dr SHO Sdn	9120	11105

OPTIONS FOR TAURUS

6 cyl 3.0 L FLEX Engine +140
6 cyl 3.8 L Engine[Opt on GL,SE] +190
Auto 4-Speed Transmission[Opt on SHO] +235
Anti-Lock Brakes[Std on SHO] +175
Climate Control for AC[Opt on LX] +50
Compact Disc W/fm/tape +95
Cruise Control[Std on SHO] +65
Keyless Entry System[Std on SHO] +55
Leather Seats +185
Power Door Locks[Opt on GL] +75
Power Drivers Seat[Opt on GL] +90
Power Moonroof +195

Don't forget to refer to the Mileage Adjustment Table at the back of this book!

FORD 95-94

Model Description	Trade-in Value	Market Value	Model Description	Trade-in Value	Market Value

Power Passenger Seat +85
Power Windows[Opt on GL] +95
Premium Sound System[Opt on LX] +115
Third Seat +50

THUNDERBIRD   1995

The trunk-mounted CD changer is deleted in favor of an in-dash CD-player. Variable-assist power steering is lost from the standard equipment list.

RATINGS (SCALE OF 1-10)

Overall	Safety	Reliability	Performance	Comfort	Value
7.8	8.7	7.3	8	7.9	7.1

Category C
2 Dr LX Cpe   5690   7335
Category F
2 Dr SC Sprchgd Cpe   8235   10025

OPTIONS FOR THUNDERBIRD

8 cyl 4.6 L Engine +185
Auto 4-Speed Transmission[Opt on SC] +235
AM/FM Compact Disc Player +105
Anti-Lock Brakes[Opt on LX] +175
Climate Control for AC[Opt on LX] +50
Keyless Entry System +55
Leather Seats[Opt on LX] +185
Power Door Locks[Opt on LX] +60
Power Moonroof +195
Power Passenger Seat +85
Premium Sound System +115

WINDSTAR   1995

This year, Ford introduces its version of the front-wheel-drive minivan. Designed to replace the archaic Aerostar, the Windstar offers a wealth of standard equipment. Dual airbags, antilock brakes, a four-speed automatic transmission and V6 power are just a few of the features included in the base price. The Windstar seats seven and has an integrated child seat: an attractive feature for the family with toddlers.

RATINGS (SCALE OF 1-10)

Overall	Safety	Reliability	Performance	Comfort	Value
7.2	8.9	5.9	6.6	7.3	7.1

Category G
2 Dr GL Pass. Van   7890   9610
1995.5 2 Dr GL Pass. Van   8580   10445
2 Dr LX Pass. Van   9035   11000
1995.5 2 Dr LX Pass. Van   10075   12270
2 Dr STD Cargo Van   7200   8770
1995.5 2 Dr STD Cargo Van   7800   9495

OPTIONS FOR WINDSTAR

6 cyl 3.8 L Engine[Opt on 1995.5] +125
AM/FM Compact Disc Player +95
Air Conditioning[Std on LX] +245

Child Seat (1) +50
Cruise Control[Std on LX] +65
Dual Air Conditioning +275
Keyless Entry System +60
Leather Seats +235
Luggage Rack +50
Power Door Locks[Std on LX] +70
Power Windows[Std on LX] +70

1994 FORD

AEROSTAR   1994

A high-mounted rear brake light is standard. No other changes to Ford's venerable minivan.

RATINGS (SCALE OF 1-10)

Overall	Safety	Reliability	Performance	Comfort	Value
7.1	6.2	7.7	6.6	7.5	7.4

Category G
2 Dr Eddie Bauer Pass. Van   7305   9075
2 Dr Eddie Bauer 4WD Pass. Van   7890   9805
2 Dr Eddie Bauer Pass. Van Ext   7550   9380
2 Dr Eddie Bauer 4WD Pass. Van Ext
                                         8170   10150
2 Dr STD Cargo Van   5055   6280
2 Dr STD 4WD Cargo Van   5865   7285
2 Dr STD Cargo Van Ext   5230   6500
2 Dr STD 4WD Cargo Van Ext   6060   7530
2 Dr Window Cargo Van   5240   6515
2 Dr Window 4WD Cargo Van   5960   7405
2 Dr Window Cargo Van Ext   5420   6735
2 Dr Window 4WD Cargo Van Ext   6155   7645
2 Dr XL Pass. Van   5035   6255
2 Dr XL 4WD Pass. Van   6160   7655
2 Dr XL Pass. Van Ext   5505   6840
2 Dr XL 4WD Pass. Van Ext   6505   8085
2 Dr XL Plus Pass. Van   5530   6875
2 Dr XL Plus 4WD Pass. Van   6510   8090
2 Dr XL Plus Pass. Van Ext   5870   7295
2 Dr XL Plus 4WD Pass. Van Ext
                                         6950   8640
2 Dr XLT Pass. Van   6800   8450
2 Dr XLT 4WD Pass. Van   6895   8570
2 Dr XLT Pass. Van Ext   6955   8645
2 Dr XLT 4WD Pass. Van Ext   7215   8970

OPTIONS FOR AEROSTAR

6 cyl 4.0 L Engine[Std on Cargo Van, 4WD, Eddie Bauer Pass. Van Ext] +110
Auto 4-Speed Transmission[Std on Eddie Bauer, XLT, 4WD] +185
AM/FM Stereo Tape +55
Air Conditioning[Std on XLT] +200
Captain Chairs (4) +150

Don't forget to refer to the Mileage Adjustment Table at the back of this book!

Model Description	Trade-in Value	Market Value
Child Seat (1) +40		
Cruise Control[Std on Eddie Bauer,XLT] +50		
Dual Air Conditioning[Std on Eddie Bauer] +225		
Leather Seats +190		
Luggage Rack[Std on Eddie Bauer] +40		
Power Door Locks[Std on Eddie Bauer] +55		
Power Windows[Std on Eddie Bauer] +60		
Premium Sound System[Opt on XLT] +85		
Trip Computer[Opt on XLT] +35		

ASPIRE 1994

Ford introduces the Aspire as a replacement for the aging Festiva. This little econobox has a 1.3-liter inline-four that produces a measly 63 horsepower. The Aspire is available with a five-speed manual or a three-speed automatic transmission.

RATINGS (SCALE OF 1-10)

Overall	Safety	Reliability	Performance	Comfort	Value
7	7.3	6.9	7.2	7.3	6.3

Category E
2 Dr SE Hbk	2205	3180
2 Dr STD Hbk	2045	2955
4 Dr STD Hbk	2195	3170

OPTIONS FOR ASPIRE
Auto 3-Speed Transmission +140
AM/FM Compact Disc Player +105
Air Conditioning +205
* Anti-Lock Brakes +160
Power Steering +60
Premium Sound System +80
Rear Window Defroster +40

BRONCO 1994

The 1994 Bronco receives a driver airbag and door guard beams. ABS now works in two-wheel drive and four-wheel drive.

RATINGS (SCALE OF 1-10)

Overall	Safety	Reliability	Performance	Comfort	Value
6.9	8.8	6	6.4	6.6	6.9

Category H
2 Dr Eddie Bauer 4WD Utility	10905	13175
2 Dr XL 4WD Utility	8870	10715
2 Dr XLT 4WD Utility	9770	11800

OPTIONS FOR BRONCO
8 cyl 5.8 L Engine +205
Auto 4-Speed Transmission[Opt on XL,XLT] +225
AM/FM Compact Disc Player +75
Air Conditioning[Opt on XL,XLT] +200
Camper/Towing Package +80
Chrome Wheels +75
Keyless Entry System +45
Leather Seats +245
Limited Slip Diff +65

Model Description	Trade-in Value	Market Value
Power Door Locks +45		
Power Windows +45		
Swing Out Tire Carrier +50		

CLUB WAGON/ECONOLINE 1994

Four-wheel antilock brakes replace previous rear-wheel antilock brakes.

RATINGS (SCALE OF 1-10)

Overall	Safety	Reliability	Performance	Comfort	Value
N/A	7.8	8.5	6.4	7.8	N/A

E-150

Category H
2 Dr Chateau Club Wagon	9615	11615
2 Dr STD Econoline	6710	8105
2 Dr XL Club Wagon	7600	9185
2 Dr XL Econoline	7265	8780
2 Dr XLT Club Wagon	8435	10195

E-250

Category H
2 Dr STD Econoline	6815	8230
2 Dr STD Econoline Ext	7095	8570
2 Dr XL Econoline	7365	8900

E-350

Category H
2 Dr Chateau Club Wagon	9880	11935
2 Dr STD Econoline	7400	8940
2 Dr STD Econoline Ext	7695	9295
2 Dr XL Club Wagon	8405	10155
2 Dr XL Club Wagon Ext	8405	10155
2 Dr XL Econoline	7860	9500
2 Dr XLT Club Wagon	9050	10935
2 Dr XLT Club Wagon Ext	9050	10935

OPTIONS FOR CLUB WAGON/ECONOLINE
8 cyl 5.0 L Engine +145
8 cyl 5.8 L Engine +205
8 cyl 7.3 L Dsl Engine +640
8 cyl 7.5 L Engine +215
Auto 4-Speed Transmission[Std on Chateau,Club Wagon Ext, E-150 XL Club Wagon,E-150 XLT Club Wagon] +75
AM/FM Stereo Tape[Std on Chateau] +50
Air Conditioning[Std on Chateau,E-150 XLT Club Wagon] +200
Anti-Lock Brakes[Opt on STD,Econoline] +120
Camper/Towing Package[Std on E-350 STD Econoline,E-350 Club Wagon,E-350 Club Wagon Ext] +80
Chrome Bumpers[Opt on STD] +30
Cruise Control +45
Dual Air Conditioning +315
Limited Slip Diff +65
Power Door Locks[Opt on STD] +45
Power Drivers Seat[Std on Chateau] +70
Power Passenger Seat +60
Power Windows[Opt on STD, XL] +45

Model Description	Trade-in Value	Market Value

Premium Sound System +90
Velour/Cloth Seats[Opt on STD, XL Club Wagon] +25

CROWN VICTORIA   1994

A passenger airbag is now standard. Air conditioning gets CFC-free refrigerant.

RATINGS (SCALE OF 1-10)

Overall	Safety	Reliability	Performance	Comfort	Value
7.9	7.8	7	7.7	8.2	8.6

Category B

	Trade-in	Market
4 Dr LX Sdn	5735	7505
4 Dr S Sdn	5335	6980
4 Dr STD Sdn	5355	7005

OPTIONS FOR CROWN VICTORIA

Preferred Equipment Pkg +200
AM/FM Stereo Tape +40
Aluminum/Alloy Wheels +80
Anti-Lock Brakes +165
Climate Control for AC +40
Cruise Control[Std on S] +55
Keyless Entry System +45
Leather Seats +165
Power Door Locks +65
Premium Sound System +90
Traction Control System +45

ESCORT   1994

A driver airbag debuts on all models. Antilock brakes are now available on the GT. The LX-E sedan is dropped from the lineup.

RATINGS (SCALE OF 1-10)

Overall	Safety	Reliability	Performance	Comfort	Value
6.9	6.2	8	6.8	7.6	5.9

Category E

	Trade-in	Market
2 Dr GT Hbk	3460	4990
2 Dr LX Hbk	2800	4040
4 Dr LX Hbk	2920	4215
4 Dr LX Sdn	2980	4300
4 Dr LX Wgn	3070	4430
2 Dr STD Hbk	2570	3705

OPTIONS FOR ESCORT

Auto 4-Speed Transmission +195
AM/FM Compact Disc Player +105
Air Conditioning +205
Anti-Lock Brakes +160
Cruise Control +55
Luggage Rack +30
Power Door Locks +60
Power Moonroof +140
Power Steering[Std on GT] +60
Power Windows +65
Premium Sound System +80
Rear Spoiler[Opt on LX] +55

EXPLORER   1994

New wheels and a power equipment group for the Eddie Bauer model are the only changes to this year's Explorer.

RATINGS (SCALE OF 1-10)

Overall	Safety	Reliability	Performance	Comfort	Value
6.8	5.2	5.5	7.4	8.3	7.4

Category G

	Trade-in	Market
2 Dr Eddie Bauer Utility	7630	9480
2 Dr Eddie Bauer 4WD Utility	8225	10220
4 Dr Eddie Bauer Utility	8385	10415
4 Dr Eddie Bauer 4WD Utility	9015	11205
4 Dr Limited Utility	9555	11870
4 Dr Limited 4WD Utility	10185	12655
2 Dr Sport Utility	6850	8510
2 Dr Sport 4WD Utility	7470	9285
2 Dr XL Utility	6465	8035
2 Dr XL 4WD Utility	7105	8825
4 Dr XL Utility	6790	8435
4 Dr XL 4WD Utility	7435	9240
4 Dr XLT Utility	7695	9560
4 Dr XLT 4WD Utility	8035	9985

OPTIONS FOR EXPLORER

Auto 4-Speed Transmission[Std on Limited] +215
Air Conditioning[Std on Limited] +200
Camper/Towing Package +70
Compact Disc W/fm/tape +110
Cruise Control[Opt on Sport,XL] +50
JBL Sound System +185
Keyless Entry System[Std on Limited] +50
Leather Seats[Std on Limited] +190
Limited Slip Diff +70
Luggage Rack[Opt on Sport,XL, XLT Wgn] +40
Power Door Locks[Opt on Sport,XL] +55
Power Windows[Opt on Sport,XL] +60
Running Boards +95

F-SERIES PICKUP   1994

A driver airbag becomes part of the standard equipment list on the light-duty trucks. Side-door beams and a high-mounted third taillight round out the safety changes for this year. New options include a CD player and a unique tri-fold seat that turns into a center armrest.

RATINGS (SCALE OF 1-10)

Overall	Safety	Reliability	Performance	Comfort	Value
N/A	7.1	6.9	6.8	7.4	N/A

F-150

Category H

	Trade-in	Market
2 Dr Lightning Std Cab SB	9685	11705
2 Dr S Ext Cab LB	6835	8260
2 Dr S Ext Cab SB	6730	8135

Don't forget to refer to the Mileage Adjustment Table at the back of this book!

Model Description	Trade-in Value	Market Value
2 Dr S Std Cab LB	6040	7300
2 Dr S 4WD Std Cab LB	7505	9065
2 Dr S Std Cab SB	5815	7025
2 Dr S 4WD Std Cab SB	7355	8885
2 Dr XL Ext Cab LB	7460	9010
2 Dr XL 4WD Ext Cab LB	8405	10155
2 Dr XL Ext Cab SB	7305	8825
2 Dr XL 4WD Ext Cab SB	8345	10080
2 Dr XL Ext Cab Stepside SB	7620	9210
2 Dr XL 4WD Ext Cab Stepside SB	8665	10465
2 Dr XL Std Cab LB	6680	8070
2 Dr XL 4WD Std Cab LB	7835	9465
2 Dr XL Std Cab SB	6575	7945
2 Dr XL 4WD Std Cab SB	7675	9270
2 Dr XL Std Cab Stepside SB	6975	8425
2 Dr XL 4WD Std Cab Stepside SB	8055	9735
2 Dr XLT Ext Cab LB	8360	10100
2 Dr XLT 4WD Ext Cab LB	9355	11300
2 Dr XLT Ext Cab SB	8250	9965
2 Dr XLT 4WD Ext Cab SB	9290	11225
2 Dr XLT Ext Cab Stepside SB	8570	10350
2 Dr XLT 4WD Ext Cab Stepside SB	9610	11610
2 Dr XLT Std Cab LB	7630	9215
2 Dr XLT 4WD Std Cab LB	9285	11220
2 Dr XLT Std Cab SB	7525	9095
2 Dr XLT 4WD Std Cab SB	8555	10335
2 Dr XLT Std Cab Stepside SB	7925	9575
2 Dr XLT 4WD Std Cab Stepside SB	8935	10795

F-250

Category H

Model Description	Trade-in Value	Market Value
2 Dr S Ext Cab LB	8265	9985
2 Dr XL Ext Cab LB	9005	10880
2 Dr XL 4WD Ext Cab LB	10185	12305
2 Dr XL Std Cab LB	7515	9075
2 Dr XL 4WD Std Cab LB	9435	11400
2 Dr XLT Ext Cab LB	10210	12335
2 Dr XLT 4WD Ext Cab LB	11190	13520
2 Dr XLT Std Cab LB	8920	10775
2 Dr XLT 4WD Std Cab LB	10385	12545

F-350

Category H

Model Description	Trade-in Value	Market Value
4 Dr XL Crew Cab LB	10405	12570
4 Dr XL 4WD Crew Cab LB	11890	14365
2 Dr XL Ext Cab LB	10710	12940
2 Dr XL Std Cab LB	9620	11625
2 Dr XL 4WD Std Cab LB	10480	12660
4 Dr XLT Crew Cab LB	11645	14070

Model Description	Trade-in Value	Market Value
4 Dr XLT 4WD Crew Cab LB	13200	15945
2 Dr XLT Ext Cab LB	11895	14375
2 Dr XLT Std Cab LB	10805	13055
2 Dr XLT 4WD Std Cab LB	11630	14055

OPTIONS FOR F-SERIES PICKUP

8 cyl 5.0 L Engine +145
8 cyl 5.8 L Engine +205
8 cyl 7.3 L Dsl Engine +640
8 cyl 7.3 L Turbodsl Engine +915
8 cyl 7.5 L Engine +215
Auto 3-Speed Transmission +170
Auto 4-Speed Transmission[Std on Lightning] +225
AM/FM Compact Disc Player +75
Air Conditioning[Opt on S,XL] +200
Camper/Towing Package +80
Cruise Control[Opt on S,XL] +45
Dual Rear Wheels +195
Keyless Entry System +45
Power Door Locks[Std on F-250,F-350,Eddie Bauer, Lightning] +45
Power Drivers Seat +70
Power Windows[Std on F-250,F-350,Eddie Bauer, Lightning] +45
Premium Sound System +90
Rear Step Bumper +35

MUSTANG   1994

New sheetmetal for the venerable pony. The LX model and hatchback are dropped. The base Mustang gets a 3.8-liter V6, and GT models receive a boost in horsepower. Four-wheel disc brakes are standard on both Mustangs and ABS finally becomes an available option. A passenger airbag, power driver's seat, and tilt steering wheel become standard in 1994. Convertibles are available with a removable hardtop.

RATINGS (SCALE OF 1-10)

Overall	Safety	Reliability	Performance	Comfort	Value
7	7.4	6.9	8.8	7.3	4.8

Category F

Model Description	Trade-in Value	Market Value
2 Dr Cobra Conv	10035	12460
2 Dr Cobra Cpe	9075	11265
2 Dr GT Conv	9475	11760
2 Dr GT Cpe	7680	9540
2 Dr STD Conv	8815	10945
2 Dr STD Cpe	6055	7515

OPTIONS FOR MUSTANG

Auto 4-Speed Transmission +195
Air Conditioning +205
Anti-Lock Brakes[Std on Cobra] +160
Compact Disc W/fm/tape +125
Cruise Control +55
Keyless Entry System +45
Leather Seats[Opt on GT,STD,Cpe] +155
Power Door Locks[Opt on STD Cpe] +50

Don't forget to refer to the Mileage Adjustment Table at the back of this book!

FORD 94

Power Windows[Opt on STD Cpe] +55
Premium Sound System +95
Rear Spoiler[Opt on STD] +60

PROBE 1994

Dual airbags are now standard on all Probes. A Sport Appearance Package is available for base models.

RATINGS (SCALE OF 1-10)

Overall	Safety	Reliability	Performance	Comfort	Value
7	7.8	7.2	9	7.4	3.4

	Trade-in	Market
Category E		
2 Dr SE Hbk	4025	5805
2 Dr STD Hbk	3815	5510
Category F		
2 Dr GT Hbk	5470	6790

OPTIONS FOR PROBE

Auto 4-Speed Transmission +195
AM/FM Compact Disc Player +105
Air Conditioning +205
Anti-Lock Brakes +160
Cruise Control +55
Keyless Entry System +40
Leather Seats +155
Power Door Locks +50
Power Drivers Seat +60
Power Sunroof +150
Power Windows +55

RANGER 1994

Side-impact door beams are installed on the Ranger to protect occupants. The Splash model is now available as a SuperCab. Look out, the Splash 2WD holds the road better than most sport coupes.

RATINGS (SCALE OF 1-10)

Overall	Safety	Reliability	Performance	Comfort	Value
N/A	4.9	7.9	7.2	7.3	N/A

	Trade-in	Market
Category G		
2 Dr STX Ext Cab SB	5760	7155
2 Dr STX 4WD Ext Cab SB	7460	9270
2 Dr STX Std Cab LB	5410	6725
2 Dr STX 4WD Std Cab LB	7245	9000
2 Dr STX Std Cab SB	5185	6440
2 Dr STX 4WD Std Cab SB	6995	8695
2 Dr Splash Ext Cab Stepside SB	6095	7575
2 Dr Splash 4WD Ext Cab Stepside SB	7875	9790
2 Dr Splash Std Cab Stepside SB	5490	6825
2 Dr Splash 4WD Std Cab Stepside SB	7380	9170
2 Dr XL Ext Cab SB	5070	6305
2 Dr XL 4WD Ext Cab SB	6545	8135
2 Dr XL Std Cab LB	4220	5240
2 Dr XL 4WD Std Cab LB	6045	7515
2 Dr XL Std Cab SB	4065	5050
2 Dr XL 4WD Std Cab SB	5745	7135
2 Dr XLT Ext Cab SB	5275	6555
2 Dr XLT 4WD Ext Cab SB	7085	8805
2 Dr XLT Std Cab LB	5000	6215
2 Dr XLT 4WD Std Cab LB	6830	8490
2 Dr XLT Std Cab SB	4775	5935
2 Dr XLT 4WD Std Cab SB	6555	8145

OPTIONS FOR RANGER

6 cyl 3.0 L Engine +150
6 cyl 4.0 L Engine +110
Auto 4-Speed Transmission +240
AM/FM Compact Disc Player +75
Air Conditioning +200
Cruise Control +50
Limited Slip Diff +70
Power Door Locks +55
Power Steering[Std on Splash,STX,Ext Cab,4WD] +70
Power Windows +60
Premium Sound System +85

TAURUS 1994

The passenger airbag is finally a standard equipment item. GL models receive 15-inch wheels and all Tauruses get a new steering wheel. Cellular phones are a new option.

RATINGS (SCALE OF 1-10)

Overall	Safety	Reliability	Performance	Comfort	Value
7.8	7.3	7.1	8	7.8	8.7

	Trade-in	Market
Category C		
4 Dr GL Sdn	4290	5880
4 Dr GL Wgn	4540	6220
4 Dr LX Sdn	4940	6770
4 Dr LX Wgn	5355	7335
Category F		
4 Dr SHO Sdn	7465	9270

OPTIONS FOR TAURUS

6 cyl 3.8 L Engine[Opt on GL,LX] +135
Auto 4-Speed Transmission[Opt on SHO] +195
Flex Fuel Option +250
Air Conditioning[Std on LX,SHO] +200
Anti-Lock Brakes[Std on SHO] +145
Climate Control for AC[Opt on LX] +40
Compact Disc W/fm/tape +80
Cruise Control[Std on SHO] +55
Keyless Entry System +45
Leather Seats[Std on SHO] +150
Power Door Locks[Std on LX,SHO] +60
Power Drivers Seat[Opt on GL,Wgn] +75
Power Moonroof +160
Power Passenger Seat +70
Power Windows[Std on LX,SHO] +80

FORD 94-93

Model Description	Trade-in Value	Market Value	Model Description	Trade-in Value	Market Value

Premium Sound System +95
Third Seat +40

TEMPO   1994

CFC-free air conditioning refrigerant and redesigned seatbelts are the only changes this year. The Tempo is mercifully retired after this model year in favor of the new Contour.

RATINGS (SCALE OF 1-10)

Overall	Safety	Reliability	Performance	Comfort	Value
6.9	5.2	7.5	7.6	7.1	7

Category C
		Trade-in	Market
2 Dr GL Sdn		2485	3405
4 Dr GL Sdn		2485	3405
4 Dr LX Sdn		2890	3960

OPTIONS FOR TEMPO

6 cyl 3.0 L Engine +165
Auto 3-Speed Transmission +130
AM/FM Stereo Tape +40
Air Bag Restraint +115
Air Conditioning +200
Cruise Control +55
Power Door Locks[Opt on GL] +60
Power Drivers Seat +75
Power Windows +80

THUNDERBIRD   1994

Dual airbags make their first appearance on the Thunderbird. An optional 4.6-liter V8 replaces last year's 5.0-liter V8. Dual cupholders complement the center console and the airbags are housed in a restyled dashboard.

RATINGS (SCALE OF 1-10)

Overall	Safety	Reliability	Performance	Comfort	Value
7.4	8.7	6.9	8	7.9	5.7

Category C
		Trade-in	Market
2 Dr LX Cpe		4545	6230

Category F
		Trade-in	Market
2 Dr SC Sprchgd Cpe		6935	8610

OPTIONS FOR THUNDERBIRD

8 cyl 4.6 L Engine +140
Auto 4-Speed Transmission[Opt on SC] +195
Anti-Lock Brakes[Opt on LX] +145
Climate Control for AC[Opt on LX] +40
Compact Disc Changer +115
Cruise Control[Opt on SC] +55
Keyless Entry System +45
Leather Seats +150
Power Door Locks[Opt on SC] +50
Power Drivers Seat[Opt on SC] +60
Power Moonroof +160
Power Passenger Seat +70
Premium Sound System +95
Traction Control System +50

1993 FORD

AEROSTAR   1993

An integrated child seat is introduced as an option.

RATINGS (SCALE OF 1-10)

Overall	Safety	Reliability	Performance	Comfort	Value
7	6.2	6.7	6.6	7.5	8.2

Category G
	Trade-in	Market
2 Dr Eddie Bauer Pass. Van	5745	7325
2 Dr Eddie Bauer 4WD Pass. Van	6220	7930
2 Dr Eddie Bauer Pass. Van Ext	5950	7585
2 Dr Eddie Bauer 4WD Pass. Van Ext	6415	8180
2 Dr STD Cargo Van	3985	5080
2 Dr STD 4WD Cargo Van	4650	5930
2 Dr STD 4WD Cargo Van Ext	4855	6195
2 Dr STD Cargo Van Ext	4185	5335
2 Dr Window Cargo Van	4065	5185
2 Dr Window 4WD Cargo Van	4730	6030
2 Dr XL Pass. Van	4020	5130
2 Dr XL 4WD Pass. Van	4955	6315
2 Dr XL Pass. Van Ext	4400	5610
2 Dr XL 4WD Pass. Van Ext	5125	6540
2 Dr XL Plus Pass. Van	4425	5640
2 Dr XL Plus 4WD Pass. Van	5230	6670
2 Dr XL Plus Pass. Van Ext	4685	5975
2 Dr XLT Pass. Van	5560	7090
2 Dr XLT Pass. Van Ext	5280	6730
2 Dr XLT 4WD Pass. Van Ext	5600	7145
2 Dr XLT Plus Pass. Van	5425	6920
2 Dr XLT Plus 4WD Pass. Van	7015	8520

OPTIONS FOR AEROSTAR

6 cyl 4.0 L Engine[Std on 4WD, Eddie Bauer] +95
Auto 4-Speed Transmission[Std on Eddie Bauer,XLT,XLT Plus,4WD] +150
Seat/Bed Pkg +210
Seat/bed Pkg +220
AM/FM Stereo Tape +45
Air Conditioning[Std on XLT,XLT Plus,Eddie Bauer] +165
Aluminum/Alloy Wheels[Std on Eddie Bauer] +65
Captain Chairs (4)[Opt on XL,XL Plus,XLT,XLT Plus,Pass. Van Ext] +125
Child Seat (1) +35
Chrome Wheels +35
Cruise Control[Opt on STD,XL,XL Plus] +40
Dual Air Conditioning[Std on Eddie Bauer] +185
Leather Seats +155
Luggage Rack[Std on Eddie Bauer] +30
Power Door Locks[Std on Eddie Bauer] +45
Power Windows[Std on Eddie Bauer] +50
Premium Sound System[Std on Eddie Bauer] +70
Trip Computer[Std on Eddie Bauer] +30

Don't forget to refer to the Mileage Adjustment Table at the back of this book!

Model Description	Trade-in Value	Market Value
BRONCO		**1993**

Four-wheel antilock brakes introduced on the 1993 Bronco.

RATINGS (SCALE OF 1-10)

Overall	Safety	Reliability	Performance	Comfort	Value
6.4	6.4	5.7	6.4	6.6	6.8

Category H

	Trade-in	Market
2 Dr Eddie Bauer 4WD Utility	8735	10720
2 Dr STD 4WD Utility	7490	9195
2 Dr XLT 4WD Utility	7890	9685

OPTIONS FOR BRONCO
8 cyl 5.8 L Engine +170
Auto 4-Speed Transmission[Opt on STD,XLT] +185
AM/FM Stereo Tape +40
Air Conditioning[Opt on STD,XLT] +165
Aluminum/Alloy Wheels[Opt on XLT] +60
Camper/Towing Package +65
Leather Seats +200
Limited Slip Diff +55
Power Door Locks +40
Power Drivers Seat +55
Power Windows +40
Swing Out Tire Carrier[Std on XLT] +40

CLUB WAGON/ECONOLINE 1993

No changes to the recently redesigned Ford Club Wagon.

RATINGS (SCALE OF 1-10)

Overall	Safety	Reliability	Performance	Comfort	Value
N/A	7.8	8.3	6.4	7.8	N/A

E-150

Category H

	Trade-in	Market
2 Dr Chateau Club Wagon	8645	10610
2 Dr Custom Club Wagon	6485	7960
2 Dr STD Econoline	5800	7120
2 Dr XL Econoline	6300	7730
2 Dr XLT Club Wagon	7590	9315
2 Dr XLT Super Club Wagon Ext	7655	9400

E-250

Category H

	Trade-in	Market
2 Dr STD Econoline	6000	7370
2 Dr STD Econoline Ext	6000	7370
2 Dr XL Econoline	6505	7990
2 Dr XL Econoline Ext	6745	8280

E-350

Category H

	Trade-in	Market
2 Dr Custom Club Wagon	6965	8555
2 Dr Custom Super Club Wagon Ext	7725	9485
2 Dr STD Econoline	6495	7975

	Trade-in	Market
2 Dr STD Econoline Ext	6460	7930
2 Dr XL Econoline	7005	8600
2 Dr XL Econoline Ext	6970	8555
2 Dr XLT Super Club Wagon Ext	8050	9885

OPTIONS FOR CLUB WAGON/ECONOLINE
8 cyl 5.0 L Engine +120
8 cyl 5.8 L Engine +170
8 cyl 7.3 L Dsl Engine +530
8 cyl 7.5 L Engine +195
Auto 4-Speed Transmission[Std on Chateau,Custom,XLT] +60
Club Wagon Seat/Bed Pkg +200
Seat/bed Combination +200
AM/FM Stereo Tape[Std on Chateau] +40
Air Conditioning[Std on Chateau] +165
Aluminum/Alloy Wheels[Std on Chateau] +60
Camper/Towing Package[Opt on Custom,STD,XL] +65
Cruise Control[Std on Chateau] +40
Limited Slip Diff +55
Power Door Locks[Std on Chateau,XLT,XLT Super] +40
Power Drivers Seat[Std on Chateau] +55
Power Windows[Std on Chateau,XLT,XLT Super] +40

CROWN VICTORIA 1993

The touring sedan is no longer available. Front-end styling changes include the addition of a grille. Cupholders finally appear in the dashboard. An express-down feature shows up for the driver's side window. An electronic overdrive lock-out debuts on the automatic transmission and a traction control system is available with the antilock brakes option. A 10-disc CD changer and an auto-dimming mirror are new options.

RATINGS (SCALE OF 1-10)

Overall	Safety	Reliability	Performance	Comfort	Value
7.6	6.8	6.8	7.5	8.2	8.5

Category B

	Trade-in	Market
4 Dr LX Sdn	4810	6400
4 Dr STD Sdn	4660	6195

OPTIONS FOR CROWN VICTORIA
AM/FM Stereo Tape +35
Air Bag Restraint[Opt on LX] +170
Aluminum/Alloy Wheels +65
Anti-Lock Brakes +135
Climate Control for AC +35
Compact Disc Changer +90
Cruise Control +45
Dual Power Seats +75
Keyless Entry System +35
Leather Seats +135
Power Door Locks +50
Premium Sound System +75
Traction Control System +35
Trip Computer +80

Model Description	Trade-in Value	Market Value

ESCORT 1993

Minor styling changes to all trim-levels include new taillights and grille. GT models receive a new spoiler and wheels. The LX models receive body-color spoilers.

RATINGS (SCALE OF 1-10)

Overall	Safety	Reliability	Performance	Comfort	Value
6.5	4.6	7	6.8	7.6	6.3

Category E

Model	Trade-in	Market
2 Dr GT Hbk	2630	4180
2 Dr LX Hbk	2090	3325
4 Dr LX Hbk	2185	3475
4 Dr LX Sdn	2235	3555
4 Dr LX Wgn	2305	3670
4 Dr LX-E Sdn	2640	4200
2 Dr STD Hbk	1875	2980

OPTIONS FOR ESCORT

Auto 4-Speed Transmission +145
AM/FM Stereo Tape[Opt on LX,STD] +60
Air Conditioning +165
Cruise Control +45
Luggage Rack +25
Power Door Locks +50
Power Moonroof +115
Power Steering[Opt on LX,STD] +50
Power Windows +55
Premium Sound System +65
Rear Spoiler[Opt on LX] +45

EXPLORER 1993

A new steering wheel and instrument panel freshen the Explorer's interior. New wheels are the only exterior changes. Explorers gain four-wheel antilock brakes that work in both two- and four-wheel-drive modes.

RATINGS (SCALE OF 1-10)

Overall	Safety	Reliability	Performance	Comfort	Value
6.4	4.2	4.9	7.4	8.3	7.4

Category G

Model	Trade-in	Market
2 Dr Eddie Bauer Utility	6395	8160
2 Dr Eddie Bauer 4WD Utility	6915	8815
4 Dr Eddie Bauer Utility	6830	8710
4 Dr Eddie Bauer 4WD Utility	7350	9375
4 Dr Limited Utility	7790	9930
4 Dr Limited 4WD Utility	8310	10595
2 Dr Sport Utility	5680	7245
2 Dr Sport 4WD Utility	6220	7930
2 Dr XL Utility	5365	6845
2 Dr XL 4WD Utility	5930	7560
4 Dr XL Utility	5635	7185
4 Dr XL 4WD Utility	6210	7920
4 Dr XLT Utility	6310	8050
4 Dr XLT 4WD Utility	6530	8330

OPTIONS FOR EXPLORER

Auto 4-Speed Transmission[Std on Limited] +175
AM/FM Compact Disc Player +65
Air Conditioning[Std on Limited] +165
Aluminum/Alloy Wheels[Opt on XL] +65
Camper/Towing Package +60
Cruise Control[Opt on Sport,XL] +40
Dual Power Seats[Opt on XLT] +85
Keyless Entry System +40
Leather Seats[Std on Limited] +155
Limited Slip Diff +55
Luggage Rack[Opt on Sport,XL,XLT] +30
Power Door Locks[Opt on Sport,XL] +45
Power Windows[Opt on Sport,XL] +50
Premium Sound System +70
Running Boards +75
Sunroof +60

F-SERIES PICKUP 1993

No changes for the 1993 F-Series.

RATINGS (SCALE OF 1-10)

Overall	Safety	Reliability	Performance	Comfort	Value
N/A	5.4	6.8	6.8	7.4	N/A

F-150

Category H

Model	Trade-in	Market
2 Dr Lightning Std Cab SB	7965	9780
2 Dr S Std Cab LB	4915	6030
2 Dr S 4WD Std Cab LB	6235	7650
2 Dr S Std Cab SB	4790	5880
2 Dr S 4WD Std Cab SB	6110	7500
2 Dr XL Ext Cab LB	6330	7770
2 Dr XL 4WD Ext Cab LB	7190	8830
2 Dr XL Ext Cab SB	6210	7620
2 Dr XL 4WD Ext Cab SB	7070	8680
2 Dr XL Ext Cab Stepside SB	6500	7975
2 Dr XL 4WD Ext Cab Stepside SB	7360	9035
2 Dr XL Std Cab LB	5745	7050
2 Dr XL 4WD Std Cab LB	6645	8160
2 Dr XL Std Cab SB	5620	6900
2 Dr XL 4WD Std Cab SB	6525	8010
2 Dr XL Std Cab Stepside SB	5970	7325
2 Dr XL 4WD Std Cab Stepside SB	6870	8435
2 Dr XLT Ext Cab LB	6965	8550
2 Dr XLT 4WD Ext Cab LB	7705	9460
2 Dr XLT Ext Cab SB	6845	8400
2 Dr XLT 4WD Ext Cab SB	7745	9510
2 Dr XLT Ext Cab Stepside SB	7135	8755

Model Description	Trade-in Value	Market Value
2 Dr XLT 4WD Ext Cab Stepside SB	8035	9865
2 Dr XLT Std Cab LB	6380	7835
2 Dr XLT 4WD Std Cab LB	7220	8865
2 Dr XLT Std Cab SB	6260	7685
2 Dr XLT 4WD Std Cab SB	7100	8715
2 Dr XLT Std Cab Stepside SB	6605	8110
2 Dr XLT 4WD Std Cab Stepside SB	7445	9140

F-250

Category H

Model Description	Trade-in Value	Market Value
2 Dr XL Ext Cab LB	7710	9460
2 Dr XL 4WD Ext Cab LB	8665	10635
2 Dr XL Std Cab LB	6660	8175
2 Dr XL 4WD Std Cab LB	8035	9860
2 Dr XLT Ext Cab LB	8740	10730
2 Dr XLT 4WD Ext Cab LB	9465	11620
2 Dr XLT Std Cab LB	7630	9370
2 Dr XLT 4WD Std Cab LB	8785	10785

F-350

Category H

Model Description	Trade-in Value	Market Value
4 Dr XL Crew Cab LB	8875	10895
4 Dr XL 4WD Crew Cab LB	10115	12415
2 Dr XL Ext Cab LB	9205	11300
2 Dr XL Std Cab LB	8295	10180
2 Dr XL 4WD Std Cab LB	8940	10975
2 Dr XL 4WD Std Cab SB	8930	10960
4 Dr XLT Crew Cab LB	9895	12150
4 Dr XLT 4WD Crew Cab LB	11160	13700
2 Dr XLT Ext Cab LB	10170	12485
2 Dr XLT Std Cab LB	9315	11435
2 Dr XLT 4WD Std Cab LB	9880	12130

OPTIONS FOR F-SERIES PICKUP

8 cyl 5.0 L Engine +120
8 cyl 5.8 L Engine +170
8 cyl 7.3 L Dsl Engine +530
8 cyl 7.3 L Turbodsl Engine +765
8 cyl 7.5 L Engine +195
Auto 3-Speed Transmission +140
Auto 4-Speed Transmission[Std on Lightning] +185
AM/FM Stereo Tape[Std on XLT] +40
Air Conditioning[Opt on Lightning,S,XL, XLT] +165
Aluminum/Alloy Wheels[Std on Lightning] +60
Camper/Towing Package +65
Cruise Control[Opt on XL, XLT] +40
Dual Rear Wheels +160
Limited Slip Diff[Std on Lightning] +55
Power Door Locks[Opt on XL, XLT] +40
Power Windows[Opt on XL, XLT] +40
Rear Step Bumper +30

FESTIVA 1993

No changes to the 1993 Festiva.

RATINGS (SCALE OF 1-10)

Overall	Safety	Reliability	Performance	Comfort	Value
6.1	4.6	7.5	6.2	6.9	5.1

Category E

Model Description	Trade-in Value	Market Value
2 Dr GL Hbk	1530	2430
2 Dr L Hbk	1355	2155

OPTIONS FOR FESTIVA

Auto 3-Speed Transmission +105
AM/FM Stereo Tape +60
Air Conditioning +165
Rear Spoiler +45
Rear Window Defroster +35
Sunroof +70

MUSTANG 1993

The Cobra is introduced to the lineup. Two hundred forty-five horsepower, a beefy suspension, and four-wheel disc brakes distinguish it from other Mustangs. Improved stereos grace all Mustangs this year.

RATINGS (SCALE OF 1-10)

Overall	Safety	Reliability	Performance	Comfort	Value
N/A	N/A	7.1	7.8	6.3	3.9

Category C

Model Description	Trade-in Value	Market Value
2 Dr LX Conv	4580	6560
2 Dr LX Cpe	2850	4085
2 Dr LX Hbk	2980	4270

Category F

Model Description	Trade-in Value	Market Value
2 Dr Cobra Hbk	6165	7760
2 Dr GT Conv	6585	8290
2 Dr GT Hbk	5300	6675
2 Dr LX 5.0 Conv	6795	8550
2 Dr LX 5.0 Cpe	4705	5925
2 Dr LX 5.0 Hbk	4965	6250

OPTIONS FOR MUSTANG

Auto 4-Speed Transmission +120
AM/FM Compact Disc Player +70
Air Conditioning +160
Aluminum/Alloy Wheels[Opt on LX] +60
Chrome Wheels +120
Cruise Control +45
Leather Seats +125
Power Door Locks[Std on Conv] +40
Power Drivers Seat +50
Power Windows[Std on Conv] +45
Rear Spoiler[Opt on Conv] +50
Sunroof +75

PROBE 1993

A driver airbag becomes standard on the restyled Probe. The Probe's wheelbase stretches four inches and its curb weight jumps 100 pounds. The slow-selling LX model is dropped. Four-cylinder engines in the base model are good for 115 horsepower; GT models get a

FORD 93

twin-cam 2.5-liter V6 engine that makes 164. Antilock brakes become optional for all Probes.

RATINGS (SCALE OF 1-10)

Overall	Safety	Reliability	Performance	Comfort	Value
6.7	6	6.7	9	7.4	4.2

Category C

	Trade-in	Market
2 Dr STD Hbk	2850	4085

Category F

	Trade-in	Market
2 Dr GT Hbk	4380	5510

OPTIONS FOR PROBE

Auto 4-Speed Transmission +145
AM/FM Compact Disc Player +70
Air Conditioning +160
Aluminum/Alloy Wheels[Std on GT] +60
Anti-Lock Brakes +120
Cruise Control +45
Keyless Entry System +35
Leather Seats +125
Power Door Locks +40
Power Drivers Seat[Std on GT] +60
Power Sunroof +135
Power Windows +45

RANGER   1993

The classy-looking Ranger Splash is introduced in 1993, offering the first flareside cargo box in the small pickup class. The rest of the Ranger lineup gets new sheetmetal.

RATINGS (SCALE OF 1-10)

Overall	Safety	Reliability	Performance	Comfort	Value
N/A	5	8.1	7.2	7.3	N/A

Category G

	Trade-in	Market
2 Dr STX Ext Cab SB	4680	5970
2 Dr STX 4WD Ext Cab SB	5925	7555
2 Dr STX Std Cab LB	3905	4975
2 Dr STX 4WD Std Cab LB	5445	6945
2 Dr STX Std Cab SB	3800	4845
2 Dr STX 4WD Std Cab SB	5340	6810
2 Dr Splash Std Cab Stepside SB	4405	5615
2 Dr Splash 4WD Std Cab Stepside SB	5890	7510
2 Dr Sport Std Cab LB	3895	4965
2 Dr Sport 4WD Std Cab LB	4865	6205
2 Dr Sport Std Cab SB	3790	4830
2 Dr Sport 4WD Std Cab SB	4760	6075
2 Dr XL Ext Cab SB	4265	5440
2 Dr XL 4WD Ext Cab SB	5470	6975
2 Dr XL Std Cab LB	3675	4685
2 Dr XL 4WD Std Cab LB	4650	5925
2 Dr XL Std Cab SB	3570	4555
2 Dr XL 4WD Std Cab SB	4580	5840
2 Dr XLT Ext Cab SB	4395	5605
2 Dr XLT 4WD Ext Cab SB	5720	7295
2 Dr XLT Std Cab LB	3925	5010
2 Dr XLT 4WD Std Cab LB	5185	6615
2 Dr XLT Std Cab SB	3800	4845
2 Dr XLT 4WD Std Cab SB	5080	6480

OPTIONS FOR RANGER

6 cyl 3.0 L Engine +130
6 cyl 4.0 L Engine +95
Auto 4-Speed Transmission +195
AM/FM Compact Disc Player +65
Air Conditioning +165
Aluminum/Alloy Wheels[Std on Splash] +65
Cruise Control +40
Limited Slip Diff +55
Power Door Locks +45
Power Steering[Opt on XL 2WD Std Cab] +55
Power Windows +50
Premium Sound System +70

TAURUS   1993

SHOs finally receive an optional automatic transmission. The base L model is dropped in favor of the new entry-level Taurus GL. Body-color bumpers and side moldings are now standard.

RATINGS (SCALE OF 1-10)

Overall	Safety	Reliability	Performance	Comfort	Value
7.2	6.4	5.2	8	7.8	8.6

Category C

	Trade-in	Market
4 Dr GL Sdn	3270	4680
4 Dr GL Wgn	3505	5025
4 Dr LX Sdn	3840	5505
4 Dr LX Wgn	4185	6000

Category F

	Trade-in	Market
4 Dr SHO Sdn	6220	7830

OPTIONS FOR TAURUS

6 cyl 3.0 L FLEX Engine +145
6 cyl 3.8 L Engine +110
Auto 4-Speed Transmission[Opt on SHO] +130
AM/FM Compact Disc Player +70
Air Conditioning[Opt on GL] +160
Aluminum/Alloy Wheels[Opt on GL] +60
Anti-Lock Brakes[Std on SHO] +120
Climate Control for AC[Opt on LX] +35
Cruise Control[Std on SHO] +45
Dual Air Bag Restraints +95
Dual Power Seats +115
Leather Seats +125
Power Door Locks[Opt on GL] +50
Power Moonroof +130
Power Windows[Opt on GL] +65
Premium Sound System +75
Third Seat +35

Don't forget to refer to the Mileage Adjustment Table at the back of this book!

TEMPO — 1993

Say goodbye to the GLS. GL and LX Tempos have removable cupholders and a leather-wrapped shift knob. A driver airbag is optional on both models.

RATINGS (SCALE OF 1-10)

Overall	Safety	Reliability	Performance	Comfort	Value
6.6	4.4*	7.1	7.6	7.1	6.8

Category C
2 Dr GL Sdn	2050	2935
4 Dr GL Sdn	2050	2935
4 Dr LX Sdn	2405	3445

OPTIONS FOR TEMPO

6 cyl 3.0 L Engine +140
Auto 3-Speed Transmission +110
AM/FM Stereo Tape +35
Air Bag Restraint +95
Air Conditioning +160
Aluminum/Alloy Wheels +60
Cruise Control +45
Power Door Locks[Opt on GL] +50
Power Drivers Seat +60
Power Windows +65

THUNDERBIRD — 1993

Base and Sport models are discontinued. Restyled alloy wheels and a new steering wheel complete the changes to the 1993 Thunderbird.

RATINGS (SCALE OF 1-10)

Overall	Safety	Reliability	Performance	Comfort	Value
6.9	5.7	7	6.8	8	6.9

Category C
2 Dr LX Cpe	3255	4940

Category F
2 Dr SC Sprchgd Cpe	5365	6755

OPTIONS FOR THUNDERBIRD

8 cyl 5.0 L Engine +225
Auto 4-Speed Transmission[Opt on SC] +120
AM/FM Compact Disc Player +70
Aluminum/Alloy Wheels[Opt on LX] +60
Anti-Lock Brakes +120
Climate Control for AC +35
Cruise Control[Opt on SC] +45
Keyless Entry System +35
Leather Seats +125
Power Door Locks[Opt on SC] +40
Power Drivers Seat +50
Power Moonroof +130
Power Passenger Seat +55
Premium Sound System +75

1992 FORD

AEROSTAR — 1992

A driver airbag becomes standard on passenger and cargo models. A new dashboard includes redesigned climate controls. On automatics, the shift lever moves from the floor to the column. High-back front bucket seats are now standard for all trim levels. Leather seats are available for the Eddie Bauer model. Outboard rear-seat passengers get a shoulder belt. A new grille and headlights appear on the exterior.

RATINGS (SCALE OF 1-10)

Overall	Safety	Reliability	Performance	Comfort	Value
7	6.2	6.6	6.6	7.5	8.1

Category G
2 Dr Eddie Bauer Pass. Van	4675	6195
2 Dr Eddie Bauer 4WD Pass. Van	5050	6695
2 Dr Eddie Bauer Pass. Van Ext	4880	6465
2 Dr Eddie Bauer 4WD Pass. Van Ext	5255	6965
2 Dr STD Cargo Van	3280	4345
2 Dr STD 4WD Cargo Van	3845	5095
2 Dr STD Cargo Van Ext	3460	4585
2 Dr STD 4WD Cargo Van Ext	4025	5335
2 Dr XL Pass. Van	3275	4340
2 Dr XL 4WD Pass. Van	4025	5335
2 Dr XL Pass. Van Ext	3270	4330
2 Dr XL 4WD Pass. Van Ext	4255	5635
2 Dr XLT Pass. Van	4250	5630
2 Dr XLT 4WD Pass. Van	4355	5770
2 Dr XLT Pass. Van Ext	4470	5925
2 Dr XLT 4WD Pass. Van Ext	4560	6040

OPTIONS FOR AEROSTAR

6 cyl 4.0 L Engine[Std on 4WD] +90
Auto 4-Speed Transmission[Opt on 2WD] +120
Plus Pkg +160
Seat/Bed Combination +155
Air Conditioning[Std on XLT] +135
Captain Chairs (4) +100
Cruise Control[Opt on STD,XL] +35
Dual Air Conditioning[Opt on XL,XLT] +150
Power Door Locks[Opt on STD,XL] +40
Power Windows[Opt on STD,XL] +40

BRONCO — 1992

Freshened front-end styling and the addition of the XLT and Eddie Bauer models are the main changes for 1992.

RATINGS (SCALE OF 1-10)

Overall	Safety	Reliability	Performance	Comfort	Value
6.2	5.6	5.5	6.4	6.6	6.7

Don't forget to refer to the Mileage Adjustment Table at the back of this book!

Model Description	Trade-in Value	Market Value
Category H		
2 Dr Custom 4WD Utility	6085	7555
2 Dr Eddie Bauer 4WD Utility	6980	8670
2 Dr XLT 4WD Utility	6225	7730

OPTIONS FOR BRONCO

8 cyl 5.0 L Engine[Opt on Custom,XLT] +95
8 cyl 5.8 L Engine +140
Auto 4-Speed Transmission +150
Air Conditioning[Opt on Custom,XLT] +135
Camper/Towing Package +55
Cruise Control[Opt on Custom,XLT] +30
Limited Slip Diff +45
Power Door Locks +30
Power Windows +30

CLUB WAGON/ECONOLINE 1992

Fully redesigned, Ford's full-size van receives a new body, lights, suspension and fuel tank. New safety features include a driver's side airbag and a high-mounted third brake light.

RATINGS (SCALE OF 1-10)

Overall	Safety	Reliability	Performance	Comfort	Value
N/A	7	7.9	6.4	7.8	N/A

E-150

Category B

	Trade-in	Market
2 Dr Chateau Club Wagon	7240	8990
2 Dr STD Club Wagon	5430	6745
2 Dr STD Econoline	4870	6050
2 Dr XL Econoline	5305	6590
2 Dr XLT Club Wagon	6205	7705

E-250

Category H

	Trade-in	Market
2 Dr STD Econoline	5185	6440
2 Dr STD Econoline Ext	5185	6440
2 Dr XL Econoline	5460	6780
2 Dr XL Econoline Ext	5460	6780

E-350

Category H

	Trade-in	Market
2 Dr Chateau Club Wagon Ext	7930	9850
2 Dr STD Club Wagon	6040	7500
2 Dr STD Econoline	6440	8000
2 Dr STD Econoline Ext	5625	6990
2 Dr Super Club Wagon Ext	6720	8345
2 Dr XL Econoline Ext	5905	7335
2 Dr XLT Club Wagon Ext	7180	8915
2 Dr XLT Pass. Van	6975	8660

OPTIONS FOR CLUB WAGON/ECONOLINE

8 cyl 5.0 L Engine +95
8 cyl 5.8 L Engine +140
8 cyl 7.3 L Dsl Engine +425
8 cyl 7.5 L Engine +155

Model Description	Trade-in Value	Market Value
Auto 4-Speed Transmission[Std on E-150 Club Wagon] +50		
Seat/Bed Combination +130		
Seat/Bed Pkg +160		
XLT Trim Pkg +145		
Air Conditioning +135		
Camper/Towing Package[Std on E-150 Econoline Ext,E-350 Econoline,E-350 Econoline Ext] +55		
Cruise Control +30		
Dual Air Conditioning +210		
Power Door Locks +30		
Power Drivers Seat +45		
Power Windows +30		

CROWN VICTORIA 1992

After a total redesign, the corny LTD moniker is dropped from name and the station wagon body style is deleted from the Crown Vic's lineup. Suspension improvements include gas-charged shock absorbers and rear stabilizer bars. Antilock brakes are optional but four-wheel disc brakes are standard.

RATINGS (SCALE OF 1-10)

Overall	Safety	Reliability	Performance	Comfort	Value
7.2	6.8	5.8	7.5	8.2	7.8

Category B

	Trade-in	Market
4 Dr LX Sdn	4075	5495
4 Dr STD Sdn	3995	5390
4 Dr Touring Sdn	4635	6250

OPTIONS FOR CROWN VICTORIA

Anti-Lock Brakes[Std on Touring] +110
Cruise Control[Std on Touring] +35
JBL Sound System +85
Leather Seats +110
Power Door Locks +45
Power Drivers Seat[Std on Touring] +50
Power Passenger Seat[Opt on LX] +60
Trip Computer +65

ESCORT 1992

A notchback sedan is introduced as an LX-E trim-level; it offers four-wheel disc brakes, the GT engine, and GT interior touches. The Pony Comfort Group option makes air conditioning and power steering available on the base model.

RATINGS (SCALE OF 1-10)

Overall	Safety	Reliability	Performance	Comfort	Value
6.3	4.5	6.9	6.8	7.6	5.8

Category E

	Trade-in	Market
2 Dr GT Hbk	2055	3625
2 Dr LX Hbk	1580	2790
4 Dr LX Hbk	1650	2920
4 Dr LX Sdn	1705	3010
4 Dr LX Wgn	1750	3090

Don't forget to refer to the Mileage Adjustment Table at the back of this book!

Model Description	Trade-in Value	Market Value
4 Dr LX-E Sdn	2065	3645
2 Dr Pony Hbk	1465	2585

OPTIONS FOR ESCORT

Auto 4-Speed Transmission +120
Air Conditioning +135
Cruise Control +35
Power Door Locks +40
Power Steering[Opt on LX,Pony] +40
Power Windows +45

EXPLORER   1992

A 3.55 axle replaces last year's 3.27 on four-wheel drive models. A one-touch-down driver's window becomes standard on all Explorers equipped with power windows. Eddie Bauer models receive color-keyed alloy wheels. A tilt-open sunroof is now available without an option package.

RATINGS (SCALE OF 1-10)

Overall	Safety	Reliability	Performance	Comfort	Value
6.2	4.3	4.8	7.4	8.3	6

Category G

Model Description	Trade-in Value	Market Value
2 Dr Eddie Bauer Utility	5445	7215
2 Dr Eddie Bauer 4WD Utility	5895	7810
4 Dr Eddie Bauer Utility	5800	7685
4 Dr Eddie Bauer 4WD Utility	6260	8295
2 Dr Sport Utility	4800	6360
2 Dr Sport 4WD Utility	5275	6985
2 Dr XL Utility	4485	5940
2 Dr XL 4WD Utility	4975	6590
4 Dr XL Utility	4715	6245
4 Dr XL 4WD Utility	5210	6905
4 Dr XLT Utility	5250	6955
4 Dr XLT 4WD Utility	5375	7125

OPTIONS FOR EXPLORER

Auto 4-Speed Transmission +145
AM/FM Compact Disc Player +50
Air Conditioning +135
Camper/Towing Package +50
Cruise Control[Std on Eddie Bauer, XLT] +35
Flip-Up Sunroof +55
Leather Seats +130
Limited Slip Diff +45
Power Door Locks[Std on Eddie Bauer, XLT] +40
Power Drivers Seat[Opt on XLT] +45
Power Windows[Std on Eddie Bauer, XLT] +40

F SUPER DUTY   1992

Category H

Model Description	Trade-in Value	Market Value
2 Dr XLT Lariat Std Cab LB	6240	7750

OPTIONS FOR F SUPER DUTY

8 cyl 7.3 L Dsl Engine +425
Air Conditioning +135
Power Windows +30

F-SERIES PICKUP   1992

New front sheetmetal, a redesigned dashboard, and the return of the Flareside mark the changes for the 1992 F-Series. Climate controls are simplified and stereo controls are moved closer to the driver.

RATINGS (SCALE OF 1-10)

Overall	Safety	Reliability	Performance	Comfort	Value
N/A	5.6	7.1	6.8	7.4	N/A

F-150

Category H

Model Description	Trade-in Value	Market Value
2 Dr S Ext Cab LB	4835	6005
2 Dr S Ext Cab SB	4730	5875
2 Dr S Std Cab LB	3985	4945
2 Dr S 4WD Std Cab LB	5095	6330
2 Dr S Std Cab SB	3875	4815
2 Dr S 4WD Std Cab SB	4990	6195
2 Dr STD Ext Cab LB	5345	6635
2 Dr STD 4WD Ext Cab LB	6095	7570
2 Dr STD Ext Cab SB	5240	6505
2 Dr STD 4WD Ext Cab SB	5990	7435
2 Dr STD Ext Cab Stepside SB	5595	6950
2 Dr STD 4WD Ext Cab Stepside SB	6345	7880
2 Dr STD Std Cab LB	4860	6035
2 Dr STD 4WD Std Cab LB	5645	7010
2 Dr STD Std Cab SB	4755	5905
2 Dr STD 4WD Std Cab SB	5540	6880
2 Dr STD Std Cab Stepside SB	5220	6480
2 Dr STD 4WD Std Cab Stepside SB	5955	7395
2 Dr XL Ext Cab LB	5480	6805
2 Dr XL 4WD Ext Cab LB	6230	7740
2 Dr XL Ext Cab SB	5375	6675
2 Dr XL 4WD Ext Cab SB	6125	7605
2 Dr XL Ext Cab Stepside SB	5735	7120
2 Dr XL 4WD Ext Cab Stepside SB	6485	8050
2 Dr XL Std Cab LB	5000	6205
2 Dr XL 4WD Std Cab LB	5765	7160
2 Dr XL Std Cab SB	4925	6120
2 Dr XL 4WD Std Cab SB	5660	7025
2 Dr XL Std Cab Stepside SB	5395	6700
2 Dr XL 4WD Std Cab Stepside SB	6125	7605
2 Dr XLT Lariat Ext Cab LB	5640	7005
2 Dr XLT Lariat 4WD Ext Cab LB	6495	8070
2 Dr XLT Lariat Ext Cab SB	5685	7060
2 Dr XLT Lariat 4WD Ext Cab SB	6390	7935
2 Dr XLT Lariat Ext Cab Stepside SB	6000	7450

Model Description	Trade-in Value	Market Value
2 Dr XLT Lariat 4WD Ext Cab Stepside SB		
	6750	8380
2 Dr XLT Lariat Std Cab LB	5305	6585
2 Dr XLT Lariat 4WD Std Cab LB	6050	7515
2 Dr XLT Lariat Std Cab SB	5200	6455
2 Dr XLT Lariat 4WD Std Cab SB	5965	7405
2 Dr XLT Lariat Std Cab Stepside SB		
	5665	7035
2 Dr XLT Lariat 4WD Std Cab Stepside SB		
	6430	7985

F-250

Category H

Model Description	Trade-in Value	Market Value
2 Dr STD Ext Cab LB	5955	7395
2 Dr STD 4WD Ext Cab LB	7055	8765
2 Dr STD Std Cab LB	5150	6400
2 Dr STD 4WD Std Cab LB	6645	8255
2 Dr XLT Lariat Ext Cab LB	6330	7860
2 Dr XLT Lariat 4WD Ext Cab LB	7115	8835
2 Dr XLT Lariat Std Cab LB	5475	6795
2 Dr XLT Lariat 4WD Std Cab LB	6970	8655

F-350

Category H

Model Description	Trade-in Value	Market Value
4 Dr STD Crew Cab LB	6650	8260
4 Dr STD 4WD Crew Cab LB	7365	9150
2 Dr STD Ext Cab LB	6830	8485
2 Dr STD Std Cab LB	6165	7660
2 Dr STD 4WD Std Cab LB	6785	8430
4 Dr XLT Lariat Crew Cab LB	7000	8695
4 Dr XLT Lariat 4WD Crew Cab LB		
	7705	9565
2 Dr XLT Lariat Ext Cab LB	7175	8910
2 Dr XLT Lariat Std Cab LB	6455	8015
2 Dr XLT Lariat 4WD Std Cab LB	7075	8785

OPTIONS FOR F-SERIES PICKUP
8 cyl 5.0 L Engine +95
8 cyl 5.8 L Engine +140
8 cyl 7.3 L Dsl Engine +425
8 cyl 7.5 L Engine +155
Auto 3-Speed Transmission +135
Auto 4-Speed Transmission +150
Nite Trim Pkg +190
Air Conditioning +135
Camper/Towing Package +55
Cruise Control +30
Dual Rear Wheels +130
Limited Slip Diff +45
Power Door Locks +30
Power Windows +30

FESTIVA 1992

The GL gets alloy wheels. Sport trim and a spoiler are part of the GL's optional Sport Package.

RATINGS (SCALE OF 1-10)

Overall	Safety	Reliability	Performance	Comfort	Value
6.1	4.6	7.9	6.2	6.9	5

Category E

Model Description	Trade-in Value	Market Value
2 Dr GL Hbk	1225	2165
2 Dr L Hbk	1070	1895

OPTIONS FOR FESTIVA
Auto 3-Speed Transmission +85
Air Conditioning +135
Sunroof +55

MUSTANG 1992

LX models receive color-keyed body side moldings and bumper rub strips. All models get a new dome lamp.

RATINGS (SCALE OF 1-10)

Overall	Safety	Reliability	Performance	Comfort	Value
N/A	N/A	7.2	7.8	6.3	4.6

Category C

Model Description	Trade-in Value	Market Value
2 Dr LX Conv	3790	5755
2 Dr LX Cpe	2330	3535
2 Dr LX Hbk	2440	3705

Category F

Model Description	Trade-in Value	Market Value
2 Dr GT Conv	5700	7415
2 Dr GT Hbk	4580	5965
2 Dr LX 5.0 Conv	5870	7635
2 Dr LX 5.0 Cpe	4050	5270
2 Dr LX 5.0 Hbk	4280	5570

OPTIONS FOR MUSTANG
Auto 4-Speed Transmission +95
Air Conditioning +135
Cruise Control +35
Leather Seats +105
Power Door Locks[Std on Conv] +35
Power Drivers Seat +40
Power Windows[Std on Conv] +40
Sunroof +60

PROBE 1992

The Sport Option Package becomes available for the LX model. A rear window defroster, interval wipers, power mirrors, tinted glass, and a tilt steering wheel are no longer standard on the GT or LX.

Category E

Model Description	Trade-in Value	Market Value
2 Dr GL Hbk	1975	3490
2 Dr LX Hbk	2135	3770

Category F

Model Description	Trade-in Value	Market Value
2 Dr GT Turbo Hbk	3515	4570

OPTIONS FOR PROBE
Auto 4-Speed Transmission +120
Air Conditioning +135
Anti-Lock Brakes +105

Don't forget to refer to the Mileage Adjustment Table at the back of this book!

Model Description	Trade-in Value	Market Value

Cruise Control +35
Leather Seats +105
Power Door Locks +35
Power Drivers Seat +40
Power Windows +40
Sunroof +55

RANGER   1992

No changes to the 1992 Ford Ranger.

Category G

Model Description	Trade-in Value	Market Value
2 Dr Custom Std Cab LB	3050	4045
2 Dr Custom 4WD Std Cab LB	4040	5355
2 Dr Custom Std Cab SB	2960	3920
2 Dr Custom 4WD Std Cab SB	3955	5240
2 Dr S Std Cab SB	2630	3485
2 Dr STD Ext Cab SB	3445	4565
2 Dr STD 4WD Ext Cab SB	4260	5645
2 Dr STX Ext Cab SB	3695	4895
2 Dr STX 4WD Ext Cab SB	4570	6055
2 Dr STX Std Cab LB	3295	4365
2 Dr STX 4WD Std Cab LB	4265	5650
2 Dr STX Std Cab SB	3205	4245
2 Dr STX 4WD Std Cab SB	4135	5475
2 Dr Sport Std Cab LB	2675	3545
2 Dr Sport 4WD Std Cab LB	3800	5030
2 Dr Sport Std Cab SB	2630	3485
2 Dr Sport 4WD Std Cab SB	3710	4920
2 Dr XLT Ext Cab SB	3700	4900
2 Dr XLT 4WD Ext Cab SB	4570	6055
2 Dr XLT Std Cab LB	3255	4310
2 Dr XLT 4WD Std Cab LB	4445	5895
2 Dr XLT Std Cab SB	3160	4190
2 Dr XLT 4WD Std Cab SB	4360	5780

OPTIONS FOR RANGER

6 cyl 2.9 L Engine +90
6 cyl 3.0 L Engine[Std on STX] +125
6 cyl 4.0 L Engine +90
Auto 4-Speed Transmission +155
Chrome Rally Bar Pkg +150
Chrome Sport Appear Pkg +140
Air Conditioning +135
Cruise Control[Opt on Custom,Sport,STD,XLT,4WD] +35
Limited Slip Diff +45
Power Door Locks +40
Power Drivers Seat +45
Power Windows +40

TAURUS   1992

A passenger airbag is now optional. Interior changes include a new dash. Restyled sheetmetal replaces everything but the doors. Antilock brakes are standard on the SHO and optional on other models. The SHO receives distinctive front-end styling. Wagons get an optional remote lift gate release.

RATINGS (SCALE OF 1-10)

Overall	Safety	Reliability	Performance	Comfort	Value
7.2	6.6	5.7	8	7.8	8.1

Category C

Model Description	Trade-in Value	Market Value
4 Dr GL Sdn	2680	4070
4 Dr GL Wgn	2850	4330
4 Dr L Sdn	2630	3990
4 Dr L Wgn	2805	4260
4 Dr LX Sdn	3105	4715
4 Dr LX Wgn	3390	5150

Category F

Model Description	Trade-in Value	Market Value
4 Dr SHO Sdn	5160	6715

OPTIONS FOR TAURUS

6 cyl 3.8 L Engine[Opt on GL] +80
AM/FM Compact Disc Player +55
Air Conditioning[Std on LX,SHO] +135
Anti-Lock Brakes[Std on SHO] +95
Cruise Control[Std on SHO] +35
Dual Air Bag Restraints +80
Leather Seats +100
Power Door Locks[Std on LX,SHO] +40
Power Drivers Seat[Std on LX,SHO] +50
Power Moonroof +105
Power Windows[Std on LX,SHO] +50

TEMPO   1992

V6 power becomes available but the four-wheel drive option departs. Rear stabilizer bars are added to V6 models and sequential-port fuel injection appears on all Tempos. The GLS model receives fog lamps, alloy wheels and 15-inch tires.

RATINGS (SCALE OF 1-10)

Overall	Safety	Reliability	Performance	Comfort	Value
6.4	4.4	6.6	7.6	7.1	6.3

Category C

Model Description	Trade-in Value	Market Value
2 Dr GL Sdn	1725	2620
4 Dr GL Sdn	1750	2655
2 Dr GLS Sdn	2165	3285
4 Dr GLS Sdn	2190	3325
4 Dr LX Sdn	1910	2900

OPTIONS FOR TEMPO

6 cyl 3.0 L Engine[Std on GLS] +115
Auto 3-Speed Transmission +90
Air Bag Restraint +75
Air Conditioning[Std on GLS] +135
Cruise Control +35
Power Door Locks[Std on LX] +40
Power Drivers Seat +50
Power Windows +50

Model Description	Trade-in Value	Market Value

THUNDERBIRD 1992

A V8 engine is available on the Base and LX Thunderbird; standard on the new Sport. The Sport has alloy wheels and V8 fender badges.

RATINGS (SCALE OF 1-10)

Overall	Safety	Reliability	Performance	Comfort	Value
6.8	5.7	6.5	6.8	8	6.9

Category C
2 Dr LX Cpe	3225	4625
2 Dr STD Cpe	2840	4315
2 Dr Sport Cpe	3225	4900

Category F
2 Dr SC Sprchgd Cpe	4760	6195

OPTIONS FOR THUNDERBIRD

8 cyl 5.0 L Engine[Std on Sport] +180
Auto 4-Speed Transmission[Opt on SC] +95
AM/FM Compact Disc Player +55
Anti-Lock Brakes[Std on SC] +95
Cruise Control[Opt on STD] +35
JBL Sound System +80
Leather Seats +100
Power Door Locks[Std on LX] +35
Power Drivers Seat[Std on LX] +40
Power Moonroof +105
Power Passenger Seat +45

1991 FORD

AEROSTAR 1991

A new sport appearance package debuts on XL and XLT models; it includes running boards and a front air dam. The towing harness is upgraded and a door ajar dummy-light appears for rear doors. The Eddie Bauer trim-level is added this year.

RATINGS (SCALE OF 1-10)

Overall	Safety	Reliability	Performance	Comfort	Value
6.4	4.4	5.7	6.6	7.3	8.1

Category G
2 Dr Eddie Bauer Pass. Van	4015	5510
2 Dr Eddie Bauer 4WD Pass. Van	4005	5500
2 Dr Eddie Bauer Pass. Van Ext	3830	5255
2 Dr Eddie Bauer 4WD Pass. Van Ext	4175	5725
2 Dr STD Cargo Van	2660	3655
2 Dr STD 4WD Cargo Van	3150	4325
2 Dr STD Cargo Van Ext	2815	3860
2 Dr STD 4WD Cargo Van Ext	3305	4535
2 Dr XL Pass. Van	2810	3890
2 Dr XL 4WD Pass. Van	3265	4480
2 Dr XL Pass. Van Ext	2980	4225
2 Dr XL 4WD Pass. Van Ext	3405	4825
2 Dr XLT Pass. Van	3290	4520
2 Dr XLT 4WD Pass. Van	3780	5185
2 Dr XLT Pass. Van Ext	3475	4770
2 Dr XLT 4WD Pass. Van Ext	3965	5440

OPTIONS FOR AEROSTAR

6 cyl 4.0 L Engine[Opt on 2WD] +80
Auto 4-Speed Transmission[Opt on XL,XLT] +90
Seat/Bed Combination +120
Air Conditioning[Std on Eddie Bauer, XLT] +110
Camper/Towing Package +40
Captain Chairs (4) +80
Cruise Control[Std on Eddie Bauer, XLT] +30
Dual Air Conditioning[Opt on STD,XL,XLT] +125
Power Door Locks +30
Power Windows +30

BRONCO 1991

A four-speed automatic transmission replaces the three-speed unit. A silver-anniversary edition is available.

Category H
2 Dr Custom 4WD Utility	4700	6035
2 Dr Eddie Bauer 4WD Utility	5230	6715
2 Dr Slvr Anniversary 4WD Utility	5970	7665
2 Dr XLT 4WD Utility	4840	6215
2 Dr XLT Nite 4WD Utility	5125	6580

OPTIONS FOR BRONCO

8 cyl 5.0 L Engine[Opt on Custom,XLT] +80
8 cyl 5.8 L Engine +110
Auto 4-Speed Transmission[Std on Slvr Anniversary] +125
Air Conditioning[Opt on Custom] +110
Camper/Towing Package +45
Cruise Control[Opt on Custom] +25
Limited Slip Diff +35
Power Door Locks[Opt on Custom] +25
Power Windows[Opt on Custom] +25

CLUB WAGON/ECONOLINE 1991

The short wheelbase model is dropped but a Heavy Duty workhorse becomes available. Optional 15-inch deep-dish wheels are available for those who want that sporty full-size van look.

E-150

Category H
2 Dr STD Econoline	3580	4600
2 Dr STD Econoline Ext	3580	4600
2 Dr XL Econoline	3750	4820
2 Dr XL Econoline Ext	4050	5120
2 Dr XLT Club Wagon	4340	5575

E-250

Category H
2 Dr STD Club Wagon	4980	6395
2 Dr STD Econoline	3960	5085

Don't forget to refer to the Mileage Adjustment Table at the back of this book!

Model Description	Trade-in Value	Market Value
2 Dr STD Econoline Ext	3960	5085
2 Dr XLT Club Wagon	5785	7430

E-350

Category H

2 Dr STD Econoline	4670	5995
2 Dr STD Econoline Ext	4645	5960
2 Dr Super Club Wagon Ext	5740	7370
2 Dr XLT Club Wagon Ext	6480	8320

OPTIONS FOR CLUB WAGON/ECONOLINE

8 cyl 5.0 L Engine +80
8 cyl 5.8 L Engine +110
8 cyl 7.3 L Dsl Engine +320
8 cyl 7.5 L Engine +115
Auto 4-Speed Transmission[Std on E-150 XLT Club Wagon] +40
Air Conditioning +110
Camper/Towing Package[Std on E-250 XLT Club Wagon] +45
Cruise Control[Std on E-250 XLT Club Wagon] +25
Dual Air Conditioning[Std on E-250 XLT Club Wagon] +170
Power Door Locks[Std on E-250 XLT Club Wagon] +25
Power Drivers Seat +40
Power Windows[Std on E-250 XLT Club Wagon] +25

CROWN VICTORIA   1991

No changes to the 1991 Crown Victoria.
Category B

4 Dr Cntry Squire Wgn	2640	3960
4 Dr Cntry Squire LX Wgn	2745	4120
4 Dr LX Sdn	2715	4070
4 Dr LX Wgn	2710	4065
4 Dr S Sdn	2535	3805
4 Dr STD Sdn	2625	3940
4 Dr STD Wgn	2605	3910

OPTIONS FOR CROWN VICTORIA

Cruise Control +30
Leather Seats +90
Power Door Locks +35
Power Drivers Seat +40
Power Passenger Seat +50

ESCORT   1991

A totally redesigned Escort bows in 1991. New engines, sheetmetal and interiors round out the changes.

RATINGS (SCALE OF 1-10)

Overall	Safety	Reliability	Performance	Comfort	Value
6	4.4	5.5	6.8	7.6	5.6

Category E

2 Dr GT Hbk	1600	3225
2 Dr LX Hbk	1220	2460
4 Dr LX Hbk	1275	2575
4 Dr LX Wgn	1355	2735
2 Dr Pony Hbk	1125	2270

OPTIONS FOR ESCORT

Auto 4-Speed Transmission +95
Air Conditioning +110
Cruise Control +30
Power Door Locks +35
Power Steering[Std on GT] +35

EXPLORER   1991

New model introduced to replace aging Bronco II. The Explorer is one of the bigger compact sport utilities and comes in two- or four-door models. A 4.0-liter V6 engine powers two- and four-wheel-drive models. Part-time four-wheel drive can be engaged with the push of a button.

RATINGS (SCALE OF 1-10)

Overall	Safety	Reliability	Performance	Comfort	Value
6	4.2	4.1	7.4	8.3	5.9

Category G

2 Dr Eddie Bauer Utility	4450	6105
2 Dr Eddie Bauer 4WD Utility	4540	6230
4 Dr Eddie Bauer Utility	4410	6055
4 Dr Eddie Bauer 4WD Utility	4795	6580
2 Dr Sport Utility	3870	5310
2 Dr Sport 4WD Utility	4115	5645
2 Dr XL Utility	3470	4760
2 Dr XL 4WD Utility	3885	5330
4 Dr XL Utility	3690	5065
4 Dr XL 4WD Utility	4110	5645
4 Dr XLT Utility	3735	5130
4 Dr XLT 4WD Utility	4505	6180

OPTIONS FOR EXPLORER

Auto 4-Speed Transmission +115
AM/FM Compact Disc Player +40
Air Conditioning +110
Camper/Towing Package +40
Cruise Control[Opt on Sport,XL] +30
JBL Sound System +100
Leather Seats +105
Power Door Locks[Opt on Sport,XL] +30
Power Drivers Seat +40
Power Windows[Opt on Sport,XL] +30
Sunroof +40

F-SERIES PICKUP   1991

A Nite Appearance Package is offered and the 5.0-liter engine is now available with the four-speed automatic transmission. F-250 and 350s receive auto-locking hubs. Ford's touch-drive transfer case replaces the older, floor-mounted system.

F-150

Category H

2 Dr S Std Cab LB	3450	4435
2 Dr S Std Cab SB	3360	4315

Model Description	Trade-in Value	Market Value
2 Dr STD Ext Cab LB	4275	5490
2 Dr STD 4WD Ext Cab LB	4930	6330
2 Dr STD Ext Cab SB	4185	5375
2 Dr STD 4WD Ext Cab SB	4830	6205
2 Dr STD Std Cab LB	3905	5015
2 Dr STD 4WD Std Cab LB	4845	6220
2 Dr STD Std Cab SB	3815	4895
2 Dr STD 4WD Std Cab SB	4450	5710
2 Dr XL Ext Cab LB	4390	5635
2 Dr XL 4WD Ext Cab LB	5035	6465
2 Dr XL Ext Cab SB	4295	5515
2 Dr XL 4WD Ext Cab SB	4940	6345
2 Dr XL Std Cab LB	4075	5235
2 Dr XL 4WD Std Cab LB	4710	6050
2 Dr XL Std Cab SB	3985	5115
2 Dr XL 4WD Std Cab SB	4620	5930
2 Dr XLT Lariat Ext Cab LB	4555	5850
2 Dr XLT Lariat 4WD Ext Cab LB	5200	6675
2 Dr XLT Lariat Ext Cab SB	4465	5730
2 Dr XLT Lariat 4WD Ext Cab SB	5110	6560
2 Dr XLT Lariat Std Cab LB	4105	5270
2 Dr XLT Lariat 4WD Std Cab LB	4740	6085
2 Dr XLT Lariat Std Cab SB	4015	5155
2 Dr XLT Lariat 4WD Std Cab SB	4650	5970

F-250

Category H

Model Description	Trade-in Value	Market Value
2 Dr STD Ext Cab LB	4950	6355
2 Dr STD 4WD Ext Cab LB	5760	7395
2 Dr STD Std Cab LB	4135	5310
2 Dr STD 4WD Std Cab LB	4775	6130
2 Dr XL Ext Cab LB	5060	6500
2 Dr XL 4WD Ext Cab LB	5870	7535
2 Dr XL Std Cab LB	4245	5450
2 Dr XL 4WD Std Cab LB	4800	6165
2 Dr XLT Lariat Ext Cab LB	5215	6695
2 Dr XLT Lariat 4WD Ext Cab LB	6005	7710
2 Dr XLT Lariat Std Cab LB	4365	5605
2 Dr XLT Lariat 4WD Std Cab LB	4920	6320

F-350

Category H

Model Description	Trade-in Value	Market Value
4 Dr STD Crew Cab LB	5495	7055
4 Dr STD 4WD Crew Cab LB	6040	7755
2 Dr STD Ext Cab LB	5430	6970
2 Dr STD Std Cab LB	4900	6290
2 Dr STD 4WD Std Cab LB	5795	7440
2 Dr XL 4WD Std Cab LB	5900	7575
4 Dr XLT Lariat Crew Cab LB	5915	7595
4 Dr XLT Lariat 4WD Crew Cab LB	6435	8260
2 Dr XLT Lariat Ext Cab LB	5770	7410

Model Description	Trade-in Value	Market Value
2 Dr XLT Lariat Std Cab LB	5240	6730
2 Dr XLT Lariat 4WD Std Cab LB	5945	7630

OPTIONS FOR F-SERIES PICKUP
8 cyl 5.0 L Engine +80
8 cyl 5.8 L Engine +110
8 cyl 7.3 L Dsl Engine +320
8 cyl 7.5 L Engine +115
Auto 3-Speed Transmission +105
Auto 4-Speed Transmission +125
Air Conditioning +110
Camper/Towing Package +45
Cruise Control +25
Dual Rear Wheels +105
Limited Slip Diff +35
Power Door Locks +25
Power Windows +25

FESTIVA   1991

The L Plus model is dropped. The LX is renamed GL and gets body-color bumpers and color-keyed wheels in the process.

RATINGS (SCALE OF 1-10)

Overall	Safety	Reliability	Performance	Comfort	Value
5.9	4.6	6.9	6.2	6.9	5

Category E

Model	Trade-in	Market
2 Dr GL Hbk	895	1800
2 Dr L Hbk	795	1605

OPTIONS FOR FESTIVA
Auto 3-Speed Transmission +70
Air Conditioning +110

MUSTANG   1991

New wheels appear on the GT and LX 5.0 Mustangs.

RATINGS (SCALE OF 1-10)

Overall	Safety	Reliability	Performance	Comfort	Value
N/A	N/A	6.2	7.8	6.3	4.1

Category C

Model	Trade-in	Market
2 Dr LX Conv	2945	4865
2 Dr LX Cpe	1870	3095
2 Dr LX Hbk	1960	3240

Category F

Model	Trade-in	Market
2 Dr GT Conv	4850	6495
2 Dr GT Hbk	3950	5290
2 Dr LX 5.0 Conv	4935	6605
2 Dr LX 5.0 Cpe	3515	4705
2 Dr LX 5.0 Hbk	3585	4795

OPTIONS FOR MUSTANG
Auto 4-Speed Transmission +80
Air Conditioning +110
Cruise Control +30
Flip-Up Sunroof +50
Leather Seats +85

Don't forget to refer to the Mileage Adjustment Table at the back of this book!

Model Description	Trade-in Value	Market Value	Model Description	Trade-in Value	Market Value

Power Door Locks[Std on Conv] +25
Power Windows[Std on Conv] +30

PROBE 1991

All Probes get revised front and rear styling. GT models lose their body-side cladding resulting in a cleaner look.

Category E

Model	Trade-in	Market
2 Dr GL Hbk	1490	3000
2 Dr LX Hbk	1680	3385

Category F

Model	Trade-in	Market
2 Dr GT Turbo Hbk	3130	4190

OPTIONS FOR PROBE

Auto 4-Speed Transmission +95
Air Conditioning +110
Anti-Lock Brakes +85
Cruise Control +30
Flip-Up Sunroof +45
Power Door Locks +25
Power Drivers Seat +30
Power Windows +30

RANGER 1991

Ford introduces a Sport model to the Ranger stable. Equipped with an optional V6 engine, alloy wheels, and snazzy graphics, the Ranger Sport promises to be one of the hottest vehicles in the high-school parking lot.

Category G

Model	Trade-in	Market
2 Dr Custom Ext Cab SB	2855	3920
2 Dr Custom 4WD Ext Cab SB	3560	4890
2 Dr Custom Std Cab LB	2555	3505
2 Dr Custom 4WD Std Cab LB	3230	4435
2 Dr Custom Std Cab SB	2515	3450
2 Dr Custom 4WD Std Cab SB	3160	4335
2 Dr S Std Cab SB	2170	2975
2 Dr STX Ext Cab SB	3055	4195
2 Dr STX 4WD Ext Cab SB	3655	5015
2 Dr STX Std Cab LB	2505	3440
2 Dr STX 4WD Std Cab LB	3200	4535
2 Dr STX Std Cab SB	2435	3340
2 Dr STX 4WD Std Cab SB	3135	4240
2 Dr Sport Std Cab LB	2410	3415
2 Dr Sport 4WD Std Cab LB	3080	4230
2 Dr Sport Std Cab SB	2370	3360
2 Dr Sport 4WD Std Cab SB	3005	4125
2 Dr XLT Ext Cab SB	2865	3930
2 Dr XLT 4WD Ext Cab SB	3665	5030
2 Dr XLT Std Cab LB	2465	3385
2 Dr XLT 4WD Std Cab LB	3140	4305
2 Dr XLT Std Cab SB	2395	3285
2 Dr XLT 4WD Std Cab SB	3065	4205

OPTIONS FOR RANGER

6 cyl 2.9 L Engine +70
6 cyl 3.0 L Engine +95
6 cyl 4.0 L Engine +80
Auto 4-Speed Transmission +125
Sport Appearance Pkg +105
Air Conditioning +110
Cruise Control +30
Limited Slip Diff +35
Power Door Locks +30

TAURUS 1991

Sequential multi-port fuel injection systems are added to the Taurus.

Category C

Model	Trade-in	Market
4 Dr GL Sdn	1935	3200
4 Dr GL Wgn	2130	3520
4 Dr L Sdn	1885	3120
4 Dr L Wgn	2085	3445
4 Dr LX Sdn	2435	4025
4 Dr LX Wgn	2545	4205

Category F

Model	Trade-in	Market
4 Dr SHO Sdn	4160	5570

OPTIONS FOR TAURUS

6 cyl 3.0 L Engine[Std on LX,SHO,Wgn] +90
6 cyl 3.8 L Engine +75
Air Conditioning[Opt on GL,L] +110
Anti-Lock Brakes[Opt on GL,L] +80
Cruise Control[Std on SHO] +30
JBL Sound System +65
Leather Seats +85
Power Door Locks[Opt on GL,L] +35
Power Drivers Seat[Opt on GL,L] +40
Power Sunroof +90
Power Windows[Opt on GL,L] +40

TEMPO 1991

No significant changes for the 1991 Tempo.

RATINGS (SCALE OF 1-10)

Overall	Safety	Reliability	Performance	Comfort	Value
6.5	4.5	6.5	7.2	7.1	7.3

Category C

Model	Trade-in	Market
2 Dr GL Sdn	1200	1980
4 Dr GL Sdn	1215	2010
2 Dr GLS Sdn	1295	2145
4 Dr GLS Sdn	1315	2175
2 Dr L Sdn	1070	1770
4 Dr L Sdn	1075	1775
4 Dr LX Sdn	1325	2195
4 Dr STD 4WD Sdn	1420	2350

Model Description	Trade-in Value	Market Value
OPTIONS FOR TEMPO		
Auto 3-Speed Transmission[Std on STD] +75		
Air Conditioning +110		
Cruise Control +30		
Power Door Locks[Std on LX] +35		
Power Drivers Seat +40		
Power Windows[Std on LX] +40		

THUNDERBIRD   1991

No changes for the 1991 Thunderbird.

RATINGS (SCALE OF 1-10)

Overall	Safety	Reliability	Performance	Comfort	Value
6.7	5.6	6.1	6.8	8	6.8

Model Description	Trade-in Value	Market Value
Category C		
2 Dr LX Cpe	2590	4285
2 Dr STD Cpe	2245	3710
Category F		
2 Dr SC Sprchgd Cpe	4060	5440

OPTIONS FOR THUNDERBIRD
8 cyl 5.0 L Engine +150
Anti-Lock Brakes[Std on SC] +80
Cruise Control[Opt on STD] +30
Leather Seats +85
Power Door Locks[Opt on STD] +35
Power Drivers Seat[Opt on STD] +40
Power Moonroof +85

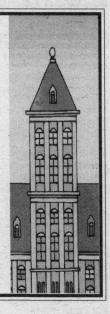
Don't forget to refer to the Mileage Adjustment Table at the back of this book!

Model Description	Trade-in Value	Market Value	Model Description	Trade-in Value	Market Value

GEO 97

GEO — Japan

1994 Geo Prizm

1997 GEO

METRO — 1997

Geo drops the base sedan variant of the Metro for 1997. A new convenience package is available on LSi models, and the LSi hatchback comes with the larger 1.3-liter engine standard. Two new colors debut.

RATINGS (SCALE OF 1-10)

Overall	Safety	Reliability	Performance	Comfort	Value
6.1	6.3	7.1	6.6	6.4	4.3

Category E

2 Dr LSi Hbk	4010	5085
4 Dr LSi Sdn	4295	5440
2 Dr STD Hbk	3760	4765

OPTIONS FOR METRO

Auto 3-Speed Transmission +265
Air Conditioning +370
Anti-Lock Brakes +295
Compact Disc W/fm/tape +215
Power Door Locks +110
Power Steering +115
Rear Window Defroster +75

PRIZM — 1997

The Prizm is essentially carried over for 1997, sporting new door trim panels, standard power steering, new exterior colors, and strengthened side-impact protection.

RATINGS (SCALE OF 1-10)

Overall	Safety	Reliability	Performance	Comfort	Value
7	6.5	8.5	8	7.8	4.4

Category E

4 Dr LSi Sdn	6685	8475
4 Dr STD Sdn	6375	8080

OPTIONS FOR PRIZM

4 cyl 1.8 L Engine +155
Auto 3-Speed Transmission +220
Auto 4-Speed Transmission +355
Air Conditioning +370
Aluminum/Alloy Wheels +150
Anti-Lock Brakes +295
Child Seat (1) +50
Compact Disc W/fm/tape +215
Cruise Control +100
Leather Seats +390
Power Door Locks +110
Power Sunroof +280
Power Windows +120
Rear Window Defroster +75

TRACKER — 1997

After a heavy makeover for 1996, changes for 1997 are limited. Convertibles get a standard fold-and-stow rear bench seat along with an enhanced evaporative emissions system. All Trackers can be painted Sunset Red Metallic or Azurite Blue Metallic for the first time. Prices have been at or near 1996 levels in an effort to make the Tracker more attractive to folks shopping Kia Sportage, Toyota RAV4 and Honda CR-V.

RATINGS (SCALE OF 1-10)

Overall	Safety	Reliability	Performance	Comfort	Value
6.1	5.5	8.6	6.4	6.8	3.2

Category G

4 Dr LSi Wgn	7175	8740
4 Dr LSi 4WD Wgn	7520	9160
2 Dr STD Conv	6445	7850
2 Dr STD 4WD Conv	6930	8445
4 Dr STD Wgn	6985	8510
4 Dr STD 4WD Wgn	7335	8940

OPTIONS FOR TRACKER

Auto 3-Speed Transmission +280
Auto 4-Speed Transmission +425
Air Conditioning +365
Aluminum/Alloy Wheels +145
Anti-Lock Brakes +260
Auto Locking Hubs (4WD) +120
Compact Disc W/fm/tape +200
Cruise Control +95
Power Door Locks +105
Power Steering[Std on LSi,Wgn,4WD] +125
Power Windows +110
Skid Plates +60

Don't forget to refer to the Mileage Adjustment Table at the back of this book!

GEO 96-95

Model Description	Trade-in Value	Market Value	Model Description	Trade-in Value	Market Value

1996 GEO

METRO 1996

A zoned rear window defroster clears the center of the Metro's tiny rear backlight first, base coupes get dual exterior mirrors, and LSi coupes get cool hubcaps and body-color bumpers that keep it from looking like a refugee from some third-world country.

RATINGS (SCALE OF 1-10)

Overall	Safety	Reliability	Performance	Comfort	Value
6.3	6.5	7.7	6.6	6.4	4.3

Category E

2 Dr LSi Hbk	3245	4185
4 Dr LSi Sdn	3580	4625
2 Dr STD Hbk	3100	4005
4 Dr STD Sdn	3440	4440

OPTIONS FOR METRO

4 cyl 1.3 L Engine[Opt on Hbk] +125
Auto 3-Speed Transmission +175
Air Conditioning +305
Anti-Lock Brakes +245
Compact Disc W/fm/tape +175
Power Door Locks +90
Power Steering +95

PRIZM 1996

An integrated child safety seat is optional on the LSi, and daytime running lights debut, making the Prizm more visible to other motorists, and radar-toting police officers. Three new exterior colors and added equipment to the base model round out the changes to this excellent compact.

RATINGS (SCALE OF 1-10)

Overall	Safety	Reliability	Performance	Comfort	Value
7.3	6.6	9.1	8	7.8	4.9

Category E

4 Dr LSi Sdn	5505	7110
4 Dr STD Sdn	5245	6770

OPTIONS FOR PRIZM

4 cyl 1.8 L Engine +120
Auto 3-Speed Transmission +170
Auto 4-Speed Transmission +275
Air Conditioning +305
Anti-Lock Brakes +245
Child Seat (1) +40
Compact Disc W/fm/tape +175
Cruise Control +85
Leather Seats +320
Power Door Locks +90
Power Steering +95
Power Sunroof +230
Power Windows +95

TRACKER 1996

A new four-door model joins the lineup, and dual airbags are standard on all Trackers. Four-wheel antilock brakes are optional. Revised styling freshens the new exterior, and daytime running lights make the Tracker more conspicuous to motorists. In a switch from tradition, tasteful exterior colors are newly available. Cruise control is a new convenience option.

RATINGS (SCALE OF 1-10)

Overall	Safety	Reliability	Performance	Comfort	Value
6.1	5.4	8.1	6.4	6.8	3.7

Category G

2 Dr LSi Conv	5720	7140
2 Dr LSi 4WD Conv	6125	7650
4 Dr LSi Wgn	6165	7695
4 Dr LSi 4WD Wgn	6460	8065
2 Dr STD Conv	5355	6685
2 Dr STD 4WD Conv	5955	7430
4 Dr STD Wgn	6000	7490
4 Dr STD 4WD Wgn	6305	7870

OPTIONS FOR TRACKER

Auto 3-Speed Transmission +215
Auto 4-Speed Transmission +275
Air Conditioning +300
Aluminum/Alloy Wheels +120
Anti-Lock Brakes +210
Auto Locking Hubs (4WD) +95
Compact Disc W/fm/tape +160
Cruise Control +75
Power Door Locks +85
Power Steering[Std on Wgn,LSi 4WD Conv] +105
Power Windows +90
Skid Plates +50

1995 GEO

METRO 1995

All-new car is larger than previous model, and comes as a two-door hatchback or four-door sedan in base or LSi trim. Dual airbags are standard. ABS is optional on all models. Hatchbacks get the carryover 1.0-liter three-cylinder motor. Optional on LSi hatchback and standard on sedans is a 70-horsepower, 1.3-liter four-cylinder engine. Daytime running lights are standard.

RATINGS (SCALE OF 1-10)

Overall	Safety	Reliability	Performance	Comfort	Value
6.3	7	7	6.6	6.4	4.7

Category E

2 Dr LSi Hbk	2400	3340
4 Dr LSi Sdn	2705	3765

Model Description	Trade-in Value	Market Value
2 Dr STD Hbk	2315	3225
4 Dr STD Sdn	2590	3610

OPTIONS FOR METRO •
4 cyl 1.3 L Engine[Opt on Hbk] +105
Auto 3-Speed Transmission +150
Air Conditioning +250
Anti-Lock Brakes +200
Compact Disc W/fm/tape +145
Power Door Locks +75
Power Steering +75
Rear Window Defroster +50

PRIZM   1995

Base 1.6-liter engine loses horsepower. All models get new wheelcovers, and leather is newly optional on LSi.

RATINGS (SCALE OF 1-10)

Overall	Safety	Reliability	Performance	Comfort	Value
7.3	7	8.1	8	7.8	5.4

Category E

	Trade-in	Market
4 Dr LSi Sdn	4180	5820
4 Dr STD Sdn	3965	5515

OPTIONS FOR PRIZM
4 cyl 1.8 L Engine +195
Auto 3-Speed Transmission +150
Auto 4-Speed Transmission +240
Air Conditioning +250
Aluminum/Alloy Wheels +100
Anti-Lock Brakes +200
Compact Disc W/fm/tape +145
Cruise Control +70
Leather Seats +260
Power Door Locks +75
Power Steering +75
Power Sunroof +185
Power Windows +80

TRACKER   1995

All 4WD models and Massachusetts-bound Trackers get 95-horsepower engine. Convertible top has been redesigned for easier operation. Expressions Packages offer color-coordinated tops and wheels.

RATINGS (SCALE OF 1-10)

Overall	Safety	Reliability	Performance	Comfort	Value
5.5	2.7	7.8	6.2	7	3.6

Category G

	Trade-in	Market
2 Dr LSi 4WD Conv	5205	6680
2 Dr LSi 4WD Utility	5270	6760
2 Dr STD Conv	4195	5385
2 Dr STD 4WD Conv	4725	6065
2 Dr STD 4WD Utility	4640	5955

OPTIONS FOR TRACKER
Auto 3-Speed Transmission +175
Air Conditioning +245
Aluminum/Alloy Wheels +95
Compact Disc W/fm/tape +130
Skid Plates +40

1994 GEO

METRO   1994

Convertible is dropped as is LSi trim level. CFC-free refrigerant is added to air conditioning systems.

RATINGS (SCALE OF 1-10)

Overall	Safety	Reliability	Performance	Comfort	Value
N/A	N/A	7.4	6.6	7.1	4.2

Category E

	Trade-in	Market
2 Dr STD Hbk	1555	2450
4 Dr STD Hbk	1660	2615
2 Dr XFi Hbk	1555	2450

OPTIONS FOR METRO
Auto 3-Speed Transmission +120
AM/FM Stereo Tape +75
Air Conditioning +205
Rear Window Defroster +40

PRIZM   1994

Passenger airbag is added. Air conditioners get CFC-free coolant.

RATINGS (SCALE OF 1-10)

Overall	Safety	Reliability	Performance	Comfort	Value
7.2	7	7.7	8	7.8	5.3

Category E

	Trade-in	Market
4 Dr LSi Sdn	3130	4940
4 Dr STD Sdn	2930	4615

OPTIONS FOR PRIZM
4 cyl 1.8 L Engine +110
Auto 3-Speed Transmission +120
Auto 4-Speed Transmission +195
Air Conditioning +205
Aluminum/Alloy Wheels +80
Anti-Lock Brakes +160
Compact Disc W/fm/tape +120
Cruise Control +55
Leather Seats +215
Power Door Locks +60
Power Steering +60
Power Sunroof +150
Power Windows +65
Premium Sound System +80

TRACKER   1994

Trackers sold in California and New York get 95-horsepower version of 1.6-liter engine to clear emissions hurdles. Four-wheel-drive models trade on-/off-road tires for better riding all-season type rubber. Alloy wheels have been restyled. Center console gets cupholders. Interior fabrics are new. Optional is a CD/cassette player.

RATINGS (SCALE OF 1-10)

Overall	Safety	Reliability	Performance	Comfort	Value
5.2	2.3	6.9	6.2	7	3.6

Category G

	Trade-in	Market
2 Dr LSi 4WD Conv	4245	5645
2 Dr LSi 4WD Utility	4325	5750
2 Dr STD Conv	3370	4480
2 Dr STD 4WD Conv	3750	4990
2 Dr STD 4WD Utility	3800	5055

OPTIONS FOR TRACKER

Auto 3-Speed Transmission +145
Air Conditioning +200
Aluminum/Alloy Wheels +80
Compact Disc W/fm/tape +110
Luggage Rack +40
Power Steering[Opt on STD] +70
Skid Plates +35

1993 GEO

METRO   1993

Automatic door locks are added. Convertibles can have an optional CD player.

RATINGS (SCALE OF 1-10)

Overall	Safety	Reliability	Performance	Comfort	Value
N/A	N/A	7.9	6.6	7.1	4.7

Category E

	Trade-in	Market
2 Dr LSi Conv	1685	2805
2 Dr LSi Hbk	1395	2320
4 Dr LSi Hbk	1460	2430
2 Dr STD Hbk	1150	1915
4 Dr STD Hbk	1230	2045
2 Dr XFi Hbk	1150	1915

OPTIONS FOR METRO

Auto 3-Speed Transmission +100
AM/FM Stereo Tape +60
Air Conditioning +165
Rear Window Defroster[Std on LSi] +35

PRIZM   1993

Totally redesigned and available in base or LSi trim in sedan configuration. A driver airbag is standard. ABS is available. Still based on Toyota Corolla design. Standard engine is a 108-horsepower, DOHC 1.6-liter engine. Available on LSi models is a twin-cam 1.8-liter engine making 115 horsepower.

RATINGS (SCALE OF 1-10)

Overall	Safety	Reliability	Performance	Comfort	Value
7.1	5.8	8.1	8 ·	7.8	5.7

Category E

	Trade-in	Market
4 Dr LSi Sdn	2515	4195
4 Dr STD Sdn	2370	3950

OPTIONS FOR PRIZM

4 cyl 1.8 L Engine +80
Auto 3-Speed Transmission +100
Auto 4-Speed Transmission +155
AM/FM Compact Disc Player +85
Air Conditioning +165
Aluminum/Alloy Wheels +65
Anti-Lock Brakes +135
Cruise Control +45
Power Door Locks +50
Power Steering +50
Power Sunroof +125
Power Windows +55
Rear Window Defroster +35

STORM   1993

Hatchback model is dropped. Base engine loses five horsepower, but peak torque is made at lower rpm. Base models can be equipped with alloys. A CD player is optional.

RATINGS (SCALE OF 1-10)

Overall	Safety	Reliability	Performance	Comfort	Value
N/A	N/A	N/A	N/A	N/A	3.3

Category E

	Trade-in	Market
2 Dr GSi Cpe	2395	3990
2 Dr STD Cpe	2055	3425

OPTIONS FOR STORM

Auto 3-Speed Transmission +110
Auto 4-Speed Transmission +150
AM/FM Compact Disc Player +85
Air Conditioning +165
Aluminum/Alloy Wheels[Opt on STD] +65

TRACKER   1993

Radios get revised controls.

RATINGS (SCALE OF 1-10)

Overall	Safety	Reliability	Performance	Comfort	Value
5.3	2.5	7.5	6.2	7	3.4

Category G

	Trade-in	Market
2 Dr LSi 4WD Conv	3485	4655
2 Dr LSi 4WD Utility	3555	4750
2 Dr STD Conv	2855	3810
2 Dr STD 4WD Conv	3190	4260
2 Dr STD 4WD Utility	3235	4320

Don't forget to refer to the Mileage Adjustment Table at the back of this book!

GEO 93-91

Model Description	Trade-in Value	Market Value	Model Description	Trade-in Value	Market Value

OPTIONS FOR TRACKER
Auto 3-Speed Transmission +120
AM/FM Stereo Tape +45
Air Conditioning +165
Aluminum/Alloy Wheels +65
Power Steering +55

1992 GEO

METRO   1992

Styling is revised front and rear. A new instrument panel is installed. New wheelcovers are installed on base and LSi models. Four-door hatchbacks get child safety rear-door locks.

RATINGS (SCALE OF 1-10)

Overall	Safety	Reliability	Performance	Comfort	Value
N/A	N/A	7.2	6.6	7.1	4.5

Category E

2 Dr LSi Conv	1475	2565
2 Dr LSi Hbk	1220	2125
4 Dr LSi Hbk	1275	2225
2 Dr STD Hbk	1060	1850
4 Dr STD Hbk	1020	1775
2 Dr XFi Hbk	1045	1825

OPTIONS FOR METRO
Auto 3-Speed Transmission +80
Air Conditioning +135

PRIZM   1992

Four-door hatchback is dropped.
Category E

4 Dr GSi Sdn	2510	4375
4 Dr LSi Sdn	2330	4060
4 Dr STD Sdn	1860	3245

OPTIONS FOR PRIZM
Auto 3-Speed Transmission +80
Auto 4-Speed Transmission +125
Air Conditioning[Opt on STD] +135
Cruise Control +35
Power Door Locks[Std on LSi] +40
Power Sunroof +100
Power Windows +45

STORM   1992

Styling is revised front and rear. GSi models get new 1.8-liter engine making 140 horsepower.

RATINGS (SCALE OF 1-10)

Overall	Safety	Reliability	Performance	Comfort	Value
N/A	N/A	N/A	N/A	N/A	4.8

Category E

2 Dr 2+2 Cpe	1675	2915
2 Dr GSi Cpe	1955	3410
2 Dr STD Hbk	1785	3110

OPTIONS FOR STORM
Auto 3-Speed Transmission +90
Auto 4-Speed Transmission +120
Air Conditioning +135

TRACKER   1992

Dashboard is slightly revised and a tilt steering column is a new option. Center console includes cupholders. New seat fabrics and cloth bolsters are added.

RATINGS (SCALE OF 1-10)

Overall	Safety	Reliability	Performance	Comfort	Value
5.5	2.4	7.9	6.2	7	3.8

Category G

2 Dr LSi 4WD Conv	2840	4065
2 Dr LSi 4WD Utility	2930	4190
2 Dr STD Conv	2185	3130
2 Dr STD 4WD Conv	2585	3695
2 Dr STD 4WD Utility	2670	3820

OPTIONS FOR TRACKER
Auto 3-Speed Transmission +95
Air Conditioning +135

1991 GEO

METRO   1991

LSi Convertible debuts, and includes driver airbag and larger tires. Convertible seats only two.

RATINGS (SCALE OF 1-10)

Overall	Safety	Reliability	Performance	Comfort	Value
N/A	N/A	7.6	6.6	7.1	4.6

Category E

2 Dr LSi Conv	1185	2260
2 Dr LSi Hbk	955	1820
4 Dr LSi Hbk	980	1870
2 Dr STD Hbk	840	1595
4 Dr STD Hbk	860	1640
2 Dr XFi Hbk	840	1595

OPTIONS FOR METRO
Auto 3-Speed Transmission +60
Air Conditioning +110

PRIZM   1991

Horsepower is up to 102 on base models and 130 on GSi models.

GEO 91

Model Description	Trade-in Value	Market Value
Category E		
4 Dr GSi Hbk	1860	3540
4 Dr GSi Sdn	1785	3405
4 Dr STD Hbk	1510	2875
4 Dr STD Sdn	1420	2700

OPTIONS FOR PRIZM

Auto 3-Speed Transmission +60
Auto 4-Speed Transmission +105
LSi Pkg +175
Air Conditioning +110
Cruise Control +30
Power Door Locks +35
Power Sunroof +85
Power Windows +35

STORM   1991

A funky-looking three-door hatchback joins the lineup with squared-off rear styling like that found on Honda Civic. New hatchback is available only in base trim.

RATINGS (SCALE OF 1-10)

Overall	Safety	Reliability	Performance	Comfort	Value
N/A	N/A	N/A	N/A	N/A	3.8

Model Description	Trade-in Value	Market Value
Category E		
2 Dr 2+2 Cpe	1275	2425
2 Dr GSi Cpe	1480	2815
2 Dr STD Hbk	1365	2600

OPTIONS FOR STORM

Auto 3-Speed Transmission +75
Auto 4-Speed Transmission +100
Air Conditioning +110

TRACKER   1991

Rear antilock brakes are standard, and work only in 2WD. Four-wheel drive LSi models get auto-locking front hubs.

RATINGS (SCALE OF 1-10)

Overall	Safety	Reliability	Performance	Comfort	Value
5.5	2.3	7.5	6.2	7	4.3

Model Description	Trade-in Value	Market Value
Category G		
2 Dr LSi 4WD Conv	2435	3605
2 Dr LSi 4WD Utility	2550	3780
2 Dr STD Conv	1840	2725
2 Dr STD 4WD Conv	2215	3280
2 Dr STD 4WD Utility	2295	3395

OPTIONS FOR TRACKER

Auto 3-Speed Transmission +75
Air Conditioning +110

Don't forget to refer to the Mileage Adjustment Table at the back of this book!

Model Description	Trade-in Value	Market Value	Model Description	Trade-in Value	Market Value

GMC USA

1995 GMC Suburban

2000 GMC

C/K 2500 — 2000

GM has refined the Sierra Classic lineup, dropping all 1500 series (half-ton) trucks in favor of workhorse 2500 (three-quarter-ton) and 3500 (one-ton) series models. The only other news is the addition of a new paint color, as this old truck platform (based on the previous-generation C/K pickup) soldiers on for a final year.

Category H

Model	Trade-in	Market
4 Dr SL Crew Cab SB	16190	18765
4 Dr SL 4WD Crew Cab SB	18285	21195
2 Dr SL Ext Cab LB	14485	16790
2 Dr SL 4WD Ext Cab LB	16620	19265
2 Dr SL 4WD Ext Cab SB	16540	19170
2 Dr SL Std Cab LB	13360	15485
2 Dr SL 4WD Std Cab LB	15180	17595
4 Dr SLE Crew Cab SB	18615	21575
4 Dr SLE 4WD Crew Cab SB	20710	24005
2 Dr SLE Ext Cab LB	15995	18540
2 Dr SLE 4WD Ext Cab LB	18130	21015
2 Dr SLE 4WD Ext Cab SB	18045	20915
2 Dr SLE Pass. Van	18575	21530
2 Dr SLE Std Cab LB	14870	17235
2 Dr SLE 4WD Std Cab LB	16690	19345
4 Dr SLT Crew Cab SB	19725	22860
4 Dr SLT 4WD Crew Cab SB	21820	25290
2 Dr SLT Ext Cab LB	16970	19670
2 Dr SLT 4WD Ext Cab LB	19110	22145
2 Dr SLT 4WD Ext Cab SB	19025	22050
2 Dr SLT Std Cab LB	15805	18315
2 Dr SLT 4WD Std Cab LB	17625	20425

OPTIONS FOR C/K 2500

8 cyl 6.5 L Turbodsl Engine +2310
8 cyl 7.4 L Engine +490
Auto 4-Speed Transmission +890
AM/FM Stereo Tape[Opt on SL,SLE Pass Van] +165
Air Conditioning[Opt on SL] +665
Bed Liner +185
Compact Disc W/fm/tape +255
Cruise Control[Opt on SL] +155
Dual Air Conditioning +1055
Dual Power Seats +385
Keyless Entry System +145
Power Door Locks[Opt on SL] +155
Power Drivers Seat[Std on SLT 4WD Ext Cab LB,SLT 4WD Ext Cab SB,SLT Ext Cab LB] +230
Sliding Rear Window +95
Tilt Steering Wheel[Opt on SL] +155
Trailer Hitch +135

C/K 3500 — 2000

GM has refined the Sierra Classic's lineup, dropping all 1500 series (half-ton) trucks in favor of workhorse 2500 (three-quarter-ton) and 3500 (one-ton) series models. The only other news is the addition of a new paint color, as this old truck platform (based on the previous-generation C/K pickup) soldiers on into its second decade.

Category H

Model	Trade-in	Market
4 Dr SL Crew Cab LB	15865	18385
4 Dr SL 4WD Crew Cab LB	17955	20810
4 Dr SL Crew Cab SB	16840	19520
4 Dr SL 4WD Crew Cab SB	18935	21945
2 Dr SL Ext Cab LB	15995	18535
2 Dr SL 4WD Ext Cab LB	17845	20685
2 Dr SL Std Cab LB	13670	15840
2 Dr SL 4WD Std Cab LB	15645	18135
4 Dr SLE Crew Cab LB	18285	21190
4 Dr SLE 4WD Crew Cab LB	20375	23615
4 Dr SLE Crew Cab SB	19260	22325
4 Dr SLE 4WD Crew Cab SB	22845	26475
2 Dr SLE Ext Cab LB	17500	20285
2 Dr SLE 4WD Ext Cab LB	19355	22430
2 Dr SLE Std Cab LB	15175	17590
2 Dr SLE 4WD Std Cab LB	17155	19880
4 Dr SLT Crew Cab LB	19390	22475
4 Dr SLT 4WD Crew Cab LB	21485	24900
4 Dr SLT Crew Cab SB	20365	23605
4 Dr SLT 4WD Crew Cab SB	22460	26035
2 Dr SLT Ext Cab LB	18475	21415
2 Dr SLT 4WD Ext Cab LB	20330	23565
2 Dr SLT Std Cab LB	16110	18670
2 Dr SLT 4WD Std Cab LB	18085	20965

Don't forget to refer to the Mileage Adjustment Table at the back of this book!

Model Description	Trade-in Value	Market Value	Model Description	Trade-in Value	Market Value

OPTIONS FOR C/K 3500
8 cyl 6.5 L Turbodsl Engine +2310
8 cyl 7.4 L Engine[Std on Crew Cab SB,] +490
Auto 4-Speed Transmission +895
Air Conditioning[Opt on SL] +665

ENVOY   2000

Upgraded seats and V6 engine improvements headline changes to GM's high-end compact SUV. There's also a new metallic paint color, and a heavy-duty battery is now standard.

Category G

Model	Trade-in	Market
4 Dr STD 4WD Wgn	25260	29520

OPTIONS FOR ENVOY
Power Moonroof +710

JIMMY   2000

For 2000, GMC is celebrating the 30th anniversary of its Jimmy nameplate with a dolled-up Diamond Edition model. Other changes center on new equipment and suspension packaging. A heavy-duty battery is now standard, and Jimmy's V6 has been upgraded with a roller timing chain, sprocket and rocker arms for improved durability and reduced noise. There are also two new exterior colors, while the SLE gets a revised cloth interior.

Category G

Model	Trade-in	Market
4 Dr Diamond Edition Wgn	21005	24545
4 Dr Diamond Edition 4WD Wgn	22395	26170
4 Dr SLE Wgn	18910	22100
4 Dr SLE 4WD Wgn	20305	23730
2 Dr SLS Utility	13680	15985
2 Dr SLS 4WD Utility	15775	18430
2 Dr SLS Convenience Utility	15705	18350
2 Dr SLS Convenience 4WD Utility	17795	20795
4 Dr SLT Wgn	19820	23160
4 Dr SLT 4WD Wgn	21210	24785

OPTIONS FOR JIMMY
Auto 4-Speed Transmission[Opt on SLS] +815
Luxury Pkg +710
AM/FM Compact Disc Player[Opt on SLS] +260
Camper/Towing Package[Std on Diamond Edition] +245
Climate Control for AC +160
Compact Disc W/fm/tape +365
Cruise Control[Opt on SLS] +170
Dual Power Seats +340
Power Door Locks[Opt on SLS] +190
Power Drivers Seat[Std on Diamond Edition,SLE,SLT] +230
Power Moonroof +710
Power Windows[Opt on SLS] +200
Rear Window Defroster[Opt on SLS] +140
Rear Window Wiper[Opt on SLS] +125
Tilt Steering Wheel[Opt on SLS] +145

SAFARI   2000

The 2000 Safari gets engineering enhancements for its 4.3-liter V6 and ABS components, a tow/haul mode for its four-speed automatic transmission, revised lighting and power locking functions, a larger (27-gallon) composite fuel tank, and a third-row seat as standard equipment.

Category G

Model	Trade-in	Market
2 Dr SL Pass. Van Ext	15590	18215
2 Dr SL 4WD Pass. Van Ext	17200	20095
2 Dr SLE Pass. Van Ext	16390	19155
2 Dr SLE 4WD Pass. Van Ext	17650	20625
2 Dr SLT Pass. Van Ext	19475	22760
2 Dr SLT 4WD Pass. Van Ext	21070	24620

OPTIONS FOR SAFARI
AM/FM Stereo Tape[Opt on SL] +180
Aluminum/Alloy Wheels[Std on SLT] +265
Cruise Control[Opt on SL] +170
Leather Seats +640
Luggage Rack[Opt on SL] +130
Power Door Locks[Opt on SL] +190
Power Mirrors[Opt on SL] +110
Power Windows[Opt on SL] +200
Privacy Glass[Opt on SL] +225
Rear Window Defroster[Std on SLT] +140
Tilt Steering Wheel[Opt on SL] +145

SAFARI CARGO   2000

The 2000 Safari gets engineering enhancements for its 4.3-liter V6 and ABS components, a tow/haul mode for its four-speed automatic transmission, revised lighting and power locking functions, a larger (27-gallon) composite fuel tank, and a third-row seat as standard equipment.

Category G

Model	Trade-in	Market
2 Dr SL Cargo Van Ext	14475	16915
2 Dr SL 4WD Cargo Van Ext	16135	18855

SAVANA   2000

GMC's full-size passenger van gets improved powertrains, increased trailer ratings, seat-mounted tether anchors for installing child safety seats and an optional rear-window defogger.

Category H

Model	Trade-in	Market
2 Dr G1500 SLE Pass. Van	17440	20215
2 Dr STD Pass. Van	16315	18910
2 Dr G2500 STD Pass. Van	18015	20880
2 Dr G2500 SLE Pass. Van Ext	19755	22895
2 Dr G2500 STD Pass. Van Ext	18625	21590
2 Dr G3500 SLE Pass. Van	19340	22415
2 Dr G3500 STD Pass. Van	18210	21110
2 Dr G3500 SLE Pass. Van Ext	19980	23160
2 Dr G3500 STD Pass. Van Ext	18855	21855

Don't forget to refer to the Mileage Adjustment Table at the back of this book!

EDMUNDS® USED CARS & TRUCKS

Model Description	Trade-in Value	Market Value

OPTIONS FOR SAVANA

8 cyl 5.0 L Engine[Opt on 1500] +400
8 cyl 5.7 L Engine[Opt on 1500] +975
8 cyl 6.5 L Turbodsl Engine +2310
8 cyl 7.4 L Engine +490
15 Passenger Seating +670
AM/FM Compact Disc Player +255
Aluminum/Alloy Wheels +255
Cruise Control[Std on SLE] +155
Dual Air Conditioning +1055
Keyless Entry System +145
Power Door Locks[Opt on STD] +155
Power Drivers Seat +230
Privacy Glass +130
Rear Heater +175

SAVANA CARGO 2000

GMC's full-size cargo van gets improved powertrains, increased trailer ratings, and an optional rear-window defogger.

Category H

Model Description	Trade-in Value	Market Value
2 Dr G1500 STD Cargo Van	13850	16055
2 Dr G2500 STD Cargo Van Ext	14690	17030
2 Dr G3500 STD Cargo Van	14105	16345
2 Dr G3500 STD Cargo Van	15265	17690
2 Dr G3500 STD Cargo Van Ext	15855	18375

OPTIONS FOR SAVANA CARGO

8 cyl 5.0 L Engine +400
8 cyl 5.7 L Engine[Std on Standard G3500 Ext. Van HD, Standard G3500 Van HD] +975
8 cyl 6.5 L Turbodsl Engine +2310
8 cyl 7.4 L Engine +490
Air Conditioning +665
Cruise Control +155
Dual Air Conditioning +1055
Power Door Locks +155
Power Drivers Seat +230
Power Windows +155
Privacy Glass +130
Rear Heater +175
Tilt Steering Wheel +155

SIERRA PICKUP 2000

SIERRA 1500

Category H

Model Description	Trade-in Value	Market Value
2 Dr SL Ext Cab LB	15545	18020
2 Dr SL 4WD Ext Cab LB	17595	20395
2 Dr SL Ext Cab SB	15345	17785
2 Dr SL 4WD Ext Cab SB	17395	20160
2 Dr SL Ext Cab Stepside SB	15945	18480
2 Dr SL 4WD Ext Cab Stepside SB	17995	20855
2 Dr SL Std Cab LB	11555	13395
2 Dr SL 4WD Std Cab LB	13615	15780
2 Dr SL Std Cab SB	11355	13160

Model Description	Trade-in Value	Market Value
2 Dr SL 4WD Std Cab SB	13415	15550
2 Dr SL Std Cab Stepside SB	11955	13855
2 Dr SL 4WD Std Cab Stepside SB	14015	16245
2 Dr SLE Ext Cab LB	17145	19870
2 Dr SLE 4WD Ext Cab LB	19195	22250
2 Dr SLE Ext Cab SB	16945	19640
2 Dr SLE 4WD Ext Cab SB	18995	22015
2 Dr SLE Ext Cab Stepside SB	17475	20255
2 Dr SLE 4WD Ext Cab Stepside SB	19525	22630
2 Dr SLE Std Cab LB	14045	16275
2 Dr SLE 4WD Std Cab LB	16090	18650
2 Dr SLE Std Cab SB	13840	16045
2 Dr SLE 4WD Std Cab SB	15890	18420
2 Dr SLE Std Cab Stepside SB	14375	16660
2 Dr SLE 4WD Std Cab Stepside SB	16425	19035
2 Dr SLT Ext Cab LB	18315	21230
2 Dr SLT 4WD Ext Cab LB	20620	23895
2 Dr SLT Ext Cab SB	18115	20995
2 Dr SLT 4WD Ext Cab SB	20415	23665
2 Dr SLT Ext Cab Stepside SB	18650	21615
2 Dr SLT 4WD Ext Cab Stepside SB	20950	24280

SIERRA 2500

Category H

Model Description	Trade-in Value	Market Value
2 Dr SL Ext Cab LB	16735	19395
2 Dr SL 4WD Ext Cab LB	18750	21730
2 Dr SL Ext Cab SB	16080	18635
2 Dr SL 4WD Ext Cab SB	18550	21505
2 Dr SL Std Cab LB	14600	16925
2 Dr SL Std Cab LB	14340	16620
2 Dr SL 4WD Std Cab LB	16355	18955
2 Dr SLE Ext Cab LB	18310	21220
2 Dr SLE 4WD Ext Cab LB	20320	23555
2 Dr SLE Ext Cab SB	17650	20460
2 Dr SLE 4WD Ext Cab SB	20125	23325
2 Dr SLE Std Cab LB	16175	18745
2 Dr SLE Std Cab LB	15915	18445
2 Dr SLE 4WD Std Cab LB	17930	20780
2 Dr SLT Ext Cab LB HD	19460	22555
2 Dr SLT 4WD Ext Cab HD LB	21720	25175
2 Dr SLT Ext Cab SB	18800	21790
2 Dr SLT 4WD Ext Cab HD SB	21525	24945

OPTIONS FOR SIERRA PICKUP

8 cyl 4.8 L Engine +570
8 cyl 5.3 L Engine +910
8 cyl 6.0 L Engine +290
Auto 4-Speed Transmission +895
AM/FM Stereo Tape +165

Don't forget to refer to the Mileage Adjustment Table at the back of this book!

Model Description	Trade-in Value	Market Value	Model Description	Trade-in Value	Market Value
Air Conditioning +665			Hinged Third Door +275		
Aluminum/Alloy Wheels +255			Keyless Entry System +160		
Camper/Towing Package +270			Leather Steering Wheel +45		
Compact Disc W/fm/tape +255			Power Door Locks +190		
Cruise Control +155			Power Windows +200		
Dual Power Seats +385			Sliding Rear Window +100		
Hinged Fourth Door +270			Sport Suspension +365		
Power Door Locks +155			Tachometer +55		
Privacy Glass +130			Tilt Steering Wheel +145		
Skid Plates +85					
Trailer Hitch +135					

SONOMA 2000

Four-wheel-drive Sonomas get a higher-output V6 and a handling/trailering suspension standard. GMC drops the 4WD long-bed and High-Rider regular-cab models and adds a new, lower-priced base-trim extended-cab model. All versions get a boost in trailer ratings and a new paint color.

Category G

Model	Trade-in	Market
2 Dr SL Ext Cab SB	11570	13520
2 Dr SL 4WD Ext Cab SB	13930	16275
2 Dr SL Std Cab LB	9740	11380
2 Dr SL Std Cab SB	9485	11085
2 Dr SL 4WD Std Cab SB	12540	14655
2 Dr SLE Ext Cab SB Ext Cab SB	12490	14590
2 Dr SLE 4WD Ext Cab SB 4WD Ext Cab SB	15485	18090
2 Dr SLE Std Cab SB	10830	12655
2 Dr SLE 4WD Std Cab SB 4WD Std Cab SB	14005	16365
2 Dr SLS Sport Ext Cab SB	11980	14000
2 Dr SLS Sport 4WD Ext Cab SB	14975	17500
2 Dr SLS Sport Ext Cab Stepside SB	12325	14400
2 Dr SLS Sport 4WD Ext Cab Stepside SB	15320	17900
2 Dr SLS Sport Std Cab LB	10575	12360
2 Dr SLS Sport Std Cab SB	10320	12060
2 Dr SLS Sport 4WD Std Cab SB	13500	15775
2 Dr SLS Sport Std Cab Stepside SB	10665	12460
2 Dr SLS Sport 4WD SC Std Cab Stepside SB	13840	16175

OPTIONS FOR SONOMA

6 cyl 4.3 L Engine +1060		
Auto 4-Speed Transmission +895		
ZR2 Highrider Suspension +1440		
AM/FM Compact Disc Player +260		
AM/FM Stereo Tape +180		
Air Conditioning +670		
Aluminum/Alloy Wheels +265		
Cruise Control +170		

YUKON 2000

Completely redesigned, Yukon is based on the new Sierra pickup platform with zippy V8 engines and a stouter chassis for a better, more isolated ride.

Category H

Model	Trade-in	Market
4 Dr SLE Wgn	23850	27640
4 Dr SLE 4WD Wgn	25965	30095
4 Dr SLT 4WD Wgn 4WD Wgn	27095	31405
4 Dr SLT Wgn	24980	28950

OPTIONS FOR YUKON

8 cyl 5.3 L Engine +910		
Camper/Towing Package +270		
Climate Control for AC +370		
Compact Disc W/fm/tape[Opt on SLE] +255		
Heated Front Seats +295		
Power Moonroof +795		
Running Boards +285		
Third Seat +515		
Traction Control System +230		

YUKON DENALI 2000

For the 2000 model year, GMC's Yukon Denali gets a new exterior color and adds GM's OnStar communications system to its already impressive standard equipment list.

Category H

Model	Trade-in	Market
4 Dr Denali 4WD Wgn	29150	33785

YUKON XL 2000

The 2000 GMC Yukon XL is a complete redesign of last year's Suburban model, adding a whole lot of mechanical and comfort upgrades.

Category H

Model	Trade-in	Market
4 Dr C1500 SLT Wgn	27540	31920
4 Dr C1500 SLE Wgn	25930	30055
4 Dr C2500 SLT Wgn	28660	33220
4 Dr C2500 SLE Wgn	27050	31350
4 Dr K1500 SLT 4WD Wgn	29660	34380
4 Dr K1500 SLE 4WD Wgn	28050	32515
4 Dr K2500 SLT 4WD Wgn	30990	35920
4 Dr K2500 SLE 4WD Wgn	29230	33880

OPTIONS FOR YUKON XL

Autoride Suspension Pkg +645		
Aluminum/Alloy Wheels[Std on C1500 SLE,K1500 SLE] +255		

Don't forget to refer to the Mileage Adjustment Table at the back of this book!

GMC 00-99

Model Description	Trade-in Value	Market Value	Model Description	Trade-in Value	Market Value

Camper/Towing Package +270
Compact Disc W/fm/tape +255
Power Moonroof +795
Running Boards +285
Traction Control System +230

1999 GMC

ENVOY 1999

After its debut as General Motors' high-end compact SUV last year, the GMC Envoy gets equipment upgrades for '99. A new mini-module for the driver's airbag allows for steering-wheel radio controls, and the turn-signal stalk now incorporates a flash-to-pass headlamp feature. Heated, eight-way power front seating is improved, thanks to available two-position memory for the driver and power recliners. A liftgate ajar telltale resides in the instrument cluster, and the outside rearview mirrors have been redesigned, featuring electrochromic dimming and power folding capability. GM's advanced AutoTrac active transfer case is now standard, while a new, shift lever-mounted button selects a Tow/Haul mode to optimize transmission shift points. There are three new metallic exterior paint colors: Topaz gold, Meadow green and Indigo blue.

RATINGS (SCALE OF 1-10)

Overall	Safety	Reliability	Performance	Comfort	Value
N/A	7.3	8.5	N/A	N/A	N/A

Category G

	Trade-in	Market
4 Dr STD 4WD Wgn	24010	28195

OPTIONS FOR ENVOY
Dual Power Seats +280
Power Moonroof +580

JIMMY 1999

There are three new colors and revised outside mirrors, but most changes to the '99 Jimmy are inside. You'll find new power-seating features, redundant radio controls and a mini-module depowered airbag in the steering wheel, as well as a new Bose premium sound system and six-disc CD changer. A vehicle content theft alarm, flash-to-pass headlamp feature, and liftgate ajar warning lamp have also been added. Four-wheel-drive versions get the new AutoTrac active transfer case and four-door models gain a Tow/Haul mode for the transmission. Finally, the optional Z85 Euro-Ride suspension has been retuned.

RATINGS (SCALE OF 1-10)

Overall	Safety	Reliability	Performance	Comfort	Value
N/A	7.2	N/A	8	7.9	N/A

Category G

	Trade-in	Market
2 Dr SL Utility	13175	15560
2 Dr SL 4WD Utility	14330	16830
4 Dr SL Wgn	15980	18765
4 Dr SL 4WD Wgn	17090	20070
4 Dr SLE Wgn	17700	20785
4 Dr SLE 4WD Wgn	18985	22295
2 Dr SLS Sport Utility	14290	16780
2 Dr SLS Sport 4WD Utility	16240	19070
4 Dr SLT Wgn	18950	22255
4 Dr SLT 4WD Wgn	20235	23765

OPTIONS FOR JIMMY
Auto 4-Speed Transmission[Std on SLE,SLS Sport,SLT, Wgn] +670
AM/FM Compact Disc Player +210
Aluminum/Alloy Wheels[Std on SL] +215
Compact Disc W/fm/tape +295
Cruise Control[Opt on SLS Sport] +140
Keyless Entry System[Std on SLT] +130
Luggage Rack[Opt on SL] +110
Power Door Locks[Std on SLE,SLT] +155
Power Drivers Seat[Std on SLE, SLT] +190
Power Moonroof +580
Power Windows[Std on SLE,SLT] +160
Rear Window Defroster[Std on SLE,SLT] +115
Tilt Steering Wheel[Std on SLE,SLT] +120

SAFARI 1999

RATINGS (SCALE OF 1-10)

Overall	Safety	Reliability	Performance	Comfort	Value
N/A	7.2	8.5	N/A	6.1	N/A

SAFARI CARGO

Category G

	Trade-in	Market
2 Dr SL Cargo Van Ext	13640	16020
2 Dr SL 4WD Cargo Van Ext	15250	17910

SAFARI PASSENGER

Category G

	Trade-in	Market
2 Dr SL Pass. Van Ext	13985	16425
2 Dr SL 4WD Pass. Van Ext	15475	18170
2 Dr SLE Pass. Van Ext	14715	17280
2 Dr SLE 4WD Pass. Van Ext	15880	18650
2 Dr SLT Pass. Van Ext	16750	19670
2 Dr SLT 4WD Pass. Van Ext	18220	21400

OPTIONS FOR SAFARI
AM/FM Stereo Tape[Std on SLE] +150
Aluminum/Alloy Wheels[Std on SLT] +215
Cruise Control[Std on SLE,SLT] +140
Dual Air Conditioning +615
Dual Power Seats +280
Power Door Locks[Std on SLE,SLT] +155
Power Drivers Seat[Std on SLT] +190
Power Mirrors[Opt on SL] +90

Model Description	Trade-in Value	Market Value
Power Windows[Std on SLE,SLT] +160		
Privacy Glass[Std on SLE,SLT] +185		
Rear Window Defroster +115		
Rear Window Wiper +105		
Tilt Steering Wheel[Std on SLE,SLT] +120		

SAVANA 1999

GMC's full-size van gets two new exterior colors, one new interior color and automatic transmission enhancements.

RATINGS (SCALE OF 1-10)

Overall	Safety	Reliability	Performance	Comfort	Value
N/A	N/A	N/A	4.8	6.5	N/A

Category H

Model Description	Trade-in Value	Market Value
2 Dr G1500 Cargo Van	13190	15370
2 Dr G1500 SLE Pass. Van	16220	18900
2 Dr G1500 Pass. Van	15160	17665
2 Dr G2500 Cargo Van	13480	15705
2 Dr G2500 Cargo Van Ext	14055	16375
2 Dr G2500 SLE Pass. Van	17820	20765
2 Dr G2500 STD Pass. Van	16760	19530
2 Dr G2500 SLE Pass. Van Ext	18400	21435
2 Dr G2500 Pass. Van Ext	17340	20200
2 Dr G3500 Cargo Van	14460	16850
2 Dr G3500 Cargo Van Ext	15040	17520
2 Dr G3500 SLE Pass. Van	18005	20980
2 Dr G3500 Pass. Van	16945	19745
2 Dr G3500 SLE Pass. Van Ext	18585	21655
2 Dr G3500 Pass. Van Ext	17525	20420

OPTIONS FOR SAVANA

8 cyl 5.0 L Engine +330	
8 cyl 5.7 L Engine[Std on G2500, G3500] +675	
8 cyl 6.5 L Turbodsl Engine +1910	
8 cyl 7.4 L Engine +400	
15 Passenger Seating +545	
AM/FM Compact Disc Player +205	
Air Conditioning[Opt on Cargo Van, Cargo Van Ext] +545	
Aluminum/Alloy Wheels +210	
Cruise Control[Opt on STD] +130	
Dual Air Conditioning +860	
Keyless Entry System +115	
Power Door Locks[Opt on STD] +125	
Power Drivers Seat +190	
Power Windows[Opt on STD] +130	
Privacy Glass +105	
Rear Heater +140	
Tilt Steering Wheel[Opt on STD] +125	

SIERRA PICKUP 1999

CLASSIC C/K 1500

Category H

Model Description	Trade-in Value	Market Value
2 Dr C1500 SL Ext Cab Stepside SB		
	14490	16885

Model Description	Trade-in Value	Market Value
2 Dr C1500 SL Std Cab Stepside SB		
	10775	12555
2 Dr C1500 SLE Ext Cab SB	14605	17015
2 Dr C1500 SLE Ext Cab Stepside SB		
	15815	18430
2 Dr C1500 SLE Std Cab Stepside SB		
	13055	15210
2 Dr C1500 SLT Ext Cab LB	16760	19530
2 Dr C1500 SLT Ext Cab SB	16575	19310
2 Dr C1500 SLT Ext Cab Stepside SB		
	16945	19745
2 Dr K1500 SL 4WD Ext Cab Stepside SB		
	16400	19110
2 Dr K1500 SL 4WD Std Cab Stepside SB		
	12690	14785
2 Dr K1500 SLE 4WD Ext Cab SB	16565	19305
2 Dr K1500 SLE 4WD Ext Cab Stepside SB		
	17725	20655
2 Dr K1500 SLE 4WD Std Cab Stepside SB		
	14960	17435
2 Dr K1500 SLT 4WD Ext Cab LB	18900	22025
2 Dr K1500 SLT 4WD Ext Cab SB	18715	21805
2 Dr K1500 SLT 4WD Ext Cab Stepside SB		
	19085	22240

CLASSIC C/K 2500

Category H

Model Description	Trade-in Value	Market Value
2 Dr C2500 HD SLE Ext Cab LB	14780	17220
2 Dr C2500 HD SLE Std Cab LB	13780	16055
2 Dr C2500 HD SLT Ext Cab LB	15700	18295
2 Dr C2500 HD SLT Ext Cab LB	18115	21105
2 Dr C2500 HD SLT Std Cab LB	14660	17085
4 Dr C2500 SL Crew Cab SB	14840	17290
2 Dr C2500 SL Ext Cab LB	13355	15560
2 Dr C2500 SL Std Cab LB	12355	14395
4 Dr C2500 SLE Crew Cab SB	15670	18260
4 Dr C2500 SLT Crew Cab SB	17125	19955
2 Dr C2500 SLT Ext Cab SB	17400	20275
2 Dr K2500 HD SL 4WD Ext Cab LB		
	15370	17910
2 Dr K2500 HD SL 4WD Ext Cab SB		
	15290	17815
2 Dr K2500 HD SL 4WD Std Cab LB		
	14070	16395
2 Dr K2500 HD SLE 4WD Ext Cab LB		
	16795	19570
2 Dr K2500 HD SLE 4WD Ext Cab SB		
	16715	19475
2 Dr K2500 HD SLE 4WD Std Cab LB		
	15495	18055
2 Dr K2500 HD SLT 4WD Ext Cab LB		
	17715	20640

Model Description	Trade-in Value	Market Value	Model Description	Trade-in Value	Market Value
2 Dr K2500 HD SLT 4WD Ext Cab SB			2 Dr SL 4WD Std Cab SB	12395	14440
	17635	20550	2 Dr SLE Ext Cab LB	15805	18420
2 Dr K2500 HD SLT 4WD Std Cab LB			2 Dr SLE 4WD Ext Cab LB	17750	20680
	16375	19085	2 Dr SLE Ext Cab SB	15615	18195
4 Dr K2500 SLE 4WD Crew Cab SB			2 Dr SLE 4WD Ext Cab SB	17560	20460
	17645	20565	2 Dr SLE Std Cab LB	13010	15160
4 Dr K2500 SLT 4WD Crew Cab SB			2 Dr SLE 4WD Std Cab LB	14940	17410
	19100	22255	2 Dr SLE Std Cab SB	12825	14940
2 Dr K2500 SLT 4WD Ext Cab LB	20255	23600	2 Dr SLE 4WD Std Cab SB	14755	17190
2 Dr K2500 SLT 4WD Ext Cab SB	20070	23385			
4 Dr K2500 STD 4WD Crew Cab SB			**SIERRA 2500**		
	16815	19595	*Category H*		
			2 Dr SL Ext Cab LB	15555	18125
CLASSIC C/K 3500			2 Dr SL 4WD Ext Cab LB	17450	20335
Category H			2 Dr SL Ext Cab SB	14845	17300
4 Dr C3500 SL Crew Cab LB	14490	16885	2 Dr SL 4WD Ext Cab SB	17265	20115
4 Dr C3500 SL Crew Cab SB	15415	17960	2 Dr SL Std Cab LB	13155	15330
2 Dr C3500 SL Ext Cab LB	14675	17100	2 Dr SL Std Cab SB	13250	15435
2 Dr C3500 SL Std Cab LB	12540	14610	2 Dr SL 4WD Std Cab LB	15050	17540
4 Dr C3500 SLE Crew Cab LB	16780	19550	2 Dr SLE Ext Cab LB	16935	19730
4 Dr C3500 SLE Crew Cab SB	17700	20625	2 Dr SLE 4WD Ext Cab LB	18830	21940
2 Dr C3500 SLE Ext Cab LB	16100	18760	2 Dr SLE Ext Cab SB	16225	18905
2 Dr C3500 SLE Std Cab LB	13965	16270	2 Dr SLE 4WD Ext Cab SB	18645	21725
4 Dr C3500 SLT Crew Cab LB	17825	20770	2 Dr SLE Std Cab LB	14555	16960
4 Dr C3500 SLT Crew Cab SB	18745	21845	2 Dr SLE Std Cab LB	14650	17070
2 Dr C3500 SLT Ext Cab LB	17020	19835	2 Dr SLE 4WD Std Cab LB	16465	19185
2 Dr C3500 SLT Std Cab LB	14845	17300			
4 Dr K3500 SL 4WD Crew Cab LB	16470	19190	*OPTIONS FOR SIERRA PICKUP*		
4 Dr K3500 SL 4WD Crew Cab SB	17390	20265	8 cyl 4.8 L Engine[Opt on Std Cab] +395		
2 Dr K3500 SL 4WD Ext Cab LB	16425	19140	8 cyl 5.3 L Engine[Std on Sierra 2500] +680		
2 Dr K3500 SL 4WD Std Cab LB	14410	16790	8 cyl 5.7 L Engine[Opt on C1500 SLE,K1500 SLE] +675		
4 Dr K3500 SLE 4WD Crew Cab LB			8 cyl 6.0 L Engine +335		
	18755	21855	8 cyl 6.5 L Turbodsl Engine +1910		
4 Dr K3500 SLE 4WD Crew Cab SB			8 cyl 7.4 L Engine +400		
	19680	22930	Auto 4-Speed Transmission[Opt on Std Cab] +665		
2 Dr K3500 SLE 4WD Ext Cab LB	17850	20800	AM/FM Compact Disc Player +205		
2 Dr K3500 SLE 4WD Std Cab LB	15835	18450	Air Conditioning[Std on SLE, SLT] +545		
4 Dr K3500 SLT 4WD Crew Cab LB			Aluminum/Alloy Wheels[Std on SLT] +210		
	19800	23075	Bed Liner +150		
4 Dr K3500 SLT 4WD Crew Cab SB			Camper/Towing Package +220		
	20725	24150	Cruise Control[Std on SLE, SLT] +130		
2 Dr K3500 SLT 4WD Ext Cab LB	18775	21875	Keyless Entry System[Std on SLE, SLT] +115		
2 Dr K3500 SLT 4WD Std Cab LB	16715	19475	Power Door Locks[Std on SLE, SLT] +125		
SIERRA 1500			Power Drivers Seat +190		
Category H			Privacy Glass +105		
2 Dr SL Ext Cab LB	14405	16780	Skid Plates +70		
2 Dr SL 4WD Ext Cab LB	16330	19030	Sliding Rear Window +80		
2 Dr SL Ext Cab SB	14215	16560			
2 Dr SL 4WD Ext Cab SB	16145	18810	**SONOMA**		**1999**
2 Dr SL Std Cab LB	10645	12405			
2 Dr SL 4WD Std Cab LB	12585	14660			
2 Dr SL Std Cab SB	10455	12185			

The '99 Sonoma touts four new exterior colors, a new steering wheel with mini-module depowered airbag, and larger, more robust outside rearview mirrors, with the uplevel power mirror gaining a heated feature. AutoTrac, GM's electronic push-button two-speed transfer case, is now standard on four-wheel-drive models, and all Sonomas get a content theft alarm with remote keyless entry as well as a flash-to-pass headlamp feature for the smart stalk. Serious four-wheelers can now order composite skid plates.

RATINGS (SCALE OF 1-10)

Overall	Safety	Reliability	Performance	Comfort	Value
N/A	N/A	N/A	6.6	8.1	N/A

Category G

Model Description	Trade-in Value	Market Value
2 Dr SL Std Cab LB	9330	10955
2 Dr SL 4WD Std Cab LB	12275	14415
2 Dr SL Std Cab SB	8865	10410
2 Dr SL 4WD Std Cab SB	12040	14140
2 Dr SLE Ext Cab SB	11740	13785
2 Dr SLE 4WD Ext Cab SB	14815	17400
2 Dr SLE Std Cab SB	10305	12100
2 Dr SLE 4WD Std Cab SB	13490	15840
2 Dr SLS Sport Ext Cab Stepside SB		
	11580	13600
2 Dr SLS Sport 4WD Ext Cab Stepside SB		
	14660	17215
2 Dr SLS Sport Std Cab Stepside SB		
	10145	11915
2 Dr SLS Sport 4WD Std Cab Stepside SB		
	13330	15655
2 Dr SLS Sport Ext Cab SB	11250	13210
2 Dr SLS Sport 4WD Ext Cab SB	14325	16825
2 Dr SLS Sport Std Cab LB	10060	11815
2 Dr SLS Sport 4WD Std Cab LB	13295	15615
2 Dr SLS Sport Std Cab SB	9815	11525
2 Dr SLS Sport 4WD Std Cab SB	13000	15265

OPTIONS FOR SONOMA

6 cyl 4.3 L Engine[Opt on 2WD] +730
6 cyl 4.3 L Vortec Engine +615
Auto 4-Speed Transmission +715
ZR2 Highrider Suspension +1095
AM/FM Compact Disc Player +210
Air Conditioning +550
Aluminum/Alloy Wheels +215
Cruise Control +140
Hinged Third Door +225
Keyless Entry System +130
Power Door Locks +155
Power Windows +160
Sliding Rear Window +80
Sport Suspension +300
Tilt Steering Wheel +120

SUBURBAN   1999

A couple of new colors are the only modifications to the Suburban.

RATINGS (SCALE OF 1-10)

Overall	Safety	Reliability	Performance	Comfort	Value
N/A	8.4	8.1	7	7.9	N/A

Category H

Model Description	Trade-in Value	Market Value
4 Dr C1500 Wgn	17885	20840
4 Dr C2500 Wgn	18965	22095
4 Dr K1500 4WD Wgn	19925	23220
4 Dr K2500 4WD Wgn	21005	24475

OPTIONS FOR SUBURBAN

8 cyl 6.5 L Turbodsl Engine[Opt on 2500] +1910
8 cyl 7.4 L Engine[Opt on 2500] +400
AM/FM Compact Disc Player +205
Air Conditioning +545
Aluminum/Alloy Wheels +210
Automatic Dimming Mirror +100
Camper/Towing Package +220
Cruise Control +130
Dual Air Conditioning +860
Heated Front Seats +240
Keyless Entry System +115
Leather Seats +670
Power Drivers Seat +190
Power Mirrors +70
Power Windows +130
Privacy Glass +105
Rear Heater +140
Rear Window Defroster +105
Rear Window Wiper +85
Running Boards +235
Tilt Steering Wheel +125

YUKON   1999

More new colors are added as Yukon cruises into 1999.

RATINGS (SCALE OF 1-10)

Overall	Safety	Reliability	Performance	Comfort	Value
N/A	N/A	N/A	7.4	8	N/A

Category H

Model Description	Trade-in Value	Market Value
4 Dr SLE Wgn	21175	24675
4 Dr SLE 4WD Wgn	23255	27100
4 Dr SLT Wgn	22660	26400
4 Dr SLT 4WD Wgn	24735	28825

OPTIONS FOR YUKON

AM/FM Compact Disc Player +205
Camper/Towing Package +220
Compact Disc W/fm/tape[Std on SLT] +210
Dual Air Conditioning[Opt on SLE] +860
Heated Front Seats +240
Running Boards +235

YUKON DENALI   1999

General Motors brand managers came up with an idea to dress up the GMC Yukon, fill it full of luxury touches and give it a special name to toss their hat into the luxury SUV arena. Enter the 1999 GMC Yukon Denali, with loads of unique features and exclusive exterior paint colors- until, that is, GM decided to spin-off a clone for Cadillac called the Escalade.

Don't forget to refer to the Mileage Adjustment Table at the back of this book!

GMC 99-98

Model Description	Trade-in Value	Market Value	Model Description	Trade-in Value	Market Value

RATINGS (SCALE OF 1-10)

Overall	Safety	Reliability	Performance	Comfort	Value
N/A	N/A	N/A	7.4	8	N/A

Category H
4 Dr Denali 4WD Wgn   26985   31445

1998 GMC

ENVOY   1998

GMC is introduces its finest luxury compact SUV to date: the Envoy.

RATINGS (SCALE OF 1-10)

Overall	Safety	Reliability	Performance	Comfort	Value
N/A	7.1	7.4	N/A	N/A	N/A

Category G
4 Dr STD 4WD Wgn   22735   26855

JIMMY   1998

A revised interior contains dual second-generation airbags, improved climate controls and available premium sound systems. Outside, the front bumper, grille and headlights are new. Side cladding is restyled and SLT models have new alloy wheels. Fresh colors inside and out sum up the changes.

RATINGS (SCALE OF 1-10)

Overall	Safety	Reliability	Performance	Comfort	Value
7.6	7.3	8	8	7.9	6.9

Category G
2 Dr SL Utility	12380	14540
2 Dr SL 4WD Utility	13250	15850
4 Dr SL Wgn	14405	17015
4 Dr SL 4WD Wgn	15355	18140
4 Dr SLE Wgn	15510	18320
4 Dr SLE 4WD Wgn	16685	19705
2 Dr SLS Sport Utility	13285	15895
2 Dr SLS Sport 4WD Utility	14945	17655
4 Dr SLS Sport Wgn	14925	17630
4 Dr SLS Sport 4WD Wgn	16080	18995
4 Dr SLT Wgn	16225	19165
4 Dr SLT 4WD Wgn	17450	20615

OPTIONS FOR JIMMY
AM/FM Compact Disc Player +175
Aluminum/Alloy Wheels[Opt on SL] +175
Cruise Control[Opt on SL] +115
Heated Front Seats +150
Keyless Entry System[Std on SLE, SLT] +105
Luggage Rack[Opt on SL] +90
Power Door Locks[Opt on SL] +130
Power Drivers Seat[Std on SLE, SLT] +155
Power Mirrors[Opt on SL] +70
Power Moonroof +475

Power Windows[Opt on SL] +135
Rear Window Defroster[Opt on SL] +95
Rear Window Wiper[Opt on SL] +85
Tilt Steering Wheel[Opt on SL] +100

SAFARI   1998

New colors, a theft deterrent system and automatic transmission refinements are the changes to the Safari. This van is one of the few GM models that retains full-power airbags for 1998.

RATINGS (SCALE OF 1-10)

Overall	Safety	Reliability	Performance	Comfort	Value
7.4	7.1	8	7	6.5	8.6

Category G
2 Dr SL Cargo Van Ext	11990	14160
2 Dr SL 4WD Cargo Van Ext	13430	15865
2 Dr SLE Pass. Van Ext	14105	16665
2 Dr SLE 4WD Pass. Van Ext	15290	18060
2 Dr SLT Pass. Van Ext	15295	18065
2 Dr SLT 4WD Pass. Van Ext	16655	19675
2 Dr SLX Pass. Van Ext	12490	14755
2 Dr SLX 4WD Pass. Van Ext	13870	16385

OPTIONS FOR SAFARI
8 Passenger Seating[Opt on SLX] +220
AM/FM Compact Disc Player[Std on SLT] +175
Aluminum/Alloy Wheels[Std on SLT] +175
Cruise Control[Opt on SL, SLX] +115
Dual Air Conditioning +505
Dual Power Seats +230
Keyless Entry System[Std on SLT] +105
Leather Seats +430
Power Door Locks[Opt on SL, SLX] +130
Power Drivers Seat[Std on SLT] +155
Power Mirrors[Std on SLT] +70
Power Windows[Opt on SL, SLX] +135
Premium Sound System +185
Privacy Glass[Opt on SL, SLX] +150
Rear Heater +105
Rear Window Defroster +95
Rear Window Wiper +85
Tilt Steering Wheel[Opt on SL, SLX] +100

SAVANA   1998

New colors, transmission enhancements, more power for the diesel engine, revised uplevel stereos and the addition of a PassLock theft deterrent system mark the changes for 1998. A mini-module driver's airbag is new, but it and the passenger airbag still deploy at full-force levels.

Category H
2 Dr G1500 Cargo Van	12345	14415
2 Dr G1500 Pass. Van	14330	16735
2 Dr G1500 SLE Pass. Van	15005	17525
2 Dr G2500 Cargo Van	12605	14720

Don't forget to refer to the Mileage Adjustment Table at the back of this book!

Model Description	Trade-in Value	Market Value	Model Description	Trade-in Value	Market Value
2 Dr G2500 Cargo Van Ext	13155	15360	2 Dr C1500 SLE Ext Cab Stepside SB		
2 Dr G2500 Pass. Van	15510	18115		14255	16645
2 Dr G2500 Pass. Van Ext	16050	18745	2 Dr C1500 SLE Std Cab LB	11475	13400
2 Dr G2500 SLE Pass. Van	16500	19270	2 Dr C1500 SLE Std Cab SB	11295	13190
2 Dr G2500 SLE Pass. Van Ext	17040	19900	2 Dr C1500 SLE Std Cab Stepside SB		
2 Dr G3500 Cargo Van	13540	15815		11640	13590
2 Dr G3500 Cargo Van Ext	14090	16455	2 Dr C1500 SLT Ext Cab LB	14345	16755
2 Dr G3500 Pass. Van	15685	18315	2 Dr C1500 SLT Ext Cab SB	13870	16200
2 Dr G3500 Pass. Van Ext	16225	18945	2 Dr C1500 SLT Ext Cab Stepside SB		
2 Dr G3500 SLE Pass. Van	16675	19470		15340	17910
2 Dr G3500 SLE Pass. Van Ext	17215	20100	2 Dr C1500 SLT Std Cab LB	12820	14970
			2 Dr C1500 SLT Std Cab SB	12640	14760
			2 Dr C1500 SLT Std Cab Stepside SB		
				12985	15160
			2 Dr C1500 Special Std Cab LB	9570	11175
			2 Dr C1500 Special Std Cab SB	9380	10955
			2 Dr K1500 SL 4WD Ext Cab LB	13685	15985
			2 Dr K1500 SL 4WD Ext Cab SB	13210	15430
			2 Dr K1500 SL 4WD Std Cab LB	12200	14245
			2 Dr K1500 SL 4WD Std Cab SB	12020	14035
			2 Dr K1500 SL 4WD Std Cab Stepside SB		
				12365	14435
			2 Dr K1500 SLE 4WD Ext Cab LB	14750	17225
			2 Dr K1500 SLE 4WD Ext Cab SB	14275	16675
			2 Dr K1500 SLE 4WD Ext Cab Stepside SB		
				16040	18735
			2 Dr K1500 SLE 4WD Std Cab LB	13265	15490
			2 Dr K1500 SLE 4WD Std Cab SB	13085	15280
			2 Dr K1500 SLE 4WD Std Cab Stepside SB		
				13430	15680
			2 Dr K1500 SLT 4WD Ext Cab LB	16135	18845
			2 Dr K1500 SLT 4WD Ext Cab SB	15660	18285
			2 Dr K1500 SLT 4WD Ext Cab Stepside SB		
				17130	20000
			2 Dr K1500 SLT 4WD Std Cab LB	14610	17060
			2 Dr K1500 SLT 4WD Std Cab SB	14430	16850
			2 Dr K1500 SLT 4WD Std Cab Stepside SB		
				14770	17250
			2 Dr K1500 Special 4WD Std Cab LB		
				11780	13755
			2 Dr K1500 Special 4WD Std Cab SB		
				11585	13530

OPTIONS FOR SAVANA

8 cyl 5.0 L Engine +270
8 cyl 5.7 L Engine[Std on G2500 Pass. Van, G2500 Pass. Van Ext., G3500] +545
8 cyl 6.5 L Turbodsl Engine +1645
8 cyl 7.4 L Engine +330
15 Passenger Seating +445
AM/FM Compact Disc Player +170
Air Conditioning[Opt on Cargo Van, Cargo Van Ext] +445
Aluminum/Alloy Wheels +170
Cruise Control[Opt on STD] +105
Dual Air Conditioning +705
Keyless Entry System +95
Power Door Locks[Opt on STD] +105
Power Drivers Seat +155
Power Windows[Opt on STD] +105
Privacy Glass +85
Rear Heater +115
Tilt Steering Wheel[Opt on STD] +105

SIERRA PICKUP 1998

With an all-new Sierra just one year away, changes are minimal. Diesel engines make more power and torque, extended cab models get rear heater ducts, a PassLock theft deterrent system is standard, 1500-series trucks get reduced rolling resistance tires and three new colors debut. Second generation airbags are standard.

RATINGS (SCALE OF 1-10)

Overall	Safety	Reliability	Performance	Comfort	Value
N/A	N/A	7.5	6.6	8.3	N/A

SIERRA 1500

Category H

	Trade-in	Market
2 Dr C1500 SL Ext Cab LB	11895	13895
2 Dr C1500 SL Ext Cab SB	11425	13340
2 Dr C1500 SL Std Cab LB	10410	12155
2 Dr C1500 SL Std Cab SB	10230	11945
2 Dr C1500 SL Std Cab Stepside SB		
	10575	12345
2 Dr C1500 SLE Ext Cab LB	12960	15135
2 Dr C1500 SLE Ext Cab SB	12490	14585

SIERRA 2500

Category H

	Trade-in	Market
2 Dr C2500 HD SL Ext Cab LB	12475	14570
2 Dr C2500 HD SL Std Cab LB	11535	13470
2 Dr C2500 HD SLE Ext Cab LB	13815	16135
2 Dr C2500 HD SLE Std Cab LB	12875	15035
2 Dr C2500 HD SLT Ext Cab LB	14680	17145
2 Dr C2500 HD SLT Std Cab LB	13705	16005
2 Dr C2500 SL Ext Cab SB	12455	14545

Model Description	Trade-in Value	Market Value
2 Dr C2500 SL Std Cab LB	10920	12750
2 Dr C2500 SLE Ext Cab SB	13795	16110
2 Dr C2500 SLE Std Cab LB	12260	14315
2 Dr C2500 SLT Ext Cab SB	14660	17120
2 Dr C2500 SLT Std Cab LB	13090	15285
2 Dr K2500 HD SL 4WD Ext Cab LB	14370	16780
2 Dr K2500 HD SL 4WD Ext Cab SB	14295	16695
2 Dr K2500 HD SL 4WD Std Cab LB	13150	15355
2 Dr K2500 HD SLE 4WD Ext Cab LB	15710	18345
2 Dr K2500 HD SLE 4WD Ext Cab SB	15635	18260
2 Dr K2500 HD SLE 4WD Std Cab LB	14490	16920
2 Dr K2500 HD SLT 4WD Ext Cab LB	16575	19360
2 Dr K2500 HD SLT 4WD Ext Cab SB	16505	19270
2 Dr K2500 HD SLT 4WD Std Cab LB	15320	17890

SIERRA 3500

Category H

Model Description	Trade-in Value	Market Value
4 Dr C3500 SL Crew Cab LB	13215	15430
2 Dr C3500 SL Ext Cab LB	13380	15625
2 Dr C3500 SL Std Cab LB	11410	13325
4 Dr C3500 SLE Crew Cab LB	15325	17900
2 Dr C3500 SLE Ext Cab LB	14700	17165
2 Dr C3500 SLE Std Cab LB	12725	14860
4 Dr C3500 SLT Crew Cab LB	16295	19030
2 Dr C3500 SLT Ext Cab LB	15550	18160
2 Dr C3500 SLT Std Cab LB	13540	15815
4 Dr K3500 SL 4WD Crew Cab LB	15040	17565
2 Dr K3500 SL 4WD Ext Cab LB	15000	17515
2 Dr K3500 SL 4WD Std Cab LB	13140	15340
4 Dr K3500 SLE 4WD Crew Cab LB	17155	20035
2 Dr K3500 SLE 4WD Ext Cab LB	16315	19055
2 Dr K3500 SLE 4WD Std Cab LB	14455	16880
4 Dr K3500 SLT 4WD Crew Cab LB	18120	21160
2 Dr K3500 SLT 4WD Ext Cab LB	17170	20050
2 Dr K3500 SLT 4WD Std Cab LB	15270	17830

OPTIONS FOR SIERRA PICKUP

8 cyl 5.0 L Engine[Std on C1500 Ext Cab, C2500, K1500 4WD Ext Cab] +270
8 cyl 5.7 L Engine[Opt on C1500, C2500, K1500] +545
8 cyl 6.5 L Turbodsl Engine +1645
8 cyl 7.4 L Engine +330

Auto 4-Speed Transmission[Std on C1500 Ext Cab Stepside] +530
AM/FM Compact Disc Player +170
Air Conditioning[Std on SLE, SLT] +445
Aluminum/Alloy Wheels[Std on SLT] +170
Bed Liner +125
Camper/Towing Package +180
Cruise Control[Std on SLE, SLT] +105
Dual Rear Wheels[Std on Ext Cab] +430
Hinged Third Door +230
Keyless Entry System[Opt on SLE] +95
Power Door Locks[Std on SLE, SLT] +105
Power Drivers Seat[Opt on SLE] +155
Privacy Glass +85
Rear Window Defroster +85
Sliding Rear Window +65
Tilt Steering Wheel[Std on SLE, SLT] +105

SONOMA   1998

Styling is re-tuned inside and out, resulting in a sleeker look and better interior ergonomics. Dual second-generation airbags are standard, and seats are upgraded for improved comfort and appearance. Four-wheel disc brakes are standard on 4WD models and uplevel stereos are new for 1998. New colors inside and out round out the changes.

RATINGS (SCALE OF 1-10)

Overall	Safety	Reliability	Performance	Comfort	Value
N/A	N/A	7.3	6.6	8.1	N/A

Category G

Model Description	Trade-in Value	Market Value
2 Dr SL Std Cab LB	8255	9750
2 Dr SL 4WD Std Cab LB	10890	12865
2 Dr SL Std Cab SB	7840	9260
2 Dr SL 4WD Std Cab SB	10685	12620
2 Dr SLE Ext Cab SB	10415	12300
2 Dr SLE 4WD Ext Cab SB	12995	15350
2 Dr SLE Std Cab SB	9130	10785
2 Dr SLE 4WD Std Cab SB	11950	14115
2 Dr SLS Sport Ext Cab SB	9975	11780
2 Dr SLS Sport 4WD Ext Cab SB	12730	15035
2 Dr SLS Sport Ext Cab Stepside SB	10270	12135
2 Dr SLS Sport 4WD Ext Cab Stepside SB	13010	15370
2 Dr SLS Sport Std Cab LB	8910	10525
2 Dr SLS Sport 4WD Std Cab LB	11810	13950
2 Dr SLS Sport Std Cab SB	8690	10265
2 Dr SLS Sport 4WD Std Cab SB	11540	13630
2 Dr SLS Sport Std Cab Stepside SB	8990	10615
2 Dr SLS Sport 4WD Std Cab Stepside SB	11825	13965

GMC 98-97

Model Description	Trade-in Value	Market Value	Model Description	Trade-in Value	Market Value

OPTIONS FOR SONOMA

6 cyl 4.3 L Engine[Opt on 2WD] +595
6 cyl 4.3 L Vortec Engine +440
Auto 4-Speed Transmission +585
Highrider Suspension Pkg +825
AM/FM Compact Disc Player +175
Air Conditioning +450
Aluminum/Alloy Wheels[Std on SLE] +175
Cruise Control +115
Heavy Duty Suspension[Opt on SL, Std Cab, 4WD] +80
Hinged Third Door +185
Keyless Entry System +105
Power Door Locks +130
Power Mirrors +70
Power Windows +135
Premium Sound System +185
Sliding Rear Window +65
Sport Suspension +245
Tilt Steering Wheel +100

SUBURBAN   1998

De-powered second-generation airbags protect front seat occupants for 1998. A new innovation called carpeted floor mats finally appears inside the big 'Burban. Standard equipment now includes PassLock theft deterrent system, electrochromic rearview mirror, and automatic four-wheel drive on K-series models.

RATINGS (SCALE OF 1-10)

Overall	Safety	Reliability	Performance	Comfort	Value
7.6	8.3	7.5	7.2	7.9	7.3

Category H
4 Dr C1500 Wgn	16615	19400
4 Dr C2500 Wgn	17630	20590
4 Dr K1500 4WD Wgn	18545	21655
4 Dr K2500 4WD Wgn	19565	22845

OPTIONS FOR SUBURBAN

8 cyl 6.5 L Turbodsl Engine[Opt on 2500] +1645
8 cyl 7.4 L Engine[Opt on 2500] +330
Air Conditioning +445
Aluminum/Alloy Wheels +170
Camper/Towing Package +180
Compact Disc W/fm/tape +170
Cruise Control +105
Dual Air Conditioning +705
Heated Front Seats +200
Keyless Entry System +95
Leather Seats +545
Power Drivers Seat +155
Power Mirrors +55
Power Windows +105
Privacy Glass +85
Rear Heater +115
Rear Window Defroster +85
Rear Window Wiper +70
Running Boards +190
Tilt Steering Wheel +105

YUKON   1998

The two-door model gets the ax this year. Rear seat passengers are cooled by a newly optional rear air conditioning system. A host of new standard features has been added, including carpeted floor mats. Three new colors spruce up the outside a bit, and second-generation airbags are standard inside.

RATINGS (SCALE OF 1-10)

Overall	Safety	Reliability	Performance	Comfort	Value
7.7	8.4	7.4	7.4	8	7.3

Category H
4 Dr SLE Wgn	20185	23575
4 Dr SLE 4WD Wgn	22190	25910
4 Dr SLT Wgn	21615	25240
4 Dr SLT 4WD Wgn	23615	27575

OPTIONS FOR YUKON

Luxury Convenience Group +465
Compact Disc W/fm/tape[Opt on SLE] +170
Dual Air Conditioning[Opt on SLE] +705
Heated Front Seats +200
Running Boards +190

1997 GMC

JIMMY   1997

Highrider off-road package deleted as GMC realigns Jimmy as luxury sport-ute. Instead, buyers can opt for a Gold Edition in one of four colors. New options include a power sunroof and HomeLink universal transmitter. In a fit of good taste, Radar Purple and Bright Teal paint colors are replaced by Fairway Green and Smoky Caramel.

RATINGS (SCALE OF 1-10)

Overall	Safety	Reliability	Performance	Comfort	Value
7.1	5.1	7.7	8	7.9	6.9

Category G
2 Dr SL Utility	11395	13535
2 Dr SL 4WD Utility	12390	14715
4 Dr SL Wgn	12220	14510
4 Dr SL 4WD Wgn	13240	15725
4 Dr SLE Wgn	13975	16600
4 Dr SLE 4WD Wgn	14955	17760
2 Dr SLS Sport Utility	12460	14795
2 Dr SLS Sport 4WD Utility	13225	15710
4 Dr SLS Sport Wgn	13280	15775
4 Dr SLS Sport 4WD Wgn	14260	16935
4 Dr SLT Wgn	14315	17000
4 Dr SLT 4WD Wgn	15295	18165

GMC 97

Model Description	Trade-in Value	Market Value	Model Description	Trade-in Value	Market Value

OPTIONS FOR JIMMY
AM/FM Compact Disc Player +140
Aluminum/Alloy Wheels[Opt on SL] +145
Camper/Towing Package +135
Cruise Control[Std on SLE,SLS Sport,SLT] +95
Keyless Entry System[Std on SLT] +85
Luggage Rack[Std on SLE,SLS Sport,SLT] +70
Power Door Locks[Std on SLE,SLS Sport,SLT] +105
Power Drivers Seat[Std on SLT] +125
Power Moonroof +385
Power Windows[Std on SLE,SLS Sport,SLT] +110
Premium Sound System[Std on SLT] +155
Skid Plates +60
Swing Out Tire Carrier +85

SAFARI   1997

Illuminated entry and daytime running lights debut this year, along with a couple of new colors and automatic transmission improvements. SLT models can be equipped with leather seating, and a HomeLink three-channel transmitter is optional. Speed-sensitive power steering makes parking easier.

RATINGS (SCALE OF 1-10)

Overall	Safety	Reliability	Performance	Comfort	Value
7.3	7	7.4	7	6.5	8.5

Category G

2 Dr SL Cargo Van Ext	10455	12420
2 Dr SL 4WD Cargo Van Ext	11625	13805
2 Dr SLE Pass. Van Ext	11825	14040
2 Dr SLE 4WD Pass. Van Ext	12735	15125
2 Dr SLT Pass. Van Ext	12965	15400
2 Dr SLT 4WD Pass. Van Ext	14110	16760
2 Dr SLX Pass. Van Ext	10765	12785
2 Dr SLX 4WD Pass. Van Ext	11935	14175

OPTIONS FOR SAFARI
Aluminum/Alloy Wheels[Std on SLT] +145
Camper/Towing Package +135
Chrome Wheels +75
Compact Disc W/fm/tape +200
Cruise Control[Opt on SL, SLX] +95
Dual Air Conditioning +410
Dual Power Seats +185
Keyless Entry System[Std on SLT] +85
Leather Seats +350
Luggage Rack[Std on SLT] +70
Power Door Locks[Opt on SL,SLX] +105
Power Drivers Seat[Std on SLT] +125
Power Windows[Opt on SL,SLX] +110

SAVANA   1997

G3500 models get dual airbags, while daytime running lights are a new standard feature. Speed-sensitive steering reduces effort at low speeds. Chrome-plated wheels are a new option. Remote keyless entry key fobs are redesigned, and automatic transmissions provide better fuel economy and smoother shifts.

Category H

2 Dr G1500 Cargo Van	11565	13550
2 Dr G1500 Pass. Van	13440	15745
2 Dr G1500 SLE Pass. Van	14090	16510
2 Dr G2500 Cargo Van	11815	13840
2 Dr G2500 Cargo Van Ext	12340	14460
2 Dr G2500 Pass. Van	14630	17140
2 Dr G2500 Pass. Van Ext	15145	17745
2 Dr G3500 Cargo Van	12620	14785
2 Dr G3500 Cargo Van Ext	13150	15405
2 Dr G3500 Pass. Van	14720	17245
2 Dr G3500 Pass. Van Ext	15240	17855
2 Dr G3500 SLE Pass. Van	15635	18315
2 Dr G3500 SLE Pass. Van Ext	16150	18920

OPTIONS FOR SAVANA
8 cyl 5.0 L Engine +220
8 cyl 5.7 L Engine[Std on G3500] +465
8 cyl 6.5 L Turbodsl Engine +1365
8 cyl 7.4 L Engine +270
Air Conditioning[Opt on Cargo Van,Cargo Van Ext] +365
Aluminum/Alloy Wheels +140
Camper/Towing Package +150
Chrome Bumpers[Std on SLE] +50
Chrome Wheels +135
Compact Disc W/fm/tape +140
Cruise Control[Std on SLE] +85
Dual Air Conditioning[Opt on G1500 Savana] +575
Dual Power Seats +210
Keyless Entry System +80
Locking Differential +115
Power Door Locks[Std on SLE] +85
Power Windows[Std on SLE] +85

SIERRA PICKUP   1997

A passenger airbag is added, along with speed sensitive steering that reduces low-speed effort. K1500 models have a tighter turning radius for better maneuverability. Automatic transmissions are refined to provide smoother shifts and improved efficiency. Three new paint colors debut.

RATINGS (SCALE OF 1-10)

Overall	Safety	Reliability	Performance	Comfort	Value
N/A	N/A	7.5	N/A	N/A	N/A

SIERRA 1500
Category H

2 Dr C1500 GT Std Cab SB	11790	13815
2 Dr C1500 SL Ext Cab LB	12120	14195
2 Dr C1500 SL Ext Cab SB	11505	13480
2 Dr C1500 SL Ext Cab Stepside SB	11860	13895
2 Dr C1500 SL Std Cab LB	10410	12195

Model Description	Trade-in Value	Market Value
2 Dr C1500 SL Std Cab SB	10225	11980
2 Dr C1500 SL Std Cab Stepside SB		
	10580	12395
2 Dr C1500 SLE Ext Cab LB	13295	15575
2 Dr C1500 SLE Ext Cab SB	12685	14860
2 Dr C1500 SLE Ext Cab Stepside SB		
	13345	15630
2 Dr C1500 SLE Std Cab LB	11590	13575
2 Dr C1500 SLE Std Cab SB	11405	13360
2 Dr C1500 SLE Std Cab Stepside SB		
	11755	13775
2 Dr C1500 SLT Ext Cab LB	14350	16815
2 Dr C1500 SLT Ext Cab SB	13740	16095
2 Dr C1500 SLT Ext Cab Stepside SB		
	14400	16870
2 Dr C1500 SLT Std Cab LB	12605	14765
2 Dr C1500 SLT Std Cab SB	12420	14550
2 Dr C1500 SLT Std Cab Stepside SB		
	12775	14965
2 Dr C1500 Special Std Cab LB	9620	11270
2 Dr C1500 Special Std Cab SB	9360	10965
2 Dr K1500 SL 4WD Ext Cab LB	13840	16210
2 Dr K1500 SL 4WD Ext Cab SB	13230	15500
2 Dr K1500 SL 4WD Ext Cab Stepside SB		
	13585	15915
2 Dr K1500 SL 4WD Std Cab LB	12255	14360
2 Dr K1500 SL 4WD Std Cab SB	12070	14140
2 Dr K1500 SL 4WD Std Cab Stepside SB		
	12425	14555
2 Dr K1500 SLE 4WD Ext Cab LB	15015	17590
2 Dr K1500 SLE 4WD Ext Cab SB	14405	16875
2 Dr K1500 SLE 4WD Ext Cab Stepside SB		
	15065	17650
2 Dr K1500 SLE 4WD Std Cab LB	13430	15735
2 Dr K1500 SLE 4WD Std Cab SB	13250	15520
2 Dr K1500 SLE 4WD Std Cab Stepside SB		
	13600	15935
2 Dr K1500 SLT 4WD Ext Cab LB	16075	18830
2 Dr K1500 SLT 4WD Ext Cab SB	15465	18115
2 Dr K1500 SLT 4WD Ext Cab Stepside SB		
	15815	18530
2 Dr K1500 SLT 4WD Std Cab LB	14450	16925
2 Dr K1500 SLT 4WD Std Cab SB	14265	16710
2 Dr K1500 SLT 4WD Std Cab Stepside SB		
	14620	17125
2 Dr K1500 Special 4WD Std Cab LB		
	11830	13860
2 Dr K1500 Special 4WD Std Cab SB		
	11635	13630

SIERRA 2500
Category H

Model Description	Trade-in Value	Market Value
2 Dr C2500 HD SL Ext Cab LB	12425	14555
2 Dr C2500 HD SL Std Cab LB	11455	13420
2 Dr C2500 HD SLE Ext Cab LB	13885	16265
2 Dr C2500 HD SLE Std Cab LB	12915	15130
2 Dr C2500 HD SLT Ext Cab LB	14770	17305
2 Dr C2500 HD SLT Std Cab LB	13765	16125
2 Dr C2500 SL Ext Cab SB	12525	14670
2 Dr C2500 SL Std Cab LB	10945	12820
2 Dr C2500 SLE Ext Cab SB	13985	16380
2 Dr C2500 SLE Std Cab LB	12400	14530
2 Dr C2500 SLT Ext Cab SB	14870	17420
2 Dr C2500 SLT Std Cab LB	13250	15525
2 Dr K2500 HD SL 4WD Ext Cab LB		
	14380	16845
2 Dr K2500 HD SL 4WD Ext Cab SB		
	14300	16755
2 Dr K2500 HD SL 4WD Std Cab LB		
	13120	15370
2 Dr K2500 HD SLE 4WD Ext Cab LB		
	15835	18555
2 Dr K2500 HD SLE 4WD Ext Cab SB		
	15760	18465
2 Dr K2500 HD SLE 4WD Std Cab LB		
	14580	17080
2 Dr K2500 HD SLT 4WD Ext Cab LB		
	16725	19595
2 Dr K2500 HD SLT 4WD Ext Cab SB		
	16650	19505
2 Dr K2500 HD SLT 4WD Std Cab LB		
	15425	18075

SIERRA 3500
Category H

Model Description	Trade-in Value	Market Value
4 Dr C3500 SL Crew Cab LB	13195	15455
2 Dr C3500 SL Ext Cab LB	13370	15660
2 Dr C3500 SL Std Cab LB	11335	13280
4 Dr C3500 SLE Crew Cab LB	15450	18100
2 Dr C3500 SLE Ext Cab LB	14800	17340
2 Dr C3500 SLE Std Cab LB	12770	14960
4 Dr C3500 SLT Crew Cab LB	16440	19260
2 Dr C3500 SLT Ext Cab LB	15675	18360
2 Dr C3500 SLT Std Cab LB	13600	15935
4 Dr K3500 SL 4WD Crew Cab LB	15075	17665
2 Dr K3500 SL 4WD Ext Cab LB	15035	17615
2 Dr K3500 SL 4WD Std Cab LB	13115	15365
4 Dr K3500 SLE 4WD Crew Cab LB		
	17330	20305
2 Dr K3500 SLE 4WD Ext Cab LB	16470	19295
2 Dr K3500 SLE 4WD Std Cab LB	14550	17045

Model Description	Trade-in Value	Market Value
4 Dr K3500 SLT 4WD Crew Cab LB		
	18325	21465
2 Dr K3500 SLT 4WD Ext Cab LB	17345	20315
2 Dr K3500 SLT 4WD Std Cab LB	15380	18020

OPTIONS FOR SIERRA PICKUP
8 cyl 5.0 L Engine +220
8 cyl 5.7 L Engine +465
8 cyl 6.5 L Turbodsl Engine +1365
8 cyl 7.4 L Engine +270
Auto 4-Speed Transmission +435
AM/FM Compact Disc Player +140
Air Conditioning[Opt on SL,Special] +365
Aluminum/Alloy Wheels[Std on SLT] +140
Bed Liner +100
Camper/Towing Package +150
Chrome Wheels[Std on GT] +135
Compact Disc W/fm/tape +140
Cruise Control[Opt on SL,Special] +85
Dual Rear Wheels +355
Hinged Third Door +185
Keyless Entry System[Opt on SLE] +80
Locking Differential +115
Power Door Locks[Opt on GT,SL] +85
Power Drivers Seat[Opt on SLE] +125
Rear Step Bumper +65
Skid Plates +50

SONOMA   1997

Nothing much. Changes are limited to new colors, availability of the Sport Suspension on extended cab models, engine and transmission improvements, lighter-weight plug-in half shafts for 4WD Sonomas, and console-mounted shifter for trucks equipped with a center console and bucket seats.

RATINGS (SCALE OF 1-10)

Overall	Safety	Reliability	Performance	Comfort	Value
N/A	4.9	6.8	6.6	8.1	N/A

Category G

Model	Trade-in	Market
2 Dr SL Std Cab LB	7465	8865
2 Dr SL 4WD Std Cab LB	10340	12280
2 Dr SL Std Cab SB	7285	8650
2 Dr SL 4WD Std Cab SB	10140	12040
2 Dr SLE Ext Cab SB	9180	10905
2 Dr SLE 4WD Ext Cab SB	11890	14120
2 Dr SLE Ext Cab Stepside SB	9910	11770
2 Dr SLE 4WD Ext Cab Stepside SB		
	12750	15145
2 Dr SLE Std Cab SB	8035	9545
2 Dr SLE 4WD Std Cab SB	10800	12830
2 Dr SLE Std Cab Stepside SB	8710	10340
2 Dr SLE 4WD Std Cab Stepside SB		
	11610	13790
2 Dr SLS Sport Ext Cab SB	9145	10860

Model Description	Trade-in Value	Market Value
2 Dr SLS Sport 4WD Ext Cab SB	11970	14215
2 Dr SLS Sport Ext Cab Stepside SB		
	9475	11255
2 Dr SLS Sport 4WD Ext Cab Stepside SB		
	12240	14535
2 Dr SLS Sport Std Cab LB	8125	9650
2 Dr SLS Sport 4WD Std Cab LB	11085	13165
2 Dr SLS Sport Std Cab SB	7945	9435
2 Dr SLS Sport 4WD Std Cab SB	10825	12860
2 Dr SLS Sport Std Cab Stepside SB		
	8215	9755
2 Dr SLS Sport 4WD Std Cab Stepside SB		
	11100	13180

OPTIONS FOR SONOMA
6 cyl 4.3 L Engine +440
6 cyl 4.3 L Vortec Engine +335
Auto 4-Speed Transmission +480
Highrider Suspension Pkg +780
AM/FM Compact Disc Player +140
AM/FM Stereo Tape +100
Air Conditioning +365
Aluminum/Alloy Wheels[Std on SLE] +145
Cruise Control +95
Power Door Locks +105
Power Windows +110
Tilt Steering Wheel +80
Tutone Paint[Opt on SLS Sport] +115

SUBURBAN   1997

GMC has added a passenger side airbag and a power lock switch in the cargo compartment. SLE and SLT trim now includes rear heat and air conditioning, as well as remote keyless entry. Uplevel SLT trim also includes a combination CD and cassette player stereo system. All Suburbans receive speed-sensitive power steering, and 4WD models have a tighter turning circle. Two new colors freshen the dated exterior design this year.

RATINGS (SCALE OF 1-10)

Overall	Safety	Reliability	Performance	Comfort	Value
7.5	8.3	7	7.2	7.9	7.1

Category H

Model	Trade-in	Market
4 Dr C1500 Wgn	16845	19730
4 Dr C2500 Wgn	17660	20690
4 Dr K1500 4WD Wgn	18570	21755
4 Dr K2500 4WD Wgn	18600	21925

OPTIONS FOR SUBURBAN
8 cyl 6.5 L Turbodsl Engine +1365
8 cyl 7.4 L Engine +270
Air Conditioning +365
Aluminum/Alloy Wheels +140
Camper/Towing Package +150

GMC 97-96

Model Description	Trade-in Value	Market Value	Model Description	Trade-in Value	Market Value

Compact Disc W/fm/tape +140
Cruise Control +85
Dual Air Conditioning +575
Keyless Entry System +80
Leather Seats +445
Luggage Rack +70
Power Drivers Seat +125
Power Windows +85
Running Boards +155
Skid Plates +50

YUKON   1997

Dual airbags, speed-sensitive steering and a tighter turning circle for 4WD models. A power lock switch is added to the cargo compartment, and SLT models have a standard CD/cassette combo stereo. Remote keyless entry is standard on four-door models, and on SLE and SLT two-door models. Newly optional on four-door models is a rear air conditioning unit.

RATINGS (SCALE OF 1-10)

Overall	Safety	Reliability	Performance	Comfort	Value
7.6	8	7.3	7.4	8	7.2

Category H

2 Dr SL Utility	14405	16875
2 Dr SL 4WD Utility	15980	18725
2 Dr SLE Utility	16845	19735
2 Dr SLE 4WD Utility	18420	21580
4 Dr SLE Wgn	17605	20625
4 Dr SLE 4WD Wgn	19150	22435
2 Dr SLT Utility	17870	20935
2 Dr SLT 4WD Utility	19450	22785
4 Dr SLT Wgn	18780	22005
4 Dr SLT 4WD Wgn	20330	23815

OPTIONS FOR YUKON

8 cyl 6.5 L Turbodsl Engine +1365
Air Conditioning[Opt on SL] +365
Aluminum/Alloy Wheels[Opt on SL] +140
Camper/Towing Package +150
Compact Disc W/fm/tape[Std on SLT] +140
Cruise Control[Opt on SL] +85
Dual Air Conditioning +575
Keyless Entry System[Opt on SL ,SLE] +80
Power Drivers Seat[Std on SLT] +125
Running Boards +155
Skid Plates +50

1996 GMC

JIMMY   1996

GMC's popular compact sport utility gets a super-duper optional off-road package called Highrider, as well as an available five-speed transmission. Either of these are available on two-door models only. All Jimmys receive glow-in-the-day headlights and long-life engine coolant. Spark plugs last 100,000 miles. All-wheel drive, which became optional in mid-1995, continues. Conspicuously absent is a passenger airbag.

RATINGS (SCALE OF 1-10)

Overall	Safety	Reliability	Performance	Comfort	Value
6.5	4.9	7.1	8	7.9	4.8

Category G

2 Dr SL 4WD Utility	11040	13225
2 Dr SL Utility	10375	12430
4 Dr SL Wgn	11005	13185
4 Dr SL 4WD Wgn	11820	14160
4 Dr SLE Wgn	11740	14070
4 Dr SLE 4WD Wgn	12555	15040
2 Dr SLS Utility	10865	13015
2 Dr SLS 4WD Utility	11485	13760
4 Dr SLS Wgn	11415	13675
4 Dr SLS 4WD Wgn	12445	14915
4 Dr SLT Wgn	12510	14985
4 Dr SLT 4WD Wgn	13320	15960
2 Dr STD Utility	9545	11435
2 Dr STD 4WD Utility	10475	12550
4 Dr STD Wgn	10355	12410
4 Dr STD 4WD Wgn	11150	13360

OPTIONS FOR JIMMY

AM/FM Compact Disc Player +115
Aluminum/Alloy Wheels[Opt on SL,STD] +120
Camper/Towing Package +110
Cruise Control[Opt on STD] +75
Keyless Entry System[Std on SLT] +70
Limited Slip Diff +100
Luggage Rack[Opt on STD] +60
Power Door Locks[Opt on STD] +85
Power Drivers Seat[Std on SLT] +105
Power Windows[Opt on STD] +90
Premium Sound System[Std on SLT] +125
Skid Plates +50
Swing Out Tire Carrier +70

SAFARI   1996

An all-new interior debuts with dual airbags, more leg and foot room, and a host of other features. Important among them are the availability of dual integrated child seats and a child-proof lock on the right side sliding door. Under seat heat ducts help warm the rear passengers, and new audio systems include a radio that can be tuned independently by rear seat passengers without disturbing the listening pleasure, or program, that the front occupants are enjoying.

RATINGS (SCALE OF 1-10)

Overall	Safety	Reliability	Performance	Comfort	Value
7.3	6.9	7.5	7	6.5	8.4

Don't forget to refer to the Mileage Adjustment Table at the back of this book!

Model Description	Trade-in Value	Market Value
Category G		
2 Dr SL Cargo Van Ext	9230	11055
2 Dr SL 4WD Cargo Van Ext	10285	12320
2 Dr SLE Pass. Van Ext	10365	12420
2 Dr SLE 4WD Pass. Van Ext	11165	13375
2 Dr SLT Pass. Van Ext	11375	13625
2 Dr SLT 4WD Pass. Van Ext	12405	14865
2 Dr SLX Pass. Van Ext	9945	11915
2 Dr SLX 4WD Pass. Van Ext	11000	13180
2 Dr STD Pass. Van Ext	9510	11390
2 Dr STD 4WD Pass. Van Ext	10565	12655

OPTIONS FOR SAFARI

Aluminum/Alloy Wheels[Std on SLT] +120
Camper/Towing Package +110
Chrome Wheels +60
Compact Disc W/fm/tape +160
Cruise Control[Opt on SL] +75
Dual Air Conditioning +335
Keyless Entry System[Opt on SLE] +70
Luggage Rack[Std on SLT] +60
Power Door Locks[Opt on SL,STD] +85
Power Drivers Seat[Std on SLT] +105
Power Passenger Seat +75
Power Windows[Opt on SL] +90

SAVANA   1996

Model Description	Trade-in Value	Market Value
Category H		
2 Dr G1500 Cargo Van	10380	12210
2 Dr G1500 Pass. Van	12100	14235
2 Dr G2500 Cargo Van	10610	12480
2 Dr G2500 Cargo Van Ext	11095	13050
2 Dr G2500 Pass. Van	13160	15480
2 Dr G2500 Pass. Van Ext	13635	16040
2 Dr G3500 Cargo Van	11350	13355
2 Dr G3500 Cargo Van Ext	11835	13925
2 Dr G3500 Pass. Van	13245	15580
2 Dr G3500 Pass. Van Ext	13715	16135

OPTIONS FOR SAVANA

8 cyl 5.0 L Engine +205
8 cyl 5.7 L Engine[Std on G35 Savana,G25 Savana] +370
8 cyl 6.5 L Turbodsl Engine +1195
8 cyl 7.4 L Engine +225
Air Conditioning[Opt on Cargo Van,Cargo Van Ext] +300
Aluminum/Alloy Wheels +115
Camper/Towing Package +120
Chrome Bumpers +40
Compact Disc W/fm/tape +115
Cruise Control +70
Dual Air Conditioning +470
Power Door Locks +70
Power Drivers Seat +105
Power Passenger Seat +95
Power Windows +70

SIERRA PICKUP   1996

Extended-cab models get a trick new side-access panel on the passenger side of the truck. Engines are dramatically improved across the board, daytime running lights debut, and long-life engine coolant gets changed about the same time you make your last payment. Spark plugs last 100,000 miles. Passenger car tires on 1500 models improve the ride and make the Sierra quieter. Heat ducts keep rear passengers' tootsies warm on extended cab models. Four-wheel-drive models get optional electronic shift-on-the-fly, and illuminated entry is a nice new touch.

RATINGS (SCALE OF 1-10)

Overall	Safety	Reliability	Performance	Comfort	Value
N/A	N/A	6.8	N/A	N/A	N/A

SIERRA 1500

Model Description	Trade-in Value	Market Value
Category H		
2 Dr C1500 SL Ext Cab LB	11315	13310
2 Dr C1500 SL Ext Cab SB	10760	12655
2 Dr C1500 SL Ext Cab Stepside SB	11000	12940
2 Dr C1500 SL Std Cab LB	9705	11415
2 Dr C1500 SL Std Cab SB	9715	11430
2 Dr C1500 SL Std Cab Stepside SB	9540	11220
2 Dr C1500 SLE Ext Cab LB	12745	14990
2 Dr C1500 SLE Ext Cab SB	12185	14335
2 Dr C1500 SLE Ext Cab Stepside SB	12490	14690
2 Dr C1500 SLE Std Cab LB	11130	13095
2 Dr C1500 SLE Std Cab SB	10965	12900
2 Dr C1500 SLE Std Cab Stepside SB	11445	13465
2 Dr C1500 SLT Ext Cab LB	13650	16060
2 Dr C1500 SLT Ext Cab SB	13195	15525
2 Dr C1500 SLT Ext Cab Stepside SB	13500	15880
2 Dr C1500 SLT Std Cab LB	12105	14240
2 Dr C1500 SLT Std Cab SB	11935	14045
2 Dr C1500 SLT Std Cab Stepside SB	12415	14605
2 Dr C1500 Special Std Cab LB	8940	10515
2 Dr C1500 Special Std Cab SB	8705	10240
2 Dr K1500 SL 4WD Ext Cab LB	12835	15100
2 Dr K1500 SL 4WD Ext Cab SB	12375	14560
2 Dr K1500 SL 4WD Ext Cab Stepside SB	12620	14845
2 Dr K1500 SL 4WD Std Cab LB	11435	13450
2 Dr K1500 SL 4WD Std Cab SB	11255	13245

GMC 96

Model Description	Trade-in Value	Market Value
2 Dr K1500 SL 4WD Std Cab Stepside SB		
	11590	13635
2 Dr K1500 SLE 4WD Ext Cab LB	14155	16655
2 Dr K1500 SLE 4WD Ext Cab SB	13700	16120
2 Dr K1500 SLE 4WD Ext Cab Stepside SB		
	14005	16475
2 Dr K1500 SLE 4WD Std Cab LB	12865	15130
2 Dr K1500 SLE 4WD Std Cab SB	12685	14925
2 Dr K1500 SLE 4WD Std Cab Stepside SB		
	13020	15315
2 Dr K1500 SLT 4WD Ext Cab LB	15160	17830
2 Dr K1500 SLT 4WD Ext Cab SB	14705	17295
2 Dr K1500 SLT 4WD Ext Cab Stepside SB		
	14945	17585
2 Dr K1500 SLT 4WD Std Cab LB	13730	16155
2 Dr K1500 SLT 4WD Std Cab SB	13555	15945
2 Dr K1500 SLT 4WD Std Cab Stepside SB		
	13885	16335
2 Dr K1500 Special 4WD Std Cab LB		
	10955	12890
2 Dr K1500 Special 4WD Std Cab SB		
	10835	12750

SIERRA 2500
Category H

Model Description	Trade-in Value	Market Value
2 Dr C2500 SL Ext Cab LB	11285	13275
2 Dr C2500 SL Ext Cab SB	11250	13235
2 Dr C2500 SL Std Cab LB	9795	11520
2 Dr C2500 SLE Ext Cab LB	12935	15215
2 Dr C2500 SLE Ext Cab SB	12600	14820
2 Dr C2500 SLE Std Cab LB	11140	13105
2 Dr C2500 SLT Ext Cab SB	13215	15545
2 Dr C2500 SLT Std Cab LB	11915	14015
2 Dr K2500 SL 4WD Ext Cab LB	12840	15105
2 Dr K2500 SL 4WD Ext Cab SB	12840	15105
2 Dr K2500 SL 4WD Std Cab LB	11945	14050
2 Dr K2500 SLE 4WD Ext Cab LB	14165	16665
2 Dr K2500 SLE 4WD Ext Cab SB	14095	16585
2 Dr K2500 SLE 4WD Std Cab LB	13095	15405
2 Dr K2500 SLT 4WD Ext Cab LB	14965	17605
2 Dr K2500 SLT 4WD Std Cab LB	13860	16305

SIERRA 3500
Category H

Model Description	Trade-in Value	Market Value
4 Dr C3500 SL Crew Cab LB	12975	15260
2 Dr C3500 SL Ext Cab LB	13145	15465
2 Dr C3500 SL Std Cab LB	11115	13080
4 Dr C3500 SLE Crew Cab LB	14660	17250
2 Dr C3500 SLE Ext Cab LB	14040	16515
4 Dr C3500 SLT Crew Cab LB	15605	18360
2 Dr C3500 SLT Ext Cab LB	14870	17490
2 Dr C3500 SLT Std Cab LB	12990	15285

Model Description	Trade-in Value	Market Value
4 Dr K3500 SL 4WD Crew Cab LB	14710	17305
2 Dr K3500 SL 4WD Ext Cab LB	14675	17265
2 Dr K3500 SL 4WD Std Cab LB	12850	15115
4 Dr K3500 SLE 4WD Crew Cab LB		
	16410	19305
2 Dr K3500 SLE 4WD Ext Cab LB	15585	18335
2 Dr K3500 SLE 4WD Std Cab LB	14545	17110
4 Dr K3500 SLT 4WD Crew Cab LB		
	17355	20415
2 Dr K3500 SLT 4WD Ext Cab LB	16415	19310
2 Dr K3500 SLT 4WD Std Cab LB	14545	17110

OPTIONS FOR SIERRA PICKUP
8 cyl 5.0 L Engine +205
8 cyl 5.7 L Engine +370
8 cyl 6.5 L Turbodsl Engine +1195
8 cyl 7.4 L Engine +225
Auto 4-Speed Transmission +355
Air Conditioning[Std on SLE,SLT] +300
Aluminum/Alloy Wheels[Std on SLT] +115
Bed Liner +85
Camper/Towing Package +120
Chrome Bumpers[Opt on SL] +40
Chrome Wheels +110
Compact Disc W/fm/tape +115
Cruise Control[Std on SLE,SLT] +70
Dual Rear Wheels +290
Hinged Third Door +155
Keyless Entry System[Opt on SLE] +65
Locking Differential +95
Power Door Locks[Opt on SL] +70
Power Drivers Seat[Opt on SLE] +105
Rear Step Bumper +50
Skid Plates +40

SONOMA   1996

Extended-cab models get an optional driver's side rear access panel. All Sonomas are now equipped with four-wheel ABS. A new sport suspension provides sporty handling, and a snazzy Sportside box ends Ford's reign as lord of compact stepsides. A new five-speed transmission improves shifter location and operation when equipped with the base four-cylinder. Still missing is the availability of a passenger airbag.

RATINGS (SCALE OF 1-10)

Overall	Safety	Reliability	Performance	Comfort	Value
N/A	5	6.3	6.6	8.1	N/A

Category G

Model Description	Trade-in Value	Market Value
2 Dr SL Std Cab LB	6155	7375
2 Dr SL 4WD Std Cab LB	8755	10490
2 Dr SL Std Cab SB	5995	7185
2 Dr SL 4WD Std Cab SB	8460	10140
2 Dr SLE Ext Cab SB	7925	9495
2 Dr SLE 4WD Ext Cab SB	10300	12340

Model Description	Trade-in Value	Market Value
2 Dr SLE Ext Cab Stepside SB	8130	9740
2 Dr SLE 4WD Ext Cab Stepside SB	10500	12580
2 Dr SLE Std Cab SB	6640	7955
2 Dr SLE 4WD Std Cab SB	9100	10900
2 Dr SLS Sport Ext Cab SB	7505	8990
2 Dr SLS Sport 4WD Ext Cab SB	9865	11815
2 Dr SLS Sport Ext Cab Stepside SB	7710	9235
2 Dr SLS Sport 4WD Ext Cab Stepside SB	10065	12060
2 Dr SLS Sport Std Cab LB	6775	8120
2 Dr SLS Sport 4WD Std Cab LB	9375	11230
2 Dr SLS Sport Std Cab SB	6640	7955
2 Dr SLS Sport 4WD Std Cab SB	9100	10900
2 Dr SLS Sport Std Cab Stepside SB	6845	8200
2 Dr SLS Sport 4WD Std Cab Stepside SB	9305	11145

OPTIONS FOR SONOMA
6 cyl 4.3 L Engine +360
6 cyl 4.3 L Vortec Engine +275
Auto 4-Speed Transmission +390
Highrider Suspension Pkg +630
AM/FM Compact Disc Player +115
Air Conditioning +300
Aluminum/Alloy Wheels[Std on SLE] +120
Camper/Towing Package +110
Cruise Control +75
Hinged Third Door +125
Keyless Entry System +70
Limited Slip Diff +100
Power Door Locks +85
Power Windows +90
Premium Sound System +125
Skid Plates +50
Tutone Paint[Opt on SLS Sport] +95

SUBURBAN   1996

Giant SUV gets daytime running lights to make it more visible to other drivers. This is akin to installing field lighting on the bow of the Queen Mary. New V8s, quieter tires, and long-life spark plugs and coolant make the Suburban more satisfying to skipper. Rear passengers get warmer faster, thanks to new rear-seat heat ducting. Illuminated entry is newly standard, and electronic 4WD controls are a new option.

RATINGS (SCALE OF 1-10)

Overall	Safety	Reliability	Performance	Comfort	Value
7.2	6.8	6.7	7.2	7.9	7.6

Category H

Model	Trade-in Value	Market Value
4 Dr C1500 Wgn	15580	18330
4 Dr C2500 Wgn	16360	19245

Model Description	Trade-in Value	Market Value
4 Dr K1500 4WD Wgn	17040	20045
4 Dr K2500 4WD Wgn	17760	20895

OPTIONS FOR SUBURBAN
8 cyl 6.5 L Turbodsl Engine +1195
8 cyl 7.4 L Engine +225
Air Conditioning +300
Camper/Towing Package[Std on C2500] +120
Compact Disc W/fm/tape +115
Cruise Control +70
Dual Air Conditioning +470
Keyless Entry System +65
Leather Seats +365
Luggage Rack +55
Power Door Locks +70
Power Drivers Seat +105
Power Windows +70
Skid Plates +40

VANDURA/RALLY WAGON 1996

RALLY WAGON
Category H

Model	Trade-in Value	Market Value
2 Dr G35 Rally Wagon	11965	14075
2 Dr G35 Rally Wagon Ext	12165	14310
2 Dr G35 STX Rally Wagon	12660	14890
2 Dr G35 STX Rally Wagon Ext	13130	15445

VANDURA
Category H

Model	Trade-in Value	Market Value
2 Dr G35 Vandura	10315	12135
2 Dr G35 Vandura Ext	10845	12760

OPTIONS FOR VANDURA/RALLY WAGON
8 cyl 6.5 L Dsl Engine +605
8 cyl 7.4 L Engine +225
AM/FM Compact Disc Player +115
Air Conditioning[Opt on STD] +300
Camper/Towing Package +120
Chrome Bumpers[Opt on Vandura, Vandura Ext] +40
Cruise Control[Opt on STD] +70
Dual Air Conditioning +470
Keyless Entry System +65
Power Door Locks[Opt on STD] +70
Power Windows[Opt on STD] +70
Premium Sound System +140

YUKON   1996

Just what we need: a two-wheel-drive two-door Yukon. A new 5700 Vortec V8 gets long-life coolant and spark plugs, as well as a hefty bump in power and torque. Passenger car tires on less stout Yukons result in a softer, quieter ride. Rear heat ducts, illuminated entry, and height-adjustable seat belts debut. Four-wheel-drive models get a newly optional electronic shift mechanism.

RATINGS (SCALE OF 1-10)

Overall	Safety	Reliability	Performance	Comfort	Value
7.4	7.1	6.9	7.4	8	7.6

Don't forget to refer to the Mileage Adjustment Table at the back of this book!

Model Description	Trade-in Value	Market Value
Category H		
2 Dr SL Utility	13145	15460
2 Dr SL 4WD Utility	14400	16940
2 Dr SLE Utility	14945	17585
2 Dr SLE 4WD Utility	16130	18975
4 Dr SLE Wgn	16150	19000
4 Dr SLE 4WD Wgn	17380	20445
2 Dr SLT Utility	15830	18620
2 Dr SLT 4WD Utility	17000	20000
4 Dr SLT Wgn	16610	19540
4 Dr SLT 4WD Wgn	17805	20945

OPTIONS FOR YUKON

8 cyl 6.5 L Turbodsl Engine +1195
Air Conditioning[Opt on SL] +300
Aluminum/Alloy Wheels[Opt on SL] +115
Camper/Towing Package +120
Compact Disc W/fm/tape +115
Cruise Control[Opt on SL] +70
Keyless Entry System[Opt on SL,SLE] +65
Power Drivers Seat[Opt on SLE, SLT] +105
Rear Window Defroster[Opt on SL] +55
Running Boards +130
Skid Plates +40

1995 GMC

JIMMY   1995

All-new SUV appears based on revamped Sonoma. Four-wheel-drive models have electronic transfer case as standard equipment. Spare tire on four-door model is mounted beneath cargo bay instead of in it. Five different suspension packages are available. One engine, a 195-horsepower 4.3-liter V6, is available. All-wheel drive is optional. Driver airbag and air conditioning are standard equipment.

RATINGS (SCALE OF 1-10)

Overall	Safety	Reliability	Performance	Comfort	Value
6.6	5.3	5.8	8	7.9	6.1

	Trade-in Value	Market Value
Category G		
2 Dr SL Utility	8745	10665
2 Dr SL 4WD Utility	9295	11340
4 Dr SLE Wgn	9480	11565
4 Dr SLE 4WD Wgn	9890	12060
2 Dr SLS Utility	9015	10990
2 Dr SLS 4WD Utility	9560	11660
4 Dr SLS Wgn	9570	11670
4 Dr SLS 4WD Wgn	10470	12770
4 Dr SLT Wgn	10470	12770
4 Dr SLT 4WD Wgn	11195	13655
2 Dr STD Utility	8120	9900
2 Dr STD 4WD Utility	8920	10880

	Trade-in Value	Market Value
4 Dr STD Wgn	8845	10785
4 Dr STD 4WD Wgn	9400	11465

OPTIONS FOR JIMMY

AM/FM Compact Disc Player +95
Camper/Towing Package +90
Cruise Control[Opt on STD] +65
Keyless Entry System[Std on SLT] +60
Limited Slip Diff +85
Luggage Rack[Opt on STD] +50
Power Door Locks[Opt on STD] +70
Power Drivers Seat[Std on SLT] +85
Power Windows[Opt on STD] +70
Premium Sound System[Std on SLT Wgn] +100
Skid Plates +40
Swing Out Tire Carrier +55

SAFARI   1995

Front sheetmetal is restyled. Regular-length versions are dropped from the lineup, leaving only the extended model. Multileaf steel springs replace single-leaf plastic springs. One engine is available, the 190-horsepower, 4.3-liter V6. Air conditioning is newly standard, and remote keyless entry is a new option.

RATINGS (SCALE OF 1-10)

Overall	Safety	Reliability	Performance	Comfort	Value
7	6	6.3	7.2	6.6	8.9

	Trade-in Value	Market Value
Category G		
2 Dr SL Cargo Van Ext	7520	9170
2 Dr SL 4WD Cargo Van Ext	8420	10265
2 Dr SLE Pass. Van Ext	8380	10220
2 Dr SLE 4WD Pass. Van Ext	8975	10945
2 Dr SLT Pass. Van Ext	9045	11030
2 Dr SLT 4WD Pass. Van Ext	9915	12090
2 Dr SLX Pass. Van Ext	7880	9610
2 Dr SLX 4WD Pass. Van Ext	8820	10755
2 Dr STD Pass. Van Ext	7765	9470
2 Dr STD 4WD Pass. Van Ext	8665	10565

OPTIONS FOR SAFARI

AM/FM Compact Disc Player +95
Camper/Towing Package +90
Cruise Control[Opt on SL] +65
Dual Air Conditioning +275
Keyless Entry System[Std on SLT] +60
Limited Slip Diff +85
Luggage Rack +50
Power Door Locks[Std on SLE,SLT] +70
Power Drivers Seat +85
Power Windows[Std on SLT] +70
Premium Sound System +100

SIERRA PICKUP   1995

New interior with driver airbag (models under 8,500 lb. GVWR) and standard four-wheel ABS debut. Sport package is dropped. New dashboard features

Model Description	Trade-in Value	Market Value
Model Description	Trade-in Value	Market Value

modular design with controls that are much easier to read and use. Power mirrors and remote keyless entry are new options. Uplevel radios come with automatic volume controls that raise or lower volume depending on vehicle speed.

RATINGS (SCALE OF 1-10)

Overall	Safety	Reliability	Performance	Comfort	Value
N/A	N/A	5.7	N/A	N/A	N/A

SIERRA 1500

Category H

2 Dr C1500 SL Ext Cab LB	9895	11750
2 Dr C1500 SL Ext Cab SB	9445	11215
2 Dr C1500 SL Ext Cab Stepside SB	9720	11545
2 Dr C1500 SL Std Cab LB	8460	10050
2 Dr C1500 SL Std Cab SB	8310	9870
2 Dr C1500 SL Std Cab Stepside SB	8750	10390
2 Dr C1500 SLE Ext Cab LB	11005	13070
2 Dr C1500 SLE Ext Cab SB	10500	12470
2 Dr C1500 SLE Ext Cab Stepside SB	10775	12795
2 Dr C1500 SLE Std Cab LB	9465	11240
2 Dr C1500 SLE Std Cab SB	9310	11060
2 Dr C1500 SLE Std Cab Stepside SB	9750	11580
2 Dr C1500 SLT Ext Cab LB	11910	14145
2 Dr C1500 SLT Ext Cab SB	11535	13700
2 Dr C1500 SLT Ext Cab Stepside SB	11810	14025
2 Dr C1500 Special Std Cab LB	7770	9225
2 Dr C1500 Special Std Cab SB	7555	8970
2 Dr K1500 SL 4WD Ext Cab LB	11105	13190
2 Dr K1500 SL 4WD Ext Cab SB	10745	12765
2 Dr K1500 SL 4WD Ext Cab Stepside SB	10970	13025
2 Dr K1500 SL 4WD Std Cab LB	9865	11715
2 Dr K1500 SL 4WD Std Cab SB	9705	11525
2 Dr K1500 SL 4WD Std Cab Stepside SB	10140	12040
2 Dr K1500 SLE 4WD Ext Cab LB	12245	14545
2 Dr K1500 SLE 4WD Ext Cab SB	11800	14015
2 Dr K1500 SLE 4WD Ext Cab Stepside SB	11895	14125
2 Dr K1500 SLE 4WD Std Cab LB	10865	12905
2 Dr K1500 SLE 4WD Std Cab SB	10705	12710
2 Dr K1500 SLE 4WD Std Cab Stepside SB	11140	13230
2 Dr K1500 SLS 4WD Ext Cab SB	10745	12765
2 Dr K1500 SLS 4WD Ext Cab Stepside SB	10970	13025
2 Dr K1500 SLT 4WD Ext Cab LB	13110	15570
2 Dr K1500 SLT 4WD Ext Cab SB	12700	15080
2 Dr K1500 SLT 4WD Ext Cab Stepside SB	12920	15340
2 Dr K1500 Special 4WD Std Cab LB	9455	11230
2 Dr K1500 Special 4WD Std Cab SB	9350	11105

SIERRA 2500

Category H

2 Dr C2500 SL Ext Cab LB	9885	11740
2 Dr C2500 SL Ext Cab SB	9855	11705
2 Dr C2500 SL Std Cab LB	8330	9895
2 Dr C2500 SLE Ext Cab LB	10955	13010
2 Dr C2500 SLE Ext Cab SB	10925	12975
2 Dr C2500 SLE Std Cab LB	9400	11165
2 Dr C2500 SLT Ext Cab LB	12450	14785
2 Dr C2500 SLT Ext Cab SB	11570	13740
2 Dr K2500 SL 4WD Ext Cab LB	11115	13200
2 Dr K2500 SL 4WD Ext Cab SB	10775	12800
2 Dr K2500 SL 4WD Std Cab LB	9460	11235
2 Dr K2500 SLE 4WD Ext Cab LB	12165	14450
2 Dr K2500 SLE 4WD Ext Cab SB	11640	13825
2 Dr K2500 SLE 4WD Std Cab LB	10530	12505
2 Dr K2500 SLT 4WD Ext Cab LB	13005	15445
2 Dr K2500 SLT 4WD Ext Cab SB	13395	15905

SIERRA 3500

Category H

4 Dr C3500 SL Crew Cab LB	11510	13670
2 Dr C3500 SL Ext Cab LB	11805	14020
2 Dr C3500 SL Std Cab LB	9975	11850
4 Dr C3500 SLE Crew Cab LB	12660	15035
2 Dr C3500 SLE Ext Cab LB	12195	14480
2 Dr C3500 SLE Std Cab LB	11140	13230
2 Dr C3500 SLT Ext Cab LB	13060	15510
4 Dr K3500 SL 4WD Crew Cab LB	13125	15585
2 Dr K3500 SL 4WD Ext Cab LB	13060	15510
2 Dr K3500 SL 4WD Std Cab LB	11415	13555
4 Dr K3500 SLE 4WD Crew Cab LB	14140	16795
2 Dr K3500 SLE 4WD Ext Cab LB	13435	15955
2 Dr K3500 SLE 4WD Std Cab LB	11825	14040
2 Dr K3500 SLT 4WD Ext Cab LB	14300	16985

OPTIONS FOR SIERRA PICKUP

8 cyl 5.0 L Engine +180
8 cyl 5.7 L Engine +225
8 cyl 6.5 L Turbodsl Engine +950
8 cyl 7.4 L Engine +170
Auto 4-Speed Transmission +275

Don't forget to refer to the Mileage Adjustment Table at the back of this book!

Model Description	Trade-in Value	Market Value
Air Conditioning[Std on SLE , SLT] +245		
Bed Liner +70		
Camper/Towing Package +100		
Chrome Bumpers[Opt on C1500,K1500] +35		
Chrome Wheels +90		
Compact Disc W/fm/tape +95		
Cruise Control[Std on SLE,SLT] +55		
Dual Rear Wheels +235		
Keyless Entry System[Opt on SL,SLE] +50		
Limited Slip Diff +80		
Locking Differential +75		
Power Door Locks[Std on SLE,SLT] +55		
Power Drivers Seat[Opt on SLE] +85		
Premium Sound System +115		
Rear Step Bumper +40		
Skid Plates +30		

SONOMA   1995

Driver airbag is added, and daytime running lights are standard. Highrider off-road package can be ordered on the Club Coupe. Power window and lock buttons are illuminated at night. Remote keyless entry is a new option. A single key operates both the door locks and the ignition. A manual transmission can now be ordered with the 191-horsepower, 4.3-liter V6.

RATINGS (SCALE OF 1-10)

Overall	Safety	Reliability	Performance	Comfort	Value
N/A	4.9	5.7	6.6	8.1	N/A

Category G

Model Description	Trade-in Value	Market Value
2 Dr SL Std Cab LB	5050	6160
2 Dr SL 4WD Std Cab LB	7195	8775
2 Dr SL Std Cab SB	4910	5990
2 Dr SL 4WD Std Cab SB	6935	8460
2 Dr SLE Ext Cab SB	6230	7600
2 Dr SLE 4WD Ext Cab SB	8370	10210
2 Dr SLE Std Cab SB	5575	6800
2 Dr SLE 4WD Std Cab SB	7540	9195
2 Dr SLS Ext Cab SB	6005	7320
2 Dr SLS 4WD Ext Cab SB	7960	9710
2 Dr SLS Std Cab LB	5700	6950
2 Dr SLS 4WD Std Cab LB	7785	9495
2 Dr SLS Std Cab SB	5520	6730
2 Dr SLS 4WD Std Cab SB	7540	9195

OPTIONS FOR SONOMA

6 cyl 4.3 L Engine +240	
6 cyl 4.3 L CPI Engine +245	
Auto 4-Speed Transmission +300	
Highrider Suspension +515	
Highrider Suspension Pkg +515	
AM/FM Compact Disc Player +95	
Air Conditioning +245	
Anti-Lock Brakes[Opt on 2WD] +175	
Camper/Towing Package +90	
Cruise Control +65	

Model Description	Trade-in Value	Market Value
Keyless Entry System +60		
Limited Slip Diff +85		
Power Door Locks +70		
Power Windows +70		
Premium Sound System +100		
Rear Step Bumper[Opt on SL] +45		
Skid Plates +40		
Velour/Cloth Seats +65		

SUBURBAN   1995

New interior with driver airbag debuts. New dashboard features modular design with controls that are much easier to read and use. 1500 models can now be ordered with turbodiesel engine. Brake/transmission shift interlock is added to automatic transmission. Seats and door panels are revised. New console on models with bucket seats features pivoting writing surface, along with rear cupholders and storage drawer. Uplevel radios come with automatic volume controls that raise or lower the volume depending on vehicle speed.

RATINGS (SCALE OF 1-10)

Overall	Safety	Reliability	Performance	Comfort	Value
6.9	7.1	5.1	7	7.9	7.5

Category H

Model Description	Trade-in Value	Market Value
4 Dr C1500 Wgn	13280	15775
4 Dr C2500 Wgn	14005	16635
4 Dr K1500 4WD Wgn	14465	17175
4 Dr K2500 4WD Wgn	15310	18185

OPTIONS FOR SUBURBAN

8 cyl 6.5 L Turbodsl Engine +950	
8 cyl 7.4 L Engine +170	
Air Conditioning +245	
Camper/Towing Package[Std on C2500] +100	
Compact Disc W/fm/tape +95	
Cruise Control +55	
Dual Air Conditioning +385	
Keyless Entry System +50	
Leather Seats +300	
Luggage Rack +45	
Power Door Locks +55	
Power Drivers Seat +85	
Power Windows +55	
Skid Plates +30	

VANDURA/RALLY WAGON 1995

No changes.

RALLY WAGON

Category H

Model Description	Trade-in Value	Market Value
2 Dr G25 Rally Wagon	9525	11310
2 Dr G25 STX Rally Wagon	10390	12340
2 Dr G35 Rally Wagon	10175	12085
2 Dr G35 Rally Wagon Ext	10385	12330
2 Dr G35 STX Rally Wagon	10700	12710
2 Dr G35 STX Rally Wagon Ext	11225	13330

Don't forget to refer to the Mileage Adjustment Table at the back of this book!

GMC 95-94

Model Description	Trade-in Value	Market Value	Model Description	Trade-in Value	Market Value

VANDURA

Category H

Model Description	Trade-in Value	Market Value
2 Dr G15 Vandura	7890	9370
2 Dr G15 Vandura Ext	7970	9470
2 Dr G25 Vandura	7875	9355
2 Dr G25 Vandura Ext	7970	9465
2 Dr G35 Vandura	8035	9545
2 Dr G35 Vandura Ext	8995	10680

OPTIONS FOR VANDURA/RALLY WAGON

8 cyl 5.0 L Engine +180
8 cyl 5.7 L Engine[Opt on G25] +225
8 cyl 6.5 L Dsl Engine +670
8 cyl 7.4 L Engine +170
AM/FM Compact Disc Player +90
Air Conditioning[Std on STX] +245
Camper/Towing Package +100
Chrome Bumpers[Opt on G15, Vandura, Vandura Ext] +35
Cruise Control[Std on STX] +55
Dual Air Conditioning +385
Keyless Entry System +50
Limited Slip Diff +80
Power Door Locks[Std on STX] +55
Power Windows[Std on STX] +55
Premium Sound System +115

YUKON 1995

New interior with driver airbag debuts. New dashboard features modular design with controls that are much easier to read and use. New four-door model is added midyear, nicely sized between Jimmy and Suburban. New model is offered only in SLE or SLT trim with a 5.7-liter V8 and an automatic transmission in either 2WD or 4WD. Brake/transmission shift interlock is added to automatic transmission. New console on models with bucket seats features pivoting writing surface, along with rear cupholders and storage drawer.

RATINGS (SCALE OF 1-10)

Overall	Safety	Reliability	Performance	Comfort	Value
7.2	7.8	5.6	7.2	8	7.6

Category H

Model Description	Trade-in Value	Market Value
2 Dr SLE 4WD Utility	13000	15435
4 Dr SLE Wgn	13925	16540
4 Dr SLE 4WD Wgn	14785	17560
2 Dr SLT 4WD Utility	13845	16440
4 Dr SLT Wgn	14135	16785
4 Dr SLT 4WD Wgn	15215	18070
2 Dr STD 4WD Utility	12070	14335

OPTIONS FOR YUKON

8 cyl 6.5 L Turbodsl Engine +950
Auto 4-Speed Transmission[Std on Wgn] +275
Air Conditioning[Opt on STD] +245
Camper/Towing Package +100
Compact Disc W/fm/tape +95

Cruise Control[Opt on STD] +55
Keyless Entry System[Opt on SLE] +50
Power Door Locks[Opt on STD] +55
Power Drivers Seat[Opt on SLE] +85
Running Boards +105
Skid Plates +30

1994 GMC

JIMMY 1994

Side-door guard beams and a high-mounted center brake light are added. Front bench seat is now standard on four-door models.

RATINGS (SCALE OF 1-10)

Overall	Safety	Reliability	Performance	Comfort	Value
6	5.1	6.6	6.8	7.1	4.6

Category G

Model Description	Trade-in Value	Market Value
2 Dr SLE Utility	7720	9540
2 Dr SLE 4WD Utility	8360	10330
4 Dr SLE Wgn	7685	9495
4 Dr SLE 4WD Wgn	8285	10240
2 Dr SLS Utility	6640	8205
2 Dr SLS 4WD Utility	7195	8890
4 Dr SLS Wgn	6615	8170
4 Dr SLS 4WD Wgn	7610	9405
2 Dr SLT Utility	8820	10900
2 Dr SLT 4WD Utility	9795	12100
4 Dr SLT Wgn	7590	9375
4 Dr SLT 4WD Wgn	8365	10335
2 Dr STD Utility	6180	7635
2 Dr STD 4WD Utility	6915	8545
4 Dr STD Wgn	6680	8255
4 Dr STD 4WD Wgn	7660	9465

OPTIONS FOR JIMMY

6 cyl 4.3 L CPI Engine +135
Auto 4-Speed Transmission +220
AM/FM Compact Disc Player +75
Air Conditioning[Opt on SLS, STD] +200
Camper/Towing Package +70
Cruise Control[Std on SLE, SLT] +50
Keyless Entry System[Std on SLT] +50
Limited Slip Diff +70
Luggage Rack[Std on SLE, SLT] +40
Power Door Locks[Std on SLT, SLE] +55
Power Drivers Seat[Opt on SLE, SLS, STD] +70
Power Windows[Std on SLT, SLE Wgn] +60
Premium Sound System +85
Skid Plates +35

SAFARI 1994

Driver airbag is made standard. Side-door guard beams are stronger, and air conditioners use CFC-free refrigerant. A high-mount center brake light is

Don't forget to refer to the Mileage Adjustment Table at the back of this book!

GMC 94

Model Description	Trade-in Value	Market Value	Model Description	Trade-in Value	Market Value

added. Analog gauges get new graphics, and carpet is treated with Scotchgard.

RATINGS (SCALE OF 1-10)

Overall	Safety	Reliability	Performance	Comfort	Value
7	5.8	6.2	7.2	6.6	9.3

Category G

Model	Trade-in	Market
2 Dr SLE Pass. Van	6650	8220
2 Dr SLE Pass. Van Ext	6850	8465
2 Dr SLE 4WD Pass. Van Ext	7615	9410
2 Dr SLT Pass. Van	7660	9465
2 Dr SLT Pass. Van Ext	7515	9285
2 Dr SLT 4WD Pass. Van Ext	7985	9865
2 Dr SLX Pass. Van	6425	7935
2 Dr SLX 4WD Pass. Van Ext	7560	9340
2 Dr SLX Pass. Van Ext	6625	8185
2 Dr STD Cargo Van	5855	7235
2 Dr STD 4WD Cargo Van	6705	8285
2 Dr STD Cargo Van Ext	5990	7405
2 Dr STD 4WD Cargo Van Ext	6880	8500
2 Dr STD Pass. Van	6250	7725
2 Dr STD 4WD Pass. Van	7105	8780
2 Dr STD Pass. Van Ext	6365	7860
2 Dr STD 4WD Pass. Van Ext	7220	8920

OPTIONS FOR SAFARI

6 cyl 4.3 L CPI Engine[Std on 4WD] +135
AM/FM Compact Disc Player +75
Air Conditioning +200
Camper/Towing Package +70
Chrome Bumpers +35
Cruise Control[Std on SLT] +50
Dual Air Conditioning +225
Keyless Entry System +50
Limited Slip Diff +70
Luggage Rack[Std on SLT Pass. Van] +40
Power Drivers Seat +70
Power Windows[Std on SLT] +60
Premium Sound System +85

SIERRA PICKUP   1994

Grilles are restyled, side-door guard beams are added, and a third brake light is installed. Leather seats are included in new SLT package. Front seatback on Club Coupe models gets memory feature to improve entry and exit to rear seat. A 6.5-liter diesel replaces last year's 6.2-liter unit.

RATINGS (SCALE OF 1-10)

Overall	Safety	Reliability	Performance	Comfort	Value
N/A	N/A	7.3	N/A	N/A	N/A

SIERRA 1500

Category H

Model	Trade-in	Market
2 Dr C1500 SL Ext Cab LB	8805	10535
2 Dr C1500 SL Ext Cab SB	8240	9855
2 Dr C1500 SL Ext Cab Stepside SB	8440	10100
2 Dr C1500 SL Std Cab LB	7675	9180
2 Dr C1500 SL Std Cab SB	7335	8775
2 Dr C1500 SL Std Cab Stepside SB	7665	9170
2 Dr C1500 SLE Ext Cab LB	9050	10825
2 Dr C1500 SLE Ext Cab SB	8635	10330
2 Dr C1500 SLE Ext Cab Stepside SB	8835	10570
2 Dr C1500 SLE Std Cab LB	7905	9455
2 Dr C1500 SLE Std Cab SB	7765	9290
2 Dr C1500 SLE Std Cab Stepside SB	8095	9685
2 Dr C1500 SLT Ext Cab SB	10590	12670
2 Dr C1500 SLT Ext Cab Stepside SB	10790	12910
2 Dr C1500 Special Std Cab LB	6575	7865
2 Dr C1500 Special Std Cab SB	6425	7690
2 Dr K1500 4WD Ext Cab LB	9765	11685
2 Dr K1500 4WD Ext Cab SB	9385	11230
2 Dr K1500 4WD Ext Cab Stepside SB	9590	11470
2 Dr K1500 SL 4WD Std Cab LB	8690	10395
2 Dr K1500 SL 4WD Std Cab SB	8425	10080
2 Dr K1500 SL 4WD Std Cab Stepside SB	8630	10325
2 Dr K1500 SLE 4WD Ext Cab LB	10215	12220
2 Dr K1500 SLE 4WD Ext Cab SB	9925	11875
2 Dr K1500 SLE 4WD Ext Cab Stepside SB	10130	12120
2 Dr K1500 SLE 4WD Std Cab LB	9205	11015
2 Dr K1500 SLE 4WD Std Cab SB	9060	10835
2 Dr K1500 SLE 4WD Std Cab Stepside SB	9265	11085
2 Dr K1500 SLT 4WD Ext Cab SB	11725	14025
2 Dr K1500 SLT 4WD Ext Cab Stepside SB	11925	14265
2 Dr K1500 Special 4WD Std Cab LB	8100	9690
2 Dr K1500 Special 4WD Std Cab SB	7950	9515

SIERRA 2500

Category H

Model	Trade-in	Market
2 Dr C2500 SL Ext Cab LB	8740	10455
2 Dr C2500 SL Ext Cab SB	8740	10455
2 Dr C2500 SL Std Cab LB	7570	9055
2 Dr C2500 SLE Ext Cab LB	9490	11355
2 Dr C2500 SLE Ext Cab SB	9080	10865
2 Dr C2500 SLE Std Cab LB	8005	9575
2 Dr K2500 4WD Ext Cab LB	11370	13605

Don't forget to refer to the Mileage Adjustment Table at the back of this book!

Model Description	Trade-in Value	Market Value
2 Dr K2500 4WD Ext Cab SB	10845	12975
2 Dr K2500 SL 4WD Std Cab LB	8510	10180
2 Dr K2500 SLE 4WD Ext Cab LB	10165	12160
2 Dr K2500 SLE 4WD Ext Cab SB	9920	11870
2 Dr K2500 SLE 4WD Std Cab LB	8895	10645

SIERRA 3500

Category H

Model Description	Trade-in Value	Market Value
4 Dr C3500 Crew Cab LB	10330	12355
2 Dr C3500 Std Cab LB	8880	10625
2 Dr C3500 SL Ext Cab LB	10740	12850
4 Dr C3500 SLE Crew Cab LB	10450	12500
2 Dr C3500 SLE Ext Cab LB	10275	12290
2 Dr C3500 SLE Std Cab LB	9565	11445
4 Dr K3500 4WD Crew Cab LB	11820	14140
2 Dr K3500 4WD Ext Cab LB	11385	13620
2 Dr K3500 SL 4WD Std Cab LB	10420	12465
4 Dr K3500 SLE 4WD Crew Cab LB	11890	14225
2 Dr K3500 SLE 4WD Ext Cab LB	11405	13640
2 Dr K3500 SLE 4WD Std Cab LB	10220	12225

OPTIONS FOR SIERRA PICKUP
8 cyl 5.0 L Engine +145
8 cyl 5.7 L Engine +175
8 cyl 6.5 L Dsl Engine +640
8 cyl 6.5 L Turbodsl Engine +755
8 cyl 7.4 L Engine +150
Auto 4-Speed Transmission +220
Air Conditioning[Std on SLE] +200
Aluminum/Alloy Wheels +75
Bed Liner +55
Camper/Towing Package +80
Chrome Wheels +75
Cruise Control[Std on SLT] +45
Dual Rear Wheels[Opt on Crew Cab,Std Cab] +195
Limited Slip Diff +65
Locking Differential +60
Power Door Locks[Std on SLT] +45
Power Drivers Seat[Std on SLT] +70
Power Windows[Std on SLT] +45
Premium Sound System[Std on SLT] +90
Rear Step Bumper +35
Skid Plates +25

SONOMA   1994

All-new truck debuts with more powerful engines and available four-wheel ABS. Side-door guard beams are standard. Rear ABS is standard on four-cylinder models; V6 trucks get the new four-wheel ABS system that works in both two- and four-wheel drive. Highrider package is for serious off-roaders. Available only on regular-cab shortbed models, the Highrider includes four-inch wider track, three-inch height increase, off-road suspension and tires, wheel flares, and thick skid plates. Base engine is 118-horse, 2.2-liter four

cylinder. Standard on 4WD models is a 165-horsepower, 4.3-liter V6. Optional on all models is a 195-horsepower, high-output 4.3-liter V6.

RATINGS (SCALE OF 1-10)

Overall	Safety	Reliability	Performance	Comfort	Value
N/A	4.9	6.5	6.6	8.1	N/A

Category G

Model Description	Trade-in Value	Market Value
2 Dr SL Std Cab LB	4300	5310
2 Dr SL 4WD Std Cab LB	6130	7570
2 Dr SL Std Cab SB	4175	5160
2 Dr SL 4WD Std Cab SB	6005	7420
2 Dr SLE Ext Cab SB	5225	6455
2 Dr SLE 4WD Ext Cab SB	7550	9330
2 Dr SLE Std Cab LB	5290	6535
2 Dr SLE 4WD Std Cab LB	7245	8955
2 Dr SLE Std Cab SB	4825	5965
2 Dr SLS Ext Cab SB	5115	6320
2 Dr SLS 4WD Ext Cab SB	6945	8580
2 Dr SLS Std Cab SB	4720	5830
2 Dr SLS 4WD Std Cab SB	6550	8090

OPTIONS FOR SONOMA
6 cyl 4.3 L Engine +205
6 cyl 4.3 L CPI Engine +135
Auto 4-Speed Transmission +225
AM/FM Compact Disc Player +75
Air Conditioning +200
Aluminum/Alloy Wheels +80
Anti-Lock Brakes[Opt on 2WD] +140
Camper/Towing Package +70
Cruise Control +50
Limited Slip Diff +70
Power Door Locks +55
Power Windows +60
Premium Sound System +85
Skid Plates +35

SUBURBAN   1994

Side-door guard beams are added, as well as a high-mounted center brake light. A turbocharged diesel is newly optional on 2500 models. A new grille appears.

RATINGS (SCALE OF 1-10)

Overall	Safety	Reliability	Performance	Comfort	Value
6.8	6.6	6.7	7	7.5	6.3

Category H

Model Description	Trade-in Value	Market Value
4 Dr C1500 Wgn	11240	13450
4 Dr C2500 Wgn	11835	14160
4 Dr K1500 4WD Wgn	12630	15115
4 Dr K2500 4WD Wgn	13020	15580

OPTIONS FOR SUBURBAN
8 cyl 6.5 L Turbodsl Engine +755
8 cyl 7.4 L Engine +150
SLE Decor Group +445

Don't forget to refer to the Mileage Adjustment Table at the back of this book!

GMC 94-93

Model Description	Trade-in Value	Market Value	Model Description	Trade-in Value	Market Value

AM/FM Stereo Tape +50
Air Conditioning +200
Camper/Towing Package +80
Cruise Control +45
Dual Air Conditioning +315
Leather Seats +245
Limited Slip Diff +65
Luggage Rack +40
Power Door Locks +45
Power Drivers Seat +70
Power Mirrors +25
Power Windows +45
Premium Sound System +90
Skid Plates +25

VANDURA/RALLY WAGON 1994

Driver airbag is added to all models under 8,500-lb. GVWR. Side-door guard beams are installed in front doors and a high-mounted center brake light is added.

RALLY WAGON

Category H

Model	Trade-in	Market
2 Dr G25 Rally Wagon	8065	9645
2 Dr G25 STX Rally Wagon	8865	10605
2 Dr G35 Rally Wagon	8535	10210
2 Dr G35 Rally Wagon Ext	8725	10435

VANDURA

Category H

Model	Trade-in	Market
2 Dr G15 Vandura	6760	8090
2 Dr G15 Vandura Ext	6835	8175
2 Dr G25 Vandura	6655	7960
2 Dr G25 Vandura Ext	6830	8170
2 Dr G35 Vandura	6855	8200
2 Dr G35 Vandura Ext	7720	9235

OPTIONS FOR VANDURA/RALLY WAGON
8 cyl 5.0 L Engine +145
8 cyl 5.7 L Engine[Opt on G25, Vandura] +175
8 cyl 6.2 L Turbodsl Engine +405
8 cyl 6.5 L Dsl Engine +640
8 cyl 7.4 L Engine +150
AM/FM Compact Disc Player +75
Air Conditioning[Std on STX] +200
Camper/Towing Package +80
Captain Chairs (2)[Std on STX] +130
Chrome Bumpers[Opt on G15, Vandura, Vandura Ext] +30
Cruise Control +45
Dual Air Conditioning +315
Keyless Entry System +45
Leather Seats +245
Limited Slip Diff +65
Power Door Locks +45
Power Windows +45
Premium Sound System +90

YUKON 1994

Air conditioning receives CFC-free coolant. Side-door guard beams are added. A new grille appears, and models equipped with a decor package get composite headlamps. A turbocharged diesel is newly optional. Third brake light is added.

Category H

Model	Trade-in	Market
2 Dr SLE 4WD Utility	10165	12160
2 Dr STD 4WD Utility	10545	12620
2 Dr Sport 4WD Utility	11880	14215

OPTIONS FOR YUKON
8 cyl 6.5 L Turbodsl Engine +755
Auto 4-Speed Transmission +215
AM/FM Stereo Tape[Std on Sport] +50
Air Conditioning[Std on Sport] +200
Camper/Towing Package +80
Cruise Control[Std on Sport] +45
Luggage Rack +40
Power Door Locks[Std on Sport] +45
Power Drivers Seat +70
Power Windows[Std on Sport] +45
Premium Sound System +90
Skid Plates +25
Tilt Steering Wheel[Std on Sport] +45

1993 GMC

JIMMY 1993

Two-door model available in SLT trim. Four-door models get monochromatic paint scheme in SLS trim. V6 engines get internal balance shaft designed to reduce vibration. Automatic transmission receives electronic shift controls and second-gear start feature. Manual lumbar adjusters are newly standard on front seats. Typhoon can be ordered in white as well as black.

RATINGS (SCALE OF 1-10)

Overall	Safety	Reliability	Performance	Comfort	Value
5.9	5.1	6.1	6.8	7.1	4.3

Category G

Model	Trade-in	Market
2 Dr SLE Utility	6170	7855
2 Dr SLE 4WD Utility	6865	8745
4 Dr SLE Wgn	5625	7165
4 Dr SLE 4WD Wgn	6405	8160
2 Dr SLS Utility	5705	7265
2 Dr SLS 4WD Utility	6345	8085
4 Dr SLS 4WD Wgn	6670	8495
2 Dr SLT Utility	7080	9020
2 Dr SLT 4WD Utility	7880	10035
4 Dr SLT Wgn	6980	8890
4 Dr SLT 4WD Wgn	7155	9115

Model Description	Trade-in Value	Market Value
2 Dr STD Utility	5290	6740
2 Dr STD 4WD Utility	5935	7560

OPTIONS FOR JIMMY

6 cyl 4.3 L CPI Engine +100
Auto 4-Speed Transmission +180
AM/FM Compact Disc Player +65
Air Conditioning[Std on SLE Wgn] +165
Aluminum/Alloy Wheels[Opt on SLE,STD] +65
Camper/Towing Package +60
Cruise Control[Std on SLT Wgn] +40
Keyless Entry System[Std on SLT Wgn] +40
Leather Seats[Std on SLT] +155
Limited Slip Diff +55
Luggage Rack[Std on SLT Wgn] +30
Power Door Locks[Std on SLT Wgn] +45
Power Drivers Seat[Std on SLT] +55
Power Windows[Std on SLT Wgn] +50
Premium Sound System +70

SAFARI 1993

Base 4.3-liter V6 gets 15 additional horsepower. Automatic transmission gets electronic shift controls and second-gear start feature. New speedometer reads to 100 mph. Driver airbag is offered as an option midyear.

RATINGS (SCALE OF 1-10)

Overall	Safety	Reliability	Performance	Comfort	Value
6.6	4	6.3	7.2	6.6	9.1

Category G

2 Dr GT Sport Pass. Van Ext	5190	6610
2 Dr SLE Pass. Van	5225	6655
2 Dr SLE 4WD Pass. Van	5920	7540
2 Dr SLE 4WD Pass. Van Ext	6020	7670
2 Dr SLE Pass. Van Ext	5345	6805
2 Dr SLT Pass. Van	5750	7325
2 Dr SLT 4WD Pass. Van	6105	7775
2 Dr SLT Pass. Van Ext	5870	7475
2 Dr SLT 4WD Pass. Van Ext	6200	7895
2 Dr STD Cargo Van	4580	5835
2 Dr STD Cargo Van Ext	4780	6090
2 Dr STD 4WD Cargo Van Ext	5465	6960
2 Dr STD Pass. Van	4900	6240
2 Dr STD 4WD Pass. Van	5595	7125
2 Dr STD Pass. Van Ext	5015	6390
2 Dr STD 4WD Pass. Van Ext	5695	7255

OPTIONS FOR SAFARI

6 cyl 4.3 L CPI Engine[Std on 4WD] +100
AM/FM Compact Disc Player +65
Air Bag Restraint[Std on Cargo Van Ext] +100
Air Conditioning +165
Aluminum/Alloy Wheels +65
Camper/Towing Package +60
Chrome Bumpers +30

Cruise Control +40
Dual Air Conditioning +185
Limited Slip Diff +55
Luggage Rack +30
Power Door Locks +45
Power Drivers Seat +55
Power Windows +50
Premium Sound System +70

SIERRA PICKUP 1993

Solar-Ray tinted glass is made standard. Cloth interior surfaces are now protected by Scotchgard fabric protection. Automatic transmissions get electronic shift controls. Base V6 gets five additional horsepower.

RATINGS (SCALE OF 1-10)

Overall	Safety	Reliability	Performance	Comfort	Value
N/A	N/A	7.4	N/A	N/A	N/A

SIERRA 1500

Category H

2 Dr C1500 Ext Cab LB	7290	8870
2 Dr C1500 Ext Cab SB	7155	8705
2 Dr C1500 Ext Cab Stepside SB	7335	8925
2 Dr C1500 Std Cab LB	6595	8025
2 Dr C1500 Std Cab SB	6460	7865
2 Dr C1500 Std Cab Stepside SB	6640	8080
2 Dr C1500 SLE Ext Cab LB	7650	9310
2 Dr C1500 SLE Ext Cab SB	7515	9145
2 Dr C1500 SLE Ext Cab Stepside SB	7695	9365
2 Dr C1500 SLE Std Cab LB	6955	8460
2 Dr C1500 SLE Std Cab SB	6820	8295
2 Dr C1500 SLE Std Cab Stepside SB	6995	8515
2 Dr C1500 SLX Ext Cab LB	7500	9130
2 Dr C1500 SLX Ext Cab SB	7365	8965
2 Dr C1500 SLX Ext Cab Stepside SB	7545	9180
2 Dr C1500 SLX Std Cab SB	6640	8080
2 Dr C1500 Special Std Cab LB	5310	6465
2 Dr K1500 4WD Ext Cab LB	8300	10100
2 Dr K1500 4WD Ext Cab SB	8165	9935
2 Dr K1500 4WD Std Cab LB	7605	9255
2 Dr K1500 4WD Std Cab SB	7470	9090
2 Dr K1500 SLE 4WD Ext Cab LB	8660	10540
2 Dr K1500 SLE 4WD Ext Cab SB	8525	10375
2 Dr K1500 SLE 4WD Ext Cab Stepside SB	8705	10595
2 Dr K1500 SLE 4WD Std Cab LB	8110	9870
2 Dr K1500 SLE 4WD Std Cab SB	7980	9705
2 Dr K1500 SLE 4WD Std Cab Stepside SB	8160	9930

Model Description	Trade-in Value	Market Value
2 Dr K1500 SLX 4WD Ext Cab LB	8510	10355
2 Dr K1500 SLX 4WD Ext Cab SB	8375	10195
2 Dr K1500 Special 4WD Std Cab LB		
	6760	8225
2 Dr K1500 Sport 4WD Std Cab SB		
	7820	9515
2 Dr STD 4WD Std Cab Stepside SB		
	7470	9090

SIERRA 2500
Category H

Model Description	Trade-in Value	Market Value
2 Dr C2500 Ext Cab LB	7680	9345
2 Dr C2500 Ext Cab SB	7680	9345
2 Dr C2500 Std Cab LB	6865	8355
2 Dr C2500 SLE Ext Cab LB	7520	9155
2 Dr C2500 SLE Ext Cab SB	7520	9155
2 Dr C2500 SLE Std Cab LB	6750	8215
2 Dr C2500 SLX Ext Cab LB	7945	9670
2 Dr C2500 SLX Ext Cab SB	7820	9515
2 Dr C2500 SLX Std Cab LB	7065	8595
2 Dr K2500 4WD Ext Cab LB	8450	10280
2 Dr K2500 4WD Ext Cab SB	8450	10280
2 Dr K2500 4WD Std Cab LB	7705	9375
2 Dr K2500 SLE 4WD Ext Cab LB	8245	10030
2 Dr K2500 SLE 4WD Ext Cab SB	8245	10030
2 Dr K2500 SLE 4WD Std Cab LB	8380	10195
2 Dr K2500 SLX 4WD Ext Cab LB	8665	10540
2 Dr K2500 SLX 4WD Ext Cab SB	8665	10540
2 Dr K2500 SLX 4WD Std Cab LB	7970	9695

SIERRA 3500
Category H

Model Description	Trade-in Value	Market Value
4 Dr C3500 Crew Cab LB	8895	10825
2 Dr C3500 Ext Cab LB	8750	10645
2 Dr C3500 Std Cab LB	7965	9695
4 Dr C3500 SLE Crew Cab LB	8680	10560
2 Dr C3500 SLE Ext Cab LB	8585	10445
2 Dr C3500 SLE Std Cab LB	8340	10150
2 Dr C3500 SLX Ext Cab LB	8970	10915
2 Dr C3500 SLX Std Cab LB	8245	10030
4 Dr K3500 4WD Crew Cab LB	10245	12465
2 Dr K3500 4WD Ext Cab LB	9825	11955
2 Dr K3500 4WD Std Cab LB	9020	10975
4 Dr K3500 SLE 4WD Crew Cab LB		
	9810	11940
2 Dr K3500 SLE 4WD Ext Cab LB	9410	11455
2 Dr K3500 SLE 4WD Std Cab LB	8680	10560
2 Dr K3500 SLX 4WD Ext Cab LB	9890	12035
2 Dr K3500 SLX 4WD Std Cab LB	9295	11315

OPTIONS FOR SIERRA PICKUP
8 cyl 5.0 L Engine +120
8 cyl 5.7 L Engine +165
8 cyl 6.2 L Dsl Engine +425
8 cyl 6.5 L Turbodsl Engine +570
8 cyl 7.4 L Engine +170
Auto 4-Speed Transmission +175
SLE Decor Pkg +160
Sport Handling Pkg +170
AM/FM Stereo Tape +40
Air Conditioning[Std on SL] +165
Aluminum/Alloy Wheels +60
Bed Liner +45
Camper/Towing Package +65
Cruise Control +40
Dual Rear Wheels +160
Locking Differential +50
Power Door Locks +40
Power Drivers Seat +55
Power Windows +40
Premium Sound System +75
Rear Step Bumper +30

SONOMA   1993

V6 engines get internal balance shaft designed to reduce vibration. Automatic transmission gets electronic shift controls. Syclone dropped.

RATINGS (SCALE OF 1-10)

Overall	Safety	Reliability	Performance	Comfort	Value
N/A	3.2	6.6	7.2	7	N/A

Category G

Model Description	Trade-in Value	Market Value
2 Dr SLE Ext Cab SB	4325	5510
2 Dr SLE 4WD Ext Cab SB	5550	7070
2 Dr SLE Std Cab LB	3935	5015
2 Dr SLE 4WD Std Cab LB	5060	6445
2 Dr SLE Std Cab SB	3835	4885
2 Dr SLE 4WD Std Cab SB	5060	6445
2 Dr SLS Ext Cab SB	4275	5445
2 Dr SLS 4WD Ext Cab SB	5505	7015
2 Dr SLS Std Cab LB	3835	4885
2 Dr SLS 4WD Std Cab LB	4915	6260
2 Dr SLS Std Cab SB	3735	4755
2 Dr SLS 4WD Std Cab SB	4915	6260
2 Dr STD Ext Cab SB	4120	5245
2 Dr STD 4WD Ext Cab SB	5310	6765
2 Dr STD Std Cab LB	3415	4350
2 Dr STD 4WD Std Cab LB	4810	6125
2 Dr STD Std Cab SB	3615	4605
2 Dr STD 4WD Std Cab SB	4810	6125
2 Dr Special Std Cab SB	3110	3960
2 Dr Special 4WD Std Cab SB	4380	5580

OPTIONS FOR SONOMA
6 cyl 2.8 L Engine +80
6 cyl 4.3 L Engine +125
6 cyl 4.3 L CPI Engine +100
Auto 4-Speed Transmission +175
AM/FM Stereo[Opt on Special] +40
AM/FM Stereo Tape +45

Don't forget to refer to the Mileage Adjustment Table at the back of this book!

Model Description	Trade-in Value	Market Value
Air Conditioning +165		
Aluminum/Alloy Wheels +65		
Cruise Control +40		
Power Mirrors[Std on SLE] +25		
Power Steering[Opt on 2WD] +55		
Tilt Steering Wheel +35		

SUBURBAN 1993

No changes.

RATINGS (SCALE OF 1-10)

Overall	Safety	Reliability	Performance	Comfort	Value
7	6.8	6.9	7	7.5	6.7

Category H

Model Description	Trade-in Value	Market Value
4 Dr C1500 Wgn	9460	11515
4 Dr C2500 Wgn	9905	12050
4 Dr K1500 4WD Wgn	10370	12615
4 Dr K2500 4WD Wgn	10935	13305

OPTIONS FOR SUBURBAN

8 cyl 7.4 L Engine +170
SLE Pkg +265
AM/FM Stereo Tape +40
Air Conditioning +165
Aluminum/Alloy Wheels +60
Camper/Towing Package +65
Cruise Control +40
Dual Air Conditioning +255
Leather Seats +200
Luggage Rack +30
Power Door Locks +40
Power Drivers Seat +55
Power Passenger Seat +50
Power Windows +40
Premium Sound System +75

TYPHOON 1993

Typhoon can be ordered in white as well as black.

Category I

Model Description	Trade-in Value	Market Value
2 Dr STD Turbo 4WD Utility	10490	12480

OPTIONS FOR TYPHOON

AM/FM Compact Disc Player +25
Luggage Rack +25

VANDURA/RALLY WAGON 1993

Solar-Ray tinted glass and Scotchgard fabric protectant are both standard. Four-wheel ABS is a new standard feature. Remote keyless entry joins the options list.

RALLY WAGON

Category H

Model Description	Trade-in Value	Market Value
2 Dr G15 Rally Wagon	5910	7195
2 Dr G15 Rally Wagon Ext	6155	7485
2 Dr G15 STX Rally Wagon	6200	7545
2 Dr G25 Rally Wagon Ext	6220	7565
2 Dr G25 STX Rally Wagon Ext	6505	7920
2 Dr G35 Dsl Rally Wagon	6910	8410
2 Dr G35 Rally Wagon Ext	6890	8385
2 Dr G35 STX Rally Wagon	6935	8435

VANDURA

Category H

Model Description	Trade-in Value	Market Value
2 Dr G15 Vandura	5630	6850
2 Dr G15 Vandura Ext	5695	6930
2 Dr G25 Vandura	5675	6905
2 Dr G25 Vandura Ext	5745	6995
2 Dr G35 Vandura	5770	7020
2 Dr G35 Vandura Ext	6685	8135

OPTIONS FOR VANDURA/RALLY WAGON

8 cyl 5.0 L Engine +120
8 cyl 5.7 L Engine[Std on G35] +165
8 cyl 6.2 L Dsl Engine +425
8 cyl 7.4 L Engine +170
AM/FM Compact Disc Player +60
Air Conditioning +165
Aluminum/Alloy Wheels +60
Camper/Towing Package +65
Cruise Control +40
Dual Air Conditioning +255
Keyless Entry System +35
Power Door Locks +40
Power Windows +40
Premium Sound System +75

YUKON 1993

No changes.

Category H

Model Description	Trade-in Value	Market Value
2 Dr SLE 4WD Utility	9295	11315
2 Dr STD 4WD Utility	9580	11655
2 Dr Sport GT 4WD Utility	10625	12930

OPTIONS FOR YUKON

Auto 4-Speed Transmission +175
AM/FM Stereo Tape[Opt on STD] +40
Air Conditioning[Opt on STD] +165
Aluminum/Alloy Wheels[Opt on STD] +60
Camper/Towing Package +65
Cruise Control[Opt on STD] +40
Luggage Rack +30
Power Door Locks +40
Power Drivers Seat +55
Power Windows +40
Premium Sound System +75

1992 GMC

JIMMY 1992

Four-wheel ABS is standard on all models. Electronic-shift transfer case is added to options list; comes standard with SLT trim. A high-performance, 4.3-liter V6 debuts with 40 additional horsepower, bringing total output to 200 ponies. Bucket seats are redesigned, a

GMC 92

Model Description	Trade-in Value	Market Value	Model Description	Trade-in Value	Market Value

new speedometer is installed, and a four-spoke steering wheel is added.

RATINGS (SCALE OF 1-10)

Overall	Safety	Reliability	Performance	Comfort	Value
5.8	3.9	6.2	6.8	7.1	4.9

Category G

	Trade-in	Market
2 Dr SLE Utility	5200	6785
2 Dr SLE 4WD Utility	5760	7515
4 Dr SLE Wgn	5175	6750
4 Dr SLE 4WD Wgn	6140	8015
4 Dr SLT Wgn	5285	6900
4 Dr SLT 4WD Wgn	6665	8695
2 Dr STD Utility	4780	6240
2 Dr STD 4WD Utility	5330	6955
4 Dr STD Wgn	5235	6830
4 Dr STD 4WD Wgn	5935	7740

OPTIONS FOR JIMMY

Auto 4-Speed Transmission +150
Air Conditioning +135
Camper/Towing Package +50
Cruise Control +35
Leather Seats +130
Limited Slip Diff +45
Power Door Locks +40
Power Windows +40

SAFARI   1992

Dutch rear door treatment is available. With Dutch doors, a rear washer/wiper and rear defogger can be ordered. All-wheel-drive models get high-output, 200-horsepower V6 standard. Engine is optional on 2WD models.

RATINGS (SCALE OF 1-10)

Overall	Safety	Reliability	Performance	Comfort	Value
6.5	4.1	6.6	7.2	6.6	8.1

Category G

	Trade-in	Market
2 Dr SLE Pass. Van	4640	6055
2 Dr SLE 4WD Pass. Van	5210	6795
2 Dr SLE Pass. Van Ext	4830	6300
2 Dr SLT Pass. Van	4650	6065
2 Dr SLT 4WD Pass. Van	5215	6805
2 Dr SLT Pass. Van Ext	4830	6305
2 Dr SLT 4WD Pass. Van Ext	6025	7860
2 Dr STD Cargo Van	3980	5190
2 Dr STD Cargo Van Ext	4160	5430
2 Dr STD 4WD Cargo Van Ext	4860	6340
2 Dr STD Pass. Van	3980	5190
2 Dr STD 4WD Pass. Van	4910	6405
2 Dr STD Pass. Van Ext	4530	5910
2 Dr STD 4WD Pass. Van Ext	5085	6635

OPTIONS FOR SAFARI

6 cyl 4.3 L CPI Engine[Std on 4WD] +70
Air Conditioning +135
Camper/Towing Package +50
Cruise Control +35
Dual Air Conditioning +150
Power Door Locks +40
Power Drivers Seat +45
Power Windows +40

SIERRA PICKUP   1992

Extended-cab models get Sportside box option. Crew Cab model is all-new, sporting same engineering and styling as rest of Sierra line. Front buckets have been redesigned. Standard gauge cluster is restyled. Integral head restraints are added for outboard passengers. A new turbocharged, 6.5-liter diesel V8 is optional in C/K 2500 and regular-cab C/K 3500 models. Four-speed manual transmission is dropped.

RATINGS (SCALE OF 1-10)

Overall	Safety	Reliability	Performance	Comfort	Value
N/A	N/A	6.8	N/A	N/A	N/A

SIERRA 1500

Category H

	Trade-in	Market
2 Dr C1500 Ext Cab LB	5225	6480
2 Dr C1500 Ext Cab SB	5120	6350
2 Dr C1500 Ext Cab Stepside SB	5260	6525
2 Dr C1500 Std Cab LB	4890	6070
2 Dr C1500 Std Cab SB	4785	5940
2 Dr C1500 SLE Ext Cab LB	5500	6825
2 Dr C1500 SLE Ext Cab SB	5430	6735
2 Dr C1500 SLE Ext Cab Stepside SB	5570	6910
2 Dr C1500 SLE Std Cab LB	5190	6440
2 Dr C1500 SLE Std Cab SB	5085	6310
2 Dr C1500 SLE Std Cab Stepside SB	5225	6480
2 Dr C1500 SLX Ext Cab LB	5455	6770
2 Dr C1500 SLX Ext Cab SB	5350	6640
2 Dr C1500 SLX Ext Cab Stepside SB	5490	6815
2 Dr C1500 SLX Std Cab LB	5115	6350
2 Dr C1500 SLX Std Cab SB	5025	6235
2 Dr C1500 SLX Std Cab Stepside SB	5165	6410
2 Dr C1500 Special Std Cab LB	3915	4855
2 Dr K1500 4WD Ext Cab LB	6010	7460
2 Dr K1500 4WD Ext Cab SB	5905	7330
2 Dr K1500 4WD Ext Cab Stepside SB	6045	7500
2 Dr K1500 4WD Std Cab LB	5680	7045
2 Dr K1500 4WD Std Cab SB	5575	6915

Model Description	Trade-in Value	Market Value
2 Dr K1500 4WD Std Cab Stepside SB	5710	7090
2 Dr K1500 SLE 4WD Ext Cab LB	6315	7835
2 Dr K1500 SLE 4WD Ext Cab SB	6210	7705
2 Dr K1500 SLE 4WD Ext Cab Stepside SB	6350	7880
2 Dr K1500 SLE 4WD Std Cab LB	5975	7415
2 Dr K1500 SLE 4WD Std Cab SB	5870	7285
2 Dr K1500 SLE 4WD Std Cab Stepside SB	6010	7460
2 Dr K1500 SLX 4WD Ext Cab LB	6245	7750
2 Dr K1500 SLX 4WD Ext Cab SB	6140	7620
2 Dr K1500 SLX 4WD Ext Cab Stepside SB	6280	7790
2 Dr K1500 SLX 4WD Std Cab LB	5915	7340
2 Dr K1500 SLX 4WD Std Cab SB	5810	7210
2 Dr K1500 SLX 4WD Std Cab Stepside SB	5950	7385
2 Dr K1500 Special 4WD Std Cab LB	4970	6165

SIERRA 2500

Category H

Model Description	Trade-in Value	Market Value
2 Dr C2500 Ext Cab LB	5640	6995
2 Dr C2500 Ext Cab SB	5540	6875
2 Dr C2500 Std Cab LB	5070	6295
2 Dr C2500 SLE Ext Cab LB	5800	7200
2 Dr C2500 SLE Ext Cab SB	5800	7200
2 Dr C2500 SLE Std Cab LB	5410	6710
2 Dr C2500 SLX Ext Cab LB	5805	7200
2 Dr C2500 SLX Ext Cab SB	5705	7080
2 Dr C2500 SLX Std Cab LB	5355	6650
2 Dr K2500 4WD Ext Cab LB	6050	7510
2 Dr K2500 4WD Ext Cab SB	6050	7510
2 Dr K2500 4WD Std Cab LB	5685	7055
2 Dr K2500 SLE 4WD Ext Cab LB	6395	7935
2 Dr K2500 SLE 4WD Ext Cab SB	6395	7935
2 Dr K2500 SLE 4WD Std Cab LB	6020	7470
2 Dr K2500 SLX 4WD Ext Cab LB	6250	7755
2 Dr K2500 SLX 4WD Ext Cab SB	6250	7755
2 Dr K2500 SLX 4WD Std Cab LB	5920	7350

SIERRA 3500

Category H

Model Description	Trade-in Value	Market Value
4 Dr C3500 Crew Cab LB	6240	7745
2 Dr C3500 Ext Cab LB	5985	7425
2 Dr C3500 Std Cab LB	5615	6970
2 Dr C3500 SLE Ext Cab LB	6265	7775
2 Dr C3500 SLE Std Cab LB	5945	7375
2 Dr C3500 SLX Ext Cab LB	6145	7630
2 Dr C3500 SLX Std Cab LB	5820	7220
4 Dr K3500 4WD Crew Cab LB	6965	8645
2 Dr K3500 4WD Ext Cab LB	6715	8330
2 Dr K3500 4WD Std Cab LB	6350	7880
4 Dr K3500 SLE 4WD Crew Cab LB	7305	9065
2 Dr K3500 SLE 4WD Ext Cab LB	6755	8380
2 Dr K3500 SLE 4WD Std Cab LB	6735	8360
2 Dr K3500 SLX 4WD Ext Cab LB	6910	8575
2 Dr K3500 SLX 4WD Std Cab LB	6585	8170

OPTIONS FOR SIERRA PICKUP

8 cyl 5.0 L Engine +95
8 cyl 5.7 L Engine +135
8 cyl 6.2 L Dsl Engine +350
8 cyl 6.5 L Turbodsl Engine +460
8 cyl 7.4 L Engine +130
Auto 4-Speed Transmission +145
SLE Pkg +150
Sport Handling Pkg +140
Air Conditioning +135
Camper/Towing Package +55
Cruise Control +30
Dual Rear Wheels +130
Limited Slip Diff +45
Power Door Locks +30
Power Windows +30

SONOMA   1992

New GT model debuts, available on regular-cab shortbed 2WD models and including many Syclone styling cues along with high-output, 4.3-liter V6. Front bucket seats are redesigned, integral head restraints are added, and Club Coupes may be equipped with leather seats. New speedometer and four-spoke steering wheel are installed. Premium sound system with CD player is added to options list. Four-wheel-drive models can be equipped with an electronic-shift transfer case.

RATINGS (SCALE OF 1-10)

Overall	Safety	Reliability	Performance	Comfort	Value
N/A	3	6.6	7.2	7	N/A

Category G

Model Description	Trade-in Value	Market Value
2 Dr GT Std Cab SB	5050	6585
2 Dr SLE Ext Cab SB	3965	5175
2 Dr SLE 4WD Ext Cab SB	4970	6485
2 Dr SLE Std Cab LB	3390	4420
2 Dr SLE 4WD Std Cab LB	4395	5735
2 Dr SLE Std Cab SB	3390	4420
2 Dr SLE 4WD Std Cab SB	4395	5735
2 Dr STD Ext Cab SB	3620	4725
2 Dr STD 4WD Ext Cab SB	4700	6130
2 Dr STD Std Cab LB	3170	4135
2 Dr STD 4WD Std Cab LB	4250	5545
2 Dr STD Std Cab SB	3170	4135
2 Dr STD 4WD Std Cab SB	4250	5545
2 Dr Special Std Cab SB	2785	3635

Don't forget to refer to the Mileage Adjustment Table at the back of this book!

EDMUNDS® USED CARS & TRUCKS   www.edmunds.com   265

Model Description	Trade-in Value	Market Value
2 Dr Special 4WD Std Cab SB	3860	5040
2 Dr Syclone Turbo 4WD Std Cab SB	7950	10370

OPTIONS FOR SONOMA
6 cyl 2.8 L Engine +65
6 cyl 4.3 L Engine +100
Auto 4-Speed Transmission[Std on GT,Syclone] +145
Air Conditioning[Std on GT] +135
Camper/Towing Package +50
Cruise Control[Opt on SLE,STD] +35
Limited Slip Diff[Opt on SLE,STD] +45
Power Door Locks[Opt on SLE,STD] +40
Power Windows[Opt on SLE,STD] +40

SUBURBAN   1992

All-new design debuts based on platform and styling of Sierra. Cargo space and towing capacity are up. ABS works on all four wheels even in 4WD. Tailgate glass is lifted up instead of powered down. No diesel is offered. GM's Instatrac 4WD system is standard on K models.

RATINGS (SCALE OF 1-10)

Overall	Safety	Reliability	Performance	Comfort	Value
6.8	6.6	6.3	7	7.5	6.6

Category H

	Trade-in	Market
4 Dr C1500 Wgn	6825	8470
4 Dr C2500 Wgn	7265	9015
4 Dr K1500 4WD Wgn	7300	9060
4 Dr K2500 4WD Wgn	7720	9580

OPTIONS FOR SUBURBAN
8 cyl 7.4 L Engine +130
SLE Pkg +320
Air Conditioning +135
Camper/Towing Package +55
Cruise Control +30
Dual Air Conditioning +210
Limited Slip Diff +45
Power Door Locks +30
Power Drivers Seat +45
Power Windows +30

TYPHOON   1992

Typhoon blows into town, featuring Syclone powertrain wrapped in two-door Jimmy body.

Category I

	Trade-in	Market
2 Dr STD Turbo 4WD Utility	8320	9905

OPTIONS FOR TYPHOON
Ground Effects Package +30

VANDURA / RALLY WAGON 1992

Minor suspension modifications improve the ride.

RALLY WAGON

Category H

Model Description	Trade-in Value	Market Value
2 Dr G15 Rally Wagon	4915	6100
2 Dr G15 Rally Wagon Ext	5190	6445
2 Dr G15 STX Rally Wagon	5155	6395
2 Dr G25 Rally Wagon Ext	5245	6510
2 Dr G25 STX Rally Wagon Ext	5485	6810
2 Dr G35 Dsl Rally Wagon	5730	7115
2 Dr G35 Rally Wagon Ext	5740	7125
2 Dr G35 STX Dsl Rally Wagon	5955	7390
2 Dr G35 STX Rally Wagon Ext	5980	7420

VANDURA

Category H

	Trade-in	Market
2 Dr G15 Vandura	4405	5465
2 Dr G15 Vandura Ext	4520	5610
2 Dr G25 Vandura	4470	5545
2 Dr G25 Vandura Ext	4555	5655
2 Dr G35 Vandura	4485	5570
2 Dr G35 Vandura Ext	5275	6550

OPTIONS FOR VANDURA/RALLY WAGON
8 cyl 5.0 L Engine +95
8 cyl 5.7 L Engine[Opt on G15,G25, Vandura] +135
8 cyl 6.2 L Dsl Engine +350
8 cyl 7.4 L Engine +130
Air Conditioning +135
Camper/Towing Package +55
Cruise Control +30
Dual Air Conditioning +210
Limited Slip Diff +45
Power Door Locks +30
Power Windows +30

YUKON   1992

Totally redesigned and based on same platform and sheetmetal as Sierra pickup, the old Jimmy becomes the Yukon to differentiate it from the Sonoma-based Jimmy. Six-passenger seating is standard. Cargo area gets fixed metal roof rather than fiberglass shell. Four-wheel ABS is standard and works in 4WD. New Sport appearance package includes two-tone paint and wheelwell flares. Diesel option is dropped. Five-speed manual is standard transmission. An automatic is optional. Shift-on-the-fly 4WD is standard.

Category H

	Trade-in	Market
2 Dr SLE 4WD Utility	7510	9320
2 Dr STD 4WD Utility	7375	9150
2 Dr Sport 4WD Utility	7625	9460

OPTIONS FOR YUKON
Auto 4-Speed Transmission +145
SLE Pkg +195
Sport Handling Pkg +260
Air Conditioning +135
Camper/Towing Package +55
Cruise Control +30

Model Description	Trade-in Value	Market Value
Limited Slip Diff +45		
Power Door Locks +30		
Power Drivers Seat +45		
Power Windows +30		

1991 GMC

JIMMY 1991

Throttle-body fuel injection is improved, and more powerful alternator is standard.

Category H

Model	Trade-in	Market
2 Dr STD 4WD Utility	5675	7165

OPTIONS FOR JIMMY

8 cyl 6.2 L Dsl Engine +315
Auto 4-Speed Transmission +115
Air Conditioning +110
Camper/Towing Package +45
Cruise Control +25
Limited Slip Diff +35
Power Door Locks +25
Power Windows +25

R35 PICKUP 1991

Category H

Model	Trade-in	Market
4 Dr SLE Crew Cab LB	5320	6720
4 Dr STD Crew Cab LB	5040	6365

OPTIONS FOR R35 PICKUP

8 cyl 6.2 L Dsl Engine +315
8 cyl 7.4 L Engine +115
Auto 4-Speed Transmission +115
Air Conditioning +110
Cruise Control +25
Dual Rear Wheels +105
Power Door Locks +25
Power Windows +25

S15 JIMMY 1991

Four-door models get new Gypsy package on the options list. It includes two-tone paint, alloy wheels and chrome trim. A heavy-duty battery is standard on all models, and 2WD Jimmys can be equipped with 15-inch alloy wheels. Front bench seat option will give four-door six passenger capacity. SLT Touring Package with softer suspension added midyear.

RATINGS (SCALE OF 1-10)

Overall	Safety	Reliability	Performance	Comfort	Value
5.5	3.7	5.4	6.8	7.1	4.3

Category G

Model	Trade-in	Market
2 Dr SLE Utility	4005	5355
2 Dr SLE 4WD Utility	4445	5940
4 Dr SLE 4WD Wgn	4190	5600
2 Dr SLS Utility	3640	4865
2 Dr SLS 4WD Utility	3985	5325
4 Dr SLS Wgn	3895	5205
4 Dr SLS 4WD Wgn	4400	5880
4 Dr SLT 4WD Wgn	4670	6245
2 Dr STD Utility	3340	4465
2 Dr STD 4WD Utility	3745	5010
4 Dr STD Wgn	3635	4855
4 Dr STD 4WD Wgn	4130	5520

OPTIONS FOR S15 JIMMY

Auto 4-Speed Transmission +115
Air Conditioning[Std on SLT] +110
Camper/Towing Package +40
Cruise Control[Std on SLT] +30
Limited Slip Diff +35
Power Door Locks[Std on SLT] +30
Power Windows[Std on SLT] +30

SAFARI 1991

Cargo models gain the 4.3-liter V6 as standard equipment. A new GT model is available with sport suspension, rally wheels, front air dam, fog lights, and a sport steering wheel. Side and rear windows now have swing-out glass. Extended-length models can now be ordered with the Sport Appearance Package. A high-output, 4.3-liter V6 option is expected midyear.

RATINGS (SCALE OF 1-10)

Overall	Safety	Reliability	Performance	Comfort	Value
6.3	3.9	6.2	7.2	6.6	7.7

Category G

Model	Trade-in	Market
2 Dr SLE Pass. Van	4035	5395
2 Dr SLE 4WD Pass. Van	4540	6065
2 Dr SLE Pass. Van Ext	4205	5620
2 Dr SLE 4WD Pass. Van Ext	4800	6410
2 Dr SLT Pass. Van	4155	5555
2 Dr SLT 4WD Pass. Van	4655	6225
2 Dr SLT Pass. Van Ext	4320	5775
2 Dr SLT 4WD Pass. Van Ext	4825	6445
2 Dr STD Cargo Van	3490	4665
2 Dr STD 4WD Cargo Van	4135	5530
2 Dr STD Cargo Van Ext	3655	4885
2 Dr STD 4WD Cargo Van Ext	4225	5645
2 Dr STD Pass. Van	3770	5035
2 Dr STD 4WD Pass. Van	4270	5705
2 Dr STD Pass. Van Ext	3935	5260
2 Dr STD 4WD Pass. Van Ext	4435	5930

OPTIONS FOR SAFARI

6 cyl 4.3 L HO Engine +55
Sport Handling Pkg +120
Air Conditioning +110
Camper/Towing Package +40
Cruise Control +30
Dual Air Conditioning +125
Power Door Locks +30
Power Drivers Seat +40
Power Windows +30

Don't forget to refer to the Mileage Adjustment Table at the back of this book!

SIERRA PICKUP   1991

7.4-liter V8 is reworked, and can be mated to four-speed automatic transmission. New gauge cluster includes a tachometer. Bucket seats are a new option. Air conditioners get a new recirculation mode. Two-wheel-drive models add tow hooks to the options list. Special gets new steering wheel and revised outside mirrors.

RATINGS (SCALE OF 1-10)

Overall	Safety	Reliability	Performance	Comfort	Value
N/A	N/A	6.3	N/A	N/A	N/A

SIERRA 1500

Category H

Model Description	Trade-in Value	Market Value
2 Dr C1500 Ext Cab LB	4075	5145
2 Dr C1500 Ext Cab SB	3980	5025
2 Dr C1500 Ext Cab Stepside SB	4355	5500
2 Dr C1500 Std Cab LB	3785	4775
2 Dr C1500 Std Cab SB	3690	4660
2 Dr C1500 Std Cab Stepside SB	3795	4795
2 Dr C1500 SLE Ext Cab LB	4255	5375
2 Dr C1500 SLE Ext Cab SB	4165	5260
2 Dr C1500 SLE Std Cab LB	3970	5010
2 Dr C1500 SLE Std Cab SB	3875	4895
2 Dr C1500 SLE Std Cab Stepside SB	3980	5025
2 Dr C1500 SLX Ext Cab LB	4380	5530
2 Dr C1500 SLX Ext Cab SB	4290	5415
2 Dr C1500 SLX Std Cab LB	4090	5165
2 Dr C1500 SLX Std Cab SB	4000	5050
2 Dr C1500 SLX Std Cab Stepside SB	4105	5180
2 Dr K1500 4WD Ext Cab LB	4760	6010
2 Dr K1500 4WD Ext Cab SB	4670	5895
2 Dr K1500 4WD Std Cab LB	4460	5630
2 Dr K1500 4WD Std Cab SB	4370	5515
2 Dr K1500 4WD Std Cab Stepside SB	4470	5645
2 Dr K1500 SLE 4WD Ext Cab LB	4945	6245
2 Dr K1500 SLE 4WD Ext Cab SB	4850	6125
2 Dr K1500 SLE 4WD Std Cab LB	4645	5865
2 Dr K1500 SLE 4WD Std Cab SB	4550	5750
2 Dr K1500 SLE 4WD Std Cab Stepside SB	4655	5880
2 Dr K1500 SLX 4WD Ext Cab LB	5075	6410
2 Dr K1500 SLX 4WD Ext Cab SB	4975	6285
2 Dr K1500 SLX 4WD Std Cab LB	4770	6020
2 Dr K1500 SLX 4WD Std Cab SB	4675	5905
2 Dr K1500 SLX 4WD Std Cab Stepside SB	4780	6035

SIERRA 2500

Category H

Model Description	Trade-in Value	Market Value
2 Dr C2500 Ext Cab LB	4280	5405
2 Dr C2500 Ext Cab SB	4550	5745
2 Dr C2500 Std Cab LB	3945	4980
2 Dr C2500 SLE Ext Cab LB	4465	5640
2 Dr C2500 SLE Ext Cab SB	4465	5640
2 Dr C2500 SLE Std Cab LB	4125	5210
2 Dr C2500 SLX Ext Cab LB	4775	6030
2 Dr C2500 SLX Ext Cab SB	4690	5920
2 Dr C2500 SLX Std Cab LB	4395	5550
2 Dr K2500 4WD Ext Cab LB	4800	6060
2 Dr K2500 4WD Ext Cab SB	4800	6060
2 Dr K2500 4WD Std Cab LB	4480	5655
2 Dr K2500 SLE 4WD Ext Cab LB	4980	6290
2 Dr K2500 SLE 4WD Ext Cab SB	4980	6290
2 Dr K2500 SLE 4WD Std Cab LB	4660	5885
2 Dr K2500 SLX 4WD Ext Cab LB	5105	6445
2 Dr K2500 SLX 4WD Ext Cab SB	5105	6445
2 Dr K2500 SLX 4WD Std Cab LB	4785	6040

SIERRA 3500

Category H

Model Description	Trade-in Value	Market Value
2 Dr C3500 Ext Cab LB	5295	6685
2 Dr C3500 Std Cab LB	4725	5970
2 Dr C3500 SLE Ext Cab LB	5485	6925
2 Dr C3500 SLE Std Cab LB	4860	6135
2 Dr C3500 SLX Ext Cab LB	5300	6695
2 Dr C3500 SLX Std Cab LB	4975	6280
2 Dr K3500 4WD Ext Cab LB	5745	7250
2 Dr K3500 4WD Std Cab LB	5675	7165
2 Dr K3500 SLE 4WD Ext Cab LB	5840	7370
2 Dr K3500 SLE 4WD Std Cab LB	5555	7015
2 Dr K3500 SLX 4WD Ext Cab LB	5750	7260
2 Dr K3500 SLX 4WD Std Cab LB	5675	7165

OPTIONS FOR SIERRA PICKUP

8 cyl 5.0 L Engine +80
8 cyl 5.7 L Engine +110
8 cyl 6.2 L Dsl Engine +315
8 cyl 7.4 L Engine +115
Auto 4-Speed Transmission +115
Sport Handling Pkg +115
Air Conditioning +110
Camper/Towing Package +45
Cruise Control +25
Dual Rear Wheels[Opt on C3500,SLE] +105
Limited Slip Diff +35
Power Door Locks +25
Power Windows +25

SONOMA   1991

Introduced in January, 1990, Sonoma is a S15 Pickup with a new name and an exterior facelift that includes a new grille, fresh trim and restyled wheels. Four-wheel drive models get the 4.3-liter V6 as standard equipment.

Model Description	Trade-in Value	Market Value	Model Description	Trade-in Value	Market Value

High Sierra trim is dropped, and Sierra Classic trim is changed to SLE. Midyear, the base four-cylinder powerplant gets more horsepower.

RATINGS (SCALE OF 1-10)

Overall	Safety	Reliability	Performance	Comfort	Value
N/A	2.9	6	7.2	7	N/A

Category G

2 Dr SLE Ext Cab SB	3300	4410
2 Dr SLE 4WD Ext Cab SB	4225	5645
2 Dr SLE Std Cab LB	2915	3900
2 Dr SLE 4WD Std Cab LB	3805	5085
2 Dr SLE Std Cab SB	2915	3900
2 Dr SLE 4WD Std Cab SB	3805	5085
2 Dr STD Ext Cab SB	3105	4145
2 Dr STD 4WD Ext Cab SB	3880	5185
2 Dr STD Std Cab LB	2760	3685
2 Dr STD 4WD Std Cab LB	3660	4890
2 Dr STD Std Cab SB	2760	3685
2 Dr STD 4WD Std Cab SB	3660	4890
2 Dr Special Std Cab SB	2400	3210
2 Dr Syclone Turbo 4WD Std Cab SB	6765	9045

OPTIONS FOR SONOMA

6 cyl 2.8 L Engine +50
6 cyl 4.3 L Engine +85
Auto 4-Speed Transmission[Opt on SLE,STD] +115
Air Conditioning[Opt on SLE,Special,STD] +110
Camper/Towing Package +40
Cruise Control[Opt on SLE,STD] +30
Limited Slip Diff[Opt on SLE,STD] +35
Power Door Locks[Opt on SLE,STD] +30
Power Windows[Opt on SLE,STD] +30

SUBURBAN   1991

Manual transmission is dropped.

Category H

4 Dr R1500 Wgn	5440	6870
4 Dr R2500 Wgn	5930	7490
4 Dr V1500 4WD Wgn	6065	7660
4 Dr V2500 4WD Wgn	6175	7800

OPTIONS FOR SUBURBAN

8 cyl 6.2 L Dsl Engine +315
8 cyl 7.4 L Engine +115
SLE Pkg +220
Air Conditioning +110
Camper/Towing Package +45
Cruise Control +25
Dual Air Conditioning +170
Limited Slip Diff +35
Power Door Locks +25
Power Windows +25
Rear Bench Seat +40

SYCLONE   1991

This Sonoma pickup is an all-wheel-drive turbocharged V6 terror with a Corvette automatic transmission, four-wheel ABS and 280 horsepower. GMC says acceleration from zero to 60 is accomplished in 4.6 seconds.

Category I

2 Dr STD Turbo 4WD Std Cab SB	7730	9765

V3500 PICKUP   1991

Category H

4 Dr STD 4WD Crew Cab LB	5880	7425

OPTIONS FOR V3500 PICKUP

8 cyl 6.2 L Dsl Engine +315
8 cyl 7.4 L Engine +115
Auto 4-Speed Transmission +115
SLE Pkg - R&v Series +120
Air Conditioning +110
Power Door Locks +25
Power Windows +25

VANDURA/RALLY WAGON 1991

7.4-liter engine can be equipped with a four-speed automatic transmission.

RALLY WAGON

Category H

2 Dr G15 Rally Wagon	4160	5250
2 Dr G15 Rally Wagon Ext	4405	5565
2 Dr G25 Rally Wagon	4445	5615
2 Dr G25 STX Rally Wagon	4675	5905
2 Dr G35 Dsl Rally Wagon	4930	6220
2 Dr G35 Rally Wagon Ext	4885	6165
2 Dr G35 STX Dsl Rally Wagon	5140	6490
2 Dr G35 STX Rally Wagon Ext	5115	6455

VANDURA

Category H

2 Dr G15 Vandura	3530	4455
2 Dr G15 Vandura Ext	3650	4610
2 Dr G25 Vandura	3575	4515
2 Dr G25 Vandura Ext	3645	4605
2 Dr G35 Vandura	4355	5500
2 Dr G35 Vandura Ext	4320	5455

OPTIONS FOR VANDURA/RALLY WAGON

8 cyl 5.0 L Engine +80
8 cyl 5.7 L Engine[Opt on G25,G15] +110
8 cyl 6.2 L Dsl Engine +315
8 cyl 7.4 L Engine +115
Air Conditioning +110
Camper/Towing Package +45
Cruise Control +25
Dual Air Conditioning +170
Power Door Locks +25
Power Windows +25

Don't forget to refer to the Mileage Adjustment Table at the back of this book!

HONDA 00

Model Description	Trade-in Value	Market Value	Model Description	Trade-in Value	Market Value

HONDA   Japan

1993 Honda Civic

2000 HONDA

ACCORD   2000

The four-cylinder engines now have a 100,000-mile no-tuneup service life. Side airbags are standard for all V6 models and EX four-cylinders with the leather interior. The feature-laden Accord SE sedan makes its debut this year. In the paint department, Nighthawk Black replaces Starlight Black, and Naples Gold Metallic replaces Heather Mist Metallic; Raisin and Currant have been dropped.

Category E

4 Dr DX Sdn	11075	12965
2 Dr EX Cpe	15080	17655
4 Dr EX Sdn	15100	17675
2 Dr EX V6 Cpe	17540	20535
4 Dr EX V6 Sdn	17540	20535
2 Dr LX Cpe	13320	15590
4 Dr LX Sdn	13320	15590
2 Dr LX V6 Cpe	15715	18395
4 Dr LX V6 Sdn	15715	18395
4 Dr SE Sdn	14705	17215

OPTIONS FOR ACCORD
Auto 4-Speed Transmission[Opt on DX,EX,LX] +655
Air Conditioning[Opt on DX] +680
Leather Seats[Opt on EX] +720
Power Drivers Seat[Opt on EX] +245

CIVIC   2000

No styling, content or trim changes for this year. The performance-oriented Si returns for 2000, and there have been paint comings and goings: Taffeta White has been added to the CX and DX Hatchback, and Dark

Amethyst has been dropped; Titanium Metallic comes to the DX, LX and EX Sedan, and Vogue Silver is gone. Vintage Plum is now available to the LX and EX Sedan, and Inza Red has been eliminated.

Category E

2 Dr CX Hbk	8610	9575
2 Dr DX Cpe	10100	11230
2 Dr DX Hbk	9730	10820
4 Dr DX Sdn	10260	11405
2 Dr EX Cpe	12335	13715
4 Dr EX Sdn	13300	14790
2 Dr HX Cpe	10735	11935
4 Dr LX Sdn	11835	13160
2 Dr Si Cpe	13870	15425
4 Dr VP Sdn Sdn	11680	12990

OPTIONS FOR CIVIC
Auto 4-Speed Transmission[Std on VP Sdn] +695
AM/FM Compact Disc Player[Opt on DX,LX] +355
AM/FM Stereo Tape +250
Air Conditioning[Opt on CX,DX,HX] +680
Aluminum/Alloy Wheels[Opt on LX,EX Coupe] +275
Power Steering[Opt on CX] +210
Rear Spoiler[Std on CX,Hbk] +180

CR-V   2000

The 2000 Honda CR-V gets a new SE (Special Edition) package.

Category G

4 Dr EX AWD Wgn	15845	18310
4 Dr LX Wgn	14405	16650
4 Dr LX AWD Wgn	14710	17000
4 Dr Special Edition 4WD Wgn	17410	20120

OPTIONS FOR CR-V
Auto 4-Speed Transmission[Opt on EX,LX AWD] +655

ODYSSEY   2000

Since it was redesigned last year, the only new feature is an optional navigation system on the EX.

Category G

4 Dr EX Pass. Van	21790	25180
4 Dr LX Pass. Van	19625	22680

OPTIONS FOR ODYSSEY
Navigation System +1635

PASSPORT   2000

The Passport receives new front and rear fascias, a modified grille, redesigned front combination lamps and a host of fresh features for a new, top-of-the-line EX-L trim level.

Category G

4 Dr EX Wgn	18850	21785
4 Dr EX 4WD Wgn	20560	23760

Model Description	Trade-in Value	Market Value
4 Dr LX Wgn	16200	18720
4 Dr LX 4WD Wgn	18400	21260

OPTIONS FOR PASSPORT
Auto 4-Speed Transmission[Std on EX] +940

PRELUDE   2000

The 2000 Prelude is a carry-over from 1999 and remains unchanged.
Category F

Model Description	Trade-in Value	Market Value
2 Dr STD Cpe	16780	19520
2 Dr Type SH Cpe	18535	21560

OPTIONS FOR PRELUDE
Auto 4-Speed Transmission +815

S2000   2000

Honda brings out the high-revving, high horsepower S2000 for 2000.
Category F

Model Description	Trade-in Value	Market Value
2 Dr STD Conv	26555	30890

1999 HONDA

ACCORD   1999

The coupes remain unchanged after their recent overhaul, but the sedans receive new seat fabric, and the LX and EX sedans now feature foldaway side mirrors.

RATINGS (SCALE OF 1-10)

Overall	Safety	Reliability	Performance	Comfort	Value
N/A	7.1	8.9	7.6	8.3	N/A

Category E

Model Description	Trade-in Value	Market Value
4 Dr DX Sdn	10320	12150
2 Dr EX Cpe	14085	16590
4 Dr EX Sdn	14085	16590
2 Dr EX V6 Cpe	16330	19235
4 Dr EX V6 Sdn	16330	19235
2 Dr LX Cpe	12425	14635
4 Dr LX Sdn	12425	14635
2 Dr LX V6 Cpe	14615	17210
4 Dr LX V6 Sdn	13955	16435

OPTIONS FOR ACCORD
Auto 4-Speed Transmission[Std on EX V6,LX V6] +535
Air Conditioning[Opt on DX] +555
Aluminum/Alloy Wheels[Std on EX,EX V6] +225
Anti-Lock Brakes[Opt on LX] +445
Keyless Entry System[Opt on LX] +110
Leather Seats[Std on EX V6] +585
Power Drivers Seat[Opt on EX] +200

CIVIC   1999

The Civic gets new front and rear styling as well as an improved instrument panel. The DX trim gets a rear wiper and washer, a cargo cover and a low-fuel warning light. A hotrod Si model is introduced mid-year with a 160-hp VTEC engine.

RATINGS (SCALE OF 1-10)

Overall	Safety	Reliability	Performance	Comfort	Value
N/A	6.8	9	8.2	7.8	N/A

Category E

Model Description	Trade-in Value	Market Value
2 Dr CX Hbk	8025	8980
2 Dr DX Cpe	9425	10545
2 Dr DX Hbk	9080	10155
4 Dr DX Sdn	9575	10715
2 Dr EX Cpe	11505	12875
4 Dr EX Sdn	12435	13915
2 Dr HX Cpe	10020	11210
4 Dr LX Sdn	11060	12370
2 Dr SI Cpe	12955	14495
4 Dr VP Sdn	10915	12210

OPTIONS FOR CIVIC
Auto 4-Speed Transmission[Std on VP] +570
AM/FM Compact Disc Player[Opt on DX,LX] +290
Air Conditioning[Opt on CX,DX,HX] +555

CR-V   1999

The CR-V gains 20 horsepower, bringing the total output to 146. Automatic transmission models have a revised column shifter with an overdrive switch. The power window buttons are illuminated, the spare tire cover has been upgraded, and the front passenger seat is equipped with an armrest. Since Honda has effectively addressed all of our previous gripes with this year's changes, we'll have to get more creative with our complaints.

RATINGS (SCALE OF 1-10)

Overall	Safety	Reliability	Performance	Comfort	Value
N/A	N/A	N/A	8	8.5	N/A

Category G

Model Description	Trade-in Value	Market Value
4 Dr EX 4WD Wgn	15235	17760
4 Dr LX Wgn	13850	16140
4 Dr LX 4WD Wgn	14140	16480

OPTIONS FOR CR-V
Auto 4-Speed Transmission[Std on 2WD] +535
AM/FM Compact Disc Player[Std on EX] +210

ODYSSEY   1999

Honda's latest masterpiece, the totally redesigned Odyssey, will finally give Chrysler's minivans a run for their money.

Don't forget to refer to the Mileage Adjustment Table at the back of this book!

Model Description	Trade-in Value	Market Value

Model Description	Trade-in Value	Market Value

RATINGS (SCALE OF 1-10)

Overall	Safety	Reliability	Performance	Comfort	Value
N/A	8.9	9.2	7.8	8	N/A

Category G
4 Dr EX Pass. Van	20875	24330
4 Dr LX Pass. Van	18645	21730

PASSPORT   1999

Last year, the Passport and the identical Isuzu Rodeo were completely redesigned, so there are no new changes this year.

RATINGS (SCALE OF 1-10)

Overall	Safety	Reliability	Performance	Comfort	Value
N/A	7.6	N/A	6.6	7.3	N/A

Category G
4 Dr EX Wgn	17805	20755
4 Dr EX 4WD Wgn	19425	22645
4 Dr LX Wgn	15410	17960
4 Dr LX 4WD Wgn	17110	19945

OPTIONS FOR PASSPORT
Auto 4-Speed Transmission[Std on EX] +770
Leather Seats +525
Limited Slip Diff[Std on EX] +185
Swing Out Tire Carrier[Std on EX] +125

PRELUDE   1999

Prelude gets another five horsepower, bringing it up to 200 horsepower with the manual transmission and 195 horsepower with the automatic. A remote keyless entry system is added, as is an air filtration system, mesh-style grille and new interior color choices.

RATINGS (SCALE OF 1-10)

Overall	Safety	Reliability	Performance	Comfort	Value
N/A	N/A	N/A	8.6	6.9	N/A

Category F
2 Dr STD Cpe	15800	18435
2 Dr Type SH Cpe	17455	20365

OPTIONS FOR PRELUDE
Auto 4-Speed Transmission +670

1998 HONDA

ACCORD   1998

Honda redesigns its best-seller for 1998. A 3.0-liter V6 engine makes its debut in LX V6 and EX V6 models, marking the first six-cylinder VTEC in the Honda lineup. The standard 2.3-liter four-banger is also re-engineered, as is the chassis. The new Accord is also larger, and the interior boasts more room inside than any of Accord's competitors.

RATINGS (SCALE OF 1-10)

Overall	Safety	Reliability	Performance	Comfort	Value
7.2	6.9	8.2	7.6	8.3	5

Category E
4 Dr DX Sdn	9685	11440
2 Dr EX Cpe	13250	15650
4 Dr EX Sdn	13250	15650
2 Dr EX V6 Cpe	15340	18125
4 Dr EX V6 Sdn	15340	18125
2 Dr LX Cpe	11680	13800
4 Dr LX Sdn	11680	13800
2 Dr LX V6 Cpe	13715	16205
4 Dr LX V6 Sdn	13715	16205

OPTIONS FOR ACCORD
Auto 4-Speed Transmission[Std on EX V6, LX V6] +435
Air Conditioning[Opt on DX] +455
Aluminum/Alloy Wheels[Std on EX, EX V6] +185
Anti-Lock Brakes[Std on EX, EX V6, LX V6] +365
Leather Seats[Std on EX V6] +480
Power Drivers Seat[Std on EX V6, LX V6] +165

CIVIC   1998

Last year's best-selling small car gets minor revisions: select models get new wheelcovers, a rear hatch handle, and map lights.

RATINGS (SCALE OF 1-10)

Overall	Safety	Reliability	Performance	Comfort	Value
7.5	6.7	8.7	8.2	7.8	6

Category E
2 Dr CX Hbk	8005	8985
2 Dr DX Cpe	9405	10560
2 Dr DX Hbk	9060	10165
4 Dr DX Sdn	9520	10685
2 Dr EX Cpe	11345	12730
4 Dr EX Sdn	12235	13730
2 Dr HX Cpe	10000	11225
4 Dr LX Sdn	10980	12325

OPTIONS FOR CIVIC
Auto 4-Speed Transmission +465
AM/FM Compact Disc Player +235
Air Conditioning[Std on EX, LX] +455
Power Steering[Opt on CX] +140

CR-V   1998

A manual transmission lowers the ante, making the CR-V a more attractive value than before. Also available is a front-wheel drive LX model, and the EX trim level now includes a CD player, anti-lock brakes, and remote keyless entry.

Don't forget to refer to the Mileage Adjustment Table at the back of this book!

HONDA 98-97

Model Description	Trade-in Value	Market Value	Model Description	Trade-in Value	Market Value

RATINGS (SCALE OF 1-10)

Overall	Safety	Reliability	Performance	Comfort	Value
N/A	7.3	8.5	7.8	8.5	N/A

Category G
4 Dr EX 4WD Wgn	13825	16185
4 Dr LX Wgn	12550	14695
4 Dr LX 4WD Wgn	12820	15010

OPTIONS FOR CR-V
Auto 4-Speed Transmission[Std on 2WD] +435

ODYSSEY 1998

The engine is upgraded to a more sophisticated 2.3-liter, good for an extra 10 horsepower and seven foot-pounds of torque. New looks up front come from a revised bumper and grille, and the interior gets dressed in new fabric.

RATINGS (SCALE OF 1-10)

Overall	Safety	Reliability	Performance	Comfort	Value
7.7	7.5	9.2	7.2	7.1	7.3

Category G
4 Dr EX Pass. Van	18110	21205
4 Dr LX Pass. Van	16800	19675

OPTIONS FOR ODYSSEY
6 Passenger Seating[Opt on LX] +280
Captain Chairs (4)[Opt on LX] +335

PASSPORT 1998

Like its Isuzu Rodeo counterpart, the Passport has been completely revised from top to bottom. The Passport gets modernized styling, a user-friendly interior, more powerful V6 and added room for passengers and cargo.

RATINGS (SCALE OF 1-10)

Overall	Safety	Reliability	Performance	Comfort	Value
7	7.3	7.1	6.6	7.3	6.6

Category G
4 Dr EX Wgn	16125	18880
4 Dr EX 4WD Wgn	17590	20600
4 Dr LX Wgn	14000	16395
4 Dr LX 4WD Wgn	15495	18145

OPTIONS FOR PASSPORT
Auto 4-Speed Transmission[Opt on LX] +630
Compact Disc W/fm/tape +240
Leather Seats +430
Limited Slip Diff[Opt on LX] +150
Swing Out Tire Carrier +100

PRELUDE 1998

The Prelude doesn't change for 1998, because you don't mess with success. (Pssst, buy this car!)

RATINGS (SCALE OF 1-10)

Overall	Safety	Reliability	Performance	Comfort	Value
N/A	N/A	8.8	8.6	6.9	4.2

Category F
2 Dr STD Cpe	14850	17365
2 Dr Type SH Cpe	16420	19200

OPTIONS FOR PRELUDE
Auto 4-Speed Transmission +545

1997 HONDA

ACCORD 1997

Changes to the ever-popular Accord include the deletion of antilock brakes on the LX five-speed models and the discontinuation of the EX coupes with leather. No other changes for the 1997 Accord.

RATINGS (SCALE OF 1-10)

Overall	Safety	Reliability	Performance	Comfort	Value
7.5	6.8	8.9	7.8	8	5.8

Category E
4 Dr DX Sdn	9295	11030
2 Dr EX Cpe	12535	14875
4 Dr EX Sdn	12655	15020
4 Dr EX Wgn	13755	16320
4 Dr EX V6 Sdn	15310	18170
2 Dr LX Cpe	11030	13090
4 Dr LX Sdn	11150	13230
4 Dr LX Wgn	11690	13870
4 Dr LX V6 Sdn	13735	16300
2 Dr Special Edition Cpe	12355	14660
4 Dr Special Edition Sdn	12475	14805
4 Dr Value Sdn	10435	12380

OPTIONS FOR ACCORD
Auto 4-Speed Transmission[Opt on DX,LX,EX Sdn,EX Cpe] +355
Air Conditioning[Opt on DX] +370
Aluminum/Alloy Wheels[Opt on LX] +150
Anti-Lock Brakes[Opt on LX] +295
Compact Disc W/fm/tape[Opt on EX,EX V6] +215
Leather Seats[Opt on EX] +390
Power Drivers Seat[Opt on EX] +135

CIVIC 1997

For some reason, Honda deletes the Civic EX Coupe five-speed with ABS model. Maybe they think that people who like to row their own gears don't worry about whether they can stop or not. DX models receive new wheel covers, all Civics get 14-inch wheels, and the LX sedan gets air conditioning.

Don't forget to refer to the Mileage Adjustment Table at the back of this book!

Model Description	Trade-in Value	Market Value

Model Description	Trade-in Value	Market Value

RATINGS (SCALE OF 1-10)

Overall	Safety	Reliability	Performance	Comfort	Value
7	6.7	8.6	8.2	7.8	3.9

Category E

	Trade-in	Market
2 Dr CX Hbk	7280	8210
2 Dr DX Cpe	8430	9505
2 Dr DX Hbk	8115	9145
4 Dr DX Sdn	8670	9770
2 Dr EX Cpe	10410	11735
4 Dr EX Sdn	11225	12655
2 Dr HX Cpe	9175	10345
4 Dr LX Sdn	10010	11285

OPTIONS FOR CIVIC

Auto 4-Speed Transmission +400
AM/FM Compact Disc Player +195
Air Conditioning[Std on EX,LX] +370
Anti-Lock Brakes[Opt on Cpe] +295
Leather Seats +390
Power Steering[Std on EX,HX,LX,DX,Sdn] +115
Rear Spoiler +100

CIVIC DEL SOL   1997

No changes to Honda's two-seater.

RATINGS (SCALE OF 1-10)

Overall	Safety	Reliability	Performance	Comfort	Value
N/A	N/A	N/A	N/A	N/A	4.1

Category F

	Trade-in	Market
2 Dr S Cpe	10250	11485
2 Dr Si Cpe	11725	13135
2 Dr VTEC Cpe	13245	14840

OPTIONS FOR CIVIC DEL SOL

Auto 4-Speed Transmission +395
Air Conditioning +375
Power Steering[Opt on S] +160

CR-V   1997

Priced competitively with mini-utes, the CR-V offers more passenger room and cargo capacity than its peers. The CR-V is available with antilock brakes.

RATINGS (SCALE OF 1-10)

Overall	Safety	Reliability	Performance	Comfort	Value
N/A	7.3	8.5	7.8	8.5	N/A

Category G

	Trade-in	Market
4 Dr STD 4WD Wgn	13555	15905

OPTIONS FOR CR-V

AM/FM Compact Disc Player +140
Aluminum/Alloy Wheels +145
Anti-Lock Brakes +260
Luggage Rack +70

ODYSSEY   1997

No changes for the 1997 Honda Odyssey.

RATINGS (SCALE OF 1-10)

Overall	Safety	Reliability	Performance	Comfort	Value
7.6	7.5	9.3	7.2	7.1	6.8

Category G

	Trade-in	Market
4 Dr EX Pass. Van	16475	19330
4 Dr LX Pass. Van	15215	17850

OPTIONS FOR ODYSSEY

AM/FM Compact Disc Player +140
Captain Chairs (4)[Opt on LX] +275
Luggage Rack +70

PASSPORT   1997

Honda drops the slow-selling DX four-cylinder Passport.

RATINGS (SCALE OF 1-10)

Overall	Safety	Reliability	Performance	Comfort	Value
7	6.8	8	6.6	7.1	6.6

Category G

	Trade-in	Market
4 Dr EX Wgn	13805	16195
4 Dr EX 4WD Wgn	14685	17230
4 Dr LX Wgn	11590	13600
4 Dr LX 4WD Wgn	12850	15080

OPTIONS FOR PASSPORT

Auto 4-Speed Transmission[Opt on LX,4WD] +485
Air Conditioning[Std on EX,4WD] +365
Limited Slip Diff[Opt on LX] +125

PRELUDE   1997

The Prelude is totally redesigned for 1997. A base model is available with a five-speed manual or four-speed automatic gearbox, but the top-of-the-line Type SH model, featuring Honda's new Active Torque Transfer System, can only be had as a manual. Both the base and Type SH Preludes feature last year's VTEC engine which produces 195-horsepower for 1997.

RATINGS (SCALE OF 1-10)

Overall	Safety	Reliability	Performance	Comfort	Value
N/A	N/A	8.6	8.6	6.9	2.6

Category F

	Trade-in	Market
2 Dr STD Cpe	14750	17395
2 Dr Type SH Cpe	15985	18850

1996 HONDA

ACCORD   1996

All Accords get revised styling, featuring new taillights and bumper covers. Wagons have a new roof rack, while sedans boast a new pass-through ski sack.

Model Description	Trade-in Value	Market Value

RATINGS (SCALE OF 1-10)

Overall	Safety	Reliability	Performance	Comfort	Value
7.3	6.8	8.8	7.8	8	5

Category E

Model	Trade-in	Market
4 Dr 25th Anniversary Sdn	9415	11295
4 Dr DX Sdn	8350	10015
2 Dr EX Cpe	11105	13320
4 Dr EX Sdn	11320	13580
4 Dr EX Wgn	12300	14755
4 Dr EX V6 Sdn	13715	16455
2 Dr LX Cpe	9850	11815
4 Dr LX Sdn	9960	11945
4 Dr LX Wgn	10445	12530
4 Dr LX V6 Sdn	12335	14800

OPTIONS FOR ACCORD

Auto 4-Speed Transmission[Opt on DX,LX,EX Cpe,EX Sdn] +290
Air Conditioning[Opt on DX] +305
Aluminum/Alloy Wheels[Opt on LX,LX V6] +125
Anti-Lock Brakes[Opt on LX] +245
Compact Disc W/fm/tape +175
Leather Seats[Opt on EX] +320

CIVIC 1996

Keeping to their legendary four-year redesign schedule, Honda engineers have created a more powerful, and more contemporary Civic for 1996. This is a great car for those concerned about reliability and value, but who don't want to sacrifice style.

RATINGS (SCALE OF 1-10)

Overall	Safety	Reliability	Performance	Comfort	Value
7.1	6.7	8.4	8.2	7.8	4.4

Category E

Model	Trade-in	Market
2 Dr CX Hbk	6235	7105
2 Dr DX Cpe	7510	8555
2 Dr DX Hbk	7000	7975
4 Dr DX Sdn	7720	8800
2 Dr EX Cpe	9225	10515
4 Dr EX Sdn	10030	11425
2 Dr HX Cpe	8115	9245
4 Dr LX Sdn	8415	9590

OPTIONS FOR CIVIC

Auto 4-Speed Transmission +330
AM/FM Stereo Tape +110
Air Conditioning[Std on EX] +305
Aluminum/Alloy Wheels[Opt on DX] +125
Anti-Lock Brakes[Opt on LX,Cpe] +245
Compact Disc Changer +175
Power Steering[Std on EX,HX,LX,DX Sdn] +95
Rear Spoiler +80

CIVIC DEL SOL 1996

No changes to the 1996 del Sol.

RATINGS (SCALE OF 1-10)

Overall	Safety	Reliability	Performance	Comfort	Value
N/A	N/A	N/A	N/A	N/A	4

Category F

Model	Trade-in	Market
2 Dr S Cpe	9260	10430
2 Dr Si Cpe	10645	11995
2 Dr VTEC Cpe	11960	13480

OPTIONS FOR CIVIC DEL SOL

Auto 4-Speed Transmission +315
Air Conditioning +305
Power Steering[Opt on S] +130

ODYSSEY 1996

Minivan-wagon hybrid carries into 1996 sans changes.

RATINGS (SCALE OF 1-10)

Overall	Safety	Reliability	Performance	Comfort	Value
7.8	7.5	9.3	7.2	7.1	7.8

Category G

Model	Trade-in	Market
4 Dr EX Pass. Van	14330	16985
4 Dr LX Pass. Van	13235	15685

OPTIONS FOR ODYSSEY

Captain Chairs (4)[Opt on LX] +225

PASSPORT 1996

New wheels, dual airbags, available ABS, and a stronger V6 engine are the changes for the 1996 Isuzu Rodeo, er, we mean Passport.

RATINGS (SCALE OF 1-10)

Overall	Safety	Reliability	Performance	Comfort	Value
7.1	6.8	7.7	6.6	7.1	7.5

Category G

Model	Trade-in	Market
4 Dr DX Wgn	8860	10500
4 Dr EX Wgn	12525	14845
4 Dr EX 4WD Wgn	13325	15795
4 Dr LX Wgn	10540	12490
4 Dr LX 4WD Wgn	11665	13820

OPTIONS FOR PASSPORT

Auto 4-Speed Transmission[Opt on LX,4WD] +400
Air Conditioning[Std on EX,4WD] +300

PRELUDE 1996

This is the last year for the current-generation Prelude. All of the really exciting stuff happens in 1997.

RATINGS (SCALE OF 1-10)

Overall	Safety	Reliability	Performance	Comfort	Value
7.1	7.4	9.2	9	6.8	3.1

Model Description	Trade-in Value	Market Value
Category F		
2 Dr S Cpe	11420	13545
2 Dr Si Cpe	12805	15190
2 Dr VTEC Cpe	14600	17315

OPTIONS FOR PRELUDE
Auto 4-Speed Transmission +290

1995 HONDA

ACCORD 1995

Finally, a V6 is offered in the midsized Honda! Unfortunately, it fails to improve performance figures because of the mandatory automatic transmission. V6 Accords gain different front styling as a result of the increased size of the engine bay. All V6 Accords come with standard antilock brakes.

RATINGS (SCALE OF 1-10)

Overall	Safety	Reliability	Performance	Comfort	Value
7.3	7.4	8.2	7.8	8	5

	Trade-in	Market
Category E		
4 Dr DX Sdn	7030	8595
2 Dr EX Cpe	9495	11605
4 Dr EX Sdn	9585	11720
4 Dr EX Wgn	10320	12615
4 Dr EX V6 Sdn	11635	14225
2 Dr LX Cpe	8305	10155
4 Dr LX Sdn	8400	10270
4 Dr LX Wgn	8845	10810
4 Dr LX V6 Sdn	10415	12735

OPTIONS FOR ACCORD
Auto 4-Speed Transmission[Opt on DX,LX,EX Cpe,EX Sdn] +225
Air Conditioning[Opt on DX] +250
Anti-Lock Brakes[Opt on LX] +200
Compact Disc W/fm/tape +145
Leather Seats[Std on EX V6] +260
Power Drivers Seat[Opt on EX] +90

CIVIC 1995

No changes for the last year of the current Civic.

RATINGS (SCALE OF 1-10)

Overall	Safety	Reliability	Performance	Comfort	Value
7.1	6.5	8.6	8	8	4.4

	Trade-in	Market
Category E		
2 Dr CX Hbk	5260	6110
2 Dr DX Cpe	6130	7120
2 Dr DX Hbk	5880	6830
4 Dr DX Sdn	6330	7355
2 Dr EX Cpe	7380	8575
4 Dr EX Sdn	8495	9865
4 Dr LX Sdn	7015	8150

	Trade-in	Market
2 Dr Si Hbk	7130	8280
2 Dr VX Hbk	6240	7245

OPTIONS FOR CIVIC
Auto 4-Speed Transmission +245
AM/FM Stereo Tape[Opt on DX] +90
Air Conditioning[Std on EX Sdn] +250
Aluminum/Alloy Wheels[Opt on EX] +100
Anti-Lock Brakes[Opt on LX,Cpe] +200
Power Steering[Opt on DX Hbk] +75
Premium Sound System +100
Rear Spoiler +65

CIVIC DEL SOL 1995

Antilock brakes are now standard on VTEC models. Power door locks are also new to the standard equipment lists of Si and VTEC models. All del Sols get a remote trunk release.

RATINGS (SCALE OF 1-10)

Overall	Safety	Reliability	Performance	Comfort	Value
N/A	N/A	N/A	N/A	N/A	4.5

	Trade-in	Market
Category F		
2 Dr S Cpe	7835	8960
2 Dr Si Cpe	8765	10020
2 Dr VTEC Cpe	9925	11350

OPTIONS FOR CIVIC DEL SOL
Auto 4-Speed Transmission +260
Air Conditioning +250
Power Steering[Opt on S] +105

ODYSSEY 1995

Honda finally gets its minivan in the form of the Odyssey. Unique to the Odyssey is five-door design that includes four passenger car-like swing-out doors. LX and EX models come standard with antilock brakes and dual airbags.

RATINGS (SCALE OF 1-10)

Overall	Safety	Reliability	Performance	Comfort	Value
7.5	8.2	8.9	7.2	7.1	6

	Trade-in	Market
Category G		
4 Dr EX Pass. Van	12455	14930
4 Dr LX Pass. Van	11370	13630

OPTIONS FOR ODYSSEY
Captain Chairs (4) +185
Luggage Rack[Opt on LX] +50

PASSPORT 1995

Midyear change gives the Passport driver and passenger airbags in a redesigned dashboard.

RATINGS (SCALE OF 1-10)

Overall	Safety	Reliability	Performance	Comfort	Value
6.9	7	7.1	6.6	7.1	6.8

Don't forget to refer to the Mileage Adjustment Table at the back of this book!

Model Description	Trade-in Value	Market Value
Category G		
4 Dr DX Wgn	6900	8270
1995.5 4 Dr DX Wgn	7480	8965
4 Dr EX 4WD Wgn	10365	12430
1995.5 4 Dr EX Wgn	10445	12525
1995.5 4 Dr EX 4WD Wgn	10870	13030
4 Dr LX Wgn	8310	9965
4 Dr LX 4WD Wgn	9120	10935
1995.5 4 Dr LX Wgn	8810	10565
1995.5 4 Dr LX 4WD Wgn	9610	11520

OPTIONS FOR PASSPORT

Auto 4-Speed Transmission +340
AM/FM Stereo Tape[Opt on DX] +65
Air Conditioning[Opt on DX,2WD] +245
Leather Seats +235
Limited Slip Diff[Opt on LX] +85
Luggage Rack +50
Running Boards +115

PRELUDE   1995

The ill-conceived Si 4WS is mercifully dropped from the Prelude lineup. The fourth-generation Prelude is nearing the end of its life. Few changes for 1995, except the addition of air conditioning to the standard equipment list of S models.

RATINGS (SCALE OF 1-10)

Overall	Safety	Reliability	Performance	Comfort	Value
7.1	8.1	9.1	9	6.8	2.6

	Trade-in	Market
Category F		
2 Dr S Cpe	9425	11345
2 Dr SE Cpe	10980	13215
2 Dr Si Cpe	10315	12420
2 Dr VTEC Cpe	11880	14300

OPTIONS FOR PRELUDE

Auto 4-Speed Transmission +225

1994 HONDA

ACCORD   1994

Once again, Honda's best-selling model is redesigned. Changes for 1994 make the vehicle more competitive with its midsize rival, the Ford Taurus. Shorter and wider than the previous generation Accord, the 1994 model is available in three trim levels. Antilock brakes are standard on the EX and are finally available on the LX and DX. New engines across the board improve horsepower figures for all Accords.

RATINGS (SCALE OF 1-10)

Overall	Safety	Reliability	Performance	Comfort	Value
7.3	7.5	8.2	7.8	8	4.8

Model Description	Trade-in Value	Market Value
Category E		
2 Dr DX Cpe	6045	7515
4 Dr DX Sdn	6125	7620
2 Dr EX Cpe	8305	10330
4 Dr EX Sdn	8390	10435
4 Dr EX Wgn	8900	11065
2 Dr LX Cpe	7255	9025
4 Dr LX Sdn	7340	9125
4 Dr LX Wgn	7815	9715

OPTIONS FOR ACCORD

Auto 4-Speed Transmission +185
AM/FM Compact Disc Player +105
Air Conditioning[Opt on DX] +205
Anti-Lock Brakes[Std on EX] +160
Leather Seats +215

CIVIC   1994

The passenger airbag is now standard on all Civics. Antilock brakes are optional on the LX sedan, EX coupe and Si hatchback.

RATINGS (SCALE OF 1-10)

Overall	Safety	Reliability	Performance	Comfort	Value
7.3	6.3	7.9	8	8	6.3

	Trade-in	Market
Category E		
2 Dr CX Hbk	4510	5330
2 Dr DX Cpe	5350	6325
2 Dr DX Hbk	5160	6095
4 Dr DX Sdn	5600	6615
2 Dr EX Cpe	6455	7625
4 Dr EX Sdn	7445	8795
4 Dr LX Sdn	6155	7270
2 Dr Si Hbk	6255	7390
2 Dr VX Hbk	5480	6475

OPTIONS FOR CIVIC

Auto 4-Speed Transmission +200
AM/FM Compact Disc Player +105
Air Conditioning[Std on EX Sdn] +205
Aluminum/Alloy Wheels[Std on VX] +80
Anti-Lock Brakes[Opt on LX,Si,Cpe] +160
Cruise Control[Opt on DX] +55
Leather Seats +215
Power Door Locks[Opt on VX] +60
Power Steering[Std on EX,LX,Si,Sdn] +60
Rear Spoiler +45

CIVIC DEL SOL   1994

VTEC technology makes its way to the del Sol, giving buyers a choice of three models. VTEC del Sols offer 35 more horsepower than the Si. A passenger airbag joins the standard equipment list for all models. VTEC del Sols gain performance-oriented upgrades that include a beefier suspension, larger tires and bigger brakes.

Don't forget to refer to the Mileage Adjustment Table at the back of this book!

Model Description	Trade-in Value	Market Value

Model Description	Trade-in Value	Market Value

RATINGS (SCALE OF 1-10)

Overall	Safety	Reliability	Performance	Comfort	Value
N/A	N/A	N/A	N/A	N/A	4.3

Category F

2 Dr S Cpe	6615	7650
2 Dr Si Cpe	7535	8710
2 Dr VTEC Cpe	8175	9450

OPTIONS FOR CIVIC DEL SOL

Auto 4-Speed Transmission +210
AM/FM Stereo Tape[Opt on S] +55
Air Conditioning +205
Power Steering[Opt on S] +85

PASSPORT   1994

Honda loyalists waiting for the launch of a Honda sport utility should be thrilled with the Passport, until they discover that it's an Isuzu. Based on the highly successful Rodeo, the Honda Passport has very little to distinguish it from its less expensive twin. Two- and four-wheel-drive models are available in three trim levels ranging from the budget-minded DX to the top-end EX.

RATINGS (SCALE OF 1-10)

Overall	Safety	Reliability	Performance	Comfort	Value
6.3	3.7	6.3	6.6	7.4	7.4

Category G

4 Dr DX Wgn	5770	7025
4 Dr EX 4WD Wgn	8470	10315
4 Dr LX Wgn	6995	8515
4 Dr LX 4WD Wgn	7505	9140

OPTIONS FOR PASSPORT

Auto 4-Speed Transmission +250
AM/FM Stereo Tape[Std on EX] +55
Air Conditioning[Opt on DX,2WD] +200
Luggage Rack +40

PRELUDE   1994

Dual airbags are standard on all Preludes this year. Improved interior ergonomics, freshened front-end styling, and environmentally conscious CFC-free air conditioning are also welcome changes to this car.

RATINGS (SCALE OF 1-10)

Overall	Safety	Reliability	Performance	Comfort	Value
7.2	8.1	9	9	6.8	3

Category F

2 Dr S Cpe	7890	9600
2 Dr Si Cpe	9065	11030
2 Dr Si 4WS Cpe	10810	13150
2 Dr VTEC Cpe	10355	12600

OPTIONS FOR PRELUDE

Auto 4-Speed Transmission +185
Air Conditioning[Opt on S] +205
Aluminum/Alloy Wheels[Opt on S] +75
Rear Spoiler[Opt on Si] +60

1993 HONDA

ACCORD   1993

The SE model is re-introduced as the top-of-the-line Accord. A passenger airbag is added.

RATINGS (SCALE OF 1-10)

Overall	Safety	Reliability	Performance	Comfort	Value
N/A	N/A	8	8	8.4	4.8

Category E

4 Dr 10th Anniversary Sdn	6820	8650
2 Dr DX Cpe	5110	6485
4 Dr DX Sdn	5185	6575
2 Dr EX Cpe	6935	8795
4 Dr EX Sdn	7010	8890
4 Dr EX Wgn	7535	9560
2 Dr LX Cpe	6055	7680
4 Dr LX Sdn	6130	7775
4 Dr LX Wgn	6645	8430
2 Dr SE Cpe	7810	9910
4 Dr SE Sdn	7885	10000

OPTIONS FOR ACCORD

Auto 4-Speed Transmission[Opt on DX,EX,LX] +150
AM/FM Stereo Tape[Opt on DX] +60
Air Conditioning[Opt on DX] +165
Aluminum/Alloy Wheels[Opt on LX] +65
Anti-Lock Brakes[Opt on LX] +135
Leather Seats[Std on SE] +175

CIVIC   1993

A coupe body style is added to the Civic stable. EX models get standard power steering and a sunroof. A passenger airbag is available on the EX coupe.

RATINGS (SCALE OF 1-10)

Overall	Safety	Reliability	Performance	Comfort	Value
6.8	5	8.1	8	8	4.8

Category E

2 Dr CX Hbk	3565	4300
2 Dr DX Cpe	4415	5320
2 Dr DX Hbk	4255	5125
4 Dr DX Sdn	4640	5590
2 Dr EX Cpe	5245	6320
4 Dr EX Sdn	6275	7560
4 Dr LX Sdn	4975	5995
2 Dr Si Hbk	5100	6145
2 Dr VX Hbk	4535	5465

OPTIONS FOR CIVIC

Auto 4-Speed Transmission +165
AM/FM Compact Disc Player +85
Air Conditioning +165
Aluminum/Alloy Wheels[Opt on EX] +65
Cruise Control[Opt on VX] +45
Dual Air Bag Restraints +125
Power Steering[Opt on DX Cpe] +50
Rear Spoiler +45

CIVIC DEL SOL   1993

The sun, that's what Honda wants you to think of when you picture the open-air replacement for the CRX. Poised to recapture some of the two-seater market from the Mazda Miata, the del Sol offers solid performance and value. Usable trunk space and improved body rigidity are the benefits the del Sol has over its rivals. We think, however, that the Miata's superior horsepower and rear-wheel drive will prove to be more fun in the long run.

RATINGS (SCALE OF 1-10)

Overall	Safety	Reliability	Performance	Comfort	Value
N/A	N/A	N/A	N/A	N/A	4.4

Category F
2 Dr S Cpe	5605	6565
2 Dr Si Cpe	6340	7430

OPTIONS FOR CIVIC DEL SOL

Auto 4-Speed Transmission +170
AM/FM Stereo Tape +45
Air Conditioning +170
Power Door Locks +40

PRELUDE   1993

More power, in the form of Honda's exclusive VTEC system, is available to the Prelude. A boost of 30 horsepower for top-end Preludes means that this car won't be the laughingstock of stoplight drags anymore.

RATINGS (SCALE OF 1-10)

Overall	Safety	Reliability	Performance	Comfort	Value
6.9	7	8.9	9	6.8	3

Category F
2 Dr S Cpe	6775	8355
2 Dr Si Cpe	7945	9800
2 Dr Si 4WS Cpe	8610	10620
2 Dr VTEC Cpe	8750	10795

OPTIONS FOR PRELUDE

Auto 4-Speed Transmission +150
AM/FM Compact Disc Player +90
Air Conditioning[Opt on S] +170

1992 HONDA

ACCORD   1992

The SE model is dropped. The EX model gains antilock brakes with rear discs instead of drums. Horsepower is up in the EX sedans, 10 more than last year's 130. A driver airbag is added to the standard equipment list.

RATINGS (SCALE OF 1-10)

Overall	Safety	Reliability	Performance	Comfort	Value
N/A	N/A	7.4	8	8.4	5.7

Category E
2 Dr DX Cpe	4245	5525
4 Dr DX Sdn	4305	5610
2 Dr EX Cpe	5845	7610
4 Dr EX Sdn	5905	7690
4 Dr EX Wgn	6435	8380
2 Dr LX Cpe	5070	6605
4 Dr LX Sdn	5135	6685
4 Dr LX Wgn	5655	7360

OPTIONS FOR ACCORD

Auto 4-Speed Transmission +120
Air Conditioning[Opt on DX] +135

CIVIC   1992

A driver airbag is standard on all new Civics. Unfortunately, the wagon body style is dropped from the lineup. VTEC power is available by way of the top-end EX model. All sedans now have power steering added to their standard equipment list.

RATINGS (SCALE OF 1-10)

Overall	Safety	Reliability	Performance	Comfort	Value
6.9	5	7.9	8	8	5.7

Category E
2 Dr CX Hbk	3065	3790
2 Dr DX Hbk	3700	4580
4 Dr DX Sdn	3955	4895
4 Dr EX Sdn	5055	6255
4 Dr LX Sdn	4340	5365
2 Dr Si Hbk	4455	5510
2 Dr VX Hbk	3960	4900

OPTIONS FOR CIVIC

Auto 4-Speed Transmission +120
Air Conditioning +135

PRELUDE   1992

Totally redesigned for 1992, the fourth generation Prelude sports a driver airbag in all models and a standard passenger airbag on the Si 4WS. Antilock brakes are still available only on Si models.

Don't forget to refer to the Mileage Adjustment Table at the back of this book!

Model Description	Trade-in Value	Market Value

RATINGS (SCALE OF 1-10)

Overall	Safety	Reliability	Performance	Comfort	Value
7.2	7	8.8	9	6.8	4.4

Category F

2 Dr S Cpe	5895	7405
2 Dr Si Cpe	6960	8750

OPTIONS FOR PRELUDE
Auto 4-Speed Transmission +120
Air Conditioning[Opt on S] +135
Leather Seats +105

1991 HONDA

ACCORD 1991

Honda introduces a leather-trimmed SE model to the lineup to compete in the upscale market.

RATINGS (SCALE OF 1-10)

Overall	Safety	Reliability	Performance	Comfort	Value
N/A	N/A	6.9	8	8.4	6.5

Category E

2 Dr DX Cpe	3660	4950
4 Dr DX Sdn	3720	5030
2 Dr EX Cpe	4895	6620
4 Dr EX Sdn	4950	6700
4 Dr EX Wgn	5645	7635
2 Dr LX Cpe	4400	5955
4 Dr LX Sdn	4460	6030
4 Dr LX Wgn	5055	6835
4 Dr SE Sdn	5750	7780

OPTIONS FOR ACCORD
Auto 4-Speed Transmission[Std on SE] +100
Air Conditioning[Opt on DX] +110
Cruise Control[Opt on DX] +30

CIVIC 1991

Few changes for Honda's popular subcompact. A complete redesign is expected for 1992.

Category E

2 Dr DX Hbk	2690	3460
4 Dr DX Sdn	2915	3745
4 Dr EX Sdn	3425	4400
4 Dr LX Sdn	3215	4135
2 Dr STD Hbk	2140	2750
4 Dr STD Wgn	3165	4065
4 Dr STD 4WD Wgn	3785	4865
2 Dr Si Hbk	3155	4055

OPTIONS FOR CIVIC
Auto 4-Speed Transmission +110
Air Conditioning +110
Cruise Control[Std on EX,LX] +30

CIVIC CRX 1991

This is the last year for the Honda CRX. Stiff competition from Toyota and Mazda are forcing this superb two-seater into obscurity. The CRX's large luggage storage and peppy performance will be missed.

Category E

2 Dr HF Cpe	2735	3515
2 Dr STD Cpe	2810	3610
2 Dr Si Cpe	3310	4255

OPTIONS FOR CIVIC CRX
Auto 4-Speed Transmission +80
Air Conditioning +110
Cruise Control +30

PRELUDE 1991

1991 is the last year for the third-generation Prelude, so no major changes in face of next year's redesign.

Category F

2 Dr 2.0 Si Cpe	4460	5930
2 Dr Si Cpe	5110	6795

OPTIONS FOR PRELUDE
Auto 4-Speed Transmission +100
Air Conditioning +110
Anti-Lock Brakes +85
Power Door Locks +25

Don't forget to refer to the Mileage Adjustment Table at the back of this book!

Model Description	Trade-in Value	Market Value

HYUNDAI   S. Korea

1995 Hyundai Sonata

Model Description	Trade-in Value	Market Value
Category D		
4 Dr GLS Sdn	11145	13670
4 Dr STD Sdn	9865	12100

OPTIONS FOR SONATA
Auto 4-Speed Transmission +410

TIBURON   2000

Hyundai's Tiburon is now offered in just one trim level. It receives new interior and exterior styling as well as alloy wheels, a power package and four-wheel disc brakes standard.

Category E		
2 Dr STD Hbk	10430	12395

OPTIONS FOR TIBURON
Auto 4-Speed Transmission +615
Compact Disc W/fm/tape +395
Power Moonroof +475
Rear Spoiler +180

2000 HYUNDAI

ACCENT   2000

The Accent has been completely redesigned for the 2000 model year.

Category E		
4 Dr GL Sdn	7330	8710
2 Dr GS Hbk	7255	8625
2 Dr L Hbk	6820	8110

OPTIONS FOR ACCENT
Auto 4-Speed Transmission +490
Air Conditioning +680

ELANTRA   2000

In an effort to mold its image into that of a serious, first-rate automobile manufacturer, Hyundai has recently added standard equipment and enhanced the performance of several of its cars. The redesigned Accent and new Sonata are proving that this South Korean automaker has finally learned how to build a good car. The current Elantra provides even more proof, and the company offers an industry-leading warranty program to back it up.

Category E		
4 Dr GLS Sdn	8505	10110
4 Dr GLS Wgn	8990	10685

OPTIONS FOR ELANTRA
Auto 4-Speed Transmission +615
Cruise Control +185

SONATA   2000

With new standard 15-inch alloy wheels, standard side airbags, and some option changes, Hyundai's 2000 Sonata maintains the same base MSRP as last year.

1999 HYUNDAI

ACCENT   1999

The L model has power steering standard, the GS and GL models have standard alloy wheels and a couple of new paint options are available. Hyundai's new, industry leading buyer assurance program is also worth taking note of.

RATINGS (SCALE OF 1-10)

Overall	Safety	Reliability	Performance	Comfort	Value
N/A	6.1	N/A	N/A	N/A	N/A

Category E		
4 Dr GL Sdn	6280	7585
2 Dr GS Hbk	6280	7585
2 Dr L Hbk	5735	6925

OPTIONS FOR ACCENT
Auto 4-Speed Transmission +535
AM/FM Compact Disc Player +290
Air Conditioning +555
Flip-Up Sunroof +230
Keyless Entry System +110

ELANTRA   1999

The 1999 Elantra boasts a more powerful engine, styling changes and the best buyer assurance program of any car in this class.

RATINGS (SCALE OF 1-10)

Overall	Safety	Reliability	Performance	Comfort	Value
N/A	6.1	N/A	N/A	N/A	N/A

Category E		
4 Dr GL Sdn	7150	8635
4 Dr GL Wgn	7690	9290

Don't forget to refer to the Mileage Adjustment Table at the back of this book!

Model Description	Trade-in Value	Market Value
4 Dr GLS Sdn	7900	9540
4 Dr GLS Wgn	8650	10445

OPTIONS FOR ELANTRA

Auto 4-Speed Transmission[Std on 4 Dr GLS Wagon] +525
AM/FM Compact Disc Player +290
Aluminum/Alloy Wheels +225
Anti-Lock Brakes +445
Cruise Control +155
Keyless Entry System +110
Power Moonroof +390

SONATA 1999

Hyundai's Sonata is completely new and much-improved for 1999.

Category D

	Trade-in Value	Market Value
4 Dr GLS Sdn	10645	12630
4 Dr STD Sdn	9425	11180

OPTIONS FOR SONATA

Auto 4-Speed Transmission +535
AM/FM Compact Disc Player[Std on GLS] +310
Anti-Lock Brakes +595
Cruise Control[Std on GLS] +165
Keyless Entry System +210
Leather Seats[Opt on GLS] +760
Power Moonroof +565

TIBURON 1999

Nothing changes on the Tiburon for 1999, but the company's all-new, industry leading buyer assurance program is worth investigation.

Category E

	Trade-in Value	Market Value
2 Dr FX Hbk	9480	11450
2 Dr STD Hbk	8675	10480

OPTIONS FOR TIBURON

Auto 4-Speed Transmission +535
AM/FM Compact Disc Player +290
Air Conditioning +555
Aluminum/Alloy Wheels[Std on FX] +225
Anti-Lock Brakes +445
Cruise Control +155
Fog Lights[Std on FX] +100
Keyless Entry System +110
Leather Seats +585
Power Sunroof +415

1998 HYUNDAI

ACCENT 1998

The Accent GSi replaces the Accent GT this year. New front and rear fascias, and new engine mounts, which reduce engine vibration and harshness, are the only other changes to Hyundai's smallest car.

Model Description	Trade-in Value	Market Value

RATINGS (SCALE OF 1-10)

Overall	Safety	Reliability	Performance	Comfort	Value
N/A	6.1	N/A	N/A	N/A	N/A

Category E

	Trade-in Value	Market Value
4 Dr GL Sdn	5490	6705
2 Dr GS Hbk	5290	6455
2 Dr GSi Hbk	5695	6955
2 Dr L Hbk	4880	5955

OPTIONS FOR ACCENT

Auto 4-Speed Transmission +410
AM/FM Compact Disc Player +235
Air Conditioning +455
Anti-Lock Brakes +365
Flip-Up Sunroof +190
Keyless Entry System +90

ELANTRA 1998

No changes to the Elantra for 1998.

RATINGS (SCALE OF 1-10)

Overall	Safety	Reliability	Performance	Comfort	Value
N/A	6.1	N/A	N/A	N/A	N/A

Category E

	Trade-in Value	Market Value
4 Dr GLS Sdn	6455	7885
4 Dr GLS Wgn	7175	8765
4 Dr STD Sdn	5935	7245
4 Dr STD Wgn	6380	7795

OPTIONS FOR ELANTRA

Auto 4-Speed Transmission[Std on GLS Wgn] +435
AM/FM Compact Disc Player +235
Air Conditioning +455
Aluminum/Alloy Wheels +185
Anti-Lock Brakes +365
Cruise Control +125
Keyless Entry System +90
Power Moonroof +320

SONATA 1998

No changes to the Sonata for 1998.

Category D

	Trade-in Value	Market Value
4 Dr GL Sdn	8305	9940
4 Dr GL V6 Sdn	8800	10535
4 Dr GLS Sdn	9395	11245
4 Dr STD Sdn	7515	8995

OPTIONS FOR SONATA

Auto 4-Speed Transmission[Opt on STD] +435
Anti-Lock Brakes +485
Cruise Control[Std on GLS] +135
Keyless Entry System +170
Leather Seats +620
Power Moonroof +460

Don't forget to refer to the Mileage Adjustment Table at the back of this book!

Model Description	Trade-in Value	Market Value

TIBURON 1998

Base Tiburons get the 2.0-liter 140-horsepower engine as standard equipment.

Category E

	Trade-in	Market
2 Dr FX Hbk	8500	10375
2 Dr STD Hbk	7775	9495

OPTIONS FOR TIBURON

Auto 4-Speed Transmission +435
Air Conditioning +455
Aluminum/Alloy Wheels[Std on FX] +185
Anti-Lock Brakes +365
Cruise Control +125
Fog Lights[Std on FX] +85
Keyless Entry System +90
Leather Seats +480
Power Sunroof +340

1997 HYUNDAI

ACCENT 1997

In the absence of truly ground-breaking improvement, Hyundai revises trim levels, adding GS hatchback and GL sedan mid-range models.

RATINGS (SCALE OF 1-10)

Overall	Safety	Reliability	Performance	Comfort	Value
N/A	5.9	N/A	N/A	N/A	N/A

Category E

	Trade-in	Market
4 Dr GL Sdn	4040	5105
2 Dr GS Hbk	3885	4905
2 Dr GT Hbk	4200	5305
2 Dr L Hbk	3565	4505

OPTIONS FOR ACCENT

Auto 4-Speed Transmission +335
AM/FM Compact Disc Player +195
AM/FM Stereo Tape +135
Air Conditioning +370
Anti-Lock Brakes +295
Flip-Up Sunroof +155
Keyless Entry System +75
Power Steering[Std on GT] +115
Rear Spoiler[Std on GT] +100

ELANTRA 1997

Elantra rolls into 1997 with zero changes, save for a slight price increase.

RATINGS (SCALE OF 1-10)

Overall	Safety	Reliability	Performance	Comfort	Value
N/A	5.8	N/A	N/A	N/A	N/A

Category E

	Trade-in	Market
4 Dr GLS Sdn	5425	6850
4 Dr GLS Wgn	6035	7620

Model Description	Trade-in Value	Market Value
4 Dr STD Sdn	4820	6085
4 Dr STD Wgn	5115	6455

OPTIONS FOR ELANTRA

Auto 4-Speed Transmission[Opt on STD] +355
AM/FM Compact Disc Player +195
Air Conditioning +370
Aluminum/Alloy Wheels +150
Anti-Lock Brakes +295
Cruise Control +100
Keyless Entry System +75
Luggage Rack[Opt on GLS] +60
Power Moonroof +260
Rear Spoiler +100

SONATA 1997

Sheetmetal is all-new, and gives Sonata a more substantial look despite somewhat controversial retro-style front fascia and grille. Flush-fitting doors and restyled exterior mirrors help quiet the ride, while horn activation switches from spoke button to center steering wheel pad.

Category D

	Trade-in	Market
4 Dr GL Sdn	6850	8385
4 Dr GLS Sdn	7745	9485
4 Dr STD Sdn	6195	7585

OPTIONS FOR SONATA

6 cyl 3.0 L Engine[Opt on GL] +445
Auto 4-Speed Transmission[Opt on STD] +355
Anti-Lock Brakes +395
Compact Disc W/fm/tape +345
Cruise Control[Opt on GL] +110
Keyless Entry System +140
Leather Seats +505
Power Moonroof +380

TIBURON 1997

Loosely based on the 1993 HCD-II concept car, the Tiburon (Spanish for shark) debuts as a budget sport coupe that promises to gobble competitors such as the Toyota Paseo like so much chum.

Category E

	Trade-in	Market
2 Dr FX Hbk	7100	8965
2 Dr STD Hbk	6450	8145

OPTIONS FOR TIBURON

Auto 4-Speed Transmission +355
Air Conditioning +370
Aluminum/Alloy Wheels[Std on FX] +150
Anti-Lock Brakes +295
Center Console[Std on FX] +40
Compact Disc W/fm/tape +215
Cruise Control +100
Fog Lights[Std on FX] +70
Keyless Entry System +75
Leather Seats +390
Power Sunroof +280
Rear Spoiler[Std on FX] +100

Don't forget to refer to the Mileage Adjustment Table at the back of this book!

HYUNDAI 96-95

Model Description	Trade-in Value	Market Value	Model Description	Trade-in Value	Market Value

1996 HYUNDAI

ACCENT 1996

Hyundai is painting the Accent in some new colors this year, and height-adjustable seatbelt anchors are standard. Front and rear center consoles with cupholders debut, and optional air conditioning is now CFC-free. A new, 105-horsepower GT hatch debuted midyear.

RATINGS (SCALE OF 1-10)

Overall	Safety	Reliability	Performance	Comfort	Value
N/A	5.8	N/A	N/A	N/A	N/A

Category E
2 Dr GT Hbk	3485	4710
2 Dr L Hbk	2940	3970
2 Dr STD Hbk	3110	4200
4 Dr STD Sdn	3280	4430

OPTIONS FOR ACCENT
Auto 4-Speed Transmission +275
AM/FM Compact Disc Player +160
Air Conditioning +305
Anti-Lock Brakes +245
Power Steering[Std on GT] +95
Rear Spoiler[Std on GT] +80
Sunroof +130

ELANTRA 1996

All-new Elantra is a slickly styled sedan or wagon featuring dual airbags, side-impact protection, and a more powerful engine. Pricing is up as well, pushing this Hyundai squarely into Dodge Neon and Honda Civic territory.

RATINGS (SCALE OF 1-10)

Overall	Safety	Reliability	Performance	Comfort	Value
N/A	5.8	N/A	N/A	N/A	N/A

Category E
4 Dr GLS Sdn	4135	5590
4 Dr GLS Wgn	4605	6225
4 Dr STD Sdn	3665	4955
4 Dr STD Wgn	3960	5345

OPTIONS FOR ELANTRA
Auto 4-Speed Transmission[Opt on STD,Sdn] +315
AM/FM Compact Disc Player +160
Air Conditioning +305
Aluminum/Alloy Wheels +125
Anti-Lock Brakes +245
Cruise Control +85
Rear Spoiler +80
Sunroof +130

SONATA 1996

Noise, vibration and harshness are quelled with the addition of insulation to the floor and cowl, and liquid-filled V6 engine mounts. ABS is available as a stand-alone option on the GLS, and Steel Gray joins the color chart. Upgraded seat fabric comes in the base and GL models, while all Sonatas get CFC-free A/C.

Category D
4 Dr GL Sdn	5085	6535
4 Dr GL V6 Sdn	5400	6940
4 Dr GLS Sdn	5810	7465
4 Dr STD Sdn	4550	5845

OPTIONS FOR SONATA
Auto 4-Speed Transmission[Opt on STD] +290
Anti-Lock Brakes +325
Compact Disc W/fm/tape +285
Cruise Control[Std on GLS] +90
Leather Seats +415
Power Moonroof +310

1995 HYUNDAI

ACCENT 1995

Dramatically improved car replaces Excel in lineup. Dual airbags are standard, and ABS is optional. Power comes from the 1.5-liter Alpha engine which debuted in 1993 Scoupe.

Category E
2 Dr L Hbk	2255	3200
2 Dr STD Hbk	2385	3385
4 Dr STD Sdn	2520	3575

OPTIONS FOR ACCENT
Auto 4-Speed Transmission +260
AM/FM Stereo Tape +90
Air Conditioning +250
Anti-Lock Brakes +200
Power Steering +75
Sunroof +105

ELANTRA 1995

No changes.
Category E
4 Dr GLS Sdn	2985	4235
4 Dr SE Sdn	2810	3990
4 Dr STD Sdn	2635	3745

OPTIONS FOR ELANTRA
4 cyl 1.8 L Engine[Std on GLS] +195
Auto 4-Speed Transmission +215
AM/FM Stereo Tape[Std on GLS] +90
Air Conditioning +250
Aluminum/Alloy Wheels +100
Anti-Lock Brakes +200
Cruise Control +70

Don't forget to refer to the Mileage Adjustment Table at the back of this book!

Model Description	Trade-in Value	Market Value
Power Moonroof +175		
Premium Sound System +100		
Rear Spoiler[Std on SE] +65		

SCOUPE 1995

No changes.

Category E

2 Dr LS Cpe	3035	4310
2 Dr STD Cpe	2665	3785
2 Dr STD Turbo Cpe	3245	4605

OPTIONS FOR SCOUPE

Auto 4-Speed Transmission +200
AM/FM Compact Disc Player +130
Air Conditioning +250
Aluminum/Alloy Wheels[Opt on LS] +100
Flip-Up Sunroof +105
Power Steering[Std on LS] +75
Premium Sound System +100

SONATA 1995

Brand-new Sonata debuted in mid-1994. Dual airbags are standard. A 137-horsepower engine powers base and GL models while a 142-horsepower V6 is optional on midlevel GL and standard on GLS. Both engines are Mitsubishi-based designs. New car meets 1997 side-impact standards. Air conditioning and cassette stereo are standard on all models.

Category D

4 Dr GL Sdn	3685	5160
4 Dr GL V6 Sdn	3920	5495
4 Dr GLS Sdn	4275	5995
4 Dr STD Sdn	3315	4645

OPTIONS FOR SONATA

Auto 4-Speed Transmission[Opt on STD] +240
Anti-Lock Brakes +265
Compact Disc W/fm/tape +230
Cruise Control[Std on GLS] +75
Leather Seats +340
Power Moonroof +250
Power Sunroof +235

1994 HYUNDAI

ELANTRA 1994

Styling is updated, and a driver airbag is standard. ABS is optional on GLS models. CFC-free refrigerant replaces freon in Elantra's air conditioning system.

Category E

4 Dr GLS Sdn	2015	3325
4 Dr STD Sdn	1800	2970

OPTIONS FOR ELANTRA

4 cyl 1.8 L Engine[Opt on STD] +110
Auto 4-Speed Transmission +175
AM/FM Compact Disc Player +105

Model Description	Trade-in Value	Market Value
Air Conditioning +205		
Aluminum/Alloy Wheels +80		
Anti-Lock Brakes +160		
Cruise Control +55		
Power Sunroof +150		

EXCEL 1994

Four-speed manual dropped from base car in favor of five-speed unit. Base sedan is discontinued. New interior fabrics and wheel covers spruce up the Excel. Air conditioners get CFC-free coolant.

Category E

4 Dr GL Sdn	1520	2505
2 Dr GS Hbk	1520	2505
2 Dr STD Hbk	1240	2045

OPTIONS FOR EXCEL

Auto 4-Speed Transmission +135
AM/FM Stereo Tape[Opt on STD] +75
Air Conditioning +205
Power Steering +60
Power Sunroof +150

SCOUPE 1994

Base and LS models receive new interior fabrics, wheel covers and revised trim molding. CFC-free refrigerant is added to the air conditioner.

Category E

2 Dr LS Cpe	2070	3415
2 Dr STD Cpe	1835	3030
2 Dr STD Turbo Cpe	2125	3505

OPTIONS FOR SCOUPE

Auto 4-Speed Transmission +165
AM/FM Compact Disc Player +105
Air Conditioning +205
Aluminum/Alloy Wheels +80
Flip-Up Sunroof +85
Power Steering[Std on LS] +60

SONATA 1994

No changes.

Category D

4 Dr GLS Sdn	2610	4290
4 Dr GLS V6 Sdn	2895	4750
4 Dr STD Sdn	2360	3880
4 Dr V6 Sdn	2645	4340

OPTIONS FOR SONATA

Auto 4-Speed Transmission[Opt on GLS,STD] +190
Aluminum/Alloy Wheels[Opt on GLS] +115
Anti-Lock Brakes +215
Compact Disc W/fm/tape +190
Cruise Control[Opt on STD,V6] +60
Leather Seats +275
Power Door Locks[Opt on STD,V6] +65
Power Sunroof +190
Power Windows[Opt on STD,V6] +65

Don't forget to refer to the Mileage Adjustment Table at the back of this book!

HYUNDAI 93-92

Model Description	Trade-in Value	Market Value	Model Description	Trade-in Value	Market Value

1993 HYUNDAI

ELANTRA 1993

Base model gets a black grille, while GLS features a body-color piece. GLS also gets new wheelcovers and steering wheel. All automatic models and the five-speed GLS get a new 1.8-liter engine good for 124 horsepower.

Category E

	Trade-in	Market
4 Dr GLS Sdn	1450	2685
4 Dr STD Sdn	1275	2355

OPTIONS FOR ELANTRA

4 cyl 1.8 L Engine[Opt on STD] +80
Auto 4-Speed Transmission +140
AM/FM Stereo Tape[Opt on STD] +60
Air Conditioning +165
Aluminum/Alloy Wheels +65
Cruise Control +45
Power Sunroof +125

EXCEL 1993

Slight styling revisions update Excel.

Category E

	Trade-in	Market
4 Dr GL Sdn	1230	2280
2 Dr GS Hbk	1135	2105
2 Dr STD Hbk	985	1825
4 Dr STD Sdn	1340	2475

OPTIONS FOR EXCEL

Auto 4-Speed Transmission +120
AM/FM Stereo Tape[Opt on STD] +60
Air Conditioning +165
Aluminum/Alloy Wheels +65
Power Steering +50
Sunroof +70

SCOUPE 1993

Styling updates, a new engine, and a new Turbo model summarize the big news for 1993. The new motor is a 1.5-liter SOHC four-cylinder designed and built by Hyundai. Called Alpha, the new engine makes 92 horsepower in base and LS Scoupes; 115 horsepower in Turbo format. Turbos are available only with a manual transmission. Dashboard is slightly revised and features rotary climate controls.

Category E

	Trade-in	Market
2 Dr LS Cpe	1435	2660
2 Dr STD Cpe	1285	2375
2 Dr STD Turbo Cpe	1545	2860

OPTIONS FOR SCOUPE

Auto 4-Speed Transmission +115
AM/FM Stereo Tape[Std on LS, Turbo] +60
Air Conditioning +165
Aluminum/Alloy Wheels[Std on Turbo] +65

Power Steering[Std on LS, Turbo] +50
Sunroof +70

SONATA 1993

Front air intake is now body-color, and new wheelcovers debut.

Category D

	Trade-in	Market
4 Dr GLS Sdn	1775	3300
4 Dr STD Sdn	1600	2975

OPTIONS FOR SONATA

6 cyl 3.0 L Engine +155
Auto 4-Speed Transmission +145
AM/FM Compact Disc Player +95
Aluminum/Alloy Wheels +95
Anti-Lock Brakes +175
Cruise Control[Opt on STD] +50
Leather Seats +225
Power Door Locks[Opt on STD] +55
Power Sunroof +155
Power Windows[Opt on STD] +55

1992 HYUNDAI

ELANTRA 1992

Brand-new compact is slotted between Excel and Sonata. All models come standard with a 113-horsepower, 1.6-liter, twin-cam four-cylinder engine. Horsepower drops to 105 with the automatic transmission.

Category E

	Trade-in	Market
4 Dr GLS Sdn	1085	2210
4 Dr STD Sdn	980	2000

OPTIONS FOR ELANTRA

Auto 4-Speed Transmission +105
Air Conditioning +135
Cruise Control +35
Power Sunroof +100

EXCEL 1992

GLS sedan dropped from lineup.

Category E

	Trade-in	Market
4 Dr GL Sdn	995	2025
2 Dr GS Hbk	895	1820
2 Dr STD Hbk	780	1590
4 Dr STD Sdn	915	1865

OPTIONS FOR EXCEL

Auto 4-Speed Transmission +95
Air Conditioning +135

SCOUPE 1992

No changes.

Category E

	Trade-in	Market
2 Dr LS Cpe	1080	2195
2 Dr STD Cpe	955	1945

Don't forget to refer to the Mileage Adjustment Table at the back of this book!

Model Description	Trade-in Value	Market Value

OPTIONS FOR SCOUPE
Auto 4-Speed Transmission +95
Air Conditioning +135
Cruise Control +35
Sunroof +55

SONATA 1992

Styling is tweaked, ABS is optional on GLS V6 models, and a new 2.0-liter, twin-cam engine replaces the less-powerful, 2.4-liter base unit.

Category D

4 Dr GLS Sdn	1435	2975
4 Dr STD Sdn	1150	2390

OPTIONS FOR SONATA
6 cyl 3.0 L Engine +225
Auto 4-Speed Transmission +120
Air Conditioning[Opt on STD] +140
Anti-Lock Brakes +145
Cruise Control[Opt on STD] +40
Power Door Locks[Opt on STD] +45
Power Moonroof +140
Power Windows[Opt on STD] +45

1991 HYUNDAI

EXCEL 1991

No changes.
Category E

4 Dr GL Sdn	560	1660
4 Dr GL SE Sdn	555	1655
4 Dr GLS Sdn	610	1815
2 Dr GS Hbk	495	1470
2 Dr GS SE Hbk	490	1455
2 Dr STD Hbk	435	1295
4 Dr STD Sdn	510	1520

OPTIONS FOR EXCEL
Auto 4-Speed Transmission +90
Air Conditioning +110

SCOUPE 1991

Sports coupe debuts based on Excel underpinnings. Car gets its own coupe styling, interior and Lotus-tuned suspension. Scoupe has a whopping 81 horsepower; a shorter final-drive ratio makes Scoupe slightly speedier than the slooooooow Excel.

Category E

2 Dr LS Cpe	625	1855
2 Dr SE Cpe	585	1735
2 Dr STD Cpe	540	1605

OPTIONS FOR SCOUPE
Auto 4-Speed Transmission +70
Air Conditioning +110
Cruise Control +30
Sunroof +45

SONATA 1991

Child-proof rear door locks are added.
Category D

4 Dr GLS Sdn	1180	2450
4 Dr GLS SE Sdn	1340	2780
4 Dr STD Sdn	960	1990

OPTIONS FOR SONATA
6 cyl 3.0 L Engine[Std on GLS SE] +100
Auto 4-Speed Transmission[Std on GLS SE] +95
Radio Option +175
Air Conditioning[Opt on STD] +115
Cruise Control[Opt on STD] +35
Power Door Locks[Opt on STD] +35
Power Windows[Opt on STD] +35

INFINITI 00-99

Model Description	Trade-in Value	Market Value	Model Description	Trade-in Value	Market Value

INFINITI   Japan

1993 Infiniti J30

2000 INFINITI

G20   2000

The G20 entry-level compact receives numerous mechanical improvements, exterior and interior enhancements and safety additions for 2000, including more horsepower, revised transmissions, and a new muffler.

Category D

4 Dr Luxury Sdn	15835	18370
4 Dr Touring Sdn	16920	19625

OPTIONS FOR G20
Auto 4-Speed Transmission +655
Infiniti Communicator +1305
Climate Control for AC[Opt on Luxury] +245
Garage Door Opener +165
Leather Seats +925
Leather Steering Wheel[Opt on Luxury] +105
Power Drivers Seat +255
Power Moonroof +690

I30   2000

2000 marks the introduction of the all-new Infiniti I30.

Category D

4 Dr STD Sdn	22085	25620
4 Dr Touring Sdn	23615	27395

OPTIONS FOR I30
Infiniti Communicator +1305
Heated Front Seats +305
Rear Spoiler +360

Q45   2000

For 2000 the Q45 celebrates a decade of production with a special 10th Anniversary model. All Qs receive a new 100,000-mile tune-up interval and special child seat tethers.

Category J

4 Dr Anniversary Sdn	35775	41095
4 Dr STD Sdn	34585	39730
4 Dr Touring Sdn	35775	41095

OPTIONS FOR Q45
Infiniti Communicator +1305

QX4   2000

Infiniti's luxury SUV gets minor improvements to its emissions system but is otherwise a carryover from the 1999 model year. A more powerful QX4 will be available soon as a 2001 model.

Category G

4 Dr STD 4WD Wgn	26365	30490

OPTIONS FOR QX4
Infiniti Communicator +1305
Compact Disc Changer +415
Power Moonroof +710
Rear Wind Deflector +105

1999 INFINITI

G20   1999

The G20 returns to the Infiniti lineup after a two-year hiatus. This entry-level compact is based on the European- and Japanese- market Primera, which has garnered a great deal of acclaim from the foreign automotive press.

RATINGS (SCALE OF 1-10)

Overall	Safety	Reliability	Performance	Comfort	Value
N/A	N/A	9.1	7.8	7.8	N/A

Category D

4 Dr STD Sdn	14955	17410
4 Dr Touring Sdn	15225	17725

OPTIONS FOR G20
Auto 4-Speed Transmission +535
Climate Control for AC[Opt on STD] +200
Garage Door Opener +135
Heated Front Seats +250
Leather Seats +760
Leather Steering Wheel[Opt on STD] +85
Power Drivers Seat +210
Power Moonroof +565

I30   1999

Traction control is available as an option, the audio faceplate has been updated and an ignition immobilizer is offered on the I30.

Don't forget to refer to the Mileage Adjustment Table at the back of this book!

Model Description	Trade-in Value	Market Value

RATINGS (SCALE OF 1-10)

Overall	Safety	Reliability	Performance	Comfort	Value
N/A	N/A	N/A	8.4	8	N/A

Category D
4 Dr STD Sdn   19855   23115
4 Dr Touring Sdn   21410   24920

OPTIONS FOR I30
Auto 4-Speed Transmission[Opt on Touring] +670
Infiniti Communicator +600
Automatic Dimming Mirror[Opt on STD] +165
Garage Door Opener[Opt on STD] +135
Heated Front Seats +250
Leather Seats[Opt on STD] +760
Power Moonroof[Opt on STD] +565

Q45   1999

Several small exterior and interior enhancements have been added to the Q for 1999, including a new sunroof, revised front styling and the return of the analog clock.

RATINGS (SCALE OF 1-10)

Overall	Safety	Reliability	Performance	Comfort	Value
N/A	N/A	N/A	8.4	9	N/A

Category J
4 Dr STD Sdn   30375   35040
4 Dr Touring Sdn   31435   36260

OPTIONS FOR Q45
Infiniti Communicator +600
Compact Disc Changer +625
Heated Front Seats +290

QX4   1999

Infiniti's luxury sport-ute enters its third year with no major changes.

RATINGS (SCALE OF 1-10)

Overall	Safety	Reliability	Performance	Comfort	Value
N/A	N/A	N/A	7	7.3	N/A

Category G
4 Dr STD 4WD Wgn   24790   28715

OPTIONS FOR QX4
Infiniti Communicator +1070
Compact Disc Changer +340
Heated Front Seats +180
Power Moonroof +580

1998 INFINITI

I30   1998

Side-impact airbags make their way into the Infiniti I30, as do new headlamps, taillamps, center console and wheels.

RATINGS (SCALE OF 1-10)

Overall	Safety	Reliability	Performance	Comfort	Value
7.5	7.9	9.3	8.4	8	4.1

Category D
4 Dr STD Sdn   17625   20590
4 Dr Touring Sdn   19185   22410

OPTIONS FOR I30
Auto 4-Speed Transmission[Opt on Touring] +545
Infiniti Communicator +490
Heated Front Seats[Opt on STD] +205
Heated Power Mirrors[Opt on STD] +45
Leather Seats[Opt on STD] +620
Power Moonroof[Opt on STD] +460

Q45   1998

The Q45 gets front seatbelt pretensioners. No other changes for Infiniti's flagship.

RATINGS (SCALE OF 1-10)

Overall	Safety	Reliability	Performance	Comfort	Value
N/A	N/A	9	8.4	9	5.3

Category J
4 Dr STD Sdn   27180   31365
4 Dr Touring Sdn   28305   32665

OPTIONS FOR Q45
Infiniti Communicator +490
Compact Disc Changer[Opt on STD] +515
Heated Front Seats[Opt on STD] +235

QX4   1998

No changes to the QX4.

RATINGS (SCALE OF 1-10)

Overall	Safety	Reliability	Performance	Comfort	Value
N/A	N/A	8.8	7	7.3	4.6

Category G
4 Dr STD 4WD Wgn   22680   26325

OPTIONS FOR QX4
Compact Disc Changer +275
Heated Front Seats +150
Power Moonroof +475

1997 INFINITI

I30   1997

A few new paint colors are the only changes to the 1997 I30.

RATINGS (SCALE OF 1-10)

Overall	Safety	Reliability	Performance	Comfort	Value
7.5	7.5	9.3	8.4	8	4.1

Model Description	Trade-in Value	Market Value
Category D		
4 Dr STD Sdn	15405	17970
4 Dr Touring Sdn	16825	19625

OPTIONS FOR I30

Auto 4-Speed Transmission +430
Heated Front Seats[Opt on STD] +165
Leather Seats[Opt on STD] +505
Limited Slip Diff[Opt on STD] +220
Power Moonroof[Opt on STD] +380

J30   1997

Last year for the J30.

RATINGS (SCALE OF 1-10)

Overall	Safety	Reliability	Performance	Comfort	Value
7.7	7.6	9.7	8.4	8.5	4.4

Category J		
4 Dr STD Sdn	18190	21155
1997.5 4 Dr STD Sdn	18190	21155
4 Dr Touring Sdn	17120	19910
1997.5 4 Dr Touring Sdn	17120	19910

Q45   1997

This totally redesigned car has almost nothing in common with its predecessor. Power now comes via a 4.1-liter V8 engine and is still delivered through the rear wheels. The Q45 no longer has aspirations to be a sports sedan, its prime duties now are interstate cruising.

RATINGS (SCALE OF 1-10)

Overall	Safety	Reliability	Performance	Comfort	Value
N/A	N/A	8.5	8.4	9	4

Category J		
4 Dr STD Sdn	23870	27760
1997.5 4 Dr STD Sdn	23870	27760
4 Dr Touring Sdn	24860	28910
1997.5 4 Dr Touring Sdn	24860	28910

OPTIONS FOR Q45

Heated Front Seats[Opt on STD] +195

QX4   1997

A version of Nissan's wonderful four-wheeler is introduced by Infiniti, aiming to compete with the Mercury Mountaineer, Acura SLX and Land Rover Discovery. Differences between the QX4 and the Pathfinder include the Q's full-time four-wheel drive system, a more luxurious interior, and some different sheetmetal.

RATINGS (SCALE OF 1-10)

Overall	Safety	Reliability	Performance	Comfort	Value
N/A	N/A	8.6	7	7.3	4.5

Model Description	Trade-in Value	Market Value
Category G		
4 Dr STD 4WD Wgn	20600	23970

OPTIONS FOR QX4

Heated Front Seats +120
Limited Slip Diff +125
Power Moonroof +385

1996 INFINITI

G20   1996

Emergency locking front and rear seatbelts have been installed, and fake wood is applied on models equipped with the Leather Appointment Package. This is the last year for the entry-level Infinti.

RATINGS (SCALE OF 1-10)

Overall	Safety	Reliability	Performance	Comfort	Value
N/A	N/A	8.9	8.6	7.8	5.9

Category D		
4 Dr STD Sdn	10125	12025
4 Dr Touring Sdn	11250	13360

OPTIONS FOR G20

Auto 4-Speed Transmission +365
Dual Power Seats[Opt on STD] +310
Keyless Entry System[Opt on STD] +115
Leather Seats[Opt on STD] +415
Power Moonroof[Opt on STD] +310

I30   1996

New luxo-sport sedan based on the Nissan Maxima arrived during 1995. Slotted between the G20 and the J30, the I30 competes with the Lexus ES 300, BMW 3-Series, and the new Acura TL-Series. If you like big chrome grilles, this is the car to buy.

RATINGS (SCALE OF 1-10)

Overall	Safety	Reliability	Performance	Comfort	Value
N/A	N/A	9.2	8.4	8	5

Category D		
4 Dr STD Sdn	13020	15455
4 Dr Touring Sdn	14955	17755

OPTIONS FOR I30

Auto 4-Speed Transmission +335
Heated Front Seats[Opt on STD] +135
Leather Seats[Opt on STD] +415
Limited Slip Diff[Opt on STD] +180
Power Moonroof[Opt on STD] +310

J30   1996

Three new colors join the paint palette.

RATINGS (SCALE OF 1-10)

Overall	Safety	Reliability	Performance	Comfort	Value
7.7	7.6	9.8	8.4	8.5	4.4

Don't forget to refer to the Mileage Adjustment Table at the back of this book!

Model Description	Trade-in Value	Market Value
Category J		
4 Dr STD Sdn	16030	18790
4 Dr Touring Sdn	16825	19725

Q45   1996

Active suspension model is canceled, but two new exterior colors are available.

RATINGS (SCALE OF 1-10)

Overall	Safety	Reliability	Performance	Comfort	Value
N/A	N/A	9.2	8.6	9.1	5.7

Category J		
4 Dr STD Sdn	19530	22890
4 Dr Touring Sdn	20920	24525

OPTIONS FOR Q45
Compact Disc W/fm/tape +260
Heated Front Seats +160
Traction Control System +425

1995 INFINITI

G20   1995

All-season tires are added to the G20. No other changes are made to the entry-level Infiniti.

RATINGS (SCALE OF 1-10)

Overall	Safety	Reliability	Performance	Comfort	Value
N/A	N/A	8.3	8.6	7.8	5.4

Category D		
4 Dr STD Sdn	8710	10560
4 Dr Touring Sdn	9870	11960

OPTIONS FOR G20
Auto 4-Speed Transmission +300
Dual Power Seats +255
Keyless Entry System[Opt on STD] +95
Leather Seats[Opt on STD] +340
Power Moonroof[Opt on STD] +250

J30   1995

Redesigned taillights, power lumbar support for the driver's seat, and an anti-glare mirror mark the changes for the 1995 J30.

RATINGS (SCALE OF 1-10)

Overall	Safety	Reliability	Performance	Comfort	Value
7.9	8.3	9.4	8.4	8.5	4.9

Category J		
4 Dr STD Sdn	13390	15785

OPTIONS FOR J30
Touring Pkg +470
Rear Spoiler +120

Q45   1995

Alloy wheels for the base model are about the only changes for the Q45.

RATINGS (SCALE OF 1-10)

Overall	Safety	Reliability	Performance	Comfort	Value
N/A	N/A	8.8	8.6	9.1	5.6

Category J		
4 Dr A Sdn	19875	23425
4 Dr STD Sdn	17565	20705

OPTIONS FOR Q45
Compact Disc Changer[Std on A] +280
Heated Front Seats[Std on A] +130
Traction Control System[Std on A] +350

1994 INFINITI

G20   1994

No changes to the G20.

RATINGS (SCALE OF 1-10)

Overall	Safety	Reliability	Performance	Comfort	Value
N/A	N/A	8.4	8.6	7.8	6.3

Category D		
4 Dr STD Sdn	7400	9060

OPTIONS FOR G20
Auto 4-Speed Transmission +245
Dual Power Seats +210
Keyless Entry System +75
Leather Seats +275
Limited Slip Diff +120
Power Moonroof +205
Rear Spoiler +110

J30   1994

Heated front seats and the addition of two speakers further pamper passengers in the J30.

RATINGS (SCALE OF 1-10)

Overall	Safety	Reliability	Performance	Comfort	Value
7.7	8.3	9	8.4	8.5	4.3

Category J		
4 Dr STD Sdn	12250	14555

OPTIONS FOR J30
Touring Pkg +490
Rear Spoiler +95

Q45   1994

A passenger airbag appears on the restyled 1994 Infiniti. Changes to the grille, bumpers and fog lights will distinguish this car from previous models.

Don't forget to refer to the Mileage Adjustment Table at the back of this book!

Model Description	Trade-in Value	Market Value

RATINGS (SCALE OF 1-10)

Overall	Safety	Reliability	Performance	Comfort	Value
N/A	N/A	8	8.6	9.1	5.5

Category J

	Trade-in	Market
4 Dr A Sdn	16225	19280
4 Dr STD Sdn	14615	17365

OPTIONS FOR Q45

Touring Pkg +560
Heated Front Seats[Std on A] +105
Traction Control System[Std on A] +285

1993 INFINITI

G20 — 1993

Driver and passenger airbags are introduced as a midyear change to the G20.

RATINGS (SCALE OF 1-10)

Overall	Safety	Reliability	Performance	Comfort	Value
N/A	N/A	8.3	8.6	7.8	6.2

Category D

	Trade-in	Market
4 Dr STD Sdn	5540	7130

OPTIONS FOR G20

Auto 4-Speed Transmission +180
Dual Power Seats +170
Keyless Entry System +60
Leather Seats +225
Power Sunroof +155

J30 — 1993

A new introduction to the Infiniti lineup, the J30 really shakes things up. Love it or hate it, this car certainly turns heads. Powered by a 210-horsepower V6 gleaned from the Nissan 300ZX, the J30 is shifted by a four-speed automatic transmission. Dual airbags are standard on the J30, as are antilock brakes.

RATINGS (SCALE OF 1-10)

Overall	Safety	Reliability	Performance	Comfort	Value
7.6	8.3	9.1	8.4	8.5	3.8

Category J

	Trade-in	Market
4 Dr STD Sdn	9920	11915

OPTIONS FOR J30

Touring Pkg +345
Rear Spoiler +80

Q45 — 1993

Interior designers get a hold of the Q, sprucing, coloring and covering everything in beautiful new materials; even the clock on this car masquerades as a hand-crafted timepiece. Additional touches include map pockets to the front seat backs.

Model Description	Trade-in Value	Market Value

RATINGS (SCALE OF 1-10)

Overall	Safety	Reliability	Performance	Comfort	Value
N/A	N/A	8.7	9	8.4	5.4

Category J

	Trade-in	Market
4 Dr A Sdn	12280	14750
4 Dr STD Sdn	11070	13300

OPTIONS FOR Q45

Touring Pkg +540
Traction Control System +230

1992 INFINITI

G20 — 1992

New tires and an automatic transmission are introduced on Infiniti junior.

RATINGS (SCALE OF 1-10)

Overall	Safety	Reliability	Performance	Comfort	Value
N/A	N/A	8.1	8.6	7.8	6.2

Category D

	Trade-in	Market
4 Dr STD Sdn	4340	5710

OPTIONS FOR G20

Auto 4-Speed Transmission +145
Leather Seats +185
Power Sunroof +125

M30 — 1992

Last year for the M30.

Category J

	Trade-in	Market
2 Dr STD Conv	7715	9475
2 Dr STD Cpe	5745	7050

Q45 — 1992

High-performance tires and new exterior colors are available on the 1992 Q45.

RATINGS (SCALE OF 1-10)

Overall	Safety	Reliability	Performance	Comfort	Value
N/A	N/A	8.5	9	8.4	5.9

Category J

	Trade-in	Market
4 Dr A Sdn	10285	12625
4 Dr STD Sdn	9340	11465

OPTIONS FOR Q45

Touring Pkg +405
Traction Control System +190

Don't forget to refer to the Mileage Adjustment Table at the back of this book!

INFINITI 91

Model Description	Trade-in Value	Market Value	Model Description	Trade-in Value	Market Value

1991 INFINITI

G20 1991

Infiniti's entry-level sedan is the new G20. Based on the Japanese market Nissan Primera, but suitably well-dressed to call itself an Infiniti, the G20 is designed to lure not-yet-affluent car buyers into the Infiniti family.

RATINGS (SCALE OF 1-10)

Overall	Safety	Reliability	Performance	Comfort	Value
N/A	N/A	6.8	8.6	7.8	5.5

Category D

	Trade-in	Market
4 Dr STD Sdn	3925	5135

OPTIONS FOR G20

Auto 4-Speed Transmission +105
Leather Seats +150
Power Sunroof +105

M30 1991

No significant changes for the midsized offering from Infiniti.

Category J

	Trade-in	Market
2 Dr STD Conv	6535	8205
2 Dr STD Cpe	5180	6505

Q45 1991

Four-wheel steering is introduced to the Infiniti flagship. Full Active Suspension is available on the Q45, enabling the car to react much more quickly to changes in car position than a vehicle with conventional shock absorbers.

RATINGS (SCALE OF 1-10)

Overall	Safety	Reliability	Performance	Comfort	Value
N/A	N/A	7.5	9	8.4	5.8

Category J

	Trade-in	Market
4 Dr A Sdn	7960	9990
4 Dr STD Sdn	7220	9060

OPTIONS FOR Q45

Touring Pkg +335

Don't forget to refer to the Mileage Adjustment Table at the back of this book!

Model Description	Trade-in Value	Market Value

Model Description	Trade-in Value	Market Value

ISUZU — Japan

1996 Isuzu Oasis

2000 ISUZU

AMIGO — 2000

Redesigned front styling and several new colors are available for the new year. The Ironman package offers the Rodeo's Intelligent Suspension Control system.

Category G

Model Description	Trade-in Value	Market Value
2 Dr S Conv	11795	13740
2 Dr S 4WD Conv	13685	15940
2 Dr S Utility	11795	13740
2 Dr S V6 Conv	13600	15845
2 Dr S V6 Utility	13600	15845
2 Dr S V6 4WD Utility	15260	17775

OPTIONS FOR AMIGO
Ironman Pkg +715
AM/FM Compact Disc Player +260
Air Conditioning +670
Alarm System +220
Aluminum/Alloy Wheels +265
Compact Disc Changer +415
Fog Lights +120
Keyless Entry System +160
Limited Slip Diff[Std on S] +225
Luggage Rack +130
Power Door Locks +190
Power Mirrors +110
Power Windows +200
Side Steps +200
Special Graphics +70
Trailer Hitch +230

HOMBRE — 2000

Hombres receive an upgraded standard suspension package and V6 engines get a horsepower boost. The three-door Space Cab gets a bare bones S trim model.

Category G

Model Description	Trade-in Value	Market Value
2 Dr S Ext Cab SB	9950	11590
2 Dr S Std Cab SB	8460	9855
2 Dr S 4WD Std Cab SB	13065	15215
2 Dr S V6 Ext Cab SB	11535	13435
2 Dr S V6 4WD Ext Cab SB	13780	16055
2 Dr XS Ext Cab SB	11420	13300
2 Dr XS 4WD Ext Cab SB	14695	17115
2 Dr XS Std Cab SB	9530	11100
2 Dr XS V6 Ext Cab SB	12885	15005

OPTIONS FOR HOMBRE
Auto 4-Speed Transmission[Opt on S,XS,4] +835
AM/FM Stereo Tape[Opt on S,S V6,Std Cab] +180
Air Conditioning[Std on XS,XS V6,S 4WD Regular Cab SB] +670

RODEO — 2000

The Rodeo marches into the 2000 model year with an aggressive exterior restyle, a collection of ergonomic and quality improvements, and interior upgrades.

Category G

Model Description	Trade-in Value	Market Value
4 Dr LS Wgn	16805	19575
4 Dr LS 4WD Wgn	18690	21770
4 Dr LSE Wgn	20565	23955
4 Dr LSE 4WD Wgn	22305	25980
4 Dr S Wgn	13045	15195
4 Dr S V6 Wgn	15085	17570
4 Dr S V6 4WD Wgn	16810	19580

OPTIONS FOR RODEO
Auto 4-Speed Transmission[Std on LSE] +815
Ironman Pkg +790
Air Conditioning[Std on LS,LSE] +670
Alarm System[Opt on S V6] +220
Aluminum/Alloy Wheels[Std on LS,LSE] +265
Luggage Rack[Std on LS,LSE] +130
Rear Spoiler +155
Rear Window Wiper[Std on LS,LSE,4] +125
Running Boards +315

TROOPER — 2000

A two-wheel drive model is available in the S trim, as well as the new mid-level LS and top-level Limited guises; all receive slight exterior restyling. The 10 year/ 120,000-mile powertrain warranty, the longest in America, ensures longevity.

Category G

Model Description	Trade-in Value	Market Value
4 Dr LS Wgn	19650	22885
4 Dr LS 4WD Wgn	20995	24455
4 Dr Limited Wgn	22375	26065
4 Dr Limited 4WD Wgn	23725	27635
4 Dr S Wgn	18500	21550
4 Dr S 4WD Wgn	18805	21905

Don't forget to refer to the Mileage Adjustment Table at the back of this book!

Model Description	Trade-in Value	Market Value	Model Description	Trade-in Value	Market Value

ISUZU 00-99

OPTIONS FOR TROOPER
Auto 4-Speed Transmission[Opt on S] +1265

VEHICROSS 2000

Fat 18-inch wheels replace the previous 16-inchers. The new year also brings standard A/C, new exterior colors and a 10-year/120,000-mile powertrain warranty, the longest in America.

Category G

2 Dr STD 4WD Utility	24050	28015

OPTIONS FOR VEHICROSS
Ironman Pkg +640

1999 ISUZU

AMIGO 1999

Two body styles are available, hardtop or softtop, and an automatic transmission is now offered with the V6 engine.

Category G

2 Dr S Conv	11325	13265
2 Dr S 4WD Conv	13075	15315
2 Dr S Utility	11325	13265
2 Dr S V6 Conv	12810	15005
2 Dr S V6 4WD Conv	13870	16245
2 Dr S V6 Utility	14415	16880
2 Dr S V6 4WD Utility	14410	16875

OPTIONS FOR AMIGO
Auto 4-Speed Transmission +520
AM/FM Compact Disc Player +210
Air Conditioning +550
Aluminum/Alloy Wheels +215
Fog Lights +95
Keyless Entry System +130
Power Door Locks +155
Power Mirrors +90
Power Windows +160

HOMBRE 1999

Hombres receive additional exterior colors and a new bumper fascia. A three-door spacecab model is now available.

RATINGS (SCALE OF 1-10)

Overall	Safety	Reliability	Performance	Comfort	Value
N/A	N/A	N/A	6.6	7.9	N/A

Category G

2 Dr S Std Cab SB	7590	8890
2 Dr S 4WD Std Cab SB	11160	13070
2 Dr XS Ext Cab SB	9895	11590
2 Dr XS 4WD Ext Cab SB	12970	15190
2 Dr XS Std Cab SB	7850	9195
2 Dr XS V6 Ext Cab SB	11295	13230

OPTIONS FOR HOMBRE
Auto 4-Speed Transmission[Std on XS V6] +715
AM/FM Compact Disc Player +210
Air Conditioning +550
Aluminum/Alloy Wheels[Std on 4WD] +215
Cruise Control +140
Power Door Locks +155
Power Windows +160
Sliding Rear Window +80
Tilt Steering Wheel +120

OASIS 1999

Only one trim level is available for 1999. Oasis has a new seating arrangement, interior and exterior refinements, and a couple of new colors.

RATINGS (SCALE OF 1-10)

Overall	Safety	Reliability	Performance	Comfort	Value
N/A	7.5	N/A	N/A	N/A	N/A

Category G

4 Dr S Pass. Van	16430	19245

OPTIONS FOR OASIS
AM/FM Compact Disc Player +210
Aluminum/Alloy Wheels +215

RODEO 1999

Isuzu juggles minor standard and optional equipment for 1999, making items from last year's S V6 preferred equipment package standard on the LS, and last year's LS equipment standard on a new trim level called LSE.

RATINGS (SCALE OF 1-10)

Overall	Safety	Reliability	Performance	Comfort	Value
N/A	7.5	N/A	7.8	7.3	N/A

Category G

4 Dr LS Wgn	15875	18595
4 Dr LS 4WD Wgn	17660	20685
4 Dr LSE Wgn	18745	21955
4 Dr LSE 4WD Wgn	20380	23870
4 Dr S Wgn	12335	14445
4 Dr S V6 Wgn	14290	16735
4 Dr S V6 4WD Wgn	15975	18710

OPTIONS FOR RODEO
Auto 4-Speed Transmission[Std on LSE 4WD] +670
AM/FM Compact Disc Player +210
Air Conditioning[Std on LS,LSE] +550
Aluminum/Alloy Wheels[Std on LSE,LS 4WD] +215
Luggage Rack[Std on LS,LSE] +110
Swing Out Tire Carrier +125

TROOPER 1999

A gold trim package is added to the Trooper's option list and Torque on Demand is now standard with the automatic transmission.

Model Description	Trade-in Value	Market Value

RATINGS (SCALE OF 1-10)

Overall	Safety	Reliability	Performance	Comfort	Value
N/A	7.6	N/A	6.8	7.6	N/A

Category G

4 Dr S 4WD Wgn	17240	20190

OPTIONS FOR TROOPER
Auto 4-Speed Transmission +1035
Luxury Pkg +1140
AM/FM Compact Disc Player +210
Dual Power Seats +280
Heated Front Seats +180
Leather Seats +525
Limited Slip Diff +185
Privacy Glass +185
Running Boards +260

VEHICROSS   1999

Isuzu imports its unique-looking, award-winning SUV to the U.S. in 1999.

Category G

2 Dr STD 4WD Utility	21410	25075

OPTIONS FOR VEHICROSS
Ironman Pkg +725

1998 ISUZU

AMIGO   1998

Isuzu reintroduces its convertible sport utility after a three-year hiatus. This model comes with a modest four-cylinder engine, but the powerful V6 from the Rodeo is available and turns this 4WD droptop into a screamer.

Category G

2 Dr S Utility	9635	11375
2 Dr S 4WD Utility	11195	13220
2 Dr S V6 4WD Utility	12350	14580

OPTIONS FOR AMIGO
AM/FM Compact Disc Player +175
Air Conditioning +450
Aluminum/Alloy Wheels +175
Cruise Control +115
Fog Lights +80
Keyless Entry System +105
Power Door Locks +130
Power Mirrors +70
Power Windows +135
Tilt Steering Wheel +100

HOMBRE   1998

Four-wheel drive arrives, finally. Also new are a theft deterrent system and dual airbags housed in a revised instrument panel, with a passenger-side airbag cutoff switch so the kiddies can ride up front.

RATINGS (SCALE OF 1-10)

Overall	Safety	Reliability	Performance	Comfort	Value
N/A	6.5	8.4	6.6	7.9	N/A

Category G

2 Dr S Std Cab SB	7395	8730
2 Dr S 4WD Std Cab SB	10900	12870
2 Dr XS Ext Cab SB	9700	11450
2 Dr XS 4WD Ext Cab SB	12805	15115
2 Dr XS Std Cab SB	7165	8460
2 Dr XS V6 Ext Cab SB	11075	13075

OPTIONS FOR HOMBRE
Auto 4-Speed Transmission[Std on XS V6] +550
AM/FM Compact Disc Player +175
Air Conditioning +450
Aluminum/Alloy Wheels[Std on S,4WD] +175
Cruise Control +115
Power Door Locks +130
Power Mirrors +70
Power Windows +135
Sliding Rear Window +65
Tilt Steering Wheel +100

OASIS   1998

The engine is upgraded to a more sophisticated 2.3-liter, good for an extra 10 horsepower and 7 foot-ponds of torque, and the transmission is revised. A tachometer is now standard, so you can better measure all that extra power.

RATINGS (SCALE OF 1-10)

Overall	Safety	Reliability	Performance	Comfort	Value
N/A	7.5	9.2	N/A	N/A	N/A

Category G

4 Dr LS Pass. Van	16190	19115
4 Dr S Pass. Van	14900	17595

OPTIONS FOR OASIS
Luggage Rack[Opt on S] +90

RODEO   1998

Though it may not look like it, Isuzu has completely revised the Rodeo from top to bottom, giving it more modern styling, a user-friendly interior, more V6 power, and added room for passengers and cargo.

RATINGS (SCALE OF 1-10)

Overall	Safety	Reliability	Performance	Comfort	Value
6.9	7.1	7.1	7.8	7.3	5.4

Category G

4 Dr LS Wgn	15770	18620
4 Dr LS 4WD Wgn	16665	19675
4 Dr S Wgn	10985	12965
4 Dr S V6 Wgn	12745	15045
4 Dr S V6 4WD Wgn	14105	16655

Model Description	Trade-in Value	Market Value

Model Description	Trade-in Value	Market Value

OPTIONS FOR RODEO
Auto 4-Speed Transmission[Std on LS] +545
AM/FM Compact Disc Player +175
Air Conditioning[Std on LS] +450
Cruise Control[Std on LS] +115
Fog Lights[Std on LS] +80
Heated Power Mirrors[Std on LS] +45
Keyless Entry System[Std on LS] +105
Power Door Locks[Std on LS] +130
Power Windows[Std on LS] +135
Swing Out Tire Carrier[Opt on S, S V6, 2WD] +100
Tilt Steering Wheel[Std on LS] +100

TROOPER   1998

A bigger and lighter engine provides huge improvements in horsepower and torque (up 13 and 22 percent, respectively). And the new Torque On Demand (TOD) drive system replaces conventional four-high mode for better performance on paved or slippery roads.

RATINGS (SCALE OF 1-10)

Overall	Safety	Reliability	Performance	Comfort	Value
7.5	7.5	8.7	6.8	7.6	6.9

Category G
4 Dr Luxury 4WD Wgn	17915	21150
4 Dr S 4WD Wgn	14995	17705

OPTIONS FOR TROOPER
Auto 4-Speed Transmission[Opt on S] +685
Leather Seating Pkg +460
Performance Pkg +910
AM/FM Compact Disc Player +175
Compact Disc Changer[Opt on S] +275
Dual Power Seats[Opt on S] +230
Heated Front Seats[Opt on S] +150
Leather Seats[Opt on S] +430
Limited Slip Diff +150
Privacy Glass +150
Running Boards +210

1997 ISUZU

HOMBRE   1997

A Spacecab model debuts, with seating for five passengers and your choice of four-cylinder or V6 power. Other news includes two fresh paint colors and revised graphics.

RATINGS (SCALE OF 1-10)

Overall	Safety	Reliability	Performance	Comfort	Value
N/A	5.6	8.2	6.6	7.9	N/A

Category G
2 Dr S Std Cab SB	6360	7550
2 Dr XS Ext Cab SB	7990	9490

2 Dr XS Std Cab SB	6590	7825
2 Dr XS V6 Ext Cab SB	9140	10850

OPTIONS FOR HOMBRE
Auto 4-Speed Transmission[Opt on S,XS] +450
AM/FM Compact Disc Player +140
Air Conditioning +365
Cruise Control +95
Power Door Locks +105
Power Windows +110
Rear Step Bumper +65

OASIS   1997

Cruise control is added to the S model's standard equipment list, and four new colors are available.

RATINGS (SCALE OF 1-10)

Overall	Safety	Reliability	Performance	Comfort	Value
7.3	7.5	9.3	7.2	7.1	5.6

Category G
4 Dr LS Pass. Van	14255	16925
4 Dr S Pass. Van	13040	15480

OPTIONS FOR OASIS
AM/FM Compact Disc Player +140
Luggage Rack[Opt on S] +70

RODEO   1997

All 4WD models get a standard shift-on-the-fly transfer case, and improvements have been made to reduce noise, vibration and harshness.

RATINGS (SCALE OF 1-10)

Overall	Safety	Reliability	Performance	Comfort	Value
6.9	6.8	7.8	7	7.1	5.7

Category G
4 Dr LS Wgn	13490	16015
4 Dr LS 4WD Wgn	14135	16785
4 Dr S Wgn	9280	11015
4 Dr S V6 Wgn	11005	13065
4 Dr S V6 4WD Wgn	12070	14330

OPTIONS FOR RODEO
Auto 4-Speed Transmission[Opt on S V6,4WD] +485
Air Conditioning[Std on LS] +365
Aluminum/Alloy Wheels[Std on LS] +145
Anti-Lock Brakes +260
Compact Disc W/fm/tape +200
Cruise Control[Std on LS] +95
Keyless Entry System +85
Leather Seats +350
Limited Slip Diff +125
Luggage Rack[Std on LS] +70
Moonroof +155
Power Door Locks[Std on LS] +105
Power Windows[Std on LS] +110
Running Boards +175
Swing Out Tire Carrier[Opt on S] +85

Don't forget to refer to the Mileage Adjustment Table at the back of this book!

Model Description	Trade-in Value	Market Value

TROOPER 1997

Antilock brakes are now standard on all models, and dealers get a wider profit margin to help increase sales. Despite delirious requests by a certain consumer group, Isuzu will not equip the Trooper with training wheels for 1997.

RATINGS (SCALE OF 1-10)

Overall	Safety	Reliability	Performance	Comfort	Value
7.3	7.1	8	6.8	7.6	7

Category G
4 Dr LS 4WD Wgn	15665	18600
4 Dr Limited 4WD Wgn	18405	21850
4 Dr S 4WD Wgn	12925	15345

OPTIONS FOR TROOPER

Auto 4-Speed Transmission[Opt on S] +560
Seat Pkg +415
AM/FM Compact Disc Player +140
Air Conditioning[Opt on S] +365
Alarm System[Opt on S] +120
Aluminum/Alloy Wheels[Opt on S] +145
Cruise Control[Opt on S] +95
Dual Power Seats[Opt on LS] +185
Heated Front Seats[Opt on LS] +120
Keyless Entry System[Opt on LS,S] +85
Leather Seats[Opt on LS] +350
Limited Slip Diff[Opt on LS,S] +125
Power Door Locks[Opt on S] +105
Power Moonroof[Opt on LS] +385
Power Windows[Opt on S] +110
Running Boards +175

1996 ISUZU

HOMBRE 1996

In a switch from history, Isuzu clones a Chevy S-10 and dumps its Japanese-built compact truck. Sheetmetal is unique to Isuzu, but everything else is pure General Motors.

RATINGS (SCALE OF 1-10)

Overall	Safety	Reliability	Performance	Comfort	Value
N/A	N/A	8	6.6	7.9	N/A

Category G
2 Dr S Std Cab SB	5495	6550
2 Dr XS Std Cab SB	6005	7155

OPTIONS FOR HOMBRE

AM/FM Stereo Tape +80
Air Conditioning +300
Rear Step Bumper[Opt on S] +55

OASIS 1996

New Isuzu minivan is a clone of the Honda Odyssey, except for the grille, badging and wheels. The Isuzu offers a better warranty, too.

RATINGS (SCALE OF 1-10)

Overall	Safety	Reliability	Performance	Comfort	Value
N/A	N/A	9.3	7.2	7.1	6.6

Category G
4 Dr LS Pass. Van	12615	15040
4 Dr S Pass. Van	11425	13620

OPTIONS FOR OASIS

AM/FM Compact Disc Player +115
Cruise Control[Opt on S] +75
Luggage Rack[Opt on S] +60

RODEO 1996

Finally, Isuzu's Rodeo can be equipped with four-wheel antilock brakes, and 4WD models get a standard shift-on-the-fly system. New style wheels debut, and the engine now makes 190 horsepower. Increased wheel track improves ride quality, and spare tire covers are redesigned.

RATINGS (SCALE OF 1-10)

Overall	Safety	Reliability	Performance	Comfort	Value
7	6.8	7.7	7	7.1	6.2

Category G
4 Dr LS Wgn	12095	14420
4 Dr LS 4WD Wgn	12680	15115
4 Dr S Wgn	8400	10010
4 Dr S V6 Wgn	9890	11790
4 Dr S V6 4WD Wgn	10855	12940

OPTIONS FOR RODEO

Auto 4-Speed Transmission[Opt on S V6,4WD] +400
AM/FM Compact Disc Player +115
Air Conditioning[Std on LS] +300
Aluminum/Alloy Wheels[Std on LS] +120
Anti-Lock Brakes +210
Cruise Control[Std on LS] +75
Keyless Entry System +70
Leather Seats +285
Limited Slip Diff +100
Luggage Rack[Std on LS] +60
Moonroof +130
Power Door Locks[Std on LS] +85
Power Windows[Std on LS] +90
Running Boards +140
Swing Out Tire Carrier[Opt on S] +70

TROOPER 1996

More standard equipment, a horsepower boost for the SOHC V6 engine, and standard shift-on-the-fly debut for 1996.

Model Description	Trade-in Value	Market Value	Model Description	Trade-in Value	Market Value

RATINGS (SCALE OF 1-10)

Overall	Safety	Reliability	Performance	Comfort	Value
7.4	6.6	7.9	6.8	7.6	7.9

Category G

4 Dr LS 4WD Wgn	13915	16590
4 Dr Limited 4WD Wgn	16705	19915
4 Dr S 4WD Wgn	11215	13370
4 Dr SE 4WD Wgn	16930	20180

OPTIONS FOR TROOPER

Auto 4-Speed Transmission[Opt on S] +455
Seat Pkg +490
AM/FM Compact Disc Player +115
Air Conditioning[Opt on S] +300
Aluminum/Alloy Wheels[Opt on S] +120
Anti-Lock Brakes[Opt on LS,S] +210
Cruise Control[Opt on S] +75
Dual Power Seats[Opt on LS] +150
Keyless Entry System[Std on SE] +70
Leather Seats[Opt on LS] +285
Limited Slip Diff[Std on SE] +100
Power Door Locks[Opt on S] +85
Power Moonroof[Opt on LS] +315
Power Windows[Opt on S] +90
Running Boards +140

1995 ISUZU

HALF TON PICKUP   1995

Spacecab, V6 power and automatic transmission are canceled for 1995. All that's left are four-cylinder regular-cab trucks in 2WD or 4WD. California didn't get any 1995 Pickups, thanks to strict emissions regulations.

Category G

2 Dr S Std Cab LB	4845	5935
2 Dr S Std Cab SB	4265	5225
2 Dr S 4WD Std Cab SB	5960	7295

OPTIONS FOR HALF TON PICKUP

Wheel Pkg +240
AM/FM Stereo Tape +65
Air Conditioning +245
Power Steering[Opt on 2WD] +85
Rear Step Bumper +45

RODEO   1995

Midyear change gives the Rodeo driver and passenger airbags in a redesigned dashboard. S V6 models can be equipped with a Bright Package that includes lots of chrome trim and aluminum wheels.

RATINGS (SCALE OF 1-10)

Overall	Safety	Reliability	Performance	Comfort	Value
6.6	7	6.4	7	7.1	5.6

Category G

4 Dr LS Wgn	10120	12395
4 Dr LS 4WD Wgn	10585	12965
4 Dr S Wgn	6915	8470
4 Dr S 4WD Wgn	8830	10815
4 Dr S V6 Wgn	8050	9860

OPTIONS FOR RODEO

Auto 4-Speed Transmission[Opt on S,S V6,4WD] +320
Bright Pkg +315
Air Conditioning[Std on LS] +245
Aluminum/Alloy Wheels[Std on LS] +95
Anti-Lock Brakes +175
Compact Disc W/frn/tape +130
Cruise Control[Std on LS] +65
Dual Air Bag Restraints[Opt on S,S V6,2WD] +130
Keyless Entry System +60
Limited Slip Diff +85
Luggage Rack[Std on LS] +50
Power Door Locks[Std on LS] +70
Power Windows[Std on LS] +70
Running Boards +115
Sunroof +90
Swing Out Tire Carrier[Opt on S] +55

TROOPER   1995

Dual airbags are standard. Styling is revised. A new top-of-the-line trim level debuts. The Limited has a power sunroof, leather upholstery, heated seats, and wood grain trim. Suspensions have been reworked to provide a better ride.

RATINGS (SCALE OF 1-10)

Overall	Safety	Reliability	Performance	Comfort	Value
7.4	7.5	8.2-	6.8	7.6	7

Category G

4 Dr LS 4WD Wgn	11235	13760
4 Dr Limited 4WD Wgn	14295	17505
2 Dr RS 4WD Utility	11100	13595
4 Dr S 4WD Wgn	9305	11395
4 Dr SE 4WD Wgn	13060	15995

OPTIONS FOR TROOPER

Auto 4-Speed Transmission[Opt on LS,RS,S] +345
AM/FM Compact Disc Player +95
Air Conditioning[Opt on S] +245
Aluminum/Alloy Wheels[Opt on S] +95
Anti-Lock Brakes[Opt on S] +175
Cruise Control[Opt on S] +65
Keyless Entry System[Opt on S] +60
Limited Slip Diff[Opt on S] +85
Power Door Locks[Opt on S] +70
Power Windows[Opt on S] +70
Premium Sound System[Opt on S] +100

1994 ISUZU

AMIGO 1994

Automatic transmission disappears from options list, and base 2.3-liter, four-cylinder engine is no longer available. Power steering, power outside mirrors, a center floor console, and 16-inch tires are all newly standard.

Category G

	Trade-in	Market
2 Dr S Utility	5315	6640
2 Dr S 4WD Utility	6000	7495
2 Dr XS Utility	5545	6925
2 Dr XS 4WD Utility	6140	7665

OPTIONS FOR AMIGO
AM/FM Stereo Tape +55
Air Conditioning +200
Sunroof[Opt on S,2WD] +70

HALF TON PICKUP 1994

Vent windows are dropped. Models with 2.6-liter engine get standard power steering. Outside mirrors are revised.

Category G

	Trade-in	Market
2 Dr S Ext Cab SB	4725	5900
2 Dr S Std Cab LB	4035	5040
2 Dr S 4WD Std Cab SB	5015	6265
2 Dr S 2.6 Ext Cab SB	4725	5900
2 Dr S 2.6 Std Cab SB	4465	5580
2 Dr STD Std Cab SB	3525	4405

OPTIONS FOR HALF TON PICKUP
6 cyl 3.1 L Engine +210
Tire/Wheel Pkg +205
AM/FM Stereo Tape +55
Air Conditioning +200
Chrome Bumpers +35
Power Steering[Std on Ext Cab,4WD] +70
Rear Step Bumper +35

RODEO 1994

S model gets standard power steering. LS models are equipped with standard air conditioning. Front vent windows are dropped. All V6 models come with standard rear wiper/washer and tailgate spare tire carrier.

RATINGS (SCALE OF 1-10)

Overall	Safety	Reliability	Performance	Comfort	Value
6.1	3.7	6.3	7	7.4	6.2

Category G

	Trade-in	Market
4 Dr LS Wgn	8470	10575
4 Dr LS 4WD Wgn	8860	11065
4 Dr S Wgn	5785	7225
4 Dr S 4WD Wgn	7470	9330
4 Dr S V6 Wgn	6750	8430

OPTIONS FOR RODEO
Auto 4-Speed Transmission[Opt on S,S V6,4WD] +250
Air Conditioning[Std on LS] +200
Compact Disc W/fm/tape +110
Cruise Control[Std on LS] +50
Keyless Entry System +50
Limited Slip Diff +70
Luggage Rack[Std on LS] +40
Power Door Locks[Std on LS] +55
Power Windows[Std on LS] +60
Sunroof +70
Swing Out Tire Carrier[Opt on 2WD] +45

TROOPER 1994

Four-wheel ABS filters down to the Trooper S options sheet. Gray leather upholstery is a new options for the LS model, and it includes heated front seats with power adjustments. RS gets new alloys.

RATINGS (SCALE OF 1-10)

Overall	Safety	Reliability	Performance	Comfort	Value
7.3	4.2	8.5	7.8	7.8	8.3

Category G

	Trade-in	Market
4 Dr LS 4WD Wgn	9345	11670
2 Dr RS 4WD Utility	8365	10450
4 Dr S 4WD Wgn	7570	9455
4 Dr SE 4WD Wgn	11475	14335

OPTIONS FOR TROOPER
Auto 4-Speed Transmission[Std on SE] +280
AM/FM Compact Disc Player +75
Air Conditioning[Opt on S] +200
Anti-Lock Brakes[Opt on S] +140
Cruise Control[Opt on S] +50
Dual Power Seats[Opt on LS] +100
Heated Front Seats[Opt on LS] +65
Leather Seats[Opt on LS] +190
Limited Slip Diff[Opt on S] +70
Power Door Locks[Opt on S] +55
Power Sunroof[Opt on LS] +195
Power Windows[Opt on S] +60

1993 ISUZU

AMIGO 1993

Amigo gets a new grille.

Category G

	Trade-in	Market
2 Dr S Utility	3605	4625
2 Dr S 4WD Utility	4525	5805
2 Dr XS Utility	4075	5225
2 Dr XS 4WD Utility	4935	6330

OPTIONS FOR AMIGO
4 cyl 2.6 L Engine[Std on XS,4WD] +165
Auto 4-Speed Transmission +180

Model Description	Trade-in Value	Market Value

Amigo Tire/Wheel Pkg +160
AM/FM Stereo Tape +45
Air Conditioning +165
Aluminum/Alloy Wheels[Opt on S,2WD] +65
Sunroof +60

HALF TON PICKUP   1993

LS trim level dropped. Two models discontinued: one-ton Longbed and 4WD Spacecab. A new grille graces the front of the Pickup.

Category G

	Trade-in	Market
2 Dr S Ext Cab SB	3640	4670
2 Dr S Std Cab LB	3245	4165
2 Dr S Std Cab SB	2860	3670
2 Dr S 4WD Std Cab SB	3980	5105
2 Dr S 2.6 Std Cab SB	3430	4395

OPTIONS FOR HALF TON PICKUP
6 cyl 3.1 L Engine +165
Pick Up 4WD Bright Pkg +240
AM/FM Stereo Tape +45
Air Conditioning +165
Aluminum/Alloy Wheels +65
Power Steering[Std on S 2.6,Ext Cab,4WD] +55
Rear Step Bumper +30

RODEO   1993

More potent V6 engine filters into Rodeo from big brother Trooper for a horsepower boost of 55 ponies. A new grille is installed up front.

RATINGS (SCALE OF 1-10)

Overall	Safety	Reliability	Performance	Comfort	Value
6.4	4	7.6	7	7.4	6.2

Category G

	Trade-in	Market
4 Dr LS Wgn	6165	7910
4 Dr LS 4WD Wgn	6530	8370
4 Dr S Wgn	4480	5745
4 Dr S 4WD Wgn	5820	7465
4 Dr S V6 Wgn	5155	6610

OPTIONS FOR RODEO
Auto 4-Speed Transmission +195
Rodeo Tire/Wheel Pkg +175
AM/FM Compact Disc Player +65
Air Conditioning +165
Aluminum/Alloy Wheels +65
Cruise Control[Std on LS] +40
Limited Slip Diff +55
Luggage Rack[Std on LS] +30
Sunroof +60

STYLUS   1993

Sporty XS model is dropped, along with its twin-cam engine.

Category E

	Trade-in	Market
4 Dr S Sdn	2355	3305

OPTIONS FOR STYLUS
AM/FM Stereo Tape +60
Air Conditioning +165
Power Steering +50

TROOPER   1993

A short-wheelbase two-door model joins the lineup in RS trim. Four-wheel ABS is optional on this stubby new model.

RATINGS (SCALE OF 1-10)

Overall	Safety	Reliability	Performance	Comfort	Value
6.8	4	8	7.8	7.8	6.4

Category G

	Trade-in	Market
4 Dr LS 4WD Wgn	7770	9965
2 Dr RS 4WD Utility	6990	8965
4 Dr S 4WD Wgn	6405	8210

OPTIONS FOR TROOPER
Auto 4-Speed Transmission +230
AM/FM Compact Disc Player +65
Air Conditioning[Opt on S] +165
Aluminum/Alloy Wheels[Opt on S] +65
Cruise Control[Opt on S] +40
Limited Slip Diff[Opt on S] +55
Power Door Locks[Opt on S] +45
Power Sunroof +160
Power Windows[Opt on S] +50
Premium Sound System[Opt on S] +70

1992 ISUZU

AMIGO   1992

Those who hate shifting their own gears are in luck; an automatic is newly optional.

Category G

	Trade-in	Market
2 Dr S Utility	3205	4170
2 Dr S 4WD Utility	4020	5225
2 Dr XS Utility	3595	4675
2 Dr XS 4WD Utility	4395	5720

OPTIONS FOR AMIGO
4 cyl 2.6 L Engine[Std on XS,4WD] +120
Auto 4-Speed Transmission +145
Air Conditioning +135
Sunroof +50

HALF TON PICKUP   1992

No changes.

Category G

	Trade-in	Market
2 Dr LS Ext Cab SB	3975	5165
2 Dr LS 4WD Ext Cab SB	4790	6225
2 Dr S Ext Cab SB	3015	3920
2 Dr S Std Cab LB	2770	3600
2 Dr S Std Cab SB	2475	3215
2 Dr S 4WD Std Cab SB	3415	4440

Don't forget to refer to the Mileage Adjustment Table at the back of this book!

Model Description	Trade-in Value	Market Value

Model Description	Trade-in Value	Market Value

OPTIONS FOR HALF TON PICKUP

4 cyl 2.6 L Engine[Std on LS,Ext Cab,4WD] +120
6 cyl 3.1 L Engine +70
Auto 4-Speed Transmission +145
Air Conditioning +135
Cruise Control +35
Power Door Locks +40
Power Windows +40

IMPULSE   1992

XS gets ten more horsepower, thanks to a larger 1.8-liter twin-cam engine.

Category E

Model	Trade-in	Market
2 Dr RS Turbo 4WD Cpe	3140	4675
2 Dr XS Cpe	2515	3750
2 Dr XS Hbk	2635	3925

OPTIONS FOR IMPULSE

Impulse Rs Pkg +135
Air Conditioning[Std on RS] +135

ONE TON   1992

Category G

Model	Trade-in	Market
2 Dr S Std Cab LB	3135	4075

OPTIONS FOR ONE TON

Air Conditioning +135

RODEO   1992

No changes.

RATINGS (SCALE OF 1-10)

Overall	Safety	Reliability	Performance	Comfort	Value
6.2	4.1	7	6.6	7.4	6.1

Category G

Model	Trade-in	Market
4 Dr LS Wgn	4850	6305
4 Dr LS 4WD Wgn	5215	6780
4 Dr LX 4WD Wgn	5365	6980
4 Dr S Wgn	3885	5050
4 Dr S 4WD Wgn	4685	6090
4 Dr S V6 Wgn	4190	5450
4 Dr XS Wgn	4460	5800
4 Dr XS 4WD Wgn	5270	6855

OPTIONS FOR RODEO

Auto 4-Speed Transmission +160
Air Conditioning +135
Cruise Control +35
Limited Slip Diff[Opt on LS] +45
Power Door Locks +40
Power Windows +40
Sunroof +50

STYLUS   1992

RS gets 10 more horsepower, thanks to a larger 1.8-liter twin-cam engine.

Category E

Model	Trade-in	Market
4 Dr RS Sdn	2100	3125
4 Dr S Sdn	1805	2690

OPTIONS FOR STYLUS

Auto 3-Speed Transmission +90
Air Conditioning +135
Cruise Control +35
Power Door Locks +40
Power Windows +45

TROOPER   1992

Beefy SUV moves upscale with total redesign that renders it longer, wider, taller and heavier. Four-wheel ABS is optional on LS models. A new Isuzu-designed 3.2-liter V6 powers Trooper; base models have an SOHC unit, while LS models get a DOHC engine good for 190 horsepower.

RATINGS (SCALE OF 1-10)

Overall	Safety	Reliability	Performance	Comfort	Value
6.9	4	8.4	7.8	7.8	6.4

Category G

Model	Trade-in	Market
4 Dr LS 4WD Wgn	6705	8720
4 Dr S 4WD Wgn	5450	7090

OPTIONS FOR TROOPER

Auto 4-Speed Transmission +185
Air Conditioning[Opt on S] +135
Anti-Lock Brakes[Std on S] +95
Limited Slip Diff[Opt on S] +45
Power Sunroof +130

1991 ISUZU

AMIGO   1991

Warranty changes from 3 years/36,000 miles to 3 years/50,000 miles. Rust coverage is extended to 6 years/100,000 miles from 3 years/unlimited mileage. New powertrain warranty is good for 5 years/60,000 miles. XS gets locking center console standard; item is optional on S. New paint colors, graphics and alloy wheels debut.

Category G

Model	Trade-in	Market
2 Dr S Utility	2680	3520
2 Dr S 4WD Utility	3440	4515
2 Dr XS Utility	3035	3990
2 Dr XS 4WD Utility	3780	4960

OPTIONS FOR AMIGO

4 cyl 2.6 L Engine[Std on XS,4WD] +75
Air Conditioning +110
Sunroof +40

HALF TON PICKUP   1991

Warranty changes from 3 years/36,000 miles to 3 years/50,000 miles. Rust coverage extended to 6 years/

Don't forget to refer to the Mileage Adjustment Table at the back of this book!

ISUZU 91

Model Description	Trade-in Value	Market Value	Model Description	Trade-in Value	Market Value

100,000 miles. New powertrain warranty is good for 5 years/60,000 miles. A 3.1-liter, GM V-6 is newly optional. Grille and tailgate graphics are revised with new lettering. LS models get standard sliding rear window. On 2WD with 2.6-liter engine, drums replace the rear discs.

Category G		
2 Dr LS Ext Cab SB	3440	4520
2 Dr LS 4WD Ext Cab SB	4155	5460
2 Dr LS 4WD Std Cab SB	4180	5490
2 Dr S Ext Cab SB	2615	3435
2 Dr S Std Cab LB	2475	3250
2 Dr S Std Cab SB	2210	2900
2 Dr S 4WD Std Cab SB	2960	3890

OPTIONS FOR HALF TON PICKUP
4 cyl 2.6 L Engine[Std on LS,Ext Cab,4WD] +75
6 cyl 3.1 L Engine[Opt on S] +45
Auto 4-Speed Transmission +110
Power Pkg +105
Air Conditioning +110
Cruise Control +30
Power Door Locks +30
Power Windows +30

IMPULSE 1991

New RS model debuts equipped with turbocharged engine and all-wheel drive, two items twin Geo Storm never received. RS turbo makes 160 horsepower and can be equipped with optional ABS. Also new is an aberration called Impulse XS hatchback. Warranty changes from 3 years/36,000 miles to 3 years/50,000 miles. Rust coverage is extended to 6 years/100,000 miles from 3 years/unlimited mileage. New powertrain warranty is good for 5 years/60,000 miles.

Category E		
2 Dr RS Turbo 4WD Cpe	2105	3515
2 Dr XS Cpe	1715	2865
2 Dr XS Hbk	1795	2990

OPTIONS FOR IMPULSE
Auto 4-Speed Transmission +100
Air Conditioning +110
Cruise Control +30
Power Door Locks +35
Power Sunroof +85
Power Windows +35

ONE TON 1991

Category G		
2 Dr S Std Cab LB	2680	3515

OPTIONS FOR ONE TON
Air Conditioning +110

RODEO 1991

New Pickup-based sport utility debuts. Built in Indiana. Available with two- or four-wheel-drive with either Isuzu-built four cylinder or GM-sourced V6. Rodeo features a long wheelbase for ride comfort and excellent rear seat legroom. Four-wheel disc brakes accompany V6 engines.

RATINGS (SCALE OF 1-10)

Overall	Safety	Reliability	Performance	Comfort	Value
6.1	4	6.9	6.6	7.4	5.6

Category G		
4 Dr LS Wgn	4200	5520
4 Dr LS 4WD Wgn	4545	5970
4 Dr S Wgn	3405	4470
4 Dr S 4WD Wgn	3910	5135
4 Dr S V6 Wgn	3650	4790
4 Dr XS Wgn	3790	4975
4 Dr XS 4WD Wgn	4305	5655

OPTIONS FOR RODEO
Auto 4-Speed Transmission +125
Air Conditioning +110
Cruise Control +30
Power Door Locks +30
Power Windows +30
Sunroof +40

STYLUS 1991

New sedan based on Impulse running gear includes standard driver airbag. XS is quite a spry sport sedan with 130-horsepower, twin-cam 1.6-liter engine.

Category E		
4 Dr S Sdn	1520	2535
4 Dr XS Sdn	1815	3030

OPTIONS FOR STYLUS
Auto 3-Speed Transmission +65
Air Conditioning +110
Cruise Control +30
Power Door Locks +35
Power Sunroof +85
Power Windows +35

TROOPER 1991

Warranty changes from 3 years/36,000 miles to 3 years/50,000 miles. Rust coverage is extended to 6 years/100,000 miles from 3 years/unlimited mileage. New powertrain warranty is good for 5 years/60,000 miles.

Category G		
4 Dr LS 4WD Wgn	4035	5300
4 Dr S 4WD Wgn	3215	4220
4 Dr SE 4WD Wgn	3585	4710
4 Dr XS 4WD Wgn	3555	4665

OPTIONS FOR TROOPER
6 cyl 2.8 L Engine[Opt on S] +50
Auto 4-Speed Transmission +145
Air Conditioning +110
Camper/Towing Package[Opt on S] +40

Don't forget to refer to the Mileage Adjustment Table at the back of this book!

JAGUAR — Britain

1995 Jaguar XJ12

2000 JAGUAR

S-TYPE — 2000

From the ground up, this is a completely new sport sedan based on the new Ford midsize platform. Lincoln worked with Jaguar to develop this platform, which is also used for Lincoln's LS sedan.

Category J

	Trade-in	Market
4 Dr 3.0L Sdn	31730	36345
4 Dr 4.0L Sdn	35780	40985

OPTIONS FOR S-TYPE
Deluxe Communications +1985
Navigation System +1455
Sport Handling Pkg +800
Automatic Dimming Mirror[Std on 4.0L] +370
Compact Disc Changer +765
Power Moonroof[Std on 4.0L] +775

XJ-SERIES — 2000

A fifth model — the supercharged Vanden Plas — has been added. All XJ8 Sedans gain all-speed traction control, improved ABS, rain-sensing windshield wipers, and child seat-anchor brackets as standard equipment. A new navigation system is being offered as optional equipment, as is an upgraded 320-watt Alpine system. The anti-theft system now has an encrypted key transponder. There are two new exterior colors and one new interior color.

Category J

	Trade-in	Market
4 Dr S/C Sprchgd Sdn	61260	70165
4 Dr XJ8 Sdn	42600	48795
4 Dr XJ8L Sedan	46425	53175
4 Dr Vanden Plas Sdn	49495	56690

OPTIONS FOR XJ-SERIES
Navigation System +1225
Compact Disc Changer[Std on S/C] +765

XJR — 2000

The XJR gains all-speed traction control, improved ABS, rain-sensing windshield wipers, child seat-anchor brackets, and an upgraded 320-watt Alpine system as standard equipment. A new navigation system is being offered as optional equipment. The anti-theft system now has an encrypted key transponder. The XJR also gets new 18-inch wheels and a different sew style for the seats.

Category L

	Trade-in	Market
4 Dr XJR Sprchgd Sdn	54140	61965

XK-SERIES — 2000

The XK8 Coupe and Convertible gain all-speed traction control, improved ABS, bigger front brakes, rain-sensing windshield wipers, and child seat-anchor brackets as standard equipment. A new navigation system is being offered as optional equipment, as is an upgraded 320-watt Alpine system. The standard audio system gets two more speakers, for a total of six. The anti-theft system has been upgraded with an encrypted key transponder. Both the standard 17-inch wheels and the optional 18-inch wheels have been restyled. The front seatbelt pre-tensioners are now electronically controlled.

Category J

	Trade-in	Market
2 Dr XK8 Conv	55050	63050
2 Dr XK8 Cpe	51215	58660

OPTIONS FOR XK-SERIES
Navigation System +1960
Compact Disc Changer +765

XKR — 2000

The performance-minded, supercharged V8 powered, XKR is new for 2000.

Category J

	Trade-in	Market
2 Dr STD Sprchgd Conv	68755	78745
2 Dr STD Sprchgd Cpe	64345	73700

OPTIONS FOR XKR
Navigation System +1960

1999 JAGUAR

XJ-SERIES — 1999

Jaguar's venerable XJ sedans enter '99 largely unchanged after a major workover in '98.

Don't forget to refer to the Mileage Adjustment Table at the back of this book!

Model Description	Trade-in Value	Market Value

RATINGS (SCALE OF 1-10)

Overall	Safety	Reliability	Performance	Comfort	Value
N/A	N/A	N/A	8	7.8	N/A

Category J

	Trade-in	Market
4 Dr XJ8 Sdn	37400	42955
4 Dr Vanden Plas Sdn	43500	49965
4 Dr XJ8L Sedan	40785	46845

Category L

	Trade-in	Market
4 Dr XJR Sprchgd Sdn	45860	52605

OPTIONS FOR XJ-SERIES
All Weather Pkg +910
Compact Disc Changer[Std on Sprchgd] +625
Harman Kardon Sound Sys[Std on Sprchgd] +920
Heated Seats[Std on Sprchgd] +335
Traction Control System[Std on Sprchgd] +780

XK-SERIES 1999

The stunning XK returns for '99 with no significant changes.

RATINGS (SCALE OF 1-10)

Overall	Safety	Reliability	Performance	Comfort	Value
N/A	N/A	N/A	8.8	7.9	N/A

Category J

	Trade-in	Market
2 Dr XK8 Conv	51170	58775
2 Dr XK8 Cpe	47585	54655

OPTIONS FOR XK-SERIES
Chrome Wheels +995
Compact Disc Changer +625
Harman Kardon Sound Sys +920
Traction Control System +780

1998 JAGUAR

XJ-SERIES 1998

A new V8 engine, taken from the XK8 coupe and convertible, makes its way into the engine bay. A revised instrument panel greatly improves interior ergonomics. Cruise and satellite stereo controls are located on the steering wheel.

Category J

	Trade-in	Market
4 Dr Vanden Plas Sdn	38745	44590
4 Dr XJ8 Sdn	33300	38320
4 Dr XJ8L Sdn	36305	41785

Category L

	Trade-in	Market
4 Dr XJR Sprchgd Sdn	40470	46510

OPTIONS FOR XJ-SERIES
All Weather Pkg +680
Compact Disc Changer +515
Harman Kardon Sound Sys +750
Heated Seats +275
Traction Control System +635

XK-SERIES 1998

The 1998 XK8 gets automatic on/off headlamps, an engine immobilizer feature as part of the security system, and a cellular phone keypad integrated into the stereo controls. Other changes include the addition of two new exterior colors.

Category J

	Trade-in	Market
2 Dr XK8 Conv	45415	52265
2 Dr XK8 Cpe	42190	48555

OPTIONS FOR XK-SERIES
Compact Disc Changer +515

1997 JAGUAR

XJ-SERIES 1997

The 1997 XJ-Series loses the V12 model that has been a mainstay of the Jaguar lineup for so many years. A long-wheelbase model becomes available this year, filling a niche between the XJ6 and the Vanden Plas. All models receive a contoured bench seat and three-point seatbelts for rear occupants. The XJ6 replaces last year's chrome-vane grille with a black-vane grille, and the convenience group becomes optional on this model. The XJR loses its rear passenger heater ducts.

Category J

	Trade-in	Market
4 Dr Vanden Plas Sdn	31660	36605
4 Dr XJ6 Sdn	27035	31260
4 Dr XJ6L Sdn	29495	34100

Category L

	Trade-in	Market
4 Dr XJR Sprchgd Sdn	33050	38060

OPTIONS FOR XJ-SERIES
All Weather Pkg +895
Chrome Wheels +665
Compact Disc Changer +420
Traction Control System +520

XK8 1997

An all-new Jaguar debuts this year, replacing the stodgy XJ-S. This new sports car boasts the first V-8 engine ever found in a Jag, as well as an all-new 5-speed manual transmission that features normal and sport modes. The XK8 is available in coupe and convertible forms, but Jaguar insiders expect a full 70% of sales to be of the convertible.

Category J

	Trade-in	Market
2 Dr XK8 Conv	39225	45350
2 Dr XK8 Cpe	36440	42135

OPTIONS FOR XK8
All Weather Pkg +895
Compact Disc Changer +420
Harman Kardon Sound Sys +615
Traction Control System +520

Don't forget to refer to the Mileage Adjustment Table at the back of this book!

Model Description	Trade-in Value	Market Value	Model Description	Trade-in Value	Market Value

1996 JAGUAR

XJ-SERIES 1996

On the XJ6, thicker side window glass insulates passengers from annoying wind noise and outside distractions. After a 20-year reign, the XJS coupe is put out to pasture. The only model offered for 1996 is the six-cylinder convertible; the most popular XJS in its unremarkable history. The changes for 1996 include new wheels, new bucket seats, additional chrome exterior trim, and an adjustable, wood-trimmed steering wheel.

Category J

4 Dr Vanden Plas Sdn	27260	31640
4 Dr XJ12 Sdn	33435	38805
4 Dr XJ6 Sdn	23865	27695
2 Dr XJS Conv	26065	30255

Category L

4 Dr XJR Sprchgd Sdn	27555	31940

OPTIONS FOR XJ-SERIES
All Weather Pkg +360
Chrome Wheels +545
Compact Disc Changer +345
Sport Suspension +155
Traction Control System +425

1995 JAGUAR

XJ-SERIES 1995

Horsepower is upped for naturally aspirated 4.0-liter engine, and inline-six and V12 engines. New sheetmetal showcases a more traditional Jaguar, ironic considering the amount of input Ford had into the creation of this car. XJS V12 models get new wheels and a plethora of standard equipment such as heated seats and a multi-disc CD changer. A supercharged XJR model is introduced.

Category J

4 Dr XJ12 Sdn	27915	32495
4 Dr XJ6 Sdn	19375	22550
4 Dr XJ6 Vanden Plas Sdn	22510	26205
2 Dr XJS Conv	22280	25935
2 Dr XJS Cpe	19355	22530
2 Dr XJS V12 Conv	29815	34710
2 Dr XJS V12 Cpe	26160	30450

Category L

4 Dr XJR Sprchgd Sdn	23090	26765

OPTIONS FOR XJ-SERIES
Luxury Pkg +375
AM/FM Compact Disc Player +115
Chrome Wheels +445
Compact Disc Changer +280

Limited Slip Diff +275
Power Sunroof +335
Rear Spoiler +120
Traction Control System +350

1994 JAGUAR

XJ-SERIES 1994

A passenger airbag joins the safety equipment roster. CFC-free air conditioning is added to the standard equipment list. For the XJ6, a five-speed manual transmission is available as a new option for the 4.0-liter inline-six engine. An XJR-S derived XJ-S 6.0-liter V12 is available, they are differentiated by a rear spoiler, mirrors, grille, and alloy wheels. The XJ-12 is available with a 301-horsepower engine and a four-speed automatic transmission.

Category J

2 Dr XJS Cpe	14330	16800
4 Dr XJ12 Sdn	19455	22810
4 Dr XJ6 Sdn	14275	16735
4 Dr XJ6 Vanden Plas Sdn	16360	19185
2 Dr XJS Conv	16510	19360
2 Dr XJS V12 Conv	21665	25400
2 Dr XJS V12 Cpe	18975	22245

OPTIONS FOR XJ-SERIES
Sport Handling Pkg +245
AM/FM Compact Disc Player +95
Limited Slip Diff +225
Power Sunroof +275

1993 JAGUAR

XJ-SERIES 1993

The XJ6 loses the Sovereign model. Comfy power seats, integrated fog lights and new wheels mark the changes for Britain's most popular luxury sedan. ON the XJS, the V12 engine is dropped in favor of a 4.0-liter inline-six. Mercifully, a four-speed automatic transmission replaces the previous three-speed. A traction control system starts the car in second gear to limit wheel-spin on slippery surfaces.

Category J

4 Dr XJ12 Sdn	17585	20690
4 Dr XJ6 Sdn	12295	14465
4 Dr XJ6 Vanden Plas Sdn	14005	16480
2 Dr XJS Conv	14005	16480
2 Dr XJS Cpe	12295	14465

OPTIONS FOR XJ-SERIES
Compact Disc Changer +185
Power Sunroof +225

Don't forget to refer to the Mileage Adjustment Table at the back of this book!

Model Description	Trade-in Value	Market Value	Model Description	Trade-in Value	Market Value
1992 JAGUAR			**1991 JAGUAR**		
XJ-SERIES		**1992**	**XJ-SERIES**		**1991**

The XJS gets a new grille and headlights. Two-driver memory is also available for the mirrors and driver's seat.

Category J

Bigger engine is available on the XJS to compete with sportier competitors. A driver airbag is added to the standard equipment list.

Category J

Model Description	Trade-in Value	Market Value	Model Description	Trade-in Value	Market Value
4 Dr XJ6 Sdn	9430	11360	4 Dr XJ6 Sdn	7440	9045
4 Dr XJ6 Majestic Sdn	12565	15140	4 Dr XJ6 Sovereign Sdn	8375	10180
4 Dr XJ6 Sovereign Sdn	10475	12620	4 Dr XJ6 Vanden Plas Sdn	9940	12085
4 Dr XJ6 Vanden Plas Sdn	11520	13880	2 Dr XJS Conv	11090	13480
2 Dr XJS Conv	14180	17085	2 Dr XJS Cpe	9975	12130
2 Dr XJS Cpe	12775	15390			

Don't forget to refer to the Mileage Adjustment Table at the back of this book!

JEEP 00-99

Model Description	Trade-in Value	Market Value	Model Description	Trade-in Value	Market Value

JEEP   USA

1997 Jeep Wrangler

2000 JEEP

CHEROKEE   2000

The 2000 Cherokee scores the '99 Grand Cherokee's redesigned 4.0-liter PowerTech inline six in addition to a new five-speed manual transmission. The Limited model sports bright chrome accents, including the front grille, the headlamp surrounds, the side graphics, the rear license-plate brow, and the 16-inch wheels.

Category G

Model	Trade-in	Market
4 Dr Classic Wgn	15840	18340
4 Dr Classic 4WD Wgn	16925	19600
4 Dr Limited Wgn	17075	19770
4 Dr Limited 4WD Wgn	18595	21535
2 Dr SE Utility	12360	14315
2 Dr SE 4WD Utility	13450	15575
4 Dr SE Wgn	13105	15180
4 Dr SE 4WD Wgn	14190	16435
2 Dr Sport Utility	14045	16265
2 Dr Sport 4WD Utility	15130	17520
4 Dr Sport Wgn	14785	17125
4 Dr Sport 4WD Wgn	15960	18480

OPTIONS FOR CHEROKEE
6 cyl 4.0 L Engine[Opt on SE] +835
Auto 3-Speed Transmission +510
Auto 4-Speed Transmission[Opt on SE,Sport] +770
Air Conditioning[Std on Limited] +670
Anti-Lock Brakes +475
Compact Disc W/fm/tape +365
Cruise Control[Std on Limited 2WD] +170
Fog Lights +120
Keyless Entry System[Std on Limited 2WD] +160
Luggage Rack[Opt on SE,Sport] +130
Power Door Locks[Std on Limited 2WD] +190

Power Drivers Seat[Opt on Classic,4] +230
Power Mirrors[Opt on SE,Sport] +110
Power Windows[Std on Limited 2WD] +200
Privacy Glass[Std on Limited] +225
Rear Window Wiper[Opt on SE,Utility,Sport 2WD 4-Door] +125
Tilt Steering Wheel[Std on Limited 2WD] +145

GRAND CHEROKEE   2000

New exterior cladding has been slapped onto the Laredo, and both models have received interior touch-ups. Two-wheel drive is available with the 4.7-liter V8. Shale Green and Silverstone are the new skin tones.

Category G

Model	Trade-in	Market
4 Dr Laredo Wgn	19585	22680
4 Dr Laredo 4WD Wgn	21000	24320
4 Dr Limited Wgn	23420	27120
4 Dr Limited 4WD Wgn	25165	29140

OPTIONS FOR GRAND CHEROKEE
8 cyl 4.7 L Engine +595
Quadra-Trac Transfer Case +815
QuadraDrive Transfer Case +815
Camper/Towing Package +245
Dual Power Seats[Opt on Laredo] +340
Keyless Entry System[Std on Limited,2] +160
Power Sunroof +645

WRANGLER   2000

A reengineered 4.0-liter PowerTech inline six-cylinder that is more refined and quiet, with reduced emissions, is standard for Sport and Sahara for 2000. Shift quality kicks up a notch, thanks to an all-new five-speed manual transmission. A radio/cassette combo with four speakers is now standard for the Sport, and the Sahara gains a radio/CD. Solar Yellow, Patriot Blue and Silverstone are additional exterior colors.

Category G

Model	Trade-in	Market
2 Dr SE 4WD Utility	11095	12850
2 Dr Sahara 4WD Utility	15600	18060
2 Dr Sport 4WD Utility	14270	16525

OPTIONS FOR WRANGLER
Auto 3-Speed Transmission +510
Color Match Dual Roofs +1250
AM/FM Stereo Tape[Opt on SE] +180
Air Conditioning +670
Aluminum/Alloy Wheels[Std on Sahara] +265
Cruise Control +170
Tilt Steering Wheel[Std on Sahara] +145

1999 JEEP

CHEROKEE   1999

The Cherokee Sport gets a revised front fascia including body-colored grille and bumpers. New exterior colors

Don't forget to refer to the Mileage Adjustment Table at the back of this book!

JEEP 99-98

Model Description	Trade-in Value	Market Value		Model Description	Trade-in Value	Market Value

include Forest Green and Desert Sand, to match the most common Cherokee surroundings.

RATINGS (SCALE OF 1-10)

Overall	Safety	Reliability	Performance	Comfort	Value
N/A	6.3	8.4	7.4	7	N/A

Category G

	Trade-in	Market
4 Dr Classic Wgn	14615	17090
4 Dr Classic 4WD Wgn	15640	18285
4 Dr Limited Wgn	15765	18435
4 Dr Limited 4WD Wgn	17060	19950
2 Dr SE Utility	11175	13065
2 Dr SE 4WD Utility	12195	14260
4 Dr SE Wgn	11875	13885
4 Dr SE 4WD Wgn	12895	15075
2 Dr Sport Utility	13010	15215
2 Dr Sport 4WD Utility	14030	16405
4 Dr Sport Wgn	13710	16030
4 Dr Sport 4WD Wgn	14730	17220

OPTIONS FOR CHEROKEE

6 cyl 4.0 L Engine[Opt on SE] +675
Auto 3-Speed Transmission +420
Auto 4-Speed Transmission[Opt on SE,Sport] +630
Air Conditioning[Std on Limited] +550
Aluminum/Alloy Wheels[Opt on SE,Sport] +215
Anti-Lock Brakes +390
Compact Disc W/fm/tape +295
Cruise Control[Std on Limited] +140
Fog Lights +95
Keyless Entry System[Std on Limited] +130
Power Door Locks[Std on Limited] +155
Power Drivers Seat[Std on Limited] +190
Power Mirrors[Opt on SE,Sport] +90
Power Windows[Std on Limited] +160
Rear Window Wiper[Opt on SE,Sport] +105
Tilt Steering Wheel[Std on Limited] +120

GRAND CHEROKEE   1999

A lot. The new-for-99 Grand Cherokee contains only 127 carryover parts from the current model, and gets a new powertrain, rear suspension, braking and steering systems, 4WD system, interior and exterior styling.

RATINGS (SCALE OF 1-10)

Overall	Safety	Reliability	Performance	Comfort	Value
N/A	N/A	8.3	7	7.6	N/A

Category G

	Trade-in	Market
4 Dr Laredo Wgn	17570	20540
4 Dr Laredo 4WD Wgn	18875	22070
4 Dr Limited Wgn	21400	25020
4 Dr Limited 4WD Wgn	23015	26910

OPTIONS FOR GRAND CHEROKEE

8 cyl 4.7 L Engine +710
QuadraDrive Transfer Case +665
AM/FM Compact Disc Player +210
Camper/Towing Package +200
Dual Power Seats[Opt on Laredo] +280
Fog Lights[Opt on Laredo] +95
Heated Front Seats +180
Leather Seats[Opt on Laredo] +525
Power Sunroof +530
Sunscreen Glass[Opt on Laredo] +250

WRANGLER   1999

The Wrangler's interior finally enters the '90s with rotary HVAC controls, replacing the old slider control system. The hard or soft top is available in Dark Tan, and new colors decorate both the exterior and the interior.

RATINGS (SCALE OF 1-10)

Overall	Safety	Reliability	Performance	Comfort	Value
N/A	7.1	8.3	7	5.6	N/A

Category G

	Trade-in	Market
2 Dr SE 4WD Utility	10220	12050
2 Dr Sahara 4WD Utility	14640	17115
2 Dr Sport 4WD Utility	13165	15390

OPTIONS FOR WRANGLER

Auto 3-Speed Transmission +420
Color Match Dual Roofs +1020
AM/FM Stereo Tape[Std on Sahara] +150
Air Conditioning +550
Aluminum/Alloy Wheels[Std on Sahara] +215
Anti-Lock Brakes +390
Cruise Control +140
Hardtop Roof +535
Rear Window Defroster +115
Rear Window Wiper +105
Tilt Steering Wheel[Std on Sahara] +120

1998 JEEP

CHEROKEE   1998

Cherokee Classic and Limited replace the Cherokee Country. A new 2.5-liter four-cylinder engine is now the base engine for the SE, available with an optional three-speed automatic. New colors include Chili Pepper Red, Emerald Green and Deep Amethyst.

RATINGS (SCALE OF 1-10)

Overall	Safety	Reliability	Performance	Comfort	Value
6.9	6.1	7.5	7.4	7	6.3

Category G

	Trade-in	Market
4 Dr Classic Wgn	13250	15585
4 Dr Classic 4WD Wgn	14195	16700
4 Dr Limited Wgn	14475	17030
4 Dr Limited 4WD Wgn	15530	18275

Don't forget to refer to the Mileage Adjustment Table at the back of this book!

Model Description	Trade-in Value	Market Value
2 Dr SE Utility	10095	11875
2 Dr SE 4WD Utility	11040	12985
4 Dr SE Wgn	10740	12640
4 Dr SE 4WD Wgn	11685	13745
2 Dr Sport Utility	11735	13810
2 Dr Sport 4WD Utility	12680	14915
4 Dr Sport Wgn	12385	14570
4 Dr Sport 4WD Wgn	13325	15675

OPTIONS FOR CHEROKEE

6 cyl 4.0 L Engine[Opt on SE] +490
Auto 3-Speed Transmission +365
Auto 4-Speed Transmission[Opt on SE, Sport] +515
Air Conditioning[Std on Limited] +450
Aluminum/Alloy Wheels[Opt on SE, Sport] +175
Anti-Lock Brakes +320
Auto Locking Hubs (4WD)[Opt on Utility] +145
Compact Disc W/fm/tape +240
Cruise Control[Std on Limited] +115
Fog Lights +80
Keyless Entry System[Std on Limited] +105
Leather Seats[Opt on Classic] +430
Power Door Locks[Std on Limited] +130
Power Drivers Seat[Std on Limited] +155
Power Mirrors[Opt on SE, Sport] +70
Power Windows[Std on Limited] +135
Rear Window Defroster[Std on Limited] +95
Rear Window Wiper[Opt on SE, Sport] +85
Sunscreen Glass[Opt on Sport] +205
Tilt Steering Wheel[Std on Limited] +100

GRAND CHEROKEE 1998

A 5.9-liter V8 making 245 horsepower and 345 foot-pounds torque powers the Grand Cherokee 5.9 Limited, making it the mightiest of all Jeeps. With the addition of the 5.9, the putrid Orvis model dies. Two new colors and "next-generation" airbags round out the changes.

RATINGS (SCALE OF 1-10)

Overall	Safety	Reliability	Performance	Comfort	Value
7.2	7.1	8.1	7	7.6	6.4

Category G

	Trade-in	Market
4 Dr 5.9 Limited 4WD Wgn	22710	26720
4 Dr Laredo Wgn	15495	18230
4 Dr Laredo 4WD Wgn	16645	19585
4 Dr Limited Wgn	18720	22025
4 Dr Limited 4WD Wgn	20145	23700
4 Dr TSi Wgn	16695	19640
4 Dr TSi 4WD Wgn	17845	20995

OPTIONS FOR GRAND CHEROKEE

8 cyl 5.2 L Engine +475
Camper/Towing Package +160
Compact Disc W/fm/tape[Opt on Laredo, TSi] +240
Dual Power Seats[Opt on Laredo,TSi] +230
Fog Lights[Opt on Laredo,TSi] +80
Heated Front Seats[Std on 5.9 Limited] +150
Heated Power Mirrors[Opt on Laredo, TSi] +45
Leather Seats[Opt on Laredo, TSi] +430
Locking Differential[Std on 5.9 Limited] +160
Power Sunroof[Std on 5.9 Limited] +430
Sunscreen Glass[Opt on Laredo, TSi] +205

WRANGLER 1998

Jeep has improved off-road capability by increasing the axle ratio offered with the 4.0-liter engine and revising the torsion bar for better steering. Optional this year are a tilting driver's seat, automatic speed control, a combination CD/cassette stereo, a new Smart Key Immobilizer theft deterrent system and two new colors.

RATINGS (SCALE OF 1-10)

Overall	Safety	Reliability	Performance	Comfort	Value
6.4	6.9	7.4	7	5.6	5.2

Category G

	Trade-in	Market
2 Dr SE 4WD Utility	9640	11340
2 Dr Sahara 4WD Utility	13770	16010
2 Dr Sport 4WD Utility	11870	13965

OPTIONS FOR WRANGLER

Auto 3-Speed Transmission +340
Color Match Dual Roofs +875
AM/FM Stereo Tape[Std on Sahara] +120
Air Conditioning +450
Aluminum/Alloy Wheels[Opt on Sport] +175
Anti-Lock Brakes +320
Compact Disc W/fm/tape +240
Cruise Control +115
Fog Lights[Opt on Sport] +80
Hardtop Roof +435
Rear Window Defroster +95
Rear Window Wiper +85
Tilt Steering Wheel[Std on Sahara] +100
Velour/Cloth Seats[Std on Sahara] +115

1997 JEEP

CHEROKEE 1997

A new interior sporting modern instrumentation debuts. Front and rear styling is refined, and the rear liftgate is now stamped from steel. Multi-plex wiring is designed to improve reliability of the electrical system, while a new paint process aims to polish the finish of all Cherokees.

RATINGS (SCALE OF 1-10)

Overall	Safety	Reliability	Performance	Comfort	Value
6.8	6	6.9	7.4	7	6.9

Category G

	Trade-in	Market
4 Dr Country Wgn	12605	14895
4 Dr Country 4WD Wgn	13280	15695

Don't forget to refer to the Mileage Adjustment Table at the back of this book!

Model Description	Trade-in Value	Market Value
2 Dr SE Utility	8895	10510
2 Dr SE 4WD Utility	9745	11515
4 Dr SE Wgn	9475	11200
4 Dr SE 4WD Wgn	10325	12200
2 Dr Sport Utility	10360	12245
2 Dr Sport 4WD Utility	11210	13250
4 Dr Sport Wgn	10945	12935
4 Dr Sport 4WD Wgn	11790	13935

OPTIONS FOR CHEROKEE
6 cyl 4.0 L Engine[Opt on SE] +365
Auto 4-Speed Transmission[Std on Country] +420
Air Conditioning +365
Aluminum/Alloy Wheels[Std on Country] +145
Anti-Lock Brakes +260
Camper/Towing Package +135
Compact Disc W/fm/tape +200
Cruise Control +95
Keyless Entry System[Opt on Sport] +85
Leather Seats +350
Locking Differential +130
Luggage Rack[Std on Country] +70
Power Door Locks[Opt on Sport] +105
Power Drivers Seat +125
Power Windows[Opt on Sport] +110
Skid Plates +60

GRAND CHEROKEE 1997

Last year's integrated child safety seat has mysteriously disappeared from press kit and dealer order sheet radar. Other big news is the availability of the optional 5.2-liter V8 engine in 2WD models, and a six-cylinder that qualifies the JGC as a Transitional Low Emissions Vehicle (TLEV) in California. Refinements have been made to the ABS system, entry-level cassette stereo, and floor carpet fit. In January, a sporty TSi model debuted with monotone paint, special aluminum wheels, and other goodies.

RATINGS (SCALE OF 1-10)

Overall	Safety	Reliability	Performance	Comfort	Value
7.1	6.8	6.9	7	7.6	7

Category G
4 Dr Laredo Wgn	13785	16295
4 Dr Laredo 4WD Wgn	14830	17525
4 Dr Limited Wgn	16865	19930
4 Dr Limited 4WD Wgn	18150	21445
4 Dr TSi Wgn	14925	17635
4 Dr TSi 4WD Wgn	15965	18870

OPTIONS FOR GRAND CHEROKEE
8 cyl 5.2 L Engine +375
Camper/Towing Package +135
Compact Disc W/fm/tape +200
Dual Power Seats[Std on Limited] +185
Infinity Sound System[Std on Limited] +195
Leather Seats[Std on Limited] +350
Limited Slip Diff +125
Locking Differential +130
Power Sunroof +355
Skid Plates +60

WRANGLER 1997

Jeep has totally redesigned this American icon. A Quadra-coil suspension improves on and off-road manners; while dual airbags and optional antilock brakes increase the Wrangler's ability to keep occupants safe. Round, retro-style headlights add a nostalgic touch to this venerable ground-pounder. Fortunately, none of these refinements soften the Wrangler's tough exterior. A restyled interior includes integrated air vents, a glovebox, and car-like stereo controls and accessory switches.

RATINGS (SCALE OF 1-10)

Overall	Safety	Reliability	Performance	Comfort	Value
6.1	7.1	6.4	7	5.6	4.6

Category G
2 Dr SE 4WD Utility	9195	10865
2 Dr Sahara 4WD Utility	12965	15320
2 Dr Sport 4WD Utility	10355	12465

OPTIONS FOR WRANGLER
Auto 3-Speed Transmission +250
AM/FM Stereo Tape[Std on Sahara] +100
Air Conditioning +365
Aluminum/Alloy Wheels[Opt on Sport] +145
Anti-Lock Brakes +260
Bucket Seats[Opt on SE] +155
Hardtop Roof +355
Locking Differential +130
Power Steering[Opt on SE] +125
Velour/Cloth Seats[Std on Sahara] +95

1996 JEEP

CHEROKEE 1996

Perennial favorite rolls into 1996 with improved engines, new colors, upgraded Selec-Trac four-wheel-drive system, more standard equipment, and the same sheetmetal that it wore on introduction day in 1983.

RATINGS (SCALE OF 1-10)

Overall	Safety	Reliability	Performance	Comfort	Value
6.8	5.7	6.7	7.4	6.6	7.5

Category G
4 Dr Country Wgn	10200	12195
4 Dr Country 4WD Wgn	10935	13075
2 Dr SE Utility	7365	8805
2 Dr SE 4WD Utility	8105	9690
4 Dr SE Wgn	7875	9415
4 Dr SE 4WD Wgn	8610	10295

Model Description	Trade-in Value	Market Value
2 Dr Sport Utility	8515	10180
2 Dr Sport 4WD Utility	9250	11060
4 Dr Sport Wgn	9015	10780
4 Dr Sport 4WD Wgn	9750	11660

OPTIONS FOR CHEROKEE

6 cyl 4.0 L Engine[Opt on SE] +280
Auto 4-Speed Transmission +325
Off-Road Suspension Pkg +280
Air Conditioning +300
Aluminum/Alloy Wheels +120
Anti-Lock Brakes +210
Camper/Towing Package +110
Compact Disc W/fm/tape +160
Cruise Control +75
Keyless Entry System +70
Leather Seats +285
Limited Slip Diff +100
Locking Differential +105
Luggage Rack[Std on Country] +60
Power Door Locks +85
Power Drivers Seat +105
Power Windows +90
Skid Plates +50

GRAND CHEROKEE   1996

Jeep turns its flagship into an Explorer killer with dual airbags, revised styling, a better V6 engine, improved front suspension, and an upgraded Selec-Trac four-wheel-drive system. Interiors have been restyled, featuring new luxury doodads and an optional integrated child safety seat. Trim levels are two: Laredo and Limited. The gaudy Orvis continues as an option on the Limited. It's almost perfect; if they could just get rid of that pesky spare tire in the cargo hold.

RATINGS (SCALE OF 1-10)

Overall	Safety	Reliability	Performance	Comfort	Value
7.2	6.9	7.1	7	7.6	7.5

Category G

	Trade-in	Market
4 Dr Laredo Wgn	11775	14080
4 Dr Laredo 4WD Wgn	12700	15185
4 Dr Limited Wgn	14530	17375
4 Dr Limited 4WD Wgn	15750	18835

OPTIONS FOR GRAND CHEROKEE

8 cyl 5.2 L Engine +270
Camper/Towing Package +110
Child Seat (1) +60
Compact Disc W/fm/tape +160
Infinity Sound System[Opt on Laredo] +160
Leather Seats[Opt on Laredo] +285
Limited Slip Diff +100
Locking Differential +105
Power Sunroof +290
Skid Plates +50
Trip Computer[Opt on 2WD] +55

1995 JEEP

CHEROKEE   1995

Driver airbag is added on all models. SE model gets reclining bucket seats.

RATINGS (SCALE OF 1-10)

Overall	Safety	Reliability	Performance	Comfort	Value
6.6	6.3	6.2	7.4	6.6	6.6

Category G

	Trade-in	Market
4 Dr Country Wgn	8285	10060
4 Dr Country 4WD Wgn	8845	10740
2 Dr SE Utility	6160	7480
2 Dr SE 4WD Utility	6810	8270
4 Dr SE Wgn	6495	7885
4 Dr SE 4WD Wgn	7140	8670
2 Dr Sport Utility	7170	8710
2 Dr Sport 4WD Utility	7820	9495
4 Dr Sport Wgn	7530	9145
4 Dr Sport 4WD Wgn	8175	9930

OPTIONS FOR CHEROKEE

6 cyl 4.0 L Engine[Opt on SE] +225
Auto 4-Speed Transmission +265
Off-Road Suspension Pkg +225
AM/FM Stereo Tape +65
Air Conditioning +245
Anti-Lock Brakes +175
Camper/Towing Package +90
Center Console[Std on Country] +50
Keyless Entry System +60
Leather Seats +235
Limited Slip Diff +85
Locking Differential +85
Luggage Rack[Std on Country] +50
Power Door Locks +70
Power Drivers Seat +85
Power Windows +70
Skid Plates +40

GRAND CHEROKEE   1995

Rear disc brakes are added to all models. An Orvis trim package is added to the Limited 4WD. New options are an integrated child safety seat and a flip-up liftgate window. Optional V8 engine gets a torque increase. A 2WD Limited model is newly available. A power sunroof is added to the options list.

RATINGS (SCALE OF 1-10)

Overall	Safety	Reliability	Performance	Comfort	Value
7.2	6.8	7.6	7	7.8	6.7

Category G

	Trade-in	Market
4 Dr Laredo Wgn	10110	12280
4 Dr Laredo 4WD Wgn	10935	13280
4 Dr Limited Wgn	12230	14855

Don't forget to refer to the Mileage Adjustment Table at the back of this book!

Model Description	Trade-in Value	Market Value
4 Dr Limited 4WD Wgn	13265	16105
4 Dr SE Wgn	10055	12210
4 Dr SE 4WD Wgn	10880	13210

OPTIONS FOR GRAND CHEROKEE
8 cyl 5.2 L Engine +220
Up Country Suspension Grp +235
AM/FM Compact Disc Player +95
Camper/Towing Package +90
Child Seat (1) +50
Dual Power Seats +125
Infinity Sound System[Std on Limited] +130
Leather Seats[Std on Limited] +235
Limited Slip Diff +85
Locking Differential +85
Power Sunroof +235
Skid Plates +40

WRANGLER   1995

S model can be equipped with new Rio Grande package. Renegade is dropped from lineup. An optional dome light can be attached to the optional sound bar.

RATINGS (SCALE OF 1-10)

Overall	Safety	Reliability	Performance	Comfort	Value
5.9	4.1	6.9	6.6	5.9	6

Category G

Model Description	Trade-in Value	Market Value
2 Dr Rio Grande 4WD Utility	7255	8810
2 Dr S 4WD Utility	6185	7510
2 Dr SE 4WD Utility	8005	9720
2 Dr Sahara 4WD Utility	9020	10955

OPTIONS FOR WRANGLER
Auto 3-Speed Transmission +185
AM/FM Stereo Tape[Opt on S] +65
Air Conditioning +245
Aluminum/Alloy Wheels +95
Anti-Lock Brakes +175
Hardtop Roof +240
Locking Differential +85
Power Steering[Opt on S] +85
Velour/Cloth Seats[Opt on S] +65

1994 JEEP

CHEROKEE   1994

Side-door guard beams have been added, and center high-mounted brake light is new. Base model gets SE nomenclature.

RATINGS (SCALE OF 1-10)

Overall	Safety	Reliability	Performance	Comfort	Value
6.2	4.6	6.5	7.4	6.6	6.1

Category G

Model Description	Trade-in Value	Market Value
2 Dr Country Utility	6695	8225
2 Dr Country 4WD Utility	7265	8930
4 Dr Country Wgn	7080	8705
4 Dr Country 4WD Wgn	7655	9410
2 Dr SE Utility	5230	6430
2 Dr SE 4WD Utility	5805	7135
4 Dr SE Wgn	5620	6910
4 Dr SE 4WD Wgn	6195	7610
2 Dr Sport Utility	6060	7450
2 Dr Sport 4WD Utility	6635	8155
4 Dr Sport Wgn	6450	7930
4 Dr Sport 4WD Wgn	7255	8920

OPTIONS FOR CHEROKEE
6 cyl 4.0 L Engine[Opt on SE] +110
Auto 4-Speed Transmission +220
AM/FM Stereo Tape +55
Air Conditioning +200
Anti-Lock Brakes +140
Camper/Towing Package +70
Cruise Control +50
Keyless Entry System +50
Leather Seats +190
Limited Slip Diff +70
Locking Differential +70
Luggage Rack[Std on Country] +40
Power Door Locks +55
Power Drivers Seat +70
Power Windows +60
Skid Plates +35

GRAND CHEROKEE   1994

Side-door guard beams are added for 1994. Grand Wagoneer trim level is dropped. Base model is now called SE. Limited gets rear disc brakes.

RATINGS (SCALE OF 1-10)

Overall	Safety	Reliability	Performance	Comfort	Value
7	6.9	7.1	7	7.8	6

Category G

Model Description	Trade-in Value	Market Value
4 Dr Laredo Wgn	8245	10135
4 Dr Laredo 4WD Wgn	8710	10710
4 Dr Limited 4WD Wgn	10940	13450
4 Dr SE Wgn	8145	10010
4 Dr SE 4WD Wgn	8210	10090

OPTIONS FOR GRAND CHEROKEE
8 cyl 5.2 L Engine +175
Auto 4-Speed Transmission[Std on Limited,2WD] +220
Camper/Towing Package[Std on Limited] +70
Compact Disc W/fm/tape +110
Dual Power Seats +100
Infinity Sound System[Std on Limited] +105
Keyless Entry System[Opt on SE] +50
Leather Seats[Std on Limited] +190
Limited Slip Diff +70

JEEP 94-93

Model Description	Trade-in Value	Market Value	Model Description	Trade-in Value	Market Value

Power Door Locks[Opt on SE] +55
Power Windows[Opt on SE] +60
Skid Plates +35
Trip Computer[Opt on Laredo] +35

WRANGLER 1994

The four-cylinder engine can be saddled with an automatic transmission this year. Base trim is now termed SE. Center high-mounted brake light is added.

RATINGS (SCALE OF 1-10)

Overall	Safety	Reliability	Performance	Comfort	Value
5.9	4	6.8	6.6	5.9	6

Category G

2 Dr Renegade 4WD Utility	8875	10910
2 Dr S 4WD Utility	5495	6755
2 Dr SE 4WD Utility *	6910	8495
2 Dr Sahara 4WD Utility	8030	9870
2 Dr Sport 4WD Utility	7670	9425

OPTIONS FOR WRANGLER

Auto 3-Speed Transmission +150
AM/FM Stereo Tape[Opt on S,SE,Sport] +55
Air Conditioning +200
Anti-Lock Brakes +140
Chrome Bumpers +35
Hardtop Roof +195
Limited Slip Diff +70
Locking Differential +70
Power Steering[Opt on S,SE] +70
Velour/Cloth Seats[Opt on SE,Sport] +50

1993 JEEP

CHEROKEE 1993

Lineup is shuffled to make room for Grand Cherokee. Country trim replaces Limited. Base prices fall substantially, but models are decontented to achieve lower price.

RATINGS (SCALE OF 1-10)

Overall	Safety	Reliability	Performance	Comfort	Value
6.1	4.6	6.1	7.4	6.6	5.9

Category G

2 Dr Country Utility	5505	6910
2 Dr Country 4WD Utility	6000	7530
4 Dr Country Wgn	5840	7335
4 Dr Country 4WD Wgn	6335	7950
2 Dr STD Utility	4210	5285
2 Dr STD 4WD Utility	4705	5905
4 Dr STD Wgn	4545	5705
4 Dr STD 4WD Wgn	5040	6325
2 Dr Sport Utility	4945	6210
2 Dr Sport 4WD Utility	5435	6825

4 Dr Sport Wgn	5280	6630
4 Dr Sport 4WD Wgn	5775	7250

OPTIONS FOR CHEROKEE

6 cyl 4.0 L Engine[Opt on STD] +95
Auto 4-Speed Transmission +180
Off-road Suspension Pkg +150
AM/FM Stereo Tape +45
Air Conditioning +165
Aluminum/Alloy Wheels[Std on Country] +65
Anti-Lock Brakes +115
Camper/Towing Package +60
Cruise Control +40
Keyless Entry System +40
Luggage Rack[Std on Country] +30
Power Door Locks +45
Power Drivers Seat +55
Power Windows +50
Premium Sound System +70
Skid Plates +25
Swing Out Tire Carrier[Std on Sport 4WD Wgn] +35

GRAND CHEROKEE 1993

Introduced in April, 1992, Grand Cherokee gets a V8-engine option and a Grand Wagoneer model that includes the V8 and fake-wood siding. Late in the year, 2WD models in Base and Laredo trim are introduced. A driver airbag and ABS that works in 2WD or 4WD are standard.

RATINGS (SCALE OF 1-10)

Overall	Safety	Reliability	Performance	Comfort	Value
6.5	6.3	5.3	7	7.8	6

Category G

4 Dr Laredo Wgn	7070	8880
4 Dr Laredo 4WD Wgn	7105	8920
4 Dr Limited 4WD Wgn	9615	12075
4 Dr STD Wgn	6665	8370
4 Dr STD 4WD Wgn	6940	8715

OPTIONS FOR GRAND CHEROKEE

8 cyl 5.2 L Engine +170
Auto 4-Speed Transmission[Std on Limited,2WD] +175
Up Country Suspension Grp +155
AM/FM Compact Disc Player +65
Air Conditioning[Std on Limited] +165
Aluminum/Alloy Wheels[Std on Limited] +65
Camper/Towing Package +60
Cruise Control[Opt on STD] +40
Keyless Entry System[Std on Limited] +40
Leather Seats[Opt on Laredo] +155
Locking Differential +60
Luggage Rack[Opt on STD] +30
Power Door Locks[Std on Limited] +45
Power Drivers Seat[Std on Limited] +55
Power Passenger Seat[Opt on Laredo] +40
Power Windows[Std on Limited] +50

Don't forget to refer to the Mileage Adjustment Table at the back of this book!

Model Description	Trade-in Value	Market Value
Premium Sound System[Std on Limited] +70		
Skid Plates +25		

GRAND WAGONEER 1993

Category G

	Trade-in	Market
4 Dr STD 4WD Wgn	8395	10540

OPTIONS FOR GRAND WAGONEER
AM/FM Compact Disc Player +65

WRANGLER 1993

ABS that works in both two- and four-wheel drive is newly optional with six-cylinder engines. Islander model disappears. Other changes include a stainless steel exhaust system, tamper-resistant odometer, and tinted plastic windows for the convertible. Sport package includes new graphics and five-spoke steel wheels.

RATINGS (SCALE OF 1-10)

Overall	Safety	Reliability	Performance	Comfort	Value
5.7	4.3	6.4	6.6	5.9	5.4

Category G

	Trade-in	Market
2 Dr Renegade 4WD Utility	7485	9400
2 Dr S 4WD Utility	4720	5930
2 Dr STD 4WD Utility	5720	7185
2 Dr Sahara 4WD Utility	6755	8485

OPTIONS FOR WRANGLER
6 cyl 4.0 L Engine[Opt on S,STD] +95
Auto 3-Speed Transmission +115
Sport Handling Pkg +235
AM/FM Stereo Tape +45
Air Conditioning +165
Aluminum/Alloy Wheels[Std on Renegade] +65
Anti-Lock Brakes +115
Hardtop Roof +160
Locking Differential +60
Power Steering[Opt on S,STD] +55

1992 JEEP

CHEROKEE 1992

Sport models gain a glass sunroof option, while Laredos get vent windows. All radios now have an integral digital clock. Leather upholstery is available on Laredo for the first time. Detachable cupholders are added to the center console.

RATINGS (SCALE OF 1-10)

Overall	Safety	Reliability	Performance	Comfort	Value
6.7	4.7	7	7.4	6.6	7.7

Category G

	Trade-in	Market
4 Dr Briarwood 4WD Wgn	6630	8560
2 Dr Laredo 4WD Utility	4970	6420
4 Dr Laredo Wgn	4840	6250

Model Description	Trade-in Value	Market Value
4 Dr Laredo 4WD Wgn	5450	7040
4 Dr Limited 4WD Wgn	6770	8745
2 Dr STD Utility	4105	5305
2 Dr STD 4WD Utility	4520	5835
4 Dr STD Wgn	3845	5125
4 Dr STD 4WD Wgn	4475	5875
2 Dr Sport 4WD Utility	4735	6120
4 Dr Sport Wgn	4605	5950
4 Dr Sport 4WD Wgn	5015	6480

OPTIONS FOR CHEROKEE
6 cyl 4.0 L Engine[Opt on Laredo,Sport,STD] +90
Auto 4-Speed Transmission[Opt on Laredo,Sport,STD] +145
Off Road Pkg +160
Sport Handling Pkg +130
AM/FM Compact Disc Player +50
Air Conditioning[Opt on Laredo,Sport,STD] +135
Anti-Lock Brakes +95
Camper/Towing Package +50
Leather Seats[Opt on Laredo,Sport,STD] +130
Locking Differential +50
Power Door Locks[Opt on Laredo,Sport,STD] +40
Power Drivers Seat[Opt on Laredo,Sport,STD] +45
Power Passenger Seat[Opt on Laredo,Sport,STD] +35
Power Windows[Opt on Laredo,Sport,STD] +40
Sunroof +50

COMANCHE 1992

Sport option group debuts. Radios have digital clocks. Detachable cupholders are added to center console.

Category G

	Trade-in	Market
2 Dr Eliminator Std Cab LB	3925	5070
2 Dr Eliminator 4WD Std Cab LB	4825	6235
2 Dr Eliminator Std Cab SB	3925	5070
2 Dr Eliminator 4WD Std Cab SB	4825	6235
2 Dr Pioneer Std Cab LB	3390	4375
2 Dr Pioneer 4WD Std Cab LB	4315	5570
2 Dr Pioneer Std Cab SB	3390	4375
2 Dr Pioneer 4WD Std Cab SB	4315	5570
2 Dr STD Std Cab LB	3000	3875
2 Dr STD 4WD Std Cab LB	4115	5320
2 Dr STD Std Cab SB	2840	3670
2 Dr STD 4WD Std Cab SB	3925	5070
2 Dr Sport Std Cab LB	3235	4180
2 Dr Sport 4WD Std Cab LB	4160	5375
2 Dr Sport Std Cab SB	3235	4180
2 Dr Sport 4WD Std Cab SB	3960	5115

OPTIONS FOR COMANCHE
6 cyl 4.0 L Engine +90
5-Speed Transmission +35
Auto 4-Speed Transmission +165
Off Road Pkg +155
Air Conditioning +135
Locking Differential +50
Power Steering +45

Don't forget to refer to the Mileage Adjustment Table at the back of this book!

Model Description	Trade-in Value	Market Value

WRANGLER 1992

Three-point seatbelts anchored to the roll bar are added. New colors round out the changes.

RATINGS (SCALE OF 1-10)

Overall	Safety	Reliability	Performance	Comfort	Value
5.6	4.2	5.9	6.6	5.9	5.3

Category G

2 Dr Islander 4WD Utility	4590	5925
2 Dr Renegade 4WD Utility	5260	6795
2 Dr S 4WD Utility	3620	4675
2 Dr STD 4WD Utility	4390	5670
2 Dr Sahara 4WD Utility	4790	6190

OPTIONS FOR WRANGLER

6 cyl 4.0 L Engine +90
Auto 3-Speed Transmission +95
Air Conditioning +135
Hardtop Roof +130
Locking Differential +50
Rear Bench Seat[Opt on S] +65

1991 JEEP

CHEROKEE 1991

Two new models, the Sport four-door and top-of-the-line Briarwood, join the lineup. Child-proof rear door locks are added to four-door models. A security alarm system is a new option. Power is increased for both engines. An automatic transmission is no longer available on the base four-cylinder engine.

RATINGS (SCALE OF 1-10)

Overall	Safety	Reliability	Performance	Comfort	Value
6	4.1	5	7.4	6.6	7.1

Category G

4 Dr Briarwood 4WD Wgn	5640	7470
2 Dr Laredo 4WD Utility	4050	5365
4 Dr Laredo Wgn	4060	5380
4 Dr Laredo 4WD Wgn	4370	5790
4 Dr Limited 4WD Wgn	5760	7625
2 Dr STD Utility	3285	4350
2 Dr STD 4WD Utility	3635	4815
4 Dr STD Wgn	3525	4665
4 Dr STD 4WD Wgn	3875	5130
2 Dr Sport Utility	3380	4475
2 Dr Sport 4WD Utility	3730	4945
4 Dr Sport Wgn	3610	4780
4 Dr Sport 4WD Wgn	4085	5410

OPTIONS FOR CHEROKEE

6 cyl 4.0 L Engine[Opt on Laredo,Sport,STD] +80
Auto 4-Speed Transmission[Opt on Laredo,Sport,STD] +115
Off Road Pkg +130

Air Conditioning[Opt on Laredo,Sport,STD] +110
Anti-Lock Brakes +75
Camper/Towing Package +40
Dual Power Seats[Opt on Laredo,Sport] +55
Leather Seats[Opt on Laredo,STD] +105
Limited Slip Diff +35
Power Door Locks[Opt on Laredo,Sport,STD] +30
Power Windows[Opt on Laredo,Sport,STD] +30
Sunroof +40

COMANCHE 1991

Power is increased for both engines, and five new colors are available.

Category G

2 Dr Eliminator Std Cab LB	2685	3555
2 Dr Eliminator 4WD Std Cab LB	3520	4665
2 Dr Eliminator Std Cab SB	2685	3555
2 Dr Eliminator 4WD Std Cab SB	3520	4665
2 Dr Pioneer Std Cab LB	2695	3570
2 Dr Pioneer 4WD Std Cab LB	3530	4675
2 Dr Pioneer Std Cab SB	2695	3570
2 Dr Pioneer 4WD Std Cab SB	3530	4675
2 Dr STD Std Cab LB	2725	3605
2 Dr STD 4WD Std Cab LB	3570	4725
2 Dr STD Std Cab SB	2505	3320
2 Dr STD 4WD Std Cab SB	3345	4425

OPTIONS FOR COMANCHE

6 cyl 4.0 L Engine[Opt on Eliminator,STD] +80
5-Speed Transmission +25
Auto 3-Speed Transmission +105
Big Ton Pkg +100
Suspension Pkg +130
Air Conditioning +110
Limited Slip Diff +35
Power Steering +40

GRAND WAGONEER 1991

Five new exterior colors and one new interior color debut.

Category H

4 Dr STD 4WD Wgn	6635	8520

OPTIONS FOR GRAND WAGONEER

Camper/Towing Package +45
Limited Slip Diff +35
Power Sunroof +200

WRANGLER 1991

New Renegade option replaces Laredo and adds fender flares, fog lights and alloy wheels. A new six-cylinder engine boosts horsepower substantially, from 112 with the old 4.2-liter unit to 180 with the new 4.0-liter motor. Four-cylinder models also get a slight bump in power. New seats with reclining backrests are new

Model Description	Trade-in Value	Market Value	Model Description	Trade-in Value	Market Value
to all models except S. A sound bar is also available on all models except S.			2 Dr S 4WD Utility	2925	3870
			2 Dr STD 4WD Utility	3570	4730
			2 Dr Sahara 4WD Utility	3905	5170

RATINGS (SCALE OF 1-10)

Overall	Safety	Reliability	Performance	Comfort	Value
5.2	3.8	4.8	6.6	5.9	4.7

Category G

Model Description	Trade-in Value	Market Value
2 Dr Islander 4WD Utility	3780	5005
2 Dr Renegade 4WD Utility	4070	5390

OPTIONS FOR WRANGLER
6 cyl 4.0 L Engine +80
Auto 3-Speed Transmission +75
Air Conditioning +110
Hardtop Roof +105
Limited Slip Diff +35
Power Steering +40

Don't forget to refer to the Mileage Adjustment Table at the back of this book!

KIA 00-99

Model Description	Trade-in Value	Market Value	Model Description	Trade-in Value	Market Value

KIA   S. Korea

1997 Kia Sephia

2000 KIA

SEPHIA   2000

The Sephia has improved seat fabric, a new audio system and two new colors for 2000.

Category E

Model	Trade-in	Market
4 Dr LS Sdn	7875	9365
4 Dr STD Sdn	7190	8545

OPTIONS FOR SEPHIA

Auto 4-Speed Transmission +795
AM/FM Stereo Tape +250
Air Conditioning +680
Power Steering[Std on LS] +210

SPECTRA   2000

The Spectra is new for 2000. Similar in size to the Sephia, Kia hopes the Spectra will attract younger buyers due to the versatile four-door hatchback design and sportier styling.

Category E

Model	Trade-in	Market
4 Dr GS Sdn	7695	9145
4 Dr GSX Sdn	9200	10935

OPTIONS FOR SPECTRA

Auto 4-Speed Transmission +910
AM/FM Compact Disc Player +355
Air Conditioning[Opt on GS] +680
Cruise Control +185
Power Mirrors +90
Rear Window Wiper +105

SPORTAGE   2000

Kia ushers in the 2000 Sportage with a new sound system, dual airbags, new colors and some additional equipment, but keeps last year's MSRP.

Category G

Model	Trade-in	Market
4 Dr EX Wgn	12580	14775
4 Dr EX 4WD Wgn	13425	15770
2 Dr STD Conv	10180	11960
2 Dr STD 4WD Conv	10535	12375
4 Dr STD Wgn	10955	12875
4 Dr STD 4WD Wgn	11805	13865

OPTIONS FOR SPORTAGE

Auto 4-Speed Transmission[Std on Conv] +815
AM/FM Compact Disc Player[Std on EX] +260
AM/FM Stereo Tape +180
Air Conditioning[Std on EX] +670
Aluminum/Alloy Wheels[Std on EX,4] +265
Luggage Rack[Std on EX] +130
Rear Window Wiper[Std on EX] +125

1999 KIA

SEPHIA   1999

The Sephia was entirely redesigned in '98 and enters '99 essentially unchanged.

RATINGS (SCALE OF 1-10)

Overall	Safety	Reliability	Performance	Comfort	Value
N/A	N/A	N/A	5.8	6.4	N/A

Category E

Model	Trade-in	Market
4 Dr LS Sdn	6775	8245
4 Dr STD Sdn	6185	7525

OPTIONS FOR SEPHIA

Auto 4-Speed Transmission +650
AM/FM Compact Disc Player +290
Air Conditioning +555
Aluminum/Alloy Wheels +225
Anti-Lock Brakes +445
Cruise Control +155
Power Door Locks +165
Power Mirrors +75
Power Steering[Std on LS] +170
Power Windows +180

SPORTAGE   1999

A new two-door convertible model joins the four-door Sportage in 1999. The convertible comes in either a 4x2 layout with automatic transmission or a 4x4 layout with five-speed manual transmission. It also boasts dual front airbags and a driver's side front knee bag.

Category G

Model	Trade-in	Market
4 Dr EX Wgn	11290	13380
4 Dr EX 4WD Wgn	12050	14280
2 Dr STD Conv	9140	10830
2 Dr STD 4WD Conv	9455	11205
4 Dr STD Wgn	9645	11430
4 Dr STD 4WD Wgn	10595	12555

Don't forget to refer to the Mileage Adjustment Table at the back of this book!

EDMUNDS® USED CARS & TRUCKS

Model Description	Trade-in Value	Market Value
OPTIONS FOR SPORTAGE		
Auto 4-Speed Transmission +670		
AM/FM Compact Disc Player[Std on EX] +210		
Air Conditioning[Std on EX] +550		
Aluminum/Alloy Wheels[Std on EX,4WD] +215		
Anti-Lock Brakes +390		
Leather Seats +525		
Rear Window Wiper[Std on EX] +105		

1998 KIA

SEPHIA 1998

The Sephia is totally redesigned for 1998.

Category E		
4 Dr LS Sdn	5600	6970
4 Dr STD Sdn	5110	6360

OPTIONS FOR SEPHIA
Auto 4-Speed Transmission +530
AM/FM Compact Disc Player +235
Air Conditioning +455
Aluminum/Alloy Wheels +185
Anti-Lock Brakes +365
Cruise Control +125
Power Door Locks +135
Power Mirrors +60
Power Steering[Std on LS] +140
Power Windows +145

SPORTAGE 1998

There are lots of improvements this year for the Sportage, including a new grille, new alloy wheels, tilt steering wheel, passenger-side airbag, better brakes, improved air conditioning and four-wheel ABS that replaces last year's rear-wheel ABS.

Category G		
4 Dr EX Wgn	10080	12045
4 Dr EX 4WD Wgn	10765	12860
4 Dr STD Wgn	8720	10415
4 Dr STD 4WD Wgn	9570	11435

OPTIONS FOR SPORTAGE
Auto 4-Speed Transmission +545
AM/FM Compact Disc Player[Std on EX] +175
Air Conditioning[Std on EX] +450
Aluminum/Alloy Wheels[Std on EX, 4WD] +175
Anti-Lock Brakes +320
Leather Seats +430

1997 KIA

SEPHIA 1997

RS models get body-color bumpers this year, and a tan interior is newly available with black exterior paint.

Category E		
4 Dr GS Sdn	4755	6230
4 Dr LS Sdn	4350	5695
4 Dr RS Sdn	3925	5140

OPTIONS FOR SEPHIA
Auto 4-Speed Transmission +405
AM/FM Compact Disc Player +195
AM/FM Stereo Tape[Std on GS] +135
Air Conditioning +370
Aluminum/Alloy Wheels +150
Anti-Lock Brakes +295
Power Steering[Opt on RS] +115
Premium Sound System +145

SPORTAGE 1997

An automatic transmission is offered on 2WD models, and the EX trim level is available in 2WD for the first time. Power door locks, a theft deterrent system, and a spare tire carrier are all standard on all Sportages for 1997. A new option is a CD player. Sportage gets a new grille. A tan interior can be combined with black paint for the first time. Base 2WD models lose their standard alloy wheels.

Category G		
4 Dr EX Wgn	8110	9765
4 Dr EX 4WD Wgn	8740	10520
4 Dr STD Wgn	7650	9215
4 Dr STD 4WD Wgn	8420	10140

OPTIONS FOR SPORTAGE
Auto 4-Speed Transmission +445
AM/FM Compact Disc Player +140
Air Conditioning +365
Aluminum/Alloy Wheels[Std on EX,4WD] +145
Leather Seats +350
Luggage Rack[Std on EX] +70
Swing Out Tire Carrier[Std on EX,4WD] +85

1996 KIA

SEPHIA 1996

Styling and suspension tweaks, dual airbags, and new twin-cam motors appeared with the introduction of the 1995.5 Sephia. These improvements, along with interior revisions and improved equipment levels, make the Kia more competitive in the compact sedan marketplace. Sephia now meets 1997 side-impact standards, and GS models can be equipped with antilock brakes. Sephia comes with 5 year/60,000 mile powertrain coverage.

Category E		
4 Dr GS Sdn	3925	5345
4 Dr LS Sdn	3630	4945
4 Dr RS Sdn	3235	4410

Don't forget to refer to the Mileage Adjustment Table at the back of this book!

KIA 96-94

Model Description	Trade-in Value	Market Value	Model Description	Trade-in Value	Market Value

OPTIONS FOR SEPHIA

Auto 4-Speed Transmission +320
AM/FM Stereo Tape[Std on GS] +110
Air Conditioning +305
Anti-Lock Brakes +245
Power Steering[Opt on RS] +95
Premium Sound System +120

SPORTAGE   1996

The world's first knee airbag arrives in conjunction with a driver airbag, and a two-wheel drive edition is available this year. A spirited twin-cam engine arrived late in 1995, and cured Sportage's power ills.

Category G

	Trade-in	Market
4 Dr EX Wgn	7400	9025
4 Dr EX 4WD Wgn	7175	8750
4 Dr STD Wgn	6040	7365
4 Dr STD 4WD Wgn	6675	8145

OPTIONS FOR SPORTAGE

4 cyl 2.0 L DOHC Engine +275
Auto 4-Speed Transmission +375
AM/FM Stereo Tape +80
Air Conditioning +300
Leather Seats +285
Luggage Rack +60
Swing Out Tire Carrier +70

1995 KIA

SEPHIA   1995

Oh no, another Korean manufacturer trying to break into the American market. But wait, this one is actually worth considering; a lot of help from Mazda and Ford mean that this little upstart is actually making fairly reliable little cars. The Sephia has plenty of Mazda parts and Kia has a long history of building durable, cheap cars.

Category E

	Trade-in	Market
4 Dr GS Sdn	3470	4675
1995.5 4 Dr GS Sdn	3005	4235
4 Dr LS Sdn	3185	4290
1995.5 4 Dr LS Sdn	2760	3890
4 Dr RS Sdn	2430	3420
1995.5 4 Dr RS Sdn	2540	3580

OPTIONS FOR SEPHIA

Auto 4-Speed Transmission +250
AM/FM Stereo Tape[Std on GS] +90
Air Conditioning +250
Cruise Control[Opt on GS] +70
Dual Air Bag Restraints +185
Power Steering[Opt on RS,RS 1995.5] +75
Premium Sound System +100

SPORTAGE   1995

Another mini-SUV is introduced, competing with everything from the Jeep Cherokee to the Geo Tracker. The Sportage offers comfortable seating for four, ample storage space, and available four-wheel drive. Designed with Ford and Mazda, with suspension tuning by Lotus, the Sportage should provide a good deal of fun and durability.

Category G

	Trade-in	Market
4 Dr EX 4WD Wgn	5870	7340
4 Dr STD Wgn	5130	6415
4 Dr STD 4WD Wgn	5500	6875

OPTIONS FOR SPORTAGE

4 cyl 2.0 L DOHC Engine +225
Auto 4-Speed Transmission +300
AM/FM Stereo Tape +65
Air Conditioning +245
Leather Seats +235
Luggage Rack +50
Swing Out Tire Carrier +55

1994 KIA

SEPHIA   1994

New subcompact sedan from South Korea based on 1990-1994 Mazda Protege platform and powered by a 1.6-liter, 88-horsepower four-cylinder engine. Sold only in the western and southwestern regions of the U.S.

Category E

	Trade-in	Market
4 Dr GS Sdn	2335	3530
4 Dr LS Sdn	2135	3230
4 Dr RS Sdn	1955	2965

OPTIONS FOR SEPHIA

Auto 4-Speed Transmission +185
AM/FM Stereo Tape[Std on GS] +75
Air Conditioning +205
Cruise Control +55
Power Steering[Opt on RS] +60
Premium Sound System +80

LAND ROVER 00-98

Model Description	Trade-in Value	Market Value	Model Description	Trade-in Value	Market Value

LAND ROVER Britain

1996 Land Rover Discovery

2000 LAND ROVER

DISCOVERY SERIES II   2000

The Discovery was completely redesigned last year and sees only minor interior trim revisions for the 2000 model year.

Category H

	Trade-in	Market
4 Dr Series II 4WD Wgn	26515	30435

OPTIONS FOR DISCOVERY SERIES II
Performance Pkg +2370
Rear Seat Pkg +1430
Dual Power Seats +385
Dual Sunroof +1275
Leather Seats +815
Luggage Rack +125

RANGE ROVER   2000

The 2000 Range Rover now qualifies as a low-emissions vehicle. Interior and exterior upgrades improve the vehicle's look and feel, and new trim levels allow buyers to further dress up their Range Rover's appearance

Category H

	Trade-in	Market
4 Dr 4.0 SE AWD Wgn	45525	52255
4 Dr 4.6 HSE AWD Wgn	51860	59530
4 Dr 4.6 Vitesse 4WD Wgn	52395	60145
4 Dr County 4WD Wgn	44990	51640

OPTIONS FOR RANGE ROVER
Navigation System +2450

1999 LAND ROVER

DISCOVERY   1999

The release of the 1999 Discovery Series II sees the first engineering redesign since the vehicle's European introduction 11 years ago. Traction Control, Active Cornering Enhancement and Hill Descent Control are new standard features.

RATINGS (SCALE OF 1-10)

Overall	Safety	Reliability	Performance	Comfort	Value
N/A	N/A	N/A	6.2	7	N/A

Category H

	Trade-in	Market
4 Dr SD 4WD Wgn	24100	27785
4 Dr Series II 4WD Wgn	24925	28740

OPTIONS FOR DISCOVERY
Performance Pkg +1935
Rear Seat Pkg +1170
Compact Disc Changer +300
Dual Air Conditioning +860
Dual Sunroof +1045
Heated Front Seats +240
Leather Seats[Std on SD] +670

RANGE ROVER   1999

Engine upgrades, new color schemes, traction control and standard side-mounted airbags are some of the additions to the 1999 Range Rovers, which will be introduced later in the year. For now, interim Range Rover models called the 4.0 and 4.0S are available.

RATINGS (SCALE OF 1-10)

Overall	Safety	Reliability	Performance	Comfort	Value
N/A	N/A	N/A	6.4	N/A	N/A

Category H

	Trade-in	Market
4 Dr 4.0 4WD Wgn	37945	43970
4 Dr 4.0 S 4WD Wgn	39410	45430
4 Dr 4.0 SE 4WD Wgn	40090	46220
4 Dr 4.6 HSE 4WD Wgn	45565	52530

OPTIONS FOR RANGE ROVER
Navigation System +2000

1998 LAND ROVER

DISCOVERY   1998

Changes to the Discovery include interior trim enhancements for the LE and LSE. The rearview mirror also features map lights for the first time.

Category H

	Trade-in	Market
4 Dr 50TH Anniversary 4WD Wgn	25255	29195
4 Dr LE 4WD Wgn	22705	26250
4 Dr LSE 4WD Wgn	24620	28460

Don't forget to refer to the Mileage Adjustment Table at the back of this book!

LAND ROVER 98-95

Model Description	Trade-in Value	Market Value	Model Description	Trade-in Value	Market Value

OPTIONS FOR DISCOVERY
Compact Disc Changer[Opt on LE] +245
Dual Air Conditioning +705
Rear Jump Seats +535
Special Factory Paint +80

RANGE ROVER   1998

Range Rover models get a new Harmon Kardon audio system this year. Other changes include a new upholstery stitch pattern and a leather-wrapped gearshift knob.

Category H

	Trade-in	Market
4 Dr 4.0 SE 4WD Wgn	34655	40060
4 Dr 4.6 HSE 4WD Wgn	39645	45835
4 Dr 50TH Anniversary 4WD Wgn	36480	42175

OPTIONS FOR RANGE ROVER
Special Factory Paint +80

1997 LAND ROVER

DEFENDER 90   1997

After a one-year hiatus, Defender 90 returns in convertible and hardtop bodystyles. A 4.0-liter V8 engine is standard, mated to a ZF four-speed automatic transmission. A redesigned center console includes cupholders, and hardtops have new interior trim. Convertibles get improved top sealing, while all Defender 90s are treated to fresh paint colors.

Category G

	Trade-in	Market
2 Dr STD 4WD Conv	22330	25740
2 Dr STD 4WD Utility	23700	27320

DISCOVERY   1997

A diversity antenna is added, and all interiors are trimmed with polished burled walnut. The sunroof has darker tinting, the airbag system benefits from simplified operation, and engine management is improved. Three new exterior colors debut: Oxford Blue, Rioja Red and Charleston Green.

Category H

	Trade-in	Market
4 Dr LSE 4WD Wgn	21045	24410
4 Dr SD 4WD Wgn	18560	21525
4 Dr SE 4WD Wgn	20220	23450
4 Dr SE7 4WD Wgn	21600	25050
4 Dr XD 4WD Wgn	19940	23130

OPTIONS FOR DISCOVERY
Auto 4-Speed Transmission[Std on SE,XD] +445
Leather Rear Jump Seats +435
Compact Disc Changer +200
Dual Power Seats[Opt on SD] +210
Leather Seats[Opt on SD] +445
Luggage Rack[Std on XD] +70
Rear Jump Seats[Std on SE7] +440

RANGE ROVER   1997

4.0 SE gets three new exterior colors (Oxford Blue, Rioja Red and White Gold, all matched to Saddle leather interior), a HomeLink transmitter, and jeweled wheel center caps. The 4.6 HSE gets three new exterior colors (British Racing Green, Monza Red, AA Yellow), one new interior color (Lightstone with contrasting piping), and a leather shift handle.

Category H

	Trade-in	Market
4 Dr 4.0 SE 4WD Wgn	29680	34420
4 Dr 4.6 HSE 4WD Wgn	33645	39020

OPTIONS FOR RANGE ROVER
Kensington Interior Pkg +1340
Vitesse Pkg +1340

1996 LAND ROVER

DISCOVERY   1996

Three new trim levels, a revised engine that gets better around-town fuel economy, new colors, increased seat travel, and new power seats sum up the changes for 1996.

Category H

	Trade-in	Market
4 Dr SD 4WD Wgn	15085	17635
4 Dr SE 4WD Wgn	17750	20750
4 Dr SE7 4WD Wgn	18455	21575

OPTIONS FOR DISCOVERY
Auto 4-Speed Transmission[Std on SE] +420
Compact Disc Changer +165
Compact Disc W/fm/tape +115
Leather Seats[Opt on SD] +365
Third Seat[Std on SE7] +230

RANGE ROVER   1996

Base 4.0 SE model is unchanged for 1996. A new, more powerful 4.6 HSE model debuts, giving buyers extra horsepower, fat wheels and tires, mud flaps, and chrome exhaust for a $7,000 premium over the 4.0 SE.

Category H

	Trade-in	Market
4 Dr 4.0 SE 4WD Wgn	25475	29785
4 Dr 4.6 HSE 4WD Wgn	28680	33530

OPTIONS FOR RANGE ROVER
AM/FM Compact Disc Player +115

1995 LAND ROVER

DEFENDER   1995

Category G

	Trade-in	Market
2 Dr STD 4WD Utility	15925	18395

Don't forget to refer to the Mileage Adjustment Table at the back of this book!

Model Description	Trade-in Value	Market Value

OPTIONS FOR DEFENDER
Full Top & Safari Cage +415
Air Conditioning +245

DISCOVERY 1995

Category H

4 Dr STD 4WD Wgn	13610	15985

OPTIONS FOR DISCOVERY
Auto 4-Speed Transmission +345
Jump Seat +260
Leather Jump Seat +290
Dual Air Conditioning +385
Leather Seats +300

RANGE ROVER 1995

The new 4.0 SE is introduced as a late '95 model. Styling is an evolution of the classic Range Rover look. A new chassis sports an electronic air suspension and a 4.0-liter V8 that produces 190 horse-power. This top-of-the-line SUV also includes luxuries such as the obligatory leather and wood trimmed cabin and a premium stereo with a 6-disc CD changer.

Category H

4 Dr 4.0 SE 4WD Wgn	21475	25220
4 Dr County Classic 4WD Wgn	17935	21065
4 Dr County LWB 4WD Wgn	20880	24525

OPTIONS FOR RANGE ROVER
Body Kit +595
Interior Trim/Light Stone +260

1994 LAND ROVER

DEFENDER 1994

Category G

2 Dr 90 4WD Utility	9785	11355

OPTIONS FOR DEFENDER
Prem. Soft Top Pkg +480
Air Conditioning +200
Aluminum/Alloy Wheels +80

DISCOVERY 1994

Category H

4 Dr STD 4WD Wgn	11995	14230

OPTIONS FOR DISCOVERY
Auto 4-Speed Transmission +270
Dual Air Conditioning +315
Leather Seats +245
Power Moonroof +235
Rear Jump Seats +240

RANGE ROVER 1994

Category H

4 Dr County LWB 4WD Wgn	15355	18210
4 Dr County SWB 4WD Wgn	14355	17030

Model Description	Trade-in Value	Market Value

OPTIONS FOR RANGE ROVER
Black Sable Edition +255

1993 LAND ROVER

DEFENDER 1993

Category G

4 Dr STD 4WD Wgn	10795	12425

OPTIONS FOR DEFENDER
AM/FM Stereo Tape +45

RANGE ROVER 1993

Category H

4 Dr County 4WD Wgn	12065	14465
4 Dr LWB 4WD Wgn	13325	15970

OPTIONS FOR RANGE ROVER
Chrome Wheels +60
Compact Disc Changer +90
Running Boards +70

1992 LAND ROVER

RANGE ROVER 1992

Category H

4 Dr County 4WD Wgn	10550	12855
4 Dr LSE 4WD Wgn	10175	12395
4 Dr STD 4WD Wgn	9240	11255

OPTIONS FOR RANGE ROVER
Third Seat +100

1991 LAND ROVER

RANGE ROVER 1991

Category H

4 Dr County SE 4WD Wgn	8780	10885
4 Dr Great Divide 4WD Wgn	8265	10250
4 Dr STD 4WD Wgn	7990	9910

OPTIONS FOR RANGE ROVER
Power Sunroof[Opt on STD] +200

Don't forget to refer to the Mileage Adjustment Table at the back of this book!

LEXUS 00

Model Description	Trade-in Value	Market Value	Model Description	Trade-in Value	Market Value

LEXUS   Japan

1994 Lexus GS 300

2000 LEXUS

ES 300   2000

The Lexus ES 300 sports new front-end styling and taillights. The rearview and driver's side mirrors are now electrochromatic for improved nighttime performance. The interior gets new colors and additional wood trim on the audio/heater panel. The mirrors are added to the memory seat function. High-intensity discharge headlights are optional, as are 16-inch wheels. Brake Assist is included in the Vehicle Skid Control option. A particle-and-odor air filter is a new option. The ES 300 also receives child seat-anchor brackets and three new colors.

Category J

4 Dr STD Sdn   22345   25645

OPTIONS FOR ES 300
Leather Seats +1025
Leather Steering Wheel +85
Power Moonroof +775

GS   2000

Both the GS 300 and GS 400 get a new brake-assist system and child seat-anchor brackets. The GS 300 is certified as a low-emission vehicle. Crystal White and Millennium Silver Metallic replace Diamond White Pearl and Alpine Silver Metallic.

Category J

4 Dr GS 300 Sdn   28945   33215
4 Dr GS 400 Sdn   35370   40585

OPTIONS FOR GS
Navigation System +2050
Platinum Series +1410
Premium Pkg +670

Compact Disc Changer +765
Heated Front Seats +355
Leather Seats[Std on GS 400] +1025
Power Moonroof +775

LS 400   2000

Only minor changes are scheduled for 2000 LS 400s. Brake assist has been added to the Vehicle Skid Control system. A new onboard refueling vapor recovery system allows the LS 400 to meet transitional low-emission vehicle status. Child seat anchor-brackets are standard.

Category L

4 Dr STD Sdn   37730   43260

OPTIONS FOR LS 400
Navigation System +1840
Compact Disc Changer +885
Power Moonroof +780

LX 470   2000

A Vehicle Stability Control system and a Brake Assist system are now standard, as are last year's optional moonroof and illuminated running boards. The LX 470 also gets an optional wood and leather steering wheel and shift knob.

Category H

4 Dr STD AWD Wgn   44865   51490

OPTIONS FOR LX 470
Nakamichi Sound System +875

RX 300   2000

The RX 300 remains mechanically unchanged. A Mineral Green Opalescent paint replaces Desert Bronze Metallic on the order sheet.

Category H

4 Dr STD Wgn   23375   26830
4 Dr STD 4WD Wgn   24495   28110

OPTIONS FOR RX 300
Automatic Dimming Mirror +120
Compact Disc Changer +365
Garage Door Opener +145
Heated Front Seats +295
Leather Seats +815
Power Moonroof +795
Rear Spoiler +230

SC   2000

The 2000 Lexus SC 300 and SC 400 are unchanged except for paint selection; Cinnabar Pearl replaces Baroque Red Metallic.

Category J

2 Dr SC300 Cpe   33075   37955
2 Dr SC400 Cpe   42410   48665

Don't forget to refer to the Mileage Adjustment Table at the back of this book!

Model Description	Trade-in Value	Market Value

Model Description	Trade-in Value	Market Value

OPTIONS FOR SC
Leather Trim Pkg +650
Leather Seats[Std on SC400] +1025
Power Moonroof +775
Rear Spoiler +325

1999 LEXUS

ES 300　　　1999

A new 3.0-liter V6 engine with VVTi (Variable Valve Timing with intelligence) gives the 1999 ES300 more horsepower, lower emissions and improved fuel economy. Optional Vehicle Skid Control (VSC) is available on the new ES as are one-touch open and close front windows and a one touch operated moonroof.

RATINGS (SCALE OF 1-10)

Overall	Safety	Reliability	Performance	Comfort	Value
N/A	8.5	9.4	8.2	8.8	N/A

Category J
4 Dr STD Sdn　　　20675　23810

OPTIONS FOR ES 300
Chrome Wheels +995
Compact Disc Changer +625
Heated Front Seats +290
Leather Seats +840
Nakamichi Sound System +940
Power Moonroof +635

GS　　　1999

The GS series was totally redesigned last year with improvements in performance and a completely new look. As a result, the 1999 model goes unchanged except for the addition of daytime running lights and standard floor mats.

RATINGS (SCALE OF 1-10)

Overall	Safety	Reliability	Performance	Comfort	Value
N/A	N/A	9.8	9.2	8.8	N/A

Category J
4 Dr GS 300 Sdn　　　26935　31020
4 Dr GS 400 Sdn　　　32775　37745

OPTIONS FOR GS
Navigation System +1675
Chrome Wheels +995
Compact Disc Changer +625
Heated Front Seats +290
Leather Seats[Std on GS400] +840
Nakamichi Sound System +940
Power Moonroof +635

LS 400　　　1999

After a number of improvements to the LS400 last year, the 1999 model sees only minor upgrades to interior trim levels. Daytime running lights are now standard equipment and Mystic Gold Metallic replaces Cashmere Beige.

RATINGS (SCALE OF 1-10)

Overall	Safety	Reliability	Performance	Comfort	Value
N/A	N/A	9.9	8.2	9.4	N/A

Category L
4 Dr STD Sdn　　　35360　40635

OPTIONS FOR LS 400
Navigation System +1505
Cellular Telephone +645
Chrome Wheels +1025
Compact Disc Changer +725
Heated Front Seats +330
Nakamichi Sound System +755
Power Moonroof +640

LX 470　　　1999

For 1999 the LX470 gets a redesigned roof rack, standard floor mats, and an optional Nakamichi audio system featuring a dash-mounted, single-feed six-disc CD changer.

RATINGS (SCALE OF 1-10)

Overall	Safety	Reliability	Performance	Comfort	Value
N/A	N/A	N/A	7	8	N/A

Category H
4 Dr STD 4WD Wgn　　　39580　45590

OPTIONS FOR LX 470
Convenience Pkg +715
Nakamichi Sound System +715
Power Moonroof +650

RX 300　　　1999

The RX300 is an all new car-based SUV from Lexus designed to compete in the luxury SUV segment.

RATINGS (SCALE OF 1-10)

Overall	Safety	Reliability	Performance	Comfort	Value
N/A	N/A	N/A	7.8	8.3	N/A

Category H
4 Dr STD Wgn　　　21085　24285
4 Dr STD 4WD Wgn　　　22005　25345

OPTIONS FOR RX 300
Compact Disc Changer +300
Heated Front Seats +240
Leather Seats +670
Power Moonroof +650

Don't forget to refer to the Mileage Adjustment Table at the back of this book!

Model Description	Trade-in Value	Market Value

SC   1999

The SC coupe gets minor enhancements this year including new, perforated leather inserts, larger brakes on the SC300, daytime running lights, and a new three-spoke steering wheel similar to the GS series sport sedans.

RATINGS (SCALE OF 1-10)

Overall	Safety	Reliability	Performance	Comfort	Value
N/A	N/A	N/A	8.6	7.9	N/A

Category J

Model Description	Trade-in Value	Market Value
2 Dr SC300 Cpe	30550	35185
2 Dr SC400 Cpe	39210	45155

OPTIONS FOR SC

Leather Seats [Std on SC400] +840
Nakamichi Sound System +940
Power Moonroof +635
Traction Control System +780

1998 LEXUS

ES 300   1998

Side-impact airbags debut on Lexus's entry-level car, as does an engine immobilizer anti-theft system and an optional Nakamichi audio system. Reduced force front airbags are also new on all 1998 Lexus models.

RATINGS (SCALE OF 1-10)

Overall	Safety	Reliability	Performance	Comfort	Value
8.1	8.5	9.3	8.2	8.8	5.8

Category J

	Trade-in	Market
4 Dr STD Sdn	19495	22510

OPTIONS FOR ES 300

Chrome Wheels +815
Compact Disc Changer +515
Heated Front Seats +235
Leather Seats +685
Nakamichi Sound System +770
Power Moonroof +520
Traction Control System +635

GS   1998

A totally redesigned GS appears for 1998. Featuring the familiar inline-six engine of the previous model in the GS300 or an overhead cam V8 with continuously variable valve timing in the GS400, the new cars live up to the promise of providing serious fun in an elegant package.

RATINGS (SCALE OF 1-10)

Overall	Safety	Reliability	Performance	Comfort	Value
N/A	N/A	9.1	9.2	N/A	4.5

Category J

	Trade-in	Market
4 Dr GS300 Sdn	25150	29040
4 Dr GS400 Sdn	30545	35270

OPTIONS FOR GS

Navigation System +1230
Chrome Wheels +815
Compact Disc Changer +515
Heated Front Seats +235
Leather Seats +685
Nakamichi Sound System +770
Power Moonroof +520

LS 400   1998

Lexus further refines its flagship by introducing a new four-cam V8 engine that features continuously variable valve timing. Also new this year is a five-speed automatic transmission, Vehicle Skid Control (VSC) and a host of interior improvements.

RATINGS (SCALE OF 1-10)

Overall	Safety	Reliability	Performance	Comfort	Value
N/A	N/A	9.8	8.2	9.4	4.2

Category L

	Trade-in	Market
4 Dr STD Sdn	34265	39420

OPTIONS FOR LS 400

Navigation System +1230
Auto Load Leveling +620
Chrome Wheels +835
Compact Disc Changer +590
Heated Front Seats +270
Nakamichi Sound System +620
Power Moonroof +520

LX 470   1998

Lexus' new LX470 luxury SUV replaces the LX450, offering a completely new body design, a more powerful engine, a roomier interior and more standard perks.

Category H

	Trade-in	Market
4 Dr STD 4WD Wgn	36770	42300

OPTIONS FOR LX 470

Power Moonroof +530

SC   1998

The SC400 gets a new four-liter four-cam aluminum V8 engine this year, while the SC300 continues with the inline-six motor from last year. Both powerplants benefit from continuously variable valve timing technology. An engine immobilizer, depowered airbags and a sophisticated five-speed automatic transmission are standard this year as well. The SC300 loses its five-speed manual transmission.

LEXUS 98-96

Model Description	Trade-in Value	Market Value	Model Description	Trade-in Value	Market Value

RATINGS (SCALE OF 1-10)

Overall	Safety	Reliability	Performance	Comfort	Value
N/A	N/A	9.7	N/A	N/A	N/A

Category J

2 Dr SC300 Cpe	28625	33050
2 Dr SC400 Cpe	35405	40875

OPTIONS FOR SC

Leather Seats[Std on SC400] +685

1997 LEXUS

ES 300 — 1997

The entry-level Lexus has been totally redesigned this year, growing in nearly every dimension. Lexus manages to eke out more power from the ES300's 3.0-liter V6 engine. No longer just a dressed-up Camry, the ES300 has finally come into its own.

RATINGS (SCALE OF 1-10)

Overall	Safety	Reliability	Performance	Comfort	Value
7.8	7.6	9.1	8.2	8.8	5.3

Category J

4 Dr STD Sdn	19250	22100

OPTIONS FOR ES 300

Chrome Wheels +665
Compact Disc Changer +420
Leather Seats +560
Power Moonroof +425
Traction Control System +520

GS 300 — 1997

Nothing at all, seriously.

RATINGS (SCALE OF 1-10)

Overall	Safety	Reliability	Performance	Comfort	Value
N/A	N/A	9.7	8.6	N/A	5.4

Category J

4 Dr GS300 Sdn	26415	30635

LS 400 — 1997

Side-impact airbags are standard.

RATINGS (SCALE OF 1-10)

Overall	Safety	Reliability	Performance	Comfort	Value
N/A	N/A	9.7	8	9.4	5.5

Category L

4 Dr Coach Sdn	31020	35825
4 Dr STD Sdn	29830	34455

OPTIONS FOR LS 400

Drivers Memory System +355
Cellular Telephone +430
Chrome Wheels +685
Compact Disc Changer[Opt on STD] +485

Nakamichi Sound System +505
Power Moonroof[Opt on STD] +425
Traction Control System +605

LX 450 — 1997

There are no changes to the 1997 LX450.

Category G

4 Dr STD 4WD Wgn	29400	33920

OPTIONS FOR LX 450

F&R Locking Diff. Axles +400
Compact Disc Changer +225
Luggage Rack +70
Power Moonroof +385
Running Boards +175
Trailer Hitch +125

SC — 1997

Minor interior and exterior enhancements update the look of the SC coupes.

RATINGS (SCALE OF 1-10)

Overall	Safety	Reliability	Performance	Comfort	Value
N/A	N/A	9.3	N/A	N/A	2.7

Category J

2 Dr SC300 Cpe	24075	27920
2 Dr SC400 Cpe	29910	34690

OPTIONS FOR SC

Leather Trim Pkg +335
Compact Disc Changer +420
Leather Seats[Std on SC400] +560
Power Moonroof +425
Rear Spoiler +180
Traction Control System +520

1996 LEXUS

ES 300 — 1996

Two new colors are available.

RATINGS (SCALE OF 1-10)

Overall	Safety	Reliability	Performance	Comfort	Value
7.9	7.7	9.4	8.4	8.1	5.8

Category J

4 Dr STD Sdn	17640	20510

OPTIONS FOR ES 300

Chrome Wheels +545
Compact Disc Changer +345
Leather Seats +460
Power Moonroof +345

GS — 1996

A five-speed automatic transmission makes the GS 300 feel more sporty, while rear styling revisions and five new exterior colors update the suave exterior. 1997 side-impact standards are met this year, and the power moonroof features one-touch operation.

RATINGS (SCALE OF 1-10)

Overall	Safety	Reliability	Performance	Comfort	Value
N/A	N/A	9.7	8.6	N/A	4.6

Category J
4 Dr GS300 Sdn   24270   28215

OPTIONS FOR GS
Chrome Wheels +545
Compact Disc Changer +345
Leather Seats +460
Nakamichi Sound System +515
Power Moonroof +345
Traction Control System +425

LS 400   1996

Deep Jewel Green Pearl is newly available on the paint palette.

RATINGS (SCALE OF 1-10)

Overall	Safety	Reliability	Performance	Comfort	Value
N/A	N/A	9.3	8	9.4	5.4

Category L
4 Dr STD Sdn   25880   30020

OPTIONS FOR LS 400
Chrome Wheels +560
Compact Disc Changer +395
Nakamichi Sound System +415
Power Moonroof +350
Traction Control System +495

LX 450   1996

Lexus clones a Toyota Land Cruiser, puts some fancy wheels on it, and slathers leather and wood all over the interior to capitalize on the booming sport-ute market.

Category G
4 Dr STD 4WD Wgn   26155   30330

OPTIONS FOR LX 450
F&R Locking Differential +330
Compact Disc Changer +185
Luggage Rack +60
Power Moonroof +315
Running Boards +140

SC   1996

SC300 boasts a larger options roster with the addition of a one-touch operation moonroof and electrochromatic rearview mirrors. The buttery V8 from the LS 400 is installed in the SC 400, and chrome wheels are available. Auto-dimming electrochromic inside and outside rearview mirrors are now standard, a new

remote keyless entry system debuts, and the optional moonroof now features one-touch operation.

RATINGS (SCALE OF 1-10)

Overall	Safety	Reliability	Performance	Comfort	Value
N/A	N/A	9.1	N/A	N/A	3.7

Category J
2 Dr SC300 Cpe   21975   25550
2 Dr SC400 Cpe   26480   30785

OPTIONS FOR SC
Compact Disc Changer +345
Leather Seats[Std on SC400] +460
Power Moonroof +345

1995 LEXUS

ES 300   1995

Styling is freshened, and chrome wheels are available. Trunk-mounted CD changer is a new option.

RATINGS (SCALE OF 1-10)

Overall	Safety	Reliability	Performance	Comfort	Value
8	8.4	9.2	8.4	8.1	5.7

Category J
4 Dr STD Sdn   15295   17905

OPTIONS FOR ES 300
Chrome Wheels +445
Compact Disc Changer +280
Leather Seats +375
Power Moonroof +285

GS   1995

No changes.

RATINGS (SCALE OF 1-10)

Overall	Safety	Reliability	Performance	Comfort	Value
N/A	N/A	9.7	8.6	N/A	6.1

Category J
4 Dr GS300 Sdn   19780   23155

OPTIONS FOR GS
Compact Disc Changer +280
Leather Seats +375
Nakamichi Sound System +420
Power Moonroof +285
Traction Control System +350

LS 400   1995

All-new car looks pretty much the same as it has for half a decade. The interior and trunk are larger, the engine more powerful, and the car is quicker than before. Six-disc CD changer is dash-mounted.

Model Description	Trade-in Value	Market Value

RATINGS (SCALE OF 1-10)

Overall	Safety	Reliability	Performance	Comfort	Value
N/A	N/A	9.3	8	9.4	6.3

Category L

	Trade-in	Market
4 Dr STD Sdn	22405	26050

OPTIONS FOR LS 400
AM/FM Compact Disc Player +265
Chrome Wheels +455
Compact Disc Changer +325
Nakamichi Sound System +340
Power Moonroof +285
Traction Control System +405

SC 1995

Revised styling and new wheels spruce up the look of these coupes. 1997 side-impact standards are met this year. A cupholder is added inside.

RATINGS (SCALE OF 1-10)

Overall	Safety	Reliability	Performance	Comfort	Value
N/A	N/A	8.9	N/A	N/A	4.9

Category J

	Trade-in	Market
2 Dr SC300 Cpe	18435	21580
2 Dr SC400 Cpe	21775	25490

OPTIONS FOR SC
Compact Disc Changer +280
Leather Seats[Std on SC400] +375
Power Moonroof +285
Rear Spoiler +120

1994 LEXUS

ES 300 1994

Passenger airbag added. New 3.0-liter engine has aluminum block and a few more horsepower. Several convenience features are now standard, including an outside temperature gauge.

RATINGS (SCALE OF 1-10)

Overall	Safety	Reliability	Performance	Comfort	Value
8	8.4	9.3	8.4	8.1	5.7

Category J

	Trade-in	Market
4 Dr STD Sdn	13510	15880

OPTIONS FOR ES 300
Cellular Telephone +445
Compact Disc Changer +230
Leather Seats +305
Power Moonroof +230

GS 1994

No changes.

RATINGS (SCALE OF 1-10)

Overall	Safety	Reliability	Performance	Comfort	Value
N/A	N/A	9.3	8.6	N/A	6.1

Category J

	Trade-in	Market
4 Dr GS300 Sdn	16800	19750

OPTIONS FOR GS
Compact Disc Changer +230
Leather Seats +305
Nakamichi Sound System +345
Power Moonroof +230
Traction Control System +285

LS 400 1994

Minor trim revisions.

RATINGS (SCALE OF 1-10)

Overall	Safety	Reliability	Performance	Comfort	Value
N/A	N/A	9.7	9	9.3	6.3

Category L

	Trade-in	Market
4 Dr STD Sdn	19100	22375

OPTIONS FOR LS 400
Electric Air Suspension +415
Memory System +195
Compact Disc Changer +265
Nakamichi Sound System +275
Power Moonroof +235
Traction Control System +330

SC 1994

Air conditioning is now CFC-free.

RATINGS (SCALE OF 1-10)

Overall	Safety	Reliability	Performance	Comfort	Value
N/A	N/A	8.9	N/A	N/A	4.9

Category J

	Trade-in	Market
2 Dr SC300 Cpe	15565	18300
2 Dr SC400 Cpe	18440	21680

OPTIONS FOR SC
Leather Seats[Std on SC400] +305
Leather Steering Wheel[Std on SC400] +25
Power Moonroof +230
Rear Spoiler +95

1993 LEXUS

ES 300 1993

A fuel cap tether and automatic-locking safety belt retractors are added.

RATINGS (SCALE OF 1-10)

Overall	Safety	Reliability	Performance	Comfort	Value
-8.1	8.4	9.1	8.4	8.1	6.7

Don't forget to refer to the Mileage Adjustment Table at the back of this book!

Model Description	Trade-in Value	Market Value
Category J		
4 Dr STD Sdn	11145	13190

OPTIONS FOR ES 300
Compact Disc Changer +185
Leather Seats +250
Power Moonroof +190

GS   1993

New sports sedan looks great, but fails to deliver much performance. Arrived late in 1993 with dual airbags, ABS and CFC-free air conditioning.

RATINGS (SCALE OF 1-10)

Overall	Safety	Reliability	Performance	Comfort	Value
N/A	N/A	9.3	N/A	N/A	6.4

Category J

4 Dr GS300 Sdn	14160	16755

OPTIONS FOR GS
Portable Plus Telephone +335
Cellular Telephone +360
Chrome Wheels +295
Compact Disc Changer +185
Leather Seats +250
Nakamichi Sound System +280
Power Moonroof +190
Traction Control System +230

LS 400   1993

Passenger airbag added. New alloy wheels debut. Brakes and tires are bigger. Styling is touched up, and interiors receive a host of upgrades. CFC-free air conditioning replaces Freon-based unit.

RATINGS (SCALE OF 1-10)

Overall	Safety	Reliability	Performance	Comfort	Value
N/A	N/A	9.9	9	9.3	4.6

Category L

4 Dr STD Sdn	15265	17950

OPTIONS FOR LS 400
Memory System +160
Cellular Telephone +190
Compact Disc Changer +215
Nakamichi Sound System +225
Power Moonroof +190
Traction Control System +270

SC   1993

Passenger airbag added. Automatic headlamp system debuts, and owners could pre-wire the car for use with a Portable Plus cellular phone.

RATINGS (SCALE OF 1-10)

Overall	Safety	Reliability	Performance	Comfort	Value
N/A	N/A	9.1	N/A	N/A	4.9

Model Description	Trade-in Value	Market Value
Category J		
2 Dr SC300 Cpe	14300	16920
2 Dr SC400 Cpe	15885	18795

OPTIONS FOR SC
Compact Disc Changer +185
Leather Seats[Std on SC400] +250
Power Moonroof +190
Rear Spoiler +80

1992 LEXUS

ES 300   1992

Camry-based replacement for ES250. ABS and driver airbag are standard.

RATINGS (SCALE OF 1-10)

Overall	Safety	Reliability	Performance	Comfort	Value
7.8	7.4	8.9	8.4	8.1	6.1

Category J

4 Dr STD Sdn	9600	11445

OPTIONS FOR ES 300
Auto 4-Speed Transmission +145
AM/FM Compact Disc Player +65
Leather Seats +205
Power Moonroof +155

LS 400   1992

No changes.

RATINGS (SCALE OF 1-10)

Overall	Safety	Reliability	Performance	Comfort	Value
N/A	N/A	9.3	9	9.3	6.1

Category L

4 Dr STD Sdn	12845	15200

OPTIONS FOR LS 400
Memory System +130
AM/FM Compact Disc Player +145
Compact Disc Changer +175
Power Moonroof +155
Premium Sound System +150
Traction Control System +220

SC   1992

Introduced in June 1991, these sleek coupes feature standard ABS and driver airbag. Traction control is optional with automatic transmission. SC300 is powered by inline six-cylinder engine.

RATINGS (SCALE OF 1-10)

Overall	Safety	Reliability	Performance	Comfort	Value
N/A	N/A	8.3	N/A	N/A	5.3

Category J

2 Dr SC300 Cpe	12105	14435
2 Dr SC400 Cpe	13855	16525

Don't forget to refer to the Mileage Adjustment Table at the back of this book!

Model Description	Trade-in Value	Market Value

OPTIONS FOR SC
Leather Seats[Std on SC400] +205
Power Moonroof +155

1991 LEXUS

ES 250   1991

No changes.
Category D
4 Dr STD Sdn .... 5585 ... 7190

OPTIONS FOR ES 250
Auto 4-Speed Transmission +100
Compact Disc W/fm/tape +105
Leather Seats +150
Power Drivers Seat +40
Power Sunroof +105

Model Description	Trade-in Value	Market Value

LS 400   1991

No changes.

RATINGS (SCALE OF 1-10)

Overall	Safety	Reliability	Performance	Comfort	Value
N/A	N/A	9.2	9	9.3	5.5

Category L
4 Dr STD Sdn .... 10470 ... 12530

OPTIONS FOR LS 400
Air Suspension System +200
Memory System +105
AM/FM Compact Disc Player +120
Leather Seats +160
Nakamichi Sound System +150
Power Moonroof +125
Premium Sound System +125
Traction Control System +180

Don't forget to refer to the Mileage Adjustment Table at the back of this book!

LINCOLN 00-99

Model Description	Trade-in Value	Market Value	Model Description	Trade-in Value	Market Value

LINCOLN — USA

1999 Lincoln Town Car

2000 LINCOLN

CONTINENTAL 2000

The Continental receives additional safety features, including side airbags, an emergency trunk release, child seat-anchor brackets, and Lincoln's Belt Minder system.

Category A

	Trade-in	Market
4 Dr STD Sdn	26620	30780

OPTIONS FOR CONTINENTAL
RESCU Pkg +1180
Steer. Whl. Radio Cntrls +125

LS 2000

From the ground up, this is a completely new sport sedan based on an all-new mid-size platform. Lincoln worked with Jaguar to develop this platform, which is also being used for Jaguar's S-type sedan. It is the first Lincoln in over two decades not classified as a full-size vehicle, and should appeal to buyers looking for something sportier and smaller than the Town Car or Continental.

Category A

	Trade-in	Market
4 Dr V6 Sdn	23510	27185
4 Dr V8 Sdn	25870	29920

OPTIONS FOR LS
5-Speed Transmission[Opt on V6] +600
Rescu System +820
Sport Handling Pkg +660
Compact Disc Changer +615
Power Moonroof +1040

NAVIGATOR 2000

The 2000 Navigator is now available with a fully integrated satellite navigation system, as well as a reverse-sensing system. Side airbags are standard, while new climate-controlled seats for the driver and front passenger are optional. The 2000 Navigator also features several exterior and interior styling changes.

Category H

	Trade-in	Market
4 Dr STD Wgn	30415	35060
4 Dr STD 4WD Wgn	33055	38105

OPTIONS FOR NAVIGATOR
Navigation System +1630
Compact Disc Changer +365
Dual Air Conditioning +1055

TOWN CAR 2000

The Town Car receives additional safety features, including an emergency trunk release, child seat-anchor brackets, and Lincoln's Belt Minder system. A new storage armrest has been placed on the front-passenger door-trim panel. One new exterior color has been added: Autumn Red Clearcoat Metallic.

Category A

	Trade-in	Market
4 Dr Cartier Sdn	29590	34220
4 Dr Executive Sdn	26555	30710
4 Dr Signature Sdn	27905	32270

OPTIONS FOR TOWN CAR
Compact Disc Changer +615
Power Moonroof +1040
Special Factory Paint +295

1999 LINCOLN

CONTINENTAL 1999

Lincoln's luxury liner gets added safety in 1999 with the addition of standard side airbags for the driver and front passenger. There's also five new exterior colors, upgraded interior trim options, two new wheel designs and an improved audio system. Otherwise the Lincoln remains unchanged after its major rework in 1998.

RATINGS (SCALE OF 1-10)

Overall	Safety	Reliability	Performance	Comfort	Value
N/A	N/A	N/A	7.6	8.3	N/A

Category A

	Trade-in	Market
4 Dr STD Sdn	24210	28075

OPTIONS FOR CONTINENTAL
RESCU Pkg +960
Cellular Telephone +470
Chrome Wheels +655
Compact Disc Changer +505
Heated Front Seats +140
Power Moonroof +850

Don't forget to refer to the Mileage Adjustment Table at the back of this book!

EDMUNDS® USED CARS & TRUCKS

Model Description	Trade-in Value	Market Value

NAVIGATOR 1999

Into its second year, Lincoln's Navigator enters 1999 with more power, adjustable pedals, speed-sensitive stereo volume, and a hands-free cellular phone. Also, the optional third row seat is mounted on rollers this year for easy installation and removal.

RATINGS (SCALE OF 1-10)

Overall	Safety	Reliability	Performance	Comfort	Value
N/A	N/A	N/A	5.6	7.5	N/A

Category H
4 Dr STD Wgn	29335	33470
4 Dr STD 4WD Wgn	29400	33940

OPTIONS FOR NAVIGATOR
Chrome Wheels +200
Compact Disc Changer +300
Dual Air Conditioning +860
Limited Slip Diff[Opt on 2WD] +175
Power Moonroof +650

TOWN CAR 1999

Standard side airbags improve the Town Car's ability to protect occupants and a new JBL audio system makes getting there even more fun.

RATINGS (SCALE OF 1-10)

Overall	Safety	Reliability	Performance	Comfort	Value
N/A	N/A	9.2	7.4	8.4	N/A

Category A
4 Dr Cartier Sdn	27200	31540
4 Dr Executive Sdn	24390	28285
4 Dr Signature Sdn	25640	29735

OPTIONS FOR TOWN CAR
Cellular Telephone +470
Chrome Wheels[Std on Cartier] +655
Compact Disc Changer +505
Power Moonroof +850

1998 LINCOLN

CONTINENTAL 1998

Lincoln's front-wheel drive luxo-barge gets a bigger grille (just what it needs) and rounded corners. It also gets an interior freshening that replaces the digital clock with an analog timepiece.

RATINGS (SCALE OF 1-10)

Overall	Safety	Reliability	Performance	Comfort	Value
N/A	N/A	8.7	7.6	8.3	5

Category A
4 Dr STD Sdn	20290	23590

OPTIONS FOR CONTINENTAL
RESCU Pkg +530
Chrome Wheels +535
Compact Disc Changer +410
Heated Front Seats +115
JBL Sound System +310
Power Moonroof +695

MARK VIII 1998

No changes to Lincoln's muscle car.

RATINGS (SCALE OF 1-10)

Overall	Safety	Reliability	Performance	Comfort	Value
N/A	N/A	8.6	8.4	7.9	4.5

Category A
2 Dr LSC Cpe	20980	24395
2 Dr STD Cpe	20200	23485

OPTIONS FOR MARK VIII
AM/FM Compact Disc Player +255
Chrome Wheels[Opt on STD] +535
Compact Disc Changer +410
Heated Front Seats +115
Power Moonroof +695

NAVIGATOR 1998

This all-new entrant into the luxury SUV market is the first truck ever sold by Lincoln. Based on the highly-acclaimed Ford Expedition, the Navigator is powered by a 5.4-liter SOHC V8 engine and has standard goodies that include illuminated running boards and a load-leveling air suspension. This truck also features one of the largest grilles this side of a Kenworth.

RATINGS (SCALE OF 1-10)

Overall	Safety	Reliability	Performance	Comfort	Value
N/A	N/A	8.5	5.4	7.5	N/A

Category H
4 Dr STD Wgn	25905	29965
4 Dr STD 4WD Wgn	27550	31870

OPTIONS FOR NAVIGATOR
Chrome Wheels +165
Compact Disc Changer +245
Dual Air Conditioning +705
Limited Slip Diff[Opt on 2WD] +145
Power Moonroof +530

TOWN CAR 1998

Lincoln redesigns its Town Car this year, making it lower, stiffer and faster. The interior is nicely improved as well, with softer seats and better positioned controls.

RATINGS (SCALE OF 1-10)

Overall	Safety	Reliability	Performance	Comfort	Value
N/A	N/A	8.4	7.4	8.4	5

Don't forget to refer to the Mileage Adjustment Table at the back of this book!

Model Description	Trade-in Value	Market Value
Category A		
4 Dr Cartier Sdn	22885	26610
4 Dr Executive Sdn	20895	24295
4 Dr Signature Sdn	21785	25330

OPTIONS FOR TOWN CAR
Chrome Wheels +535
Compact Disc Changer +410
Heated Front Seats[Std on Cartier] +115
JBL Sound System[Std on Cartier] +310
Leather Seats[Std on Cartier] +375
Power Moonroof +695
Traction Control System[Std on Cartier] +115

1997 LINCOLN

CONTINENTAL   1997

The changes to the 1997 Continental are minor this year. The first is the addition of a single-key locking system that locks the doors, glove box, and trunk with a turn of the wrist. The second is the addition of all-speed traction control. Lastly, the Continental receives a minor interior and exterior facelift.

RATINGS (SCALE OF 1-10)

Overall	Safety	Reliability	Performance	Comfort	Value
N/A	N/A	8.7	7.6	8.1	6.1

	Trade-in	Market
Category A		
4 Dr STD Sdn	16630	19465

OPTIONS FOR CONTINENTAL
RESCU Pkg +570
Cellular Telephone +315
Chrome Wheels +440
Compact Disc Changer +335
Power Moonroof +570

MARK VIII   1997

Lincoln thoroughly updates this personal coupe, lighting the darn thing up like a Christmas tree in the process. The Mark now has high-intensity discharge front headlamps, cornering lamps, a neon rear applique, and puddle lamps. Wow, you'll see this thing from miles away. The hood, grille and interior have also been slightly redesigned.

RATINGS (SCALE OF 1-10)

Overall	Safety	Reliability	Performance	Comfort	Value
N/A	N/A	8.6	8.4	7.9	5.2

	Trade-in	Market
Category A		
2 Dr LSC Cpe	17980	21050
2 Dr STD Cpe	17255	20195

OPTIONS FOR MARK VIII
AM/FM Compact Disc Player +210
Cellular Telephone +315
Chrome Wheels[Opt on STD] +440

Compact Disc Changer +335
Power Moonroof +570

TOWN CAR   1997

The Town Car's power steering has been improved. Watch out, Mario!

RATINGS (SCALE OF 1-10)

Overall	Safety	Reliability	Performance	Comfort	Value
7.7	8.2	8.1	7.4	8.4	6.3

	Trade-in	Market
Category A		
4 Dr Cartier Sdn	20660	24185
4 Dr Executive Sdn	17835	20880
4 Dr Signature Sdn	18945	22180

OPTIONS FOR TOWN CAR
Cellular Telephone +315
Chrome Wheels +440
Compact Disc Changer +335
JBL Sound System[Std on Cartier] +250
Leather Seats[Std on Cartier] +310
Power Moonroof +570
Traction Control System[Std on Cartier] +95

1996 LINCOLN

CONTINENTAL   1996

The big news for Continental is an optional gee-whiz rescue unit that uses a Global Positioning Satellite to pinpoint your location for roadside assistance, medical, and law enforcement personnel in the event of an emergency. Likely the greatest safety advance since airbags and antilock brakes. Also new are run-flat Michelin tires, a 75th Diamond Anniversary Edition, and a standard anti-theft system. It's getting there.

RATINGS (SCALE OF 1-10)

Overall	Safety	Reliability	Performance	Comfort	Value
N/A	N/A	8.1	7.6	8.1	6.5

	Trade-in	Market
Category A		
4 Dr STD Sdn	14680	17320

OPTIONS FOR CONTINENTAL
Personal Security Pkg +320
Cellular Telephone +260
Chrome Wheels +360
Compact Disc Changer +275
JBL Sound System +205
Power Moonroof +465
Traction Control System +75

MARK VIII   1996

Last year's limited-edition LSC model goes full-time for 1996. Eight new colors are available, and borderless floor mats debut. A Touring Package and 75th Diamond Anniversary model are offered.

Don't forget to refer to the Mileage Adjustment Table at the back of this book!

Model Description	Trade-in Value	Market Value

Model Description	Trade-in Value	Market Value

RATINGS (SCALE OF 1-10)

Overall	Safety	Reliability	Performance	Comfort	Value
N/A	N/A	8.7	8.4	7.9	5.7

Category A

2 Dr LSC Cpe	14915	17600
2 Dr STD Cpe	14265	16835

OPTIONS FOR MARK VIII

Cellular Telephone +260
Chrome Wheels[Opt on STD] +360
Compact Disc Changer +275
Power Moonroof +465
Traction Control System +75

TOWN CAR   1996

Engine upgrades, new automatic climate controls, and real wood on the dashboard in Cartier models sum up the changes to the Town Car.

RATINGS (SCALE OF 1-10)

Overall	Safety	Reliability	Performance	Comfort	Value
7.6	8	7.5	7.4	8.4	6.7

Category A

4 Dr Cartier Sdn	16735	19745
4 Dr Executive Sdn	14750	17405
4 Dr Signature Sdn	15565	18365

OPTIONS FOR TOWN CAR

Limousine Builder's Pkg +315
Cellular Telephone +260
Compact Disc Changer +275
JBL Sound System[Std on Cartier] +205
Leather Seats[Std on Cartier] +250
Power Moonroof +465
Traction Control System[Std on Cartier] +75

1995 LINCOLN

CONTINENTAL   1995

An all-new Continental is released with a V8 DOHC engine. A new suspension system that adjusts the shock absorbers to the prevailing driving conditions debuts, as does a memory seat system that will retain the seating preferences for two people. The new Continental has swoopier styling which is geared towards attracting a more youthful audience.

RATINGS (SCALE OF 1-10)

Overall	Safety	Reliability	Performance	Comfort	Value
N/A	N/A	8.1	7.6	8.1	5.7

Category A

4 Dr STD Sdn	11655	13970

OPTIONS FOR CONTINENTAL

Cellular Telephone +210
Chrome Wheels +295

Compact Disc Changer +225
Power Moonroof +380
Traction Control System +65

MARK VIII   1995

Lincoln's premium touring coupe receives significant changes across the board. A new instrument panel houses a new stereo with larger buttons. A feature called retained accessory power makes an appearance on the Mark VIII, allowing passengers 10 seconds to close the window after the car is turned off.

RATINGS (SCALE OF 1-10)

Overall	Safety	Reliability	Performance	Comfort	Value
N/A	N/A	7.8	8.4	7.9	6.1

Category A

2 Dr LSC Cpe	12065	14460
2 Dr STD Cpe	11620	13925

OPTIONS FOR MARK VIII

Cellular Telephone +210
Chrome Wheels +295
Compact Disc Changer +225
Power Moonroof +380
Traction Control System +65

TOWN CAR   1995

Exterior changes on the Town Car include new headlights, grille, taillights, bumpers, and bodyside molding. The outside mirrors have been moved forward slightly to increase visibility. An electronic steering switch selector allows the driver to select the type of steering effort they want. The instrument panel includes a redesigned two-spoke steering wheel, illuminated switches, and improved stereos with larger controls. Signature and Cartier models get steering wheel-mounted stereo and climate controls. A gate access unit integrated into the driver's side visor allows up to three frequencies to be programmed into its memory.

RATINGS (SCALE OF 1-10)

Overall	Safety	Reliability	Performance	Comfort	Value
7.7	8.7	6.5	7.4	8.4	7.7

Category A

4 Dr Cartier Sdn	13360	16015
4 Dr Executive Sdn	11840	14195
4 Dr Signature Sdn	12505	14990

OPTIONS FOR TOWN CAR

Touring Pkg +225
Cellular Telephone +210
Compact Disc Changer +225
JBL Sound System[Std on Cartier] +170
Leather Seats[Std on Cartier] +205
Power Moonroof +380
Traction Control System[Std on Cartier] +65

Don't forget to refer to the Mileage Adjustment Table at the back of this book!

1994 LINCOLN

CONTINENTAL 1994

Suspension changes improve the Continental's ride. A memory feature on the remote keyless entry automatically adjusts the driver's seat to a pre-set position each time it's activated. Exterior changes include revised taillamps, grille and rocker moldings. A retractable trunk cord is standard on all Continentals; it is designed to keep the trunk from bouncing around when it has to be left open for large loads.

RATINGS (SCALE OF 1-10)

Overall	Safety	Reliability	Performance	Comfort	Value
N/A	N/A	6.3	7.6	7.6	6.4

Category A

4 Dr Executive Sdn	7740	9550
4 Dr Signature Sdn	8155	10065

OPTIONS FOR CONTINENTAL

AM/FM Compact Disc Player +115
Cellular Telephone +170
Keyless Entry System[Opt on Executive] +65
Power Moonroof +310
Power Passenger Seat[Opt on Executive] +75

MARK VIII 1994

Chrome wheels are now an available option on the Mark VIII. There is a memory feature for the seats and outside mirrors.

RATINGS (SCALE OF 1-10)

Overall	Safety	Reliability	Performance	Comfort	Value
N/A	N/A	8.7	8.4	7.9	6.1

Category A

2 Dr STD Cpe	9055	11175

OPTIONS FOR MARK VIII

AM/FM Compact Disc Player +115
Cellular Telephone +170
Chrome Wheels +240
Compact Disc Changer +185
Power Moonroof +310
Traction Control System +50

TOWN CAR 1994

A dual exhaust system on the Town Car is made standard this year, upping horsepower to 210. All models receive solar tinted glass. The Jack Nicklaus Special Edition has been dropped.

RATINGS (SCALE OF 1-10)

Overall	Safety	Reliability	Performance	Comfort	Value
N/A	N/A	7.7	7	8	7.1

Category A

4 Dr Cartier Sdn	9715	11990
4 Dr Executive Sdn	8970	11070
4 Dr Signature Sdn	9300	11475

OPTIONS FOR TOWN CAR

Cellular Telephone +170
Compact Disc Changer +185
JBL Sound System[Std on Cartier] +140
Keyless Entry System[Opt on Executive] +65
Leather Seats[Std on Cartier] +170
Power Moonroof +310
Traction Control System +50

1993 LINCOLN

CONTINENTAL 1993

Bucket seats are available this year with a handy center console. The Signature series gets remote keyless entry, aluminum wheels, and the Comfort and Convenience Group added to its standard features list. Both models receive adjustable seatbelt anchor points.

RATINGS (SCALE OF 1-10)

Overall	Safety	Reliability	Performance	Comfort	Value
N/A	N/A	6.9	7.6	7.6	5.8

Category A

4 Dr Executive Sdn	5920	7555
4 Dr Signature Sdn	6270	8000

OPTIONS FOR CONTINENTAL

AM/FM Compact Disc Player +95
Cellular Telephone +140
Dual Power Seats[Opt on Executive] +95
Keyless Entry System[Opt on Executive] +55
Power Sunroof +305
Premium Sound System[Opt on Executive] +45

MARK VIII 1993

The Mark VIII debuts replacing the dated Mark VII. Based on the Thunderbird platform, the new Mark has a sportier feel than previous models. A twin-cam, 4.6-liter V8 produces 280 horsepower in the Mark VIII, and the transmission is an electronically controlled four-speed automatic.

RATINGS (SCALE OF 1-10)

Overall	Safety	Reliability	Performance	Comfort	Value
N/A	N/A	7.6	8.4	7.9	4.3

Category A

2 Dr STD Cpe	7230	9225

OPTIONS FOR MARK VIII

Cellular Telephone +140
Compact Disc Changer +150
Compact Disc W/fm/tape +125
Power Sunroof +305

Model Description	Trade-in Value	Market Value

TOWN CAR 1993

Styling changes and an optional Handling Package mark the differences in this year's Town Car. The formerly optional geometric aluminum wheels are made standard and the grille and headlights are slightly altered. The Handling Package consists of a firmer suspension and larger tires. The Executive series gains some features that were standard on the other models.

RATINGS (SCALE OF 1-10)

Overall	Safety	Reliability	Performance	Comfort	Value
N/A	N/A	8.2	7	8	6.6

Category A

4 Dr Cartier Sdn	7835	10000
4 Dr Executive Sdn	7315	9330
4 Dr Signature Sdn	7585	9680

OPTIONS FOR TOWN CAR

Heavy Duty Pkg +155
Cellular Telephone +140
Compact Disc Changer +150
Leather Seats[Std on Cartier] +140
Power Sunroof +305
Premium Sound System[Std on Cartier] +45

OPTIONS FOR MARK VII

AM/FM Compact Disc Player +75
Cellular Telephone +115
Power Moonroof +205

TOWN CAR 1992

Transmission adaptations include electronic shift controls, overdrive lockout, and a feature that won't allow the car to be shifted out of "Park" unless the brake is on.

RATINGS (SCALE OF 1-10)

Overall	Safety	Reliability	Performance	Comfort	Value
N/A	N/A	7.3	7	8	6.9

Category A

4 Dr Cartier Sdn	6160	8120
4 Dr Executive Sdn	5570	7340
4 Dr Signature Sdn	6100	8040

OPTIONS FOR TOWN CAR

AM/FM Compact Disc Player +75
Cellular Telephone +115
JBL Sound System[Std on Cartier] +90
Leather Seats +115
Power Moonroof +205
Power Passenger Seat[Opt on Executive] +50

1992 LINCOLN

CONTINENTAL 1992

The passenger airbag is revived this year and two trim-levels are available, the Signature and the Executive. Several optional safety features debut this year, such as an electrochromatic rearview mirror and a remote keyless entry system with a panic button.

RATINGS (SCALE OF 1-10)

Overall	Safety	Reliability	Performance	Comfort	Value
N/A	N/A	6.5	7.6	7.6	5.7

Category A

4 Dr Executive Sdn	4810	6345
4 Dr Signature Sdn	5105	6725

OPTIONS FOR CONTINENTAL

Cellular Telephone +115
Compact Disc W/fm/tape +105
Power Moonroof +205

MARK VII 1992

The final year for the Mark VII, changes are limited to minor alterations of the interior.

Category A

2 Dr Bill Blass Cpe	5160	6805
2 Dr LSC Cpe	5140	6775

1991 LINCOLN

CONTINENTAL 1991

A passenger airbag is available only in a portion of these cars since they ran out of propellant halfway through the production run.

RATINGS (SCALE OF 1-10)

Overall	Safety	Reliability	Performance	Comfort	Value
N/A	N/A	5.3	7.6	7.6	7.1

Category A

4 Dr STD Sdn	3715	5180
4 Dr Signature Sdn	3945	5500

OPTIONS FOR CONTINENTAL

AM/FM Compact Disc Player +65
Cellular Telephone +95
Power Passenger Seat[Opt on STD] +40
Power Sunroof +200

MARK VII 1991

No significant changes to the Mark VII.

Category A

2 Dr Bill Blass Cpe	4195	5850
2 Dr LSC Cpe	4180	5825

OPTIONS FOR MARK VII

AM/FM Compact Disc Player +65
Cellular Telephone +95
Power Sunroof +200

Don't forget to refer to the Mileage Adjustment Table at the back of this book!

Model Description	Trade-in Value	Market Value	Model Description	Trade-in Value	Market Value
TOWN CAR **1991**			*Category A*		
			4 Dr Cartier Sdn	4875	6800
			4 Dr STD Sdn	4155	5795
			4 Dr Signature Sdn	4580	6385

An impressive 4.6-liter, overhead-cam V8 engine debuts in the Town Car. Offering 40 to 60 more horsepower, depending on the exhaust system, than the previous 5.0-liter V8. The new Town Car has quite a bit more pizzazz than many luxo-barges.

OPTIONS FOR TOWN CAR
AM/FM Compact Disc Player +65
Cellular Telephone +95
Leather Seats[Std on Cartier] +90
Power Passenger Seat[Opt on STD] +40
Power Sunroof +200
Traction Control System +30

RATINGS (SCALE OF 1-10)

Overall	Safety	Reliability	Performance	Comfort	Value
N/A	N/A	6.3	7	8	6.9

Don't forget to refer to the Mileage Adjustment Table at the back of this book!

Model Description	Trade-in Value	Market Value

MAZDA — Japan

1995 Mazda Millenia

2000 MAZDA

626 — 2000

Improvements in styling, handling, steering, interior content, and options are the highlights of the 2000 626.

Category D

	Trade-in	Market
4 Dr ES Sdn	14460	16925
4 Dr ES V6 Sdn	15830	18530
4 Dr LX Sdn	12950	15160
4 Dr LX V6 Sdn	13775	16125

OPTIONS FOR 626
Auto 4-Speed Transmission[Std on ES] +655
Alarm System[Std on ES V6] +430
Aluminum/Alloy Wheels[Std on ES,ES V6] +380
Anti-Lock Brakes +725
Power Drivers Seat[Std on ES V6] +255

B-SERIES — 2000

Two B3000 regular-cab models are added—SX and SE. The B2500 Troy Lee edition has been discontinued. Fog lights are standard on all 4x4 models. A CD-equipped audio system is standard on all B4000 models. P225/70R15 tires are standard on SX models, and air conditioning is standard on SE and Troy Lee edition models. A 6,000-pound trailer hitch is standard on B4000 4x4s and optional on B4000 4x2 models. Troy Lee editions get standard leather-wrapped steering wheels.

Category G

	Trade-in	Market
2 Dr B2500 SE Ext Cab SB	11590	13645
2 Dr B2500 SE Std Cab SB	10065	11845
2 Dr B2500 SX Std Cab SB	8455	9950
2 Dr B3000 SE Ext Cab SB	11920	14030
4 Dr B3000 SE Ext Cab SB	12435	14635
4 Dr B3000 SE 4WD Ext Cab SB	14530	17100
2 Dr B3000 SE Std Cab SB	10340	12170
2 Dr B3000 SE 4WD Std Cab SB	12795	15065
2 Dr B3000 SX Std Cab SB	8730	10275
4 Dr B3000 TL Ext Cab SB	13415	15790
4 Dr B4000 SE Ext Cab SB	14820	17445
4 Dr B4000 SE 4WD Ext Cab SB	16150	19015
4 Dr B4000 TL 4WD Ext Cab SB	16920	19915

OPTIONS FOR B-SERIES
Auto 4-Speed Transmission +895
Auto 5-Speed Transmission[Opt on B4000 4WD] +935
Air Conditioning[Opt on B2500 SX,B3000 SX] +670
Bed Liner[Std on B4000 SE,B4000 TL] +230
Cruise Control[Std on B4000 SE,B4000 TL] +170
Sliding Rear Window[Std on B4000 SE,B4000 TL] +100
Tilt Steering Wheel[Std on B4000 SE,B4000 TL] +145

MILLENIA — 2000

Millenia models receive considerable price reductions to make them more competitive in the market. Mazda is also offering a special 2000 Millenium edition of the Millenia. This version comes with 17-inch chrome wheels, an in-dash six-disc CD changer, suede seat and door trim, and a choice of either Highlight Silver Mica or Millennium Red Mica paint.

Category D

	Trade-in	Market
4 Dr Millennium Sdn	22400	26225
4 Dr S Sdn	21870	25600
4 Dr STD Sdn	18340	21470

OPTIONS FOR MILLENIA
Heated Front Seats +305
Heated Power Mirrors +65

MPV — 2000

The MPV has been completely redesigned from top to bottom. Several unique features, like hinged rear doors and all-wheel drive, have disappeared. At the same time, items like roll-down windows in the sliding doors and tailgate seating in the third-row seats certify the MPV as a standout vehicle.

Category G

	Trade-in	Market
4 Dr DX Pass. Van	14900	17540
4 Dr ES Pass. Van	18940	22295
4 Dr LX Pass. Van	16440	19355

OPTIONS FOR MPV
GFX Pkg +575
Aluminum/Alloy Wheels[Std on ES] +265
Power Moonroof +710
Rear Heater +155
Rear Window Defroster +140

Don't forget to refer to the Mileage Adjustment Table at the back of this book!

MX-5 MIATA — 2000

The Miata's option packages have been simplified. There are now two models — Miata and Miata LS — and three option packages. A six-speed Miata Special-Edition will also be available by spring 2000.

Category F

	Trade-in	Market
2 Dr MX-5 Conv	16160	18780
2 Dr MX-5 LS Conv	18210	21165
2 Dr MX-5 Special ED. Conv	18995	22080

OPTIONS FOR MX-5 MIATA

Auto 4-Speed Transmission +735
Air Conditioning[Opt on MX-5,MX-5 LS] +690
Anti-Lock Brakes +530
Hardtop Roof +1180
Sport Suspension +155

PROTEGE — 2000

Front-seat side airbags and an improved ABS system are new to the LX premium and ES premium packages. The LX and ES also get illuminated power window switches. Chrome plating has been added to the inner door handles, and a Mazda symbol now appears on the steering wheel, the parking brake button, and the automatic transmission shift-lever button. The Twilight Blue Mica exterior color has been discontinued and replaced with Midnight Blue Mica.

Category E

	Trade-in	Market
4 Dr DX Sdn	9725	11930
4 Dr ES Sdn	10955	13725
4 Dr LX Sdn	9760	12230

OPTIONS FOR PROTEGE

Auto 4-Speed Transmission +655
AM/FM Compact Disc Player[Opt on DX] +355
Air Conditioning[Std on ES] +680
Power Moonroof +475

1999 MAZDA

626 — 1999

After a major makeover in '98, the 626 slides into '99 with only one major change: a new height-adjustable seat for the driver.

RATINGS (SCALE OF 1-10)

Overall	Safety	Reliability	Performance	Comfort	Value
N/A	7.2	8.7	9	7.9	N/A

Category D

	Trade-in	Market
4 Dr ES Sdn	14495	16735
4 Dr ES V6 Sdn	14490	17030
4 Dr LX Sdn	11565	13595
4 Dr LX V6 Sdn	13845	16035

OPTIONS FOR 626

Auto 4-Speed Transmission[Std on ES] +535
Aluminum/Alloy Wheels[Std on ES V6] +310
Anti-Lock Brakes +595
Bose Sound System[Std on ES V6] +520
Power Moonroof[Std on ES V6] +565

B-SERIES — 1999

The B-Series now comes with a four-door option called the Cab Plus 4. Option packages have been consolidated and simplified this year to reduce buyer confusion. A class III frame mounted hitch receiver is available with V6 applications.

RATINGS (SCALE OF 1-10)

Overall	Safety	Reliability	Performance	Comfort	Value
N/A	N/A	N/A	6.8	7.4	N/A

Category G

	Trade-in	Market
2 Dr B2500 SE Ext Cab SB	10470	12410
4 Dr B2500 SE Ext Cab SB	10895	12915
2 Dr B2500 SE Std Cab SB	9215	10920
2 Dr B2500 SX Std Cab SB	7610	9020
2 Dr B2500 TL Std Cab SB	9765	11575
2 Dr B3000 SE Ext Cab SB	10840	12850
2 Dr B3000 SE 4WD Ext Cab SB	12850	15235
4 Dr B3000 SE Ext Cab SB	11265	13355
4 Dr B3000 SE 4WD Ext Cab SB	12720	15080
2 Dr B3000 SE 4WD Std Cab SB	11655	13815
4 Dr B3000 TL Ext Cab SB	12230	14500
2 Dr B4000 SE Ext Cab SB	13000	15410
2 Dr B4000 SE 4WD Ext Cab SB	14285	16935
4 Dr B4000 SE Ext Cab SB	13425	15915
4 Dr B4000 SE 4WD Ext Cab SB	14710	17440
2 Dr B4000 SE Std Cab SB	10945	12970
4 Dr B4000 TL 4WD Ext Cab SB	15485	18355

OPTIONS FOR B-SERIES

Auto 4-Speed Transmission +730
Auto 5-Speed Transmission[Std on B4000 SE 2WD Cab Plus/Cab Plus 4] +755
Air Conditioning[Opt on B2500 SX] +550
Anti-Lock Brakes +390
Bed Liner[Std on B4000 SE, B4000 TL] +185
Cruise Control[Std on B4000 SE,B4000 TL] +140
Keyless Entry System +130
Power Door Locks +155
Power Mirrors +90
Power Windows +160
Sliding Rear Window[Std on B4000 SE,B4000 TL] +80
Tilt Steering Wheel[Std on B4000 SE,B4000 TL] +120

MIATA — 1999

Mazda cautiously redesigns the Miata, improving the car in every way without bumping up the price or diluting the car's personality. Very nice job.

Don't forget to refer to the Mileage Adjustment Table at the back of this book!

Model Description	Trade-in Value	Market Value

RATINGS (SCALE OF 1-10)

Overall	Safety	Reliability	Performance	Comfort	Value
N/A	N/A	9	9	7.1	N/A

Category F
2 Dr MX-5 Conv	13860	16235
2 Dr MX-5 10TH Anniv. Conv	18735	21940

OPTIONS FOR MIATA

Auto 4-Speed Transmission +505
Leather Pkg +960
Sports Pkg +525
Air Conditioning +565
Aluminum/Alloy Wheels[Opt on MX-5] +205
Anti-Lock Brakes +435
Cruise Control[Opt on MX-5] +150
Hardtop Roof +965
Leather Seats[Opt on MX-5] +425
Limited Slip Diff[Opt on MX-5] +220
Power Door Locks[Opt on MX-5] +135
Power Mirrors[Opt on MX-5] +75
Power Steering[Opt on MX-5] +235
Power Windows[Opt on MX-5] +155
Rear Spoiler[Opt on MX-5] +160
Sport Suspension[Opt on MX-5] +130

MILLENIA 1999

Revised front- and rear-end styling, plus an optional two-tone color scheme, separate the '99 Millenia from past models.

RATINGS (SCALE OF 1-10)

Overall	Safety	Reliability	Performance	Comfort	Value
N/A	8	N/A	8.2	7.9	N/A

Category D
4 Dr S Sdn	19775	23245
4 Dr STD Sdn	16950	19925

OPTIONS FOR MILLENIA

Bose Sound System[Std on S] +520
Heated Front Seats +250
Keyless Entry System[Std on S] +210
Leather Seats[Std on S] +760
Power Moonroof[Std on S] +565
Traction Control System[Std on S] +355

PROTEGE 1999

The Protege gets an extensive makeover for '99 that includes new exterior and interior styling, a more powerful engine lineup, additional luxury options, and five new colors.

RATINGS (SCALE OF 1-10)

Overall	Safety	Reliability	Performance	Comfort	Value
N/A	6.6	8.5	7.6	7.8	N/A

Category E
4 Dr DX Sdn	8690	10345
4 Dr ES Sdn	10760	12805
4 Dr LX Sdn	9500	11310

OPTIONS FOR PROTEGE

Auto 4-Speed Transmission +535
AM/FM Compact Disc Player[Opt on DX] +290
Air Conditioning[Std on ES] +555
Aluminum/Alloy Wheels +225
Anti-Lock Brakes +445
Keyless Entry System[Std on ES] +110
Power Moonroof +390

1998 MAZDA

626 1998

Mazda redesigns the 626, giving it more upscale styling, more powerful engines, a tighter body and increased cargo and people space while retaining the sedan's distinctive sporting nature.

RATINGS (SCALE OF 1-10)

Overall	Safety	Reliability	Performance	Comfort	Value
7.7	7	7.9	9	7.9	6.5

Category D
4 Dr DX Sdn	9370	11065
4 Dr ES Sdn	12975	15480
4 Dr LX Sdn	10600	12515
4 Dr LX V6 Sdn	12365	14600

OPTIONS FOR 626

Auto 4-Speed Transmission +435
AM/FM Compact Disc Player[Opt on DX] +255
Air Conditioning[Opt on DX] +470
Aluminum/Alloy Wheels[Std on ES] +255
Anti-Lock Brakes[Opt on LX] +485
Bose Sound System[Std on ES] +425
Keyless Entry System[Opt on LX] +170
Leather Seats[Opt on LX] +620
Power Drivers Seat[Std on ES] +170
Power Moonroof[Std on ES] +460

B-SERIES PICKUP 1998

Fresh styling, a revised front suspension, a larger regular cab, a more powerful 2.5-liter four-cylinder engine, a stiffer frame and a new 4WD system ensure that Mazda's compact truck will remain competitive through the end of the century.

RATINGS (SCALE OF 1-10)

Overall	Safety	Reliability	Performance	Comfort	Value
N/A	7.3	8.5	7.2	7.4	N/A

Category G
2 Dr B2500 SE Ext Cab SB	9495	11235
4 Dr B2500 SE Ext Cab SB	9860	11670

Don't forget to refer to the Mileage Adjustment Table at the back of this book!

MAZDA 98-97

Model Description	Trade-in Value	Market Value
2 Dr B2500 SE Std Cab SB	8180	9680
2 Dr B2500 SX Std Cab SB	7060	8355
2 Dr B3000 SE Ext Cab SB	10080	11925
2 Dr B3000 SE 4WD Ext Cab SB	11635	13770
2 Dr B3000 SE 4WD Std Cab SB	10725	12690
2 Dr B3000 SX 4WD Std Cab SB	9785	11575
2 Dr B4000 SE Ext Cab SB	10495	12415
2 Dr B4000 SE 4WD Ext Cab SB	12050	14260

OPTIONS FOR B-SERIES PICKUP
Auto 4-Speed Transmission +585
Auto 5-Speed Transmission[Opt on B4000] +605
AM/FM Compact Disc Player +175
Air Conditioning +450
Aluminum/Alloy Wheels +175
Anti-Lock Brakes +320
Bed Liner +155
Cruise Control +115
Fog Lights +80
Keyless Entry System +105
Power Door Locks +130
Power Mirrors +70
Power Windows +135
Sliding Rear Window +65
Tilt Steering Wheel +100

MILLENIA — 1998

Millenia carries over into 1998 with no changes.

RATINGS (SCALE OF 1-10)

Overall	Safety	Reliability	Performance	Comfort	Value
7.5	8	9	8.4	7.9	4.1

Category D
4 Dr S Sdn	17855	21510
4 Dr STD Sdn	16085	18995

OPTIONS FOR MILLENIA
Premium Pkg +470
Bose Sound System[Std on S] +425
Dual Power Seats[Std on S] +465
Heated Front Seats +205
Heated Power Mirrors +45
Keyless Entry System[Std on S] +170
Leather Seats[Std on S] +620
Power Moonroof[Std on S] +460
Traction Control System[Std on S] +290

MPV — 1998

A CD player is now standard.

RATINGS (SCALE OF 1-10)

Overall	Safety	Reliability	Performance	Comfort	Value
7.4	7.7	8.4	7.6	7.6	5.6

Category G
2 Dr ES Pass. Van	15960	18880
2 Dr ES 4WD Pass. Van	17445	20640

Model Description	Trade-in Value	Market Value
2 Dr LX Pass. Van	14210	16815
2 Dr LX 4WD Pass. Van	16255	19235

OPTIONS FOR MPV
Air Conditioning +450
Aluminum/Alloy Wheels[Std on ES,4WD] +175
Auto Load Leveling[Opt on LX] +130
Dual Air Conditioning +505
Keyless Entry System +105
Leather Seats[Opt on LX] +430
Power Moonroof +475
Privacy Glass +150

PROTEGE — 1998

A CD player is standard on ES and LX. It also comes on DX models equipped with an option package.

RATINGS (SCALE OF 1-10)

Overall	Safety	Reliability	Performance	Comfort	Value
N/A	N/A	8.4	8	7.4	5.4

Category E
4 Dr DX Sdn	7630	9170
4 Dr ES Sdn	9540	11460
4 Dr LX Sdn	8480	10185

OPTIONS FOR PROTEGE
Auto 4-Speed Transmission +435
AM/FM Compact Disc Player[Opt on DX] +235
Air Conditioning[Std on ES] +455
Aluminum/Alloy Wheels +185
Anti-Lock Brakes +365
Keyless Entry System +90
Power Moonroof +320

1997 MAZDA

626 — 1997

LX V6 and ES models gain power and torque, while the four-cylinder LX gets a Lexus-like trim package that includes two-tone paint, chrome wheel covers, leather interior, and other creature comforts. Audio systems are revised and two new colors debut.

RATINGS (SCALE OF 1-10)

Overall	Safety	Reliability	Performance	Comfort	Value
7.6	7	8	8.8	8.1	5.9

Category D
4 Dr DX Sdn	8415	10005
4 Dr ES Sdn	12220	14530
4 Dr LX Sdn	9565	11370
4 Dr LX V6 Sdn	10660	12675

OPTIONS FOR 626
Auto 4-Speed Transmission +345
AM/FM Stereo Tape[Opt on DX] +160
Air Conditioning[Opt on DX] +385
Aluminum/Alloy Wheels[Opt on LX] +210

Don't forget to refer to the Mileage Adjustment Table at the back of this book!

Model Description	Trade-in Value	Market Value

Anti-Lock Brakes[Std on ES] +395
Chrome Wheels +255
Keyless Entry System[Std on ES] +140
Leather Seats[Std on ES] +505
Power Antenna[Std on ES] +55
Power Drivers Seat[Std on ES] +140
Power Moonroof[Std on ES] +380

B-SERIES PICKUP   1997

The lineup is trimmed, leaving just B2300 and B4000 models available. SE-5 designation returns to bolster marketing efforts. B4000 pickups can be equipped with a new five-speed automatic transmission.

RATINGS (SCALE OF 1-10)

Overall	Safety	Reliability	Performance	Comfort	Value
N/A	6.5	8.7	7.2	7.3	N/A

Category G

Model	Trade-in	Market
2 Dr B2300 Std Cab SB	5895	7020
2 Dr B2300 SE Ext Cab SB	8480	10035
2 Dr B2300 SE Std Cab SB	6900	8220
2 Dr B4000 4WD Ext Cab SB	10070	11990
2 Dr B4000 4WD Std Cab SB	9055	10785
2 Dr B4000 SE Ext Cab SB	8860	10550
2 Dr B4000 SE 4WD Ext Cab SB	10785	12845

OPTIONS FOR B-SERIES PICKUP

Auto 4-Speed Transmission +480
Auto 5-Speed Transmission +495
AM/FM Compact Disc Player +140
Air Conditioning +365
Aluminum/Alloy Wheels +145
Anti-Lock Brakes +260
Bed Liner +125
Compact Disc Changer +225
Cruise Control +95
Keyless Entry System +85
Limited Slip Diff +125
Power Door Locks +105
Power Steering[Std on B4000,B4000 SE,Ext Cab] +125
Power Windows +110
Premium Sound System +155
Rear Step Bumper[Opt on Ext Cab] +65

MIATA   1997

Mazda adds a Touring Package to the options list, consisting of alloy wheels, power steering, leather-wrapped steering wheel, power mirrors, power windows, and door map pockets. Midyear a new M-Edition debuts, sporting Marina Green paint and chromed alloy wheels. Summertime brings the limited-production STO-Edition, of which 1,500 were produced.

RATINGS (SCALE OF 1-10)

Overall	Safety	Reliability	Performance	Comfort	Value
7.3	6.3	9	9	7.1	5

Category F

Model	Trade-in	Market
2 Dr MX-5 Conv	10985	13000
2 Dr MX-5 M-Edition Conv	13715	16230
2 Dr MX-5 STO Conv	12890	15250

OPTIONS FOR MIATA

Auto 4-Speed Transmission +395
Leather Pkg +405
Air Conditioning[Opt on MX-5] +375
Aluminum/Alloy Wheels[Opt on MX-5] +135
Anti-Lock Brakes +290
Compact Disc W/fm/tape[Opt on MX-5] +225
Cruise Control[Opt on MX-5] +100
Hardtop Roof +645
Leather Seats[Opt on MX-5] +285
Limited Slip Diff[Opt on MX-5] +145
Power Steering[Opt on MX-5] +160
Power Windows[Opt on MX-5] +105
Rear Spoiler +105
Sport Suspension +85

MILLENIA   1997

Models equipped with leather are upgraded this year with an eight-way power passenger seat, 16-inch alloy wheels, and revised final drive ratio for better low-end response. S models also get the power passenger seat. All Millenias have a new rear-window-mounted diversity antenna, a new sound system with in-dash CD player, revised center console design, and Michelin tires.

RATINGS (SCALE OF 1-10)

Overall	Safety	Reliability	Performance	Comfort	Value
7.5	8	8.9	8.4	7.9	4.5

Category D

Model	Trade-in	Market
4 Dr L Sdn	16315	19400
4 Dr S Sdn	18070	21485
4 Dr STD Sdn	14365	17080

OPTIONS FOR MILLENIA

Bose Sound System +350
Traction Control System[Std on S] +235

MPV   1997

Four-wheel ABS is standard across the board, and all but the LX 2WD model are dressed in dorky All-Sport exterior trim.

RATINGS (SCALE OF 1-10)

Overall	Safety	Reliability	Performance	Comfort	Value
7.4	7.7	8.3	7.6	7.6	6

Category G

Model	Trade-in	Market
2 Dr ES Pass. Van	13955	16620
2 Dr ES 4WD Pass. Van	15250	18165
2 Dr LX Pass. Van	12520	14915
2 Dr LX 4WD Pass. Van	14210	16930

Don't forget to refer to the Mileage Adjustment Table at the back of this book!

OPTIONS FOR MPV

Air Conditioning +365
Aluminum/Alloy Wheels[Std on ES,4WD] +145
Compact Disc W/fm/tape +200
Dual Air Conditioning +410
Keyless Entry System +85
Luggage Rack[Std on ES,4WD] +70
Power Moonroof +385

MX6   1997

All LS models get a rear spoiler.

RATINGS (SCALE OF 1-10)

Overall	Safety	Reliability	Performance	Comfort	Value
7.5	7.2	8.6	9	7.9	4.6

Category F
2 Dr LS Cpe	12790	15135
2 Dr STD Cpe	11085	13115

OPTIONS FOR MX6

Auto 4-Speed Transmission +355
Air Conditioning[Std on LS] +375
Aluminum/Alloy Wheels[Std on LS] +135
Anti-Lock Brakes +290
Keyless Entry System[Std on LS] +80
Leather Seats +285
Power Drivers Seat +110
Power Sunroof[Std on LS] +300
Rear Spoiler[Std on LS] +105

PROTEGE   1997

Styling revisions inside and out update this roomy compact nicely.

RATINGS (SCALE OF 1-10)

Overall	Safety	Reliability	Performance	Comfort	Value
N/A	N/A	8.1	8	7.4	5.3

Category E
4 Dr DX Sdn	6815	8300
4 Dr ES Sdn	8515	10375
4 Dr LX Sdn	7570	9225

OPTIONS FOR PROTEGE

Auto 4-Speed Transmission +355
AM/FM Stereo Tape[Opt on DX] +135
Air Conditioning[Std on ES] +370
Aluminum/Alloy Wheels +150
Anti-Lock Brakes +295
Power Moonroof +260

1996 MAZDA

626   1996

Chrome is tacked on front and rear, and the hood is raised a bit to give the 626 a more substantial look. ABS is available as a stand alone option on LX and LX

V6 models for the first time (formerly, you had to buy an option package), and side-impact protection meets 1997 standards.

RATINGS (SCALE OF 1-10)

Overall	Safety	Reliability	Performance	Comfort	Value
7.5	7.1	8.1	8.8	8.1	5.4

Category D
4 Dr DX Sdn	6880	8355
4 Dr ES Sdn	9785	11890
4 Dr LX Sdn	7825	9510
4 Dr LX V6 Sdn	8775	10660

OPTIONS FOR 626

Auto 4-Speed Transmission +290
AM/FM Stereo Tape[Opt on DX] +130
Air Conditioning[Opt on DX] +315
Anti-Lock Brakes[Std on ES] +325
Keyless Entry System[Std on ES] +115
Power Drivers Seat[Std on ES] +115
Power Moonroof[Std on ES] +310

B-SERIES PICKUP   1996

A passenger side airbag comes with SE Plus and LE trim levels, and it can be deactivated in the event that a rear facing child safety seat is installed. SE models also get new chrome bumpers.

RATINGS (SCALE OF 1-10)

Overall	Safety	Reliability	Performance	Comfort	Value
N/A	6.5	8.5	7.2	7.3	N/A

Category G
2 Dr B2300 Ext Cab SB	6515	7910
2 Dr B2300 Std Cab LB	5130	6230
2 Dr B2300 Std Cab SB	4950	6005
2 Dr B2300 4WD Std Cab SB	7500	9100
2 Dr B2300 SE Ext Cab SB	7200	8725
2 Dr B2300 SE Std Cab SB	5900	7160
2 Dr B3000 4WD Ext Cab SB	8630	10475
2 Dr B3000 SE Ext Cab SB	7355	8925
2 Dr B4000 LE Ext Cab SB	8265	10035
2 Dr B4000 LE 4WD Ext Cab SB	10075	12225
2 Dr B4000 SE 4WD Ext Cab SB	9475	11500
2 Dr B4000 SE 4WD Std Cab SB	8875	10770

OPTIONS FOR B-SERIES PICKUP

Auto 4-Speed Transmission +380
Air Conditioning[Std on B4000 LE] +300
Aluminum/Alloy Wheels[Std on B4000 LE] +120
Anti-Lock Brakes +210
Bed Liner +100
Compact Disc Changer +185
Cruise Control +75
Lighted Entry System +55
Power Door Locks +85
Power Windows +90

Don't forget to refer to the Mileage Adjustment Table at the back of this book!

MAZDA 96

Model Description	Trade-in Value	Market Value	Model Description	Trade-in Value	Market Value

Premium Sound System +125
Rear Jump Seats[Std on B4000 LE] +85

MIATA 1996

Side-impact standards for 1997 are met a year early, and to offset the added weight, Mazda boosts power and torque.

RATINGS (SCALE OF 1-10)

Overall	Safety	Reliability	Performance	Comfort	Value
7.3	6.3	9.1	9	7.1	5

Category F

2 Dr MX-5 Conv	9375	11210
2 Dr MX-5 M-Edition Conv	12175	14555

OPTIONS FOR MIATA

Auto 4-Speed Transmission +335
Sensory Sound System +320
Air Conditioning[Opt on MX-5] +305
Aluminum/Alloy Wheels[Opt on MX-5] +110
Anti-Lock Brakes[Opt on MX-5] +235
Cruise Control[Opt on MX-5] +80
Hardtop Roof +525
Leather Seats[Opt on MX-5] +230
Limited Slip Diff[Opt on MX-5] +120
Power Steering[Opt on MX-5] +130
Power Windows[Opt on MX-5] +85
Rear Spoiler +90
Sport Suspension +70

MILLENIA 1996

The Millenia S gets revised bright-finish alloy wheels.

RATINGS (SCALE OF 1-10)

Overall	Safety	Reliability	Performance	Comfort	Value
7.5	8	8.8	8.4	7.9	4.5

Category D

4 Dr L Sdn	13610	16530
4 Dr S Sdn	14890	18090
4 Dr STD Sdn	12155	14765

OPTIONS FOR MILLENIA

Bose Sound System +285
Traction Control System[Std on S] +195

MPV 1996

New styling up front, a fourth door on the driver's side, and a revised instrument panel with dual airbags sum up the changes to Mazda's attempt at a minivan.

RATINGS (SCALE OF 1-10)

Overall	Safety	Reliability	Performance	Comfort	Value
7.5	7.7	8.3	7.6	7.6	6.2

Category G

2 Dr DX Pass. Van	10530	12780
2 Dr ES Pass. Van	11770	14285
2 Dr ES 4WD Pass. Van	13130	15935
2 Dr LX Pass. Van	10910	13240
2 Dr LX 4WD Pass. Van	12055	14630

OPTIONS FOR MPV

AM/FM Compact Disc Player +115
Air Conditioning +300
Aluminum/Alloy Wheels[Opt on 2WD] +120
Dual Air Conditioning +335
Keyless Entry System +70
Power Moonroof +315

MX6 1996

No changes for 1995.

RATINGS (SCALE OF 1-10)

Overall	Safety	Reliability	Performance	Comfort	Value
7.3	7.2	8.5	9	7.9	4.1

Category F

2 Dr LS Cpe	10945	13085
2 Dr M-Edition Cpe	12585	15050
2 Dr STD Cpe	9685	11580

OPTIONS FOR MX6

Auto 4-Speed Transmission +290
Air Conditioning[Opt on STD] +305
Aluminum/Alloy Wheels[Opt on STD] +110
Anti-Lock Brakes[Opt on LS,STD] +235
Keyless Entry System[Opt on STD] +65
Leather Seats[Opt on LS] +230
Power Drivers Seat[Opt on LS] +90
Power Sunroof[Opt on STD] +245
Rear Spoiler[Opt on LS,STD] +90

PROTEGE 1996

No changes for 1996.

RATINGS (SCALE OF 1-10)

Overall	Safety	Reliability	Performance	Comfort	Value
N/A	N/A	8	8	7.4	5.8

Category E

4 Dr DX Sdn	5575	6920
4 Dr ES Sdn	6955	8630
4 Dr LX Sdn	6175	7665

OPTIONS FOR PROTEGE

Auto 4-Speed Transmission +290
AM/FM Stereo Tape[Opt on DX] +110
Air Conditioning[Std on ES] +305
Anti-Lock Brakes +245
Keyless Entry System +60
Power Moonroof +215

1995 MAZDA

626 — 1995

ES gets remote keyless entry, which is available on LX and LX-V6 models. New wheels and wheelcovers are added across the board.

RATINGS (SCALE OF 1-10)

Overall	Safety	Reliability	Performance	Comfort	Value
7.7	7.7	7.4	8.8	8.1	6.3

Category D

Model	Trade-in	Market
4 Dr DX Sdn	5625	6905
4 Dr ES Sdn	8130	9975
4 Dr LX Sdn	6495	7970
4 Dr LX V6 Sdn	7300	8955

OPTIONS FOR 626
Auto 4-Speed Transmission +240
AM/FM Stereo Tape[Opt on DX] +105
Air Conditioning[Opt on DX] +255
Aluminum/Alloy Wheels[Opt on LX] +140
Anti-Lock Brakes[Std on ES] +265
Keyless Entry System[Std on ES] +95
Power Drivers Seat[Std on ES] +95
Power Moonroof[Std on ES] +250

929 — 1995

Leather seats, wood trim and remote keyless entry are standard. Final year for sleek executive sedan.

RATINGS (SCALE OF 1-10)

Overall	Safety	Reliability	Performance	Comfort	Value
N/A	N/A	8.5	8.2	8.4	3.8

Category D

Model	Trade-in	Market
4 Dr STD Sdn	11900	14600

OPTIONS FOR 929
Limited Slip Diff +145

B-SERIES PICKUP — 1995

Redesigned dashboard with driver airbag debuts. Four-wheel ABS is standard on 4WD and 2WD B4000 models.

RATINGS (SCALE OF 1-10)

Overall	Safety	Reliability	Performance	Comfort	Value
N/A	6.7	8.5	7.2	7.3	N/A

Category G

Model	Trade-in	Market
2 Dr B2300 Ext Cab SB	5660	6965
2 Dr B2300 Std Cab LB	4620	5685
2 Dr B2300 Std Cab SB	4455	5485
2 Dr B2300 4WD Std Cab SB	6620	8150
2 Dr B2300 SE Ext Cab SB	6150	7490
2 Dr B2300 SE Std Cab SB	5245	6455
2 Dr B3000 SE Ext Cab SB	6080	7485
2 Dr B3000 SE 4WD Ext Cab SB	7410	9125
2 Dr B3000 SE Std Cab SB	5520	6795
2 Dr B4000 LE Ext Cab SB	6915	8515
2 Dr B4000 LE 4WD Ext Cab SB	8595	10580
2 Dr B4000 SE Ext Cab SB	6305	7760
2 Dr B4000 SE 4WD Ext Cab SB	8070	9930
2 Dr B4000 SE 4WD Std Cab SB	7680	9455

OPTIONS FOR B-SERIES PICKUP
Auto 4-Speed Transmission +310
AM/FM Stereo Tape[Opt on B2300] +65
Air Conditioning[Std on B4000 LE] +245
Aluminum/Alloy Wheels +95
Auto Locking Hubs (4WD)[Std on B4000 SE] +80
Bed Liner +85
Compact Disc Changer +150
Cruise Control +65
Keyless Entry System +60
Limited Slip Diff +85
Power Door Locks +70
Power Drivers Seat +85
Power Steering[Std on SE,LE,Ext Cab,4WD] +85
Power Windows +70
Premium Sound System +100

MIATA — 1995

Option packages are revised, and a gorgeous M-Edition with Merlot Mica paint, tan top, tan leather interior, and 15-inch BBS rims is available.

RATINGS (SCALE OF 1-10)

Overall	Safety	Reliability	Performance	Comfort	Value
7.3	6.9	8	9	7.1	5.4

Category F

Model	Trade-in	Market
2 Dr MX-5 Conv	7725	9345
2 Dr MX-5 M-Edition Conv	9955	12040

OPTIONS FOR MIATA
Auto 4-Speed Transmission +255
Leather Pkg +665
Sensory Sound System +260
Air Conditioning[Opt on MX-5] +250
Aluminum/Alloy Wheels[Opt on MX-5] +90
Anti-Lock Brakes[Opt on MX-5] +195
Compact Disc W/fm/tape +150
Cruise Control[Opt on MX-5] +65
Hardtop Roof +430
Limited Slip Diff +100
Power Steering[Opt on MX-5] +105
Power Windows[Opt on MX-5] +70
Rear Spoiler +70
Sport Seats +140
Sport Suspension +55

MILLENIA — 1995

Luxury-oriented model that was to be in Mazda's aborted upscale Amati luxury division. Positioned to do battle with entry-level Lexus, Infiniti and BMW

Don't forget to refer to the Mileage Adjustment Table at the back of this book!

MAZDA 95

Model Description	Trade-in Value	Market Value	Model Description	Trade-in Value	Market Value

models. S models have 2.3-liter V6 with Miller-cycle technology and 210 horsepower. Dual airbags and ABS are standard on all models. The Millenia S adds traction control.

RATINGS (SCALE OF 1-10)

Overall	Safety	Reliability	Performance	Comfort	Value
7.4	8	8.3	8.4	7.9	4.4

Category D
4 Dr S Sdn	11460	14060
4 Dr STD Sdn	10085	12370

OPTIONS FOR MILLENIA

Bose Sound System +235
Compact Disc Changer +195
Keyless Entry System[Std on S] +95
Leather Seats[Std on S] +340
Power Moonroof[Std on S] +250
Power Passenger Seat[Std on S] +95
Traction Control System[Std on S] +160

MPV   1995

New lineup includes L, LX and LXE trim levels. All come with seven-passenger seating. Four-cylinder engine has been dropped.

RATINGS (SCALE OF 1-10)

Overall	Safety	Reliability	Performance	Comfort	Value
7.5	6.5	8.9	7.8	7.6	6.5

Category G
2 Dr L Pass. Van	8400	10340
2 Dr LX Pass. Van	8355	10285
2 Dr LX 4WD Pass. Van	9615	11835
2 Dr LXE Pass. Van	9240	11375
2 Dr LXE 4WD Pass. Van	10465	12885

OPTIONS FOR MPV

Air Conditioning +245
Aluminum/Alloy Wheels +95
Camper/Towing Package[Opt on LX] +90
Dual Air Conditioning +275
Keyless Entry System +60
Power Moonroof +260

MX3   1995

GS model, and its cool 1.8-liter, V6 engine, vanishes. ABS is available only with manual transmission.

Category E
2 Dr STD Hbk	5080	6660

OPTIONS FOR MX3

Auto 4-Speed Transmission +240
Air Conditioning +250
Aluminum/Alloy Wheels +100
Anti-Lock Brakes +200
Cruise Control +70
Power Door Locks +75

Power Sunroof +185
Power Windows +80

MX6   1995

No changes for 1995.

RATINGS (SCALE OF 1-10)

Overall	Safety	Reliability	Performance	Comfort	Value
7.4	7.9	8.3	9	7.9	4

Category F
2 Dr LS Cpe	8825	10675
2 Dr STD Cpe	7595	9185

OPTIONS FOR MX6

Auto 4-Speed Transmission +240
Air Conditioning[Std on LS] +250
Aluminum/Alloy Wheels +90
Anti-Lock Brakes +195
Keyless Entry System +55
Leather Seats +190
Power Sunroof[Std on LS] +200
Rear Spoiler +70

PROTEGE   1995

Totally redesigned, the Protege grows substantially in interior volume. Has 10 more cubic feet of volume than Honda Civic. Dual airbags are finally added. ABS is standard on ES trim level; optional on LX.

RATINGS (SCALE OF 1-10)

Overall	Safety	Reliability	Performance	Comfort	Value
N/A	N/A	6.8	8	7.4	5.6

Category E
4 Dr DX Sdn	4575	6000
4 Dr ES Sdn	6105	8005
4 Dr LX Sdn	5090	6675

OPTIONS FOR PROTEGE

Auto 4-Speed Transmission +240
AM/FM Stereo Tape[Opt on DX] +90
Air Conditioning[Std on ES] +250
Aluminum/Alloy Wheels +100
Anti-Lock Brakes[Opt on LX] +200
Power Moonroof +175

RX-7   1995

CFC-free refrigerant is added to air conditioner. Touring package ousted. Red leather option dumped. Last year for RX-7.

Category F
2 Dr STD Turbo Rotary Cpe	17065	20640

OPTIONS FOR RX-7

Auto 4-Speed Transmission +270
Leather Seats +190
Power Sunroof +200
Rear Spoiler +70
Sport Suspension +55

Don't forget to refer to the Mileage Adjustment Table at the back of this book!

MAZDA 94

Model Description	Trade-in Value	Market Value	Model Description	Trade-in Value	Market Value

1994 MAZDA

323 — 1994

No changes. Final year for homely, slow-selling hatchback.

RATINGS (SCALE OF 1-10)

Overall	Safety	Reliability	Performance	Comfort	Value
6.2	4.3	7.2	6.8	7	5.8

Category E

	Trade-in	Market
2 Dr STD Hbk	2810	3870

OPTIONS FOR 323
Auto 4-Speed Transmission +185
AM/FM Stereo Tape +75
Air Conditioning +205
Power Steering +60

626 — 1994

Passenger airbag added. LX-V6 debuts. Four-cylinder models get new Ford transmission for smoother shifting than previous Mazda unit. ABS becomes standard on ES trim level, as well as leather seats and power sunroof.

RATINGS (SCALE OF 1-10)

Overall	Safety	Reliability	Performance	Comfort	Value
7.6	7.9	8	8.8	8.1	5.2

Category D

	Trade-in	Market
4 Dr DX Sdn	4515	5795
4 Dr ES Sdn	6485	8325
4 Dr LX Sdn	5220	6700
4 Dr LX V6 Sdn	5885	7555

OPTIONS FOR 626
Auto 4-Speed Transmission +195
Air Conditioning[Opt on DX] +210
Aluminum/Alloy Wheels +115
Anti-Lock Brakes[Std on ES] +215
Cruise Control[Opt on DX] +60
Power Door Locks[Opt on DX] +65
Power Drivers Seat[Std on ES] +75
Power Moonroof[Std on ES] +205
Power Windows[Opt on DX] +65

929 — 1994

Trimmed to one model. Console cupholder added, height-adjustable seatbelts debut, and a limited-slip differential is included with the Cold Package. Premium Package adds remote keyless entry. New alloy wheels are standard.

RATINGS (SCALE OF 1-10)

Overall	Safety	Reliability	Performance	Comfort	Value
N/A	N/A	8	8.2	8.4	5.4

Category D

	Trade-in	Market
4 Dr STD Sdn	9145	11735

OPTIONS FOR 929
Premium Pkg +435
Cellular Telephone +200
Compact Disc Changer +160
Leather Seats +275
Power Passenger Seat +75

B-SERIES PICKUP — 1994

Mazda revises the styling of Ford's Ranger, slaps its name on the tailgate, and has a new compact pickup to sell. Base, SE and LE trim levels are offered in two- or four-wheel drive and two bodystyles.

RATINGS (SCALE OF 1-10)

Overall	Safety	Reliability	Performance	Comfort	Value
N/A	4.9	7.9	7.2	7.3	N/A

Category G

	Trade-in	Market
2 Dr B2300 Ext Cab SB	4655	5815
2 Dr B2300 Std Cab SB	3675	4590
2 Dr B2300 SE Std Cab SB	4355	5435
2 Dr B3000 Ext Cab SB	5080	6340
2 Dr B3000 4WD Ext Cab SB	6170	7700
2 Dr B3000 4WD Std Cab SB	5760	7190
2 Dr B3000 SE Ext Cab SB	5085	6350
2 Dr B3000 SE Std Cab LB	4945	6170
2 Dr B3000 SE Std Cab SB	4530	5655
2 Dr B4000 LE Ext Cab SB	5900	7365
2 Dr B4000 LE 4WD Ext Cab SB	7450	9300
2 Dr B4000 SE 4WD Ext Cab SB	6625	8270
2 Dr B4000 SE Std Cab LB	5010	6255
2 Dr B4000 SE 4WD Std Cab SB	6300	7865

OPTIONS FOR B-SERIES PICKUP
Auto 4-Speed Transmission[Std on B4000 LE] +350
AM/FM Compact Disc Player +75
Air Conditioning +200
Aluminum/Alloy Wheels +80
Bed Liner +70
Power Door Locks[Std on B4000 LE] +55
Power Steering[Opt on B2300 Std Cab SB] +70
Power Windows[Std on B4000 LE] +60

MIATA — 1994

Dual airbags arrive, and a 1.8-liter four cylinder making 128 horsepower replaces the original 1.6-liter engine. Sharp new alloy wheels debut. Optional automatic gets electronic shift controls. Larger diameter disc brakes are standard. Bigger gas tank added. New R package debuts with sportier suspension. Superman Blue replaced by Montego Blue. M-Edition is painted Montego Blue with chromed alloys.

RATINGS (SCALE OF 1-10)

Overall	Safety	Reliability	Performance	Comfort	Value
7.5	6.9	8.5	9	7.1	5.9

Don't forget to refer to the Mileage Adjustment Table at the back of this book!

Model Description	Trade-in Value	Market Value
Category F		
2 Dr MX-5 Conv	6605	8130
2 Dr MX-5 M-Edition Conv	8075	9940

OPTIONS FOR MIATA

Auto 4-Speed Transmission +160
Air Conditioning[Opt on MX-5] +205
Aluminum/Alloy Wheels[Opt on MX-5] +75
Anti-Lock Brakes +160
Compact Disc W/fm/tape +125
Cruise Control[Opt on MX-5] +55
Hardtop Roof +350
Leather Seats[Opt on MX-5] +155
Limited Slip Diff[Opt on MX-5] +80
Power Steering[Opt on MX-5] +85
Power Windows[Opt on MX-5] +55
Rear Spoiler +60
Sport Suspension +45

MPV   1994

Side-door impact beams are added. Four-wheel disc brakes are new. Standard tire size increases.

RATINGS (SCALE OF 1-10)

Overall	Safety	Reliability	Performance	Comfort	Value
7.2	6.3	7.8	7.8	7.6	6.3

	Trade-in	Market
Category G		
2 Dr STD Pass. Van	6150	7680
2 Dr STD 4WD Pass. Van	7420	9265

OPTIONS FOR MPV

6 cyl 3.0 L Engine[Opt on 2WD] +150
Luxury Pkg +255
7 Passenger Seating[Opt on 2WD] +125
AM/FM Compact Disc Player +75
Air Conditioning +200
Aluminum/Alloy Wheels +80
Camper/Towing Package +70
Cruise Control +50
Dual Air Conditioning +225
Keyless Entry System +50
Leather Seats +190
Power Door Locks +55
Power Moonroof +210
Power Windows +60

MX3   1994

Base model gets more power, and a passenger airbag is added. ABS can be ordered on base models for the first time. Can't get ABS on GS with automatic transmission. Base cars can be equipped with power sunroof. Both models get new wheels.

Category E		
2 Dr GS Hbk	5165	7120
2 Dr STD Hbk	4235	5840

OPTIONS FOR MX3

Auto 4-Speed Transmission +215
Air Conditioning +205
Aluminum/Alloy Wheels +80

Model Description	Trade-in Value	Market Value

Anti-Lock Brakes +160
Cruise Control +55
Power Door Locks +60
Power Sunroof +150
Power Windows +65

MX6   1994

Passenger airbag debuts. Air conditioning and power sunroof become standard on LS.

RATINGS (SCALE OF 1-10)

Overall	Safety	Reliability	Performance	Comfort	Value
7.2	7.9	7.7	9	7.9	3.3

Category F		
2 Dr LS Cpe	7260	8940
2 Dr STD Cpe	6265	7710

OPTIONS FOR MX6

Auto 4-Speed Transmission +195
Air Conditioning[Std on LS] +205
Aluminum/Alloy Wheels +75
Anti-Lock Brakes +160
Leather Seats +155
Power Drivers Seat +60
Power Sunroof[Std on LS] +165
Rear Spoiler +60

NAVAJO   1994

Restyled alloy wheels are new. Since Ford won't give Mazda a four-door version of Explorer to sell, this is final year for Navajo as Mazda picks up its toys and goes home to pout.

RATINGS (SCALE OF 1-10)

Overall	Safety	Reliability	Performance	Comfort	Value
7.2	5.7	5.9	7.6	8.3	8.4

Category G		
2 Dr DX Utility	6940	8665
2 Dr DX 4WD Utility	7620	9515
2 Dr LX Utility	7405	9245
2 Dr LX 4WD Utility	8085	10090

OPTIONS FOR NAVAJO

Auto 4-Speed Transmission +215
AM/FM Compact Disc Player +75
Air Conditioning +200
Camper/Towing Package +70
Cruise Control +50
Leather Seats +190
Limited Slip Diff +70
Luggage Rack +40
Moonroof +85
Power Drivers Seat +70

PROTEGE   1994

Minor styling revisions include new grille, headlamps, hood and front fascia.

MAZDA 94-93

Model Description	Trade-in Value	Market Value

RATINGS (SCALE OF 1-10)

Overall	Safety	Reliability	Performance	Comfort	Value
N/A	N/A	6.8	8.2	7.4	5

Category E

	Trade-in Value	Market Value
4 Dr DX Sdn	3575	4925
4 Dr LX Sdn	4085	5630
4 Dr Special Sdn	2980	4110

OPTIONS FOR PROTEGE

Auto 4-Speed Transmission +185
AM/FM Stereo Tape[Opt on DX] +75
Air Conditioning +205
Aluminum/Alloy Wheels +80
Power Door Locks[Opt on DX] +60
Power Sunroof +150
Power Windows[Opt on DX] +65
Tilt Steering Wheel[Opt on DX] +35

RX-7 1994

Dual airbags appear, and softer suspension settings are available. Seatbacks get map pockets, and power windows have a driver express-down feature.

Category F

	Trade-in	Market
2 Dr STD Turbo Rotary Cpe	13865	17070

OPTIONS FOR RX-7

Auto 4-Speed Transmission +220
R-2 Pkg +395
Touring Pkg +385
AM/FM Compact Disc Player +115
Bose Sound System +110
Leather Seats +155
Power Moonroof +160
Rear Spoiler +60
Sport Suspension +45

1993 MAZDA

323 1993

No changes.

RATINGS (SCALE OF 1-10)

Overall	Safety	Reliability	Performance	Comfort	Value
6.3	4.3	7.9	6.8	7	5.7

Category E

	Trade-in	Market
2 Dr SE Hbk	2350	3245
2 Dr STD Hbk	1930	2670

OPTIONS FOR 323

Auto 4-Speed Transmission +145
AM/FM Stereo Tape +60
Air Conditioning +165
Power Steering +50

626 1993

Completely redesigned for 1993. First import-badged car to be classified domestic by EPA. Driver airbag is standard, and ABS is optional. Top-end ES model gets 2.5-liter V6 engine. DX and LX powered by four-cylinder motor.

RATINGS (SCALE OF 1-10)

Overall	Safety	Reliability	Performance	Comfort	Value
7.1	6.1	7.5	8.8	8.1	5.1

Category D

	Trade-in	Market
4 Dr DX Sdn	3705	4920
4 Dr ES Sdn	4840	6430
4 Dr LX Sdn	4260	5660

OPTIONS FOR 626

Auto 4-Speed Transmission +155
AM/FM Compact Disc Player +95
Air Conditioning[Opt on DX] +170
Alarm System[Opt on LX] +105
Aluminum/Alloy Wheels[Opt on LX] +95
Anti-Lock Brakes +175
Compact Disc W/fm/tape +155
Cruise Control[Opt on DX] +50
Leather Seats +225
Power Door Locks[Opt on DX] +55
Power Drivers Seat +60
Power Moonroof +170
Power Windows[Opt on DX] +55

929 1993

Glass moonroof replaces steel offering. Revised alloy wheels, optional wood trim and optional power passenger's seat are new for 1993.

RATINGS (SCALE OF 1-10)

Overall	Safety	Reliability	Performance	Comfort	Value
N/A	N/A	8	8.2	8.4	5.4

Category D

	Trade-in	Market
4 Dr STD Sdn	6970	9265

OPTIONS FOR 929

Premium Pkg +325
Compact Disc Changer +130
Leather Seats +225
Power Passenger Seat +65
Premium Sound System +75

B-SERIES PICKUP 1993

No changes.

Category G

	Trade-in	Market
2 Dr B2200 Ext Cab SB	3730	4785
2 Dr B2200 Std Cab LB	3225	4140
2 Dr B2200 Std Cab SB	3155	4050
2 Dr B2600i Ext Cab SB	3850	4940
2 Dr B2600i 4WD Ext Cab SB	4750	6095
2 Dr B2600i 4WD Std Cab SB	4230	5430

Don't forget to refer to the Mileage Adjustment Table at the back of this book!

Model Description	Trade-in Value	Market Value

Model Description	Trade-in Value	Market Value

OPTIONS FOR B-SERIES PICKUP

Auto 4-Speed Transmission +160
AM/FM Stereo Tape +45
Air Conditioning +165
Aluminum/Alloy Wheels +65
Bed Liner +55
Chrome Wheels +35
Power Steering[Std on B2600i, Ext Cab] +55
Rear Step Bumper +30

MIATA 1993

Limited Edition available with black paint and red leather interior; just 1,500 were produced. Yellow dropped from paint roster. Tan roof and leather interior optional on red and white cars. A 130-watt Sensory Sound System is newly optional.

RATINGS (SCALE OF 1-10)

Overall	Safety	Reliability	Performance	Comfort	Value
7.3	6.2	8.6	8.8	7.1	5.9

Category F
2 Dr MX-5 Conv	5475	6870
2 Dr MX-5 Limited Conv	7750	9730

OPTIONS FOR MIATA

Auto 4-Speed Transmission +150
AM/FM Compact Disc Player +90
Air Conditioning[Opt on MX-5] +170
Aluminum/Alloy Wheels[Opt on MX-5] +60
Anti-Lock Brakes[Opt on MX-5] +130
Cruise Control[Opt on MX-5] +45
Hardtop Roof +285
Leather Seats[Opt on MX-5] +125
Limited Slip Diff[Opt on MX-5] +65
Power Steering[Opt on MX-5] +70
Power Windows[Opt on MX-5] +45

MPV 1993

Keyless entry system added to options list. Driver airbag added midyear.

RATINGS (SCALE OF 1-10)

Overall	Safety	Reliability	Performance	Comfort	Value
7	5.3	8.1	7.8	7.6	6.2

Category G
2 Dr STD Pass. Van	5435	6980
2 Dr STD 4WD Pass. Van	6040	7755

OPTIONS FOR MPV

6 cyl 3.0 L Engine[Opt on 2WD] +130
Air Conditioning +165
Aluminum/Alloy Wheels[Opt on 2WD] +65
Camper/Towing Package +60
Compact Disc W/fm/tape +90
Cruise Control +40
Dual Air Conditioning +185
Keyless Entry System +40

Leather Seats +155
Power Door Locks +45
Power Moonroof +175
Power Windows +50

MX3 1993

A cassette stereo is made standard, and Laguna Blue Metallic is a new color.

Category E
2 Dr GS Hbk	3955	5465
2 Dr STD Hbk	3225	4455
2 Dr Special Hbk	4440	6130

OPTIONS FOR MX3

Auto 4-Speed Transmission +145
AM/FM Compact Disc Player +85
Air Conditioning +165
Aluminum/Alloy Wheels[Opt on STD] +65
Anti-Lock Brakes +135
Cruise Control[Opt on GS] +45
Power Door Locks[Opt on GS, STD] +50
Power Sunroof[Opt on GS] +125
Power Windows[Opt on GS, STD] +55

MX6 1993

All-new this year, sporting dramatically swept bodywork and a speedy LS model with 2.5-liter V6 engine. EPA says MX-6 is a domestic car. Driver airbag standard, while ABS is optional.

RATINGS (SCALE OF 1-10)

Overall	Safety	Reliability	Performance	Comfort	Value
N/A	N/A	7	9	7.9	4.7

Category F
2 Dr LS Cpe	5970	7500
2 Dr STD Cpe	5255	6600

OPTIONS FOR MX6

Auto 4-Speed Transmission +160
AM/FM Compact Disc Player +90
Air Conditioning +170
Aluminum/Alloy Wheels[Std on LS] +60
Anti-Lock Brakes +130
Leather Seats +125
Power Drivers Seat +50
Power Sunroof +135
Rear Spoiler +50

NAVAJO 1993

Four-wheel ABS is newly standard.

RATINGS (SCALE OF 1-10)

Overall	Safety	Reliability	Performance	Comfort	Value
7	5	4.9	7.6	8.3	9.3

Category G
2 Dr DX Utility	5305	6805
2 Dr DX 4WD Utility	5860	7525

Don't forget to refer to the Mileage Adjustment Table at the back of this book!

MAZDA 93-92

Model Description	Trade-in Value	Market Value
2 Dr LX Utility	5800	7445
2 Dr LX 4WD Utility	6360	8160

OPTIONS FOR NAVAJO
Auto 4-Speed Transmission +175
Navajo LX Leather Pkg +410
AM/FM Compact Disc Player +65
Air Conditioning +165
Camper/Towing Package +60
Cruise Control +40
Leather Seats +155
Luggage Rack +30
Power Drivers Seat +55
Sunroof +60

PROTEGE   1993

Trim and equipment revisions.

RATINGS (SCALE OF 1-10)

Overall	Safety	Reliability	Performance	Comfort	Value
N/A	N/A	7.7	8.2	7.4	5.6

Category E

	Trade-in	Market
4 Dr DX Sdn	2895	4000
4 Dr LX Sdn	3285	4535

OPTIONS FOR PROTEGE
Auto 4-Speed Transmission +145
AM/FM Stereo Tape[Opt on LX] +60
Air Conditioning +165
Aluminum/Alloy Wheels +65
Power Sunroof +125
Tilt Steering Wheel[Opt on DX] +30

RX-7   1993

All-new supercar designed with a singular purpose: speed. Convertible dropped. 2+2 version canceled. Twin-turbo rotary engine is standard. Driver airbag and ABS are standard.

Category F

	Trade-in	Market
2 Dr STD Turbo Rotary Cpe	10825	13590

OPTIONS FOR RX-7
Auto 4-Speed Transmission +170
R-1 Pkg +240
Touring Pkg +230
AM/FM Compact Disc Player +90
Bose Sound System +90
Leather Seats +125
Power Sunroof +135
Premium Sound System +75
Rear Spoiler +50

1992 MAZDA

323   1992

New taillights debut.

RATINGS (SCALE OF 1-10)

Overall	Safety	Reliability	Performance	Comfort	Value
6.3	4.3	7.7	6.8	7	5.6

Category E

	Trade-in	Market
2 Dr SE Hbk	1795	2730
2 Dr STD Hbk	1525	2320

OPTIONS FOR 323
Auto 4-Speed Transmission +115
Air Conditioning +135
Power Steering +40

626   1992

Touring Sedan is dropped.

Category D

	Trade-in	Market
4 Dr DX Sdn	2535	3850
4 Dr LX Sdn	2835	4305

OPTIONS FOR 626
Auto 4-Speed Transmission +130
Air Conditioning +140
Anti-Lock Brakes +145
Power Moonroof +140

929   1992

Completely redesigned. Dual airbags and antilock brakes are standard.

RATINGS (SCALE OF 1-10)

Overall	Safety	Reliability	Performance	Comfort	Value
N/A	N/A	7.3	8.2	8.4	5.8

Category D

	Trade-in	Market
4 Dr STD Sdn	5290	8040

OPTIONS FOR 929
Compact Disc Changer +105
Leather Seats +185
Power Moonroof +140
Power Passenger Seat +50

B-SERIES PICKUP   1992

New steering wheel and minor trim changes. Extended-cab models get new rear lap/shoulder seatbelts.

Category G

	Trade-in	Market
2 Dr B2200 Ext Cab SB	3105	4055
2 Dr B2200 Std Cab LB	2715	3545
2 Dr B2200 Std Cab SB	2655	3470
2 Dr B2600i Ext Cab SB	3210	4195
2 Dr B2600i 4WD Ext Cab SB	4020	5250
2 Dr B2600i Std Cab SB	2845	3715
2 Dr B2600i 4WD Std Cab SB	3570	4665

OPTIONS FOR B-SERIES PICKUP
Auto 4-Speed Transmission +130
Air Conditioning +135
Power Steering[Std on B2600i,Ext Cab] +45

Don't forget to refer to the Mileage Adjustment Table at the back of this book!

Model Description	Trade-in Value	Market Value

MIATA 1992

Silver paint dropped in favor of yellow and black. Remote trunk release added. Optional hardtop gets rear window defogger. Brilliant Black special edition available.

RATINGS (SCALE OF 1-10)

Overall	Safety	Reliability	Performance	Comfort	Value
7	6.2	8.5	8.8	7.1	4.3

Category F
2 Dr MX-5 Conv	4680	6170

OPTIONS FOR MIATA
Auto 4-Speed Transmission +120
Pkg C +125
AM/FM Compact Disc Player +75
Air Conditioning +135
Anti-Lock Brakes +105
Hardtop Roof +235
Leather Seats +105
Limited Slip Diff +55
Power Steering +60
Power Windows +40

MPV 1992

Eight-passenger seating and power moonroof added to options list. Five-speed manual transmission dropped. V6 engine gets five additional horsepower. New alloy wheels debut.

RATINGS (SCALE OF 1-10)

Overall	Safety	Reliability	Performance	Comfort	Value
7.2	4.9	7.5	7.8	7.6	8.4

Category G
2 Dr STD Pass. Van	4300	5615
2 Dr STD 4WD Pass. Van	4930	6440

OPTIONS FOR MPV
6 cyl 3.0 L Engine[Opt on 2WD] +125
Luxury Pkg +215
AM/FM Compact Disc Player +50
Air Conditioning +135
Camper/Towing Package +50
Dual Air Conditioning +150
Leather Seats +130
Power Door Locks +40
Power Moonroof +140
Power Windows +40

MX3 1992

All-new sport coupe takes over where Honda CRX left off. A 1.8-liter V6 engine, the industry's smallest, is standard on GS models. ABS optional on GS.

Category E
2 Dr GS Hbk	3065	4660
2 Dr STD Hbk	2460	3740

OPTIONS FOR MX3
Auto 4-Speed Transmission +115
AM/FM Compact Disc Player +70
Air Conditioning +135
Anti-Lock Brakes +110
Power Door Locks +40
Power Sunroof +100
Power Windows +45

MX6 1992

No changes.
Category F
2 Dr DX Cpe	3545	4670
2 Dr GT Turbo Cpe	4490	5915
2 Dr LX Cpe	3885	5120

OPTIONS FOR MX6
Auto 4-Speed Transmission +130
AM/FM Compact Disc Player +75
Air Conditioning +135
Anti-Lock Brakes +105
Power Sunroof +110

NAVAJO 1992

A base model joins the lineup, called DX. Upper trim level becomes LX. Two-wheel drive is now available in either trim level.

RATINGS (SCALE OF 1-10)

Overall	Safety	Reliability	Performance	Comfort	Value
6.4	5.1	4.8	7.6	8.3	6.4

Category G
2 Dr DX Utility	4625	6045
2 Dr DX 4WD Utility	5140	6710
2 Dr LX Utility	5110	6675
2 Dr LX 4WD Utility	5620	7345

OPTIONS FOR NAVAJO
Auto 4-Speed Transmission +140
Air Conditioning +135
Camper/Towing Package +50
Leather Seats +130
Moonroof +55
Power Drivers Seat +45

PROTEGE 1992

New taillights are added, and the all-wheel-drive model is dropped.

RATINGS (SCALE OF 1-10)

Overall	Safety	Reliability	Performance	Comfort	Value
N/A	N/A	7.6	8.2	7.4	5.5

Category E
4 Dr DX Sdn	2225	3380
4 Dr LX Sdn	2590	3935

Don't forget to refer to the Mileage Adjustment Table at the back of this book!

OPTIONS FOR PROTEGE
Auto 4-Speed Transmission +115
Air Conditioning +135
Power Steering[Opt on DX] +40
Power Sunroof +100

1991 MAZDA

323 — 1991

No changes.

RATINGS (SCALE OF 1-10)

Overall	Safety	Reliability	Performance	Comfort	Value
6	4.3	7	6.8	7	5

Category E

	Trade-in	Market
2 Dr SE Hbk	1405	2365
2 Dr STD Hbk	1170	1970

OPTIONS FOR 323
Auto 4-Speed Transmission +95
Air Conditioning +110
Power Steering +35

626 — 1991

New option packages added.
Category D

	Trade-in	Market
4 Dr DX Sdn	1790	2990
4 Dr GT Turbo Hbk	3490	4985
4 Dr LE Sdn	3360	4800
4 Dr LX Hbk	3180	4540
4 Dr LX Sdn	2340	3625

OPTIONS FOR 626
Auto 4-Speed Transmission +100
Air Conditioning[Std on LE] +115
Anti-Lock Brakes +120
Power Sunroof[Std on LE] +105

929 — 1991

Lace alloys standard on all models. Two new option packages are available.
Category D

	Trade-in	Market
4 Dr S Sdn	3730	5325
4 Dr STD Sdn	3505	5010

OPTIONS FOR 929
Compact Disc W/fm/tape +105
Leather Seats +150
Power Passenger Seat +40

B-SERIES PICKUP — 1991

Four-wheel-drive models get new grille and fender flares. Regular-cab models get headrests.
Category G

	Trade-in	Market
2 Dr B2200 Ext Cab SB	2595	3670
2 Dr B2200 Std Cab LB	2255	3190
2 Dr B2200 Std Cab SB	2205	3115
2 Dr B2600i Ext Cab SB	2655	3755
2 Dr B2600i 4WD Ext Cab SB	3385	4790
2 Dr B2600i Std Cab SB	2335	3300
2 Dr B2600i 4WD Std Cab SB	2985	4225

OPTIONS FOR B-SERIES PICKUP
Auto 4-Speed Transmission +105
Air Conditioning +110
Power Steering[Std on B2600i,Ext Cab] +40

MIATA — 1991

Special edition painted British Racing Green; 4,000 units produced. ABS is a new option.

RATINGS (SCALE OF 1-10)

Overall	Safety	Reliability	Performance	Comfort	Value
6.9	6	7.7	8.8	7.1	4.9

Category F

	Trade-in	Market
2 Dr MX-5 Conv	4130	5555
2 Dr MX-5 Special Conv	5100	6860

OPTIONS FOR MIATA
Auto 4-Speed Transmission +80
Air Conditioning[Opt on MX-5] +110
Anti-Lock Brakes +85
Hardtop Roof +190
Limited Slip Diff[Opt on MX-5 Conv] +45
Power Steering[Opt on MX-5 Conv] +45
Power Windows[Opt on MX-5 Conv] +30

MPV — 1991

Luxury package with lace alloy wheels, leather seats and two-tone paint debuts.

RATINGS (SCALE OF 1-10)

Overall	Safety	Reliability	Performance	Comfort	Value
7	4.7	6.4	7.8	7.6	8.3

Category G

	Trade-in	Market
2 Dr STD Cargo Van	2860	4050
2 Dr STD Pass. Van	3155	4460
2 Dr STD 4WD Pass. Van	4060	5745

OPTIONS FOR MPV
6 cyl 3.0 L Engine[Opt on 2WD] +95
Auto 4-Speed Transmission[Std on Cargo Van,4WD] +95
Value Pkg +230
AM/FM Compact Disc Player +40
Air Conditioning +110
Camper/Towing Package[Opt on 2WD] +40
Dual Air Conditioning +125
Leather Seats +105
Power Door Locks +30
Power Windows +30

MX6 — 1991

GT 4WS dropped.

Don't forget to refer to the Mileage Adjustment Table at the back of this book!

Model Description	Trade-in Value	Market Value
Category F		
2 Dr DX Cpe	3090	4160
2 Dr GT Turbo Cpe	3860	5195
2 Dr LE Cpe	3500	4705
2 Dr LX Cpe	3370	4535

OPTIONS FOR MX6
Auto 4-Speed Transmission +95
AM/FM Compact Disc Player +60
Air Conditioning[Std on LE] +110
Anti-Lock Brakes +85
Power Sunroof[Std on LE] +90

NAVAJO 1991

Reskinned two-door Ford Explorer gives Mazda its first sport-utility vehicle. Single trim level with 4WD and rear antilock brakes available.

RATINGS (SCALE OF 1-10)

Overall	Safety	Reliability	Performance	Comfort	Value
6.3	5	4.1	7.6	8.3	6.4

Model Description	Trade-in Value	Market Value
Category G		
2 Dr STD 4WD Utility	4660	6590

OPTIONS FOR NAVAJO
Auto 4-Speed Transmission +115
Air Conditioning +110
Camper/Towing Package +40
Leather Seats +105
Sunroof +40

PROTEGE 1991

No changes.

RATINGS (SCALE OF 1-10)

Overall	Safety	Reliability	Performance	Comfort	Value
N/A	N/A	7.2	8.2	7.4	5

Model Description	Trade-in Value	Market Value
Category E		
4 Dr DX Sdn	1815	3060
4 Dr LX Sdn	2015	3395
4 Dr STD 4WD Sdn	2085	3510

OPTIONS FOR PROTEGE
Auto 4-Speed Transmission +95
Air Conditioning +110
Power Steering[Opt on DX] +35
Power Sunroof +85

RX-7 1991

Lineup trimmed to three models: base, Turbo and convertible. ABS is standard on Turbo. A driver airbag is standard on the convertible.

Model Description	Trade-in Value	Market Value
Category F		
2 Dr STD Rotary Conv	6045	8130
2 Dr STD Rotary Cpe	4305	5790
2 Dr Turbo Rotary Cpe	5680	7640

OPTIONS FOR RX-7
Auto 4-Speed Transmission +100
Leather Seats[Std on Conv] +85
Power Sunroof[Opt on Cpe] +90

Don't forget to refer to the Mileage Adjustment Table at the back of this book!

MERCEDES-BENZ 00

Model Description	Trade-in Value	Market Value	Model Description	Trade-in Value	Market Value

MERCEDES   Germany

1997 Mercedes-Benz C230

2000 MERCEDES-BENZ

C-CLASS   2000

TeleAid, which can assist in summoning help if you're ill or involved in a crash, is a brilliant new standard feature. A Touch Shift automanual transmission is added to all C-Class models, and stability control is standard this year. C-Class now comes with free scheduled service for the duration of the warranty period.

Category L

4 Dr C230 Komp Sdn	26475	30295
4 Dr C280 Sdn	29910	34225

OPTIONS FOR C-CLASS
Full Leather Seat Trim +1100
Option Pkg K2 +780
Dual Power Seats [Std on C280] +645
Power Moonroof +780

C43   2000

TeleAid, which can assist in summoning help if you're ill or involved in a crash, is a new standard feature. A Touch Shift automanual transmission is added to simulate the thrill of shifting gears manually. Free scheduled service for the duration of the warranty period has been added to the lengthy standard equipment list.

Category L

4 Dr C43 Sdn	44640	51085

OPTIONS FOR C43
Option Pkg K2 +780

CL-CLASS   2000

2000 marks the introduction of an all-new CL500 that is lighter, less expensive, and more advanced than the previous version.

Category L

2 Dr CL500 Cpe	71685	82030

OPTIONS FOR CL-CLASS
CL1 Pkg +1265
Dual Multi-contour Seats +860
Parktronic System +795

CLK-CLASS   2000

The CLK430 Convertible debuts, reminding us, for a premium price, what a drop-top muscle car from the '70s was like. Turn-signal indicators have been added to exterior mirrors, stability control is standard on all models, automatics get Touch Shift manual gear selection, and TeleAid emergency cellular service is standard. A new instrument cluster and multi-function steering wheel are added, and buyers can opt for the confusing COMAND navigation/phone/trip computer/sound system. CLK320s benefit from exterior cosmetic changes including new wheels, while 430s are enhanced inside with new black birdseye maple wood trim. Free maintenance for the duration of the warranty is now included.

Category J

2 Dr CLK430 Conv	46800	53560
2 Dr CLK430 Cpe	41390	47370

Category L

2 Dr CLK320 Conv	40565	46420
2 Dr CLK320 Cpe	35155	40230

OPTIONS FOR CLK-CLASS
COMAND System +1535
K2 Option Pkg +780
K2a Option Pkg +1100
AM/FM Compact Disc Player +320
Compact Disc Changer +765
Heated Front Seats +355
Power Moonroof +775
Xenon Headlamps +590

E-CLASS   2000

Though it might not look different, the E-Class receives a substantial freshening for 2000, with an entirely new front end and a revised interior. Stability control, a Touch Shift automanual transmission, and side airbags for all outboard seating positions are now standard. A multi-function steering wheel debuts, and E430 models can be equipped with 4matic all-wheel drive. TeleAid, a cellular emergency service, is standard and the confounding COMAND system is optional. For 2000, free maintenance is provided for the duration of the

Model Description	Trade-in Value	Market Value	Model Description	Trade-in Value	Market Value

warranty period. The E300 turbodiesel model has been dropped. Other changes are limited to minor cosmetic and functional upgrades.

Category L

	Trade-in	Market
4 Dr E320 Sdn	37345	42735
4 Dr E320 4WD Sdn	39535	45240
4 Dr E320 Wgn	38010	43495
4 Dr E320 4WD Wgn	40200	46000
4 Dr E430 Sdn	41530	47520
4 Dr E430 4WD Sdn	43720	50025

OPTIONS FOR E-CLASS

COMAND System +1630
Full Leather Seat Trim +1100
Nappa Leather Seat Trim +1670
Option Pkg K2 +780
Option Pkg K2a +1100
Parktronic System +795
Sport Pkg E3 +1640
Bose Sound System[Std on E430] +455
Compact Disc Changer +885
Heated Front Seats +405
Metallic Paint +480
Power Moonroof +780

E55 — 2000

Though it might not look different, the E55 receives the same substantial freshening for 2000 that other E-Class models get, which includes an entirely new front end and a revised interior. A Touch Shift automanual transmission and side airbags for all outboard seating positions are now standard. A multi-function steering wheel debuts, and TeleAid, a cellular emergency service, comes with the package for 2000. Thankfully, the confounding COMAND system is optional. Hard-charging drivers will be happy to learn that free maintenance is provided for the duration of the warranty period.

Category L

	Trade-in	Market
4 Dr E55 Sdn	58620	67080

OPTIONS FOR E55

Option Pkg K2 +780
Option Pkg K2a +1100

M-CLASS — 2000

All M-Class models get an interior facelift available in one of three new colors, optional third-row seating and a Touch Shift automanual transmission. ML320 buyers get body-color bumpers and trim, real walnut inside, leather-wrapped steering wheel and gearshift knob, revised interior fabric, seatback map pockets and footwell lamps. In addition to these items, a standard navigation system, high-grade leather, and heated seats come on all ML430s.

Category G

	Trade-in	Market
4 Dr ML320 4WD Wgn	29030	33280

OPTIONS FOR M-CLASS

M7 Third Row Seat Pkg +1105
Skyview Roof +1960
Automatic Dimming Mirror +145
Bose Sound System +640
Compact Disc Changer +415
Dual Power Seats +340
Heated Front Seats +225
Leather Seats +640
Power Moonroof +710
Privacy Glass +225
Trip Computer +125

ML55 — 2000

Mercedes goes overboard on power and performance with the new ML55. Correct us if we're wrong, but weren't SUVs originally designed for rugged off-road travel?

Category H

	Trade-in	Market
4 Dr ML55 AWD Wgn	54400	62415

S-CLASS — 2000

An all-new S-Class debuts for the millennium with enhanced performance and a snazzy COMAND system.

Category L

	Trade-in	Market
4 Dr S430 Sdn	58240	66645
4 Dr S500 Sdn	64990	74370

OPTIONS FOR S-CLASS

Climate Comfort Rear Seat +1160
Four Place Seating Pkg +4530
Parktronic System +755
Power Rear Seat Adjusters +1350
S1 Audio Pkg +635
S2 Lighting Pkg +555
S3 Comfort Pkg +1500
S4 Convenience Pkg +2915
Cellular Telephone +785
Compact Disc Changer +885

SL-CLASS — 2000

Designo editions debut in Slate Blue and Black Diamond with special color-coordinated interior trim. Non-designo versions can be painted in Desert Silver. TeleAid is standard, as is a StarTAC digital phone with voice-recognition technology on the SL600. Free maintenance now covers you during the warranty period. For more than 80 grand, it oughta cover you for the life of the car.

Category J

	Trade-in	Market
2 Dr SL500 STD Conv	66975	76645
2 Dr SL600 STD Conv	104260	119320

Don't forget to refer to the Mileage Adjustment Table at the back of this book!

MERCEDES-BENZ 00-99

Model Description	Trade-in Value	Market Value	Model Description	Trade-in Value	Market Value

OPTIONS FOR SL-CLASS
Adapt Damping System +3270
Removable Panorama Roof +3085
Sport Option Pkg SL1 +4060

SLK   2000

Designo editions debut and include special paint and trim in either Copper or Electric Green hues.

Category J

	Trade-in	Market
2 Dr Kompressor Sprchgd Conv	32870	37615

OPTIONS FOR SLK
Auto 5-Speed Transmission +735
Designo Copper Edition +3840
Electric Green Edition +3475
Option Pkg K2 +925
Option Pkg K2a +1250

1999 MERCEDES-BENZ

C-CLASS   1999

The SLK's 2.3-liter supercharged engine gets dropped into the C-Class, replacing the normally-aspirated engine of the last C230. Performance has been turned up a notch. In addition, leather seating surfaces are now standard across the C-Class line.

RATINGS (SCALE OF 1-10)

Overall	Safety	Reliability	Performance	Comfort	Value
N/A	8.5	9	8.6	8.1	N/A

Category L

	Trade-in	Market
4 Dr C230 Komp Sdn	24805	28490
4 Dr C280 Sdn	28240	32430
4 Dr C43 Sdn	41205	47320

OPTIONS FOR C-CLASS
Full Leather Seat Trim +885
Option Pkg C1 +570
Bose Sound System[Opt on Kompressor] +370
Dual Power Seats[Opt on Kompressor] +530
Heated Front Seats[Std on C43] +330
Leather Seats[Opt on Kompressor] +815
Power Moonroof[Std on C43] +640
Telescopic Steering Whl[Std on C43] +120
Traction Control System[Std on C43] +905

CL-CLASS   1999

The CL coupes are carryover models for 1999 with no changes.

Category L

	Trade-in	Market
2 Dr CL500 Cpe	64915	74550
2 Dr CL600 Cpe	96780	111145

OPTIONS FOR CL-CLASS
Adapt Damping System +1350

CLK320   1999

These guys are still on a roll. Last year, Mercedes introduced an all-new sport coupe that is an amalgamation of C- and SLK-Class technologies, available this year with a larger engine in the CLK 430 model, and now they're rolling out the CLK 320 Cabriolet, a convertible version of the fabulous little car.

RATINGS (SCALE OF 1-10)

Overall	Safety	Reliability	Performance	Comfort	Value
N/A	N/A	N/A	8.4	8	N/A

Category L

	Trade-in	Market
2 Dr CLK320 Conv	36755	42210
2 Dr CLK320 Cpe	31680	36380

OPTIONS FOR CLK320
Compact Disc Changer +725
Heated Front Seats +330
Power Moonroof +640
Traction Control System +905
Xenon Headlamps +615

CLK430   1999

These guys are still on a roll. Last year, Mercedes introduced an all-new sport coupe that is an amalgamation of C- and SLK-Class technologies, available this year with a larger engine in the CLK 430 model, and now they're rolling out the CLK 320 Cabriolet, a convertible version of the fabulous little car.

RATINGS (SCALE OF 1-10)

Overall	Safety	Reliability	Performance	Comfort	Value
N/A	N/A	N/A	8.6	8	N/A

Category J

	Trade-in	Market
2 Dr CLK430 Cpe	37345	42825

OPTIONS FOR CLK430
Navigation System +1665
Option Pkg K4 +675
Compact Disc Changer +625
Heated Front Seats +290
Power Moonroof +635
Xenon Headlamps +480

E-CLASS   1999

More airbags find room in the E-Class, which now features a full curtain side airbag protection system. The E300 Turbodiesel and E320 wagon are enhanced with leather seat inserts, and all E-Class cars get fiber-optic technology in their sound system/optional telephone unit. A performance-oriented E55 model is also available, bringing with it a fire-breathing V8.

Don't forget to refer to the Mileage Adjustment Table at the back of this book!

Model Description	Trade-in Value	Market Value

RATINGS (SCALE OF 1-10)

Overall	Safety	Reliability	Performance	Comfort	Value
N/A	N/A	8.7	9.4	8.6	N/A

Category L

4 Dr E300TD Turbodsl Sdn	31705	36410
4 Dr E320 Sdn	34510	39630
4 Dr E320 4WD Sdn	36565	41995
4 Dr E320 Wgn	35245	40475
4 Dr E320 4WD Wgn	37305	42840
4 Dr E430 Sdn	38270	43950
4 Dr E55 Sdn	51395	59025

OPTIONS FOR E-CLASS

Elect. Stability Program +670
Option Pkg E1 +635
Parktronic System +650
Pkg K2 +565
Sport Pkg E3 +1050
Bose Sound System[Std on E430, E55] +370
Compact Disc Changer +725
Heated Front Seats[Std on E55] +330
Leather Seats[Opt on Wgn, Turbodsl] +815
Power Moonroof[Std on E55] +640
Traction Control System[Opt on Turbodsl, E320 Sedan] +905
Xenon Headlamps[Std on E55] +615

M-CLASS 1999

Mercedes expands its M-Class with the addition of the more powerful and luxurious ML430 and gives the 320 more standard equipment.

RATINGS (SCALE OF 1-10)

Overall	Safety	Reliability	Performance	Comfort	Value
N/A	N/A	N/A	7.8	8.1	N/A

Category G

4 Dr ML320 4WD Wgn	27835	32075

Category H

4 Dr ML430 4WD Wgn	33750	38850

OPTIONS FOR M-CLASS

Pkg M1 +660
Pkg M4 +675
Compact Disc Changer +300
Dual Power Seats[Std on ML430] +280
Heated Front Seats +180
Leather Seats[Std on ML430] +525
Power Moonroof +580
Privacy Glass[Std on ML430] +185
Trip Computer[Std on ML430] +100

S-CLASS 1999

The folks at the three-pointed star unleash an S-Class Mercedes that offers freshened styling, unstoppable engines and a host of luxuries. A limited-production Grand Edition S500 also debuts.

RATINGS (SCALE OF 1-10)

Overall	Safety	Reliability	Performance	Comfort	Value
N/A	N/A	N/A	8	9	N/A

Category L

4 Dr S320 LWB Sdn	50465	57950
4 Dr S320 SWB Sdn	48070	55205
4 Dr S420 Sdn	54805	62935
4 Dr S500 Sdn	63375	72780
4 Dr S600 Sdn	97005	111405

OPTIONS FOR S-CLASS

Adapt Damping System +1350
Four Place Power Seating +3290
Grand Edition Pkg +800
Parktronic System +580
Power Rear Seat Adjusters +1040
Compact Disc Changer[Std on S600] +725
Dual Air Conditioning[Std on S600] +1260
Heated Front Seats[Std on S500,S600] +330
Traction Control System[Std on S600] +905
Xenon Headlamps[Std on S500,S600] +615

SL-CLASS 1999

The SL500 gets a brand-spankin'-new 5.0-liter V8 that delivers better performance than ever before. Both SL models get side view mirrors from the SLK, body-colored door handles and new side molding, new taillights, new exterior colors, a new instrument panel, new shifter and shift gate, and a new four-spoke steering wheel.

RATINGS (SCALE OF 1-10)

Overall	Safety	Reliability	Performance	Comfort	Value
N/A	N/A	N/A	9.6	7.9	N/A

Category J

2 Dr SL500 STD Conv	62905	72140
2 Dr SL600STD Conv	98170	112580

OPTIONS FOR SL-CLASS

Removable Panorama Roof +2470
Sport Option Pkg SL1 +3320
Heated Front Seats[Std on SL600] +290
Xenon Headlamps[Std on SL600] +480

SLK230 1999

This year, Mercedes gives the SLK a standard five-speed manual transmission, optional Sport Package, a new-generation stereo with cassette that uses fiber-optic technology, and integrated controls for a cellular phone.

RATINGS (SCALE OF 1-10)

Overall	Safety	Reliability	Performance	Comfort	Value
N/A	N/A	N/A	8	7.9	N/A

Category J

2 Dr STD Sprchgd Conv	31850	36525
2 Dr Sport Sprchgd Conv	33955	38935

Don't forget to refer to the Mileage Adjustment Table at the back of this book!

MERCEDES-BENZ 99-98

Model Description	Trade-in Value	Market Value	Model Description	Trade-in Value	Market Value

OPTIONS FOR SLK230
Auto 5-Speed Transmission +600
Heated Front Seats +290

1998 MERCEDES-BENZ

C-CLASS   1998

The C280 is the lucky recipient of Mercedes' new V-type engine technology, receiving a 2.8-liter unit for the engine bay. BabySmart car seats, Brake Assist and side airbags also debut on the C-Class this year. For the C43, think BMW M3 without all the fun of a stick shift. The C43 is fast and stylish, but the automatic transmission robs plenty of the fun.

RATINGS (SCALE OF 1-10)

Overall	Safety	Reliability	Performance	Comfort	Value
7.9	8.5	8.9	8.6	8.1	5.2

Category L

4 Dr C230 Sdn	22095	25410
4 Dr C280 Sdn	25620	29465
4 Dr C43 Sdn	37550	43180

OPTIONS FOR C-CLASS
Bose Sound System[Opt on C230] +305
Compact Disc Changer +590
Dual Power Seats[Opt on C230] +430
Heated Front Seats +270
Leather Seats +665
Power Moonroof +520
Sport Suspension +90
Telescopic Steering Whl +100
Traction Control System +740

CL-CLASS   1998

In keeping with Mercedes' somewhat odd habit of changing their cars' names just as people are getting the hang of them, the former S-Class coupes are now dubbed the CL-Class. Other than that confusing switch, the only changes to these big coupes are the addition of BabySmart airbag technology and Brake Assist to the standard equipment lists.

Category L

2 Dr CL500 Cpe	60400	69460
2 Dr CL600 Cpe	88740	102050

OPTIONS FOR CL-CLASS
Adapt Damping System +1240
Traction Control System[Std on CL600] +740

CLK320   1998

Mercedes rolls out an all-new sport coupe that is an amalgamation of C- and SLK-Class technologies, with E-Class style up front. The CLK is infused with the same 3.2-liter V6 that has made its way into the ML320 and E320.

Category L

2 Dr STD Cpe	29470	33890

OPTIONS FOR CLK320
Pkg K4 +880
Compact Disc Changer +590
Heated Front Seats +270
Power Moonroof +520

E-CLASS   1998

All-wheel drive comes to the Mercedes' E-Class lineup via the E320 sedan and all-new E320 wagon. Like the rest of Mercedes' model lineup, E-Class cars formerly powered by an inline-six engine now receive a more fuel efficient V6 unit that is also supposed to improve the cars' low-end torque. The 1998 E-Class cars receive the benefit of BabySmart airbags which are able to detect the presence of a Mercedes' car seat in the front passenger seat and disable the front passenger airbag. Brake Assist is also a new feature, which aids drivers' stopping distance in a panic stop situation.

RATINGS (SCALE OF 1-10)

Overall	Safety	Reliability	Performance	Comfort	Value
N/A	N/A	9.1	9.4	8.6	5.3

Category L

4 Dr E300TD Turbodsl Sdn	31205	35885
4 Dr E320 Sdn	33925	39015
4 Dr E320 4WD Sdn	35950	41345
4 Dr E320 Wgn	34665	39860
4 Dr E320 4WD Wgn	36685	42190
4 Dr E430 Sdn	37680	43330

OPTIONS FOR E-CLASS
Option Pkg E1 +800
Parktronic System +530
Pkg K2 +460
Sport Pkg E3 +1945
Bose Sound System[Std on E430] +305
Compact Disc Changer +590
Leather Seats[Opt on E300TD, Wgn] +665
Luggage Rack +175
Metallic Paint +320
Power Moonroof +520

M-CLASS   1998

Mercedes enters the sport-ute fray with the introduction of the ML320. Designed from a clean sheet of paper, the ML320 offers the best of the car and truck worlds.

RATINGS (SCALE OF 1-10)

Overall	Safety	Reliability	Performance	Comfort	Value
N/A	N/A	7.6	7.2	8.1	N/A

Category G

4 Dr ML320 4WD Wgn	24815	28715

Don't forget to refer to the Mileage Adjustment Table at the back of this book!

Model Description	Trade-in Value	Market Value

Model Description	Trade-in Value	Market Value

OPTIONS FOR M-CLASS

Pkg M1 +855
Pkg M4 +440
Automatic Dimming Mirror +95
Bose Sound System +430
Dual Power Seats +230
Heated Front Seats +150
Leather Seats +430
Power Moonroof +475
Privacy Glass +150
Trip Computer +80

S-CLASS 1998

The uber-Mercedes are not changed much in anticipation of the cars' imminent replacement. Brake Assist and BabySmart appear in the lineup, but the S320s don't receive the V6 engines that have empowered lesser Mercedes, like the C280 and E320.

Category L

	Trade-in	Market
4 Dr S320 LWB Sdn	44335	50985
4 Dr S320 SWB Sdn	42180	48505
4 Dr S420 Sdn	47515	54640
4 Dr S500 Sdn	56190	64615
4 Dr S600 Sdn	84730	97435

OPTIONS FOR S-CLASS

Adapt Damping System +1240
Four Place Power Seating +3025
Parktronic System +530
Power Rear Seat Adjusters +955
Auto Load Leveling[Std on S500,S600] +620
Compact Disc Changer[Std on S600] +590
Dual Air Conditioning[Std on S600] +1030
Headlight Washers[Opt on S320 SWB] +180
Heated Front Seats[Std on S500,S600] +270
Traction Control System[Std on S600] +740
Xenon Headlamps[Std on S500,S600] +500

SL-CLASS 1998

The bargain basement, ha ha, SL320 has been discontinued this year, leaving only the wallet busting SL500 and SL600. The big news is the $10,000 price reduction of the SL500; this car cost only $79,900 when new.

Category J

	Trade-in	Market
2 Dr SL500 Conv	58345	66120
2 Dr SL500 SL1 Sport Conv	61070	69385
2 Dr SL600 Conv	80930	93060
2 Dr SL600 SL1 Sport Conv	84135	96740

OPTIONS FOR SL-CLASS

Adapt Damping System +2395
Removable Panorama Roof +1965
Heated Front Seats[Opt on SL500] +235
Traction Control System +635

SLK230 1998

Mercedes-Benz releases an all-new retractable-hardtop roadster. Powered by a supercharged 2.3-liter engine, which is hooked to a five-speed automatic transmission, the SLK races to 60 mph in just over seven seconds.

Category J

	Trade-in	Market
2 Dr STD Sprchgd Conv	30605	35190

OPTIONS FOR SLK230

Compact Disc Changer +515
Heated Front Seats +235

1997 MERCEDES-BENZ

C-CLASS 1997

The C220 is replaced by a more powerful C230. The C36 gains more horsepower. All C-Class models have redesigned headlamps.

RATINGS (SCALE OF 1-10)

Overall	Safety	Reliability	Performance	Comfort	Value
7.6	7.5	8.8	8.6	8.1	5.2

Category L

	Trade-in	Market
4 Dr C230 Sdn	19805	22815
4 Dr C280 Sdn	22965	26455
4 Dr C36 Sdn	33165	38200

OPTIONS FOR C-CLASS

Bose Sound System[Opt on C230] +250
Cellular Telephone +430
Compact Disc Changer +485
Dual Power Seats[Opt on C230] +355
Leather Seats[Std on C36] +545
Limited Slip Diff +640
Power Moonroof[Std on C36] +425
Sport Suspension +75
Telescopic Steering Whl +80
Traction Control System +605

E-CLASS 1997

The Mercedes-Benz E300D and E320 receive the driver-adaptable five-speed automatic transmission. The E-Class also has a smart sensor to determine if anyone is sitting in the passenger seat and to determine whether or not to deploy the air bag. The E420 can be had with a Sport Package.

RATINGS (SCALE OF 1-10)

Overall	Safety	Reliability	Performance	Comfort	Value
N/A	N/A	8.9	9.4	8.6	5.1

Category L

	Trade-in	Market
4 Dr E300D Dsl Sdn	27120	31240
4 Dr E320 Sdn	30340	34950
4 Dr E420 Sdn	33750	38880

Don't forget to refer to the Mileage Adjustment Table at the back of this book!

MERCEDES-BENZ 97-96

Model Description	Trade-in Value	Market Value	Model Description	Trade-in Value	Market Value

OPTIONS FOR E-CLASS
Option Pkg E4 +655
Sport Pkg E6 +1245
Bose Sound System[Std on E420] +250
Cellular Telephone +430
Chrome Wheels +685
Compact Disc Changer +485
Compact Disc W/fm/tape +280
Leather Seats[Opt on E300D] +545
Limited Slip Diff[Opt on E320] +640
Power Moonroof +425

S-CLASS   1997

It's a big year for the big Benz. After a few years of relatively minor changes, the S-Class gets its share of the fun that has been flying around the Stuttgart design studios. Side impact air bags debut in all S-Class cars this year. S-Class coupes get new front bumpers. All cars get new alloy wheels. A Parktronic system is available for those who aren't comfortable parking their $100,000 car in a narrow space. Mercedes' outstanding Automatic Slip Reduction (ASR) traction control system is finally available on the S320s. Lastly, a rain sensor system is now standard on all models. (It adjusts the speed of the wipers to the intensity of the rain.)

Category L

4 Dr S320 LWB Sdn	38875	44785
4 Dr S320 SWB Sdn	36970	42585
4 Dr S420 Sdn	42060	48450
2 Dr S500 Cpe	52225	60160
4 Dr S500 Sdn	49740	57300
2 Dr S600 Cpe	75600	87085
4 Dr S600 Sdn	73905	85135

OPTIONS FOR S-CLASS
Adapt Damping System +1000
Four Place Power Seating +2435
Parktronic System +430
Power Rear Seat Adjusters +770
Auto Load Leveling[Opt on S320,S420] +505
Traction Control System[Opt on S420,S500] +605

SL-CLASS   1997

A Panorama hardtop is now available, and it helps improve top-up visibility. ASR traction control is now standard on the SL320. A rain sensor is now standard on all models as well.

Category J

2 Dr SL320 Conv	48685	55855
2 Dr SL500 Conv	52940	61035
2 Dr SL500 SL1 Sport Conv	55915	64445
2 Dr SL600 Conv	75155	86225

OPTIONS FOR SL-CLASS
Adapt Damping System +1930
Removable Panorama Roof +1560
SI1 Sport Pkg +2000
Traction Control System[Opt on SL500] +520

1996 MERCEDES-BENZ

C-CLASS   1996

An infrared remote security system, dual cupholders in the console, a delayed headlamp dousing system, and reconfigured option packages mark the changes to the baby Benz.

RATINGS (SCALE OF 1-10)

Overall	Safety	Reliability	Performance	Comfort	Value
7.7	7.4	8.5	8.6	8.1	5.7

Category L

4 Dr C220 Sdn	17435	20125
4 Dr C280 Sdn	20495	23655
4 Dr C36 Sdn	29190	33695

OPTIONS FOR C-CLASS
Bose Sound System[Opt on C220] +205
Cellular Telephone +350
Compact Disc Changer +395
Leather Seats[Std on C36] +445
Limited Slip Diff +525
Power Moonroof[Std on C36] +350
Power Passenger Seat +175
Telescopic Steering Whl[Std on C36] +65
Traction Control System +495

E-CLASS   1996

All-new and sporting a face anybody's mother could love, the E-Class comes in three flavors: E300 Diesel, E320 and E420. A new front suspension and larger wheels and tires provide better handling response, while optional gas-discharge headlamps mark new technology. Side-impact airbags are included in the doors of all E-Class models. E420's can be had with ESP, which is a new safety system that makes sure the E420 is under control at all times. The E420 also gets a new five-speed transmission.

RATINGS (SCALE OF 1-10)

Overall	Safety	Reliability	Performance	Comfort	Value
N/A	N/A	8.6	9.4	8.6	5.1

Category L

4 Dr E300D Dsl Sdn	24940	28790
4 Dr E320 Sdn	27160	31350

OPTIONS FOR E-CLASS
Bose Sound System +205
Cellular Telephone +350
Compact Disc Changer +395

Don't forget to refer to the Mileage Adjustment Table at the back of this book!

Leather Seats[Std on E320] +445
Limited Slip Diff +525
Power Moonroof +350

S-CLASS 1996

No cosmetic improvements to the S-Class this year; everything new is under the skin. ESP is standard on the S600 and optional on V8 models. ESP is a stability control system designed to help the driver keep the S-Class under control at all times. V8 and V12 versions get a new five-speed automatic, and all models get a standard power glass sunroof and smog-sensing climate control system. The S350 Turbodiesel is history.

Category L

Model	Trade-in	Market
4 Dr S320 LWB Sdn	32940	38025
4 Dr S320 SWB Sdn	31355	36195
4 Dr S420 Sdn	35790	41315
2 Dr S500 Cpe	44380	51230
4 Dr S500 Sdn	42040	48525
2 Dr S600 Cpe	64750	74745
4 Dr S600 Sdn	62600	72265

OPTIONS FOR S-CLASS

Adapt Damping System +900
Elect. Stability Program +680
Four Place Power Seating +1730
Rear Axle Level Control +325
Cellular Telephone +350
Power Moonroof +350

SL-CLASS 1996

Tweaked styling and new alloys freshen the exterior of the SL roadster. Underneath, ESP keeps drivers on track in lousy driving conditions. It comes standard on the SL600; can be ordered for the SL320 and SL500. Side airbags are standard across the board. A five-speed automatic is included with SL500 and SL600. Cool gas-discharge headlamps are not available on the SL320.

Category J

Model	Trade-in	Market
2 Dr SL320 Conv	39935	45895
2 Dr SL500 Conv	45510	52300
2 Dr SL600 Conv	61755	70975

OPTIONS FOR SL-CLASS

Adapt Damping System +1530
Slip Control +440
Cellular Telephone +665

1995 MERCEDES-BENZ

C-CLASS 1995

The AMG-prepared C36 is introduced to the C-Class family. This little mighty mouse runs circles around its lesser siblings and gives BMW M3 owners something to think about. Only 300 copies of the C36 are available in 1995; get one if you can.

RATINGS (SCALE OF 1-10)

Overall	Safety	Reliability	Performance	Comfort	Value
7.4	7.5	8.6	8.6	8.1	4.3

Category L

Model	Trade-in	Market
4 Dr C220 Sdn	16005	18540
4 Dr C280 Sdn	18730	21695
4 Dr C36 Sdn	25270	29275

OPTIONS FOR C-CLASS

Option Pkg C1 +490
Bose Sound System[Opt on C220] +165
Leather Seats[Std on C36] +365
Limited Slip Diff +430
Power Moonroof +285
Power Passenger Seat[Opt on C220] +145
Telescopic Steering Whl +55
Traction Control System +405

E-CLASS 1995

No changes for the last year of this rendition of the E-Class.

RATINGS (SCALE OF 1-10)

Overall	Safety	Reliability	Performance	Comfort	Value
N/A	N/A	8.3	8.8	8.4	5

Category L

Model	Trade-in	Market
4 Dr E300D Dsl Sdn	19325	22385
2 Dr E320 Conv	36495	42275
2 Dr E320 Cpe	29580	34260
4 Dr E320 Sdn	20490	23735
4 Dr E320 Wgn	22355	25895
4 Dr E420 Sdn	24685	28595

OPTIONS FOR E-CLASS

Option Pkg E1 +520
Sportline Pkg +325
Cellular Telephone +285
Compact Disc Changer +325
Leather Seats[Opt on E300D, Wgn] +365
Limited Slip Diff +430
Premium Sound System[Std on E420, Cpe] +275
Telescopic Steering Whl[Opt on E300D, Wgn] +55

S-CLASS 1995

Minuscule exterior changes and a drop in price are about the only changes to the S-Class.

Category L

Model	Trade-in	Market
4 Dr S320 LWB Sdn	29655	34355
4 Dr S320 SWB Sdn	28225	32695
4 Dr S350D Turbodsl Sdn	29655	34355
4 Dr S420 Sdn	32350	37475
2 Dr S500 Cpe	40180	46545
4 Dr S500 Sdn	38265	44325

Don't forget to refer to the Mileage Adjustment Table at the back of this book!

Model Description	Trade-in Value	Market Value
2 Dr S600 Cpe	58190	67405
4 Dr S600 Sdn	56885	65890

OPTIONS FOR S-CLASS
Adapt Damping System +770
Four Place Power Seating +1415
Rear Axle Level Control +265
Cellular Telephone +285
Power Moonroof +285

SL-CLASS 1995

Traction control is now standard on the SL320. Price cuts are the only other change for the Mercedes roadster.

Category J

Model Description	Trade-in Value	Market Value
2 Dr SL320 Conv	35455	40775
2 Dr SL500 Conv	40675	46780
2 Dr SL600 Conv	54270	62415

OPTIONS FOR SL-CLASS
Adapt Damping System +1235
Slip Control +490
Cellular Telephone +540

1994 MERCEDES-BENZ

C-CLASS 1994

This peppy replacement for the 190 is long-awaited. Longer and wider than the 190, the C-Class gives rear seat passengers more room. Standard on the C-Class are dual airbags, a wood-trimmed interior, four-wheel antilock brakes and a power sunroof. The C-Class cars are available in four- or six-cylinder flavors with a standard automatic transmission.

RATINGS (SCALE OF 1-10)

Overall	Safety	Reliability	Performance	Comfort	Value
7.8	7.4	8.7	8.6	8.1	6.1

Category L

Model Description	Trade-in Value	Market Value
4 Dr C220 Sdn	14250	16530
4 Dr C280 Sdn	16595	19250

OPTIONS FOR C-CLASS
Leather Seats +295
Limited Slip Diff +350
Power Moonroof +235
Power Passenger Seat[Opt on C220] +115
Premium Sound System +225
Traction Control System +330

E-CLASS 1994

In an effort at simplification, Mercedes renames its 300-Class, now calling it the E-Class. Like the new C-Class, the numeral after the E indicates the engine's size. Pretty cool, huh? Coupe, convertible, sedan and wagon body styles are still offered.

RATINGS (SCALE OF 1-10)

Overall	Safety	Reliability	Performance	Comfort	Value
N/A	N/A	8.3	8.8	8.4	5

Category L

Model Description	Trade-in Value	Market Value
2 Dr E320 Conv	31660	36730
2 Dr E320 Cpe	25665	29780
4 Dr E320 Sdn	17770	20615
4 Dr E320 Wgn	19300	22390
4 Dr E420 Sdn	21285	24695
4 Dr E500 Sdn	33085	38385

OPTIONS FOR E-CLASS
Sportline Pkg +335
Leather Seats[Opt on Wgn] +295
Premium Sound System[Opt on E320 STD Sdn] +225
Sport Suspension +40
Tilt Steering Wheel[Opt on Wgn] +75
Traction Control System[Std on E500] +330

S-CLASS 1994

The big Benz gains Mercedes's new alphanumeric nomenclature that makes it easier to identify the vehicle family and engine size. Fuel economy is improved for the S-Class, and all but the S600 switch to H-rated tires for increased traction in inclement weather.

Category L

Model Description	Trade-in Value	Market Value
4 Dr S320 Sdn	26890	31200
4 Dr S350D Turbodsl Sdn	26890	31200
4 Dr S420 Sdn	30255	35105
2 Dr S500 Cpe	37940	44015
4 Dr S500 Sdn	36235	42040
2 Dr S600 Cpe	50610	58720
4 Dr S600 Sdn	49475	57405

OPTIONS FOR S-CLASS
Adapt Damping System +600
Four Place Seating +1190
Level Control Suspension +210
Rear Power Seatback +255
Cellular Telephone[Opt on S500] +235
Power Sunroof +235
Traction Control System[Opt on S320,S420] +330

SL-CLASS 1994

The 300SL becomes the SL320 as a new powerplant slips into the engine bay. Offering the same horsepower as the previous engine, the SL320 throws out considerably more torque than last year's model. A Bose stereo is added to the standard equipment lists of the entire SL-Class.

Category J

Model Description	Trade-in Value	Market Value
2 Dr SL320 Conv	33390	38480
2 Dr SL500 Conv	38965	44905
2 Dr SL600 Conv	46990	54160

Don't forget to refer to the Mileage Adjustment Table at the back of this book!

Model Description	Trade-in Value	Market Value

OPTIONS FOR SL-CLASS
Adapt Damping System +980
Traction Control System[Opt on SL320] +285

1993 MERCEDES-BENZ

190 — 1993

No changes for the little Mercedes that could; still a good car at a relatively good price. A new model replaces the 190 for 1994.

Category L

Model	Trade-in	Market
4 Dr 190E Sdn	9985	11655
4 Dr 190E 2.6 Sdn	11700	13660

OPTIONS FOR 190
Auto 4-Speed Transmission +180
190E 2.6 Sportline Pkg +310
Cellular Telephone +190
Compact Disc W/fm/tape +125
Dual Power Seats[Opt on STD] +155
Leather Seats +245
Limited Slip Diff +285
Power Sunroof +190
Sport Suspension +35
Traction Control System +270

300 — 1993

All but the turbo models receive a larger engine. A driver airbag is finally standard on the 300-Class Mercedes. A 300 CE cabriolet model is brought into the fold; it has a power top and a pop-up roll bar similar to the one found on the SL-roadsters.

Category L

Model	Trade-in	Market
2 Dr 300CE Conv	26245	30640
2 Dr 300CE Cpe	21590	25200
4 Dr 300D Turbodsl Sdn	15540	18140
4 Dr 300E Sdn	17685	20645
4 Dr 300E 2.8 Sdn	17685	20645
4 Dr 300E 4matic 4WD Sdn	20425	23845
4 Dr 300SD Turbodsl Sdn	23995	28010
4 Dr 300SE Sdn	23995	28010
2 Dr 300SL Conv	28565	33350
4 Dr 300TE Wgn	19270	22495
4 Dr 300TE 4matic 4WD Wgn	21835	25490

OPTIONS FOR 300
Auto 5-Speed Transmission[Opt on 300SL] +220
300E Sportline Pkg +340
Adapt Damping System +625
CE Sportline Pkg +210
Four Place Seating +1030
Power Rear Seat Back +205
Rear Axle Level Cntrl Sus +170
AM/FM Compact Disc Player +180
Cellular Telephone +190

Leather Seats[Opt on 300D,300TE,2.8] +245
Power Moonroof +190
Premium Sound System[Opt on 300D,2.8] +185
Sport Suspension +35
Third Seat +225
Traction Control System +270

400 — 1993

The 400SE becomes the 400SEL in order to compete with the longer wheelbase sedans from BMW.

Category L

Model	Trade-in	Market
4 Dr 400E Sdn	18240	21290
4 Dr 400SEL Sdn	24375	28460

OPTIONS FOR 400
Adapt Damping System +545
Four Place Seating +1030
Power Rear Seat Back +205
Rear Axle Level Cntrl Sus +170
Cellular Telephone +190
Compact Disc Changer +215
Power Moonroof +190
Traction Control System +270

500 — 1993

No changes to 500-Series models.

Category L

Model	Trade-in	Market
4 Dr 500E Sdn	27105	31640
2 Dr 500SEC Cpe	33475	39080
4 Dr 500SEL Sdn	31960	37310
2 Dr 500SL Conv	33340	38920

OPTIONS FOR 500
Adapt Damping System +530
Four Place Seating +1030
Cellular Telephone +190
Power Moonroof +190

600 — 1993

600SEL
Category L

Model	Trade-in	Market
4 Dr STD Sdn	36110	42155

600SL
Category L

Model	Trade-in	Market
2 Dr STD Conv	39400	45360

OPTIONS FOR 600
Four Place Seating +785
Power Sunroof +190

600SEC — 1993

Category L

Model	Trade-in	Market
2 Dr STD Cpe	40580	47375

OPTIONS FOR 600SEC
Four Place Seating +785

MERCEDES-BENZ 92-91

Model Description	Trade-in Value	Market Value	Model Description	Trade-in Value	Market Value

1992 MERCEDES-BENZ

190 — 1992

A sportline package is now available on the six-cylinder 190E 2.6. The package consists of go-fast goodies like V-rated tires, a sport-tuned suspension and quicker steering.

Category L

4 Dr 190E Sdn	8940	10515
4 Dr 190E 2.6 Sdn	10480	12325

OPTIONS FOR 190
Auto 4-Speed Transmission +145
Sportline Pack +205
Auto Load Leveling +185
Dual Power Seats +130
Leather Seats +200
Power Sunroof +155

300 — 1992

Mercedes brings out a new S-Class lineup. The 300SE and 300SD are more powerful and sleeker than their forebears. Safety and comfort have also been improved in these big sedans. The rest of the 300 numbered cars are unchanged.

Category L

2 Dr 300CE Cpe	18035	21215
4 Dr 300D Turbodsl Sdn	12855	15120
4 Dr 300E Sdn	14800	17410
4 Dr 300E 2.6 Sdn	12855	15120
4 Dr 300E 4matic 4WD Sdn	17055	20065
4 Dr 300SD Turbodsl Sdn	19750	23230
4 Dr 300SE Sdn	19750	23230
2 Dr 300SL Conv	23460	27595
4 Dr 300TE Wgn	16105	18945
4 Dr 300TE 4matic 4WD Wgn	18245	21460

OPTIONS FOR 300
Auto 4-Speed Transmission[Opt on 300SL] +165
Adapt Damping System +505
Four Place Seating Pkg +835
Rear Power Seats +165
Sportline Pkg +290
Alarm System[Opt on 300D,300E STD Sdn] +95
Auto Load Leveling[Std on 300TE] +185
Dual Air Bag Restraints[Std on 300SD,300SL] +110
Leather Seats[Opt on 300D,300TE,300E STD Sdn] +200
Power Sunroof +155
Premium Sound System[Opt on 300D,300E STD Sdn] +150
Third Seat +185

400 — 1992

A new model is introduced to the lineup of midsize Mercedes: the 400E. It offers V8 power, a first in this line of cars, and comes standard with an automatic transmission. Dual airbags are now standard on these pricey sedans, as are neat features like traction control, a five-speed automatic transmission, heated front seats, double paned side-windows, and a self-leveling system.

Category L

4 Dr 400E Sdn	16155	19000
4 Dr 400SE Sdn	21470	25255

OPTIONS FOR 400
Adapt Damping System +440
Four Place Seating Pkg +835
Power Seatback Recliner +165
Auto Load Leveling +185
Power Passenger Seat +80
Power Sunroof +155
Traction Control System +220

500 — 1992

A new 500E model is introduced to the Mercedes top-drawer lineup.

Category L

4 Dr 500E Sdn	24655	29005
4 Dr 500SEL Sdn	29090	34215
2 Dr 500SL Conv	30325	35675

OPTIONS FOR 500
Adapt Damping System +485
Four Place Seating +775
Air Bag Restraint[Std on 500E] +180
Cellular Telephone +155
Power Moonroof +155

600 — 1992

600SEL

Category L

4 Dr STD Sdn	30735	36155

OPTIONS FOR 600
Four Place Seating Pkg +635

1991 MERCEDES-BENZ

190 — 1991

A four-cylinder gas powered model is reintroduced to the 190 lineup.

Category L

4 Dr 190E Sdn	8025	9510
4 Dr 190E 2.6 Sdn	9455	11200

OPTIONS FOR 190
Auto 4-Speed Transmission +120
Dual Power Seats[Opt on STD] +105
Leather Seats +160
Limited Slip Diff +190
Power Drivers Seat +65
Power Sunroof +130
Traction Control System +180

Don't forget to refer to the Mileage Adjustment Table at the back of this book!

Model Description	Trade-in Value	Market Value
300		**1991**

No major changes for this recently overhauled Mercedes.

Category L

Model Description	Trade-in Value	Market Value
2 Dr 300CE Cpe	15000	17775
4 Dr 300D Turbodsl Sdn	10750	12735
4 Dr 300E Sdn	12490	14800
4 Dr 300E 2.6 Sdn	10750	12735
4 Dr 300E 4matic 4WD Sdn	14170	16790
4 Dr 300SE Sdn	14105	16710
4 Dr 300SEL Sdn	15115	17910
2 Dr 300SL Conv	18930	22430
4 Dr 300TE Wgn	13390	15865
4 Dr 300TE 4matic 4WD Wgn	15145	17945

OPTIONS FOR 300
Auto 4-Speed Transmission[Opt on 300SL] +135
Adapt Damping System +505
Four Place Seating Pkg +410
Dual Air Bag Restraints[Std on 300SL] +90
Leather Seats[Opt on 300D,2.6,300E STD Sdn] +160
Power Sunroof +130
Premium Sound System[Opt on 300D,2.6,300E
    STD Sdn] +125
Third Seat +150

Model Description	Trade-in Value	Market Value
350		**1991**

No changes.

Category L

Model Description	Trade-in Value	Market Value
4 Dr 350SD Turbodsl Sdn	15230	18050
4 Dr 350SDL Turbodsl Sdn	16325	19345

OPTIONS FOR 350
Four Place Seating Pkg +410
Leather Seats +160
Power Sunroof +130

Model Description	Trade-in Value	Market Value
420		**1991**

No changes.

Category L

Model Description	Trade-in Value	Market Value
4 Dr 420SEL Sdn	14165	16785

OPTIONS FOR 420
Four Place Seating Pkg +410
Power Sunroof +130

Model Description	Trade-in Value	Market Value
500		**1991**

We wait in anticipation as Mercedes readies its new flagship. Unfortunately, there are no major changes in the interim.

Category L

Model Description	Trade-in Value	Market Value
2 Dr 500SL Conv	24850	29445

OPTIONS FOR 500
Adapt Damping System +505

Model Description	Trade-in Value	Market Value
560		**1991**

We wait in anticipation as Mercedes readies its new flagship. Unfortunately, there are no major changes in the interim.

Category L

Model Description	Trade-in Value	Market Value
2 Dr 560SEC Cpe	18245	21615
4 Dr 560SEL Sdn	16535	19590

OPTIONS FOR 560
Four Place Seating Pkg +320

Don't forget to refer to the Mileage Adjustment Table at the back of this book!

MERCURY 00

Model Description	Trade-in Value	Market Value	Model Description	Trade-in Value	Market Value

MERCURY   USA

1995 Mercury Sable

2000 MERCURY

COUGAR   2000

All Cougars receive an emergency trunk release as standard equipment, as well as a redesigned floor console. Citrus Gold, Light Blue, and Light Sapphire are the three new clearcoat metallic paints available.

Category C

	Trade-in	Market
2 Dr I4 Cpe	11975	14030
2 Dr V6 Cpe	12330	14445

OPTIONS FOR COUGAR
Auto 4-Speed Transmission +665
AM/FM Compact Disc Player +285
Cruise Control +180
Keyless Entry System +150
Leather Steering Wheel +80
Power Drivers Seat +245
Rear Spoiler +145
Rear Window Wiper +120

GRAND MARQUIS   2000

The Marquis receives additional safety features, including an emergency trunk release, child seat-anchor brackets, and Mercury's Belt Minder system. The interior gets a new trim color, Dark Charcoal. One new exterior color will be offered, Tropic Green. The handling package's rear-axle ratio changes from 3.27 to 3.55. The Grand Marquis Limited will be offered later in the 2000 model year.

Category B

	Trade-in	Market
4 Dr GS Sdn	16085	18745
4 Dr LS Sdn	17470	20360

OPTIONS FOR GRAND MARQUIS
Aluminum/Alloy Wheels +270
Anti-Lock Brakes +550
Climate Control for AC +140
Dual Power Seats +320
Leather Seats +560

MOUNTAINEER   2000

Mountaineer is uprated with new Premier and Monterey trim packages, which include tan leather upholstery, special paint, upgraded alloy wheels and wood-grain dash trim.

Category H

	Trade-in	Market
4 Dr STD Wgn	19455	22595
4 Dr STD 4WD Wgn	20845	24205

OPTIONS FOR MOUNTAINEER
8 cyl 5.0 L Engine +400
Automatic Dimming Mirror +120
Compact Disc W/fm/tape +255
Dual Power Seats +385
Keyless Entry System +145
Leather Seats +815
Overhead Console +110

MYSTIQUE   2000

The Mystique comes standard with an emergency glow-in-the-dark trunk release, designed to allow a child or adult trapped in the trunk to open it from the inside. Two new exterior colors debut.

Category C

	Trade-in	Market
4 Dr GS Sdn	11210	13135
4 Dr LS Sdn	12075	14150

OPTIONS FOR MYSTIQUE
Auto 4-Speed Transmission +665
Aluminum/Alloy Wheels[Std on LS] +255
Anti-Lock Brakes +485
Rear Spoiler +145

SABLE   2000

The 2000 Mercury Sable gains new sheetmetal and additional refinements. The freshened styling includes a raised hood and decklid, a larger grille, improved headlamps and taillights, and new mirrors. The instrument panel has been updated, and the new integrated control panel provides better functionality. The Sable also gains significant improvements to its safety and powertrain components.

Category C

	Trade-in	Market
4 Dr GS Sdn	13685	16035
4 Dr GS Wgn	14945	17510
4 Dr LS Sdn	14455	16935
4 Dr LS Premium Sdn	15365	18005
4 Dr LS Premium Wgn	16135	18905

Don't forget to refer to the Mileage Adjustment Table at the back of this book!

MERCURY 00-99

Model Description	Trade-in Value	Market Value	Model Description	Trade-in Value	Market Value

OPTIONS FOR SABLE
6 cyl 3.0 L DOHC Engine[Opt on LS,Wgn] +545
Anti-Lock Brakes +485
Power Drivers Seat[Opt on GS] +245

VILLAGER   2000

The convenience, comfort, and luxury option packages have been simplified. All 2000 Villagers meet federal low-emission vehicle status and come standard with a child seat-anchor system. A new rear-seat video entertainment system is now optional.

Category G

2 Dr Estate Pass. Van	19445	22565
2 Dr STD Pass. Van	16165	18755
2 Dr Sport Pass. Van	18260	21190

OPTIONS FOR VILLAGER
Entertainment System +1060
Anti-Lock Brakes +475
Dual Air Conditioning[Opt on STD] +755
Overhead Console[Opt on STD] +130
Power Drivers Seat[Opt on STD] +230
Privacy Glass[Opt on STD] +225

1999 MERCURY

COUGAR   1999

Mercury reintroduces the Cougar this year after a one-year hiatus that saw the departure of most of Ford Motor Co.'s personal coupes. The new model is built on the Mondeo global platform that is also the basis for the Ford Contour and Mercury Mystique. This new coupe is powered by the same engine choices as the Contour/Mystique, which means that buyers can choose between a zippy Zetec four-cylinder and a high-revving Duratec V6.

RATINGS (SCALE OF 1-10)

Overall	Safety	Reliability	Performance	Comfort	Value
N/A	N/A	8.4	7.2	7.1	N/A

Category C

2 Dr I4 Cpe	11010	13010
2 Dr V6 Cpe	11340	13395

OPTIONS FOR COUGAR
Auto 4-Speed Transmission +545
AM/FM Compact Disc Player +235
Anti-Lock Brakes +395
Cruise Control +145
Keyless Entry System +125
Leather Seats +415
Power Drivers Seat +200
Traction Control System +140

GRAND MARQUIS   1999

Not much. This traditional American sedan got a revised rear suspension and exterior styling last year. This year all it gets are some new color options.

RATINGS (SCALE OF 1-10)

Overall	Safety	Reliability	Performance	Comfort	Value
N/A	8.3	8.7	7.6	8.3	N/A

Category B

4 Dr GS Sdn	14490	16975
4 Dr LS Sdn	15755	18450

OPTIONS FOR GRAND MARQUIS
AM/FM Compact Disc Player +220
Aluminum/Alloy Wheels +220
Anti-Lock Brakes +450
Dual Power Seats +260
Keyless Entry System[Std on LS] +120
Leather Seats +460
Traction Control System +115

MOUNTAINEER   1999

For '99 the Mountaineer gets optional rear load leveling and a reverse parking aid. It also receives a new seat design.

RATINGS (SCALE OF 1-10)

Overall	Safety	Reliability	Performance	Comfort	Value
N/A	N/A	N/A	7.4	7.3	N/A

Category H

4 Dr STD Wgn	18290	21315
4 Dr STD 4WD Wgn	19675	22930

OPTIONS FOR MOUNTAINEER
8 cyl 5.0 L Engine +330
Alarm System +130
Chrome Wheels +200
Climate Control for AC +300
Compact Disc W/fm/tape +210
Dual Power Seats +315
Keyless Entry System +115
Leather Seats +670
Power Drivers Seat +190
Power Moonroof +650

MYSTIQUE   1999

The Mystique gets a revised instrument panel and redesigned front seats this year. A six-way power adjustable seat is now standard on the LS model and all Mystiques benefit from a revised suspension and larger fuel tank. Medium Steel Blue replaces Light Denim Blue as an exterior color. A final note to family-oriented shoppers: the optional integrated child safety seat is no longer available.

Model Description	Trade-in Value	Market Value

RATINGS (SCALE OF 1-10)

Overall	Safety	Reliability	Performance	Comfort	Value
N/A	6.9	7.5	N/A	N/A	N/A

Category C

4 Dr GS Sdn	10285	12150
4 Dr LS Sdn	11045	13050

OPTIONS FOR MYSTIQUE

Auto 4-Speed Transmission +545
AM/FM Compact Disc Player +235
Aluminum/Alloy Wheels[Std on LS] +205
Anti-Lock Brakes +395
Keyless Entry System[Std on LS] +125
Power Drivers Seat[Std on LS] +200
Power Moonroof +460

SABLE   1999

Still smarting from that 1996 "redesign" that had many longtime Sable fans running to the competition, Mercury performed some minor cosmetic surgery in '98 to help soften the Sable's front end. This year's changes are limited to new wheel designs, a revised gauge cluster and interior console, as well as suspension alterations designed to improve overall ride quality. The particulate filtration system has been deleted from this year's models.

RATINGS (SCALE OF 1-10)

Overall	Safety	Reliability	Performance	Comfort	Value
N/A	7.8	7.9	7.8	8.1	N/A

Category C

4 Dr GS Sdn	11855	14005
4 Dr LS Sdn	12475	14745
4 Dr LS Wgn	13160	15550

OPTIONS FOR SABLE

6 cyl 3.0 L DOHC Engine +350
Aluminum/Alloy Wheels[Std on LS] +205
Anti-Lock Brakes +395
Climate Control for AC +110
Compact Disc Changer +315
Dual Power Seats +390
Keyless Entry System[Std on LS] +125
Leather Seats +415
Power Drivers Seat[Std on LS] +200
Power Moonroof +460

TRACER   1999

The Tracer gets a new sport wagon model to help extend its appeal to young buyers. The LS Sport Wagon model comes standard with leather seating surfaces and 15-inch wheels. Other changes include a standard interior trunk release on all sedans. A remote, keyless entry and AM/FM cassette player is standard on LS models.

RATINGS (SCALE OF 1-10)

Overall	Safety	Reliability	Performance	Comfort	Value
N/A	6.3	8.6	6.6	7.3	N/A

Category E

4 Dr GS Sdn	7385	8865
4 Dr LS Sdn	8335	10000
4 Dr LS Wgn	9075	10890

OPTIONS FOR TRACER

Auto 4-Speed Transmission +545
AM/FM Stereo Tape[Std on LS] +200
Air Conditioning[Std on LS] +555
Aluminum/Alloy Wheels +225
Anti-Lock Brakes +445
Cruise Control +155
Keyless Entry System[Std on LS] +110
Power Door Locks +165
Power Mirrors[Std on LS] +75
Power Windows +180
Tilt Steering Wheel +100

VILLAGER   1999

The Mercury Villager is completely redesigned for '99. Improvements range from a more powerful engine to a larger interior to a second sliding door on the driver's side. New styling features include larger headlights and a distinctive front grille. Inside, ergonomics have been addressed with easier to reach controls and an innovative storage shelf located behind the third seat.

RATINGS (SCALE OF 1-10)

Overall	Safety	Reliability	Performance	Comfort	Value
N/A	N/A	8.6	6.8	7.4	N/A

Category G

2 Dr Estate Pass. Van	17170	20040
2 Dr STD Pass. Van	14440	17035
2 Dr Sport Pass. Van	17170	20040

OPTIONS FOR VILLAGER

Aluminum/Alloy Wheels[Opt on STD] +215
Anti-Lock Brakes +390
Climate Control for AC +130
Compact Disc W/fm/tape +295
Dual Air Conditioning +615
Dual Power Seats +280
Keyless Entry System +130
Leather Seats +525
Power Drivers Seat +190
Power Moonroof +580
Privacy Glass +185

1998 MERCURY

GRAND MARQUIS   1998

Vive le Grand Marquis! The last of the American rear-drive sedans gets substantial improvements this year,

---

Don't forget to refer to the Mileage Adjustment Table at the back of this book!

MERCURY 98

Model Description	Trade-in Value	Market Value	Model Description	Trade-in Value	Market Value

including a new instrument panel, new steering gear and an improved ride, thanks to a Watt's linkage suspension. All-speed traction control debuts this year as well.

RATINGS (SCALE OF 1-10)

Overall	Safety	Reliability	Performance	Comfort	Value
8.2	8.3	8.5	7.6	8.3	8.4

Category B

4 Dr GS Sdn	13375	15710
4 Dr LS Sdn	14555	17100

OPTIONS FOR GRAND MARQUIS

AM/FM Compact Disc Player +180
Aluminum/Alloy Wheels +180
Anti-Lock Brakes +365
Climate Control for AC +90
Dual Power Seats +210
Keyless Entry System[Opt on GS] +95
Leather Seats +375
Traction Control System +95

MOUNTAINEER   1998

The Mountaineer gets minor front and rear styling tweaks as it enters its second year of production. In addition, a new model, with full-time four-wheel drive, receives the SOHC V6 and five-speed automatic transmission that became available on the Explorer last year.

RATINGS (SCALE OF 1-10)

Overall	Safety	Reliability	Performance	Comfort	Value
N/A	N/A	8.4	6.6	7.3	8.2

Category H

4 Dr STD Wgn	16825	19665
4 Dr STD 4WD Wgn	18060	21110

OPTIONS FOR MOUNTAINEER

8 cyl 5.0 L Engine +270
Chrome Wheels +165
Climate Control for AC +245
Compact Disc Changer +245
Compact Disc W/fm/tape +170
Dual Power Seats +255
Keyless Entry System +95
Leather Seats +545
Power Drivers Seat +155
Power Moonroof +530
Running Boards +190

MYSTIQUE   1998

The 1998 Mystique receives a freshened interior and exterior that includes new wheels and a new front end. Mechanical enhancements include 100,000-mile maintenance intervals for the 2.0-liter Zetec engine, improved manual transmission shifter feel, improved NVH and improved air conditioning performance. New

interior pieces are intended to distinguish the Mystique from its otherwise-identical twin, the Ford Contour.

RATINGS (SCALE OF 1-10)

Overall	Safety	Reliability	Performance	Comfort	Value
7.4	6.7	6.7	8.2	7.9	7.5

Category C

4 Dr GS Sdn	9020	10835
4 Dr LS Sdn	9785	11760

OPTIONS FOR MYSTIQUE

Auto 4-Speed Transmission +445
AM/FM Compact Disc Player +190
Aluminum/Alloy Wheels[Opt on GS] +170
Anti-Lock Brakes +325
Keyless Entry System[Opt on GS] +100
Leather Seats +340
Power Drivers Seat[Opt on GS] +165
Power Moonroof +375

SABLE   1998

A mild facelift and fewer options are the only change to Mercury's mid-size sedan.

RATINGS (SCALE OF 1-10)

Overall	Safety	Reliability	Performance	Comfort	Value
8.1	7.9	8.1	7.8	8.1	8.6

Category C

4 Dr GS Sdn	10755	12920
4 Dr LS Sdn	11315	13595
4 Dr LS Wgn	12330	14815

OPTIONS FOR SABLE

6 cyl 3.0 L DOHC Engine +270
Aluminum/Alloy Wheels[Opt on GS] +170
Anti-Lock Brakes +325
Chrome Wheels +330
Climate Control for AC +90
Compact Disc Changer +255
Dual Power Seats +315
Heated Power Mirrors +55
Keyless Entry System[Opt on GS] +100
Leather Seats +340
Power Drivers Seat[Opt on GS] +165
Power Moonroof +375

TRACER   1998

No changes to Mercury's recently redesigned entry-level car.

RATINGS (SCALE OF 1-10)

Overall	Safety	Reliability	Performance	Comfort	Value
7.4	6.3	8.5	6.6	7.3	8.2

Category E

4 Dr GS Sdn	6715	8115
4 Dr LS Sdn	7480	9040
4 Dr LS Wgn	8320	10055

Don't forget to refer to the Mileage Adjustment Table at the back of this book!

MERCURY 98-97

Model Description	Trade-in Value	Market Value	Model Description	Trade-in Value	Market Value

OPTIONS FOR TRACER

Auto 4-Speed Transmission +445
Air Conditioning[Opt on GS] +455
Aluminum/Alloy Wheels +185
Anti-Lock Brakes +365
Cruise Control +125
Keyless Entry System[Opt on GS] +90
Power Door Locks +135
Power Mirrors[Opt on GS] +60
Power Windows +145
Rear Window Defroster[Opt on GS] +90
Tilt Steering Wheel +80

VILLAGER   1998

No changes to the 1998 Villager as Mercury readies a replacement.

RATINGS (SCALE OF 1-10)

Overall	Safety	Reliability	Performance	Comfort	Value
7.7	7.3	8.2	6.8	7.5	8.7

Category G

2 Dr GS Cargo Van	12795	15015
2 Dr GS Pass. Van	13015	15270
2 Dr LS Pass. Van	15445	18125
2 Dr Nautica Pass. Van	16545	19415

OPTIONS FOR VILLAGER

7 Passenger Seating[Opt on GS] +285
Air Conditioning[Opt on GS] +450
Aluminum/Alloy Wheels[Opt on GS, LS] +175
Anti-Lock Brakes[Opt on GS] +320
Climate Control for AC +105
Compact Disc W/fm/tape +240
Cruise Control +115
Dual Air Conditioning +505
Dual Power Seats +230
Keyless Entry System +105
Leather Seats[Opt on LS] +430
Power Door Locks[Opt on GS] +130
Power Drivers Seat +155
Power Mirrors[Opt on GS] +70
Power Moonroof +475
Power Windows[Opt on GS] +135
Premium Sound System +185
Privacy Glass[Opt on GS] +150
Rear Window Defroster[Opt on GS] +95

1997 MERCURY

COUGAR XR7   1997

Mercury gives you the chance to buy a special anniversary edition replete with plenty of badges, a special interior and a few luxury doo-dads.

RATINGS (SCALE OF 1-10)

Overall	Safety	Reliability	Performance	Comfort	Value
7.6	7.9	8.2	8	7.8	6.3

Category C

2 Dr XR7 Cpe	9060	10890

OPTIONS FOR COUGAR XR7

8 cyl 4.6 L Engine +330
AM/FM Compact Disc Player +155
Aluminum/Alloy Wheels +140
Anti-Lock Brakes +265
Cruise Control +95
Dual Power Seats +260
Keyless Entry System +85
Power Door Locks +115
Power Drivers Seat +135
Power Moonroof +305
Premium Sound System +170
Sport Suspension +95
Traction Control System +95

GRAND MARQUIS   1997

After a mild facelift last year, the Grand Marquis soldiers on with a few color changes, improved power steering and the addition of rear air suspension to the handling package.

RATINGS (SCALE OF 1-10)

Overall	Safety	Reliability	Performance	Comfort	Value
8	7.9	7.7	7.6	8.3	8.3

Category B

4 Dr GS Sdn	11555	13690
4 Dr LS Sdn	12225	14480

OPTIONS FOR GRAND MARQUIS

Aluminum/Alloy Wheels +150
Anti-Lock Brakes +300
Cruise Control +100
Keyless Entry System +80
Leather Seats +305
Power Door Locks +115
Premium Sound System +165
Traction Control System +80
Trip Computer +175

MOUNTAINEER   1997

The all-new Mercury Mountaineer is yet another entrant into the booming luxury sport-utility market. Based on the wildly successful Ford Explorer, the Mountaineer is intended to appeal to outdoor sophisticates rather than true roughnecks. Distinguishing characteristics of the Mountaineer include four-wheel antilock brakes, a pushrod V8 engine and optional all-wheel drive.

RATINGS (SCALE OF 1-10)

Overall	Safety	Reliability	Performance	Comfort	Value
N/A	N/A.	8	7.6	7.3	8.6

Model Description	Trade-in Value	Market Value
Category H		
4 Dr STD Wgn	15055	17695
4 Dr STD 4WD Wgn	16135	18970

OPTIONS FOR MOUNTAINEER
Camper/Towing Package +150
Child Seat (1) +90
Compact Disc Changer +200
Compact Disc W/fm/tape +140
Keyless Entry System +80
Leather Seats +445
Luggage Rack +70
Power Drivers Seat +125
Power Moonroof +435
Running Boards +155

MYSTIQUE 1997

The addition of a Spree Package for the GS model and the inclusion of a tilt steering wheel and standard trunk light are the only changes for the 1997 Mystique.

RATINGS (SCALE OF 1-10)

Overall	Safety	Reliability	Performance	Comfort	Value
7.5	6.8	7.1	8.2	7.9	7.4

Model	Trade-in	Market
Category C		
4 Dr GS Sdn	7355	8840
4 Dr LS Sdn	8015	9630
4 Dr STD Sdn	6960	8370

OPTIONS FOR MYSTIQUE
6 cyl 2.5 L Engine +405
Auto 4-Speed Transmission +365
AM/FM Compact Disc Player +155
AM/FM Stereo Tape[Std on LS] +75
Air Conditioning +365
Aluminum/Alloy Wheels[Opt on GS] +140
Anti-Lock Brakes +265
Cruise Control +95
Keyless Entry System +85
Leather Seats +275
Power Door Locks +115
Power Drivers Seat[Opt on GS] +135
Power Moonroof +305
Power Windows +140
Premium Sound System +170

SABLE 1997

The 1997 Sable LS can now be had with Ford's outstanding Mach audio system. Other changes, occurring at the end of the 1996 model year, include the addition of a mass airflow sensor to the Vulcan V6, and improvements to the Duratec V6 to improve responsiveness.

RATINGS (SCALE OF 1-10)

Overall	Safety	Reliability	Performance	Comfort	Value
8	7.8	7.5	7.8	8.1	9

Model	Trade-in	Market
Category C		
4 Dr GS Sdn	9635	11580
4 Dr GS Wgn	9635	11580
4 Dr LS Sdn	10870	13070
4 Dr LS Wgn	10870	13070

OPTIONS FOR SABLE
Leather Bucket Seats +440
AM/FM Stereo Tape[Opt on GS] +75
Aluminum/Alloy Wheels[Opt on GS] +140
Anti-Lock Brakes +265
Child Seat (1) +55
Chrome Wheels +270
Compact Disc Changer +210
Cruise Control +95
Keyless Entry System +85
Leather Seats[Opt on GS] +275
Power Door Locks[Opt on GS] +115
Power Moonroof +305

TRACER 1997

The Mercury Tracer is totally redesigned this year with enhancements across the board. The most noticeable improvements are in the powertrain and in the ride quality. New sheetmetal gives the Tracer a rounder, more aerodynamic appearance as well. The speedy LTS sedan is discontinued.

RATINGS (SCALE OF 1-10)

Overall	Safety	Reliability	Performance	Comfort	Value
7	6.3	8.3	7.2	7.3	6.1

Model	Trade-in	Market
Category E		
4 Dr GS Sdn	5600	6885
4 Dr LS Sdn	5990	7365
4 Dr LS Wgn	6335	7790

OPTIONS FOR TRACER
Auto 4-Speed Transmission +340
AM/FM Stereo Tape +135
Air Conditioning +370
Aluminum/Alloy Wheels +150
Anti-Lock Brakes +295
Child Seat (1) +50
Compact Disc Changer +215
Cruise Control +100
Keyless Entry System +75
Power Door Locks +110
Power Windows +120

VILLAGER 1997

For 1997, the Villager offers a few more luxury items to distinguish it from the Nissan Quest. Quad captain's chairs are a nice alternative to the middle-row bench, and the addition of rear radio controls and rear air conditioning should also make rear seat passengers happy.

Model Description	Trade-in Value	Market Value	Model Description	Trade-in Value	Market Value

RATINGS (SCALE OF 1-10)

Overall	Safety	Reliability	Performance	Comfort	Value
7.4	7.2	7.6	6.8	7.5	8.1

Category G

	Trade-in	Market
2 Dr GS Cargo Van	11065	13065
2 Dr GS Pass. Van	11205	13225
2 Dr LS Pass. Van	13590	16040
2 Dr Nautica Pass. Van	14560	17185

OPTIONS FOR VILLAGER

7 Passenger Seating[Opt on GS] +235
Air Conditioning[Opt on GS Cargo Van] +365
Aluminum/Alloy Wheels[Opt on GS] +145
Anti-Lock Brakes[Opt on GS] +260
Captain Chairs (4)[Opt on LS] +275
Child Seats (2) +115
Compact Disc W/fm/tape +200
Cruise Control +95
Dual Air Conditioning +410
Dual Power Seats +185
Keyless Entry System +85
Leather Seats[Opt on LS] +350
Luggage Rack[Opt on GS] +70
Power Door Locks[Opt on GS Cargo Van] +105
Power Drivers Seat +125
Power Moonroof +385
Power Windows[Opt on GS Cargo Van] +110
Premium Sound System +155

1996 MERCURY

COUGAR   1996

New styling and powertrain improvements highlight the 1996 Cougar. Some formerly standard equipment is now optional. New options include a revamped cruise control system and a Total Anti-theft System. Four new colors debut.

RATINGS (SCALE OF 1-10)

Overall	Safety	Reliability	Performance	Comfort	Value
N/A	7.9	7.9	8	N/A	6.6

Category C

	Trade-in	Market
2 Dr XR7 Cpe	7495	9195

OPTIONS FOR COUGAR

AM/FM Compact Disc Player +130
Anti-Lock Brakes +215
Chrome Wheels +220
Cruise Control +80
Keyless Entry System +70
Leather Seats +225
Power Door Locks +95
Power Drivers Seat +110
Power Moonroof +250
Power Passenger Seat +105
Premium Sound System +140
Traction Control System +80

GRAND MARQUIS   1996

This distant descendant of the Turnpike Cruiser gets engine and transmission upgrades, a new steering wheel and a new gas cap design. Passenger power lumbar support has been deleted.

RATINGS (SCALE OF 1-10)

Overall	Safety	Reliability	Performance	Comfort	Value
7.8	7.7	6.9	7.6	8.3	8.7

Category B

	Trade-in	Market
4 Dr GS Sdn	9605	11515
4 Dr LS Sdn	10115	12130

OPTIONS FOR GRAND MARQUIS

Anti-Lock Brakes +245
Cruise Control +80
Keyless Entry System +65
Leather Steering Wheel +30
Power Door Locks +95
Power Passenger Seat +130
Premium Sound System +135

MYSTIQUE   1996

More rear seat room is the big story for Mystique in 1996. Gearshift effort has been improved on manual transmissions, a new Sport Appearance Package is available, and five new colors are on the palette. Alloy wheels have been restyled on LS models.

RATINGS (SCALE OF 1-10)

Overall	Safety	Reliability	Performance	Comfort	Value
7.2	6.8	6.5	8.2	7.9	6.8

Category C

	Trade-in	Market
4 Dr GS Sdn	6030	7395
4 Dr LS Sdn	6585	8080

OPTIONS FOR MYSTIQUE

6 cyl 2.5 L Engine +365
Auto 4-Speed Transmission +285
AM/FM Compact Disc Player +130
Air Conditioning +295
Anti-Lock Brakes +215
Cruise Control +80
Keyless Entry System +70
Leather Seats +225
Power Antenna[Opt on GS] +30
Power Door Locks +95
Power Drivers Seat[Opt on GS] +110
Power Moonroof +250
Power Windows +115

SABLE   1996

Fresh off the drawing boards for 1996, and it seems the drawing boards were poorly lit. Styling is heavy-handed and homely, but definitely not dull. Otherwise, the new Sable is an excellent car, powered by new engines, suspended by new components, and innovative in nearly every way. Longer and wider sedan and wagon bodystyles are offered in GS and LS trim.

RATINGS (SCALE OF 1-10)

Overall	Safety	Reliability	Performance	Comfort	Value
7.8	7.7	6.5	7.8	8.1	8.8

Category C
4 Dr G Sdn	7710	9455
4 Dr GS Sdn	7965	9770
4 Dr GS Wgn	8380	10280
4 Dr LS Sdn	8905	10920
4 Dr LS Wgn	9335	11450

OPTIONS FOR SABLE
Preferred Equipment Pkg +265
AM/FM Stereo Tape[Std on LS] +60
Anti-Lock Brakes +215
Child Seat (1) +45
Chrome Wheels +220
Compact Disc Changer +170
Cruise Control +80
Keyless Entry System +70
Leather Seats +225
Power Door Locks[Opt on GS] +95
Power Drivers Seat[Opt on GS] +110
Power Moonroof +250

TRACER 1996

Automatic transmission modifications make base Tracers more responsive, and the standard 1.9-liter engine now goes 100,000 miles between tune-ups. Last year's integrated child seat continues, and Trio models are now available in all colors, including a new one called Toreador Red.

RATINGS (SCALE OF 1-10)

Overall	Safety	Reliability	Performance	Comfort	Value
7.2	6.8	8.3	7.6	7.1	6.4

Category E
4 Dr LTS Sdn	5110	6530
4 Dr STD Sdn	4430	5660
4 Dr STD Wgn	4620	5910

OPTIONS FOR TRACER
Auto 4-Speed Transmission +285
AM/FM Compact Disc Player +160
Air Conditioning +305
Anti-Lock Brakes +245
Child Seat (1) +40
Cruise Control[Opt on STD] +85
Luggage Rack +45
Power Door Locks +90
Power Moonroof +215
Power Windows +95

VILLAGER 1996

A passenger-side airbag is installed in a redesigned dashboard for 1996, and fresh front and rear styling updates this versatile van. Villager also gets an optional integrated child seat, automatic climate control system, and remote keyless entry system. Substantial trim and functional changes make Villager competitive once again.

RATINGS (SCALE OF 1-10)

Overall	Safety	Reliability	Performance	Comfort	Value
7.3	7	6.8	6.8	7.5	8.5

Category G
2 Dr GS Cargo Van	9405	11200
2 Dr GS Pass. Van	9670	11515
2 Dr LS Pass. Van	11430	13615
2 Dr Nautica Pass. Van	12390	14755

OPTIONS FOR VILLAGER
7 Passenger Seating[Opt on GS] +190
Air Conditioning[Opt on GS Cargo Van] +300
Captain Chairs (4)[Opt on LS] +225
Child Seats (2) +90
Compact Disc W/fm/tape +160
Cruise Control +75
Dual Air Conditioning +335
Keyless Entry System +70
Leather Seats[Opt on LS] +285
Luggage Rack[Opt on GS] +60
Power Door Locks[Opt on GS Cargo Van] +85
Power Drivers Seat +105
Power Moonroof +315
Power Passenger Seat +75
Power Windows[Opt on GS Cargo Van] +90
Premium Sound System +125

1995 MERCURY

COUGAR 1995

A Sport Appearance Package is offered to spruce up the Cougar with BBS wheels and a luggage rack. Unfortunately, the trunk-mounted CD-changer is deleted from the option list. Antilock brakes and a traction-lock axle are available as separate options for the first time this year.

RATINGS (SCALE OF 1-10)

Overall	Safety	Reliability	Performance	Comfort	Value
N/A	8.7	7.3	8	N/A	7.1

Category C
2 Dr XR7 Cpe	6005	7570

OPTIONS FOR COUGAR
8 cyl 4.6 L Engine +185
AM/FM Compact Disc Player +105
Anti-Lock Brakes +175

Don't forget to refer to the Mileage Adjustment Table at the back of this book!

Model Description	Trade-in Value	Market Value	Model Description	Trade-in Value	Market Value

Climate Control for AC +50
Cruise Control +65
Keyless Entry System +55
Leather Seats +185
Power Door Locks +75
Power Drivers Seat +90
Power Moonroof +205
Power Passenger Seat +85
Premium Sound System +115

GRAND MARQUIS   1995

Updated styling and an increased number of convenience features improve upon last year's model. A battery saver shuts off power to accessories or lights 10 minutes after the ignition is switched off. The mast antenna has been replaced by an integrated rear window antenna. Interior updates include a 12-volt outlet in a redesigned dashboard. Enlarged stereo controls improve ease of operation and bigger gauges improve the instrument panel.

RATINGS (SCALE OF 1-10)

Overall	Safety	Reliability	Performance	Comfort	Value
7.6	8.1	5.4	7.6	8.3	8.7

Category B

				Trade-in	Market
4 Dr GS Sdn				7800	9535
4 Dr LS Sdn				8155	9975

OPTIONS FOR GRAND MARQUIS

Anti-Lock Brakes +200
Climate Control for AC +50
Cruise Control +65
Keyless Entry System +50
Leather Seats +205
Power Door Locks +80
Power Passenger Seat +110
Power Sunroof +320
Premium Sound System +110

MYSTIQUE   1995

Introduced to replace the aging Topaz, the Mystique is a virtual twin to the Ford Contour. Euro-styling combined with German engineering results in a $20,000 American car that can compete with import sedans that cost nearly twice as much. You may choose between two trim levels, the base GS or the more luxurious LS. A 170-horsepower V6 engine is optional.

RATINGS (SCALE OF 1-10)

Overall	Safety	Reliability	Performance	Comfort	Value
7.1	7	5.3	8.2	7.9	7.2

Category C

				Trade-in	Market
4 Dr GS Sdn				4825	6080
4 Dr LS Sdn				5285	6660

OPTIONS FOR MYSTIQUE

6 cyl 2.5 L Engine +290
Auto 4-Speed Transmission +245
AM/FM Compact Disc Player +105
Air Conditioning +245
Anti-Lock Brakes +175
Cruise Control +65
Keyless Entry System +55
Leather Seats +185
Power Door Locks +75
Power Drivers Seat[Opt on GS] +90
Power Moonroof +205
Power Windows +95
Premium Sound System +115

SABLE   1995

Last year for the Sable in its current form. New cylinder heads and crankshafts are intended to decrease engine noise by reducing vibration. Solar control window glass makes a brief appearance on the sedan and wagon.

RATINGS (SCALE OF 1-10)

Overall	Safety	Reliability	Performance	Comfort	Value
7.9	7.4	7.4	8	7.8	8.7

Category C

				Trade-in	Market
4 Dr GS Sdn				6165	7765
4 Dr GS Wgn				6540	8245
4 Dr LS Sdn				6905	8705
4 Dr LS Wgn				7275	9165

OPTIONS FOR SABLE

6 cyl 3.8 L Engine +190
AM/FM Compact Disc Player +105
Anti-Lock Brakes[Opt on GS] +175
Chrome Wheels +180
Cruise Control +65
Dual Power Seats +175
Keyless Entry System +55
Leather Seats +185
Power Door Locks[Opt on GS] +75
Power Moonroof +205
Power Windows[Opt on GS] +95

TRACER   1995

A passenger airbag is finally available for the Tracer. Unfortunately, some engineering genius decided to retain the annoying motorized shoulder belts. An integrated child seat is introduced as an optional safety feature. The Trio package is introduced, designed to give budget shoppers the option of purchasing some of the more popular LTS features such as the spoiler, aluminum wheels and leather-wrapped steering wheel.

RATINGS (SCALE OF 1-10)

Overall	Safety	Reliability	Performance	Comfort	Value
7.2	7.2	7.7	7.6	7.1	6.4

Model Description	Trade-in Value	Market Value
Category E		
4 Dr LTS Sdn	4265	5790
4 Dr STD Sdn	3645	4950
4 Dr STD Wgn	3810	5175

OPTIONS FOR TRACER
Auto 4-Speed Transmission +245
AM/FM Compact Disc Player +130
Air Conditioning +250
Anti-Lock Brakes +200
Child Seat (1) +35
Cruise Control[Opt on STD] +70
Luggage Rack +40
Power Door Locks +75
Power Moonroof +175
Power Windows +80

VILLAGER   1995

No changes for the Villager.

RATINGS (SCALE OF 1-10)

Overall	Safety	Reliability	Performance	Comfort	Value
7.2	7	6	6.8	7.1	9

Model Description	Trade-in Value	Market Value
Category G		
2 Dr GS Cargo Van	7625	9200
2 Dr GS Pass. Van	7870	9490
2 Dr LS Pass. Van	9430	11375
2 Dr Nautica Pass. Van	10000	12060

OPTIONS FOR VILLAGER
Supersound System +260
7 Passenger Seating[Opt on GS] +155
Air Conditioning +245
Captain Chairs (4)[Opt on LS] +185
Compact Disc W/fm/tape +130
Cruise Control +65
Keyless Entry System +60
Leather Seats[Opt on LS] +235
Luggage Rack[Opt on GS] +50
Power Door Locks +70
Power Drivers Seat +85
Power Moonroof +260
Power Passenger Seat +60
Power Windows +70
Premium Sound System +100

1994 MERCURY

CAPRI   1994

A passenger airbag is added. A new suspension on the XR2 improves handling. Both trim levels get a freshened exterior. Slow sales make this the final year for this car.

Model Description	Trade-in Value	Market Value
Category F		
2 Dr STD Conv	4495	5725
2 Dr XR2 Turbo Conv	5065	6450

OPTIONS FOR CAPRI
Auto 4-Speed Transmission +195
AM/FM Stereo Tape[Opt on STD] +55
Air Conditioning +205
Aluminum/Alloy Wheels +75
Cruise Control +55
Leather Seats +155
Power Door Locks +50

COUGAR   1994

Dual airbags are finally available on the Cougar. The standard four-speed automatic transmission gains electronic shift controls and an overdrive lockout switch. Optional traction control joins the lineup of safety features. Updated front and rear fascias, taillamps and headlights round out the changes.

RATINGS (SCALE OF 1-10)

Overall	Safety	Reliability	Performance	Comfort	Value
N/A	8.7	7.6	8	N/A	7.5

Model Description	Trade-in Value	Market Value
Category C		
2 Dr XR7 Cpe	4730	6225

OPTIONS FOR COUGAR
8 cyl 4.6 L Engine +140
Aluminum/Alloy Wheels +75
Anti-Lock Brakes +145
Climate Control for AC +40
Compact Disc Changer +115
Cruise Control +55
Keyless Entry System +45
Leather Seats +150
Power Door Locks +60
Power Drivers Seat +75
Power Moonroof +165
Power Passenger Seat +70
Premium Sound System +95
Traction Control System +50

GRAND MARQUIS   1994

The Grand Marquis passes the stringent 1997 side-impact standards this year. Wire-spoke wheelcovers are now part of the standard equipment package.

RATINGS (SCALE OF 1-10)

Overall	Safety	Reliability	Performance	Comfort	Value
7.8	7.8	6.9	7.6	8.3	8.6

Model Description	Trade-in Value	Market Value
Category B		
4 Dr GS Sdn	6255	7800
4 Dr LS Sdn	6440	8030

OPTIONS FOR GRAND MARQUIS
Anti-Lock Brakes +165
Cruise Control +55

MERCURY 94

Model Description	Trade-in Value	Market Value	Model Description	Trade-in Value	Market Value

Keyless Entry System +45
Leather Seats +165
Power Door Locks +65
Power Passenger Seat +90
Premium Sound System +90
Rear Window Defroster +40
Traction Control System +45

SABLE   1994

Rear window defroster becomes standard equipment on the sedan and wagon. The wagon gets a standard rear window wiper as well. CFC-free air conditioning is introduced to the Sable.

RATINGS (SCALE OF 1-10)

Overall	Safety	Reliability	Performance	Comfort	Value
7.7	7.3	6.7	8	7.8	8.7

Category C
4 Dr GS Sdn	4915	6470
4 Dr GS Wgn	5195	6840
4 Dr LS Sdn	5490	7225
4 Dr LS Wgn	5785	7615

OPTIONS FOR SABLE
6 cyl 3.8 L Engine +135
AM/FM Compact Disc Player +85
Anti-Lock Brakes[Opt on GS] +145
Cruise Control +55
Keyless Entry System +45
Leather Seats +150
Power Door Locks +60
Power Drivers Seat[Opt on GS] +75
Power Moonroof +165
Power Passenger Seat +70
Power Windows[Opt on GS] +80

TOPAZ   1994

The Topaz receives CFC-free air conditioning. This will be the last year for the Topaz; Mercury is replacing it with an all-new compact called the Mystique.

RATINGS (SCALE OF 1-10)

Overall	Safety	Reliability	Performance	Comfort	Value
6.9	5.4	7.5	7.6	7.1	7

Category C
2 Dr GS Sdn	2840	3740
4 Dr GS Sdn	2840	3740

OPTIONS FOR TOPAZ
6 cyl 3.0 L Engine +165
Auto 3-Speed Transmission +130
AM/FM Stereo Tape +40
Air Bag Restraint +115
Air Conditioning +200
Cruise Control +55
Power Door Locks +60
Power Drivers Seat +75

Power Windows +80
Tilt Steering Wheel +35

TRACER   1994

A driver's side airbag is introduced on all models. New alloy wheels and optional antilock brakes show up on the LTS.

RATINGS (SCALE OF 1-10)

Overall	Safety	Reliability	Performance	Comfort	Value
6.9	6.2	7.5	7.6	7.1	6.3

Category E
4 Dr LTS Sdn	3410	4790
4 Dr STD Sdn	2805	3935
4 Dr STD Wgn	2875	4035

OPTIONS FOR TRACER
Auto 4-Speed Transmission +195
AM/FM Compact Disc Player +105
Air Conditioning +205
Anti-Lock Brakes[Opt on LTS] +160
Cruise Control[Opt on STD] +55
Luggage Rack +30
Power Door Locks +60
Power Moonroof +140
Power Windows +65
Premium Sound System +80

VILLAGER   1994

A driver airbag is installed in the Villager and a special edition luxury model debuts. Borrowing the name of an upscale men's clothier, the Nautica edition of the Villager includes such niceties as two-tone paint, alloy wheels and leather upholstery; all tastefully done in blue and white befitting a nautical theme.

RATINGS (SCALE OF 1-10)

Overall	Safety	Reliability	Performance	Comfort	Value
7.4	7.3	7.2	6.8	7.1	8.5

Category G
2 Dr GS Cargo Van	6470	7960
2 Dr GS Pass. Van	6680	8215
2 Dr LS Pass. Van	8000	9840
2 Dr Nautica Pass. Van	8495	10450

OPTIONS FOR VILLAGER
7 Passenger Seating[Opt on GS] +125
Air Conditioning[Opt on GS Cargo Van] +200
Captain Chairs (4)[Opt on LS] +150
Compact Disc W/fm/tape +110
Cruise Control[Opt on GS Cargo Van] +50
Dual Air Conditioning +225
Keyless Entry System +50
Leather Seats[Opt on LS] +190
Luggage Rack[Opt on GS] +40
Power Door Locks[Opt on GS Cargo Van] +55
Power Drivers Seat +70

Don't forget to refer to the Mileage Adjustment Table at the back of this book!

Model Description	Trade-in Value	Market Value

Power Moonroof +210
Power Passenger Seat +50
Power Windows[Opt on GS Cargo Van] +60
Premium Sound System +85

1993 MERCURY

CAPRI   1993

A new radio is introduced as the only change on the 1993 Capri.

Category F

2 Dr STD Conv	3405	4785
2 Dr XR2 Turbo Conv	4045	5690

OPTIONS FOR CAPRI
Auto 4-Speed Transmission +145
AM/FM Stereo Tape[Opt on STD] +45
Air Conditioning[Opt on STD] +170
Aluminum/Alloy Wheels[Opt on STD] +60
Cruise Control[Opt on STD] +45
Hardtop Roof +285
Leather Seats +125
Premium Sound System +75

COUGAR   1993

The LS trim level is dropped in favor of the XR7. The XR7 is decontented for 1993, losing the V8 engine, limited-slip axle and antilock brakes from the standard equipment lists. Split-fold rear seats are no longer available.

RATINGS (SCALE OF 1-10)

Overall	Safety	Reliability	Performance	Comfort	Value
7	5.7	7.1	6.8	7.8	7.4

Category C

2 Dr XR7 Cpe	3355	4790

OPTIONS FOR COUGAR
8 cyl 5.0 L Engine +225
AM/FM Compact Disc Player +70
Aluminum/Alloy Wheels +60
Anti-Lock Brakes +120
Cruise Control +45
Dual Power Seats +115
Keyless Entry System +35
Leather Seats +125
Power Door Locks +50
Power Moonroof +135
Premium Sound System +75

GRAND MARQUIS   1993

A passenger airbag, an overdrive-lockout selector on the automatic gearshift, a stainless steel exhaust system, an express-down driver's window, and dual front cupholders appear on the Grand Marquis's extensive standard equipment list this year.

RATINGS (SCALE OF 1-10)

Overall	Safety	Reliability	Performance	Comfort	Value
7.6	6.8	6.8	7.4	8.3	8.5

Category B

4 Dr GS Sdn	5415	6870
4 Dr LS Sdn	5545	7030

OPTIONS FOR GRAND MARQUIS
Aluminum/Alloy Wheels +65
Anti-Lock Brakes +135
Cruise Control +45
Keyless Entry System +35
Leather Seats +135
Power Door Locks +50
Power Passenger Seat +70
Premium Sound System +75
Traction Control System +35

SABLE   1993

The lower body-side cladding and bumpers become body colored for 1993. Bucket seats become an option on both body styles.

RATINGS (SCALE OF 1-10)

Overall	Safety	Reliability	Performance	Comfort	Value
7.2	6.9	4.9	8	7.8	8.2

Category C

4 Dr GS Sdn	3610	5155
4 Dr GS Wgn	3810	5440
4 Dr LS Sdn	3805	5430
4 Dr LS Wgn	4010	5725

OPTIONS FOR SABLE
6 cyl 3.8 L Engine +110
AM/FM Compact Disc Player +70
Aluminum/Alloy Wheels +60
Anti-Lock Brakes +120
Cruise Control +45
Keyless Entry System +35
Leather Seats +125
Power Door Locks +50
Power Drivers Seat +60
Power Passenger Seat +55
Power Sunroof +135
Power Windows[Opt on GS] +65
Premium Sound System +75

TOPAZ   1993

Mercury offers only one trim level for the Topaz this year: the lowly GS.

RATINGS (SCALE OF 1-10)

Overall	Safety	Reliability	Performance	Comfort	Value
6.7	4.5	7.3	7.6	7.1	6.8

Category C

2 Dr GS Sdn	2155	3075
4 Dr GS Sdn	2190	3125

Don't forget to refer to the Mileage Adjustment Table at the back of this book!

MERCURY 93-92

Model Description	Trade-in Value	Market Value	Model Description	Trade-in Value	Market Value

OPTIONS FOR TOPAZ

6 cyl 3.0 L Engine +140
Auto 3-Speed Transmission +110
AM/FM Stereo Tape +35
Air Bag Restraint +95
Air Conditioning +160
Aluminum/Alloy Wheels +60
Cruise Control +45
Power Door Locks +50
Power Drivers Seat +60
Power Windows +65
Premium Sound System +75

Compact Disc W/fm/tape +90
Cruise Control[Opt on GS Cargo Van] +40
Keyless Entry System +40
Leather Seats +155
Luggage Rack[Opt on GS] +30
Power Door Locks[Opt on GS Cargo Van] +45
Power Drivers Seat +55
Power Passenger Seat +40
Power Sunroof +160
Power Windows[Opt on GS Cargo Van] +50
Trip Computer +30

TRACER   1993

Beefy stabilizer arms on all trim levels improve handling. Base models receive a new fascia and the LTS receives a one-piece spoiler. All models get new interior fabrics and tail lamps.

RATINGS (SCALE OF 1-10)

Overall	Safety	Reliability	Performance	Comfort	Value
6.4	4.7	7	7.6	7.1	5.8

Category E
4 Dr LTS Sdn	2475	3785
4 Dr STD Sdn	2180	3335
4 Dr STD Wgn	2265	3465

OPTIONS FOR TRACER

Auto 4-Speed Transmission +145
AM/FM Stereo Tape[Opt on STD] +60
Air Conditioning +165
Cruise Control[Opt on STD] +45
Luggage Rack +25
Power Door Locks +50
Power Moonroof +115
Power Steering[Std on LTS,Wgn] +50
Power Windows +55

VILLAGER   1993

Mercury joins the minivan fray by introducing a vehicle designed jointly with Nissan. Attractive styling and standard features such as antilock brakes are certainly commendable, but the absence of airbags would lead us toward another model.

RATINGS (SCALE OF 1-10)

Overall	Safety	Reliability	Performance	Comfort	Value
6.2	5.5	4.5	6.8	7.1	7.3

Category G
2 Dr GS Cargo Van	5280	6585
2 Dr GS Pass. Van	5430	6775
2 Dr LS Pass. Van	6655	8305

OPTIONS FOR VILLAGER

Air Conditioning[Opt on GS Cargo Van] +165
Aluminum/Alloy Wheels +65
Captain Chairs (4) +125

1992 MERCURY

CAPRI   1992

The XR2 receives 15-inch wheels, new tires and updated cabin trim. Power door locks are no longer available but cruise control is added to the options list.
Category F
2 Dr STD Conv	3190	4410
2 Dr XR2 Turbo Conv	3790	5245

OPTIONS FOR CAPRI

Auto 4-Speed Transmission +120
Air Conditioning[Opt on STD] +135
Hardtop Roof +235
Leather Seats +105

COUGAR   1992

The 25th anniversary edition debuts. A unique LS model becomes available this year equipped with 5.0-liter V8 engine, monochromatic colors, BBS aluminum wheels, and special trim. White sidewall tires and the anti-theft system are no longer available.

RATINGS (SCALE OF 1-10)

Overall	Safety	Reliability	Performance	Comfort	Value
6.8	5.7	7	6.8	7.8	6.9

Category C
2 Dr LS Cpe	2870	4590
2 Dr XR7 Cpe	3600	5760

OPTIONS FOR COUGAR

8 cyl 5.0 L Engine[Opt on LS] +180
AM/FM Compact Disc Player +55
Anti-Lock Brakes[Opt on LS] +95
Leather Seats +100
Power Door Locks +40
Power Drivers Seat +50
Power Moonroof +110
Power Passenger Seat +45

GRAND MARQUIS   1992

New sheetmetal debuts on the Grand Marquis. Rounded styling and two additional inches in length give the car a sleeker appearance. The old V8 engine is replaced with a 4.6-liter V8 that makes between 40

Don't forget to refer to the Mileage Adjustment Table at the back of this book!

Model Description	Trade-in Value	Market Value

and 60 more horsepower, depending on the exhaust system. A new passenger airbag is added to the options list. Antilock brakes are available in the performance and handling package. The wagon is discontinued.

RATINGS (SCALE OF 1-10)

Overall	Safety	Reliability	Performance	Comfort	Value
N/A	6.8	5.8	7.4	N/A	7.8

Category B

	Trade-in	Market
4 Dr GS Sdn	4190	5495
4 Dr LS Sdn	4275	5605

OPTIONS FOR GRAND MARQUIS

Anti-Lock Brakes +110
Dual Air Bag Restraints +80
Leather Seats +110
Power Door Locks +45
Power Drivers Seat +50
Power Passenger Seat +60

SABLE   1992

Sable gets dual airbags for front seat occupants. New sheetmetal does little to change the looks of the car. Fifteen-inch wheels replace last year's 14-inchers. Additional radio controls have been placed near the steering wheel and the power window buttons have been moved to the armrest. Variable-assist power steering becomes standard and the heated windshield is dropped from the options list.

RATINGS (SCALE OF 1-10)

Overall	Safety	Reliability	Performance	Comfort	Value
7.2	6.7	5.5	8	7.8	8

Category C

	Trade-in	Market
4 Dr GS Sdn	2670	4275
4 Dr GS Wgn	2825	4520
4 Dr LS Sdn	2820	4515
4 Dr LS Wgn	2985	4775

OPTIONS FOR SABLE

6 cyl 3.8 L Engine +90
Anti-Lock Brakes +95
Leather Seats +100
Power Door Locks +40
Power Drivers Seat +50
Power Moonroof +110
Power Passenger Seat +45
Power Windows[Opt on GS] +50

TOPAZ   1992

V6 is available for those who need a little more horsepower. Unfortunately the all-wheel-drive system is dropped from the option list.

RATINGS (SCALE OF 1-10)

Overall	Safety	Reliability	Performance	Comfort	Value
6.7	4.5	6.6	7.6	7.1	7.5

Category C

	Trade-in	Market
2 Dr GS Sdn	1705	2730
4 Dr GS Sdn	1730	2770
4 Dr LS Sdn	1995	3190
4 Dr LTS Sdn	2340	3745
2 Dr XR5 Sdn	2215	3545

OPTIONS FOR TOPAZ

6 cyl 3.0 L Engine[Opt on GS,LS] +115
Auto 3-Speed Transmission +90
Air Bag Restraint +75
Air Conditioning[Opt on GS,LS] +135
Power Door Locks[Opt on GS,XR5] +40
Power Drivers Seat[Std on LTS] +50
Power Windows[Opt on GS] +50

TRACER   1992

No changes.

RATINGS (SCALE OF 1-10)

Overall	Safety	Reliability	Performance	Comfort	Value
6.5	4.6	7.6	7.6	7.1	5.8

Category E

	Trade-in	Market
4 Dr LTS Sdn	2050	3380
4 Dr STD Sdn	1675	2765
4 Dr STD Wgn	1845	3045

OPTIONS FOR TRACER

Auto 4-Speed Transmission +120
Air Conditioning +135
Power Door Locks +40
Power Moonroof +95
Power Steering[Std on LTS,Wgn] +40
Power Windows +45

1991 MERCURY

CAPRI   1991

This Australian-built convertible is based on the Mazda 323 platform. The 1.6-liter engine is available in turbo or regularly aspirated versions good for either 132 or 100 horsepower. An optional lift-off hardtop with a rear window defroster and interior lights is also available.

Category F

	Trade-in	Market
2 Dr STD Conv	2310	3550
2 Dr XR2 Turbo Conv	2830	4355

OPTIONS FOR CAPRI

Auto 4-Speed Transmission +95
Air Conditioning[Opt on STD] +110
Hardtop Roof +190
Power Door Locks[Opt on STD] +25

Model Description	Trade-in Value	Market Value

COUGAR 1991

No significant changes to the Mercury Cougar.

RATINGS (SCALE OF 1-10)

Overall	Safety	Reliability	Performance	Comfort	Value
6.7	5.7	6.5	6.8	7.8	6.8

Category C

	Trade-in	Market
2 Dr LS Cpe	2225	3820
2 Dr XR7 Cpe	2805	4810

OPTIONS FOR COUGAR

8 cyl 5.0 L Engine[Opt on LS] +150
Anti-Lock Brakes[Opt on LS] +80
Leather Seats +85
Power Door Locks +35
Power Drivers Seat +40
Power Passenger Seat +40
Power Sunroof +90

GRAND MARQUIS 1991

No major changes to the 1991 Grand Marquis.

Category B

	Trade-in	Market
4 Dr Colony Park GS Wgn	2955	4245
4 Dr Colony Park LS Wgn	3045	4375
4 Dr GS Sdn	2930	4205
4 Dr LS Sdn	3005	4320

OPTIONS FOR GRAND MARQUIS

Leather Seats +90
Power Door Locks +35
Power Drivers Seat +40
Power Passenger Seat +50

SABLE 1991

No significant changes to the 1991 Sable.

Category C

	Trade-in	Market
4 Dr GS Sdn	2095	3595
4 Dr GS Wgn	2225	3820
4 Dr LS Sdn	2215	3795
4 Dr LS Wgn	2345	4025

OPTIONS FOR SABLE

6 cyl 3.8 L Engine +75
Anti-Lock Brakes +80
Leather Seats +85
Power Door Locks +35
Power Drivers Seat +40
Power Passenger Seat +40
Power Sunroof +90
Power Windows[Opt on GS] +40

TOPAZ 1991

No changes for the 1991 Topaz.

RATINGS (SCALE OF 1-10)

Overall	Safety	Reliability	Performance	Comfort	Value
6.6	4.6	6.8	7.2	7.1	7.3

Category C

	Trade-in	Market
2 Dr GS Sdn	1355	2325
2 Dr GS 4WD Sdn	1480	2540
4 Dr GS Sdn	1375	2360
4 Dr GS 4WD Sdn	1645	2825
4 Dr LS Sdn	1565	2680
4 Dr LS 4WD Sdn	1685	2890
4 Dr LTS Sdn	1700	2915
4 Dr LTS 4WD Sdn	1810	3105
2 Dr XR5 Sdn	1490	2555

OPTIONS FOR TOPAZ

Auto 3-Speed Transmission +75
Air Bag Restraint +65
Air Conditioning[Std on LTS] +110
Power Door Locks[Opt on GS, XR5] +35
Power Drivers Seat[Std on LTS] +40
Power Windows[Opt on GS] +40

TRACER 1991

Tracer receives a mighty makeover. Base notchback and wagon body styles share the Escort's base engine, but the up-level LTS receives a much more powerful Mazda DOHC engine that produces 127 horsepower.

RATINGS (SCALE OF 1-10)

Overall	Safety	Reliability	Performance	Comfort	Value
6.2	4.5	6	7.6	7.1	5.6

Category E

	Trade-in	Market
4 Dr LTS Sdn	1740	2880
4 Dr STD Sdn	1400	2325
4 Dr STD Wgn	1555	2575

OPTIONS FOR TRACER

Auto 4-Speed Transmission +95
Air Conditioning +110
Power Door Locks +35
Power Steering[Std on LTS, Wgn] +35
Power Sunroof +85
Power Windows +35

Don't forget to refer to the Mileage Adjustment Table at the back of this book!

MITSUBISHI 00

Model Description	Trade-in Value	Market Value	Model Description	Trade-in Value	Market Value

MITSUBISHI *Japan*

1994 Mitsubishi Diamante

2000 MITSUBISHI

DIAMANTE 2000

This Mitsubishi model doesn't change much from last year, but product planners add a couple of standard features, replace four colors, and offer a new all-weather package for the LS buyer.

Category D

	Trade-in	Market
4 Dr ES Sdn	17815	20780
4 Dr LS Sdn	19795	23085

ECLIPSE 2000

Mitsubishi's 2000 Eclipse is redesigned inside and out and based on the Galant sedan platform, embodying a youthful image and providing a sporty drive. V6 power is now available, but the spunky turbocharged engine is gone as is the all-wheel drive model.

Category F

	Trade-in	Market
2 Dr GS Hbk	14205	16540
2 Dr GT Hbk	15105	17590
2 Dr RS Hbk	13225	15400

OPTIONS FOR ECLIPSE

Auto 4-Speed Transmission +690
Anti-Lock Brakes +530
Compact Disc W/fm/tape +410
Infinity Sound System +505
Leather Seats +520
Power Moonroof[Std on GS] +535
Rear Spoiler[Std on GT] +195
Rear Window Wiper[Std on GS] +130

GALANT 2000

After a '99 redesign, Mitsubishi's fourth-generation Galant features some new standard and optional equipment, like cruise-control memory function, an in-dash CD player, larger tires and four new colors.

Category D

	Trade-in	Market
4 Dr DE Sdn	12865	15005
4 Dr ES Sdn	12865	15005
4 Dr ES V6 Sdn	14165	16525
4 Dr GTZ Sdn	16635	19405
4 Dr LS Sdn	16570	19325

OPTIONS FOR GALANT

Alarm System[Std on GTZ,LS] +430
Aluminum/Alloy Wheels[Std on GTZ,LS] +380
Power Moonroof[Std on GTZ,LS] +690

MIRAGE 2000

The DE Sedan now comes with the more powerful 1.8-liter engine in place of last year's base 1.5-liter powerplant. All DE models (sedans and coupes) get a host of luxury items and larger brakes as standard equipment. The LS Sedan also gets a few more standard goodies for 2000.

Category E

	Trade-in	Market
2 Dr DE Cpe	8245	9730
4 Dr DE Sdn	9745	11500
2 Dr LS Cpe	10160	11995
4 Dr LS Sdn	11735	13855

OPTIONS FOR MIRAGE

Auto 4-Speed Transmission[Opt on DE,Cpe] +655
AM/FM Compact Disc Player[Std on LS,Sdn] +355
Air Conditioning[Std on LS,Sdn] +680
Power Door Locks[Std on LS,Sdn] +205
Power Windows[Std on LS,Sdn] +215

MONTERO 2000

The Montero's list of standard features has been lengthened, and a new Endeavor package adds even more luxury items to Mitsubishi's largest SUV.

Category G

	Trade-in	Market
4 Dr STD 4WD Wgn	23700	27570

OPTIONS FOR MONTERO

Endeavor Pkg +745

MONTERO SPORT 2000

The 2000 Montero Sport receives significant interior and exterior styling updates like a new grille, revised headlights, body-colored bumpers and new center console design, as well as several technical improvements, including a limited-slip differential on XLS and Limited models, and 16-inch alloy wheels.

Don't forget to refer to the Mileage Adjustment Table at the back of this book!

MITSUBISHI 00-99

Model Description	Trade-in Value	Market Value	Model Description	Trade-in Value	Market Value

Category G

4 Dr ES Wgn	16335	19005
4 Dr LS Wgn	17930	20860
4 Dr LS 4WD Wgn	19155	22285
4 Dr Limited Wgn	21335	24820
4 Dr Limited 4WD Wgn	22350	26000
4 Dr XLS Wgn	19585	22785
4 Dr XLS 4WD Wgn	20925	24345

OPTIONS FOR MONTERO SPORT

Alarm System[Opt on ES,LS] +220
Leather Seats +640
Luggage Rack[Opt on ES,LS] +130
Rear Wind Deflector[Opt on ES,LS] +105
Side Steps[Opt on LS] +200

1999 MITSUBISHI

3000GT   1999

The 1999 3000GT sees some styling changes and a few choice pieces of standard equipment, including antilock brakes and a power sunroof for the SL.

RATINGS (SCALE OF 1-10)

Overall	Safety	Reliability	Performance	Comfort	Value
N/A	N/A	N/A	8.8	6.6	N/A

Category F

2 Dr SL Cpe	22480	26265
2 Dr STD Cpe	17205	20100
2 Dr VR-4 Turbo 4WD Cpe	30630	35790

OPTIONS FOR 3000GT

Auto 4-Speed Transmission +605
AM/FM Compact Disc Player +310

DIAMANTE   1999

Only one Diamante model is available, replacing the ES and LS models. Mitsubishi also adds some new standard features, options and exterior colors to this top-level model.

RATINGS (SCALE OF 1-10)

Overall	Safety	Reliability	Performance	Comfort	Value
N/A	N/A	N/A	7.4	7.5	N/A

Category D

4 Dr STD Sdn	17300	20300

OPTIONS FOR DIAMANTE

Aluminum/Alloy Wheels +310
Dual Power Seats +570
Fog Lights +165
Infinity Sound System +285
Leather Seats +760
Power Drivers Seat +210
Power Moonroof +565

ECLIPSE   1999

For 1999, the Eclipse gets a host of new standard equipment, and there is a new Sports Value Option Package for buyers of the GS.

RATINGS (SCALE OF 1-10)

Overall	Safety	Reliability	Performance	Comfort	Value
N/A	6.8	N/A	8.4	6.6	N/A

Category F

2 Dr GS Hbk	12655	14790
2 Dr GS-T Turbo Hbk	16315	19060
2 Dr GSX Turbo 4WD Hbk	18450	21555
2 Dr RS Hbk	11165	13045

OPTIONS FOR ECLIPSE

Auto 4-Speed Transmission +535
AM/FM Compact Disc Player[Opt on GS, RS] +310
Air Conditioning[Opt on GS,RS] +565
Aluminum/Alloy Wheels[Std on GSX] +205
Anti-Lock Brakes[Std on GSX] +435
Cruise Control[Opt on GS,RS] +150
Keyless Entry System[Opt on GS,RS] +120
Leather Seats[Std on GSX] +425
Power Door Locks[Opt on GS,RS] +135
Power Moonroof[Opt on GS,RS] +440
Power Windows[Opt on GS,RS] +155

ECLIPSE SPYDER   1999

Sundance Plum Pearl exterior paint replaces Magenta Gray Pearl, black leather interior replaces the gray, and the GS-T model gets white-faced instrumentation.

RATINGS (SCALE OF 1-10)

Overall	Safety	Reliability	Performance	Comfort	Value
N/A	N/A	N/A	8.4	6.6	N/A

Category F

2 Dr Spyder GS Conv	14290	16695
2 Dr Spyder GS-T Turbo Conv	17390	20320

OPTIONS FOR ECLIPSE SPYDER

Auto 4-Speed Transmission +535
Anti-Lock Brakes +435
Cruise Control[Opt on Spyder GS] +150
Infinity Sound System[Opt on Spyder GS] +415
Keyless Entry System[Opt on Spyder GS] +120
Leather Seats[Opt on Spyder GS] +425

GALANT   1999

The all-new '99 Galant lineup features a new V6 engine option, more standard equipment and a GTZ model with a sport-tuned suspension.

RATINGS (SCALE OF 1-10)

Overall	Safety	Reliability	Performance	Comfort	Value
N/A	7.3	8	7.4	7.9	N/A

Don't forget to refer to the Mileage Adjustment Table at the back of this book!

MITSUBISHI 99-98

Model Description	Trade-in Value	Market Value
Category D		
4 Dr DE Sdn	11040	12955
4 Dr ES Sdn	11675	13700
4 Dr ES V6 Sdn	12940	15185
4 Dr GTZ Sdn	15705	18430
4 Dr LS Sdn	15640	18355

OPTIONS FOR GALANT
Auto 4-Speed Transmission[Opt on ES] +520
AM/FM Compact Disc Player +310
Aluminum/Alloy Wheels[Std on GTZ,LS] +310
Anti-Lock Brakes[Opt on ES] +595
Leather Seats[Std on GTZ,LS] +760
Power Moonroof[Std on GTZ,LS] +565
Side Air Bag Restraint[Std on GTZ,LS] +195

MIRAGE   1999

A new rear deck lid and taillamps, new seat fabric and some different exterior colors premier on the Mirage. The LS trim level also gets a few interior enhancements.

RATINGS (SCALE OF 1-10)

Overall	Safety	Reliability	Performance	Comfort	Value
N/A	N/A	N/A	7.4	6.4	N/A

Model Description	Trade-in Value	Market Value
Category E		
2 Dr DE Cpe	7070	8490
4 Dr DE Sdn	7865	9445
2 Dr LS Cpe	9180	11020
4 Dr LS Sdn	8445	10140

OPTIONS FOR MIRAGE
Auto 4-Speed Transmission +485
AM/FM Compact Disc Player[Std on LS Coupe] +290
Air Conditioning[Std on LS Coupe] +555
Aluminum/Alloy Wheels[Std on Cpe] +225
Anti-Lock Brakes +445
Cruise Control +155
Keyless Entry System +110
Power Door Locks +165
Power Mirrors +75
Power Moonroof +390
Power Windows +180
Tilt Steering Wheel[Std on LS] +100

MONTERO   1999

Nothing changes on the Montero this year, but one less paint color is available.

RATINGS (SCALE OF 1-10)

Overall	Safety	Reliability	Performance	Comfort	Value
N/A	N/A	N/A	6.6	7.5	N/A

Model Description	Trade-in Value	Market Value
Category G		
4 Dr STD 4WD Wgn	21790	25430

OPTIONS FOR MONTERO
Premium Pkg +560
AM/FM Compact Disc Player +210

Model Description	Trade-in Value	Market Value
Alarm System +180		
Chrome Wheels +110		
Compact Disc Changer +340		
Heated Front Seats +180		
Infinity Sound System +295		
Keyless Entry System +130		
Leather Seats +525		
Power Drivers Seat +190		
Power Moonroof +580		

MONTERO SPORT   1999

A new Limited model joins the Montero Sport lineup and with it comes a powerful new V6 engine.

Model Description	Trade-in Value	Market Value
Category G		
4 Dr ES Wgn	12260	14310
4 Dr LS Wgn	16380	19120
4 Dr LS 4WD Wgn	17140	20005
4 Dr Limited Wgn	19790	23100
4 Dr Limited 4WD Wgn	21330	24900
4 Dr XLS Wgn	16085	19035
4 Dr XLS 4WD Wgn	18925	22090

OPTIONS FOR MONTERO SPORT
Auto 4-Speed Transmission[Opt on LS] +575
AM/FM Compact Disc Player[Opt on LS, XLS] +210
Keyless Entry System[Std on Limited,XLS] +130
Power Moonroof[Std on Limited] +580

1998 MITSUBISHI

3000GT   1998

SL and VR-4 models get a standard power sunroof this year.

RATINGS (SCALE OF 1-10)

Overall	Safety	Reliability	Performance	Comfort	Value
N/A	N/A	7.8	8.8	6.6	N/A

Model Description	Trade-in Value	Market Value
Category F		
2 Dr SL Cpe	20930	24510
2 Dr STD Cpe	16575	19410
2 Dr VR-4 Turbo 4WD Cpe	26715	31285

OPTIONS FOR 3000GT
Auto 4-Speed Transmission[Opt on STD, SL] +495
Anti-Lock Brakes[Opt on SL] +355
Compact Disc W/fm/tape[Opt on STD] +275
Fog Lights[Opt on STD] +100
Leather Seats[Opt on STD] +345

DIAMANTE   1998

All Diamantes get standard ABS and remote keyless entry for 1998.

RATINGS (SCALE OF 1-10)

Overall	Safety	Reliability	Performance	Comfort	Value
N/A	N/A	8.6	7.4	7.5	4

Don't forget to refer to the Mileage Adjustment Table at the back of this book!

Model Description	Trade-in Value	Market Value	Model Description	Trade-in Value	Market Value

Category D

4 Dr ES Sdn	14790	17465
4 Dr LS Sdn	17630	20815

OPTIONS FOR DIAMANTE

Luxury Group +1440
Aluminum/Alloy Wheels[Opt on ES] +255
Chrome Wheels +310
Dual Power Seats +465
Fog Lights[Opt on ES] +135
Infinity Sound System +235
Leather Seats[Opt on ES] +620
Power Drivers Seat[Opt on ES] +170
Power Moonroof[Opt on ES] +460

ECLIPSE   1998

The GSX gets a standard sunroof, power driver's seat and remote keyless entry.

RATINGS (SCALE OF 1-10)

Overall	Safety	Reliability	Performance	Comfort	Value
6.4	6.4	6.3	8.4	6.6	4.2

Category F

2 Dr GS Hbk	11315	13250
2 Dr GS-T Turbo Hbk	13835	16205
2 Dr GSX Turbo 4WD Hbk	15670	18350
2 Dr RS Hbk	9995	11705

OPTIONS FOR ECLIPSE

Auto 4-Speed Transmission +420
AM/FM Compact Disc Player[Opt on GS, RS] +255
Air Conditioning[Opt on GS, RS] +460
Aluminum/Alloy Wheels[Opt on GS, RS] +170
Anti-Lock Brakes +355
Cruise Control[Opt on GS, RS] +120
Infinity Sound System +340
Keyless Entry System[Std on GSX] +100
Leather Seats[Std on GSX] +345
Power Door Locks[Opt on GS, RS] +110
Power Moonroof[Std on GSX] +360
Power Windows[Opt on GS, RS] +125

ECLIPSE SPYDER   1998

Eclipse Spyder GS gets air conditioning, AM/FM stereo with CD player and wheel locks. The Spyder GS-T is now flashier than ever before thanks to standard 16-inch chrome-plated alloy wheels. All models have a fresh black interior appearance with gray cloth.

RATINGS (SCALE OF 1-10)

Overall	Safety	Reliability	Performance	Comfort	Value
N/A	N/A	6.3	N/A	N/A	N/A

Category F

2 Dr Spyder GS Conv	12810	15000
2 Dr Spyder GS-T Turbo Conv	15735	18425

OPTIONS FOR ECLIPSE SPYDER

Cruise Control[Opt on Spyder GS] +120
Rear Spoiler[Opt on Spyder GS] +130

GALANT   1998

Solar tinted glass makes it harder to tan in the new Galant. The ES gets a standard manual transmission, and the ES and LS have a new black grille with chrome accents. The LS also benefits from standard antilock brakes. All models have a new heavy-duty starter and battery.

RATINGS (SCALE OF 1-10)

Overall	Safety	Reliability	Performance	Comfort	Value
7.4	6.5	7.8	8	8.3	6.5

Category D

4 Dr DE Sdn	8370	9880
4 Dr ES Sdn	9400	11100
4 Dr LS Sdn	13075	15435

OPTIONS FOR GALANT

Auto 4-Speed Transmission[Std on LS] +450
AM/FM Compact Disc Player +255
Air Conditioning[Opt on DE] +470
Aluminum/Alloy Wheels[Opt on ES] +255
Anti-Lock Brakes[Opt on ES] +485
Fog Lights[Opt on ES] +135
Leather Seats[Opt on ES] +620
Power Moonroof[Opt on ES] +460

MIRAGE   1998

Some new colors to choose from and a new heavy duty starter and battery make the Mirage more reliable.

RATINGS (SCALE OF 1-10)

Overall	Safety	Reliability	Performance	Comfort	Value
N/A	N/A	7.8	7.4	6.4	5.4

Category E

2 Dr DE Cpe	6160	7545
4 Dr DE Sdn	6995	8570
2 Dr LS Cpe	8075	9895
4 Dr LS Sdn	7510	9200

OPTIONS FOR MIRAGE

Auto 4-Speed Transmission +380
AM/FM Compact Disc Player[Opt on Sdn] +235
Air Conditioning[Opt on DE, Sdn] +455
Anti-Lock Brakes +365
Cruise Control +125
Keyless Entry System +90
Power Door Locks +135
Power Mirrors +60
Power Moonroof +320
Power Windows +145
Tilt Steering Wheel[Opt on DE] +80

MONTERO — 1998

A revised front bumper and grille, new fenders and new rear quarter panels mark the exterior changes. Inside is a new steering wheel, while the standard equipment list now includes ABS, air conditioning, third row seats and alloy wheels.

Category G

	Trade-in	Market
4 Dr STD 4WD Wgn	20345	23805

OPTIONS FOR MONTERO

Premium Pkg +435
AM/FM Compact Disc Player +175
Chrome Wheels +90
Compact Disc Changer +275
Heated Front Seats +150
Infinity Sound System +240
Keyless Entry System +105
Leather Seats +430
Power Drivers Seat +155
Power Moonroof +475

MONTERO SPORT — 1998

Montero Sports get lots of features added to their option packages, and 4WD models now come with standard ABS.

RATINGS (SCALE OF 1-10)

Overall	Safety	Reliability	Performance	Comfort	Value
N/A	N/A	8.4	6	7.5	N/A

Category G

	Trade-in	Market
4 Dr ES Wgn	11280	13200
4 Dr LS Wgn	13865	16220
4 Dr LS 4WD Wgn	14875	17405
4 Dr XLS Wgn	14665	17620
4 Dr XLS 4WD Wgn	17345	20695

OPTIONS FOR MONTERO SPORT

Auto 4-Speed Transmission[Std on XLS, 2WD] +470
Appearance Pkg +650
AM/FM Compact Disc Player +175
Air Conditioning[Std on XLS] +450
Aluminum/Alloy Wheels[Opt on LS] +175
Cruise Control[Opt on LS] +115
Keyless Entry System +105
Limited Slip Diff[Opt on LS, 2WD] +150
Power Door Locks[Opt on LS] +130
Power Mirrors +70
Power Moonroof[Opt on LS] +475
Power Windows[Opt on LS] +135
Rear Heater[Opt on LS] +105
Tutone Paint[Opt on LS] +140

1997 MITSUBISHI

3000GT — 1997

A value-leader base model is introduced. It has less than stellar performance and we think that it's embarrassing that this car is in the same lineup as the earth-scorching VR-4.

RATINGS (SCALE OF 1-10)

Overall	Safety	Reliability	Performance	Comfort	Value
N/A	7.9	7.7	8.8	6.6	N/A

Category F

	Trade-in	Market
2 Dr SL Cpe	17250	20330
2 Dr STD Cpe	14150	16675
2 Dr VR-4 Turbo 4WD Cpe	22545	26570

OPTIONS FOR 3000GT

Auto 4-Speed Transmission +400
Anti-Lock Brakes[Opt on SL] +290
Compact Disc W/fm/tape[Opt on STD] +225
Keyless Entry System[Std on VR-4] +80
Leather Seats[Opt on STD] +285
Power Sunroof +300

DIAMANTE — 1997

After a one-year hiatus, the Diamante returns to the Mitsubishi lineup sporting clean, crisp styling, a full-load of luxury features, and a lower price. The old car barely registered on near-luxury car buyers' radar; this new one deserves consideration and a close inspection.

RATINGS (SCALE OF 1-10)

Overall	Safety	Reliability	Performance	Comfort	Value
N/A	N/A	8.5	7.4	7.5	3.9

Category D

	Trade-in	Market
4 Dr ES Sdn	12505	14885
4 Dr LS Sdn	14445	17195

OPTIONS FOR DIAMANTE

Luxury Group +625
Aluminum/Alloy Wheels[Opt on ES] +210
Anti-Lock Brakes +395
Fog Lights[Opt on ES] +110
Infinity Sound System +190
Keyless Entry System +140
Leather Seats[Opt on ES] +505
Leather Steering Wheel[Opt on ES] +55
Power Drivers Seat[Opt on ES] +140
Power Moonroof +380

ECLIPSE — 1997

Revised styling makes the attractive Eclipse drop-dead gorgeous. New interior fabrics and paint colors debut as well. Antilock brakes are now available on the GS model, and a CD player joins its standard equipment

MITSUBISHI 97

Model Description	Trade-in Value	Market Value	Model Description	Trade-in Value	Market Value

list. Two new exterior colors, new seat fabrics and a new interior color combination round out the changes.

RATINGS (SCALE OF 1-10)

Overall	Safety	Reliability	Performance	Comfort	Value
6.6	6.5	6.3	8.4	6.6	5

Category F

2 Dr GS Hbk	10500	12375
2 Dr GS-T Turbo Hbk	12625	14880
2 Dr GSX Turbo 4WD Hbk	13815	16280
2 Dr RS Hbk	9090	10715
2 Dr STD Hbk	8325	9810

OPTIONS FOR ECLIPSE

Auto 4-Speed Transmission +335
Air Conditioning[Opt on GS,RS,STD] +375
Aluminum/Alloy Wheels[Opt on GS,RS] +135
Anti-Lock Brakes +290
Compact Disc W/fm/tape[Opt on GS] +225
Keyless Entry System +80
Leather Seats +285
Power Door Locks[Opt on GS,RS] +90
Power Drivers Seat[Opt on GSX] +110
Power Moonroof +290
Power Windows[Opt on GS,RS] +105

ECLIPSE SPYDER   1997

The 1997 Spyder gets revised front and rear styling. Anti-lock brakes are now available on the GS model. Two new exterior colors, new seat fabrics, and a new interior color combination round out the changes.

RATINGS (SCALE OF 1-10)

Overall	Safety	Reliability	Performance	Comfort	Value
N/A	N/A	6.3	N/A	N/A	N/A

Category F

2 Dr Spyder GS Conv	11430	13470
2 Dr Spyder GS-T Turbo Conv	14465	17045

OPTIONS FOR ECLIPSE SPYDER

Air Conditioning[Opt on Spyder GS] +375
Cruise Control[Opt on Spyder GS] +100
Rear Spoiler[Opt on Spyder GS] +105

GALANT   1997

Mitsubishi shuffles the Galant lineup, replacing the S sedan with a base model called the DE. Front and rear fascias have been redesigned, and the interiors of all models have been upgraded by the addition of more ergonomically correct center armrests, upgraded upholstery, additional sound deadening material, and a new steering wheel.

RATINGS (SCALE OF 1-10)

Overall	Safety	Reliability	Performance	Comfort	Value
7.1	6.5	7.4	8	8.3	5.3

Category D

4 Dr DE Sdn	7605	9055
4 Dr ES Sdn	8900	10595
4 Dr LS Sdn	11160	13285

OPTIONS FOR GALANT

Auto 4-Speed Transmission[Opt on DE] +390
AM/FM Compact Disc Player +210
Air Conditioning[Opt on DE] +385
Aluminum/Alloy Wheels[Opt on ES] +210
Anti-Lock Brakes +395
Fog Lights[Opt on ES] +110
Keyless Entry System[Opt on ES] +140
Leather Seats[Opt on ES] +505
Power Moonroof[Opt on ES] +380

MIRAGE   1997

The Mirage is totally redesigned for 1997, sharing little with the model it replaces. Mitsubishi claims that interior size has been increased and that NVH have been reduced.

RATINGS (SCALE OF 1-10)

Overall	Safety	Reliability	Performance	Comfort	Value
N/A	N/A	8.3	7.4	6.4	5.4

Category E

2 Dr DE Cpe	5340	6580
4 Dr DE Sdn	6170	7605
2 Dr LS Cpe	6720	8285
4 Dr LS Sdn	6620	8165

OPTIONS FOR MIRAGE

Auto 4-Speed Transmission +305
Air Conditioning +370
Aluminum/Alloy Wheels[Opt on Sdn] +150
Anti-Lock Brakes +295
Compact Disc W/fm/tape +215
Cruise Control +100
Keyless Entry System +75
Power Door Locks +110
Power Moonroof +260
Power Steering[Opt on DE Cpe] +115
Power Windows +120

MONTERO   1997

This all-new entry from Mitsubishi is poised to steal sales in the ever-growing midsized sport-utility segment. Based on the same floorpan as the full-sized Montero, the Montero Sport is shorter in length, lighter in weight, and generally more nimble than its big brother.

RATINGS (SCALE OF 1-10)

Overall	Safety	Reliability	Performance	Comfort	Value
N/A	N/A	N/A	N/A	N/A	3.5

Don't forget to refer to the Mileage Adjustment Table at the back of this book!

Model Description	Trade-in Value	Market Value
Category G		
4 Dr LS 4WD Wgn	15865	18645
4 Dr SR 4WD Wgn	19685	23140

OPTIONS FOR MONTERO
Air Conditioning[Opt on LS] +365
Alarm System +120
Aluminum/Alloy Wheels[Opt on LS] +145
Anti-Lock Brakes +260
Chrome Wheels +75
Heated Front Seats +120
Keyless Entry System +85
Leather Seats[Opt on LS] +350
Luggage Rack +70
Power Drivers Seat[Opt on LS] +125
Power Moonroof[Opt on LS] +385
Running Boards +175
Third Seat +320
Trailer Hitch +125

MONTERO SPORT   1997

This all-new entry from Mitsubishi is poised to steal sales in the ever-growing midsized sport-utility segment. Based on the same floorpan as the full-sized Montero, the Montero Sport is shorter in length, lighter in weight, and generally more nimble than its big brother.

RATINGS (SCALE OF 1-10)

Overall	Safety	Reliability	Performance	Comfort	Value
N/A	N/A	8.1	6	7.5	N/A

	Trade-in	Market
Category G		
4 Dr ES Wgn	10230	12025
4 Dr LS Wgn	12605	14820
4 Dr LS 4WD Wgn	13350	15690
4 Dr XLS 4WD Wgn	17630	20725

OPTIONS FOR MONTERO SPORT
Auto 4-Speed Transmission[Std on XLS,2WD] +410
Appearance Pkg +675
LS Appearance Pkg +675
Premium Pkg +585
Air Conditioning[Std on XLS] +365
Aluminum/Alloy Wheels[Opt on LS] +145
Anti-Lock Brakes +260
Compact Disc W/fm/tape +200
Cruise Control[Opt on LS] +95
Infinity Sound System[Opt on LS] +195
Leather Seats[Opt on LS] +350
Limited Slip Diff +125
Luggage Rack +70
Power Door Locks[Opt on LS] +105
Power Moonroof[Opt on LS] +385
Power Windows[Opt on LS] +110
Rear Heater +85
Rear Window Wiper[Opt on ES] +70

1996 MITSUBISHI

3000GT   1996

Base model gets new cloth interior, while upper trim levels receive a choice of black or tan leather. Remote keyless entry gets panic feature, and several new colors are available.

RATINGS (SCALE OF 1-10)

Overall	Safety	Reliability	Performance	Comfort	Value
N/A	7.9	7.6	8.8	6.6	N/A

	Trade-in	Market
Category F		
2 Dr SL Cpe	16410	19405
2 Dr STD Cpe	12615	15185
2 Dr VR-4 Turbo 4WD Cpe	20505	24250

OPTIONS FOR 3000GT
Auto 4-Speed Transmission +320
Chrome Wheels[Opt on SL] +215
Compact Disc Changer +235
Power Sunroof +245

DIAMANTE   1996

The only Diamantes sold this year were for fleet sales. So unless you see one at a rental car auction, chances are not good that you'll find a used 1996 model.

Category D		
4 Dr ES Sdn	11080	13430

ECLIPSE   1996

The "Spyder" (convertible) version debuts, as do three new colors.

Audio systems are revised, and RS models can be ordered with a rear spoiler. Remote keyless entry systems get a new panic feature.

RATINGS (SCALE OF 1-10)

Overall	Safety	Reliability	Performance	Comfort	Value
6.6	6.5	6.3	8.4	6.6	5

	Trade-in	Market
Category F		
2 Dr GS Hbk	8895	10520
2 Dr GS-T Turbo Hbk	10705	12660
2 Dr GSX Turbo 4WD Hbk	11890	14060
2 Dr RS Hbk	7715	9120
2 Dr STD Hbk	7020	8305
2 Dr Spyder GS Conv	9875	11675
2 Dr Sypder GS-T Turbo Conv	12415	14685

OPTIONS FOR ECLIPSE
Auto 4-Speed Transmission +275
Air Conditioning[Std on GS-T,GSX] +305
Aluminum/Alloy Wheels[Std on GS-T,GSX] +110
Anti-Lock Brakes +235
Cruise Control[Std on GS-T,GSX] +80

Don't forget to refer to the Mileage Adjustment Table at the back of this book!

MITSUBISHI 96-95

Model Description	Trade-in Value	Market Value	Model Description	Trade-in Value	Market Value

Keyless Entry System[Opt on GS,GSX,Spyder GS] +65
Leather Seats[Std on GSX,GS-T Turbo Conv] +230
Power Drivers Seat[Std on GSX] +90
Power Sunroof +245
Rear Window Wiper[Opt on GS] +60

GALANT   1996

A Homelink transmitter is available, and a panic feature debuts on keyless entry systems. New two-tone interiors debut, and four fresh exterior colors join the palette. Other changes include new wheelcovers, expanded availability of alloy wheels, and a heavy duty defroster with timer. LS models have standard leather seating and antilock brakes are available across the line.

RATINGS (SCALE OF 1-10)

Overall	Safety	Reliability	Performance	Comfort	Value
7.2	6.5	7.3	8	8.3	5.8

Category D
4 Dr ES Sdn	8465	10260
4 Dr LS Sdn	9495	11505
4 Dr S Sdn	6425	7785

OPTIONS FOR GALANT

Auto 4-Speed Transmission[Opt on S] +325
AM/FM Compact Disc Player +170
AM/FM Stereo Tape[Opt on S] +130
Air Conditioning[Opt on S] +315
Aluminum/Alloy Wheels[Opt on ES] +170
Anti-Lock Brakes +320
Cruise Control[Opt on S] +90
Keyless Entry System +115
Power Door Locks[Opt on S] +100
Power Moonroof[Opt on ES] +310
Power Windows[Opt on S] +100

MIGHTY MAX PICKUP   1996

No changes this year, the Mighty Max's last.

Category G
2 Dr STD Std Cab SB	4650	5570

OPTIONS FOR MIGHTY MAX PICKUP

Auto 4-Speed Transmission +520
AM/FM Stereo Tape +80
Air Conditioning +300
Power Steering +105
Rear Step Bumper +55

MIRAGE   1996

Four colors debut, and the Preferred Equipment Packages are revised a bit.

RATINGS (SCALE OF 1-10)

Overall	Safety	Reliability	Performance	Comfort	Value
6.6	5.3	8.1	8.2	7	4.6

Category E
2 Dr LS Cpe	5010	6635
2 Dr S Cpe	3965	5255
4 Dr S Sdn	4975	6590

OPTIONS FOR MIRAGE

Auto 3-Speed Transmission[Opt on Cpe] +195
Auto 4-Speed Transmission +240
AM/FM Compact Disc Player +160
AM/FM Stereo Tape[Opt on S] +110
Air Conditioning +305
Power Steering[Std on LS,Sdn] +95

MONTERO   1996

Refinements result in a better SUV this year. A passenger airbag has been installed, optional side steps make it easier to clamber aboard, and split-fold second row seats increase versatility. New colors, new seat fabrics and better audio systems round out the package.

RATINGS (SCALE OF 1-10)

Overall	Safety	Reliability	Performance	Comfort	Value
N/A	N/A	N/A	N/A	N/A	3.8

Category G
4 Dr LS 4WD Wgn	13415	16070
4 Dr SR 4WD Wgn	17740	21250

OPTIONS FOR MONTERO

Auto 4-Speed Transmission[Opt on LS] +325
Leather/Wood Pkg +275
Air Conditioning[Opt on LS] +300
Aluminum/Alloy Wheels[Opt on LS] +120
Anti-Lock Brakes[Opt on LS] +210
Chrome Wheels +60
Compact Disc Changer +185
Keyless Entry System[Opt on LS] +70
Leather Seats +285
Luggage Rack +60
Power Moonroof[Opt on LS] +315
Power Sunroof +290
Running Boards +140
Trailer Hitch +105

1995 MITSUBISHI

3000GT   1995

The VR-4 gains chrome-plated alloy wheels as standard equipment.

RATINGS (SCALE OF 1-10)

Overall	Safety	Reliability	Performance	Comfort	Value
N/A	8.7	7.5	8.8	6.6	N/A

Category F
2 Dr SL Cpe	14040	16730
2 Dr STD Cpe	11865	14140

Don't forget to refer to the Mileage Adjustment Table at the back of this book!

Model Description	Trade-in Value	Market Value
2 Dr Spyder SL Conv	23090	27510
2 Dr Spyder VR-4 Turbo 4WD Conv	25855	30810
2 Dr VR-4 Turbo 4WD Cpe	17330	20655

OPTIONS FOR 3000GT

Auto 4-Speed Transmission[Opt on SL,STD] +260
Chrome Wheels[Opt on SL] +175
Compact Disc Changer[Opt on SL,STD,VR-4] +190
Power Sunroof +200

DIAMANTE   1995

The base Diamante sedan is sent out to pasture, available only to fleet purchasers such as rental car agencies. No other changes for the Mitsubishi flagship.

RATINGS (SCALE OF 1-10)

Overall	Safety	Reliability	Performance	Comfort	Value
7.3	7	8.2	8.4	8.4	4.3

Category D
4 Dr ES Sdn	8490	10580
4 Dr LS Sdn	10690	13325
4 Dr STD Wgn	8595	10710

OPTIONS FOR DIAMANTE

Compact Disc Changer +195
Power Moonroof +250
Power Passenger Seat +95
Traction Control System +160

ECLIPSE   1995

Radically redesigned, the new Eclipse sports bulging shoulders and no-nonsense looks, particularly in GSX guise. Engine ratings are improved for all models, while the turbocharged GS-T and GSX produce a mighty 210 horsepower at 6,000 rpm. Antilock brakes are optional on all models. Dual airbags are finally standard on the Eclipse.

RATINGS (SCALE OF 1-10)

Overall	Safety	Reliability	Performance	Comfort	Value
6.4	6.9	5.7	8.4	6.6	4.2

Category F
2 Dr GS Hbk	7135	8505
2 Dr GS-T Turbo Hbk	8700	10365
2 Dr GSX Turbo 4WD Hbk	9570	11405
2 Dr RS Hbk	6295	7505

OPTIONS FOR ECLIPSE

Auto 4-Speed Transmission +225
AM/FM Compact Disc Player +140
Air Conditioning[Opt on GS,RS] +250
Aluminum/Alloy Wheels[Opt on GS,RS] +90
Cruise Control[Opt on GS] +65
Infinity Sound System[Opt on GS] +185
Leather Seats[Std on GSX] +190
Power Door Locks[Opt on GS] +60

Power Drivers Seat[Std on GSX] +70
Power Sunroof +200
Power Windows[Opt on GS] +70

EXPO   1995

This is the last year for the Expo.
Category E
4 Dr STD Hbk	5905	7725
4 Dr STD 4WD Hbk	6390	8360

OPTIONS FOR EXPO

AM/FM Stereo Tape +90
Air Conditioning +250
Anti-Lock Brakes +200
Cruise Control +70
Luggage Rack +40
Power Door Locks +75
Power Windows +80

GALANT   1995

The much anticipated V6 engine never transpired in the 1995 Galant due to the increased costs and complexity involved in making the model. The 1995 Galants are available in three trim-levels, all with the 141-horsepower four-cylinder.

RATINGS (SCALE OF 1-10)

Overall	Safety	Reliability	Performance	Comfort	Value
6.8	7	6.7	8	8.3	4.1

Category D
4 Dr ES Sdn	6410	7990
4 Dr LS Sdn	6950	8660
4 Dr S Sdn	4960	6180

OPTIONS FOR GALANT

Auto 4-Speed Transmission[Opt on S] +270
AM/FM Compact Disc Player +140
Air Conditioning[Opt on S] +255
Aluminum/Alloy Wheels[Opt on ES] +140
Anti-Lock Brakes +265
Cruise Control[Opt on S] +75
Keyless Entry System +95
Leather Seats +340
Power Door Locks[Opt on S] +80
Power Drivers Seat +95
Power Windows[Opt on S] +80

MIGHTY MAX PICKUP   1995

The Mighty Max line is drastically reduced. Remaining is a four-cylinder two-wheel-drive regular-cab model.
Category G
2 Dr STD Std Cab SB	3845	4760

OPTIONS FOR MIGHTY MAX PICKUP

Auto 4-Speed Transmission +275
AM/FM Stereo Tape +65
Air Conditioning +245

Don't forget to refer to the Mileage Adjustment Table at the back of this book!

MITSUBISHI 95-94

Model Description	Trade-in Value	Market Value	Model Description	Trade-in Value	Market Value

Power Steering +85
Rear Step Bumper +45

MIRAGE 1995

The often changing Mitsubishi Mirage is once again revised, this time with dual airbags. LS versions get bigger alloy wheels.

RATINGS (SCALE OF 1-10)

Overall	Safety	Reliability	Performance	Comfort	Value
6.8	5.8	7.7	8.2	7	5.2

Category E

2 Dr ES Cpe	3900	5105
4 Dr ES Sdn	4305	5635
2 Dr LS Cpe	4020	5260
2 Dr S Cpe	3270	4285
4 Dr S Sdn	4010	5245

OPTIONS FOR MIRAGE

Auto 3-Speed Transmission[Opt on Cpe] +220
Auto 4-Speed Transmission +160
AM/FM Compact Disc Player +130
AM/FM Stereo Tape[Opt on S] +90
Air Conditioning +250
Cruise Control[Opt on ES] +70
Power Door Locks +75
Power Steering[Std on ES,LS,Sdn] +75
Power Windows +80

MONTERO 1995

The Montero LS gets a more powerful V6 that offers a 26-horsepower boost over last year's marginal 151-horsepower rating. Towing capacity increases to 5,000 pounds for all models. Tricky, electronic shock absorbers return to the Montero SR's standard equipment list, letting drivers choose between soft, medium or hard setting depending on their preferences.

RATINGS (SCALE OF 1-10)

Overall	Safety	Reliability	Performance	Comfort	Value
N/A	N/A	N/A	N/A	N/A	4.3

Category G

4 Dr LS 4WD Wgn	11025	13645
4 Dr SR 4WD Wgn	13770	17050

OPTIONS FOR MONTERO

Auto 4-Speed Transmission[Opt on LS] +255
Leather & Wood Pkg +350
Anti-Lock Brakes[Opt on LS] +175
Chrome Wheels +50
Compact Disc W/fm/tape +130
Keyless Entry System[Opt on LS] +60
Leather Seats +235
Luggage Rack +50
Power Drivers Seat +85
Power Sunroof[Opt on LS] +235

1994 MITSUBISHI

3000GT 1994

The 3000GT gets a passenger airbag. The 3000GT VR-4 gets a totally unnecessary 20 extra horsepower. But, hey, you won't find us complaining. To harness the extra power, the VR-4 switches to a six-speed manual gearbox. Freshened styling and CFC-free air conditioning round out the changes for all models.

RATINGS (SCALE OF 1-10)

Overall	Safety	Reliability	Performance	Comfort	Value
N/A	8.7	7.5	8.8	6.6	N/A

Category F

2 Dr SL Cpe	10640	13535
2 Dr STD Cpe	9160	11650
2 Dr VR-4 Turbo 4WD Cpe	13125	16700

OPTIONS FOR 3000GT

Auto 4-Speed Transmission +215
Compact Disc Changer +155
Leather Seats[Opt on SL] +155
Sunroof +95

DIAMANTE 1994

A passenger airbag and CFC-free air conditioning make the Diamante much friendlier to its passengers and the environment. A five-door wagon model introduced late last year comes with the 175-horsepower engine that is standard in the ES sedan. New wood trim and an upgraded Infinity stereo debut on the 1994 Diamante.

RATINGS (SCALE OF 1-10)

Overall	Safety	Reliability	Performance	Comfort	Value
7	6.8	7.5	8.4	8.4	3.8

Category D

4 Dr ES Sdn	6545	8370
4 Dr LS Sdn	8300	10615
4 Dr STD Wgn	6625	8475

OPTIONS FOR DIAMANTE

AM/FM Compact Disc Player +115
Anti-Lock Brakes[Std on LS] +215
Infinity Sound System[Opt on ES] +105
Keyless Entry System[Std on LS] +75
Leather Seats[Std on LS] +275
Power Drivers Seat[Std on LS] +75
Power Passenger Seat[Opt on ES] +75
Power Sunroof +190
Traction Control System +130

ECLIPSE 1994

Last year for the current edition of the Diamond Star sport coupe. Turbo engines gain a minimal boost in

Model Description	Trade-in Value	Market Value	Model Description	Trade-in Value	Market Value

horsepower. Several of the models get more standard equipment in an attempt to increase sales in this edition's final year.

RATINGS (SCALE OF 1-10)

Overall	Safety	Reliability	Performance	Comfort	Value
N/A	N/A	8	8.4	6.8	3.9

Category F

	Trade-in	Market
2 Dr GS Turbo Hbk	5790	7370
2 Dr GS 1.8 Hbk	4435	5640
2 Dr GS 2.0 Hbk	4965	6315
2 Dr GSX Turbo 4WD Hbk	6145	7815

OPTIONS FOR ECLIPSE

Auto 4-Speed Transmission +180
Air Conditioning[Opt on GS 1.8] +205
Anti-Lock Brakes[Opt on GS] +160
Compact Disc W/fm/tape[Opt on GS 2.0] +125
Cruise Control[Opt on GS 1.8] +55
Keyless Entry System[Std on GS 2.0] +45
Leather Seats +155
Power Door Locks[Std on GS,GSX] +50
Power Windows[Std on GS,GSX] +55
Sunroof +95

EXPO   1994

The Expo and LRV receive a driver airbag this year. Unfortunately, the Expo loses its up-level SP model, but base models do receive better standard equipment as a result. LRVs are available only as two-wheel-drive models in 1994; the AWD has been axed. This is the last year for the Expo LRV, although it will live on as the Eagle Summit wagon.

Category E

	Trade-in	Market
2 Dr LRV 1.8 Hbk	4065	5715
2 Dr LRV 2.4 Hbk	4315	6070
2 Dr LRV Sport Hbk	5155	7250
4 Dr STD Hbk	4475	6295
4 Dr STD 4WD Hbk	4875	6860

OPTIONS FOR EXPO

Auto 4-Speed Transmission +170
AM/FM Stereo Tape +75
Air Conditioning +205
Aluminum/Alloy Wheels +80
Anti-Lock Brakes +160
Cruise Control +55
Keyless Entry System +40
Luggage Rack +30
Power Door Locks +60
Power Sunroof +150
Power Windows +65

GALANT   1994

Dual airbags debut on this totally redesigned sedan. Four trim-levels are offered, ranging from the low-level S to the luxury ES and sporty GS models. An automatic transmission is standard on the ES and LS models. GS Galants come with a twin-cam engine rated at 160 horsepower.

RATINGS (SCALE OF 1-10)

Overall	Safety	Reliability	Performance	Comfort	Value
7	7	6.9	8	8.3	4.7

Category D

	Trade-in	Market
4 Dr ES Sdn	5195	6640
4 Dr GS Sdn	6455	8260
4 Dr LS Sdn	5630	7200
4 Dr S Sdn	4135	5285

OPTIONS FOR GALANT

Auto 4-Speed Transmission[Opt on GS,S] +205
Air Conditioning[Opt on S] +210
Anti-Lock Brakes +215
Compact Disc W/fm/tape[Std on GS] +190
Keyless Entry System +75

MIGHTY MAX PICKUP   1994

The Mighty Max gains a few safety features such as a high-mounted rear stop light and side-impact door guard beams. The vehicle is otherwise unchanged.

Category G

	Trade-in	Market
2 Dr STD Ext Cab SB	3655	4695
2 Dr STD Std Cab SB	3075	3950
2 Dr STD 4WD Std Cab SB	4725	6070

OPTIONS FOR MIGHTY MAX PICKUP

Auto 4-Speed Transmission +195
AM/FM Stereo Tape +55
Air Conditioning +200
Limited Slip Diff +70
Power Steering[Std on 4WD] +70
Rear Step Bumper +35
Sliding Rear Window +30
Velour/Cloth Seats[Std on 4WD] +50

MIRAGE   1994

The Mirage finally gains a standard driver airbag, but the LS loses its optional antilock brakes. The LS coupe gets the 1.8-liter engine that was formerly available only on the LS and ES sedans. S and ES coupes get power steering added to their standard equipment lists, and LS sedans get alloy wheels.

RATINGS (SCALE OF 1-10)

Overall	Safety	Reliability	Performance	Comfort	Value
N/A	N/A	7.8	8.2	7	5.7

Category E

	Trade-in	Market
2 Dr ES Cpe	2835	3990
4 Dr ES Sdn	3250	4570
2 Dr LS Cpe	3235	4550
4 Dr LS Sdn	3935	5530

Don't forget to refer to the Mileage Adjustment Table at the back of this book!

Model Description	Trade-in Value	Market Value
2 Dr S Cpe	2475	3480
4 Dr S Sdn	3100	4365

OPTIONS FOR MIRAGE

Auto 3-Speed Transmission +115
Auto 4-Speed Transmission[Opt on ES,Cpe] +150
AM/FM Compact Disc Player +105
AM/FM Stereo Tape[Std on LS] +75
Air Conditioning +205
Cruise Control[Opt on ES] +55
Power Door Locks[Std on LS] +60
Power Windows[Std on LS] +65

MONTERO   1994

Deciding to go the luxury sport-ute route, Mitsubishi drops its entry-level Monteros. The remaining models are the luxury-oriented LS and sporty SR. A driver airbag is standard on the 1994 Montero. Antilock brakes move from the standard equipment list to the option list of both trucks. CFC-free air conditioning, a third-row bench seat, heated outside mirrors, and a leather-wrapped steering wheel become standard equipment. SR models finally receive a gutsier engine to move this scale-tipping SUV around; a 215-horsepower V6 engine is now standard on that model.

RATINGS (SCALE OF 1-10)

Overall	Safety	Reliability	Performance	Comfort	Value
N/A	N/A	N/A	N/A	N/A	4.3

Category G
4 Dr LS 4WD Wgn	8390	10775
4 Dr SR 4WD Wgn	10970	14085

OPTIONS FOR MONTERO

Auto 4-Speed Transmission[Opt on LS] +205
Air Conditioning[Opt on LS] +200
Aluminum/Alloy Wheels +80
Anti-Lock Brakes[Opt on LS] +140
Chrome Wheels +40
Compact Disc W/fm/tape +110
Keyless Entry System[Opt on LS] +50
Leather Seats +190
Limited Slip Diff +70
Luggage Rack +40
Power Drivers Seat +70
Power Sunroof +195
Running Boards +95

PRECIS   1994

Category E
2 Dr STD Hbk	1630	2290

OPTIONS FOR PRECIS

Auto 4-Speed Transmission +160
AM/FM Stereo Tape +75
Air Conditioning +205
Power Steering +60

1993 MITSUBISHI

3000GT   1993

Leather makes its way into the top-of-the-line VR-4. Base models get bigger and better standard equipment lists that include air conditioning, power windows, power door locks, and cruise control (to name a few).

RATINGS (SCALE OF 1-10)

Overall	Safety	Reliability	Performance	Comfort	Value
N/A	6.9	7.4	8.8	6.6	N/A

Category F
2 Dr SL Cpe	7665	9995
2 Dr STD Cpe	6340	8265
2 Dr VR-4 Turbo 4WD Cpe	9185	11975

OPTIONS FOR 3000GT

Auto 4-Speed Transmission +170
Compact Disc Changer +125
Leather Seats[Opt on SL] +125
Sunroof +80

DIAMANTE   1993

Base models are now called ES and gain cruise control, a power trunk opener and steering wheel mounted stereo controls.

RATINGS (SCALE OF 1-10)

Overall	Safety	Reliability	Performance	Comfort	Value
N/A	N/A	7	8.4	8.4	3.7

Category D
4 Dr ES Sdn	4760	6350
4 Dr ES Wgn	4880	6510
4 Dr LS Sdn	6310	8425

OPTIONS FOR DIAMANTE

Diamante Euro Handling Pkg +335
Diamante Leather Seat Pkg +175
AM/FM Compact Disc Player +95
Aluminum/Alloy Wheels[Opt on ES] +95
Anti-Lock Brakes[Opt on ES] +175
Keyless Entry System[Opt on ES] +60
Leather Seats[Opt on ES] +225
Power Drivers Seat[Opt on ES] +60
Power Sunroof +155
Premium Sound System[Opt on ES] +75
Traction Control System +105

ECLIPSE   1993

The GS model gets a rear spoiler. GSX Eclipses now have standard antilock brakes. Some interior changes include new seat stitching and a new manual shift knob. Exterior changes are limited to new wheels and optional graphics.

Don't forget to refer to the Mileage Adjustment Table at the back of this book!

Model Description	Trade-in Value	Market Value

RATINGS (SCALE OF 1-10)

Overall	Safety	Reliability	Performance	Comfort	Value
N/A	N/A	7.6	8.4	6.8	4.2

Category F

2 Dr GS 2.0 Hbk	3945	5145
2 Dr GSX Turbo 4WD Hbk	5200	6780

OPTIONS FOR ECLIPSE

Auto 4-Speed Transmission +150
Air Conditioning +170
Aluminum/Alloy Wheels +60
Cruise Control +45
Keyless Entry System +35
Leather Seats +125
Power Door Locks +40
Power Windows +45
Premium Sound System +75
Rear Window Wiper +30
Sunroof +80

EXPO 1993

Mitsubishi increases the number of valves on the Expo's 2.4-liter engine, improving horsepower by 12 percent. Sport and AWD Sport Expo LRVs get the larger 2.4-liter engine found on the Expo. More equipment is now standard on the LRV Sport models.

Category E

2 Dr LRV Hbk	2910	4100
2 Dr LRV 4WD Hbk	3340	4700
2 Dr LRV Sport Hbk	3610	5080
4 Dr SP Hbk	3955	5565
4 Dr SP 4WD Hbk	4285	6035
4 Dr STD Hbk	3435	4840
4 Dr STD 4WD Hbk	3760	5295

OPTIONS FOR EXPO

Auto 4-Speed Transmission +135
AM/FM Stereo Tape[Std on SP] +60
Air Conditioning +165
Anti-Lock Brakes +135
Cruise Control[Std on SP] +45
Luggage Rack +25
Power Door Locks[Std on SP] +50
Power Sunroof +125
Power Windows[Std on SP] +55
Premium Sound System +65

GALANT 1993

Sporty VR-4 model goes the way of the buffalo. GS and GSR models are combined into the previously named luxury LS. The former LS model is now the ES model. Base Galants are now called S models. Confused? So are we. All 1993 Galants use the SOHC 2.0-liter engine, which makes 121-horsepower this year with the addition of an extra two valves per cylinder.

Model Description	Trade-in Value	Market Value

RATINGS (SCALE OF 1-10)

Overall	Safety	Reliability	Performance	Comfort	Value
N/A	N/A	8.6	7.4	7.9	5.8

Category D

4 Dr ES Sdn	3445	4595
4 Dr LS Sdn	3665	4895
4 Dr S Sdn	2815	3755

OPTIONS FOR GALANT

Auto 4-Speed Transmission[Opt on S] +305
AM/FM Compact Disc Player +95
Air Conditioning +170
Aluminum/Alloy Wheels[Opt on ES] +95
Cruise Control[Opt on S] +50
Power Door Locks[Opt on S] +55
Power Sunroof +155
Power Windows[Opt on S] +55
Premium Sound System +75

MIGHTY MAX PICKUP 1993

The Mighty Max is unchanged for 1993.

Category G

2 Dr STD Ext Cab SB	3035	3845
2 Dr STD Std Cab SB	2575	3265
2 Dr STD 4WD Std Cab SB	3935	4995

OPTIONS FOR MIGHTY MAX PICKUP

Auto 4-Speed Transmission +165
AM/FM Stereo Tape +45
Air Conditioning +165
Bed Liner +55
Limited Slip Diff +55
Power Steering[Std on 4WD] +55

MIRAGE 1993

The Mirage is totally redesigned this year, gaining size but losing weight. A coupe and sedan are offered in Base, S, ES and LS trim-levels. A five-speed manual transmission is standard on all vehicles, although an automatic is available on all Mirages except the S coupe. Antilock brakes make their first appearance on the Mirage, becoming an available option on the LS sedan.

RATINGS (SCALE OF 1-10)

Overall	Safety	Reliability	Performance	Comfort	Value
N/A	N/A	6.5	8.2	7	6.6

Category E

2 Dr ES Cpe	2165	3050
4 Dr ES Sdn	2545	3585
2 Dr LS Cpe	2475	3490
4 Dr LS Sdn	2915	4105
2 Dr S Cpe	1870	2630
4 Dr S Sdn	2305	3245

Don't forget to refer to the Mileage Adjustment Table at the back of this book!

MITSUBISHI 93-92

Model Description	Trade-in Value	Market Value	Model Description	Trade-in Value	Market Value

OPTIONS FOR MIRAGE

Auto 3-Speed Transmission +95
Auto 4-Speed Transmission +130
Air Conditioning +165
Aluminum/Alloy Wheels[Opt on Sdn] +65
Anti-Lock Brakes +135
Compact Disc W/fm/tape +95
Cruise Control[Opt on ES] +45
Power Door Locks[Opt on ES,S,LS,Cpe] +50
Power Steering[Opt on S,ES Cpe] +50
Power Windows[Opt on ES,S,LS,Cpe] +55
Tilt Steering Wheel[Opt on ES] +30

MONTERO   1993

Shift-on-the-fly four-wheel drive is introduced in the 1993 Montero. Antilock brakes become standard equipment for the SR and optional for the RS; they were formerly standard only on the LS. Top-of-the-line Monteros may now be ordered with a leather and wood package, for those who really want to get down and dirty.

RATINGS (SCALE OF 1-10)

Overall	Safety	Reliability	Performance	Comfort	Value
N/A	N/A	N/A	N/A	N/A	4.2

Category G

4 Dr LS 4WD Wgn	7945	10080
4 Dr RS 4WD Wgn	7270	9220
4 Dr SR 4WD Wgn	8135	10320
4 Dr STD 4WD Wgn	6845	8680

OPTIONS FOR MONTERO

Auto 4-Speed Transmission[Std on LS,SR] +165
Montero Lthr & Wood Pkg +235
AM/FM Compact Disc Player +65
Air Conditioning +165
Cruise Control[Opt on RS] +40
Leather Seats +155
Limited Slip Diff +55
Luggage Rack +30
Power Door Locks[Opt on RS] +45
Power Sunroof +160
Power Windows[Opt on RS] +50

PRECIS   1993

No changes for the last year of this little hatchback.
Category E

2 Dr STD Hbk	1415	1990

OPTIONS FOR PRECIS

Auto 4-Speed Transmission +130
AM/FM Stereo Tape +60
Air Conditioning +165
Power Steering +50

1992 MITSUBISHI

3000GT   1992

New paint. That's the only change for the highly touted 3000GT.

RATINGS (SCALE OF 1-10)

Overall	Safety	Reliability	Performance	Comfort	Value
N/A	6.9	7.4	8.8	6.6	N/A

Category F

2 Dr SL Cpe	6305	8390
2 Dr STD Cpe	5210	6935
2 Dr VR-4 Turbo 4WD Cpe	7865	10470

OPTIONS FOR 3000GT

Auto 4-Speed Transmission +135
Air Conditioning[Opt on STD] +135
Anti-Lock Brakes[Opt on STD] +105
Compact Disc W/fm/tape +80
Leather Seats +105
Sunroof +65

DIAMANTE   1992

As a replacement for the low-tech Sigma, the Diamante offers V6 power delivering 175-horsepower in the base model, 202-horsepower in the LS. Antilock brakes are standard on the LS and optional on the base, and a driver airbag is standard on both models. A Euro Handling Package and an electronically controlled suspension that includes traction control is an available option on the LS.

RATINGS (SCALE OF 1-10)

Overall	Safety	Reliability	Performance	Comfort	Value
N/A	N/A	7.1	8.4	8.4	4.2

Category D

4 Dr LS Sdn	4560	6360
4 Dr STD Sdn	4075	5680

OPTIONS FOR DIAMANTE

Euro Handling Pkg +270
Luxury Pkg +125
AM/FM Compact Disc Player +75
Anti-Lock Brakes[Std on LS] +145
Leather Seats +185
Power Passenger Seat +50
Power Sunroof +125

ECLIPSE   1992

Freshened front-end styling includes aero headlights and a new air dam. The GS-X model loses leather trim from its options list.

RATINGS (SCALE OF 1-10)

Overall	Safety	Reliability	Performance	Comfort	Value
N/A	N/A	7.8	8.4	6.8	3.3

Don't forget to refer to the Mileage Adjustment Table at the back of this book!

Model Description	Trade-in Value	Market Value
Category F		
2 Dr GS Hbk	3035	4040
2 Dr GS Turbo Hbk	3570	4755
2 Dr GSX Turbo 4WD Hbk	4570	6080
2 Dr STD Hbk	2735	3640

OPTIONS FOR ECLIPSE
Auto 4-Speed Transmission +115
Air Conditioning[Std on GSX] +135
Anti-Lock Brakes +105
Power Door Locks[Opt on GS] +35
Power Steering[Opt on STD] +60
Power Windows[Opt on GS] +40
Sunroof +65

EXPO   1992

Mitsubishi creates a van/station wagon hybrid. Designed to compete with everything from the Dodge Caravan to the Subaru Legacy wagon, the Expo seats seven while the Expo LRV seats five. Three models are available including a Sport all-wheel drive, a logical choice for residents of bad-weather states.

Model Description	Trade-in Value	Market Value
Category E		
2 Dr LRV Hbk	2325	3550
2 Dr LRV Sport Hbk	2490	3800
2 Dr LRV Sport 4WD Hbk	2875	4385
4 Dr SP Hbk	3000	4575
4 Dr SP 4WD Hbk	3265	4985

OPTIONS FOR EXPO
Auto 4-Speed Transmission +110
Air Conditioning +135
Anti-Lock Brakes +110
Power Door Locks +40
Power Sunroof +100
Power Windows +45

GALANT   1992

The GS-X model is discontinued in favor of ultra-high performance VR-4. A 195-horsepower engine lurks under its sedate exterior. Standard antilock brakes, four-wheel steering, and leather seating surfaces are a few of the standard equipment items found on this very competent sedan. A Euro Handling Package and an Electronically Controlled Suspension are available options on the LS model.

RATINGS (SCALE OF 1-10)

Overall	Safety	Reliability	Performance	Comfort	Value
N/A	N/A	7.9	7.4	7.9	5.2

Model Description	Trade-in Value	Market Value
Category D		
4 Dr GS Sdn	2990	4175
4 Dr GSR Sdn	3280	4580
4 Dr GSX 4WD Sdn	3480	4855
4 Dr LS Sdn	2865	4000

Model Description	Trade-in Value	Market Value
4 Dr STD Sdn	2320	3240
4 Dr VR-4 Turbo 4WD Sdn	4060	5665

OPTIONS FOR GALANT
Auto 4-Speed Transmission[Opt on GS,STD] +180
AM/FM Compact Disc Player +75
Air Conditioning[Std on VR4] +140
Anti-Lock Brakes[Std on VR4] +145
Leather Seats +185
Power Door Locks[Opt on STD] +45
Power Sunroof +125
Power Windows[Opt on STD] +45

MIGHTY MAX PICKUP   1992

Safety-interlocks are now standard on manual transmission models, requiring the clutch to be fully depressed before the vehicle will start. The automatic transmission also gets a shift-interlock, requiring the brake to be depressed before the car can be shifted out of park. Two-wheel-drive Mighty Max models lose their rear-wheel antilock brakes.

Model Description	Trade-in Value	Market Value
Category G		
2 Dr Mighty Max Std Cab SB	2335	2995
2 Dr Mighty Max 4WD Std Cab SB	3495	4490
2 Dr Mighty Max Macro Ext Cab SB	2690	3455

OPTIONS FOR MIGHTY MAX PICKUP
Auto 4-Speed Transmission +125
Air Conditioning +135
Limited Slip Diff +45
Power Steering[Std on 4WD] +45

MIRAGE   1992

Base models finally lose the sticky vinyl interior in favor of full-cloth seats. LS models receive minor exterior trim changes.

Model Description	Trade-in Value	Market Value
Category E		
4 Dr GS Sdn	2110	3225
4 Dr LS Sdn	1795	2740
2 Dr STD Hbk	1510	2300
4 Dr STD Sdn	1695	2585
2 Dr VL Hbk	1400	2135

OPTIONS FOR MIRAGE
Auto 3-Speed Transmission +85
Auto 4-Speed Transmission +105
Air Conditioning +135

MONTERO   1992

An all-new Montero is introduced. The new Montero features new wheels, a new grille, more interesting sheetmetal, more curves around the edges, and a very serious-looking blackout treatment on the formerly chrome accessories. Horsepower is upped but only

---

Don't forget to refer to the Mileage Adjustment Table at the back of this book!

MITSUBISHI 92-91

Model Description	Trade-in Value	Market Value	Model Description	Trade-in Value	Market Value

enough to keep pace with its 125-pound weight gain. Antilock brakes are standard on the LS and optional on the SR model, working in both two- and four-wheel-drive mode.

RATINGS (SCALE OF 1-10)

Overall	Safety	Reliability	Performance	Comfort	Value
N/A	N/A	N/A	N/A	N/A	5.2

Category G

4 Dr LS 4WD Wgn	6955	8930
4 Dr RS 4WD Wgn	5955	7645
4 Dr SR 4WD Wgn	6790	8720
4 Dr STD 4WD Wgn	5705	7325

OPTIONS FOR MONTERO
Auto 4-Speed Transmission[Std on LS,SR] +130
Air Conditioning +135
Anti-Lock Brakes[Opt on SR] +95
Compact Disc W/fm/tape +70
Leather Seats +130
Limited Slip Diff[Opt on SR] +45
Power Door Locks[Opt on RS] +40
Power Sunroof +130
Power Windows[Opt on RS] +40

ONE TON   1992

Category G

2 Dr Mighty Max Std Cab SB	2400	3080

OPTIONS FOR ONE TON
Air Conditioning +135

PRECIS   1992

The bargain-basement Precis gets a nose job.

Category E

2 Dr STD Hbk	1095	1670

OPTIONS FOR PRECIS
Auto 4-Speed Transmission +105
Air Conditioning +135
Power Steering +40

1991 MITSUBISHI

3000GT   1991

Dumping the Starion in favor of the 3000GT is one of the better decisions made by Mitsubishi this decade. Gorgeous styling, exceptional handling, and available all-wheel drive characterize the improvements the 3000GT has over Mitsubishi's previous sports cars. A driver airbag is standard on all models; antilock brakes are standard on the SL and VR-4 models.

RATINGS (SCALE OF 1-10)

Overall	Safety	Reliability	Performance	Comfort	Value
N/A	6.8	6.9	8.8	6.6	N/A

Category F

2 Dr SL Cpe	5075	7410
2 Dr STD Cpe	4230	6175
2 Dr VR-4 Turbo 4WD Cpe	6300	9200

OPTIONS FOR 3000GT
Auto 4-Speed Transmission +110
Anti-Lock Brakes[Opt on STD] +85
Compact Disc W/fm/tape +65
Leather Seats +85
Power Windows[Opt on STD] +30

ECLIPSE   1991

Antilock brakes are offered on the GS-T and GSX models.

RATINGS (SCALE OF 1-10)

Overall	Safety	Reliability	Performance	Comfort	Value
N/A	N/A	7.3	8.4	6.8	4.2

Category F

2 Dr GS Hbk	2520	3675
2 Dr GS Turbo Hbk	3120	4555
2 Dr GSX Turbo 4WD Hbk	3435	5015
2 Dr STD Hbk	2405	3515

OPTIONS FOR ECLIPSE
4 cyl 2.0 L 16V Engine +120
Auto 3-Speed Transmission +85
Auto 4-Speed Transmission +90
Turbo Pkg +400
Air Conditioning +110
Anti-Lock Brakes +85
Power Door Locks +25
Power Steering[Opt on STD] +45
Power Windows +30

GALANT   1991

A sporty GSR model is added to the lineup.

RATINGS (SCALE OF 1-10)

Overall	Safety	Reliability	Performance	Comfort	Value
N/A	N/A	7.6	7.4	7.9	5.2

Category D

4 Dr GS Sdn	2585	3925
4 Dr GSR Sdn	2650	4030
4 Dr GSX 4WD Sdn	2900	4405
4 Dr LS Sdn	2420	3680
4 Dr STD Sdn	2255	3430
4 Dr VR-4 Turbo 4WD Sdn	3255	4950

OPTIONS FOR GALANT
Auto 4-Speed Transmission[Opt on GS,STD] +140
AM/FM Compact Disc Player +60
Air Conditioning[Std on VR4] +115
Anti-Lock Brakes[Opt on GS,GSX] +120
Power Door Locks[Opt on STD] +35

Don't forget to refer to the Mileage Adjustment Table at the back of this book!

Model Description	Trade-in Value	Market Value	Model Description	Trade-in Value	Market Value

Power Sunroof +105
Power Windows[Opt on STD] +35

MIGHTY MAX PICKUP 1991

A Special Edition Package is added to the option list, featuring wide-spoke wheels, upgraded seats, better carpet, and a tachometer for four-wheel-drive models.

Category G

2 Dr Mighty Max Std Cab SB	1790	2580
2 Dr Mighty Max 4WD Std Cab SB		
	2680	3870
2 Dr Mighty Max Macro Ext Cab SB		
	2060	2975

OPTIONS FOR MIGHTY MAX PICKUP
Auto 3-Speed Transmission +100
Air Conditioning +110
Anti-Lock Brakes +75
Limited Slip Diff +35
Power Steering[Std on 4WD] +40

MIRAGE 1991

No changes for the Mirage.
Category E

4 Dr GS Sdn	1360	2725
4 Dr LS Sdn	1185	2370
2 Dr STD Hbk	1040	2080
4 Dr STD Sdn	1230	2455
2 Dr VL Hbk	970	1945

OPTIONS FOR MIRAGE
Auto 3-Speed Transmission +75
Auto 4-Speed Transmission +85
Air Conditioning +110
Power Door Locks +35
Power Windows +35

MONTERO 1991

The slow-selling two-door Montero is dropped in favor of the popular four-door. Base models are no longer available with an automatic transmission. RS models now come standard with an automatic. The top-end LS model is available with a manual or automatic transmission.

Category G

4 Dr LS 4WD Wgn	4330	6245
4 Dr RS 4WD Wgn	3845	5550
4 Dr STD 4WD Wgn	3580	5165

OPTIONS FOR MONTERO
Auto 4-Speed Transmission[Opt on LS] +95
Air Conditioning +110
Power Sunroof +105
Power Windows[Opt on RS] +30
Theft Deterrent System +40

ONE TON 1991

Category G

2 Dr Mighty Max Std Cab LB	1830	2640

OPTIONS FOR ONE TON
Air Conditioning +110

PRECIS 1991

No changes for the Hyundai-twin.
Category E

2 Dr RS Hbk	780	1555
2 Dr STD Hbk	720	1440

OPTIONS FOR PRECIS
Auto 4-Speed Transmission +80
Air Conditioning +110
Power Steering +35

Don't forget to refer to the Mileage Adjustment Table at the back of this book!

Model Description	Trade-in Value	Market Value	Model Description	Trade-in Value	Market Value

NISSAN   Japan

1996 Nissan 300ZX

2000 NISSAN

ALTIMA   2000

2000 Altimas receive fresh sheetmetal, comfort and convenience enhancements, engine refinements, and a revised suspension.

Category D

	Trade-in	Market
4 Dr GLE Sdn	14815	17310
4 Dr GXE Sdn	12945	14955
4 Dr SE Sdn	13575	15860
4 Dr XE Sdn	11095	12965

OPTIONS FOR ALTIMA
Auto 4-Speed Transmission[Std on GLE] +655
XE Option Pkg +1230
AM/FM Compact Disc Player +380
Air Conditioning[Std on GLE,SE] +705
Cruise Control[Std on GLE,SE] +205
Power Door Locks[Opt on GXE] +220
Power Moonroof +690

FRONTIER   2000

Nissan's pickup line expands to 11 models, including the new Desert Runner and a four-door Frontier Crew Cab.

Category G

	Trade-in	Market
2 Dr Desert Runner SE Ext Cab SB	13510	15690
2 Dr Desert Runner XE Ext Cab SB	11935	13860
4 Dr SE Crew Cab SB	14025	16285
4 Dr SE 4WD Crew Cab SB	16725	19425
2 Dr SE 4WD Ext Cab SB	15420	17905
4 Dr XE Crew Cab SB	13070	15180
4 Dr XE 4WD Crew Cab SB	14980	17395
2 Dr XE Ext Cab SB	10320	11985
2 Dr XE 4WD Ext Cab SB	13110	15220
2 Dr XE Std Cab SB	8890	10320
2 Dr XE V6 4WD Ext Cab SB	13845	16075

OPTIONS FOR FRONTIER
Auto 4-Speed Transmission +830
AM/FM Compact Disc Player[Std on Desert Runner SE, SE] +260
AM/FM Stereo Tape +180
Air Conditioning[Std on Desert Runner SE,SE, Crew Cab] +670
Alarm System +220
Aluminum/Alloy Wheels[Std on Desert Runner SE,SE] +265
Bed Liner +230
Cruise Control[Opt on Desert Runner XE,XE,XE V6, Crew Cab] +170
Flip-Up Sunroof +270
Keyless Entry System +160
Limited Slip Diff +225
Power Door Locks +190
Power Mirrors +110
Power Windows +200
Privacy Glass[Std on Desert Runner SE,SE,Crew Cab] +225
Sliding Rear Window[Std on Desert Runner SE, Desert Runner XE,SE,Crew Cab] +100
Tilt Steering Wheel[Std on Desert Runner SE,SE] +145

MAXIMA   2000

The Maxima has been (controversially) redesigned, providing more power, more room and more amenities to the luxury/performance sedan buyer. Key among the improvements is 222 horsepower from the standard V6, a boost in rear-seat legroom and an available 200-watt Bose audio system.

Category D

	Trade-in	Market
4 Dr GLE Sdn	21075	24320
4 Dr GXE Sdn	17805	20420
4 Dr SE Sdn	17375	20305

OPTIONS FOR MAXIMA
Auto 4-Speed Transmission[Std on GLE] +840
Aluminum/Alloy Wheels[Opt on GXE] +380
Power Drivers Seat +255
Power Moonroof +690

PATHFINDER   2000

After a substantial update in the middle of the 1999 model year, the Pathfinder soldiers into the new millennium without change. However, rumor has it that later in 2000 the Pathfinder will get a massive power upgrade.

Category G

	Trade-in	Market
4 Dr LE Wgn	21495	24960
4 Dr LE 4WD Wgn	22935	26635
4 Dr SE Wgn	20090	23330

Don't forget to refer to the Mileage Adjustment Table at the back of this book!

Model Description	Trade-in Value	Market Value
4 Dr SE 4WD Wgn	21530	25000
4 Dr XE Wgn	19405	22535
4 Dr XE 4WD Wgn	20845	24205

OPTIONS FOR PATHFINDER
Auto 4-Speed Transmission[Opt on SE] +815
Cruise Control[Opt on XE] +170
Garage Door Opener[Std on LE] +120
Heated Power Mirrors[Opt on XE] +65
Leather Seats +640
Power Door Locks[Opt on XE] +190
Power Drivers Seat +230
Power Moonroof +710
Power Windows[Opt on XE] +200
Side Air Bag Restraint +320

QUEST 2000

A stabilizer bar is now standard on the GLE model while new titanium-colored accents have been added to the 16-inch SE and 15-inch GXE alloy wheels. The SE gets auto on/off headlights and all Quests now come with a video entertainment system at no extra cost.

Category G

	Trade-in	Market
2 Dr GLE	18700	21715
2 Dr GXE	15825	18375
2 Dr SE	17310	20100

OPTIONS FOR QUEST
Aluminum/Alloy Wheels[Opt on GXE] +265
Dual Air Conditioning[Opt on GXE] +755
Garage Door Opener[Opt on SE] +120
Leather Seats[Opt on SE] +640
Power Drivers Seat +230

SENTRA 2000

The Sentra has been completely overhauled for the 2000 model year. A better ride, more powerful engines, and a new enviro-friendly version top the bill, and we likes what we sees.

Category E

	Trade-in	Market
4 Dr GXE Sdn	10525	12380
4 Dr SE Sdn	11575	13615
4 Dr XE Sdn	9135	10745

OPTIONS FOR SENTRA
Auto 4-Speed Transmission +640
AM/FM Stereo Tape +250
Air Conditioning[Opt on XE] +680

XTERRA 2000

A truck-based mini-SUV, the athletic new Xterra competes with several smaller vehicles built on car platforms.

Category G

	Trade-in	Market
4 Dr SE Wgn	17940	20830
4 Dr SE 4WD Wgn	19480	22615

Model Description	Trade-in Value	Market Value
4 Dr XE Wgn	13940	16185
4 Dr XE V6 4WD Wgn	16360	19000

OPTIONS FOR XTERRA
Auto 4-Speed Transmission +765
AM/FM Compact Disc Player[Opt on XE] +260
Alarm System[Std on SE] +220
Aluminum/Alloy Wheels[Std on SE] +265
Cruise Control[Std on SE] +170
Fog Lights[Std on SE] +120
Keyless Entry System[Std on SE] +160
Limited Slip Diff[Std on SE] +225
Luggage Rack[Std on SE] +130
Power Door Locks[Std on SE] +190
Power Mirrors[Std on SE] +110
Power Windows[Std on SE] +200
Rear Window Wiper[Std on SE] +125
Tilt Steering Wheel[Std on SE] +145

1999 NISSAN

ALTIMA 1999

All 1999 models get two new exterior colors, improved speakers and a new head unit for the three-in-one stereo combo. The GLE trim level gets alloy wheels added to its standard equipment list, and all alloy wheels now have a bright finish instead of a painted finish. All SE trim levels are now called SE Limited (SE-L) models and come with additional equipment.

RATINGS (SCALE OF 1-10)

Overall	Safety	Reliability	Performance	Comfort	Value
N/A	N/A	N/A	8	7.8	N/A

Category D

	Trade-in	Market
4 Dr GLE Sdn	13280	15590
4 Dr GXE Sdn	11465	13465
4 Dr SE Sdn	12800	15030
4 Dr SE Limited Sdn	13340	15660
4 Dr XE Sdn	11670	13420

OPTIONS FOR ALTIMA
Auto 4-Speed Transmission[Std on GLE] +535
Air Conditioning[Opt on XE] +575
Cruise Control[Opt on XE] +165
Keyless Entry System[Opt on GXE] +210
Leather Seats[Std on GLE] +760
Power Drivers Seat[Std on GLE] +210
Power Moonroof +565

FRONTIER 1999

Two new King Cab models debut with a powerful V6 engine under the hood, and new standard and optional equipment is available.

RATINGS (SCALE OF 1-10)

Overall	Safety	Reliability	Performance	Comfort	Value
N/A	N/A	N/A	6	7.3	N/A

Model Description	Trade-in Value	Market Value
Category G		
2 Dr SE Ext Cab SB	10945	12810
2 Dr SE 4WD Ext Cab SB	14615	17105
2 Dr XE Ext Cab SB	9890	11570
2 Dr XE 4WD Ext Cab SB	12570	14710
2 Dr XE Std Cab SB	9275	10915
2 Dr XE 4WD Std Cab SB	11650	13635
2 Dr XE V6 4WD Ext Cab SB	13275	15535

OPTIONS FOR FRONTIER

Auto 4-Speed Transmission +700
Air Conditioning[Std on SE] +550
Aluminum/Alloy Wheels[Std on SE] +215
Bed Liner +185
Compact Disc W/fm/tape +295
Cruise Control +140
Keyless Entry System +130
Power Door Locks +155
Power Mirrors +90
Power Windows +160
Sliding Rear Window[Std on SE] +80
Tilt Steering Wheel[Std on SE] +120

MAXIMA   1999

Traction Control is now available on models with automatic transmissions and, in addition to minor interior enhancements, four new colors debut. The SE trim level has been renamed SE-Limited (SE-L) and offers new standard features.

RATINGS (SCALE OF 1-10)

Overall	Safety	Reliability	Performance	Comfort	Value
N/A	7.5	9.1	8	7.8	N/A

	Trade-in	Market
Category D		
4 Dr GLE Sdn	18495	21715
4 Dr GXE Sdn	14835	17420
4 Dr SE Sdn	16185	19000
4 Dr SE Limited Sdn	16185	19000

OPTIONS FOR MAXIMA

Auto 4-Speed Transmission[Std on GLE] +835
Aluminum/Alloy Wheels[Opt on GXE] +310
Anti-Lock Brakes +595
Bose Sound System[Std on GLE] +520
Compact Disc W/fm/tape[Opt on GXE] +520
Dual Power Seats[Std on GLE] +570
Heated Front Seats +250
Keyless Entry System[Std on GLE] +210
Leather Seats[Std on GLE] +760
Power Drivers Seat +210
Power Moonroof +565
Side Air Bag Restraint +195

PATHFINDER   1999

Only the LE trim level sees change in 1999, with new body-color fender flares and SE-style alloy wheels, tires and tubular step rails.

RATINGS (SCALE OF 1-10)

Overall	Safety	Reliability	Performance	Comfort	Value
N/A	7	8.7	7.4	8.3	N/A

	Trade-in	Market
Category G		
4 Dr LE Wgn	20910	24545
4 Dr LE 4WD Wgn	22565	26470
1999.5 4 Dr LE Wgn	20480	23965
1999.5 4 Dr LE 4WD Wgn	21860	25580
4 Dr SE 4WD Wgn	20515	24005
1999.5 4 Dr SE Limited Wgn	19135	22395
1999.5 4 Dr SE Limited 4WD Wgn	20515	24005
4 Dr XE Wgn	17080	19985
4 Dr XE 4WD Wgn	18380	21505
1999.5 4 Dr XE Wgn	18485	21625
1999.5 4 Dr XE 4WD Wgn	19860	23240

OPTIONS FOR PATHFINDER

Auto 4-Speed Transmission[Std on LE] +690
Aluminum/Alloy Wheels[Opt on XE] +215
Bose Sound System[Std on LE] +525
Compact Disc W/fm/tape[Std on LE] +295
Cruise Control[Opt on XE] +140
Dual Power Seats +280
Fog Lights[Opt on XE] +95
Heated Front Seats[Std on LE 4WD] +180
Keyless Entry System[Opt on XE] +130
Leather Seats[Std on LE, SE Limited] +525
Limited Slip Diff[Std on LE 4WD] +185
Power Door Locks[Opt on XE] +155
Power Moonroof +580
Power Windows[Opt on XE] +160

QUEST   1999

Nissan redesigns its minivan for 1999 and adds a new SE trim level, standard driver-side sliding rear door and a more powerful engine.

RATINGS (SCALE OF 1-10)

Overall	Safety	Reliability	Performance	Comfort	Value
N/A	N/A	8.6	6.8	7.5	N/A

	Trade-in	Market
Category G		
2 Dr GLE Pass. Van	17250	20185
2 Dr GXE Pass. Van	14740	17250
2 Dr SE Pass. Van	16405	19195

OPTIONS FOR QUEST

Compact Disc W/fm/tape +295
Dual Air Conditioning[Opt on GXE] +615
Dual Power Seats[Opt on SE] +280
Leather Seats[Std on GLE] +525
Power Moonroof +580

SENTRA   1999

Fresh front-end styling, a Limited Edition Option Package for GXE models, and some new paint colors constitute the changes for 1999.

Don't forget to refer to the Mileage Adjustment Table at the back of this book!

Model Description	Trade-in Value	Market Value

RATINGS (SCALE OF 1-10)

Overall	Safety	Reliability	Performance	Comfort	Value
N/A	6.4	N/A	6.4	6.9	N/A

Category E

Model	Trade-in	Market
4 Dr GXE Sdn	9080	11025
4 Dr SE Sdn	10660	12715
4 Dr SE Limited Sdn	10860	12915
4 Dr XE Sdn	8475	10085

OPTIONS FOR SENTRA

Auto 4-Speed Transmission +535
AM/FM Compact Disc Player[Opt on GXE,SE] +290
Air Conditioning[Opt on XE] +555
Anti-Lock Brakes +445
Keyless Entry System[Std on SE Limited] +110
Power Moonroof +390

1998 NISSAN

200SX   1998

Exterior enhancements include new headlights, taillights, front and rear bumpers and revised grille. Three new colors are available for 1998.

RATINGS (SCALE OF 1-10)

Overall	Safety	Reliability	Performance	Comfort	Value
N/A	6.6	8.6	7.8	6.8	N/A

Category F

Model	Trade-in	Market
2 Dr SE Cpe	9570	11440
2 Dr SE-R Cpe	10385	12410
2 Dr STD Cpe	8215	9820

OPTIONS FOR 200SX

Auto 4-Speed Transmission +435
AM/FM Compact Disc Player[Opt on STD] +255
Air Conditioning[Opt on STD] +460
Anti-Lock Brakes +355
Keyless Entry System +100
Power Moonroof +360

240SX   1998

No changes to Nissan's sporty coupe.

RATINGS (SCALE OF 1-10)

Overall	Safety	Reliability	Performance	Comfort	Value
6.8	6.5	8.7	8.4	7.6	2.7

Category F

Model	Trade-in	Market
2 Dr LE Cpe	14990	17920
2 Dr SE Cpe	13705	16380
2 Dr STD Cpe	11485	13730

OPTIONS FOR 240SX

Auto 4-Speed Transmission +435
AM/FM Compact Disc Player +255
Air Conditioning[Opt on STD] +460
Aluminum/Alloy Wheels[Opt on STD] +170

Anti-Lock Brakes +355
Cruise Control[Opt on STD] +120
Power Door Locks[Opt on STD] +110
Power Mirrors[Opt on STD] +65
Power Moonroof[Std on LE] +360
Tilt Steering Wheel[Opt on STD] +150

ALTIMA   1998

Altima is totally, and unnecessarily, redesigned for 1998. The Altima's new look is more wedge-shaped, with a trunk that looks like it has met the business end of a band saw. Standard equipment is up, including a CD player on every model except the XE.

RATINGS (SCALE OF 1-10)

Overall	Safety	Reliability	Performance	Comfort	Value
N/A	N/A	9	8	7.8	N/A

Category D

Model	Trade-in	Market
4 Dr GLE Sdn	12055	14205
4 Dr GXE Sdn	10985	12940
4 Dr SE Sdn	11790	13890
4 Dr XE Sdn	9615	11330

OPTIONS FOR ALTIMA

Auto 4-Speed Transmission[Std on GLE] +435
Air Conditioning[Opt on XE] +470
Aluminum/Alloy Wheels[Std on SE] +255
Anti-Lock Brakes +485
Compact Disc W/fm/tape[Opt on GXE] +425
Cruise Control[Opt on XE] +135
Keyless Entry System[Opt on GXE] +170
Leather Seats[Opt on SE] +620
Power Drivers Seat[Std on GLE] +170
Power Moonroof +460

FRONTIER   1998

Nissan introduces an all-new truck for 1998. This model, named the Frontier, is larger than the model it replaces, and has improved interior ergonomics.

RATINGS (SCALE OF 1-10)

Overall	Safety	Reliability	Performance	Comfort	Value
N/A	N/A	8.9	6	7.3	N/A

Category G

Model	Trade-in	Market
2 Dr SE Ext Cab SB	9080	11125
2 Dr SE 4WD Ext Cab SB	13185	15560
2 Dr STD Cab SB	7660	9040
2 Dr XE Ext Cab SB	9285	10960
2 Dr XE 4WD Ext Cab SB	11465	13530
2 Dr XE Std Cab SB	8395	9910
2 Dr XE 4WD Std Cab SB	10730	12665

OPTIONS FOR FRONTIER

Auto 4-Speed Transmission[Opt on 2WD] +575
Aluminum/Alloy Wheels[Std on SE, XE 2WD Ext Cab SB] +175

NISSAN 98

Model Description	Trade-in Value	Market Value	Model Description	Trade-in Value	Market Value

Bed Liner[Opt on STD, XE, 2WD] +155
Compact Disc W/fm/tape[Opt on XE] +240
Cruise Control[Opt on XE] +115
Keyless Entry System[Opt on XE] +105
Power Door Locks[Opt on XE] +130
Power Mirrors[Opt on XE] +70
Power Windows[Opt on XE] +135
Sliding Rear Window[Opt on XE] +65
Tilt Steering Wheel[Opt on XE] +100

MAXIMA   1998

Side-impact airbags are added to the optional equipment lists of the SE and GLE models. Sterling Mist is a new color choice for this sporty sedan.

RATINGS (SCALE OF 1-10)

Overall	Safety	Reliability	Performance	Comfort	Value
7.3	7.5	9	8	7.8	4.1

Category D
4 Dr GLE Sdn	16955	19975
4 Dr GXE Sdn	13610	16035
4 Dr SE Sdn	14850	17495

OPTIONS FOR MAXIMA

Auto 4-Speed Transmission[Std on GLE] +750
Aluminum/Alloy Wheels[Opt on GXE] +255
Anti-Lock Brakes +485
Bose Sound System +425
Climate Control for AC[Opt on SE] +165
Compact Disc W/fm/tape[Opt on GXE] +425
Dual Power Seats[Opt on SE] +465
Heated Front Seats +205
Keyless Entry System[Std on GLE] +170
Leather Seats[Opt on SE] +620
Power Drivers Seat +170
Power Moonroof +460
Side Air Bag Restraint +160

PATHFINDER   1998

The only changes to the 1998 Pathfinder include chrome bumpers for the XE model, the addition of air conditioning to XE and SE standard equipment lists and additions to the XE Sport Package equipment.

RATINGS (SCALE OF 1-10)

Overall	Safety	Reliability	Performance	Comfort	Value
7	7	8.8	7.4	8.3	3.5

Category G
4 Dr LE Wgn	18620	21980
4 Dr LE 4WD Wgn	20065	23685
4 Dr SE 4WD Wgn	17810	21020
4 Dr XE Wgn	14740	17395
4 Dr XE 4WD Wgn	15945	18820

OPTIONS FOR PATHFINDER

Auto 4-Speed Transmission[Std on LE] +545
Aluminum/Alloy Wheels[Opt on XE] +175

Bose Sound System[Opt on SE] +430
Compact Disc W/fm/tape[Opt on SE] +240
Cruise Control[Opt on XE] +115
Dual Power Seats +230
Fog Lights[Opt on XE] +80
Heated Front Seats[Opt on SE] +150
Heated Power Mirrors[Opt on XE] +45
Keyless Entry System[Opt on XE] +105
Leather Seats[Opt on SE] +430
Limited Slip Diff[Std on LE] +150
Power Door Locks[Opt on XE] +130
Power Moonroof +475
Power Windows[Opt on XE] +135

QUEST   1998

No changes to the 1998 Quest.

RATINGS (SCALE OF 1-10)

Overall	Safety	Reliability	Performance	Comfort	Value
7.5	6.8	8.2	6.2	7.5	8.7

Category G
2 Dr GXE Pass. Van	15435	18215
2 Dr XE Pass. Van	13910	16420

OPTIONS FOR QUEST

Aluminum/Alloy Wheels[Opt on XE] +175
Anti-Lock Brakes[Opt on XE] +320
Captain Chairs (4)[Opt on XE] +335
Climate Control for AC +105
Compact Disc W/fm/tape[Opt on XE] +240
Dual Air Conditioning[Opt on XE] +505
Dual Power Seats +230
Leather Seats +430
Power Moonroof +475

SENTRA   1998

A new Sentra SE debuts, sporting the same 140-horespower engine and styling cues found in the 200SX SE-R coupe. Other changes include an exterior freshening that features new front and rear fascias.

RATINGS (SCALE OF 1-10)

Overall	Safety	Reliability	Performance	Comfort	Value
6.7	6.3	8.7	6.4	6.9	5.4

Category E
4 Dr GLE Sdn	9615	11540
4 Dr GXE Sdn	9110	10935
4 Dr SE Sdn	10205	12250
4 Dr STD Sdn	7095	8520
4 Dr XE Sdn	7185	8865

OPTIONS FOR SENTRA

Auto 4-Speed Transmission +435
Air Conditioning[Opt on STD] +455
Anti-Lock Brakes +430
Compact Disc W/fm/tape[Std on GLE] +265
Keyless Entry System[Opt on SE] +90
Power Moonroof +320

Don't forget to refer to the Mileage Adjustment Table at the back of this book!

Model Description	Trade-in Value	Market Value	Model Description	Trade-in Value	Market Value

1997 NISSAN

200SX — 1997

A spoiler is now standard on all models. An additional exterior color is the only other change for 1997.

RATINGS (SCALE OF 1-10)

Overall	Safety	Reliability	Performance	Comfort	Value
6.9	6.6	7.7	7.8	6.8	5.5

Category F

2 Dr SE Cpe	8920	10645
2 Dr SE-R Cpe	9710	11585
2 Dr STD Cpe	7595	9065

OPTIONS FOR 200SX

Auto 4-Speed Transmission +355
AM/FM Compact Disc Player +205
AM/FM Stereo Tape[Opt on STD] +100
Air Conditioning[Opt on STD] +375
Anti-Lock Brakes +290
Compact Disc Changer +285
Power Moonroof +290

240SX — 1997

Extensive exterior changes update the look of the 240SX. A luxury model is introduced midyear.

RATINGS (SCALE OF 1-10)

Overall	Safety	Reliability	Performance	Comfort	Value
6.7	6.5	8.5	8.4	7.6	2.6

Category F

2 Dr LE Cpe	12705	15160
2 Dr SE Cpe	11770	14045
2 Dr STD Cpe	9865	11770

OPTIONS FOR 240SX

Auto 4-Speed Transmission +365
Air Conditioning[Opt on STD] +375
Aluminum/Alloy Wheels[Opt on STD] +135
Anti-Lock Brakes +290
Cruise Control[Opt on STD] +100
Leather Seats[Opt on SE] +285
Limited Slip Diff +145
Power Door Locks[Opt on STD] +90
Power Mirrors[Opt on STD] +50
Power Moonroof[Std on LE] +290

ALTIMA — 1997

1997 models are virtually identical to 1996 models, except for the addition of new emissions equipment.

RATINGS (SCALE OF 1-10)

Overall	Safety	Reliability	Performance	Comfort	Value
7.3	7	8.5	8	7.5	5.4

Category D

4 Dr GLE Sdn	11125	13245
1997.5 4 Dr GLE Sdn	11075	13185
4 Dr GXE Sdn	9050	10780
1997.5 4 Dr GXE Sdn	9260	11025
4 Dr SE Sdn	10245	12195
1997.5 4 Dr SE Sdn	10450	12445
4 Dr XE Sdn	8350	9945
1997.5 4 Dr XE Sdn	8455	10070

OPTIONS FOR ALTIMA

Auto 4-Speed Transmission[Std on GLE] +350
Air Conditioning[Opt on GXE,XE] +385
Aluminum/Alloy Wheels[Opt on GXE] +210
Anti-Lock Brakes +395
Compact Disc W/fm/tape[Std on GLE] +345
Cruise Control[Opt on GXE,XE] +110
Keyless Entry System +140
Leather Seats[Std on GLE] +505
Leather Steering Wheel[Opt on GLE] +55
Power Moonroof[Std on GLE] +380
Rear Spoiler[Std on SE] +195

MAXIMA — 1997

The Nissan Maxima gets a new grille, headlights, bumpers and taillights. New alloy wheels and fog lights on the SE, new wheel covers on the GXE, and new aluminum wheels on the GLE round out the changes.

RATINGS (SCALE OF 1-10)

Overall	Safety	Reliability	Performance	Comfort	Value
7.2	7.1	8.9	8	7.8	4

Category D

4 Dr GLE Sdn	15180	18075
4 Dr GXE Sdn	12215	14545
4 Dr SE Sdn	13185	15695

OPTIONS FOR MAXIMA

Auto 4-Speed Transmission[Std on GLE] +615
Aluminum/Alloy Wheels[Opt on GXE] +210
Anti-Lock Brakes +395
Bose Sound System +350
Climate Control for AC[Opt on SE] +135
Compact Disc W/fm/tape[Opt on GXE] +345
Dual Power Seats[Opt on SE] +380
Heated Front Seats +165
Keyless Entry System[Std on GLE] +140
Leather Seats[Opt on SE] +505
Power Moonroof +380

PATHFINDER — 1997

Changes to the 1997 Nissan Pathfinder include storage pockets added at all doors, a new exterior color and an available Bose sound system.

Don't forget to refer to the Mileage Adjustment Table at the back of this book!

Model Description	Trade-in Value	Market Value

Model Description	Trade-in Value	Market Value

RATINGS (SCALE OF 1-10)

Overall	Safety	Reliability	Performance	Comfort	Value
7	7	8.5	7.4	8.3	3.9

Category G

	Trade-in	Market
4 Dr LE Wgn	17150	20320
4 Dr LE 4WD Wgn	18480	21900
4 Dr SE 4WD Wgn	15765	18680
4 Dr XE Wgn	13135	15565
4 Dr XE 4WD Wgn	14070	16675

OPTIONS FOR PATHFINDER

Auto 4-Speed Transmission[Std on LE] +445
Air Conditioning[Std on LE] +365
Aluminum/Alloy Wheels[Opt on XE] +145
Bose Sound System[Opt on SE] +350
Climate Control for AC[Opt on SE] +85
Cruise Control[Opt on SE] +95
Dual Power Seats +185
Fog Lights[Opt on XE] +65
Heated Front Seats[Opt on SE] +120
Keyless Entry System[Opt on XE] +85
Leather Seats[Opt on SE] +350
Limited Slip Diff[Std on LE] +125
Luggage Rack[Opt on XE] +70
Power Door Locks[Opt on XE] +105
Power Moonroof +385
Power Windows[Opt on XE] +110
Swing Out Tire Carrier +85

QUEST   1997

A few new colors are the only changes to the 1997 Quest.

RATINGS (SCALE OF 1-10)

Overall	Safety	Reliability	Performance	Comfort	Value
7.2	6.8	7.6	6.2	7.5	8.1

Category G

	Trade-in	Market
2 Dr GXE Pass. Van	14175	16800
2 Dr XE Pass. Van	11795	13975

OPTIONS FOR QUEST

Aluminum/Alloy Wheels[Opt on XE] +145
Anti-Lock Brakes[Opt on XE] +260
Captain Chairs (4)[Opt on XE] +275
Child Seat (1) +75
Compact Disc W/fm/tape +200
Cruise Control[Opt on XE] +95
Dual Air Conditioning[Opt on XE] +410
Keyless Entry System[Opt on XE] +85
Leather Seats +350
Luggage Rack[Opt on XE] +70
Power Door Locks[Opt on XE] +105
Power Moonroof +385
Power Windows[Opt on XE] +110
Steer. Whl. Radio Cntrls[Opt on XE] +70

SENTRA   1997

The base model is now simply called "Base" instead of S. Nissan works to quiet the Sentra's interior by using a bigger muffler and reducing the number of suspension-mounting points.

RATINGS (SCALE OF 1-10)

Overall	Safety	Reliability	Performance	Comfort	Value
6.6	6.1	7.6	6.4	6.9	5.8

Category E

	Trade-in	Market
4 Dr GLE Sdn	8630	10445
4 Dr GXE Sdn	8175	9890
4 Dr STD Sdn	6405	7755
4 Dr XE Sdn	7560	9145

OPTIONS FOR SENTRA

Auto 4-Speed Transmission +320
AM/FM Compact Disc Player +195
Air Conditioning[Opt on STD] +370
Alarm System[Opt on GXE] +185
Anti-Lock Brakes +295
Power Moonroof +260
Rear Spoiler +100

TRUCK   1997

HALF TON

Category G

	Trade-in	Market
2 Dr STD Std Cab SB	6305	7475
2 Dr XE Std Cab SB	7405	8775
2 Dr XE 4WD Std Cab SB	9165	10860

KING CAB

Category G

	Trade-in	Market
2 Dr SE Ext Cab SB	9955	11795
2 Dr SE 4WD Ext Cab SB	11630	13780
2 Dr XE Ext Cab SB	8590	10180
2 Dr XE 4WD Ext Cab SB	10520	12470

OPTIONS FOR TRUCK

AM/FM Stereo Tape[Std on SE] +100
Air Conditioning[Std on SE] +365
Aluminum/Alloy Wheels[Std on SE] +145
Bed Liner[Std on SE] +125
Power Steering[Opt on STD] +125

1996 NISSAN

200SX   1996

Body-color door handles and outside mirrors are newly standard on SE and SE-R models.

RATINGS (SCALE OF 1-10)

Overall	Safety	Reliability	Performance	Comfort	Value
6.9	6.5	7.5	7.8	6.8	6

Don't forget to refer to the Mileage Adjustment Table at the back of this book!

Model Description	Trade-in Value	Market Value
Category F		
2 Dr SE Cpe	7510	8910
2 Dr SE-R Cpe	8100	9610
2 Dr STD Cpe	6320	7500

OPTIONS FOR 200SX

Auto 4-Speed Transmission +280
AM/FM Stereo Tape[Opt on STD] +80
Air Conditioning[Opt on STD] +305
Anti-Lock Brakes +235
Power Moonroof +240
Rear Spoiler[Opt on SE] +90

240SX   1996

Sporty new fabrics and a new grille are the only changes to the attractive 240SX.

RATINGS (SCALE OF 1-10)

Overall	Safety	Reliability	Performance	Comfort	Value
7	6.5	8.3	8.4	7.6	4

Model Description	Trade-in Value	Market Value
Category F		
2 Dr SE Cpe	10720	12715
2 Dr STD Cpe	8880	10535

OPTIONS FOR 240SX

Auto 4-Speed Transmission +290
Air Conditioning[Std on SE] +305
Aluminum/Alloy Wheels[Std on SE] +110
Anti-Lock Brakes +235
Cruise Control[Std on SE] +80
Keyless Entry System +65
Leather Seats +230
Limited Slip Diff +120
Power Door Locks[Std on SE] +75
Power Sunroof +245
Steer. Whl. Radio Cntrls +65

300ZX   1996

It's the end of the world as we know it. The final Z-car is produced for 1996.

RATINGS (SCALE OF 1-10)

Overall	Safety	Reliability	Performance	Comfort	Value
N/A	N/A	N/A	N/A	N/A	4.2

Model Description	Trade-in Value	Market Value
Category F		
2 Dr 2+2 Cpe	19175	22745
2 Dr STD Conv	21295	25260
2 Dr STD Cpe	18470	21915
2 Dr STD Turbo Cpe	20965	24870

OPTIONS FOR 300ZX

Auto 4-Speed Transmission +330
Glass Panel T-tops[Std on 2+2, Turbo] +360
Leather Seats[Std on Conv] +230
Power Drivers Seat[Std on Turbo] +90

ALTIMA   1996

New wheelcovers, power lock logic and fresh GXE upholstery update this hot-selling sedan.

RATINGS (SCALE OF 1-10)

Overall	Safety	Reliability	Performance	Comfort	Value
7.4	7	8.8	8	7.5	5.9

Model Description	Trade-in Value	Market Value
Category D		
4 Dr GLE Sdn	9540	11455
4 Dr GXE Sdn	7760	9315
4 Dr SE Sdn	8785	10545
4 Dr XE Sdn	7155	8590

OPTIONS FOR ALTIMA

Auto 4-Speed Transmission[Std on GLE] +305
AM/FM Stereo Tape[Std on SE] +130
Air Conditioning[Opt on GXE,XE] +315
Anti-Lock Brakes +325
Cruise Control[Opt on GXE,XE] +90
Leather Seats +415
Power Moonroof +310

MAXIMA   1996

All new for 1995, the excellent Maxima receives few changes for 1996. A four-way power passenger seat is available, a new center console cupholder will hold a Big Gulp, and two new colors grace the Maxima's decidedly dull flanks. Taillights are as ugly as ever.

RATINGS (SCALE OF 1-10)

Overall	Safety	Reliability	Performance	Comfort	Value
7.2	7.1	8.9	8	7.8	4

Model Description	Trade-in Value	Market Value
Category D		
4 Dr GLE Sdn	12765	15330
4 Dr GXE Sdn	10340	12415
4 Dr SE Sdn	11045	13260

OPTIONS FOR MAXIMA

Auto 4-Speed Transmission[Std on GLE] +465
Aluminum/Alloy Wheels[Opt on GXE] +170
Anti-Lock Brakes +325
Bose Sound System +285
Climate Control for AC[Opt on SE] +110
Compact Disc W/fm/tape[Opt on GXE] +285
Heated Front Seats +135
Keyless Entry System[Std on GLE] +115
Leather Seats[Opt on SE] +415
Power Moonroof +310

PATHFINDER   1996

Outstanding new Pathfinder debuts with dual airbags and great interior styling. Engine output is up, but the Pathfinder is still not going to win any drag races. The new interior is open, airy, and much more comfortable than most of its competitors.

Model Description	Trade-in Value	Market Value	Model Description	Trade-in Value	Market Value

RATINGS (SCALE OF 1-10)

Overall	Safety	Reliability	Performance	Comfort	Value
7.4	6.8	7.5	7.4	8.3	7

Category G

	Trade-in	Market
4 Dr LE Wgn	14800	17735
4 Dr LE 4WD Wgn	15995	19165
4 Dr SE 4WD Wgn	13745	16470
4 Dr XE Wgn	11415	13680
4 Dr XE 4WD Wgn	12195	14615

OPTIONS FOR PATHFINDER

Auto 4-Speed Transmission[Std on LE] +365
Air Conditioning[Std on LE] +300
Climate Control for AC[Opt on SE] +70
Cruise Control[Opt on XE] +75
Dual Power Seats +150
Fog Lights[Opt on XE] +55
Heated Front Seats[Opt on SE] +100
Keyless Entry System[Opt on XE] +70
Leather Seats[Opt on SE] +285
Limited Slip Diff[Std on LE] +100
Luggage Rack[Opt on XE] +60
Power Door Locks[Opt on XE] +85
Power Moonroof +315
Power Windows[Opt on XE] +90
Swing Out Tire Carrier +70

QUEST   1996

Substantial upgrades include dual airbags, integrated child safety seats, side-impact protection meeting 1997 passenger car standards, revamped fabrics, new colors, freshened styling, and a cool, in-dash six-disc CD changer. The Quest is still in the hunt.

RATINGS (SCALE OF 1-10)

Overall	Safety	Reliability	Performance	Comfort	Value
7.1	6.6	6.8	6.2	7.5	8.5

Category G

	Trade-in	Market
2 Dr GXE Pass. Van	12270	14700
2 Dr XE Pass. Van	10230	12260

OPTIONS FOR QUEST

Aluminum/Alloy Wheels[Opt on XE] +120
Anti-Lock Brakes[Opt on XE] +210
Child Seat (1) +60
Climate Control for AC +70
Cruise Control[Opt on XE] +75
Dual Air Conditioning[Opt on XE] +335
Keyless Entry System[Opt on XE] +70
Leather Seats +285
Luggage Rack[Opt on XE] +60
Power Door Locks[Opt on XE] +85
Power Passenger Seat +75
Power Windows[Opt on XE] +90
Privacy Glass[Opt on XE] +100

SENTRA   1996

Prices have crept up, making the Sentra a hard sell against the Neon, Prizm and Cavalier. Still, you may be able to find a good deal on a former rental vehicle. We've seen tons of them at the Alamo rental lots.

RATINGS (SCALE OF 1-10)

Overall	Safety	Reliability	Performance	Comfort	Value
6.7	6.2	7.7	6.4	6.9	6.2

Category E

	Trade-in	Market
4 Dr GLE Sdn	7030	8795
4 Dr GXE Sdn	6685	8360
4 Dr STD Sdn	5355	6695
4 Dr XE Sdn	6265	7835

OPTIONS FOR SENTRA

Auto 4-Speed Transmission +290
AM/FM Stereo Tape[Opt on STD] +110
Air Conditioning[Opt on STD] +305
Anti-Lock Brakes +245

TRUCK   1996

No changes for the Truck.

RATINGS (SCALE OF 1-10)

Overall	Safety	Reliability	Performance	Comfort	Value
N/A	5.2	7.5	6	6.1	N/A

HALF TON
Category G

	Trade-in	Market
2 Dr STD Std Cab SB	5190	6220
2 Dr XE Std Cab SB	5875	7040
2 Dr XE 4WD Std Cab SB	7330	8785

KING CAB
Category G

	Trade-in	Market
2 Dr SE Ext Cab SB	8460	10140
2 Dr SE 4WD Ext Cab SB	9930	11895
2 Dr XE Ext Cab SB	7240	8680
2 Dr XE 4WD Ext Cab SB	8935	10705

OPTIONS FOR TRUCK

Auto 4-Speed Transmission +365
AM/FM Stereo Tape +80
Air Conditioning[Std on SE] +300
Aluminum/Alloy Wheels[Std on SE] +120
Center Console[Std on 2WD] +60
Chrome Bumpers[Std on SE] +55
Chrome Wheels +60
Cruise Control[Std on SE] +75
Flip-Up Sunroof[Opt on 4WD] +120
Power Steering[Opt on STD] +105
Power Windows[Opt on 4WD] +90
Privacy Glass[Std on SE] +100
Tilt Steering Wheel[Opt on Half Ton] +65

Don't forget to refer to the Mileage Adjustment Table at the back of this book!

NISSAN 95

Model Description	Trade-in Value	Market Value	Model Description	Trade-in Value	Market Value

1995 NISSAN

200SX — 1995

A Sentra derived 200SX is introduced to the sporting public. Basically a two-door version of the redesigned Sentra, the 200SX comes equipped with dual airbags. The 200SX has two available powerplants, a 1.6-liter four-cylinder that produces 115-horsepower or a 2.0-liter four that is good for 140 ponies.

RATINGS (SCALE OF 1-10)

Overall	Safety	Reliability	Performance	Comfort	Value
7.1	7.2	8.1	7.8	6.8	5.5

Category F
2 Dr SE Cpe	6410	7760
2 Dr SE-R Cpe	6845	8290
2 Dr STD Cpe	5415	6560

OPTIONS FOR 200SX
Auto 4-Speed Transmission +240
AM/FM Stereo Tape[Opt on STD] +65
Air Conditioning[Opt on STD] +250
Anti-Lock Brakes +195
Power Moonroof +195
Rear Spoiler[Opt on SE] +70

240SX — 1995

Totally redesigned, the 240SX loses its hatchback and convertible body styles. Available as a base or SE model, the 240 uses the same engine as the previous generation model. Dual airbags are standard on the new 240SX as are side door beams that help the car meet federal side-impact standards.

RATINGS (SCALE OF 1-10)

Overall	Safety	Reliability	Performance	Comfort	Value
6.8	7.1	7.3	8.4	7.6	3.5

Category F
2 Dr SE Cpe	8955	10845
2 Dr STD Cpe	7605	9210

OPTIONS FOR 240SX
Auto 4-Speed Transmission +255
Air Conditioning[Std on SE] +250
Aluminum/Alloy Wheels[Std on SE] +90
Anti-Lock Brakes +195
Cruise Control[Std on SE] +65
Leather Seats +190
Leather Steering Wheel[Opt on SE] +50
Limited Slip Diff +100
Power Door Locks[Std on SE] +60
Power Moonroof +195

300ZX — 1995

No changes for the 300ZX.

RATINGS (SCALE OF 1-10)

Overall	Safety	Reliability	Performance	Comfort	Value
N/A	N/A	N/A	N/A	N/A	4.1

Category F
2 Dr 2+2 Cpe	16720	20245
2 Dr STD Conv	18010	21810
2 Dr STD Cpe	15530	18805
2 Dr STD Turbo Cpe	17720	21455

OPTIONS FOR 300ZX
Auto 4-Speed Transmission +270
Glass Panel T-tops[Std on 2+2, Turbo] +295
Leather Seats[Std on Conv] +190
Power Drivers Seat[Opt on STD Cpe] +70

ALTIMA — 1995

Minor exterior tweaks to the grille, taillights and wheels are the only changes for this attractive compact from Tennessee.

RATINGS (SCALE OF 1-10)

Overall	Safety	Reliability	Performance	Comfort	Value
7.4	7.7	7.9	8	7.5	5.8

Category D
4 Dr GLE Sdn	7835	9635
4 Dr GXE Sdn	6460	7950
4 Dr SE Sdn	7440	9150
4 Dr XE Sdn	5865	7220

OPTIONS FOR ALTIMA
Auto 4-Speed Transmission[Std on GLE] +245
Air Conditioning[Opt on GXE, XE] +255
Anti-Lock Brakes +265
Cruise Control[Opt on GXE, XE] +75
Power Moonroof[Opt on GXE] +250

MAXIMA — 1995

Wow, what a beauty. The redesigned Maxima bows with an aerodynamic shape and a lengthened wheelbase. The new Maxima is available as a budget-minded GXE, sporty SE or luxurious GLE. All Maximas get the 190-horsepower engine previously exclusive to the SE.

RATINGS (SCALE OF 1-10)

Overall	Safety	Reliability	Performance	Comfort	Value
7.4	7.7	8.5	8	7.8	5

Category D
4 Dr GLE Sdn	10205	12550
4 Dr GXE Sdn	8385	10315
4 Dr SE Sdn	9045	11125

OPTIONS FOR MAXIMA
Auto 4-Speed Transmission[Std on GLE] +390
Aluminum/Alloy Wheels[Opt on GXE] +140
Anti-Lock Brakes +265

Don't forget to refer to the Mileage Adjustment Table at the back of this book!

NISSAN 95

Model Description	Trade-in Value	Market Value

Climate Control for AC[Opt on SE] +90
Compact Disc W/fm/tape[Std on GLE] +230
Heated Front Seats +110
Keyless Entry System[Std on GLE] +95
Leather Seats[Std on GLE] +340
Power Drivers Seat[Std on GLE] +95
Power Moonroof +250
Rear Spoiler[Std on SE] +130

PATHFINDER 1995

Whoopee. A two-wheel-drive version of Nissan's ancient sport utility is now available in LE flavor.

RATINGS (SCALE OF 1-10)

Overall	Safety	Reliability	Performance	Comfort	Value
6.7	4.3	9.1	7.6	7.5	4.8

Category G

4 Dr LE Wgn	11430	13995
4 Dr LE 4WD Wgn	12505	15310
4 Dr SE 4WD Wgn	10820	13250
4 Dr XE Wgn	8700	10655
4 Dr XE 4WD Wgn	9085	11125

OPTIONS FOR PATHFINDER

Auto 4-Speed Transmission[Std on LE] +365
Air Conditioning[Std on LE] +245
Camper/Towing Package +90
Compact Disc W/fm/tape[Opt on SE] +130
Cruise Control[Opt on XE] +65
Fog Lights[Opt on XE] +45
Heated Front Seats[Opt on SE] +80
Intermittent Wipers[Opt on XE] +25
Keyless Entry System[Opt on XE] +60
Leather Seats[Opt on SE] +235
Limited Slip Diff[Std on LE] +85
Power Door Locks[Opt on XE] +70
Power Windows[Opt on XE] +70
Swing Out Tire Carrier[Opt on XE] +55

QUEST 1995

GXE models get standard captain's chairs for second-row occupants. The Extra Performance Package is renamed the Handling Package. No other significant changes for the Quest.

RATINGS (SCALE OF 1-10)

Overall	Safety	Reliability	Performance	Comfort	Value
7	6.5	6	6.2	7.1	9

Category G

2 Dr GXE Pass. Van	9955	12190
2 Dr XE Pass. Van	8310	10175

OPTIONS FOR QUEST

Anti-Lock Brakes[Opt on XE] +175
Cruise Control[Opt on XE] +65
Dual Air Conditioning[Opt on XE] +275
Keyless Entry System +60

Leather Seats +235
Lighted Entry System +45
Luggage Rack[Opt on XE] +50
Power Door Locks[Opt on XE] +70
Power Moonroof +260
Power Passenger Seat +60
Power Windows[Opt on XE] +70
Privacy Glass[Opt on XE] +80

SENTRA 1995

An all-new Sentra is released featuring aero styling and a stubby trunk. The 1995 Sentra is available only as a four-door sedan, the two-door model now being called the 200SX. Increased interior space is the most noticeable feature of the redesign. The engines remain unchanged from previous models.

RATINGS (SCALE OF 1-10)

Overall	Safety	Reliability	Performance	Comfort	Value
N/A	N/A	7.4	6.4	6.9	5.6

Category E

4 Dr GLE Sdn	5825	7385
4 Dr GXE Sdn	5430	6885
4 Dr STD Sdn	4470	5670
4 Dr XE Sdn	5155	6540

OPTIONS FOR SENTRA

Auto 4-Speed Transmission +240
Air Conditioning[Opt on STD] +250
Anti-Lock Brakes +200

TRUCK 1995

The two-wheel-drive Nissan trucks finally get rear-wheel antilock brakes.

RATINGS (SCALE OF 1-10)

Overall	Safety	Reliability	Performance	Comfort	Value
N/A	4.3	8.6	6	6.1	N/A

HALF TON

Category G

2 Dr HD Std Cab LB	5360	6565
2 Dr STD Std Cab SB	4185	5125
2 Dr XE Std Cab SB	4620	5660
2 Dr XE 4WD Std Cab SB	6295	7705

KING CAB

Category G

2 Dr SE V6 4WD Ext Cab SB	9375	11480
2 Dr XE Ext Cab SB	5840	7155
2 Dr XE 4WD Ext Cab SB	7675	9400
2 Dr XE V6 Ext Cab SB	6390	7825
2 Dr XE V6 4WD Ext Cab SB	8220	10070

OPTIONS FOR TRUCK

Auto 4-Speed Transmission +350
AM/FM Stereo Tape[Std on SE V6] +65

Don't forget to refer to the Mileage Adjustment Table at the back of this book!

Model Description	Trade-in Value	Market Value

Air Conditioning[Std on SE V6] +245
Chrome Bumpers[Std on SE V6] +45
Chrome Wheels[Std on XE V6,King Cab XE 4WD Ext Cab SB] +50
Cruise Control[Opt on XE V6] +65
Flip-Up Sunroof +100
Limited Slip Diff[Opt on XE V6] +85
Power Door Locks +70
Power Steering[Std on HD,SE V6,XE V6,4WD] +85
Power Windows +70
Rear Step Bumper[Opt on STD] +45
Tilt Steering Wheel[Opt on XE V6] +55

1994 NISSAN

240SX — 1994

A convertible body style is the sole offering this year as the coupe is set for a complete redesign.

RATINGS (SCALE OF 1-10)

Overall	Safety	Reliability	Performance	Comfort	Value
N/A	N/A	8	8	7.3	3.4

Category F
2 Dr SE Conv	7945	9420

OPTIONS FOR 240SX
Air Conditioning +205

300ZX — 1994

A passenger airbag is a new safety feature on the 300ZX, which allows the use of manual seatbelts. Remote keyless entry is another new feature for the 300ZX.

RATINGS (SCALE OF 1-10)

Overall	Safety	Reliability	Performance	Comfort	Value
N/A	N/A	N/A	N/A	N/A	3.6

Category F
2 Dr 2+2 Cpe	14725	17455
2 Dr STD Conv	15770	18695
2 Dr STD Cpe	13610	16135
2 Dr STD Turbo Cpe	15470	18340

OPTIONS FOR 300ZX
Auto 4-Speed Transmission +235
Alarm System +45
Compact Disc W/fm/tape +125
Glass Panel T-tops[Opt on STD] +240
Leather Seats[Std on Conv] +155

ALTIMA — 1994

A passenger-side airbag is added to this hot-selling Tennessee-built compact. SE models gain a standard sunroof and GLEs have it as an available option.

RATINGS (SCALE OF 1-10)

Overall	Safety	Reliability	Performance	Comfort	Value
7.5	7.7	8.4	8	7.5	5.8

Category D
4 Dr GLE Sdn	6740	8430
4 Dr GXE Sdn	5255	6570
4 Dr SE Sdn	6400	8000
4 Dr XE Sdn	4865	6085

OPTIONS FOR ALTIMA
Auto 4-Speed Transmission[Std on GLE] +210
Air Conditioning[Opt on GXE,XE] +210
Aluminum/Alloy Wheels[Opt on GXE] +115
Anti-Lock Brakes +215
Compact Disc W/fm/tape +190
Cruise Control[Opt on GXE,XE] +60
Leather Seats +275
Power Antenna[Opt on GXE] +30
Power Sunroof[Opt on GXE] +190
Premium Sound System +90

MAXIMA — 1994

No changes for the 1994 Maxima.

RATINGS (SCALE OF 1-10)

Overall	Safety	Reliability	Performance	Comfort	Value
N/A	N/A	8.1	8.8	7.9	4.3

Category D
4 Dr GXE Sdn	7020	8780
4 Dr SE Sdn	7365	9205

OPTIONS FOR MAXIMA
Auto 4-Speed Transmission[Opt on SE] +230
AM/FM Compact Disc Player +115
Anti-Lock Brakes +215
Bose Sound System[Std on SE] +190
Climate Control for AC +75
Leather Seats +275
Power Drivers Seat +75
Power Passenger Seat +75
Power Sunroof +190

PATHFINDER — 1994

The LE model is introduced for the country-club crowd. Standard equipment on the LE includes leather upholstery, heated seats, a CD player, and a luggage rack. All 1994 Pathfinders sport a redesigned dashboard and instrument panel. SE models get new alloy wheels and a sunroof.

RATINGS (SCALE OF 1-10)

Overall	Safety	Reliability	Performance	Comfort	Value
6.5	4.2	8.3	7.6	7.5	4.7

Category G
4 Dr LE 4WD Wgn	10540	13075
4 Dr SE 4WD Wgn	9110	11300

Model Description	Trade-in Value	Market Value
4 Dr XE Wgn	7365	9135
4 Dr XE 4WD Wgn	7985	9905

OPTIONS FOR PATHFINDER
Auto 4-Speed Transmission[Std on LE] +300
Air Conditioning[Std on LE] +200
Alarm System[Opt on XE] +65
Cruise Control[Opt on XE] +50
Fog Lights[Opt on XE] +35
Heated Front Seats +65
Leather Seats[Opt on SE] +190
Limited Slip Diff[Std on LE] +70
Luggage Rack[Opt on SE] +40
Power Door Locks[Opt on XE] +55
Power Windows[Opt on XE] +60
Theft Deterrent System[Opt on XE] +70

QUEST   1994

The Quest gets a driver airbag added to its standard equipment list for 1994. GXE models can now be had with a premium audio package that includes a CD player.

RATINGS (SCALE OF 1-10)

Overall	Safety	Reliability	Performance	Comfort	Value
7.1	6.8	6.9	6.2	7.1	8.5

Category G
	Trade-in	Market
2 Dr GXE Pass. Van	8295	10290
2 Dr XE Pass. Van	6935	8600

OPTIONS FOR QUEST
Aluminum/Alloy Wheels +80
Anti-Lock Brakes[Opt on XE] +140
Camper/Towing Package +70
Captain Chairs (2) +130
Compact Disc W/fm/tape +110
Cruise Control[Opt on XE] +50
Dual Air Conditioning[Opt on XE] +225
Keyless Entry System +50
Leather Seats +190
Lighted Entry System +35
Luggage Rack[Opt on XE] +40
Power Door Locks[Opt on XE] +55
Power Moonroof +210
Power Passenger Seat +50
Power Windows[Opt on XE] +60

SENTRA   1994

CFC-free coolant is now standard on vehicles equipped with air conditioning. XE models get more standard equipment that includes air conditioning, cruise control and a stereo with cassette player.

RATINGS (SCALE OF 1-10)

Overall	Safety	Reliability	Performance	Comfort	Value
N/A	N/A	8.2	7.2	7.9	5.6

Category E
	Trade-in	Market
2 Dr E Sdn	3160	4255
4 Dr E Sdn	3330	4475
4 Dr GXE Sdn	4560	6135
1994.5 2 Dr Limited Sdn	3950	5315
1994.5 4 Dr Limited Sdn	4015	5405
2 Dr SE Sdn	3935	5295
2 Dr SE-R Sdn	4300	5780
2 Dr XE Sdn	3785	5090
4 Dr XE Sdn	3845	5170

OPTIONS FOR SENTRA
Auto 4-Speed Transmission +220
AM/FM Stereo Tape[Opt on E,SE] +75
Air Bag Restraint[Std on GXE] +140
Air Conditioning[Opt on E,SE,SE-R] +205
Aluminum/Alloy Wheels[Std on GXE,SE-R] +80
Anti-Lock Brakes +160
Cruise Control[Opt on SE,SE-R] +55
Power Steering[Opt on E] +60
Power Sunroof +150
Tilt Steering Wheel[Opt on E] +35

TRUCK   1994

The Nissan pickup gets a redesigned dashboard and a new model for 1994. The new model is called the XE.

RATINGS (SCALE OF 1-10)

Overall	Safety	Reliability	Performance	Comfort	Value
N/A	4.3	7.9	6	6.1	N/A

HALF TON

Category G
	Trade-in	Market
2 Dr STD Std Cab SB	3560	4415
2 Dr V6 Std Cab LB	4560	5655
2 Dr XE Std Cab SB	3840	4760
2 Dr XE 4WD Std Cab SB	5115	6345

KING CAB

Category G
	Trade-in	Market
2 Dr SE V6 Ext Cab SB	5870	7285
2 Dr SE V6 4WD Ext Cab SB	6715	8330
2 Dr XE Ext Cab SB	4830	5990
2 Dr XE 4WD Ext Cab SB	6195	7685
2 Dr XE V6 4WD Ext Cab SB	6515	8080

OPTIONS FOR TRUCK
Auto 4-Speed Transmission +275
Sport Handling Pkg +280
AM/FM Stereo Tape[Std on SE V6,XE Std Cab SB] +55
Air Conditioning +200
Aluminum/Alloy Wheels +80
Bed Liner +70
Chrome Bumpers[Std on SE V6] +35
Chrome Wheels[Std on SE V6] +40
Cruise Control[Opt on XE V6] +50
Flip-Up Sunroof +80

Don't forget to refer to the Mileage Adjustment Table at the back of this book!

Limited Slip Diff +70
Power Door Locks +55
Power Steering[Std on SE V6,XE V6,4WD] +70
Power Windows +60
Rear Jump Seats[Opt on XE] +55
Sliding Rear Window[Opt on STD] +30
Tilt Steering Wheel[Opt on XE V6] +45

1993 NISSAN

240SX   1993

The luxury-oriented LE is dropped from the 240SX lineup due to poor sales. Don't worry, those with a penchant for leather can still get their kicks in a cowhide-equipped SE model. Half of the 240SXs produced this year have CFC-free air conditioning.

RATINGS (SCALE OF 1-10)

Overall	Safety	Reliability	Performance	Comfort	Value
N/A	N/A	8.2	8	7.3	4

Category F
2 Dr SE Conv	6525	8135
2 Dr SE Cpe	5390	6720
2 Dr SE Hbk	5530	6895
2 Dr STD Cpe	4630	5780
2 Dr STD Hbk	4855	6055

OPTIONS FOR 240SX

Auto 4-Speed Transmission[Std on Conv] +165
Air Conditioning +170
Anti-Lock Brakes +130
Flip-Up Sunroof +80
Leather Seats +125
Limited Slip Diff +65
Power Sunroof +135
Sport Suspension +40

300ZX   1993

The first chop-top Z-car debuts this year. A basket handle behind the seats reduces body flex in the 300ZX and gives the seatbelts an anchor point. No changes for the other models.

RATINGS (SCALE OF 1-10)

Overall	Safety	Reliability	Performance	Comfort	Value
N/A	N/A	N/A	N/A	N/A	3.1

Category F
2 Dr 2+2 Cpe	11295	14090
2 Dr STD Conv	12100	15095
2 Dr STD Cpe	10150	12660
2 Dr STD Turbo Cpe	11715	14610

OPTIONS FOR 300ZX

Auto 4-Speed Transmission +190
AM/FM Stereo Tape[Opt on Cpe] +45
Glass Panel T-tops[Std on 2+2, Turbo] +195

Leather Seats +125
Premium Sound System[Std on 2+2, Turbo] +75

ALTIMA   1993

The Infiniti-inspired Altima replaces the aging Stanza. Swooping sheetmetal, a longer wheelbase, and increased cabin size distinguish the Altima from its lackluster predecessor. The Altima is powered by a twin-cam four-cylinder that produces 150 horsepower. A driver airbag is standard on the Altima, as are motorized seatbelts.

RATINGS (SCALE OF 1-10)

Overall	Safety	Reliability	Performance	Comfort	Value
N/A	N/A	7.7	8	7.5	6.2

Category D
4 Dr GLE Sdn	5590	7210
4 Dr GXE Sdn	4300	5545
4 Dr SE Sdn	5045	6510
4 Dr XE Sdn	3990	5150

OPTIONS FOR ALTIMA

Auto 4-Speed Transmission[Std on GLE] +165
Air Conditioning[Opt on GXE,XE] +170
Alarm System[Opt on SE] +105
Anti-Lock Brakes +175
Compact Disc W/fm/tape[Opt on SE] +155
Cruise Control[Opt on GXE,XE] +50
Leather Seats +225
Leather Steering Wheel[Std on SE] +25
Power Moonroof +170
Theft Deterrent System +120

MAXIMA   1993

The driver airbag is now standard on Nissan's front-wheel drive midsize sedan. Both cars have CFC-free air conditioning and SE models get a trick new stereo, compliments of Bose.

RATINGS (SCALE OF 1-10)

Overall	Safety	Reliability	Performance	Comfort	Value
N/A	N/A	7.8	8.8	7.9	5.6

Category D
4 Dr GXE Sdn	5640	7275
4 Dr SE Sdn	5925	7640

OPTIONS FOR MAXIMA

Auto 4-Speed Transmission[Opt on SE] +185
Luxury Pkg +175
Anti-Lock Brakes +175
Bose Sound System[Std on SE] +155
Climate Control for AC +60
Compact Disc W/fm/tape +155
Dual Power Seats +170
Leather Seats +225
Power Sunroof +155   •

Model Description	Trade-in Value	Market Value	Model Description	Trade-in Value	Market Value

NX 1993

The 2000 gets a standard T-top. New interior fabrics mark the only other changes for the NX line.

RATINGS (SCALE OF 1-10)

Overall	Safety	Reliability	Performance	Comfort	Value
N/A	N/A	N/A	N/A	N/A	4.6

Category E
2 Dr 1600 Cpe	3005	4140
2 Dr 2000 Cpe	3780	5205

OPTIONS FOR NX

Auto 4-Speed Transmission +165
AM/FM Stereo Tape[Opt on 1600] +60
Air Conditioning +165
Anti-Lock Brakes +135
Cruise Control +45
Power Door Locks +50
Power Windows +55
T-Bar Roof[Opt on 1600] +180

PATHFINDER 1993

CFC-free air conditioning is standard and side-impact door beams are introduced to protect occupants. The Pathfinder's standard stereo gets its wattage increased and the SE's leather seats are now heated. How cozy.

RATINGS (SCALE OF 1-10)

Overall	Safety	Reliability	Performance	Comfort	Value
6.5	4.3	8.9	7.6	6.8	4.8

Category G
4 Dr SE 4WD Wgn	7775	9825
4 Dr XE Wgn	6320	7980
4 Dr XE 4WD Wgn	6900	8720

OPTIONS FOR PATHFINDER

Auto 4-Speed Transmission +250
Sport Handling Pkg +230
Air Conditioning[Opt on XE] +165
Aluminum/Alloy Wheels +65
Heated Front Seats +55
Leather Seats +155
Limited Slip Diff +55
Luggage Rack +30
Power Door Locks[Opt on XE] +45
Power Windows[Opt on XE] +50
Sunroof +60

QUEST 1993

After messing around with the Axxess and Nissan Van, Nissan finally gets it right on this joint project with Mercury. The Quest is a front-engine, front-wheel-drive minivan that is built alongside the Villager at the Ford plant in Avon Lake, Ohio. The Quest is powered by a 3.0-liter V6 engine that produces 150-horsepower. The Quest seats seven and has standard air conditioning, a tilt steering wheel, and a stereo with cassette. Antilock brakes are optional on the Quest.

RATINGS (SCALE OF 1-10)

Overall	Safety	Reliability	Performance	Comfort	Value
6.1	5	5	6.2	7.1	7.4

Category G
2 Dr GXE Pass. Van	6735	8505
2 Dr STD Cargo Van	5530	6985
2 Dr XE Pass. Van	5655	7145

OPTIONS FOR QUEST

7 Passenger Seating[Opt on XE] +105
AM/FM Stereo Tape[Std on XE] +45
Aluminum/Alloy Wheels[Opt on XE] +65
Anti-Lock Brakes +115
Cruise Control[Opt on XE] +40
Dual Air Conditioning[Opt on XE] +185
Keyless Entry System +40
Leather Seats +155
Lighted Entry System +30
Luggage Rack[Opt on XE] +30
Power Door Locks[Opt on XE] +45
Power Passenger Seat +40
Power Sunroof +160
Power Windows[Opt on XE] +50
Premium Sound System[Opt on XE] +70

SENTRA 1993

A driver airbag is now standard on the GXE model. Base models ditch the Flintstone transmissions, gaining a standard five-speed manual or optional four-speed automatic in place of the archaic four-speed manual and three-speed automatic that was formerly available. All Sentras receive minor nose work that includes a redesigned grille, headlights and front fascia.

RATINGS (SCALE OF 1-10)

Overall	Safety	Reliability	Performance	Comfort	Value
N/A	N/A	8.4	7.2	7.9	4.5

Category E
2 Dr E Sdn	2490	3430
4 Dr E Sdn	2800	3855
4 Dr GXE Sdn	3860	5315
2 Dr SE Sdn	2995	4125
2 Dr SE-R Sdn	3410	4695
2 Dr XE Sdn	2890	3980
4 Dr XE Sdn	3070	4235

OPTIONS FOR SENTRA

Auto 4-Speed Transmission +185
AM/FM Stereo Tape[Std on GXE] +60
Air Bag Restraint[Std on GXE] +115
Air Conditioning[Std on GXE] +165
Anti-Lock Brakes +135
Cruise Control[Std on GXE] +45

Don't forget to refer to the Mileage Adjustment Table at the back of this book!

Model Description	Trade-in Value	Market Value
Power Steering[Opt on E] +50		
Power Sunroof +125		

TRUCK 1993

CFC-free air conditioning debuts. No other changes to this mini-bruiser.

RATINGS (SCALE OF 1-10)

Overall	Safety	Reliability	Performance	Comfort	Value
N/A	4.3	8.1	6	6.5	N/A

HALF TON

Category G

	Trade-in	Market
2 Dr STD Std Cab LB	3700	4670
2 Dr STD Std Cab SB	3190	4035
2 Dr STD 4WD Std Cab SB	4485	5670

KING CAB

Category G

	Trade-in	Market
2 Dr SE Ext Cab SB	5315	6715
2 Dr SE 4WD Ext Cab SB	6085	7690
2 Dr STD Ext Cab SB	4400	5560
2 Dr STD 4WD Ext Cab SB	5490	6935

OPTIONS FOR TRUCK

6 cyl 3.0 L Engine +130
Auto 4-Speed Transmission +195
2WD Sport Pkg +175
4WD Sport Pkg +165
AM/FM Stereo Tape[Std on SE,4WD] +45
Air Conditioning +165
Aluminum/Alloy Wheels +65
Bed Liner +55
Camper/Towing Package +60
Chrome Bumpers[Std on SE] +30
Chrome Wheels[Std on King Cab,4WD] +35
Flip-Up Sunroof +65
Limited Slip Diff +55
Power Door Locks +45
Power Steering[Std on King Cab,4WD] +55
Power Windows +50

1992 NISSAN

240SX 1992

Nissan chops the top off the 240SX, adding a convertible to this versatile line of cars. Antilock brakes are made available on the LE model.

RATINGS (SCALE OF 1-10)

Overall	Safety	Reliability	Performance	Comfort	Value
N/A	N/A	8.3	8	7.3	4

Category F

	Trade-in	Market
2 Dr LE Hbk	5140	6615
2 Dr SE Conv	5605	7215
2 Dr SE Cpe	4590	5910

Model Description	Trade-in Value	Market Value
2 Dr SE Hbk	4640	5975
2 Dr STD Cpe	4000	5150
2 Dr STD Hbk	4075	5245

OPTIONS FOR 240SX

Auto 4-Speed Transmission[Std on Conv] +135
Air Conditioning[Std on LE] +135
Anti-Lock Brakes +105
Flip-Up Sunroof +65
Leather Seats[Opt on SE] +105
Limited Slip Diff +55
Power Sunroof +110

300ZX 1992

The driver airbag is moved to the standard equipment list this year. No other changes to this fine car.

RATINGS (SCALE OF 1-10)

Overall	Safety	Reliability	Performance	Comfort	Value
N/A	N/A	N/A	N/A	N/A	3.5

Category F

	Trade-in	Market
2 Dr 2+2 Cpe	9160	11790
2 Dr STD Cpe	8230	10595
2 Dr STD Turbo Cpe	9175	11810

OPTIONS FOR 300ZX

Auto 4-Speed Transmission +155
Bose Sound System[Std on 2+2,Turbo] +75
Glass Panel T-tops[Std on Turbo] +160
Leather Seats +105
Power Drivers Seat[Std on 2+2,Turbo] +40

MAXIMA 1992

The Maxima gets an available driver airbag and a bigger engine for the SE. The SE's new engine is a DOHC, 190-horsepower V6. Unfortunately, the SE loses its standard sunroof. All Maximas receive a new grille and taillights for 1992.

RATINGS (SCALE OF 1-10)

Overall	Safety	Reliability	Performance	Comfort	Value
N/A	N/A	7.5	8.8	7.9	6.4

Category D

	Trade-in	Market
4 Dr GXE Sdn	5085	6505
4 Dr SE Sdn	5180	6630

OPTIONS FOR MAXIMA

Auto 4-Speed Transmission[Opt on SE] +150
Luxury Pkg +145
Air Bag Restraint +90
Anti-Lock Brakes +145
Bose Sound System[Std on SE] +125
Climate Control for AC +50
Dual Power Seats +140
Leather Seats +185
Power Sunroof +125

Model Description	Trade-in Value	Market Value

NX   1992

The optional T-tops are now available on the 1600. The NX 2000 is available this year with a power package that adds power windows, power door locks and cruise control.

RATINGS (SCALE OF 1-10)

Overall	Safety	Reliability	Performance	Comfort	Value
*N/A	N/A	N/A	N/A	N/A	4.5

Category E

2 Dr 1600 Cpe	2465	3525
2 Dr 2000 Cpe	2930	4185

OPTIONS FOR NX

Auto 4-Speed Transmission +135
Air Conditioning +135
Anti-Lock Brakes +110
Power Door Locks +40
Power Windows +45
T-Tops (solid/Colored) +145

PATHFINDER   1992

Safari Green paint is a new exterior color choice for this aging veteran of the sport-ute wars. No other changes are made.

RATINGS (SCALE OF 1-10)

Overall	Safety	Reliability	Performance	Comfort	Value
6.7	4.3	8.7	7.6	6.8	6.2

Category G

4 Dr SE 4WD Wgn	6540	8320
4 Dr XE Wgn	5370	6830
4 Dr XE 4WD Wgn	5870	7465

OPTIONS FOR PATHFINDER

Auto 4-Speed Transmission +185
AM/FM Compact Disc Player +50
Air Conditioning[Opt on XE] +135
Flip-Up Sunroof +55
Leather Seats +130
Limited Slip Diff +45
Power Door Locks[Opt on XE] +40
Power Windows[Opt on XE] +40

SENTRA   1992

A passenger's side vanity mirror and black body-side moldings are now standard on the two-door Sentra. The Value Option Package (includes air conditioning, cruise control, and a stereo) is extended to the SE Sentras this year.

RATINGS (SCALE OF 1-10)

Overall	Safety	Reliability	Performance	Comfort	Value
N/A	N/A	8.1	7.2	7.9	4.9

Category E

2 Dr E Sdn	2075	2970
4 Dr E Sdn	2325	3325
4 Dr GXE Sdn	3130	4470
2 Dr SE Sdn	2570	3670
2 Dr SE-R Sdn	2870	4100
2 Dr XE Sdn	2405	3435
4 Dr XE Sdn	2565	3665

OPTIONS FOR SENTRA

Auto 4-Speed Transmission +135
Air Conditioning[Std on GXE] +135
Anti-Lock Brakes +110
Power Steering[Opt on E] +40
Power Sunroof +100

STANZA   1992

A sporty SE model joins the roster of available Stanzas this year. Distinguished by a blacked-out grille, fog lights, rear spoiler, and leather-wrapped steering wheel and shift knob, the SE is attempting to draw in customers who want more from their compact family sedan.

Category E

4 Dr GXE Sdn	3750	5360
4 Dr SE Sdn	3670	5245
4 Dr XE Sdn	2820	4030

OPTIONS FOR STANZA

Auto 4-Speed Transmission[Std on GXE] +145
Air Conditioning[Opt on XE] +135
Anti-Lock Brakes +110
Power Door Locks[Opt on XE] +40
Power Sunroof +100
Power Windows[Opt on XE] +45

TRUCK   1992

No changes for the Nissan Pickup.

RATINGS (SCALE OF 1-10)

Overall	Safety	Reliability	Performance	Comfort	Value
N/A	4	7.9	6	6.5	N/A

HALF TON

Category G

2 Dr STD Std Cab LB	3340	4250
2 Dr STD Std Cab SB	2830	3595
2 Dr STD 4WD Std Cab SB	3760	4780

KING CAB

Category G

2 Dr SE Ext Cab SB	4450	5660
2 Dr SE 4WD Ext Cab SB	5135	6525
2 Dr STD Ext Cab SB	3490	4440
2 Dr STD 4WD Ext Cab SB	4535	5765

OPTIONS FOR TRUCK

6 cyl 3.0 L Engine +125
Auto 4-Speed Transmission +150

Don't forget to refer to the Mileage Adjustment Table at the back of this book!

Model Description	Trade-in Value	Market Value	Model Description	Trade-in Value	Market Value

NISSAN 92-91

Air Conditioning +135
Flip-Up Sunroof +55
Limited Slip Diff +45
Power Door Locks +40
Power Steering[Std on SE,4WD] +45
Power Windows +40

1991 NISSAN

240SX — 1991

More gadgets for the Nissan sport coupe. Four-wheel steering and antilock brakes are the latest additions to Nissan's spry pocket-rocket. The 2.4-liter DOHC inline-four produces 15 more horsepower than last year.

RATINGS (SCALE OF 1-10)

Overall	Safety	Reliability	Performance	Comfort	Value
N/A	N/A	7.6	8	7.3	4.4

Category F

	Trade-in	Market
2 Dr LE Hbk	4475	5810
2 Dr Limited Hbk	5050	6555
2 Dr SE Cpe	3995	5185
2 Dr SE Hbk	4045	5245
2 Dr STD Cpe	3485	4525
2 Dr STD Hbk	3550	4605

OPTIONS FOR 240SX

Auto 4-Speed Transmission +110
Air Conditioning[Opt on SE,STD] +110
Anti-Lock Brakes +85
Flip-Up Sunroof +55
Leather Seats[Opt on SE] +85
Power Sunroof +90

300ZX — 1991

The 300ZX is available with the four-wheel steering and antilock brakes. A driver airbag joins the options list this year.

RATINGS (SCALE OF 1-10)

Overall	Safety	Reliability	Performance	Comfort	Value
N/A	N/A	N/A	N/A	N/A	3.9

Category F

	Trade-in	Market
2 Dr 2+2 Cpe	7775	10090
2 Dr STD Cpe	7010	9100
2 Dr STD Turbo Cpe	8590	11145

OPTIONS FOR 300ZX

Auto 4-Speed Transmission +105
Air Bag Restraint +65
Bose Sound System +60
Glass Panel T-tops +130
Leather Seats +85
Power Drivers Seat +30

MAXIMA — 1991

Antilock brakes are added to the options list of the capable Maxima.

RATINGS (SCALE OF 1-10)

Overall	Safety	Reliability	Performance	Comfort	Value
N/A	N/A	7.3	8.8	7.9	6.9

Category D

	Trade-in	Market
4 Dr GXE Sdn	4050	5460
4 Dr SE Sdn	4055	5465

OPTIONS FOR MAXIMA

Auto 4-Speed Transmission[Opt on SE] +125
Anti-Lock Brakes +120
Bose Sound System[Std on SE] +105
Compact Disc W/fm/tape +105
Leather Seats +150
Power Drivers Seat +40
Power Sunroof[Std on SE] +105

NX — 1991

The replacement for the Nissan Pulsar appears in the guise of the NX twins. Available with the same engines found in the Nissan Sentra, the NX duo are designed to be a sportier alternative to their pedestrian cousins. Both models feature a driver airbag, a two-door body style and front-wheel drive. Antilock brakes are available on the NX 2000 equipped with a manual transmission.

RATINGS (SCALE OF 1-10)

Overall	Safety	Reliability	Performance	Comfort	Value
N/A	N/A	N/A	N/A	N/A	4.9

Category E

	Trade-in	Market
2 Dr 1600 Cpe	2170	3150
2 Dr 2000 Cpe	2535	3685

OPTIONS FOR NX

Auto 4-Speed Transmission +110
Air Conditioning +110
Anti-Lock Brakes +90
T-Tops (solid/Colored) +120

PATHFINDER — 1991

The two-door version of Nissan's sport-utility wagon is dropped in favor of the much better selling four-door. Reaching a new level of refinement, Nissan makes leather seating surfaces available on the top-end SE model. All '91 Pathfinders get rear-wheel antilock brakes.

RATINGS (SCALE OF 1-10)

Overall	Safety	Reliability	Performance	Comfort	Value
6.6	4.2	8.1	7.6	6.8	6.5

Don't forget to refer to the Mileage Adjustment Table at the back of this book!

NISSAN 91

Model Description	Trade-in Value	Market Value
Category G		
4 Dr SE 4WD Wgn	5350	7090
4 Dr XE Wgn	4410	5840
4 Dr XE 4WD Wgn	4990	6610

OPTIONS FOR PATHFINDER
Auto 4-Speed Transmission +145
AM/FM Compact Disc Player +40
Air Conditioning[Opt on XE] +110
Leather Seats +105
Limited Slip Diff +35
Power Door Locks[Opt on XE] +30
Power Windows[Opt on XE] +30
Sunroof +40

SENTRA 1991

The Nissan Sentra is totally redesigned for 1991. Edges are smoothed out and corners are rounded, giving the '91 Sentra a more substantial feel. A racy SE-R is introduced with an outstanding little 140-horsepower engine. All other Sentras get a 110-horsepower engine that is about average for this class. A four-speed automatic transmission is available on all Sentras but the SE-R.

RATINGS (SCALE OF 1-10)

Overall	Safety	Reliability	Performance	Comfort	Value
N/A	N/A	7.1	7.2	7.9	5.9

Model Description	Trade-in Value	Market Value
Category E		
2 Dr E Sdn	1795	2610
4 Dr E Sdn	1995	2895
4 Dr GXE Sdn	2675	3890
2 Dr SE Sdn	2180	3165
2 Dr SE-R Sdn	2535	3680
2 Dr XE Sdn	2035	2960
4 Dr XE Sdn	2180	3165

OPTIONS FOR SENTRA
Auto 3-Speed Transmission +120
Auto 4-Speed Transmission +95
Air Conditioning[Std on GXE] +110
Anti-Lock Brakes +90
Power Steering[Opt on E] +35
Power Sunroof +85

STANZA 1991

Four-wheel antilock brakes are a new option on the Stanza GXE. No other changes for the recently redesigned sedan from Nissan.

Model Description	Trade-in Value	Market Value
Category E		
4 Dr GXE Sdn	3120	4535
4 Dr XE Sdn	2450	3560

OPTIONS FOR STANZA
Auto 4-Speed Transmission +100
Air Conditioning[Opt on XE] +110
Anti-Lock Brakes +90

Power Door Locks[Opt on XE] +35
Power Sunroof +85
Power Windows[Opt on XE] +35

TRUCK 1991

The regular cab six-cylinder four-wheel-drive model is dropped. The remaining Nissan four-wheel drives are equipped with rear-wheel antilock brakes.

RATINGS (SCALE OF 1-10)

Overall	Safety	Reliability	Performance	Comfort	Value
N/A	3.9	7.5	6	6.5	N/A

HALF TON

Model Description	Trade-in Value	Market Value
Category G		
2 Dr STD Std Cab LB	2800	3710
2 Dr STD Std Cab SB	2355	3120
2 Dr STD 4WD Std Cab SB	3140	4155

KING CAB

Model Description	Trade-in Value	Market Value
Category G		
2 Dr SE Ext Cab SB	3760	4985
2 Dr SE 4WD Ext Cab SB	4355	5770
2 Dr STD Ext Cab SB	2935	3890
2 Dr STD 4WD Ext Cab SB	3835	5080

OPTIONS FOR TRUCK
6 cyl 3.0 L Engine[Std on King Cab,LB] +95
Auto 4-Speed Transmission +115
Chrome Pkg +110
Air Conditioning +110
Limited Slip Diff +35
Power Door Locks +30
Power Steering[Std on King Cab,4WD] +40
Power Windows +30
Sunroof +40

Don't forget to refer to the Mileage Adjustment Table at the back of this book!

OLDSMOBILE 00-99

Model Description	Trade-in Value	Market Value	Model Description	Trade-in Value	Market Value

OLDSMOBILE USA

1996 Oldsmobile Achieva

2000 OLDSMOBILE

ALERO   2000

A performance suspension is newly optional on GL models. The four-cylinder gets a composite intake manifold, while all models benefit from the addition of three rear-shelf anchors for child safety-seat restraints. If glitz is your thing, you can now opt for a new gold package on GL and GLS versions.

Category C		
2 Dr GLS Cpe	15470	18240
4 Dr GLS Sdn	15470	18240
2 Dr GX Cpe	11590	13665
4 Dr GX Sdn	11590	13665
Category E		
2 Dr GL Cpe	12860	15165
4 Dr GL Sdn	12860	15165

OPTIONS FOR ALERO
Auto 4-Speed Transmission[Std on GLS] +640
AM/FM Stereo Tape[Std on GL] +135
Aluminum/Alloy Wheels[Std on GLS] +255
Compact Disc W/fm/tape[Std on GLS] +265
Cruise Control[Opt on GX] +180
Power Moonroof +475
Rear Spoiler +145

BRAVADA   2000

GM's OnStar communications system is now available as a dealer-installed option, and a new cargo management system is expected sometime this year. Special color treatments include a new Jewelcoat Red option that features a deep red base color finished with a red-tinted final top coat in place of the usual clearcoat. There's also a Platinum Edition option that adds pewter-colored lower body cladding.

Category G		
4 Dr STD AWD Wgn	20930	24425

OPTIONS FOR BRAVADA
Camper/Towing Package +245
Dual Power Seats +340
Heated Front Seats +225
Power Moonroof +710

INTRIGUE   2000

All Intrigues get restyled six-spoke 16-inch alloy wheels in either silver argent paint or chrome, and the option of adding Oldsmobile's Precision Control System (PCS). The full-function traction-control unit that's standard on the GL and GLS is now available on the GX. Retained accessory power becomes standard, and GL buyers can opt for the revised heated seats on the GLS.

Category B		
4 Dr GL Sdn	16020	18720
4 Dr GLS Sdn	17340	20260
4 Dr GX Sdn	14955	17470

OPTIONS FOR INTRIGUE
Chrome Wheels +555
Compact Disc W/fm/tape[Std on GLS] +305
Power Drivers Seat[Std on GL] +260
Rear Spoiler +95

SILHOUETTE   2000

Olds has canned its 112-inch wheelbase GS, meaning all 2000 Silhouettes (GL, GLS and Premiere) are now extended-length (120-inch wheelbase), seven-passenger models. The traction-control system has been improved, and heated front seats are available in leather. There's also a redesigned instrument cluster with dual trip odometers, as well as upgraded radios, interior lighting and electrical system functions.

Category G		
4 Dr GL Pass. Van Ext	17710	20670
4 Dr GLS Pass. Van Ext	20005	23345
4 Dr Premiere Pass. Van Ext	21965	25635

OPTIONS FOR SILHOUETTE
Aluminum/Alloy Wheels[Opt on GL] +265
Camper/Towing Package +245

1999 OLDSMOBILE

ALERO   1999

Oldsmobile has dropped the slow-selling Achieva in favor of this new clean-sheet design patterned after the successful Intrigue midsize sedan. Available in both two- and four-door configurations with three well-

OLDSMOBILE 99

Model Description	Trade-in Value	Market Value

equipped trim levels the Alero represents a quantum leap forward over previous small Olds models.

RATINGS (SCALE OF 1-10)

Overall	Safety	Reliability	Performance	Comfort	Value
N/A	N/A	N/A	7.6	8	N/A

Category C

	Trade-in	Market
2 Dr GL Cpe	11450	13530
4 Dr GL Sdn	11220	13255
2 Dr GLS Cpe	12980	15335
4 Dr GLS Sdn	12980	15335
2 Dr GX Cpe	10220	12075
4 Dr GX Sdn	10220	12075

OPTIONS FOR ALERO
6 cyl 3.4 L Engine[Opt on GL] +415
Aluminum/Alloy Wheels[Opt on GL] +205
Compact Disc W/fm/tape[Std on GLS] +220
Cruise Control[Opt on GX] +145
Keyless Entry System[Opt on GL] +125
Power Drivers Seat[Opt on GL] +200
Power Moonroof +460

AURORA 1999

It's the status quo again in Auroraville, except this year Olds has added two more hydraulic engine mounts (for a total of three to better isolate engine vibrations. Other than that, a few new colors have been added (Galaxy Silver, Copper Nightmist and Dark Bronzemist).

RATINGS (SCALE OF 1-10)

Overall	Safety	Reliability	Performance	Comfort	Value
N/A	7.1	N/A	8.8	9	N/A

Category A

	Trade-in	Market
4 Dr STD Sdn	21935	25810

OPTIONS FOR AURORA
Bose Sound System +410
Chrome Wheels +655
Heated Front Seats +140
Power Moonroof +850

BRAVADA 1999

In the wake of last year's restyle, Bravada sees feature refinements for '99. The driver-side airbag has been redesigned into a mini-module to permit a clearer view of the instruments, while the turn signal stalk now provides a flash-to-pass feature. A telltale warning lamp has been added to alert the driver when the tailgate lift glass is ajar. And an anti-theft alarm system is now standard. There's also an option package that combines a driver-side memory seat and a power passenger-side seat, as well as sound system upgrades across the board.

RATINGS (SCALE OF 1-10)

Overall	Safety	Reliability	Performance	Comfort	Value
N/A	7.3	N/A	8	8	N/A

Category G

	Trade-in	Market
4 Dr STD 4WD Wgn	19245	22485

OPTIONS FOR BRAVADA
Bose Sound System +525
Heated Front Seats +180
Power Moonroof +580

CUTLASS 1999

No changes to Oldsmobile's fresh-in-'97 bread-and butter sedan, except for two new colors, Bronze Mist and Dark Cherry, and the addition of a Gold Package.

RATINGS (SCALE OF 1-10)

Overall	Safety	Reliability	Performance	Comfort	Value
N/A	7.5	8.6	N/A	8.3	N/A

Category C

	Trade-in	Market
4 Dr GL Sdn	11145	13170
4 Dr GLS Sdn	12100	14300

OPTIONS FOR CUTLASS
Aluminum/Alloy Wheels[Opt on GL] +205
Compact Disc W/fm/tape +220
Keyless Entry System[Opt on GL] +125
Power Drivers Seat[Opt on GL] +200
Power Mirrors[Opt on GL] +70
Power Moonroof +460
Power Windows[Opt on GL] +215

EIGHTY EIGHT 1999

Nothing, unless you count the fact the Eighty-Eight gets two new exterior colors, Champagne and Evergreen, and the LS model gets the option of white-stripe 16-inch tires. Oh, wait. Oldsmobile is celebrating the nameplate's golden anniversary with a special 50th Anniversary Edition Eighty Eight. It has 16-inch aluminum wheels fitted with 215/65SR blackwalls, a highly contented leather interior package and special badging finished in, what else? gold.

RATINGS (SCALE OF 1-10)

Overall	Safety	Reliability	Performance	Comfort	Value
N/A	7.6	8.9	8.6	8.5	N/A

Category B

	Trade-in	Market
4 Dr 50TH Anniversary Sdn	16690	19635
4 Dr LS Sdn	15350	18060
4 Dr STD Sdn	14425	16970

OPTIONS FOR EIGHTY EIGHT
Aluminum/Alloy Wheels[Opt on STD] +220
Compact Disc W/fm/tape[Opt on LS,STD] +250
Dual Power Seats[Opt on LS] +260
Keyless Entry System[Opt on STD] +120
Leather Seats[Std on 50TH Anniversary] +460

Don't forget to refer to the Mileage Adjustment Table at the back of this book!

OLDSMOBILE 99-98

Model Description	Trade-in Value	Market Value	Model Description	Trade-in Value	Market Value

INTRIGUE 1999

Last year, Oldsmobile dumped the stodgy Cutlass Supreme for the Intrigue; a suave, sophisticated sporty sedan designed to take on the best of the imports. For '99 Olds is dumping the 3800 Series II V6 that powers the Intrigue for an all-new, 24-valve 3.5-liter twin cam V6. Until production of the 3.5 liter (a design based on the Aurora V8) can be ramped up to meet the Intrigue build schedule, the new 215-horsepower engine will come standard only in the new top-line GLS model, and optional in the base GX and mid-line GL series. Full function traction control is now available in models equipped with the new powerplant. Minor feature revisions, one new color and new badging rounds out the changes this year.

RATINGS (SCALE OF 1-10)

Overall	Safety	Reliability	Performance	Comfort	Value
N/A	N/A	N/A	8.2	8	N/A

Category B
4 Dr GL Sdn	13950	16410
4 Dr GLS Sdn	15375	18090
4 Dr GX Sdn	13105	15415

OPTIONS FOR INTRIGUE

6 cyl 3.5 L Engine[Std on GLS] +265
Bose Sound System +330
Chrome Wheels +455
Compact Disc W/fm/tape[Std on GLS] +250
Keyless Entry System[Opt on GX] +120
Leather Seats[Std on GLS] +460
Power Drivers Seat[Opt on GX] +210
Power Moonroof +650

LSS 1999

The LSS gets two new exterior colors (Champagne and Evergreen) for '99. Olds has also upgraded the standard radio to an AM/FM stereo cassette with CD player and seek-scan, auto tone control, digital clock and power antenna.
Category C
4 Dr STD Sdn	17665	20870
4 Dr STD Sprchgd Sedan	18295	21615

OPTIONS FOR LSS

Chrome Wheels +405
Power Moonroof +460

SILHOUETTE 1999

Olds is headlining its Premiere Edition, a loaded-up model that debuted in mid-'98 with a standard integrated video entertainment system in back. But other news for 1999 includes a horsepower and torque increase for Silhouette's 3.4-liter V6, plus the addition of a theft-deterrent system and heated outside rearview

mirrors as standard equipment. And if four new exterior colors (Sky, Ruby, Silvermist and Cypress) weren't enough, then consider the availability of a new Gold Package (but only if you must).

RATINGS (SCALE OF 1-10)

Overall	Safety	Reliability	Performance	Comfort	Value
N/A	8	8.5	7.8	7.9	N/A

Category G
4 Dr GL Pass. Van Ext	16145	18865
4 Dr GLS Pass. Van Ext	18305	21390
4 Dr GS Pass. Van	16200	18930
4 Dr Premiere Pass. Van Ext	20165	23565

OPTIONS FOR SILHOUETTE

Aluminum/Alloy Wheels[Opt on GL,GS] +215
Captain Chairs (4)[Opt on GL,GS] +410
Compact Disc W/fm/tape[Std on Premiere] +295
Dual Air Conditioning[Opt on GL] +615
Keyless Entry System[Opt on GL] +130
Leather Seats[Std on GLS, Premiere] +525
Traction Control System[Opt on GL,GS] +180

1998 OLDSMOBILE

ACHIEVA 1998

Oldsmobile limited sales of the Achieva to fleets for 1998, so if you're considering one, it's probably a former rental car.
Category C
4 Dr SL Sdn	8910	10635

AURORA 1998

Status quo in Auroraville, but second-generation airbags have been added.

RATINGS (SCALE OF 1-10)

Overall	Safety	Reliability	Performance	Comfort	Value
8.4	7.1	8.4	8.8	9	8.7

Category A
4 Dr STD Sdn	18340	21460

OPTIONS FOR AURORA

Bose Sound System +335
Chrome Wheels +535
Heated Front Seats +115
Power Moonroof +695

BRAVADA 1998

Front styling is revised, and new body-side cladding alters the Bravada's profile. Inside, dual second generation airbags are housed in a new dashboard. A heated driver's side exterior mirror is newly standard, while heated front seats have been added to the options roster. Battery rundown protection and a theft deterrent system are new standard features.

Don't forget to refer to the Mileage Adjustment Table at the back of this book!

OLDSMOBILE 98

Model Description	Trade-in Value	Market Value

RATINGS (SCALE OF 1-10)

Overall	Safety	Reliability	Performance	Comfort	Value
7.7	7.1	7.4	8	8	8.1

Category G

4 Dr STD 4WD Wgn	17455	20410

OPTIONS FOR BRAVADA
Compact Disc W/fm/tape +240
Heated Front Seats +150
Power Moonroof +475

CUTLASS   1998

No changes to Oldsmobile's fresh bread-and butter sedan, except for the addition of second-generation airbags.

RATINGS (SCALE OF 1-10)

Overall	Safety	Reliability	Performance	Comfort	Value
7.9	7.5	8.2	8.4	8.3	7.3

Category C

4 Dr GL Sdn	9720	11600
4 Dr GLS Sdn	10585	12630

OPTIONS FOR CUTLASS
Aluminum/Alloy Wheels[Opt on GL] +170
Compact Disc W/fm/tape +180
Keyless Entry System[Opt on GL] +100
Power Drivers Seat[Opt on GL] +165
Power Mirrors[Opt on GL] +60
Power Moonroof +375
Power Windows[Opt on GL] +175

EIGHTY EIGHT   1998

Virtually nothing, unless you find a new fuel cap, better access to rear seat belts, new ABS wheel-speed sensors and a couple of new colors intriguing. Second-generation airbags are standard.

RATINGS (SCALE OF 1-10)

Overall	Safety	Reliability	Performance	Comfort	Value
8.4	7.6	8.6	8.6	8.5	8.8

Category B

4 Dr LS Sdn	12570	14870
4 Dr STD Sdn	11950	14140

OPTIONS FOR EIGHTY EIGHT
Aluminum/Alloy Wheels[Std on LS] +180
Compact Disc W/fm/tape +205
Dual Power Seats +210
Keyless Entry System[Std on LS] +95
Leather Seats +375

INTRIGUE   1998

Oldsmobile dumps the stodgy Cutlass Supreme for the Intrigue: a suave, sophisticated, sporty sedan designed to take on the best of the imports. Too bad refinement

issues exist. Second-generation airbags are standard equipment.

RATINGS (SCALE OF 1-10)

Overall	Safety	Reliability	Performance	Comfort	Value
N/A	N/A	8.3	8.2	8	N/A

Category B

4 Dr GL Sdn	12145	14365
4 Dr GLS Sdn	13065	15455
4 Dr STD Sdn	11400	13485

OPTIONS FOR INTRIGUE
Bose Sound System +270
Chrome Wheels +370
Compact Disc W/fm/tape[Std on GLS] +205
Keyless Entry System[Opt on STD] +95
Leather Seats[Opt on GL] +375
Power Drivers Seat[Std on GL] +175
Power Moonroof +530

LSS   1998

New colors, improved ABS, a revised electrochromic rearview mirror, second-generation airbags and a redesigned fuel cap are the major changes for 1998.

RATINGS (SCALE OF 1-10)

Overall	Safety	Reliability	Performance	Comfort	Value
8.4	7.6	8.6	8.4	8.6	8.8

Category C

4 Dr STD Sdn	13980	16685
4 Dr STD Sprchgd Sdn	14480	17280

OPTIONS FOR LSS
Chrome Wheels +330
Power Moonroof +375

REGENCY   1998

Minor changes to this retirement village special for '98. The ABS is upgraded, it's easier to get at the rear seat belts, colors are revised and the "unleaded fuel only" label is removed from the inside of the fuel door.

RATINGS (SCALE OF 1-10)

Overall	Safety	Reliability	Performance	Comfort	Value
N/A	7.6	8.7	8.6	N/A	N/A

Category A

4 Dr STD Sdn	15195	17780

OPTIONS FOR REGENCY
Power Moonroof +695

SILHOUETTE   1998

Side-impact airbags are standard for front seat passengers, and Oldsmobile is building more short-wheelbase vans with dual sliding doors. Front airbags get second generation technology, which results in slower deployment speeds. Midyear, a Premiere

Don't forget to refer to the Mileage Adjustment Table at the back of this book!

OLDSMOBILE 98-97

Model Description	Trade-in Value	Market Value	Model Description	Trade-in Value	Market Value

Edition debuted, loaded with standard features including a TV/VCP setup in back.

RATINGS (SCALE OF 1-10)

Overall	Safety	Reliability	Performance	Comfort	Value
7.6	7.8	7.4	7.8	7.9	6.9

Category G

2 Dr GL Pass. Van Ext	14735	17230
2 Dr GLS Pass. Van Ext	16685	19505
2 Dr GS Pass. Van	14955	17485
2 Dr Premiere Pass. Van Ext	18650	21805

OPTIONS FOR SILHOUETTE

Aluminum/Alloy Wheels[Opt on GL, GS] +175
Auto Load Leveling[Opt on GL, GS] +130
Captain Chairs (2) +285
Compact Disc W/fm/tape[Std on Premiere] +240
Dual Air Conditioning[Opt on GL, GLS] +505
Dual Power Seats[Opt on GL] +230
Keyless Entry System[Opt on GL] +105
Leather Seats +430
Privacy Glass[Opt on GL] +150
Traction Control System[Std on Premiere] +145

1997 OLDSMOBILE

ACHIEVA   1997

Side-impact standards are met, and standard equipment lists are enhanced. Series II Coupe gets new alloy wheels, and the lineup has been simplified.

RATINGS (SCALE OF 1-10)

Overall	Safety	Reliability	Performance	Comfort	Value
7.7	7.5	8.3	8.4	7.6	6.7

Category C

2 Dr SC Series II Cpe	7745	9315
4 Dr SL Series II Sdn	7660	9205

OPTIONS FOR ACHIEVA

6 cyl 3.1 L Engine +190
Compact Disc W/fm/tape +145
Keyless Entry System +85
Leather Steering Wheel[Opt on SL Series II] +45
Power Drivers Seat +135
Power Moonroof +305
Rear Spoiler[Opt on SL Series II] +80

AURORA   1997

Larger front brakes, an in-dash CD player for the Bose sound system, a tilt-down right-hand exterior mirror for backing assistance, an integrated rearview mirror compass, and a three-channel garage door opener are added this year.

RATINGS (SCALE OF 1-10)

Overall	Safety	Reliability	Performance	Comfort	Value
8.3	7.1	8	8.8	9	8.5

Category A

4 Dr STD Sdn	15680	18430

OPTIONS FOR AURORA

Bose Sound System +275
Chrome Wheels +440
Compact Disc Changer +335
Heated Front Seats +95
Power Moonroof +570

BRAVADA   1997

Bravada drops the split-tailgate arrangement at the rear in favor of a top-hinged liftgate with separately lifting glass. So, tailgate parties aren't as convenient, but loading cargo sure is easier. Also new to the options list is a power tilt and slide sunroof. Included with the hole in the roof are a mini-overhead console, a pop-up wind deflector, and a sun shade. Rear disc brakes replace the former drums, combining with the front discs to provide better stopping ability.

RATINGS (SCALE OF 1-10)

Overall	Safety	Reliability	Performance	Comfort	Value
7.1	5.3	7.2	8	8	6.8

Category G

4 Dr STD 4WD Wgn	15460	18260

OPTIONS FOR BRAVADA

AM/FM Compact Disc Player +140
Camper/Towing Package +135
Gold Package +155
Power Moonroof +385

CUTLASS   1997

Oldsmobile retires the Ciera and introduces the Cutlass, based on the same platform as Chevy's new Malibu. Cutlass is more upscale that its Chevrolet counterpart, offering a slightly more powerful V-6 engine on all models, and a sunroof option, standard leather interior, and larger wheels on the GLS.

RATINGS (SCALE OF 1-10)

Overall	Safety	Reliability	Performance	Comfort	Value
7.8	7.5	7.6	8.4	8.3	7.1

Category C

4 Dr GLS Sdn	9460	11375
4 Dr STD Sdn	8780	10555

OPTIONS FOR CUTLASS

Aluminum/Alloy Wheels[Opt on STD] +140
Compact Disc W/fm/tape +145
Keyless Entry System[Opt on STD] +85
Power Drivers Seat[Opt on STD] +135
Power Moonroof +305
Power Windows[Opt on STD] +140

Don't forget to refer to the Mileage Adjustment Table at the back of this book!

CUTLASS SUPREME   1997

Alloy wheels and a power trunk release are added to the standard equipment list, while coupes gain side-impact protection that meets federal safety standards. The 3.4-liter DOHC V-6 engine is dropped from the options list.

RATINGS (SCALE OF 1-10)

Overall	Safety	Reliability	Performance	Comfort	Value
7.9	7.6	8	8.2	8.3	7.6

Category C
2 Dr SL Series III Cpe	10095	12140
4 Dr SL Series III Sdn	10095	12140

OPTIONS FOR CUTLASS SUPREME
Compact Disc W/fm/tape +145
Power Moonroof +305

EIGHTY EIGHT   1997

Side-impact protection is upgraded to federal safety standards, interiors are improved, and new Oldsmobile logos adorn the body.

RATINGS (SCALE OF 1-10)

Overall	Safety	Reliability	Performance	Comfort	Value
8.3	7.6	8.6	8.6	8.5	8.3

Category B
4 Dr LS Sdn	10575	12645
4 Dr STD Sdn	10155	12145

OPTIONS FOR EIGHTY EIGHT
Aluminum/Alloy Wheels[Std on LS] +150
Compact Disc W/fm/tape +165
Dual Power Seats +175
Leather Seats +305

LSS   1997

Minor changes accompany Oldsmobile's euro-flavored sedan into 1997. The center console and shifter are new, and other interior upgrades have been made. New, more prominent badging has been added to the exterior. Finally, the final-drive ratio has been changed to 2.93:1 from 2.97:1.

RATINGS (SCALE OF 1-10)

Overall	Safety	Reliability	Performance	Comfort	Value
8.3	7.6	8.6	8.4	8.6	8.3

Category C
4 Dr STD Sdn	12255	14730
4 Dr STD Sprchgd Sdn	12695	15265

OPTIONS FOR LSS
Chrome Wheels +270
Power Moonroof +305

REGENCY   1997

New name for an old concept. Look closely...see the old Eighty Eight before 1996's restyle? Regency takes over where the Ninety Eight left off, satisfying traditional Oldsmobile buyers.

RATINGS (SCALE OF 1-10)

Overall	Safety	Reliability	Performance	Comfort	Value
N/A	N/A	8.7	8.6	N/A	N/A

Category A
4 Dr STD Sdn	13080	15375

OPTIONS FOR REGENCY
Power Moonroof +570

SILHOUETTE   1997

Completely redesigned, the new Silhouette comes in several trim levels and two sizes, each with a healthy load of standard equipment.

RATINGS (SCALE OF 1-10)

Overall	Safety	Reliability	Performance	Comfort	Value
7.4	7	7.5	7.8	7.9	6.8

Category G
2 Dr GL Pass. Van Ext	12820	15140
2 Dr GLS Pass. Van Ext	13685	16165
2 Dr STD Pass. Van	11815	13955
2 Dr STD Pass. Van Ext	12260	14475

OPTIONS FOR SILHOUETTE
Aluminum/Alloy Wheels[Opt on GL] +145
Auto Load Leveling[Opt on GL] +105 .
Child Seats (2) +115
Compact Disc W/fm/tape +200
Dual Air Conditioning[Opt on GL] +410
Leather Seats +350
Power Moonroof +385
Privacy Glass[Opt on STD] +120
Sliding Driver Side Door +235
Traction Control System[Opt on GL] +120

1996 OLDSMOBILE

ACHIEVA   1996

Substantial upgrades make the Achieva palatable for 1996. A new interior with dual airbags, standard air conditioning, a new base engine, daytime running lights, a theft-deterrent system and optional traction control make this Oldsmobile an excellent value in the compact class.

RATINGS (SCALE OF 1-10)

Overall	Safety	Reliability	Performance	Comfort	Value
7.4	7.1	6.7	8.4	7.6	7.2

Model Description	Trade-in Value	Market Value
Category C		
2 Dr SC Series III Cpe	6405	7825
4 Dr SL Series III Sdn	6405	7825

OPTIONS FOR ACHIEVA

6 cyl 3.1 L Engine +170
Auto 4-Speed Transmission[Opt on SC Series II, SL Series II] +290
Compact Disc W/fm/tape +120
Keyless Entry System +70
Power Drivers Seat +110
Power Sunroof +245

AURORA   1996

Daytime running lights are added, and looking through the backlight won't make your eyes water from distortions anymore. We knew it was only a matter of time before some goofball decided chrome wheels and a gold package would look great on the otherwise classy Aurora. The new Oldsmobile? What's that? When do we get the fake convertible roof, guys?

RATINGS (SCALE OF 1-10)

Overall	Safety	Reliability	Performance	Comfort	Value
8	7	7.7	8.8	9	7.3

Category A

4 Dr STD Sdn	13075	15500

OPTIONS FOR AURORA

Bose Sound System +225
Chrome Wheels +360
Compact Disc Changer +275
Heated Front Seats +75
Power Moonroof +465

BRAVADA   1996

Nice truck, but how many luxury SUV's do we really need? The only thing different about the Bravada to differentiate it from the Chevy Blazer and GMC Jimmy are the seats, front styling, trim — and the price tag.

RATINGS (SCALE OF 1-10)

Overall	Safety	Reliability	Performance	Comfort	Value
6.7	4.9	6.8	8	8	5.8

Category G

4 Dr STD 4WD Wgn	13325	15780

OPTIONS FOR BRAVADA

AM/FM Compact Disc Player +115
Camper/Towing Package +110
Gold Package +130

CIERA   1996

Bestseller prepares for retirement at the end of the year, receiving badge revisions, some additional standard equipment and an improved, optional V6 engine.

RATINGS (SCALE OF 1-10)

Overall	Safety	Reliability	Performance	Comfort	Value
7.5	6.5	7.3	7.4	7.6	8.5

Category C

4 Dr SL Wgn	7225	8825
4 Dr SL Series II Sdn	6825	8335

OPTIONS FOR CIERA

Cruise Control[Std on SL Series II] +80
Keyless Entry System +70
Luggage Rack +40
Power Drivers Seat +110
Power Windows[Std on SL Series II] +115
Third Seat +60

CUTLASS SUPREME   1996

The convertible has been retired. The sedan and coupe enjoy their last year in production, receiving engine upgrades for 1996.

RATINGS (SCALE OF 1-10)

Overall	Safety	Reliability	Performance	Comfort	Value
7.9	7.6	7.8	8.2	8.3	7.5

Category C

2 Dr SL Series IV Cpe	8640	10555
4 Dr SL Series IV Sdn	8640	10555

OPTIONS FOR CUTLASS SUPREME

6 cyl 3.4 L Engine +445
Power Moonroof +250
Rear Spoiler +65

EIGHTY EIGHT   1996

Royale designation dropped, and the Eighty Eight gets fresh Aurora-inspired styling front and rear. Standard equipment levels go up, and daytime running lights are added.

RATINGS (SCALE OF 1-10)

Overall	Safety	Reliability	Performance	Comfort	Value
8.2	7.5	8	8.6	8.5	8.3

Category B

4 Dr LS Sdn	8965	10770
4 Dr LSS Sdn	10190	12240
4 Dr LSS Sprchgd Sdn	10585	12715
4 Dr STD Sdn	8180	9830

OPTIONS FOR EIGHTY EIGHT

Chrome Wheels +250
Compact Disc W/fm/tape +135
Cruise Control[Opt on STD] +80
Leather Seats[Std on LSS] +250
Power Drivers Seat[Opt on STD] +115
Power Moonroof +355
Traction Control System[Opt on LS] +65

Don't forget to refer to the Mileage Adjustment Table at the back of this book!

OLDSMOBILE 96-95

Model Description	Trade-in Value	Market Value	Model Description	Trade-in Value	Market Value

NINETY-EIGHT   1996

Supercharged engine dropped from this model, and daytime running lamps have been added. Don't expect a 1997 Ninety Eight.

RATINGS (SCALE OF 1-10)

Overall	Safety	Reliability	Performance	Comfort	Value
8	7.5	8.4	7.9	8.1	8.3

Category A

4 Dr Series II Sdn	11440	13560

OPTIONS FOR NINETY-EIGHT
Compact Disc W/fm/tape +230
Power Sunroof +555

SILHOUETTE   1996

New 180-horsepower 3.4-liter V6 makes the Silhouette even better able to imitate Japan's bullet train.

RATINGS (SCALE OF 1-10)

Overall	Safety	Reliability	Performance	Comfort	Value
7.4	6.4	7.8	7.2	7.3	8.5

Category G

2 Dr Series II Pass. Van	10065	11915

OPTIONS FOR SILHOUETTE
AM/FM Compact Disc Player +115
Auto Load Leveling +85
Child Seats (2) +90
Dual Air Conditioning +335

1995 OLDSMOBILE

ACHIEVA   1995

Fewer options and powertrains are available; SOHC and high-output Quad 4 engines are gone. Standard engine makes 150 horsepower this year, up from 115 in 1994. A V6 is optional. Air conditioning is standard.

RATINGS (SCALE OF 1-10)

Overall	Safety	Reliability	Performance	Comfort	Value
7.6	6.6	7.8	8.4	7.9	7.1

Category C

4 Dr S Sdn	4590	5760
2 Dr S Series II Cpe	5140	6450

OPTIONS FOR ACHIEVA
6 cyl 3.1 L Engine +145
Auto 3-Speed Transmission +165
Auto 4-Speed Transmission[Std on S Series II] +225
AM/FM Stereo Tape[Std on S Series II] +50
Air Conditioning[Std on S Series II] +245
Cruise Control[Std on S Series II] +65
Keyless Entry System +55
Power Windows[Std on S Series II] +95
Rear Spoiler +55

AURORA   1995

World-class V8 front-drive luxury sedan features cutting-edge styling, dual airbags, ABS and traction control.

RATINGS (SCALE OF 1-10)

Overall	Safety	Reliability	Performance	Comfort	Value
8	7.8	7.5	8.8	9	7.1

Category A

4 Dr STD Sdn	10265	12340

OPTIONS FOR AURORA
Bose Sound System +185
Heated Front Seats +60
Power Moonroof +380

CIERA   1995

Offered in a single trim level this year. Rear defroster and cassette player are standard. Brake/transmission shift interlock is new.

RATINGS (SCALE OF 1-10)

Overall	Safety	Reliability	Performance	Comfort	Value
7.7	7.1	7.4	7.4	7.6	8.9

Category C

4 Dr SL Sdn	5070	6365
4 Dr SL Wgn	5950	7465

OPTIONS FOR CIERA
6 cyl 3.1 L Engine[Opt on Sdn] +145
AM/FM Stereo Tape[Opt on Wgn] +50
Aluminum/Alloy Wheels +90
Cruise Control[Opt on Wgn] +65
Keyless Entry System +55
Luggage Rack +35
Power Drivers Seat +90
Power Windows +95
Third Seat +50
Woodgrain Applique +95

CUTLASS SUPREME   1995

Redesigned dashboard equipped with dual airbags debuts. Single trim level offered this year. Front bench seat is no longer available. Front seatbelts are mounted to door pillars instead of doors. Air conditioning, power windows, power locks, tilt steering, and cassette player are standard on all models.

RATINGS (SCALE OF 1-10)

Overall	Safety	Reliability	Performance	Comfort	Value
7.9	8.1	6.8	8.2	8.3	7.9

Category C

2 Dr S Cpe	6240	7830
4 Dr S Sdn	6240	7830
2 Dr STD Conv	8800	11040

Don't forget to refer to the Mileage Adjustment Table at the back of this book!

Model Description	Trade-in Value	Market Value

Model Description	Trade-in Value	Market Value

OPTIONS FOR CUTLASS SUPREME
6 cyl 3.4 L Engine +370
Compact Disc W/fm/tape +95
Cruise Control[Opt on Sdn] +65
Keyless Entry System[Opt on Sdn] +55
Leather Seats[Opt on S] +185
Power Drivers Seat[Opt on S] +90
Power Moonroof +205

EIGHTY-EIGHT ROYALE   1995

Engine upgraded to 3800 Series II status, and supercharged 3.8-liter V6 is a new option on LSS models. New on-board navigation system called Guidestar was a $1,995 option, originally available only in California.

RATINGS (SCALE OF 1-10)

Overall	Safety	Reliability	Performance	Comfort	Value
N/A	8.3	7.2	8.5	N/A	N/A

	Trade-in	Market
Category B		
4 Dr LS Sdn	7545	9210
4 Dr LSS Sdn	7965	9720
4 Dr LSS Sprchgd Sdn	8425	10285
4 Dr STD Sdn	7100	8670

OPTIONS FOR EIGHTY-EIGHT ROYALE
Compact Disc W/fm/tape +110
Cruise Control[Opt on STD] +65
Leather Seats[Std on LSS] +205
Power Drivers Seat[Opt on STD] +95
Traction Control System[Std on LSS] +50

NINETY-EIGHT   1995

Engine upgraded to 3800 Series II status. Alloy wheels are standard. Flash-to-pass is new standard feature.

RATINGS (SCALE OF 1-10)

Overall	Safety	Reliability	Performance	Comfort	Value
7.8	8.2	7.3	7.9	8.1	7.6

	Trade-in	Market
Category A		
4 Dr STD Sdn	9120	10960
4 Dr STD Sprchgd Sdn	9465	11375

OPTIONS FOR NINETY-EIGHT
Compact Disc W/fm/tape +190
Keyless Entry System +80
Power Moonroof +380
Traction Control System +65

SILHOUETTE   1995

3.1-liter V6 engine dropped in favor of more powerful 3.8-liter V6.

RATINGS (SCALE OF 1-10)

Overall	Safety	Reliability	Performance	Comfort	Value
7	6.6	5.9	7.2	7.3	7.8

	Trade-in	Market
Category G		
2 Dr STD Pass. Van	7650	9325

OPTIONS FOR SILHOUETTE
AM/FM Compact Disc Player +95
Child Seats (2) +75
Dual Air Conditioning +275
Keyless Entry System +60
Leather Seats +235
Power Drivers Seat +85
Traction Control System +80

1994 OLDSMOBILE

ACHIEVA   1994

Driver airbag debuts. 3.1-liter V6 replaces 3.3-liter V6 on options sheet. Hot-rod SCX gone from lineup.

RATINGS (SCALE OF 1-10)

Overall	Safety	Reliability	Performance	Comfort	Value
7.6	6.5	8	8.4	7.9	7.1

	Trade-in	Market
Category C		
2 Dr S Cpe	3835	4935
4 Dr S Sdn	3860	4970
2 Dr SC Cpe	4725	6090
4 Dr SL Sdn	4725	6090

OPTIONS FOR ACHIEVA
6 cyl 3.1 L Engine +125
Auto 3-Speed Transmission +135
Auto 4-Speed Transmission +185
AM/FM Stereo Tape[Opt on S] +40
Air Conditioning[Opt on S] +200
Astro Roof +170
Cruise Control[Opt on S] +55
Leather Seats +150
Power Drivers Seat +75
Power Mirrors[Opt on S] +25
Power Windows +80

BRAVADA   1994

New Special Edition model has gold trim. Doors get guard beams. Shock absorbers are softened for a better ride.

RATINGS (SCALE OF 1-10)

Overall	Safety	Reliability	Performance	Comfort	Value
6.1	5	6.5	6.8	7.1	5.2

	Trade-in	Market
Category G		
4 Dr STD 4WD Wgn	9360	11290
4 Dr Special Edition 4WD Wgn	8840	10660

OPTIONS FOR BRAVADA
AM/FM Compact Disc Player +75
Camper/Towing Package[Opt on STD] +70
Electronic Gauges[Opt on STD] +65
Gold Package[Opt on STD] +85

Don't forget to refer to the Mileage Adjustment Table at the back of this book!

OLDSMOBILE 94

Model Description	Trade-in Value	Market Value	Model Description	Trade-in Value	Market Value

Leather Seats[Opt on STD] +190
Swing Out Tire Carrier[Opt on STD] +45

CUTLASS CIERA   1994

Driver airbag and ABS standard for all models. Four-cylinder engine back in base models, producing 120 horsepower. A 3.1-liter V6 replaces last year's 3.3-liter V6. Variable-assist steering is a new option on sedans. SL replaced by Special Edition models.

RATINGS (SCALE OF 1-10)

Overall	Safety	Reliability	Performance	Comfort	Value
7.3	7.1	6.1	7.4	7.6	8.3

Category C

	Trade-in	Market
4 Dr S Sdn	4550	5865
4 Dr S Wgn	4965	6395
4 Dr Special Edition Sdn	3895	5015
4 Dr Special Edition Wgn	4715	6075

OPTIONS FOR CUTLASS CIERA

6 cyl 3.1 L Engine[Opt on S Sdn] +125
AM/FM Stereo Tape[Opt on S] +40
Cruise Control[Opt on S] +55
Keyless Entry System +45
Leather Seats +150
Power Drivers Seat[Opt on S] +75
Power Windows[Opt on S] +80
Premium Sound System +95
Third Seat[Opt on S] +40
Woodgrain Applique +80

CUTLASS SUPREME   1994

Driver airbag added and ABS is made standard on all models. International Series dropped. Special Editions are on sale, carrying one-price stickers and a healthy load of standard equipment. 3.1-liter V6 makes 20 more horsepower. 3.4-liter V6 makes 15 more horsepower. New standard features include tilt steering, intermittent wipers, Pass-Key theft deterrent system, and rear defogger.

RATINGS (SCALE OF 1-10)

Overall	Safety	Reliability	Performance	Comfort	Value
7.7	7.4	6.5	8.2	8	8.4

Category C

	Trade-in	Market
2 Dr S Cpe	5175	6665
4 Dr S Sdn	5200	6700
2 Dr STD Conv	7075	9115
2 Dr Special Edition Cpe	4890	6300
4 Dr Special Edition Sdn	4920	6335

OPTIONS FOR CUTLASS SUPREME

6 cyl,3.4 L Engine +320
Climate Control for AC[Opt on S Cpe] +40
Cruise Control[Opt on S] +55
Keyless Entry System +45

Leather Seats[Std on STD] +150
Lighted Entry System[Opt on STD] +40
Power Drivers Seat[Std on STD] +75
Power Moonroof +165
Power Passenger Seat +70
Power Windows[Opt on S] +80
Premium Sound System +95

EIGHTY-EIGHT ROYALE   1994

Passenger airbag is housed in a new dashboard featuring more compact layout and new four-spoke steering wheel. Grille is body-color. Headlamps and turn signals are restyled. Traction control system can now reduce engine power as well as apply brakes to slipping wheel. New Special Edition model is available.

RATINGS (SCALE OF 1-10)

Overall	Safety	Reliability	Performance	Comfort	Value
N/A	8.3	7.7	8.3	N/A	N/A

Category B

	Trade-in	Market
4 Dr LS Sdn	6095	7740
4 Dr LSS Sdn	5980	7590
4 Dr STD Sdn	5755	7310
4 Dr Special Edition Sdn	5365	6815

OPTIONS FOR EIGHTY-EIGHT ROYALE

Compact Disc W/fm/tape +90
Cruise Control[Opt on STD] +55
Keyless Entry System +45
Leather Seats[Std on LS Special Edit.] +165
Power Drivers Seat[Opt on LS,STD] +75
Traction Control System +45

NINETY-EIGHT   1994

Passenger airbag is housed in a new dashboard featuring more compact layout. Touring Sedan is dropped, and a Special Edition is added. Supercharged engine is now available on the Elite, and it gains horsepower and torque. Traction control system can now reduce engine power as well as apply brakes to slipping wheel. There is an additional inch of seat travel. The grille and headlamps are restyled.

RATINGS (SCALE OF 1-10)

Overall	Safety	Reliability	Performance	Comfort	Value
8.1	8.3	7.7	7.7	8.1	8.5

Category A

	Trade-in	Market
4 Dr Elite Sdn	7275	9105
4 Dr Elite Sprchgd Sdn	7695	9630
4 Dr STD Sdn	6840	8560
4 Dr Special Edition Sdn	6460	8085

OPTIONS FOR NINETY-EIGHT

Astro Roof +355
Compact Disc W/fm/tape +155
Keyless Entry System[Opt on STD] +65
Leather Seats[Opt on Elite,STD] +170

Don't forget to refer to the Mileage Adjustment Table at the back of this book!

OLDSMOBILE 94-93

Model Description	Trade-in Value	Market Value	Model Description	Trade-in Value	Market Value

Power Passenger Seat[Opt on STD] +75
Traction Control System +50

SILHOUETTE   1994

Driver airbag added to standard equipment list. Traction control and integrated child seats are new options. Power sliding side door debuts. New Special Edition model is available.

RATINGS (SCALE OF 1-10)

Overall	Safety	Reliability	Performance	Comfort	Value
7	6.5	5.9	7.2	7.3	8.3

Category G
2 Dr STD Pass. Van — 6870 — 8285
2 Dr Special Edition Pass. Van — 6660 — 8030

OPTIONS FOR SILHOUETTE

6 cyl 3.8 L Engine[Opt on STD] +100
Auto 4-Speed Transmission[Opt on STD] +50
AM/FM Compact Disc Player +75
AM/FM Stereo Tape[Opt on STD] +55
Child Seats (2) +60
Cruise Control[Opt on STD] +50
Keyless Entry System +50
Leather Seats +190
Luggage Rack[Opt on STD] +40
Power Door Locks[Opt on STD] +55
Power Drivers Seat +70
Power Windows[Opt on STD] +60
Traction Control System +65

1993 OLDSMOBILE

ACHIEVA   1993

All four-cylinder engines lose five horsepower, thanks to emissions regulations. They also get new engine mounts and other revisions aimed at making them smoother and quieter. Battery rundown protection is new standard feature.

RATINGS (SCALE OF 1-10)

Overall	Safety	Reliability	Performance	Comfort	Value
7	4.3	7.6	8.4	7.9	6.9

Category C
2 Dr S Cpe — 2650 — 3645
4 Dr S Sdn — 2670 — 3670
2 Dr SL Cpe — 3015 — 4145
4 Dr SL Sdn — 3025 — 4155

OPTIONS FOR ACHIEVA

4 cyl 2.3 L Quad 4 Engine +80
6 cyl 3.3 L Engine[Opt on S,Sdn] +105
Auto 3-Speed Transmission[Opt on S] +110
Achieva SCX Performance Pkg +430
AM/FM Stereo Tape[Opt on S] +35
Air Conditioning +160

Aluminum/Alloy Wheels +60
Cruise Control +45
Keyless Entry System +35
Power Drivers Seat +60
Power Windows +65

BRAVADA   1993

Electronic shift controls added to transmission. Gold Package is new option. Driver's seat gets six-way power adjustment. Both front seats gain power lumbar adjusters. Sun visors get extender panels, and a new overhead console with compass is added.

RATINGS (SCALE OF 1-10)

Overall	Safety	Reliability	Performance	Comfort	Value
6.3	5.1	7	6.8	7.1	5.6

Category G
4 Dr STD 4WD Wgn — 6700 — 8535

OPTIONS FOR BRAVADA

AM/FM Compact Disc Player +65
Camper/Towing Package +60
Electronic Gauges +50
Leather Seats +155
Swing Out Tire Carrier +35

CUTLASS CIERA   1993

Driver airbag is standard on SL; optional on S. Four-cylinder engine dropped in favor of standard V6 power. Air conditioning also makes the standard equipment list. SL sedans get a trunk cargo net; SL wagons get a cargo cover. Leather is new option on base model.

RATINGS (SCALE OF 1-10)

Overall	Safety	Reliability	Performance	Comfort	Value
7.4	6.1	6.9	7.4	7.6	8.8

Category C
4 Dr S Sdn — 3210 — 4410
4 Dr S Cruiser Wgn — 3360 — 4620
4 Dr SL Sdn — 4015 — 5520
4 Dr SL Cruiser Wgn — 4125 — 5670

OPTIONS FOR CUTLASS CIERA

6 cyl 3.3 L Engine[Opt on S,S Cruiser] +105
Auto 4-Speed Transmission[Std on SL Cruiser] +40
AM/FM Stereo Tape[Opt on S,S Cruiser] +35
Air Bag Restraint[Opt on S,S Cruiser] +95
Aluminum/Alloy Wheels +60
Cruise Control +45
Keyless Entry System +35
Leather Seats +125
Power Drivers Seat +60
Power Windows +65
Premium Sound System +75
Third Seat[Opt on S Cruiser] +35
Woodgrain Applique +65

Don't forget to refer to the Mileage Adjustment Table at the back of this book!

OLDSMOBILE 93-92

CUTLASS SUPREME 1993

3.4-liter, twin-cam engine now available in convertible, but can't be ordered with five-speed transmission anymore. International Series gets new alloys, and all models are equipped with automatic power door locks.

RATINGS (SCALE OF 1-10)

Overall	Safety	Reliability	Performance	Comfort	Value
7.2	5.3	6.9	8.2	8	7.8

Category C
2 Dr International Cpe	4950	6805
4 Dr International Sdn	4970	6835
2 Dr S Cpe	3615	4970
4 Dr S Sdn	3640	5000
2 Dr STD Conv	4930	6775
2 Dr Special Cpe	3570	4910
4 Dr Special Sdn	3595	4940

OPTIONS FOR CUTLASS SUPREME

6 cyl 3.4 L Engine[Opt on S,STD] +265
Auto 4-Speed Transmission[Opt on S] +35
AM/FM Stereo Tape[Opt on S] +35
Aluminum/Alloy Wheels[Opt on S] +60
Anti-Lock Brakes[Opt on S,STD] +120
Climate Control for AC[Opt on S,STD] +35
Cruise Control[Opt on S,STD] +45
Leather Seats +125
Power Drivers Seat[Opt on S,STD] +60
Power Sunroof +135
Power Windows[Std on Special,STD] +65
Premium Sound System +75
Steer. Whl. Radio Cntrls[Opt on S,STD] +30

EIGHTY-EIGHT ROYALE 1993

ABS is standard on all models. Engine makes more torque. LSS gets new alloy wheels and variable-assist power steering.

RATINGS (SCALE OF 1-10)

Overall	Safety	Reliability	Performance	Comfort	Value
N/A	6.8	7.1	8.3	N/A	N/A

Category B
4 Dr LS Sdn	4610	5990
4 Dr STD Sdn	4315	5605

OPTIONS FOR EIGHTY-EIGHT ROYALE

LSS Pkg +225
AM/FM Stereo Tape[Std on LS] +35
Aluminum/Alloy Wheels +65
Auto Load Leveling +35
Cruise Control[Std on LS] +45
Leather Seats +135
Power Door Locks[Std on LS] +50
Power Drivers Seat +65
Premium Sound System +75
Traction Control System +35

NINETY-EIGHT 1993

Base V6 makes more torque. Touring Sedan gets body-color grille and headlight trim. Base model loses standard cassette player.

RATINGS (SCALE OF 1-10)

Overall	Safety	Reliability	Performance	Comfort	Value
N/A	N/A	7.3	7.7	7.7	8.4

Category A
4 Dr Regency Sdn	5410	6795
4 Dr Regency Elite Sdn	5830	7325
4 Dr Regency Touring Sdn	6400	8040
4 Dr Regency Touring Sprchgd Sdn		
	6620	8310
4 Dr Special Sdn	5070	6370

OPTIONS FOR NINETY-EIGHT

AM/FM Stereo Tape[Opt on Regency] +30
Aluminum/Alloy Wheels[Opt on Regency] +90
Keyless Entry System[Opt on Regency] +55
Leather Seats[Opt on Regency,Regency Elite] +140
Power Passenger Seat +65
Power Sunroof +305
Premium Sound System[Std on Regency Touring] +45
Steer. Whl. Radio Cntrls[Opt on Regency] +30

SILHOUETTE 1993

Subtle restyle includes front and rear fascias, as well as alloy wheels. Optional V6 makes more power.

RATINGS (SCALE OF 1-10)

Overall	Safety	Reliability	Performance	Comfort	Value
7	5.6	6.5	7.2	7.3	8.3

Category G
2 Dr STD Pass. Van	5350	6815

OPTIONS FOR SILHOUETTE

6 cyl 3.8 L Engine +110
Auto 4-Speed Transmission +100
AM/FM Compact Disc Player +65
Auto Load Leveling +45
Cruise Control +40
Dual Air Conditioning +185
Leather Seats +155
Luggage Rack +30
Power Door Locks +45
Power Drivers Seat +55
Power Windows +50
Sunroof +60

1992 OLDSMOBILE

ACHIEVA 1992

Cutlass Calais replacement. SCX coupe is hot-rod of the bunch, featuring a 190-horsepower Quad 4 engine. ABS is standard. Computer Command Ride is optional on SL and SC, and allows driver to select one of three suspension settings.

RATINGS (SCALE OF 1-10)

Overall	Safety	Reliability	Performance	Comfort	Value
6.9	4.4	7.1	8.4	7.9	6.8

Category C

Model	Trade-in	Market
2 Dr S Cpe	2205	3140
4 Dr S Sdn	2220	3165
2 Dr SCX Cpe	2620	3730
2 Dr SL Cpe	2500	3565
4 Dr SL Sdn	2520	3590

OPTIONS FOR ACHIEVA

4 cyl 2.3 L Quad 4 Engine[Opt on S] +65
6 cyl 3.3 L Engine +90
Auto 3-Speed Transmission[Opt on S] +90
Sport Performance Pkg +215
Air Conditioning +135
Power Drivers Seat +50
Power Windows +50

BRAVADA   1992

CD player and outside spare tire carrier are new options. New speedometer placed in dashboard. Midyear, a 200-horsepower V6 is added.

RATINGS (SCALE OF 1-10)

Overall	Safety	Reliability	Performance	Comfort	Value
5.8	3.8	6.7	6.4	7.1	5

Category G

Model	Trade-in	Market
4 Dr STD 4WD Wgn	5935	7700

OPTIONS FOR BRAVADA

AM/FM Compact Disc Player +50
Camper/Towing Package +50
Leather Seats +130
Swing Out Tire Carrier +30

CUSTOM CRUISER   1992

A more powerful 5.7-liter V8 is newly optional.
Category C

Model	Trade-in	Market
4 Dr STD Wgn	4085	5820

OPTIONS FOR CUSTOM CRUISER

8 cyl 5.7 L Engine +40
Power Door Locks +40
Power Drivers Seat +50
Power Windows +50

CUTLASS CIERA   1992

Coupe and base sedan are given the axe. Automatic door locks made standard.

RATINGS (SCALE OF 1-10)

Overall	Safety	Reliability	Performance	Comfort	Value
7	4.7	6.7	7.4	7.6	8.7

Category C

Model	Trade-in	Market
4 Dr S Sdn	2345	3340
4 Dr S Cruiser Wgn	2540	3620
4 Dr SL Sdn	3075	4385
4 Dr SL Cruiser Wgn	3165	4510

OPTIONS FOR CUTLASS CIERA

6 cyl 3.3 L Engine[Opt on S, S Cruiser] +90
Auto 4-Speed Transmission[Std on SL Cruiser] +35
Air Conditioning[Opt on S, S Cruiser] +135
Leather Seats +100
Power Drivers Seat[Opt on S] +50
Power Windows +50
Third Seat[Opt on S Cruiser] +30

CUTLASS SUPREME   1992

Styling is updated front and rear. Four-cylinder engine dropped. International Series models get 3.4-liter twin-cam engine, heads-up instrument display and ABS standard. Sedans get folding rear seatback. Alloys are standard on SL models.

RATINGS (SCALE OF 1-10)

Overall	Safety	Reliability	Performance	Comfort	Value
7.4	5.4	7	8.2	8	8.3

Category C

Model	Trade-in	Market
2 Dr International Cpe	3690	5255
4 Dr International Sdn	3705	5280
2 Dr S Cpe	2980	4250
4 Dr S Sdn	3000	4275
2 Dr STD Conv	3895	5550

OPTIONS FOR CUTLASS SUPREME

6 cyl 3.4 L Engine +195
Auto 4-Speed Transmission[Std on STD] +30
Anti-Lock Brakes[Opt on S, STD] +95
Astro Roof +110
Auto Load Leveling +45
Keyless Entry System[Opt on S, STD] +30
Leather Seats +100
Power Door Locks[Opt on S, STD] +40
Power Windows[Std on STD] +50

EIGHTY-EIGHT ROYALE   1992

Redesigned and based on Ninety-Eight platform. Available only as a sedan; coupe dropped from lineup. Driver airbag is standard. LS models have standard ABS; this feature is optional on base models. 3.8-liter V6 makes 170 horsepower. Passenger and cargo volume are both up. Traction control is optional on LS models. Midyear, an LSS model debuted with FE3 suspension, alloy wheels and bucket seats.

RATINGS (SCALE OF 1-10)

Overall	Safety	Reliability	Performance	Comfort	Value
N/A	6.8	6.9	8.3	N/A	N/A

Don't forget to refer to the Mileage Adjustment Table at the back of this book!

Model Description	Trade-in Value	Market Value

Category B

4 Dr LS Sdn	3865	5115
4 Dr STD Sdn	3525	4665

OPTIONS FOR EIGHTY-EIGHT ROYALE

Anti-Lock Brakes[Std on LS] +110
Auto Load Leveling +30
Leather Seats +110
Power Door Locks[Std on LS] +45
Power Drivers Seat +50
Power Passenger Seat +60
Traction Control System +30

NINETY-EIGHT   1992

Supercharged engine is optional on Touring Sedan. Traction control is optional on any model.

RATINGS (SCALE OF 1-10)

Overall	Safety	Reliability	Performance	Comfort	Value
N/A	N/A	7	7.7	7.7	7.9

Category A

4 Dr Regency Sdn	4565	5815
4 Dr Regency Elite Sdn	4855	6180
4 Dr Regency Touring Sdn	5365	6830
4 Dr Regency Touring Sprchgd Sdn	5550	7065

OPTIONS FOR NINETY-EIGHT

AM/FM Compact Disc Player +75
Astro Roof +240
Dual Power Seats +80
Leather Seats[Std on Regency Touring] +115
Traction Control System +35

SILHOUETTE   1992

Newly optional 165-horsepower, 3.8-liter V6 is highly recommended. ABS is made standard. Larger wheels and tires are standard. New options include sunroof, remote keyless entry and rear climate controls.

RATINGS (SCALE OF 1-10)

Overall	Safety	Reliability	Performance	Comfort	Value
7	5.7	6.6	7.2	7.3	8.3

Category G

2 Dr STD Pass. Van	4625	6000

OPTIONS FOR SILHOUETTE

6 cyl 3.8 L Engine +110
Auto 4-Speed Transmission +35
AM/FM Compact Disc Player +50
Auto Load Leveling +40
Dual Air Conditioning +150
Leather Seats +130
Power Door Locks +40
Power Windows +40

TORONADO   1992

Trofeo gets firmer suspension and bigger wheels and tires.

Category B

2 Dr STD Cpe	4110	5440
2 Dr Trofeo Cpe	4535	6000

OPTIONS FOR TORONADO

Visual Info System +210
Visual Information System +210
AM/FM Compact Disc Player +55
Astro Roof +220
Leather Seats[Opt on STD] +110
Power Passenger Seat[Opt on STD] +60

1991 OLDSMOBILE

BRAVADA   1991

Olds markets a gussied-up S10 Blazer. Features all-wheel drive and four-wheel ABS. Remote keyless entry is standard.

RATINGS (SCALE OF 1-10)

Overall	Safety	Reliability	Performance	Comfort	Value
5.5	3.6	5.8	6.4	7.1	4.5

Category G

4 Dr STD 4WD Wgn	4930	6685

OPTIONS FOR BRAVADA

Camper/Towing Package +40
Leather Seats +105

CUSTOM CRUISER   1991

Behemoth wagon based on same chassis and bodywork as Caprice and Roadmaster joins lineup. Features eight-passenger seating, glass Vista Roof treatment, ABS and driver airbag. Leather is optional.

Category B

4 Dr STD Wgn	3060	4785

OPTIONS FOR CUSTOM CRUISER

Leather Seats +90
Power Door Locks +35
Power Drivers Seat +40
Power Passenger Seat +50
Power Windows +40

CUTLASS CALAIS   1991

Quad 442 gets performance tires. International Series has standard ABS.

Category C

2 Dr International Cpe	2280	3570
4 Dr International Sdn	2295	3590
2 Dr S Cpe	1630	2545
4 Dr S Sdn	1640	2570
2 Dr SL Cpe	2120	3315

Don't forget to refer to the Mileage Adjustment Table at the back of this book!

Model Description	Trade-in Value	Market Value
4 Dr SL Sdn	2130	3335
2 Dr STD Cpe	1465	2290
4 Dr STD Sdn	1465	2290

OPTIONS FOR CUTLASS CALAIS
4 cyl 2.3 L Quad 4 Engine[Opt on S,STD] +90
6 cyl 3.3 L Engine +85
Auto 3-Speed Transmission[Std on SL] +70
Quad 442 Performance Pkg +230
Air Conditioning[Opt on S,STD] +110
Leather Seats +85
Power Door Locks +35
Power Drivers Seat +40
Power Windows +40

CUTLASS CIERA   1991
No changes.

RATINGS (SCALE OF 1-10)

Overall	Safety	Reliability	Performance	Comfort	Value
6.8	4.6	5.9	7.4	7.6	8.3

Category C
2 Dr S Cpe	1930	3015
4 Dr S Sdn	1875	2930
4 Dr S Cruiser Wgn	1995	3125
4 Dr SL Sdn	2210	3455
4 Dr SL Cruiser Wgn	2375	3710
4 Dr STD Sdn	1805	2820

OPTIONS FOR CUTLASS CIERA
6 cyl 3.3 L Engine[Std on SL,SL Cruiser] +85
Auto 4-Speed Transmission[Opt on S,SL] +25
Sport Appearance Pkg +110
Air Conditioning[Std on SL,SL Cruiser] +110
Leather Seats +85
Power Door Locks +35
Power Drivers Seat +40
Power Windows +40

CUTLASS SUPREME   1991
3.4-liter, twin-cam V6 debuts on options list, equipped with a five-speed in coupes and an automatic in sedans.

RATINGS (SCALE OF 1-10)

Overall	Safety	Reliability	Performance	Comfort	Value
7.2	5.3	6.3	8.2	8	8.1

Category C
2 Dr International Cpe	2660	4165
4 Dr International Sdn	2675	4185
2 Dr SL Cpe	2470	3870
4 Dr SL Sdn	2485	3890
2 Dr STD Conv	2830	4430
2 Dr STD Cpe	2205	3445
4 Dr STD Sdn	2215	3470

OPTIONS FOR CUTLASS SUPREME
6 cyl 3.1 L Engine[Std on International,SL,Conv] +70
6 cyl 3.4 L Engine +100
Anti-Lock Brakes +80
Leather Seats +85
Power Door Locks[Opt on SL,STD] +35
Power Drivers Seat +40
Power Sunroof +90
Power Windows[Std on Conv] +40

EIGHTY-EIGHT ROYALE   1991
No changes.
Category B
2 Dr Brougham Cpe	2950	4040
4 Dr Brougham Sdn	2965	4060
2 Dr STD Cpe	2705	3705
4 Dr STD Sdn	2720	3725

OPTIONS FOR EIGHTY-EIGHT ROYALE
Touring Suspension +105
Air Bag Restraint +115
Anti-Lock Brakes +90
Leather Seats +90
Power Door Locks +35
Power Drivers Seat[Opt on STD] +40
Power Passenger Seat +50
Power Windows +40

NINETY-EIGHT   1991
Total redesign gives Ninety-Eight nine inches of additional length. Automatic load leveling, ABS, child-proof rear door locks, driver airbag, and automatic climate controls are standard. Touring Sedan again available.

RATINGS (SCALE OF 1-10)

Overall	Safety	Reliability	Performance	Comfort	Value
N/A	N/A	6.9	7.7	7.7	8

Category A
4 Dr Regency Elite Sdn	3920	5150
4 Dr Touring Sdn	4710	6190

OPTIONS FOR NINETY-EIGHT
AM/FM Compact Disc Player +65
Astro Roof +195
Leather Seats[Std on Touring] +90
Power Passenger Seat[Std on Touring] +40

SILHOUETTE   1991
No changes.

RATINGS (SCALE OF 1-10)

Overall	Safety	Reliability	Performance	Comfort	Value
6.7	4.8	6.8	6.8	7.3	7.7

Category G
2 Dr STD Pass. Van	3705	5025

Don't forget to refer to the Mileage Adjustment Table at the back of this book!

OLDSMOBILE 91

Model Description	Trade-in Value	Market Value	Model Description	Trade-in Value	Market Value
OPTIONS FOR SILHOUETTE			*Category B*		
AM/FM Compact Disc Player +40			2 Dr STD Cpe	3330	4565
Auto Load Leveling +30			2 Dr Trofeo Cpe	3700	5070
Leather Seats +105			*OPTIONS FOR TORONADO*		
Power Door Locks +30			*Visual Info System +135*		
Power Drivers Seat +40			*AM/FM Compact Disc Player +45*		
Power Windows +30			*Leather Seats[Opt on STD] +90*		
			Power Sunroof +145		

TORONADO   1991

Remote keyless entry standard. Hands-free mobile phone is optional.

Don't forget to refer to the Mileage Adjustment Table at the back of this book!

PLYMOUTH 00-99

PLYMOUTH   USA

1995 Plymouth Neon

2000 PLYMOUTH

BREEZE   2000

New colors and child-seat tether anchorages update the Breeze for 2000.

Category C
4 Dr STD Sdn	10825	12785

OPTIONS FOR BREEZE
4 cyl 2.4 L Engine +370
Auto 4-Speed Transmission +860
AM/FM Stereo Tape +135
Cruise Control +180
Power Door Locks +210
Power Drivers Seat +245
Power Windows +260

NEON   2000

Side-impact airbags and leather seats are now available in Plymouth's economy car. If you've got a hankering for the Plymouth nameplate, act fast; as of 2002 Plymouth will be closing shop and subsuming its identity to the gods of DaimlerChrysler.

Category E
4 Dr Highline Sdn	8970	10650
4 Dr LX Sedan Sdn	10240	12155

OPTIONS FOR NEON
Auto 3-Speed Transmission +430
Air Conditioning[Std on LX Sedan] +680
Bucket Seats[Std on LX Sedan] +95

PROWLER   2000

Prowler Purple is discontinued, replaced by Prowler Silver for 2000. Chrome wheels are standard, as is a

new leather shift boot and speed-sensitive volume for the stereo.

Category F
2 Dr STD Conv	36100	41425

OPTIONS FOR PROWLER
Woodward Edition Group +1225

VOYAGER   2000

Four new colors and a new T-Plus option package that includes a V6 and power goodies for about $20,000 are new this year.

Category G
4 Dr Grand Pass. Van	15630	18235
4 Dr Grand SE Pass. Van	17190	20050
4 Dr SE Pass. Van	16500	19245
4 Dr STD Pass. Van	13455	15695

OPTIONS FOR VOYAGER
6 cyl 3.0 L Engine[Opt on STD] +655
6 cyl 3.3 L Engine +465
6 cyl 3.3 L FLEX Engine[Opt on STD] +795
Auto 4-Speed Transmission[Opt on STD] +165
7 Passenger Seating[Opt on STD] +425
Air Conditioning[Opt on STD] +670
Aluminum/Alloy Wheels +265
Captain Chairs (4) +505
Cruise Control[Opt on Grand,STD] +170
Heated Power Mirrors[Opt on Grand,STD] +65
Keyless Entry System +160
Luggage Rack +130
Overhead Console +130
Power Door Locks[Opt on Grand,STD] +190
Power Windows[Opt on Grand,STD] +200
Rear Window Defroster[Opt on Grand,STD] +140
Sunscreen Glass[Opt on Grand,STD] +310
Tilt Steering Wheel[Opt on Grand,STD] +145
Trip Computer +125

1999 PLYMOUTH

BREEZE   1999

Power windows, locks and mirrors, along with floor mats and a driver's seat height adjuster are now standard on the Breeze. In addition, the suspension has been revised for a more pleasant ride. What more could you ask? Oh yeah: the Noise, Vibration and Harshness levels have also been reduced.

RATINGS (SCALE OF 1-10)
Overall	Safety	Reliability	Performance	Comfort	Value
N/A	6.4	N/A	6.6	7.1	N/A

Category C
4 Dr Expresso Sdn	9675	11520
4 Dr STD Sdn	9310	11085

OPTIONS FOR BREEZE

4 cyl 2.4 L Engine +300
Auto 4-Speed Transmission +700
AM/FM Compact Disc Player +235
Aluminum/Alloy Wheels +205
Anti-Lock Brakes +395
Cruise Control +145
Keyless Entry System +125

NEON   1999

The Neon is now based on the same platform as the Viper. No, just kidding. Nothing's changed for '99.

RATINGS (SCALE OF 1-10)

Overall	Safety	Reliability	Performance	Comfort	Value
N/A	6	7.6	7.4	7.6	N/A

Category E

2 Dr Competition Cpe	7400	8905
4 Dr Competition Sdn	7525	9055
2 Dr Expresso Cpe	8395	10105
4 Dr Expresso Sdn	8520	10260
2 Dr Highline Cpe	7655	9215
4 Dr Highline Sdn	7710	9280

OPTIONS FOR NEON

4 cyl 2.0 L DOHC Engine[Opt on Highline] +100
Auto 3-Speed Transmission +400
Competition Pkg +1010
AM/FM Compact Disc Player +290
Air Conditioning[Std on Expresso] +555
Aluminum/Alloy Wheels +225
Anti-Lock Brakes +445
Cruise Control +155
Keyless Entry System +110
Power Door Locks +165
Power Mirrors +75
Power Windows +180
Rear Window Defroster[Opt on Competition] +110
Tilt Steering Wheel +100

PROWLER   1999

A brand-new 3.5-liter engine under the hood creates performance more fitting a hot rod. Also new for '99 is one more color option: Prowler Yellow.

RATINGS (SCALE OF 1-10)

Overall	Safety	Reliability	Performance	Comfort	Value
N/A	N/A	N/A	8.6	7.6	N/A

Category K

2 Dr STD Conv	31335	36040

VOYAGER   1999

SE trim levels get body-colored door and liftgate handles, as well as a body-colored front grille. All models add a cargo net between the front seats, and the new exterior color this year is Light Cypress Green.

RATINGS (SCALE OF 1-10)

Overall	Safety	Reliability	Performance	Comfort	Value
N/A	6.4	8.8	6.6	7.4	N/A

Category G

2 Dr Expresso Pass. Van	15790	18500
2 Dr Grand Pass. Van	14380	16845
2 Dr Grand Expresso Pass. Van	16450	19270
2 Dr Grand SE Pass. Van	14880	17435
2 Dr SE Pass. Van	14250	16695
2 Dr STD Pass. Van	11790	13815

OPTIONS FOR VOYAGER

6 cyl 3.0 L Engine[Opt on STD] +375
6 cyl 3.3 L Engine +650
6 cyl 3.8 L Engine +245
Auto 4-Speed Transmission[Opt on STD] +135
Air Conditioning[Opt on Grand,STD] +550
Aluminum/Alloy Wheels +215
Anti-Lock Brakes[Opt on Grand,STD] +390
Compact Disc W/fm/tape[Opt on Grand SE,SE] +295
Cruise Control[Opt on Grand,STD] +140
Keyless Entry System +130
Power Door Locks +155
Power Windows +160
Rear Window Defroster[Opt on Grand,STD] +115
Sliding Driver Side Door[Opt on STD] +350
Sunscreen Glass[Std on Expresso,Grand Expresso] +250
Tilt Steering Wheel[Opt on Grand,STD] +120

1998 PLYMOUTH

BREEZE   1998

Availability of a 2.4-liter engine brings 150 horsepower and 167 foot-pounds of torque, and that's just what the Breeze needs to live up to its name. Both engines can meet California emissions regulations, and new engine mounts helps make them quieter. An Expresso package adds some aesthetic changes, a power sunroof is now optional and there are six new colors to choose from.

RATINGS (SCALE OF 1-10)

Overall	Safety	Reliability	Performance	Comfort	Value
N/A	6.3	7.5	6.6	7.1	N/A

Category C

4 Dr Expresso Sdn	8430	10125
4 Dr STD Sdn	8280	9950

OPTIONS FOR BREEZE

4 cyl 2.4 L Engine +245
Auto 4-Speed Transmission +575
AM/FM Compact Disc Player +190
Aluminum/Alloy Wheels +170
Anti-Lock Brakes +325
Cruise Control +120
Keyless Entry System +100

PLYMOUTH 98-97

Model Description	Trade-in Value	Market Value	Model Description	Trade-in Value	Market Value

Power Door Locks +140
Power Sunroof +365
Power Windows +175

NEON   1998

California and other emission-regulating states get an LEV (Low Emission Vehicle) engine calibration. Also changed this year are ABS, a new ignition key lock and the addition of four new colors.

RATINGS (SCALE OF 1-10)

Overall	Safety	Reliability	Performance	Comfort	Value
7.1	6.1	7.7	7.4 ⊕	7.6	6.8

Category E

	Trade-in	Market
2 Dr Competition Cpe	6500	7905
4 Dr Competition Sdn	6615	8040
2 Dr Expresso Cpe	7445	9050
4 Dr Expresso Sdn	7375	8965
2 Dr Highline Cpe	6645	8080
4 Dr Highline Sdn	6755	8215
4 Dr Style Sdn	7845	9535

OPTIONS FOR NEON

Auto 3-Speed Transmission +330
Competition Pkg +860
AM/FM Compact Disc Player +235
Air Conditioning[Std on Expresso, Style] +455
Aluminum/Alloy Wheels[Std on Style] +185
Anti-Lock Brakes +365
Cruise Control +125
Keyless Entry System +90
Power Door Locks +135
Power Mirrors +60
Power Moonroof +320
Power Windows +145
Rear Window Defroster[Opt on Competition] +90
Tilt Steering Wheel +80

VOYAGER   1998

Expresso Decor Package, four new exterior colors, and "next generation" depowered airbags sum up the changes this year.

RATINGS (SCALE OF 1-10)

Overall	Safety	Reliability	Performance	Comfort	Value
7.5	6.3	8	6.6	7.4	9.2

Category G

	Trade-in	Market
2 Dr Expresso Pass. Van	13600	16030
2 Dr Grand Pass. Van	12255	14440
2 Dr Grand Expresso Pass. Van	14190	16725
2 Dr Grand SE Pass. Van	13605	16035
2 Dr SE Pass. Van	13015	15340
2 Dr STD Pass. Van	10725	12640

OPTIONS FOR VOYAGER

6 cyl 3.0 L Engine[Opt on STD] +270
6 cyl 3.3 L Engine +185
6 cyl 3.3 L FLEX Engine +110
Auto 4-Speed Transmission[Opt on Grand,STD] +135
Air Conditioning[Opt on Grand, Grand SE, SE, STD] +450
Aluminum/Alloy Wheels +175
Anti-Lock Brakes[Opt on Grand, STD] +320
Compact Disc W/fm/tape[Opt on Grand SE,SE] +240
Cruise Control[Opt on Grand, STD] +115
Keyless Entry System +105
Power Door Locks +130
Power Mirrors[Opt on Grand, STD] +70
Power Windows +135
Rear Window Defroster[Opt on Grand, Grand SE, SE, STD] +95
Sliding Driver Side Door[Opt on STD] +290
Sunscreen Glass[Opt on Grand, Grand SE, SE, STD] +205
Tilt Steering Wheel[Opt on Grand, STD] +100

1997 PLYMOUTH

BREEZE   1997

Plymouth is inching the Breeze up-market in both price and content. This year sees a fairly sizable price hike and the addition of luxury options such as an in-dash CD changer. Changes to the standard equipment list bring a nicer center console, improved basic stereos, and increased flow rear seat heater ducts.

RATINGS (SCALE OF 1-10)

Overall	Safety	Reliability	Performance	Comfort	Value
N/A	N/A	6.3	6.6	7.1	6.7

Category C

	Trade-in	Market
4 Dr STD Sdn	7365	8955

OPTIONS FOR BREEZE

Auto 4-Speed Transmission +455
AM/FM Compact Disc Player +155
Aluminum/Alloy Wheels +140
Anti-Lock Brakes +265
Child Seat (1) +55
Cruise Control +95
Keyless Entry System +85
Power Door Locks +115
Power Windows +140

NEON   1997

1997 Neons are made quieter with the addition of a structural oil pan. Other changes include new optional radios, a new seat fabric, new wheels and wheel covers, and a few new paint colors.

RATINGS (SCALE OF 1-10)

Overall	Safety	Reliability	Performance	Comfort	Value
6.9	6	7.1	7.4	7.6	6.6

Don't forget to refer to the Mileage Adjustment Table at the back of this book!

Model Description	Trade-in Value	Market Value
Category E		
2 Dr Expresso Cpe	6310	7800
4 Dr Expresso Sdn	6405	7920
2 Dr Highline Cpe	6170	7625
4 Dr Highline Sdn	6265	7745
2 Dr STD Cpe	5180	6405
4 Dr STD Sdn	5275	6525

OPTIONS FOR NEON
4 cyl 2.0 L DOHC Engine +65
Auto 3-Speed Transmission +260
Competition Pkg +560
AM/FM Compact Disc Player +195
Air Conditioning[Opt on STD] +370
Aluminum/Alloy Wheels +150
Anti-Lock Brakes +295
Child Seat (1) +50
Keyless Entry System +75
Power Door Locks +110
Power Moonroof +260
Power Windows +120

PROWLER   1997
Category K

Model Description	Trade-in Value	Market Value
2 Dr STD Conv	23150	26570

VOYAGER   1997
For 1997, the Plymouth minivans receive a cornucopia of changes. This year brings new wheel covers, improved antilock braking systems, an accident response system that unlocks the doors and turns on the interior lights if the air bags deploy, better radios, a quieter interior, and more optional equipment for Base and SE models.

RATINGS (SCALE OF 1-10)

Overall	Safety	Reliability	Performance	Comfort	Value
6.9	6	6.4	6.6	7.4	8

Model Description	Trade-in Value	Market Value
Category G		
2 Dr Grand Pass. Van	10730	12660
2 Dr Grand SE Pass. Van	11945	14100
2 Dr SE Pass. Van	11130	13135
2 Dr STD Pass. Van	9670	11410

OPTIONS FOR VOYAGER
6 cyl 3.0 L Engine +310
6 cyl 3.3 L Engine +410
Auto 4-Speed Transmission[Opt on Grand,STD] +110
7 Passenger Seating[Opt on STD] +235
Air Conditioning +365
Aluminum/Alloy Wheels +145
Anti-Lock Brakes[Opt on Grand,STD] +260
Auto Load Leveling +105
Captain Chairs (4) +275
Child Seats (2) +115
Compact Disc W/fm/tape +200

Cruise Control[Opt on Grand,STD] +95
Dual Air Conditioning +410
Keyless Entry System +85
Luggage Rack +70
Power Door Locks +105
Power Drivers Seat +125
Power Windows +110
Sliding Driver Side Door +235

1996 PLYMOUTH

BREEZE   1996
The Breeze is introduced this year as Chrysler Corporation's bargain-basement midsize sedan. Nicely equipped with air conditioning and a decent stereo, the Breeze has a surprising amount of interior room.

RATINGS (SCALE OF 1-10)

Overall	Safety	Reliability	Performance	Comfort	Value
N/A	N/A	5.3	6.6	7.1	6.2

Model Description	Trade-in Value	Market Value
Category C		
4 Dr STD Sdn	6025	7485

OPTIONS FOR BREEZE
Auto 4-Speed Transmission +385
Anti-Lock Brakes +215
Child Seat (1) +45
Compact Disc W/fm/tape +120
Keyless Entry System +70
Power Door Locks +95
Power Sunroof +245
Power Windows +115

NEON   1996
Antilock brakes are optional across the line, and base models get more standard equipment for 1996. A value-packed Expresso package is aimed at twenty-something first-time buyers. A base coupe is newly available, and all Neons are supposedly quieter than last year. A power moonroof joins the options list, and a remote keyless entry system with panic alarm is available.

RATINGS (SCALE OF 1-10)

Overall	Safety	Reliability	Performance	Comfort	Value
6.6	5.9	6.3	7.4	7.6	5.9

Model Description	Trade-in Value	Market Value
Category E		
2 Dr Highline Cpe	5045	6375
4 Dr Highline Sdn	5130	6480
2 Dr STD Cpe	4275	5400
4 Dr STD Sdn	4485	5670
2 Dr Sport Cpe	5560	7020
4 Dr Sport Sdn	5645	7130

Don't forget to refer to the Mileage Adjustment Table at the back of this book!

Model Description	Trade-in Value	Market Value

OPTIONS FOR NEON

4 cyl 2.0 L DOHC Engine +55
Auto 3-Speed Transmission +220
Competition Pkg +375
AM/FM Compact Disc Player +160
Air Conditioning +305
Aluminum/Alloy Wheels +125
Anti-Lock Brakes +245
Child Seat (1) +40
Cruise Control +85
Keyless Entry System +60
Power Door Locks[Std on Sport] +90
Power Moonroof +215
Power Windows +95
Rear Spoiler +80
Tilt Steering Wheel[Std on Sport] +55

VOYAGER   1996

Chrysler's stylists and engineers have achieved what many thought was impossible: they substantially improved upon their original formula in every way. Interior comfort is top-notch, and the left-hand passenger door is an industry first.

RATINGS (SCALE OF 1-10)

Overall	Safety	Reliability	Performance	Comfort	Value
6.7	5.8	5	6.6	7.4	8.8

Category G

Model	Trade-in	Market
2 Dr Grand Pass. Van	8860	10620
2 Dr Grand SE Pass. Van	9915	11885
2 Dr SE Pass. Van	9560	11455
2 Dr STD Pass. Van	8260	9900

OPTIONS FOR VOYAGER

6 cyl 3.0 L Engine[Std on Grand] +265
6 cyl 3.3 L Engine +315
7 Passenger Seating[Opt on STD] +190
Air Conditioning +300
Aluminum/Alloy Wheels +120
Anti-Lock Brakes[Opt on Grand,STD] +210
Captain Chairs (4) +225
Child Seats (2) +90
Compact Disc W/fm/tape +160
Cruise Control[Opt on Grand,STD] +75
Dual Air Conditioning +335
Keyless Entry System +70
Luggage Rack +60
Power Door Locks +85
Power Windows +90
Premium Sound System +125
Sliding Driver Side Door +190

1995 PLYMOUTH

ACCLAIM   1995

The Acclaim is into the home stretch of its career.

RATINGS (SCALE OF 1-10)

Overall	Safety	Reliability	Performance	Comfort	Value
7	6.7	7.5	6.8	7.4	6.6

Category C

Model	Trade-in	Market
4 Dr STD Sdn	4085	5835

OPTIONS FOR ACCLAIM

6 cyl 3.0 L Engine +240
Aluminum/Alloy Wheels +90
Power Door Locks +75
Power Drivers Seat +90
Power Windows +95

NEON   1995

The all-new Neon is introduced as Plymouth's entry in the compact car class. Roomy, cute and quick are three of the best adjectives we can find for this car. Unfortunately, Chrysler Corporation is still grappling with reliability and noise issues. The Neon is available in coupe and sedan bodystyles in three trim-levels. Safety equipment includes standard dual airbags, optional antilock brakes and an optional integrated child seat.

RATINGS (SCALE OF 1-10)

Overall	Safety	Reliability	Performance	Comfort	Value
6.5	5.6	4.8	7.4	7.6	6.9

Category E

Model	Trade-in	Market
2 Dr Highline Cpe	3870	5095
4 Dr Highline Sdn	3870	5095
4 Dr STD Sdn	3295	4340
2 Dr Sport Cpe	4635	6110
4 Dr Sport Sdn	4535	5980

OPTIONS FOR NEON

4 cyl 2.0 L DOHC Engine[Std on Sport] +50
Auto 3-Speed Transmission +180
AM/FM Compact Disc Player +130
Air Conditioning +250
Anti-Lock Brakes[Std on Sport] +200
Child Seat (1) +35
Cruise Control +70
Power Door Locks[Std on Sport] +75
Power Windows +80
Tilt Steering Wheel[Std on Sport] +45

VOYAGER   1995

A 3.3-liter V6 natural gas engine is available this year. Plymouth introduces a snazzy Rallye package for those trying to disguise the fact that they are driving a minivan.

RATINGS (SCALE OF 1-10)

Overall	Safety	Reliability	Performance	Comfort	Value
7.7	8.2	6.4	7.4	8.3	8.4

Don't forget to refer to the Mileage Adjustment Table at the back of this book!

Model Description	Trade-in Value	Market Value
Category G		
2 Dr Grand Pass. Van	7140	8880
2 Dr Grand LE Pass. Van	8635	10740
2 Dr Grand LE 4WD Pass. Van	9375	11660
2 Dr Grand SE Pass. Van	7510	9340
2 Dr Grand SE 4WD Pass. Van	8130	10115
2 Dr LE Pass. Van	8525	10605
2 Dr SE Pass. Van	7235	9000
2 Dr STD Pass. Van	6230	7750

OPTIONS FOR VOYAGER

6 cyl 3.0 L Engine[Opt on STD] +215
6 cyl 3.3 L Engine[Opt on LE,SE,STD] +70
6 cyl 3.8 L Engine +125
Auto 4-Speed Transmission[Opt on SE,STD] +60
7 Passenger Seating[Opt on STD] +155
Air Conditioning[Std on Grand LE,LE] +245
Anti-Lock Brakes[Std on Grand LE,LE,4WD] +175
Captain Chairs (4) +185
Child Seats (2) +75
Compact Disc W/fm/tape +130
Cruise Control[Opt on Grand,STD] +65
Dual Air Conditioning +275
Keyless Entry System[Opt on Grand SE,SE] +60
Leather Seats +235
Luggage Rack +50
Power Door Locks[Std on Grand LE,LE] +70
Power Drivers Seat +85
Power Windows +70
Trip Computer[Opt on Grand SE] +45

1994 PLYMOUTH

ACCLAIM 1994

The Acclaim gains a motorized passenger seatbelt. The flexible-fuel model is now available to retail customers.

RATINGS (SCALE OF 1-10)

Overall	Safety	Reliability	Performance	Comfort	Value
7.2	6.6	7.8	6.8	7.4	7.4

	Trade-in	Market
Category C		
4 Dr STD Sdn	3400	4355

OPTIONS FOR ACCLAIM

6 cyl 3.0 L Engine +165
Auto 4-Speed Transmission +40
AM/FM Stereo Tape +40
Air Conditioning +200
Anti-Lock Brakes +145
Cruise Control +55
Power Door Locks +60
Power Drivers Seat +75
Power Windows +80
Rear Window Defroster +40
Tilt Steering Wheel +35

COLT 1994

A driver's airbag is now standard on the Colt. CFC-free air conditioning optional.

RATINGS (SCALE OF 1-10)

Overall	Safety	Reliability	Performance	Comfort	Value
6.6	5.5	7.4	8	7.4	4.7

	Trade-in	Market
Category E		
2 Dr GL Sdn	2955	4090
4 Dr GL Sdn	3555	4915
4 Dr SE Wgn	4160	5760
2 Dr STD Sdn	2690	3725
4 Dr STD Sdn	3340	4625
4 Dr STD Wgn	3815	5280
4 Dr STD 4WD Wgn	4350	6020

OPTIONS FOR COLT

4 cyl 1.8 L Engine[Opt on GL Sdn] +110
4 cyl 2.4 L Engine[Opt on STD Wgn] +45
Auto 3-Speed Transmission +125
Auto 4-Speed Transmission +170
AM/FM Stereo Tape +75
Air Conditioning +205
Aluminum/Alloy Wheels +80
Anti-Lock Brakes +160
Cruise Control +55
Keyless Entry System +40
Power Door Locks[Std on SE] +60
Power Windows +65
Rear Window Wiper[Std on SE,4WD] +30

LASER 1994

The final year for the Laser brings automatic-locking retractors for rear seats, making them more compatible for child seats.

RATINGS (SCALE OF 1-10)

Overall	Safety	Reliability	Performance	Comfort	Value
N/A	N/A	7.5	8.4	6.8	4

	Trade-in	Market
Category C		
2 Dr RS Hbk	4290	5495
2 Dr RS Turbo Hbk	4745	6080
2 Dr RS Turbo 4WD Hbk	5385	6895
2 Dr STD Hbk	3580	4585

OPTIONS FOR LASER

Auto 4-Speed Transmission +190
AM/FM Compact Disc Player +85
Air Conditioning +200
Aluminum/Alloy Wheels[Opt on 2WD] +75
Anti-Lock Brakes +145
Cruise Control +55
Power Door Locks +60
Power Windows +80
Premium Sound System +95
Rear Spoiler[Std on RS] +45

Model Description	Trade-in Value	Market Value
Rear Window Wiper +35		
Sunroof +90		

SUNDANCE · 1994

The Sundance gets a motorized passenger shoulder belt and CFC-free air conditioning.

RATINGS (SCALE OF 1-10)

Overall	Safety	Reliability	Performance	Comfort	Value
6.4	6.5	6.7	7.2	6.8	5

Category E

Model Description	Trade-in Value	Market Value
2 Dr Duster Hbk	2920	4040
4 Dr Duster Hbk	3030	4190
2 Dr STD Hbk	2530	3500
4 Dr STD Hbk	2635	3650

OPTIONS FOR SUNDANCE

4 cyl 2.5 L Engine[Opt on STD] +70
6 cyl 3.0 L Engine +195
Auto 3-Speed Transmission +135
Auto 4-Speed Transmission +180
AM/FM Compact Disc Player +105
Air Conditioning +205
Aluminum/Alloy Wheels +80
Anti-Lock Brakes +160
Cruise Control +55
Power Door Locks +60
Power Drivers Seat +75
Power Windows +65
Premium Sound System +80

VOYAGER · 1994

New safety features include a passenger airbag and side-impact door beams that meet federal 1997 passenger car standards. Other changes include a new dashboard, optional integrated child seats and new body moldings.

RATINGS (SCALE OF 1-10)

Overall	Safety	Reliability	Performance	Comfort	Value
7.5	8.2	5.9	7.4	8.3	7.8

Category G

Model Description	Trade-in Value	Market Value
2 Dr Grand Pass. Van	5715	7440
2 Dr Grand LE Pass. Van	6735	8765
2 Dr Grand LE 4WD Pass. Van	7500	9770
2 Dr Grand SE Pass. Van	6055	7885
2 Dr Grand SE 4WD Pass. Van	6475	8430
2 Dr LE Pass. Van	6470	8425
2 Dr SE Pass. Van	5700	7425
2 Dr STD Pass. Van	4720	6145

OPTIONS FOR VOYAGER

6 cyl 3.0 L Engine[Opt on STD] +150
6 cyl 3.3 L Engine +25
6 cyl 3.8 L Engine +100
Auto 3-Speed Transmission[Opt on STD] +145
Auto 4-Speed Transmission[Opt on Grand,LE,SE,STD] +85
7 Passenger Seating[Std on Grand SE,SE] +125
AM/FM Compact Disc Player +75
AM/FM Stereo Tape[Opt on Grand,STD] +55
Air Conditioning[Std on Grand LE,LE] +200
Aluminum/Alloy Wheels +80
Anti-Lock Brakes[Std on 4WD] +140
Captain Chairs (4) +150
Child Seats (2) +60
Cruise Control[Opt on Grand,STD] +50
Dual Air Conditioning +225
Infinity Sound System +105
Keyless Entry System[Opt on Grand SE,SE] +50
Leather Seats +190
Luggage Rack +40
Power Door Locks[Std on Grand LE,LE] +55
Power Drivers Seat +70
Power Windows[Std on LE] +60

1993 PLYMOUTH

ACCLAIM · 1993

The Acclaim is now available to fleet purchasers as a flexible-fuel vehicle, able to run on a fuel mix that is 85 percent methanol.

RATINGS (SCALE OF 1-10)

Overall	Safety	Reliability	Performance	Comfort	Value
7.1	6.1	8	6.8	7.4	7.4

Category C

Model Description	Trade-in Value	Market Value
4 Dr STD Sdn	2510	3515

OPTIONS FOR ACCLAIM

6 cyl 3.0 L Engine +140
Auto 3-Speed Transmission +110
Auto 4-Speed Transmission +135
AM/FM Stereo Tape +35
Air Conditioning +160
Aluminum/Alloy Wheels +60
Anti-Lock Brakes +120
Cruise Control +45
Power Door Locks +50
Power Drivers Seat +60
Power Windows +65

COLT · 1993

The Colt is redesigned for 1993. The hatchback is dropped in favor of two- and four-door notchback styles and the GL model is equipped with a 113-horsepower engine that is optional on the base.

RATINGS (SCALE OF 1-10)

Overall	Safety	Reliability	Performance	Comfort	Value
N/A	N/A	6	8	7.4	6.6

Category E

Model Description	Trade-in Value	Market Value
2 Dr GL Sdn	1965	3120
4 Dr GL Sdn	2305	3660

Don't forget to refer to the Mileage Adjustment Table at the back of this book!

Model Description	Trade-in Value	Market Value
4 Dr SE Wgn	2680	4255
2 Dr STD Sdn	1740	2765
4 Dr STD Sdn	2100	3335
4 Dr STD Wgn	2490	3950
4 Dr STD 4WD Wgn	2925	4645

OPTIONS FOR COLT
4 cyl 1.8 L Engine[Std on GL,Wgn] +80
4 cyl 2.4 L Engine[Std on SE] +35
Auto 3-Speed Transmission +105
Auto 4-Speed Transmission +140
AM/FM Stereo Tape +60
Air Conditioning +165
Aluminum/Alloy Wheels +65
Anti-Lock Brakes +135
Cruise Control +45
Keyless Entry System +30
Power Door Locks +50
Power Steering[Opt on GL,Sdn] +50
Power Windows +55
Rear Window Wiper +25

LASER 1993

The all-wheel drive Laser is now available with an automatic transmission. New alloy wheels are introduced to all but the base Laser. A gold package is available for those of you wanting the ever-popular midlife crisis look.

RATINGS (SCALE OF 1-10)

Overall	Safety	Reliability	Performance	Comfort	Value
N/A	N/A	7.3	8.4	6.8	4.2

Category C		
2 Dr RS Hbk	2900	4065
2 Dr RS Turbo Hbk	3210	4500
2 Dr RS Turbo 4WD Hbk	3645	5100
2 Dr STD Hbk	2425	3390

OPTIONS FOR LASER
Auto 4-Speed Transmission +155
Air Conditioning +160
Aluminum/Alloy Wheels[Opt on 2WD] +60
Anti-Lock Brakes +120
Compact Disc W/fm/tape +65
Cruise Control +45
Power Door Locks +50
Power Windows +65
Premium Sound System +75
Sunroof +75

SUNDANCE 1993

The Sundance is available with antilock brakes in 1993.

RATINGS (SCALE OF 1-10)

Overall	Safety	Reliability	Performance	Comfort	Value
6.6	6.5	7.5	7.2	6.8	5

Model Description	Trade-in Value	Market Value
Category E		
2 Dr Duster Hbk	2170	3445
4 Dr Duster Hbk	2250	3570
2 Dr STD Hbk	1755	2785
4 Dr STD Hbk	1835	2910

OPTIONS FOR SUNDANCE
4 cyl 2.5 L Engine[Opt on STD] +55
6 cyl 3.0 L Engine +140
Auto 3-Speed Transmission +110
Auto 4-Speed Transmission +135
AM/FM Compact Disc Player +85
Air Conditioning +165
Aluminum/Alloy Wheels +65
Anti-Lock Brakes +135
Cruise Control +45
Power Door Locks +50
Power Drivers Seat +60
Power Windows +55
Premium Sound System +65

VOYAGER 1993

Front shoulder belts are now height adjustable on the Voyager. All-wheel drive models gain new exterior and interior options.

RATINGS (SCALE OF 1-10)

Overall	Safety	Reliability	Performance	Comfort	Value
6.9	6	4.7	7.4	8.3	8.2

Category G		
2 Dr Grand Pass. Van	4615	6105
2 Dr Grand LE Pass. Van	5245	6935
2 Dr Grand LE 4WD Pass. Van	5735	7590
2 Dr Grand SE Pass. Van	4715	6235
2 Dr Grand SE 4WD Pass. Van	5245	6940
2 Dr LE Pass. Van	5000	6615
2 Dr LE 4WD Pass. Van	5585	7390
2 Dr SE Pass. Van	4250	5620
2 Dr SE 4WD Pass. Van	5310	7025
2 Dr STD Pass. Van	3735	4940

OPTIONS FOR VOYAGER
6 cyl 3.0 L Engine[Opt on SE,STD] +130
6 cyl 3.3 L Engine[Std on Grand LE,Grand SE,4WD] +85
Auto 3-Speed Transmission +120
Auto 4-Speed Transmission +45
7 Passenger Seating +105
AM/FM Compact Disc Player +65
Air Conditioning[Std on Grand LE,LE] +165
Aluminum/Alloy Wheels +65
Anti-Lock Brakes +115
Captain Chairs (4) +125
Child Seats (2) +50
Cruise Control[Std on Grand LE,LE] +40
Dual Air Conditioning +185
Luggage Rack +30
Power Door Locks[Std on Grand LE] +45

Model Description	Trade-in Value	Market Value

Model Description	Trade-in Value	Market Value

Power Drivers Seat +55
Power Windows[Std on LE] +50
Premium Sound System +70
Velour/Cloth Seats[Opt on STD] +40
Woodgrain Applique +65

1992 PLYMOUTH

ACCLAIM   1992

Plymouth trims the fat, offering the Acclaim in only one trim level for 1992. The remaining Acclaim can be had with four-cylinder or V6 power.

RATINGS (SCALE OF 1-10)

Overall	Safety	Reliability	Performance	Comfort	Value
7	6	7.3	6.8	7.4	7.7

Category C
4 Dr STD Sdn	1980	2960

OPTIONS FOR ACCLAIM
6 cyl 3.0 L Engine +115
Auto 3-Speed Transmission +90
Auto 4-Speed Transmission +105
Air Conditioning +135
Anti-Lock Brakes +95
Power Door Locks +40
Power Drivers Seat +50
Power Windows +50

COLT   1992

Factory options list is pared in a cost-savings measure. A 113-horsepower engine is standard and a 118-horsepower engine is optional.
Category E
2 Dr GL Hbk	1835	2850
4 Dr SE Wgn	2460	3815
2 Dr STD Hbk	1660	2575
4 Dr STD Wgn	2320	3600
4 Dr STD 4WD Wgn	2730	4235

OPTIONS FOR COLT
4 cyl 2.4 L Engine +30
Auto 3-Speed Transmission +90
Auto 4-Speed Transmission +120
Air Conditioning +135
Anti-Lock Brakes +110
Power Door Locks +40
Power Windows +45

LASER   1992

The Laser gains all-wheel drive as an option that greatly improves handling. Front and rear styling changes include headlights, taillamps, and a new rear spoiler on turbo models.

RATINGS (SCALE OF 1-10)

Overall	Safety	Reliability	Performance	Comfort	Value
N/A	N/A	7.1	8.4	6.8	3.2

Category C
2 Dr RS Hbk	2405	3595
2 Dr RS Turbo Hbk	2665	3985
2 Dr RS Turbo 4WD Hbk	3025	4520
2 Dr STD Hbk	2030	3030

OPTIONS FOR LASER
Auto 4-Speed Transmission +120
Air Conditioning +135
Anti-Lock Brakes +95
Power Door Locks +40
Power Windows +50
Sunroof +60

SUNDANCE   1992

The RS trim level is dropped due to poor sales. No other changes to the Sundance.

RATINGS (SCALE OF 1-10)

Overall	Safety	Reliability	Performance	Comfort	Value
6.3	5.7	6.4	7.2	6.8	5.4

Category E
2 Dr America Hbk	1585	2460
4 Dr America Hbk	1660	2580
2 Dr Duster Hbk	1935	3005
4 Dr Duster Hbk	2010	3120
2 Dr Highline Hbk	1825	2830
4 Dr Highline Hbk	1900	2945

OPTIONS FOR SUNDANCE
4 cyl 2.5 L Engine[Std on Duster] +45
6 cyl 3.0 L Engine +120
Auto 3-Speed Transmission +90
Auto 4-Speed Transmission +110
AM/FM Compact Disc Player +70
Air Conditioning +135
Power Door Locks +40
Power Drivers Seat +50
Power Windows +45
Sunroof +55

VOYAGER   1992

The driver airbag first seen on the 1991 model becomes standard in 1992. An integrated child seat is available for those with toddlers.

RATINGS (SCALE OF 1-10)

Overall	Safety	Reliability	Performance	Comfort	Value
6.6	5.3	3.9	7.4	8.3	8.1

Category G
2 Dr Grand Pass. Van	4105	5530
2 Dr Grand LE Pass. Van	4555	6135
2 Dr Grand LE 4WD Pass. Van	4980	6710

PLYMOUTH 92-91

Model Description	Trade-in Value	Market Value
2 Dr Grand SE Pass. Van	4160	5600
2 Dr Grand SE 4WD Pass. Van	4620	6220
2 Dr LE Pass. Van	4385	5905
2 Dr LE 4WD Pass. Van	4755	6400
2 Dr LX Pass. Van	4530	6100
2 Dr LX 4WD Pass. Van	4970	6690
2 Dr SE Pass. Van	3705	4985
2 Dr SE 4WD Pass. Van	4410	5935
2 Dr STD Pass. Van	3215	4325

OPTIONS FOR VOYAGER

6 cyl 3.0 L Engine[Opt on SE,STD] +125
6 cyl 3.3 L Engine[Std on Grand LE,Grand SE,4WD] +65
Auto 3-Speed Transmission +95
Auto 4-Speed Transmission +30
7 Passenger Seating[Opt on STD] +85
Air Conditioning[Std on Grand LE,LE,LX] +135
Power Door Locks[Std on Grand LE,LE,LX] +40
Power Windows +40

1991 PLYMOUTH

ACCLAIM   1991

Four-wheel antilock brakes are introduced as an option on the 1991 Acclaim.

RATINGS (SCALE OF 1-10)

Overall	Safety	Reliability	Performance	Comfort	Value
6.9	5.8	6.2	6.8	7.4	8.2

Category C

	Trade-in	Market
4 Dr LE Sdn	1730	2990
4 Dr LX Sdn	1925	3325
4 Dr STD Sdn	1465	2530

OPTIONS FOR ACCLAIM

6 cyl 3.0 L Engine[Std on LX] +90
Auto 3-Speed Transmission[Opt on STD] +75
Auto 4-Speed Transmission[Opt on LE] +50
Air Conditioning +110
Anti-Lock Brakes +80
Power Door Locks +35
Power Drivers Seat +40
Power Windows +40

COLT   1991

No changes to the Colt.

Category E

	Trade-in	Market
2 Dr GL Hbk	1290	2360
2 Dr STD Hbk	1145	2105
4 Dr Vista Wgn	1940	3560
4 Dr Vista 4WD Wgn	2135	3910

OPTIONS FOR COLT

Auto 3-Speed Transmission +70
Air Conditioning +110
Power Door Locks +35

Power Steering[Std on 4WD] +35
Power Windows +35

LASER   1991

No major changes for the '91 Laser.

RATINGS (SCALE OF 1-10)

Overall	Safety	Reliability	Performance	Comfort	Value
N/A	N/A	6.7	8.4	6.8	3.2

Category C

	Trade-in	Market
2 Dr RS Hbk	1750	3025
2 Dr RS Turbo Hbk	1910	3295
2 Dr STD Hbk	1495	2585

OPTIONS FOR LASER

Auto 4-Speed Transmission +90
Air Conditioning +110
Anti-Lock Brakes +80
Power Door Locks +35
Power Windows +40
Sunroof +50

SUNDANCE   1991

No major changes to the bargain-basement Sundance.

RATINGS (SCALE OF 1-10)

Overall	Safety	Reliability	Performance	Comfort	Value
6.3	5.6	5.7	7.4	6.8	5.8

Category E

	Trade-in	Market
2 Dr America Hbk	1060	1945
4 Dr America Hbk	1100	2020
2 Dr Highline Hbk	1225	2250
4 Dr Highline Hbk	1270	2325
2 Dr RS Hbk	1390	2550
2 Dr RS Turbo Hbk	1490	2735
4 Dr RS Hbk	1435	2635
4 Dr RS Turbo Hbk	1535	2820

OPTIONS FOR SUNDANCE

4 cyl 2.5 L Engine[Std on RS] +40
Auto 3-Speed Transmission +75
Air Conditioning +110
Power Door Locks +35
Power Drivers Seat +40
Power Windows +35
Sunroof +45

VOYAGER   1991

Big changes for the all-new Plymouth Voyager. New sheetmetal, available antilock brakes and optional all-wheel drive are new features for the Voyager. A driver airbag also debuts on the Voyager. An LX model joins the Voyager lineup sporting a front air dam, fog lights and alloy wheels.

Don't forget to refer to the Mileage Adjustment Table at the back of this book!

444   www.edmunds.com   EDMUNDS® USED CARS & TRUCKS

Model Description	Trade-in Value	Market Value

RATINGS (SCALE OF 1-10)

Overall	Safety	Reliability	Performance	Comfort	Value
6.6	4.8	3.7	7.4	8.3	8.6

Category G

Model Description	Trade-in Value	Market Value
2 Dr Grand LE Pass. Van	3785	5535
2 Dr Grand LE 4WD Pass. Van	3775	5530
2 Dr Grand SE Pass. Van	3180	4650
2 Dr Grand SE 4WD Pass. Van	3535	5170
2 Dr LE Pass. Van	3475	5085
2 Dr LE 4WD Pass. Van	3675	5380
2 Dr LX Pass. Van	3760	5505
2 Dr LX 4WD Pass. Van	3765	5515
2 Dr SE Pass. Van	2845	4160
2 Dr SE 4WD Pass. Van	3400	4975
2 Dr STD Pass. Van	2630	3845

OPTIONS FOR VOYAGER
6 cyl 3.0 L Engine[Std on LX] +95
6 cyl 3.3 L Engine[Std on Grand LE,Grand SE,4WD] +80
Luxury Pkg +150
7 Passenger Seating[Opt on STD] +70
Air Bag Restraint[Std on STD] +65
Air Conditioning[Std on Grand LE,LE,LX] +110
Anti-Lock Brakes +75
Captain Chairs (4) +80
Dual Air Conditioning +125
Leather Seats +105
Power Door Locks[Std on Grand LE,LE,LX] +30
Power Drivers Seat +40
Power Windows +30

PONTIAC 00

Model Description	Trade-in Value	Market Value

PONTIAC   USA

1996 Pontiac Firebird Coupe

2000 PONTIAC

BONNEVILLE   2000

Brand-new from the ground up, Pontiac's flagship sedan moves onto a stiffer platform with rakish styling and high-tech goodies such as an integrated chassis control system.
Category B

Model	Trade-in	Market
4 Dr SE Sdn	16940	19670
4 Dr SLE Sdn	19635	22800
4 Dr SSEi Sprchgd Sdn	22620	26265

OPTIONS FOR BONNEVILLE
AM/FM Compact Disc Player +270
Aluminum/Alloy Wheels[Opt on SE] +270
Leather Seats[Std on SSEi] +560
Power Drivers Seat[Opt on SE] +260
Power Moonroof +795

FIREBIRD   2000

New wheels, exterior and interior colors, and engine revisions for improved emissions and better throttle response on manual-transmission-equipped cars top the list of Firebird changes for 2000.
Category F

Model	Trade-in	Market
2 Dr Formula Cpe	17455	20225
2 Dr SLP Firehawk Cpe	22645	26245
2 Dr STD Conv	18485	21425
2 Dr STD Cpe	13735	15920
2 Dr Trans Am Conv	22605	26200
2 Dr Trans Am Cpe	19775	22920

OPTIONS FOR FIREBIRD
Auto 4-Speed Transmission[Opt on STD] +665
17 Inch Chrome Wheels +655
Bilstein Suspension Systm +815

High Torque Differential +735
Performance Differential +735
Ram Air Performance Pkg +2575
Sport Appearance Pkg +850
Alarm System[Std on Trans Am,Conv] +150
Chrome Wheels +480
Glass Panel T-tops[Std on Trans Am] +810
Leather Seats[Std on Trans Am] +520
Power Antenna[Opt on Base Coupe] +65
Power Door Locks[Opt on Base Coupe] +170
Power Drivers Seat[Std on Trans Am,Conv] +195
Power Mirrors[Opt on Base Coupe] +95
Power Windows[Opt on Base Coupe] +190
Rear Spoiler[Opt on SLP Firehawk Cpe] +195
Traction Control System +300

GRAND AM   2000

In the wake of its 1999 redesign, Grand Am gets engine improvements, interior upgrades (including a revamped center console), new exterior appearance packages and revised paint choices.
Category C

Model	Trade-in	Market
2 Dr GT Cpe	14355	16835
4 Dr GT Sdn	14570	17085
2 Dr GT1 Cpe	15420	18085
4 Dr GT1 Sdn	15635	18335
2 Dr SE Cpe	11780	13815
4 Dr SE Sdn	11990	14065
2 Dr SE1 Cpe	12640	14820
4 Dr SE1 Sdn	12895	15120
2 Dr SE2 Cpe	14295	16760
4 Dr SE2 Sdn	14505	17010

OPTIONS FOR GRAND AM
6 cyl 3.4 L Engine[Opt on SE1] +450
Auto 4-Speed Transmission[Opt on SE,SE1] +640
AM/FM Compact Disc Player[Std on GT1,SE2] +285
Aluminum/Alloy Wheels[Opt on SE,SE1 Coupe] +255
Cruise Control[Opt on SE] +180
Power Drivers Seat[Opt on GT,SE2] +245
Power Moonroof[Std on GT1] +560
Rear Spoiler[Std on GT,GT1] +145

GRAND PRIX   2000

Improvements to the base 3.1-liter V6 net a gain of 15 horsepower, as well as improved durability, reduced noise and lower emissions. A limited run (2000 coupes) of Daytona Pace Car replicas will be built, featuring unique exterior and interior details. Also new are a revised antitheft system, five-spoke silver-painted wheels, three new exterior colors and Cyclone cloth upholstery.
Category C

Model	Trade-in	Market
2 Dr GT Cpe	15795	18525
4 Dr GT Sdn	16040	18810
2 Dr GTP Sprchgd Cpe	17930	21030

Don't forget to refer to the Mileage Adjustment Table at the back of this book!

446   www.edmunds.com   **EDMUNDS® USED CARS & TRUCKS**

Model Description	Trade-in Value	Market Value
4 Dr GTP Sprchgd Sdn	17880	20970
4 Dr SE Sdn	14665	17200

OPTIONS FOR GRAND PRIX
AM/FM Compact Disc Player[Std on GTP] +285
Alarm System[Std on GTP] +135
Aluminum/Alloy Wheels[Opt on SE] +255
Automatic Dimming Mirror +90
Cruise Control[Opt on SE] +180
Heads-up Display +205
Keyless Entry System[Std on GTP] +150
Leather Seats +505
Leather Steering Wheel[Std on GTP] +80
Overhead Console[Std on GTP] +280
Power Drivers Seat[Std on GTP] +245
Power Moonroof +560
Steer. Whl. Radio Cntrls[Std on GTP] +125

MONTANA   2000

The 2000 Montana boasts improvements to its V6 and antilock brakes, an upgraded electrical system, a revised instrument cluster and radios, a quieter climate-control blower motor, the option of heated leather seats, reading lamps and oil-life monitoring as well as new paint schemes.

Category G

	Trade-in	Market
4 Dr STD Pass. Van	17320	20185
4 Dr STD Pass. Van Ext	18640	21720
4 Dr Vision Pass. Van Ext	19955	23250

OPTIONS FOR MONTANA
Aluminum/Alloy Wheels +265
Auto Load Leveling +190
Compact Disc W/fm/tape +365
Dual Air Conditioning +755
Keyless Entry System +160
Luggage Rack +130
Overhead Console +130
Power Drivers Seat +230
Power Sliding Door +340
Power Windows +200
Privacy Glass +225
Sport Suspension +365
Traction Control System +220

SUNFIRE   2000

Redesigned front and rear fascias for a sportier appearance, a new five-speed manual transmission and the availability of the premium Monsoon audio system lead Sunfire's upgrade list for 2000. There are also restyled rocker-panel moldings, new wheels and exterior colors, as well as a revised instrument panel cluster, floor console and upholstery.

Category E

	Trade-in	Market
2 Dr GT Conv	15500	18325
2 Dr GT Cpe	11705	13840

Model Description	Trade-in Value	Market Value
2 Dr SE Cpe	10115	11960
4 Dr SE Sdn	10180	12035

OPTIONS FOR SUNFIRE
4 cyl 2.4 L Engine[Std on GT] +370
Auto 3-Speed Transmission +530
Auto 4-Speed Transmission[Std on Conv] +660
AM/FM Compact Disc Player[Std on GT] +355
Cruise Control[Std on GT] +185
Power Door Locks[Std on Conv] +205
Power Mirrors[Std on Conv] +90
Power Windows[Std on Conv] +215
Rear Spoiler[Opt on Sdn] +180
Tilt Steering Wheel[Std on GT] +125

1999 PONTIAC

BONNEVILLE   1999

All the '99 model year has to offer the rapidly aging Bonneville is a couple of new exterior colors and the availability of GM's dealer-installed OnStar mobile communications system.

RATINGS (SCALE OF 1-10)

Overall	Safety	Reliability	Performance	Comfort	Value
N/A	7.6	8.8	8.4	7.8	N/A

Category B

	Trade-in	Market
4 Dr SE Sdn	14260	16670
4 Dr SLE Sdn	16160	18895
4 Dr SSE Sdn	18585	21725
4 Dr SSEi Sprchgd Sdn	19220	22465

OPTIONS FOR BONNEVILLE
AM/FM Compact Disc Player[Opt on SE,SLE] +220
Aluminum/Alloy Wheels[Opt on SE] +220
Chrome Wheels +455
Keyless Entry System[Opt on SE] +120
Power Drivers Seat[Opt on SE] +210
Power Mirrors[Opt on SE] +65
Power Moonroof +650
Premium Sound System[Opt on SE] +250
Traction Control System[Opt on SE,SLE] +115

FIREBIRD   1999

After last year's freshening, Firebird gets minor revisions and a few new standard items. Electronic traction control is now available on all models, with a bigger gas tank and an oil life monitor standard. A Torsen limited-slip rear axle comes with V8 models (and V6 cars with the performance package), while an eight-speaker Delco/Monsoon sound system goes into the convertible. A power-steering cooler is now available for V8s, and a Hurst shifter is optional on the six-speed manual transmission. The Ram Air WS6 package now sports dual outlet exhaust, and two new exterior colors debut, Pewter and Medium Blue metallic.

Model Description	Trade-in Value	Market Value

Model Description	Trade-in Value	Market Value

RATINGS (SCALE OF 1-10)

Overall	Safety	Reliability	Performance	Comfort	Value
N/A	8	N/A	N/A	7.3	N/A

Category F

2 Dr Formula Cpe	16405	19100
2 Dr STD Conv	17450	20320
2 Dr STD Cpe	12995	15135
2 Dr Trans Am Conv	21215	24700
2 Dr Trans Am Cpe	18410	21435

OPTIONS FOR FIREBIRD

Auto 4-Speed Transmission[Opt on STD] +545
30th Anniversary Pkg +1050
AutoCross Performance Pkg +785
Ram Air Performance Pkg +2105
Sport Appearance Pkg +695
Chrome Wheels +395
Glass Panel T-tops[Std on Trans Am] +660
Keyless Entry System[Std on Trans Am,Conv] +120
Leather Seats[Std on Trans Am] +425
Power Door Locks[Opt on Base Coupe] +135
Power Drivers Seat[Std on Trans Am,Conv] +160
Power Mirrors[Opt on Base Coupe] +75
Power Windows[Opt on Base Coupe] +155
Traction Control System +245

GRAND AM   1999

New for 1999, the Grand Am offers a host of standard and optional equipment as well as a completely redesigned exterior.

RATINGS (SCALE OF 1-10)

Overall	Safety	Reliability	Performance	Comfort	Value
N/A	7.3	8.8	7.8	8	N/A

Category C

2 Dr GT Cpe	12640	14915
4 Dr GT Sdn	12935	15265
2 Dr GT1 Cpe	13605	16055
4 Dr GT1 Sdn	13865	16360
2 Dr SE Cpe	10705	12630
4 Dr SE Sdn	10965	12935
2 Dr SE1 Cpe	11610	13695
4 Dr SE1 Sdn	11865	14000
2 Dr SE2 Cpe	11775	14005
4 Dr SE2 Sdn	12835	15140

OPTIONS FOR GRAND AM

6 cyl 3.4 L Engine[Opt on SE1] +415
AM/FM Compact Disc Player[Std on GT1,SE2] +235
Cruise Control[Opt on SE] +145
Keyless Entry System[Std on GT1,SE2] +125
Leather Seats +415
Power Drivers Seat +200
Power Moonroof[Std on GT1] +460

GRAND PRIX   1999

The Grand Prix gets more muscle for '99 with low-restriction air-induction components giving the naturally aspirated 3.8-liter V6 five more horsepower, to 200. This engine is standard on the GT (sedan and coupe) and optional on the SE sedan. A traction control indicator and on/off button are now standard on GTP models. Minor revisions are in order inside, with front-door courtesy lamps and a six-speaker sound system now standard, with an eight-speaker Bose audio unit and OnStar mobile communications system optional. Outside, a rear deck spoiler is standard on the GT model, and two colors have been added to the 1999 exterior paint chart.

RATINGS (SCALE OF 1-10)

Overall	Safety	Reliability	Performance	Comfort	Value
N/A	7.7	8.5	8.8	7.9	N/A

Category C

2 Dr GT Cpe	14255	16820
4 Dr GT Sdn	14355	16935
2 Dr GTP Sprchgd Cpe	16085	18975
4 Dr GTP Sprchgd Sdn	16185	19095
4 Dr SE Sdn	13210	15585

OPTIONS FOR GRAND PRIX

6 cyl 3.8 L Engine[Std on GT] +275
AM/FM Compact Disc Player[Std on GTP] +235
Aluminum/Alloy Wheels[Opt on SE] +205
Climate Control for AC[Opt on GT] +110
Cruise Control[Opt on SE] +145
Heads-up Display +170
Keyless Entry System[Std on GTP] +125
Leather Seats +415
Power Drivers Seat[Std on GTP] +200
Power Moonroof +460
Trip Computer[Opt on GT] +125

MONTANA   1999

After a ground-up redesign in 1997, the entire line gets a name change this year, from Trans Sport to Montana (the name pulled from 98's sporty trim package). Regular-wheelbase models come with one or two sliding doors, while extended wheelbase vans get two only with a right-side power sliding door option. Side-impact airbags are standard, as are 15-inch 215-70R white-letter puncture sealant tires. New two-tone paint jobs are available and four new exterior colors are offered, as are options for front-row leather seats and an overhead video system. Better still, a special sport performance package adds cast aluminum wheels, traction control and a specially tuned sport suspension for soccer dads (and moms) who are sport sedan wannabees.

Model Description	Trade-in Value	Market Value

Model Description	Trade-in Value	Market Value

RATINGS (SCALE OF 1-10)

Overall	Safety	Reliability	Performance	Comfort	Value
N/A	8	8.5	7.8	7.9	N/A

Category G

	Trade-in	Market
2 Dr STD Pass. Van	14810	17335
4 Dr STD Pass. Van	15900	18610
4 Dr STD Pass. Van Ext	16575	19400

OPTIONS FOR MONTANA

Aluminum/Alloy Wheels +215
Captain Chairs (4) +410
Compact Disc W/fm/tape +295
Dual Air Conditioning +615
Keyless Entry System +130
Leather Seats +525
Power Drivers Seat +190
Power Sliding Door +275
Power Windows +160
Privacy Glass +185
Traction Control System +180

SUNFIRE   1999

After Sunfire coupes got a rear spoiler last year, this year it's the sedan's turn, only as an option. The top-line 2.4-liter twin-cam engine is revised to improve breathing, including new fuel injectors, injection rails, exhaust manifold and catalytic converter. Fern Green Metallic is added to the paint color chart.

RATINGS (SCALE OF 1-10)

Overall	Safety	Reliability	Performance	Comfort	Value
N/A	6.8	9	6.8	7.1	N/A

Category E

	Trade-in	Market
2 Dr GT Conv	13875	16530
2 Dr GT Cpe	10415	12410
2 Dr SE Cpe	8495	10120
4 Dr SE Sdn	8560	10195

OPTIONS FOR SUNFIRE

4 cyl 2.4 L Engine[Std on GT] +300
Auto 3-Speed Transmission +400
Auto 4-Speed Transmission[Std on Conv] +540
AM/FM Compact Disc Player[Std on GT] +290
Air Conditioning[Std on GT] +555
Aluminum/Alloy Wheels[Std on GT] +225
Cruise Control[Std on Conv] +155
Keyless Entry System[Std on Conv] +110
Power Door Locks[Std on Conv] +165
Power Mirrors[Std on Conv] +75
Power Moonroof +390
Power Windows[Std on Conv] +180
Premium Sound System +220
Rear Window Defroster[Std on GT] +110
Tilt Steering Wheel[Std on GT] +100

BONNEVILLE   1998

Second-generation airbags are standard, the SE comes with a standard decklid spoiler, and the SSE gets more standard equipment. New colors freshen the rapidly aging Bonneville.

RATINGS (SCALE OF 1-10)

Overall	Safety	Reliability	Performance	Comfort	Value
8.2	7.6	8.6	8.4	7.8	8.8

Category B

	Trade-in	Market
4 Dr SE Sdn	12305	14515
4 Dr SLE Sdn	13920	16420
4 Dr SSE Sdn	15980	18850
4 Dr SSEi Sprchgd Sdn	16600	19585

OPTIONS FOR BONNEVILLE

AM/FM Compact Disc Player[Opt on SE, SLE] +180
Aluminum/Alloy Wheels[Opt on SE] +180
Chrome Wheels +370
Dual Power Seats[Opt on SE, SLE] +210
Keyless Entry System[Opt on SE] +95
Power Drivers Seat[Opt on SE] +175
Power Mirrors[Opt on SE] +55
Power Moonroof +530
Premium Sound System[Opt on SE] +205
Traction Control System[Opt on SE, SLE] +95

FIREBIRD   1998

Firebirds get a minor restyle that is most evident from the front end. Also on tap for Formula and Trans Am models is a de-tuned Corvette engine making 305 horsepower without Ram Air induction. Base models can be equipped with a new Sport Appearance Package, and two new exterior colors debut. Second-generation airbags are standard.

RATINGS (SCALE OF 1-10)

Overall	Safety	Reliability	Performance	Comfort	Value
N/A	8	8	N/A	7.3	4.1

Category F

	Trade-in	Market
2 Dr Formula Cpe	15260	17845
2 Dr STD Conv	16075	18795
2 Dr STD Cpe	12095	14145
2 Dr Trans Am Conv	19575	22890
2 Dr Trans Am Cpe	17155	20060

OPTIONS FOR FIREBIRD

Auto 4-Speed Transmission[Opt on STD] +445
AutoCross Performance Pkg +640
Performance Handling Pkg +1695
Performance/Handling Pkg +1695
Sport Appearance Pkg +540
Chrome Wheels +320
Glass Panel T-tops[Std on Trans Am] +540

Don't forget to refer to the Mileage Adjustment Table at the back of this book!

PONTIAC 98

Model Description	Trade-in Value	Market Value	Model Description	Trade-in Value	Market Value

Keyless Entry System[Std on Trans Am, Conv] +100
Leather Seats[Std on Trans Am] +345
Power Door Locks[Opt on STD Cpe] +110
Power Drivers Seat[Std on Trans Am] +130
Power Mirrors[Opt on STD Cpe] +65
Power Windows[Opt on STD Cpe] +125
Traction Control System +200

GRAND AM 1998

Second generation airbags are newly standard, and option groups are simplified.

RATINGS (SCALE OF 1-10)

Overall	Safety	Reliability	Performance	Comfort	Value
7.6	7.3	8.6	8.2	7.4	6.3

Category C

2 Dr GT Cpe	9895	11745
4 Dr GT Sdn	9980	11850
2 Dr SE Cpe	9045	10735
4 Dr SE Sdn	9130	10840

OPTIONS FOR GRAND AM

6 cyl 3.1 L Engine +245
Auto 4-Speed Transmission +440
AM/FM Compact Disc Player +190
Aluminum/Alloy Wheels[Opt on SE] +170
Cruise Control +120
Keyless Entry System +100
Leather Seats +340
Power Drivers Seat +165
Power Mirrors +60
Power Moonroof +375
Power Windows +175
Premium Sound System +210
Rear Window Defroster +90
Tilt Steering Wheel[Opt on SE] +85
Traction Control System +115

GRAND PRIX 1998

Supercharged GTP models get traction control, and new colors are available inside and out. Second-generation airbags debut as standard equipment.

RATINGS (SCALE OF 1-10)

Overall	Safety	Reliability	Performance	Comfort	Value
8.3	7.7	8.5	8.8	7.9	8.7

Category C

2 Dr GT Cpe	12865	15270
4 Dr GT Sdn	13020	15455
2 Dr GTP Sprchgd Cpe	13855	16445
4 Dr GTP Sprchgd Sdn	14005	16625
4 Dr SE Sdn	11870	14090

OPTIONS FOR GRAND PRIX

6 cyl 3.8 L Engine[Opt on SE] +235
AM/FM Compact Disc Player +190
Aluminum/Alloy Wheels[Opt on SE] +170

Climate Control for AC +90
Cruise Control[Opt on SE] +120
Heads-up Display +140
Keyless Entry System +100
Leather Seats +340
Power Drivers Seat +165
Power Moonroof +375
Premium Sound System[Opt on SE] +210
Trip Computer[Std on GTP] +100

SUNFIRE 1998

All coupes have a rear spoiler, a new six-speaker sound system is available, the base four-cylinder gets some additional low-end punch, and Topaz Gold Metallic is added to the paint color chart. Second-generation airbags are added as standard equipment.

RATINGS (SCALE OF 1-10)

Overall	Safety	Reliability	Performance	Comfort	Value
7.2	6.8	8.5	6.8	7.1	6.8

Category E

2 Dr GT Cpe	9530	11425
2 Dr SE Conv	11840	14195
2 Dr SE Cpe	7755	9295
4 Dr SE Sdn	7815	9365

OPTIONS FOR SUNFIRE

4 cyl 2.4 L Engine[Opt on SE] +245.
Auto 3-Speed Transmission +330
Auto 4-Speed Transmission[Std on Conv] +440
AM/FM Compact Disc Player[Std on GT, Conv] +235
Air Conditioning[Std on GT, Conv] +455
Aluminum/Alloy Wheels[Opt on SE] +185
Cruise Control[Std on Conv] +125
Keyless Entry System +90
Power Door Locks +135
Power Mirrors +60
Power Moonroof +320
Power Windows +145
Premium Sound System +180
Rear Window Defroster[Std on GT, Conv] +90
Tilt Steering Wheel[Std on GT, Conv] +80

TRANS SPORT 1998

Short-wheelbase models get the dual sliding doors and power sliding door options. Side-impact airbags are standard, and a white two-tone paint job is new. Second generation airbags are standard for front seat occupants.

RATINGS (SCALE OF 1-10)*

Overall	Safety	Reliability	Performance	Comfort	Value
7.5	7.9	7.4	7.6	7.9	6.9

Category G

2 Dr Montana Pass. Van	15115	17760
2 Dr Montana Pass. Van Ext	15405	18100

Don't forget to refer to the Mileage Adjustment Table at the back of this book!

| 2 Dr STD Pass. Van | 13385 | 15730 |
| 2 Dr STD Pass. Van Ext | 14795 | 17380 |

OPTIONS FOR TRANS SPORT
Aluminum/Alloy Wheels[Opt on STD] +175
Auto Load Leveling[Opt on STD] +130
Captain Chairs (4) +335
Compact Disc W/fm/tape +240
Cruise Control[Std on Pass. Van Ext] +115
Dual Air Conditioning +505
Dual Power Seats +230
Keyless Entry System +105
Leather Seats +430
Power Drivers Seat +155
Power Windows +135
Premium Sound System +185
Privacy Glass +150
Rear Window Defroster +95
Sliding Driver Side Door[Std on Montana, Pass. Van Ext] +290
Traction Control System[Opt on STD] +145

1997 PONTIAC

BONNEVILLE 1997

Changes for 1997 are few. Supercharged Bonnevilles get a new transmission, a new Delco/Bose premium sound system is optional on the SSE, and the EYE CUE head-up display has a new motorized adjustment feature. Two new exterior colors, a new interior color and a new interior fabric liven the aging Bonneville visually.

RATINGS (SCALE OF 1-10)

Overall	Safety	Reliability	Performance	Comfort	Value
8	7.5	8.2	8.4	7.8	8.2

Category B
4 Dr SE Sdn	11255	13300
4 Dr SE Sprchgd Sdn	11885	14045
4 Dr SSE Sdn	13640	16115
4 Dr SSEi Sprchgd Sdn	14300	16895

OPTIONS FOR BONNEVILLE
Computer Command Ride Pkg +370
Aluminum/Alloy Wheels[Opt on SE] +150
Chrome Wheels +305
Compact Disc W/fm/tape +165
Dual Power Seats +175
Keyless Entry System[Opt on SE] +80
Leather Seats +305
Power Moonroof +435
Premium Sound System[Opt on SE] +165
Steer. Whl. Radio Cntrls[Opt on SE] +65
Traction Control System +80

FIREBIRD 1997

Pontiac upgrades the Firebird in several ways for 1997. Performance freaks will appreciate the addition of Ram Air induction to the options list of the Formula and Trans Am convertibles. Audiophiles will be blown away by the newly optional 500-watt Monsoon sound system. Luxury intenders can get power seats swathed in leather this year. Safety-conscious buyers will find daytime running lights. Additional cosmetic and comfort items keep the fourth-generation Firebird fresh for its fifth year.

RATINGS (SCALE OF 1-10)

Overall	Safety	Reliability	Performance	Comfort	Value
N/A	7.8	7.1	N/A	7.3	4

Category F
2 Dr Formula Conv	16000	18790
2 Dr Formula Cpe	12705	14920
2 Dr STD Conv	14115	16575
2 Dr STD Cpe	10580	12425
2 Dr Trans Am Conv	17135	20125
2 Dr Trans Am Cpe	13995	16435

OPTIONS FOR FIREBIRD
Auto 4-Speed Transmission[Opt on STD] +365
Performance Handling Pkg +1235
Performance Pkg +525
Sport Appearance Pkg +600
AM/FM Compact Disc Player +205
Chrome Wheels +265
Cruise Control[Std on Trans Am, Conv] +100
Glass Panel T-tops +440
Keyless Entry System[Opt on Formula, STD] +80
Leather Seats +285
Power Door Locks[Std on Trans Am, Conv] +90
Power Drivers Seat +110
Power Windows[Std on Trans Am, Conv] +105
Steer. Whl. Radio Cntrls[Opt on Formula, STD] +80
Traction Control System +165

GRAND AM 1997

Very minimal changes this year as Pontiac concentrates on Grand Prix and Trans Sport launches. Air conditioning is now standard. Also, three new colors are added.

RATINGS (SCALE OF 1-10)

Overall	Safety	Reliability	Performance	Comfort	Value
7.5	7.2	7.9	8.2	7.4	6.6

Category C
2 Dr GT Cpe	8705	10395
4 Dr GT Sdn	8705	10395
2 Dr SE Cpe	8050	9615
4 Dr SE Sdn	8050	9615

PONTIAC 97-96

Model Description	Trade-in Value	Market Value

OPTIONS FOR GRAND AM

6 cyl 3.1 L Engine +190
Auto 4-Speed Transmission +360
Aluminum/Alloy Wheels[Opt on SE] +140
Compact Disc W/fm/tape +145
Cruise Control +95
Keyless Entry System +85
Leather Seats +275
Power Drivers Seat +135
Power Moonroof +305
Power Windows +140
Premium Sound System +170

GRAND PRIX 1997

Pontiac redesigns the Grand Prix for 1997, giving buyers slick new styling, a longer and wider wheelbase, and available supercharged V6 power on GT models. Traction control, antilock brakes, dual airbags and side-impact protection are standard. Optional is a built-in child safety seat.

RATINGS (SCALE OF 1-10)

Overall	Safety	Reliability	Performance	Comfort	Value
8	7.7	8.2	8.8	7.9	7.6

Category C

2 Dr GT Cpe	11055	13205
4 Dr GT Sdn	11565	13810
2 Dr GTP Sprchgd Cpe	11910	14225
4 Dr GTP Sprchgd Sdn	12370	14770
4 Dr SE Sdn	10510	12555

OPTIONS FOR GRAND PRIX

6 cyl 3.8 L Engine[Opt on SE] +185
Aluminum/Alloy Wheels[Opt on SE] +140
Child Seat (1) +55
Climate Control for AC +75
Compact Disc W/fm/tape +145
Cruise Control[Opt on SE,Cpe] +95
Keyless Entry System +85
Leather Seats +275
Power Drivers Seat +135
Power Moonroof +305
Premium Sound System +170
Trip Computer[Std on GTP] +85

SUNFIRE 1997

SE Convertible gets a higher level of standard equipment, including an automatic transmission. Coupes get a new front seatbelt guide loop, and a new Sports Interior trim debuts called Patina/Redondo cloth.

RATINGS (SCALE OF 1-10)

Overall	Safety	Reliability	Performance	Comfort	Value
6.6	6.6	7.5	6.8	7.1	5.1

Category E

2 Dr GT Cpe	7790	9390
2 Dr SE Conv	10630	12815

Model Description	Trade-in Value	Market Value
2 Dr SE Cpe	6880	8295
4 Dr SE Sdn	6960	8390

OPTIONS FOR SUNFIRE

4 cyl 2.4 L Engine[Opt on SE] +190
Auto 3-Speed Transmission +245
Auto 4-Speed Transmission[Std on Conv] +360
AM/FM Compact Disc Player +195
Air Conditioning[Std on Conv] +370
Aluminum/Alloy Wheels[Opt on SE] +150
Cruise Control[Std on Conv] +100
Keyless Entry System +75
Overhead Console[Std on Conv] +55
Power Door Locks +110
Power Moonroof +260
Power Windows +120
Premium Sound System +145
Rear Spoiler[Std on GT,Conv] +100
Tilt Steering Wheel[Std on GT,Conv] +65

TRANS SPORT 1997

After years of taking it on the chin, Pontiac redesigns the Trans Sport and lands one squarely in Chrysler's face. This van is good-looking, loaded with features and fun to drive. Wait. Did we say fun to drive?

RATINGS (SCALE OF 1-10)

Overall	Safety	Reliability	Performance	Comfort	Value
7.4	7.2	7.5	7.6	7.9	6.8

Category G

2 Dr SE Pass. Van	11895	14035
2 Dr SE Pass. Van Ext	12435	14675

OPTIONS FOR TRANS SPORT

7 Passenger Seating[Opt on Pass. Van] +235
Aluminum/Alloy Wheels +145
Auto Load Leveling +105
Captain Chairs (4) +275
Child Seats (2) +115
Compact Disc W/fm/tape +200
Cruise Control +95
Dual Power Seats +185
Keyless Entry System +85
Leather Seats +350
Luggage Rack +70
Power Windows +110
Premium Sound System +155
Rear Heater +85
Sliding Driver Side Door +235

1996 PONTIAC

BONNEVILLE 1996

The Series II V6 has been supercharged for 1996, pumping out 240 horsepower. Styling front and rear has been tweaked, and daytime running lights debut.

Don't forget to refer to the Mileage Adjustment Table at the back of this book!

EDMUNDS® USED CARS & TRUCKS

Model Description	Trade-in Value	Market Value

RATINGS (SCALE OF 1-10)

Overall	Safety	Reliability	Performance	Comfort	Value
7.9	7.5	7.8	8.4	7.8	8.2

Category B

	Trade-in	Market
4 Dr SE Sdn	9425	11285
4 Dr SE Sprchgd Sdn	9920	11880
4 Dr SLE Sdn	10635	12735
4 Dr SSE Sdn	11440	13700
4 Dr SSE Sprchgd Sdn	11440	13700

OPTIONS FOR BONNEVILLE

Computer Command Ride Pkg +335
SSEi Supercharger Pkg +405
Chrome Wheels +250
Climate Control for AC[Opt on SE] +60
Compact Disc W/fm/tape +135
Keyless Entry System[Opt on SE] +65
Leather Seats +250
Power Drivers Seat[Opt on SE] +115
Power Moonroof +355
Power Passenger Seat +130
Premium Sound System[Opt on SE] +135
Traction Control System +65

FIREBIRD 1996

A new standard V6 makes 40 more horsepower than the old one. The LT1 V8 also makes more power, particularly when equipped with Ram Air induction. A new color livens up the exterior, as if it needed it.

RATINGS (SCALE OF 1-10)

Overall	Safety	Reliability	Performance	Comfort	Value
N/A	8	7.3	N/A	7.3	4.3

Category F

	Trade-in	Market
2 Dr Formula Conv	13370	15850
2 Dr Formula Cpe	10530	12490
2 Dr STD Conv	12105	14355
2 Dr STD Cpe	8500	10080
2 Dr Trans Am Conv	14445	17130
2 Dr Trans Am Cpe	11560	13710

OPTIONS FOR FIREBIRD

Auto 4-Speed Transmission +275
Performance Handling Pkg +945
AM/FM Compact Disc Player +170
Air Conditioning[Opt on STD Cpe] +305
Chrome Wheels +215
Cruise Control[Std on Trans Am,Conv] +80
Glass Panel T-tops +360
Keyless Entry System[Opt on Formula,STD,Cpe] +65
Leather Seats +230
Power Door Locks[Std on Trans Am,Conv] +75
Power Drivers Seat +90
Power Windows[Std on Trans Am,Conv] +85
Premium Sound System[Std on Trans Am,Conv] +140
Steer. Whl. Radio Cntrls[Opt on Formula,STD,Cpe] +65

GRAND AM 1996

New styling, a new base engine, and ... what's this? Dual airbags and body-mounted seatbelts? Will wonders never cease?

RATINGS (SCALE OF 1-10)

Overall	Safety	Reliability	Performance	Comfort	Value
7.3	6.9	6.8	8.2	7.4	7

Category C

	Trade-in	Market
2 Dr GT Cpe	7145	8775
4 Dr GT Sdn	7145	8775
2 Dr SE Cpe	6255	7675
4 Dr SE Sdn	6255	7675

OPTIONS FOR GRAND AM

6 cyl 3.1 L Engine +170
Auto 4-Speed Transmission +275
Air Conditioning[Opt on SE] +295
Compact Disc W/fm/tape +120
Cruise Control +80
Keyless Entry System +70
Leather Seats +225
Power Drivers Seat +110
Power Moonroof +250
Power Windows +115
Premium Sound System +140

GRAND PRIX 1996

Minor trim and powertrain improvements to the only car in GM's stable that still has those stupid door-mounted seatbelts. Do yourself a favor. Buy the 1997 GP.

RATINGS (SCALE OF 1-10)

Overall	Safety	Reliability	Performance	Comfort	Value
7.7	7.2	8	8	7.3	8

Category C

	Trade-in	Market
4 Dr GT Sdn	8545	10490
2 Dr GTP Cpe	8815	10825
2 Dr SE Cpe	8115	9960
4 Dr SE Sdn	7570	9295

OPTIONS FOR GRAND PRIX

GT Performance Pkg +335
AM/FM Compact Disc Player +130
Aluminum/Alloy Wheels[Opt on SE] +115
Anti-Lock Brakes[Opt on SE] +215
Cruise Control[Opt on GT,Sdn] +80
Keyless Entry System +70
Leather Seats +225
Power Drivers Seat +110
Power Moonroof +250
Premium Sound System +140
Sport Suspension[Opt on SE] +80
Trip Computer +70

Don't forget to refer to the Mileage Adjustment Table at the back of this book!

PONTIAC 96-95

Model Description	Trade-in Value	Market Value	Model Description	Trade-in Value	Market Value

SUNFIRE 1996

Traction control, remote keyless entry and steering wheel radio controls are newly available. Old Quad 4 engine dumped in favor of new 2.4-liter twin-cam engine. Two new paint choices spiff up the exterior.

RATINGS (SCALE OF 1-10)

Overall	Safety	Reliability	Performance	Comfort	Value
6.6	6.4	6.7	6.8	7.1	6

Category E

	Trade-in	Market
2 Dr GT Cpe	6390	7935
2 Dr SE Conv	8530	10590
2 Dr SE Cpe	5595	6945
4 Dr SE Sdn	5765	7155

OPTIONS FOR SUNFIRE

4 cyl 2.4 L Engine[Opt on SE] +125
Auto 3-Speed Transmission[Std on Conv] +190
Auto 4-Speed Transmission +230
AM/FM Compact Disc Player +160
Air Conditioning[Std on Conv] +305
Cruise Control +85
Keyless Entry System +60
Power Door Locks +90
Power Sunroof +230
Power Windows +95
Premium Sound System +120

TRANS SPORT 1996

A 180-horsepower 3.4-liter V6 replaces last year's pathetic base engine as well as the optional 3.8-liter V6. Front air conditioning is standard equipment for 1996.

RATINGS (SCALE OF 1-10)

Overall	Safety	Reliability	Performance	Comfort	Value
7.4	6.5	7.6	7.2	7.1	8.5

Category G

	Trade-in	Market
2 Dr SE Pass. Van	9320	11255

OPTIONS FOR TRANS SPORT

7 Passenger Seating +190
Air Conditioning +300
Auto Load Leveling +85
Child Seats (2) +90
Cruise Control +75
Dual Air Conditioning +335
Keyless Entry System +70
Leather Seats +285
Power Door Locks +85
Power Drivers Seat +105
Power Sliding Door +150
Power Windows +90
Premium Sound System +125
Traction Control System +100

1995 PONTIAC

BONNEVILLE 1995

Base engine is upgraded to 3800 Series II status, gaining 35 horsepower in the process. SE models with the SLE package can be ordered with the supercharged 3.8-liter V6. Computer Command Ride is made available on SE models.

RATINGS (SCALE OF 1-10)

Overall	Safety	Reliability	Performance	Comfort	Value
7.9	8.3	7.3	8.4	7.8	7.9

Category B

	Trade-in	Market
4 Dr SE Sdn	7625	9210
4 Dr SE Sprchgd Sdn	7915	9560
4 Dr SSE Sdn	9250	11175
4 Dr SSEi Sprchgd Sdn	9660	11670

OPTIONS FOR BONNEVILLE

Articulating Lthr Seats +330
Climate Control for AC +50
Dual Power Seats +115
Keyless Entry System +50
Leather Seats +205
Power Moonroof +290
Premium Sound System[Opt on SE] +110
Steer. Whl. Radio Cntrls +40

FIREBIRD 1995

Traction control is added as an option on Formula and Trans Am. Trans Am GT is dropped from lineup. Californians get a 3.8-liter V6 equipped with an automatic transmission on base models instead of the 3.4-liter V6. The new engine meets strict emissions standards in that state, and makes 40 additional horsepower.

RATINGS (SCALE OF 1-10)

Overall	Safety	Reliability	Performance	Comfort	Value
N/A	8.7	6.9	N/A	7.3	4.4

Category F

	Trade-in	Market
2 Dr Formula Conv	11415	13640
2 Dr Formula Cpe	8965	10715
2 Dr STD Conv	9995	11940
2 Dr STD Cpe	7025	8395
2 Dr Trans Am Conv	12310	14710
2 Dr Trans Am Cpe	9865	11790

OPTIONS FOR FIREBIRD

Auto 4-Speed Transmission +230
AM/FM Compact Disc Player +140
Air Conditioning[Std on Trans Am,Conv] +250
Cruise Control[Std on Trans Am,Conv] +65
Glass Panel T-tops +295
Keyless Entry System[Opt on Formula,STD] +55

Don't forget to refer to the Mileage Adjustment Table at the back of this book!

Model Description	Trade-in Value	Market Value
Leather Seats[Opt on Formula,STD] +190		
Power Door Locks[Std on Trans Am,Conv] +60		
Power Windows[Std on Trans Am,Conv] +70		
Premium Sound System[Opt on Formula,STD] +115		
Steer. Whl. Radio Cntrls +50		
Traction Control System +110		

GRAND AM 1995

Base engine upgraded to a 150-horsepower version of the Quad 4. High-output Quad 4 motor is dropped from the GT, which now uses the same standard and optional powerplants as the SE. Variable-effort power steering is a new option on GT models, rear suspensions are redesigned, and SE models get restyled wheelcovers and alloy wheels.

RATINGS (SCALE OF 1-10)

Overall	Safety	Reliability	Performance	Comfort	Value
7.2	6.6	7.8	8.2	7.3	6

Category C
Model	Trade-in	Market
2 Dr GT Cpe	5550	7070
4 Dr GT Sdn	5660	7210
2 Dr SE Cpe	4845	6170
4 Dr SE Sdn	4880	6220

OPTIONS FOR GRAND AM
6 cyl 3.1 L Engine +145
Auto 3-Speed Transmission +165
Auto 4-Speed Transmission +225
AM/FM Compact Disc Player +105
Air Conditioning[Opt on SE] +245
Cruise Control +65
Keyless Entry System +55
Leather Seats +185
Power Drivers Seat +90
Power Moonroof +205
Power Windows +95
Premium Sound System +115

GRAND PRIX 1995

Brake/transmission shift interlock is added. GT coupe dropped in favor of GTP Package. GT sedan continues. Variable-effort steering is added to GTP and GT. New alloys debut on GT and GTP. Coupes can be equipped with a White Appearance Package, which includes color-keyed alloys and special pinstriping. Floor consoles are redesigned on models with bucket seats.

RATINGS (SCALE OF 1-10)

Overall	Safety	Reliability	Performance	Comfort	Value
7.6	7.6	7.3	8	7.3	7.9

Category C
Model	Trade-in	Market
4 Dr GT Sdn	7145	9100
2 Dr GTP Cpe	7410	9440
2 Dr SE Cpe	6585	8385
4 Dr SE Sdn	6310	8035

OPTIONS FOR GRAND PRIX
AM/FM Compact Disc Player +105
Anti-Lock Brakes[Opt on SE] +175
Cruise Control +65
Keyless Entry System +55
Leather Seats +185
Power Drivers Seat +90
Power Moonroof +205
Premium Sound System +115
Sport Suspension[Opt on SE] +65
Trip Computer +55

SUNFIRE 1995

All-new replacement for aged Sunbird comes in SE coupe or sedan, and GT coupe trim levels. An SE convertible debuted midyear. Dual airbags, ABS, tilt steering and tachometer are standard. Base engine is a 2.2-liter four cylinder good for 120 horsepower. GT models get a 150-horsepower Quad 4 engine, which is optional on SE. Order the four-speed automatic transmission, and you'll get traction control.

RATINGS (SCALE OF 1-10)

Overall	Safety	Reliability	Performance	Comfort	Value
7	7.1	6.8	6.8	7.1	7.1

Category E
Model	Trade-in	Market
2 Dr GT Cpe	5475	6800
2 Dr SE Conv	7095	8805
2 Dr SE Cpe	4755	5900
4 Dr SE Sdn	4815	5975

OPTIONS FOR SUNFIRE
4 cyl 2.3 L Quad 4 Engine[Opt on SE] +120
Auto 3-Speed Transmission[Std on Conv] +150
Auto 4-Speed Transmission[Opt on GT only] +140
AM/FM Compact Disc Player +130
Air Conditioning +250
Cruise Control +70
Power Door Locks +75
Power Sunroof +185
Power Windows +80
Premium Sound System +100
Tilt Steering Wheel[Std on GT,Conv] +45

TRANS SPORT 1995

A brake/transmission shift interlock is added. New overhead console includes outside temperature gauge, compass and storage bin.

RATINGS (SCALE OF 1-10)

Overall	Safety	Reliability	Performance	Comfort	Value
7	6.8	5.8	7.2	7.1	8.3

Category G
Model	Trade-in	Market
2 Dr SE Pass. Van	7545	9360

Don't forget to refer to the Mileage Adjustment Table at the back of this book!

PONTIAC 95-94

Model Description	Trade-in Value	Market Value	Model Description	Trade-in Value	Market Value

OPTIONS FOR TRANS SPORT

6 cyl 3.8 L Engine +125
Auto 4-Speed Transmission +60
7 Passenger Seating +155
AM/FM Compact Disc Player +95
Air Conditioning +245
Auto Load Leveling +70
Child Seats (2) +75
Cruise Control +65
Dual Air Conditioning +275
Keyless Entry System +60
Leather Seats +235
Luggage Rack +50
Power Door Locks +70
Power Windows +70
Premium Sound System +100
Traction Control System +80

1994 PONTIAC

BONNEVILLE   1994

Dual airbags are standard. SE and SSE trim levels are available. Californians get SLE model. SSEi is an option package on SSE. Supercharged engine in SSEi package gets 20 more horsepower. Automatic transmission gains Normal and Performance shift modes when hooked to supercharged engine. Traction control gains ability to retard engine power as well as apply brakes to slow spinning wheel(s). Get traction control on the SSE, and you can opt for Computer Command Ride, a suspension package that automatically adjusts the suspension to meet the demands of the driver.

RATINGS (SCALE OF 1-10)

Overall	Safety	Reliability	Performance	Comfort	Value
8.2	8.4	8	8.2	7.8	8.5

Category B
4 Dr SE Sdn	6210	7675
4 Dr SSE Sdn	7635	9425
4 Dr SSEi Sprchgd Sdn	8005	9885

OPTIONS FOR BONNEVILLE

Compact Disc W/fm/tape +90
Cruise Control[Opt on SE] +55
Keyless Entry System +45
Leather Seats +165
Power Drivers Seat[Opt on SE] +75
Power Moonroof +235
Power Passenger Seat +90
Premium Sound System[Opt on SE] +90
Sport Suspension +75
Traction Control System +45

FIREBIRD   1994

Trans Am GT debuts. Six-speed transmission is saddled with a first-to-fourth skip shift feature designed to improve fuel economy. Automatic is new electronically controlled unit with the V8 engine, and it features Normal and Performance modes. Remote keyless entry, cassette player, and leather-wrapped steering wheel move from the Trans Am standard equipment list to the options sheet. T/A also loses Batwing rear spoiler to GT, taking Formula's more subdued rear treatment. Convertible debuts at midyear.

RATINGS (SCALE OF 1-10)

Overall	Safety	Reliability	Performance	Comfort	Value
N/A	8.7	7.2	N/A	7.3	4.9

Category F
2 Dr Formula Conv	10025	12105
2 Dr Formula Cpe	7620	9200
2 Dr STD Conv	8765	10580
2 Dr STD Cpe	5970	7210
2 Dr Trans Am Cpe	8405	10145
2 Dr Trans Am 25th Anniv. Cpe	9320	11250
2 Dr Trans Am GT Conv	10905	13170
2 Dr Trans Am GT Cpe	8750	10565

OPTIONS FOR FIREBIRD

Auto 4-Speed Transmission +175
Air Conditioning[Opt on STD Cpe] +205
Compact Disc W/fm/tape +125
Cruise Control[Opt on Formula Cpe,STD Cpe] +55
Glass Panel T-tops +240
Keyless Entry System[Opt on Formula,STD,Trans Am] +45
Leather Seats[Std on Trans Am GT Conv] +155
Power Door Locks[Opt on Formula Cpe,STD Cpe] +50
Power Drivers Seat +60
Power Windows[Opt on STD Cpe,Formula Cpe] +55
Premium Sound System[Opt on Formula,STD,Trans Am] +95
Steer. Whl. Radio Cntrls +45

GRAND AM   1994

Driver airbag added. A 3.1-liter V6 replaces last year's optional 3.3-liter V6. Four-speed automatic debuts; standard with V6 and optional on four-cylinder models.

RATINGS (SCALE OF 1-10)

Overall	Safety	Reliability	Performance	Comfort	Value
7.1	6.5	7.7	8.2	7.3	6

Category C
2 Dr GT Cpe	4905	6365
4 Dr GT Sdn	4935	6405
2 Dr SE Cpe	4110	5340
4 Dr SE Sdn	4145	5380

Don't forget to refer to the Mileage Adjustment Table at the back of this book!

Model Description	Trade-in Value	Market Value	Model Description	Trade-in Value	Market Value

OPTIONS FOR GRAND AM

6 cyl 3.1 L Engine +125
Auto 3-Speed Transmission +135
Auto 4-Speed Transmission +185
AM/FM Compact Disc Player +85
Air Conditioning[Opt on SE] +200
Cruise Control +55
Keyless Entry System +45
Leather Seats +150
Power Drivers Seat +75
Power Windows +80
Premium Sound System +95

GRAND PRIX   1994

Interior is redesigned to accommodate dual airbags. LE and STE sedans are dropped; GT and GTP become option packages on SE coupe. A GT package is available on SE sedan, and includes 3.4-liter V6, alloys, low-profile tires, ABS, and sport suspension. Front seatbelts are anchored to pillars instead of doors on sedan; coupe retains door-mounted belts. 3.1-liter V6 is up 20 horsepower. Twin-cam 3.4-liter V6 is up ten horsepower. Five-speed manual and three-speed automatic transmissions are dropped in favor of four-speed automatic. Coupes gain standard equipment, including 16-inch alloys, cruise, and leather-wrapped steering wheel with integral radio controls.

RATINGS (SCALE OF 1-10)

Overall	Safety	Reliability	Performance	Comfort	Value
7.7	7.8	6.9	8	7.3	8.3

Category C

				Trade-in	Market
2 Dr SE Cpe				5300	6880
4 Dr SE Sdn				5160	6695

OPTIONS FOR GRAND PRIX

6 cyl 3.4 L Engine +275
AM/FM Compact Disc Player +85
AM/FM Stereo Tape[Opt on Sdn] +40
Anti-Lock Brakes +145
Cruise Control[Opt on Sdn] +55
Keyless Entry System +45
Leather Seats +150
Power Drivers Seat +75
Power Sunroof +160
Premium Sound System +95
Sport Suspension +50
Trip Computer +45

SUNBIRD   1994

GT coupe, SE convertible and SE sedan vanish. Surviving are LE models and an SE coupe that comes standard with the GT's old body work. Convertibles get alloys and rear spoiler standard. SE comes with a 3.1-liter V6 standard.

RATINGS (SCALE OF 1-10)

Overall	Safety	Reliability	Performance	Comfort	Value
6.5	5.5	7.5	6.6	6.8	5.9

Category E

				Trade-in	Market
2 Dr LE Conv				4835	6345
2 Dr LE Cpe				3095	4060
4 Dr LE Sdn				3125	4100
2 Dr SE Cpe				3900	5115

OPTIONS FOR SUNBIRD

6 cyl 3.1 L Engine[Opt on LE] +180
Auto 3-Speed Transmission +120
AM/FM Compact Disc Player +105
Air Conditioning +205
Aluminum/Alloy Wheels +80
Cruise Control +55
Power Windows[Std on Conv] +65
Sunroof +85

TRANS SPORT   1994

Driver airbag debuts and new front styling improves doorstop looks. Dashboard gets styling tweak to shorten visual acreage on top. A power sliding side door and integrated child seats are newly optional. Automatic power door locks are added, and rear seats gain a fold-and-stow feature. Traction control is made available at midyear; requires 3.8-liter engine.

RATINGS (SCALE OF 1-10)

Overall	Safety	Reliability	Performance	Comfort	Value
7	6.7	5.8	7.2	7.1	8.3

Category G

				Trade-in	Market
2 Dr SE Pass. Van				6050	7715

OPTIONS FOR TRANS SPORT

6 cyl 3.8 L Engine +100
7 Passenger Seating +125
AM/FM Compact Disc Player +75
Air Conditioning +200
Auto Load Leveling +55
Child Seats (2) +60
Cruise Control +50
Dual Air Conditioning +225
Keyless Entry System +50
Leather Seats +190
Luggage Rack +40
Power Door Locks +55
Power Drivers Seat +70
Power Windows +60
Premium Sound System +85
Traction Control System +65

1993 PONTIAC

BONNEVILLE 1993

SSE gets supercharged engine option. ABS is standard on all models. Sport Luxury Edition (SLE) for SE includes chrome grille, decklid spoiler, cross-lace alloy wheels, bigger tires, leather seats, and performance-oriented transaxle ratio.

RATINGS (SCALE OF 1-10)

Overall	Safety	Reliability	Performance	Comfort	Value
7.7	7.3	7.3	8.2	7.8	8

Category B

	Trade-in	Market
4 Dr SE Sdn	4965	6305
4 Dr SSE Sdn	6115	7760
4 Dr SSE Sprchgd Sdn	6365	8080
4 Dr SSEi Sprchgd Sdn	7220	9165

OPTIONS FOR BONNEVILLE

Aluminum/Alloy Wheels[Opt on SE] +65
Cruise Control[Opt on SE] +45
Leather Seats[Std on SSEi] +135
Power Drivers Seat[Opt on SE] +65
Power Sunroof +215
Premium Sound System[Opt on SE] +75

FIREBIRD 1993

Brand new car debuts, marking first redesign since 1982. Base, Formula and Trans Am trim levels are available. Base car powered by 160-horsepower 3.4-liter V6. Formula and T/A get 5.7-liter V8 worth 275 horsepower. Formula and T/A get a standard six-speed manual transmission. Dual airbags and ABS are standard.

RATINGS (SCALE OF 1-10)

Overall	Safety	Reliability	Performance	Comfort	Value
N/A	8.7	7	N/A	7.3	3.8

Category F

	Trade-in	Market
2 Dr Formula Cpe	6450	8035
2 Dr STD Cpe	5055	6300
2 Dr Trans Am Cpe	7325	9125

OPTIONS FOR FIREBIRD

Auto 4-Speed Transmission +120
AM/FM Compact Disc Player +90
Air Conditioning[Opt on STD] +170
Cruise Control[Std on Trans Am] +45
Keyless Entry System[Opt on STD] +35
Leather Seats[Std on Trans Am] +125
Power Door Locks[Std on Trans Am] +40
Power Drivers Seat +50
Power Windows[Std on Trans Am] +45
Premium Sound System[Opt on STD] +75

GRAND AM 1993

Four-cylinder engines lose five horsepower, but gain modifications designed to reduce engine noise. Climate controls are revised, instrument panel graphics are revised on the SE, and battery-saver protection is added.

RATINGS (SCALE OF 1-10)

Overall	Safety	Reliability	Performance	Comfort	Value
6.7	4.3	7.1	8.2	7.3	6.7

Category C

	Trade-in	Market
2 Dr GT Cpe	3635	4860
4 Dr GT Sdn	3660	4895
2 Dr SE Cpe	3280	4385
4 Dr SE Sdn	3305	4420

OPTIONS FOR GRAND AM

4 cyl 2.3 L Quad 4 Engine[Opt on SE] +80
6 cyl 3.3 L Engine +105
Auto 3-Speed Transmission +110
AM/FM Compact Disc Player +70
Air Conditioning +160
Aluminum/Alloy Wheels[Opt on SE] +60
Cruise Control +45
Power Drivers Seat +60
Power Windows +65
Premium Sound System +75

GRAND PRIX 1993

An electronically-controlled four-speed automatic is optional on LE sedan and SE coupe. A Sport Appearance Package for the LE sedan includes aero body panels, heads-up display, and bucket seats with console. Automatic door locks are standard. Chime added to warn driver if turn signal has been left on.

RATINGS (SCALE OF 1-10)

Overall	Safety	Reliability	Performance	Comfort	Value
7.2	5.4	7.3	8	7	8.3

Category C

	Trade-in	Market
2 Dr GT Cpe	4995	6685
4 Dr LE Sdn	3690	4935
2 Dr SE Cpe	3810	5095
4 Dr SE Sdn	4000	5350
4 Dr STE Sdn	5060	6765

OPTIONS FOR GRAND PRIX

6 cyl 3.4 L Engine +200
Auto 4-Speed Transmission[Opt on LE,SE] +45
Aero Performance Pkg +385
AM/FM Compact Disc Player +70
Aluminum/Alloy Wheels[Opt on LE,SE Cpe] +60
Anti-Lock Brakes[Opt on LE,SE] +120
Cruise Control[Opt on LE,SE] +45
Keyless Entry System[Std on STE] +35
Leather Seats +125

Don't forget to refer to the Mileage Adjustment Table at the back of this book!

PONTIAC 93-92

Model Description	Trade-in Value	Market Value	Model Description	Trade-in Value	Market Value

Power Sunroof +135
Power Windows[Opt on LE,SE] +65
Premium Sound System[Opt on LE,SE] +75

LE MANS 1993

New front styling and revised taillights debut. New moldings and wheelcovers complete the minor makeover.

Category E

	Trade-in	Market
2 Dr SE Cpe	1850	2775
4 Dr SE Sdn	2005	3010
2 Dr Value Leader Cpe	1675	2510

OPTIONS FOR LE MANS

Auto 3-Speed Transmission +95
AM/FM Stereo Tape +60
Air Conditioning +165
Power Steering +50
Sunroof +70

SUNBIRD 1993

Base models can be equipped with a V6, and midline coupe gets Sport Appearance Package, which includes GT styling.

RATINGS (SCALE OF 1-10)

Overall	Safety	Reliability	Performance	Comfort	Value
6.4	5.4	6.6	6.6	6.8	6.7

Category E

	Trade-in	Market
2 Dr GT Cpe	3100	4650
2 Dr LE Cpe	2300	3445
4 Dr LE Sdn	2320	3480
2 Dr SE Conv	3700	5550
2 Dr SE Cpe	2530	3795
4 Dr SE Sdn	2555	3830

OPTIONS FOR SUNBIRD

6 cyl 3.1 L Engine[Std on GT] +120
Auto 3-Speed Transmission +100
AM/FM Compact Disc Player +85
Air Conditioning +165
Aluminum/Alloy Wheels[Std on GT] +65
Cruise Control +45
Power Windows[Std on Conv] +55
Rear Spoiler[Std on GT] +45
Sunroof +70
Tilt Steering Wheel +30

TRANS SPORT 1993

GT model canceled. SE is only trim level. Leather seats and steering wheel controls for the radio have been added to the options sheet. Climate controls are bigger. Sunroof becomes optional midyear.

RATINGS (SCALE OF 1-10)

Overall	Safety	Reliability	Performance	Comfort	Value
6.9	5.6	6.1	7.2	7.1	8.3

Category G

	Trade-in	Market
2 Dr SE Pass. Van	4875	6505

OPTIONS FOR TRANS SPORT

6 cyl 3.8 L Engine +110
AM/FM Compact Disc Player +65
Air Conditioning +165
Aluminum/Alloy Wheels +65
Cruise Control +40
Dual Air Conditioning +185
Keyless Entry System +40
Leather Seats +155
Power Door Locks +45
Power Drivers Seat +55
Power Windows +50
Premium Sound System +70

1992 PONTIAC

BONNEVILLE 1992

Earns restyle that swaps stodgy, three-box design theme for flowing lines reminiscent of the Jaguar XJ6. LE trim level dies. 3.8-liter V6 gets five additional horsepower. SSEi has a supercharged V6 worth 205 horsepower and standard traction control. Traction control is optional on other Bonnevilles. ABS is standard on SSE and SSEi; optional on SE with Sport Appearance Package. A passenger airbag is standard on SSEi, optional on SSE. A heads-up display is standard on SSEi and optional on SSE.

RATINGS (SCALE OF 1-10)

Overall	Safety	Reliability	Performance	Comfort	Value
7.4	6.6	6.3	8.2	7.8	7.9

Category B

	Trade-in	Market
4 Dr SE Sdn	3875	5115
4 Dr SSE Sdn	4765	6295
4 Dr SSE Sprchgd Sdn	4970	6565
4 Dr SSEi Sprchgd Sdn	5555	7330

OPTIONS FOR BONNEVILLE

Premium Equipment Pkg +150
Anti-Lock Brakes[Opt on SE] +110
Leather Seats +110
Power Drivers Seat[Opt on SE] +50
Power Moonroof +160
Power Sunroof +175

FIREBIRD 1992

Pontiac takes great pains to reduce the number of squeaks and rattles in the Firebird. Body has been stiffened for a tighter feel. Performance Equipment Group is available on Formula and Trans Am coupes, and boosts tuned-port 5.0-liter to 230 horsepower.

Category F

	Trade-in	Market
2 Dr Formula Cpe	5015	6305
2 Dr STD Conv	5970	7505

Don't forget to refer to the Mileage Adjustment Table at the back of this book!

Model Description	Trade-in Value	Market Value
2 Dr STD Cpe	3905	4910
2 Dr Trans Am Conv	6920	8700
2 Dr Trans Am Cpe	5590	7025
2 Dr Trans Am GTA Cpe	7340	9230

OPTIONS FOR FIREBIRD

8 cyl 5.0 L Engine[Opt on STD] +60
8 cyl 5.0 L TPI Engine[Opt on Formula] +120
8 cyl 5.7 L Engine[Std on Trans Am GTA] +75
Auto 4-Speed Transmission +85
AM/FM Compact Disc Player +75
Air Conditioning[Opt on STD] +135
Glass Panel T-tops +160
Leather Seats +105
Limited Slip Diff[Opt on Formula, STD] +55
Power Door Locks[Std on Trans Am GTA] +35
Power Windows[Std on Trans Am GTA] +40

GRAND AM   1992

Redesign nets Grand Am swoopy look, standard ABS and optional V6 power. Car is now based on same platform as Chevy Corsica/Beretta. SE and GT models are available. Standard engine is a 120-horsepower SOHC engine. GT gets 180-horsepower Quad 4. Optional on both is a 3.3-liter V6. Hook an automatic to the Quad 4 engine and horsepower drops to 160.

RATINGS (SCALE OF 1-10)

Overall	Safety	Reliability	Performance	Comfort	Value
6.3	4.1	6.2	8.2	7.3	5.7

Category C

	Trade-in	Market
2 Dr GT Cpe	3050	4145
4 Dr GT Sdn	3075	4175
2 Dr SE Cpe	2665	3620
4 Dr SE Sdn	2685	3650

OPTIONS FOR GRAND AM

6 cyl 3.3 L Engine +90
Auto 3-Speed Transmission +90
AM/FM Compact Disc Player +55
Air Conditioning +135
Power Drivers Seat +50
Power Windows +50

GRAND PRIX   1992

All sedans get STE light-bar front styling treatment. Base 160-horsepower Quad 4 motor replaced by 140-horsepower 3.1-liter V6. GTP coupe still has 210-horsepower twin-cam V6 standard. ABS is standard on GT, GTP, and STE; optional on LE and SE. Base SE coupes can be dressed in GT lower-body extensions.

RATINGS (SCALE OF 1-10)

Overall	Safety	Reliability	Performance	Comfort	Value
7.1	5.4	7.2	8	7	8

Model Description	Trade-in Value	Market Value
Category C		
2 Dr GT Cpe	4090	5560
4 Dr LE Sdn	3190	4335
2 Dr SE Cpe	3295	4475
4 Dr SE Sdn	3460	4700
4 Dr STE Sdn	4345	5905

OPTIONS FOR GRAND PRIX

6 cyl 3.4 L Engine +160
Auto 4-Speed Transmission[Opt on LE, SE] +35
Aero Performance Pkg +355
Anti-Lock Brakes[Opt on LE, SE] +95
Leather Seats +100
Power Door Locks[Opt on LE, SE] +40
Power Drivers Seat[Std on STE] +50
Power Sunroof +110
Power Windows[Opt on LE, SE] +50

LE MANS   1992

LE designation swapped for SE nomenclature. Coupe gets amber turn signals.

Category E

	Trade-in	Market
2 Dr SE Cpe	1365	2360
4 Dr SE Sdn	1475	2545
2 Dr Value Leader Cpe	1260	2180

OPTIONS FOR LE MANS

Auto 3-Speed Transmission +75
Air Conditioning +135
Sunroof +55

SUNBIRD   1992

ABS is standard. LE designation extended to base coupe and sedan. 2.0-liter four-cylinder engine gets 15 more horsepower. Brake/transmission shift interlock is added. Fuel capacity jumps to 15.2 gallons. Automatic door locks lock doors when automatic is shifted from "Park" or manually shifted car begins moving forward. Convertible gets glass rear window at midyear.

RATINGS (SCALE OF 1-10)

Overall	Safety	Reliability	Performance	Comfort	Value
6	5.3	6.3	6.6	6.8	5.2

	Trade-in	Market
Category E		
2 Dr GT Cpe	2300	3965
2 Dr LE Cpe	1745	3010
4 Dr LE Sdn	1765	3040
2 Dr SE Conv	2745	4740
2 Dr SE Cpe	1875	3240
4 Dr SE Sdn	1895	3270

OPTIONS FOR SUNBIRD

6 cyl 3.1 L Engine[Opt on SE] +100
Auto 3-Speed Transmission +80
AM/FM Compact Disc Player +70
Air Conditioning +135

Don't forget to refer to the Mileage Adjustment Table at the back of this book!

PONTIAC 92-91

Model Description	Trade-in Value	Market Value	Model Description	Trade-in Value	Market Value

Power Windows[Std on Conv] +45
Sunroof +55

TRANS SPORT 1992

ABS is standard. SE becomes base model; new top-of-the-line is the GT. GT gets a standard 3.8-liter V6 good for 165 horsepower. SE retains old 3.1-liter, but offers the bigger motor as an option. 15-inch wheels replace 14-inch wheels on both models. Remote keyless entry and rear climate controls are added to the options list.

RATINGS (SCALE OF 1-10)

Overall	Safety	Reliability	Performance	Comfort	Value
6.9	5.7	6.2	7.2	7.1	8.2

Category G
2 Dr GT Pass. Van	4765	6475
2 Dr SE Pass. Van	4005	5445

OPTIONS FOR TRANS SPORT
6 cyl 3.8 L Engine[Opt on SE] +110
7 Passenger Seating +85
AM/FM Compact Disc Player +50
Air Conditioning[Opt on SE] +135
Auto Load Leveling[Opt on SE] +40
Dual Air Conditioning +150
Power Door Locks +40
Power Drivers Seat +45
Power Windows +40

1991 PONTIAC

6000 1991

No changes.
Category C
4 Dr LE Sdn	2055	3235
4 Dr LE Wgn	2620	4125
4 Dr SE Sdn	2880	4530

OPTIONS FOR 6000
6 cyl 3.1 L Engine[Std on SE,Wgn] +70
Auto 4-Speed Transmission[Std on SE,Wgn] +25
Air Conditioning[Std on SE,Wgn] +110
Power Door Locks[Opt on LE] +35
Power Drivers Seat +40
Power Windows[Opt on LE] +40

BONNEVILLE 1991

Brake/transmission shift interlock is added.
Category B
4 Dr LE Sdn	2725	4035
4 Dr SE Sdn	3145	4660
4 Dr SSE Sdn	3860	5720

OPTIONS FOR BONNEVILLE
Anti-Lock Brakes[Std on SSE] +90
Leather Seats +90
Power Door Locks[Opt on LE] +35

Power Drivers Seat[Opt on LE] +40
Power Moonroof +130
Power Windows[Opt on LE] +40

FIREBIRD 1991

Top level V8 engines get more horsepower. Front and rear styling is freshened. Rocker panel extensions are restyled. Base coupes get new Sport Appearance Package.
Category F
2 Dr Formula Cpe	4235	5460
2 Dr STD Conv	5200	6705
2 Dr STD Cpe	3695	4765
2 Dr Trans Am Conv	5820	7505
2 Dr Trans Am Cpe	4900	6320
2 Dr Trans Am GTA Cpe	6070	7830

OPTIONS FOR FIREBIRD
8 cyl 5.0 L Engine[Opt on STD] +45
8 cyl 5.7 L Engine[Std on Trans Am GTA] +65
Auto 4-Speed Transmission[Std on STD Conv] +70
AM/FM Compact Disc Player +60
Air Conditioning[Opt on STD] +110
Leather Seats +85
Limited Slip Diff[Opt on Formula,STD] +45
Power Door Locks[Std on Trans Am GTA] +25
Power Windows[Std on Trans Am GTA] +30
T-Tops (solid/Colored) +125

GRAND AM 1991

ABS is standard on SE. Larger, vented front rotors increase stopping ability on SE. LE with Sport Performance Package adds several SE goodies, like high-output Quad 4 engine, alloy wheels, exterior trim, and a revised suspension.
Category C
2 Dr LE Cpe	1730	2720
4 Dr LE Sdn	1945	3065
2 Dr SE Cpe	2590	4075
4 Dr SE Sdn	2620	4125
2 Dr STD Cpe	1775	2795
4 Dr STD Sdn	1805	2840

OPTIONS FOR GRAND AM
4 cyl 2.3 L Quad 4 Engine[Opt on LE] +90
Auto 3-Speed Transmission +70
Sport Performance Pkg +120
AM/FM Compact Disc Player +45
Air Conditioning[Std on SE] +110
Power Door Locks[Opt on LE] +35
Power Drivers Seat +40
Power Windows[Opt on LE] +40
Sunroof +50

GRAND PRIX 1991

LE and Turbo coupes dropped; GT coupe added. A twin-cam V6 with five-speed transmission is optional.

Don't forget to refer to the Mileage Adjustment Table at the back of this book!

Model Description	Trade-in Value	Market Value

RATINGS (SCALE OF 1-10)

Overall	Safety	Reliability	Performance	Comfort	Value
6.8	5.2	5.8	8	7	8.1

Category C

Model	Trade-in	Market
2 Dr GT Cpe	3190	5020
4 Dr LE Sdn	2400	3775
2 Dr SE Cpe	2495	3930
4 Dr SE Sdn	2560	4030
4 Dr STE Sdn	3145	4950

OPTIONS FOR GRAND PRIX

6 cyl 3.1 L Engine[Opt on LE,SE] +70
6 cyl 3.4 L Engine +125
Auto 4-Speed Transmission[Opt on LE,SE] +25
Aero Performance Pkg +310
Anti-Lock Brakes +80
Leather Seats +85
Power Door Locks[Opt on LE,SE] +35
Power Drivers Seat[Opt on LE,SE] +40
Power Sunroof +90
Power Windows[Opt on LE,SE] +40

LE MANS   1991

Sporty GSE dropped.

Category E

Model	Trade-in	Market
2 Dr LE Cpe	1160	2115
4 Dr LE Sdn	1220	2225
2 Dr Value Leader Cpe	1065	1940

OPTIONS FOR LE MANS

Auto 3-Speed Transmission +60
Air Conditioning +110
Power Steering +35
Sunroof +45

SUNBIRD   1991

Turbo engine dropped in favor of 3.1-liter V6. Six-cylinder makes 25 fewer horsepower than previous turbo. GT gets new alloys.

RATINGS (SCALE OF 1-10)

Overall	Safety	Reliability	Performance	Comfort	Value
5.9	4.4	6.6	6.6	6.8	5.2

Category E

Model	Trade-in	Market
2 Dr GT Cpe	2025	3690
2 Dr LE Conv	2310	4205
2 Dr LE Cpe	1595	2905
4 Dr LE Sdn	1610	2930
2 Dr SE Cpe	1410	2870
2 Dr STD Cpe	1485	2705
4 Dr STD Sdn	1500	2730

OPTIONS FOR SUNBIRD

6 cyl 3.1 L Engine[Std on GT] +90
Auto 3-Speed Transmission +60
AM/FM Compact Disc Player +55
Air Conditioning +110
Power Door Locks[Std on Conv] +35
Power Windows[Std on Conv] +35
Sunroof +45

TRANS SPORT   1991

No changes.

RATINGS (SCALE OF 1-10)

Overall	Safety	Reliability	Performance	Comfort	Value
6.6	4.8	6.5	6.8	7.1	7.7

Category G

Model	Trade-in	Market
2 Dr SE Pass. Van	4265	5865
2 Dr STD Pass. Van	3545	4875

OPTIONS FOR TRANS SPORT

7 Passenger Seating +70
Air Conditioning[Std on SE] +110
Power Door Locks +30
Power Drivers Seat +40
Power Windows +30

Don't forget to refer to the Mileage Adjustment Table at the back of this book!

PORSCHE 00-99

Model Description	Trade-in Value	Market Value	Model Description	Trade-in Value	Market Value

PORSCHE   Germany

1997 Porsche 911

AM/FM Compact Disc Player +320
Dual Power Seats +605
Metallic Paint +530

BOXSTER   2000

The big news for 2000 is the Boxster S. This more powerful version of the Boxster features a bigger engine that generates 250 horsepower. The regular Boxster (if you can call it that) also gets a horsepower boost in 2000, going from 201 to 217. Both models feature upgraded interior materials and new exterior colors.

Category J

	Trade-in	Market
2 Dr S Conv	42255	48275
2 Dr STD Conv	35170	40180

OPTIONS FOR BOXSTER

Auto Manual Transmission +2625
18 In. Sport Classic Whls +3410
Boxster Design Wheels +1100
Digital Sound Processing +960
Dyno Wheels +1900
F & R Aerokit Spoilers +5090
GPS Navigation System +2895
Leather Seat/Interior Trm +1625
Litronic Headlamps +875
Power Seats With Memory +1240
Special Leather Seat Trim +1935
Sport Classic Wheels +2035
Sport Design Radial Whls +3410
Sport Handling Pkg +1675
Technic Sport Pkg +1120
Turbo Look Alloy Wheels +2235
AM/FM Compact Disc Player +320
Cruise Control +400
Headlight Washers +195
Rear Wind Deflector +295
Roll/Light Bar +435
Traction Control System +955

2000 PORSCHE

911   2000

A new exhaust system bumps horsepower from 296 to 300. Already featured on Carrera 4 models, two-wheel-drive Carreras now get an electronic drive-by-wire throttle and optional PSM stability control. All models receive an upgraded interior console and materials. The formerly optional charcoal odor filter is now standard. There are two new standard and one new optional exterior colors.

Category J

	Trade-in	Market
2 Dr Carrera Conv	63130	72120
2 Dr Carrera Cpe	55310	63185
2 Dr Carrera 4 AWD Conv	67655	77290
2 Dr Carrera 4 AWD Cpe	59835	68360

OPTIONS FOR 911

Auto Manual Transmission +2795
Alloy Instrument Dials +745
Aluminum & Chrome Pkg +1590
Carbon Door Sill Insignia +625
Carbon/Alloy Brake/Shiftr +705
Carbon/Lthr Steer Wheel +1440
Digital Sound Radio +960
Front & Rear Aero Kit +6515
Full Leather Interior +2630
Leather Dashboard Pkg +2385
Leather Interior Trim +2630
Litronic Headlamps +875
PCM Info/Navigation Systm +2895
Painted Instrument Dials +625
Special Interior Trim +2985
Sport Classic Wheels +2175
Sport Design Radial Whls +2175
Turbo Look Alloy Wheels +975

1999 PORSCHE

911   1999

Everything just got better with the totally redesigned 911, internally named the 996. The 911 Coupe, Cabriolet and Carrera 4 (available as either a coupe or cabrio) are all available for the 1999 model year.

RATINGS (SCALE OF 1-10)

Overall	Safety	Reliability	Performance	Comfort	Value
N/A	N/A	N/A	9	7	N/A

Category J

	Trade-in	Market
2 Dr Carrera Conv	59240	67780
2 Dr Carrera Cpe	51810	59285
2 Dr Carrera 4 4WD Conv	63535	72700
2 Dr Carrera 4 4WD Cpe	56105	64195

Don't forget to refer to the Mileage Adjustment Table at the back of this book!

Model Description	Trade-in Value	Market Value

OPTIONS FOR 911

Auto Manual Transmission +2285
Aluminum & Chrome Pkg +1295
Carbon Door Sill Insignia +510
Carbon/Alum. Brake Shiftr +590
Carbon/Leather Door Grip +765
Carbon/Lthr Steer Wheel +1110
Digital Sound Radio +785
F&R Aero Spoilers Kit +4710
Front & Rear Aero Kit +5325
Leather Dashboard Pkg +1950
Leather Interior Trim +2150
Litronic Headlamps +715
PCM Info/Navigation Systm +2365
Rear Carbon Console +1065
Rear Window Washer +720
Rootwood Steering Wheel +1240
Sport Classic Wheels +1700
Sport Design Radial Whls +1775
Targa Wheels +620
Technology Alloy Wheels +1190
Turbo Look Alloy Wheels +795
AM/FM Compact Disc Player +260
Compact Disc Changer +625
Dual Power Seats +495
Hardtop Roof +2105
Heated Front Seats +290
Limited Slip Diff[Opt on Carrera] +620
Onboard Computer +290
Premium Sound System +860
Special Factory Paint +1180
Traction Control System[Opt on Carrera] +780

BOXSTER   1999

The Boxster is slowly adding features and options. This year, a Classic Package includes metallic paint and all-leather seats, and adds special highlights to the interior. The gas tank is increased from a 12.5- to a 14.1- gallon capacity, and gas-discharge Litronic headlights are optional. All the features in the Sport Package are individually optional this year, and 18-inch wheels are now available.

RATINGS (SCALE OF 1-10)

Overall	Safety	Reliability	Performance	Comfort	Value
N/A	N/A	N/A	9.2	7.8	N/A

Category J
2 Dr STD Conv   32890   37635

OPTIONS FOR BOXSTER

Auto Manual Transmission +2145
Boxster Design Wheels +990
Leather Seat/Interior Trm +1330
Light Alloy Turbo Wheels +1825
Special Leather Seat Trim +1585
Sport Classic Wheels +1665
Sport Design Wheels +2785
Sport Handling Pkg +1370

Technic Sport Pkg +915
AM/FM Compact Disc Player +260
Compact Disc Changer +625
Cruise Control +325
Heated Front Seats +290
Onboard Computer +290

1998 PORSCHE

911   1998

The current-generation 911 goes the way of the dodo at year's end, when it will be replaced by the next evolutionary step toward the perfect driving machine.
Category J

	Trade-in	Market
2 Dr Carrera Conv	57185	65230
2 Dr Carrera 4WD Conv	58970	67640
2 Dr Carrera 4S 4WD Cpe	54985	63070
2 Dr Carrera S Cpe	48090	55160
2 Dr Targa Cpe	53305	61145

OPTIONS FOR 911

5-Spoke Cast Alloy Wheels +790
Aero Kit +3850
Digital Sound Radio Equip +1135
F&R Aero Spoilers Kit +3605
Hi-Fi Sound Radio Equip. +510
Leather Door Panels +1035
Leather Interior Trim +2180
Leather/Vinyl Inter. Trim +845
Litronic Headlamps +840
Rear Window Washer +590
Rootwood Steering Wheel +1015
Special Chassis +875
Special Leather Int. Trim +2560
Sport Chassis W/18" Whls +1340
Sport Classic Wheels +1115
Targa Wheels +770
Technology Alloy Wheels +1370
Technology Pressure Whls. +975
Wood Dash +3555
AM/FM Compact Disc Player +215
Compact Disc Changer +515
Dual Power Seats +405
Hardtop Roof[Opt on Cabriolet] +1720
Heated Front Seats +235
Leather Seats +685
Limited Slip Diff[Std on Carrera 4S, 4WD] +505
Onboard Computer +240
Premium Sound System +705
Special Factory Paint +965
Traction Control System[Opt on 2WD] +635

BOXSTER   1998

Side air bags are standard for 1998.
Category J
2 Dr STD Conv   31130   35710

Don't forget to refer to the Mileage Adjustment Table at the back of this book!

Model Description	Trade-in Value	Market Value

OPTIONS FOR BOXSTER

Boxster Design Wheels +810
Leather Seat/Interior Trm +1085
Special Leather Seat Trim +1295
Sport Classic Wheels +1360
Sport Handling Pkg +1095
Technic Sport Pkg +660
AM/FM Compact Disc Player +215
Compact Disc Changer +515
Cruise Control +265
Heated Front Seats +235
Onboard Computer +240

1997 PORSCHE

911   1997

The only change to this year's Porsche 911 is the availability of a Porsche-engineered child seat that will deactivate the passenger airbag when it is in place.
Category J

Model Description	Trade-in Value	Market Value
2 Dr Carrera Conv	54570	62540
2 Dr Carrera 4WD Conv	56680	65235
2 Dr Carrera Cpe	48195	55235
2 Dr Carrera 4S 4WD Cpe	54570	62540
2 Dr Targa Cpe	51275	59005
2 Dr Turbo 4WD Cpe	78240	89670
2 Dr Turbo S 4WD Cpe	111530	127825

OPTIONS FOR 911

17 Inch Cup Design Wheels +645
17 Inch Targa Wheels +1060
5 Spoke Light Alloy Whls +615
Aero Kit +3140
Aluminum/Chrome Pkg +925
Carbon/Alloy Brake and Shifter +370
Carbon/Lth Steering Wheel +705
Digital Sound Radio +510
Hi-Fi Sound Radio +415
Leather Door Panels +845
Leather Headliner +695
Leather Interior Trim +1780
Leather Sun Visors +375
Pearlescent White Paint +5465
Technology Wheels +1440
Wood Dash +1945
AM/FM Compact Disc Player +175
Compact Disc Changer +420
Dual Power Seats[Std on Turbo, Turbo S] +330
Hardtop Roof +1405
Heated Front Seats[Std on Turbo, Turbo S] +195
Leather Seats[Std on Turbo, Turbo S] +560
Limited Slip Diff[Opt on Targa, 2WD] +415
Onboard Computer[Std on Turbo, Turbo S] +195

BOXSTER   1997

This all-new roadster is introduced to compete in the revitalized midpriced sports car category. The Boxster features a 2.5-liter six-cylinder engine, a five-speed manual or five-speed Tiptronic transmission, and a power top that closes in an impressive 12 seconds.
Category J

Model Description	Trade-in Value	Market Value
2 Dr STD Conv	28755	32960

OPTIONS FOR BOXSTER

Aerokit +2585
Boxster-design Wheels +600
Color Keyed Rear Spoiler +710
Leather Seat Trim +980
Rain Sensing Windshield +680
Special Leather Seat Trim +1165
Sport Classic Wheels +1220
Sport Handling Pkg +1480
Compact Disc Changer[Opt on STD] +420
Compact Disc W/fm/tape +320
Cruise Control +220
Hardtop Roof +1405
Heated Front Seats +195
Onboard Computer[Opt on STD] +195
Traction Control System +520

1996 PORSCHE

911   1996

Trick Targa model joins the lineup, and power is up in midrange revs. New Carrera 4S model provides Turbo looks without Turbo price or performance. Bigger wheels are standard across the line, as well as Litronic headlights. New stereos and exterior colors compliment one new interior color this year. Remote keyless entry system gets an immobilizer feature.
Category J

Model Description	Trade-in Value	Market Value
2 Dr Carrera Conv	49205	56390
2 Dr Carrera 4WD Conv	52775	60480
2 Dr Carrera Cpe	43505	49860
2 Dr Carrera 4WD Cpe	46600	53410
2 Dr Carrera 4S 4WD Cpe	49205	56390
2 Dr Turbo 4WD Cpe	70555	80860
2 Dr Targa Cpe	47700	54670

OPTIONS FOR 911

5 Spoke Light Alloy Whls +505
Color To Sample Leather +2240
Digital Sound System +395
Door Panel Pkg +645
Hi-fi Sound +340
Leather Door Panels +690
Pearl White Metallic Pnt. +3995
Pearlescent White Paint +4470
Seat Pkg +665
Steering Wheel Pkg +440
Technology Wheels +650
Wood Dash +1590
AM/FM Compact Disc Player +145
Compact Disc Changer +345

Model Description	Trade-in Value	Market Value	Model Description	Trade-in Value	Market Value

Dual Power Seats[Std on STD] +270
Heated Front Seats +160
Leather Seats[Std on Turbo] +460
Limited Slip Diff[Opt on 2WD] +340
Onboard Computer +160
Premium Sound System +470

1995 PORSCHE

911 — 1995

Category J

Model	Trade-in	Market
2 Dr Carrera Conv	40500	46635
2 Dr Carrera 4WD Conv	44025	50695
2 Dr Carrera Cpe	36160	41640
2 Dr Carrera 4WD Cpe	39740	45765

OPTIONS FOR 911

5 Spoke Light Alloy Whls +410
Active Brake Differential +270
Color To Sample Paint +745
Digital Sound Radio Equip +620
Door Panel Pkg +565
Hi-fi Sound W/amplifier +275
LT Rootwood Door Trim Pnl +435
Leather Door Panels +565
Leather Headliner +585
Light Rootwood Dashboard +1300
Pearlescent White Paint +3650
Pressure Cast Alloy Whls +410
Seat Pkg +520
Steering Wheel Pkg +360
Telephone Handset Kit +285
Wood Dash +1300
AM/FM Compact Disc Player +115
Compact Disc Changer +280
Dual Power Seats +220
Heated Front Seats +130
Leather Seats +375
Limited Slip Diff[Opt on 2WD] +275
Onboard Computer +130
Rear Window Wiper +105

928 — 1995

Category J

Model	Trade-in	Market
2 Dr GTS Cpe	45775	52710

OPTIONS FOR 928

Door Pkg +710
Leather Seat Pkg +590
Pkg 1 +390
Pkg 2 +320
Pkg 3 +585
Pkg 4 +325

968 — 1995

Category J

Model	Trade-in	Market
2 Dr STD Conv	27325	31465
2 Dr STD Cpe	21120	24320

OPTIONS FOR 968

17 Inch 5-Spoke Wheels +410
Compact Disc Changer +280
Compact Disc W/fm/tape +215
Heated Front Seats +130
Leather Seats +375
Limited Slip Diff +275
Power Drivers Seat +105
Power Passenger Seat +105

1994 PORSCHE

911 — 1994

Porsche modernizes the 911, updating and improving the car without killing its character. A more aerodynamic body and various tweaks to the engine and suspension make this old favorite even better.

Category J

Model	Trade-in	Market
2 Dr America Roadster Conv	49525	57090
2 Dr Cabriolet Conv	40325	46490
2 Dr Carrera Cpe	35375	40780
2 Dr Carrera Turbo Cpe	53680	61885
2 Dr Carrera 4WD Cpe	42635	49145
2 Dr RS America Cpe	30355	34995
2 Dr Speedster Conv	36135	41655
2 Dr Targa Cpe	36240	41780
2 Dr Wide Body Cpe	36450	42020
2 Dr Wide Body 4WD Cpe	42620	49130

OPTIONS FOR 911

5-Spoke 17 Inch Wheels +335
5-spoke 17 Inch Wheels +335
Boot Cover +630
Leather Headliner +330
Rootwood Dashboard +1060
Special Leather Console +645
AM/FM Compact Disc Player +95
Air Conditioning[Std on Cabriolet,Carrera,Targa, Wide Body] +685
Climate Control for AC[Opt on RS America,Speedster] +70
Compact Disc Changer +230
Cruise Control[Opt on Speedster] +120
Hardtop Roof +765
Headlight Washers[Opt on Targa] +60
Heated Front Seats +105
Limited Slip Diff[Std on Turbo] +225
Onboard Computer[Std on Turbo] +105
Power Drivers Seat +85
Power Passenger Seat +85
Power Sunroof[Opt on RS America] +275
Rear Window Wiper[Std on Turbo] +85

911S — 1994

Category J

Model	Trade-in	Market
2 Dr STD Turbo Cpe	58515	67455

Model Description	Trade-in Value	Market Value
928		**1994**
Category J		
2 Dr GTS Cpe	33200	38270

OPTIONS FOR 928
Leather Door Pkg +580
Leather Seat Pkg +480
Pkg 1 +320
Pkg 2 +260
Pkg 3 +480
Pkg 4 +265

968		**1994**
Category J		
2 Dr Cabriolet Conv	24555	28310
2 Dr STD Cpe	18980	21880

OPTIONS FOR 968
5-Spoke 17-Inch Wheels +335
Leather Boot Cover +630
Rootwood Pkg +585
Sport Chassis +490
AM/FM Compact Disc Player +95
Compact Disc Changer +230
Heated Front Seats +105
Leather Seats +305
Limited Slip Diff +225
Power Drivers Seat +85
Power Passenger Seat +85
Premium Sound System +315

1993 PORSCHE

Model Description	Trade-in Value	Market Value
911		**1993**
Category J		
2 Dr America Roadster Conv	38070	43900
2 Dr Cabriolet Conv	31645	36490
2 Dr Cabriolet 4WD Conv	36760	42390
2 Dr Carrera Cpe	27775	32030
2 Dr Carrera 4WD Cpe	32870	37905
2 Dr RS America Cpe	24480	28230
2 Dr Targa Cpe	28455	32810
2 Dr Targa 4WD Cpe	33550	38690

OPTIONS FOR 911
Leather Interior Trim +465
AM/FM Compact Disc Player +80
Air Conditioning[Std on Cabriolet Conv, Carrera 4WD Cpe] +560
Climate Control for AC[Opt on RS America] +55
Compact Disc Changer +185
Dual Power Seats +150
Hardtop Roof +625
Headlight Washers[Opt on Carrera] +45
Heated Front Seats +85
Leather Seats[Opt on Cabriolet] +250
Limited Slip Diff +185

Onboard Computer +85
Power Sunroof[Std on Carrera] +225

928		**1993**
Category J		
2 Dr GTS Cpe	30155	34775

OPTIONS FOR 928
AM/FM Stereo Tape +195

968		**1993**
Category J		
2 Dr STD Conv	19680	22695
2 Dr STD Cpe	14405	16610

OPTIONS FOR 968
5-Spoke 17-Inch Wheels +275
968 Special Chassis +400
Leather Piping All Seats +290
Lthr Interior W/Blck Belt +1095
Lthr Interior W/Lthr Belt +690
Metallic Paint To Sample +340
Painted Rims +215
Special Leather Upholstry +775
Compact Disc Changer +185
Heated Front Seats +85
Leather Seats +250
Limited Slip Diff +185
Sport Seats +145

1992 PORSCHE

Model Description	Trade-in Value	Market Value
911		**1992**
Category J		
2 Dr America Roadster Conv	29435	34155
2 Dr Cabriolet Conv	24450	28375
2 Dr Carrera Cpe	21460	24905
2 Dr Carrera 4 4WD Conv	28395	32955
2 Dr Carrera 4 4WD Cpe	25405	29485
2 Dr Carrera 4 Targa 4WD Cpe	25940	30100
2 Dr STD Turbo Cpe	33080	38390
2 Dr Targa Cpe	21990	25520

OPTIONS FOR 911
Lthr Instrument Housing +140
Rear Window Washing Systm +130
Special Leather Seat Trim +640
AM/FM Compact Disc Player +65
Compact Disc Changer +155
Dual Power Seats[Std on STD] +120
Hardtop Roof +515
Leather Seats[Opt on America Roadster] +205
Limited Slip Diff +150

968		**1992**

944 replacement arrives, sporting 928-inspired front end and the most powerful (naturally aspirated) 4-cylinder engine available anywhere.

Don't forget to refer to the Mileage Adjustment Table at the back of this book!

PORSCHE 92-91

Model Description	Trade-in Value	Market Value
Category J		
2 Dr Cabriolet Conv	16685	19365
2 Dr STD Cpe	13090	15190

OPTIONS FOR 968
AM/FM Compact Disc Player +65
Compact Disc Changer +155
Leather Seats +205
Limited Slip Diff +150
Power Drivers Seat +60
Power Passenger Seat +55

1991 PORSCHE

911   1991

Model Description	Trade-in Value	Market Value
Category J		
2 Dr Carrera Cpe	18525	21420
2 Dr Carrera 4 4WD Cpe	21930	25365
2 Dr Carrera 4 Cabrio 4WD Conv	30240	34975
2 Dr Carrera 4 Targa 4WD Cpe	22385	25890
2 Dr Carrera Cabrio Conv	26555	30710
2 Dr Carrera Targa Cpe	23395	27060
2 Dr STD Turbo Cpe	28870	33390

OPTIONS FOR 911
All Leather Interior +1285
Car Color Rims +130
Forged Alloy Wheels +215
Leather Boot Cover +300

Leather Headliner +135
Leather Instr Panel +180
AM/FM Compact Disc Player +50
Compact Disc W/fm/tape +95
Leather Seats[Std on STD] +165
Limited Slip Diff +125
Power Drivers Seat[Std on STD] +45
Power Passenger Seat[Std on STD] +45

928   1991

Model Description	Trade-in Value	Market Value
Category J		
2 Dr STD Cpe	25005	28920

OPTIONS FOR 928
All Leather Interior +1285
Passenger Memory Seat +135
Pwr Lumbar Supports +145

944 S2   1991

Model Description	Trade-in Value	Market Value
Category F		
2 Dr Cabriolet Conv	15385	18215
2 Dr STD Cpe	13275	15715

OPTIONS FOR 944 S2
16-Inch Disc Wheels +265
Sport Chassis +265
AM/FM Compact Disc Player +60
Dual Power Seats +110
Leather Seats +85
Limited Slip Diff +45

Don't forget to refer to the Mileage Adjustment Table at the back of this book!

SAAB 00-99

Model Description	Trade-in Value	Market Value	Model Description	Trade-in Value	Market Value

SAAB   Sweden

1997 Saab 900 Convertible

and traction-control system (TCS) have been added to the standard equipment list.

Category J

	Trade-in	Market
4 Dr 2.3t Turbo Sdn	25775	29740
4 Dr 2.3t Turbo Wgn	25775	29740
4 Dr Aero Turbo Sdn	31175	35965
4 Dr Aero Turbo Wgn	31175	35965
4 Dr Gary Fisher ED. Turbo Wgn	28740	33160
4 Dr SE V6t Turbo Sdn	29625	34180
4 Dr SE V6t Turbo Wgn	29625	34180

OPTIONS FOR 9-5
Auto 4-Speed Transmission[Std on SE V6t] +980
BBS Wheel Upgrade +1350
OnStar Telematic System +730
Ventilated Seats +785
Wheel And Tire Pkg +1595

2000 SAAB

9-3   2000

The base model gets restyled 15-inch alloy wheels, while the SE version gains performance enhancements and increased horsepower. The sporty 9-3 Viggen offers even more power, and is available as a five-door or convertible in addition to the coupe. All engines are now LEV compliant and GM's OnStar "Telematics" System becomes optional across the model lineup.

Category J

	Trade-in	Market
2 Dr SE HO Turbo Conv	34155	39410
4 Dr SE HO Turbo Hbk	25525	29450
2 Dr STD Turbo Conv	31410	36240
2 Dr STD Turbo Hbk	20790	23990
4 Dr STD Turbo Hbk	21180	24435
2 Dr Viggen Turbo Conv	35515	40980
2 Dr Viggen Turbo Hbk	30060	34685
4 Dr Viggen Turbo Hbk	30060	34685

OPTIONS FOR 9-3
Auto 4-Speed Transmission +980
OnStar Telematic System +730
AM/FM Compact Disc Player +320
Power Moonroof[Opt on STD] +775

9-5   2000

Intended to do for the 9-5 line what the Viggen does for the 9-3, Saab debuts the high-performance 9-5 Aero Sedan and Wagon with 230 horsepower. Entry-level sedans and wagons sport new 16-inch 10-spoke alloy wheels, and all SE versions offer a turbo V6 and auto-dimming rearview mirror. The 9-5 Wagon Gary Fisher Edition offers a sportier exterior design and a Saab Limited Edition Gary Fisher mountain bike. A sunroof

1999 SAAB

9-3   1999

Saab changed about 1,000 suspension, steering and interior pieces on the 900 and decided to change the car's name to the 9-3, giving it a mild exterior freshening to boot. Around mid-year, a high-output version of its 2.0-liter turbo four-cylinder (making an amazing 200 horsepower) becomes the standard engine in the uplevel SE five-door and SE Convertible models equipped with a manual transmission. All SE's also get new five-speed 16-inch alloy wheels. All five-speed manual 9-3s get revised gearbox ratios and a numerically higher (4.05:1) final drive ratio for better off-the-line feel. A revised 9-3 interior headliner provides more padding for increased protection in the event of a crash. And five-door SE variants add an integrated driver-seat armrest and a centrally located cupholder that swings out from the instrument panel.

RATINGS (SCALE OF 1-10)

Overall	Safety	Reliability	Performance	Comfort	Value
N/A	8.1	8.7	8	7.8	N/A

Category J

	Trade-in	Market
2 Dr SE Turbo Conv	28875	33490
4 Dr SE Turbo Hbk	22010	25525
2 Dr SE HO Turbo Conv	29920	34700
4 Dr SE HO Turbo Hbk	22165	25705
2 Dr STD Turbo Conv	25460	29525
2 Dr STD Turbo Hbk	17890	20745
4 Dr STD Turbo Hbk	18235	21145
2 Dr Viggen Turbo Hbk	26320	30520

OPTIONS FOR 9-3
Auto 4-Speed Transmission +680
Styling Value Pkg +1645

Don't forget to refer to the Mileage Adjustment Table at the back of this book!

Model Description	Trade-in Value	Market Value	Model Description	Trade-in Value	Market Value

Compact Disc Changer +625
Heated Front Seats +290
Leather Seats[Std on SE, SE HO, Viggen, Conv] +840
Power Moonroof[Opt on STD] +635

9-5 — 1999

Saab's 9-5 model replaces the 9000 line for 1999. Available as a sedan or a station wagon with turbocharged four-cylinder or V6 engines, the new 9-5 is designed to showcase three Saab "world-first" technologies: an active head-restraint system, ventilated seats, and an "asymmetrically turbocharged" V6. Saab has added two-stage head- and chest-protecting side airbags and its new force-reducing front seatbelt pre-tensioners as standard equipment. Also available on all 9-5 models is GM's dealer-installed OnStar mobile communications system.

RATINGS (SCALE OF 1-10)

Overall	Safety	Reliability	Performance	Comfort	Value
N/A	N/A	8.8	7.8	8.3	N/A

Category J

	Trade-in	Market
4 Dr SE V6 Turbo Sdn	25170	29190
4 Dr SE Turbo Sdn	23305	27025
4 Dr STD Turbo Sdn	20590	23875
4 Dr STD Turbo Wgn	21840	25325
4 Dr V6 Turbo Wgn	25240	29270

OPTIONS FOR 9-5
Auto 4-Speed Transmission[Std on SE V6, V6 Turbo Wagon] +720
Power Ventilated Seats +595
Styling Value Pkg +1550
Heated Seats +335
Leather Seats[Opt on STD, STD Turbo Wagon] +840
Power Moonroof[Opt on STD] +635

1998 SAAB

900 — 1998

The Saab 900 three-door hatchback gets the same turbocharged engine as the SE models this year. Other changes include the addition of body-color front and rear bumpers.

RATINGS (SCALE OF 1-10)

Overall	Safety	Reliability	Performance	Comfort	Value
7.4	7	7.7	8.6	7.9	6

Category J

	Trade-in	Market
2 Dr S Conv	21555	25140
4 Dr S Hbk	16045	18720
2 Dr S Turbo Hbk	14615	17045
2 Dr SE Turbo Conv	24170	28190
2 Dr SE Turbo Hbk	18405	21465
4 Dr SE Turbo Hbk	18985	22150

OPTIONS FOR 900
Auto 4-Speed Transmission +555
Leather Seats[Std on SE, Conv] +685
Power Moonroof[Opt on S] +520

9000 — 1998

No changes to the aging 9000.

RATINGS (SCALE OF 1-10)

Overall	Safety	Reliability	Performance	Comfort	Value
7.8	7.4	8.5	8.8	8.4	6.1

Category J

	Trade-in	Market
4 Dr CSE Turbo Hbk	22830	26630

OPTIONS FOR 9000
Auto 4-Speed Transmission +570

1997 SAAB

900 — 1997

No changes to this aging model.

RATINGS (SCALE OF 1-10)

Overall	Safety	Reliability	Performance	Comfort	Value
7.5	6.9	7	8.6	7.9	7.1

Category J

	Trade-in	Market
2 Dr S Conv	18865	22100
2 Dr S Hbk	13550	15870
4 Dr S Hbk	14070	16480
2 Dr SE Turbo Conv	21235	24875
2 Dr SE Turbo Hbk	16155	18925
4 Dr SE Turbo Hbk	16675	19535
2 Dr SE Talladega Turbo Conv	21500	25185
2 Dr SE Talladega Turbo Hbk	16430	19245
4 Dr SE Talladega Turbo Hbk	16950	19855
2 Dr SE V6 Conv	21995	25760
4 Dr SE V6 Hbk	17465	20455

OPTIONS FOR 900
Auto 4-Speed Transmission[Std on SE V6] +450
Child Seats (2) +115
Leather Seats[Opt on S Hbk] +560
Power Moonroof[Opt on S] +425

9000 — 1997

No changes to this aging model.

RATINGS (SCALE OF 1-10)

Overall	Safety	Reliability	Performance	Comfort	Value
7.7	7.4	8	8.8	8.4	6.1

Category J

	Trade-in	Market
4 Dr Aero Turbo Hbk	20445	23950
4 Dr CS Turbo Hbk	16175	18945
4 Dr CSE Turbo Hbk	19435	22765

Don't forget to refer to the Mileage Adjustment Table at the back of this book!

Model Description	Trade-in Value	Market Value
4 Dr CSE Anniversary Turbo Hbk	19840	23235
4 Dr CSE V6 Hbk	19965	23380

OPTIONS FOR 9000

Auto 4-Speed Transmission[Std on CSE V6] +465
Dual Power Seats[Opt on CS] +330
Leather Seats[Opt on CS] +560
Power Moonroof[Opt on CS] +425

1996 SAAB

900   1996

The popular Saab 900 SE five-door is available this year with the amazing turbocharged four-cylinder engine. An automatic transmission is now optional on turbos. V6 models come only with an automatic. Adjustable driver's lumbar support is now standard on all 900 models.

RATINGS (SCALE OF 1-10)

Overall	Safety	Reliability	Performance	Comfort	Value
7.3	6.9	6.7	8.6	7.9	6.5

Category J

	Trade-in	Market
2 Dr S Conv	15450	18220
2 Dr S Hbk	10970	12935
4 Dr S Hbk	11285	13305
2 Dr SE Turbo Conv	17500	20635
2 Dr SE Turbo Hbk	13210	15580
4 Dr SE Turbo Hbk	13670	16120
2 Dr SE V6 Conv	18580	21910
4 Dr SE V6 Hbk	14195	16740

OPTIONS FOR 900

Auto 4-Speed Transmission[Opt on S,SE] +365
Child Seats (2) +90
Leather Seats[Std on SE,SE V6,Conv] +460
Power Moonroof[Opt on S] +345

9000   1996

The 9000 sedans are dropped, leaving only the hatchback bodystyle. Cupholders for rear seat passengers, new upholstery for the CS, and new three-spoke alloy wheels for the CS and CSE round out the major developments for this year's model.

RATINGS (SCALE OF 1-10)

Overall	Safety	Reliability	Performance	Comfort	Value
7.9	7.5	8.2	8.8	8.4	6.7

Category J

	Trade-in	Market
4 Dr Aero Turbo Hbk	17235	20325
4 Dr CS Turbo Hbk	13745	16210
4 Dr CSE Turbo Hbk	16460	19415
4 Dr CSE V6 Hbk	16820	19840

OPTIONS FOR 9000

Auto 4-Speed Transmission[Opt on CS,CSE] +380
Dual Power Seats[Opt on CS] +270
Leather Seats[Opt on CS] +460
Power Moonroof[Opt on CS] +345

1995 SAAB

900   1995

Saab adds a light-pressure turbo and a V6 to their large-car engine roster. V6 cars come only with an automatic transmission. Daytime running lights (DRLs) become standard on all 9000s this year.

RATINGS (SCALE OF 1-10)

Overall	Safety	Reliability	Performance	Comfort	Value
6.7	7.3	5.7	8.6	7.9	4.1

Category J

	Trade-in	Market
2 Dr S Conv	13035	15455
2 Dr S Hbk	9415	11160
4 Dr S Hbk	9290	11010
2 Dr SE Conv	15135	17940
2 Dr SE Turbo Conv	14930	17700
2 Dr SE Turbo Hbk	11475	13605
4 Dr SE Hbk	11355	13460

OPTIONS FOR 900

Auto 4-Speed Transmission +295
AM/FM Compact Disc Player +115
Aluminum/Alloy Wheels[Std on SE,Conv] +115
Compact Disc Changer[Opt on Hbk] +280
Leather Seats[Std on SE,Conv] +375
Power Moonroof[Opt on S] +285

9000   1995

Saab adds a light-pressure turbo and a V6 to their large-car engine roster. V6 cars come only with an automatic transmission. Daytime running lights (DRLs) become standard on all 9000s this year.

RATINGS (SCALE OF 1-10)

Overall	Safety	Reliability	Performance	Comfort	Value
8	8.2	8	8.8	8.4	6.7

Category J

	Trade-in	Market
4 Dr Aero Turbo Hbk	14535	17230
4 Dr CDE Sdn	13730	16280
4 Dr CS Turbo Hbk	11115	13175
4 Dr CSE Hbk	13610	16135
4 Dr CSE Turbo Hbk	13560	16075

OPTIONS FOR 9000

Auto 4-Speed Transmission[Opt on Aero,CS,Turbo] +310
Leather Seats[Opt on CS] +375
Power Moonroof[Opt on CS] +285

Don't forget to refer to the Mileage Adjustment Table at the back of this book!

SAAB 94-93

Model Description	Trade-in Value	Market Value	Model Description	Trade-in Value	Market Value

1994 SAAB

900 — 1994

Dual airbags for the 9000! CS models get front and rear fog lights. Unfortunately, traction control is dropped for all models.

RATINGS (SCALE OF 1-10)

Overall	Safety	Reliability	Performance	Comfort	Value
6.5	7.1	5.1	8.6	7.9	3.6

Category J

	Trade-in	Market
2 Dr Commemorative Turbo Conv	13130	15810
2 Dr S Conv	11425	13755
2 Dr S Hbk	7930	9550
4 Dr S Hbk	7825	9425
2 Dr SE Turbo Hbk	9670	11645
4 Dr SE Hbk	9570	11525
2 Dr STD Turbo Conv	12485	15035

OPTIONS FOR 900

6 cyl 2.5 L Engine[Opt on S] +560
Auto 3-Speed Transmission +170
Auto 4-Speed Transmission +220
Aluminum/Alloy Wheels[Opt on S Hbk] +95
Child Seats (2) +60
Compact Disc W/fm/tape[Opt on S] +175
Leather Seats[Opt on S] +305
Power Drivers Seat[Opt on S Hbk, SE Hbk] +85
Power Moonroof[Opt on S] +230
Power Passenger Seat[Opt on SE Hbk, S Hbk] +85
Power Sunroof +275
Traction Control System[Opt on S] +285

9000 — 1994

Dual airbags for the 9000! CS models get front and rear fog lights. Unfortunately, traction control is dropped for all models.

RATINGS (SCALE OF 1-10)

Overall	Safety	Reliability	Performance	Comfort	Value
7.6	7.9	6.6	8.8	8.4	6.1

Category J

	Trade-in	Market
4 Dr Aero Turbo Hbk	12065	14530
4 Dr CD Turbo Sdn	10240	12335
4 Dr CDE Sdn	10835	13045
4 Dr CDE Turbo Sdn	12550	15115
4 Dr CS Hbk	9860	11875
4 Dr CS Turbo Hbk	10540	12690
4 Dr CSE Hbk	10950	13190
4 Dr CSE Turbo Hbk	11950	14390

OPTIONS FOR 9000

Auto 4-Speed Transmission +230
Compact Disc W/fm/tape +175
Leather Seats[Opt on CD, CS] +305
Power Moonroof[Opt on CD] +230
Rear Spoiler[Opt on CSE] +95
Traction Control System +285

1993 SAAB

900 — 1993

New nomenclature reflects Saab's current identity crisis. Base models are now called the CS and CD; luxury models are called CSE and CDE. Hatchbacks get more sedan-like styling that increases their length by four inches. A new Aero hatchback enters the lineup. The Aero is the fastest vehicle in the large-car class. It is powered by a 225-horsepower version of the inline-four found in the other turbo models, and it offers exceptional handling.

RATINGS (SCALE OF 1-10)

Overall	Safety	Reliability	Performance	Comfort	Value
N/A	N/A	7.7	8.4	7.5	4.1

Category J

	Trade-in	Market
2 Dr Commemorative Turbo Hbk	9045	11020
2 Dr S Conv	8795	10720
2 Dr S Hbk	5975	7280
4 Dr S Sdn	5855	7130
2 Dr S Luxury Hbk	6625	8070
4 Dr S Luxury Sdn	6850	8345
2 Dr STD Turbo Conv	9695	11810
2 Dr STD Turbo Hbk	8360	10185

OPTIONS FOR 900

Auto 3-Speed Transmission +135

9000 — 1993

New nomenclature reflects Saab's current identity crisis. Base models are now called the CS and CD; luxury models are called CSE and CDE. Hatchbacks get more sedan-like styling that increases their length by four inches. A new Aero hatchback enters the lineup. The Aero is the fastest vehicle in the large-car class. It is powered by a 225-horsepower version of the inline-four found in the other turbo models, and it offers exceptional handling.

RATINGS (SCALE OF 1-10)

Overall	Safety	Reliability	Performance	Comfort	Value
7.6	6.4	6.4	8.8	8.4	8

Category J

	Trade-in	Market
4 Dr Aero Turbo Hbk	9905	12145
4 Dr CD Sdn	7305	8955
4 Dr CD Turbo Sdn	8415	10315
4 Dr CDE Sdn	8980	11010
4 Dr CDE Turbo Sdn	10095	12375
4 Dr CS Hbk	7560	9270

Don't forget to refer to the Mileage Adjustment Table at the back of this book!

Model Description	Trade-in Value	Market Value
4 Dr CS Turbo Hbk	8670	10630
4 Dr CSE Hbk	9050	11090
4 Dr CSE Turbo Hbk	9355	11465

OPTIONS FOR 9000
Auto 4-Speed Transmission[Std on CD Sdn] +185
Leather Seats[Opt on CD,CS] +250
Power Sunroof[Opt on CD,CS] +225

1992 SAAB

900 — 1992

A limited-edition Griffin Edition is introduced as the *crhme de la crhme* 9000 for 1992. It is available only as a four-door turbo sedan. All turbo models get traction control for 1992. All Saab 9000s get a sunroof as well.

RATINGS (SCALE OF 1-10)

Overall	Safety	Reliability	Performance	Comfort	Value
N/A	N/A	7.7	8.4	7.5	3.6

Category J

	Trade-in	Market
2 Dr S Conv	6530	8330
2 Dr S Hbk	5015	6400
4 Dr S Sdn	5140	6560
2 Dr STD Turbo Conv	6880	8780
2 Dr STD Hbk	4485	5720
2 Dr STD Turbo Hbk	6120	7805
4 Dr STD Sdn	4300	5485

OPTIONS FOR 900
Auto 3-Speed Transmission +110
Auto 4-Speed Transmission +110

9000 — 1992

A limited-edition Griffin Edition is introduced as the *crhme de la crhme* 9000 for 1992. It is available only as a four-door turbo sedan. All turbo models get traction control for 1992. All Saab 9000s get a sunroof as well.

RATINGS (SCALE OF 1-10)

Overall	Safety	Reliability	Performance	Comfort	Value
7.3	6.5	6.6	8.8	8.4	6.4

Category J

	Trade-in	Market
4 Dr CD Sdn	6495	8285
4 Dr CD Turbo Sdn	7205	9190
4 Dr CD Griffin Turbo Sdn	8655	10930
4 Dr S Hbk	6050	7715
4 Dr STD Hbk	5360	6835
4 Dr STD Turbo Hbk	7080	9030

OPTIONS FOR 9000
Auto 4-Speed Transmission[Std on CD] +145

1991 SAAB

900 — 1991

Turbo CD Sedan is introduced.

RATINGS (SCALE OF 1-10)

Overall	Safety	Reliability	Performance	Comfort	Value
N/A	N/A	7	8.4	7.5	3.5

Category J

	Trade-in	Market
2 Dr S Conv	5445	7350
2 Dr S Hbk	4075	5500
4 Dr S Sdn	4175	5635
2 Dr SE Turbo Conv	5785	7810
2 Dr SPG Turbo Hbk	5315	7175
2 Dr STD Turbo Conv	6040	8155
2 Dr STD Hbk	3575	4825
2 Dr STD Turbo Hbk	4770	6440
4 Dr STD Sdn	3675	4965

OPTIONS FOR 900
Auto 3-Speed Transmission +80

9000 — 1991

Turbo CD Sedan is introduced.

RATINGS (SCALE OF 1-10)

Overall	Safety	Reliability	Performance	Comfort	Value
7.6	6.7	7.4	8.8	8.4	6.9

Category J

	Trade-in	Market
4 Dr CD Sdn	5285	7135
4 Dr CD Turbo Sdn	6200	8365
4 Dr S Hbk	4920	6645
4 Dr STD Hbk	4175	5635
4 Dr STD Turbo Hbk	6015	8120

OPTIONS FOR 9000
Auto 4-Speed Transmission[Std on CD] +105

SATURN

USA

1998 Saturn SL2

2000 SATURN

L-SERIES 2000

The L-Series is a new midsize line of sedans and wagons that was developed for Saturn customers moving up from the smaller cars. Offered in three trim levels, with two engines and manual or automatic transmissions (depending on model), the L-Series is based on the European-market Opel Vectra platform, and consequently carries a distinct import feel.

Category E

Model Description	Trade-in Value	Market Value
4 Dr LS Sdn	11640	13710
4 Dr LS1 Sdn	12950	15255
4 Dr LS2 Sdn	15500	18260
4 Dr LW1 Wgn	14520	17105
4 Dr LW2 Wgn	16420	19345

OPTIONS FOR L-SERIES
Auto 4-Speed Transmission[Std on Wgn,LS2 Sedan] +705
Aluminum/Alloy Wheels[Std on LS2 Sedan,LW2 Wagon] +275
Compact Disc W/fm/tape[Std on LS2 Sedan, LW2 Wagon] +395
Power Drivers Seat +245
Rear Spoiler[Std on Wgn] +180

S-SERIES 2000

Saturn has redesigned the body panels and cockpit of its S-Series SL Sedan and SW Wagon this year. GM's OnStar communications system will now be available as a dealer-installed option across the Saturn line.

Category E

Model Description	Trade-in Value	Market Value
3 Dr SC1 Cpe	10175	11985
3 Dr SC2 Cpe	12220	14395
4 Dr SL Sdn	8720	10275
4 Dr SL1 Sdn	9350	11015
4 Dr SL2 Sdn	10455	12315
4 Dr SW2 Wgn	11550	13605

OPTIONS FOR S-SERIES
Auto 4-Speed Transmission +700
AM/FM Compact Disc Player +355
AM/FM Stereo Tape +250
Air Conditioning[Std on Wgn,SC2 Coupe,SL2 Sedan] +680
Alarm System +340
Aluminum/Alloy Wheels +275
Compact Disc W/fm/tape +395
Cruise Control +185
Power Door Locks +205
Power Mirrors +90
Power Sunroof +510
Power Windows[Std on Wgn] +215
Rear Spoiler[Std on SC2 Coupe] +180

1999 SATURN

SC 1999

Saturn continues on its refinement theme for 1999. Refined powertrain performance, interior upgrades and new wheel selections top the list of changes for SC1 and SC2 models. New later this year on all coupes is a standard driver's-side third door to improve access to the rear seats. Improvements to both the single- and dual-overhead cam engines (including new pistons, connecting rods and crankshafts) are designed to reduce noise, vibration and harshness while improving fuel economy about one mpg across the board. The SC2 gets redesigned standard wheel covers and new optional 15-inch aluminum wheels. Interior cloth fabrics have been revised, the capacity of the windshield washer solvent bottle has been increased to one gallon, and there's a new Green exterior paint. In a move backward, all Coupes will revert to rear drum brakes, replacing the once-available rear discs on SC2 with ABS.

RATINGS (SCALE OF 1-10)

Overall	Safety	Reliability	Performance	Comfort	Value
N/A	N/A	8.6	7.8	N/A	N/A

Category E

Model Description	Trade-in Value	Market Value
2 Dr SC1 Cpe	8845	10545
3 Dr SC1 Cpe	9200	10970
2 Dr SC2 Cpe	10670	12725
3 Dr SC2 Cpe	11030	13150

OPTIONS FOR SC
Auto 4-Speed Transmission +575
AM/FM Compact Disc Player +290
Air Conditioning[Std on SC2] +555
Aluminum/Alloy Wheels +225
Cruise Control +155
Keyless Entry System +110

Don't forget to refer to the Mileage Adjustment Table at the back of this book!

SATURN 99-98

Model Description	Trade-in Value	Market Value	Model Description	Trade-in Value	Market Value

Leather Seats +585
Power Door Locks +165
Power Mirrors +75
Power Sunroof +415
Power Windows +180
Premium Sound System +220
Traction Control System +35

SL   1999

Powertrain components in both the single- and dual-overhead cam engines (such as pistons, connecting rods, crankshaft and timing chain) have been revised to reduce noise, vibration and harshness, while returning an increase of about one mpg across the board. Three new exterior colors debut: Dark Blue on SL, Green and Blackberry on SL1 and SL2. Front seatbelts have been repositioned, and the windshield washer solvent bottle's capacity has been upped to one full gallon. Sadly, Saturn has moved to rear drum brakes on all models, replacing the rear discs that had been available on SL2s with ABS.

RATINGS (SCALE OF 1-10)

Overall	Safety	Reliability	Performance	Comfort	Value
N/A	7.4	8.7	7.8	7	N/A

Category E
4 Dr SL Sdn	7875	9390
4 Dr SL1 Sdn	8375	9985
4 Dr SL2 Sdn	9415	11230

OPTIONS FOR SL

Auto 4-Speed Transmission +575
AM/FM Compact Disc Player +290
Air Conditioning[Std on SL2] +555
Aluminum/Alloy Wheels +225
Anti-Lock Brakes +445
Cruise Control +155
Keyless Entry System +110
Leather Seats +585
Power Door Locks +165
Power Mirrors +75
Power Sunroof +415
Power Windows +180
Premium Sound System +220
Traction Control System +35

SW   1999

As with the rest of the 1999 Saturn line, SW models are sure to benefit from revised powertrain components in both the single- and dual-overhead cam engines. The pistons, connecting rods, crankshaft and timing chain in these motors have been redesigned to reduce noise, vibration and harshness, while returning an increase of about one mpg across the board. Wagons have a new Green exterior color. The only other changes are repositioned front seatbelts for easier access and increased windshield washer solvent bottle capacity, which is now one full gallon.

RATINGS (SCALE OF 1-10)

Overall	Safety	Reliability	Performance	Comfort	Value
N/A	7.4	8.7	7.8	N/A	N/A

Category E
4 Dr SW1 Wgn	9165	10930
4 Dr SW2 Wgn	10575	12610

OPTIONS FOR SW

Auto 4-Speed Transmission +575
AM/FM Compact Disc Player +290
Air Conditioning[Std on SW2] +555
Aluminum/Alloy Wheels +225
Anti-Lock Brakes +445
Cruise Control +155
Keyless Entry System +110
Leather Seats +585
Power Door Locks +165
Power Mirrors +75
Power Windows +180
Premium Sound System +220
Traction Control System +35

1998 SATURN

SC   1998

Refinement is the name of the game for 1998. Improvements to the suspension, transmission and engine blocks are designed to smooth the ride, reduce noise, increase durability and provide slick shifts. Second-generation airbags deploy with less force than the old ones. A child seatbelt comfort guide has been added in the back seat, and SC1 models have a new wheel design. Dark Blue is the single new color.

RATINGS (SCALE OF 1-10)

Overall	Safety	Reliability	Performance	Comfort	Value
N/A	N/A	8.6	7.8	7	7.8

Category E
2 Dr SC1 Cpe	8040	9850
2 Dr SC2 Cpe	9435	11560

OPTIONS FOR SC

Auto 4-Speed Transmission +470
AM/FM Compact Disc Player +235
Air Conditioning[Opt on SC1] +455
Aluminum/Alloy Wheels +185
Anti-Lock Brakes +365
Cruise Control +125
Keyless Entry System +90
Leather Seats +480
Power Door Locks +135
Power Mirrors +60
Power Sunroof +340
Power Windows +145

SATURN 98-97

Model Description	Trade-in Value	Market Value	Model Description	Trade-in Value	Market Value

Premium Sound System +180
Traction Control System +25

SL   1998

Minor trim modifications, reduced force airbags, and hardware improvements to stifle unwanted noise, vibration and harshness are on tap for 1998.

RATINGS (SCALE OF 1-10)

Overall	Safety	Reliability	Performance	Comfort	Value
7.9	7.4	8.7	8.2	7.4	8

Category E

4 Dr SL1 Sdn	7240	8870
4 Dr SL2 Sdn	8140	9970
4 Dr STD Sdn	6805	8340

OPTIONS FOR SL

Auto 4-Speed Transmission +470
AM/FM Compact Disc Player +235
Air Conditioning[Std on SL2] +455
Aluminum/Alloy Wheels +185
Anti-Lock Brakes +365
Cruise Control +125
Keyless Entry System +90
Leather Seats +480
Power Door Locks +135
Power Mirrors +60
Power Sunroof +340
Power Windows +145
Premium Sound System +180
Traction Control System +25

SW   1998

1998 brings fresh colors, revised fabrics, redesigned wheels, reduced force airbags and more attempts at reducing noise and vibration levels.

RATINGS (SCALE OF 1-10)

Overall	Safety	Reliability	Performance	Comfort	Value
7.9	7.4	8.7	7.8	7.5	8.1

Category E

4 Dr SW1 Wgn	7855	9625
4 Dr SW2 Wgn	9065	11105

OPTIONS FOR SW

Auto 4-Speed Transmission +470
AM/FM Compact Disc Player +235
Air Conditioning[Opt on SW1] +455
Aluminum/Alloy Wheels +185
Anti-Lock Brakes +365
Cruise Control +125
Keyless Entry System +90
Leather Seats +480
Power Door Locks +135
Power Mirrors +60
Power Windows +145
Premium Sound System +180
Traction Control System +25

1997 SATURN

SC   1997

Saturn restyles its sport coupe, moving it to the SL/SW platform in the process. The result is a larger, roomier and heavier car. Dashboard is carried over, but interior trim is new. Newly optional is an in-dash CD player. More steps are taken to reduce noise, vibration and harshness.

RATINGS (SCALE OF 1-10)

Overall	Safety	Reliability	Performance	Comfort	Value
N/A	N/A	7.4	7.8	7	8.9

Category E

2 Dr SC1 Cpe	7550	9225
2 Dr SC2 Cpe	8255	10085

OPTIONS FOR SC

Auto 4-Speed Transmission +355
AM/FM Compact Disc Player +195
Air Conditioning +370
Aluminum/Alloy Wheels +150
Anti-Lock Brakes +295
Cruise Control +100
Leather Seats +390
Power Door Locks +110
Power Sunroof +280
Power Windows +120
Premium Sound System +145
Rear Spoiler[Opt on SC1] +100

SL   1997

Once again, Saturn attempts to quell noise, vibration, and harshness (NVH) with improved engine mounts, revised torque struts, thicker dash mat, and non-asbestos organic front brake pads. Other changes are limited to new colors, an optional in-dash CD player, a panic mode for the security system, and a low-fuel indicator.

RATINGS (SCALE OF 1-10)

Overall	Safety	Reliability	Performance	Comfort	Value
7.9	7.2	7.5	8.2	7.4	9

Category E

4 Dr SL1 Sdn	7025	8580
4 Dr SL2 Sdn	7550	9225
4 Dr STD Sdn	6440	7865

OPTIONS FOR SL

Auto 4-Speed Transmission +375
AM/FM Compact Disc Player +195
Air Conditioning +370
Aluminum/Alloy Wheels +150
Anti-Lock Brakes +295
Cruise Control +100
Keyless Entry System +75

Don't forget to refer to the Mileage Adjustment Table at the back of this book!

Model Description	Trade-in Value	Market Value	Model Description	Trade-in Value	Market Value

Leather Seats +390
Power Door Locks +110
Power Sunroof +280
Power Windows +120
Premium Sound System +145

SW 1997

Once again, Saturn attempts to quell noise, vibration, and harshness (NVH) with improved engine mounts, revised torque struts, thicker dash mat, and non-asbestos organic front brake pads. Other changes are limited to a new color, an optional in-dash CD player, a panic mode for the security system, and a low-fuel indicator.

RATINGS (SCALE OF 1-10)

Overall	Safety	Reliability	Performance	Comfort	Value
7.8	7.2	7.5	7.8	7.5	9.1

Category E
4 Dr SW1 Wgn 7375 9010
4 Dr SW2 Wgn 7905 9655

OPTIONS FOR SW

Auto 4-Speed Transmission +375
AM/FM Compact Disc Player +195
Air Conditioning +370
Aluminum/Alloy Wheels +150
Anti-Lock Brakes +295
Cruise Control +100
Keyless Entry System +75
Leather Seats +390
Power Door Locks +110
Power Windows +120
Premium Sound System +145

1996 SATURN

SC 1996

Coupe carries over in anticipation of all-new styling to arrive for 1997. Traction control can now be ordered with the manual transmission and antilock brake system.

RATINGS (SCALE OF 1-10)

Overall	Safety	Reliability	Performance	Comfort	Value
7.5	6.5	7.8	8.5	7.1	7.5

Category E
2 Dr SC1 Cpe 6360 7835
2 Dr SC2 Cpe 6915 8520

OPTIONS FOR SC

Auto 4-Speed Transmission +290
AM/FM Stereo Tape +110
Air Conditioning +305
Aluminum/Alloy Wheels +125
Anti-Lock Brakes +245
Compact Disc Changer +175

Cruise Control +85
Keyless Entry System +60
Leather Seats +320
Power Door Locks +90
Power Sunroof +230
Power Windows +95
Premium Sound System +120

SL 1996

New bodywork and interior improvements make the SL an excellent value in the compact sedan class. SL's meet 1997 side-impact standards for the first time. A five-speed and traction control are no longer mutually exclusive items. The back seat is actually livable this year. Daytime running lights are standard, and rain water won't leak all over your stuff anymore when you open the trunk.

RATINGS (SCALE OF 1-10)

Overall	Safety	Reliability	Performance	Comfort	Value
7.7	7.3	7.9	8.2	7.4	7.7

Category E
4 Dr SL1 Sdn 5945 7325
4 Dr SL2 Sdn 6400 7885
4 Dr STD Sdn 5490 6765

OPTIONS FOR SL

Auto 4-Speed Transmission +290
AM/FM Compact Disc Player +160
Air Conditioning +305
Aluminum/Alloy Wheels +125
Anti-Lock Brakes +245
Cruise Control +85
Keyless Entry System +60
Leather Seats +320
Power Door Locks +90
Power Sunroof +230
Power Windows +95
Premium Sound System +120

SW 1996

Sporty wagon gets more conventional, but more attractive, plastic panels for 1996. Wagon meets 1997 side-impact standards this year, and five-speed models can be equipped with traction control. The rear seat is more comfortable, and head room is improved. Daytime running lights debut. Avoid new purple color, unless you want the kids calling your car the Barneymobile in front of friends and relatives.

RATINGS (SCALE OF 1-10)

Overall	Safety	Reliability	Performance	Comfort	Value
7.7	7.3	7.9	7.8	7.5	7.8

Category E
4 Dr SW1 Wgn 6365 7845
4 Dr SW2 Wgn 6830 8415

Don't forget to refer to the Mileage Adjustment Table at the back of this book!

Model Description	Trade-in Value	Market Value

OPTIONS FOR SW

Auto 4-Speed Transmission +290
AM/FM Stereo Tape +110
Air Conditioning +305
Aluminum/Alloy Wheels +125
Anti-Lock Brakes +245
Cruise Control +85
Keyless Entry System +60
Leather Seats +320
Power Door Locks +90
Power Windows +95
Premium Sound System +120

1995 SATURN

SC   1995

Dashboard is redesigned and now contains two airbags. Base engine is rated at 100 horsepower, up 15 from last year. With the automatic transmission, traction control is included with optional ABS. Styling is cleaned up front and rear. Manual three-point front seatbelts replace automatic type. SC1 gets new bucket seats.

RATINGS (SCALE OF 1-10)

Overall	Safety	Reliability	Performance	Comfort	Value
7.4	7.1	7.1	8.5	7.1	7.4

Category E

Model Description	Trade-in Value	Market Value
2 Dr SC1 Cpe	5110	6525
2 Dr SC2 Cpe	5565	7115

OPTIONS FOR SC

Auto 4-Speed Transmission +245
AM/FM Stereo Tape +90
Air Conditioning +250
Aluminum/Alloy Wheels +100
Anti-Lock Brakes +200
Cruise Control +70
Keyless Entry System +50
Leather Seats +260
Power Door Locks +75
Power Sunroof +185
Power Windows +80
Premium Sound System +100

SL   1995

Dashboard is redesigned and now contains two airbags. Base engine is rated at 100 horsepower, up 15 from last year. With the automatic transmission, traction control is included with optional ABS. Styling is cleaned up front and rear. Manual three-point front seatbelts replace automatic type.

RATINGS (SCALE OF 1-10)

Overall	Safety	Reliability	Performance	Comfort	Value
7.5	7.1	7.3	8.2	7.5	7.6

Category E

Model Description	Trade-in Value	Market Value
4 Dr SL1 Sdn	4695	6000
4 Dr SL2 Sdn	5110	6530
4 Dr STD Sdn	4285	5475

OPTIONS FOR SL

Auto 4-Speed Transmission +245
AM/FM Stereo Tape +90
Air Conditioning +250
Aluminum/Alloy Wheels +100
Anti-Lock Brakes +200
Compact Disc Changer +145
Cruise Control +70
Leather Seats +260
Power Door Locks +75
Power Mirrors +35
Power Sunroof +185
Power Windows +80
Premium Sound System +100

SW   1995

Dashboard is redesigned and now contains two airbags. Base engine is rated at 100 horsepower, up 15 from last year. With the automatic transmission, traction control is included with optional ABS. Styling is cleaned up front and rear. Manual three-point front seatbelts replace automatic type.

RATINGS (SCALE OF 1-10)

Overall	Safety	Reliability	Performance	Comfort	Value
7.5	7.1	7.3	7.8	7.5	7.8

Category E

Model Description	Trade-in Value	Market Value
4 Dr SW1 Wgn	5075	6485
4 Dr SW2 Wgn	5495	7025

OPTIONS FOR SW

Auto 4-Speed Transmission +245
AM/FM Stereo Tape +90
Air Conditioning +250
Aluminum/Alloy Wheels +100
Anti-Lock Brakes +200
Cruise Control +70
Leather Seats +260
Power Door Locks +75
Power Windows +80
Premium Sound System +100

1994 SATURN

SC   1994

CFC-free refrigerant is added to air conditioning system. Automatic transmission's Performance mode is recalibrated to give smoother shifts. New central unlocking feature on power door locks allows all doors to be unlocked with a twist of the key. New alloy wheels are optional on SC1.

Don't forget to refer to the Mileage Adjustment Table at the back of this book!

Model Description				Trade-in Value	Market Value

RATINGS (SCALE OF 1-10)

Overall	Safety	Reliability	Performance	Comfort	Value
7.1	5.5	7.5	8.3	7.3	6.9

Category E

Model	Trade-in Value	Market Value
2 Dr SC1 Cpe	4250	5620
2 Dr SC2 Cpe	4670	6180

OPTIONS FOR SC

Auto 4-Speed Transmission +195
AM/FM Compact Disc Player +105
Air Conditioning +205
Aluminum/Alloy Wheels +80
Anti-Lock Brakes +160
Cruise Control +55
Leather Seats +215
Power Door Locks +60
Power Sunroof +150
Power Windows +65
Premium Sound System +80

SL 1994

CFC-free refrigerant is added to air conditioning system. Automatic transmission's Performance mode is recalibrated to give smoother shifts. New central unlocking feature on power door locks allows all doors to be unlocked with a twist of the key. New alloy wheels are optional on SL2.

RATINGS (SCALE OF 1-10)

Overall	Safety	Reliability	Performance	Comfort	Value
7.3	5.5	8.1	8	7.6	7.1

Category E

Model	Trade-in Value	Market Value
4 Dr SL1 Sdn	3890	5145
4 Dr SL2 Sdn	4240	5610
4 Dr STD Sdn	3610	4775

OPTIONS FOR SL

Auto 4-Speed Transmission +195
AM/FM Compact Disc Player +105
Air Conditioning +205
Aluminum/Alloy Wheels +80
Anti-Lock Brakes +160
Cruise Control +55
Leather Seats +215
Power Door Locks +60
Power Sunroof +150
Power Windows +65
Premium Sound System +80

SW 1994

CFC-free refrigerant is added to air conditioning system. Automatic transmission's Performance mode is recalibrated to give smoother shifts. New central unlocking feature on power door locks allows all doors to be unlocked with a twist of the key. New alloy wheels are optional on SW2.

RATINGS (SCALE OF 1-10)

Overall	Safety	Reliability	Performance	Comfort	Value
7.2	5.5	8.1	7.4	7.6	7.2

Category E

Model	Trade-in Value	Market Value
4 Dr SW1 Wgn	3810	5040
4 Dr SW2 Wgn	4095	5420

OPTIONS FOR SW

Auto 4-Speed Transmission +195
AM/FM Compact Disc Player +105
AM/FM Stereo Tape +75
Air Conditioning +205
Aluminum/Alloy Wheels +80
Anti-Lock Brakes +160
Cruise Control +55
Leather Seats +215
Power Door Locks +60
Power Windows +65
Premium Sound System +80

1993 SATURN

SC 1993

Driver airbag added. Cars with ABS and automatic transmission can be ordered with traction control. SC coupe equipped with same 85-horsepower 1.9-liter engine as in SL.

RATINGS (SCALE OF 1-10)

Overall	Safety	Reliability	Performance	Comfort	Value
7	5.3	7.1	8.3	7.3	6.8

Category E

Model	Trade-in Value	Market Value
2 Dr SC1 Cpe	3180	4505
2 Dr SC2 Cpe	3690	5225

OPTIONS FOR SC

Auto 4-Speed Transmission +150
AM/FM Compact Disc Player +85
AM/FM Stereo Tape +60
Air Conditioning +165
Aluminum/Alloy Wheels[Opt on SC1] +65
Anti-Lock Brakes +135
Cruise Control +45
Leather Seats +175
Power Door Locks +50
Power Sunroof +125
Power Windows +55
Premium Sound System +65

SL 1993

Driver airbag added. SL2 gets new front fascia and optional fog lights. Cars with ABS and automatic transmission can be ordered with traction control. SL2 suspension provides softer ride.

SATURN 93-91

Model Description	Trade-in Value	Market Value

RATINGS (SCALE OF 1-10)

Overall	Safety	Reliability	Performance	Comfort	Value
7.1	5.3	7.5	8	7.6	7.1

Category E

	Trade-in	Market
4 Dr SL1 Sdn	3025	4290
4 Dr SL2 Sdn	3395	4810
4 Dr STD Sdn	2795	3960

OPTIONS FOR SL

Auto 4-Speed Transmission +150
AM/FM Compact Disc Player +85
Air Conditioning +165
Aluminum/Alloy Wheels[Opt on SL1] +65
Anti-Lock Brakes +135
Cruise Control +45
Leather Seats +175
Power Door Locks +50
Power Moonroof +115
Power Sunroof +125
Power Windows +55
Premium Sound System +65

SW   1993

Driver airbag added, and is standard on SW. Cars with ABS and automatic transmission can be ordered with traction control. New station wagon model comes in SW1 and SW2 trim, and rear wiper/washer and defogger are standard. SW1 equipped with same 85-horsepower 1.9-liter engine as in SL. SW2 gets twin-cam 124-horsepower engine and SL2's sport suspension.

RATINGS (SCALE OF 1-10)

Overall	Safety	Reliability	Performance	Comfort	Value
7	5.3	7.5	7.4	7.6	7.2

Category E

	Trade-in	Market
4 Dr SW1 Wgn	3030	4295
4 Dr SW2 Wgn	3385	4795

OPTIONS FOR SW

Auto 4-Speed Transmission +150
AM/FM Compact Disc Player +85
Air Conditioning +165
Aluminum/Alloy Wheels +65
Anti-Lock Brakes +135
Cruise Control +45
Power Door Locks +50
Power Windows +55
Premium Sound System +65

1992 SATURN

SC   1992

New engine and transmission mounting system supposedly cuts down on noise and vibration.

Passenger compartment gets added acoustic insulation. Alloy wheels are redesigned.

RATINGS (SCALE OF 1-10)

Overall	Safety	Reliability	Performance	Comfort	Value
6.6	4.4	7.3	8.6	7.3	5.3

Category E

	Trade-in	Market
2 Dr SC2 Cpe	3115	4370

OPTIONS FOR SC

Auto 4-Speed Transmission +140
AM/FM Compact Disc Player +70
Air Bag Restraint +95
Air Conditioning +135
Anti-Lock Brakes +110
Leather Seats +145
Power Door Locks +40
Power Sunroof +100
Power Windows +45

SL   1992

New engine and transmission mounting system supposedly cuts down on noise and vibration. Passenger compartment gets added acoustic insulation. Leather and a rear deck spoiler are new for SL2 models. Alloy wheels are redesigned.

RATINGS (SCALE OF 1-10)

Overall	Safety	Reliability	Performance	Comfort	Value
6.5	4.4	7.2	8	7.6	5.5

Category E

	Trade-in	Market
4 Dr SL1 Sdn	2500	3510
4 Dr SL2 Sdn	2790	3915
4 Dr STD Sdn	2230	3130

OPTIONS FOR SL

Auto 4-Speed Transmission +120
Air Bag Restraint +95
Air Conditioning +135
Anti-Lock Brakes +110
Leather Seats +145
Power Door Locks +40
Power Sunroof +100
Power Windows +45

1991 SATURN

SC   1991

Saturn coupe comes with a dual overhead cam engine, sport-tuned suspension, alloy wheels, and speed rated tires. All body panels except hood, roof and trunk lid are made of plastic composite materials on all models, and ABS is optional.

RATINGS (SCALE OF 1-10)

Overall	Safety	Reliability	Performance	Comfort	Value
6.4	3.5	7.6	8.6	7.3	5.2

Model Description	Trade-in Value	Market Value	Model Description	Trade-in Value	Market Value

Category E
2 Dr SC2 Cpe   2595   3820

OPTIONS FOR SC
Auto 4-Speed Transmission +90
AM/FM Compact Disc Player +55
Air Conditioning +110
Anti-Lock Brakes +90
Power Door Locks +35
Power Sunroof +85
Power Windows +35

SL 1991

Featuring an underpowered 1.9-liter engine and uninspired ergonomics, first Saturn sedan isn't all it's cracked up to be. The SL is very basic, with manual steering and transmission. Variable-effort steering, adjustable steering column, tachometer, and remote fuel door and trunk lid releases are standard on SL1. SL2 adds more powerful engine, sport-tuned suspension, alloy wheels, body-color bumpers, and speed-rated tires. All body panels except hood, roof and trunk lid are made of plastic composite materials on all models, and ABS is optional.

RATINGS (SCALE OF 1-10)

Overall	Safety	Reliability	Performance	Comfort	Value
6.4	3.5	7.5	8	7.6	5.4

Category E
4 Dr SL1 Sdn   2030   2995
4 Dr SL2 Sdn   2420   3565
4 Dr STD Sdn   1895   2790

OPTIONS FOR SL
Auto 4-Speed Transmission +90
AM/FM Compact Disc Player +55
Air Conditioning +110
Anti-Lock Brakes +90
Power Door Locks +35
Power Sunroof +85
Power Windows +35

Don't forget to refer to the Mileage Adjustment Table at the back of this book!

SUBARU 00-99

Model Description	Trade-in Value	Market Value	Model Description	Trade-in Value	Market Value

SUBARU · Japan

1997 Subaru Legacy

2000 SUBARU

FORESTER 2000

This year, Forester L gets standard cruise control and Forester S receives a viscous limited-slip rear differential at base price increases of $100.

Category G

	Trade-in	Market
4 Dr L AWD Wgn	14730	17150
4 Dr S AWD Wgn	16520	19235

OPTIONS FOR FORESTER
Auto 4-Speed Transmission +655

IMPREZA 2000

For 2000, Subaru introduces the new Impreza 2.5 RS Sedan, a cross between an aggressive driver's car and a sedan. More standard equipment comes on the 2.5 Coupe and Sedan while the L model remains unchanged. All Impreza models now come with 24-hour roadside assistance.

Category E

	Trade-in	Market
2 Dr L AWD Cpe	12175	14265
4 Dr L AWD Sdn	12175	14265
4 Dr L AWD Wgn	12470	14610
2 Dr RS 4WD Cpe	14700	17225
4 Dr RS 4WD Sdn	14700	17225

OPTIONS FOR IMPREZA
Auto 4-Speed Transmission +655
AM/FM Compact Disc Player +355
Compact Disc W/fm/tape +395
Keyless Entry System +135
Luggage Rack +105

IMPREZA OUTBACK 2000

For 2000, Subaru's Impreza Outback Sport receives some exterior design changes and 24-hour roadside assistance.

Category E

	Trade-in	Market
4 Dr Outback Sport 4WD Wgn	13800	16170

OPTIONS FOR IMPREZA OUTBACK
Auto 4-Speed Transmission +655

LEGACY 2000

Subaru's Legacy is completely redesigned for the millennium.

Category D

	Trade-in	Market
4 Dr Brighton AWD Wgn	13835	16065
4 Dr GT AWD Sdn	17055	19805
4 Dr GT AWD Wgn	17715	20570
4 Dr GT Limited AWD Sdn	18155	21080
4 Dr L AWD Sdn	14420	16745
4 Dr L AWD Wgn	14930	17340

OPTIONS FOR LEGACY
Auto 4-Speed Transmission[Std on Outback Limited AWD Sedan] +655
Luggage Rack[Std on Limited,STD] +220
Rear Spoiler[Std on GT Limited,Wgn] +360

OUTBACK 2000

As with the Legacy platform it's based on, Subaru's hot-selling Outback is completely redesigned for the millennium.

Category D

	Trade-in	Market
4 Dr Limited 4WD Sdn	19375	22500
4 Dr Limited 4WD Wgn	19520	22670
4 Dr STD 4WD Wgn	17025	19770

1999 SUBARU

FORESTER 1999

This year, Forester's engine makes more torque and the automatic transmission has been improved. L and S models have longer lists of standard equipment and two new colors are available.

RATINGS (SCALE OF 1-10)

Overall	Safety	Reliability	Performance	Comfort	Value
N/A	N/A	N/A	7	7.5	N/A

Category G

	Trade-in	Market
4 Dr L 4WD Wgn	14240	16635
4 Dr S 4WD Wgn	15975	18665
4 Dr STD 4WD Wgn	13335	15580

OPTIONS FOR FORESTER
Auto 4-Speed Transmission +535
AM/FM Compact Disc Player +210

SUBARU 99-98

Model Description	Trade-in Value	Market Value
Aluminum/Alloy Wheels[Std on S] +215		
Cruise Control[Std on S] +140		
Keyless Entry System +130		
Leather Seats +525		

IMPREZA 1999

More horsepower, more torque and a more efficient automatic transmission is the big news this year. Multi-reflector halogen headlights are new and Outback Sport gets a revised grille. The 2.5 RS gets silver alloy wheels, a new front bumper, white gauge faces and more torque, as well as an upgraded leather-wrapped steering wheel and shift knob. Two new colors are available for 1999.

RATINGS (SCALE OF 1-10)

Overall	Safety	Reliability	Performance	Comfort	Value
N/A	6.8	9.1	7.8	7.4	N/A

Category E
2 Dr L 4WD Cpe	11620	13660
4 Dr L 4WD Sdn	11760	13830
4 Dr L 4WD Wgn	11900	13995
4 Dr Outback Sport 4WD Wgn	13105	15410
2 Dr RS 4WD Cpe	13960	16415

OPTIONS FOR IMPREZA
Auto 4-Speed Transmission +525
AM/FM Compact Disc Player +290
Aluminum/Alloy Wheels[Std on RS] +225
Cruise Control +155
Keyless Entry System +110

LEGACY 1999

Subaru celebrates 30 years of selling cars in the United States by adding special editions to the Legacy lineup. The L sedan and wagon are available with a package of goodies that includes power moonroof, alloy wheels, rear spoiler or roof rack, body-color trim, power antenna, and seat height adjuster. New colors include Sandstone Metallic and Winestone Pearl. The 2.5GT Limited is newly available with a manual transmission, while all 2.5GT, Limited and Outback models receive standard remote keyless entry.

RATINGS (SCALE OF 1-10)

Overall	Safety	Reliability	Performance	Comfort	Value
N/A	7.4	8.3	7.6	7.5	N/A

Category D
4 Dr 30th Anniversary 4WD Sdn	16600	19410
4 Dr Brighton 4WD Wgn	12080	14130
4 Dr GT 4WD Sdn	16180	18920
4 Dr GT 4WD Wgn	16670	19490
4 Dr GT Ltd. 30th Ann 4WD Sdn	17085	19975
4 Dr L 4WD Sdn	13680	15995
4 Dr L 4WD Wgn	14165	16565

Model Description	Trade-in Value	Market Value
4 Dr Limited 30TH ANN 4WD Sdn	18190	21270
4 Dr Outback 4WD Wgn	15975	18680
4 Dr Outback Ltd 30th 4WD Wgn	17430	20385

OPTIONS FOR LEGACY
Auto 4-Speed Transmission +535
30th Ann. Edition L Pkg +670
AM/FM Compact Disc Player[Std on GT Lim 30th An, Outback Lim 30th An, SUS Lim 30th An] +310
Aluminum/Alloy Wheels[Opt on Brighton,L] +310
Dual Sunroof +800
Fog Lights[Opt on Brighton,L] +165
Heated Front Seats[Opt on Outback] +250
Keyless Entry System[Opt on Brighton, L] +210
Leather Seats[Opt on 30TH Anniversary,GT,Outback] +760

1998 SUBARU

FORESTER 1998

Subaru attacks the mini-SUV market head-on with the Forester, which actually constitutes an SUV body on an Impreza platform with a Legacy engine under the hood. The most car-like of the mini-utes, Forester is also the most powerful. Airbags remain the full power variety, despite new rules allowing lower deployment speeds.

RATINGS (SCALE OF 1-10)

Overall	Safety	Reliability	Performance	Comfort	Value
N/A	N/A	8.5	7	7.5	N/A

Category G
4 Dr L 4WD Wgn	13095	15325
4 Dr S 4WD Wgn	14500	16970
4 Dr STD 4WD Wgn	12265	14350

OPTIONS FOR FORESTER
Auto 4-Speed Transmission +435
AM/FM Compact Disc Player +175
Aluminum/Alloy Wheels[Std on S] +175
Cruise Control[Std on S] +115
Heated Front Seats +150
Heated Power Mirrors +45
Keyless Entry System +105
Leather Seats +430

IMPREZA 1998

Impreza gets a new dashboard and revised door panels. The entry-level Brighton coupe is dropped, and the high-end 2.5RS coupe is added. No depowered airbags here.

RATINGS (SCALE OF 1-10)

Overall	Safety	Reliability	Performance	Comfort	Value
7.6	6.8	9	7.8	7.4	6.9

Category E
2 Dr L 4WD Cpe	10555	12665
4 Dr L 4WD Sdn	10680	12820

Don't forget to refer to the Mileage Adjustment Table at the back of this book!

Model Description	Trade-in Value	Market Value
4 Dr L 4WD Wgn	10810	12975
4 Dr Outback Sport 4WD Wgn	11905	14285
2 Dr RS 4WD Cpe	12680	15215

OPTIONS FOR IMPREZA

Auto 4-Speed Transmission +435
AM/FM Compact Disc Player +235
Aluminum/Alloy Wheels[Std on RS] +185
Cruise Control +125
Fog Lights[Std on RS] +85
Keyless Entry System +90

LEGACY   1998

Prices remain stable while equipment is shuffled and the LSi model is dropped. All Legacy sedans and wagons except the Outback sport the grille and multi-reflector halogen lights found on the 2.5GT. A new Limited model joins the 2.5GT lineup, and a dual power moonroof package is available for the Outback Limited wagon. Outbacks get new alloy wheels, an overhead console and longer splash guards, while mid-year Outback Limiteds with revised trim and added content were dubbed 30th Anniversary models. The cold weather package has heated windshield wiper nozzles this year instead of an engine block heater. The Brighton wagon's stereo loses half its wattage, Limited models have a standard CD player and the base Outback comes with a Weatherband radio. Full power airbags continue, despite new government rules allowing automakers to install reduced force bags to better protect small adults.

RATINGS (SCALE OF 1-10)

Overall	Safety	Reliability	Performance	Comfort	Value
7.5	7.3	7.8	7.6	7.5	7.2

Category D

Model Description	Trade-in Value	Market Value
4 Dr Brighton 4WD Wgn	10485	12270
4 Dr GT 4WD Sdn	14045	16435
4 Dr GT 4WD Wgn	14470	16925
4 Dr GT Limited 4WD Sdn	15235	17825
4 Dr L 4WD Sdn	11875	13895
4 Dr L 4WD Wgn	12295	14385
4 Dr Outback 4WD Wgn	13865	16220
4 Dr Outback Limited 4WD Wgn	15055	17615

OPTIONS FOR LEGACY

Auto 4-Speed Transmission[Std on GT Limited] +435
AM/FM Compact Disc Player[Std on Limited] +255
Aluminum/Alloy Wheels[Opt on Brighton, L] +255
Cruise Control[Opt on Brighton] +135
Dual Sunroof[Opt on Outback Limited] +655
Fog Lights[Opt on Brighton, L] +135
Heated Front Seats[Opt on Outback] +205
Heated Power Mirrors[Opt on Outback] +45
Keyless Entry System +170
Leather Seats[Opt on GT, Outback] +620

1997 SUBARU

IMPREZA   1997

Imprezas receive a facelifted front end that includes a Hemi-sized hood scoop. A new Outback Sport Wagon debuts, with nearly six-inches of additional ground clearance, fog lights, and a slightly raised roof. LX model disappears, which means only the Outback is equipped with ABS. Power and torque for both Impreza engines is up for 1997, and some new colors are available. HVAC controls are revised.

RATINGS (SCALE OF 1-10)

Overall	Safety	Reliability	Performance	Comfort	Value
7.4	6.8	9.1	7.8	7.4	5.9

Category E

Model Description	Trade-in Value	Market Value
2 Dr Brighton 4WD Cpe	7760	9340
2 Dr L 4WD Cpe	8900	10710
4 Dr L 4WD Sdn	9005	10840
4 Dr L 4WD Wgn	9115	10970
4 Dr Outback Sport 4WD Wgn	10035	12080

OPTIONS FOR IMPREZA

4 cyl 2.2 L Engine[Opt on Brighton] +90
Auto 4-Speed Transmission +355
AM/FM Compact Disc Player +195
Aluminum/Alloy Wheels +150
Compact Disc Changer +215
Cruise Control +100
Fog Lights[Std on L 4WD Cpe] +70
Keyless Entry System +75
Luggage Rack[Opt on L] +60
Rear Spoiler[Opt on Brighton, Sdn] +100

LEGACY   1997

Front-wheel drive models are given the ax as Subaru returns to its all-wheel drive roots. Power and torque are up marginally with the base 2.2-liter engine. The 2.5-liter motor (also stronger this year and now available with a manual transmission) is now the only engine mated to the Outback. L models gain cruise control, anti-lock brakes, and power door locks as standard equipment. GT's get a manual transmission, larger tires, and revised styling. The Outback lineup is expanded with the introduction of a Limited model, which includes a leather interior, new alloy wheels, fresh exterior colors, and woodgrain interior trim.

RATINGS (SCALE OF 1-10)

Overall	Safety	Reliability	Performance	Comfort	Value
7.3	7.2	7.2	7.6	7.5	7.1

Category D

Model Description	Trade-in Value	Market Value
4 Dr Brighton 4WD Wgn	9375	10990
4 Dr GT 4WD Sdn	12555	14720

Model Description	Trade-in Value	Market Value
4 Dr GT 4WD Wgn	12805	15020
4 Dr L 4WD Sdn	10610	12445
4 Dr L 4WD Wgn	10990	12885
4 Dr LSi 4WD Sdn	13610	15955
4 Dr LSi 4WD Wgn	13980	16395
4 Dr Outback 4WD Sdn	12555	14725
4 Dr Outback 4WD Wgn	12390	14530
4 Dr Outback Limited 4WD Wgn	13180	15455

OPTIONS FOR LEGACY

Auto 4-Speed Transmission[Std on LSi] +355
AM/FM Compact Disc Player +210
Alarm System[Std on LSi] +235
Aluminum/Alloy Wheels[Opt on Brighton,L] +210
Compact Disc Changer[Std on LSi] +290
Compact Disc W/fm/tape +345
Cruise Control[Opt on Brighton] +110
Heated Front Seats[Opt on Outback] +165
Keyless Entry System +140
Leather Seats[Opt on GT,Outback] +505
Luggage Rack[Opt on Brighton,L,LSi] +120

SVX   1997

A body-color grille debuts, along with P215/55VR16 tires. You wanted an SVX in Laguna Blue? Tough rocks, pal. That color vanishes this year.

Category F

	Trade-in	Market
2 Dr L 4WD Cpe	15455	18140
2 Dr LSi 4WD Cpe	18245	21415

OPTIONS FOR SVX

Alarm System[Opt on L] +80

1996 SUBARU

IMPREZA   1996

The formerly optional 2.2-liter engine is standard across the board, except in the new budget-minded Brighton AWD Coupe. A new grille accompanies the bigger engine, and a five-speed is available as well.

RATINGS (SCALE OF 1-10)

Overall	Safety	Reliability	Performance	Comfort	Value
7.3	6.6	9	7.8	7.4	5.9

Category E

	Trade-in	Market
2 Dr Brighton 4WD Cpe	6695	8080
2 Dr L 4WD Cpe	7700	9290
4 Dr L 4WD Sdn	7795	9405
4 Dr L 4WD Wgn	7890	9520
2 Dr LX 4WD Cpe	8515	10270
4 Dr LX 4WD Sdn	8755	10560
4 Dr LX 4WD Wgn	8945	10790
4 Dr Outback 4WD Wgn	8660	10445

OPTIONS FOR IMPREZA

Auto 4-Speed Transmission[Opt on L,Outback,Cpe] +290
AM/FM Compact Disc Player +160
Aluminum/Alloy Wheels[Std on LX 4WD Cpe] +125
Anti-Lock Brakes[Opt on L] +245
Compact Disc Changer +175
Cruise Control +85
Luggage Rack[Opt on L,LX] +45

LEGACY   1996

A new sport model debuts, with a larger, more powerful engine. The 2.5GT is available in sedan or wagon format. The luxury-oriented LSi model also gets the new motor. A knobby-tired, raised-roof Outback wagon appears, offering 7.3 inches of ground clearance and an optional 2.5-liter engine. Designed specifically for American consumers, the Outback provides a car-like ride with light-duty off-road ability.

RATINGS (SCALE OF 1-10)

Overall	Safety	Reliability	Performance	Comfort	Value
7.7	7.4	7.9	7.4	7.5	8.3

Category D

	Trade-in	Market
4 Dr Brighton 4WD Wgn	8015	9585
4 Dr GT 4WD Sdn	10755	12855
4 Dr GT 4WD Wgn	10930	13065
4 Dr L Sdn	8345	9975
4 Dr L 4WD Sdn	8820	10540
4 Dr L Wgn	8675	10370
4 Dr L 4WD Wgn	9195	10995
4 Dr LS 4WD Sdn	10660	12740
4 Dr LS 4WD Wgn	10835	12955
4 Dr LSi 4WD Sdn	11770	14065
4 Dr LSi 4WD Wgn	12095	14455
4 Dr Outback 4WD Wgn	10615	12685

OPTIONS FOR LEGACY

4 cyl 2.5 L DOHC Engine[Std on GT,LSi] +70
Auto 4-Speed Transmission[Std on GT,LS,LSi] +275
Aluminum/Alloy Wheels[Opt on L] +170
Anti-Lock Brakes[Opt on L] +325
Compact Disc W/fm/tape +285
Cruise Control[Opt on Brighton,L] +90
Heated Front Seats +135
Keyless Entry System +115
Luggage Rack[Opt on Brighton] +100

SVX   1996

Umm ... the L model gets standard solar-reduction glass this year. Whoopee.

Category F

	Trade-in	Market
2 Dr L 4WD Cpe	13380	15780
2 Dr LSi 4WD Cpe	15795	18625

OPTIONS FOR SVX

AM/FM Compact Disc Player +170

Don't forget to refer to the Mileage Adjustment Table at the back of this book!

SUBARU 95-94

Model Description	Trade-in Value	Market Value	Model Description	Trade-in Value	Market Value

1995 SUBARU

IMPREZA 1995

An Impreza coupe and an Outback Wagon are added to Subaru's subcompact line of cars in an attempt to broaden their appeal with sporting and outdoor enthusiasts. Top-of-the-line LX model is introduced, replacing the LS trim-level, with an available 2.2-liter engine taken from the Legacy. Unfortunately it is available only with an automatic transmission.

RATINGS (SCALE OF 1-10)

Overall	Safety	Reliability	Performance	Comfort	Value
7.4	7.3	7.9	7.8	7.4	6.8

Category E

	Trade-in	Market
2 Dr L Cpe	6105	7550
2 Dr L 4WD Cpe	6530	8075
4 Dr L Sdn	6105	7550
4 Dr L 4WD Sdn	6530	8075
4 Dr L 4WD Wgn	6605	8165
4 Dr L Spec. Edition Sdn	6380	7885
4 Dr L Special Edit. 4WD Sdn	6800	8410
4 Dr L Special Edit. 4WD Wgn	6885	8515
2 Dr LX 4WD Cpe	7510	9285
4 Dr LX 4WD Sdn	7385	9130
4 Dr LX 4WD Wgn	7555	9340
4 Dr Outback 4WD Wgn	6940	8585
4 Dr Outback Spec. Ed. 4WD Wgn	6885	8515
2 Dr STD Cpe	5305	6560
4 Dr STD Sdn	5305	6560

OPTIONS FOR IMPREZA

4 cyl 2.2 L Engine[Std on LX] +290
Auto 4-Speed Transmission[Std on L Spec. Edition,LX,L Special Edit. 4WD Sdn] +240
4-WD Active Safety Group +535
AM/FM Compact Disc Player +130
Air Conditioning[Opt on STD,L 4WD Cpe] +250
Aluminum/Alloy Wheels[Std on LX 4WD Sdn] +100
Anti-Lock Brakes[Opt on L] +200
Cruise Control +70
Luggage Rack[Opt on L,L Special Edit.,LX] +40

LEGACY 1995

New sheetmetal freshens the flanks of one of our favorite compact sedans and wagons. Unfortunately the turbocharged engine has been dropped, leaving the Legacy with a rather anemic 2.2-liter four-cylinder that produces a meager 135 horsepower. The value leader Brighton wagon is introduced for budding naturalists. It includes all-wheel drive, air conditioning and a stereo with cassette. The Outback Wagon is also introduced as an alternative to the burgeoning SUV market.

RATINGS (SCALE OF 1-10)

Overall	Safety	Reliability	Performance	Comfort	Value
7.4	7.7	7.7	7.4	7.5	6.5

Category D

	Trade-in	Market
4 Dr Brighton 4WD Wgn	6935	8455
4 Dr L Sdn	7200	8775
4 Dr L 4WD Sdn	7620	9290
4 Dr L Wgn	7495	9135
4 Dr L 4WD Wgn	7915	9650
4 Dr LS 4WD Sdn	9095	11085
4 Dr LS 4WD Wgn	9390	11445
4 Dr LSi 4WD Sdn	9995	12185
4 Dr LSi 4WD Wgn	10285	12540
4 Dr Outback 4WD Wgn	8545	10420
4 Dr STD Sdn	6250	7615

OPTIONS FOR LEGACY

Auto 4-Speed Transmission[Std on LS,LSi] +240
AM/FM Compact Disc Player[Std on LSi] +140
Air Conditioning[Opt on STD] +255
Aluminum/Alloy Wheels[Opt on Brighton,L,STD] +140
Anti-Lock Brakes[Opt on L] +265
Compact Disc Changer +195
Cruise Control[Opt on Brighton,L,STD] +75
Luggage Rack[Std on LSi,Outback] +80
Power Antenna[Opt on L] +35
Power Moonroof[Opt on L] +250

SVX 1995

Dual airbags are extended to the base model.

Category F

	Trade-in	Market
2 Dr L Cpe	10585	12645
2 Dr L 4WD Cpe	10965	13100
2 Dr LS Cpe	10585	12645
2 Dr LSi 4WD Cpe	13270	15850

1994 SUBARU

IMPREZA 1994

A passenger airbag joins the driver's airbag on all models. LS Imprezas have standard antilock brakes, automatic transmission and sunroof.

RATINGS (SCALE OF 1-10)

Overall	Safety	Reliability	Performance	Comfort	Value
7.4	6.8	8.6	7.6	7.4	6.8

Category E

	Trade-in	Market
4 Dr L Sdn	4185	5585
4 Dr L 4WD Sdn	4690	6255
4 Dr L Wgn	4320	5765
4 Dr L 4WD Wgn	4825	6435
4 Dr LS 4WD Sdn	6390	8525
4 Dr LS 4WD Wgn	6525	8705
4 Dr STD Sdn	3915	5225

Don't forget to refer to the Mileage Adjustment Table at the back of this book!

Model Description	Trade-in Value	Market Value

OPTIONS FOR IMPREZA
Auto 4-Speed Transmission[Std on LS] +195
AM/FM Stereo Tape[Std on LS] +75
Air Conditioning[Std on LS] +205
Anti-Lock Brakes[Std on LS] +160
Dual Air Bag Restraints[Std on LS] +150
Power Door Locks[Std on LS] +60
Power Sunroof[Std on LS] +150
Power Windows[Std on LS] +65

JUSTY   1994

Continuously variable transmission is no longer available. Base models gain a standard rear-window defroster. Last year for the Justy runabout.

Category E

2 Dr DL Hbk	2600	3470
4 Dr GL 4WD Hbk	3190	4255

OPTIONS FOR JUSTY
Air Conditioning +205

LEGACY   1994

Antilock brakes become optional on the L sedan.

RATINGS (SCALE OF 1-10)

Overall	Safety	Reliability	Performance	Comfort	Value
N/A	N/A	8.2	8.3	7.8	6.5

Category D

4 Dr L Sdn	5170	6345
4 Dr L 4WD Sdn	6655	7935
4 Dr L Wgn	5210	6510
4 Dr L 4WD Wgn	6985	8335
4 Dr LS Sdn	6795	8395
4 Dr LS 4WD Sdn	7090	8765
4 Dr LS Wgn	7030	8690
4 Dr LS 4WD Wgn	7320	9050
4 Dr LSi 4WD Sdn	7270	8990
4 Dr LSi 4WD Wgn	7595	9390
4 Dr Sport Turbo 4WD Sdn	7125	8805
4 Dr Touring Turbo 4WD Wgn	7710	9530

OPTIONS FOR LEGACY
Auto 4-Speed Transmission[Opt on L] +195
AM/FM Compact Disc Player +115
Air Conditioning[Opt on L] +210
Aluminum/Alloy Wheels[Opt on L] +115
Anti-Lock Brakes[Opt on L] +215
Cruise Control[Opt on L] +60
Graphic Equalizer[Opt on L] +45
Heated Seats +115
Keyless Entry System +75
Luggage Rack +65
Power Door Locks[Opt on L] +65
Power Moonroof[Opt on L,LS 4WD Sdn] +205
Power Windows[Opt on L] +65
Premium Sound System +90

LOYALE   1994

The Loyale is available only in the wagon bodystyle and is seeing its last year as the Impreza is set to take over the duties of all-wheel drive subcompact in Subaru's lineup.

Category D

4 Dr STD 4WD Wgn	5180	6405

OPTIONS FOR LOYALE
Auto 3-Speed Transmission +135
AM/FM Stereo Tape +90
Cruise Control +60
Luggage Rack +65

SVX   1994

Subaru introduces two-wheel drive "value leaders" to the SVX lineup called the L and LS. These new SVXs offer the same 3.3-liter Flat-6 found in the LSi, and antilock brakes are standard on the LS . A passenger airbag becomes standard on the uplevel LS and LSi models.

Category F

2 Dr L Cpe	7495	9110
2 Dr LS Cpe	8925	10845
2 Dr LSi 4WD Cpe	10555	12830

OPTIONS FOR SVX
Dual Air Bag Restraints[Opt on L] +120

1993 SUBARU

IMPREZA   1993

Designed as a replacement for the aging Loyale, the Impreza is a subcompact available as a sedan or wagon. A driver airbag and available antilock brakes are important safety features included on the Impreza that never found their way to the Loyale. The Impreza is powered by a 1.8-liter 118-horsepower engine. Front-wheel drive and full-time all-wheel drive models are offered.

RATINGS (SCALE OF 1-10)

Overall	Safety	Reliability	Performance	Comfort	Value
N/A	N/A	8.8	7.6	7.4	6.8

Category E

4 Dr L Sdn	3420	4935
4 Dr L 4WD Sdn	3805	5485
4 Dr L Wgn	3525	5085
4 Dr L 4WD Wgn	3905	5635
4 Dr LS Sdn	4110	5930
4 Dr LS 4WD Sdn	4490	6480
4 Dr LS Wgn	4210	6075
4 Dr LS 4WD Wgn	4590	6625
4 Dr STD Sdn	2910	4200

Model Description	Trade-in Value	Market Value

Model Description	Trade-in Value	Market Value

OPTIONS FOR IMPREZA

Auto 4-Speed Transmission[Opt on L] +160
AM/FM Stereo Tape +60
Air Conditioning[Opt on STD] +165
Aluminum/Alloy Wheels +65

JUSTY   1993

The base Justy gets a larger engine that increases horsepower to GL standards.

Category E

2 Dr GL Hbk	2160	3115
4 Dr GL Hbk	2340	3375
4 Dr GL 4WD Hbk	2240	3235
2 Dr STD Hbk	1760	2535

OPTIONS FOR JUSTY

Auto 3-Speed Transmission[Opt on 4WD] +85
AM/FM Stereo Tape +60
Air Conditioning +165

LEGACY   1993

A driver airbag is now standard on all Legacys. Touring wagons and LSi wagons were introduced in 1992 as upscale versions of the Legacy. Commendably, antilock brakes are now standard on all Legacys except the L models. Several new trim-levels of the Legacy are available for 1993. Based on the L wagon, these models are geared to appeal to different groups of outdoor enthusiasts such as skiers, beach combers and campers. The standard equipment lists of these models reflects the differences in their target market, such as heated seats and a ski rack on the Alpine model.

RATINGS (SCALE OF 1-10)

Overall	Safety	Reliability	Performance	Comfort	Value
N/A	N/A	7.8	8.3	7.8	6.4

Category D

4 Dr L Sdn	4225	5835
4 Dr L 4WD Sdn	4925	6690
4 Dr L Wgn	4385	6000
4 Dr L 4WD Wgn	5115	6945
4 Dr LS Sdn	5275	7165
4 Dr LS 4WD Sdn	5480	7440
4 Dr LS Wgn	5465	7420
4 Dr LS 4WD Wgn	5660	7685
4 Dr LSi 4WD Sdn	5710	7755
4 Dr LSi 4WD Wgn	6010	8165
4 Dr Sport Turbo 4WD Sdn	5505	7475
4 Dr Touring Turbo 4WD Wgn	6010	8165

OPTIONS FOR LEGACY

Auto 4-Speed Transmission[Opt on L,Sport] +160
Anti-Lock Brakes[Opt on L Wgn] +175
Compact Disc W/fm/tape[Opt on LS] +155
Cruise Control[Opt on L Wgn] +50
Luggage Rack[Std on L] +55

LOYALE   1993

New colors are the only changes to the Loyale.

Category D

4 Dr FWD Sdn	2540	3450
4 Dr FWD Wgn	2740	3720
4 Dr STD 4WD Sdn	2855	3880
4 Dr STD 4WD Wgn	3085	4195

OPTIONS FOR LOYALE

Auto 3-Speed Transmission +110
AM/FM Stereo Tape +70
Luggage Rack +55

SVX   1993

No changes for Subaru's quirky sports car.

Category F

2 Dr 25th Anniversary 4WD Cpe	9920	12010
2 Dr LS Cpe	7725	9350
2 Dr LS-L Cpe	8590	10400
2 Dr XR Cpe	8690	10520

1992 SUBARU

JUSTY   1992

The Subaru Justy is unchanged.

Category E

2 Dr GL Hbk	1460	2580
2 Dr GL 4WD Hbk	1570	2780
4 Dr GL 4WD Hbk	1615	2855
2 Dr STD Hbk	1220	2155

OPTIONS FOR JUSTY

Air Conditioning +135

LEGACY   1992

A driver airbag is now standard on the Legacy LS and LSi; it is optional on L model. A trunk pass-through opening in the rear seats, rear heater ducts, and cupholders integrated into the dashboard give more utility to the passengers.

RATINGS (SCALE OF 1-10)

Overall	Safety	Reliability	Performance	Comfort	Value
N/A	N/A	7.1	8.3	7.8	5.7

Category D

4 Dr L Sdn	2985	4155
4 Dr L 4WD Sdn	3295	4585
4 Dr L Wgn	3095	4305
4 Dr L 4WD Wgn	3435	4780
4 Dr LE Turbo 4WD Wgn	4440	6180
4 Dr LS Sdn	4305	5985
4 Dr LS 4WD Sdn	4270	5940
4 Dr LS Wgn	4240	5900
4 Dr LS 4WD Wgn	4440	6180

Model Description	Trade-in Value	Market Value
4 Dr LSi Sdn	4250	5915
4 Dr LSi 4WD Sdn	4550	6335
4 Dr Sport Turbo 4WD Sdn	4140	5760

OPTIONS FOR LEGACY
Auto 4-Speed Transmission[Opt on L,Sport] +130
Air Bag Restraint[Std on Sport,LS Sdn] +90
Air Conditioning[Opt on L] +140
Anti-Lock Brakes[Opt on L] +145
Compact Disc W/fm/tape[Opt on L] +125
Power Door Locks[Opt on L] +45
Power Windows[Opt on L] +45

LOYALE   1992

Still no changes for the Loyale.
Category D

Model Description	Trade-in Value	Market Value
4 Dr STD Sdn	2205	3070
4 Dr STD 4WD Sdn	2415	3360
4 Dr STD Wgn	2390	3325
4 Dr STD 4WD Wgn	2625	3650

OPTIONS FOR LOYALE
Auto 3-Speed Transmission +90

SVX   1992

Subaru replaces the odd XT6 with the equally unusual SVX. Performance numbers are quite good with the standard 3.3-liter Flat-6 engine and standard all-wheel drive. The strange two-piece side windows, designed to decrease interior turbulence when the window is opened, leave something to be desired. Antilock brakes and a driver airbag are standard.
Category F

Model Description	Trade-in Value	Market Value
2 Dr STD 4WD Cpe	6390	8050

OPTIONS FOR SVX
Compact Disc W/fm/tape +80
Leather Seats +105
Power Drivers Seat +40
Power Sunroof +110

1991 SUBARU

JUSTY   1991

The Subaru Justy is unchanged.
Category E

Model Description	Trade-in Value	Market Value
2 Dr GL Hbk	1105	2145
2 Dr GL 4WD Hbk	1165	2255
4 Dr GL 4WD Hbk	1235	2395
2 Dr STD Hbk	905	1760

OPTIONS FOR JUSTY
Auto 3-Speed Transmission +70
Air Conditioning +110

LEGACY   1991

Turbo power is now available on the Legacy Sport sedan. The boosted engine produces 160-horsepower and 180 ft-lbs. of torque; not too shabby for a family hauler.

RATINGS (SCALE OF 1-10)

Overall	Safety	Reliability	Performance	Comfort	Value
N/A	N/A	6.5	8.3	7.8	6.2

Category D

Model Description	Trade-in Value	Market Value
4 Dr L Sdn	2480	3635
4 Dr L 4WD Sdn	2785	4085
4 Dr L Wgn	2590	3800
4 Dr L 4WD Wgn	2765	4055
4 Dr LS Sdn	3315	4865
4 Dr LS 4WD Sdn	3665	5375
4 Dr LS Wgn	3430	5035
4 Dr LS 4WD Wgn	3760	5515
4 Dr LSi Sdn	3640	5340
4 Dr LSi 4WD Sdn	3705	5430
4 Dr Sport Turbo 4WD Sdn	3680	5395

OPTIONS FOR LEGACY
Auto 4-Speed Transmission[Std on LSi] +100
Air Conditioning[Opt on L] +115
Anti-Lock Brakes[Opt on L,L Plus] +120
*Power Windows[Std on L Plus,LS,LSi,Sport,
L 4WD Wgn] +35*

LOYALE   1991

No changes to the ever-popular Loyale.
Category D

Model Description	Trade-in Value	Market Value
4 Dr STD Sdn	1825	2680
4 Dr STD 4WD Sdn	1955	2870
4 Dr STD Wgn	1975	2895
4 Dr STD 4WD Wgn	2085	3060

OPTIONS FOR LOYALE
Auto 3-Speed Transmission +75
Sunroof +60

XT   1991

The car with the weirdest steering wheel in the world enters its final year of production with no changes.
Category F

Model Description	Trade-in Value	Market Value
2 Dr GL Cpe	2255	3615
2 Dr XT6 Cpe	2935	4700
2 Dr XT6 4WD Cpe	3070	4915

OPTIONS FOR XT
Auto 4-Speed Transmission[Opt on GL,4WD] +100
Air Conditioning[Opt on GL] +110

Don't forget to refer to the Mileage Adjustment Table at the back of this book!

Model Description	Trade-in Value	Market Value

Model Description	Trade-in Value	Market Value

SUZUKI — Japan

1998 Suzuki Esteem

2000 SUZUKI

ESTEEM — 2000

All Esteems get the 1.8-liter engine starting with the September 1999 production run. GLX and GLX+ models receive 15-inch wheels and tires as standard equipment. Two new paint colors, Bluish Black Pearl and Cassis Red Pearl, replace Mars Red and Midnight Black.

Category E

	Trade-in	Market
4 Dr GL Sdn	8845	10470
4 Dr GL Wgn	9535	11280
4 Dr GLX Sdn	9880	11690
4 Dr GLX Wgn	10225	12095

OPTIONS FOR ESTEEM
4 cyl 1.8 L Engine[Opt on GL] +410
Auto 4-Speed Transmission +815
Cruise Control +185

GRAND VITARA — 2000

The 2000 Limited Edition Grand Vitara comes with leather seats, privacy glass, fog lamps, a hard spare tire cover, an armrest, gold emblems, and a special black-and-white paint scheme. The spare tire cover on regular Grand Vitaras features a new design. The '99 model's base trim levels JS and JS+ have been renamed JLS and JLS+. A CD changer is standard equipment on JLS+ and JLX+ models.

Category G

	Trade-in	Market
4 Dr JLS Hardtop	13205	15445
4 Dr JLX 4WD Hardtop	13910	16265
4 Dr Limited Hardtop	15600	18245
4 Dr Limited 4WD Hardtop	16305	19070

OPTIONS FOR GRAND VITARA
Auto 4-Speed Transmission[Std on Limited] +815
Aluminum/Alloy Wheels[Std on Limited] +265

SWIFT — 2000

The 2000 Suzuki Swift remains mechanically unchanged. Two new exterior colors - Brilliant Blue Metallic and Catseye Blue Metallic - are offered.

Category E

	Trade-in	Market
2 Dr GA Hbk	6320	7480
2 Dr GL Hbk	6985	8270

OPTIONS FOR SWIFT
Auto 3-Speed Transmission +530
AM/FM Stereo Tape[Std on GL] +250
Air Conditioning[Std on GL] +680

VITARA — 2000

Four-door models receive a new luggage cover for 2000. The Vitara two-door JLS/JLX is equipped with air conditioning as standard equipment. There are three new paint colors, and four-wheel-drive models have a "4x4" sticker in the rear-quarter windows.

Category G

	Trade-in	Market
2 Dr JLS Conv	11490	13435
4 Dr JLS Wgn	12465	14580
2 Dr JLX 4WD Conv	12830	15005
4 Dr JLX 4WD Wgn	13655	15970
2 Dr JS Conv	10375	12130
4 Dr JS Wgn	11870	13880
2 Dr JX 4WD Conv	11715	13700
4 Dr JX 4WD Wgn	13060	15275

OPTIONS FOR VITARA
Auto 4-Speed Transmission +815

1999 SUZUKI

ESTEEM — 1999

A restyled front end with multi-reflector headlights and an overall smoother body distinguishes the 1999 Esteem line from its predecessors. Base GL models now come with the 14-inch wheels that were standard on GLX models. Interior surfaces have been upgraded and a Clarion AM/FM cassette is now available. But the exciting news comes in the form of an all-new, 1.8-lite inline four that makes 122 horsepower.

RATINGS (SCALE OF 1-10)

Overall	Safety	Reliability	Performance	Comfort	Value
N/A	N/A	N/A	6.2	7	N/A

Category E

	Trade-in	Market
4 Dr GL Sdn	8050	9710
4 Dr GL Wgn	8370	10095

Model Description	Trade-in Value	Market Value
4 Dr GLX Sdn	8755	10555
4 Dr GLX Wgn	9070	10940

OPTIONS FOR ESTEEM
4 cyl 1.8 L Engine +335
Auto 4-Speed Transmission +670
Anti-Lock Brakes +445
Cruise Control +155

GRAND VITARA 1999

The Grand Vitara is a completely new design from Suzuki and offers plenty of passenger room along with a standard V6 engine.

RATINGS (SCALE OF 1-10)

Overall	Safety	Reliability	Performance	Comfort	Value
N/A	N/A	N/A	7.2	7.4	N/A

Category G

	Trade-in	Market
4 Dr JLX 4WD Hardtop	12420	14725
4 Dr JS Hardtop	12305	14590

OPTIONS FOR GRAND VITARA
Auto 4-Speed Transmission +670
Aluminum/Alloy Wheels +215
Anti-Lock Brakes +390

SWIFT 1999

With the exception of some color changes, the Suzuki Swift remains unchanged for '99.

RATINGS (SCALE OF 1-10)

Overall	Safety	Reliability	Performance	Comfort	Value
N/A	N/A	N/A	6.4	6.4	N/A

Category E

	Trade-in	Market
2 Dr STD Hbk	6155	7425

OPTIONS FOR SWIFT
Auto 3-Speed Transmission +435
AM/FM Stereo Tape +200
Air Conditioning +555

VITARA 1999

The Vitara is an all-new model that replaces the Sidekick as Suzuki's entry into the mini SUV class.

RATINGS (SCALE OF 1-10)

Overall	Safety	Reliability	Performance	Comfort	Value
N/A	N/A	N/A	6.6	7.4	N/A

Category G

	Trade-in	Market
4 Dr JS Wgn	10215	12110
2 Dr JS 1.6 Conv	8980	10650
2 Dr JS 2.0 Conv	9500	11265
4 Dr JX 4WD Wgn	11250	13335
2 Dr JX 1.6 4WD Conv	10145	12030
2 Dr JX 2.0 4WD Conv	10660	12640

OPTIONS FOR VITARA
Auto 4-Speed Transmission +670
Air Conditioning +550
Cruise Control +140
Keyless Entry System +130

1998 SUZUKI

ESTEEM 1998

A wagon adds diversity to the Esteem lineup.
Category E

	Trade-in	Market
4 Dr GL Sdn	6995	8560
4 Dr GL Wgn	7275	8905
4 Dr GL SE Wgn	8175	10010
4 Dr GLX Sdn	7610	9320
4 Dr GLX Wgn	7895	9665
4 Dr GLX SE Wgn	8795	10765

OPTIONS FOR ESTEEM
Auto 4-Speed Transmission[Opt on GL, GLX] +545
Anti-Lock Brakes +365
Cruise Control +125

SIDEKICK 1998

A couple of new colors debut.

RATINGS (SCALE OF 1-10)

Overall	Safety	Reliability	Performance	Comfort	Value
6.3	5.5	8.9	6.4	6.6	4.2

Category G

	Trade-in	Market
2 Dr JS Conv	7470	9005
4 Dr JS Wgn	8190	9880
2 Dr JX 4WD Conv	8445	10185
4 Dr JX 4WD Wgn	9075	10945
4 Dr JX FLT 4WD Wgn	10520	12685
2 Dr JX SE 4WD Conv	9225	11125
4 Dr Sport JLX 4WD Wgn	10955	13210
4 Dr Sport JS Wgn	9575	11545
4 Dr Sport JX 4WD Wgn	10125	12210
4 Dr Sport JX SE 4WD Wgn	10675	12875

OPTIONS FOR SIDEKICK
Auto 3-Speed Transmission +330
Auto 4-Speed Transmission +535
Air Conditioning[Opt on JS, JX] +450
Anti-Lock Brakes[Std on Sport JLX] +320

SWIFT 1998

Swift's engine makes nine more horsepower this year, and one more pound of torque.

RATINGS (SCALE OF 1-10)

Overall	Safety	Reliability	Performance	Comfort	Value
6.5	6.3	8.3	6.4	6.4	4.9

Don't forget to refer to the Mileage Adjustment Table at the back of this book!

Category E

2 Dr STD Hbk	5020	6145

OPTIONS FOR SWIFT
Auto 3-Speed Transmission +355
Air Conditioning +455
Anti-Lock Brakes +365

X-90   1998

The VIN number is new for 1998.
Category G

2 Dr SE 4WD Utility	9020	10875
2 Dr STD Utility	7290	8790
2 Dr STD 4WD Utility	8030	9680

OPTIONS FOR X-90
AM/FM Stereo Tape[Opt on 2WD] +120
Air Conditioning[Std on SE] +450

1997 SUZUKI

ESTEEM   1997

No changes to the economical Esteem.
Category E

4 Dr GL Sdn	5435	7165
4 Dr GLX Sdn	5920	7805

OPTIONS FOR ESTEEM
Auto 4-Speed Transmission +445
Anti-Lock Brakes +295
Cruise Control +100

SIDEKICK   1997

A JS Sport 2WD model is added to the Sidekick lineup. It has a DOHC engine that makes 120 horsepower at 6500 rpm. There are no changes to the rest of the Sidekick line.

RATINGS (SCALE OF 1-10)

Overall	Safety	Reliability	Performance	Comfort	Value
6	5.5	8.6	6.4	6.6 ↑	3.1

Category G

2 Dr JS Conv	6175	7640
4 Dr JS Wgn	6880	8510
2 Dr JX 4WD Conv	6995	8655
4 Dr JX 4WD Wgn	7620	9430
4 Dr Sport JLX 4WD Wgn	9105	11265
4 Dr Sport JS Wgn	7945	9830
4 Dr Sport JX 4WD Wgn	8410	10405

OPTIONS FOR SIDEKICK
Auto 3-Speed Transmission +270
Auto 4-Speed Transmission +435
AM/FM Stereo Tape[Opt on Conv] +100
Air Conditioning[Opt on JS,JX] +365
Anti-Lock Brakes[Std on Sport JLX] +260

SWIFT   1997

New paint colors (Victory Red and Bright Teal Metallic) and new seat coverings are the only changes to the 1996 Swift.

RATINGS (SCALE OF 1-10)

Overall	Safety	Reliability	Performance	Comfort	Value
6.4	6.3	8.1	6.4	6.4	4.8

Category E

2 Dr STD Hbk	4085	5385

OPTIONS FOR SWIFT
Auto 3-Speed Transmission +290
AM/FM Stereo Tape +135
Air Conditioning +370
Anti-Lock Brakes +295

X-90   1997

No changes to Suzuki's interesting alternative to AWD vehicles.
Category G

2 Dr STD Utility	6350	7855
2 Dr STD 4WD Utility	7000	8660

OPTIONS FOR X-90
Auto 4-Speed Transmission +425
AM/FM Stereo Tape[Opt on 2WD] +100
Air Conditioning +365
Anti-Lock Brakes +260
Cruise Control +95

1996 SUZUKI

ESTEEM   1996

New for 1996 are daytime running lights, standard air conditioning and body-color bumpers on the GL.
Category E

4 Dr GL Sdn	4470	6210
4 Dr GLX Sdn	4955	6885

OPTIONS FOR ESTEEM
Auto 4-Speed Transmission +365
AM/FM Stereo Tape[Opt on GL] +110
Anti-Lock Brakes +245
Cruise Control +85

SIDEKICK   1996

Lots of changes to this mini SUV: the 16-valve, 95-horsepower engine is available across the board (except in the Sport), and dual airbags are housed in a revised instrument panel. New fabrics, colors and styling revisions update the Sidekick nicely. All-new for 1996 is a Sport variant, equipped with lots of exclusive standard equipment, a 120-horsepower twin-cam motor, a wider track, two-tone paint and a dorky chrome grille.

Don't forget to refer to the Mileage Adjustment Table at the back of this book!

Model Description	Trade-in Value	Market Value

RATINGS (SCALE OF 1-10)

Overall	Safety	Reliability	Performance	Comfort	Value
6	5.4	8	6.4	6.6	3.6

Category G

2 Dr JS Conv	5725	7055
4 Dr JS Wgn	6380	7865
2 Dr JX 4WD Conv	6490	8000
4 Dr JX 4WD Wgn	7070	8715
4 Dr Sport JLX 4WD Wgn	8365	10310
4 Dr Sport JX 4WD Wgn	7935	9775

OPTIONS FOR SIDEKICK
Auto 3-Speed Transmission +220
Auto 4-Speed Transmission +355
Air Conditioning[Opt on JS,JX] +300
Anti-Lock Brakes[Opt on JS,JX] +210

SWIFT   1996

Oh boy. Two new colors and new seat fabrics. Whoopee.

RATINGS (SCALE OF 1-10)

Overall	Safety	Reliability	Performance	Comfort	Value
6.4	6.3	8	6.4	6.4	4.8

Category E

2 Dr STD Hbk	3495	4855

OPTIONS FOR SWIFT
Auto 3-Speed Transmission +235
AM/FM Stereo Tape +110
Air Conditioning +305
Anti-Lock Brakes +245

X-90   1996

Based on Sidekick platform, this new concept features a two-seat cockpit, T-top roof, conventional trunk, and available four-wheel drive. Loaded with standard equipment, the X-90 is an interesting vehicle indeed.

Category G

2 Dr STD Utility	5680	7000
2 Dr STD 4WD Utility	6290	7755

OPTIONS FOR X-90
Auto 4-Speed Transmission +345
Air Conditioning +300

1995 SUZUKI

ESTEEM   1995

The 1995 Esteem is Suzuki's latest entry in the hotly contested subcompact car market. The Esteem has standard antilock brakes and dual airbags but is saddled with a 1.6-liter engine. Competition from Toyota, Geo and Honda is stiff, but low resale values may make this car worthwhile.

Category E

4 Dr GL Sdn	3645	4890
4 Dr GLX Sdn	4045	5430

OPTIONS FOR ESTEEM
Auto 4-Speed Transmission +300
Air Conditioning +250
Anti-Lock Brakes +200
Cruise Control +70

SAMURAI   1995

The Samurai is retired this year with no changes.

Category G

2 Dr JL 4WD Conv	3565	4550

OPTIONS FOR SAMURAI
Air Conditioning +245

SIDEKICK   1995

The convertible model gets a new top.

RATINGS (SCALE OF 1-10)

Overall	Safety	Reliability	Performance	Comfort	Value
5.7	2.7	8	6.6	6.6	4.6

Category G

4 Dr JLX 4WD Wgn	6270	8000
2 Dr JS Conv	4525	5775
4 Dr JS Wgn	5210	6650
2 Dr JX 4WD Conv	5200	6640
4 Dr JX 4WD Wgn	5705	7280

OPTIONS FOR SIDEKICK
Auto 3-Speed Transmission +180
Auto 4-Speed Transmission +270
Air Conditioning +245
Luggage Rack +50

SWIFT   1995

The sedan is dropped and dual airbags are added. Antilock brakes become a much appreciated option. The two-door, GT hatchback has also been dropped.

RATINGS (SCALE OF 1-10)

Overall	Safety	Reliability	Performance	Comfort	Value
6.4	6.9	7.8	6.4	6.4	4.7

Category E

2 Dr STD Hbk	2650	3560

OPTIONS FOR SWIFT
Auto 3-Speed Transmission +345
AM/FM Stereo Tape +90
Air Conditioning +250
Anti-Lock Brakes +200

Model Description	Trade-in Value	Market Value	Model Description	Trade-in Value	Market Value

1994 SUZUKI

SAMURAI 1994

Another Samurai commits Hari-Kari; the two-wheel drive model is no longer available. Other changes are limited to the addition of a high-mounted rear brake light.

Category G

	Trade-in	Market
2 Dr JL 4WD Conv	2970	3885

OPTIONS FOR SAMURAI
Air Conditioning +200

SIDEKICK 1994

All Sidekicks get an alarm and a tilt steering wheel as standard equipment this year. A high-mounted rear brake light is a new safety item found on all Sidekicks.

RATINGS (SCALE OF 1-10)

Overall	Safety	Reliability	Performance	Comfort	Value
5.2	2.3	6.8	6.6	6.6	3.5

Category G

	Trade-in	Market
4 Dr JLX 4WD Wgn	5245	6860
2 Dr JS Conv	3920	5130
4 Dr JS Wgn	4475	5855
2 Dr JX 4WD Conv	4385	5735
4 Dr JX 4WD Wgn	4795	6270

OPTIONS FOR SIDEKICK
Auto 3-Speed Transmission +145
Auto 4-Speed Transmission +245
Air Conditioning +200
Flip-Up Sunroof +80

SWIFT 1994

The GA hatchback gets a cargo cover and both GA models get a right sideview mirror. Will wonders never cease?

Category E

	Trade-in	Market
2 Dr GA Hbk	1700	2655
4 Dr GA Sdn	1890	2955
4 Dr GS Sdn	2210	3450
2 Dr GT Hbk	2345	3660

OPTIONS FOR SWIFT
Auto 3-Speed Transmission +155
AM/FM Stereo Tape[Opt on GA] +75
Air Conditioning +205

1993 SUZUKI

SAMURAI 1993

When are they going to retire this thing? The Samurai continues unchanged.

Category G

	Trade-in	Market
2 Dr JA Conv	2015	2640
2 Dr JL 4WD Conv	2410	3160

OPTIONS FOR SAMURAI
AM/FM Stereo Tape +45
Air Conditioning +165

SIDEKICK 1993

No changes for the Sidekick.

RATINGS (SCALE OF 1-10)

Overall	Safety	Reliability	Performance	Comfort	Value
5.3	2.5	7.5	6.6	6.6	3.5

Category G

	Trade-in	Market
4 Dr JLX 4WD Wgn	4535	5950
2 Dr JS Conv	3410	4475
4 Dr JS Wgn	3795	4980
2 Dr JX 4WD Conv	3835	5030
4 Dr JX 4WD Wgn	4145	5440

OPTIONS FOR SIDEKICK
Auto 3-Speed Transmission +120
Auto 4-Speed Transmission +180
AM/FM Stereo Tape[Opt on Conv] +45
Air Conditioning +165
Hardtop Roof +160

SWIFT 1993

The doors lock when the Swift reaches speeds of 8 mph or more; apparently Suzuki thinks that anyone crazy enough to buy this car won't be able to figure out how to do this on their own.

Category E

	Trade-in	Market
2 Dr GA Hbk	1410	2325
4 Dr GA Sdn	1540	2535
4 Dr GS Sdn	1800	2965
2 Dr GT Hbk	1915	3150

OPTIONS FOR SWIFT
Auto 3-Speed Transmission +120
AM/FM Stereo Tape[Opt on GA] +60
Air Conditioning +165

1992 SUZUKI

SAMURAI 1992

The Samurai loses a trim-level, making it available only as a two-wheel drive JA or four-wheel drive JL. The JL model loses its back seat.

Category G

	Trade-in	Market
2 Dr JA Conv	1715	2295
2 Dr JL 4WD Conv	2080	2785

OPTIONS FOR SAMURAI
AM/FM Stereo Tape +35
Air Conditioning +135

Don't forget to refer to the Mileage Adjustment Table at the back of this book!

Model Description	Trade-in Value	Market Value

SIDEKICK 1992

Four-door models receive an increase of 15 horsepower and a four-speed automatic transmission. All Sidekicks get a redesigned instrument panel.

RATINGS (SCALE OF 1-10)

Overall	Safety	Reliability	Performance	Comfort	Value
5.4	2.4	7.8	6.6	6.6	3.8

Category G

Model	Trade-in	Market
4 Dr JLX 4WD Wgn	3590	4800
2 Dr JS Conv	2820	3770
4 Dr JS Wgn	3065	4100
2 Dr JX 4WD Conv	3155	4215
4 Dr JX 4WD Wgn	3285	4390

OPTIONS FOR SIDEKICK
Auto 3-Speed Transmission +140
Air Conditioning +135
Hardtop Roof +130
Leather Seats +130

SWIFT 1992

All Swifts get a redesigned front and rear fascia as well as a new dashboard. GS sedans receive power steering and new hub caps.

Category E

Model	Trade-in	Market
2 Dr GA Hbk	1170	2015
4 Dr GA Sdn	1300	2240
4 Dr GS Sdn	1530	2635
2 Dr GT Hbk	1610	2775

OPTIONS FOR SWIFT
Auto 3-Speed Transmission +100
Air Conditioning +135

1991 SUZUKI

SAMURAI 1991

The Samurai receives a freshened front-end that includes a new grille.

Category G

Model	Trade-in	Market
2 Dr JL 4WD Conv	1905	2635
2 Dr STD Conv	1850	2555

OPTIONS FOR SAMURAI
Js Option +135
Air Conditioning +110

SIDEKICK 1991

A four-door Sidekick is introduced, offering more passenger and cargo room.

RATINGS (SCALE OF 1-10)

Overall	Safety	Reliability	Performance	Comfort	Value
5.4	2.3	7.1	6.6	6.6	4.3

Category G

Model	Trade-in	Market
2 Dr JL 4WD Conv	2705	3740
4 Dr JLX 4WD Wgn	3090	4270
2 Dr JS Conv	2460	3400
2 Dr JX 4WD Conv	2805	3880
4 Dr JX 4WD Wgn	2855	3950

OPTIONS FOR SIDEKICK
Auto 3-Speed Transmission +80
AM/FM Stereo Tape[Opt on JL,JS] +30
Air Conditioning +110

SWIFT 1991

A GS sedan is introduced to the Swift lineup, offering first-time buyers a touch more luxury than is found in the base model.

Category E

Model	Trade-in	Market
2 Dr GA Hbk	910	1750
4 Dr GA Sdn	1060	2040
4 Dr GS Sdn	1210	2325
2 Dr GT Hbk	1320	2535

OPTIONS FOR SWIFT
Auto 3-Speed Transmission +80
AM/FM Stereo Tape[Opt on GA] +40
Air Conditioning +110

Don't forget to refer to the Mileage Adjustment Table at the back of this book!

TOYOTA

Japan

1994 Toyota Corolla

2000 TOYOTA

4RUNNER — 2000

Optional color-coordinated fender flares are available on the SR5. An AM/FM/Cassette/CD is now available on base models, and is standard on SR5 and Limited models. Daytime running lights are now included with the antilock brake package.

Category G

Model	Trade-in	Market
4 Dr Limited Wgn	24470	28585
4 Dr Limited 4WD Wgn	26230	30640
4 Dr SR5 Wgn	18835	22005
4 Dr SR5 4WD Wgn	19645	22950
4 Dr STD Wgn	16010	18705
4 Dr STD 4WD Wgn	17530	20480

OPTIONS FOR 4RUNNER

Auto 4-Speed Transmission[Opt on STD,SR5 V6 4WD] +735
Black Elite Pkg +720
Exterior Pkg +690
Gold Elite Pkg +765
Sport Handling Pkg +695
Air Conditioning[Std on Limited] +670
Aluminum/Alloy Wheels[Std on Limited] +265
Anti-Lock Brakes[Opt on STD] +475
Compact Disc W/fm/tape[Opt on STD,SR5 V6 2WD] +365
Cruise Control[Opt on STD] +170
Fog Lights[Opt on SR5] +120
Keyless Entry System[Opt on SR5] +160
Leather Seats[Opt on SR5] +640
Power Door Locks[Opt on STD,SR5 V6 2WD] +190
Power Mirrors +110
Power Moonroof +710
Power Windows[Std on Limited] +200
Privacy Glass[Opt on STD] +225

Rear Wind Deflector +105
Running Boards[Std on Limited] +315
Tilt Steering Wheel[Opt on STD] +145

AVALON — 2000

Entering its second generation, the 2000 Avalon is roomier, more powerful and more technically advanced. The Kentucky-built Avalon features new styling inside and out, enhanced safety features, increased engine performance, and more comfort and convenience than its predecessor.

Category D

Model	Trade-in	Market
4 Dr XL Sdn	19295	22500
4 Dr XLS Sdn	22605	26360

OPTIONS FOR AVALON

Aluminum/Alloy Wheels[Opt on XL] +380
Dual Power Seats[Opt on XL] +695
Leather Seats +925
Power Moonroof +690
Traction Control System +435

CAMRY — 2000

The Camry sedan receives minor updates for the 2000 model year. The exterior benefits from new front and rear styling. Camry LE models get 15-inch tires with new wheel covers while the XLE gets standard 16-inch tires. Four-cylinder models make three more horsepower than last year. Interior upgrades include an available JBL premium audio system, automatic climate control, larger buttons on the audio faceplate, imitation wood trim on XLE models, optional leather seats with driver-side power on LE models, and new LE model seat fabric. The hood is now supported with struts and dampers.

Category D

Model	Trade-in	Market
4 Dr CE Sdn	12275	14315
4 Dr LE Sdn	14235	16600
4 Dr LE V6 Sdn	15580	18170
4 Dr XLE Sdn	16750	19530
4 Dr XLE V6 Sdn	18200	21225

OPTIONS FOR CAMRY

Auto 4-Speed Transmission[Opt on CE,LE V6] +655
Black Elite Pkg +715
Air Conditioning[Opt on CE] +705
Aluminum/Alloy Wheels[Std on XLE,XLE V6] +380
Anti-Lock Brakes[Opt on CE,LE] +725
Compact Disc W/fm/tape[Opt on CE] +635
Cruise Control[Opt on CE] +205
Keyless Entry System[Opt on LE,LE V6] +255
Leather Seats +925
Power Door Locks[Opt on CE] +220
Power Drivers Seat +255
Power Mirrors[Opt on CE] +130
Power Moonroof +690
Power Windows[Opt on CE] +220

Don't forget to refer to the Mileage Adjustment Table at the back of this book!

TOYOTA 00

Model Description	Trade-in Value	Market Value	Model Description	Trade-in Value	Market Value

Side Air Bag Restraint +240
Traction Control System +435

CAMRY SOLARA 2000

Solara four-cylinder models will achieve ultra-low-emission vehicle (ULEV) status. A convertible version is now offered for topless fun. SLE models get a JBL premium audio system as standard equipment, and a six-disc in-dash CD changer is optional. Two new exterior colors are offered.

Category D

Model	Trade-in	Market
2 Dr SE Conv	19330	22540
2 Dr SE Cpe	14685	17125
2 Dr SE V6 Conv	21555	25135
2 Dr SE V6 Cpe	16740	19520
2 Dr SLE Conv	23435	27325
2 Dr SLE Cpe	19760	23045

OPTIONS FOR CAMRY SOLARA

Auto 4-Speed Transmission[Std on SLE,Conv] +655
Aluminum/Alloy Wheels[Std on SLE] +380
Anti-Lock Brakes[Opt on SE] +725
Keyless Entry System[Std on SLE] +255
Leather Seats[Std on SLE] +925
Power Drivers Seat[Std on SLE] +255
Power Moonroof +690
Side Air Bag Restraint +240
Traction Control System +435

CELICA 2000

The all-new 2000 Celica is considerably more performance-oriented than the previous model. Highlights include an exciting exterior, a 180-horsepower engine and six-speed gearbox for the GT-S, and sharp handling.

Category F

Model	Trade-in	Market
2 Dr GT Hbk	12060	14065
2 Dr GT-S Hbk	15170	17690

OPTIONS FOR CELICA

Auto 4-Speed Transmission +615
Aluminum/Alloy Wheels[Opt on GT] +250
Anti-Lock Brakes +530
Cruise Control[Opt on GT] +180
Leather Seats +520
Power Door Locks[Opt on GT] +170
Power Moonroof +535
Power Windows[Opt on GT] +190
Rear Spoiler +195

COROLLA 2000

The Corolla receives increased performance from VVT-i engine technology. Horsepower jumps from 120 to 125. The Corolla also achieves low-emission vehicle status this year.

Category E

Model	Trade-in	Market
4 Dr CE Sdn	9880	11685
4 Dr LE Sdn	11080	13050
4 Dr VE Sdn	9190	10820

OPTIONS FOR COROLLA

Auto 3-Speed Transmission +410
Auto 4-Speed Transmission +655
Air Conditioning[Std on LE] +680
Cruise Control +185
Power Door Locks[Std on LE] +205
Power Windows[Std on LE] +215
Rear Window Defroster[Opt on VE] +135

ECHO 2000

The 2000 Toyota Echo brings a new name and a fresh concept to the Toyota lineup. Designed to attract youthful buyers, the Echo features a roomy and comfortable interior, superb gas mileage, and an affordable price.

Category E

Model	Trade-in	Market
2 Dr STD Cpe	8015	9440
4 Dr STD Sdn	8325	9805

OPTIONS FOR ECHO

Auto 4-Speed Transmission +655
AM/FM Compact Disc Player +355
Air Conditioning +680
Compact Disc W/fm/tape +395
Digital Clock +60
Intermittent Wipers +50
Power Steering +210
Rear Window Defroster +135

LAND CRUISER 2000

The Land Cruiser receives new standard equipment features, such as vehicle skid control and an Active TRAC electronic four-wheel-drive system with torque transfer capability. Additional newly standard equipment includes illuminated entry for the remote keyless-entry system, power tilt/slide moonroof and a leather interior. The optional third-row seat now includes rear air conditioning.

Category G

Model	Trade-in	Market
4 Dr STD 4WD Wgn	35920	41960

OPTIONS FOR LAND CRUISER

Convenience Pkg +705
Dual Air Conditioning +755
Luggage Rack +130
Rear Wind Deflector +105
Running Boards +315
Third Seat +585
Trailer Hitch +230

MR2 SPYDER 2000

Toyota revives the MR2 nameplate on a minimalist two-seat roadster, set to compete directly with the ever-

TOYOTA 00

Model Description	Trade-in Value	Market Value	Model Description	Trade-in Value	Market Value

popular Mazda Miata. Only 5,000 are being built and sold, so if you want one, be prepared for some hair-grabbing at the dealer.

Category F

2 Dr Spyder Conv	19350	22430

RAV4   2000

The RAV4 SUV remains largely unchanged for 2000. A new cupholder design and the extinction of the two-door RAV4 convertible are the big news for '00.

Category G

4 Dr L Special Edit. Wgn	14195	16585
4 Dr L Special Edit. 4WD Wgn	15210	17770
4 Dr STD Wgn	12475	14570
4 Dr STD 4WD Wgn	13485	15755

OPTIONS FOR RAV4

Auto 4-Speed Transmission +860
AM/FM Compact Disc Player[Opt on STD] +260
Air Conditioning[Opt on STD] +670
Aluminum/Alloy Wheels[Opt on STD] +265
Cruise Control[Opt on STD] +170
Power Door Locks[Opt on STD] +190
Power Mirrors[Opt on STD] +110
Power Windows[Opt on STD] +200

SIENNA   2000

New for Sienna are two exterior colors and various audio enhancements. All grades feature a standard AM/FM/cassette audio system. XLE models add a CD deck and offer an optional in-dash six-disc changer.

Category G

4 Dr CE Pass. Van	16685	19495
4 Dr LE Pass. Van	18825	21990
4 Dr XLE Pass. Van	20310	23730

OPTIONS FOR SIENNA

Aluminum/Alloy Wheels[Std on XLE] +265
Captain Chairs (4)[Opt on LE] +505
Cruise Control[Opt on CE] +170
Dual Air Conditioning[Opt on CE] +755
Keyless Entry System[Std on XLE] +160
Luggage Rack[Std on XLE] +130
Power Door Locks[Opt on CE] +190
Power Windows[Opt on CE] +200
Privacy Glass[Opt on CE] +225
Rear Window Defroster[Opt on CE] +140

TACOMA   2000

Tacomas with four-cylinder engines and four-wheel drive achieve improved performance from an enhanced gear ratio. Base-grade Tacomas feature new designs for the interior fabric and exterior mirrors. Daytime running lights are now included with the antilock brake package. There are also two new colors

as well as a color-keyed package for those who like the monochrome look.

Category G

2 Dr Limited 4WD Ext Cab SB	17845	20850
2 Dr Prerunner Ext Cab SB	13175	15295
2 Dr Prerunner Std Cab SB	10120	11825
2 Dr Prerunner V6 Ext Cab SB	13945	16125
2 Dr SR5 Ext Cab SB	12910	14880
2 Dr SR5 V6 Ext Cab SB	12515	14620
2 Dr SR5 4WD Ext Cab SB	13945	16335
2 Dr SR5 V6 4WD Ext Cab SB	14430	16930
2 Dr STD Ext Cab SB	11350	13110
2 Dr STD 4WD Ext Cab SB	13160	15370
2 Dr STD Std Cab SB	8620	10070
2 Dr STD 4WD Std Cab SB	11810	13795
2 Dr V6 Ext Cab SB	13615	15520
2 Dr V6 4WD Ext Cab SB	15040	17385

OPTIONS FOR TACOMA

Auto 4-Speed Transmission[Std on Prerunner,Prerunner V6] +695
TRD Off-Road Pkg +725
AM/FM Compact Disc Player +260
AM/FM Stereo Tape[Std on Prerunner V6] +180
Air Conditioning[Opt on Limited,STD,V6,Std Cab] +670
Aluminum/Alloy Wheels[Std on Limited] +265
Bed Liner +230
Center Console[Std on Limited,SR5 V6 4WD Ext Cab SB] +135
Compact Disc W/fm/tape[Opt on Prerunner,Prerunner V6,STD] +365
Cruise Control[Std on Limited] +170
Power Door Locks[Std on Limited] +190
Power Steering[Opt on Base 2WD Regular Cab] +230
Power Windows[Std on Limited] +200
Sliding Rear Window[Opt on Prerunner,Prerunner V6, STD,V6] +100
Tilt Steering Wheel[Std on Limited] +145

TUNDRA   2000

This is an all-new, full-size pickup truck designed to compete with the Ford F-150, Chevrolet Silverado 1500, GMC Sierra 1500 and Dodge Ram 1500. It features an optional V8 engine and can be ordered in a two or four-door, regular- or extended-cab configuration.

Category H

4 Dr Limited Ext Cab SB	18265	21245
4 Dr Limited 4WD Ext Cab SB	20645	24015
4 Dr SR5 V6 Ext Cab SB	15000	17450
4 Dr SR5 V6 4WD Ext Cab SB	17285	20105
2 Dr SR5 V6 4WD Std Cab LB	14765	17175
4 Dr SR5 V8 Ext Cab SB	16480	19175
4 Dr SR5 V8 4WD Ext Cab SB	18865	21945

Don't forget to refer to the Mileage Adjustment Table at the back of this book!

Model Description	Trade-in Value	Market Value
2 Dr SR5 V8 4WD Std Cab LB	16810	19555
2 Dr STD Std Cab LB	11300	13145

OPTIONS FOR TUNDRA
Auto 4-Speed Transmission[Opt on SR5 V6,STD] +625
Air Conditioning[Opt on STD] +665
Alarm System +160
Aluminum/Alloy Wheels[Std on Limited] +255
Anti-Lock Brakes +400
Bed Liner +185
Compact Disc Changer +365
Compact Disc W/fm/tape[Std on Limited] +255
Cruise Control[Opt on SR5 V6] +155
Fog Lights[Std on Limited] +105
Leather Seats +815
Lighted Entry System[Std on Limited] +110
Power Door Locks[Std on Limited] +155
Power Drivers Seat +230
Power Mirrors[Std on Limited] +85
Power Windows[Std on Limited] +155
Sliding Rear Window[Std on Limited] +95
Tilt Steering Wheel[Opt on STD] +155
Trailer Hitch +135

1999 TOYOTA

4RUNNER 1999

The 4Runner receives a number of upgrades this year, starting with a new and improved four-wheel drive system equipped with a center differential and featuring a full-time 4WD mode in addition to the current two-high, four-high and four-low modes. New exterior features include a front bumper redesign, multi-reflector headlamps, and an enhanced sport package with fender flares and a hood scoop on the SR5 model. Inside, a new center console/cupholder design will improve beverage-carrying capacity of the 4Runner and an automatic climate control system will be featured on the Limited models.

RATINGS (SCALE OF 1-10)

Overall	Safety	Reliability	Performance	Comfort	Value
N/A	7.8	9.4	6.6	6.9	N/A

Category G

	Trade-in	Market
4 Dr Limited Wgn	23055	26995
4 Dr Limited 4WD Wgn	24675	28895
4 Dr SR5 Wgn	17695	20720
4 Dr SR5 4WD Wgn	18480	21640
4 Dr STD Wgn	14630	17130
4 Dr STD 4WD Wgn	16105	18860

OPTIONS FOR 4RUNNER
Auto 4-Speed Transmission[Opt on STD,SR5 V6 4WD] +600
Black Elite Pkg +595
Sport Handling Pkg +570

Air Conditioning[Std on Limited] +550
Aluminum/Alloy Wheels[Std on Limited] +215
Anti-Lock Brakes[Std on Limited,SR5] +390
Compact Disc Changer +340
Compact Disc W/fm/tape +295
Cruise Control[Opt on STD] +140
Fog Lights[Std on Limited] +95
Keyless Entry System[Std on Limited] +130
Leather Seats[Opt on SR5] +525
Power Door Locks[Std on Limited] +155
Power Mirrors[Opt on STD] +90
Power Moonroof +580
Power Windows[Std on Limited] +160
Privacy Glass[Opt on STD] +185
Rear Window Defroster[Opt on STD] +115
Rear Window Wiper[Opt on STD] +105
Running Boards[Std on Limited] +260
Tilt Steering Wheel[Opt on STD] +120

AVALON 1999

After a body makeover and safety improvements (side airbags) last year, the Avalon heads into '99 with only minor updates. Daytime running lights with auto-off color-keyed foglamp covers and dual heated color keyed power mirrors are new this year. A new three-in-one ETR/cassette/CD sound system is optional on the XL model and Lunar Mist metallic replaces Golden Sand metallic.

RATINGS (SCALE OF 1-10)

Overall	Safety	Reliability	Performance	Comfort	Value
N/A	N/A	N/A	8.2	8.4	N/A

Category D

	Trade-in	Market
4 Dr XL Sdn	17600	20565
4 Dr XLS Sdn	20410	23850

OPTIONS FOR AVALON
Aluminum/Alloy Wheels[Opt on XL] +310
Compact Disc W/fm/tape[Opt on XL] +520
Heated Front Seats +250
Leather Seats +760
Power Moonroof +565
Traction Control System +355

CAMRY 1999

If it ain't broken, don't fix (or change) it. The Camry is already Toyota's best-selling car so changes to the '99 are minimal. Two new audio systems are available and both include three-in-one ETR/cassette/CD features. Also available are daytime running lights with auto-off. Vintage Red Pearl, Sable Pearl, and Woodland Pearl replace Sunfire Red Pearl, Ruby Red and Classic Green Pearl.

RATINGS (SCALE OF 1-10)

Overall	Safety	Reliability	Performance	Comfort	Value
N/A	7.9	8.7	8.6	8.1	N/A

Model Description	Trade-in Value	Market Value
Category D		
4 Dr CE Sdn	11260	13155
4 Dr LE Sdn	13240	15425
4 Dr LE V6 Sdn	15285	17895
4 Dr XLE Sdn	14950	17465
4 Dr XLE V6 Sdn	16390	19155

OPTIONS FOR CAMRY

Auto 4-Speed Transmission[Opt on CE] +535
Black Elite Pkg +550
Air Conditioning[Opt on CE] +575
Aluminum/Alloy Wheels[Std on XLE,XLE V6] +310
Anti-Lock Brakes[Opt on CE,LE] +595
Compact Disc W/fm/tape +520
Cruise Control[Opt on CE] +165
Keyless Entry System[Std on XLE,XLE V6] +210
Leather Seats +760
Power Door Locks[Opt on CE] +180
Power Drivers Seat +210
Power Mirrors[Opt on CE] +110
Power Moonroof +565
Power Windows[Opt on CE] +180
Side Air Bag Restraint +195
Traction Control System +355

CAMRY SOLARA   1999

Everything. This all-new coupe is based on the Camry platform. Designed jointly by the Toyota Motor Corporation in Japan and the Toyota Technical Center in Ann Arbor, Michigan, the Solara is targeted at consumers who want the style of a sports car but the room and comfort of a larger, more practical vehicle.

RATINGS (SCALE OF 1-10)

Overall	Safety	Reliability	Performance	Comfort	Value
N/A	N/A	N/A	8.6	8.1	N/A

	Trade-in	Market
Category D		
2 Dr SE Cpe	13670	15975
2 Dr SE V6 Cpe	15495	18105
2 Dr SLE Cpe	18215	21285

OPTIONS FOR CAMRY SOLARA

Auto 4-Speed Transmission[Std on SLE] +525
Aluminum/Alloy Wheels[Std on SLE] +310
Anti-Lock Brakes[Opt on SE] +595
Compact Disc W/fm/tape +520
Keyless Entry System[Std on SLE] +210
Power Drivers Seat[Std on SLE] +210
Power Moonroof +565
Side Air Bag Restraint +195
Traction Control System +355

CELICA   1999

The Celica GT Sport Coupe has been discontinued along with the color Galaxy Blue Metallic.

RATINGS (SCALE OF 1-10)

Overall	Safety	Reliability	Performance	Comfort	Value
N/A	N/A	N/A	8.2	7.6	N/A

	Trade-in	Market
Category F		
2 Dr GT Conv	16640	19440
2 Dr GT Hbk	14290	16700

OPTIONS FOR CELICA

Auto 4-Speed Transmission +535
Aluminum/Alloy Wheels[Std on Conv] +205
Anti-Lock Brakes +435
Compact Disc W/fm/tape[Std on Conv] +335
Leather Seats +425
Power Moonroof +440

COROLLA   1999

A major makeover in '98 means only minor updates to the Corolla in '99. The VE model will feature a Deluxe AM/FM ETR four-speaker audio system as standard equipment. A Touring Package will be standard equipment on the Corolla LE model. Five new exterior colors include Silver Stream Opal, Venetian Red Pearl, Dark Emerald Pearl, Aqua Blue Metallic and Twilight Blue Pearl.

RATINGS (SCALE OF 1-10)

Overall	Safety	Reliability	Performance	Comfort	Value
N/A	7.2	9.6	7.6	8.1	N/A

	Trade-in	Market
Category E		
4 Dr CE Sdn	9005	10700
4 Dr LE Sdn	10215	12160
4 Dr VE Sdn	8440	10055

OPTIONS FOR COROLLA

Auto 3-Speed Transmission +335
Auto 4-Speed Transmission +535
AM/FM Compact Disc Player +290
Air Conditioning[Std on LE] +555
Aluminum/Alloy Wheels +225
Anti-Lock Brakes +445
Cruise Control +155
Keyless Entry System +110
Power Door Locks[Std on LE] +165
Power Moonroof +390
Power Windows[Std on LE] +180
Rear Window Defroster[Opt on VE] +110
Side Air Bag Restraint +190

LAND CRUISER   1999

The Land Cruiser was reintroduced in '98 with major upgrades. As such, it enters '99 completely unchanged.

RATINGS (SCALE OF 1-10)

Overall	Safety	Reliability	Performance	Comfort	Value
N/A	N/A	N/A	7	7.9	N/A

Don't forget to refer to the Mileage Adjustment Table at the back of this book!

Model Description	Trade-in Value	Market Value
Category G		
4 Dr STD 4WD Wgn	31465	36845

OPTIONS FOR LAND CRUISER

Convenience Pkg +515
Third Seat Pkg +745
Dual Air Conditioning +615
Leather Seats +525
Locking Differential +195
Power Moonroof +580
Running Boards +260
Third Seat +480

RAV4   1999

Toyota promises minor upgrades for it's mini-SUV in '99. Leather seats and color-keyed body cladding are now available as part of the "L Special Edition" package. Color-keyed mirrors and door handles can also be had this year and the spare tire is now a full-size steel wheel with a soft cover.

RATINGS (SCALE OF 1-10)

Overall	Safety	Reliability	Performance	Comfort	Value
N/A	6.6	8.3	7	6.4	N/A

Model Description	Trade-in Value	Market Value
Category G		
2 Dr STD Conv	11240	13165
2 Dr STD 4WD Conv	12225	14315
4 Dr STD Wgn	11725	13730
4 Dr STD 4WD Wgn	12710	14880
4 Dr Special Edition 4WD Wgn	14245	16680

OPTIONS FOR RAV4

Auto 4-Speed Transmission +700
AM/FM Compact Disc Player +210
Air Conditioning[Opt on STD] +550
Aluminum/Alloy Wheels[Opt on STD] +215
Anti-Lock Brakes +390
Cruise Control[Opt on STD] +140
Power Door Locks[Opt on STD] +155
Power Mirrors[Opt on STD] +90
Power Windows[Opt on STD] +160

SIENNA   1999

Entering its second full model year of production at Toyota's Kentucky plant, the Sienna minivan gets a right side power sliding door. An engine immobilizer system has been added to the keyless-entry security system and all Siennas will be equipped with daytime running lights. Selected models have a full size spare tire and Woodland Pearl replaces Classic Green Pearl as an exterior color option.

RATINGS (SCALE OF 1-10)

Overall	Safety	Reliability	Performance	Comfort	Value
N/A	N/A	N/A	7	7.9	N/A

Model Description	Trade-in Value	Market Value
Category G		
2 Dr CE Pass. Van	15570	18235
4 Dr LE Pass. Van	17595	20605
4 Dr XLE Pass. Van	19170	22445

OPTIONS FOR SIENNA

AM/FM Compact Disc Player[Std on XLE] +210
Aluminum/Alloy Wheels[Std on XLE] +215
Captain Chairs (4)[Std on XLE] +410
Cruise Control[Opt on CE] +140
Dual Air Conditioning[Opt on CE] +615
Keyless Entry System[Std on XLE] +130
Leather Seats +525
Power Door Locks[Opt on CE] +155
Power Mirrors[Opt on CE] +90
Power Moonroof +580
Power Sliding Door +275
Power Windows[Opt on CE] +160
Privacy Glass[Opt on CE] +185
Rear Window Defroster[Opt on CE] +115

TACOMA   1999

Toyota adds new front seat belt pretensioners and force limiters. Newly optional on Xtra Cab models is an AM/FM four-speaker CD audio system while 4x4s get 15"x7" inch steel wheels. The PreRunner adds a regular cab option to its model mix. Natural White, Imperial Jade Mica and Horizon Blue Metallic replace White, Copper Canyon Mica, Evergreen Pearl, and Cool Steel Metallic as color options.

RATINGS (SCALE OF 1-10)

Overall	Safety	Reliability	Performance	Comfort	Value
N/A	N/A	N/A	7.2	7	N/A

Model Description	Trade-in Value	Market Value
Category G		
2 Dr Limited 4WD Ext Cab SB	16625	19630
2 Dr Prerunner Ext Cab SB	12185	14400
2 Dr Prerunner V6 Ext Cab SB	13235	15495
2 Dr Prerunner Std Cab SB	10600	12415
2 Dr SR5 Ext Cab SB	11335	13275
2 Dr SR5 V6 Ext Cab SB	12120	14195
2 Dr SR5 4WD Ext Cab SB	12840	15205
2 Dr SR5 V6 4WD Ext Cab SB	12645	15125
2 Dr STD Ext Cab SB	10280	12180
2 Dr STD 4WD Ext Cab SB	13585	15905
2 Dr STD Std Cab SB	9155	10725
2 Dr STD 4WD Std Cab SB	12570	14720
2 Dr V6 Ext Cab SB	12105	14030
2 Dr V6 4WD Ext Cab SB	13845	16220

OPTIONS FOR TACOMA

Auto 4-Speed Transmission[Std on Prerunner, Prerunner V6] +570
TRD Off-Road Pkg +635
AM/FM Compact Disc Player[Std on Limited] +210
Air Conditioning[Opt on Limited, STD, V6] +550

Don't forget to refer to the Mileage Adjustment Table at the back of this book!

TOYOTA 99-98

Model Description	Trade-in Value	Market Value	Model Description	Trade-in Value	Market Value

Aluminum/Alloy Wheels[Std on Limited] +215
Anti-Lock Brakes +390
Auto Locking Hubs (4WD)[Std on Limited] +180
Bed Liner +185
Cruise Control[Std on Limited] +140
Flip-Up Sunroof +220
Keyless Entry System +130
Power Door Locks[Std on Limited] +155
Power Steering[Opt on STD 4 cyl.] +190
Power Windows[Std on Limited] +160
Sliding Rear Window[Std on Limited, SR5] +80
Tilt Steering Wheel[Std on Limited] +120

1998 TOYOTA

4RUNNER   1998

For 1998, the Toyota 4Runner gets rotary HVAC controls, a new four-spoke steering wheel and revised audio control head units.

RATINGS (SCALE OF 1-10)

Overall	Safety	Reliability	Performance	Comfort	Value
6.8	7.8	9.3	6.6	6.9	3.6

Category G
4 Dr Limited Wgn	20555	24170
4 Dr Limited 4WD Wgn	22045	25915
4 Dr SR5 Wgn	16105	18930
4 Dr SR5 4WD Wgn	16825	19780
4 Dr STD Wgn	13225	15545
4 Dr STD 4WD Wgn	14580	17140

OPTIONS FOR 4RUNNER

Auto 4-Speed Transmission[Std on Limited, SR5 2WD] +490
Black Elite Pkg +500
Sports Pkg +435
Air Conditioning[Std on Limited] +450
Aluminum/Alloy Wheels[Std on Limited] +175
Anti-Lock Brakes[Opt on STD] +320
Compact Disc Changer +275
Compact Disc W/fm/tape +240
Cruise Control[Std on Limited] +115
Fog Lights +80
Keyless Entry System +105
Leather Seats[Opt on SR5] +430
Power Door Locks[Opt on STD] +130
Power Mirrors[Opt on STD] +70
Power Moonroof +475
Power Windows[Std on Limited] +135
Privacy Glass[Opt on STD] +150
Rear Window Defroster[Opt on STD] +95
Rear Window Wiper[Opt on STD] +85
Running Boards[Opt on SR5, STD] +210
Tilt Steering Wheel[Opt on STD] +100

AVALON   1998

The Avalon gets side-impact airbags, new headlights and taillamps, a new grille, a new trunk lid and pretension seatbelts with force limiters.

RATINGS (SCALE OF 1-10)

Overall	Safety	Reliability	Performance	Comfort	Value
8	8.8	8.8	8.2	8.4	5.7

Category D
4 Dr XL Sdn	16655	19520
4 Dr XLS Sdn	19260	22570

OPTIONS FOR AVALON

Leather Bucket Seat Pkg +425
AM/FM Compact Disc Player[Opt on XL] +255
Aluminum/Alloy Wheels[Opt on XL] +255
Dual Power Seats[Opt on XL] +465
Heated Front Seats +205
Heated Power Mirrors[Opt on XL] +45
Leather Seats +620
Power Moonroof +460
Traction Control System +290

CAMRY   1998

Side-impact airbags debut on the recently redesigned Camry. Depowered front airbags further enhance this car's ability to protect its occupant in a crash. An engine immobilizer feature is now part of the theft-deterrent package.

RATINGS (SCALE OF 1-10)

Overall	Safety	Reliability	Performance	Comfort	Value
7.4	7.9	8.5	8.6	8.1	4

Category D
4 Dr CE Sdn	9220	11105
4 Dr CE V6 Sdn	12770	14965
4 Dr LE Sdn	12715	14920
4 Dr LE V6 Sdn	14190	16785
4 Dr XLE Sdn	14535	17035
4 Dr XLE V6 Sdn	15990	18740

OPTIONS FOR CAMRY

Auto 4-Speed Transmission[Opt on CE] +435
Black Elite Pkg +450
AM/FM Compact Disc Player[Std on XLE, XLE V6] +255
Air Conditioning[Opt on CE, CE V6] +470
Aluminum/Alloy Wheels[Std on XLE, XLE V6] +255
Anti-Lock Brakes[Opt on CE 4 cyl.] +485
Cruise Control[Opt on CE, CE V6] +135
Keyless Entry System[Std on XLE, XLE V6] +170
Leather Seats +620
Power Door Locks[Opt on CE, CE V6] +150
Power Drivers Seat +170
Power Mirrors[Opt on CE, CE V6] +90
Power Moonroof +460
Power Windows[Opt on CE, CE V6] +150

Don't forget to refer to the Mileage Adjustment Table at the back of this book!

TOYOTA 98

Model Description	Trade-in Value	Market Value	Model Description	Trade-in Value	Market Value

Side Air Bag Restraint +160
Traction Control System +290

CELICA   1998

Celica ST is eliminated. GT's get more standard features and one new color: Caribbean Green Metallic.

RATINGS (SCALE OF 1-10)

Overall	Safety	Reliability	Performance	Comfort	Value
N/A	N/A	9.7	8.2	7.6	N/A

Category F
2 Dr GT Conv   15595   18195
2 Dr GT Cpe   12820   14960
2 Dr GT Hbk   13090   15270

OPTIONS FOR CELICA
Aluminum/Alloy Wheels[Std on Conv] +170
Compact Disc W/fm/tape[Opt on Hbk] +275
Leather Steering Wheel +90
Power Moonroof +360
Rear Spoiler[Opt on Cpe] +130

COROLLA   1998

The Toyota Corolla is completely redesigned this year with a new engine, new sheetmetal and a new standard for safety in compact cars: optional front passenger side-impact airbags.

RATINGS (SCALE OF 1-10)

Overall	Safety	Reliability	Performance	Comfort	Value
7.5	7.2	9.4	7.6	8.1	5.4

Category E
4 Dr CE Sdn   7995   9840
4 Dr LE Sdn   9820   11800
4 Dr VE Sdn   7955   9560

OPTIONS FOR COROLLA
Auto 3-Speed Transmission +275
Auto 4-Speed Transmission +435
AM/FM Compact Disc Player +235
Air Conditioning[Opt on VE] +455
Aluminum/Alloy Wheels +185
Anti-Lock Brakes +365
Cruise Control +125
Keyless Entry System +90
Power Door Locks[Opt on CE] +135
Power Moonroof +320
Power Windows[Opt on CE] +145
Rear Window Defroster[Opt on VE] +90
Side Air Bag Restraint +155
Tachometer[Opt on CE] +40

LAND CRUISER   1998

For 1998, Land Cruiser gets a more powerful V8 engine, standard ABS, an increase in structural rigidity, an improved suspension system, increased passenger and cargo room and a slew of new colors.

Category G
4 Dr STD 4WD Wgn   28460   33460

OPTIONS FOR LAND CRUISER
Convenience Pkg +420
Third Seat Pkg +600
Leather Seats +430
Locking Differential +160
Power Moonroof +475
Running Boards +210
Third Seat +390

RAV4   1998

Toyota's jellybean enters its third year of production with minor changes to the grille, headlights, taillamps and interior. Four-door RAV4s get new seat fabric. A late-year introduction of the new RAV4 convertible makes this sport-ute more appealing for those who live in the sunbelt.

RATINGS (SCALE OF 1-10)

Overall	Safety	Reliability	Performance	Comfort	Value
N/A	6.6	8.2	7	6.4	N/A

Category G
4 Dr L Special Edition Wgn   12185   14325
2 Dr STD Conv   10835   12735
2 Dr STD 4WD Conv   11735   13800
2 Dr STD Utility   10160   11945
2 Dr STD 4WD Utility   11065   13010
4 Dr STD Wgn   10910   12715
4 Dr STD 4WD Wgn   11615   13655

OPTIONS FOR RAV4
Auto 4-Speed Transmission +575
Luxury Pkg +1120
AM/FM Compact Disc Player +175
Air Conditioning +450
Aluminum/Alloy Wheels +175
Anti-Lock Brakes +320
Cruise Control +115
Keyless Entry System +105
Power Door Locks +130
Power Mirrors +70
Power Windows +135
Tilt Steering Wheel[Std on Wgn] +100

SIENNA   1998

A new minivan from Toyota brings some innovation to the family truckster market. A powerful 194-horsepower V6 engine rests under the hood of all models. Safety equipment includes standard anti-lock brakes, low tire pressure warning systems and five mph front and rear bumpers. Sienna boasts outstanding crash test scores.

RATINGS (SCALE OF 1-10)

Overall	Safety	Reliability	Performance	Comfort	Value
N/A	N/A	8.7	7	7.9	N/A

Model Description	Trade-in Value	Market Value
Category G		
2 Dr CE Pass. Van	14120	16605
2 Dr LE Pass. Van	15670	18420
2 Dr XLE Pass. Van	18015	21180

OPTIONS FOR SIENNA

AM/FM Compact Disc Player[Std on XLE] +175
Aluminum/Alloy Wheels[Std on LE] +175
Captain Chairs (4)[Opt on LE] +335
Cruise Control[Opt on CE] +115
Dual Air Conditioning[Opt on CE] +505
Heated Power Mirrors[Std on XLE] +45
Keyless Entry System[Std on XLE] +105
Leather Seats +430
Power Door Locks[Opt on CE] +130
Power Mirrors[Opt on CE] +70
Power Moonroof +475
Power Windows[Opt on CE] +135
Privacy Glass[Opt on CE] +150
Rear Window Defroster[Opt on CE] +95
Sliding Driver Side Door +290

SUPRA   1998

Variable Valve Timing with Intelligence appears on the new Supra. No other changes to Toyota's bargain basement exotic.

Model Description	Trade-in Value	Market Value
Category F		
2 Dr STD Hbk	24685	28040
2 Dr STD Turbo Hbk	28400	32685

OPTIONS FOR SUPRA

Sport Roof +1680
Leather Seats[Std on Turbo] +345
Power Drivers Seat[Std on Turbo] +130

T100   1998

No changes to Toyota's full-size truck.

RATINGS (SCALE OF 1-10)

Overall	Safety	Reliability	Performance	Comfort	Value
N/A	N/A	9.3	7	7.5	N/A

Model Description	Trade-in Value	Market Value
Category H		
2 Dr DX Ext Cab SB	12155	14250
2 Dr DX 4WD Ext Cab SB	14580	17100
2 Dr SR5 Ext Cab SB	13185	15460
2 Dr SR5 4WD Ext Cab SB	15695	18405
2 Dr STD Std Cab LB	9640	11305

OPTIONS FOR T100

Auto 4-Speed Transmission +490
AM/FM Compact Disc Player +170
Air Conditioning +445
Aluminum/Alloy Wheels +170
Anti-Lock Brakes +270
Bed Liner +125
Cruise Control +105
Keyless Entry System +95
Power Door Locks +105

Model Description	Trade-in Value	Market Value
Power Mirrors +55		
Power Windows +105		
Privacy Glass[Opt on DX] +85		
Sliding Rear Window[Std on SR5] +65		
Tilt Steering Wheel[Std on SR5] +105		
Velour/Cloth Seats[Opt on STD] +60		

TACOMA   1998

The 1998 four-wheel drive Tacomas receive fresh front-end styling that makes them more closely resemble their two-wheel drive brothers. A new option package appears for 1998 as well; the TRD (no, not short for "turd") Off-Road Package for extended cab models is designed to make the Tacoma appeal to would-be Baja 1000 racers. On the safety front, Toyota introduces a passenger's side airbag that can be deactivated with a cut-off switch, making the Tacoma somewhat safer for children and short adults. Toyota also offers a new Tacoma PreRunner for 1998, billing it as a two-wheel drive truck with four-wheel drive performance.

RATINGS (SCALE OF 1-10)

Overall	Safety	Reliability	Performance	Comfort	Value
N/A	7.1	9.5	7.2	7	N/A

Model Description	Trade-in Value	Market Value
Category G		
2 Dr Limited 4WD Ext Cab SB	15660	18410
2 Dr Prerunner Ext Cab SB	11310	13295
2 Dr Prerunner V6 Ext Cab SB	11905	14000
2 Dr SR5 Ext Cab SB	10270	12075
2 Dr SR5 4WD Ext Cab SB	12625	14840
2 Dr SR5 V6 Ext Cab SB	10970	12900
2 Dr SR5 V6 4WD Ext Cab SB	13320	15660
2 Dr STD Ext Cab SB	9690	11390
2 Dr STD 4WD Ext Cab SB	13060	15325
2 Dr STD Std Cab SB	8300	9760
2 Dr STD 4WD Std Cab SB	11430	13440
2 Dr V6 Ext Cab SB	10760	12620
2 Dr V6 4WD Ext Cab SB	12760	15000

OPTIONS FOR TACOMA

Auto 4-Speed Transmission[Std on Prerunner, Prerunner V6] +455
TRD Off-Road Pkg +665
AM/FM Compact Disc Player +175
Air Conditioning[Opt on Limited, STD, V6] +450
Aluminum/Alloy Wheels[Std on Limited] +175
Anti-Lock Brakes +320
Auto Locking Hubs (4WD)[Std on Limited] +145
Bed Liner +155
Cruise Control[Std on Limited] +115
Flip-Up Sunroof +180
Keyless Entry System +105
Power Door Locks[Std on Limited] +130
Power Steering[Opt on STD 4 cyl.] +155

Don't forget to refer to the Mileage Adjustment Table at the back of this book!

TOYOTA 98-97

Model Description	Trade-in Value	Market Value	Model Description	Trade-in Value	Market Value

Power Windows[Std on Limited] +135
Sliding Rear Window[Opt on STD, V6] +65
Tilt Steering Wheel[Std on Limited] +100

TERCEL   1998

For 1998, the Tercel is available exclusively as a two-door CE model with additional standard features like color-keyed grille and bumpers, rear seat headrests, AM/FM stereo with cassette, air conditioning, digital clock and power steering.

RATINGS (SCALE OF 1-10)

Overall	Safety	Reliability	Performance	Comfort	Value
6.9	6.1	9.3	6.6	7	5.5

Category E
2 Dr CE Sdn			8385	10070

OPTIONS FOR TERCEL

Auto 3-Speed Transmission +275
AM/FM Compact Disc Player +235
Anti-Lock Brakes +365
Keyless Entry System +90
Power Door Locks +135
Power Windows +145
Rear Window Defroster +90

1997 TOYOTA

4RUNNER   1997

Toyota's hot-selling redesign receives minor changes. The most noticeable is the addition of the 2WD Limited to the model lineup. SR5 models receive new interior fabrics.

RATINGS (SCALE OF 1-10)

Overall	Safety	Reliability	Performance	Comfort	Value
6.9	7.8	9.3	6.6	6.9	4.1

Category G
Model	Trade-in	Market
4 Dr Limited Wgn	19070	22330
4 Dr Limited 4WD Wgn	20455	23955
4 Dr SR5 Wgn	14955	17515
4 Dr SR5 4WD Wgn	15630	18300
4 Dr STD Wgn	12160	14240
4 Dr STD 4WD Wgn	13920	16235

OPTIONS FOR 4RUNNER

Auto 4-Speed Transmission[Opt on STD,SR5 4WD Wgn] +400
Elite Pkg +490
Walnut Wood Dash +355
Air Conditioning[Opt on SR5,STD] +365
Aluminum/Alloy Wheels[Opt on SR5,STD] +145
Anti-Lock Brakes[Opt on STD] +260
Compact Disc W/fm/tape +200
Cruise Control[Opt on SR5,STD] +95
Keyless Entry System +85

Leather Seats[Opt on SR5,STD] +350
Locking Differential +130
Luggage Rack +70
Power Door Locks[Opt on STD] +105
Power Moonroof +385
Power Windows[Opt on SR5,STD] +110
Rear Heater +85
Running Boards[Opt on SR5,STD] +175

AVALON   1997

More power, more torque, and added standard features make the Avalon one of the most appealing full-sized sedans

RATINGS (SCALE OF 1-10)

Overall	Safety	Reliability	Performance	Comfort	Value
8.2	8	8.7	8.2	8.4	7.9

Category D
Model	Trade-in	Market
4 Dr XL Sdn	14635	17210
4 Dr XLS Sdn	16780	19735

OPTIONS FOR AVALON

Power Bench Seat +365
Aluminum/Alloy Wheels[Opt on XL] +210
Compact Disc W/fm/tape +345
Dual Power Seats[Opt on XL] +380
Leather Seats +505
Power Moonroof +380
Traction Control System +235

CAMRY   1997

Toyota plays the market conservatively with the all-new Camry, giving consumers exactly what they want; a roomy, attractive, feature-laden car with available V6 performance and the promise of excellent reliability as well as resale value. The Camry is the new standard for midsized sedans.

RATINGS (SCALE OF 1-10)

Overall	Safety	Reliability	Performance	Comfort	Value
7.5	7.4	8.2	8.6	8.1	5

Category D
Model	Trade-in	Market
4 Dr CE Sdn	9105	10695
4 Dr CE V6 Sdn	11700	13755
4 Dr LE Sdn	11765	13890
4 Dr LE V6 Sdn	13435	15800
4 Dr XLE Sdn	13220	15545
4 Dr XLE V6 Sdn	14610	17180

OPTIONS FOR CAMRY

Auto 4-Speed Transmission[Opt on CE] +355
6-disc CD Autochanger +355
Elite Pkg +595
Air Conditioning[Opt on CE,CE V6] +385
Aluminum/Alloy Wheels[Std on XLE,XLE V6] +210
Anti-Lock Brakes[Opt on CE] +395
Child Seat (1) +70

TOYOTA 97

Model Description	Trade-in Value	Market Value	Model Description	Trade-in Value	Market Value

Compact Disc W/fm/tape +345
Cruise Control[Opt on CE,CE V6] +110
Keyless Entry System[Std on XLE,XLE V6] +140
Leather Seats +505
Power Door Locks[Opt on CE,CE V6] +120
Power Moonroof +380
Power Windows[Opt on CE,CE V6] +120
Traction Control System +235

CELICA   1997

GT Coupe is gone, and Fiesta Blue Metallic can be specified for cars equipped with black sport cloth interior.

RATINGS (SCALE OF 1-10)

Overall	Safety	Reliability	Performance	Comfort	Value
N/A	N/A	9.5	8.2	7.6	4.3

Category F

		Trade-in	Market
2 Dr GT Conv		14550	17095
2 Dr GT Hbk		12585	14680
2 Dr GT Limited Edit. Conv		15500	18210
2 Dr ST Cpe		10695	12425
2 Dr ST Hbk		10710	12535
2 Dr ST Limited Edit. Hbk		11750	13805

OPTIONS FOR CELICA

Auto 4-Speed Transmission +360
Air Conditioning[Opt on GT,ST] +375
Aluminum/Alloy Wheels[Opt on GT,ST] +135
Anti-Lock Brakes +290
Compact Disc W/fm/tape[Opt on GT] +225
Cruise Control[Opt on GT,ST] +100
Leather Seats +285
Power Door Locks[Opt on ST] +90
Power Moonroof +290
Power Windows[Opt on ST] +105
Premium Sound System +170
Sport Suspension +85

COROLLA   1997

The Classic Edition (CE) debuts and the slow-selling DX Wagon gets the ax.

RATINGS (SCALE OF 1-10)

Overall	Safety	Reliability	Performance	Comfort	Value
7.1	6.5	8.9	7.4	8.1	4.4

Category E

		Trade-in	Market
4 Dr CE Sdn		7140	8730
4 Dr DX Sdn		9185	10770
4 Dr STD Sdn		8455	9915

OPTIONS FOR COROLLA

Auto 3-Speed Transmission +225
Auto 4-Speed Transmission +355
Air Conditioning[Std on CE] +370
Aluminum/Alloy Wheels +150
Anti-Lock Brakes +295

Child Seat (1) +50
Compact Disc W/fm/tape +215
Cruise Control +100
Power Door Locks[Opt on DX] +110
Power Sunroof +280
Power Windows[Opt on DX] +120

LAND CRUISER   1997

The Black Package is discontinued, but black paint becomes an available color choice. A 40th-Anniversary Package lets buyers slather their Cruiser in leather and choose one of two unique paint schemes.

Category G

		Trade-in	Market
4 Dr 40th Anniv. Ltd. 4WD Wgn		29360	34380
4 Dr STD 4WD Wgn		25895	30325

OPTIONS FOR LAND CRUISER

Burlwood Dash +355
Convenience Pkg +355
Leather Trim Pkg +1235
Third Seat Pkg +535
Aluminum/Alloy Wheels +145
Compact Disc Changer +225
Compact Disc W/fm/tape +200
Dual Power Seats[Opt on STD] +185
Keyless Entry System +85
Leather Seats[Opt on STD] +350
Locking Differential +130
Luggage Rack +70
Power Moonroof +385
Running Boards +175
Third Seat[Opt on STD] +320

PASEO   1997

For some reason, Toyota product planners took a look at the cheap convertible market and thought, "Hmmm...a convertible Tercel with fancy styling will just kill the Sunfire SE Convertible's sales and make us rich." Coupes get dual-visor vanity mirrors, fresh door trim and rotary-heater controls.

RATINGS (SCALE OF 1-10)

Overall	Safety	Reliability	Performance	Comfort	Value
6.8	6.6	9.5	7	6.9	4.2

Category E

		Trade-in	Market
2 Dr STD Conv		10625	12460
2 Dr STD Cpe		8445	9900

OPTIONS FOR PASEO

Auto 4-Speed Transmission +355
AM/FM Compact Disc Player +195
Air Conditioning +370
Aluminum/Alloy Wheels +150
Anti-Lock Brakes +295
Cruise Control +100
Flip-Up Sunroof +155
Power Door Locks +110
Power Windows +120

TOYOTA 97

Model Description	Trade-in Value	Market Value	Model Description	Trade-in Value	Market Value

PREVIA   1997

RATINGS (SCALE OF 1-10)

Overall	Safety	Reliability	Performance	Comfort	Value
7.4	6.7	8.7	7.7	7.3	6.7

Category G

2 Dr DX Sprchgd Pass. Van	15205	17805
2 Dr DX Sprchgd 4WD Pass. Van	17385	20360
2 Dr LE Sprchgd Pass. Van	18000	21080
2 Dr LE Sprchgd 4WD Pass. Van	20050	23480

OPTIONS FOR PREVIA

Aluminum/Alloy Wheels +145
Anti-Lock Brakes +260
Captain Chairs (4) +275
Compact Disc W/fm/tape +200
Cruise Control[Opt on DX] +95
Dual Air Conditioning[Opt on DX] +410
Keyless Entry System +85
Leather Seats +350
Luggage Rack +70
Power Door Locks[Opt on DX] +105
Power Moonroof +385
Power Windows[Opt on DX] +110
Premium Sound System +155
Running Boards +175

RAV4   1997

New fabric debuts on the two-door RAV, and a sunroof is finally available on the four-door. Improvements have also been made by using sound deadening material in the dash area, reducing engine noise in the passenger compartment.

RATINGS (SCALE OF 1-10)

Overall	Safety	Reliability	Performance	Comfort	Value
N/A	6.8	9.2	7	6.4	N/A

Category G

2 Dr STD Utility	9980	11685
2 Dr STD 4WD Utility	10880	12740
4 Dr STD Wgn	10230	12010
4 Dr STD 4WD Wgn	11325	13265

OPTIONS FOR RAV4

Auto 4-Speed Transmission +470
AM/FM Compact Disc Player +140
Air Conditioning +365
Aluminum/Alloy Wheels +145
Anti-Lock Brakes +260
Cruise Control +95
Keyless Entry System +85
Leather Seats +350
Power Door Locks +105
Power Moonroof +385
Power Windows +110
Tilt Steering Wheel +80

SUPRA   1997

Turbo models get the six-speed manual transmission back, but the bigger news details massive price cuts. Turbos with automatics are $12,000 dollars less expensive than last year! All Supras commemorate the nameplate's 15th anniversary with a rear spoiler, premium sound and special badging. Despite price cuts, equipment levels are enhanced across the board.

Category F

2 Dr STD Hbk	23325	26415
2 Dr STD Turbo Hbk	24095	28005

OPTIONS FOR SUPRA

6-Speed Transmission +760
Auto 4-Speed Transmission[Std on Turbo] +400
Sport Roof +1650
Compact Disc Changer +285
Compact Disc W/fm/tape[Std on Turbo] +225
Keyless Entry System +80
Leather Seats[Std on Turbo] +285
Power Drivers Seat[Std on Turbo] +110

T100   1997

Two new colors debut and the optional wheel and tire packages are larger this year. Standard models get radio pre-wiring, midlevel models get fabric door trim panels, and SR5 models get chrome wheel arches.

RATINGS (SCALE OF 1-10)

Overall	Safety	Reliability	Performance	Comfort	Value
N/A	6.4	9.2	7	7.5	N/A

Category H

2 Dr SR5 Ext Cab SB	13145	15300
2 Dr SR5 4WD Ext Cab SB	15180	17835
2 Dr STD Ext Cab SB	12370	14240
2 Dr STD 4WD Ext Cab SB	13650	16035
2 Dr STD Std Cab LB	1025	11545

OPTIONS FOR T100

Auto 4-Speed Transmission +400
AM/FM Compact Disc Player +140
Air Conditioning +365
Aluminum/Alloy Wheels +140
Anti-Lock Brakes +220
Bed Liner +100
Chrome Wheels +135
Cruise Control +85
Keyless Entry System +80
Power Door Locks +85
Power Windows +85
Premium Sound System +170
Rear Step Bumper +65
Running Boards +155
Velour/Cloth Seats[Opt on Std Cab] +50

Don't forget to refer to the Mileage Adjustment Table at the back of this book!

TOYOTA 97-96

Model Description	Trade-in Value	Market Value	Model Description	Trade-in Value	Market Value

TACOMA 1997

The 1997 Tacoma receives several new value packages that make optioning the truck easier. A locking rear-wheel differential is now available on all 4WD models. Bucket seats can be had on all Xtracab Tacomas this year; not just the SR5. Two-wheel drive models have new headlamps and a new grille that make the vehicle look more like the T100.

RATINGS (SCALE OF 1-10)

Overall	Safety	Reliability	Performance	Comfort	Value
N/A	5.7	9.4	7.2	7	N/A

Category G
2 Dr SR5 4WD Ext Cab SB	14675	17185
2 Dr STD Ext Cab SB	8785	10410
2 Dr STD 4WD Ext Cab SB	12155	14235
2 Dr STD Std Cab SB	8100	9485
2 Dr STD 4WD Std Cab SB	11225	13145
2 Dr V6 Ext Cab SB	9245	11040
2 Dr V6 4WD Ext Cab SB	11780	13980
2 Dr V6 4WD Std Cab SB	11955	14000

OPTIONS FOR TACOMA
Auto 4-Speed Transmission +380
Air Conditioning +365
Aluminum/Alloy Wheels[Std on SR5] +145
Anti-Lock Brakes +260
Auto Locking Hubs (4WD)[Std on SR5] +120
Bed Liner +125
Compact Disc W/fm/tape +200
Cruise Control +95
Power Door Locks +105
Power Steering[Std on SR5,V6,4WD] +125
Power Windows +110
Rear Step Bumper[Std on V6,Ext Cab,4WD] +65
Running Boards +175

TERCEL 1997

Standard and DX trim levels are shelved in favor of CE trim for all Tercels. All models have upgraded cloth trim, new rotary heater controls, a trip odometer, and a storage console. New wheelcovers adorn standard 14-inch wheels.

RATINGS (SCALE OF 1-10)

Overall	Safety	Reliability	Performance	Comfort	Value
6.9	6.1	9.2	6.6	7	5.5

Category E
2 Dr CE Sdn	6905	8095
4 Dr CE Sdn	8085	9480
2 Dr Limited Edition Sdn	7110	8340

OPTIONS FOR TERCEL
Auto 3-Speed Transmission +230
Auto 4-Speed Transmission +310
AM/FM Compact Disc Player +195

Air Conditioning +370
Anti-Lock Brakes +295
Keyless Entry System +75
Power Door Locks +110
Power Steering +115
Power Windows +120

1996 TOYOTA

4RUNNER 1996

A cool new 4Runner with a potent V6, big bruiser styling, and lots more interior room debuts. This thing annihilates most compact off-road vehicles.

RATINGS (SCALE OF 1-10)

Overall	Safety	Reliability	Performance	Comfort	Value
6.9	7.7	8.8	6.6	6.9	4.5

Category G
4 Dr Limited 4WD Wgn	17965	21730
4 Dr SR5 Wgn	12240	15000
4 Dr SR5 4WD Wgn	12835	15720
4 Dr STD Wgn	10845	13005
4 Dr STD 4WD Wgn	12980	15420

OPTIONS FOR 4RUNNER
Auto 4-Speed Transmission[Opt on STD,SR5 4WD Wgn] +330
Walnut Wood Dash +290
Air Conditioning[Opt on SR5,STD] +300
Aluminum/Alloy Wheels[Opt on SR5,STD] +120
Anti-Lock Brakes[Opt on STD] +210
Compact Disc W/fm/tape +160
Cruise Control[Opt on SR5,STD] +75
Keyless Entry System +70
Leather Seats[Opt on SR5] +285
Locking Differential +105
Luggage Rack +60
Power Door Locks[Opt on STD] +85
Power Moonroof +315
Power Windows[Opt on 2WD] +90
Rear Heater +70
Running Boards +140
Trailer Hitch +105

AVALON 1996

No changes as cloud car floats into its second year.

RATINGS (SCALE OF 1-10)

Overall	Safety	Reliability	Performance	Comfort	Value
8.1	7.6	8.3	8.2	8.4	7.8

Category D
4 Dr XL Sdn	12635	14975
4 Dr XLS Sdn	14775	17510

OPTIONS FOR AVALON
Power Bench Seat +295
Aluminum/Alloy Wheels[Opt on XL] +170

Don't forget to refer to the Mileage Adjustment Table at the back of this book!

Model Description	Trade-in Value	Market Value
Anti-Lock Brakes[Opt on XL] +325		
Compact Disc W/fm/tape +285		
Dual Power Seats[Opt on XL] +310		
Leather Seats +415		
Power Moonroof +310		
Premium Sound System[Opt on XL] +135		

CAMRY 1996

The 1996 Camry remains virtually unchanged from last year's model. Minor engine adjustments mean that the four-cylinder is fully compliant with all On-Board Diagnostic standards, and is now certified as a Transitional Low Emission Vehicle powerplant. Additionally, the interior of the DX line gets a new seat fabric, the LE Sedan is available with a leather package, and the Wagon can now be ordered with a power-operated driver seat.

RATINGS (SCALE OF 1-10)

Overall	Safety	Reliability	Performance	Comfort	Value
7.6	6.6	8.6	8.6	8.4	5.9

Category D

Model	Trade-in	Market
4 Dr Collector Sdn	14495	17175
2 Dr DX Cpe	8795	10425
4 Dr DX Sdn	8945	10605
2 Dr LE Cpe	10570	12530
4 Dr LE Sdn	10915	12935
4 Dr LE Wgn	11475	13595
2 Dr LE V6 Cpe	11760	13935
4 Dr LE V6 Sdn	11910	14115
4 Dr LE V6 Wgn	12665	15010
2 Dr SE Cpe	12620	14955
4 Dr SE Sdn	12770	15135
4 Dr XLE Sdn	11820	14010
4 Dr XLE V6 Sdn	13250	15700

OPTIONS FOR CAMRY

Auto 4-Speed Transmission[Opt on DX] +290
Air Conditioning[Opt on DX] +315
Anti-Lock Brakes[Std on XLE,XLE V6] +325
Compact Disc W/fm/tape[Std on Collector] +285
Cruise Control[Opt on DX] +90
Keyless Entry System +115
Leather Seats[Std on Collector] +415
Power Door Locks[Opt on DX] +100
Power Drivers Seat[Opt on LE,LE V6] +115
Power Moonroof +310
Power Passenger Seat +115
Power Windows[Opt on DX] +100
Premium Sound System +135

CELICA 1996

Minor front end freshening doesn't help much. A new spoiler, new wheelcovers, two new colors, and revised fabrics debut this year.

RATINGS (SCALE OF 1-10)

Overall	Safety	Reliability	Performance	Comfort	Value
N/A	N/A	9.2	8.2	7.6	4.3

Category F

Model	Trade-in	Market
2 Dr GT Conv	13175	15675
2 Dr GT Cpe	11465	13455
2 Dr GT Hbk	11355	13425
2 Dr GT 25th Anniv. Conv	15115	17740
2 Dr ST Cpe	9415	11110
2 Dr ST Hbk	9860	11640
2 Dr ST 25th Anniv. Hbk	11980	14065

OPTIONS FOR CELICA

Auto 4-Speed Transmission +290
Leather Sport Pkg +385
Air Conditioning[Opt on GT,ST] +305
Anti-Lock Brakes +235
Compact Disc W/fm/tape[Opt on GT] +185
Cruise Control[Opt on GT,ST] +80
Keyless Entry System +65
Leather Seats +230
Power Door Locks[Opt on ST] +75
Power Moonroof[Opt on GT,ST] +240
Power Windows[Opt on ST] +85
Premium Sound System +140
Sport Suspension +70

COROLLA 1996

The Toyota Corolla heads into 1996 with a redesigned front and rear fascia, three new colors, new wheel covers, an optional integrated child seat, and a revised interior. Additionally, the five-speed manual transmission has been revised for a better feel and more positive gear engagement.

RATINGS (SCALE OF 1-10)

Overall	Safety	Reliability	Performance	Comfort	Value
7.3	6.5	9.2	7.4	8.1	5.1

Category E

Model	Trade-in	Market
4 Dr DX Sdn	7620	9315
4 Dr DX Wgn	8230	10060
4 Dr STD Sdn	7325	8955

OPTIONS FOR COROLLA

Auto 3-Speed Transmission +175
Auto 4-Speed Transmission +290
Air Conditioning +305
Anti-Lock Brakes +245
Child Seat (1) +40
Cruise Control +85
Keyless Entry System +60
Power Door Locks +90
Power Sunroof +230
Power Windows +95

Model Description	Trade-in Value	Market Value

LAND CRUISER 1996

The Black Paint Package debuts, for those who enjoy spending long hours maintaining the finish on their truck.

Category G

4 Dr STD 4WD Wgn	22375	26565

OPTIONS FOR LAND CRUISER

Burlwood Dash +290
Leather Trim Pkg +1120
Third Seat Pkg +555
Compact Disc Changer +185
Compact Disc W/fm/tape +160
Dual Power Seats +150
Keyless Entry System +70
Leather Seats +285
Power Moonroof +315
Running Boards +140
Third Seat +260

PASEO 1996

All new Paseo looks like last year's car, but is much improved. It now meets 1997 passenger car safety standards. It has a split-fold rear seat.

RATINGS (SCALE OF 1-10)

Overall	Safety	Reliability	Performance	Comfort	Value
6.8	6.6	9.4	7	6.9	4.2

Category E

2 Dr STD Cpe	6985	8540

OPTIONS FOR PASEO

Auto 4-Speed Transmission +290
AM/FM Stereo Tape +110
Air Conditioning +305
Rear Spoiler +80
Rear Window Defroster +60

PREVIA 1996

Supercharged engines for everyone!

RATINGS (SCALE OF 1-10)

Overall	Safety	Reliability	Performance	Comfort	Value
7.6	6.8	8.8	7.7	7.3	7.2

Category G

2 Dr DX Sprchgd Pass. Van	12980	15410
2 Dr DX Sprchgd 4WD Pass. Van	14835	17615
2 Dr LE Sprchgd Pass. Van	15360	18235
2 Dr LE Sprchgd 4WD Pass. Van	17110	20320

OPTIONS FOR PREVIA

Aluminum/Alloy Wheels +120
Anti-Lock Brakes +210
Captain Chairs (4) +225
Compact Disc W/fm/tape +160
Cruise Control[Opt on DX] +75
Dual Air Conditioning[Opt on DX] +335

Keyless Entry System +70
Leather Seats +285
Luggage Rack +60
Power Door Locks[Opt on DX] +85
Power Moonroof +315
Power Windows[Opt on DX] +90
Premium Sound System +125
Running Boards +140

RAV4 1996

A cool new mini-ute based on passenger car mechanicals debuts this year. Available as a two-door or four-door, the RAV4 has a gutsy powerplant and cute-as-can-be styling. We like the RAV, but think that the Jeep Cherokee offers more bang-for-the-buck.

RATINGS (SCALE OF 1-10)

Overall	Safety	Reliability	Performance	Comfort	Value
N/A	N/A	9	7	6.4	N/A

Category G

2 Dr STD Utility	9140	10850
2 Dr STD 4WD Utility	9975	11840
4 Dr STD Wgn	9555	11345
4 Dr STD 4WD Wgn	10390	12335

OPTIONS FOR RAV4

Auto 4-Speed Transmission +385
AM/FM Compact Disc Player +115
Air Conditioning +300
Aluminum/Alloy Wheels +120
Anti-Lock Brakes +210
Cruise Control +75
Keyless Entry System +70
Luggage Rack +60
Power Door Locks +85
Power Windows +90

SUPRA 1996

Manual transmission Turbo models are history, thanks to stringent emission regulations. Don't worry, they're back for 1997.

Category F

2 Dr STD Hbk	21315	25020
2 Dr STD Turbo Hbk	22270	26860

OPTIONS FOR SUPRA

Auto 4-Speed Transmission[Std on Turbo] +330
Sport Roof +910
Compact Disc Changer +235
Compact Disc W/fm/tape +185
Dual Power Seats +305
Keyless Entry System +65
Leather Seats +230
Limited Slip Diff[Std on Turbo] +120

Don't forget to refer to the Mileage Adjustment Table at the back of this book!

TOYOTA 96-95

Model Description	Trade-in Value	Market Value	Model Description	Trade-in Value	Market Value

T100 1996

Essentially a carryover, but DX models are scrapped. Strangely, regular cabs can't be equipped with cruise control anymore. A new shade of red is offered, and tan interiors are offered in a wider variety of trucks.

RATINGS (SCALE OF 1-10)

Overall	Safety	Reliability	Performance	Comfort	Value
N/A	6.5	8.7	7	7.5	N/A

Category H

	Trade-in	Market
2 Dr SR5 Ext Cab SB	12000	14245
2 Dr SR5 4WD Ext Cab SB	14115	16755
2 Dr STD Ext Cab SB	10975	13030
2 Dr STD 4WD Ext Cab SB	13290	15780
2 Dr STD Std Cab LB	8850	10505

OPTIONS FOR T100

Auto 4-Speed Transmission +325
AM/FM Compact Disc Player +115
Air Conditioning +300
Aluminum/Alloy Wheels +115
Anti-Lock Brakes +180
Bed Liner +85
Chrome Wheels +110
Cruise Control +70
Keyless Entry System +65
Power Door Locks +70
Power Windows +70
Premium Sound System +140
Rear Step Bumper +50
Running Boards +130
Velour/Cloth Seats[Opt on Std Cab] +40

TACOMA 1996

Regular Cab 4WD models can be equipped with a new Off-Road Package.

RATINGS (SCALE OF 1-10)

Overall	Safety	Reliability	Performance	Comfort	Value
N/A	5.7	8.8	7.2	7	N/A

Category G

	Trade-in	Market
2 Dr SR5 4WD Ext Cab SB	13450	15970
2 Dr STD Ext Cab SB	8670	10295
2 Dr STD 4WD Ext Cab SB	11140	13225
2 Dr STD Std Cab SB	7390	8775
2 Dr STD 4WD Std Cab SB	10290	12220
2 Dr V6 Ext Cab SB	9445	11215
2 Dr V6 4WD Ext Cab SB	11780	13985
2 Dr V6 4WD Std Cab SB	10955	13005

OPTIONS FOR TACOMA

Auto 4-Speed Transmission +310
Off Road Pkg +495
Wheel Pkg +360
AM/FM Compact Disc Player +115
Air Conditioning +300

Aluminum/Alloy Wheels +120
Anti-Lock Brakes +210
Auto Locking Hubs (4WD)[Std on SR5] +95
Bed Liner +100
Cruise Control +75
Keyless Entry System +70
Power Door Locks +85
Power Steering[Std on SR5,V6,4WD] +105
Power Windows +90
Rear Step Bumper +55
Running Boards +140

TERCEL 1996

Base cars can be equipped with fabric seats, and a ... ha,ha,ha ... "Sports" package is available.

RATINGS (SCALE OF 1-10)

Overall	Safety	Reliability	Performance	Comfort	Value
6.8	6.1	8.9	6.6	7	5.4

Category E

	Trade-in	Market
2 Dr DX Sdn	6290	7685
4 Dr DX Sdn	6450	7885
2 Dr STD Sdn	5635	6890

OPTIONS FOR TERCEL

Auto 3-Speed Transmission +255
Auto 4-Speed Transmission +255
AM/FM Compact Disc Player +160
Air Conditioning +305
Anti-Lock Brakes +245
Electric Sunroof +150
Keyless Entry System +60
Power Door Locks +90
Power Steering +95
Power Windows +95
Rear Window Defroster +60

1995 TOYOTA

4RUNNER 1995

V6 models get new tape stripes. Whoo-hoo!

RATINGS (SCALE OF 1-10)

Overall	Safety	Reliability	Performance	Comfort	Value
6.3	3.9	9.1	7	7	4.4

Category G

	Trade-in	Market
4 Dr Limited 4WD Wgn	14420	17320
4 Dr SR5 Wgn	11650	13990
4 Dr SR5 4WD Wgn	11355	13640
4 Dr SR5 V6 4WD Wgn	12385	14880

OPTIONS FOR 4RUNNER

Auto 4-Speed Transmission[Std on 2WD] +315
Value Pkg +285
Air Conditioning[Std on Limited] +245
Anti-Lock Brakes +175
Compact Disc W/fm/tape +130

Don't forget to refer to the Mileage Adjustment Table at the back of this book!

TOYOTA 95

Model Description	Trade-in Value	Market Value	Model Description	Trade-in Value	Market Value

Cruise Control[Std on Limited] +65
Leather Seats[Opt on SR5 V6] +235
Luggage Rack[Std on Limited] +50
Power Door Locks[Std on Limited] +70
Power Moonroof +260
Power Windows[Opt on SR5 V6,2WD] +70
Premium Sound System +100
Rear Heater +55 •
Running Boards +115

AVALON 1995

Marginally larger than the Camry, the Avalon is a true six-passenger sedan set to conquer Buick LeSabre and Ford Crown Victoria. Dual airbags, power windows, power mirrors, and power locks are standard. ABS is optional. Mechanicals are mostly Camry-based.

RATINGS (SCALE OF 1-10)

Overall	Safety	Reliability	Performance	Comfort	Value
8	8.3	8.5	8.2	8.4	6.6

Category D
4 Dr XL Sdn   10660 12785
4 Dr XLS Sdn 12470 14960

OPTIONS FOR AVALON

Power Bench Seat +235
Aluminum/Alloy Wheels[Opt on XL] +140
Anti-Lock Brakes[Opt on XL] +265
Compact Disc W/fm/tape +230
Dual Power Seats +255
Leather Seats +340
Power Moonroof +250
Premium Sound System[Opt on XL] +110

CAMRY 1995

Front and rear styling is updated, ABS is standard on XLE model, and Camry now meets 1997 side-impact protection standards. DX wagon dumped from lineup.

RATINGS (SCALE OF 1-10)

Overall	Safety	Reliability	Performance	Comfort	Value
7.9	7.4	9.1	8.6	8.4	6.1

Category D
2 Dr DX Cpe   7510 9005
4 Dr DX Sdn   7640 9165
2 Dr LE Cpe   8935 10720
4 Dr LE Sdn   9070 10875
4 Dr LE Wgn   9710 11645
2 Dr LE V6 Cpe   9990 11985
4 Dr LE V6 Sdn 10125 12140
4 Dr LE V6 Wgn 10710 12845
2 Dr SE Cpe   10780 12930
4 Dr SE Sdn   10915 13090
4 Dr XLE Sdn   10005 12000
4 Dr XLE V6 Sdn 11200 13435

OPTIONS FOR CAMRY

Auto 4-Speed Transmission[Opt on DX] +240
Elite Pkg +380
Air Conditioning[Opt on DX] +255
Anti-Lock Brakes[Std on XLE,XLE V6] +265
Compact Disc W/fm/tape +230
Cruise Control[Opt on DX] +75
Leather Seats +340
Power Door Locks[Opt on DX] +80
Power Drivers Seat[Std on XLE,XLE V6] +95
Power Moonroof +250
Power Passenger Seat +95
Power Windows[Opt on DX] +80
Premium Sound System +110

CELICA 1995

GT convertible returns to lineup, available in red, white, blue or black.

RATINGS (SCALE OF 1-10)

Overall	Safety	Reliability	Performance	Comfort	Value
N/A	N/A	8.9	8.2	7.6	4.3

Category F
2 Dr GT Conv 12380 14650
2 Dr GT Cpe   10115 11970
2 Dr GT Hbk   10370 12265
2 Dr ST Cpe   8885 10510
2 Dr ST Hbk   9065 10720

OPTIONS FOR CELICA

Auto 4-Speed Transmission +240
Air Conditioning +250
Anti-Lock Brakes +195
Compact Disc W/fm/tape +150
Cruise Control +65
Leather Seats +190
Power Door Locks[Opt on ST] +60
Power Moonroof +195
Power Windows[Opt on ST] +70
Premium Sound System +115
Sport Suspension +55

COROLLA 1995

1.8-liter engine loses ten horsepower to meet stricter emissions regulations. Torque is up, though. DX models get new interior fabric.

RATINGS (SCALE OF 1-10)

Overall	Safety	Reliability	Performance	Comfort	Value
7.1	7	8.1	7.4	8.1	5.1

Category E
4 Dr DX Sdn   6030 7565
4 Dr DX Wgn   6520 8180
4 Dr LE Sdn   7415 9305
4 Dr STD Sdn 5545 6960

Don't forget to refer to the Mileage Adjustment Table at the back of this book!

TOYOTA 95

Model Description	Trade-in Value	Market Value	Model Description	Trade-in Value	Market Value

OPTIONS FOR COROLLA
Auto 3-Speed Transmission +150
Auto 4-Speed Transmission[Opt on DX] +240
AM/FM Compact Disc Player +130
Air Conditioning[Std on LE] +250
Aluminum/Alloy Wheels +100
Anti-Lock Brakes +200
Cruise Control[Opt on DX] +70
Power Door Locks[Opt on DX] +75
Power Sunroof +185
Power Windows[Opt on DX] +80
Premium Sound System +100

LAND CRUISER 1995
Redesigned dashboard carries dual airbags, and ABS is now standard. Revised grille carries Toyota logo rather than nameplate.
Category G

4 Dr STD 4WD Wgn	19120	22965

OPTIONS FOR LAND CRUISER
Leather Trim Pkg +700
Third Seat Pkg +330
Compact Disc Changer +150
Compact Disc W/fm/tape +130
Dual Power Seats +125
Leather Seats +235
Locking Differential +85
Luggage Rack +50
Power Moonroof +260
Running Boards +115
Third Seat +215

MR2 1995
Final year for Mister Two. Several states lose Turbo model, which wouldn't pass emissions regulations. Base models with T-bar roof get power windows and locks standard.
Category F

2 Dr STD Cpe	9860	11660
2 Dr STD Turbo Cpe	11955	14145

OPTIONS FOR MR2
Auto 4-Speed Transmission +240
T-Bar Roof Pkg +320
Air Conditioning +250
Anti-Lock Brakes +195
Compact Disc W/fm/tape +150
Cruise Control[Std on Turbo] +65
Flip-Up Sunroof +125
Leather Seats +190
Limited Slip Diff +100
Power Door Locks[Std on Turbo] +60
Power Drivers Seat +70
Power Windows[Std on Turbo] +70

PASEO 1995
Several states with strict emissions laws get detuned Paseo for 1995.

RATINGS (SCALE OF 1-10)
Overall	Safety	Reliability	Performance	Comfort	Value
6.8	5.9	9.3	7.8	7.1	4.1

Category E

2 Dr STD Cpe	6070	7615

OPTIONS FOR PASEO
Auto 4-Speed Transmission +240
AM/FM Stereo Tape +90
Air Conditioning +250

PICKUP 1995
No changes.
HALF TON
Category G

2 Dr DX Ext Cab SB	6485	7790
2 Dr DX 4WD Ext Cab SB	8370	10055
2 Dr DX Std Cab SB	5700	6845
2 Dr DX 4WD Std Cab SB	7580	9100
2 Dr DX V6 Ext Cab SB	7070	8490
2 Dr DX V6 4WD Ext Cab SB	8995	10800
2 Dr DX V6 4WD Std Cab SB	8220	9870
2 Dr SR5 Ext Cab SB	8055	9670
2 Dr SR5 4WD Ext Cab SB	9980	11990
2 Dr STD Std Cab SB	5260	6315

OPTIONS FOR PICKUP
Auto 4-Speed Transmission +285
AM/FM Stereo Tape +65
Air Conditioning +245
Aluminum/Alloy Wheels +95
Anti-Lock Brakes +175
Auto Locking Hubs (4WD) +80
Bed Liner +85
Chrome Wheels +50
Cruise Control +65
Intermittent Wipers[Opt on DX] +25
Power Door Locks +70
Power Steering[Opt on DX,STD] +85
Power Windows +70
Premium Sound System +100
Rear Step Bumper +45
Running Boards +115

PREVIA 1995
Seatback map pockets and an illuminated driver's visor vanity mirror are standard on all models.

RATINGS (SCALE OF 1-10)
Overall	Safety	Reliability	Performance	Comfort	Value
7.7	7.4	8.4	7.7	7.3	7.6

Don't forget to refer to the Mileage Adjustment Table at the back of this book!

TOYOTA 95

Model Description	Trade-in Value	Market Value
Category G		
2 Dr DX Pass. Van	10660	12805
2 Dr DX Sprchgd Pass. Van	10895	13090
2 Dr DX 4WD Pass. Van	12225	14685
2 Dr DX Sprchgd 4WD Pass. Van	12460	14965
2 Dr LE Pass. Van	12660	15205
2 Dr LE Sprchgd Pass. Van	12895	15490
2 Dr LE 4WD Pass. Van	14410	17310
2 Dr LE Sprchgd 4WD Pass. Van	14645	17590

OPTIONS FOR PREVIA
Aluminum/Alloy Wheels +95
Anti-Lock Brakes +175
Captain Chairs (2) +155
Compact Disc W/fm/tape +130
Cruise Control[Opt on DX] +65
Dual Air Conditioning[Opt on DX] +275
Leather Seats +235
Luggage Rack +50
Power Door Locks[Opt on DX] +70
Power Moonroof +260
Power Windows[Opt on DX] +70
Premium Sound System +100
Running Boards +115

SUPRA   1995

No changes.

Model Description	Trade-in Value	Market Value
Category F		
2 Dr STD Hbk	18295	21640
2 Dr STD Turbo Hbk	21750	25735

OPTIONS FOR SUPRA
Auto 4-Speed Transmission +315
Sport Roof +345
Compact Disc W/fm/tape +150
Leather Seats +190
Limited Slip Diff[Std on Turbo] +100
Power Drivers Seat[Std on Turbo] +70

T100   1995

The 1995 T100 adds an extended-cab body style to fill out this midsized truck's lineup. A much more powerful DOHC V6 engine is introduced this year as are four-wheel antilock brakes. The antilock brakes are available only on DX and Xtracab models equipped V6 engine.

RATINGS (SCALE OF 1-10)

Overall	Safety	Reliability	Performance	Comfort	Value
N/A	7.1	9	7	7.5	N/A

Model Description	Trade-in Value	Market Value
Category H		
2 Dr DX Ext Cab SB	9010	10965
2 Dr DX 4WD Ext Cab SB	10915	13285
2 Dr DX Std Cab LB	8295	10095
2 Dr DX 4WD Std Cab LB	10005	12175

Model Description	Trade-in Value	Market Value
2 Dr DX 1 Ton Std Cab LB	8705	10590
2 Dr SR5 Ext Cab SB	9855	11990
2 Dr SR5 4WD Ext Cab SB	11480	13970
2 Dr STD Std Cab LB	7250	8825
2 Dr V6 Std Cab LB	7765	9445

OPTIONS FOR T100
Auto 4-Speed Transmission +270
AM/FM Compact Disc Player +90
Air Conditioning +245
Aluminum/Alloy Wheels +95
Anti-Lock Brakes +145
Bed Liner +70
Chrome Wheels +90
Cruise Control +55
Power Door Locks +55
Power Windows +55
Premium Sound System +115
Rear Step Bumper +40
Running Boards +105
Velour/Cloth Seats[Opt on STD] +35

TACOMA   1995

Toyota puts a city on wheels. No. New compact pickup with a real name debuted in March, 1995. Optional four-wheel ABS, a driver airbag, and potent new engines are highlights of the new design. Rack and pinion steering replaces the old recirculating ball-type on the old truck. Front seatbelts are height adjustable.

RATINGS (SCALE OF 1-10)

Overall	Safety	Reliability	Performance	Comfort	Value
N/A	6.3	8.7	7.2	7	N/A

Model Description	Trade-in Value	Market Value
Category G		
2 Dr SR5 4WD Ext Cab SB	12060	14485
2 Dr STD Ext Cab SB	7935	9530
2 Dr STD 4WD Ext Cab SB	9745	11700
2 Dr STD Std Cab SB	6620	7950
2 Dr STD 4WD Std Cab SB	8985	10795
2 Dr V6 Ext Cab SB	8240	9900
2 Dr V6 4WD Ext Cab SB	10305	12380
2 Dr V6 4WD Std Cab SB	8490	10200

OPTIONS FOR TACOMA
Auto 4-Speed Transmission +255
Wheel Pkg +295
AM/FM Stereo Tape +65
Air Conditioning +245
Anti-Lock Brakes +175
Auto Locking Hubs (4WD) +80
Bed Liner +85
Chrome Bumpers[Std on SR5] +45
Cruise Control +65
Power Door Locks +70
Power Windows +70

Model Description	Trade-in Value	Market Value

TERCEL 1995

Redesigned, but based on 1991-1994 generation. Coupe and sedan body styles. Coupe available in Standard and DX trim; sedan comes in DX flavor only. Dual airbags are standard. Height-adjustable seat belts are new. Car now meets 1997 side-impact standards. Engine is more powerful than before.

RATINGS (SCALE OF 1-10)

Overall	Safety	Reliability	Performance	Comfort	Value
6.9	6.7	9	6.6	7	5.4

Category E

2 Dr DX Sdn	5170	6490
4 Dr DX Sdn	5305	6660
2 Dr STD Sdn	4700	5905

OPTIONS FOR TERCEL

Auto 3-Speed Transmission +210
Auto 4-Speed Transmission +210
AM/FM Compact Disc Player +130
Air Conditioning +250
Anti-Lock Brakes +200
Power Door Locks +75
Power Steering +75
Power Windows +80

1994 TOYOTA

4RUNNER 1994

Four-wheel ABS available on models with V6 engine. Side-door guard beams added. Air conditioners get CFC-free refrigerant. Optional leather can be had in new Oak color.

RATINGS (SCALE OF 1-10)

Overall	Safety	Reliability	Performance	Comfort	Value
6.1	3.9	8.5	7	7	4.2

Category G

4 Dr SR5 4WD Wgn	9650	11700
4 Dr SR5 V6 Wgn	10435	12645
4 Dr SR5 V6 4WD Wgn	10675	12940

OPTIONS FOR 4RUNNER

Auto 4-Speed Transmission[Std on 2WD] +255
Air Conditioning +200
Anti-Lock Brakes +140
Compact Disc W/fm/tape +110
Cruise Control +50
Leather Seats +190
Luggage Rack +40
Power Door Locks +55
Power Moonroof +210
Power Windows +60
Premium Sound System +85
Rear Heater +45
Running Boards +95

CAMRY 1994

Coupe body style debuts in DX, LE and SE form. All Camrys get passenger airbag. V6 engine is tweaked for more power. New fuzzy logic controls govern automatic transmission. SE models get standard power windows, locks, mirrors and cruise control.

RATINGS (SCALE OF 1-10)

Overall	Safety	Reliability	Performance	Comfort	Value
7.9	7.3	8.4	8.6	8.4	6.6

Category D

2 Dr DX Cpe	6395	7825
4 Dr DX Sdn	6505	7960
4 Dr DX Wgn	7485	9160
2 Dr LE Cpe	7470	9145
4 Dr LE Sdn	7585	9280
4 Dr LE Wgn	8135	9955
2 Dr LE V6 Cpe	8355	10220
4 Dr LE V6 Sdn	8350	10220
4 Dr LE V6 Wgn	8890	10880
2 Dr SE Cpe	8630	10560
4 Dr SE Sdn	8740	10695
4 Dr XLE Sdn	8370	10240
4 Dr XLE V6 Sdn	9295	11375

OPTIONS FOR CAMRY

Auto 4-Speed Transmission[Opt on DX Sdn, DX Cpe] +195
Elite Pkg +280
Air Conditioning[Opt on DX] +210
Anti-Lock Brakes +215
Compact Disc W/fm/tape +190
Cruise Control[Opt on DX] +60
Leather Seats +275
Power Door Locks[Opt on DX] +65
Power Drivers Seat[Opt on LE,LE V6] +75
Power Moonroof[Std on XLE,XLE V6] +205
Premium Sound System +90

CELICA 1994

Redesigned coupe and liftback debut. Turbocharged All-Trac is gone. ST and GT are only trim levels. Dual airbags are standard; ABS is optional. Power mirrors and driver's seat height adjuster are standard.

RATINGS (SCALE OF 1-10)

Overall	Safety	Reliability	Performance	Comfort	Value
N/A	N/A	9.3	8.2	7.6	5.2

Category F

2 Dr GT Cpe	8555	10220
2 Dr GT Hbk	8765	10480
2 Dr ST Cpe	7525	8995
2 Dr ST Hbk	7680	9180

OPTIONS FOR CELICA

Auto 4-Speed Transmission +195
Air Conditioning +205
Anti-Lock Brakes +160
Compact Disc W/fm/tape +125
Cruise Control +55
Leather Seats +155
Power Door Locks[Opt on ST] +50
Power Drivers Seat +60
Power Sunroof +165
Power Windows[Opt on ST] +55
Premium Sound System +95
Sport Suspension +45

COROLLA   1994

Passenger airbag added. Passenger seatbelts have automatic locking retractors. CFC-free refrigerant is added to air conditioning system.

RATINGS (SCALE OF 1-10)

Overall	Safety	Reliabiliy	Performance	Comfort	Value
7.1	6.9	7.7	7.4	8.1	5.5

Category E

	Trade-in	Market
4 Dr DX Sdn	5290	6810
4 Dr DX Wgn	5720	7365
4 Dr LE Sdn	6510	8385
4 Dr STD Sdn	4860	6260

OPTIONS FOR COROLLA

Auto 3-Speed Transmission +120
Auto 4-Speed Transmission[Opt on DX] +195
AM/FM Compact Disc Player +105
Air Conditioning[Std on LE] +205
Aluminum/Alloy Wheels +80
Anti-Lock Brakes +160
Cruise Control[Opt on DX] +55
Power Door Locks[Opt on DX] +60
Power Sunroof +150
Power Windows[Opt on DX] +65
Premium Sound System +80

LAND CRUISER   1994

Standard sound system has nine speakers instead of five. Passenger seatbelts have automatic locking retractors.

Category G

	Trade-in	Market
4 Dr STD 4WD Wgn	16100	19520

OPTIONS FOR LAND CRUISER

Leather Trim Pkg +510
Third Rear Seat Pkg +340
Anti-Lock Brakes +140
Compact Disc W/fm/tape +110
Leather Seats +190
Limited Slip Diff +70
Luggage Rack +40
Power Drivers Seat +70
Power Moonroof +210

Power Passenger Seat +50
Running Boards +95
Third Seat +175

MR2   1994

Passenger airbag debuts. ABS made standard. Taillights are revised, and the suspension gets further fine-tuning. Base models get standard air conditioning (made standard last year on turbo), which is CFC-free on both models.

Category F

	Trade-in	Market
2 Dr STD Cpe	8595	10275
2 Dr STD Turbo Cpe	10490	12535

OPTIONS FOR MR2

Auto 4-Speed Transmission +195
Anti-Lock Brakes +160
Compact Disc W/fm/tape +125
Cruise Control[Std on Turbo] +55
Flip-Up Sunroof +100
Leather Seats +155
Limited Slip Diff +80
Power Door Locks[Std on Turbo] +50
Power Windows[Std on Turbo] +55
Premium Sound System[Std on Turbo] +95
T-Bar Roof[Std on Turbo] +210

PASEO   1994

CFC-free A/C added. Passenger seatbelts get automatic locking retractors.

RATINGS (SCALE OF 1-10)

Overall	Safety	Reliability	Performance	Comfort	Value
7.2	5.9	8.9	7.8	7.1	6.1

Category E

	Trade-in	Market
2 Dr STD Cpe	4470	5760

OPTIONS FOR PASEO

Auto 4-Speed Transmission +195
AM/FM Stereo Tape +75
Air Conditioning +205
Anti-Lock Brakes +160
Cruise Control +55
Pop-Up Moonroof +95

PICKUP   1994

Longbed models dropped. Side-door guard beams have been added.

RATINGS (SCALE OF 1-10)

Overall	Safety	Reliability	Performance	Comfort	Value
N/A	4.5	9.2	7.1	7.1	N/A

HALFTON

Category G

	Trade-in	Market
2 Dr DX Ext Cab SB	5740	6960
2 Dr DX 4WD Ext Cab SB	7320	8870
2 Dr DX Std Cab SB	5050	6120

Don't forget to refer to the Mileage Adjustment Table at the back of this book!

Model Description	Trade-in Value	Market Value
2 Dr DX 4WD Std Cab SB	6645	8055
2 Dr DX V6 Ext Cab SB	6255	7580
2 Dr DX V6 4WD Ext Cab SB	8030	9735
2 Dr DX V6 4WD Std Cab SB	7205	8730
2 Dr SR5 V6 Ext Cab SB	7385	8950
2 Dr SR5 V6 4WD Ext Cab SB	9045	10965
2 Dr STD Std Cab SB	4560	5530

OPTIONS FOR PICKUP
Auto 4-Speed Transmission +235
AM/FM Stereo Tape +55
Air Conditioning +200
Anti-Lock Rear Brakes[Std on SR5 V6] +65
Auto Locking Hubs (4WD)[Opt on DX V6] +65
Bed Liner +70
Cruise Control +50
Power Door Locks +55
Power Steering[Opt on DX,STD] +70
Power Windows +60
Premium Sound System +85
Rear Jump Seats +55
Rear Step Bumper +35
Running Boards +95
Tilt Steering Wheel[Std on SR5 V6] +45

PREVIA   1994

Passenger airbag added. Supercharged engine included on S/C models. Manual transmission is dropped. CFC-free air conditioning is new. Leather is available on LE models. New front bucket seats are installed.

RATINGS (SCALE OF 1-10)

Overall	Safety	Reliability	Performance	Comfort	Value
7.6	7.4	8.5	7.7	7.3	7.2

Category G
2 Dr DX Pass. Van	8840	10715
2 Dr DX 4WD Pass. Van	10110	12255
2 Dr LE Pass. Van	10270	12450
2 Dr LE Sprchgd Pass. Van	11195	13575
2 Dr LE 4WD Pass. Van	11465	13900
2 Dr LE Sprchgd 4WD Pass. Van	12430	15065

OPTIONS FOR PREVIA
Anti-Lock Brakes +140
Captain Chairs (2) +130
Compact Disc W/fm/tape +110
Cruise Control[Opt on DX] +50
Dual Air Conditioning[Opt on DX] +225
Leather Seats +190
Luggage Rack +40
Power Door Locks[Opt on DX] +55
Power Moonroof +210
Power Windows[Opt on DX] +60
Premium Sound System +85
Running Boards +95

SUPRA   1994

Base model gets revised final-drive ratio for improved launch.
Category F
2 Dr STD Hbk	16195	19355
2 Dr STD Turbo Hbk	18080	21610

OPTIONS FOR SUPRA
Auto 4-Speed Transmission +220
Sport Roof +270
Compact Disc W/fm/tape +125
Leather Seats +155
Limited Slip Diff[Std on Turbo] +80

T100   1994

Driver airbag is added, and base models get four-cylinder engine. Side-door guard beams are installed, and beds get cargo tie-down hooks. Formerly standard rear ABS is now optional on base and DX trucks.

RATINGS (SCALE OF 1-10)

Overall	Safety	Reliability	Performance	Comfort	Value
N/A	6.9	8.9	6.8	7.5	N/A

Category H
2 Dr DX Std Cab LB	7090	8695
2 Dr DX 4WD Std Cab LB	8725	10695
2 Dr DX 1 Ton Std Cab LB	7550	9255
2 Dr SR5 Std Cab LB	8530	10460
2 Dr SR5 4WD Std Cab LB	10060	12330
2 Dr STD Std Cab LB	6295	7715

OPTIONS FOR T100
Auto 4-Speed Transmission +220
AM/FM Compact Disc Player +75
Air Conditioning +200
Anti-Lock Rear Brakes[Std on SR5] +60
Bed Liner +55
Cruise Control +45
Power Door Locks +45
Power Windows +45
Premium Sound System +90
Rear Step Bumper +35

TERCEL   1994

CFC-free refrigerant added to optional A/C. Passenger seatbelts get automatic locking retractors. LE sedan is dropped.

RATINGS (SCALE OF 1-10)

Overall	Safety	Reliability	Performance	Comfort	Value
N/A	N/A	9	7.2	7.1	5.3

Category E
2 Dr DX Sdn	3765	4845
4 Dr DX Sdn	3800	4895
2 Dr STD Sdn	3245	4180

Model Description	Trade-in Value	Market Value
OPTIONS FOR TERCEL		
Auto 3-Speed Transmission +120		
AM/FM Stereo Tape +75		
Air Conditioning +205		
Anti-Lock Brakes +160		
Power Steering +60		

1993 TOYOTA

4RUNNER 1993

Two-door model is dropped from lineup, a victim of import tariffs. Four-wheel drive models come standard with 4WDemand system. Alloy wheels available only on V6 models, and now include chrome package.

RATINGS (SCALE OF 1-10)

Overall	Safety	Reliability	Performance	Comfort	Value
6.3	3.9	8.9	7	7	4.8

Model Description	Trade-in Value	Market Value
Category G		
4 Dr SR5 4WD Wgn	8320	10275
4 Dr SR5 V6 Wgn	8740	10795
4 Dr SR5 V6 4WD Wgn	9030	11155

OPTIONS FOR 4RUNNER
Auto 4-Speed Transmission[Opt on 4WD] +210
Air Conditioning +165
Aluminum/Alloy Wheels +65
Anti-Lock Rear Brakes[Opt on SR5] +55
Compact Disc W/frn/tape +90
Cruise Control +40
Leather Seats +155
Luggage Rack +30
Power Door Locks +45
Power Moonroof +175
Power Windows +50
Premium Sound System +70
Rear Heater +40
Running Boards +75

CAMRY 1993

DX models get color-keyed bodyside moldings. Oak is a new interior color.

RATINGS (SCALE OF 1-10)

Overall	Safety	Reliability	Performance	Comfort	Value
N/A	N/A	8.8	8.6	8.4	6.5

Model Description	Trade-in Value	Market Value
Category D		
4 Dr DX Sdn	5545	6860
4 Dr DX Wgn	6310	7805
4 Dr DX V6 Sdn	6650	8225
4 Dr LE Sdn	6530	8080
4 Dr LE Wgn	7010	8670
4 Dr LE V6 Sdn	7235	8950
4 Dr LE V6 Wgn	7625	9435
4 Dr SE Sdn	6975	8630

Model Description	Trade-in Value	Market Value
4 Dr XLE Sdn	7240	8955
4 Dr XLE V6 Sdn	7860	9725

OPTIONS FOR CAMRY
Auto 4-Speed Transmission[Opt on SE,DX Sdn] +160
AM/FM Compact Disc Player +95
Air Conditioning[Opt on DX,DX V6] +170
Anti-Lock Brakes +175
Cruise Control[Opt on DX,DX V6,SE] +50
Leather Seats +225
Power Door Locks[Opt on SE] +55
Power Moonroof[Std on XLE,XLE V6] +170
Power Windows[Opt on SE] +55
Premium Sound System +75

CELICA 1993

ABS is standard on All-Trac model; optional for first time on GT convertible.

Category F		
2 Dr GT Conv	8225	9960
2 Dr GT Cpe	6555	7940
2 Dr GT Hbk	6610	8005
2 Dr GT-S Hbk	7220	8745
2 Dr ST Cpe	5595	6775
2 Dr STD Turbo 4WD Hbk	10650	12900

OPTIONS FOR CELICA
Auto 4-Speed Transmission +155
Air Conditioning[Std on STD] +170
Aluminum/Alloy Wheels[Opt on GT] +60
Anti-Lock Brakes[Std on STD] +130
Cruise Control[Std on STD] +45
Leather Seats[Std on STD] +125
Power Door Locks[Std on STD] +40
Power Drivers Seat[Std on STD] +50
Power Sunroof[Std on STD,Conv] +135
Power Windows[Std on STD] +45

COROLLA 1993

All-new Corolla arrives with driver airbag. Sedan and wagon body styles available. All-Trac wagon dies. Interior volume increases enough to move Corolla out of subcompact classification. Height-adjustable seat belts are standard. ABS optional on all models.

RATINGS (SCALE OF 1-10)

Overall	Safety	Reliability	Performance	Comfort	Value
7.1	5.7	8.3	7.4	8.1	5.9

Model Description	Trade-in Value	Market Value
Category E		
4 Dr DX Sdn	4585	6035
4 Dr DX Wgn	4830	6360
4 Dr LE Sdn	5645	7430
4 Dr STD Sdn	4185	5510

OPTIONS FOR COROLLA
Auto 3-Speed Transmission +100
Auto 4-Speed Transmission[Opt on DX] +160
AM/FM Stereo Tape +60

Don't forget to refer to the Mileage Adjustment Table at the back of this book!

Model Description	Trade-in Value	Market Value	Model Description	Trade-in Value	Market Value

Air Conditioning[Std on LE] +165
Aluminum/Alloy Wheels +65
Anti-Lock Brakes +135
Cruise Control[Opt on DX] +45
Power Door Locks[Opt on DX] +50
Power Sunroof +125
Power Windows[Opt on DX] +55

LAND CRUISER 1993

New 4.5-liter inline six pumps out 57 more horsepower than last year's engine; output is up to 212. Air conditioning and cruise control are added to the standard equipment list. Front and rear differential locks are newly optional. New leather package is available. Side-door guard beams added.

Category G

	Trade-in	Market
4 Dr STD 4WD Wgn	13705	16930

OPTIONS FOR LAND CRUISER

Leather Trim Pkg +405
Alarm System +55
Aluminum/Alloy Wheels +65
Anti-Lock Brakes +115
Compact Disc Changer +100
Compact Disc W/fm/tape +90
Dual Power Seats +85
Leather Seats +155
Locking Differential +60
Luggage Rack +30
Power Moonroof +175
Running Boards +75
Third Seat +145

MR2 1993

Suspension revisions aim to cure quirky cornering characteristics. All Turbos come with a standard T-bar roof. Base MR2s get V-rated tires, and alloy wheels have been redesigned. An eight-speaker stereo, air conditioning, cruise, power windows, and power door locks are all newly standard on Turbo.

Category F

	Trade-in	Market
2 Dr STD Cpe	6905	8360
2 Dr STD Turbo Cpe	8600	10410

OPTIONS FOR MR2

Auto 4-Speed Transmission +160
Air Conditioning +170
Anti-Lock Brakes +130
Compact Disc W/fm/tape +100
Cruise Control[Std on Turbo] +45
Leather Seats +125
Limited Slip Diff +65
Power Door Locks[Std on Turbo] +40
Power Windows[Std on Turbo] +45
Premium Sound System +75
T-Tops (solid/Colored)[Std on Turbo] +190

PASEO 1993

Driver airbag added, and ABS is now optional. Interior fabrics are revised. Two new colors.

RATINGS (SCALE OF 1-10)

Overall	Safety	Reliability	Performance	Comfort	Value
7.1	5.9	9	7.8	7.1	5.5

Category E

	Trade-in	Market
2 Dr STD Cpe	3715	4890

OPTIONS FOR PASEO

Auto 4-Speed Transmission +160
AM/FM Stereo Tape +60
Air Conditioning +165
Aluminum/Alloy Wheels +65
Anti-Lock Brakes +135
Cruise Control +45
Moonroof +75

PICKUP 1993

One-ton and 4WD longbed dropped.

RATINGS (SCALE OF 1-10)

Overall	Safety	Reliability	Performance	Comfort	Value
N/A	4.4	8.7	7.1	7.1	N/A

HALF TON

Category G

	Trade-in	Market
2 Dr Deluxe Ext Cab SB	5330	6585
2 Dr Deluxe 4WD Ext Cab SB	6810	8410
2 Dr Deluxe Std Cab LB	5375	6640
2 Dr Deluxe Std Cab SB	4680	5780
2 Dr Deluxe 4WD Std Cab SB	6165	7615
2 Dr Deluxe V6 Ext Cab SB	5835	7210
2 Dr Deluxe V6 4WD Ext Cab SB	7325	9045
2 Dr SR5 V6 Ext Cab SB	6425	7935
2 Dr SR5 V6 4WD Ext Cab SB	7855	9700
2 Dr STD Std Cab SB	3940	4865

OPTIONS FOR PICKUP

6 cyl 3.0 L Engine[Opt on Deluxe] +130
Auto 4-Speed Transmission +185
AM/FM Stereo Tape +45
Air Conditioning +165
Aluminum/Alloy Wheels +65
Anti-Lock Rear Brakes[Std on SR5 V6] +55
Auto Locking Hubs (4WD) +55
Bed Liner +55
Cruise Control +40
Power Door Locks +45
Power Steering[Opt on Deluxe,STD] +55
Power Windows +50
Premium Sound System +70
Rear Step Bumper +30
Velour/Cloth Seats[Opt on STD] +40

PREVIA 1993

All Previas seat seven instead of five. Only 2WD DX can be equipped with manual transmission. All-Tracs and 2WD LE get rear disc brakes.

RATINGS (SCALE OF 1-10)

Overall	Safety	Reliability	Performance	Comfort	Value
7	5.4	8.8	7.5	7.3	5.9

Category G

	Trade-in	Market
2 Dr Deluxe Pass. Van	7105	8775
2 Dr Deluxe 4WD Pass. Van	8300	10250
2 Dr LE Pass. Van	8630	10660
2 Dr LE 4WD Pass. Van	9660	11930

OPTIONS FOR PREVIA

Auto 4-Speed Transmission[Std on LE,4WD] +160
Aluminum/Alloy Wheels +65
Anti-Lock Brakes +115
Captain Chairs (2) +105
Compact Disc W/fm/tape +90
Cruise Control[Std on LE] +40
Dual Air Conditioning[Std on LE] +185
Luggage Rack +30
Power Door Locks[Std on LE] +45
Power Sunroof +160
Power Windows[Std on LE] +50

SUPRA 1993

Debuted in summer 1993. All-new car features dual airbags and ABS. Twin Turbo model has 320 horsepower and traction control.

Category F

	Trade-in	Market
2 Dr STD Hbk	14090	17065
2 Dr STD Turbo Hbk	15295	18525

OPTIONS FOR SUPRA

Auto 4-Speed Transmission +180
AM/FM Compact Disc Player +90
Leather Seats +125
Limited Slip Diff[Std on Turbo] +65
Power Sunroof +135
T-Tops (solid/Colored) +190

T100 1993

New full-size Toyota pickup designed to battle Chevy C/K, Ford F-Series and Dodge Ram. 150-horsepower V6 is only powerplant. One-ton model handles 2,570 lbs.

RATINGS (SCALE OF 1-10)

Overall	Safety	Reliability	Performance	Comfort	Value
N/A	N/A	8.8	6.8	7.5	N/A

Category H

	Trade-in	Market
2 Dr 1 Ton Std Cab LB	6435	7965
2 Dr SR5 Std Cab LB	6860	8495
2 Dr SR5 4WD Std Cab LB	8275	10245

	Trade-in	Market
2 Dr STD Std Cab LB	6125	7585
2 Dr STD 4WD Std Cab LB	7565	9370

OPTIONS FOR T100

Auto 4-Speed Transmission +180
AM/FM Compact Disc Player +60
Air Conditioning +165
Aluminum/Alloy Wheels +60
Bed Liner +45
Cruise Control +40
Power Door Locks +40
Power Windows +40
Premium Sound System +75
Rear Step Bumper +30

TERCEL 1993

Driver airbag added, and ABS is optional for first time. Sedans get height-adjustable seatbelts. Exteriors get a new grille. DX models get body-color bumpers and moldings. Airbag is housed in new steering wheel. LE gets standard power steering.

RATINGS (SCALE OF 1-10)

Overall	Safety	Reliability	Performance	Comfort	Value
N/A	N/A	8.5	7.2	7.1	5.2

Category E

	Trade-in	Market
2 Dr DX Sdn	3230	4250
4 Dr DX Sdn	3330	4385
4 Dr LE Sdn	3980	5240
2 Dr STD Sdn	2690	3540

OPTIONS FOR TERCEL

Auto 3-Speed Transmission +100
AM/FM Stereo Tape +60
Air Conditioning +165
Anti-Lock Brakes +135
Power Steering +50

1992 TOYOTA

4RUNNER 1992

New grille, front bumper and aero headlights debut. Power steering and a rear wiper/washer are standard on all models. Spare tire is moved underneath body of truck. Leather seats are newly optional on four-door models with a V6 engine.

RATINGS (SCALE OF 1-10)

Overall	Safety	Reliability	Performance	Comfort	Value
6.3	3.9	8.4	7	7	5.1

Category G

	Trade-in	Market
2 Dr SR5 4WD Utility	8475	10570
4 Dr SR5 Wgn	7995	9970
4 Dr SR5 4WD Wgn	7165	8935

Don't forget to refer to the Mileage Adjustment Table at the back of this book!

Model Description	Trade-in Value	Market Value

OPTIONS FOR 4RUNNER
6 cyl 3.0 L Engine[Std on Utility,2WD] +125
Auto 4-Speed Transmission[Opt on 4WD] +180
Air Conditioning +135
Anti-Lock Rear Brakes +45
Auto Locking Hubs (4WD) +45
Compact Disc W/fm/tape +70
Leather Seats +130
Power Door Locks +40
Power Sunroof +130
Power Windows +40

CAMRY 1992
Redesign nets a driver airbag, larger engines, more interior volume and a sporty SE model. All-Trac has been dropped. ABS is optional across all trim levels and body styles.

RATINGS (SCALE OF 1-10)

Overall	Safety	Reliability	Performance	Comfort	Value
N/A	N/A	8.2	8.6	8.4	6.9

Category D

Model	Trade-in	Market
4 Dr Deluxe Sdn	4845	6050
4 Dr Deluxe Wgn	5680	7090
4 Dr LE Sdn	5715	7135
4 Dr LE Wgn	6310	7875
4 Dr SE Sdn	6220	7765
4 Dr XLE Sdn	6325	7895

OPTIONS FOR CAMRY
6 cyl 3.0 L Engine[Std on SE] +225
Auto 4-Speed Transmission[Std on LE,XLE,Wgn] +130
Bicentennial Pkg +210
Air Conditioning[Opt on Deluxe] +140
Anti-Lock Brakes +145
Compact Disc W/fm/tape +125
Leather Seats +185
Power Door Locks[Opt on SE] +45
Power Moonroof[Std on XLE] +140
Power Windows[Opt on SE] +45

CELICA 1992
Subtle restyling, larger wheels and tires, and wider availability of ABS.
Category F

Model	Trade-in	Market
2 Dr GT Conv	6640	8285
2 Dr GT Cpe	5330	6655
2 Dr GT Hbk	5375	6710
2 Dr GT-S Hbk	5870	7330
2 Dr ST Cpe	4555	5685
2 Dr STD Turbo 4WD Hbk	7140	8915

OPTIONS FOR CELICA
Auto 4-Speed Transmission +120
Air Conditioning +135
Anti-Lock Brakes +105
Compact Disc W/fm/tape +80

Leather Seats +105
Power Door Locks[Std on STD] +35
Power Drivers Seat +40
Power Sunroof +110
Power Windows[Std on STD] +40

COROLLA 1992
LE sedan comes with an automatic only. Coupe body style is dropped.
Category E

Model	Trade-in	Market
4 Dr Deluxe Sdn	3105	4330
4 Dr Deluxe Wgn	3300	4600
4 Dr Deluxe 4WD Wgn	3770	5255
4 Dr LE Sdn	3740	5220
4 Dr STD Sdn	2820	3930

OPTIONS FOR COROLLA
Auto 3-Speed Transmission +80
Auto 4-Speed Transmission[Std on LE] +130
Air Conditioning +135
Power Door Locks +40
Power Steering[Std on LE] +40
Power Sunroof +100
Power Windows +45

CRESSIDA 1992
No changes.
Category D

Model	Trade-in	Market
4 Dr STD Sdn	7185	8970

OPTIONS FOR CRESSIDA
Anti-Lock Brakes +145
Dual Power Seats +140
Leather Seats +185
Power Moonroof +140

LAND CRUISER 1992
Power windows, locks and outside mirrors are standard this year.
Category G

Model	Trade-in	Market
4 Dr STD 4WD Wgn	10120	12625

OPTIONS FOR LAND CRUISER
Air Conditioning +135
Compact Disc W/fm/tape +70
Leather Seats +130
Power Sunroof +130
Third Seat +115

MR2 1992
ABS is optional.
Category F

Model	Trade-in	Market
2 Dr STD Cpe	5325	6645
2 Dr STD Turbo Cpe	6410	8000

OPTIONS FOR MR2
Auto 4-Speed Transmission +130
Air Conditioning +135
Anti-Lock Brakes +105

TOYOTA 92

Model Description	Trade-in Value	Market Value	Model Description	Trade-in Value	Market Value

Compact Disc W/fm/tape +80
Leather Seats +105
Power Door Locks +35
Power Windows +40
T-Tops (solid/Colored) +155

PASEO   1992

Sporty version of the Tercel offers more horsepower, stiffer suspension, and racier bodywork than its more pedestrian counterpart.

RATINGS (SCALE OF 1-10)

Overall	Safety	Reliability	Performance	Comfort	Value
6.3	3.6	8.6	7.8	7.1	4.3

Category E

	Trade-in	Market
2 Dr STD Cpe	2940	4100

OPTIONS FOR PASEO
Auto 4-Speed Transmission +130
Air Conditioning +135
Moonroof +60

PICKUP   1992

New front grille debuts. Storage compartment is added to dashboard. Two-wheel drive models get full wheelcovers. Four-wheel drive models get new steel wheels and passenger assist grip.

RATINGS (SCALE OF 1-10)

Overall	Safety	Reliability	Performance	Comfort	Value
N/A	3.7	8.9	7.1	7.1	N/A

HALF TON

Category G

	Trade-in	Market
2 Dr Deluxe Ext Cab SB	4430	5525
2 Dr Deluxe 4WD Ext Cab SB	5580	6960
2 Dr Deluxe Std Cab LB	4180	5215
2 Dr Deluxe 4WD Std Cab LB	5330	6650
2 Dr Deluxe Std Cab SB	3975	4960
2 Dr Deluxe 4WD Std Cab SB	5095	6355
2 Dr SR5 Ext Cab SB	5575	6955
2 Dr SR5 4WD Ext Cab SB	6715	8375
2 Dr STD Std Cab SB	3495	4360

ONE TON

Category G

	Trade-in	Market
2 Dr STD Std Cab LB	4375	5455

OPTIONS FOR PICKUP
6 cyl 3.0 L Engine[Opt on Deluxe] +125
Auto 4-Speed Transmission +145
Air Conditioning +135
Anti-Lock Brakes[Std on SR5] +95
Auto Locking Hubs (4WD)[Std on SR5] +45
Power Door Locks +40
Power Steering[Std on One Ton,SR5] +45
Power Windows +40

PREVIA   1992

Driver airbag is added, and with new knee bolsters under the dash and a third brake light, the 1992 Previa becomes the first minivan to meet passenger car safety requirements, including standards for roof crush and side-impact protection. ABS is newly optional on DX models. LE models get standard power windows, locks and mirrors.

RATINGS (SCALE OF 1-10)

Overall	Safety	Reliability	Performance	Comfort	Value
6.9	5.2	8.2	7.5	7.3	6.1

Category G

	Trade-in	Market
2 Dr Deluxe Pass. Van	5755	7180
2 Dr Deluxe 4WD Pass. Van	6650	8290
2 Dr LE Pass. Van	7225	9010
2 Dr LE 4WD Pass. Van	8090	10090

OPTIONS FOR PREVIA
Auto 4-Speed Transmission[Std on LE] +140
Anti-Lock Brakes +95
Captain Chairs (2) +85
Dual Air Conditioning[Std on LE] +150
Power Door Locks[Std on LE] +40
Power Windows[Std on LE] +40

SUPRA   1992

Automatic transmission gets revised shift points.

Category F

	Trade-in	Market
2 Dr STD Hbk	7765	9695
2 Dr STD Turbo Hbk	8815	11010

OPTIONS FOR SUPRA
Auto 4-Speed Transmission +120
AM/FM Compact Disc Player +75
Anti-Lock Brakes[Std on Turbo] +105
Leather Seats +105
Limited Slip Diff[Std on Turbo] +55
Solid Targa Top +135

TERCEL   1992

No changes.

RATINGS (SCALE OF 1-10)

Overall	Safety	Reliability	Performance	Comfort	Value
N/A	N/A	8.5	7.2	7.1	5.1

Category E

	Trade-in	Market
2 Dr DX Sdn	2515	3510
4 Dr DX Sdn	2545	3550
4 Dr LE Sdn	2945	4105
2 Dr STD Sdn	2105	2935

OPTIONS FOR TERCEL
Auto 3-Speed Transmission +80
Air Conditioning +135
Power Steering +40

Don't forget to refer to the Mileage Adjustment Table at the back of this book!

Model Description	Trade-in Value	Market Value

1991 TOYOTA

4RUNNER — 1991

No changes.

RATINGS (SCALE OF 1-10)

Overall	Safety	Reliability	Performance	Comfort	Value
6.1	3.9	8.1	7	7	4.7

Category G

Model Description	Trade-in Value	Market Value
2 Dr SR5 4WD Utility	6225	7910
4 Dr SR5 Wgn	5925	7525
4 Dr SR5 4WD Wgn	6220	7905
4 Dr SR5 V6 4WD Wgn	7060	8970

OPTIONS FOR 4RUNNER

6 cyl 3.0 L Engine[Opt on SR5] +95
Auto 4-Speed Transmission[Std on 2WD] +125
Air Conditioning +110
Anti-Lock Brakes[Opt on SR5] +75
Compact Disc W/fm/tape +60
Power Door Locks +30
Power Moonroof +115
Power Windows +30

CAMRY — 1991

No changes.
Category D

Model Description	Trade-in Value	Market Value
4 Dr Deluxe Sdn	3300	4380
4 Dr Deluxe 4WD Sdn	3980	5280
4 Dr Deluxe Wgn	3605	4780
4 Dr LE Sdn	3830	5075
4 Dr LE 4WD Sdn	4405	5840
4 Dr LE Wgn	4590	6215
4 Dr LE V6 Sdn	4505	5975
4 Dr STD Sdn	3580	4745

OPTIONS FOR CAMRY

6 cyl 2.5 L Engine[Opt on Deluxe] +170
Auto 4-Speed Transmission[Std on LE,LE V6,Wgn,4WD] +90
Air Conditioning[Std on LE V6,LE Wgn] +115
Anti-Lock Brakes +120
Leather Seats +150
Power Door Locks[Std on LE V6,LE Wgn] +35
Power Drivers Seat +40
Power Sunroof +105
Power Windows[Std on LE V6,LE Wgn] +35

CELICA — 1991

Driver airbag added.
Category F

Model Description	Trade-in Value	Market Value
2 Dr GT Conv	6010	7675
2 Dr GT Cpe	5045	6440
2 Dr GT Hbk	4505	5755
2 Dr GT-S Hbk	5140	6560
2 Dr ST Cpe	4000	5105
2 Dr STD Turbo 4WD Hbk	6330	8080

OPTIONS FOR CELICA

Auto 4-Speed Transmission +90
Air Conditioning +110
Anti-Lock Brakes +85
Compact Disc W/fm/tape +65
Leather Seats +85
Power Door Locks[Std on STD] +25
Power Sunroof +90
Power Windows[Std on STD] +30

COROLLA — 1991

All-Trac sedan dropped.
Category E

Model Description	Trade-in Value	Market Value
4 Dr Deluxe Sdn	2740	3920
4 Dr Deluxe Wgn	2915	4175
4 Dr Deluxe 4WD Wgn	3370	4825
2 Dr GT-S Cpe	3695	5290
4 Dr LE Sdn	3060	4380
2 Dr SR5 Cpe	3120	4465
4 Dr STD Sdn	2470	3540

OPTIONS FOR COROLLA

Auto 3-Speed Transmission +65
Auto 4-Speed Transmission +95
Air Conditioning +110
Power Door Locks +35
Power Steering[Std on GT-S,LE] +35
Power Sunroof +85
Power Windows +35

CRESSIDA — 1991

No changes.
Category D

Model Description	Trade-in Value	Market Value
4 Dr Luxury Sdn	5870	7785

OPTIONS FOR CRESSIDA

Anti-Lock Brakes +120
Leather Seats +150
Power Drivers Seat +40
Power Passenger Seat +40
Power Sunroof +105

LAND CRUISER — 1991

All-new design debuted in March, 1990. Features permanent 4WD. Coil springs replace leaf springs. 4.0-liter inline six makes 155 horsepower. Optional third seat allows truck to carry seven passengers.
Category G

Model Description	Trade-in Value	Market Value
4 Dr STD 4WD Wgn	8350	10605

OPTIONS FOR LAND CRUISER

Air Conditioning +110
Compact Disc W/fm/tape +60
Power Door Locks +30
Power Sunroof +105

Don't forget to refer to the Mileage Adjustment Table at the back of this book!

TOYOTA 91

Model Description	Trade-in Value	Market Value	Model Description	Trade-in Value	Market Value

Power Windows +30
Third Seat +95

MR2   1991

Back after one-year hiatus. Ferrari styling themes, driver airbag and optional turbocharged power make this one a winner.

Category F

2 Dr STD Cpe	4585	5850
2 Dr STD Turbo Cpe	5590	7140

OPTIONS FOR MR2

Auto 4-Speed Transmission +100
Air Conditioning +110
Anti-Lock Brakes +85
Compact Disc W/fm/tape +65
Leather Seats +85
Power Door Locks +25
Power Windows +30

PICKUP   1991

Wider availability of shift-on-the-fly 4WD and rear ABS. All engines have fuel injection. Four-speed manual transmission dropped. SR5 trim available only with V6 engine, and SR5s get new graphics and seat fabric.

RATINGS (SCALE OF 1-10)

Overall	Safety	Reliability	Performance	Comfort	Value
N/A	3.7	8.7	7.1	7.1	N/A

HALF TON

Category G

2 Dr Deluxe Ext Cab SB	3795	4820
2 Dr Deluxe 4WD Ext Cab SB	4740	6025
2 Dr Deluxe Std Cab LB	3630	4610
2 Dr Deluxe 4WD Std Cab LB	4480	5695
2 Dr Deluxe Std Cab SB	3440	4365
2 Dr Deluxe 4WD Std Cab SB	4290	5450
2 Dr SR5 Ext Cab SB	4875	6195
2 Dr SR5 4WD Ext Cab SB	5835	7415
2 Dr STD Std Cab SB	3045	3865

ONE TON

Category G

2 Dr STD Std Cab LB	3730	4740

OPTIONS FOR PICKUP

6 cyl 3.0 L Engine[Opt on Deluxe] +95
Auto 4-Speed Transmission +110
Air Conditioning +110
Anti-Lock Brakes +75
Auto Locking Hubs (4WD)[Std on SR5] +35
Power Door Locks +30
Power Steering[Std on One Ton,SR5] +40
Power Windows +30

PREVIA   1991

Replaced Van in March, 1990. Employs midengine design driving the rear or all four wheels. ABS is optional on LE models.

RATINGS (SCALE OF 1-10)

Overall	Safety	Reliability	Performance	Comfort	Value
6.8	4.1	7	7.5	7.3	7.9

Category G

2 Dr Deluxe Pass. Van	4670	5930
2 Dr Deluxe 4WD Pass. Van	5500	6990
2 Dr LE Pass. Van	6230	7915
2 Dr LE 4WD Pass. Van	6855	8710

OPTIONS FOR PREVIA

Auto 4-Speed Transmission[Std on LE] +105
7 Passenger Seating[Std on LE] +70
Air Conditioning +110
Anti-Lock Brakes +75
Captain Chairs (4) +80
Dual Air Conditioning[Std on LE] +125
Power Door Locks[Std on LE] +30
Power Windows +30

SUPRA   1991

ABS made standard on Turbo.

Category F

2 Dr STD Hbk	6450	8235
2 Dr STD Turbo Hbk	7390	9435

OPTIONS FOR SUPRA

Auto 4-Speed Transmission +100
Sport Handling Pkg +105
AM/FM Compact Disc Player +60
Anti-Lock Brakes[Std on Turbo] +85
Leather Seats +85
Power Drivers Seat +30
Power Sunroof +90
Solid Targa Top +110

TERCEL   1991

Redesigned Tercel available in coupe and sedan versions only.

RATINGS (SCALE OF 1-10)

Overall	Safety	Reliability	Performance	Comfort	Value
N/A	N/A	8.5	7.2	7.1	4.6

Category E

2 Dr DX Sdn	2140	3065
4 Dr DX Sdn	2165	3100
4 Dr LE Sdn	2585	3700
2 Dr STD Sdn	1795	2565

OPTIONS FOR TERCEL

Auto 3-Speed Transmission +65
Air Conditioning +110
Power Steering[Opt on DX] +35

Don't forget to refer to the Mileage Adjustment Table at the back of this book!

VOLKSWAGEN 00

VOLKSWAGEN Germany

1996 Volkswagen Cabrio

2000 VOLKSWAGEN

CABRIO 2000

Volkswagen's Cabrio gets minor equipment updates for the millennium.

Category F

Model Description	Trade-in Value	Market Value
2 Dr GL Conv	15770	18395
2 Dr GLS Conv	18310	21360

OPTIONS FOR CABRIO
Auto 4-Speed Transmission +715
Aluminum/Alloy Wheels[Opt on GL] +250
Cruise Control[Opt on GL] +180
Heated Front Seats[Opt on GL] +315
Heated Power Mirrors[Opt on GL] +170
Keyless Entry System +150
Power Windows[Opt on GL] +190

EUROVAN 2000

For its second year back in the U.S., Volkswagen's EuroVan receives minor equipment updates.

Category G

Model Description	Trade-in Value	Market Value
2 Dr GLS Pass. Van	22845	26500
2 Dr MV Pass. Van	23920	27745

OPTIONS FOR EUROVAN
Weekender Pkg +2855
Heated Front Seats +225
Power Moonroof +710

GOLF 2000

VW's Golf arrives for 2000 with several equipment updates. But the big news is that the 150-horsepower, turbocharged engine found in the New Beetle Turbo is standard for the GTI and optional on the Golf GLS.

Category E

Model Description	Trade-in Value	Market Value
2 Dr GL Hbk	11500	13450
2 Dr GL TDI Turbodsl Hbk	12465	14580
4 Dr GLS Hbk	12580	14715
4 Dr GLS Turbo Hbk	13735	16065
4 Dr GLS TDI Turbodsl Hbk	13365	15630

Category F

Model Description	Trade-in Value	Market Value
2 Dr GTI GLS Hbk	13605	15870
2 Dr GTI GLS Turbo Hbk	14765	17220
2 Dr GTI GLX Hbk	17300	20185

OPTIONS FOR GOLF
Auto 4-Speed Transmission +715
AM/FM Compact Disc Player +380
Aluminum/Alloy Wheels[Std on GTI, GLX] +275
Leather Seats[Std on GLX] +520
Power Moonroof[Std on GTI, GLX] +475

JETTA 2000

VW's 2000 Jetta arrives with an optional turbocharged 1.8T engine on the GLS for that extra zip-a-dee-doo-dah as well as minor equipment updates.

Category D

Model Description	Trade-in Value	Market Value
4 Dr GL Sdn	13260	15440
4 Dr GL TDI Turbodsl Sdn	14255	16605
4 Dr GLS Sdn	13990	16295
4 Dr GLS Turbo Sdn	15185	17685
4 Dr GLS TDI Turbodsl Sdn	14800	17235
4 Dr GLS VR6 Sdn	15760	18355
4 Dr GLX VR6 Sdn	19010	22140

OPTIONS FOR JETTA
Auto 4-Speed Transmission +715
AM/FM Compact Disc Player +380
Aluminum/Alloy Wheels[Std on GLX VR6] +380
Heated Front Seats[Std on GLX VR6] +305
Leather Seats[Std on GLX VR6] +925
Leather Steering Wheel[Std on GLX VR6] +105
Power Moonroof[Std on GLX VR6] +690

NEW BEETLE 2000

Several minor equipment upgrades, such as improved theft protection, debut on the 2000 New Beetle.

Category E

Model Description	Trade-in Value	Market Value
2 Dr GL Sdn	12795	14965
2 Dr GLS Sdn	13535	15830
2 Dr GLS Turbo Sdn	15210	17790
2 Dr GLS TDI Turbodsl Sdn	14350	16785
2 Dr GLX Turbo Sdn	16825	19680

OPTIONS FOR NEW BEETLE
Auto 4-Speed Transmission +715
Aluminum/Alloy Wheels[Std on GLX] +275
Leather Seats[Std on GLX] +720
Power Moonroof[Std on GLX] +475

Don't forget to refer to the Mileage Adjustment Table at the back of this book!

Model Description	Trade-in Value	Market Value	Model Description	Trade-in Value	Market Value

PASSAT   2000

The radio display and anti-theft system have been updated. A brake-wear indicator is now standard on all models.

Category D

	Trade-in	Market
4 Dr GLS V6 Sdn	18420	21450
4 Dr GLS Turbo Sdn	16450	19155
4 Dr GLS V6 4WD Sdn	20480	23855
4 Dr GLS V6 Wgn	19025	22155
4 Dr GLS Turbo Wgn	17055	19865
4 Dr GLS V6 4WD Wgn	21085	24560
4 Dr GLX Sdn	21335	24850
4 Dr GLX 4WD Sdn	23400	27250
4 Dr GLX Wgn	21940	25555
4 Dr GLX 4WD Wgn	24005	27955

OPTIONS FOR PASSAT

Auto Manual Transmission[Std on AWD] +880
Aluminum/Alloy Wheels[Std on GLX, AWD] +380
Compact Disc Changer +535
Leather Seats[Std on GLX,] +925
Power Moonroof[Std on GLX,] +690

1999 VOLKSWAGEN

CABRIO   1999

Volkswagen imparts new Euro-styling on the '99 Cabrios, making them more aerodynamic and adding twin headlights that show interior elements through the lens. Cabrio interiors also receive makeovers.

RATINGS (SCALE OF 1-10)

Overall	Safety	Reliability	Performance	Comfort	Value
N/A	N/A	N/A	7.8	6.4	N/A

Category F

	Trade-in	Market
2 Dr NEW GL Conv	14870	17405
2 Dr GL Conv	13395	15675
2 Dr NEW GLS Conv	17270	20215
2 Dr GLS Conv	16520	19335

OPTIONS FOR CABRIO

Auto 4-Speed Transmission +585
Air Conditioning[Opt on GL] +565
Aluminum/Alloy Wheels[Opt on GL,NEW GL] +205
Cruise Control[Opt on GL,NEW GL] +150
Heated Front Seats[Std on NEW GLS] +260
Keyless Entry System +120
Power Windows[Opt on GL,NEW GL] +155
Side Air Bag Restraint[Opt on GL,GLS] +265

EUROVAN   1999

After a five-year hiatus, the funky EuroVan passenger van returns to the U.S. with a six-cylinder engine, structural improvements and new safety features.

RATINGS (SCALE OF 1-10)

Overall	Safety	Reliability	Performance	Comfort	Value
N/A	N/A	N/A	6.2	6.4	N/A

Category G

	Trade-in	Market
2 Dr GLS Pass. Van	20645	24030
2 Dr MV Pass. Van	21635	25180

OPTIONS FOR EUROVAN

Weekender Pkg +2295
Heated Front Seats +180
Power Moonroof +580

GOLF   1999

The four-cylinder GTI is dropped in favor of a four-door Wolfsburg Edition during the final year for the current Golf.

RATINGS (SCALE OF 1-10)

Overall	Safety	Reliability	Performance	Comfort	Value
N/A	6.3	N/A	8	7.6	N/A

Category E

	Trade-in	Market
4 Dr GL Hbk	11555	13250
4 Dr Wolfsburg Hbk	11070	13015

Category F

	Trade-in	Market
2 Dr GTI VR6 Hbk	15850	18500

OPTIONS FOR GOLF

Auto 4-Speed Transmission +585
AM/FM Compact Disc Player +310
Air Conditioning[Opt on GL] +555
Anti-Lock Brakes[Std on VR6] +445
Leather Seats +425
Power Moonroof[Std on VR6] +390
Side Air Bag Restraint +190

GTI   1999

VW's all-new Golf GTIs arrive in 1999 with new interior and exterior designs and more powerful engines.

Category F

	Trade-in	Market
2 Dr NEW GLS Hbk	12455	14575
2 Dr NEW GLX Hbk	15670	18340

OPTIONS FOR GTI

Auto 4-Speed Transmission +585
AM/FM Compact Disc Player +310
Heated Front Seats[Std on NEW GLX] +260
Leather Seats[Std on NEW GLX] +425

JETTA   1999

Volkswagen trims model availability, killing the GLS and GT in favor of the Wolfsburg Edition.

RATINGS (SCALE OF 1-10)

Overall	Safety	Reliability	Performance	Comfort	Value
N/A	6.3	N/A	8.6	7.6	N/A

Don't forget to refer to the Mileage Adjustment Table at the back of this book!

Model Description	Trade-in Value	Market Value

Category D

Model Description	Trade-in Value	Market Value
4 Dr GL Sdn	11375	13315
4 Dr GLX Sdn	15905	18620
4 Dr TDI Turbodsl Sdn	12065	14120
4 Dr Wolfsburg Sdn	12605	14755

OPTIONS FOR JETTA

Auto 4-Speed Transmission +585
Air Conditioning[Opt on GL,TDI] +575
Aluminum/Alloy Wheels[Opt on GL,TDI] +310
Anti-Lock Brakes[Std on GLX] +595
Cruise Control[Opt on GL] +165
Leather Seats +760
Power Moonroof[Std on GLX] +565
Side Air Bag Restraint +195

NEW BEETLE   1999

A high-performance turbo model debuts this year. A small spoiler over the rear window is the only exterior telltale that the Slug Bug next to you has the 150-horsepower 1.8-liter turbocharged inline-four from the larger Passat sedan under the hood.

RATINGS (SCALE OF 1-10)

Overall	Safety	Reliability	Performance	Comfort	Value
N/A	N/A	N/A	6.8	7.9	N/A

Category E

	Trade-in	Market
2 Dr GL Sdn	11610	13880
2 Dr GLS Sdn	13055	15350
2 Dr GLS Turbo Sdn	14695	17275
2 Dr GLS TDI Turbodsl Sdn	13865	16305
2 Dr GLX Turbo Sdn	16125	18955

OPTIONS FOR NEW BEETLE

Auto 4-Speed Transmission +585
Aluminum/Alloy Wheels[Std on GLX] +225
Leather Seats[Std on GLX] +585
Power Moonroof[Std on GLX] +390

NEW GOLF   1999

VW's all-new Golf arrives in 1999 with new interior and exterior designs and more powerful engines.

RATINGS (SCALE OF 1-10)

Overall	Safety	Reliability	Performance	Comfort	Value
N/A	N/A	N/A	8	7.9	N/A

Category E

	Trade-in	Market
2 Dr NEW GL Hbk	10610	12475
2 Dr NEW GL TDI Turbodsl Hbk	11500	13520
4 Dr NEW GLS Hbk	11605	13645
4 Dr NEW GLS TDI Turbodsl Hbk	12330	14495

OPTIONS FOR NEW GOLF

Auto 4-Speed Transmission +585
Aluminum/Alloy Wheels +225
Power Moonroof +390

NEW JETTA   1999

VW's all-new 1999 Jetta arrives with bigger engines, updated styling and new standard equipment.

RATINGS (SCALE OF 1-10)

Overall	Safety	Reliability	Performance	Comfort	Value
N/A	N/A	N/A	8	7.6	N/A

Category D

	Trade-in	Market
4 Dr NEW GL Sdn	12235	14320
4 Dr NEW GL TDI Turbodsl Sdn	13155	15400
4 Dr NEW GLS Sdn	12910	15110
4 Dr NEW GLS TDI Turbodsl Sdn	13655	15985
4 Dr NEW GLS VR6 Sdn	14545	17025
4 Dr NEW GLX VR6 Sdn	17065	19975

OPTIONS FOR NEW JETTA

Auto 4-Speed Transmission +585
Aluminum/Alloy Wheels[Std on NEW GLX VR6] +310
Power Moonroof[Std on NEW GLX VR6] +565

PASSAT   1999

After promising the availability of all-wheel drive this year, Volkswagen, in a last-minute product change, has cancelled the Synchro all-wheel drive option on all Passats for 1999 and will not be offering the GLS wagon with a V6 engine.

RATINGS (SCALE OF 1-10)

Overall	Safety	Reliability	Performance	Comfort	Value
N/A	N/A	8.8	8.6	8.3	N/A

Category D

	Trade-in	Market
4 Dr GLS V6 Sdn	17470	20445
4 Dr GLS Turbo Sdn	15600	18260
4 Dr GLS Turbo Wgn	15995	18725
4 Dr GLX Sdn	19690	23215

OPTIONS FOR PASSAT

Auto Manual Transmission[Std on GLX] +720
AM/FM Compact Disc Player +310
Aluminum/Alloy Wheels +310
Power Moonroof[Std on GLX] +565

1998 VOLKSWAGEN

CABRIO   1998

The Highline trim designation is replaced by more sensible GLS nomenclature, though we'd prefer to see something like GTI grace the rear flanks of this drop-top. New GLS model gets a power top, making the Cabrio easier to live with. Optional are side impact airbags mounted inside the seats. Newly standard on both base and GLS are door pocket liners, a trunk cargo net and sport seats with height adjustment. Still no much-needed power boost.

Don't forget to refer to the Mileage Adjustment Table at the back of this book!

Model Description	Trade-in Value	Market Value

Model Description	Trade-in Value	Market Value

RATINGS (SCALE OF 1-10)

Overall	Safety	Reliability	Performance	Comfort	Value
7	5.9	9	7.8	6.4	5.7

Category F

2 Dr GL Conv	12635	14825
2 Dr GLS Conv	15585	18285

OPTIONS FOR CABRIO

Auto 4-Speed Transmission +480
Air Conditioning[Opt on GL] +460
Aluminum/Alloy Wheels[Opt on GL] +170
Compact Disc Changer +350
Cruise Control[Opt on GL] +120
Heated Front Seats +210
Heated Power Mirrors[Opt on GL] +115
Keyless Entry System +100
Power Windows[Opt on GL] +125
Side Air Bag Restraint +215

GOLF   1998

GTI VR6 receives several cosmetic upgrades taken from the 1997 Driver's Edition. Among them are a chrome-tipped exhaust pipe, silver/white-faced instruments, embossed sill covers, leather-wrapped steering wheel, shift boot and handbrake lever (with stitching designed to coordinate with new Sport-Jacquard seat fabric) and the aluminum ball shift knob. Exclusive to the VR6 for 1998 are the Speedline 15-inch alloys from the Driver's Edition and one-touch up power windows with pinch protection. All GTIs get standard remote keyless entry.

RATINGS (SCALE OF 1-10)

Overall	Safety	Reliability	Performance	Comfort	Value
7.3	6.3	8.2	8.6	7.6	6

Category E

4 Dr GL Hbk	9470	11185
4 Dr K2 Hbk	10415	12305
4 Dr Wolfsburg Hbk	10675	12610

Category F

2 Dr GTI Hbk	11620	13725
2 Dr GTI VR6 Hbk	14490	17000

OPTIONS FOR GOLF

Auto 4-Speed Transmission +480
AM/FM Stereo Tape[Opt on GL] +165
Air Conditioning[Opt on GL,K2] +455
Leather Seats +345
Power Moonroof[Opt on GL,K2] +320
Power Windows[Opt on Wolfsburg] +145

JETTA   1998

The TDI has finally arrived. New wheel covers and colors spruce up the exterior for another year, while remote keyless entry makes it easier to lock and unlock the Jetta. GLX models have new one-touch up power windows with pinch protection.

RATINGS (SCALE OF 1-10)

Overall	Safety	Reliability	Performance	Comfort	Value
7.3	6.3	8.2	8.6	7.6	6

Category D

4 Dr GL Sdn	10345	12155
4 Dr GLS Sdn	11955	14050
4 Dr GLX Sdn	14705	17280
4 Dr GT Sdn	10615	12475
4 Dr K2 Sdn	11305	13285
4 Dr TDI Turbodsl Sdn	11150	13100
4 Dr Wolfsburg Sdn	11650	13690

OPTIONS FOR JETTA

Auto 4-Speed Transmission +485
Air Conditioning[Opt on GL, GT, TDI] +470
Aluminum/Alloy Wheels[Opt on GL, TDI] +255
Anti-Lock Brakes[Std on GLX] +485
Bose Sound System[Opt on GLS] +425
Compact Disc Changer[Std on Wolfsburg] +360
Cruise Control[Std on GLS, GLX, TDI] +135
Heated Front Seats +205
Heated Power Mirrors[Std on GLS, GLX] +45
Leather Seats +620
Power Moonroof[Std on GLX, Wolfsburg] +460
Power Windows[Std on GLS, GLX] +150
Side Air Bag Restraint +160

NEW BEETLE   1998

Volkswagen attempts to revive a legend using retro styling touches wrapped around Golf underpinnings.

RATINGS (SCALE OF 1-10)

Overall	Safety	Reliability	Performance	Comfort	Value
N/A	8.3	8.3	N/A	N/A	N/A

Category E

2 Dr STD Sdn	11530	13620
2 Dr TDI Turbodsl Sdn	12465	14725

OPTIONS FOR NEW BEETLE

Auto 4-Speed Transmission +510
Aluminum/Alloy Wheels +185
Anti-Lock Brakes +365
Compact Disc Changer +265
Cruise Control[Std on TDI] +125
Fog Lights +85
Heated Front Seats +80
Power Windows +145

PASSAT   1998

An all-new Passat arrives wearing stylish sheetmetal over a stretched Audi A4 platform. Engine choices include a spunky turbocharged four or a silky V6.

VOLKSWAGEN 98-97

Model Description	Trade-in Value	Market Value

RATINGS (SCALE OF 1-10)

Overall	Safety	Reliability	Performance	Comfort	Value
7.9	8.4	8.1	8.6	8.3	6.1

Category D

	Trade-in	Market
4 Dr GLS Turbo Sdn	13980	16430
4 Dr GLS Turbo Wgn	15160	17815
4 Dr GLS V6 Sdn	15590	18315
4 Dr GLX Sdn	17660	20755

OPTIONS FOR PASSAT

Heated Front Seats[Std on GLX] +205
Leather Seats[Std on GLX] +620
Power Moonroof[Std on GLX] +460

1997 VOLKSWAGEN

CABRIO 1997

Cabrio comes in two trim levels for 1997: Base and Highline. Base models are decontented versions of last year's car, priced a couple thousand dollars lower to entice young drivers. Highline models have standard alloy wheels, fog lights and leather seats. Engines have a redesigned cylinder head resulting in quieter operation.

RATINGS (SCALE OF 1-10)

Overall	Safety	Reliability	Performance	Comfort	Value
6.9	5.9	8.7	7.8	6.4	5.6

Category F

	Trade-in	Market
2 Dr Highline Conv	13765	16200
2 Dr STD Conv	11935	13900

OPTIONS FOR CABRIO

Auto 4-Speed Transmission +390
Air Conditioning[Opt on STD] +375
Aluminum/Alloy Wheels[Opt on STD] +135
Compact Disc Changer +285
Cruise Control[Opt on STD] +100
Heated Front Seats +175
Power Windows[Opt on STD] +105

EUROVAN 1997

Category G

	Trade-in	Market
2 Dr Campmobile Pass.Van	20635	23810

OPTIONS FOR EUROVAN

AM/FM Stereo Tape +100

GOLF 1997

GTI VR6 gets a lowered suspension for improved handling, and a redesigned cylinder head quiets GL and GTI models. A K2 edition debuted in December, 1996, sporting heated front seats, premium sound, and a rack with either skis or a snowboard attached. Spring, 1997, brought a slick Trek model with alloys and a bike up top.

RATINGS (SCALE OF 1-10)

Overall	Safety	Reliability	Performance	Comfort	Value
7.1	5.9	7.9	8.6	7.6	5.3

Category E

	Trade-in	Market
2 Dr GL Hbk	8015	9595
4 Dr GL Hbk	8310	9950
4 Dr K2 Hbk	8790	10525
4 Dr Trek Hbk	8835	10580

Category F

	Trade-in	Market
2 Dr GTI Hbk	10005	11980
2 Dr GTI VR6 Hbk	12595	14830

OPTIONS FOR GOLF

Auto 4-Speed Transmission +390
AM/FM Stereo Tape[Opt on GL,Trek] +135
Air Conditioning[Opt on GL,K2,Trek] +370
Leather Seats +285
Power Moonroof[Opt on GL,K2,Trek] +260

JETTA 1997

Wolfsburg models are gone, and the Jetta GT arrives sporting the look of the GLX without that darn expensive VR6 engine. Trek gets alloy wheels. GL, GLS, Trek and GT run more quietly, thanks to a new cylinder head design.

RATINGS (SCALE OF 1-10)

Overall	Safety	Reliability	Performance	Comfort	Value
7.1	5.9	7.9	8.6	7.6	5.3

Category D

	Trade-in	Market
4 Dr GL Sdn	9250	10935
4 Dr GLS Sdn	10690	12640
4 Dr GLX Sdn	13150	15550
4 Dr GT Sdn	9490	11220
4 Dr TDI Turbodsl Sdn	9970	11790
4 Dr Trek Sdn	9835	11630

OPTIONS FOR JETTA

Auto 4-Speed Transmission +395
AM/FM Compact Disc Player +210
Air Conditioning[Std on GLS,GLX] +385
Aluminum/Alloy Wheels[Opt on GL] +210
Anti-Lock Brakes[Std on GLX] +395
Bose Sound System[Opt on GLS] +350
Cruise Control[Opt on GL,GT,Trek] +110
Heated Front Seats +165
Heated Power Mirrors[Opt on Trek] +35
Leather Seats +505
Power Moonroof[Std on GLX] +380
Power Windows[Opt on Trek] +120

PASSAT 1997

GLS model vanishes from radar as Volkswagen prepares for launch of all-new Passat in mid-1997.

Don't forget to refer to the Mileage Adjustment Table at the back of this book!

Model Description	Trade-in Value	Market Value	Model Description	Trade-in Value	Market Value

RATINGS (SCALE OF 1-10)

Overall	Safety	Reliability	Performance	Comfort	Value
6.7	7.2	7.7	7.8	8	3

Category D

4 Dr GLX Sdn	13230	15645
4 Dr GLX Wgn	13485	15945
4 Dr TDI Turbodsl Sdn	11775	13925
4 Dr TDI Turbodsl Wgn	12030	14225

OPTIONS FOR PASSAT

Auto 4-Speed Transmission +395
Anti-Lock Brakes[Opt on TDI] +395
Compact Disc Changer +290
Heated Front Seats +165
Leather Seats +505
Power Moonroof +380

1996 VOLKSWAGEN

CABRIO   1996

Daytime running lights and new body-color side moldings alter the exterior appearance of the 1996 Cabrio. A new color scheme also livens things up. Central locking and unlocking switch is dash mounted.

RATINGS (SCALE OF 1-10)

Overall	Safety	Reliability	Performance	Comfort	Value
7	5.9	9	7.8	6.4	5.9

Category F

2 Dr STD Conv	10645	12825

OPTIONS FOR CABRIO

Auto 4-Speed Transmission +310
Air Conditioning +305
Aluminum/Alloy Wheels +110
Leather Seats +230

GOLF   1996

The Golf Sport becomes the GTI, powered by a 2.0-liter four-cylinder with alloys, sport seats, and smoke-tinted taillights. GTI VR6 continues, with firmer front suspension, three new colors, and new "Pininfarina" style alloy wheels. Black leather seats are newly optional on GTI VR6. Automatic transmissions are smoother this year.

RATINGS (SCALE OF 1-10)

Overall	Safety	Reliability	Performance	Comfort	Value
7	5.8	7.3	8.6	7.6	5.7

Category E

4 Dr GL Hbk	7230	8740
4 Dr TDI Turbodsl Hbk	7710	9320

OPTIONS FOR GOLF

Auto 4-Speed Transmission +320
AM/FM Stereo Tape +110

Air Conditioning +305
Anti-Lock Brakes +245
Compact Disc Changer +175
Power Moonroof +215

GTI   1996

Category F

2 Dr STD Hbk	8355	10095
2 Dr VR6 Hbk	10750	12800

OPTIONS FOR GTI

Auto 4-Speed Transmission +320
Compact Disc Changer +235
Leather Seats +230

JETTA   1996

A new grille is added up front. GLX models get a firmer front suspension and new "Bugatti" style wheels. New colors sum up the changes.

RATINGS (SCALE OF 1-10)

Overall	Safety	Reliability	Performance	Comfort	Value
7	5.8	7.3	8.6	7.6	5.7

Category D

4 Dr City Sdn	7425	8885
4 Dr GL Sdn	7855	9400
4 Dr GLS Sdn	8920	10675
4 Dr GLX Sdn	11220	13430
4 Dr TDI Turbodsl Sdn	8000	9575
4 Dr Trek Limited Ed. Sdn	7990	9560
4 Dr Wolfsburg Sdn	7940	9500

OPTIONS FOR JETTA

Auto 4-Speed Transmission +320
AM/FM Compact Disc Player[Std on TDI] +170
Air Conditioning[Std on GLS,GLX] +315
Aluminum/Alloy Wheels[Opt on GL] +170
Anti-Lock Brakes[Std on GLX] +325
Bose Sound System[Opt on GLS] +285
Cruise Control[Std on GLS,GLX] +90
Heated Front Seats +135
Leather Seats +415
Power Moonroof[Std on GLX,Wolfsburg] +310

PASSAT   1996

Daytime running lights debut, two new colors are added to the palette, and a new price-leader GLS model powered by a 2.0-liter, 115-horsepower, four-cylinder engine is introduced. Midyear, a Turbo Direct Injection (TDI) diesel model appears in sedan and wagon form.

RATINGS (SCALE OF 1-10)

Overall	Safety	Reliability	Performance	Comfort	Value
6.8	7.2	7.5	7.8	8	3.4

Category D

4 Dr GLS Sdn	9670	11570
4 Dr GLX Sdn	11405	13650

Don't forget to refer to the Mileage Adjustment Table at the back of this book!

Model Description	Trade-in Value	Market Value	Model Description	Trade-in Value	Market Value
4 Dr GLX Wgn	11625	13910	4 Dr STD Hbk	5540	6870
4 Dr TDI Turbodsl Sdn	10150	12145	2 Dr Sport Hbk	6725	8335
4 Dr TDI Turbodsl Wgn	10395	12440	*Category F*		
			2 Dr GTI VR6 Hbk	8925	10710

OPTIONS FOR PASSAT

Auto 4-Speed Transmission +290
Anti-Lock Brakes[Std on GLX] +325
Compact Disc Changer +240
Heated Front Seats +135
Leather Seats +415
Power Moonroof +310

1995 VOLKSWAGEN

CABRIO   1995

Dual airbags, ABS, and 115-horsepower engine are standard on this Golf derivative. Manual top only.

RATINGS (SCALE OF 1-10)

Overall	Safety	Reliability	Performance	Comfort	Value
6.4	5.9	6.8	7.8	6.4	4.9

Category F
2 Dr STD Conv		9775	11730

OPTIONS FOR CABRIO

Auto 4-Speed Transmission +260
Air Conditioning +250
Aluminum/Alloy Wheels +90
Compact Disc Changer +190
Leather Seats +190

EUROVAN   1995

Category G
2 Dr Campmobile Pass. Van	16970	19805

OPTIONS FOR EUROVAN

Auto 4-Speed Transmission +300

GOLF   1995

GTI VR6 debuts, with 2.8-liter V6, ABS, and traction control. Entry-level City trim level introduced for four-door models. Two-door Golf switches from GL to Sport designation, and includes spoked alloy wheels and blacked out taillights. Golf meets 1997 side-impact standards. Front seatbelts have height adjusters and emergency tensioners. Daytime running lights are standard on all Golf models.

RATINGS (SCALE OF 1-10)

Overall	Safety	Reliability	Performance	Comfort	Value
6.6	6	5.7	8.6	7.6	5.1

Category E
4 Dr Celebration Hbk	5705	7075
4 Dr City Hbk	5120	6350
2 Dr GL Hbk	6135	7605
4 Dr GL Hbk	6290	7800

OPTIONS FOR GOLF

Auto 4-Speed Transmission +260
AM/FM Stereo Tape[Opt on City,STD] +90
Air Conditioning[Std on GTIVR6,GL,Sport] +250
Aluminum/Alloy Wheels[Opt on GL] +100
Anti-Lock Brakes[Std on GTIVR6] +200
Compact Disc Changer +145
Power Moonroof[Std on GTIVR6,Sport] +175
Premium Sound System +100

JETTA   1995

Entry-level City trim level introduced. Jetta meets 1997 side-impact standards. Front seatbelts have height adjusters and emergency tensioners. Daytime running lights are standard on all Jetta models.

RATINGS (SCALE OF 1-10)

Overall	Safety	Reliability	Performance	Comfort	Value
6.6	6	5.7	8.6	7.6	5.1

Category D
4 Dr Celebration Sdn	6290	7720
4 Dr City Sdn	5650	6940
4 Dr GL Sdn	6340	8030
4 Dr GLS Sdn	7620	9355
4 Dr GLX Sdn	8910	10940
4 Dr STD Sdn	6065	7450

OPTIONS FOR JETTA

Auto 4-Speed Transmission +260
AM/FM Stereo Tape[Std on GL,GLS,GLX] +105
Air Conditioning[Std on GL,GLS,GLX,STD] +255
Alarm System[Opt on Celebration] +155
Anti-Lock Brakes[Std on GLX] +265
Compact Disc Changer +195
Leather Seats +340
Power Moonroof[Std on GLS,GLX] +250

PASSAT   1995

Reskinned for 1995, VW adds dual airbags, three-point seatbelts, and side-impact protection that meets 1997 safety standards. Climate control system gains dust and pollen filter. GLX is only trim level.

RATINGS (SCALE OF 1-10)

Overall	Safety	Reliability	Performance	Comfort	Value
6.8	7.7	6.7	7.8	8	3.8

Category D
4 Dr GLS Sdn	7735	9495
4 Dr GLX Sdn	8935	10970
4 Dr GLX Wgn	9115	11195

Don't forget to refer to the Mileage Adjustment Table at the back of this book!

VOLKSWAGEN 95-93

Model Description	Trade-in Value	Market Value	Model Description	Trade-in Value	Market Value

OPTIONS FOR PASSAT

Auto 4-Speed Transmission +240
Anti-Lock Brakes[Opt on GLS] +265
Compact Disc Changer +195
Heated Front Seats +110
Leather Seats +340
Power Moonroof +250

1994 VOLKSWAGEN

CORRADO 1994

Adaptive dual-mode automatic transmission debuts. Meets 1997 side-impact standards. Speed-activated spoiler rises at 55 mph instead of 45 mph.
Category F

2 Dr SLC Cpe	10380	12315

GOLF 1994

Two-door GL debuts. ABS is optional. Dual airbags are phased in shortly after 1994 production begins.

RATINGS (SCALE OF 1-10)

Overall	Safety	Reliability	Performance	Comfort	Value
6.6	5.9	5	8.6	7.6	6

Category E

2 Dr GL Hbk	4955	6190
4 Dr GL Hbk	4790	5985
2 Dr Limited Hbk	5385	6730

OPTIONS FOR GOLF

Auto 4-Speed Transmission +215
AM/FM Stereo Tape +75
Air Conditioning +205
Aluminum/Alloy Wheels +80
Anti-Lock Brakes +160
Dual Air Bag Restraints +150
Power Moonroof +140

JETTA 1994

GLS and GLX models arrive this year. ABS is optional on GL and GLS; standard on GLX. Dual airbags are phased in shortly after 1994 production begins. GLX features 2.8-liter V6 and traction control.

RATINGS (SCALE OF 1-10)

Overall	Safety	Reliability	Performance	Comfort	Value
6.6	5.9	5	8.6	7.6	6

Category D

4 Dr GL Sdn	5300	6535
4 Dr GLS Sdn	6310	7780
4 Dr GLX Sdn	7990	9845
4 Dr Limited Edition Sdn	5625	6935

OPTIONS FOR JETTA

Auto 4-Speed Transmission +225
AM/FM Stereo Tape[Opt on GL] +90

Air Conditioning[Std on GLS,GLX] +210
Aluminum/Alloy Wheels[Std on GLX] +115
Anti-Lock Brakes[Std on GLX] +215
Compact Disc Changer +160
Cruise Control[Std on GLS,GLX] +60
Dual Air Bag Restraints +150
Leather Seats +275
Power Moonroof +205
Premium Sound System +90

PASSAT 1994

GL dropped, leaving only the V6 GLX. ABS and traction control are standard. Adaptive dual-mode transmission debuts.

RATINGS (SCALE OF 1-10)

Overall	Safety	Reliability	Performance	Comfort	Value
6.6	4.9	8.1	7.8	8	4.4

Category D

4 Dr GLX Sdn	8260	10185
4 Dr GLX Wgn	8410	10370

OPTIONS FOR PASSAT

Auto 4-Speed Transmission +215
Compact Disc Changer +160
Heated Front Seats +90
Leather Seats +275

1993 VOLKSWAGEN

CABRIOLET 1993

Carat replaced by Classic. Base models get leatherette upholstery option. Audio systems are upgraded, and CD player joins options list.
Category F

2 Dr Classic Conv	6825	8390
2 Dr STD Conv	6305	7750

OPTIONS FOR CABRIOLET

Auto 3-Speed Transmission +120
Air Conditioning[Opt on STD] +170
Compact Disc Changer +125

CORRADO 1993

In mid-1992, supercharged four-cylinder engine was replaced by 2.8-liter V6. V6 model designated SLC. ABS and traction control are standard. BBS wheels dumped in favor of five-spoke VW design. Fuel capacity up four gallons, and front styling is tweaked. A/C is CFC-free. Radio turns off with ignition switch.
Category F

2 Dr SLC Cpe	7935	9755

OPTIONS FOR CORRADO

Auto 4-Speed Transmission +175
Heated Front Seats +75

Don't forget to refer to the Mileage Adjustment Table at the back of this book!

VOLKSWAGEN 93-92

Model Description	Trade-in Value	Market Value	Model Description	Trade-in Value	Market Value

Leather Seats +125
Power Sunroof +135

EUROVAN 1993

The EuroVan is introduced as a replacement for the aging Vanagon. Major differences over the previous generation Volkswagen van are the switch to a front-engine/front-wheel drive platform. Antilock brakes are available on the EuroVan, and it has a 2.5-liter four-cylinder engine that produces 109-horsepower. A five-speed manual transmission is standard, a four-speed automatic is optional.

Category G
2 Dr CL Pass. Van	5330	6650
2 Dr GL Pass. Van	6510	8115
2 Dr MV Pass. Van	6585	8210

OPTIONS FOR EUROVAN
Auto 4-Speed Transmission +180
Weekender Pkg +505
AM/FM Stereo Tape[Opt on CL] +45
Anti-Lock Brakes +115
Cruise Control +40
Dual Air Conditioning[Opt on CL] +185
Power Door Locks +45
Power Windows +50

FOX 1993

Air conditioning is standard. Five-speed transmission replaces four-speed unit on Base coupe. Base model gets wheelcovers, dual outside mirrors, body-color bumpers and bigger tires. GL model gets upgraded interior trim.

Category E
2 Dr Wolfsburg Sdn	1950	2850
4 Dr Wolfsburg GL Sdn	2285	3345

OPTIONS FOR FOX
AM/FM Stereo Tape +60

GOLF 1993

All new Golf debuts, but a strike at the assembly plant in Mexico restricts sales to Southern California and parts of New England.

Category E
4 Dr GL Hbk	3620	5295

OPTIONS FOR GOLF
Auto 4-Speed Transmission +175
AM/FM Stereo Tape +60
Air Conditioning +165
Power Sunroof +125

JETTA 1993

All new Jetta debuts, but a strike at the assembly plant in Mexico restricts sales to Southern California and parts of New England.

Category D
4 Dr GL Sdn	4425	5635

OPTIONS FOR JETTA
Auto 4-Speed Transmission +175
AM/FM Stereo Tape +70
Air Conditioning +170
Power Sunroof +155

PASSAT 1993

GLX trim level introduced, with 2.8-liter V6, ABS and traction control. Fog lamps and six-spoke alloys indicate GLX model. CL trim dropped. GL gets suspension modifications. All models get trip computer and CFC-free air conditioning.

RATINGS (SCALE OF 1-10)

Overall	Safety	Reliability	Performance	Comfort	Value
6.1	4.7	6.6	7.8	8	3.4

Category D
4 Dr GL Sdn	5305	6755
4 Dr GL Wgn	5435	6920
4 Dr GLX Sdn	6085	7750
4 Dr GLX Wgn	6205	7905

OPTIONS FOR PASSAT
Auto 4-Speed Transmission +175
Leather Seats +225
Power Sunroof[Opt on GL] +155

1992 VOLKSWAGEN

CABRIOLET 1992

Etienne Aigner edition dropped. Three-point seatbelts are added to the back seat. Base model gets full wheelcovers. Radio turns off with ignition switch.

Category F
2 Dr Carat Conv	5865	7510
2 Dr STD Conv	5370	6875
2 Dr Wolfsburg Class. Conv	6035	7720

OPTIONS FOR CABRIOLET
Auto 3-Speed Transmission +90
Auto 4-Speed Transmission +90
Power Converible Top +140
Air Conditioning[Opt on Carat,STD] +135

CORRADO 1992

No changes.
Category F
2 Dr SLC Cpe	6770	8665
2 Dr STD Sprchgd Cpe	6375	8160

OPTIONS FOR CORRADO
Auto 4-Speed Transmission +130
Anti-Lock Brakes[Opt on STD] +105

Don't forget to refer to the Mileage Adjustment Table at the back of this book!

Model Description	Trade-in Value	Market Value	Model Description	Trade-in Value	Market Value

Leather Seats +105
Power Sunroof +110

FOX 1992

Radio turns off with ignition switch.

Category E

4 Dr GL Sdn	1755	2760
2 Dr STD Sdn	1510	2370

OPTIONS FOR FOX
Air Conditioning[Std on GL] +135

GOLF 1992

Radio turns off with ignition switch.

Category E

2 Dr GL Hbk	2315	3635
4 Dr GL Hbk	2385	3750

Category F

2 Dr GTI Hbk	3480	4455
2 Dr GTI 16V Hbk	4330	5540

OPTIONS FOR GOLF
Auto 3-Speed Transmission +90
Air Conditioning +135
Sunroof +55

JETTA 1992

ECOdiesel debuts, featuring turbocharging and fewer pollutants. Two-door model dropped. GL models get new wheelcovers. Radio turns off with ignition switch.

Category D

4 Dr Carat Sdn	3195	4295
4 Dr GL Sdn	2940	3950
4 Dr GL ECO Dsl Sdn	3015	4050
4 Dr GLI Sdn	3970	5335

OPTIONS FOR JETTA
Auto 3-Speed Transmission +90
Air Conditioning +140
Aluminum/Alloy Wheels[Opt on GL] +75
Anti-Lock Brakes +145
Power Windows[Opt on GLI] +45
Sunroof +75

PASSAT 1992

New entry-level CL trim level introduced.

RATINGS (SCALE OF 1-10)

Overall	Safety	Reliability	Performance	Comfort	Value
6.2	4.4	7.1	7.4	8	4.3

Category D

4 Dr CL Sdn	3635	4885
4 Dr GL Sdn	4195	5635
4 Dr GL Wgn	4290	5765

OPTIONS FOR PASSAT
Auto 4-Speed Transmission +130
Air Conditioning[Opt on CL] +140
Aluminum/Alloy Wheels +75
Anti-Lock Brakes +145
Compact Disc Changer +105
Leather Seats +185
Power Sunroof +125

1991 VOLKSWAGEN

CABRIOLET 1991

Airbag added to steering wheel. Etienne Aigner edition debuts.

Category F

2 Dr STD Conv	4305	5835

OPTIONS FOR CABRIOLET
Auto 3-Speed Transmission +70
Air Conditioning +110
Leather Seats +85

CORRADO 1991

BBS alloy wheels are added as standard equipment.

Category F

2 Dr STD Sprchgd Cpe	4875	6610

OPTIONS FOR CORRADO
Auto 4-Speed Transmission +105
Anti-Lock Brakes +85
Leather Seats +85
Power Sunroof +90

FOX 1991

Restyled front end features flush headlamps. Wagon dropped. Lineup trimmed to Base coupe and GL sedan.

Category E

4 Dr GL Sdn	1270	2435
2 Dr STD Sdn	1100	2110

OPTIONS FOR FOX
Air Conditioning +110

GOLF 1991

BBS wheels added to GTI 16V as standard equipment.

Category E

2 Dr GL Hbk	1635	3140
4 Dr GL Hbk	1690	3240

Category F

2 Dr GTI Hbk	2840	3850
2 Dr GTI 16V Hbk	3570	4840

OPTIONS FOR GOLF
Auto 3-Speed Transmission +70
Air Conditioning +110
Sunroof +45

Don't forget to refer to the Mileage Adjustment Table at the back of this book!

Model Description	Trade-in Value	Market Value

JETTA 1991

GLI 16V gets standard BBS alloys.

Category D

Model Description	Trade-in Value	Market Value
4 Dr Carat Sdn	2535	3670
2 Dr GL Dsl Sdn	2480	3595
2 Dr GL Sdn	2415	3500
4 Dr GL Sdn	2375	3440
4 Dr GL Dsl Sdn	2420	3505
4 Dr GLI 16V Sdn	3145	4555

OPTIONS FOR JETTA

Auto 3-Speed Transmission +70
Air Conditioning +115
Anti-Lock Brakes +120
Power Windows[Std on Carat] +35
Sunroof +60

PASSAT 1991

No changes.

RATINGS (SCALE OF 1-10)

Overall	Safety	Reliability	Performance	Comfort	Value
6.5	4.4	7.2	7.4	8	5.3

Category D

4 Dr GL Sdn	3145	4560
4 Dr GL Wgn	3230	4680

OPTIONS FOR PASSAT

Auto 4-Speed Transmission +105
Anti-Lock Brakes +120
Leather Seats +150
Power Door Locks +35
Power Sunroof +105
Power Windows +35

VANAGON 1991

No changes. Final year for Vanagon.

Category G

2 Dr Carat Pass. Van	5935	7335
2 Dr GL Pass. Van	5650	6985
2 Dr GL Camper Pass. Van	7655	9220
2 Dr GL Syncro 4WD Pass. Van	8440	10430
2 Dr Multi Pass. Van	6495	8025
2 Dr STD Pass. Van	4640	5735
2 Dr Syncro 4WD Pass. Van	5775	7140

OPTIONS FOR VANAGON

Auto 3-Speed Transmission +70
Auto 4-Speed Transmission +70
Air Conditioning[Opt on STD,Syncro] +110
Power Door Locks[Std on Carat,GL Syncro,Multi] +30
Power Windows[Std on Carat,GL Syncro,Multi] +30

VOLVO 00

Model Description	Trade-in Value	Market Value

VOLVO — Sweden

1997 Volvo 960

2000 VOLVO

C70 — 2000

Engine improvements, a new transmission, and equipment upgrades constitute the changes for these 2000 Volvos. The V70 AWD and V70 T-5 have been discontinued. Volvo has added the S70 SE Sedan, the S70 GLT SE Sedan, the V70 SE Wagon, and the V70 XC SE AWD Wagon. These Special Edition models feature more standard luxury equipment.

Category L

Model Description	Trade-in Value	Market Value
2 Dr HT Turbo Conv	35830	41305
2 Dr HT Turbo Cpe	30775	35475
2 Dr LT Turbo Conv	34275	39510
2 Dr LT Turbo Cpe	28090	32100

OPTIONS FOR C70
17 In. Multi-Spoke Alloys +1225
Dolby Pro Logic Radio +1105
Full Soft Leather Seating +1310

S40 — 2000

The S40 is Volvo's completely new entry-level sedan. Along with its wagon variant, the V40, this car rounds out Volvo's vehicle lineup. Safety, styling, and comfort are its main attributes.

Category L

Model Description	Trade-in Value	Market Value
4 Dr STD Turbo Sdn	17960	20700

OPTIONS FOR S40
Touring Pkg +655

S70 — 2000

Engine improvements, a new transmission, and equipment upgrades constitute the changes for these 2000 Volvos. The V70 AWD and V70 T-5 have been discontinued. Volvo has added the S70 SE Sedan, the S70 GLT SE Sedan, the V70 SE Wagon, and the V70 XC SE AWD Wagon. These Special Edition models feature more standard luxury equipment.

Category L

Model Description	Trade-in Value	Market Value
4 Dr GLT Turbo Sdn	25100	28935
4 Dr GLT SE Turbo Sdn	25720	29650
4 Dr SE Sdn	22610	26065
4 Dr STD Sdn	21835	25170
4 Dr STD Turbo 4WD Sdn	26575	30635
4 Dr T-5 Turbo Sdn	26345	30365

S80 — 2000

The 2.9 and T-6 models go unchanged, save a few new colors and options.

Category L

Model Description	Trade-in Value	Market Value
4 Dr 2.9 Sdn	28335	32660
4 Dr T-6 Turbo Sdn	31820	36680

OPTIONS FOR S80
Dynamic Stability Control +900
Navigation System +2045
Headlight Washers +265
Heated Front Seats +405
Leather Seats +995
Power Moonroof +780

V40 — 2000

The S40 is Volvo's completely new entry-level sedan. Along with its wagon variant, the V40, this car rounds out Volvo's vehicle lineup. Safety, styling, and comfort are its main attributes.

Category L

Model Description	Trade-in Value	Market Value
4 Dr STD Turbo Wgn	18710	21565

OPTIONS FOR V40
Sport Plus Pkg +945
Touring Pkg +615

V70 — 2000

Engine improvements, a new transmission, and equipment upgrades constitute the changes for these 2000 Volvos. The V70 AWD and V70 T-5 have been discontinued. Volvo has added the S70 SE Sedan, the S70 GLT SE Sedan, the V70 SE Wagon, and the V70 XC SE AWD Wagon. These Special Edition models feature more standard luxury equipment.

Category L

Model Description	Trade-in Value	Market Value
4 Dr GLT Turbo Wgn	26110	30100
4 Dr R Turbo 4WD Wgn	32720	37720
4 Dr SE Wgn	23775	27410
4 Dr STD Wgn	22845	26335
4 Dr XC Turbo 4WD Wgn	28520	32875
4 Dr XC SE Turbo 4WD Wgn	29220	33685

Don't forget to refer to the Mileage Adjustment Table at the back of this book!

1999 VOLVO

70-SERIES 1999

Volvo's first all-wheel drive sedan debuts, vehicle options and color choices have been simplified, and S70/V70 models get new standard equipment.

RATINGS (SCALE OF 1-10)

Overall	Safety	Reliability	Performance	Comfort	Value
N/A	9.5	8.8	7.8	8.1	N/A

Category L

	Trade-in	Market
4 Dr GLT Turbo Sdn	24265	28090
4 Dr GLT Turbo Wgn	25240	29225
4 Dr R Turbo 4WD Wgn	31610	36595
4 Dr STD Sdn	21060	24380
4 Dr STD Turbo 4WD Sdn	25680	29730
4 Dr STD Wgn	22035	25515
4 Dr STD Turbo 4WD Wgn	26655	30865
4 Dr T-5 Turbo Sdn	25445	29460
4 Dr T-5 Turbo Wgn	26425	30595
4 Dr XC Turbo 4WD Wgn	27545	31890

OPTIONS FOR 70-SERIES

Auto 4-Speed Transmission[Std on GLT,R,XC,4WD] +650
Climate Control for AC[Opt on STD] +200
Compact Disc W/fm/tape[Std on R,T-5] +420
Dual Power Seats[Std on R,T-5] +530
Heated Front Seats[Std on R,XC,4] +330
Leather Seats[Std on R] +815
Power Moonroof[Std on R] +640
Traction Control System[Std on R,XC,4WD] +905
Trip Computer[Opt on GLT,STD] +190

C70 1999

Volvo offers a light pressure turbocharged engine in the coupe to entice consumers looking for a lower-priced ticket. Both coupes and convertibles get a bit of new standard and optional equipment.

RATINGS (SCALE OF 1-10)

Overall	Safety	Reliability	Performance	Comfort	Value
N/A	N/A	N/A	8.4	7.9	N/A

Category L

	Trade-in	Market
2 Dr HT Turbo Cpe	28625	33140
2 Dr LT Turbo Conv	30920	35795
2 Dr LT Turbo Cpe	24870	29115

OPTIONS FOR C70

Auto 4-Speed Transmission[Std on LT] +650
Dolby Pro Logic Radio +890
Heated Front Seats +330
Traction Control System +905
Trip Computer[Std on HT] +190

S80 1999

This long overdue redesign of the S90 counts several firsts to its credit: first with a transverse inline six, first with fully integrated GSM phone, first to carry an environmental specification (Europe only at introduction), and the S80 boasts the world's smallest manual transmission. Whoo-hoo!

RATINGS (SCALE OF 1-10)

Overall	Safety	Reliability	Performance	Comfort	Value
N/A	N/A	N/A	8.4	8.6	N/A

Category L

	Trade-in	Market
4 Dr 2.9 Sdn	26975	31230
4 Dr T-6 Turbo Sdn	30360	35150

OPTIONS FOR S80

Navigation System +1665
Compact Disc Changer +725
Heated Front Seats[Std on T-6] +330
Leather Seats +815
Power Moonroof +640

1998 VOLVO

C70 1998

Volvo performs a slam-dunk with its first new coupe in years; the convertible is somewhat less thrilling. Modeled on the S70 chassis, the C70 shares sheetmetal with the S70 from the windshield forward, and is powered by the same set of turbocharged powerplants.

Category L

	Trade-in	Market
2 Dr STD Turbo Cpe	23975	27855

OPTIONS FOR C70

Auto 4-Speed Transmission +530
Heated Front Seats +270
Traction Control System +740

S70 1998

Volvo's 850 sedan gets a new name, new nose, body-color trim, stronger side-impact protection, more powerful turbo engines, redesigned interior, and revised suspension. A great car has been made better.

RATINGS (SCALE OF 1-10)

Overall	Safety	Reliability	Performance	Comfort	Value
8.6	9.5	8.6	8.4	8.4	8.1

Category L

	Trade-in	Market
4 Dr GLT Turbo Sdn	20580	23905
4 Dr GT Sdn	18770	21805
4 Dr STD Sdn	17180	19955
4 Dr T-5 Turbo Sdn	21555	25045

Don't forget to refer to the Mileage Adjustment Table at the back of this book!

VOLVO 98-97

| Model Description | Trade-in Value | Market Value | Model Description | Trade-in Value | Market Value |

OPTIONS FOR S70

Auto 4-Speed Transmission[Std on GLT] +530
Aluminum/Alloy Wheels[Opt on STD] +230
Compact Disc W/fm/tape[Std on T-5] +345
Dual Power Seats[Std on T-5] +430
Heated Front Seats +270
Leather Seats +665
Sport Suspension +90
Traction Control System +740
Trip Computer[Std on T-5] +155

S90   1998

Absolutely nothing changes on this aged warhorse.

RATINGS (SCALE OF 1-10)

Overall	Safety	Reliability	Performance	Comfort	Value
N/A	N/A	9.3	7.8	8.1	6.6

Category L
4 Dr STD Sdn   21240   24675

OPTIONS FOR S90

Compact Disc W/fm/tape +345
Heated Front Seats +270

V70   1998

Volvo's 850 wagon gets a new name, new nose, body-color trim, stronger side-impact protection, more powerful turbo engines, redesigned interior and revised suspension. A great car has been made better. All-wheel drive versions arrive to battle luxury SUVs.

RATINGS (SCALE OF 1-10)

Overall	Safety	Reliability	Performance	Comfort	Value
N/A	N/A	8.6	8	8.4	8.3

Category L
4 Dr GLT Turbo Wgn   22650   26315
4 Dr GT Wgn   20735   24090
4 Dr R Turbo 4WD Wgn   27440   31875
4 Dr STD Wgn   19055   22140
4 Dr STD Turbo 4WD Wgn   23100   26835
4 Dr T-5 Turbo Wgn   23685   27520
4 Dr XC Turbo 4WD Wgn   23875   27735

OPTIONS FOR V70

Auto 4-Speed Transmission[Std on GLT, R, XC, 4WD] +530
Aluminum/Alloy Wheels[Opt on STD] +230
Auto Load Leveling[Std on R, XC, 4WD] +620
Compact Disc W/fm/tape[Std on T-5] +345
Dual Power Seats[Std on R, T-5, XC] +430
Heated Front Seats[Std on R, XC, 4WD] +270
Leather Seats[Std on R, XC] +665
Power Drivers Seat[Std on GLT, GT, 4WD] +275
Power Moonroof[Opt on STD, XC] +520
Sport Suspension +90
Traction Control System[Std on R, XC, 4WD] +740
Trip Computer[Std on R, T-5, XC] +155

V90   1998

Absolutely nothing changes on this aged warhorse.

RATINGS (SCALE OF 1-10)

Overall	Safety	Reliability	Performance	Comfort	Value
N/A	N/A	9	7.8	8.3	6.6

Category L
4 Dr STD Wgn   22820   26510

OPTIONS FOR V90

Auto Load Leveling +620
Compact Disc W/fm/tape +345
Heated Front Seats +270

1997 VOLVO

850   1997

Looking for the Turbo? Inexplicably, Volvo tossed two decades of tradition and the Turbo nameplate out the door. The Turbo is now known as the T-5. GLT models get a new engine that makes 22 more horsepower than last year, and peak torque at a low 1,800 rpm. Base and GLT models meet Transitional Low Emission Vehicle (TLEV) regulations this year.

RATINGS (SCALE OF 1-10)

Overall	Safety	Reliability	Performance	Comfort	Value
8.4	8.6	8.3	8.8	8.3	8

Category L
4 Dr GLT Turbo Sdn   18255   21320
4 Dr GLT Turbo Wgn   18990   22180
4 Dr R Turbo Sdn   22125   25840
4 Dr R Turbo Wgn   22945   26795
4 Dr STD Sdn   15360   17940
4 Dr STD Wgn   16095   18800
4 Dr T-5 Turbo Sdn   19760   23080
4 Dr T-5 Turbo Wgn   20495   23935

OPTIONS FOR 850

Auto 4-Speed Transmission[Opt on STD] +435
Grand Touring Pkg +445
Wood Trim Pkg +360
Aluminum/Alloy Wheels[Opt on STD] +185
Auto Load Leveling[Std on R] +505
Compact Disc W/fm/tape[Std on R, T-5] +280
Dual Power Seats[Std on R, T-5] +355
Leather Seats[Std on R] +545
Power Moonroof[Opt on STD] +425
Sport Suspension[Std on R] +75
Traction Control System[Std on R] +605
Trip Computer[Std on R, T-5] +125

960   1997

Automatic load leveling joins the options list for the wagon, while tailored leather seating is no longer available on the wagon.

Model Description	Trade-in Value	Market Value

RATINGS (SCALE OF 1-10)

Overall	Safety	Reliability	Performance	Comfort	Value
8.1	8.5	8.4	8.8	8	6.9

Category L
4 Dr STD Sdn	18815	21975
4 Dr STD Wgn	19655	22955

OPTIONS FOR 960

Auto Load Leveling +505
Compact Disc W/fm/tape +280

S90   1997

Midyear, Volvo went and switched names for the 960. The sedan is now known as S90, while the wagon is now the V90.

RATINGS (SCALE OF 1-10)

Overall	Safety	Reliability	Performance	Comfort	Value
N/A	N/A	N/A	N/A	N/A	7.2

Category L
4 Dr STD Sdn	19515	22795

V90   1997

Midyear, Volvo went and switched names for the 960. The sedan is now known as S90, while the wagon is now the V90.

RATINGS (SCALE OF 1-10)

Overall	Safety	Reliability	Performance	Comfort	Value
N/A	N/A	N/A	N/A	N/A	7.2

Category L
4 Dr STD Wgn	20385	23805

1996 VOLVO

850   1996

This year all Volvo 850s are equipped with front seat side-impact airbags, optional traction control (TRACS), and a life insurance policy that pays $250,000 to the estate of any occupant who loses their life in the 850 as the result of an accident.

RATINGS (SCALE OF 1-10)

Overall	Safety	Reliability	Performance	Comfort	Value
8.4	8.6	8.1	8.6	8.3	8.4

Category L
4 Dr GLT Sdn	15135	17695
4 Dr GLT Wgn	15795	18465
4 Dr Platinum Ltd. Ed. Turbo Sdn	19050	22270
4 Dr Platinum Ltd. Ed. Turbo Wgn	19790	23135
4 Dr R Turbo Sdn	19580	22890
4 Dr R Turbo Wgn	20320	23755
4 Dr STD Sdn	13655	15965
4 Dr STD Turbo Sdn	16890	19750

4 Dr STD Wgn	14230	16635
4 Dr STD Turbo Wgn	17555	20525

OPTIONS FOR 850

Auto 4-Speed Transmission[Opt on GLT,Non-turbo models] +355
Grand Touring Pkg +420
Aluminum/Alloy Wheels[Opt on STD Sdn,STD Wgn] +155
Auto Load Leveling[Opt on GLT,STD] +415
Dual Power Seats[Std on R] +290
Leather Seats[Opt on GLT,STD] +445
Sport Suspension[Std on R] +60
Traction Control System[Opt on GLT,STD] +495
Trip Computer[Opt on Non-turbo models] +105

960   1996

This year all Volvo 960s are equipped with front seat side-impact airbags, a multi-step power door locking system that increases driver safety when entering the vehicle in parking lots, and a life insurance policy that pays $250,000 to the estate of any occupant who loses their life in the 960 as a result of a car accident.

RATINGS (SCALE OF 1-10)

Overall	Safety	Reliability	Performance	Comfort	Value
8.2	8.5	8.2	8.8	8	7.3

Category L
4 Dr STD Sdn	16590	19395
4 Dr STD Wgn	17215	20125

OPTIONS FOR 960

AM/FM Compact Disc Player +325

1995 VOLVO

850   1995

Side airbags are standard on all 850 Turbos this year; optional on other 850s. All models get Turbo's rounded front styling.

RATINGS (SCALE OF 1-10)

Overall	Safety	Reliability	Performance	Comfort	Value
8.3	8.5	7.8	8.6	8.3	8.4

Category L
4 Dr GLT Sdn	12655	14920
4 Dr GLT Wgn	13560	15990
4 Dr STD Sdn	11540	13605
4 Dr STD Turbo Sdn	14465	17050
4 Dr STD Wgn	12255	14450
4 Dr STD Turbo Wgn	15400	18160
4 Dr T-5R Turbo Sdn	16530	19485
4 Dr T-5R Turbo Wgn	17240	20325

OPTIONS FOR 850

Auto 4-Speed Transmission[Std on T-5R,Turbo] +270
Grand Lux Pkg +340

Don't forget to refer to the Mileage Adjustment Table at the back of this book!

Grand Touring Pkg +250
Aluminum/Alloy Wheels[Std on GLT,T-5R,Turbo] +125
Climate Control for AC[Std on T-5R,Turbo] +90
Compact Disc W/fm/tape +190
Leather Seats[Std on T-5R,STD Turbo Sdn] +365
Power Drivers Seat[Std on GLT,T-5R,Turbo] +150
Power Passenger Seat[Opt on STD,GLT Wgn] +145
Side Air Bag Restraint[Std on T-5R,Turbo,GLT Sdn] +150
Traction Control System[Std on T-5R] +405
Trip Computer[Opt on GLT] +85

940   1995

Daytime running lights debut. Level I and Level II trim is dropped in favor of less confusing base and Turbo designations.

RATINGS (SCALE OF 1-10)

Overall	Safety	Reliability	Performance	Comfort	Value
7.8	8	7.5	8	7.9	7.5

Category L
4 Dr STD Sdn	10975	12940
4 Dr STD Turbo Sdn	11440	13485
4 Dr STD Wgn	11575	13645
4 Dr STD Turbo Wgn	12035	14190

OPTIONS FOR 940

Aluminum/Alloy Wheels +125
Leather Seats +365
Power Drivers Seat +150
Power Moonroof +285

960   1995

Substantially revised with new sheetmetal and detuned powertrain. Horsepower is down to 181 from 201, thanks to emissions standards. Daytime running lights are added. The dashboard is softened with more curves and contours. Suspensions are revised, and larger tires are standard. Other new standard equipment includes remote locking, an alarm system, headlight wipers and washers, and wood interior trim.

RATINGS (SCALE OF 1-10)

Overall	Safety	Reliability	Performance	Comfort	Value
7.9	8.2	7.2	8.8	8	7.3

Category L
4 Dr STD Sdn	13095	15440
4 Dr STD Wgn	13660	16100

OPTIONS FOR 960

Compact Disc Changer +325
Leather Seats +365

850   1994

Turbo model debuts with 222-horsepower 2.3-liter five-cylinder engine, and a wagon body style is introduced with standard integrated child seat. Turbo is available in either sedan or wagon format. Warranty is upped to 4 years/50,000 miles.

RATINGS (SCALE OF 1-10)

Overall	Safety	Reliability	Performance	Comfort	Value
8.3	8.5	7.7	8.6	8.3	8.4

Category L
4 Dr GLT Sdn	9985	11950
4 Dr GLTS Sdn	10955	13105
4 Dr GLTS Wgn	11360	13590
4 Dr STD Turbo Sdn	12285	14695
4 Dr STD Turbo Wgn	12685	15180

OPTIONS FOR 850

Auto 4-Speed Transmission[Opt on GLT,GLTS,Sdn] +220
Aluminum/Alloy Wheels[Std on GLTS,Wgn] +100
Auto Load Leveling +275
Climate Control for AC[Std on STD] +70
Leather Seats[Opt on GLT,GLTS,Sdn] +295
Power Drivers Seat[Std on GLTS,Wgn] +125
Power Passenger Seat +115
Sport Suspension +40
Traction Control System +330
Trip Computer[Std on STD] +70

940   1994

940 gets passenger airbag. Level I 940s have 114-horsepower 2.3-liter engine; equip a 940 with Level II trim and you get a turbocharged version of this engine.

RATINGS (SCALE OF 1-10)

Overall	Safety	Reliability	Performance	Comfort	Value
7.9	8.2	7.7	8	8	7.4

Category L
4 Dr STD Sdn	8735	10450
4 Dr STD Turbo Sdn	10005	11970
4 Dr STD Wgn	9150	10945
4 Dr STD Turbo Wgn	10380	12420

OPTIONS FOR 940

Aluminum/Alloy Wheels[Std on Turbo] +100
Leather Seats[Std on Turbo] +295
Power Drivers Seat[Std on Turbo] +125
Power Passenger Seat +115
Power Sunroof[Std on Turbo] +235

960   1994

Base 960 is heavily decontented, and is available only in sedan format. Level II 960 adds leather, moonroof and other nice stuff.

Model Description	Trade-in Value	Market Value

RATINGS (SCALE OF 1-10)

Overall	Safety	Reliability	Performance	Comfort	Value
8	8.4	7.4	8.8	8.1	7.2

Category L
4 Dr Level II Sdn	12380	14810
4 Dr Level II Wgn	12745	15250
4 Dr STD Sdn	10735	12845

OPTIONS FOR 960

Aluminum/Alloy Wheels[Opt on STD] +100
Compact Disc Changer +265
Compact Disc W/fm/tape +155
Leather Seats[Opt on STD] +295
Power Moonroof +235
Power Passenger Seat[Std on Wgn] +115
Premium Sound System +225

1993 VOLVO

240   1993

GL model dropped, again. Metallic paint doesn't cost extra this year, air conditioning gets CFC-free refrigerant, and plush floormats are standard.

Category L
4 Dr STD Sdn	8350	10145
4 Dr STD Wgn	8725	10600

OPTIONS FOR 240

Auto 4-Speed Transmission +135
Aluminum/Alloy Wheels +85
Heated Front Seats +100
Leather Seats +245
Limited Slip Diff +285

850   1993

740 replacement arrives with 168-horsepower inline five-cylinder engine. Dual airbags and ABS are standard. Automatic transmission has Economy and Sport shift modes, as well as a winter second-gear start feature. Car meets 1997 side-impact standards, traction control is optional, and sedans have standard integrated child safety seats. Wagon not available.

RATINGS (SCALE OF 1-10)

Overall	Safety	Reliability	Performance	Comfort	Value
8.1	8.6	7.5	8.6	8.3	7.3

Category L
4 Dr GLT Sdn	8235	10005
4 Dr GLTS Sdn	9130	11095

OPTIONS FOR 850

Auto 4-Speed Transmission +150
Leather Seats[Opt on GLT] +245
Traction Control System +270
Trip Computer +55

940   1993

Wagons have integrated child seats. All stereos have anti-theft feature, and air conditioning is free of CFCs. Wagons have an extra four gallons of fuel capacity and a revised rear seat. 940 GL dropped, but a base sedan and wagon continue.

RATINGS (SCALE OF 1-10)

Overall	Safety	Reliability	Performance	Comfort	Value
7.5	7.6	7.4	8	8	6.7

Category L
4 Dr S Sdn	8590	10435
4 Dr S Wgn	8910	10820
4 Dr STD Sdn	8060	9795
4 Dr STD Turbo Sdn	9160	11130
4 Dr STD Wgn	8370	10165
4 Dr STD Turbo Wgn	9480	11515

OPTIONS FOR 940

Aluminum/Alloy Wheels[Std on S, Sdn, Turbo] +85
Power Passenger Seat +95

960   1993

960 gets passenger airbag. Wagons have integrated child seats. All stereos have anti-theft feature, and air conditioning is free of CFCs. Wagons have an extra four gallons of fuel capacity and a revised rear seat.

RATINGS (SCALE OF 1-10)

Overall	Safety	Reliability	Performance	Comfort	Value
7.7	7.6	7.3	8.8	8.1	6.7

Category L
4 Dr STD Sdn	10135	12315
4 Dr STD Wgn	9660	11735

1992 VOLVO

240   1992

ABS is newly standard. GL model returns as top-of-the-line, and adds a sunroof and heated mirrors, among other items, over the base car. GL grille is chrome rather than matte black.

Category L
4 Dr GL Sdn	6625	8135
4 Dr STD Sdn	6420	7885
4 Dr STD Wgn	6570	8070

OPTIONS FOR 240

Auto 4-Speed Transmission +110
Anti-Lock Brakes[Std on Wgn] +160
Heated Front Seats[Std on GL] +80
Leather Seats +200
Limited Slip Diff[Std on GL] +235

Don't forget to refer to the Mileage Adjustment Table at the back of this book!

VOLVO 92-91

Model Description	Trade-in Value	Market Value

740   1992

ABS is standard across the board. A locking differential is newly standard. Turbo sedan and 780 coupe have been dropped. Turbo wagon continues.

Category L

	Trade-in	Market
4 Dr GL Wgn	7700	9460
4 Dr STD Sdn	7290	8955
4 Dr STD Wgn	7490	9205
4 Dr STD Turbo Wgn	8330	10230

OPTIONS FOR 740
Aluminum/Alloy Wheels[Std on Turbo] +70
Leather Seats +200

940   1992

940 GLE, and its twin-cam engine, is discontinued for 1992.

RATINGS (SCALE OF 1-10)

Overall	Safety	Reliability	Performance	Comfort	Value
N/A	N/A	7.7	8	8	7.2

Category L

	Trade-in	Market
4 Dr GL Sdn	7130	8760
4 Dr STD Turbo Sdn	8760	10760
4 Dr STD Turbo Wgn	8950	10995

OPTIONS FOR 940
Aluminum/Alloy Wheels[Opt on GL] +70
Leather Seats[Opt on GL] +200
Power Drivers Seat[Opt on GL] +85
Power Passenger Seat +80

960   1992

960 model replaces 940 SE in lineup; is powered by 2.9-liter twin-cam inline-six good for 201 horsepower.

RATINGS (SCALE OF 1-10)

Overall	Safety	Reliability	Performance	Comfort	Value
N/A	N/A	7.7	8.8	8.1	7.1

Category L

	Trade-in	Market
4 Dr STD Sdn	8450	10385
4 Dr STD Wgn	8620	10590

1991 VOLVO

240   1991

SE wagon added to lineup. DL trim dropped, leaving base trim.

Category L

	Trade-in	Market
4 Dr SE Wgn	6155	7725
4 Dr STD Sdn	5490	6885
4 Dr STD Wgn	5520	6930

OPTIONS FOR 240
Auto 4-Speed Transmission[Std on SE] +90
Anti-Lock Brakes[Std on SE] +130
Leather Seats[Std on SE] +160
Sunroof +85

740   1991

DOHC motor dropped from lineup.

Category L

	Trade-in	Market
4 Dr SE Turbo Sdn	6490	8145
4 Dr SE Turbo Wgn	6650	8340
4 Dr STD Sdn	5285	6630
4 Dr STD Turbo Sdn	5760	7225
4 Dr STD Wgn	5440	6825
4 Dr STD Turbo Wgn	5920	7425

OPTIONS FOR 740
Auto 4-Speed Transmission[Std on SE, Non-turbo models] +90
Anti-Lock Brakes[Std on SE, Turbo] +130
Leather Seats +160
Limited Slip Diff[Std on SE, Turbo] +190
Sunroof +85

940   1991

New series of cars is basically renamed 760 series from last year. Base GLEs have twin-cam engine. Turbos and SE Turbos have slightly more powerful 162-horsepower engine.

RATINGS (SCALE OF 1-10)

Overall	Safety	Reliability	Performance	Comfort	Value
N/A	N/A	7.1	8	8	7.8

Category L

	Trade-in	Market
4 Dr GLE Sdn	6590	8265
4 Dr GLE Wgn	6750	8465
4 Dr SE Turbo Sdn	7085	8890
4 Dr SE Turbo Wgn	7215	9055
4 Dr STD Turbo Sdn	6920	8685
4 Dr STD Turbo Wgn	7080	8885

OPTIONS FOR 940
Leather Seats[Opt on GLE] +160

COUPE   1991

Renamed 780. Final year for Bertone-designed Volvo.

Category L

	Trade-in	Market
2 Dr STD Turbo Cpe	8615	10805

Don't forget to refer to the Mileage Adjustment Table at the back of this book!

8V	8-valve		LWB	long wheelbase
12V	12-valve		M&S	mud and snow
16V	16-valve		mpg	miles per gallon
24V	24-valve		mph	miles per hour
2WD	two-wheel drive		MPI	multi-port injection
4WD	four-wheel drive		MSRP	manufacturer's suggested retail price
ABS	antilock braking system		N/A	not available OR not applicable
A/C	air conditioning		NC	no charge
ALR	automatic locking retractor		NHTSA	National Highway and Traffic Safety
Amp	ampere			Administration
A/S	all-season		NVH	noise, vibration and harshness
ASR	automatic slip regulation		OD	overdrive
AT	automatic		OHC	overhead cam
Auto	automatic		OHV	overhead valve
AWD	all-wheel drive		Opt.	option OR optional
BSW	black sidewall		OWL	outline white-letter
Cass.	cassette		Pass.	passenger
CD	compact disc		Pkg.	package
CFC	chloroflourocarbon		PRNDL	Park, Reverse, Neutral, Drive, Low
Conv.	convertible		RBL	raised black-letter
Cpe	coupe		Reg.	regular
Cu. Ft.	cubic foot (feet)		RH	right hand
Cyl.	cylinder		r/l	right and left
DOHC	dual overhead cam		rpm	revolutions per minute
DRL	daytime running light(s)		RWD	rear-wheel drive
DRW	dual rear wheels		SB	shortbed
DSC	dynamic stability control		SBR	steel-belted radial
EDL	electronic differential lock		Sdn	sedan
EFI	electronic fuel injection		SFI	sequential fuel injection
ELR	emergency locking retractor		SLA	short/long arm
EQ	equalizer		SMPI	sequential multi-port injection
ETR	electronically-tuned radio		SOHC	single overhead cam
Ext.	extended		SPI	sequential port injection
ft-lbs.	foot-pounds (measurement of torque)		SRW	single rear wheels
FWD	front-wheel drive		Std.	standard
Gal.	gallon(s)		SUV	sport utility vehicle
GAWR	gross axle weight rating		SWB	short wheelbase
GVW	gross vehicle weight		TDI	turbocharged direct injection
GVWR	gross vehicle weight rating		TOD	torque on demand
GPS	global positioning satellite		TMV^{sm}	True Market Value^{sm}
Hbk.	hatchback		V6	V-type six
HD	heavy duty		V8	V-type eight
Hp	horsepower		V10	V-type ten
HUD	heads-up display		V12	V-type twelve
HVAC	heating, ventilation and air conditioning		VR	v-rated
I-4	inline four		VSC	vehicle skid control
I-5	inline five		VTEC	variable valve timing and lift electronic
I-6	inline six			control
L	liter		VVT-i	variable valve timing, intelligence
LB	longbed		Wgn.	wagon
lb(s).	pound(s)		WOL	white outline-letter
LCD	liquid crystal display		WS	work series
LED	light emitting diode		WSW	white sidewall
LEV	low emission vehicle		W/T	work truck
LH	left hand		X-cab	extended cab

1999
OLDSMOBILE ALERO

A NEW BEGINNING

INGRID LOEFFLER PALMER

Beginnings are wonderful times, full of hope and anticipation. They give us a burst of energy to face the unknown and they inspire us to start anew with fresh ideas. Of course, beginnings can be scary, too, since they represent a change in the familiar, comfortable status quo. Yet those who embrace change are often rewarded with exciting life experiences and opportunities to learn new things. It is with this attitude that Oldsmobile, after celebrating its 100th birthday, is approaching the new millenium.

A fleet of new, distinct vehicles branded with Oldsmobile seals have been steadily seeping into dealer showrooms since 1995. The latest addition to the company's all-new Centennial Product lineup is the 1999 Alero, which arrived on our doorstep with shiny black paint coating its chiseled sheetmetal. The pretty styling on our Alero GLS test car reminded us of its bigger Oldsmobile siblings, with low-mounted dual air intakes, fluted side sculpting, large taillights and plump wheel openings.

Characteristics of the compact sedan were designed to appeal to import-oriented buyers looking for style, functionality and refinement at a low

price. Oldsmobile decided that unique exterior styling was an essential element in their efforts to best competitors like Nissan, Toyota and Honda, whose cars offer reliability, quality and performance but fail to excite consumers with their look-alike sheetmetal.

In our opinion, Oldsmobile succeeded. "This is a nice car," complimented a woman who works at the dry cleaners as she helped load my clothes into the back seat. "I used to have an Oldsmobile," she added fondly.

"I love this car!" exclaimed a friend as we picked her up to go shopping. "What do you think of it? It feels pretty powerful. How much is it? Where can I get one? I really like how it looks."

But what lies beneath the sheetmetal is important, too. Our GLS model came equipped with a standard 170-horsepower, 3.4-liter V6 engine that made sprinting around town on errands more fun than should be legal. Though

the engine was noisier than we'd have liked, the car hopped to attention when the pedal hit the floor, sending us quickly through pockets in traffic and accelerating adequately on the highway. The Alero's V6 makes 200 foot-pounds of torque @ 4,000 rpm-providing a nice burst of power off the line. Like most small cars, the Alero was breathless in the higher altitudes of Colorado, but despite its unrefined noise when pushed to the limit, the speedometer needle remained steady.

We had a blast driving the Alero on our test loop, which wound up Highway 285 through Turkey Creek Canyon and into Conifer, Colo. Wind noise was kept to a minimum, road noise would never quell a conversation, the suspension soaked up road quirks and potholes like a sponge, steering was responsive, the interior was blissfully void of squeaks and rattles, and the car handled the twisty mountain turns with finesse. Alero's chassis also boasts a stiff body structure with a vibration frequency of 25Hz, making for sporty, nimble performance. Built with a four-wheel independent suspension system, antilock brakes and traction control (which engages liberally), the Alero was impressive on both dry and wet pavement.

Inside, we found more to praise. Sitting in the driver's seat is a nice experience overall, with power adjustable leather seats that are soft on top and supportive underneath, and a thick steering wheel that is easy to grip. Our six-foot-plus editor-in-chief noted that the car's narrowness made the interior seem small and made him feel a bit claustrophobic, while his wife found it difficult to turn around to

comfort their crying daughter in the back. The main complaint for smaller drivers, however, was the obstructed visibility. Despite a high seating position, the cab-forward design coupled with thick B- and C-pillars made changing lanes a nerve-racking experience. Because it was impossible to judge the rear corners of the car, parking or maneuvering in lots was also difficult. To top it off, the sun visors are too short to block the glare when flipped to the side in sunny Colorado.

On the upside, controls are intuitive and simple in layout. Door locks, mirror adjusters and window controls are well-laid out on the driver's side door, along with a trunk release button that is out of the way but easy to find. We were happy to discover a one-touch down driver window button and long door cubbies that are perfect for storing maps, treats or books. Stereo and climate control knobs are large, uncluttered and easy to grip, contributing to the Alero's user-friendly interior.

On the way to the car in a dark parking lot one evening, we discovered that neither the remote keyless entry nor the panic button worked until we were approximately six feet from the car. Whether the battery was worn down, other vehicles were blocking the way or the remote range itself was limited, we don't know, but it did not elicit a feeling of safety. Upon reaching the vehicle, we were delighted with the car's trunk space, however, managing to fit 21 bags of groceries into the Alero's trunk with room to spare.

Our biggest pet peeve with the vehicle had to do with its cupholders. There are two in the front center console-one is directly behind the gear shifter with a pop-up lid and one is in front of it. The rear cupholder works fine and holds a multitude of cup sizes and shapes, but the front cupholder is simply worthless. It is hard to reach because the gear shifter is in the way and it can hold nothing taller than a soda can. We ended up using the space as a cubby for keys and money, but became irritated when more than one person was enjoying a beverage in the car.

Other complaints centered on the extremely loud blinkers, which were annoying to listen to at traffic lights or stop signs, and a hard-to-reach cubby, which extended way under the radio and climate control panel. Finally, the horn works only if you hit it in a specific spot; test it out before you need to bang on it in an emergency situation.

Despite these grievances, Oldsmobile's Alero is an entertaining drive, smartly styled, and respectably priced. It is more appealing than the domestic Malibu/Cutlass, Cirrus/Stratus and Contour/Mystique models it competes against, and, though mechanically identical to the Pontiac Grand Am, the Olds exudes much better taste. With a distinct flavor all its own and a brand-new century around the corner, Oldsmobile's new Alero has a promising future. ∎

Vehicle Tested: 1999 Oldsmobile Alero GLS Sedan
Base Price of Vehicle: $21,400 (including destination charge)
Options on Test Vehicle: None
Price of Test Vehicle: $21,400 (including destination charge)

Photos courtesy of General Motors Corporation

Frequently Asked Questions

Edmunds.com solicits email queries from consumers who visit our Web site at http://www.edmunds.com. Below are 20 commonly asked questions regarding used cars and the buying process.

1. How do I determine a fair price for a used car?

Edmunds.com publishes a Market Value, which is based on average asking and transaction prices by dealers and private owners nationwide. As a buyer or seller, you'll want to get as close to Market Value as possible.

2. How can I determine what a dealer paid for a used car at auction or in trade?

Unless the dealer discloses this amount honestly, you can't determine an exact "invoice" price. However, by pushing for the best deal you will find the point where the dealer firms up on price. When this happens, you've gotten about as low as you can go; any lower and the dealer figures it would be better to just hang on to the car.

3. Do you have pricing for used cars more than a decade old?

No, we do not. After a decade on the road, most cars have depreciated to the point where fluctuations in values are slight and do not have much impact on the transaction price. Older models will sell easily and for top-dollar if they are in excellent condition. Specialty models are covered by a variety of guides that you can buy in your local bookstore, or you can consult the classifieds in such publications as AutoWeek, Hemmings Motor News, and The DuPont Registry. Online used-car classifieds include classifieds2000.com and traderonline.com.

4. Why does Edmunds.com's used-car pricing differ from other price guides?

Each guide uses different sources to determine pricing. You must keep in mind that these publications, and Edmunds.com, are to be considered guides. The values contained within are not absolute; they are intended to give the user a range of values to consider when determining a fair price. Used-car values depend on mileage, vehicle condition, geographic location, model popularity, seasonal demand, and even color.

Keep in mind that the dealer will use whatever pricing guide works to their advantage in the deal. By providing pricing that favors the dealer, other guides make big bucks on subscriptions to industry personnel. Some even publish two different pricing guides; one for consumers, and one for dealers. Rarely do dealers use values found at Edmunds.com. We believe that speaks volumes about the fairness of our published pricing to the consumer.

The most important thing to remember about buying, selling, or trading a used car is this: a used car is only worth as much as somebody is willing to pay for it.

5. How often is Edmunds.com's used-car pricing updated?

We update our used-car pricing quarterly.

6. The new model year rollout is occurring. How will this affect used-car values?

When you buy a new car, and it doesn't matter if it's an Acura or a Chevy, it depreciates the second it is titled in your name. Why? It has become a used car. Used cars age and accumulate mileage, and as they age and accumulate mileage they lose value. This is a constant process. Almost all used cars lose their value at a relatively steady rate, it's just that some makes, like Acura, lose value at a slower rate then other makes, like Chevy.

Just because our value guides are published quarterly doesn't mean that a car isn't losing value during that quarter. Used-car prices are never static. That's why we tell people that used-car values supplied by ANY publication are to be used simply as a guide to help you determine a fair price.

Because used-car prices are not static, the introduction of a new model year doesn't alter them much, if at all. Depreciation of used cars is almost always a steady, predictable process. Factor in climate, geographic region, supply and demand, etc., and that's where you get most of the fluctuation. Other factors, such as the release of a redesigned, and less expensive, new model and the whole Acura SLX/Isuzu Trooper rollover scare from a few years ago, can further alter valuations. And what would happen to Expedition/Suburban values if gas prices ever doubled? They'd drop in the toilet.

The bottom line is that the introduction of new model-year vehicles generally doesn't alter used-vehicle pricing much, if at all.

7. How do manufacturer-certified used-car programs affect used-car values?

Remember that our data samples include several sources, including advertised and selling prices from dealers who sell manufacturer-certified used cars. However, our data is also representative of a given vehicle in average condition, and most manufacturer-certified used cars are in good to excellent condition. Furthermore, the dealership spends anywhere from $500 to $1,000 to certify a used car to manufacturer specification. If you are shopping for a manufacturer-certified used car, you will need to take vehicle condition and the costs associated with the certification process into account when trying to determine a fair price.

8. Why won't the dealer give me wholesale value for my trade-in?

When a dealership takes a car in on trade, it is responsible for the car. Before the trade-in can be sold, it must be inspected and often repaired. Sometimes, emissions work is necessary. All this inspection and repair work costs the dealership money. If the trade is in good condition and has low miles, the dealer will put the car on the used-car lot for retail price. When the car sells, it is rarely for retail price, so the profit margin is shaved. The less you accept for the trade-in, the more room the dealer has to make a deal with a prospective buyer, and the more money the dealer will make, thanks to increased profit margins.

If the car doesn't sell, if it has high miles, or it is in poor condition, the dealer will have to wholesale it. The dealer will likely sell the car for below wholesale value at the auction, and expects to recoup some of the money spent reconditioning and inspecting the car. If the dealer offered you wholesale price when you traded in the car, he wouldn't make the money back in the event that the trade-in went to auction.

Regardless of the condition of your car, the dealer will anticipate taking the car to auction, and will leave room to make money in that event. Your best bet is to sell your car on your own to a private party, and forget about trading in.

9. Is it fair for a dealer to ask if my trade has ever been wrecked, or damaged in any way?

Certainly. If you were buying a car from a used-car dealer, you'd want to know the same thing, wouldn't you?

10. When is the best time to purchase a car from a dealer?

There's as much advice about when to visit a dealer as there are days in a year. Some say that Mondays are good because business is slower on Monday than on the weekend. Some say holidays like Thanksgiving are good for the same reason: nobody else will be there, and the sales team will be hungry for a sale. Others advise to go when it's raining or snowing; after all, who wants to look at a car and get wet? Then there's the advice that the end of the month is the best time because the dealership needs to make its "quota" of car sales and will be more willing to cut a deal.

Our advice is don't buy a car until you're ready. That's usually the best time. By then you have saved enough for a substantial down payment, and you've had plenty of time to do your research for the lowest interest rate.

If a dealer has already made his target sales for the month, you're not going to have any advantage by showing up on the 31st of the month. While there may be something to say for going to a dealership on a weekday near the end of the month on Thanksgiving at five o'clock during a raging blizzard, your best bet is to buy when you're ready.

11. I want to pay cash for my car. Do I have an advantage?

Not necessarily. You must remember that no matter how you pay for your car, it's all cash to the dealer. In the old days when dealers carried your note, you could save money by paying cash because there was no risk to the dealer. Today, dealerships finance through one of several lending institutions (banks, credit unions, or the automaker's captive financing division) that pay them cash when the contract is presented. In fact, if dealerships do the financing on your behalf, they tend to make more money on your contract in the form of a reserve; anywhere from a one-half to a one point spread on the interest. For example, if the published rate is 8.75 percent, the lender to dealer rate may be discounted to 8 percent; the .75 percent is the reserve held by the dealer as additional profit. This may not sound like much, but it adds up to hundreds of thousands of dollars a year at larger dealerships. This is the reason you should always arrange financing before going to the dealership, and then ask the dealer if they can beat your pre-approved rate. In most cases, they cannot, because of the reserve.

Paying cash is an advantage if you suffer from poor credit or bankruptcy, because it allows you to avoid the higher interest rates charged on loans to people with past credit problems. The bottom line is that if you think you can invest your money at a higher return than the interest rate of the car loan, you could actually save money by not paying cash.

12. Can I negotiate price at Saturn, Daewoo and no-haggle dealerships?

You cannot negotiate price on used cars at Saturn dealerships, but you can haggle over your trade-in and shop aggressively for the lowest-rate financing to keep costs down. Daewoo dealers also use a one-price philosophy, but the company wants to expand quickly and sell lots of cars, so the climate is favorable for negotiation.

No-haggle dealerships might wiggle a little on price, but if they're smart, they'll tell you to get lost. If you want to duke it out over $100, why would you shop at a no-haggle dealership wasting their time and yours? Think about this. If the no-haggle dealer caves and drops the price to sell you the car, you're gonna tell your buddies, and they're gonna tell their buddies, and pretty soon the whole town will be haggling over cars with the no-haggle dealer, and the no-haggle dealer isn't a no-haggle dealer anymore. Get it?

13. Who sets the residual value for a lease?

The financing institution that is handling the lease for the dealership sets the residual value, which can be affected by market forces and vehicle popularity. When shopping leases, it is important to shop different financing institutions for the highest residual value and the lowest interest rate.

14. Why don't you have a listing for the late-model used car I want to buy or sell?

To generate an accurate value for any given used car, there must be enough used examples on the market to include in the sample. Most often, the reason we don't provide a listing is because there aren't enough examples to generate an accurate value. For special interest models, such as anniversary models, try consulting a specialty-car value guide at your local bookstore, or contact a dealer who specializes in these types of cars for information.

15. Why did the used car I'm considering take a nasty drop in the ratings recently?

Edmunds.com updates used-car ratings annually, usually early in the summer. We also tend to modify the formulas that create the ratings, in an effort to make the ratings more accurate. If you find that the rating has changed recently, it's only because fresh data is available and we've finished our annual update.

Keep in mind that pricing is different from ratings. Pricing is updated quarterly throughout the year; ratings are updated once per year.

16. How much does an extended warranty cost the warranty company?

The cost of an extended warranty is based upon the degree of probability that any given vehicle will require repairs during the extended warranty period. Reliability records and repair cost information for a vehicle are evaluated to forecast potential future repair costs, and the extended warranty company will then charge a premium adequate enough to cover the potential cost of repairing the vehicle during the warranty period, while still making a profit. It is important to note that the cost of an extended warranty includes administrative costs for handling paperwork and claims, and insurance to guarantee that claims will be paid.

Extended warranty costs are based on averages, so the cost of applying an extended warranty to any given make and model of car can vary from consumer to consumer. Let's say you bought a $1,000 extended warranty for two identical Brand X vehicles: Car A and Car B. During the extended warranty period, Car A never breaks, so the extended warranty is never used. At the same time, Car B suffers bills amounting to $1,200 for transmission and valve problems. Profit on the warranty sold for Car A will counterbalance the loss suffered on Car B. Extended warranty companies sell thousands of warranties annually, and are able to make a profit when the actual loss experience is lower than the forecast potential for future repair. In other words, when sales exceed overhead the company makes money.

17. What is a secret warranty, and how can I find out if any exist for my car?

A secret warranty, actually called a technical service bulletin (TSB), is a notice that dealer service departments receive from manufacturers regarding suggested repairs to solve common complaints. The dealer is instructed to replace or repair these parts free of charge while the vehicle is under warranty or if the customer complains about a problem while the car is under warranty, but the TSB repair is not available at the time of the complaint. By law, TSB repairs covering emissions equipment are free of charge to the customer for up to 100,000 miles. If a TSB has been issued for your vehicle, but your situation does not meet any of the three listed criteria, then you are responsible for the cost of the repairs. You can get a list of TSBs for your car by contacting the National Highway Traffic Safety Administration (NHTSA) at www.nhtsa.dot.gov and conducting a search for the information.

18. What's the difference between a demo car and a program car?

A demo car is one used by the dealership as a demonstrator to potential buyers. Often, dealership personnel will use the car as personal transportation. A program car is a former rental car, purchased at auction by the dealership. Either type of car is more likely to have been abused than a used car offered for sale by a private owner.

19. When should a car be considered used?

Technically, a vehicle is considered used if it has been titled. However, some dealers can rack up hundreds or thousands of miles on a new car without titling it. In these cases, the ethical definition of a used car should include any car used for extensive demonstration or personal use by dealership staff members. The only miles a new car should have on the odometer when purchased are those put on during previous test drives by prospective buyers (at dealerships where demonstrators are not used), and any miles driven during a dealer trade, within a reasonable limit. If the car has more than 300 miles on the odometer, you should question how the car accumulated so many miles, and request a discount for the excessive mileage. We think a discount amounting to a dime a mile is a fair charge for wear and tear inflicted by the dealership.

A car should not be considered used if it is a brand-new leftover from a previous model year. However, it should be discounted, because many manufacturers offer dealers incentives designed to help the dealer lower prices and clear out old stock.

20. What is a trim level?

Most cars and trucks on the market today are available in various levels of trim with various levels of standard equipment. To distinguish between base models and better appointed or sporty models, manufacturers will add a numeric or alphabetic designation after the model name. For example, the Ford Taurus was sold in LX, SE and SHO trim levels. Similarly, the Nissan Maxima is sold in GXE, SE and GLE trim levels. Not all trim-level designations appear after the model name. Acura sells a 3.2TL and a 3.5RL. BMW's 3 Series model is available in several alphanumeric trim levels: 318ti, 323i, 323is, 323iC, 328i, 328is, 328iC and M3.

edmunds.com
where smart car buyers start

BUYER'S DECISION GUIDES
SCHEDULED RELEASE DATES
FOR 2001/2002*

VOL. 35/36		RELEASE DATE	COVER DATE
N3501	NEW CARS: Prices & Reviews [American & Import]	MAR 01	SPRING 01
S3501	NEW TRUCKS: Prices & Reviews [American & Import]	MAR 01	SPRING 01
U3502	USED CARS & TRUCKS: Prices & Ratings	APR 01	SUMMER 01
N3502	NEW CARS: Prices & Reviews [American & Import]	JUN 00	SUMMER 01
S3502	NEW TRUCKS: Prices & Reviews [American & Import]	JUN 00	SUMMER 01
U3503	USED CARS & TRUCKS: Prices & Ratings	JUL 00	FALL 01
N3503	NEW CARS: Prices & Reviews [American & Import]	SEPT 01	FALL 01
S3503	NEW TRUCKS: Prices & Reviews [American & Import]	SEPT 01	FALL 01
U3504	USED CARS & TRUCKS: Prices & Ratings	OCT 01	WINTER 01
N3504	NEW CARS: Prices & Reviews [American & Import]	DEC 01	WINTER 02
S3504	NEW TRUCKS: Prices & Reviews [American & Import]	DEC 01	WINTER 02
U3601	USED CARS & TRUCKS: Prices & Ratings	JAN 02	SPRING 02

*Subject to Change

 **SINGLE COPIES / ORDER FORM**

Please send me:

☐ **USED CARS & TRUCKS: PRICES & RATINGS** *(includes S&H)* **$14.99**

☐ **NEW CARS**
—American & Import *(includes S&H)* **$14.99**

☐ **NEW TRUCKS [PICKUPS, VANS & SPORT UTILITIES]**
—American & Import *(includes S&H)* **$14.99**

Name _____

Address _____

City, State, Zip _____

Phone _____

PAYMENT: __ MASTERCARD __ VISA __ CHECK or MONEY ORDER $_____

Make check or money order payable to:

Edmunds.com, Inc. *P.O.Box 338, Shrub Oaks, NY 10588*

For more information or to order by phone, call **(914) 962-6297**

Credit Card # _____ Exp. Date: _____

Cardholder Name: _____

Signature _____

Prices above include shipping within the U.S. and Canada only. Other countries, please add $7.00 to the price ($14.99+7.00) per book (via air mail) and $2.00 to the price ($14.99+2.00) per book (surface mail). Please pay through an American Bank or with American Currency. Rates subject to change without notice.

SUBSCRIPTIONS / ORDER FORM

BUYER'S PRICE GUIDES

Please send me a one year subscription for:

☐ **USED CARS & TRUCKS: PRICES & RATINGS**
AMERICAN & IMPORT (package price includes $10.00 S&H) **$36.80**
Canada $42.80/Foreign Countries $50.80 (includes air mail S&H)
<u>4 issues/yr</u>

☐ **NEW CARS**
AMERICAN & IMPORT (package price includes $10.00 S&H) **$36.80**
Canada $42.80/Foreign Countries $50.80 (includes air mail S&H)
<u>4 issues/yr</u>

☐ **NEW TRUCKS [PICKUPS, VANS & SPORT UTILITIES]**
AMERICAN & IMPORT (package price includes $10.00 S&H) **$36.80**
Canada $42.80/Foreign Countries $50.80 (includes air mail S&H)
<u>4 issues/yr</u>

Name _____

Address _____

City, State, Zip _____ - _____

PAYMENT: __ MC __ VISA __ Check or Money Order-Amount $_____ Rates subject to change without notice

Make check or money order payable to:
Edmunds.com, Inc. *P.O.Box 338, Shrub Oaks, NY 10588*
For more information or to order by phone, call **(914) 962-6297**

Credit Card # _____ Exp. Date: _____
Cardholder Name: _____
Signature _____

Notes

Notes

MILEAGE TABLE

Top Two Rows: Average Mileage Range
Bottom Row: Cents per mile to add/subtract if mileage is outside of range

Category	00	99	98	97	96	95	94	93	92	91
A	11,300- 15,300 +/- 11 cents	24,700- 28,700 +/- 11 cents	36,800- 40,800 +/- 10 cents	49,200- 53,200 +/- 10 cents	62,400- 66,400 +/- 9 cents	76,300- 80,300 +/- 9 cents	88,300- 92,300 +/- 8 cents	99,700- 103,700 +/- 8 cents	111,200- 115,200 +/- 7 cents	121,100- 125,100 +/- 7 cents
B&C	12,800- 16,800 +/- 10 cents	28,000- 32,000 +/- 10 cents	40,700- 44,700 +/- 9 cents	54,800- 58,800 +/- 9 cents	69,100- 73,100 +/- 8 cents	83,800- 87,800 +/- 8 cents	95,900- 99,900 +/- 7 cents	106,900- 110,900 +/- 7 cents	117,900- 121,900 +/- 6 cents	127,900- 131,900 +/- 6 cents
D&E	10,700- 14,700 +/- 9 cents	23,400- 27,400 +/- 9 cents	35,800- 39,800 +/- 8 cents	51,000- 55,000 +/- 8 cents	66,700- 70,700 +/- 7 cents	82,300- 86,300 +/- 7 cents	94,500- 98,500 +/- 6 cents	108,200- 112,200 +/- 6 cents	121,400- 125,400 +/- 5 cents	127,200- 131,200 +/- 5 cents
F	9,300- 13,300 +/- 9 cents	21,600- 25,600 +/- 9 cents	32,700- 36,700 +/- 8 cents	44,700- 48,700 +/- 8 cents	60,300- 64,300 +/- 7 cents	74,200- 78,200 +/- 7 cents	85,400- 89,400 +/- 6 cents	97,300- 101,300 +/- 6 cents	109,900- 113,900 +/- 5 cents	117,600- 121,600 +/- 5 cents
G&H	11,200- 15,200 +/- 9 cents	24,400- 28,400 +/- 9 cents	38,700- 42,700 +/- 8 cents	53,200- 57,200 +/- 8 cents	68,600- 72,600 +/- 7 cents	85,100- 89,100 +/- 7 cents	98,600- 102,600 +/- 6 cents	112,100- 116,100 +/- 6 cents	125,800- 129,800 +/- 5 cents	132,500- 136,500 +/- 5 cents
J	7,400- 11,400 +/- 11 cents	16,600- 20,600 +/- 11 cents	26,300- 30,300 +/- 10 cents	38,100- 42,100 +/- 10 cents	52,000- 56,000 +/- 9 cents	65,700- 69,700 +/- 9 cents	76,500- 80,500 +/- 8 cents	87,100- 91,100 +/- 8 cents	95,100- 99,100 +/- 7 cents	98,800- 102,800 +/- 7 cents
K	3,700- 5,700 +/- 14 cents	7,500- 9,500 +/- 14 cents	12,800- 14,800 +/- 14 cents	19,000- 21,000 +/- 14 cents	26,200- 28,200 +/- 13 cents	32,800- 34,800 +/- 13 cents	36,500- 38,500 +/- 13 cents	41,900- 43,900 +/- 13 cents	45,300- 47,300 +/- 12 cents	51,100- 53,100 +/- 12 cents
L	9,600- 13,600 +/- 14 cents	21,200- 25,200 +/- 14 cents	33,000- 37,000 +/- 14 cents	46,300- 50,300 +/- 14 cents	59,200- 63,200 +/- 13 cents	72,600- 76,600 +/- 13 cents	84,200- 88,200 +/- 13 cents	98,200- 102,200 +/- 13 cents	109,700- 113,700 +/- 12 cents	120,200- 124,200 +/- 12 cents

edmunds.com

* Mileage adjustment is not to exceed 50% of vehicle's adjusted trade-in value!